The Routledge Encyclopedia of Films

The Routledge Encyclopedia of Films comprises nearly 200 essays by leading film scholars analysing the most important, influential, innovative and interesting films of all time. Arranged alphabetically, each entry explores why each film is significant for those who study film and explores the social, historical and political contexts in which the film was produced. Ranging from Hollywood classics to international bestsellers to lesser-known representations of national cinema, this collection is deliberately broad in scope, crossing decades, boundaries and genres. The encyclopedia thus provides an introduction to the historical range and scope of cinema produced throughout the world.

Sarah Barrow is Head of Lincoln School of Media, University of Lincoln. She is co-editor of *Fifty Key British Films* (2008), author of *Mediawise: Film* (2002) and co-editor of a special journal issue on *Latin American Cinemas Today* (2013).

Sabine Haenni is Associate Professor in Film and American Studies at Cornell University. She is co-editor of *Fifty Key American Films* (2009) and author of *The Immigrant Scene* (2008).

John White is Senior Lecturer in Film and Media at Anglia Ruskin University. He co-edited *Fifty Key British Films* (2008) and *Fifty Key American Films* (2009) and is the author of *Westerns* (2011).

The Routledge Encyclopedia of Films

Edited by
Sarah Barrow, Sabine Haenni and
John White

Routledge
Taylor & Francis Group
LONDON AND NEW YORK

First published 2015
by Routledge
2 Park Square, Milton Park, Abingdon, Oxon OX14 4RN

and by Routledge
711 Third Avenue, New York, NY 10017

Routledge is an imprint of the Taylor & Francis Group, an informa business

British Library Cataloguing in Publication Data
A catalogue record for this book is available from the British Library

Library of Congress Cataloging-in-Publication Data
The Routledge encyclopedia of films / edited by Sarah Barrow, Sabine Haenni and John White.
Includes bibliographical references and index.
1. Motion pictures–Philosophy. 2. Motion pictures–History. I. White, John, 1956- editor of compilation. II. Barrow, Sarah, editor of compilation. III. Haenni, Sabine, editor of compilation.
PN1995.R6857 2014
791.4301–dc23
2013046597

ISBN: 978-0-415-68893-2 (hbk)
ISBN: 978-1-315-77383-4 (ebk)

Typeset in Baskerville
by Taylor & Francis Books

MIX
Paper from
responsible sources
FSC® C013604
FSC www.fsc.org

Printed and bound by CPI Group (UK) Ltd, Croydon, CR0 4YY

Contents

A–Z Film List (in language of origin)

4 luni, 3 saptamâni si 2 zile/4 Months, 3 Weeks and 2 Days (2007)
8 ½ (1963)
10 (2002)
À bout de souffle/Breathless (1959)
À nous la liberté/Freedom is ours (1931)
The Adventures of Priscilla, Queen of the Desert (1994)
Aguirre, der Zorn Gottes/Aguirre, Wrath of God (1972)
Ai no corrida/L'empire des sens/In the Realm of the Senses (1976)
Alexander Nevsky (1938)
Allá en el Rancho Grande/Out on the Big Ranch (1936)
Amar Akbar Anthony (1977)
Amores Perros (2000)
Angst essen Seele auf/Fear Eats the Soul (1974)
Antonia's Line (1995)
Apocalypse Now (1979)
Asfour Stah/Halfaouine: Boy of the Terraces (1990)
L'Atalante (1934)
Atanarjuat: the Fast Runner (2001)
L'Avventura (1960)
Awāra (1951)
Away from Her (2007)
Bab al-Hadid/Cairo Station aka *Cairo: Central Station* (1958)
Bab El-Oued City (1994)
Badkonake sefid/The White Balloon (1995)
Bamako (2006)
El baño del papa/The Pope's Toilet (2007)
Bashu, gharibeye koochak/Bashu: The Little Stranger (1989)
La battaglia di Algeri/The Battle of Algiers (1966)
Birth of a Nation (1915)
Blade Runner (1982, 1992)
Der blaue Engel/The Blue Angel (1930)
Blue Velvet (1986)
Bob le Flambeur (1956)
La boca del lobo/The Lion's Den (1988)
Bonnie and Clyde (1967)
Das Boot (1981); *Das Boot: The Director's Cut* (1997)
Boudu sauvé des eaux/Boudu Saved from Drowning (1932)
Brief Encounter (1945)
Die Büchse der Pandora/Pandora's Box (1929)
Caché/Hidden (2005)
Casablanca (1942)
La caza/The Hunt (1965)
Central do Brasil/Central Station (1998)
Chinatown (1974)
Chocolat (1988)
Chuncan/Spring Silkworms (1933)
Cidade de Deus/City of God (2002)
Cinema Paradiso (1989)
Citizen Kane (1941)
A Clockwork Orange (1971)
Como agua para chocolate/Like Water for Chocolate (1991)
Un condamné à mort s'est échappé ou Le vent souffle où il veut/A Man Escaped (1956)
Il Conformista/The Conformist (1970)
The Cook, The Thief, His Wife & Her Lover (1989)
Crna mačka, beli mačor/Black Cat, White Cat (1998)
Csillagosok, katonák/The Red and the White (1967)
Da hong denglong gaogao gua/Raise the Red Lantern (1991)

A–Z Film List (in English)

4 Months, 3 Weeks and 2 Days/4 luni, 3 saptamâni si 2 zile (2007)
8 ½ (1963)
10 (2002)
The 400 Blows/Les quatre cents coups (1959)
The Adventures of Priscilla, Queen of the Desert (1994)
Aguirre, Wrath of God/ Aguirre, der Zorn Gottes (1972)
Alexander Nevsky (1938)
All About My Mother/Todo sobre mi madre (1999)
Amar Akbar Anthony (1977)
Amores Perros (2000)
Antonia's Line (1995)
Apocalypse Now (1979)
The Ascent/Voskhozhdenie (1977)
Ashes and Diamonds/Popiól i diament (1958)
L'Atalante (1934)
Atanarjuat, the Fast Runner (2001)
L'Avventura (1960)
Awāra (1951)
Away from Her (2007)
Bab El-Oued City (1994)
Bamako (2006)
Bashu: The Little Stranger/Bashu, gharibeye koochak (1989)
The Battle of Algiers/La battaglia di Algeri (1966)
Bicycle Thieves/Ladri di biciclette (1948)
Birth of a Nation (1915)
Black Cat, White Cat/Crna mačka, beli mačor (1998)
Black Girl/La Noire de … (1966)
Blade Runner (1982, 1992)
The Blue Angel/Der blaue Engel (1930)
Blue Velvet (1986)
Bob le Flambeur (1956)
Bonnie and Clyde (1967)
Das Boot (1981); *Das Boot: The Director's Cut* (1997)
Boudu Saved from Drowning/Boudu sauvé des eaux (1932)
The Brave-Hearted Will Take Away the Bride/Dilwale dulhania le jayenge (1995)
Breathless/À bout de souffle (1959)
Brief Encounter (1945)
Burnt By The Sun/Utomlennye solntsem (1994)
The Cabinet of Dr Caligari/Das Kabinett des Dr Caligari (1919)
Cairo Station aka *Cairo: Central Station/Bab al-Hadid* (1958)
Casablanca (1942)
The Celebration/Festen (1998)
Central Station/Central do Brasil (1998)
Children of Paradise/Les enfants du paradis (1945)
Chinatown (1974)
Chocolat (1988)
Cinema Paradiso (1989)
Citizen Kane (1941)
City of God/Cidade de Deus (2002)
A Clockwork Orange (1971)
Closely Observed Trains/Ostře sledované vlaky (1966)
The Cloud-Capped Star/Meghe dhaka tara (1960)
The Colour of Pomegranates/Nran guyne (1969)
The Colours Trilogy/Trois couleurs (1993/4)
The Conformist/Il Conformista (1970)
The Cook, The Thief, His Wife & Her Lover (1989)
Crows and Sparrows/Wuya yu maque (1949)
Daughters of the Dust (1991)
Daybreak/Tianming (1933)

Days of Santiago/Días de Santiago (2004)
The Decline of the American Empire/Le déclin de l'empire américain (1986)
The Deer/Gavaznha (1976)
Deewaar (1975)
Delicatessen (1991)
Devdas (1935)
Distant/Uzak (2002)
Do The Right Thing (1989)
Double Indemnity (1944)
Earth/Zemlya (1930)
Eat Drink Man Woman/Yǐn shí nán nǚ (1994)
Elena (2011)
Europa Europa (1990)
Fanny and Alexander/Fanny och Alexander (1982)
Fear Eats the Soul/Angst essen Seele auf (1974)
Freaks (1932)
Freedom is ours/À nous la liberté (1931)
The Goddess/Shennu (1934)
The Godfather (1972)
Gone with the Wind (1939)
The Gospel According to St. Matthew/Il vangelo secondo Matteo (1964)
Halfaouine: Boy of the Terraces/Asfour Stah (1990)
Hatred/La Haine (1995)
Head-On/Gegen die Wand (2004)
The Headless Woman/La mujer sin cabeza (2008)
Hidden/Caché (2005)
Hiroshima mon amour (1959)
His Girl Friday (1940)
House of Flying Daggers/Shi mian mai fu (2004)
The Hunt/La caza (1965)
The Idiots/Idioterne (1998)
If … (1968)
In the Mood for Love/Hua yang nian hua (2000)
In the Realm of the Senses/Ai no corrida/L'empire des sens (1976)
The Insect Woman/Nippon konchūki (1963)
Invasion of the Body Snatchers (1956)
It Happened One Night (1934)
Jamón, Jamón (1992)
The Journey of the Hyena/Touki-Bouki (1973)
Kings of the Road/Im Lauf der Zeit (1976)
Kolya (originally released as *Kolja*) (1996)
Kukuli (1961)
Lady with a Lapdog/Dama s sobachkoi (1960)
The Ladykillers (1955)
The Last Wave (1977)
Let the Right One in/Låt den rätte komma in (2009)
Like Water for Chocolate/Como agua para chocolate (1991)
The Lion's Den/La boca del lobo (1988)
The Lodger (1926)
M (1931)
A Man Escaped/Un condamné à mort s'est échappé ou Le vent souffle où il veut (1956)
Machuca (2004)
Mad Max (1979)
Man without a Past/Mies vailla menneisyyttä (2002)
Manila, in the Claws of Neon/Maynila, Sa mga Kuko ng Liwanag (1975)
Memories of Underdevelopment/Memorias del subdesarrollo (1968)
Mildred Pierce (1945)
Milk of Sorrow/La teta asustada (2009)
Mirror/Zerkalo (1974)
The Misfits (1961)
Modern Times (1936)
Mother India (1957)
Moulin Rouge! (2001)
My Life Without Me (2003)
My Uncle/Mon Oncle (1958)
Night of the Living Dead (1968)
Nosferatu, A Symphony of Horrors/Nosferatu, eine Symphonie des Grauens (1922)
Obsession/Ossessione (1942)
Oldboy (2003)
Om Shanti Om (2007)
On The Waterfront (1954)
Once Were Warriors (1994)
Out on the Big Ranch/Allá en el Rancho Grande (1936)
A Page of Madness/Kurutta ichipeiji; sometimes *Kurutta ippeiji* (1926)
Pan's Labyrinth (2006)
Pandora's Box/Die Büchse der Pandora (1929)
The Passion of Joan of Arc/La passion de Jeanne d'Arc (1928)
Pépé le Moko (1937)
Persepolis (2007)
The Piano (1993)
The Pope's Toilet/El baño del papa (2007)
The Postman/Il Postino (1994)
Psycho (1960)
Pulp Fiction (1994)

Rabbit-Proof Fence (2002)
Raise the Red Lantern/Da hong denglong gaogao gua (1991)
Rebel without a Cause (1955)
The Red and the White/Csillagosok, katonák (1967)
The Red Shoes (1948)
The Red Violin/Le violon rouge (1998)
Redupers: the All-Round Reduced Personality/Redupers: die allseitig reduzierte Persönlichkeit (1977)
Roma, città aperta/Rome, Open City (1945)
Run Lola Run/Lola rennt (1998)
Sankofa (1993)
Satan's Tango/Sátántangó (1991–1994)
Saturday Night and Sunday Morning (1960)
The Searchers (1956)
Seven Samurai/Shichinin no samurai (1953)
Silences of the Palace/Samt el qusur (1994)
Singin' in the Rain (1952)
Song of the Little Road/Pather Panchali (1955)
The Spirit of the Beehive/El espíritu de la colmena (1973)
Spring Silkworms/Chuncan (1933)
Star Wars aka *Star Wars, Episode IV: A New Hope* (1977)
The Stolen Death/Varastettu kuolema (1938)
The Story of the Last Chrysanthemum/Zangiku monogatari (1939)
Street Angel/Malu tianshi (1937)
Strike/Stachka (1925)
Sunrise (1927)
The Sweet Hereafter (1997)
Sweet Sweetback's Baadasssss Song (1971)
Taxi Driver (1976)
Thelma and Louise (1991)
Thesis/Tesis (1996)
The Third Man (1949)
Tilaï (1990)
Tokyo Story/Tokyo monogatari (1953)
A Touch of Zen/Xia nu (1971)
Tsotsi (2005)
Twilight Samurai/Tasogare Seibei/(2002)
Two Stage Sisters/Wutai jiemei (1965)
Ugetsu/Ugetsu monogatari (1953)
Variety/Varieté (1925)
Videodrome (1983)
Viridiana (1961)
Voyage to the Beginning of the World/Viagem ao princípio do mundo (1997)
West Side Story (1961)
Whale Rider (2002)
The Wheel/La Roue (1923)
When a Woman Ascends the Stairs/Onna ga kaidan o agaru toku/(1960)
Whisky (2004)
The White Balloon/Badkonake sefid (1995)
The Wild Bunch (1969)
WR: Mysteries of the Organism/W. R.: Misterije organizma (1971)
Y Tu Mamá También (2001)
Yeelen (1987)

Chronological Film List

Birth of a Nation (1915)
Das Kabinett des Dr Caligari/The Cabinet of Dr Caligari (1919)
Nosferatu, eine Symphonie des Grauens/Nosferatu, A Symphony of Horrors (1922)
La Roue/The Wheel (1923)
Stachka/Strike (1925)
Varieté/Variety (1925)
Kurutta ichipeiji; sometimes *Kurutta ippeiji/A Page of Madness* (1926)
The Lodger (1926)
Sunrise (1927)
La passion de Jeanne d'Arc/The Passion of Joan of Arc (1928)
Die Büchse der Pandora/Pandora's Box (1929)
Der blaue Engel/The Blue Angel (1930)
Zemlya/Earth (1930)
À nous la liberté/Freedom is ours (1931)
M (1931)
Boudu sauvé des eaux/Boudu Saved from Drowning (1932)
Freaks (1932)
Chuncan/Spring Silkworms (1933)
Tianming/Daybreak (1933)
L'Atalante (1934)
It Happened One Night (1934)
Shennu/The Goddess (1934)
Devdas (1935)
Allá en el Rancho Grande/Out on the Big Ranch (1936)
Modern Times (1936)
Malu tianshi/Street Angel (1937)
Pépé le Moko (1937)
Alexander Nevsky (1938)
Varastettu kuolema/The Stolen Death (1938)
Gone with the Wind (1939)
Zangiku monogatari/The Story of the Last Chrysanthemum (1939)
His Girl Friday (1940)
Citizen Kane (1941)
Casablanca (1942)
Ossessione/Obsession (1942)
Double Indemnity (1944)
Brief Encounter (1945)
Les enfants du paradis/Children of Paradise (1945)
Mildred Pierce (1945)
Roma, città aperta/Rome, Open City (1945)
Ladri di biciclette/Bicycle Thieves (1948)
The Red Shoes (1948)
The Third Man (1949)
Wuya yu maque/Crows and Sparrows (1949)
Awāra (1951)
Singin' in the Rain (1952)
Shichinin no samurai/Seven Samurai (1953)
Tokyo monogatari/Tokyo Story (1953)
Ugetsu monogatari/Ugetsu (1953)
On The Waterfront (1954)
The Ladykillers (1955)
Pather Panchali/Song of the Little Road (1955)
Rebel without a Cause (1955)
Bob le Flambeur (1956)
Un condamné à mort s'est échappé ou Le vent souffle où il veut/A Man Escaped (1956)
Invasion of the Body Snatchers (1956)
The Searchers (1956)

Mother India (1957)
Bab al-Hadid/Cairo Station aka *Cairo: Central Station* (1958)
Mon Oncle/My Uncle (1958)
Popiół i diament/Ashes and Diamonds (1958)
À bout de souffle/Breathless (1959)
Hiroshima mon amour (1959)
Les quatre cents coups/The 400 Blows (1959)
L'Avventura (1960)
Dama s sobachkoi/Lady with a Lapdog (1960)
Meghe dhaka tara/The Cloud-Capped Star (1960)
Onna ga kaidan o agaru toku/When a Woman Ascends the Stairs (1960)
Psycho (1960)
Saturday Night and Sunday Morning (1960)
Kukuli (1961)
The Misfits (1961)
West Side Story (1961)
Viridiana (1961)
8 ½ (1963)
Nippon konchūki/The Insect Woman (1963)
Il vangelo secondo Matteo/The Gospel According to St. Matthew (1964)
La caza/The Hunt (1965)
Wutai jiemei/Two Stage Sisters (1965)
La battaglia di Algeri/The Battle of Algiers (1966)
Ostře sledované vlaky/Closely Observed Trains (1966)
La Noire de … /Black Girl (1966)
Bonnie and Clyde (1967)
Csillagosok, katonák/The Red and the White (1967)
If … (1968)
Memorias del subdesarrollo/Memories of Underdevelopment (1968)
Night of the Living Dead (1968)
Nran guyne/The Colour of Pomegranates (1969)
The Wild Bunch (1969)
Il Conformista/The Conformist (1970)
A Clockwork Orange (1971)
Sweet Sweetback's Baadasssss Song (1971)
Xia nu/A Touch of Zen (1971)
W. R.: Misterije organizma/WR: Mysteries of the Organism (1971)
Aguirre, der Zorn Gottes/Aguirre, Wrath of God (1972)
The Godfather (1972)
El espíritu de la colmena/The Spirit of the Beehive (1973)
Touki-Bouki/The Journey of the Hyena (1973)
Angst essen Seele auf/Fear Eats the Soul (1974)
Chinatown (1974)
Zerkalo/Mirror (1974)
Deewaar (1975)
Maynila, Sa mga Kuko ng Liwanag/Manila, in the Claws of Neon (1975)
Ai no corrida/L'empire des sens/In the Realm of the Senses (1976)
Gavaznha/The Deer (1976)
Im Lauf der Zeit/Kings of the Road (1976)
Taxi Driver (1976)
Amar Akbar Anthony (1977)
Voskhozhdenie/The Ascent (1977)
The Last Wave (1977)
Redupers: die allseitig reduzierte Persönlichkeit/Redupers: the All-Round Reduced Personality (1977)
Star Wars aka *Star Wars, Episode IV: A New Hope* (1977)
Apocalypse Now (1979)
Mad Max (1979)
Das Boot (1981); *Das Boot: The Director's Cut* (1997)
Blade Runner (1982, 1992)
Fanny och Alexander/Fanny and Alexander (1982)
Videodrome (1983)
Blue Velvet (1986)
Le déclin de l'empire américain/The Decline of the American Empire (1986)
Yeelen (1987)
La boca del lobo/The Lion's Den (1988)
Chocolat (1988)
Bashu, gharibeye koochak/Bashu: The Little Stranger (1989)
Cinema Paradiso (1989)
The Cook, The Thief, His Wife & Her Lover (1989)
Do The Right Thing (1989)
Asfour Stah/Halfaouine: Boy of the Terraces (1990)
Europa Europa (1990)
Tilaï (1990)
Como agua para chocolate/Like Water for Chocolate (1991)
Da hong denglong gaogao gua/Raise the Red Lantern (1991)
Daughters of the Dust (1991)
Delicatessen (1991)
Sátántangó/Satan's Tango (1991–1994)
Thelma and Louise (1991)
Jamón, Jamón (1992)
The Piano (1993)
Sankofa (1993)
Trois couleurs/The Colors Trilogy (1993/4)
The Adventures of Priscilla, Queen of the Desert (1994)
Bab El-Oued City (1994)

Once Were Warriors (1994)
Il Postino/The Postman (1994)
Pulp Fiction (1994)
Samt el qusur/Silences of the Palace (1994)
Yǐn shí nán nǚ/Eat Drink Man Woman (1994)
Utomlennye solntsem/Burnt By The Sun (1994)
Antonia's Line (1995)
Badkonake sefid/The White Balloon (1995)
Dilwale dulhania le jayenge/The Brave-Hearted Will Take Away the Bride (1995)
La Haine/Hatred (1995)
Kolya (originally released as *Kolja*) (1996)
Tesis/Thesis (1996)
The Sweet Hereafter (1997)
Viagem ao princípio do mundo/Voyage to the Beginning of the World (1997)
Central do Brasil/Central Station (1998)
Crna mačka, beli mačor/Black Cat, White Cat (1998)
Festen/The Celebration (1998)
Idioterne/The Idiots (1998)
Lola rennt/Run Lola Run (1998)
Le violon rouge/The Red Violin (1998)
Todo sobre mi madre/All About My Mother (1999)
Amores Perros (2000)
Hua yang nian hua/In the Mood for Love (2000)
Atanarjuat, the Fast Runner (2001)
Moulin Rouge! (2001)
Y Tu Mamá También (2001)
10 (2002)
Cidade de Deus/City of God (2002)
Mies vailla menneisyyttä/Man without a Past (2002)
Rabbit-Proof Fence (2002)
Tasogare Seibei/Twilight Samurai (2002)
Whale Rider (2002)
Uzak/Distant (2002)
My Life Without Me (2003)
Oldboy (2003)
Días de Santiago/Days of Santiago (2004)
Gegen die Wand/Head-On (2004)
Machuca (2004)
Shi mian mai fu/House of Flying Daggers (2004)
Whisky (2004)
Caché/Hidden (2005)
Tsotsi (2005)
Bamako (2006)
Pan's Labyrinth (2006)
4 luni, 3 saptamâni si 2 zile/4 Months, 3 Weeks and 2 Days (2007)
Away from Her (2007)
El baño del papa The Pope's Toilet (2007)
Om Shanti Om (2007)
Persepolis (2007)
La mujer sin cabeza/The Headless Woman (2008)
Låt den rätte komma in/Let the Right One in (2009)
La teta asustada/Milk of Sorrow (2009)
Elena (2011)

List of contributors

Niki Akhavan
Assistant Professor of Media Studies, The Catholic University of America

Jude G. Akudinobi
Lecturer, Department of Black Studies, University of California, Santa Barbara

Irina Anisimova
PhD candidate, Department of Slavic Languages and Literatures, University of Pittsburgh

Neil Archer
Lecturer in Film Studies, Keele University

Daniel Armogathe
President, Cinémathèque de Marseille (France), former maître de conferences, University of Provence

Doris Baltruschat
SSHRC Research Fellow in the Department of Theatre and Film and the Centre for Cinema Studies, University of British Columbia

Sarah Casey Benyahia
Film and media studies teacher

José B. Capino
Associate Professor of English and Conrad Humanities Scholar, University of Illinois, Urbana-Champaign

Shi-Yan Chao
Postdoctoral Fellow, Weatherhead East Asian Institute, Columbia University

Irene Depetris Chauvin
Assistant Researcher, University of Buenos Aires and the National Research Council of Argentina (CONICET)

Nataša Ďurovičová
Editor, International Writing Program and adjunct faculty, Department of Cinema and Comparative Literature, University of Iowa

Anna Dzenis
Lecturer in the Media: Screen + Sound program, La Trobe University, Australia

Austin Fisher
Senior Lecturer in Media Arts, University of Bedfordshire

Jaimey Fisher
Associate Professor of German and Cinema and Technocultural Studies, University of California, Davis and UC Faculty Director of Northern Europe

Terri Francis
Associate Professor of Communication and Culture, Indiana University

Alisa Freedman
Associate Professor of Japanese Literature and Film, University of Oregon

Freddie Gaffney
Subject Leader for Digital Film Production and Screenwriting at Ravensbourne, London

Dan Gao
PhD candidate, Department of Cinema Studies, New York University

Oliver Gaycken
Assistant Professor, Department of English, Program in Film Studies, University of Maryland, College Park

Lincoln Geraghty
Reader in Popular Media Cultures in the School of Creative Arts, Film and Media and Director of the Centre for Cultural and Creative Research at the University of Portsmouth

Michael B. Gillespie
Assistant Professor of Film, School of Film, School of Interdisciplinary Arts, and the Department of African American Studies, Ohio University

Katherine Groo
Lecturer of Film and Visual Culture, University of Aberdeen

Brían Hanrahan
Visiting Assistant Professor, Department of Performing and Media Arts, Cornell University

Veena Hariharan
Assistant Professor, Cinema Studies at the School of Arts and Aesthetics, Jawaharlal Nehru University, New Delhi

Joanne Hershfield
Professor and Chair, Department of Women's and Gender Studies, UNC-Chapel Hill

Brian Hoyle
Lecturer in the English and Film Studies Programme, University of Dundee

Tanya Jones
Head of Media Studies, Long Road Sixth Form College, Cambridge, UK

Anupama Kapse
Assistant Professor of Film and Media Studies, Queens College, CUNY

Janice Kearns
Senior Lecturer and Programme Leader for Documentary and Media Production, University of Lincoln

Patricia M. Keller
Assistant Professor, Romance Studies Department, Cornell University

Tina Kendall
Senior Lecturer and Course Leader for Film Studies, Anglia Ruskin University, Cambridge

Hossein Khosrowjah
Visiting Scholar, Department of Visual Studies, California College of the Arts

Chika Kinoshita
Associate Professor of Film Studies, Tokyo Metropolitan University

Olga Klimova
PhD, University of Pittsburgh

Jamicia Lackey
PhD candidate in African American Studies and Film Studies, Yale University

Phil Lloyd
Head of Film Studies at Hinchingbrooke School, Huntingdon, UK

André Loiselle
Professor of Film Studies and Associate Dean of Graduate Studies, Carleton University, Ottawa

Adam Lowenstein
Associate Professor of English and Film Studies and Director of Film Studies Program, University of Pittsburgh

Paula J. Massood
Professor of Film Studies at Brooklyn College and The Graduate Center, CUNY

Ranjani Mazumdar
Associate Professor of Cinema Studies at the School of Arts & Aesthetics, Jawaharlal Nehru University, New Delhi

Dave McCaig
Senior Lecturer in Media Theory, University of Lincoln

Ben McCann
Associate Professor in French, University of Adelaide

Paul Melo e Castro
Lecturer in Portuguese,University of Leeds

Saša Milić
Assistant Professor, Academy of Fine Arts in Belgrade, Serbia

Nima Naghibi
Associate Professor of English, Ryerson University, Toronto

Antonella Palmieri
Lecturer in Film, Television and Media Studies, University of Lincoln

Lisa Patti
Assistant Professor, Media and Society Program, Hobart and William Smith Colleges

Jennifer Peterson
Associate Professor, Film Studies Program, University of Colorado at Boulder

Nick Potamitis
Media and Film Studies teacher, Long Road Sixth Form College, Cambridge

Alexander Prokhorov
Russian Studies Program Director, Associate Professor of Russian, College of William and Mary

Yiping Qin
Program Associate, Asian American International Film Festival in New York

Thomas Redwood
Research Associate, Flinders University of South Australia

Anthony Reed
Assistant Professor of English and African American Studies, Yale University

Julian Ross
PhD candidate, Centre for World Cinemas, University of Leeds, and editor for Vertigo, an online publication by Close-Up Film Centre

Miriam Ross
Lecturer in Film Studies, Victoria University of Wellington

Dawn Seckler
PhD, Russian and Soviet Film, University of Pittsburgh

Sambudha Sen
Professor of English, University of Delhi

Robert Shail
Senior Lecturer in Film and Visual Culture, University of Wales, Trinity St David

Elliot Shapiro
Senior Lecturer and Director of Writing in the Majors Program, Cornell University

Gabriel Shapiro
PhD candidate, Department of Cultural Studies and Comparative Literature, University of Minnesota

Trish Sheil
Education Officer for the Cambridgeshire Film Consortium and guest lecturer in Film Studies, Anglia Ruskin University

Neil Sinyard
Emeritus Professor of Film Studies, University of Hull and Visiting Professor of Film at Lincoln University, UK

Michael Smith
PhD, University of Leeds

Jon Snyder
Visiting Scholar, Department of Spanish and Portuguese Literatures, New York University

Tytti Soila
Professor in Cinema Studies and Associate Dean of the Faculty of Humanities, Stockholm University

David Sorfa
Senior Lecturer and Programme Director of the MSc Film Studies, University of Edinburgh

Myra Sun
PhD candidate, Department of East Asian Languages and Cultures, Columbia University

Holly Taylor
Media Studies and Film Studies teacher, Long Road Sixth Form College, Cambridge

Martyn Thayne
Lecturer in Media Theory and Production, University of Lincoln, UK

Lilla Tőke
Assistant Professor, English, LaGuardia Community College, CUNY

Evan Torner
Andrew W. Mellon Postdoctoral Fellow and Lecturer in German, Grinnell College

Lynda Townsend
Former lecturer with the Open University and a freelance writer on film and art

Monique Tschofen
Associate Professor of English, Ryerson University, Toronto

Simon Ward
Deputy Director, Independent Cinema Office

Jean Welsh
Head of Media Studies and Film Studies, Hills Road Sixth Form College, Cambridge

Nigel Wheale
Former lecturer at Anglia Ruskin University who has written widely on the arts

David Williams
DAAD Postdoctoral Research Fellow, University of Konstanz, Germany

Melanie Williams
Senior Lecturer in Film Studies, University of East Anglia

Paul Young
Associate Professor of Film and Media Studies, Dartmouth College

Introduction

This book is not an attempt to assert that the films discussed here are the 'greatest' or 'best' films ever made by film-makers from around the world. The suggestion is more simply that this selection of films operates to provide an initial appreciation of world, classical ('classic') and independent cinema over the past 100 years. As an introductory survey focusing on individual texts, several other sets of films would serve equally as well. There is neither effort, nor wish, to promote a particular canon of world cinema. The very nature of a 'canon' is that it is exclusive and this list is not designed to be that (other than in the sense that we only have room for a little under 200 essays in this book). Nor is this list ranked in order of merit; there are three contents lists, one in alphabetical order according to original titles, one in date order, and the other in alphabetical order according to English titles.

It is true, however, that compiling lists of films according to various criteria has always been a favourite pastime of both cinephiles and moviegoers. It is fun; and film, like all storytelling and artforms, is built around pleasure of different forms. Therefore, beyond the theoretical seriousness of discussions about the potential elitism, exclusivity and political manoeuvrings associated with the notion of canons, hopefully you will also simply find pleasure in the acts of agreeing and disagreeing with the inclusions and exclusions you find here.

What were our benchmarks for deciding on these particular films? We wanted to include a spread that extended from the early twentieth century (the earliest film here was released in 1915) to the contemporary. We wanted to have a range of mainstream genres but also a range of titles that took us beyond commercial cinema. We wanted readers to see that certain titles that have reached 'classic' status had been included and were present for their consideration, but we also wanted a range of other films to be included that might encourage the adoption of a wider viewing experience. We wanted the selection to be useful to the widest possible readership looking for stimulating and lively writing about films from around the world, some of which may be familiar, others far less so.

We cannot speak for each of our contributors,[1] but for ourselves in the writing we wanted to stress that film form, narrative structure, genre, authorship and other technical approaches to film analysis only have significance within the social experience of making and reading film; that the crucial context of film and film studies is that of producers and audiences making films and making sense of films within a social context. We wished to stress the historical, social and cultural, as well as the cinematic contexts. Films are clearly not created in isolation from what is happening in society during the period in which they come into being. They are products of particular societies and each is made at a particular moment in that society's history, often serving as a cultural response to specific events and debates. In viewing them, for us, it is crucial to see them as determinedly exploring, purposefully commenting upon, or unwittingly reflecting issues relevant to their particular socio-historical moment, but also to see them as being continually reframed and reconstituted by their reception at different times. Films do not exist cut off from the world in splendid isolation within the cinema auditorium, or behind the drawn curtains of the home cinema experience or blackout facilities of the university or college screening room. In their conception, their production, their distribution, their exhibition and their reception, they take their place within the social sphere; and, to be properly understood, they need to be seen within this context. Although it is the case that films are recreated in every act of viewing by the individual spectator, and although any social action and historical moment can be seen and understood in a plurality of ways, still each film does finally exist within this social dimension. Every interpretation of the films offered here, argued clearly from the evidence of the social and historical context, is contestable. The contesting of interpretations is, after all, also the testing of interpretations and this process is at the heart of both academic debate and everyday political engagement.

To be truthful, as our emphasis on social context suggests, as editors, we cannot escape charges of 'canon building'.

> That canons exist in film studies and that canon formation is involved with the political sphere is evident. Much less evident is the shifting politics, past and present, of the factors contributing to canon formation.[2]

However lacking in political 'malice aforethought' we assure you the process has been, we have ultimately chosen this list of films over all other possibilities and in doing so we are displaying vested interests; but that is merely in the nature of all social exchange. What matters is that as viewers of film we should engage in this social exchange with critical awareness. As Barbara Klinger has suggested, there are 'competing voices involved in a particular film's public signification.'[3] We should not attempt to stand apart from this creation of 'public signification', detached from this discussion, aware of each of these 'competing voices' but never entering into the fray; rather we should 'get our hands dirty', become involved in discussing the implications of these voices and through this action arrive at our own voice and political position.

Despite our strong initial focus on the films themselves we agree with Janet Staiger when she suggests that:

> interpreting texts or films is a historical reality determined by context, not an inherent or automatic act due to some essential human process …

and would emphasise with her that it is at this point that the critical debate can begin, because:

> once interpretation becomes historical rather than universal, then claims for privileging some interpretations can be refuted. Interpretations-in-history become politicized since they relate to historical social struggles, not to essences.[4]

In discussing her concept of a 'totalised view', Staiger talks of achieving an approach to texts in which the discovery of meaning and significance has been displaced from text to context. More accurately for us, in an alert reading, context is recognised as being fully sutured into text.

With essays of the length offered here (around 2,000 words), the number of questions raised is always going to be greater than the number successfully answered, but that is as it should be. Hopefully, these short essays will encourage you as readers to return to, or seek out for the first time, at least some of these films with the enthusiasm to explore further and with one or two questions for which you are determined to seek answers. Each entry aims to be suggestive rather than exhaustive, attempting to introduce selected aspects of film form and thematic content in relation to the focus text, as well as considering historical and cultural contexts. A brief synopsis is given so as to situate the analysis that follows into its narrative context. Details of a film's production history may not be supplied unless this is in some way relevant to ideas at the core of the film. Several entries discuss the films as the 'first' to do certain things, for example to win an award, to establish a movement, to launch a groundbreaking career, and these achievements had an obvious bearing on their selection. There is, as we have emphasized, a strong underlying concern throughout to place these films within social, historical and political contexts, and not simply to analyze the 'look' of a film, but those aspects of cinematic 'language' remain important nonetheless. Concepts and debates relevant to film studies as an academic subject are considered within individual entries, where appropriate. So, ideas relating to genre, narrative structure, auteur theory, representation and identity, spectatorship and performance, national and transnational importance, for example, are dealt with at various points.

In summary, this book offers brief introductions to a range of films, some of which have gained 'classic' status through critical and/or popular acclaim and debate. The contents pages provided give both date-ordered and alphabetical listings allowing readers to use it as a reference work, and the extensive index of key names, institutions and topics has been designed to help with more specific research activities. The effort throughout is to offer entries that are accessible to the well-informed general reader but also sufficiently exploratory and analytical as models that should be useful to film scholars.

Notes

1. The central feature of a book structured around individual contributions from colleagues working in film education, research and the film industry is that it allows for a diversity of approaches, and is likely to absorb within itself something of this core aspect of film studies.
2. Janet Staiger, 'The Politics of Film Canons', *Cinema Journal*, 24 (3), Spring 1985, pp. 4–23.
3. Barbara Klinger, 'Film History Terminable and Interminable: Recovering the Past in Reception Studies', *Screen*, 38 (2), 1997, pp. 107–28.
4. Janet Staiger, *Interpreting Films: Studies in the Historical Reception of American Cinema*, Princeton, NJ, Princeton University Press, 1992, p. 18.

4 luni, 3 saptamâni si 2 zile/4 Months, 3 Weeks and 2 Days (2007)

[Country: Romania, Belgium. Production company: Mobra Films, Centrul National al Cinematografiei (CNC), Mindshare Media. Producers: Daniel Burlac, Cristian Mungiu, Oleg Mutu, Alex Teodorescu. Director: Cristian Mungiu. Screenwriters: Cristian Mungiu and Razvan Radulescu. Cinematographer: Oleg Mutu. Editor [including sound]: Dana Bunescu. Cast: Anamaria Marinca (Otilia), Laura Vasiliu (Găbiţa), Vlad Ivanov (Viarel 'Domnu' Bebe).]

Synopsis: Mungiu's second feature film follows the story of Otilia Mihartescu (Anamaria Marinca) and Gabriela 'Găbiţa' Dragut (Laura Vasiliu), two university friends in an unnamed Romanian town. The film is set in 1987, at the end of the oppressive Ceauşescu regime. When Găbiţa becomes pregnant, the two girls arrange a meeting with Mr Bebe (Vlad Ivanov) in a hotel, where he is to perform an illegal abortion. After visiting her boyfriend to borrow money, Otilia heads to a hotel where Găbiţa has booked a room, only to be informed by an unfriendly receptionist that there is no reservation under Găbiţa's last name. After much begging and haggling, they book a room at an expensive rate at a different hotel. Mr Bebe discovers that Găbiţa's claim that her pregnancy was in its third month is a lie; in fact, it has been at least four months. The two women were certain that they would pay no more than 3,000 lei (equivalent to less than 10 pence in UK currency) for the abortion. However, it slowly becomes clear to them that he expects both women to have sex with him. Otilia reluctantly has sex with Mr Bebe so that he will not walk out on them, and eventually Găbiţa does as well. Mr Bebe then performs the abortion and leaves instructions on how to dispose of the foetus when it comes out. Otilia is exasperated by Găbiţa's lies, yet continues to help her and care for her. Otilia leaves Găbiţa at the hotel to go to her boyfriend's mother's birthday, but then returns to help Găbiţa dispose of the foetus. In the film's closing sequence, Otilia looks at the camera, leaving the audience to decide what will happen to the two friends.

Anne Jäckel wrote in 2000 that '[f]or all its long history, Romanian cinema has rarely been seen before' (2000: 409). And yet, according to *Variety* (online) just seven years later, *4 Months, 3 Weeks and 2 Days* was 'further proof of Romania's new prominence in the film world' (2007).[1] In fact, the film may be considered as indicative of a broader renaissance in Romanian cinema in the 2000s, particularly in light of other successful Romanian films, including Cristi Puiu's *The Death of Mr. Lazarescu* (2005), which won the Prix un certain regard at the Cannes Film Festival, Corneliu Porumboiu's *12:08 East of Bucharest* (2006), which won the *Camera d'Or* at the Festival a year later, and Cristian Nemescu's *California Dreamin'* (2007), which won the Prix un certain regard at Cannes one year after that.

The bleakness of the storyline and brutality of the action in Mungiu's film convey a dark socio-political critique in the final years of a repressive dictatorship and contrasts starkly with the comedic approach he adopted for his feature debut, *Occident* (2002). The setting for this grippingly horrible movie is Romania, in 1987: that is, 2 years before Nicolae Ceauşescu was executed, and 20 years after he had outlawed abortion in Romania to increase the birth rate. As Peter Bradshaw suggested in his review at the time of the film's UK release, 'without ever being overtly political, it makes you feel humanity itself being coarsened and degraded by the state' (2008). He also referred to it as 'part of that emerging twenty-first-century phenomenon, ordeal cinema: a cinema that with great formal technique makes you live through a horrendous experience in what seems like real time' (2008). As a drama, it observes every subtle detail of the ordeal suffered by the young women, and it is ripe with tension as the unbearable climax is reached.

Anamaria Marinca and Laura Vasiliu play Otilia and Gabriela (Găbiţa), two students in their early twenties who share a room in a provincial Romanian town. Otilia is relatively experienced with a steady boyfriend; Gabriela, by contrast, is naïve and vulnerable, misjudging most situations. Their friendship is sorely tested by the decision to end Găbiţa's pregnancy; it is only when these two scared young women are alone with the abortionist in the charmless hotel room that the awfulness of their situation reveals itself, and their commitment to one another is put on the line.

A sense of horror seeps into almost every scene around the film's central event. For example, when Otilia meets the pompous and patronising Bebe for the first time, he complains about the way in which the young women have misunderstood the furtive arrangements. The camera fixes on Otilia in his car, revealing her distress via her facial expression, while Bebe gets out to bully an old woman about her accommodation. The scene continues until an unexplained explosive noise is heard off-screen, and Bebe returns to Otilia.

Overall, the film reveals the end of innocence in a brutal tale of coming of age. Otilia is angry, with no way of expressing her anger. She has seen what humans are capable of, and she is left to wonder what protection she would have, were she to be in the same state. She appears to wonder whether anyone would step up for her, the way she stepped up for her friend, after such a violation? These questions are eloquently suggested by Marinca's stricken face, in an outstandingly subtle performance of utter distress.

The horror of the hotel scenes climaxes with a sequence in which Otilia must contain her torment and go through with a long-arranged visit to her boyfriend's parents' for an event that would have been excruciating under any circumstances. Her face shows that she has gone into shock, and yet has to keep things together for a birthday tea party. Mungiu shoots this scene in virtually one static tableau, with the family and neighbours crowded round the table, sneering at the irresponsibility of youth. Patriarchal dominance in the form of medical men remind Otilia of the awful scene she has just left behind. From her frightened perspective, everyone, from the hotel waiter to the receptionist, to the abortionist and the party guests, seems to adopt the same air of condemnation and judgement. The family party seems friendly and harmless at first, but soon becomes intensely suffocating for the young woman who suffers the experience as if in a traumatised trance, a controlled display of intimate desperation.

'We'll never speak of this again', promise the protagonists at the end of their nightmare. As Xan Brooks remarked in his review of some of the best films of the first decade of the new millennium, the film comes with a 'wider resonance – spotlighting the collective amnesia of those who lived through Ceauşescu-era Romania and [who] are now keen to move on quickly, without a backward glance' (2009). Those oppressive years seem to have shaped the world view of this director. *4 Months, 3 Weeks and 2 Days* is a lean, social realist masterpiece that put new Romanian cinema on the map and drew sharp attention to both the nastiness and kindness of human beings.

Note

1. Winner of the Palme d'Or and FIPRESCI (critics) prize at Cannes Film Festival in 2007, and the Great Prize at the European Film Academy, Berlin, also in 2007.

Further reading

Peter Bradshaw, 'Review', *Guardian online*, 11 Jan 2008, www.theguardian.com/film/2008/jan/11/worldcinema.drama (accessed 14 August 2013).

Xan Brooks, 'Best Films of the Noughties', *Guardian online*, 24 Dec 2009, www.theguardian.com/film/filmblog/2009/dec/24/best-films-noughties-cristian-mungiu (accessed 14 August 2013).

Peter Hames (ed.), *The Cinema of Central Europe*, London, Wallflower Press, 2004.

Anne Jäckel, 'France and Romanian Cinema, 1899–1999', *French Cultural Studies*, 11, 33, 2000, 409–24.

Doru Pop, 'The Grammar of the New Romanian Cinema', *Film and Media Studies*, 3, 2010, 19–40.

Jay Weissberg, 'Review: *4 Months, 3 Weeks & 2 Days*', *Variety*, 17 May 2007.

Sarah Barrow

8 ½ (1963)

[Country: Italy, France. Production Company: Cineriz, and Francinex. Director: Federico Fellini. Producer: Angelo Rizzoli. Screenwriters: Federico Fellini, Ennio Flaiano, Tullio Pinelli and Brunello Rondi. Cinematographer: Gianni di Venanzo. Music: Nino Rota. Editor: Leo Catozzo. Production Designer: Piero Gheradi. Cast: Marcello Mastroianni (Guido Anselmi), Claudia Cardinale (Claudia), Anouk Aimée (Luisa Anselmi), Sandra Milo (Carla), Rosella Falk (Rosella).]

Synopsis: Federico Fellini's *8 ½* portrays a key juncture in the life of the fictional film director, Guido Anselmi (as played by Marcello Mastroianni). Guido is successful with audiences and well regarded by the critics, but he is having problems with his ideas for his latest work, a strange piece that seems to combine autobiographical elements with science fiction. The latter element has led to the construction of a large space rocket which has then become a sort of vast visual symbol for his escalating difficulties. As his sense of panic and paranoia grows, he is increasingly pressurised and harassed by his collaborators who are confused by his seeming indecision. To add to his woes, his marriage to Luisa (Anouk Aimée) is in trouble and his attempts to resolve this are hampered by the appearance of his demanding mistress, Carla (Sandra Milo). Ensconced at a spa resort where he is taking the cure for his nervous exhaustion, he is assailed by memories and distracted by fantasies which add to his feelings of confusion and inertia.

Any attempted plot synopsis of *8 ½* has to struggle with the considerable difficulty of trying to sum up a film in which conventional narrative plays little part. As D.A. Miller puts it, 'any argument about *8 ½*, I soon understood, ran the constant risk of being swamped by an incomparable visual spectacle' (Miller 2008: 74). What is immediately evident is that this is a highly personal work. Guido seems to bare an uncanny resemblance to the film's creator, Federico Fellini. The very title of the film refers to the fact that Fellini had previously shot six feature films, as well as co-directing one and making two shorter pieces (each counting for a half), therefore making this one count as number 8 ½ in his output. With a wonderfully circular logic, the film which Guido struggles to make is actually the film we are watching; process and outcome have become one and the same thing. The intensely personal nature of the film has led to accusations of obscurity and self-indulgence from some critics, a view which Fellini rejected. He told one interviewer: 'It doesn't seem to me that *8 ½* is a difficult film to understand. For me it was a liberating experience and I also hope it liberates the viewers' (Costantini 1995: 62).

8 ½ marked a particularly crucial moment in Fellini's own development as a filmmaker. Born in Rimini in 1920, he had begun his professional career in a striking range of occupations including as a cub reporter, humorous writer and caricature artist working for magazines, newspapers and radio, as well as acting as a gag writer for one of Italy's foremost variety performers. By the mid-1940s he had come to know many of the key creative figures in Italy and had formed a friendship with the director Roberto Rossellini for whom he co-wrote the screenplay of *Rome, Open City* (1945), one of the masterpieces of postwar Italian neo-realism. He continued to write for Rossellini, including *Paisà* (1946), as well as for other filmmakers such as Alberto Lattuada and Pietro Germi, becoming closely associated with the naturalistic, socially aware style dominating Italian cinema of the period. However, when he came to direct himself, he quickly moved away from realism. *Lights of Variety* (1950, co-directed with Alberto Lattuada) was set in the backstage world of travelling performers, while his debut as a solo director, *The White Sheik* (1952), showed the influence of his earlier career as a cartoonist.

La Strada (1954) marked the beginning of his international success; it was the first of four Fellini films to win the Academy Award as Best Foreign Language Film. Its comic-tragic story of the destructive love affair between a circus strongman and a Chaplinesque female clown, played by Fellini's wife Giulietta Masini, took him further towards the stylisation which was to become a major feature of his work. The gradual shift in Fellini's output towards a modernist mode was mirrored in the output of other Italian directors of the 1950s such as Michelangelo Antonioni and Luchino Visconti. This change of emphasis moved viewers from the exterior world of contemporary Italian society into the interior lives of the characters on screen, and of the filmmakers themselves. As Pierre Sorlin describes it, 'Filmmakers could successively, disturb and then re-establish a chronological order. Modernism was therefore an enquiry on the potentialities of cinema, not a struggle to describe the world' (1996: 132). Experimentation and international success continued to follow for Fellini with *Nights of Cabiria* (1957) and *La Dolce Vita* (1960). The latter melded Fellini's increasing interest in formal effects with a critique of the amorality of a newly affluent Italy, but it was *8 ½* which most decisively marked the director's transition into a cinema of self-reflexivity. In this way it also prefigures Fellini's later work which moved further into visual experimentation, subjectivity and memory with *Juliet of the Spirits* (1965), *Roma* (1972) and *Amarcord* (1974).

If *8 ½* is partly a film about the creative process of making cinema, then it is also about the behind the scenes world of film production itself, and the image we are presented with is hardly a flattering one. Poor Guido is pursued by a horde of demanding executives, writers, and production staff who are impatient for him to produce another popular masterpiece but who also greet his ideas, such as they are, with scepticism and incredulity. Everywhere he goes there are hangers-on, aspirant stars, and budding starlets. These people demand answers which he cannot provide. The press add to his woes with their own expectations and questions. In its depiction of the strains of contemporary filmmaking it served as a precursor to other films on the same theme, including Truffaut's *Day for Night* (1974), as well as cinematic considerations of the creative process from Woody Allen's near homage *Stardust Memories* (1980) to Bob Fosse's *All That Jazz* (1979).

However, the film we are actually watching is essentially Fellini's own riposte to any negative thoughts about the nature of filmmaking. While Guido puzzles over what ideas to pursue, his own self-doubts become the very subject of the film and they are realised with a cinematic panache which becomes a visual demonstration of the power of the medium. The opening sequence is a perfect case in point. The first shot finds us positioned just behind Guido inside his car as he is trapped in the traffic jam from hell. The camera pans left and right, with the image occasionally freezing into a still, as his neighbours stare blankly at him or are preoccupied with their own concerns. As exhaust fumes begin to fill the car and suffocate him, Guido suddenly escapes and floats away miraculously into the sky, until his pursuers lasso him and he is pulled to earth. Only at this point does Guido suddenly wake with a scream and the audience simultaneously realises that we have actually been witnessing a dream. Conventional cinema would have signalled his dream-state from the beginning, but it is part of Fellini's self-conscious formalism that he denies us explanation, leaving the audience to experience the images and sounds in front of them as pure cinema.

A few moments later we find ourselves at the spa where Guido is taking his rest cure. The camera pans and tracks around an extraordinary exterior where elderly visitors queue for the spring waters. Bright sunlight produces eye-dazzling overexposure and the movement of figures is choreographed to the music of an orchestra playing Wagner. Grotesque faces appear in close-up and acknowledge the presence of the camera by smiling at us or shyly turning away. Only after a few moments do we realise they are greeting Guido. Suddenly the beautiful Claudia appears and the music is momentarily silenced as Guido, and the audience, are held spellbound by her appearance. We are again made aware of the power of the cinematic form itself, but we are also drawn into the world of subjective experience, that of Guido, of Fellini and of the audience.

Subjectivity is signalled by sudden, unannounced switches into fantasy, again eschewing the more obvious signalling devices used by mainstream narrative films. Most notorious of these is the extended sequence in which Guido compensates for his long record of troubled relationships with women by imagining his home life as a chauvinist's paradise. Here an assortment of women from his past and present form an ever-willing harem, waiting on him hand and foot. However, Guido's imagination never allows him to stray too far from reality and his desires are quickly supplanted by his fears as the passive inmates of his harem suddenly turn on him. He quickly takes on the role of circus ringmaster as he corrals his female attackers armed with a chair and a whip, taming them like wild lions and tigers. Fantasy becomes an ironic commentary on his own attitudes.

Similarly, transitions between the past and present take place without any of the devices normally required in conventional mainstream cinema. Guido's deceased parents simply appear to him as he flicks between material reality and the interior world of his thoughts. As he calls out, they move away from him back into the past. In his confusion it is his childhood which draws him most strongly. He remembers skipping school so that he could visit La Saraghina, a broken-down, middle-aged prostitute who performs a magical dance for him and his friends on the beach. Despite her grotesque appearance, she has a strange, sensual loveliness in her movements. His Jesuit tutors are far from pleased and chase him in speeded-up motion. In another mesmerising sequence full of warmth and nostalgia, he recalls helping with the grape harvest, crushing the fruits with his bare feet, and then being bathed and wrapped in towels by another harem of loving women. The function of these memory scenes is partly to remind Guido of the happiness he has experienced, but also to form part of the film's complex mosaic of images, visually replicating the way in which the subjective mind functions.

Guido's personal crisis is to a degree one of creative block, but it is also one brought about by a sense of purposelessness, equated here with the dilemmas of modern living. However, Guido does find an answer and he does make his film. In the final sequence he is suddenly surrounded by all the most significant people in his life, who encircle him with love. Many of the individuals who have been exhausting him with their demands are there but now he sees them differently. As Fellini himself described it, 'at the end of *8 ½* the protagonist realises that his fear, complexes and anxiety are in fact a kind of wealth' (Costantini 1995: 67). Guido tells his long-suffering wife of his realisation that life is simply a party that is there to be enjoyed. Suddenly, all the things that have worried him are reversed and he views the same circumstances with a feeling of contentment. Led by a circus ringmaster, a role he often seems to play himself (as does Fellini, by implication), he joins with everyone else in the magical dance. For all its depiction of personal doubt and turmoil, *8 ½* is ultimately a joyful celebration of life and cinema.

Further reading

Peter Bondanella, *The Cinema of Federico Fellini*, Boston: Princeton University Press, 1992.

Costanzo Costantini, (ed.) *Conversations with Fellini*, New York and San Diego: Harcourt Brace, 1995.

Tullio Kezich, *Federico Fellini: His Life and Work*, London: I.B. Tauris, 2007.

D.A. Miller, (2008) *8 ½*, London: Palgrave/BFI, 2008.

Pierre Sorlin, *Italian National Cinema 1896–1996*, London and New York: Routledge, 1996.

Angel Quintana, *Federico Fellini: Masters of Cinema*, London: Cahier du Cinema, 2011.

Robert Shail

10 (2002)

[Country: Iran. Production Company: Abbas Kiarostami Productions, MK2 Productions. Director: Abbas Kiarostami. Screenwriter: Abbas Kiarostami. Cinematographer: Abbas Kiarostami. Editors: Vahid Ghazi, Abbas Kiarostami and Bahman Kiarostami. Cast: Mania Akbari (Driver), Amin Maher (Amin).]

Synopsis: Ten sequences examine the emotional lives of women at significant junctures.

'I am unable to grasp the greatness of Abbas Kiarostami … Two digital cameras, a car and your actors, and off you go.' When the great American film critic Roger Ebert dismissed *10* with these words (quoted in Andrew 2005: 8) he was swimming against a tide of critical consensus. The Iranian filmmaker was after all a familiar figure in critics' polls for the Greatest Living Director, on the back of films such as *Close Up* (1990) and *The Wind Will Carry Us* (1999).[1] Ebert's view is nevertheless important for the way it raises key questions surrounding this film and how we assess it; but it also sheds light on the way we continue to talk in general about filmmaking and filmmakers.

Ebert's main concern was with the way the film is viewed and discussed through the prism of Kiarostami's 'greatness'. Given that the idea of the *auteur* has dominated discussions of world cinema since the 1960s, and is still a main way through which we read and classify films, this is hardly surprising. *10*, though, forces us to rethink the concept of the director as the film's main creative vision. What Ebert found problematic about the film may therefore be what makes it most interesting.

The film's credits give equal prominence to all cast and crew, with Kiarostami listed as merely the first of 25 names. While Kiarostami is technically in control of all aspects of the film (scripting, cinematography, editing), the emphasis here is on a more democratic process, within which the 'director' is just one presence among many. In the case of *10*, this is actually a reflection of the film's production, as the film literally undoes the notion of a director 'behind the camera': virtually the entire film is shot on two digital cameras fixed to the dashboard of a moving car, one facing the passenger seat, the other facing the driver. While theories of art cinema have tended to focus on aspects of style as an authorial signature, the distinctive feature of *10* is its apparent *lack* of style. Movement in the image is produced only by the city streets through which the car travels, or in the editing between one camera and the other; the only sound is that of dialogue and the ambient city noise caught by the cameras themselves.

The narrative of *10* seems initially just as unembellished as its shooting style. We are in present-day Tehran. A young boy, Amin, gets into the passenger seat of a car, en route for the local swimming pool. Over the course of 15 minutes, in a virtually unbroken shot, the boy harangues his off-screen mother – at this point only a voice from the driver's side of the car – about her selfishness in divorcing his father and remarrying. It is only when the boy finally leaves the car in a rage that we have a reverse shot, revealing the source of the maternal voice: an elegant, subtly made-up woman in fashionable sunglasses (Mania Akbari, the boy's real-life mother). Several (male) reviewers of the film make the point that the woman's appearance comes as a surprise: her sophistication and attractiveness do not seem to match the shrill, hectoring voice through which, up to this point, we have perceived her.

Whether or not we agree with these inferences, the deliberate withholding of a face to go with the voice can only be a rhetorical decision on the part of the filmmaker(s); a deliberate teasing out of our visual expectations, which in turn prompts a set of questions: Why might our visual expectations prove so misguided? What is the history to this mother–son relationship, and what is the real power relationship between the two? Changing the shot at the very end of this first long sequence, and forcibly shifting our viewpoint, also marks a structural shift in the narrative, which from this point takes the mother's point of view across nine further encounters and dialogues. Mostly these are with other female friends or women met on the road, thematically linked by the dominance of men in female lives (two of the women are experiencing unhappy relationships; one, unseen, is a prostitute). But these dialogues are also punctuated – and, significantly, ended – by further arguments between Mania and Amin.

The presence of a woman here in the literal and figurative driving seat may not seem remarkable to many viewers, but it is significant in the context of Kiarostami's cinema: as Geoff Andrew points out, the character of Mania marks a radical shift in Iranian screen representation (Andrew 2005: 44–5). But the fact that Mania is apparently just a typical busy mother, trying to negotiate both her son's mood swings and the Tehran traffic, begs the question of why this shift is so notable. In an essay written just before the making of *10*, Azadeh

Farahmand reminds us that Iranian cinema, with its strict codes regarding the representation of women, makes realistic representation almost impossible. For instance, because females on screen are considered to be in public view, they are obliged to wear the *chador* (full body cloak) and headscarf even in private, domestic scenes (Farahmand 2002: 99). While Kiarostami cannot challenge these codes within Iran's Islamic Republic, Farahmand's main criticism of his work prior to *10* is that he avoids the issue altogether, focusing instead on male protagonists and safer, 'exotic' films destined to succeed with international critics, and at festivals such as Cannes (where, in 1997, Kiarostami won the Palme d'Or for *A Taste of Cherry*).

In *10*, however, Kiarostami addresses these criticisms with deceptive cinematic intelligence. The director has shown his fondness for the road movie format in previous films such as *Life and Nothing More …* (1992), but in *10* the choice of form has special connotations. Kiarostami's choice to locate the 10 dialogues in a car is an economical means of creating visual interest from a static premise, given that the genre permits a permanently moving background. But, as Andrew points out, the car interior is also a distinctive social space, at once public and private (2005: 59–60). This would be less relevant in a male-centred film, but, in *10*, it means that the female performers can be natural, intimate and believable, while still operating within the strict dress codes. The one moment of transgression occurs in the film's penultimate sequence (the nearest thing to a climactic moment), where Mania's friend, recently separated from her boyfriend, pulls back her headscarf to reveal her shaved head: a sequence that was consequently censored when the film was screened in Iran.

The decision to film with two digital cameras, besides the democratic and pragmatic virtues of being cheap and simple, also allows for other advantageous effects. While it is speculative to say that the performances are enhanced by the director's non-presence, the fact that they are not directed or observed in any strict sense possibly helped to achieve the convincing blend of frankness and familiarity between its main performers. This would have been helped by the fact that digital cameras, unlike traditional film cameras, allow long takes such as that in the first sequence. But the invisible nature of the filmmaking in *10* also gives rise to marvellous intrusions of chance, which at once add to the film's dramatic themes and bring the film closer to the feel of a documentary, be this the unplanned meeting with an old woman on her way to the temple (a meeting which partly determines the content of ensuing sequences), or the occasional leering, chauvinist comments elicited from passing male drivers.

10 in this way achieves the apparent spontaneity that a formative generation of great film theorists – chiefly amongst them André Bazin and Siegfried Kracauer – saw as the medium's strength and purpose. Because the recorded incidents and discussions happened without the immediate intervention of a director, and seemed to have shaped the direction of the overall narrative, *10* exemplifies what Kracauer called 'the found story': a story that is 'discovered rather than contrived … part and parcel of the raw material in which it lies dormant' (Kracauer 1960: 246). It also appears to exemplify the aesthetic and philosophical goals of neorealism, as argued for by Bazin in his famous essay on Vittorio de Sica's *Umberto D*: 'to make cinema the asymptope of reality … in order that it should ultimately be life itself that becomes spectacle, in order that life might in this perfect mirror be visible poetry' (Bazin 1971: 82). Neither Bazin nor Kracauer, however, driven as they are by an essentially religious belief in the redemptive possibilities of cinematic realism, are particularly interested in the *politics* of representation, especially from the point of view of gender.

The first thing to note in this respect is that the 'found' nature of *10*, as already seen, is specifically bound up with the issue of female representation and visibility. The female protagonists of *10* remain consistently prescribed by the actions of men – whether it be a partner or husband that has left or died, or in Mania's case, a son she must repeatedly collect and deposit – and consequently the private space of the car is a kind of temporary utopia at best. But then films themselves are inherently utopian, especially when their movement across borders affects the way they are perceived. Indeed, what is so problematic about the climactic unveiling sequence, described above, is that it only 'exists' *outside* its country of origin;[2] both reflective of its place and social contexts, but non-representative of the national cinema culture from which it emerges. We might speculatively argue that the acting-out that takes place is a form of cathartic process for its protagonists, most of whom are apparently discussing their own lives and concerns; but this itself underlines the point that such catharsis is a result of the film, and the film cannot fully transcend the world it depicts. This is further suggested by the decision to end the film not with the cathartic conclusion, but with a coda that repeats an earlier sequence of Amin getting into the car, demanding to be taken to his grandmother's. Indeed, the fact that the tyrannical patriarchal figure is actually a child makes the film's reflection on gender roles and power truly unsettling.

Returning to the original point about authorship, then, the idea of a shaping creative vision is important, but only inasmuch as the ability to shape filmed footage towards poetic or rhetorical ends is a necessary one. Kiarostami's skill is reflected in the way he selects and structures the material: how each sequence is juxtaposed with another, and how the rhythm within each sequence – what to leave out, when to cut between the two actors – is honed to particular cinematic effect (note for example the elegant way that, in the penultimate scene, silence and the movement back and forth between faces allows for a crucial moment of reflection and shared understanding). This judicious use is what gives the film its understated dramatic unity and emotional power. Given the film's simplicity and generosity to its main subjects, though, attributing such effects to Kiarostami's greatness, correctly or not, seems largely beside the point.

Notes

1. See for example the *Guardian*'s 2002 poll of 'World's Best Directors', which placed Kiarostami sixth: http://film.guardian.co.uk/features/page/0,11456,1082823,00.html (accessed 26 August 2012).
2. It is worth pointing out that *10*, like most of Kiarostami's output since the late 1990s, is co-produced by the French company MK2. His work's 'nationality' is consequently a debatable issue, as his recent films have benefitted from mainly European structures of investment and distribution.

Further reading

Geoff Andrew, *10*, London: BFI, 2005.

André Bazin, '*Umberto D*: A Great Work', in *What is Cinema? Volume II*, trans. Hugh Gray, Berkeley, University of California Press, 1971, pp. 79–82.

Azadeh Farahmand, 'Perspectives on Recent (International Acclaim for) Iranian Cinema', in Richard Tapper (ed.), *The New Iranian Cinema: Politics, Representation and Identity*, London and New York, I.B. Tauris, 2002, pp. 86–108.

Siegfried Kracauer, *Theory of Film: The Redemption of Physical Reality*, Princeton, Princeton University Press, 1960.

Neil Archer

À bout de souffle/Breathless (1959)

[Country: France. Production Company: Les Productions Georges de Beauregard. Director and Screenwriter: Jean-Luc Godard (story from Francois Truffaut). Cinematographer: Raoul Coutard. Music: Martial Solal. Cast: Jean-Paul Belmondo (Michel Poiccard/Laszlo Kovacs), Jean Seberg (Patricia Franchini), Daniel Boulanger (Police Inspector Vital), Jean-Pierre Melville (Parvulesco).]

Synopsis: A small-time crook, Michel, who we initially see stealing a car in Marseille, shoots a policeman. On the run in Paris he spends time with a casual girlfriend, Patricia, an American trying to make her way in journalism. She eventually betrays him to the police and he is shot and killed while trying to flee.

In terms of story content, this film is very straightforward; we simply view the last few days in the life of a small-time criminal in Paris. But, the narrative with which we are presented is rather fragmented and disjointed; certainly it lacks the lean narrative drive and the meticulously mapped plot structure of a Hollywood production. The viewer feels she is observing something more like a simple slice of life. A scene in a small studio flat between Patricia and Michel meanders its way between the light horseplay of lovers and deeper philosophical musings with little or no sense of drama or heightened urgency. And when we reach the ending it is conclusive and yet inconclusive, things remain ambiguous and uncertain rather than finally resolved. *À bout de souffle* is, therefore, particularly in the context of the period in which it was made, a challenge to both the individual reader and the mainstream cinema establishment.[1]

Godard outlined his attitude in preparing for the film in an interview in *Cahiers du Cinema* in 1962:

> I said to myself: there has already been Bresson, we just had *Hiroshima*, a certain kind of cinema has just ended – well, then, let's put the final period to it: let's show that anything goes.
>
> (Andrew 1987: 173)

And so we have a film that uses location shooting rather than studio sets, available light rather than studio lighting, direct sound rather than dubbed sound, and allows things forbidden in mainstream cinema such as speech direct to camera. In addition, the dialogue tends towards being rambling, repetitive, and apparently inconsequential rather than tightly honed and narrative-driven; the camerawork aims to be fluid, mobile and handheld rather than steady and more obviously carefully set up; and, in the editing, jump cuts not only draw attention to the process but also result in noticeable abrupt dislocations of time or place.

Beyond these technical elements, we are presented with a film that is happy to mix aspects of various genres and depends on an almost postmodern knowingness on the part of the reader. Primarily, the film grows out of film noir but with a strong awareness of other gangster movies, and a streak of black comedy that derives from the theatre of the absurd: a moment such as that in which Patricia closes her eyes and says, 'I'm trying to shut them very hard so that everything goes black. But I can't manage to. It's never completely black,' could come straight from a play by Samuel Beckett. The actions that take place often seem rather arbitrary, so that they dislocate any sense of a smooth cause and effect chain of events; and there is a lack of any clear goal orientation with characters apparently drifting aimlessly and acting on the spur of the moment. Again, these aspects exist in relation to lived experience while at the same time commenting on the normally taken for granted aspects of mainstream film narrative. Similarly, the representation of the central female character, although in some sense giving us a traditional femme fatale portrayal also displays a new, liberated woman who is challenging gender stereotypes.

There is, in all of this, an obvious fascination with American culture and in particular Hollywood, but there is also a determination to examine modern society and scrutinise human experience, particularly in relation to emerging youth culture and traditionally accepted social values, and a joyous enthusiasm for contradicting conventional cinematic norms at every available opportunity. This is a film that sets itself up as a popular movie but contains, easily (rather than uneasily) within its knowing address to film fans, a constant stream of highbrow literary and artistic references alongside challenging philosophical thoughts.

Contained within the film is the realisation that challenging the various elements of mainstream cinema will also inevitably result in a questioning of received notions of what life is actually like. Ultimately, what this amounts to is that it is never the case outside of Hollywood-style cinema that the problems, confusions and uncertainties of life are resolved, or resolvable, in any clear-cut way. The component parts, of what maybe we can describe as the French New Wave approach as initially conceived, come together to continually undercut the reader's expectations and thereby demand thoughtful reader participation in the filmic process. It might be said that as an audience we are reminded that film can soothe and comfort in a way that promotes a lack of thought, or it can be disconcerting and uncomfortable in a way that encourages reflection and debate.

Our central characters, Michel and Patricia, are distinctive individuals and yet they are also used by Godard as in some sense representative of everyman and everywoman. Patricia is, beyond this, also the 'new woman' of the period with her cropped hair, no bra and socks. Both are presented as determinedly independent and yet, contained within that, they are also the opposite, isolated and alone. We are returned time and again to the complex, problematic concept of love and, in particular, whether it is possible to move beyond the self in this context.

Questions form the very heart of the position in which Godard places us as a reader of his film. Film-related questions, such as: Is Michel a hero, or anti-hero, or, are such terms simply not appropriate for this film? Questions about human nature, such as: What is the nature of male/female sexuality? Little questions about small details that somehow feel important, such as: Why does Michel shoot at the sun? Perhaps the main question placed before us is whether Michel has any control over what happens to him, or whether he is simply the victim of fate.

One of the most interesting things is that we never really know when either of the central characters is telling the truth, when they are themselves (whatever that might mean) and when they are playing (or trying out) a role. Where does the Bogart-inspired performance end and Michel begin? Or, is the performance Michel? To what extent is Patricia playing a series of roles? Is she no more than a succession of poses? Are we each just a series of masks? 'I want to know what's behind your face,' says Patricia to Michel; and then, a little later, 'We're looking into each other's eyes and it's useless.'

Faced with the novelist, William Faulkner's choice between grief and nothing (posed in *The Wild Palms*[2]), Michel defiantly (heroically?) says he would choose nothingness. ('Grief is idiotic; I'd choose nothingness. It's not any better, but grief, it's a compromise.') Jean-Paul Sartre's *Existentialism and Humanism* was published in 1948 and his *Being and Nothingness* in 1956. The philosophy of existentialism put forward in these works sees wo/man not as the victim of fate or destiny but as the embodiment of freedom. The wo/man who defines herself, or himself, as a victim of fate renders herself, or himself, an object. According to Sartre, 'Man is nothing else but that which he makes of himself' (1982: 28). Explaining the same point a little further, he says, 'Life is nothing until it is lived; but it is yours to make sense of, and the value of it is nothing else but the sense that you choose' (ibid: 54).

To what extent could we say Michel is the victim of fate and to what extent does he exert freedom of choice in deciding his destiny? Certainly, *À bout de souffle* could be seen as investigating this freedom problematic. But there is another concept that recurs in Godard's script and that is the idea of 'sadness', and the two seem to be linked: 'I don't know if I'm unhappy because I'm not free, or if because I'm not free I'm unhappy,' says Patricia. Is the individual at the mercy of life, or does she have the potential to assert herself even in the face of seemingly overwhelming external forces? Around this time, Godard was very clear that the key question was to do with 'engagement' with life. In an article in *Arts* in 1960, he says, 'Catholicism and Marxism, they're the same thing: it's just a matter of how you are engaged in life. *À bout de souffle* is a film about the necessity of engagement' (Andrew

1987: 168). If Godard's central character, Michel, is a hero, he is perhaps a hero of consciousness.

And, engagement within the field of consciousness is what Godard also seeks to make available to the viewer. His effort is to create and maintain a critical, analytical distance between the spectator and the action. Instinctively, he wishes to transform the spectator from a consumer of the text into a producer of the text, and thereby to question the institution of mainstream cinema. Dominant cinema attempts to fix the spectator in a comfortably escapist relationship with the text: Godard attempts to make the spectator aware of, and therefore part of, the process that is the construction of meaning. The 'action' is interrupted by captions, slogans, book covers and poster art, there are digressions and other disorientations, and in this way the apparently seamless representation of the world of the classic realist text is brought into question. According to Robert Lapsley and Michael Westlake, 'Confronted by the contradictions of the Godardian text the spectator is constantly required to work on its meanings, required to produce meaning' (1992: 195).

Godard, we might note, did not prepare a complete script in advance but wrote day by day as filming was progressing. He tended, during this period, to film chronologically with actors often not knowing until each morning's filming what lines they were to deliver. Bertolt Brecht saw traditional theatre as encouraging unconscious participation in the progression of the narrative and worked to create a thinking, engaged audience. Godard would seem to be following the same trajectory in film. Although he would later see his work before 1968 as being stamped by the mindset of the bourgeois intellectual, Godard does, it seems, want to create an audience that is asking itself, 'Why did this happen in this way?' rather than simply being driven by the desire to know, 'And what happens next?'

Having said all of this, it is true that Godard's New Wave work is focused more on individual characters than the sweep of history. Furthermore, in the context of what was to emerge in Paris in 1968 it might seem incredible that just a few years earlier there is little or no reference to contemporary French politics, despite the fact that this was a time of tension and social upheaval both at home and in the various French colonies.

Notes

1. Peter Wollen (in *Readings and Writings*, London, Verso, 1982) identified seven central differences between what has been termed counter-cinema and mainstream cinema:
   - narrative continuity is disrupted by interruptions, digressions and an absence of apparent contradictions;
   - identification is challenged, for instance by having actors directly address the audience;
   - attention is drawn to the film process as a construction of meaning;
   - spatial and temporal continuity is broken making the text composite, contradictory, and plural;
   - an open rather than closed text is created where a variety of conflicting voices makes authorial intention uncertain;
   - a collective working relationship between filmmaker and audience is created rather than Hollywood pleasure;
   - fictional representation is exposed as an illusion.
2. William Faulkner, *The Wild Palms*, London, Vintage, 2000, p. 273 ('Yes, he thought, between grief and nothing I will take grief').

Further reading

Dudley Andrew (ed.), *Breathless*, New Brunswick, NJ, Rutgers University Press, 1987.

Robert Lapsley and Michael Westlake, *Film Theory: An Introduction*, Manchester, Manchester University Press, 1992.

Jean Paul Sartre, *Existentialism and Humanism*, London, Methuen, 1982.

Colin MacCabe, *Godard: A Portrait of the Artist at Seventy*, New York, Faber & Faber, 2005.

John White

À nous la liberté/Freedom is ours (1931)

[Country: France. Production Company: Tobis. Director and screenwriter: René Clair. Cinematographer: Georges Périnal. Music: Georges Auric. Production Designer: Lazare Meerson. Editor: René Le Hénaff. Cast: Henri Marchand (Emile), Raymond Cordy (Louis), Rolla France (Jeanne), Paul Ollivier (Jeanne's uncle).]

Synopsis: Two friends, Emile (Marchand) and Louis (Cordy), plot a prison break. Only Louis escapes. He works his way from record salesman to become the wealthy owner of a phonograph factory (a clear nod to French industrialist Charles Pathé and his career trajectory). He oversees a production line, where workers are reduced to automatons. Emile eventually makes it out of prison and gets work at the factory. At first, he is unaware who the owner is, but eventually the two are reunited. Fearful of his past being exposed by former convicts from the prison, now gangsters, Louis decides to give his factory to the workers. The final scene shows the now idyllic factory – it has become completely automated, and so the workers sit and play cards. Louis and Emile leave for the freedom of the open road as the title song plays.

À nous la liberté is a landmark in the history of film comedy. Its deft use of sound and its pioneering production design combine to create a scathingly satirical critique of the dehumanising nature of industrialisation and the iniquities of the capitalist system. Filmed when the world was feeling the biting effects of the Great Depression, Clair's work now seems remarkably prescient – anticipating not just Charlie Chaplin's *Modern Times* (1936), but also Jacques Tati's similar satires of modernisation in *My Uncle* (1958) and *Playtime* (1967). By exposing the myths of mechanical efficiency that swept across Europe after the First World War, *À nous la liberté* is one of a number of films released in the early 1930s that reflect France's climate of economic austerity (*Toni* (1934), *L'Atalante* (1934)). Moreover, it proposes a radical ideological alternative – only by liberating oneself from the pressures of social and economic oppression can one find true happiness.

Like Clair's earlier silent works, *The Crazy Ray* (1924) and *An Italian Straw Hat* (1927), and his three other early sound films – *Under the Roofs of Paris* (1930), *Le Million* (1931) and *Bastille Day* (1932) – *À nous la liberté* shows an impeccable sense of comic timing. Clair would often shoot long sequences without a script, giving his actors freedom to improvise and invent. The film may seem loose, and its narrative slight, almost insubstantial (like *Le Million*, with its search for a lost lottery ticket, or best friends involved with the same girl in *Under the Roofs*), but there's an exuberance and a universality in all of Clair's films. *À nous la liberté* may be an elegant *divertissement*, but is a rich storehouse of breezy satire, recurring character types, balletic camera moves, and above all glinting humanism. Add a bit of slapstick – Emile's pursuit of Jeanne is a whir of ingenuity – and it's clear that Clair always sides with ordinary people and their simple predicaments.[1]

Clair's work is rich with sound and choreographed movement, comprising 'a window on a particular lost black and white neverworld – bouncy with melody, soaked in spring light, wistful about the conflicted relationship between serendipity and love' (Atkinson 2012). The commercial and critical success of these works cemented Clair's position in the post-silent French film industry, and in their *History of the Film*, first published in French in 1935, critics Maurice Bardèche and Robert Brasillach described him as 'the only film man in France whose work displayed both purpose and progress' (Bardèche and Brasillach 1938: 334).

It is worth remembering Clair was deeply sceptical about the arrival of sound. He feared industrial centralisation and commercial imperatives would lead to the eclipse of the dreamy surreal images of French 1920 impressionist cinema and replace the visual with incessant, banal chatter, and archly theatrical dialogue. Yet, while many of his contemporaries were content with synchronising sound to recorded dialogue, Clair saw the potential of sound to enhance a film's visual fabric, and not diminish it. He became resourceful with sound, understanding its implications and possibilities, and experimenting with music and aural effects despite the rudimentary nature of sound recording and synchronisation. His early sound films do not sacrifice visual virtuosity to sound; instead, the inclusion of popular songs, sound effects and dialogue lend a deeper texture. They are transitional films, bridging the post-silent, pre-talkie world, and sketching out the direction French cinema might wish to take.

À nous la liberté is a musical in the sense that the characters sing at various times, but the songs and the music are fully integrated into the narrative in an unobtrusive, organic way. In this sense, the term 'musical' doesn't quite capture the aural complexity of the film. It might better be described as a *film sonore* – a sound film rather than a talking film. There's very little dialogue, and aside from a few brief song sequences – including the film's catchy title track – the film relies more on the aural cues and motifs of Georges Auric's score, who had previously composed Jean Cocteau's dreamlike *Blood of a Poet* (1931). We hear odd sound effects and uses of recorded sound throughout: the sound of assembly-line mechanisation is achieved musically, and the sound of prisoners in wooden clogs becomes a rhythmic beat. Clair also riffs on the visual possibilities of sound, such as the scene when Jeanne's shoe sounds like a ringing alarm clock, or when a flower appears to start singing to Emile. These surreal juxtapositions maintain Clair's link to the visual, while simultaneously exploring the newfound capabilities of sound technology. Sound, for Clair, is not just background scene-setting or romantic accompaniment, but something that can be incorporated into the narrative to create moments of genuine astonishment. Take the scene when Emile is reproached by a prison guard with the words 'You're not working? Don't you know that.' The sentence is then completed by a teacher, telling his bored pupils that 'one must work, because work is freedom.' This is the very definition of a 'shock cut' – space and time are elided through the imaginative deployment of sound editing. The school, like the factory, and the prison, are repositories of the dominant ideology, and are governed by the technological possibilities of sound: not only are the workers dictated to via recorded messages and unseen button-pushing masters, but, as Kramer notes, the very process of reproducing sound (the phonograph) represents the immediate cause of the workers' enslavement (Kramer 1984: 144).

The Kafkaesque production design was created by Russian-born designer, Lazare Meerson, who collaborated extensively with Clair on his early sound films and became a key instigator of the look of French film in the 1930s. The factory exterior in *À nous la liberté* is replicated in full Art Deco mode. Art Deco was not just beloved by Hollywood producers – many French films of this period incorporate the stylish, uncluttered aesthetics of Deco as a shorthand symbol for modernity and urban sophistication. In *À nous la liberté* Meerson's use of strong geometric linearity and Deco's intimidating reliance upon glass and steel is integrated into both the factory and the prison sets. Meerson's enormous sets often dwarf the humans lost in them, making explicit the link between work and imprisonment.

For Clair, industrial society not only made you unhappy, but it led to a life of anonymous regimentation. The opening sequence of *À nous la liberté* takes place in a prison. We see inmates assembling toy horses while sitting behind a vast table. Clair uses a series of lateral tracking shots down tables of workers – this is dehumanising labour, but not much different from working in the phonograph factory. Indeed, the later factory scenes are deliberately framed and edited to remind us of these initial exchanges – this, says Clair, is the 'worker as prisoner' at the start of the 1930s. Such political undertones are explicit throughout: indeed, *À nous la liberté* plays out like a socialist tract, poking fun at the rich. Sometimes the symbolism can be a little heavy-handed: employees trudge through the factory like the slave class from *Metropolis* (1927), and when they eat they move their hands to their mouths in rhythmic synchronisation. Later, Louis offers Emile a large wad of cash, only for blood to drip onto the money from a cut on Emile's hand. On other occasions, scenes come complete with more acerbic satirical inflections. Nowhere is this clearer than in the finale, when Louis makes an inaugural speech at his newly mechanised factory in a strong wind. A suitcase full of money is blown open, and tuxedoed dignitaries clamour after the notes, rather than listen to the remainder of the ceremony. It's a giddily choreographed sequence, worthy of Keaton, and a reminder that Clair's characters resembled marionettes in a comic dance, with the director visibly pulling the strings, orchestrating the set-up and the punch-line.[2]

Clair's humanist streak asserts itself at the end, and *À nous la liberté* becomes an ode to friendship. The reappearance of a long-lost friend is sufficient to reawaken Louis's love of life, and, as he throws a bottle of wine through the ridiculous life-size portrait he has had commissioned, bonds of friendship are reasserted. For Clair, the end result of mechanisation is a vision of utopia that may seem naive to modern audiences, but perfectly in tune with its socially concerned times. *À nous la liberté* ends with the factory fully automated, which allows the workers (but, crucially, not the industrialists who now own it) to while away the hours singing and fishing. Emile and Louis' final gesture – handing over the factory to the workers, and then heading off into the sunset – is an anarchist one. From now on, the simplicity of the open road, with its promises of mateship and freedom, bright skies and inviting horizons, is the preferred way of life.

À nous la liberté was influential. The next year, Jean Renoir made *Boudu Saved from Drowning*, in which Michel Simon's hirsute *clochard* collided with a bourgeois world but floated off down the river as the credits rolled, happy to remain penniless, but free. Renoir returned to similar themes again in 1936, in *The Crime of Monsieur Lange*, with the workers controlling the means of production in a printing plant collective. Hollywood also took notice: Ernst Lubitsch's *Trouble in Paradise* (1932) took a satirical swipe at capitalism through a comic look at a perfume business in Paris and its wealthy owners. In 1933 Lewis Milestone directed Al Jolson's embrace of the hobo lifestyle in *Hallelujah, I'm a Bum*, romanticising the Great Depression; then came *Modern Times* (1936), which repeated some of Clair's visual gags. It isn't difficult to see why Clair's production company Tobis filed a plagiarism lawsuit against the film. Chaplin argued he had never seen Clair's film, while Clair – thoroughly embarrassed by the whole affair – simply noted that 'all of us flow from Chaplin'.

Notes

1. Liam O'Leary, '*À nous la liberté*', *Film Reference*, www.filmreference.com/Films-A-An/A-Nous-la-Libert.html (accessed 27 April 2012).
2. Edward Baron Turk has compared Clair to the eighteenth-century French dramatist, Marivaux: the works of both are characterised by verbal wit, ironic distance, easy grace, and elegance. See Edward Baron Turk, *Child of Paradise: Marcel Carné and the Golden Age of French Cinema*, Cambridge, MA, and London, Harvard University Press, pp. 29–34.

Further reading

Michael Atkinson, 'À nous la liberté', *The Criterion Collection*, www.criterion.com/current/posts/216 (accessed 27 April 2012).

Barthélemy Amengual, *René Clair*, Paris, Seghers, 1969.

Maurice Bardèche and Robert Brasillach, *History of the Film*, trans. Iris Barry, London, Allen & Unwin, 1938.

Pierre Billard, *Le Mystère René Clair*, Paris, Plon, 1998.

R. C. Dale, *The Films of René Clair*, 2 volumes, Metuchen, New Jersey, Scarecrow, 1986.

Christopher Faulkner, 'René Clair, Marcel Pagnol and the Social Dimension of Speech', *Screen*, 35 (2), 1994, pp. 157–70.

Naomi Greene, *René Clair: A Guide to References and Resources*, Boston, G. K. Hall, 1985.

Steven Philip Kramer, 'René Clair: Situation and Sensibility in *À Nous la Liberté*', *Literature/Film Quarterly* 12 (2), 1984, pp. 142–4.

Ben McCann

The Adventures of Priscilla, Queen of the Desert (1994)

[Country: Australia. Production Company: Polygram. Director and screenwriter: Stephan Elliott. Cinematographer: Brian J. Breheny. Music: Guy Cross. Editor: Sue Blainey. Costume designer: Tim Chappel and Lizzy Gardiner. Cast: Hugo Weaving (Anthony 'Tick' Belrose/Mitzi Del Bra), Guy Pearce (Adam Whitely/Felicia Jollygoodfellow), Terence Stamp (Ralph Waite/Bernadette Bassenger), Bill Hunter (Robert 'Bob' Spart), Sarah Chadwick (Marion).]

Synopsis: 'Tick'/Mitzi is contacted to perform a drag show in Alice Springs. Feeling disheartened by the boorish behaviour of his audience in Sydney, he decides to go. He contacts transsexual Bernadette about being part of the act and finds her bereaved and looking for some time away from Sydney. Loud and precocious Adam/Felicia makes up the troupe. The three travel into the outback and encounter both bigotry and acceptance along the way. They meet Bob, who decides to accompany them when his Filipino wife leaves him. In Alice Springs, Bernadette and Adam discover that not only is 'Tick' married, but that he also has a son, Benji. The film ends with 'Tick' accepting both himself and his new role of a father, Bernadette and Bob becoming even closer and Adam realising, through his new friendship with 'Tick's' son, that he can be a positive role model for someone else.

Priscilla is a camp road movie that is often critically situated as part of a 'Glitter Cycle' of 1990s Australian films. This 'cycle' includes Baz Luhrmann's 1992 film *Strictly Ballroom* and P. J. Hogan's 1994 *Muriel's Wedding*. 'Glitter Cycle' films celebrate Australian popular culture, are characterised by excess and seek to present a different representation of Australian identity than more conservative cinematic counterparts. In 'Glitter' films the outback can be liberating and even transformative for the individuals who are placed within it. Protagonists within these films reject cultural restrictions and offer a more fluid representation of gender and sexuality. These films are far removed from the hyper-masculinised drive that underpins the *Mad Max* films, for example. *Priscilla* fits all of the above criteria. It is exuberant, camp and excessive. In terms of *Priscilla's* road movie credentials, it has a journey, protagonists on a trip of self-discovery, characters who are met along the way, who reflect an aspect of the main protagonists' self-questioning and an end destination in which some degree of transformation is possible.

Drag as performance and performative is an important element within *Priscilla*. The costumes within the film are incredible creations that led to a best Costume Design Oscar in 1994. In the film, a distinction is made between the varying ways the characters use costume. For 'Tick'/Mitzi and Adam/Felicia, getting dragged up is at once a job, but also a counter-culture challenge to social restrictions. It is these two characters that parade their drag performance through the streets of small town outback Australia in order to challenge the locals and what the two protagonists perceive the local values to be. Bernadette has 'show' costumes for her drag performances, but her day-to-day dress is much more conservative. Bernadette doesn't perform a gender; she lives it. Whether it is the full-scale excess of the drag costumes or the more demure clothes that Bernadette wears, the costumes in *Priscilla* help the film to fulfil part of its agenda: to reject cultural stereotypes, archetypes and a white, middle-class, over-masculinised male agenda.

In terms of representation of gender in *Priscilla*, there has been much debate. As a film that explores the nature of identity, both how it is constructed and how fluid it can possibly be, *Priscilla* locates much of the more complex characterisation with its three male protagonists. Apart from Bob and possibly Marion, the other characters in the film are quite peripheral and function purely to allow the narrative to move forward. Outback white heterosexual males are invariably homophobic: either immediately so or after they realise that these aren't actually 'sheilas'. Adam is initially an object of desire at the 'Roo' BBQ until desire turns to aggression. The female character of Shirl voices the homophobia latent within her town, when she states, 'We have nothing here for people like you. Nothing' and is not silenced by those she is speaking for rejecting what she says as homophobic, but by the witty (and sexist) put down of Bernadette. Bernadette, Mitzi and Adam are then 'allowed' to stay in the bar in order to perform for the amused, but no less homophobic, locals. In Shirl the viewer finds a character that seeks acceptance through presenting herself as the mouthpiece of her town's bigotry. Whether she is supposed to be gay or not is not fully explored. The men in the bar enjoy Bernadette's verbal attack on Shirl. She cannot even redeem her status in the town by beating Bernadette at a drinking game. Shirl's characterisation is blunt. She is a stereotype at best and a sexist stereotype at worst.

The other female character who has come under much scrutiny is Cynthia, Bob's Filipino wife. In flashback scenes we see that she has manipulated him into marriage in order to escape a squalid life of stripping (and possibly prostitution). Cynthia is a performer, but hers is presented as the much less valid type. When Cynthia is able to liberate her ping-pong balls from a locked cupboard, she goes straight to the local bar to upstage Bernadette, Mitzi and Felicia with a sex show. When Cynthia exits the narrative, it clears the way for Bernadette and Bob. Her role as hyper-sexualised woman is representative of what Bob does not want and presents him as a victim of female manipulation. Critics of the representation of women in *Priscilla* have labelled Cynthia as not only a sexist stereotype, but also a racist stereotype.

In the brightly coloured world of *Priscilla*, Marion occupies the position of the 'good woman'. She has brought up Benji (her son with 'Tick') to reject gender- and sexuality-based parameters. She is fluid in her own sexual behaviour. Benji states that his mother had a girlfriend but also implies that she might at some point have a boyfriend too. Marion is confident and has a strong voice that rejects Tick's concerns and helps him to become a father. Marion is the instigator of the film's road trip narrative and also the voice of wisdom often found at the end of a journey. Marion is more thoroughly drawn than any of the other female characters, but her legitimacy in the narrative does seem dependent on her voicing of counter-culture views on sexual identity. If she didn't so completely share the film's rejection of cultural stereotypes and its lauding of gender flexibility, would she, too, have been relegated to the position of stereotype?

Marion gives agency to the male protagonists by providing them with a modern day quest. Initially, the quest is 'Tick'/Mitzi's, a journey towards meeting his son and becoming a father. However, as with the road movie format, any other protagonists who join the journey then embark on their own transformative journey. Figuratively and literally, Alice Springs is in the middle of nowhere and thus provides an appropriate destination in which to make a self-discovery. The three main characters' journey is from urban to outback. They encounter intolerance and tolerance on the way, and come to a greater understanding of their own roles within both their friendships and own lives. The narrative is punctuated by scenes of performance, sometimes accompanied by music and sometimes not. These performances in the desert are not just for decoration. They are visually striking, pitching the expansiveness, monotony and natural beauty of the desert against the sparkles, spangles and artificiality of the costumes. However, it is the fact that the visual differences are so stark and the attendant implication that, therefore, this environment will be most transformative for the central protagonists that creates the depth within these scenes. As with most fictional journeys, however, the journey only really ends when the newly 'transformed' character goes back to where they started, with a new understanding of themselves, their situation and the value of the home they left in the first place. As the character of Bob states, he spent '30 years wandering around the world, only to find that I was better off where I started'.

En route to Alice Springs, 'Tick', Adam and Bernadette encounter Aboriginal culture. As is the structure of a road movie, scenes that occur along the way are individual vignettes that have their own thematic purpose and do not need to be linked to each other. After the three main characters have been stranded in the outback, a young Aboriginal man who takes them to his camp and involves them in a party helps them. The 'encounter' is brief, but its significance comes from the contrast between the acceptance they find with the Aborigines and the bigotry that they have encountered from mainstream white Australia so far on their journey. *Priscilla* seems to be presenting equivalence between two marginalised groups and an almost wordless understanding of the similarities between their experiences of dominant cultures. This ideological connection is relatively unexplored, however, and has received criticism over its reductive nature.

This is a film in which both individual and national identities are explored. Australia in the 1980s came alive in terms of gay culture. Sydney, especially, flourished as a gay centre and clubs sprung up all over the city. The director, Stephan Elliott states in the DVD extras to the film that the Australian drag scene is different from that of the USA or Britain, because it is more theatrical. *Priscilla* presents an Australia that in the mid-1990s still has a burgeoning gay culture, especially in Sydney, but is home to some extremely reactionary attitudes outside the city. The fact that Australian drag culture might lean towards the more theatrical and excessive allows for even more contrasts to be made with small town attitudes in outback Australia. These attitudes are perhaps most brutally expressed in the graffiti that is daubed on the bus, Priscilla. The three protagonists exit their hotel to find 'Aids fuckers go home' painted down the bus's side.

Priscilla's casting is an essential element within its overall success. For Guy Pearce the film constituted his breakout film after years acting in the Australian soap *Neighbours*. Pearce's Felicia is uber-camp and the film's character most likely to indulge in excess. Felicia is a far cry from the dull and reliable Mike in *Neighbours*. Pearce effectively shattered his association with Mike through the high camp of his performance as Felicia. Hugo Weaving had worked with Stephan Elliott before and was a trusted collaborator for the director. His portrayal of Tick/Mitzi effectively presents a character who is about to encounter a new identity. Terence Stamp's portrayal of Bernadette is a subtle and dignified portrait of a 'woman' recuperating her sense of optimism.

In terms of the visual spectacle of *Priscilla*, the impact is never greater than when the three drag queens perform in the desert. The scale and grandeur of the setting, evoking not only road movies of the past, but also more epic Westerns, is a fitting stage for the visual excesses of the drag costumes the characters wear. When, at the end of the film, Mitzi and Bernadette help Felicia to fulfil 'her' lifelong ambition of climbing to the top of King's Canyon in full drag, the full impact of placing drag queens in the outback is realised. As an iconic counter-culture moment, this scene is very powerful. The moment has an Abba soundtrack and, to use Bernadette's initial 'reading' of Adam's dream, presents 'a cock, on a rock, in a frock'. It is camp spectacle, but it is also an exuberant finale to a journey right to the heart of 1990s Australian culture and an investigation of the conflicting values that can be found within it.

Further reading

Jack Babuscio, 'Camp and the Gay Sensibility', in Harry Benshoff and Sean Griffin (eds), *Queer Cinema: the Film Reader*, London and New York, Routledge, 2004, pp. 121–36.

Philip Brophy, *The Adventures of Priscilla, Queen of the Desert [Australian Screen Classics]*, Strawberry Hills, Currency Press, 2008.

Ian Craven (ed.), *Australian Cinema in the 1990s*, London & New York, Routledge, 2000.

Kelly Farrell, '(Foot)Ball Gowns: Masculinities, Sexualities and the Politics of Performance', *Journal of Australian Studies*, 23 (63), 1999, pp. 157–64.

Emily Rustin, 'Romance and Sensation in the "Glitter Cycle", in Ian Craven (ed.) *Australian Cinema in the 1990s*, New York, Frank Cass Publishers, 2001, pp. 131–48.

Tanya Jones

Aguirre, der Zorn Gottes/Aguirre, Wrath of God (1972)

[Country: West Germany. Production Company: Werner Herzog Filmproduktion. Director and screenwriter: Werner Herzog. Cinematographer: Thomas Mauch. Music: Popol Vuh. Cast: Klaus Kinski (Don Lope de Aguirre), Ruy Guerra (Don Pedro de Ursua), Del Negro (Brother Gaspar de Carvajal), Helena Rojo (Inez), Cecilia Rivera (Flores), Peter Berling (Don Fernando de Guzman), Daniel Ades (Perucho), Armando Polanah (Armando), Edward Roland (Okello).]

Synopsis: Faced with difficult conditions, an expedition in search of the (mythical) city of El Dorado under Gonzalo Pizarro in 1560 sends an advanced party down the Amazon on rafts. A power struggle quickly develops between the leader of this group, Ursua, and his second-in-command, Aguirre. Describing himself as 'the wrath of God' and employing a series of increasingly brutal strategies, Aguirre, usurps authority and leads the small band on towards total destruction.

Why does Aguirre suggest he should be seen as 'the wrath of God' (and why does Herzog choose this as the title for his film)? Is it that Aguirre is an agent of God, bringing the anger of an Old Testament God down on his avaricious people? Is it that, more than an agent, he actually is a god on earth, not a Christ-like persuasive god but a violent god who enforces his will? ('The earth I walk upon sees me and quakes,' he claims.) Certainly, Aguirre destroys without mercy those who oppose him and commands obedience through fear. But, he comes to this position during the course of the film; we see him journeying towards this vision of himself.

For a character commonly seen as mad he is actually more reasoned in his approach than anyone else in the expedition. From the outset because he is not driven by either religious fervour or financial greed he knows the score: 'No-one can get down that river alive'. From the beginning he is marked out by Herzog as different to the other leaders of the expedition: in two-shots there is always a distance between him and either Ursua or Pizarro; when they look towards him he looks away; when they look off into the distance and make some grand statement he scrutinises them with a piercing stare; when they gather the men and make a speech we cut to Aguirre who is somewhere else both physically and mentally. He knows, and states within the first few minutes of the film, that 'We're all going to go under'. Later, after he has effectively become leader of the group, he has the priest, Brother Gaspar de Carvajal, read a statement of their position in which he says, 'We have decided to put an end to the quirks of fate'. His decision it seems is to embrace destiny, to throw himself headlong into his fate in such a way that he is no longer at the mercy of fate; to become the wrath of God in order that he should no longer be at the mercy of that terrible anger. As a god he 'despises' mere mortals. 'My men measure riches in gold', he says. 'It is more. It is power and fame. I despise them for it.' For him (maybe) his journey, that from an apparently rational standpoint would seem to have been a descent ever further into delusion and madness, has been a success, a statement of the capability of man to attain transcendence, because for him it has never been about gold but instead has always been about leaving your mark on history.[1]

On the one hand, of course, as we view the film Aguirre remains a madman whose delusion defies reason and becomes all the more outrageous as the inevitability of the doom that will engulf the group becomes ever more obvious. On the other hand, he is the ultimate rebel against authority, refusing to accept the power of the leader of the small advanced party, Don Pedro de Ursua, or of the leader of the expedition, Pizarro, or, even, of the Spanish king, Philip II. As a rebel he is Promethean, even Satanic, a bringer of fire and an embodiment of evil, with echoes of Friedrich Nietzsche's (or a Nazi version of Nietzsche's) Übermensch, or superman. For Nietzsche the most basic human drive was the will to power embodied most spectacularly in individuals who transcended common social norms. Aguirre, in this sense, is the tragic hero who succeeds in creating meaning out of the meaninglessness of existence. He is not without rationality ('What is a throne but a plank of wood covered with velvet?') or gentleness (see him with his daughter, Flores[2]), but as Übermensch he exerts power over nobody so strongly as over himself.

Aguirre sees himself as the very essence of treachery: 'I am the great traitor. There can be no greater!' Ironically, although he calls himself the wrath of God, by those who believe absolutely in the established order of mid-sixteenth-century Christian society such as Ursua he would be viewed as Satan-like in his rebellion against God's order. In refusing to accept the authority of the King of Spain he is, in terms of the dominant beliefs of the age, rebelling against God's authority on earth; that is, he is in open revolt against the person who 'truly' is God's agent on earth.

And, the levels of irony, paradox and complexity need to be extended still further. Although there was an actual historical figure called Don Lope de Aguirre who was a conquistador and did seize control of an expedition down the Amazon and did renounce allegiance to the Spanish throne, despite the grandeur of his gesture, the audacity of his rebellion and the scope of his manic vision, this Aguirre was still lost in the mists of the past until Herzog decided to make a film about him.[3] However big your efforts might be to make your mark, to forge a portion of history in your own image, time and the passage of time will reduce your attempts to nothing. Until that is, perhaps, somebody else with the drive to create meaning out of the meaninglessness of existence comes along and brings about your resurrection.

The film was shot on location in the jungles of Peru with a cast and crew of 500 working in difficult conditions that might be gauged by the shots of a river in spate that are shown in some scenes. The drive and determination of Herzog (and Kinski[4]) that might be described as manic, succeed in bringing the vision into being. In working in dangerous, isolated regions, rejecting not only the studio but also exotic but safe locations, Herzog turns the process itself of filming into a physically dangerous journey/quest/search. According to him, 'Put under extreme pressure, people give you many more insights into their innermost being and tell us about who we really are'.[5]

Visually, we are given a beautiful and haunting film. The opening sequence, for example, shows in extreme long shot what appears to be simply the imposing grandeur of a mountain scene. Slowly we become aware of the heavily burdened expedition snaking its way step-by-step down the side of this vast mountain. Man is immediately positioned as minute, ant-like against the vast scale of the natural world. And then, when we move in closer, the handheld camera brings out the full clumsiness of human movement. Maybe from a distance the rivulet flow of a train of people down this majestic mountain has its own beauty, but move closer and the reality of the use and abuse of slaves, for example, becomes unavoidable. At several points the long-handled, double-axe-bladed pike being carried by a soldier sways above the people like a cross; at other moments iron chains on the Indian porters clank heavily across the screen. With a depth of symbolism again reaching into the religious context and the social order, one native porter is shown carrying a massive cannon wheel on his back. And finally, the insanity of it all becomes apparent as we realise there are also two sedan chairs making their precarious passage down this Andean mountainside.

The film may be based on the journal of the real Gaspar de Carvajal, who accompanied an expedition to Peru under Gonzalo Pizarro (half-brother of the brutal Francisco Pizarro who conquered the Incas), but it is a fiction conflating the story of the historical Aguirre with de Carvajal's account of a different expedition. The search for a legendary city and the gold it supposedly contains provides a classic scenario for the quest structure found at the heart of so many narratives. In these tales, while the supposed 'El Dorado' proves to be illusory the journey itself is full of significance in what it suggests about the nature of the human experience.

In one sense, the whole history of expansionist, imperialist Germany, as well as Spain, is embodied in this journey. More precisely, it is possible to read the film as an allegory of what happened to Germany under Hitler and fascism. Like Hitler, Aguirre announces at one point, 'I don't turn back', and the way in which he is increasingly isolated at the end might at some level recall Hitler's last days. Certainly, for the post-war generation of Germans in the early 1970s, dealing with the legacy of the Second World War, the comparisons would have been apparent. But, Aguirre also consciously identifies himself with other conquerors from the past such as Cortes. The whole history of European 'civilisation' might be seen to be embodied in this journey. As we move out and away from 'civilisation', it is not only the nature of the 'primitive' that comes into view but also the essence of 'civilisation'. There is man's determination to conquer (not only others but also the natural world), man's belief in his own godlike strength, the greed of man, the ambition of man, the brutality of man, the treachery of man and, ultimately, the utter madness of man. There is death, disease, murder, execution and the destruction of families. There are also men stranded, trapped, irresistibly carried forward in a direction not necessarily of their choosing, and going round in circles.

In the end, to read this film on any single level is to fail to appreciate the depth of the examination of the human condition that is being undertaken. This is an investigation into the heart of man. The physical journey may be downriver towards the sea but the psychological journey mirrors Marlow's upriver in the novella, *The Heart of Darkness*, and Willard's (Martin Sheen) in the film *Apocalypse Now*.[6] Marlow and Willard are narrators who take us on a journey towards a meeting with a character (called Kurtz in both the novella and the film) who has driven himself on into megalomania, but here we follow the Kurtz-like character, Aguirre, more directly. Still, there is a narrator, Brother Gaspar, who is in many ways the classic model of an unreliable narrator. Like Aguirre, Gaspar sees himself as an agent of God on earth but also perhaps as something of a god in himself. His opening words tell us that on Christmas Day 1560 he read Mass and then 'we descended through the clouds'. Faced by a native who fails to understand the concept of the word of God being contained in a book, Gaspar's response is to run him through with his sword and note in his journal that, 'These savages are hard to convert'. He brings with him, it seems, not the love of God but the wrath of God; and when Aguirre takes control, Gaspar makes clear that the historical position of the Church 'was always on the side of the strong'.

Notes

1. See Gregory A. Waller, '*Aguirre, Wrath of God*: History, Theater, and the Camera', *South Atlantic Review*, Vol. 46, No. 2, May 1981, pp. 55–69.
2. At one point he offers Flores a slow loris he has found. The short scene seems odd, and unrelated to the narrative, unless we reflect on how he describes this creature to his daughter: 'This animal sleeps its whole life away. It is never really awake'.
3. In relation to *Aguirre* and the nature of history and truth, and the creation of narratives of the past, see Luisela Alvaray, 'Filming the Discovery of America: How and Whose History is Being Told', *Film-Historia*, Vol. 5, No. 1, 1995, pp. 35–44.
4. Gilberto Perez ('Film in Review: Bad Boys – Klaus Kinski and Werner Herzog', *The Yale Review*, Vol. 88, Issue 2, April 2000, pp. 185–94) sees the director and the actor as 'two versions of the same madness, barely under control' (p. 193).
5. Werner Herzog and Paul Cronin, *Herzog on Herzog*, London, Macmillan, 2002, p. 19.
6. See Beate West-Leuer, 'Film Essay Colonial Aggression and Collective Aggressor Trauma', *The International Journal of Psychoanalysis*, Vol. 90, Issue 5, Oct 2009, pp. 1157–68.

Further reading

Cynthia L. Stone, 'Aguirre Goes to the Movies: Twentieth-Century Visions of Colonial-Era "Relaciones"', *Chasqui: revista de literatura latinoamericana*, Vol. 34, No. 2, 2005, pp. 24–35.

John White

Ai no corrida/L'empire des sens/In the Realm of the Senses (1976)

[Country: Japan, France. Production Company: Argos Films, Oshima Productions, Shibata Organisation. Director: Nagisa Ōshima. Producer: Anatole Dauman. Screenwriter: Nagisa Ōshima. Cinematographer: Hideo Itoh. Music: Minoru Miki. Editors: Patrick Sauvion, Keiichi Uraoka. Cast: Tatsuya Itoh (Kichizō Ishida), Eiko Matsuda (Sada Abe), Aoi Nakajima (Toku), Meika Seri (Matsuko), Kanae Kobayashi (Old Geisha Kikiryū), Yasuko Matsui (Tagawa Inn Manager), Taiji Tonoyama (Old Beggar), Kyōji Kokonoe (Teacher Ōmiya).]

Synopsis: Based on a well-known high-profile criminal case from 1936, *In the Realm of the Senses* is a biopic on Sada Abe, a geisha-cum-courtesan, and her lecherous relationship with Kichizō Ishida, the owner of an inn she worked for as a maid. The two engaged in a prurient and obsessive bond where they isolated themselves for six days to partake in uninterrupted intercourse that came to an end with Kichizō's death from asphyxiation. The infatuated Abe severed her partner's penis, which is where the film concludes, but her story continued as she was arrested a few days later with Kichizō's genitals in her bag.

Erotic asphyxiation, sitophilia, rape, paedophilia and castration: when the sexual intimations and intimidations put on view in *In the Realm of the Senses* are listed out of context, the perverse acts may be mistaken for scenes from an unruly hardcore and frankly depraved pornographic feature. The reading may not be too far from the truth.

Yet, what sets aside Ōshima's film is its radical treatment of its subject matter and the ways it sparked debates around one question the film anchored as its pivot – can sex ever be considered to have a place amongst the pantheon of high art? Ever since the film's release, the question has laid the foundation upon where much of its critical analysis has hinged: the candid exhibition of real sex and penetration provoked a reconsideration of realism in cinema; its subversion of codes of both pornography and cinema demanded analysis that accommodated gender politics, psychoanalysis and spectatorship; and, finally, the numerous battles with state control in different national contexts provoked vital questions on the validity of censorship. Suffice to say, *In the Realm of the Senses* titillated critical issues far beyond any porn film of customary standards.

Sada Abe's unique life has become a source of inspiration for novels, plays and films, including Noboru Tanaka's *A Woman Called Abe Sada* (1975), Nobuhiko Ōbayashi's more recent *Sada* (1998) and Teruo Ishii's docudrama *Love and Crime* (1969). Although all drawn from the same real-life story of overdriven passion, *In the Realm of the Senses* stood out for its desire to foster an affinity with direct reality by cultivating a mode of realism where representation became presentation and re-enactment was abandoned for enactment. The two main actors who performed Kichizō Ishida and Sada Abe engaged in real and unadulterated sex in front of camera and crew, marking previously uncharted territory for the portrayal of sex in narrative cinema. Nikkatsu action film star Tatsuya Itoh (Kichi) and Eiko Matsuda (Sada), whose previous credentials included participation in Shūji Terayama's avant-garde theatre troupe Tenjō Sajiki, together joined forces to fulfil Ōshima's aspiration to shoot real sex, something the director had contemplated since his third feature *Sun's Burial* (1960). With *In the Realm of the Senses*, portrayals of sex reached a new pinnacle regarding realism in the cinematic medium.

Resonating with the rise of feminism in the 1970s for film studies and beyond, the film's narrative and representational politics called out to be discussed in this context. The pleasures Sada attained from sex displayed on-screen, on the one hand, has been celebrated for radically subverting gender representations and eschewing the privilege usually subscribed to the masculine gaze. On the other hand, some readings have asserted the prevailing presence of phallocentrism, suggesting Sada's final act to be an acknowledgement of her 'lack' and a display of her dependence on the male gender (Lehman 1987;

Allsop 2004; Standish 2007). The film was taken up by the emerging wave of psychoanalysis in film studies, with the climactic moments becoming a literal presentation of the allegory of castration. Nonetheless, such readings have also been turned on their head as the threatened loss could imply a remodelling of Jacques Lacan's 'lack' into Sada Abe's 'gain' (Williams 2008). The androcentrism of fetishism was substituted with a phallic obsession and the film's play on voyeurism, another recurrent feature in psychoanalytic film studies, similarly disavowed standard templates. In the film's unusual demonstration of scopophilia, the all-female voyeurs are acknowledged by the subjects of their gaze and encouraged to join by Sada and Kichi, who are visibly aroused in response to being watched (Sharp 2008). In extension, the position of the film's spectators has also been explored in relation to Bertolt Brecht's theories of distanciation that were in critical vogue in the 1970s, an approach where the audience is encouraged to recognise their position as spectators (Heath 1977; Polan 1983; Mellen 2004; Richie 2009). In the case of *In the Realm of the Senses*, Ōshima's on-screen voyeurs and his use of repetition, high-angle shots and withdrawn camera positions achieves this. On the other hand, the film's persistence on accounting for the senses has probed some to argue against a Brechtian reading, suggesting the invitations to join the sex for the on-screen voyeurs also extend to the film's audience (Turim 1998; Williams 2008; Nagib 2011). Described as a cocoon by actor Tatsuya Itoh, the closed universe of the inn room where much of the film is set strips the film bare to encourage such range in the spectrum of interpretations. The formal rigour of Hideo Itoh's camerawork and compositional balance in Jūshō Toda's production design equally support this. Any overt exploration of politics is subdued, limited to an invocation of the rise of imperialism in the 1930s in the shape of minor hints – one, a celebrated scene where Kichi walks unperturbed against a wave of marching soldiers and, the other, the setting of the year 1936 recalling a failed military coup on 26 February of the same year. Politics, instead, is positioned in the film's relationship it begets with its audience.

A calculated and explicit attack on censorship, *In the Realm of the Senses* provoked state responses of unprecedented measures. When we assemble the reactions across countries for the film's release in theatres and home-movie formats, we are provided with insights into the politics of culture in various guises. Irrespective of his longstanding troubles with the Japanese censors Eirin, the following indictments must have felt merciless for Ōshima: a print was confiscated by customs before its North American premiere at the New York Film Festival in 1976; a print was also impounded in Germany, but screened uncut a year later; the uncut version only screened in Britain for the first time in 2011; and Japanese audiences have yet to see the film uncensored. Furthermore, Ōshima faced obscenity charges in Japan for the publication of the script that included stills photographed on set, from which he was only acquitted in 1982 (Cather 2012). In the proceedings and his essay 'Theory of Experimental Pornographic Film' (1976), Ōshima decried the concept of obscenity itself as indefinable and ultimately meaningless especially when, such as in the case of his own film, taboos are unconditionally liberated and all expressions of desire are embraced.

It was the lifting of censorship regulations in France, however, that had ultimately encouraged the film to be made in the first place. A transnational, even transcontinental, collaboration began when the adventurous French producer Anatole Dauman, capitalising on the changes in law, came up with the idea to offer Ōshima unrestrained freedom to shoot a sex film. As one of the producers for Alain Resnais' *Hiroshima Mon Amour* (1959) that was partially shot in Japan, his partnership with Ōshima became one of the many transnational projects Dauman undertook with Japanese filmmakers that continued with the equally erotic *Fruits of Passion* (1981) by Shūji Terayama. Shot in Japan, the footage of *In the Realm of the Senses* was sent unprocessed to France where the negatives were developed and the film was edited. The film's production and reception history begs for it to be discussed in the context of transnational cinema as a collaboration born out of more than monetary necessities.

Indeed financial and state considerations were not the only traits that marked the transnationality of *In the Realm of the Senses*. A close analysis suggests the film bridged across East–West binaries to accumulate an array of influences in the shaping of the film. The portrayals of sex in European culture, especially the candid depictions of sex with political subtext seen in the literature of Georges Bataille

(*The Story of the Eye*) and Marquis de Sade (*120 Days of Sodom*), are indisputable stimuli for the film. More contemporarily, Europe was in the process of undergoing a renaissance in the serious treatment of sex on film, with Dušan Makavejev's *WR: Mysteries of the Organism* (1971), Bernardo Bertolucci's *Last Tango in Paris* (1972), and Pier Paolo Pasolini's adaptation of de Sade, *Salò, or the 120 Days of Sodom* (1975) setting high standards. *In the Realm of the Senses*, nonetheless, was also undoubtedly and inescapably a Japanese film. Despite purporting a disdain for his country's cinema – 'My hatred of Japanese film includes absolutely all of it' (Ōshima 1970) – Ōshima sought inspiration from pink cinema, Japan's developing soft-core film industry that had begun spawning new talents in filmmaking. Ōshima invited director and producer Kōji Wakamatsu, a rebel even within pink cinema, to take charge of the film as executive producer. Wakamatsu also brought together luminaries from his own industry, such as cinematographer Hideo Itoh and director Yōichi Sai in an early role as an assistant. Sharing his admiration for Nikkatsu studio's directors Tatsumi Kumashiro and Noboru Tanaka who made soft-core flicks that were dubbed *roman porno*, Ōshima paid homage by casting Nikkatsu actresses Aoi Nakajima and Meika Seri as geishas. Beyond cinema, moreover, Ōshima drew from Japan's past prior to modernisation in the Meiji period where uninhibited sex was practiced and explored artistically, a praxis that was later suppressed under pressures to assimilate to foreign standards. Specifically, the aesthetic tradition of *shunga* and *ukiyo-e* prints of the Edo period imparted substantial influence on the film's visual composition and forthright display of lust, as discerned more recently by scholars attuned to developments in the academic field of intermediality (Williams 2008; Nagib 2011). The mixing of influences for the film's title similarly induced a range of resonations: the literal translation of the Japanese title, *Ai no Corrida*, is 'love's bullfight', which borrows the Spanish term *corrida*; *L'Empire des Sens* (Empire of Senses), the French title, appropriates and challenges Roland Barthes' *L'Empire des signes* (Empire of Signs, 1970) where, in a post-structuralist semiotic reading of Japan as a 'fictive nation', Barthes gave signs primacy over what they may signify; and the English title, *In the Realm of the Senses*, offers a less Orientalist connotation with the replacement of 'empire' with 'realm'.

Although Ōshima has been described as an anti-auteur for his resistance to repetition throughout his filmmaking practice, the film, in many ways, signalled a turning point in the trajectory of his career. From there on, Ōshima would carry on his collaboration with producer Dauman to make *Empire of Passion* (1978) and continued to take part in international co-productions until *Taboo* (1999) took him back to Shōchiku studios where he had started his career in film. Having dealt with the immediate present for the most part, his subsequent films after *In the Realm of the Senses* began to engage with Japan's feudal past. Ōshima, however, never let go of his interest in different shades of sexuality and stories of crime and punishment, a career-long obsession that reached an apex with the film. *In the Realm of the Senses* remains his most profound achievement and still continues to dumbfound audiences and critics for its uninhibited radicalism.

Further reading

Samara Lea Allsop, '*Ai No Corrida: In The Realm Of The Senses*', in Justin Bowyer (ed.), *The Cinema of Japan and Korea*, London, Wallflower, 2004, pp. 103–9.

Kirsten Cather, 'A Picture's Worth a Thousand Words: *In the Realm of the Senses* (1976–1982)', in *The Art of Censorship in Postwar Japan*, Honolulu, University of Hawaii Press, 2012, pp. 197–220.

Stephen Heath, 'The Question Oshima', *Wide Angle*, Vol. 2, No. 1, 1977, pp. 49–57.

Peter Lehman, 'Oshima: The avant-garde artist without an avant-garde style', *Wide Angle*, Vol. 9, No. 2, 1987, pp. 18–31.

Christine Marran, 'Cinematic Sexualities: The Two Faces of Abe Sada in Japanese "Poruno" Film' *Asian Cinema*, Vol. 8, No. 2, 1996/97, pp. 81–90.

Joan Mellen, *In the Realm of Senses*, London, BFI, 2004.

Lúcia Nagib, '*The Realm of the Senses*, The Ethical Imperative and the Politics of Pleasure', *World Cinema and the Ethics of Realism*, New York; London, Continuum, 2011.

Nagisa Ōshima, 'Interview', *Cahiers du cinéma*, 218, March, 1970, pp. 30–4.
Nagisa Ōshima, *Cinema, Censorship and the State: The Writings of Nagisa Oshima*, ed. Annette Michelson, trans. Dawn Lawson, Cambridge, MA, 1992.
Dana Polan, 'Politics as Process in Three Films by Nagisa Oshima,' *Film Criticism*, Vol. 8, No. 1, Fall, 1983, pp. 33–41.
Donald Richie, '*In the Realm of the Senses*: Some Notes on Oshima and Pornography', *Criterion*, 30 April 2009, www.criterion.com/current/posts/1108-in-the-realm-of-the-senses-some-notes-on-oshima-and-pornography (accessed 8 October 2013). Originally published in *Neppu*, December 2006.
Jasper Sharp, *Behind the Pink Curtain: The Complete History of Japanese Sex Cinema*, Surrey, FAB Press, 2008.
Isolde Standish, 'Transgression and the Politics of Porn: Ōshima Nagisa's *In the Realm of the Sense* (1976)', in Alastair Philips and Julian Stringer (eds), *Japanese Cinema: Texts and Contexts*, New York and London, Routledge, 2007, pp. 217–28.
Maureen Turim, *The Films of Oshima Nagisa: Images of a Japanese Iconoclast*, Berkeley, CA and London, University of California Press, 1998.
Linda Williams, 'Hard-Core Eroticism: *In the Realm of the Senses* (1976)', in *Screening Sex*, Durham, NC, Duke University Press, 2008.

Julian Ross

Alexander Nevsky (1938)

[Country: USSR. Production Company: Mosfilm. Director: Sergei Eisenstein. Screenwriters: Sergei Eisenstein and Pyotr Pavlenko. Cinematographer: Eduard Tisse. Music: Sergei Prokofiev. Cast: Nikolai Cherkasov (Alexander Nevsky), Nikolai Okhlopkov (Vasili), Andrei Abrikosov (Gavrilo).]

Synopsis: The Teutonic Knights invade the city of Pskov and massacre its population. In the face of resistance, Nevsky rallies the common people of Novgorod and in a decisive Battle of the Ice, they defeat the enemy and retake the city.

The USSR of the 1920s had witnessed an explosion of creativity in the visual arts. The heady rush to find new Soviet forms of creative expression with a social function (the philosophy of constructivism) led to thrilling cinematic experimentation. Directors such as Vsevelod Pudovkin and Dziga Vertov had exposed the Hollywood style of continuity editing as just one bourgeois method of film construction. Sergei Eisenstein had been the most prominent of these Soviet filmmakers. His mastery of intellectual montage had led to international approval for *Battleship Potemkin* (1925) for its rhythm, use of juxtaposition and overall impact.

Eisenstein had also insisted on limiting the role of the individual at the centre of narrative; instead favouring the masses as united in proletarian heroism. For this, he utilised typage, a style that rejected 'acting' in favour of casting an appropriate-looking figure to play a particular part. The emotional impact of 'performance' was instead created through the dynamics of editing. Eisenstein's strong sense of compositional geometry and use of the shocking image were also key techniques. Scenes such as the horse hung from a rising bridge in *October* (1928), or the runaway pram amid Tsarist brutality in *Battleship Potemkin* are bold, memorable and terrifying. These films dripped with political intent in both form and content.

By 1938, the age of experimentation was over. Joseph Stalin's cult of personality was firmly established and the stylistic experimentation of the 1920s had been banned. All Soviet filmmaking was overseen by Boris Shumyatsky, who answered directly to Stalin. Shumyatsky's 'Soviet Hollywood' insisted on a doctrine of socialist realism: no more formalist adventures, only depictions of idealised socialist goals starring positive, proletarian heroes.

The result was a period of light comedies and 'tractor musicals' – entertainment that was ideologically Marxist and unchallenging to comprehend. Bureaucratic control of film production strangled invention, projects were expensively shelved and making the wrong film could result in executions. 'Dissident' thinkers (essentially, anyone who thought differently from the paranoid and capricious Stalin) could expect life to be made difficult, leading perhaps to imprisonment or death.[1] Eisenstein was singled out for attack and had to admit to 'past mistakes'. Perhaps inevitably in this dangerous era, Shumayatsky himself was executed in 1938.

By the time he came to make *Alexander Nevsky*, Eisenstein had not been able to complete a film for nine years. However, if the title implies a break from Eisenstein's earlier style, suggesting a central figure who dominates the action, *Alexander Nevsky* is far from a straight capitulation to the socialist realist mould.

The film's events are set in thirteenth-century Russia. Already under the control of the Mongols, there is a fresh threat from Germany: the Teutonic Knights. After a brutal sacking of the city of Pskov, the citizens of Novgorod ask the eponymous hero to come to their aid. Nevsky makes the symbolic decision to fight the invaders on the frozen Lake Peipus, rather than on Russian soil. After a bloody battle, the German knights are defeated. They retreat and the ice breaks under the combined weight of their heavy armour, drowning the defeated army. The metonymy for a strong Russia united behind a 'divine' leader facing what seemed an imminent Nazi invasion is unsubtle. In 1938, this threat was very real, so the account of a successful rout of a seemingly invincible foreign army is unmistakable propaganda.

At this time, Stalin had taken to approving films concerning the daring, though often cruel, acts of Tsars and royalists from Russia's past. Official endorsement was given for films of the lives of Peter the Great or Eisenstein's later *Ivan the Terrible*. Clearly, Stalin was casting himself in the role of the benign leader, faced with the hard choice of imposing tyranny for the greater good. The figure of Nevsky is therefore problematic for the modern viewer. Unlike the following *Ivan the Terrible* films where a dictatorial central figure is presented warts and all, Nevsky is the Premier's uncritical stand-in.

Eisenstein bolsters Nevsky's nobility with use of Christian symbolism: he is first seen among fishermen, for example, and his banishment of the Novgorod wealthy echoes Christ's expulsion of the temple money lenders (O'Mahony 2008: 168). Christian imagery occurs throughout the work of the avowedly anti-religious Eisenstein, proving ripe for compositional plunder when required by the lapsed Catholic director seeking dramatic effect. His films are littered with examples of borrowed church iconography used to emphasise grandness in composition or build on emotional impact. Contemporary Soviet images of its leaders already utilised quasi-religious symbolism to represent both Lenin and Stalin. Nevsky, frequently framed in low angle and given to wise proclamations, is cast as leader, saviour and saint – exactly the representation desired by Stalin for himself.

However, religion itself is presented as destructive and treacherous. The monks are sinister and self-serving, and Eisenstein mischievously includes swastikas among the devout symbolism on the costumes of some of the German priests, whose actions are inhuman and cruel. Conversely, while speechifying to backdrops of churches, the Russians speak of their land and humanity, not the will of God. Their visible faces contrast with the robotic, alarmingly helmeted invading army. The usual semiotic convention is reversed by having the heroic characters clothed in black versus the villainous oppressors in white. There is sense in this: the Russians are 'of the earth', opposed to the Catholic enemy, the bringers of 'salvation' through death.

The ordinary people are thus rendered heroic and defined by their earthiness, appropriate for the communist ideal of collective labour. Eisenstein opens the film with shots of Russian skulls scattered across the ground from a previous battle. Later, the Russian soldiers 'seem to be springing out of the land itself' (Scherr 2001: 221) when roused to combat. Eisenstein frequently frames the soldiers low in the shot, often allowing the sky to dominate the composition, emphasising their connection to the land.

Conversely, as a purely symbolic figure of great courage, Nevsky himself is never presented with any depth, being reduced to a series of gestures, valiant proclamations and little else. He never fears defeat nor experiences anything like a dramatic setback throughout the entire film, thus rendering him a remote figure. Similarly, the Teutonic Knights are never presented with any greater detail than manifest villainy.

If the film's hero is too remote and the villains too machine-like, then it is the proletariat who bring the film to life. All the human interaction is left to the ordinary soldiers and peasants. The friendly rivalry between Vasili and Gavrilo and the sacrifice of Ignat give the film its human face and hark back to the contrast between the crudely drawn ruling class and the naturalistic portrayal of the proletariat from Eisenstein's silent period. The result is a film whose warmth comes largely from the scenes where the title character is absent (Scherr 2001: 213), recalling a link to Eisenstein's 1920s direction of performance and his earlier use of typage.

Alexander Nevsky is justly lauded for its organisation of spectacle during the magnificent battle on the ice sequence. The rhythmic cutting between long shots and close-ups, the dynamic composition and the mobile camera carry what is largely 37 minutes of dialogue-free scrapping. If the battle seems less than astonishing to the contemporary viewer, it is because Eisenstein's technique has been imitated endlessly ever since. Random examples range from Orson Welles' *Chimes at Midnight* (1966) to Miike Takashi's *13 Assassins* (2010).

What is less imitated is Eisenstein's approach to continuity. The Russian army seems to face a charging enemy that is shot from multiple angles, rather than using the more logical consistency of shot–reverse shot so the Germans appear to make an omnidirectional assault. What Eisenstein loses in temporal logic, he gains in dramatic impact.

The sacking of Pskov is the film's most brutal sequence and is reminiscent of Eisenstein's climax to his debut film *Strike* (1925) in its shock effect. The contrast between the defeated but dignified Russian citizens and the malicious Teutonic Knights is emphasised by the invaders' dehumanising helmets and sinister stillness. Eisenstein frames them in low angle, contrasting with their terrified prisoners. The sequence builds to one of cinema's most awful atrocities as naked children are thrown onto a burning pyre.

Discussing Eisenstein's 'socialist realism' period, the critic David Bordwell considers how this sequence is structured as 'always establishing a set of elements and then rearranging them, eliminating some and introducing others, putting some in the background while promoting others' (in Scherr 2001: 25). The consequence for the spectator is alarming as characters seem to appear out of nowhere. Ever the formalist, Eisenstein's brutal editing underscores the violence of the sequence using the axial cut, the 'cutting in or back straight along the lens axis' (ibid: 15–16) instead of the more conventional edit to an angle greater than 30 degrees away, or a forward or backward track or zoom. When using this technique, the actors tend to remain stationary within a static frame while Eisenstein relies on the sudden cuts, rather than character or camera movement to create action through movement. The result of this is startling, creating a diegetic space that is dependent entirely on Eisenstein's dogmatic organisation of montage.

Likewise, the film's approach to the soundtrack is extraordinary. Eisenstein found himself in appropriate company with the composer Sergei Prokofiev, who was also considered ideologically suspect by the Soviet authorities. The extent to which the visuals and music in *Alexander Nevsky* are intertwined is a real meeting of minds. Eisenstein worked closely with Prokofiev throughout the shooting, holding discussions as to mood and effect. Several sequences are cut to a previously recorded music-track. Eisenstein was strict with himself about which types of shot he could or couldn't use, dictated by the structure of the music. In his writings, Eisenstein reveals his methods behind the scene where pipes and drums are played for the victorious Russian soldiers:

> I couldn't find a way to explain to Prokofiev what precise effect should be 'seen' in his music for this joyful moment. Seeing that we were getting nowhere, I ordered some 'prop' instruments constructed, shot these being played (without sound) visually, and projected the results for Prokofiev – who almost immediately handed me an exact 'musical equivalent' to that visual image of pipers and drummers which I had shown.
>
> (1943: 124)

Throughout, Prokofiev uses musical themes to emphasise the contrast between the rival armies. Russian identity is evoked through folk melodies and consonant harmonies; the Germans are signified with severe tones and intimidating rhythms. During the battle, these elements in the soundtrack collide, each seeking to dominate within the score. The score for the film is highly regarded as a separate entity, though it is within the context of the film itself that it truly flies. The ice battle is an astonishing choreography of image and sound.

The fate of the *Alexander Nevsky's* exhibition is typical of Eisenstein's fortunes during the decade. Released to initial acclaim in 1938, the August 1939 Soviet non-aggression pact with Hitler saw the film withdrawn. Come the 1941 Nazi invasion, it was rereleased with additional relevance. Chillingly, the sacking of Pskov sequence accurately predicts the real Nazi atrocities that were to be visited upon the city during the war. Fortunately for Russia, the film's victorious outcome also proved prophetic.

Note

1. See Kristin Thompson and David Bordwell, *Film History: An Introduction*, New York, McGraw-Hill, 1994, p. 295.

Further reading

David Bordwell, 'Eisenstein, Socialist Realism and the Charms of Mizanstsena' in Al LaValley and Barry Scherr (eds), *Eisenstein at 100*, New Brunswick, New Jersey & London, Rutgers University Press, 2001, pp. 13–37.

Sergei Eisenstein, *The Film Sense*, London, Faber & Faber, 1943.

Jay Leyda, *Kino A History of the Russian and Soviet Film*, Sydney, Allen & Unwin, 1960.

Mike O'Mahony, *Sergei Eisenstein*, London, Reaktion, 2008.

Barry Scherr, 'Alexander Nevsky: A Film Without a Hero', in Al LaValley and Barry P. Scherr (eds), *Eisenstein at 100*, New Brunswick, New Jersey & London, Rutgers University Press, 2001, pp. 207–26.

Phil Lloyd

Allá en el Rancho Grande/Out on the Big Ranch (1936)

[Country: Mexico. Production Company: Lombardo Films. Director: Fernando de Fuentes. Producers: Fernando de Fuentes and Alfonso Rivas Bustamante. Screenwriters: Fernando de Fuentes, Antonio Guzmán Aguilar and Luz Guzmán De Arellano. Cinematographer: Gabriel Figueroa. Music: Lorenzo Barcelata. Cast: Tito Guízar (José Francisco Ruelas), René Cardona (Felipe), Esther Fernandez (Cruz), Margarita Cortés (Eulalia).]

Synopsis: In flashback, Esperanza tells her son, a young military cadet, the story of his father. Esperanza falls in love with José Luis Castro, the son of wealthy *hacendados*. Despite his high-class status, José Luis is an idealistic supporter of the Mexican Revolution and its goal to bring political, economic and social justice to the peasants. His parents reject Esperanza and the Revolution because they threaten the foundations on which their wealth and status rest. The couple secretly marry and their son is born at the outbreak of armed conflict. José Luis joins the revolutionary forces and goes off to fight against the government forces. In his absence, a pair of bandit brothers, posing as revolutionary soldiers, murder José Luis' father and take Esperanza and her son hostage. José Luis returns to rescue his family but is killed trying to save them.

Two decades after the end of the Mexican Revolution, the wildly successful film by Fernando de Fuentes, *Allá en el Rancho Grande* (Out on the Big

Ranch), made its debut in Mexico City on 12 October 1936. Its national and international success signalled the beginning of a robust national film industry and the emergence of Mexican cinema into the global marketplace. Although Hollywood films dominated Mexican and other Latin American screens and US-owned companies controlled a significant percentage of the distribution side of the industry, Mexico realised significant profits by exporting films like *Allá en el Rancho Grande*. De Fuentes' film introduced one of the most popular genres in Mexican film history to the world, the *comedia ranchera*, a Mexican cowboy musical that incorporates elements of comedy, tragedy, Mexican popular music, and folkloric costumes and dances. The *comedia ranchera* resonated with domestic audiences as well as Mexican migrants in the USA.[1] In 1937, just one year after the release of *Allá en el Rancho Grande*, over half of the 38 Mexican films released were modelled on de Fuentes' film.

The setting of the *comedia ranchera* was the pre-revolutionary hacienda, a vast tract of rural ranch and farming land – thousands of acres rich in natural resources such as oil and silver that had been expropriated from peasant communities by the government and given to wealthy *criollo* (Mexicans of Spanish descent) families. The workers who lived and worked on the hacienda were the Indians and *mestizo* (people of mixed race) who had originally been displaced from the land. The hacienda system was a paternalistic feudalism that governed what were essentially self-contained communities. The peasants worked the land and in return were given food, shelter and protection by the *hacendado* (hacienda owner). Theoretically free, in reality, the workers were tenant farmers, bound by indebtedness to the *hacendado*.

During the 1930s, the government of President Lázaro Cárdenas (1934–1940) recognised the value of supporting cultural industries in the development of a coherent post-revolutionary national identity. Cárdenas nationalised the film industry, established a protectionist policy that included tax exemptions for domestic production, created the Financiadora de Películas, a state institution whose mandate it was to find private financing for films, and instituted a system of loans for the establishment of major film studios. During his administration, the first modern studio, CLASA (Cinematográfica Latino Americana, S.A.) was built with private money and outfitted with the most modern production equipment available. Film production grew from six films in 1932 to 57 films by 1938 (García Riera 1963: 25). By 1934, there were five motion picture studios in Mexico City: the Compañía Nacional Productora de Películas, Universidad Cinematográfica, México-Films de Jorge Stahl, Industrial Cinematográfica, and CLASA.

Drawing on Mexican literature, theatrical traditions, and contemporary Mexican themes, commercial films were generally conservative in terms of their cinematic strategies and the social and political articulated through their narratives. Whether they were set in historical or contemporary contexts, these films exalted Mexican patriarchy, celebrated the nuclear family, the macho hero, and virtuous and submissive women. The *comedia ranchera* was one of the more conservative film genres. For example, nationalisation policies instituted by Cárdenas included sweeping land reforms that expropriated land owned by the *hacendados* and redistributed this land to the huge population of landless rural peasants. However, the *comedia ranchera* ignored these reforms and, instead, celebrated the pre-revolutionary hacienda system as a pastoral utopia in which the *hacendados* and his workers lived like one big happy family governed by a patriarchal but caring father. The *comedia ranchera* may thus be read as a thinly disguised challenge, in the form of a musical love story, to Cárdenas' social, cultural, and economic transformations.

The box office triumph of these films confirmed a certain public weariness with a revolutionary rhetoric that was now over a decade old. The success of this popular cinema also revealed the presence of a nostalgic longing for the mythical past this rhetoric had created. Films like *La boda de Rosario, Juarez y Maximiliano* (Miguel Contreras Torres, 1933), which celebrated the reign of the French emperor, Maximilian and his empress, Carlota; *Madre querida* (Juan Orol, 1935), a film that introduced the melodramatic genre of the sacrificial mother, and *La Adelita* (Guillermo Hernández Gómez, 1937), a revolutionary melodrama, looked back fondly on the pre-revolutionary Porfirian regime, on the repressive structures of the hacienda system, on the romantic ideal of a populist revolution, and on the centrality of the family and the Catholic Church in public and private life.

The *comedia ranchera* is not the same kind of film as American backstage musicals of the 1930s, whose narratives were about the production of a grand Broadway production and whose songs and dances were central to story development. In the Mexican musical, songs and dances are presentational. The forward movement of the narrative is brought to a standstill so that a character or group of characters can perform a musical interlude in order to entertain the film audience. The title song, *Allá en el Rancho Grande*, comes from a traditional Mexican musical genre called the *ranchera* that originated in the central Mexican state of Jalisco and became widely popular after the Mexican revolution. The lyrics of *Allá en el Rancho Grande*, like the majority of *ranchera* songs, celebrate love of country, rural live, romantic love, and socio-political commentary. As depicted in a de Fuentes film, *rancheras* were performed by *mariachi* bands with guitars, trumpets, and violins.

Songs featured in *comedia ranchera* do not always specifically refer to the narrative; instead, the lyrics express the feelings of particular characters, articulate romantic yearnings, or convey a longing for the feeling of belonging to a community, most often the community of the *ranchera*. The opening scene of *Allá en el Rancho Grande*, for example, presents a grand fiesta or party that includes all the inhabitants of el Rancho Grande, including the *padrone* and his family and all the workers and their families. A *mariachi* band plays the title song, which expresses a ranch hand's fond reminisces of a love affair on the big ranch where he lived. In a later scene, one of the ranch hands requests a song from Cruz and she sings a well-known *Canción mixteca* that articulates the longing for the pastoral provinces celebrated by the comedia ranchera: 'How far away I am from the place where I was born, an immense nostalgia invades my thoughts and finds me so sad and alone, like a leaf in the wind.'[2] Occasionally, a particular song will develop a narrative plot point as in the scene in the cantina where Jose Francisco, the ranch foreman, engages in a singing dual with Martín, a ranch hand, and discovers that the reputation of Cruz, his sweetheart, has been compromised by the attentions of his best friend Felipe, the owner of el Rancho Grande.

Allá en el Rancho Grande envisioned a mythical agrarian paradise and celebrated *hispanismo*, the rallying cry of an unlikely alliance of right-wing land-owning groups who opposed post-revolutionary reforms, and the Catholic Church and Catholic peasants who resented the new regime's anti-clerical position and opposed its socialist programmes.[3] Needing a people who could personify hispanismo, its proponents found them in *los altos de Jalisco*, the isolated northwestern mountain region of Mexico whose inhabitants were devoutly Catholic, anti-Cárdenas, had never intermarried with Indians, and played mariachi music.

The hero of hispanismo was the *charro* as exemplified by Tito Guízar, who stars in the role of José Francisco, and was a well-known popular singer who had a successful career in music in the United States, and Jorge Negrete, the aspiring opera singer who became the first Mexican 'superstar', when he premiered in the *comedia ranchera*, *Ay, Jalisco, no te rajes!* (Joselita Rodríguez, 1941) and who starred in de Fuentes' 1948 remake of *Allá en el Rancho Grande*. The *charro*, originally an expert horseman on large landed estates owned by families of Spanish heritage, was a symbol of Hispanic masculinity, light-skinned, handsome, and respectful of the celebrated inherent divisions within Mexican society. Mexican cinema relied on earlier depictions of the charro introduced in nineteenth-century novels and the *orquesta típica* (national folkloric orchestra) popularised in the early twentieth century. Although the Mexican *charro* was only a ranch hand, his role was to protect the workers against the powerful *hacendado* or ranch owner. However, he was also required to uphold the patriarchal hacienda system that kept classes, races, and genders in their places on *el rancho grande*.

How was it that such a reactionary genre achieved domestic and international success? García Riera suggests that it was because Mexican as well as Latin American audiences adored characters with 'humble origins, big peasant-style skirts and hair bows, and virile-filled workers as mates' (1995: 130). The box office success of films like *Allá en el Rancho Grande*, *Bajo el cielo de México* (de Fuentes, 1937), *La Zandunga* (de Fuentes, 1938), *Nobleza ranchera* (Alfredo de Diestro, 1938) and *La tierra del mariachi* (Raúl de Anda, 1938) at home and abroad convinced Mexican producers that they had stumbled upon a safe and lucrative product.[4] In addition, the popularity confirmed the role the cinema played in the reconstruction of

Mexican nationalism. The film's cinematography, photographed by Gabriel Figueroa, who would go on to become the premiere cinematographer in Mexico, its cast of characters, its acting style, its use of popular songs, its mise en scéne, and its stars set the standards for the immediate future of the Mexican film industry.

Notes

1. De Fuentes directed a remake of *Allá en el Rancho Grande* in 1958 that starred Jorge Negrete, a contemporary of Guízar.
2. Que lejos estoy del suelo donde he nacido, inmensa nostalgia invade mi pensamiento, y al ver me tan solo y triste qual hoja al viento.
3. See Marjorie Becker, *Setting the Virgin on Fire: Lázaro Cárdenas, Michoacán Peasants, and the Redemption of the Mexican Revolution*, Berkeley, University of California Press, 1995; Alan Knight, 'Weapons and Arches in the Mexican Revolutionary Landscape', in Gilbert M. Joseph and Daniel Nugent (eds), *Everyday Forms of State Formation: Revolution and the Negotiation of Rule in Modern Mexico*, Durham, Duke University Press, 1994, pp. 24–66; and Jean Meyer, *The Cristero Rebellion: The Mexican People Between Church and State, 1926–1929*, London, Cambridge University Press, 1976.
4. For a few years, the *comedia ranchera* was the most recognisable, and thus exportable, Mexican film genre. García Riera notes that 'of the 38 Mexican films produced in 1937, over half were folkloric or nationalistic.' (1995: 131).

Further reading

Desirée Garcia, 'The Soul of a People: Mexican Spectatorship and Transnational *Comedia Ranchera*', *Journal of American Ethnic History*, Vol. 30, No. 1, 2010, pp. 72–98.

Emilio García Riera, 'The Impact of *Rancho Grande*', in Paulo Antonio Paranaguá (ed.), *Mexican Cinema*, trans. Ana M. López, London, British Film Institute, 1995, pp. 128–32.

Emilio García Riera, *El cine Mexicano*, Mexico City, ERA, 1963.

Carl J. Mora, *Mexican Cinema: Reflections of a Society, 1896–1988*, Berkeley, University of California Press, 1982.

Olga Najera-Ramírez, 'Engendering Nationalism: Identity, Discourse, and the Mexican *Charro*', Working Paper No. 3, Santa Cruz, CA, Chicano/Latino Research Center, University of California, 1993.

Aurelio de los Reyes, *Medio Siglo de Cine Mexicana (1896–1947)*, Mexico City, Editorial Trillas, 1987.

Joanne Hershfield

Amar Akbar Anthony (1977)

[Country: India. Production Company: Hirawat Jain and Company, MKD Films and Manmohan Films. Director: Manmohan Desai. Producer: Manmohan Desai. Screenwriter: Prayag Raj. Dialogue: Kader Khan. Cinematographer: Peter Pereira. Music: Laxmikant Pyarelal. Editor: Kamlakar Karkhaine. Art Director: A Rangaraj. Cast: Vinod Khanna (Amar), Amitabh Bachchan (Anthony), Rishi Kapoor (Akbar), Parveen Babi (Jenny), Neetu Singh (Salma), Shabana Aazmi (Laxmi), Pran (Kishen Lal), Nirupa Roy (Bharti), Jeevan (Robert), Mukri (Salma's father).]

Synopsis: *Amar Akbar Anthony* narrates the story of three brothers separated at birth. Kishen Lal, who works as a driver for a smuggler, Robert, takes the blame for an accident committed by his master in return for monetary compensation for his wife and three small boys. On his release, Kishen Lal discovers that Robert has not helped his family. His wife Bharti is suffering from tuberculosis and the children are in a state of destitution. He confronts Robert and is humiliated, but escapes in a car that unknown to him contains a box of gold biscuits. Kishan Lal picks up his sons and leaves them under a statue of Gandhi with the intention of returning after he has dealt with the chasing mob. Meanwhile, his wife has left home because she does not want to be a burden on the family. Kishan Lal's car goes over a mountain but he escapes and discovers the box of gold. When he returns to the statue to pick up his sons, they are gone. The children have been picked up by men belonging to three different religions and grow up as Amar, Akbar and Anthony. Kishan Lal becomes a major smuggler himself while Bharti, now blind, is told her family is dead. The rest of the film is a roller-coaster ride of gags, action, comedy, romance, revenge, coincidences and reunion. Amar grows up to follow the footsteps of the Hindu police officer who adopts him. Akbar is picked up by a Muslim tailor and brought up as a singer and a believing Muslim. Anthony is found outside a church by a priest and grows up to become a small-time Christian bootlegger. All three enter into romantic liaisons with women from their respective religious communities. Anthony's girlfriend Jenny, unbeknown to her, is Robert's daughter kidnapped and brought up by Kishan Lal. Akbar is in love with Salma, a doctor whose father is opposed to the match. Amar falls in love with a woman named Laxmi, whom he rescues from a crooked stepmother and brother. All these parallel narratives unfold and intersect via a series of coincidences. This was Manmohan Desai's special talent, to flout all norms of plausibility and yet create a narrative that contained a core value system close to his heart. In the case of *AAA* through the popular idiom of the lost and found tale, three characters are placed in the midst of different religious faiths not in any overt pious way but through an irreverent play with stereotypes.

In 1976 the word 'secular' was included as an amendment to the Indian constitution with a vision to protect all religions equally. The Indian notion of secularism has always been different from the original use of the term by the French Revolution, which was envisioned as a clear separation of the Church from the State. Secularism and secular discourse in a multi-religious country like India has had a complicated and chequered history.[1] It is therefore interesting that many have pointed to and commented on Desai's audacious vision of secularism in *Amar Akbar Anthony*.[2] The simple story of a family separated at the beginning of the film and reunited at the end was not new when *AAA* was released. The film's novelty lay in its obliquely posed vision of secularism via a comic structure where the story remained simple but the narrative was filled with chaotic and wild constructions. Films such as *AAA* remain testimonials to the limits of the framework of secular nationalism adopted by Indian society. In *AAA* there is a strong projection of minority identities that despite stereotyping is extremely conscious of posing the question of religious tolerance (Virdi 2003: 36). In line with the three different religious identities on display, Desai gave special attention to the minority communities of Christians and Muslims. One of the specific modes adopted here is that of music and its spatial imaginations conveyed through the characters of Akbar and Anthony.

Akbar is popularly known as Akbar Allahabadi in the film (named after a modern Urdu poet from Allahabad), a singer who in the film performs a well-known *Qawwali* on stage. *Qawwalis* are Sufi devotional songs that position themselves against any kind of orthodoxy, sectarianism and ritual practices.[3] These songs promote visions of transcendental and personal devotion to the Prophet and God, generally performed by groups of men where the singing tends to build to a crescendo. These performances have a long association with the everyday lives of Muslims in South Asia. As Morcom notes, the *Qawwali* is often found in 'scenes of spectacle' in Hindi films with visual stereotyping of Muslims that are now identified with these performances.[4] Akbar's 'Purda hai' song is performed as a romantic song for his lady love sitting with her father in the front row of a large auditorium filled to capacity. The erotic and yet comical charge of the song with bursts of colour, sheer curtains descending rhythmically into the frame, and stereotypical accoutrements associated with imagined notions of Muslim culture, are all deployed with confidence in the sequence. As Morcom says, no one seeing this song 'would ever guess that this genre is originally a spiritual and devotional one' (2007: 82–3). Desai could take great liberties like this in the service of harmony without hurting any religious sentiments.

If Akbar's cultural association with Islamic culture is presented through the *Qawwali* then, for Anthony, Easter celebrations become the stage for a highly performative song. 'My name is Anthony Gonzalves', a hugely popular song of the film, showcases Anthony dressed in a black tailcoat popping out of a giant-sized Easter egg to sing for his lady love, Jenny. While the song is sung by playback singer, Kishore Kumar, Bachchan alternates the song with nonsensical verse in his own voice. Some of the words of the verse are, 'Wait, wait, wait! You see the whole country of the system is juxtapositioned by the haemoglobin in the atmosphere because you are a sophisticated rhetorician intoxicated by the exuberance of your own verbosity!!' Bachchan, arguably Hindi cinema's biggest actor to date, was at that time known for his 'angry man' persona which he had played in a number of films.[5] Though he had performed a comic character in Hrishikesh Mukherjee's *Chupke Chupke* (1975), it was *Amar Akbar Anthony* that showcased Bachhan's talent for comedy. As a boy adopted by a Christian priest, Anthony always wears a cross and has the swagger of a typical Bombay *Tapori* with a hybrid street speech popularly known as *Bambayya*.[6] His collection of tight leather jackets and hats and his one-liners made him hugely popular after *AAA*. The Easter song sequence ends with Anthony drunk and beaten by Jenny's bodyguard. Anthony's display of masculinity here is not that of the 'angry man' persona. Rather he appears as a loveable victim who then proceeds to have a memorable drunken monologue with himself in front of a mirror at home. Desai's style of filmmaking depended on an aggressive and wild mobilisation of stereotypes. Thus, Anthony's Christian identity is presented through his playful use of English, his costume, and his freedom to drink and dance at a night club. These scenes and moments are etched in popular memory and remain central to the star biography built up by Bachchan.

As in many lost and found tales, objects of memory play an important role in the film. The Santoshi Ma locket becomes a connecting thread between the past and present, identifying and connecting people.[7] There is also a letter written by Bharti which Anthony carries in his pocket all the time. Amar buries a toy pistol outside his house as a child, the memory of which returns to him as an adult when he visits the neighbourhood during his investigations. It is here that Kishan Lal spots Amar digging to recover the gun and realises that this police officer must be his long-lost eldest son. Akbar's childhood photo on the wall of his house is what Bharti recognises as that of her youngest son. But there is another thread typical of Bombay films of the 1970s and significant for the Bombay crime world of the time that circulates throughout the narrative, constantly changing hands. This is the movement of gold biscuits signifying Bombay's peculiar status as a city of gold. First, Kishan Lal becomes a smuggler with the gold he discovers in the car and uses to escape from Robert's men at the beginning of the film. Many years later, Robert steals a similar box of gold from Kishan Lal's men and runs with it to trip over Anthony with whom he must share the fortunes. The second encounter between Robert and Anthony was used as a situation for an extremely popular dialogue that has been used several times in other films – 'aisa ich life me admi do hi time bhagta hai – police ka case ho ya Olympic ka race ho' ('Only two kinds of situations in life can make a man run like this – an Olympic race or a police case!'). Thus both the figure of the smuggler and the larger context of gold are parodied by Desai throughout the narrative of *Amar Akbar Anthony*.

The film's script and screenplay revel in chance occurrences and every problem posed is solved by a coincidence. A wild example of this is the way Bharti becomes blind early in the film when a tree falls on her. Many years later, after a second accident, Bharati crawls into a temple and miraculously regains her eyesight. With such miracles and coincidences strewn through the narrative, *AAA* builds up to a final climax in Robert's den with the entire cast now under one roof. This was the one sequence for which the entire cast had to be present together. Amar, Akbar and Anthony arrive at Robert's den in disguise but in keeping with their religious identity. Amar is dressed as a band master, Anthony as a priest and Akbar as a Muslim tailor. Jenny is being forced to marry her bodyguard but the arrival of the three brothers throws a spanner in the works. This fun-filled climax had the most unique slapstick action following the well-known song '*unhonee ko honee kar de honee kar de, honee ko unhonee, ek jagah jab jama ho teeno, Amar, Akbar, Anthony*' ('The impossible is possible and the possible made impossible when Amar, Akbar and Anthony come together'). This song has multiplied well beyond the film into the domain of sports, politics and advertising. Popular versions of the song have played in political rallies to promote anti-corruption campaigns and for jingles to promote cricket players. The climax leads up to the arrival of the cops and a reuniting of the entire family.

The unique quality of *AAA* was its explicit desire for comedy and a distance from overt sentimentality. All sentiments in the film are channelled and played out through comic gestures, one-liners, stereotypes and gags. At one level a tragic story with a revenge theme, but a film that turned Indian melodrama's powerful universe of emotions on its head, maintaining a lightness that only Desai could pull off so well.

Notes

1. Rajeev Bhargava (ed.), *Secularism and its Critics: Themes in Indian Politics*, Oxford India Paperbacks, 2000 and Bhargava, *The Promise of India's Secular Democracy*, Oxford University Press, USA, 2010.
2. Mayank Chaya, 'Hindi Cinema has greatly contributed to a secular idea of India', *Indian Express*, August 18, 2013.
3. Peter Manuel, 'North Indian Sufi Popular Music in the Age of Hindu and Muslim Fundamentalism', *Ethnomusicology*, Vol. 52, No. 3, Fall 2008, pp. 378–400.
4. Anna Morcom, *Hindi Film Songs and the Cinema*, Farnham, Ashgate, 2007.
5. Amitabh Bachchan's 'superstar' status has been documented by both journalists and academics. Imagined as the 'angry man' in the 1970s by the writer duo, Salim Khan and Javed Akhtar, Bachchan found himself catapulted into a strikingly new cinematic imagination of political turbulence. His image as the 'angry man' circulated widely and gained the currency of a modern myth. Never before had an actor had this kind of presence, embodying the social and political turbulence of his time. (See, Madhava Pasad, *The Ideology of the Hindi Film: A Historical Reconstruction*, New Delhi, Oxford University Press, 1998, pp. 117–59; Vijay Mishra, *Bollywood Cinema: Temples of Desire*, New York and London, Routledge, 2002; Ranjani Mazumdar, *Bombay Cinema: An Archive of the City*, Minneapolis, MN and London, University of Minnesota Press, 2007, pp. 1–40; Sushmita Dasgupta, *Amitabh: The Making of a Superstar*, New York, Penguin Global, 2007; Valentina Vitali, *Hindi Action Cinema: Industries, Narratives, Bodies*, New Delhi, Oxford University Press, 2008, pp. 184–229.)
6. The term *Tapori* is used for a typical vagabond figure belonging to the street cultures of Bombay. (See, Mazumdar, 2007: 41–78.)
7. Santoshi Ma is a recently invented goddess of the Hindu pantheon that emerged in the 1960s. She was a little known figure until a popular film titled, *Jai Santoshi Ma*, was released in 1975. (For an anthropological take on this cult goddess see, Veena Das, 'The Mythological Film and its Framework of Meaning: An Analysis of *Jai Santoshi Ma*', India International Centre Quarterly, Vol. 8, No. 1, March 1981.)

Further reading

Siddharth Bhatia, *Amar Akbar Anthony: Masala, Madness and Manmohan Desai*, Noida, UP, Harper Collins India, 2013.

Connie Haham, *Enchantment of the Mind: Manmohan Desai's Films*, University of Michigan Press, Ann Arbor, MI, Roli Books Pvt., 2006.

Jyotika Virdi, *The Cinematic Imagination: Indian Popular Films as Social History*, New Brunswick, NJ, Rutgers University Press, 2003.

Ranjani Mazumdar

Amores Perros (2000)

[Country: Mexico. Production Company: Altavista Films, Zeta Films. Director: Alejandro González Iñárritu. Screenwriter: Guillermo Arriaga. Cinematographer: Rodrigo Prieto. Editors: Alejandro González Iñárritu, Luis Carballar, Fernando Pérez Unda. Cast: Gael García Bernal (Octavio), Vanessa Bauche (Susana), Alvaro Guerrero (Daniel), Goya Toledo (Valeria), Emilio Echeverría (El Chivo).]

Synopsis: After the tragic crash which occurs in the opening scene the film is divided into three parts; three separate stories edited together, each dealing with characters from different social backgrounds. The first story, *Octavio y Susana*, focuses on characters from the Mexican lower class. Octavio is infatuated with his teenage sister-in-law Susana, who, along with Octavio's mother, brother and Susana's baby son, live together in a crowded apartment. Upon discovering that Susana has yet again become pregnant Octavio vows to protect her from his abusive brother, Ramiro, and they soon begin a love affair. After Cofi, the family Rottweiler, kills a prize-fighting dog belonging to El Jaricho, a violent street thug, Octavio is forced to enter Cofi into a number of illegal dogfights. Cofi becomes a successful prize-fighter himself and makes a substantial amount of money for Octavio. After agreeing to one last big-money fight Octavia realises that Susana has betrayed him by stealing the money he had saved for their new life together. Octavio enters Cofi into the agreed fight but, after seemingly getting the better of his opponent, Cofi is shot by Jaricho. In a fit of rage Octavio stabs Jaricho in retaliation, which results in a return to the car chase and subsequent crash the film opens with. In the second story, *Daniel y Valeria*, Daniel, a successful middle-aged magazine publisher, leaves his wife and family to live in a new apartment with supermodel Valeria, who we recognise as one of the victims of the crash in the opening sequence. After the accident Valeria suffers a serious leg injury, putting her new modelling contract in jeopardy. To make matters worse, Valeria's dog Richie gets trapped after falling through a hole in the floorboards. Indeed, the broken floorboards in their expensive apartment may symbolise the complexities of Mexican society, suggesting that even the most privileged have been affected by cultural and political instability. Confined to a wheelchair, Valeria gets increasingly anxious about Richie's safety and her own helpless predicament, and upon hearing the dog's distress she makes a futile attempt to prise up the floorboards to rescue him. This leads to a complication of her injuries, the amputation of her leg and the end of her modelling career. The final story, *El Chivo y Maru*, follows El Chivo, a vagrant and former revolutionary guerrilla who now acts as a gun for hire. Throughout the film El Chivo is seen caring for a group of stray dogs, whilst also appearing at the funeral of his ex-wife where he sees his daughter Mura for the first time since he abandoned his family to 'set the world right'. El Chivo, therefore, embodies the Left's various movements for social change which occurred during the 1960s and 1970s. He is hired by the wealthy Gustavo to kill a business partner (and incidentally, brother-in-law). During his reconnaissance of 'the mark', El Chivo witnesses the aforementioned car crash. In the aftermath he steals Cofi and retreats to care for the wounded dog, only for Cofi to turn on the other animals, killing them all. This act sparks somewhat of a redemption in El Chivo's character, as 'unlike Octavio and Valeria, El Chivo is shrewd enough to recognise something of himself in the killer dog, and to begin to make peace with his haunted past' (Schickel 2001). Rather than killing the businessman he was hired to assassinate he kidnaps both men, placing a gun between them, leaving them to resolve the situation themselves. He cleans himself up, cuts his hair and nails before breaking into Mura's home to leave her money and a voicemail apologising for his abandonment. The film closes with El Chivo and Cofi walking off into Desierto de los Leones – a vast, disparate landscape on the outskirts of the city. This ending underscores the film's social context; symbolising contemporary Mexico where marginalisation and inequality still exist, offering no indication this way of life will change in the near future.

Amores Perros is a captivating yet unnerving portrayal of social inequality, urban violence and the fragility of the human condition, which Marvin D'Lugo (2003: 224) describes as 'a new moral and cultural landscape of spiritual desolation rooted in the modern megalopolis'. The debut feature film of Mexican director Alejandro González Iñárritu opens with a frantic car chase and brutal crash that connects three narratives about contemporary Mexican society. The adoption of a *cinema vérité* shooting style adds an air of authenticity, whilst the inter-connected narrative structure is utilised to 'generate meaningful insight into everyday life' (Peters 2008). Iñárritu insists it is 'a movie about pain, love and redemption – and about Mexico City. ... a very complex, contradictory mosaic that's fascinating and electric and ugly and painful all at once' (Swart 2001). *Amores Perros* emphasises the uneven development and overcrowded landscape of Mexico City, which plays host to nearly nine million inhabitants. Here, depictions of extreme wealth and poverty converge (quite literally), epitomising a country which up until a few weeks after the film's international release had been suffering under the rule of the (largely corrupt) 'Institutional Revolutionary Party'.

True to the film's title, which roughly translates to 'love is like a dog', the three narratives centre around the relationship between dogs and their owners. According to Geoffrey Kantaris (2003: 186–7), the film uses dog-fighting as a displaced metaphor for human violence and impeded human relationships. Whilst dogs are culturally synonymous with loyalty and devotion, Iñárritu juxtaposes this symbolism with stories of infidelity and deceit, expressing the ferocity of 'dog-eat-dog' contemporary urban life. The dogs mirror the psyche of the central protagonists and their fates within the film, with El Chivo remarking in one scene that, 'Masters take after their dogs'; the allegory being that owners are just as helpless as their animals to change their situation. Much like Cofi who was trained to inflict terrible acts of violence, by the end of the film Octavio has undergone a transformation from baby-faced adolescent to gaunt, violent thug. Here, Octavio's lack of social mobility and poor quality of life force him to seek wealth through illegal means, with his aggression intensifying as he and Cofi fall deeper into the world of dog-fighting. Valeria's dog Richie, meanwhile, is cute, fluffy and petite – an apt choice for a glamorous supermodel. After Richie gets trapped in the floorboards his plight reflects Valeria's own feelings of helplessness, loneliness and loss after her accident. Likewise, El Chivo looks after abandoned strays that are just as marginalised as he is. After Cofi kills the other dogs El Chivo contemplates killing him but decides against it, realising that the animal knows no better. For Maria San Filippo (2001), *Amores Perros* questions whether those who are taught cruelty and oppression (i.e. forced to accept oppression in order to survive) are to be blamed for exacting that same cruelty, delivering a cynical examination of the human condition and contemporary social milieu.

Although the film in many ways serves to reinforce typical social conventions, most notably gender representations, it is clear that Iñárritu wishes to highlight the complexities of Mexican national identity:

> I am not a Mexican with a moustache and a sombrero, nor am I a corrupt cop or drug trafficker. There are millions like me. And this is the world I live in and the one I want to show.
>
> (Patterson 2001)

In doing so, *Amores Perros* interrogates what it means to be Mexican on a thematic level by reflecting on the effects of cultural modernity in Latin American society. By portraying the tensions that persist for millions of Mexicans (rigid class division, lack of political agency, etc.), Iñárritu shifts the focus from pre-established national stereotypes to represent contemporary Mexico in a phase of political and cultural transition. This is perhaps most apparent in the representation of family, with the film's most malicious acts (adultery, physical violence, even planned assassination) being carried out by kin. Besides offering a critical treatment of issues such as teenage pregnancy, absent father figures and domestic violence, the dissolution of the family unit throughout signifies a crisis of national identity. As De La Garza suggests, 'The family, often drawn upon as a metaphor for the nation in nationalist discourses, is under siege in the film by both the poor and the rich' (De La

Garza 2006: 152). Furthermore, Iñárritu offers no discernible positive resolution to the anguish of both the lower and middle classes, presenting a stark realisation that the continued urbanisation of Mexico heightens socio-political tensions.

One of the film's central themes, loss and regret, reflects feelings of unease and insecurity which permeated Mexican society during the film's production. In fact, as De La Garza (2006: 152–3) argues, the film exposes the 'contingency of identities' by showing them as 'unfixed'. Throughout the film, characters gaze upon photographs of themselves or their families (the picture of a youthful Octavio and Ramiro in Octavio's wallet, the billboard poster of Valeria that can be seen from her and Daniel's apartment, the family portraits El Chivo examines whilst at Mura's home); here, characters are defined by what they have lost as they look upon these photographs with yearning nostalgia:

> It's as if in this 'post modern' Mexico, characters need to have their identities confirmed by the photographs, as if they were relying on them as aids for telling themselves the stories of their lives.
>
> (De La Garza 2006: 153)

The style and structure of the film further emphasises this notion, depicting a country formally bound to tradition and heritage amidst a period of rapid cultural change; the outcome of which is a society 'characterized by the continuous juxtapositions between the modern and primitive, between a glamorous world of televisual images and the leitmotifs of animalistic violence' (D'Lugo 2003: 224). Iñárritu's blend of *avant-garde* techniques (use of multiple film-stocks, disjointed narrative, extreme close-ups) with more commercial and internationally appealing elements (rapid editing style, contemporary soundtrack, themes of sex and violence) highlights the complexities of Mexico's cinematic identity. For D'Lugo (2003: 222), *Amores Perros* embodies the contradictions of contemporary urban life at the end of the century. Importantly, it manages to do this in ways that also engage non-Mexican audiences. Indeed, the film was produced by Altavista Films, a relatively new company whose stated policy is to produce films that reach a midpoint between commercial crowd-pleasers and art-house movies (Malcolm 2002). Given its success both nationally and internationally, *Amores Perros* has been associated with a revival of Mexican cinema, with an increase of private funding being made available to support films of a more commercial, yet artistically innovative, nature (Tierney 2009: 101). Consequently, the range of visual, stylistic and narrative strategies utilised by Mexican filmmakers to appeal to both national and international markets expresses the effects of globalisation and the complexities of cultural modernity within contemporary Mexican society.

Further reading

Armida De La Garza, *Mexico on Film: National Identity & International Relations*, Bury St Edmunds, Arena Books, 2006.

Marvin D'Lugo, '*Amores perros/Love's a Bitch*', in A. Elena and M. Díaz López (eds), *The Cinema of Latin America*, London, Wallflower Press, 2003, pp. 221–9.

Geoffrey Kantaris, 'The Young and the Damned: Street Visions in Latin American Cinema', in S. Hart and R. Young (eds), *Contemporary Latin American Cultural Studies*, London, Arnold, 2003, pp. 177–89.

Derek Malcolm, 'Mexico Lit up by Dog's Star', *The Guardian*, April 7, 2002. www.guardian.co.uk/film/2002/apr/07/features.mexico.

John Patterson, 'Aztec Cameras', *The Guardian*, May 18, 2001. www.guardian.co.uk/film/2001/may/18/culture.features2.

Lindsay Peters, 'Private Fears in Public Places: Network Narrative and the Post-"Smart" American Melodrama', *Synoptique*, Vol. 12, October 28, 2008. www.synoptique.ca/core/articles/private_fears_in_public_places.

Maria San Filippo, 'Amores Perros', *Senses of Cinema* 13: April 10, 2001. http://sensesofci nema.com/2001/13/amores.

Richard Schickel, 'A Bite As Tough As Its Bark: Dogs are humans' best friends in the superb *Amores Perros*', *Time Magazine*, 16 April, 2001, Vol. 157 (15), p. 78.

S. Swart, 'Alejandro Gonzalez Iñárritu: Helmer gets raw with *Amores Perros*', *Variety*, 15 January 2001, https://variety.com/2001/film/news/alejandro-gonzalez-inarritu-1117792068/

Dolores Tierney, 'Alejandro Gonzalez Iñárritu: Director without Borders', *New Cinemas: Journal of Contemporary Film* Vol. 7 (2), 2009, pp. 101–17.

Martyn Thayne

Angst essen Seele auf/Fear Eats the Soul (1974)

[Country: West Germany. Production Company: Tango-Film. Director: Rainer Werner Fassbinder. Producer: Rainer Werner Fassbinder. Screenwriter: Rainer Werner Fassbinder. Cinematographer: Jürgen Jürges. Designers: Kurt Raab, Rainer Werner Fassbinder. Editor: Thea Eymèsz. Cast: Brigitte Mira (Emmi Kurowski), El Hedi Ben Salem (Ali), Barbara Valentin (Barbara, the bar owner), Irm Hermann (Krista), Rainer Werner Fassbinder (Eugen).]

Synopsis: After a chance meeting in a bar in Munich, Emmi, a cleaning woman (Mira) and Ali (El Hedi Ben Salem), a much younger Moroccan guest worker, fall in love and marry. Family, neighbours and work colleagues respond with horror and disgust, ostracising the couple. In despair, they take a vacation to escape social disapproval. On their return, they find attitudes have changed somewhat: their former persecutors now hypocritically look to take advantage of either Emmi or Ali. Gradually the couple's relationship starts to fall apart. At a moment of apparent reconciliation, in the same bar where they met, Ali collapses with an acute ulcer, a condition typical of immigrant workers, unlikely to be curable.

Fear Eats the Soul is among Rainer Werner Fassbinder's most canonical films. Along with *The Marriage of Maria Braun* (1979), it is the one that appears in lists of '100 best films' and is most often assigned on undergraduate film studies syllabi. The film falls into the 'domestic melodrama' phase of Fassbinder's production, the period in the early-to-mid 1970s when, under the influence of Douglas Sirk, he introduced an affective directness into his work, a directness until then rare in the Godardian genre re-workings and austere comedies of his already substantial oeuvre. But while Sirk may have given Fassbinder a taste for simpler stories, his staging of sentiment was never simple, nor did it mark a softening of his outlook. In Fassbinder's worldview, at once cynically clear-eyed and utopian, power pervades all social relations from the ground up. Individuals are locked into and exploited by large-scale systems of power and money, and interpersonal relations offer only the mirage of escape. Even on the level of – especially on the level of – personal, emotional and sexual relations, there can be no equality, motives are never innocent, and the question of *who whom* can never be escaped.

Fassbinder's films of this period – *Fear Eats the Soul*, but also *The Bitter Tears of Petra von Kant*, *Mother Küsters Journey to Heaven*, *Fox and his Friends*, *The Merchant of Four Seasons* and others – relentlessly lead their principal characters through downward spirals of emotional suffering. In doing so, they also excoriate the smugness, conformism, hypocrisy and unacknowledged violence of post-war West German society, shown to be founded on vulgar materialism, psychic repression and historical guilt. However, although there is much melodramatic suffering, there are few entirely innocent victims: affliction can be noble, but it is rarely pure. The central figures – who often die with or from their unhappiness – are frequently complicit with their situation, sometimes abjectly so, and often inflict a portion of suffering on others in turn. In compiling this compendium of distress and exploitation, Fassbinder returned time and again, with particular vehemence, to the institutions of the *family* and *couple*. The former is depicted as an inescapable site of violent socialisation, the latter as a nexus of bitterness, co-dependency, frustration and mutual manipulation.

For all that, there is a deep strain of utopianism and even romanticism at work in Fassbinder. Desire and love are constant threads through all his works, albeit ultimately in thwarted, aborted, abused, betrayed or otherwise impossible forms. A bleak but nuanced picture, and one that was, for the director, ultimately political. As he put it in a late interview: 'In the exploitative system under which we live, love too is exploited and exploitative. [Thus] I can recommend the desire to love, but not love itself. But perhaps if that desire were made to grow ever larger and ever clearer – then maybe something would change' (Fischer 2004: 600). While sympathetic to many currents of the 1960s and 70s counter-culture, Fassbinder refused to put forward overarching solutions to the problems he diagnosed, suggesting his role lay rather in forcing audiences to pose difficult questions about their own lives, to sensitise audiences through the knotted problems his films present (Fischer 2004: 324). This combination of social critique and apparent fatalism led some critics to diagnose a pernicious passivity in his work. For Richard Dyer, Fassbinder's films were suffused with 'left melancholy', wallowing in suffering, acknowledging social determinants while disavowing practical action (Dyer 1980: 54–65). Others since, however, have detected more subtle modes of resistance, seeing in the dismantled masculinities and affirmation of abjection a promise of new modes of social, emotional and erotic being.[1]

Whatever the place of passivity in his films, Fassbinder himself was a prodigiously active and productive figure. It was not unusual for him to produce up to several features a year, writing and directing, as well as frequently acting, and with a hand in editing, production and design. *Fear Eats the Soul* was produced in 15 shooting days. The speed of production is partly explicable by the great clarity of Fassbinder's artistic vision and partly by the efficiency of his close-knit group of regular collaborators. The group included a substantial number of family, acolytes, friends and former and current lovers: the director's work and tumultuous life were intimately related on the level of production and of casting, and sometimes in narrative allusions. El Hedi Ben Salem, who plays Ali, was Fassbinder's then partner. The director's complicated personal life and the multiple interconnections of biography and films were a favourite topic for West German tabloids during his life and after his early death.

Like Sirk's *All That Heaven Allows* (1956), of which it is a partial re-make, *Fear Eats the Soul* shows a scandalous love story across social divides, centring on a couple faced with the disapproval and outright sabotage of family and neighbours. However, in transposing the action from New England to Munich, Fassbinder also changes the constellation of social conflicts and taboos. Where Sirk's wealthy widow falls in love with her gardener, Fassbinder locates both his main characters at the bottom of the social scale, lessening their class difference while emphasising their common marginalisation. Above all, Fassbinder amplifies the scandalousness of the match – its impossibility and impropriety in the eyes of society, and perhaps in the eyes of the audience – by adding a difference in race and nationality, and a radical disjuncture in age and sexual attractiveness.

On paper, this compounding of 'issues' – prejudice, racism, exploitation, the loneliness of the marginalised – is reminiscent of what in German is referred to as the *Problemfilm*, contemporary dramas worthily addressing social problems. But the exacting formalism of its visual style, along with Fassbinder's writing and staging, takes the film far from banal realism. Already in the extraordinary opening scene, the meticulously constructed mise en scène – careful analysis of space; garish colour in costumes and design; stylised, almost ritualised blocking of the actors – reveals a key aspect of the film: the way it uses relations of vision and looking to demonstrate and allegorise how personal relations are constituted in a web of coercive social relations. Throughout, relations and emotions are staged through a complex exchange of gazes and glances, including the camera's look – we are never allowed to forget that we *too* are staring, along with the hostile neighbours.

Thus, when Emmi takes shelter in the bar, she is subject to the steady, cold gaze of all those present. But the starers do not have to turn to look: in Fassbinder's staging, they are *already* looking even as she enters. Likewise, the dance between Emmi and Ali, which inaugurates their scandalously inappropriate romance ('it's just not *natural*' says one character), is initially a product of the mockery, jealousy and resentment of others: a woman at the bar, her advances spurned by Ali, puts money in the jukebox and scornfully suggests he dance with the old woman.

The opening scenes conjure one of Fassbinder's moments of utopian hope. On the space of the empty dance floor, an unlikely bond between mismatched outsiders comes to pass. To an old jazz-tango, the two dance simply, with mutual respect and unexpected equality of esteem, and they speak straightforwardly and honestly. Here, the subtlety of the performances is key – although Brigitte Mira, as Emmi, tells Ali she 'hasn't danced in twenty years', she is unfazed to be asked, and gets up to dance with no sense of subordination or surprise.

Both here and later – when Ali walks her home with a kind of self-evident gallantry, and she invites him in – the dialogue does standard narrative work, giving information about the characters. But, in addition, the vocal performances (added later in voice-over) lend simplicity and dignity to their words, making of the encounter less a seduction and more a continuation of their dance. The dynamic between the two has an emphatic ordinariness and a childlike unintendedness about it. Nonetheless, by morning, there is an incorporeal moment of transformation; something has happened, a horizon of possibility has opened. As the film unfolds, we observe their relation to be primarily composed of a mixture of tenderness and solidarity: what lends it eroticism and romanticism is less a chemistry of bodies, than its sense of inevitability in a place of improbability.

Once the relation is established, inviting the viewer's investment in the story, all begins to go horribly wrong. But the problems are of more than one kind. As many observers have pointed out, the story divides neatly in two. In the first half, the couple's problems largely come from outside, while in the second – both a recapitulation and a development of the first – the relation erodes from within. The schematism and abstraction of this structure – as if the narrative is systematically testing their love under different conditions – is aligned with the coolness of the camera's gaze, which has many shots that hold characters within door or window frames, or fix them through the bars of stairwells. In part, this device visually underlines their isolation, but it also serves to frame them for *us*, showing them almost as exhibits.

In the first half, thus, the film foregrounds the comments of racist neighbours, the greed and hypocrisy of family members, the hostility of the local shopkeeper, the shameless stares of strangers. This all takes its toll: for Emmi in particular, the ostracism becomes unbearable. Although old and lonely, she still has social ties to family, colleagues and neighbours, and in that sense more to lose. However, the hostility also strengthens the couple, making marginalisation their common bond and the foundation of their relation. This simultaneous isolation and togetherness is highlighted in a famous sequence, with Ali and Emmi seated alone in a large café garden, the camera – in a rare break from its usual carefully composed static framings – moving around them, as if to trace the circle of their exclusion. As the waiting staff stands and stares in cold impassiveness, they affirm their love, but Emmi breaks down, wishing aloud that they could leave and come back to find everyone 'nice'.

Emmi's wish for acceptance comes true, but without happy consequences. Returning from vacation, the couple finds a radically changed situation. Social rejection is replaced by manipulative acceptance, as the same figures who shunned or condemned them now find reason – they all want something – to re-establish ties. When outside pressure is reduced, the couple collapses internally. Emmi finds a route back into society, but at the price of collaborating in the exclusion of others, including a new Yugoslavian worker, now ostracised in her turn. Ali becomes more and more the Other in the home. Echoing the racist banalities of her co-workers, Emmi shows him off as an exotic–erotic exhibit. Ali, whose social connection is far more limited, escapes the stifling marital home through heavy drinking and sex with other women. He too can be shockingly cruel: in a bitter scene, he laughs along as his co-workers mock the unhappy Emmi as his 'grandmother from Morocco'.

If the division into two parts represents a kind of thesis and antithesis, the conclusion offers little redeeming synthesis. The penultimate scene, the narrative climax, repeats elements from Emmi's and Ali's history, and at first seems to offer the possibility of resolution. Emmi arrives at the bar to rescue Ali, who is recklessly gambling and drinking. Dressed in their wedding clothes, the couple dance again to the music of their first meeting. Here, in the space where the relation began, they attempt – as in the liberal model of relationships – to *talk through* their problems. All seems set for a third start, a higher and happier synthesis of understanding and honesty. Ali admits to sleeping around, Emmi forgives him; it doesn't matter, she says, she knows she is old, mutual kindness is more important.

At this point, Fassbinder violently aborts the reconciliation. Ali collapses with an ulcer, a condition that, we learn, is endemic and recurrent among immigrant workers. All easy hope is dispelled: the film stages the futility of interpersonal goodwill in the face of social conditions, conditions which burrow deep into the bodies of the poor. The film ends downbeat and ambivalent, with Emmi weeping by Ali's hospital bed, vowing to take care of him. Some see this as a kind of happy ending; if so, then only in the spirit of the film's sober motto, a quotation from Godard's *Vivre sa vie*: 'Happiness is not always fun'.

Note

1. For a good summary of these readings, see Gorfinkel 2012.

Further reading

Richard Dyer, 'Reading Fassbinder's Sexual Politics', in Tony Rayns (ed.), *Fassbinder*, London, British Film Institute, 1980, pp. 54–65.

Thomas Elsaesser, *Fassbinder's Germany: History, Identity, Subject*, Amsterdam, Amsterdam University Press, 1996.

Rainer Werner Fassbinder, Michael Töteberg, Leo A. Lensing, *The Anarchy of the Imagination: Interviews, Essays, Notes*, Baltimore, Johns Hopkins University Press, 1992.

Robert Fischer (ed.), *Rainer Werner Fassbinder: Fassbinder über Fassbinder*, Frankfurt am Main, Verlag der Autoren, 2004.

Elena Gorfinkel, 'Impossible, Impolitic: *Ali: Fear Eats the Soul* and Fassbinder's Asynchronous Bodies', in Brigitte Peucker (ed.), *A Companion to Rainer Werner Fassbinder*, Hoboken, Wiley Blackwell, 2012, pp. 502–15.

Judith Mayne, 'Fassbinder and Spectatorship', *New German Critique*, Vol. 12, 1977, pp. 61–74.

Laura Mulvey, 'Notes on Sirk and Melodrama', in *Visual and Other Pleasures*, Bloomington, Indiana University Press, 1989, pp. 39–44.

Brían Hanrahan

Antonia's Line (1995)

[Country: Netherlands, Belgium, UK. Production Company: Bergen. Director and screenwriter: Marleen Gorris. Cinematographer: Willy Stassen. Editors: Wim Louwrier, Michiel Reichwein. Music: Ilona Sekacz. Cast: Willeke van Ammelrooy (Antonia), I Els Dottermans (Danielle), Veerle van Overloop (Therese), Marina de Graaf (Deedee), Jan Decleir (Farmer Bas), Mil Seghers (Crooked Finger).]

Synopsis: A Dutch matron oversees a close-knit, matriarchal community where feminism and liberalism thrive.

Antonia's Line won the Oscar for the best foreign language film of 1995, the first film by a female director ever to accomplish this feat. The woman in question was the Dutch filmmaker Marleen

Gorris, who had sprung to prominence with her sensational debut film, *A Question of Silence* (1982). Under the guise of a thriller about the seemingly motiveless murder of a male boutique owner by three women previously unknown to each other, that first film was an audacious feminist polemic that stormed the citadels of oppressive patriarchy. Made almost as a kind of avant-garde movie which therefore pulled no punches, the film's uncompromising originality propelled it into the mainstream, where it became hugely controversial. Rather like the legal figures at the end of the film who fail to see that the huge explosion of derisive female laughter is directed at them, hypersensitive male critics missed the film's mode of black comedy and were offended by its seeming proposition that the solution to patriarchy might be murder. (It was not proposing that, any more than cannibalism was being seriously offered as a solution to poverty and starvation in Jonathan Swift's political pamphlet, *A Modest Proposal:* both satirists were taking up an extreme position and suggesting a metaphor that highlighted the horror of a particular social situation in the hope that the oppressors might feel some guilt and shame.) Possibly goaded by the angry accusations of an anti-male bias that bordered on hatred, Gorris's second film was the even more ferocious *Broken Mirrors* (1984), whose main setting is a brothel in a city where a serial killer is on the loose. 'They're all bastards', says the proprietor about the clientele of her Happy House brothel to a new girl, who, significantly, has become a prostitute out of economic necessity. 'Even the nice ones aren't nice.' Ironically, the only sympathetic male character in the film is literally a dirty old man, a harmless, unseen hermit who is befriended by the brothel-keeper, but who, to her dismay, is expelled from his hideaway because he is not 'normal', the implication being that the 'normal' male is much more of a threat.

The vehemence of Gorris's feminism in her first two films even discomfited some feminists, who accused her of being not so much provocative as paranoid (see, for example, Pam Cook's (1985: 114) review of *Broken Mirrors*). Nevertheless, *The Last Island* (1990) continued in much the same vein, being a feminine *Lord of the Flies* for grown-ups, in which a motley group of men and women are shipwrecked on an island, fall out, turn violent, and where only the women survive. Still, the characterisation of the men is more complex than before; and this strain is continued in *Antonia's Line,* which is mellower and even upbeat in effect and allows some males to exhibit such hitherto unacknowledged characteristics as kindness, unselfishness and compassion. Here the nice ones *stay* nice. Admittedly, the narrative is still unashamedly female-driven and dominated, and the most sympathetic man is a philosophical recluse who would make even Schopenhauer look cheerful by comparison. Yet there is a greater generosity of spirit to all humankind, and an exuberant relish for life's variety that sweeps up everything in its path. When it was shown at the Toronto Festival, the film was given a standing ovation.

The story is told in flashback by Antonia (a superb performance from Willeke van Ammelrooy), remembering her past on what she has decided is to be the last day of her life; and also by a narrator who only at the end reveals herself to be Antonia's great-granddaughter, Sarah. The point of view is important, for, whereas at the beginning it is said of their community that 'men's noise rode roughshod over [a woman's] silence', the women will gradually be given a voice; will insist on making themselves heard; and will assume power over their own lives and, crucially, their own sexuality. When Antonia and her daughter Danielle have first returned to Antonia's home village just after the war to attend to her dying mother and take over the family farm, they have walked past a wall which has the sign 'Welcome To Our Liberators' scrawled over it. It no doubt refers to the Allied soldiers who have liberated the village after the war, but, in retrospect, it will apply equally to Antonia and Danielle, who will go some way towards liberating the community from its chauvinism, prejudice and conformity.

Over a number of years Antonia's farm will become a kind of benevolent matriarchy, a haven for the misfits and the maltreated of the village. These include the retarded Deedee, who, in an early scene reminiscent of Thomas Hardy, has been offered up for sale by her brutish father. When she is being sexually abused in a barn by her brother, Pitte, Danielle leaps to her defence by impaling Pitte with a pitchfork and taking her back to the farm. Deedee will bond with Loony Lips, who was taken under Antonia's wing when he was being persecuted by the sons of Farmer Bas, a relative newcomer to the village (he has only been there 20 years). Bas will be impressed by Antonia's humanity and courage and will propose marriage. 'The sons need a mother', he says. 'But I don't need your sons', says Antonia, who will refuse his offer but will later enter into a relationship with him of deep mutual affection. In the meantime, the growing Danielle decides she wants a baby. 'And what about a husband to go with it?' asks Antonia. 'I don't think so', she replies. Danielle will have a daughter, Therese, who will turn out to be a mathematical genius. Danielle herself will become a gifted painter and fall in love at first sight with Therese's teacher, a moment signalled when Danielle, who has always had a vivid imagination, immediately transforms her in her mind's eye into a vision of Botticelli's Venus.

And so it goes on. A friend, who has helped Antonia find a suitable young man to father Danielle's child, turns up at the farm and immediately falls for a curate, who has just left the church because he found it too constricting for his innate sense of happiness; and together they will produce 12 children. If all this sounds impossibly idyllic, one should add that the film is not blind to the darker sides of life. Although a kindly and much-loved tutor to Antonia's offspring, the hermit Crooked Finger can never shake himself free from his conviction of the fundamental cruelty and futility of existence, and he will commit suicide. Loony Lips will die in an accident and Deedee will be inconsolable, until reminded that 'life wants to live' and she must carry on. In the most disturbing section of the film, Deedee's contemptible brother, Pitte returns to the village and, in retaliation for Danielle's attack on him all those years before, pays her back by raping (off-screen) her daughter, Therese. All out for revenge, Antonia will arm herself with a shotgun, but, on confronting the rapist, she curses rather than kills him, saying that killing is not in her nature. Women give life, not take it; to do the latter would be fighting a monster like him with the very weapons they deplore. Curiously, though, the curse casts its spell. Later that night, Pitte is to be beaten up by the sons of Farmer Bas; and when he returns home, he is murdered by his brother, who has always hated him.

The fulfilment of Antonia's curse seems like an element in a fairy tale, and is an example of the film's narrative and stylistic fluidity. Although grounded mainly in earthy naturalism, paying particular attention to collective enterprise and the women's domestic labour on the farm, the film also has whimsical flights of fantasy and surrealism. Antonia's mother sits up in her coffin to sing 'My Blue Heaven' at her own funeral; a statue of Mary suddenly smiles; a stone angel uses its wing to clobber an unholy priest who has refused the last rites to a man who sheltered Jews during the war. This rich stew of disparate elements – magical realism, bucolic revelry, Europeanised gloom – was not to everyone's taste; and even an admirer of the film like Robin Wood thought that the film's Utopian fantasy, 'miraculously exempt from the incursions of corporate capitalism' (1998: 315) was inconsistent with other details of the film, such as the fact that this village, which seems removed from most of the trappings of modern civilisation, is nevertheless situated in close proximity to a large modern university. 'We need empowering utopian fantasies', he wrote, but added that 'they must take into account the conditions within which we actually today exist and struggle, for how can we strive to reach a utopia in which it is impossible to believe?' (Wood 1998: 316–17). However, it is possible to take the film as essentially a folk-tale or matriarchal fable with, in the words of a *Sight and Sound* review, 'all the magic of a Chagall painting' (McNab and Tunney 1997: 59). Certainly the film is less concerned with social realism and evolution than with the eternal life-cycle of birth and death. This is nicely conveyed in the circling camera movement as Therese's new-born baby girl is handed from villager to villager in an act of communal blessing; and also suggested in the narrator's summation that 'as this long chronicle draws to a conclusion, nothing has ended'.

Since *Antonia's Line*, Gorris has moved from filming her own original screenplays and tended to specialise more in heavyweight literary adaptations. She crafted a fine cinematic interpretation of Virginia Woolf's feminist classic *Mrs Dalloway* (1997), starring Vanessa Redgrave; and an interesting version of Vladimir Nabokov's *The Luzhin Project* (2000), with John Turturro and Emily Watson. With Emily Watson again, she also made a compelling adaptation of Eugenia Ginzburg's harrowing but ultimately heroic personal memoir as a literary professor in the Stalinist era sentenced to ten years hard labour in Siberia, *Within the Whirlwind* (2009), which has had only a limited worldwide release. Recently she has directed a television mini-series about the life of Rembrandt. *Antonia's Line* remains her biggest international success thus far, with audiences relishing its warm vitality, lusty femininity and gutsy resilience in the face of patriarchal prejudice and pressure, though, in my view, Robin Wood is right in suggesting that *A Question of Silence* still stands as 'her finest achievement to date' (Wood 1998: 317). In that film, the women's laughter in the courtroom that concludes the trial, undermining the confidence and certainty of arrogant male authority, is as liberating as Ibsen's notorious and resonant slammed door that concludes *A Doll's House*. *A Question of Silence* alone will ensure that Gorris remains a permanent icon of feminist film at its most powerful, provocative and pertinent.

Further reading

Pam Cook, 'Review: *Broken Mirrors*,' *Monthly Film Bulletin*, April, 1985, p. 114.

Maggie Humm, 'Author/Auteur: Feminist Literary Theory and Feminist Film' in *Feminism and Film*, Edinburgh, Edinburgh University Press, 1999, pp. 90–111.

Barbara Koenig Quart, *Women Directors: The Emergence of a New Cinema*, New York, Praeger, 1988.

Geoffrey McNab and Tom Tunney 'Review: *Antonia's Line*', *Sight and Sound*, May, 1997, p. 59.

Neil Sinyard, 'A Question of Gorris', *Dutch Crossing*, Winter, 1997, pp. 100–16.

Robin Wood, *Sexual Politics and Narrative Film*, Columbia University Press, 1998, pp. 315–17.

Neil Sinyard

Apocalypse Now (1979)

[Country: USA. Production Company: Zoetrope Studios. Director and producer: Francis Ford Coppola. Screenwriters: John Milius and Coppola. Cinematographer: Vittorio Storaro. Music: Carmine Coppola and Coppola. Editors: Lisa Fruchtman, Gerald Greenberg and Walter Murch. Cast: Marlon Brando (Colonel Walter E. Kurtz), Martin Sheen (Captain Willard), Robert Duvall (Lieutenant Colonel Kilgore), Frederic Forrest (Jay 'Chef' Hicks), Sam Bottoms (Lance B. Johnson), Albert Hall (Chief Phillips), Laurence Fishburne (Tyrone 'Clean' Miller), Dennis Hopper (photojournalist).]

Synopsis: Special Forces operative, Captain Willard, is given the task of journeying up the Mekong River during the Vietnam War to find and kill a US army officer, Colonel Kurtz, who has set up his own kingdom deep in the jungle where he is worshipped as a god by the local people. A series of episodes along the way highlight in various ways the insanities of the war before Willard locates and assassinates the enigmatic Kurtz.

Heavily indebted to Joseph Conrad's novella *Heart of Darkness*, it might be argued that this film wears its literary credentials rather too pretentiously. When we first meet Dennis Hopper's photojournalist character,[1] for example, he seems to attribute god-like stature to Kurtz (Marlon Brando) partly on the basis that he quotes lines from T. S. Eliot's *The Love*

Song of J. Alfred Prufrock; hardly the most likely piece of verse to be quoted by a US army officer who in the late 1960s/early 1970s has set himself up as a small-time, ultra-authoritarian dictator deep inside South East Asia. When we eventually meet Kurtz himself there is further use of Eliot's verse; this time perhaps more appropriately from *The Hollow Men* but still rather lacking in originality.[2]

But it is not the range of literary allusions, from the placing of a copy of James Frazer's *The Golden Bough* on Willard's bedside table during the opening to the photojournalist scuttling from Kurtz's presence towards the end reciting the final words from Eliot's *The Hollow Men*,

> This is the way the world ends
> Not with a bang but a whimper,

that makes this an important film. These somewhat forced attempts to express profound insights into the wider nature of the human experience are probably the weakest part of the whole. The most interesting aspect of this film is the way in which it offers, just four years after the fall of Saigon, a complex set of responses to the American experience of Vietnam.

In Conrad's book the narrator, Marlow, takes the reader ever deeper into the depths of the late nineteenth-century European colonial enterprise, on a journey that operates as a metaphor for an examination of the (dark) heart of man:[3] in *Apocalypse Now* we follow our narrator, Willard, as he is drawn with fatalistic inevitability ever further into an exploration of the American imperialist venture in Vietnam and Cambodia. Through him we experience both the historical realities of this particular war and its psychological ramifications for those individuals (and maybe a whole society) ensnared in the ongoing nightmare of that moment. Both Marlow and Willard move towards a mysterious man called Kurtz, who seems to offer the possibility of some insight into not only the particular expansionist enterprise under examination but also the psychological (even, the spiritual) state of man. Both the novella and the film move towards their culmination in the final words of Kurtz, 'The horror, the horror', and both abandon the reader to their own devices to decide the significance (if any) of these words.

Apocalypse Now utilises a very basic episodic narrative with no great sense of new complications or developments – we are simply and inevitably moving towards the climactic rendezvous with Kurtz. A sequence of events may occur which reveal an ever stronger sense of the madness at the heart of the American GI's experience of Vietnam but these are merely sights along the way. A lieutenant colonel, Kilgore (Robert Duvall), who loves 'the smell of napalm in the morning' leads a helicopter charge scudding across the sky to the sound of Wagner's *Ride of the Valkyries*;[4] troops at an army base riot at the sight of the tantalising glimpses of home offered by Playgirls during a surreal 'girlie' stage show; soldiers in a forward base surrounded by Viet Cong and abandoned by their commanders survive in a drug-induced haze; and, in between, a routine search of a sampan results in the slaughter of an innocent Vietnamese family by inexperienced, nervous US 'kids' abroad. There is no connection between these events other than that they occur during Willard's journey towards Kurtz. And this sense of a disjointed, dislocated picaresque narrative is entirely fitting for a film about the madness of war and the insanity of man.

However, despite this episodic approach there is some sense of steady incremental change as the story progresses. We move from daylight and vast tracts of open water at the start of the journey towards an ever-narrowing funnel of a river, ever more night-time episodes, and ever darker and more death-filled events. Not only that but Willard and those who are unfortunate enough to find themselves accompanying him into the jungle darkness lose their innocence in a remorseless delving ever deeper into their self and away from 'civilisation'. For Willard this culminates in a shot of him emerging at night from a swamp, half-naked and with his face blackened, on his way towards carrying out the ritual slaughter of Kurtz.

In one sense Willard might be said to kill his alter ego, in another he plays the endgame as Kurtz seems to require it to be played, but in a further narrative sense he simply operates as the traditional hero who successfully reaches the inner cave where the final test must be endured and emerges triumphant and therefore able to return to the world changed but also ritually cleansed. What this has to say about the American experience in Nam, about war in general (and about the human condition) is open to interpretation.[5] If as Kurtz asserts he has seen through to the purity of action that is required in order to win such a war, then in showing this as unacceptable to the US authorities the film might be seen to be critical of the armed forces (and perhaps a democratic country) that was not prepared to go far enough. However, Willard's comment that he can see no method in what Kurtz is engaged in positions him as the restorer of not only order but also reason (and, therefore, sanity).

In keeping with the episodic nature of the whole, the initial exposition phase effectively operates as a self-contained short film. Jim Morrison's lyrics playing over images of a verdant jungle devastated by the explosive intrusion of human technology followed by a scene in a claustrophobic hotel room effectively brings together the external socio-political world and the interior human psychology. And these dual aspects of the film come together in the superimposed image of the jungle fires playing around Willard's head. The war and its effects are inescapable. Willard's response as he peers between the slats of the blind, 'Saigon: shit', represents at several levels what within a few years of the deployment of troops came to be the dominant American response to Vietnam. Our guide is immediately disconcertingly positioned as observing this place but yet cut off from it and unable to comprehend it. We begin with a contradiction which is also a statement: 'This is the end'. This film is in its entirety going to be about 'the end': the end of civilisation, the end in terms of the death of the individual, and most of all, the end in terms of a reaching of the extremes of human experience.

The resolution phase too 'works' in the same way; from the moment Willard reaches Kurtz's kingdom we find ourselves in a section from the whole that has its own sense of narrative structure with its own exposition, development, complication, climax and resolution phases. The only element holding the whole together is the presence of Willard, just as Marlow is the only link maintaining any sense of coherence within Conrad's *Heart of Darkness*. This is entirely appropriate: the creative impulse behind both the film and the novella is the idea that the only thing enabling any sense to be made of the world at large is the connectedness achieved through the individual consciousness (and storytelling).

To be more critical, this film is American-centred and highly masculine[6] in its outlook. However, this would be to criticise it for what it is not rather than to recognise it for what it is, to judge it in terms that are beyond its terms of reference. This is a key US film because it attempts to deal with a national disaster that was at the time very recent. That it explores this period in such a way as to convert a naïve (if not idiotic) foreign policy into a heroic if doomed effort to come to some understanding of the human condition might be a valid criticism; but the fact that it does this at precisely this point in American history demonstrates the strength of the US desire to see its efforts prevail and to envision even its failures as Hollywood, even epic, in scale.

This film is a reflection of complex contradictions found in the USA in the period, and not simply, as some commentators have suggested, a condemnation of the war. In its bold approach it embodies the emergence into the cultural arena of the confidence of a younger generation taking on the perceived failings of their parents. It attempts to confront the arrogance of US foreign policy and yet remains firmly and confidently US-centred in its offering of solutions. The sequence showing Kilgore's attack on the Vietnamese village is entirely conventional in Hollywood terms in its use of sound and cinematography to engender an atmosphere of gung-ho excitement; and yet it also employs the powerful juxtaposition of the cut to the peace, tranquillity and innocence of the village that is about to be attacked. We are given a full-on Hollywood experience only to end in the shadows of a cave with a madman searching for truth in an insane world ('Horror has a face and you must make a friend of horror.' 'To kill without judgement because it is judgement that defeats us.'). It is not just that war is pointless and inhumane (and yet horribly human), but that there is something sick at the very heart of man; and this evil cannot be escaped but only faced and accepted.

Notes

1. Several photojournalists simply disappeared into the jungle in South East Asia in the period US forces were operating in the region. One of them, Sean Flynn, as the son of actors Errol Flynn and Lili Damita, had a slightly higher profile than the others. He worked in both Vietnam and Cambodia, but was captured in Cambodia by the Viet Cong or Khmer Rouge in 1970 and is believed to have been killed in 1971.
2. Kurtz reading from *The Hollow Men* was added during shooting and was not in the original script from Milius.
3. There are few representations of women in the film. The Playboy 'chicks' 'choppered' in and then swiftly out of the first American base visited on the Mekong are conventional sex objects and the disembodied, taped female voice playing at the death of 'Mr Clean' is that of the other traditional female figure of the mother.
4. The handmaidens of Odin who in Old Norse mythology rush into the confusion of battle on horseback and with swords drawn in order to carry off those selected for death; who are then taken to Valhalla as heroes.
5. See Frank P. Tomasulo, 'The Politics of Ambivalence: *Apocalypse Now* as a Prowar and Antiwar Film' in Linda Dittmar and Gene Michaud (eds), *From Hanoi to Hollywood: the Vietnam War in American Film*, New Brunswick, Rutgers University Press, 1990, pp. 145–58.
6. See the shot of the hand caressing the missile slung on the side of a helicopter as Kilgore's attack commences.

Further reading

James Clarke, *Coppola*, London, Virgin, 2003.

Eleanor Coppola, *Notes: On the Making of 'Apocalypse Now'*, London, Faber, 1995.

Peter Cowie, *The 'Apocalypse Now' Book*, London, Faber, 2000.

Linda Dittmar and Gene Michaud (eds), *From Hanoi to Hollywood: the Vietnam War in American Film*, New Brunswick, Rutgers University Press, 1990.

John White

Asfour Stah/Halfaouine: Boy of the Terraces (1990)

[Country: Tunisia, France. Production Company: Cinétéléfilms, Scarabée Films, France-Media, La SEPT, RTT, WDR. Producers: Ahmed Attia, Hassen Daldoul, Eliane Stutterheim. Director: Ferid Boughedir. Screenwriters: Ferid Boughedir, Nouri Bouzid, Taoufik Jebali, Maryse León García. Cinematographer: Georges Barsky. Music: Anouar Braham. Editor: Moufida Tlatli. Cast: Selim Boughedir (Noura), Mustapha Adouani (Si Azzouz), Rabia Ben Abdallah (La Jamila), Mohamed Driss (Salih), Hélène Catzaras (Latifa), Fatima Ben Saidane (Salouha), Abdelhamid Gayess (Cheikh Mokhtar), Jamel Sassi (Moncef), Radhouane Meddeb (Mounir), Carolyn Chelby (Leila).]

Synopsis: With his mother's agreement, 12-year-old Noura, looking younger than his age, is still admitted to the women's hammam in Halfaouine, a neighbourhood in Tunis. His older friends ask him to provide licentious details on the life in the hammam and on the bodies of the women taking baths there. On the day of his brother's circumcision, an act that repulses him, Noura is excluded from the hammam because he approaches a bather too closely. After this he is obliged to visit the men's baths with his father. He approaches the young servant Leila sensually, which results in her dismissal. He also loses the complicity of Salih, a libertarian poet arrested by the police for his anti-conformist political propositions. He dwells on fantastic images from his childhood; that of a disturbing, bearded ogre and that of a man with castrating scissors. Practically isolated, as if chased from paradise, finding himself between a rock and a hard place, not knowing any longer if he should join the adult world or if he wants to stay young so as not to be far from women, he responds with a mocking laughter to his father's prohibitions and escapes onto the terraces of the neighbourhood toward an uncertain future.

The film is a fairy tale (the director's father was a librarian and a storyteller), that of a difficult passage from the world of children to the world of adults, a traumatising initiation into the formation of the libido, into the desire for women. The hammam, which Western literature and painting have portrayed since the eighteenth century, offers Noura an opportunity to approach with an indiscrete gaze the bodies of women, without veils, in a sensuous atmosphere where the vaporous warmth puts reason to sleep, where one puts one's guard down and where social etiquette is weakened.

These modern odalisques have the taste of forbidden fruit. The film tells with fervour, without discourse, how a sexual initiation happens, against the forces forbidding all liberation, against the Islamist precepts of religious master Mokhtar, against the advice of his father ('a man never cries, a man doesn't hang around with women'), bothered by the vulgar questions posed by his two macho friends.

Largely inspired by the life of a perfectly Westernised director, but also inscribed within a culture where in 1990 the crude description of sexuality is still impossible, this films locates itself on a territory that Western filmmakers have evoked more crudely, in particular that of a young man's sexual initiation into brothels, sometimes recommended and organised by the parents themselves (nothing better than professionalism in this matter!). The films of François Truffaut starring Jean-Pierre Léaud as Antoine Doinel come to mind.

Boughedir also evokes the Western myth of the harem here, liberally described and painted in Europe in the eighteenth century. We discover the very modern idea that the female body captured in opacity and an aesthetically seductive tepidness evokes more desire than complete, realistic and anatomical nudity.

Thus the hammam invokes the harem by inversion, this confined space of women (recalling the gynaecium of antiquity) where the master and lord comes to choose a mistress who will be prepared in the baths by the servants (cf. *1001 Nights*). Noura will have known the ancestral desire for the harem without having had a chance to satisfy it. Expulsed from the body of the woman, and having symbolically killed the father, he will topple into another story, another culture, unknown and intimidating.

'I am fascinated by the women in my country. They have a kind of genius of life. They have managed, despite everything, to have fewer constraints than men .... I wanted to show that the laughter of women is the most powerful thing in the world. In this moment [when they laugh after the husband enters and leaves the courtyard], they are in charge of the house. The joy of women is stronger than any dogma.'[1] The body of the women in the hammam is sublimated by the vision of the still innocent preadolescent. They have an appearance of freedom, but only in the domestic space, not in public.

There are four female figures in the film:

1. Noura's mother, young and pretty, her son's accomplice, lies in order to allow him to enter the hammam with her, and defends him when his father mistreats him.
2. Latifa, young and sexy, dressed in Western fashion, divorced and thus free, provocative, goes to secretly get her 'shot' (i.e. see her lover) every day!
3. Salouha, emotionally unhappy, close to insanity, is at the mercy of the fundamentalist chief, a victim of the intolerance against women.
4. Leila, in a welcoming corset, provides Noura with a practical substitute for the buxom nudities of the hammam.

Ferid Boughedir is a perfect representative of an artist and intellectual with close ties to Western culture. A regular at the Cinémathèque française, assistant to Alain Robbe-Grillet and Francisco Arrabal, film critic and author of a dissertation on African cinemas, he sees this Tunisian society in the midst of transformation from a modern Western point of view: 'these were things I didn't feel until I was in Paris'.[2] He both manages to escape censorship in Tunisia and knows how to satisfy an international audience.

The women in the hammam are extras, French *beurettes* (French women of North African origin) who accepted the roles because of a certain integrity of the film's gaze, which did not shock them, and which also convinced Tunisian censorship.

The question of Islamic fundamentalism is present but there is neither a political analysis nor an answer to the problem of fundamentalism itself. The film is not anti-religious; it only stigmatises taboos that lead to hypocrisy and intolerance. It depicts an 'Arab society where everything is taboo and where real life transpires via a succession of small transgressions'.[3] It gives the shoemaker, the 'clown' of the neighbourhood, the only one who secretly tells the truth because he is a poet, who is under the surveillance of a still moderate police, a gentle hint of freedom. Cohabitation is still possible between the generations and between political positions; conflicts will emerge later.

There is however a social truth in the depiction of the inhabitants' behaviour which could usefully interest anthropologists and sociologists. Halfaouine represents a small microcosm that recalls the films of French filmmaker Marcel Pagnol, a theatre of the everyday where people exchange things, observe each other without hate (at the barber's, at the market), where the women of the men who claim authority exchange saucy stories about them, and where everyday life is above all peaceful. The scene of the circumcision, even if it repulses Noura, is treated like a secular religious custom difficult to condemn.

Let us add that despite the film's Mediterranean setting, a touristic vision, an exotic Tunisia of *souks*, is absent. The only concession to an architectural geography of the South can be found in the omnipresence of the terraces which have a double symbolic function, as they facilitate a 'horizontal communication' floating above the vaporous roundness of the hammam, as well as an escape towards a world above, dissident, still to be reached, a symbolism also found in other films, such as *Pépé le Moko* (Julien Duvivier, 1937) and *A Special Day* (Ettore Scola, 1977).

Notes

1. Bernard Génin, 'L'hymne à la joie', interview with Ferid Boughedir, *Télérama*, 26 September 1990.
2. Nicolas Saada, 'Halfaouine', *Les Cahiers du cinéma*, No. 433, June 1990, p. 61.
3. Ferid Boughedir in *L'Evénement du jeudi*, 27 September 1990.

Further reading

Ferid Boughedir interview, You Tube, www.youtube.com/watch?v=5BAOyBEI9lI.

Sonia Chamkhi, *Le cinéma tunisien à la lumière de la modernité (1996–2006)*, Tunis, Centre de publication universitaire, 2009.

Jean-Michel Frodon, 'Regard d'enfance', *Le Monde*, 27 September 1990.

Jacques Grant, *Halfaouine*, Ministère de l'Education nationale, Collège au cinéma, Dossier 40, Paris, C.N.C., 1992.

Sélim Nassib, 'Sexe, Femmes et Halfaouine', *Libération*, 27 September 1990.

Vinent Ostria, 'L'œil du désir, *Cahiers du cinéma*, No. 435, September 1990, 67–8.

www.cinematunisien.com

Daniel Armogathe (translated by Sabine Haenni)

L'Atalante (1934)

[Country: France. Production Company: Gaumont. Director: Jean Vigo. Screenwriters: Jean Guinée, Jean Vigo, and Albert Riéra. Producer: Jacques-Louis Nounez. Cinematographers: Boris Kaufman and Louis Merger. Music: Maurice Jaubert. Editor: Louis Chavance. Cast: Jean Dasté (Jean), Dita Parlow (Juliette), Michel Simon (Père Jules), Gilles Margaritis (the showman), Louis Lefebvre (the kid).]

Synopsis: Jean, a barge captain, marries Juliette in her rural village. The newlyweds depart for Paris to complete Jean's cargo delivery. They are joined on the boat by Père Jules and 'le gosse', a cabin boy. Jean promises Juliette a night away from the monotony of the barge once they reach their destination. However, their shipmates thwart these plans. Père Jules and the cabin boy escape into the streets of Paris before them and Jean cannot leave the boat unattended. Juliette eventually sneaks away to explore the city on her own and Jean responds to the betrayal by leaving her behind. The two reunite with the help of Père Jules. He discovers Juliette in a music shop and returns her to the boat and her beloved.

By nearly all accounts, including Jean Vigo's, *L'Atalante* killed its director. Vigo was just 29 years old. *L'Atalante* was only his fourth film and his first feature-length project. The film depicts the first days of marriage between Jean (Jean Dasté) and Juliette (Dita Parlow) – a barge captain and a young woman from the countryside – as they sail along the waterways with a small and peculiar crew. *L'Atalante* was shot on location between November 1933 and January 1934 in the expansive network of canals that stretch from Paris northward to Le Havre. Vigo had suffered from respiratory illnesses throughout his life and the harsh winter accelerated his already deteriorating health. He spent the final weeks of production directing from his sickbed. His cinematographer, Boris Kaufman, shot the concluding scene – a startling aerial view of barges and canals – without him. Vigo never saw the footage. Three weeks before his death, the Gaumont studio imposed a final indignity upon his work. *L'Atalante* premiered in September 1934 at the Colisée cinema in Paris as *Le Chaland qui passe* (the passing barge), a mangled version of Vigo's original. The film had been re-edited, renamed and rescored to satisfy popular tastes and a set of spectators who never arrived. *Le Chaland qui passe* quietly disappeared from public view and Vigo died on October 5 1934, eight months after completing *L'Atalante.*

It is difficult to extricate *L'Atalante* from the tragic biography of Jean Vigo and the mythologies that have emerged in the aftermath of his early death. Vigo has come to occupy a monumental position in the history of French cinema, at once genius, martyr and patron saint of the French New Wave. Successive rounds of archival research and restoration (by Gaumont in 1940 and the Cinémathèque française in the 1950s) brought *L'Atalante* into contact with the energetic post-war cinephiles and critics in France. Just a few short years after his death, Vigo was resurrected as 'cinema incarnate', the model of radical and rebellious experimentation to which all filmmakers should aspire (Temple 2005: 2).

In *L'Atalante,* however, another mythology circulates, one that offers a framework – beyond Vigo's talent and sacrifice – for reading and understanding the film. The title refers to the name of the barge that floats Jean and Juliette towards marital conflict and resolution in Paris, but it also refers to a minor figure from Greek mythology: Atalanta, the daughter of Iasus, abandoned on a mountain and raised by bears (in one version of the myth) or hunters (in another). Atalanta is trained to fight and hunt. She refuses to marry and sails with the Argonauts as the only woman in their crew. She is an orphan and an oddity, at once animal and human, male and female, mortal and goddess. Her mixed history and genealogy challenge tidy taxonomies of both gender and metaphysics. One can easily find points of comparison between the figure of Atalanta and the character of Juliette, the barge *patronne* who leaves her rural home at the start of Vigo's film and sets sails as the only woman on board. But more interesting is the way in which this foundational myth prefigures the visual, narrative, and socio-historical mixtures that make *L'Atalante* such a remarkable and uncategorisable work.

L'Atalante combines the diverse modes of experimental filmmaking that constitute the European avant-garde in the 1920s and 30s. The film brings together the city symphony, surrealism, and poetic realism; it is at once an exploration of the labour and lives of the French working class and a study of *cinematic* work and ways of seeing. *L'Atalante* likewise intersects with cinema's transition to sound, a moment of visual and industrial flux that manifests itself within Vigo's film as yet another site of experimentation and play. The first scene exemplifies the film's composite form. *L'Atalante* begins with the sound of ringing bells and a montage of establishing shots: an image of the barge's stern; an enigmatic burst of mist that covers and conceals the canal; and an extreme low-angle shot of a church's spires. This opening sequence asks us to consider: Where is the sound coming from? And what does it mean? The bells ring out across these shots, attaching to each in turn. The sound seems to emanate from the ship, the clouds, and, finally, the spires. We soon see Jean and Juliette exit the church and can perhaps retroactively read the sound as wedding bells and the film's first images as a map of the processional to come. The young couple will make their way from the ceremony to the awaiting barge, with the villagers trailing behind them. From here, however, the narrative ambiguities and visual associations continue to gather. Jean and Juliette glide through the village streets, then a field of haystacks, a forest of flowers, and a barren field before finally arriving at the ship. As spectators, we never know where they are, how much progress they have made, or how these distinct spaces are connected. Each cut introduces a radically new geography and a different cinematographic style. Jean and Juliette move across, away from, and into the frame; they are close, distant, and fragmented into parts. The first shot recalls the absurd processional of *Entr'acte* (René Clair, 1924), while the last approximates the strict formalism of Hans Richter or Walter Ruttman. Rather than adhering to a particular visual school, Vigo and Kaufman cycle through approaches. Each shot reframes and rethinks the relationship between human figures and the land.

In this introduction, Vigo crosscuts between the wedding processional and the frantic movements of another set of bodies: Père Jules (Michel Simon) and the young shipmate (Louis Lefebvre). The two men exit the church before our first encounter with Jean and Juliette, holding hands as they race back to the barge and prepare for the new *patronne*. The substitution of two men (one old, the other young) for the beautiful couple is a visual gag – one of many scattered throughout the film and the surrealist canon; however, it also signals the film's much broader play with bodies, genders and types. As Jean crawls on all fours to greet his new wife and characters dissolve in heavy fog, *L'Atalante* questions the stability of visual knowledge and rigid visual forms. Père Jules is an important example of this epistemic flexibility and uncertainty. Among the crew of domestic travellers, he is the spectre of colonialism and the embodiment of the exotic threat. Beneath his tattered clothes, he reveals a sprawling map of tattoos, including a male face (that 'smokes' from his belly button) and a female figure that stretches out across his back. Adorned in Juliette's skirt, he transforms into a woman, a member of a primitive tribe, and a matador in Seville. And he describes a photograph of a nude black woman hanging on his cabin wall as 'Me, when I was young'. Another set of gags, to be sure, but also something more. Like so many aspects of the film, Père Jules is fluid, mercurial, a patchwork of other times and places. For Michael Temple, Père Jules and *L'Atalante* are inextricably, symbiotically joined: 'Père Jules becomes the film's decentred centre, everywhere and nowhere, palpably dispersed in every sound and image, as if Simon's body and voice had somehow got into the grain of the film-stock' (2005: 132). The comparison speaks to the unstructured and ephemeral qualities that define Père Jules – torn and dispersed across the celluloid – as well as the collage of influences and inscriptions that *L'Atalante* shares with the ageing sailor.

Technically, *L'Atalante* is a narrative film. It contains a skeletal set of plot points, inherited from a script written by Jean Guinée. Love is found in the countryside, lost in the modern city, and eventually regained on the canal. But when 'L'Atalante' initially departs, the film and its characters go almost nowhere (that is, until they dock in Paris).

There are no recognisable landmarks: just water, a boat, and an indiscriminate shoreline. Meaning emerges out of the mise-en-scène, or the physical and material world of the film, rather than the clarity or accumulation of narrative events. *L'Atalante* draws our attention to the barge's cramped interiors, overflowing with dirty dishes and laundry to be done, broken-down machines, and dozens of cats that scratch, breed and blur with the dishevelled Père Jules. The camera squeezes in between objects and bodies, and presents the domestic spaces in awkward, proximate views. Truffaut accused *L'Atalante* of having smelly feet, an assessment that foregrounds both the corporeal and extra-visual aspects of the film (1978: 27). *L'Atalante* is tactile, textured, and scented with the grime of the working everyday. But for all of its investments in the sensory-material experience of life spent and worked along the canals, *L'Atalante* shares in the surrealist search for the marvellous and the magical in the most common of matter. For surrealist poet and novelist Louis Aragon, cinema was privileged in its ability to 'endow with a poetic value that which does not yet possess it, to wilfully restrict the field of vision so as to intensify its expression' (2000: 52). In Père Jules's cabin (and the film's most famous scene), Juliette uncovers his stash of trinkets, an oasis of memory and global travel. For Jean, the cabin is filled with disgusting junk. For Jules, it is a collection of the 'most beautiful things'. But for Juliette, the objects liberate her from the drudgery of life on the canals, sending her imagination to the open sea.

This division between the everyday and the extraordinary gives shape to the film's most abundant visual resource: water. As many critics have noted, *L'Atalante* is a very damp film (Andrew 1985; Conley 2006). Water encircles the barge and dominates the exterior shots (in the form of mist, fog, cloud, and snow). The atmosphere along the canals, like the filth inside the cabins, appeals to our skin and sense of touch. It also contributes to some of the most superlative compositions in the film (and, some might well argue, the entire history of cinema). But within the narrative of *L'Atalante*, water transcends its physical and aesthetic attributes. Vigo explicitly joins this element to a form of supernatural and cinematic vision. In the first days of their marriage, Juliette holds Jean's head beneath the wash water and asks, 'Don't you know you can see your beloved's face in water?... When I was little I saw things like that. And last year, I saw your face in the water.' After Juliette leaves the barge behind for a life in Paris, Jean jumps in the canal, broken-hearted and searching for his beloved. He swims against the sounds of Maurice Jaubert's haunting score, his body flowing into and out of frame. Juliette appears, angel-like, suspended in her wedding dress and superimposed upon Jean's body. On the one hand, the image belongs to Jean. It is his vision of Juliette, conjured in her absence. And yet, on the other, it cannot belong to him. It is an image *of* Jean and Juliette, a multilayered projection of bodies and frames that delights in the material and marvels of cinema itself.

When Père Jules and Juliette sit together at her sewing table, he says, holding up his palms, 'Look at these hands. You'd never guess all the things they've done.' Of course, everyone aboard the barge works with his or her hands. They are a band of tinkerers, or *bricoleurs*, collecting, cobbling, making magic, and playing music with the scraps of modern life. Dudley Andrew describes hands and handiwork in *L'Atalante* as a 'symbolic cluster' (1985: 64). There are scenes of hands, comments about hands, and, most remarkably, a set of pickled hands on a shelf. However, the symbolic content of these hands at work (or in jars) extends beyond the diegesis. *L'Atalante* is a *handmade* film, like the objects packed into Père Jules's cabin ('all handmade', he insists). It is rough around the edges, made by a band of tinkerers and bricoleurs who borrowed, gathered, and experimented with whatever was at hand. Beneath its messy and imperfect surface, one finds an open text, a dense collection of images and ideas, and a radically mixed *Atalanta*.

Further reading

James Dudley Andrew, 'The Fever of an Infectious Film: *L'Atalante* and the Aesthetics of Spontaneity', in *Film in the Aura of Art*, Princeton, Princeton University Press, 1985, pp. 59–77.

Louis Aragon, 'On Décor', in Paul Hammond (ed.), *The Shadow and Its Shadow*, New York: City Lights Books, 2000 [1918], pp. 50–4.

Tom Conley, 'Getting Lost on the Waterways of *L'Atalante*', in Murray Pomerance (ed.), *Cinema and Modernity*, Piscataway, NJ, Rutgers University Press, 2006, pp. 253–72.
Paul Emilio Salles Gomes, *Jean Vigo*, London, Faber & Faber, 1998.
Michael Temple, *Vigo*, Manchester and New York, University of Manchester Press, 2005.
François Truffaut, 'Jean Vigo is Dead at Twenty-Nine', in *The Films of My Life*, trans. Leonard Mayhew, New York: Simon & Schuster, 1978 [1975].
Jean Vigo, 'Toward a Social Cinema', in Richard Abel (ed.), trans. Stuart Liebman, *French Film Theory and Criticism: A History/Anthology, 1907–1939*, volume II, Princeton, NJ, Princeton University Press, 1988 [1930], pp. 60–3.
Marina Warner, *L'Atalante*, London, British Film Institute, 1993.

Katherine Groo

Atanarjuat: the Fast Runner (2001)

[Country: Canada. Production Company: Aboriginal Peoples Television Network, Canada Television and Cable Production Fund License Program, Canadian Television, Channel 24 Igloolik, Igloolik Isuma Productions, National Film Board of Canada. Director: Zacharias Kunuk. Producers: Paul Apak Angilirq, Norman Cohn and Zacharias Kunuk. Co-producer: National Film Board of Canada. Screenwriters: Apak Angilirq, Norman Cohn, Zacharias Kunuk, Herve Paniaq, Pauloosie Qulitalik. Cinematographer: Cohn. Cast: Natar Ungalaaq (Atanarjuat), Pakak Innuksuk (Amajuat), Sylvia Ivalu (Atuat), Peter-Henry Arnatsiaq (Oki), Lucy Tulugarjuk (Puja).]

Synopsis: The story of *Atanarjuat: the Fast Runner* is based on an ancient Inuit legend that deals with the dangers of setting personal desires above the needs of a whole community. The film's narrative unfolds at the dawn of the first millennium, when Atanarjuat is still an infant. Inside a large igloo, families have gathered for a celebration. However, festivities are marred by evil spirits, and the camp leader and shaman, Kumaglak, is killed. His cruel son Sauri takes the reins of power, and as a result Atanarjuat's family is excluded from central activities in the camp. Nonetheless, Atanarjuat and his brother Amajuat grow to be healthy young men and skilled hunters. When Atanarjuat and his rival Oki both court the beautiful Atuat, new tensions arise. Atuat chooses Atanarjuat and for several years they remain happily married – until the treacherous Puja sets murderous events in motion. She betrays the brothers to Oki and several hunters, who kill Amajuat but fail to capture Atanarjuat. In an iconic scene, Atanarjuat runs naked over the broken spring ice to escape. He stays with friends, but then returns to the camp to confront Oki and his allies. He does not kill them but instead banishes them from the community, thus breaking the cycle of violence and revenge.

Atanarjuat: the Fast Runner was produced and directed by Zacharias Kunuk and Norman Cohn from Isuma Productions, an Inuit film company with offices in Montreal and Igloolik, Canada. The film received international acclaim and won a 'Camera d'Or' award for best feature at the 2001 Cannes film festival. As one of the first feature films, written, produced and directed by Inuit filmmakers, it represents a unique stage in Canadian and Aboriginal cinema. Its international success led to increased awareness of the importance of Indigenous filmmaking, especially in regards to presenting a necessary counterpoint to widespread stereotypical portrayals of Inuit and Native peoples in mainstream media. In *Atanarjuat* the filmmakers combined a community-based approach to storytelling with digital production technologies to create an authentic portrayal of life and customs in the Arctic.

The film's adaptation reveals a key difference from the Inuit legend that centres on Atanarjuat's escape and his miraculous survival. Instead of Atanarjuat killing Oki and his allies, he pardons them. This shifts the focus to the importance of the peaceful coexistence amongst members of an Inuit community, which ultimately ensures their survival in the harsh Arctic climate. According to filmmaker Cohn (as cited in Evans 2008: 94), *Atanarjuat* 'is about how to communicate the right way to behave and live. You learn by being told how to behave through stories. There is restitution and moral authority by restoring the value of community as superior to the value of the individual. That's an Inuit value.'

For *Atanarjuat* Kunuk and his partners used historical records and museum exhibits to explore traditional Inuit ways of life. Isuma's approach is therefore fundamentally different from mainstream filmmaking practices, starting with community involvement in every aspect of the production process. From costume making, set construction and make-up, to actors, scriptwriters and technicians, over a hundred Igloolik residents took part in the film; thus, generating important employment opportunities for local residents. Paul Apak wrote the script in Inuktitut, which Norman Cohn translated into English. *Atanarjuat* received public funding from agencies such as Telefilm Canada, after a lengthy process of convincing the government that the filmmakers should be able to access the funding stream marked for Canadian productions, rather than a smaller envelope designated for Aboriginal films. Isuma's persistence was rewarded: not only did the filmmakers augment the production budget for *Atanarjuat* they also increased awareness of in-built discriminatory perceptions of Aboriginal filmmaking practices and expectations of financial returns. The international success resulted in the recognition of Inuit filmmaking – including its unique aesthetic form of representation – in Canada and abroad. It imploded previously held stereotypes about Aboriginal media and consequently made it easier for Isuma to develop other feature films like *The Journals of Knud Rasmussen* (2006) and *Before Tomorrow* (2010).

The key to Isuma's philosophy is to create films which accurately reflect Inuit history and daily life. For Zacharias Kunuk the 'Inuit point of view' in filmmaking is based on the authentic representation of Arctic settings, peoples and their environment. In *Atanarjuat* this is reflected in portraying traditional Inuit skills, from using the right tools for building an igloo, to hunting skills and attending oil lamps. The film also introduces audiences to traditional childcare, food preparations, music, dance and the art of facial adornments and sewing clothes. These depictions show audiences that an ancient culture continues to thrive. In turn, community involvement in filmmaking processes allows participants to learn about ancient customs and communicate their insights to local and international audiences.

Films like *Atanarjuat: The Fast Runner* are an important response to colonial depictions of Inuit communities in literature, photographs, films and documentaries. The most well known of these portrayals is exemplified by Robert Flaherty's documentary *Nanook of the North* from 1922, in which he created a romanticised image of an Inuit family living in a pre-industrial setting amidst a hostile natural world. Flaherty constructed an image of the 'happy Inuit', a reality that was far removed from the social and political conditions of the time. On the contrary, Alakariallak, who played Nanook, and his family were from the same Inukjuamiut community that would be relocated 30 years later to the barren High Arctic by the Canadian government. Similar stereotypes of the noble and stoic Native can be found in Doug Wilkinson's documentary *Land of the Long Day* from 1952. In establishing an important counter movement, Aboriginal filmmakers began to produce audiovisual works in the 1960s, often through the use of community-based radio and television outlets. Kunuk started experimenting with independent video productions in 1981, and co-founded Igloolik Isuma Productions with screenwriter Paul Apak Angilirq, cinematographer Norman Cohn and actor Paul Qulitalik in 1990. Their goal was to develop independent film and media projects in order to enhance local culture and language traditions.

During that time, video and lightweight camera equipment sparked a revolution in independent video productions. As a result, Inuit storytelling values, which are based on collective and community-based activities, could be combined with alternative video to create films that allow for insights into an 'authentic world'. The third vector in this equation is digital media and their development into user-friendly applications, which provide access to portable recording and editing equipment. Isuma's feature films are shot on high definition (HD), a format, which allows for digital post-production on site. Digital technologies greatly enhance independent filmmaking, especially in regions where post-production facilities are hundreds of kilometres away. Rushes from a daily shoot in Igloolik can be screened on location and do not have to be sent to Montreal, which would result in lengthy delays and increased production costs. Digital technologies therefore allow Isuma producers to complete most of their film production in Igloolik.

Atanarjuat exemplifies the confluence of traditional storytelling, community-based independent filmmaking practices and new media technologies, which resulted in a film that is fundamentally different from mainstream productions. It represents an approach, which transforms 'media that dissolve and homogenise cultures into tools of cultural preservation' (Scott 2002). The success of films like *Atanarjuat* led Isuma to pioneer several other media projects such as Isuma TV, which uses the internet as a digital distribution platform for a wide variety of indigenous programming. Isuma also launched the SILA project (ww.sila.nu), an interactive website that functions as a narrative map for entry points into traditional Inuit songs, stories and historical events. In addition, Kunuk and Cohn use their public platform to raise issues of concern for Inuit communities and the world in general. For one, they have increased awareness of the high suicide rates amongst Inuit youth and the desperate living conditions many Inuit communities face due to unemployment and health risks, especially diabetes. On an international scale, Isuma is working with environmental groups to relate observations and insights from Inuit elders to researchers investigating climate change connected to global warming. The results of these collaborations were presented at the UN Climate Change Conference in 2009 and culminated in Isuma's documentary *Inuit Knowledge & Climate Change* (2010).

Isuma's feature film narratives are rooted in Inuit spirituality and symbolism, which are not explained or 'translated' for non-Inuit viewers so they can attain easier access to their meaning. *Atanarjuat* is in Inuktitut and is, in every aspect, a representation of Inuit life and customs in the Igloolik region. As a result, *Atanarjuat* and other Isuma films are as much a celebration of cultural continuity as they are mnemonic devices to reconnect to memories of the past. Their purpose goes beyond educational aims as they allow Inuit participants and audiences to engage and reflect upon issues that are important to the community. Within the context of colonial legacies and unresolved land claims, Isuma's films also represent a political voice for Indigenous rights that extend beyond national borders.

In *Atanarjuat*, Kunuk and Cohn combined traditional storytelling with digital technology to create a unique film. Digital media production promotes participatory forms of communication because it allows smaller communities to access film production technologies. It enables Aboriginal and Inuit communities to explore issues of concern and to tell their stories in dramatic ways. Independent film practices and alternative media therefore provide the basis for Indigenous peoples to pursue social change through politics of identity and representation. Within this paradigm, cultural production is transformed into political mobilisation. According to Ginsburg (2003) this 'cultural activism' defines indigenous media as promoting differences rather than assimilation.

Furthermore, the decentralisation of media practices is an exercise in empowerment, which at various points intersects with mainstream media to redirect nationwide foci and international debates. Interest in Northern communities, its lands and peoples, is intensifying in scientific research, especially in regards to the environment and global warming; in international politics (i.e. sovereignty claims on the North), as well as in the popular imagination of the public, which ranges from animal preservation to tourism and using the image of the polar bear in advertising campaigns. Films like *Atanarjuat* therefore play a key role in contributing to a vital international cross-cultural dialogue about climate change, cultural identity and globalisation.

Further reading

Paul Apak Angilirq, Zacharias Kunuk, Herve Paniaq, Norman Cohn, Pauloosie Quilitalik, and B. Saladin d'Anglure, *Atanarjuat: the fast runner: inspired by a traditional Inuit legend of Igloolik*, Toronto, Coach House Books & Isuma Publishing, 2002.

Doris Baltruschat, 'Television and Canada's Aboriginal Communities: Seeking Opportunities through Digital Technologies', *Canadian Journal of Communication*, 29 (1), 2004, pp. 47–59.

Kimberly Chun, 'Storytelling in the Arctic Circle: An Interview with Zacharias Kunuk', *CINEASTE*, 28 (1), 2002, pp. 21–3.

Michael Robert Evans, *Isuma: Inuit video art*, Montréal, McGill-Queen's University Press, 2008.

Faye Ginsburg, '*Atanarjuat* Off-Screen: From "Media Reservations" to the World Stage', *American Anthropologist*, 105 (4), 2003, pp. 827–31.

Sigurjon Baldur Hafsteinsson and Marian Bredin, *Indigenous screen cultures in Canada*. Winnipeg, University of Manitoba Press, 2010.

Sophie McCall, '"I Can Only Sing This Song to Someone Who Understands It": Community Filmmaking and the Politics of Partial Translation in *Atanarjuat, the Fast Runner*', *Essays on Canadian Writing*, 83, 2004, pp. 19–46.

Michelle Raheja, 'Reading Nanook's Smile: Visual Sovereignty, Indigenous Revisions of Ethnography, and *Atanarjuat (The Fast Runner)*', *American Quarterly*, 59 (4), 2007, pp. 1159–85.

A.O. Scott, 'Reel Change', *New York Times*, July 14, 2002, pp. 11–12.

Monika Siebert, 'Atanarjuat and the Ideological Work of Contemporary Indigenous Filmmaking', *Public Culture*, 18 (3), 2006, pp. 531–50.

Doris Baltruschat

L'Avventura (1960)

[Country: Italy, France. Production Company: Cino del Duca. Director: Michelangelo Antonioni. Producer: Amato Pennasilico. Screenwriters: Michelangelo Antonioni, Elio Bartolini and Tonino Guerra. Cinematographer: Aldo Scavarda. Music: Giovanni Fusco. Editor: Eraldo da Roma. Cast: Gabriele Ferzetti (Sandro), Monica Vitti (Claudia), Lea Massari (Anna), Dominique Blanchar (Giulia), James Addams (Corrado), Lelio Luttazzi (Raimondo), Esmerelda Ruspoli (Patrizia).]

Synopsis: A group of wealthy friends leaves Rome for a yachting trip to an island off the coast of Sicily. They loiter on the island coast while the boat is docked, and then they realise that their friend Anna has disappeared at some point during the day. After an unfocused search for her, they summon her father and local law enforcement. Most of Anna's friends quickly lose interest in the search, but Sandro (her boyfriend) and Claudia (her closest friend) continue to look for her throughout the neighbouring islands. They pursue a series of vague leads, but their attention soon shifts to the romance developing between them. The search for Anna gradually recedes into the background of the film as the characters resume their involvements in various romantic liaisons, social events and (minimal) professional concerns. At the end of the film, the mystery of Anna's disappearance remains unresolved.

At the notorious premiere of *L'Avventura* at the Cannes International Film Festival in May 1960, the audience booed. Frustrated by the film's listless pacing and ambiguous ending, the crowd erupted in catcalls that reportedly rattled the film's director, Michelangelo Antonioni. In response, a group of influential filmmakers and film critics circulated an open letter expressing their support of the film: 'Aware of the exceptional importance of

Michelangelo Antonioni's film, *L'Avventura*, and appalled by the displays of hostility it has aroused, the undersigned critics and members of the profession are anxious to express their admiration for the maker of this film'.[1] *L'Avventura* was ultimately recognised with a special jury prize at the festival in recognition of its introduction of a 'new cinematic language'. After its rocky debut, *L'Avventura* quickly secured both enduring critical acclaim and modest box office success in the international art cinema exhibition circuit. On the occasion of the 2012 *Sight and Sound* 'Greatest Films of All Time' poll, Robert Koehler described *L'Avventura* as 'the film that – more than any other at that moment – redefined the landscape of the artform, and mapped a new path that still influences today's most venturesome and radical young filmmakers'.[2]

Antonioni's painterly landscapes in *L'Avventura*, and later films such as *Il deserto rosso/Red Desert* (1964) and *Professione: Reporter/The Passenger* (1975), are one hallmark of Antonioni's new cinematic language and the challenge his films posed to audiences. *L'Avventura* features a series of open landscapes, including the deserted volcanic island where Anna disappears. The long scene that follows the discovery of her disappearance unfolds as if in slow motion. Sandro, Claudia, and her other friends explore the craggy shore with no apparent urgency. Alone and in pairs, they wander for a minute or two before stopping to contemplate a nearby object or a distant view that arrests their attention not because it offers a clue to Anna's location but because it interests them. The characters and the camera frequently shift from concentration to distraction. Favouring long shots and long takes, the camera moves from character to character without establishing any narrative connection between their individual investigations and without establishing their relation to one another in space. As a consequence of this open style, when the party aborts their search, the viewer is left without a clear understanding of how much terrain they covered or how much time has elapsed. Instead, Antonioni and his cinematographer, Aldo Scavarda, offer an immersive (yet fragmented) experience of the landscape, at once beautiful and inhospitable. The camera isn't anchored to a character's point of view nor does it omnisciently reveal information to the viewer that the characters can't access. Instead it concentrates on unfamiliar framing strategies: positioning the characters at the edges of the frame, tracking a character intently before abruptly shifting direction and focus, and framing empty space without assigning perspective or meaning to each shot.

L'Avventura was released at a turning point in film history when a series of innovative films were charting new aesthetic and narrative paths. Like *À bout de souffle/Breathless* (1959) and *Hiroshima Mon Amour* (1959), both released the year before, *L'Avventura* marked an emphatic turn away from the standards of Hollywood studio production and the international cinemas that imitated Hollywood and toward an emerging cinematic modernism. The narrative premise of Anna's disappearance could have generated a conventional Hollywood mystery (or even an action film), but Antonioni transforms the mystery at the (presumed) centre of the film into a spectral narrative event. Anna haunts the film (and psychically haunts Claudia who is the only character who suffers from Anna's disappearance – first because of concern for her and then because of her guilt for not wanting her to return), but her narrative presence is suggestive rather than suspenseful, intellectual rather than emotional. Her absence structures the narrative development in the film in much the same way that open space structures the framing of individual shots. Antonioni's formal innovations and narrative innovations resonate with each other, but they don't invite symbolic readings or conclusions.

The common assertion that there is no action in *L'Avventura* misses one of the film's most important cinematic interventions. There is a lot of 'action' in the film, but it doesn't advance the plot in a cause-and-effect chain. *L'Avventura* includes a series of dramatically engaging events: Anna and Sandro reunite after a long separation, and Anna immediately shares her ambivalence about their relationship. They embark on an 'adventure' with their friends during which Anna is at the centre of two key dramas – first the minor drama of her false reporting of a shark sighting while she is swimming, and then the major drama of her disappearance (an event that she may or may not have engineered). The ensuing investigation, while slack and half-hearted by the standards of a conventional genre film, involves a series of intriguing encounters with various locals on the nearby islands who share rumours and speculations about what may have happened to Anna. Sandro and Claudia begin an intense affair, and Sandro immediately betrays Claudia who catches him with a prostitute before tacitly forgiving him with a tender yet ambivalent gesture of affection in the final scene of the film. These events generate a degree of ambiguous suspense, but Antonioni's direction doesn't signpost the importance of each event for the audience through the use of close-ups or swelling musical cues or explicit bits of dialogue. Furthermore, these events don't build toward an inexorable (or even an unpredictable) conclusion.

The lack of narrative closure forced audiences (and critics) to find new terms for describing the film as a whole. 'Antoniennui' was used by contemporary critics to describe the prevalence of the themes of alienation and indolence in *L'Avventura* and the three films that completed Antonioni's loosely connected 'tetralogy' – *La Notte* (1961), *L'Eclisse* (1962) and *Il deserto rosso/Red Desert* (1964). While these films pursue a very different set of aesthetic and narrative preoccupations than the Italian neorealist films that still exerted stylistic influence in this late postwar period, Antonioni's tetralogy is less apolitical and indulgent than his harshest critics suggest. The later films in the tetralogy offer more direct engagements with Italy's economic and industrial modernisation and its consequences for the physical, cultural and social environments his characters inhabit. *L'Avventura*, however, already reveals Antonioni's interest in a philosophical investigation of contemporary life and the jarring juxtapositions it produces. For example, an early scene in the film presents Anna verbally sparring with her father before she leaves for her trip. The meticulously composed mise en scène positions Anna and her father in the foreground on a dirt road that appears to lead straight to Saint Peter's Basilica which looms in the right background of the shot while a collection of newly constructed apartment buildings hovers in the left background of the shot. The featured characters in the film may be wealthy and may enjoy a decadent lifestyle that contrasts starkly with the representations of poverty and labour that dominate neorealist films, but Antonioni positions these characters not only in open landscapes but also in crowded settings that capture the uneasy coexistence of modernity and tradition, secularism and religion, and glamour and abjection.

The character of Claudia – arguably the narrative centre of the film, offering the perspective that shapes most of the audience's impressions and attachments – embodies Antonioni's approach to character development and the importance of visual style to that approach. We learn more about Claudia by watching her change from one outfit to another (including a dress borrowed from Anna), make funny faces in the mirror while she is alone in her hotel room, or wander through an art gallery than we do during the brief exchanges of dialogue between her and Sandro, by turns opaque and clichéd. Monica Vitti appears in important roles in all of the films in the tetralogy, and her performance style – a combination of organic sensuality and self-conscious posing, like a fashion model captured in a documentary – is a key element in the new cinematic grammar that Antonioni develops during this period. Prior to *L'Avventura*, Vitti had been a stage actress, unknown to film audiences. Her experience on stage lends itself to Antonioni's cinematic style; she performs without directly engaging the camera, permitting Antonioni to position her at the periphery of the frame without undermining the audience's interest in her.

In Italian, *'l'avventura'* holds two meanings – an 'adventure' in the broad sense of the term and a romantic 'affair'. The film plays with this doubleness, moving between two possible narrative strands – the adventure of solving the mystery of Anna's disappearance and the adventure of Sandro and Claudia's romance. For Antonioni, the concept of the 'adventure' also suggests a new cinematic approach to developing characters. In his 'Cannes statement', Antonioni famously reported, 'Eros is sick'. Antonioni's diagnosis leads to a broader declaration about the importance of moving beyond the emphasis on individual psychology that defines most commercial films:

> To be critically aware of the vulgarity and the futility of such an overwhelming erotic impulse, as is the case with the protagonist in *L'Avventura*, is not enough or serves no

> purpose. And here we witness the crumbling of a myth, which proclaims it is enough for us to know, to be critically conscious of ourselves, to analyze ourselves, in all our complexities and in every facet of our personality. The fact that matters is that such an examination is not enough. It is only a preliminary step. Every day, every emotional encounter gives rise to a new adventure.[3]

To the extent that art cinema functions as a coherent genre, one of its features has been an emphasis on the interiority of characters. Antonioni externalises interiority. *L'Avventura* is a turning point in film history not only because it marks a radical break from the narrative and aesthetic conventions of commercial cinema but also because it marks a new movement within art cinema – an exploration of interiority through an emphasis on the visual surface of the film.

Notes

1. The complete letter and list of signatures, originally circulated by the *Bulletin du Festival de Cannes*, is included in the booklet accompanying the Region 1 DVD release of *L'Avventura* by The Criterion Collection.
2. Robert Koehler, 'Great Wide Open: *L'Avventura*', www.bfi.org.uk/news/great-wide-open-l-avventura.
3. The complete statement has been reprinted in English in the Criterion DVD booklet.

Further reading

Michelangelo Antonioni, *The Architecture of Vision: Writings and Interviews on Cinema*, Chicago, University of Chicago Press, 2007.

Seymour Chatman, *Antonioni, or, The Surface of the World*, Berkeley, University of California Press, 1985.

Geoffrey Nowell-Smith, *L'Avventura*, London, British Film Institute, 1997.

Laura Rascaroli and John David Rhodes (eds), *Antonioni: Centenary Essays*, London, British Film Institute, 2011.

Angelo Restivo, *The Cinema of Economic Miracles: Visuality and Modernization in the Italian Art Film*, Durham, Duke University Press, 2002.

Lisa Patti

Awāra (1951)

[Country: India. Production Company: R. K. Studios. Director: Raj Kapoor. Screenwriter: K. A. Abbas. Lyrics: Hasrat Jaipuri. Music: Shanker Jaikishan, Sunny Castellino. Playback singers: Lata Mangeshkar, Mukesh, Rafi, Manna Dey, Shamshad Begum. Cinematographer: Radhu Karmakar. Art Director: M. R. Achrekar. Editor: G. G. Mayekar. Choreographer: Madame Simkie, Krishna Kumar, Surya Kumar. Costumes: Om Prakash, Madame Chorosch. Cast: Raj Kapoor (Raj), Nargis (Rita), Prithviraj Kapoor (Judge Raghunath), Leela Chitnis (Leela), K. N. Singh (Jagga), Shashi Kapoor (young Raj), Zubeida (young Rita), Cuckoo (nightclub dancer), Leela Mishra (sister-in-law), B. M. Vyas (Rita's father), D. Bashesharnath (Judge).]

Synopsis: The bandit Jagga kidnaps Leela, Judge Raghunath's wife. Upon learning that Leela is pregnant, Jagga lets her go. People believe that Jagga is the father. Though she is already pregnant when Jagga kidnaps her, the easily swayed Judge Raghunath doubts Leela and throws her out. Leela gives birth to a baby boy near a gutter on the street. She hopes that Raj will grow up to be a judge like his real father. Raj is attracted to Rita, his playmate at school, but they are separated by circumstances. Leela struggles to make ends meet. Jagga forces Raj into a life of crime. Raj grows up with ambivalent feelings for his missing father. Judge Raghunath becomes Rita's guardian after she is orphaned. Raj and Rita meet again as grown-ups. They fall in love and recognise each other as childhood sweethearts. Rita attempts to reform Raj. Raj struggles to redeem himself and become worthy of Rita.

Awāra is often referred to as Raj Kapoor's most accomplished film. Its smooth narrative style and elegant production design brought instant recognition to Kapoor as an actor and director, not to mention the notoriety he achieved for his on- and off-screen romance with his co-star Nargis. The film opens with the image of a starving mongrel feeding on crumbs from a street urchin on a dark, shadowy street as the credits roll out – a defining image of urban squalor and destitution. The scene takes place in the metropolitan setting of Bombay (now Mumbai), where the protagonist Raj is kicked around on empty, dangerous streets, like the homeless dog in the title sequence. As the rest of the film unfolds, the dog emerges as a symbol of social disparagement, unemployment and poverty in post-independence India.

Like *Mother India*, *Awāra* influenced an entire gamut of Indian films, be it through its use of courtroom scenarios, flashbacks or lavishly choreographed dream sequences. The dream sequence where Raj moves from purgatory to heaven is a case in point. Often cited for its glittering, white set, the number *Ghar aaya mera Pardesi* (*'My foreigner has come home'*) features a spiralling staircase with fog machines that evoke the hallucinatory but distant euphoria of a celestial space. Unafraid to experiment with new narrative techniques within what is broadly conceived as a mass-medium, Kapoor came to be known as a master scenarist and showman. He opens *Awāra* with a flashback, with Rita defending Raj in court. The flashback may be a nod to *Citizen Kane* (1941), whose influence is apparent in Kapoor's use of grand interiors and light and shadow to evoke social dysfunction and psychological alienation.[1] Kapoor adapted Hollywood-style continuity editing (eyeline matches that follow the 180-degree rule; match-cuts that join disparate planes of action) to tell an essentially Indian story based on popular conceptions of the vagrant as a seer imbued with worldly-wise insight. His use of rhythmic montage offers a striking example of his recasting of European art-house idioms in a popular Indian mould. Take the song *Naiyya teri Majhdar, Hoshiyaar* (*'Your boat is midstream, beware'*). Kapoor interrupts the smooth flow of action as a chorus sings about impending danger. He ends the song abruptly with a scene where Jagga kidnaps Leela to take revenge on Judge Raghunath (who has sentenced him for a crime he has not committed because Jagga's father was a convict). Soviet-style editing produces an overall effect that is jerky and unsettling but entirely convincing within the edgy narrative.

Elsewhere Jagga towers as the villain who browbeats the innocent Raj into stealing bread in a low-angle shot that came to be known as the 'Russian angle'. With his fair skin and blue eyes, Kapoor was considered rakishly attractive: his moustache and hairstyle recall Clark Gable – he assumes his wry, ironic posture in several close-ups. Indeed, Kapoor was so light-skinned that he could pass off as a European gentleman: the question of 'whiteness' comes up several times in the film.[2] Though poor, Raj *looks* so wealthy and privileged that he is never mistaken for a thief: '[It's] not your fault ... it's just the way I look (*tumhara kusoor nahin, meri soorat hi aisi hai*)', he tells Rita when she finally learns about his true identity. As Raj, Kapoor often plays himself and even retains his off-screen name. He often frames himself in soft-focus close-ups that function as reminders of his illustrious off-screen life. His father Prithviraj Kapoor was a prominent actor, who had begun his career in the silent era and was well respected for his work on the Bombay stage. Claiming that theatre was the real school, Kapoor left his formal education and worked as a stagehand and bit actor before making his first film *Aag* (*The Fire*, 1948) when he was just 24.[3] Prithviraj agreed to play the role of the father in *Awāra* as well. Raj Kapoor cast his younger brother Shashi as the child Raj: *Awāra* is, in every sense of the word, a family drama. Raghunath may forget his son, but the audience is not allowed to forget who the father is and who the son. The adroit casting alleviates Raj's culpability while amplifying the father's injustice several times over. The audience's sympathy for Raj is left intact at every opportunity, so much so that his 'lineage' is consistently preserved through his star image, even when he plays the rogue. Kapoor drew significantly on Charlie Chaplin in the song '*Awāra Hoon*' ('I am a vagabond'), appearing in the tramp's baggy pants and bowler hat, an element that became even more pronounced in his next film *Shree 420* (*Mr 420*, 1955). He was indebted to Chaplin for creating the image of a vagabond as an everyman. However, the Indian tramp also varies significantly: witty repartee replaces Chaplin's physical comic routines. The narrative is steered by an unprecedented sexual frankness and the burning pathos of song and dance numbers that go well beyond Chaplin's use of mime and humour.[4]

The plot is regulated by a set of ironic reversals and traumatic setbacks: Raj is well born but ends up with Jagga the bandit, who, in howsoever twisted a form, nurtures him. Judge Raghunath lacks judgement and ruins Jagga because of his unfair sentence. The 'judge' fails to fulfil his legal obligations to his family – *Awāra* often portrays the father as the real criminal. Raghunath's gait is heavy and cumbersome – in the opening sequences the camera frames him in low angles that represent his girth, megalomania and hypocrisy. As the film progresses, the camera reverses this position to frame Raghunath in high angles that dwarf his position and make him look very small: father and son see eye to eye by the end of the film as Raj grows in stature. It is clear that Raghunath treats Leela brutally, literally kicking his heavily pregnant wife out on a stormy night, an incident that alludes to the epic *Ramayana*, where Ram casts his wife Sita out after she is kidnapped by the demon Ravana. Kapoor incorporates numerous references to the *Ramayana*: Raghunath is another name for Ram but with an important difference in that *Awāra*'s setting is urban. He foregrounds Leela's relentless suffering – Raghunath's car knocks Leela out in a fatal accident that leaves her blind and unable to recognise him. Like her mythical counterpart Sita, Leela continues to worship her husband in spite of his 'crime' in an unrelenting display of faith. But unlike Sita, Leela lacks true strength and fortitude – perhaps the reason why Raghunath is named after Ram but Leela is not named after Sita. In the epic, Sita asks mother earth to swallow her up in a final demonstration of strength that proves her innocence. Leela, on the other hand, is utterly powerless – she is destroyed by forces that are too large and beyond her control.

While he abandons his son, Raghunath dotes on his ward Rita. In contrast to Leela, Rita, as her name suggests, is modern, Westernised, educated and strong. She turns against her mentor by falling in love with Raj, a criminal or an *awāra* (literally, a vagabond); the very person a judge must punish. Both Raj and his symbolic father Jagga are victims of circumstance and injustice. Nothing underscores this problem more effectively than the fact that Rita grows up to be a lawyer and puts the patriarch Raghunath himself on trial for ill-treating and almost murdering his wife. Confrontations ensue as father and son fight each other, vying for Rita's affection. On Rita's twenty-first birthday, Raghunath buys Rita an expensive necklace but Raj steals it from him. Visually, the episode borders on incest: father and son 'woo' Rita as each tries to deck her with the glittering necklace. The entire sequence culminates in Rita's bedroom, where Raj eventually confronts Raghunath as the man who has caused his mother's death. A childhood photograph of Rita shatters as Raj raises a knife to his father and literally hits the wall. The shattered photograph looms large on the screen, serving as a shocking reminder of Rita's threatened integrity. Raj recognises Rita's moral and intellectual supremacy as the photograph – a leitmotif that appears at several critical moments – halts the drama of possession, showing Raj the way. In fact, the entire climax is organised according to Rita's 'honourable' point of view, where the judge is finally judged. Like the girl in the photograph, Rita directs the audience in and outside the film towards the truth. In the final analysis, *Awāra* is driven by an altruistic imperative which shows that criminals are not born but made; they are victims of social injustice, prejudice and indifference.

Nargis's collaboration with Raj Kapoor played a significant part in *Awāra*'s success. Her portrayal of Rita is effortless: like Kapoor, she incorporates several elements of her star persona into her performance, which is notable for its ease of expression and sexual intensity. In a marked departure from the sublimation and transcendence that is typical of films from this period, the Nargis–Raj Kapoor romance is characterised by its frank eroticism and free-spiritedness. Nargis wore her hair in a bold bob that emphasised her Westernised, broad-minded outlook. She ignored gossip about her intimacy with Kapoor and assisted him in almost all aspects of filmmaking, including set design, camerawork, the staging of song and dance numbers and the running of R. K. Studios.[5] The couple was wildly popular not only in India but in the Soviet Union as well, where 'babies were christened after them'.[6] Above all, *Awāra* is remembered for its socialist vision and the searing intensity of the Raj Kapoor–Nargis duo, which emerged as an enduring icon of love in modern India.[7]

Notes

1. Raj Kapoor admired Orson Welles and was particularly fond of his use of low-key lighting. See Madhu Jain, *The Kapoors: The First Family of Indian Cinema*, New Delhi, Penguin, 2005, p. 98.
2. Kapoor plays on the symbolic meanings of whiteness, treating it is a sign of the purity of character, while marshalling a more complex association with whiteness as a sign of deceit and exploitation, particularly during India's colonisation. For further details, see Gayatri Chatterjee, 'Rita and Raghunath: Pursuits of Whiteness/Incest', in *Awāra*, New Delhi, Wiley-Eastern Limited, 1992, pp. 111–118.
3. K. A. Abbas's screenplay is influenced by the Indian People's Theatre Association (IPTA), which echoes Prime Minister Jawahar Lal Nehru's socialist objectives (as also Kapoor's extension of the tramp figure). Several Marxist intellectuals were associated with this influential organisation, including Abbas.
4. Malti Sahai includes a persuasive analysis of these differences in her article 'Raj Kapoor and the Indianization of Chaplin', *East-West Film Journal*, Vol. 2, No. 1, 1987, pp. 62–76.
5. Raj Kapoor established his own production company after the enormous success of *Barsaat* (Rain, 1949). The studio logo was based on a scene from *Barsaat*, where Kapoor leans over Nargis in an erotic pose, as if to kiss her, and Nargis arches her back seductively.
6. T. J. S. George, *The Life and Times of Nargis*, Chennai, East-West Books, 1994, p. 77.
7. The Kapoors are often referred to as the first family of Indian cinema. Cousins Ranbir and Kareena Kapoor now represent the fourth generation of actors descended from great-grandfather Prithviraj Kapoor.

Further reading

Paul Willemen and Ashish Rajadhyaksha, *Encyclopedia of Indian Cinema*, New Delhi and London, Oxford University Press, 1995.

Anupama Kapse

Away from Her (2007)

[Country: Canada. Production Company: Film Farm, Foundry Films, Capri Releasing, HanWay Films, Echo Lake Productions. Director and Screenwriter: Sarah Polley. Executive Producer: Atom Egoyan. Cinematographer: Luc Montpellier. Editor: David Wharnsby. Cast: Julie Christie (Fiona Anderson), Gordon Pinsent (Grant Anderson), Michael Murphy (Aubrey), Olympia Dukakis (Marian).]

Synopsis: The film addresses a timely subject matter: the onset of Alzheimer's disease – increasingly prevalent in an ageing North American population – and its impact on the personal life of a married couple. Fiona and Grant face the gradual unravelling of their life together when her memory begins to fail. She gets lost near their cottage in Brant County, Ontario, and is found wandering in a nearby town. She forgets simple daily chores and the names for ordinary things elude her. Yet, in spite of her growing confusion, Fiona seems able to recall long-term memories, in particular Grant's philandering and past betrayals. When her condition deteriorates, Fiona and Grant decide to place her in Meadowlake, a nursing home for the elderly, where she becomes attached to a fellow resident, Aubrey. Fiona's budding love for Aubrey angers Grant and seems to him like an act of revenge. The film ends with a twist that brings the story full circle: in a moment of clarity Fiona recalls Grant's kindness since she moved to Meadowlake and they are united in their enduring love for each other.

Away from Her is an adaptation of a short story by Alice Munro, 'The Bear Came Over the Mountain', originally published in the *New Yorker* magazine in 1999. Sarah Polley wrote the screenplay and directed the film, which was released in 2007. In Canada, *Away from Her* won seven Genie Awards, including Best Motion Picture, Best Director and Best Adapted Screenplay. It also received the Claude Jutra Award for best feature film by a first-time director. In addition, it garnered two Oscar nominations, for Best Actress (Julie Christie) and Best Adapted Screenplay.

The film is about love, betrayal, loss, forgiveness and reunion. It is also about memory as reflected, for one in the topic of Alzheimer's, but also through stylistic means in the form of frequent flashbacks throughout the film. These flashbacks recall Grant's memories as he relives past events like meeting Fiona over 40 years ago and his duplicity, for which he now seems to be paying the price. The story is filled with ambiguity: Grant wonders if Fiona is not play-acting in order to get back at him for his extra-marital affairs. As the story plays out through Grant's eyes, his feelings of guilt and remorse are intermingled with his despair in loosing Fiona forever. He states, he 'never wanted to be away from her', yet his separation from his wife is inevitable as she leaves to live at Meadowlake and her mind gradually fades into oblivion.

In the study of adaptations of popular novels or short stories for film, equivalences are often drawn between the adapted script and its original source to ascertain 'fidelity'. Consequently, certain story elements such as themes, characters, point of view, overall narrative development, contexts, imagery and symbols become the focus for analysis. Many adaptation theories make distinctions depending on a film's distance from its source, resulting in three distinct classifications: a literal or close reading of the source text; a general correspondence between the source text and its adaptation; and, a distant referencing between the original story and the movie adaptation (Boozer 2008). Within these paradigms *Away from Her* classifies as an adaptation that exhibits a strong correspondence between Munro's short story, Polley's screenplay and the actual film.

Away from Her is filled with rich metaphors: the winter landscape connoting the late stage in the couple's lives, tracks made in the snow by Grant and Fiona cross-country skiing – tracks that are mostly parallel but at times also diverge. The depiction of pink sunsets over snowy plains, rivers and frozen lakes follows descriptions in Munro's story and reflects the (stereo)typical portrayal of 'Canadianess' in literature and film. There are other equivalences between the original story and the film as characters, settings, dialogue and the overall narrative development show many similarities between the source text and its adaptation. Polley, however, chose to create a film based on a non-linear editing style, where story sequences are interspersed, interrupted and continued later. This is accomplished through frequent flashbacks, which provide the background story of events that occurred months or even years ago. As a result, the overall structure of the film's narrative reflects the erratic and sporadic nature of memory itself, with its tendency to wander, distort, evoke and efface.

In spite of similarities between Munro's story and *Away from Her*, creative processes involved in story writing are fundamentally different from the political-economic context of producing films. Commercial aspects of film production determine budgets, sites for production and post-production, advertising campaigns, promotional tie-ins (from clothing to toys) and the number of opening theatres for a film's release. Adapting a story for a film is therefore a highly complex process, which the following adaptation theories take into account. For example, adaptation can be conceptualised as a formal product, which entails the transposition or 'transcoding' of a particular work. This process might involve a significant shift in medium (literature adapted for film, as in *Away from Her*), genre (an epic as the basis for a novel) or contexts (i.e. a different point of view). Adaptation can also be defined as a creative and interpretive practice, which involves the appropriation *or* salvaging of a work (i.e. the adaptation of oral legends in literature and/or film). And from a reception and consumption point of view, adaptation is a form of intertextual engagement, in which audiences experience a work as palimpsests through the memory of multiple other works and texts that resonate through repetition with variation (Hutcheson 2006).

At closer inspection, fundamental differences exist between literature and audiovisual media, which are especially evident in the multi-layered textual and aesthetic composition of a film. The myriad choices available to a director, during production and post-production processes, will therefore inevitably result in the reinterpretation of a source text (Stam and Raengo 2005). In *Away from Her* this is visible in the mise-en-scène and the use of lighting and sound. Throughout the film, Polley chose to create a stark contrast in lighting the hallway at Meadowlake. For example, when Fiona pushes Aubrey's wheelchair down the hallway, part of the space is saturated with light, almost overexposed, while another section remains in darkness. This visual composition reflects the state of mind of the characters, especially their inability to clearly discern between current and past realities – their sense of time and space is skewed. Polley also experimented with the colour temperature for different scenes, in particular the flashbacks. *Away for Her* begins and ends with a light-saturated grainy image of a young Fiona looking into the camera. In turning this scene into a slow-motion sequence, it resembles a fading memory. Other flashbacks exhibit a distinct green colour-tint and diffused images of several women, which embody recollections of Grant's betrayals and his remaining guilt for his extra-marital affairs.

One scene in particular exemplifies the creative use of diegetic sound to underscore the emotional atmosphere of unfolding events. When Grant sees Fiona for the first time since her move into the nursing home, she appears not to recognise him. As she treats Grant politely like a stranger, her attention remains on her new friend Aubrey, who jealously guards her interaction with her husband. The encounter between the central characters is accompanied by an inharmonious piano key, struck repeatedly on the same note, creating a discordant mood. The repetition of this singular sound also connotes Fiona's state of mind and her current relationship to Grant which cannot evolve towards a satisfying resolution. Fiona is 'stuck' in the moment.

The film is about Grant's journey from selfishness in love to selflessness in love. His point of view is established at the beginning when he drives down a road in small-town Ontario to visit Aubrey's wife, Marian. Since Aubrey has moved back home, Fiona has fallen into deep despair. Grant tries to convince Marian to send Aubrey back to Meadowlake so Fiona can recover. His encounter with Marion develops into one of the main narrative strands, which unfolds at different intervals, but in linear fashion, throughout the film. It becomes the key frame for time and space and therefore an essential marker for the story's continuity. In contrast, Grant's flashbacks depict past events that are intertwined with non-linear sequences of Fiona's loss of memory and progressing illness. Fiona inevitably has to surrender to the present. It is therefore left to Grant to advance the story and bring it to its conclusion.

The foregrounding of Grant's point of view differs from the original short story by Munro. The film focuses on the love and healing of Grant and Fiona's relationship rather than a couple's struggle to cope with Alzheimer's. When Grant persuades Marian to let Aubrey return to Meadowlake, his journey has come full circle. In this selfless act of reuniting the two, he confirms his love for Fiona: his only desire is to see her happy and content again.

The final scene is built around a carefully crafted cinematography of shadow and light. The mise-en-scène depicts Fiona sitting in a chair by the window, saturated in diffused sunlight. In a moment of clarity, she remembers Grant and greets him with familiar gestures. With an extreme close-up of her face, she says: 'You could have just driven away. Just driven away without a care in the world and forsook me. Forsooken me. Forsaken.' Fiona's ability to find and express the right words at this moment not only shows her lucidity, but also indicates the progression of their journey together as a couple, as well as the resolution of the story and its conclusion. In a reverse shot, Grant reveals his surprise and tender love for his wife. He responds: 'Not a chance', as the camera encircles the two holding each other in a tender embrace. The scene fades to a grainy shot of a young Fiona looking directly at the camera. As she turns away the scene dissolves into white.

Polley's interpretation of Munro's story is filled with ambiguities. Throughout the film it remains unclear how much Fiona can recall of past events and Grant's infidelities. It seems that Grant's recollections of his betrayals become the main focus because of his guilt and fear of loosing Fiona. Because the story is told predominantly through Grant's eyes, his experiences and feelings are foregrounded as is his transformation from a selfish individual to a selfless husband. In comparison to Munro's focus on old age and Alzheimer's disease, *Away from Her* becomes a love story of two people who, in spite of tumultuous events and life's ultimate challenge, remain committed to each other until the end. This shift in story focus and point of view emphasises Polley's creative interpretation of the source text, which is achieved predominantly through stylistic and cinematic means. As a result, the screen adaptation of *Away from Her* reveals fundamental differences between literature and the language of film.

Further reading

Jack Boozer (ed.), *Authorship in Film Adaptation*, Austin, University of Texas Press, 2008.

Linda Hutcheson, *A Theory of Adaptation*, New York, Routledge, 2006.

Colin MacCabe, Kathleen Murray and Rick Warner (eds), *True to the Spirit: Film Adaptation and the Question of Fidelity*, Oxford, Oxford University Press, 2011.

Brian McFarlane, *Novel to Film: an Introduction to the Theory of Adaptation*, Oxford and New York, Oxford University Press, 1996.

Alice Murno, 'The Bear Came Over the Mountain', *New Yorker*, Dec 27, 1999, pp. 110–27.

Simone Murray, *The Adaptation Industry: the Cultural Economy of Contemporary Literary Adaptation*, New York, Routledge, 2011.

Sarah Polley, *Away from Her. The Screenplay*, 2006. Available at http://awayfromherscript.com.

Robert Stam and Alessandra Raengo (eds), *Literature and Film: a Guide to the Theory and Practice of Film Adaptation*, Malden, MA, Blackwell, 2005.

Doris Baltruschat

Bab al-Hadid/Cairo Station aka Cairo: Central Station (1958)

[Country: Egypt. Production Company: Gabriel Talhami Productions. Director: Youssef Chahine. Screenwriters: Youssef Chahine and Abdel Hay Adib. Cinematographer: Alvise Orfanelli. Editor: Kamal Abu al-Ela. Music: Fouad al-Zahri. Cast: Youssef Chahine (Kenaoui), Hind Rostom (Hanouma), Farid Chaouqi (Abu Seri).]

Synopsis: During a hot day in Cairo's main station, Kenaoui, a disabled rural migrant, is offered a job peddling papers and magazines. He becomes obsessed with Hanouma, a beautiful, vivacious woman who sells soft drinks to commuters, working without official permission. She is already committed to Abu Seri, a porter fighting to unionise the exploited workers in the station. Hanouma rejects Kenaoui's desperate proposal of marriage, and, as night falls, he attempts to murder her in a fit of thwarted jealousy.

Gabriel Youssef Chahine (Shahine) was born 25 January 1926 in Alexandria, to a Greek mother and a Lebanese father, who worked as a lawyer. Chahine was one of three children in the non-observant Melkite Catholic family, struggling to maintain their middle-class status. His parents made strenuous sacrifices for his education, and he attended Victoria College, a mediocre imitation of Eton, surviving from the recent period of British rule. From 1946 to 1948, and very much against his parents' wishes, Chahine left to study 'Method' acting in theatre and television (but not film) at the Pasadena Playhouse, Los Angeles.

On his return to Egypt, still resisting his father's wish that he should become an engineer, Chahine began working with cinematographer Alvise Orfanelli, a creative presence in the vigorous Alexandrian film industry, and who would be cinematographer for *Cairo Station.* By 1950 Chahine was already directing his first feature, *Baba Amin* (*Daddy Amin*). Early cinematic influences included American musicals and Douglas Sirk's melodramas. Egyptian cinema did not figure for Chahine at this point, but his films quickly began to reflect the radical developments in Egyptian society and politics of the 1950s, and to draw on European modernist film conventions as well as the Hollywood paradigm. During the 1990s Chahine's films increasingly reflected his preoccupation with the rise of Islamic fundamentalism in Egypt and his growing disenchantment with American 'late capitalism', culminating in his contribution to the multi-authored *11/09/01* (2002).

Chahine remained by choice and circumstance an outsider: a (non-believing) Christian in a predominantly Muslim society, child of an immigrant family, and a product of the complex cosmopolitan culture of pre-war Alexandria. He can also be seen as an actor manqué who came reluctantly to the role of director. Though married to Colette Favaudon for over 50 years, herself the daughter of a French immigrant family, bisexuality was also an element in Chahine's complex character. During the development of his long, often embattled career, Chahine produced 36 feature and short films and six documentaries (Murphy and Williams 2007: 30). Acknowledged as probably the most significant 'auteur' in Arab cinema, he is one of the few directors to have received the Cannes Film Festival Award for Lifetime Achievement (1997). He died in Cairo, 27 July 2008.

Chahine was fortunate that the beginning of his career coincided with the transformation of his country brought about by Gamal Abdel Nasser's overthrow of King Farouk and the establishment of the Republic of Egypt in July 1952. Nasser's revolution encouraged the adoption of nationalist social and political agendas in film, and 'by the early 1950s Egyptian cinema was integrating a loose adaptation of various realist cinematic trends including French poetic realism, Italian neorealism, and socialist realism' (Khouri 2010: 10). Drawing on some of these cinematic conventions, *Bab al-Hadid* (*Cairo Station*), Chahine's eleventh film, provoked outrage among Egyptian audiences on release, and it is not difficult to see why.

Cairo Station has an urgent pace, with striking camerawork by Chahine's early patron, Alvise Orfanelli: the editing, sound- and image track, drive the narrative forward, in contrast to conventional Egyptian films of the time, which relied on lengthier scenes and dialogue. The casting of *Cairo Station* was also outrageous: Chahine himself plays the tragic central role of the disabled Kanaoui with powerful conviction, by turns ridiculous, disgusting, pathetic and murderous. Hind Rostom, the 'Marilyn of the Arab screen', plays Hanouma, a soft-drinks seller, a part in complete contrast to her usual romantic roles, which were typecasting she fiercely resented. She recalled that working for Chahine was immensely challenging; he was 'soft moving sands that hide a volcano' (Fawal 2001: 19). Hanouma's lover, Abu Seri ('Speedy'), is played by heart-throb male lead, Farid Chaouqi, also very much against type. To cast these stars in such tragic, 'low-life' roles was daring, and one of the reasons for the film's notoriety on release. Chahine had effectively created a unique fusion between neorealist convention, Egyptian melodrama and Hollywood narrative style, through which he began to portray contemporary Egypt. But this uneasy alliance of such distinctive elements also meant that *Cairo Station* could easily disconcert audiences.

Cairo Station can be viewed as a film made in the immediate aftermath of the 'Suez crisis', more accurately described as 'the Tripartite Aggression', as it is known in Egypt, when Britain and France joined with Israel in an abortive invasion to seize the canal zone. Chahine's film portrays the tensions and divisions growing within Egyptian society between the emergent, consumerist urban commuter classes, who were adopting Western dress, popular culture and values, and those Egyptians still adhering to more traditional ways of life – the *fellahin* (rural labourers), the urban poor and the strict adherents of Islam (Chahine was prosecuted for supposedly contravening Islamic laws of representation in *al-Muhajir, The Emigrant*, 1994). The concourse and platforms of the city transport hub provide a locale that enables Chahine effectively to represent a wide range of Egyptian society. The protagonists are the marginal groups who are confined to the station precincts in a desperate struggle to survive – street children, platform hawkers, unlicensed porters and economic migrants from the countryside.

Cairo Station observes the 'unities' of time, place and action, perhaps a legacy of Chahine's first love of theatre: the action unfolds in the course of a single day, within the bounds of Bab al-Hadid (except for one significant excursion), and the narrative pursues a tragic nemesis. The first sequence, after an establishing, pre-title opening, is purely 'New Wave': a waist-down shot of a young woman wearing extremely tight, above-the-ankle floral slacks, which inevitably attract attention from the male commuter crowds in the station ticket queues. The presence and representation of women throughout *Cairo Station* is striking, and for a relatively uninformed Western audience, conditioned by mistaken assumptions about the historical 'place of women in Islamic society', often frankly startling.

The accelerating pace of mid-twentieth-century culture is evident everywhere in *Cairo Station*, and its impact on women is dramatic. A cleric and his follower watch appalled as a line of young men and women jive through the station concourse: the imam exclaims, 'It's new! All that is new leads straight to Hell!' Hanouma is delighted with her trade among the crowd attending a feminist demonstration, where the president of the Association of Women's Rights (dressed in what seems to be a distinctly 'manly' way) denounces the life of slavery endured by rural Egyptian women. A young girl waiting desperately to make an assignation with her lover, who is leaving for Europe, is harassed by the porters on the station steps; as she paces to and fro they call her 'Sputnik' and 'little Laika' (the name of the dog sent into orbit by the Soviets in 1957, and from which it could not return).

Hanouma and the other 'cola'-girls are unlicensed vendors, hounded by the official refreshment seller with his hygienic modern trolley, and by the police. They carry re-filled Coke bottles in garishly painted buckets of water, and dice with death as they are chased through freight yards by the ineffectual police. Hanouma captivates an entire carriage in a self-reflexive parody of the 'song-and-dance' routines for which conventional Egyptian films were enjoyed, but the routine is presented critically, in several ways; she rewards her audience by selling more iced lemonade. Kenaoui watches her obsessively from below on the track beside the carriage. Hanouma takes pity on him, caught in the power of her own seductive performance, and proffers a penile, Cola-shaped bottle to his lips.

In a confrontation with her enraged lover, who also witnessed her performance, she sprays him with the contents of a bottle as she desperately tries to channel his aggression into desire. Kenaoui listens fixated, outside the warehouse, to Hanouma's screams; in one shot, on a wall poster behind him, is a voluptuous figure and the fragmentary words 'rilyn Monroe, *Niagar...*', advertising Henry Hathaway's *Niagara* (1953). As he hears the couple begin to make love, in fact a violent attack by Abu Seri on Hanouma, the camera pans in to Kenaoui's stunned face, and we see that he is still gripping the re-filled Coca-Cola bottle that Hanouma gave him. As the lovers leave, apparently reconciled, he smashes the bottle against the wall, and goes in search of a knife.

Chahine's *Bab al-Hadid* anticipates the disturbing sexual violence explored in contemporary American and European films such as Hitchcock's *Psycho* (1960) and Michael Powell's *Peeping Tom* (1961), like them making explicit connection between (male) voyeurism, the performance of the 'feminine', and sadistic-erotic compulsion. Kenaoui's fingers are stained with his blood after he has been chased away from a disused carriage where he has spied on Hanouma changing her clothes; he stares at 'glamour' pictures scattered at his feet as he rubs his bloody fingers. In the abandoned workshop where he lives, he pins up centre-folds from the bundle of papers and magazines that he is supposed to be selling, and on the arm of a smiling blonde he pathetically sketches a bucket containing a bottle.

The only scene in which the protagonists manage to escape from the confines of Bab al-Hadid is when Kenaoui attempts to win Hanouma's love with his hopeless proposal of marriage and the gift of a gold necklace that belonged to his mother. Kenaoui's pathetic insignificance is emphasised in a tilt-up shot of his head and shoulders, dominated by a monumental statue of the 'great pharaoh', Ramesses II, the only image of 'Heritage Egypt' in the entire film. The pitiful mid-twentieth-century urban *fellah* remains as insignificant as any of his ancestors in pharaonic Egypt three millennia before him. Hanouma mocks and rejects his desire for a return to peasant life, which she knows would be for her an inescapable round of child rearing and animal husbandry.

Kenaoui is finally tricked by his compassionate but substitute father, Madboui, who invites him to dress in his wedding robe for marriage to Hanouma that evening, but the proffered robe is a strait jacket. The final, poignant image of *Bab al-Hadid* is the face of the nameless young woman as she gazes in the direction of the train that carried off her lover to Europe.

Chahine would surely have celebrated the uprisings and revolutions of the 'Arab Spring' in 2011. Hosni Mubarak's Emergency Act, which had suppressed critical opinion in Egypt for over two decades, was a continual target of Chahine's outrage. In a comment made in 2006 that applies perfectly to the achievement of *Bab al-Hadid*, he said, responding to a question about 'the role of the artist in the contemporary political situation': 'You must participate. You can't be an artist if you don't know the social, political, and the economic context. If you talk about the Egyptian people, you must know about their problems. Either you are with modernity or you don't know what the hell you are doing' (Murphy and Williams 2007: 37).

Note

1. Grateful thanks to Dr Walid Abdul Hamid for material and advice.

Further reading

Ibrahim Fawal, *Youssef Chahine*, BFI World Directors Series, London, BFI, 2001.

Terri Ginsberg and Chris Lippard, *Historical Dictionary of Middle Eastern Cinema*, Lanham MA, Scarecrow Press, 2010.

Lina Khatib, '*Bab El-Hadid/Cairo Station*', in Gönül Dönmez-Colin (ed.), *The Cinema of North Africa and the Middle East*, New York, Wallflower Press, 2007, pp. 23–31.

Malek Khouri, *The Arab National Project in Youssef Chahine's Cinema*, Cairo, The American University in Cairo Press, 2010.

David Murphy and Patrick Williams, *Postcolonial African Cinema: Ten Directors*, Manchester, Manchester University Press, 2007.

'The Birth of the Seventh Art in Alexandria', www.bibalex.org/alexcinema/index.html (accessed 12 November 2012).

'The Official Website of Youssef Chahine', www.-youssefchahine.us/index2.html (accessed 12 November 2012).

Nigel Wheale

Bab El-Oued City (1994)

[Country: Algeria, France, Germany. Production Company: Les Matins Films, Flashback Audiovisuel, La Sept Cinéma, Zweites Deutsches Fernsehen, Thelma Film AG. Screenwriter and Director: Merzak Allouache. Producers: Tahar Harhoura, Jean-Pierre Gallèpe, Jacques Bidou, Yacine Djadi. Cinematographer: Jean-Jacques Mréjen. Sound: Philippe Sénéchal. Editor: Marie Colonna. Cast: Hassan Abidou (Boualem), Mohammed Ourdache (Saïd), Nadia Kaci (Yamina), Nadia Samir (Ouardya), Messaoud Hatta (Mess), Mebrouk Ait Amara (Mebrouk), Ahmed Benaissa (the Imam).]

Synopsis: A young baker, Boualem, steals a speaker from the rooftop of his apartment building in the working-class Algerian neighbourhood of Bab El-Oued. The speaker belongs to the community's mosque; it spreads the disembodied voice of the Imam across the neighbourhood and keeps Boualem from sleeping in the early hours before his shift. The theft enrages Saïd, the leader of a fundamentalist gang and a local hero of the October Riots. Saïd and his gang begin terrorising the community in their search for the guilty. Boualem loses his job, gets attacked by Saïd, and finally flees Algeria on a ship bound for Marseille. He leaves behind Yamina, Saïd's sister and the woman he secretly loves, with the promise to return for her.

In October 1988, a series of violent protests against President Chadli Bendjedid and the socialist *Front de Libération Nationale* (FLN) government erupted on the streets of Algiers and quickly spread to cities and towns across Algeria. The FLN had led the revolution against French colonialism and maintained political power after the Évian Accords and independence in 1962. During the protests, students and workers united against rising prices, high unemployment, and decades of single-party political rule. The government responded to the demonstrators with brutal force: hundreds were killed by their own military. The October Riots consolidated Islamist opposition to the FLN and sparked the Algerian civil war, a bloody conflict that stretched across the 1990s. The entire period would come to be known as the 'black decade' or 'décennie noire'.

The narrative events of *Bab El-Oued City* unfold in the aftermath of the riots, amid the swell of Islamic fundamentalism and the ominous signs of a conflict to come, or already underway. The film traces a set of growing tensions between moderates and fundamentalists, Western influences and Algerian autonomy, and revolutions past and present. *Bab El-Oued City* begins with a radical provocation to the new political class – a local baker, Boualem, steals one of the mosque speakers and tosses it into the sea – and ends with multiple departures. Boualem flees Algeria on a ship bound for Marseille; Mess leaves the fundamentalist gang and returns home to France; and the Imam, too, leaves the city, in search of purer hearts. Once Saïd and his thugs have installed a new speaker – 'this'll pop their ears off!' – the Imam sends a prophetic final message beyond the diegesis to the streets of Algiers: 'Violence breeds violence. There will be no more peace in Bab El-Oued. You are responsible for what will happen in the future.'

Merzak Allouache filmed *Bab El-Oued City* within the very context of socio-political instability and everyday violence that the film represents. This context encompasses a series of radical upheavals in the Algerian film industry. In 1993, the cinema office (CAAIC) cancelled all of its contracts with state-funded filmmakers. The shift forced Algerian directors to either establish their own independent production companies or secure funds from other, often European sources; state funding was reserved for those who were willing to submit their scripts for state approval (Armes 2006: 55). As conflict in Algeria intensified, many filmmakers simply fled the country. Fundamentalist groups attacked cinemas, attempted to kill and kidnap those who worked in the industry, and threatened any citizens caught attending a screening. Throughout the 1990s, both making and watching film became an increasingly dangerous activity. This era of violence and censorship had marked effects on film production, distribution, and spectatorship: 'cinema audiences had declined from nine million in 1980 to just half a million in 1992, while the number of cinemas declined from 453 at the time of independence to a bare dozen in 1999' (Armes 2006: 56).

Bab El-Oued City bears the traces of these unstable conditions. Allouache made the film in Algeria with financial support from French and German production companies. He gathered his footage in secret, using a 16mm camera and the homes of family and friends for interiors. When Algiers became too dangerous, he moved his small cast and crew to cities and towns outside the capital (Khalil 2005: 152). The film thus sews these disparate spaces together, constructing a fictional Bab El-Oued out of its political realities. As a result, the film often feels fragmented and hurried. Scenes are short, unpolished, caught on the run. Remarkably, Allouache published a novel based on his film in 1995. The book does not repeat or transcribe the film (as so many film novelisations often do), but rather expands upon and deepens the narrative and its characters, as well as the tableau of civil-war era Algiers. Writing the book, Allouache explains, allowed him 'to exorcise the many frustrations that arose when making the film. It gave me a sense of freedom not possible with the constraints of the camera, especially when shooting in a hostile environment, as was the case there' (1998: 133).

In its representation of Algeria's historical and national crises, *Bab El-Oued City* reflects the permeability and ambiguity of national boundaries, particularly in the post-colonial era. As a European co-production made on location in Algeria, the film also troubles the concept of a national cinema. For Will Higbee, 'Allouache is a transnational filmmaker for whom the distinction between "here" and "there" has little fixed currency: for both the filmmaker and the protagonists of his films, the relationship between France and Algeria is defined by continuity and difference, and remains in constant flux' (2007: 62). Indeed, like so many of his characters, Allouache ferries between Algeria and France. In the 1960s, he trained at the *Institut National de Cinéma d'Alger* and the *Institut des Hautes Études Cinématographiques* in Paris. He worked for the *Office des Actualités Algériennes*, as well as the French *Centre National de la Cinématographie* (Khalil 2005: 143). The narrative of *Bab El-Oued City* further complicates these geopolitical dividing lines. The dialogue oscillates between French and a local Algerian dialect, with some figures moving flexibly between the two. Almost all of the characters, save perhaps Saïd, indulge in Western popular culture. Boualem's friend and co-worker, Mebrouk sells European imports on the black market, while (almost always) wearing a Public Enemy baseball cap, his Walkman, and an LA Lakers basketball jersey. The women watch French cinema and secretly swap romance novels. And even members of Saïd's gang of thugs gather together to discuss the places they have travelled and the merits of Cat Stevens (before and after his conversion to Islam). In this way, Allouache presents both a city and a cinema torn between Europe and an impossibly impure Algeria.

Bab El-Oued City is also a transhistorical film. It intervenes in film history and representations of the Maghreb through the eras of French colonialism, anti-colonial revolution, and post-colonial independence. The film counters the depictions of North Africa that dominated French colonial cinema in the 1920s and 30s, including Julien Duvivier's iconic portrayal of Jean Gabin as a criminal ex-pat in

Algiers, *Pépé Le Moko* (1937). Duvivier's film, among so many others, transformed the Casbah into an Orientalist fantasy of veiled bodies, exotic shadows, and labyrinthine passageways. The cinematic genealogy of *Bab El-Oued City* also includes *The Battle of Algiers* (1966), Gillo Pontecorvo's neo-realist portrayal of the FLN and anti-colonial resistance. Allouache's Algiers crucially reworks these picturesque and political engagements with the city. *Bab El-Oued City* lacks the visual appeal and rhythmic precision of its former cinematic selves. This Algiers is dirty and decayed, covered in the daily laundry and concealed beneath a palette of black, brown, and beige. In her analysis of this cinematic constellation, Mary Jean Green understands this shift as a challenge to colonial ways of seeing the city. She writes, 'Allouache turns his back on the traditional French views of Algiers as seen from the port, the gaze of the colonial authorities, which have dominated the cityscapes. Instead, he assumes the gaze of the contemporary resident, filming an unbroken line of crowded apartment buildings stretching to the sea' (2007: 75). But Allouache also turns his back on the collectivities and unities that defined the revolution and its images. *Bab El-Oued City* displaces the stark visual and ideological divisions (between the French military and the Algerian revolutionaries, for example) that shaped the anti-colonial era and Pontecorvo's film. In *Bab El-Oued City*, nearly every scene offers a distinct 'residential' perspective on the city and a new dividing line that developed in the aftermath of independence.

Bab El-Oued City embeds within its narrative several diachronic perspectives on the city and its history. One of these perspectives belongs to Ouardya, a former student radical who 'used to believe in beautiful things: the revolution, helping the Third World, Marxism'. In contemporary Algiers, however, she lives alone and drinks away these memories. Another of these perspectival sites emerges in the figure of an elderly blind woman who wanders into and out of the film, led by her middle-aged nephew, Monsieur Paulo. This couple represents the *pieds-noirs* who lived in Algeria during colonialism and escaped to France just before and after independence. Together, Monsieur Paolo and his aunt visit the catholic cemetery (now overgrown), their old building in Bab El-Oued (now in disrepair), and the seaside (now deserted). At each of these sites, the nephew describes the Algiers of his Aunt's memory, rather than the one that we actually see: 'Padovani Beach hasn't changed, Auntie. You should see the bright umbrellas and the pedal boats. Remember the pedal boats?... It's almost like Miami Beach. I don't know why it's empty.' The nephew, however, cannot conceal the smell of open sewers that his Aunt detects everywhere they go. The blind woman interrupts the Algerian present with its complex colonial past. She is one of the many interstitial characters who circulate between Algeria and France, belonging somewhere in between. The blind woman, like Ouardya, also straddles historical moments, at once a reminder of the way things used to be and a forecast of Algeria's future. Indeed, in her ageing, sightless body, we find a symbol of another era's conflicts, now crippled and weak.

The *pied-noir* couple further exemplifies one of the most important formal aspects of the film, namely the disjunctive interplay between sound and image. The film's entire narrative axis turns around the loss of (speaker) sound, a conceit that simultaneously establishes and destabilises the relationship between sound and socio-political power. This narrative instability nevertheless extends to the sound structures of the actual film. In *Bab El-Oued City*, we hear voices from sources we cannot see and from bodies that do not speak. Allouache layers images of the Algiers skyline with the voice of the Imam – that is, the voice of god – and joins a slow tilting shot of a dark and dirty courtyard to the collective murmur of the women who trade gossip as they wash their families' clothes. The film thus invites us to compare and confuse these distinct combinations of sound and image (the powerful and the powerless), to perhaps imagine other audiovisual possibilities, other sites of political control. The film is bookended by the voice of Yamina, reading from the letters she has written to Boualem three years after his departure. In the film's first scene, we see her writing and hear her internal diegetic sound: 'Why am I writing to you? You left three years ago. Where are you? In what country?' The film's final moments redefine Yamina's voice as a closed circuit, going nowhere, heard by no one (except us). Her letters have never been sent and Boualem has not returned. However, framed in this way, the film belongs to Yamina, begins and ends with her unspoken voice, three years after Boulaem's departure and Algeria's burgeoning conflict. Like the collective babble that counters the singularity of the Imam, this sound structure imagines an altogether different source of civil authority and a future for Algeria that is feminine.

Further reading

Merzak Allouache, *Bab El-Oued*, trans. Angela M. Brewer, Boulder, Colorado, Lynne Rienner Publishers, 1998 [1995].

Roy Armes, *African Filmmaking: North and South of the Sahara*, Edinburgh, Edinburgh University Press, 2006.

Nataša Durovicová and Kathleen Newman, *World Cinemas, Transnational Perspectives*, New York, Routledge, 2010.

Mary Jean Green, 'Echoes of the Casbah: From *Pépé le Moko* to *Bab el-Oued City*', *Nottingham French Studies*, Vol. 46, No. 1, 2007, pp. 68–83.

Will Higbee, 'Locating the Postcolonial in Transnational Cinema: The Place of Algerian Émigré Directors in Contemporary French Film', *Modern & Contemporary France*, Vol. 15, Issue 1, 2007, pp. 51–64.

Andrea Flores Khalil, 'Interview with Merzak Allouache', *The Journal of North African Studies*, Vol. 10, Issue 2, 2005, pp. 143–56.

Edward Said, *Orientalism*, New York, Vintage Books, 1979.

Katherine Groo

Badkonake sefid/The White Balloon (1995)

[Country: Iran. Production Company: Children's Division of IRIB Channel 2 and Ferdos Films. Director: Jafar Panahi. Producer: Korush Mazkouri. Screenwriter: Abbas Kiarostami (based on an original idea by Parviz Shahbazi and Jafar Panahi). Cinematographer: Farzad Joudat. Sound engineers: Mojtaba Mortazavi and Saeed Ahmadi. Sound mixing: Mehdi Dejbodi. Editor: Jafar Panahi. Cast: Fereshteh Sadr Orafaiy (Mother), Ana Bourkowska (Elder Woman), Aida Mohammadkhani (Razieh), Mohsen Kafili (Ali), Mohammad Bakhtiari (Tailor), Mohammad Shahani (Soldier), Ali-Asghar Samadi (Afghan balloon vendor).]

Synopsis: *The White Balloon* unfolds during the countdown to the New Year. The plot revolves around seven-year-old Razieh, who has her heart set on a particular goldfish. Goldfish are an essential element of a table of various items Iranians set out in celebration of the New Year, and Razieh is not satisfied with the 'skinny' fish her family cultivates in their yard. After managing to receive money from her mother for the fish, the film unfolds like an anxiety dream with a series of drawn-out obstacles standing in the way of Razieh and her goldfish.

The White Balloon (1995) is Jafar Panahi's first feature film, with a screenplay by the better-known and celebrated director Abbas Kiarostami. Funded by Iranian sources, including the Islamic Republic of Iran's Broadcasting Channel 2, the film was screened inside Iran but found its most enthusiastic audience abroad. Like his subsequent work such as *The Mirror* (1997), *Circle* (2000), *Crimson Gold* (2003) and *Offside* (2006), Panahi's *The White Balloon* was the recipient of international praise and awards. It also received critical acclaim inside Iran and was Iran's official submission to the Academy Awards. However, the Iranian government later attempted to withdraw the nomination due to political tensions with the United States.

The White Balloon stands out as among the best known of a number of other Iranian films in the 1990s which signalled a revival of Iranian cinema. Following the 1979 Revolution and the eight-year war with Iraq that began within a year, the film industry suffered along with other sectors of Iranian society.[1] With a few exceptions, such as Nader's *The Runner* (1986), Beizai's *Bashu, the Little Stranger* (1989), and Kiarostami's *Where is the Friend's House* (1987) and *Close-Up* (1990), the cinema of 1980s Iran was largely unremarkable. As the country eased into the relative stability of the post-war years following the August 1988 ceasefire, the possibilities for films and other forms of expression expanded. At the same time, films in particular and cultural production more broadly became a site of increasing political contestation. The result was a vibrant, if volatile, film industry.

Panahi's work has been noted for its neo-realist aspects,[2] and some of these elements are evident in *The White Balloon*. Employing a mix of professional and nonprofessional actors, the majority of the action takes place in the main streets and back alleys of Tehran. The film is set in a working-class neighbourhood, and while the film revolves around the protagonist's desire, rather than need, for a goldfish, the lengths she must go through to fulfil her wish for a fish that costs less than one dollar underscores the economic hardships of her family. Panahi does not gratuitously toy with the audience's emotions; he avoids close-ups, and several long takes provide an occasional sense that one is watching an observational documentary. The opening sequence of the film provides one such example.

Approximately two minutes in length, the first long take of the film captures a busy Tehran street on the eve of the Iranian New Year celebration: a radio host stating that the New Year is one hour and 28 minutes away opens the film, and the announcement of the New Year's arrival brings the film to a close, with the story time approximating the film's run time. The excitement of the countdown to the New Year is intensified by the stress of the protagonist's main obstacles. In the course of Razieh's misadventures, Panahi reveals the diversity of Tehran and ultimately tells a touching tale about human connections in a big city. At the same time, the film provides subtle social commentary, a feature that becomes overt in his later films.

Razieh's compounding difficulties in reaching her goldfish bring her into contact with a range of Tehran's permanent and transient residents, providing Panahi the opportunity to show Tehran in all its strangeness and dynamism. First, snake charmers that her mother had warned against earlier take her money as part of their act for several stressful moments. Soon thereafter, she realises that she has lost her money after leaving the snake charmers for the fish store. Seconds after spotting the money with the help of a kindly, elderly woman who speaks Persian with a foreign accent, a motorcycle rushes by, pushing the bill – already precariously perched on a gutter – into the cellar below. Razieh's nightmare continues for nearly another hour of screen time, as she tries to recover the money on her own and soon thereafter with her brother's help. Others she encounters in her attempts to recover the money include the cranky tailor with a shop next to where the money was lost, a soldier on furlough who cannot afford to go home for the New Year, and the Afghan balloon vendor who is not much older than her and her brother and who is ultimately their salvation. As is apparent from their accented Persian, the tailor and the soldier are not Tehran natives, and the Afghan boy, though he may well have been born in the city, is marked as being on the margins of Iranian society.

It is the Afghan boy who obtains chewing gum for the kids, which they adhere to the bottom of the stick holding his balloon and successfully retrieve the money. After nearly an hour and a half of immersion in Razieh's obstacle-ridden quest for the desired goldfish, the film does not end with the happy siblings rushing home to be with their family. Rather, it concludes with a focus on the Afghan boy, alone after Ali and Razieh buy their fish and pass him by without acknowledgement, much less an expression of gratitude for his help. Various characters introduced throughout the film also stroll by, likely heading out to join their loved ones for the turn of the New Year. The friendly shop owner whose cellar the money had fallen into but who had arrived after the children had already retrieved their money, pats the Afghan boy on the back and tells him that it is time to go home. But the boy does not budge, raising the question of what kind of home life – if any – he has. The film comes to a close with the Afghan vendor sitting alone with his single white balloon stirring almost imperceptibly as the clock ticking toward the New Year beats on. After the New Year is announced, he gets up; and this is where the film concludes, with the freeze frame of the boy turning to walk away.

In these last few seconds, Panahi manages to provide a new layer of complexity to his film. The audience has to this point been invested in Razieh's fate. The lengths she has to go through to obtain the money for the goldfish, including bribing and then colluding with her brother, point to the family's financial hardships. Her father, never seen but heard yelling and complaining from the shower early in the film, signals additional family tension. Talking to a soldier on furlough, while waiting for her brother to return with help for getting the money out of the gutter, Razieh tells him that her father has two jobs, one which she is allowed to speak about, and one which she is not. The unspeakable job both points to their financial problems and provides some explanation for the father's bad disposition. It also leads the viewer to conclude that the bruise on Ali's face is likely a result of the father's ill temper.

Despite the difficulties they might face, the film's conclusion suggests that others in their city fare worse. In the film's opening scenes, their mother is shown with bags full of groceries and is later seen preparing the house for New Year; the siblings' joyous run home indicates their excitement for the coming festivities. In contrast, the Afghan boy does not appear to have a place to go to. Present in the opening sequence with lots of balloons, he is down to the white one by the end: parents of happy children have presumably bought them in celebration of the New Year. The Afghan boy contributes to the festivities of the New Year but is not included in them.

In Panahi's later films, the political resonance of his work is unmistakable. This is particularly the case in his third and fifth films, *The Circle* (2000) and *Offside* (2006), which cast light on restrictions faced by women under the Islamic Republic.[3] Unlike his first two films, which centred on children, the latter faced a ban inside Iran. Yet the stark contrasts between *The White Balloon* and the later films in his oeuvre do not mean that his first work is bereft of social commentary or political implications. The final focus on the Afghan balloon seller is a poignant illustration of the hard-working yet excluded Afghan minority in Iran. Unlike other Iranian films about Afghans in Iran or Afghanistan, most notably those of the Makhmalbaf Production House, which often exoticise and are condescending to their subject, Panahi treats the Afghan boy with respect and humour.

While some have criticised the sentimental portrayal of children in 1990s Iranian cinema, contrasting them to the resilient children appearing in the films of the previous decade,[4] the kids of *The White Balloon* cannot be dismissed as romanticised innocents. At his first appearance on screen, Ali is rushing out of the house to buy soap for his father, and is later yelled at for not paying attention and buying soap instead of shampoo. The film later suggests that Ali bears the brunt of his father's physical anger as well. He is also the one sent to look for Razieh when she delays in returning from the fish store, and he acts as her protector when he finds her on the street. Razieh too is clever beyond her years and spends much of the film variously negotiating with adults. After attempting to barter with her mother in exchange for money for the fish, her mother confirms Razieh's headstrong defiance when she responds with: 'Not only have you put on your new clothes before the New Year, but you've also given your gifts away before getting them'. Finally, there is the Afghan balloon vendor, a working child who is not even able to celebrate the New Year. In short, the film's children, all charming in their own ways, nonetheless reflect the social and economic difficulties that have contributed to their strong characters.

While the political resonance of Panahi's later works have somewhat overshadowed his first film, *The White Balloon* remains a seminal work in both Panahi's oeuvre and in Iranian cinema. It was one of the key works signalling the ascendancy of Iranian cinema in the 1990s, and remains remarkable in its own right as a well-told story with cleverly understated social commentary.

Notes

1. For an overview of the state of Iranian cinema in the first decade after the 1979 revolution, see Hamid Naficy, 'Iranian Cinema Under the Islamic Republic', *American Anthropologist*, Vol. 97, No. 3, 1995, pp. 548–58.
2. For Panahi's own comments on the neo-realism of his films, see Saverio Giovacchini and Robert Sklar, 'The Geography and History of Neo-realism', in Saverio Giovacchini and Robert Sklar (eds), *Global Neo-Realism: The Transnational History of a Film Style*, Jackson, MS, University of Mississippi Press, 2012, p. 3. Hamid Naficy's essay, 'Neo-realism: Iranian Style', included in the same collection, may also be of interest.
3. The depiction of the realities of women's lives in post-revolutionary Iran is not without its downsides in the international arena. For an example and critical intervention into how some celebrations of Panahi's *Circle* have fed into troubling generalisations and erroneous assumptions about women and Iran by journalists and film reviewers, see Hossein Khosrowjah, 'Neither a Victim nor a Crusading Heroine: Kiarostami's Feminist Turn in 10', *Situations*, Vol. 4, No. 1, 2011, pp. 53–65.
4. Azadeh Farahmand has argued that the children of 1980s Iranian cinema had a 'strong and proud presence, fighting and surviving the injustices of their surroundings' whereas the children of 1990s cinema were 'purified prototypes'. See Azadeh Farahmand, 'Perspectives on Recent (International Acclaim for) Iranian Cinema', in Richard Tapper (ed.), *The New Iranian Cinema: Politics, Representation and Identity*, London and New York, I.B. Tauris, 2002, p. 105. Hamdi Reza Sadr's essay, 'Children in Contemporary Iranian Cinema: When we Were Children', also included in this collection, is also relevant for its overview of children in Iranian cinema.

Further reading

Hamid Naficy, *A Social History of Iranian Cinema: The Globalizing Era, 1984–2010*, Durham, NC, Duke University Press, 2012.

Sarah Niazi, 'Urban Imagination and the Cinema of Jafar Panahi', *Wide Screen*, Vol. 2, No. 1, 2010.

Richard Tapper (ed.), *The New Iranian Cinema: Politics, Representation and Identity*, London, I.B. Tauris, 2002.

Niki Akhavan

Bamako (2006)

[Country: Mali, France, USA. Production Company: Archipel 33, Chinguitty Films, Mali Images, arte France Cinéma, Louverture Films. Director and Screenwriter: Abderrahmane Sissako. Cinematographer: Jacques Besse. Cast: Aissa Maiga (Mele), Maimouna Helene Diarra (Saramba), Mamadou Kanoute (lawyer), Danny Glover (cowboy), Elia Suleiman (cowboy).]

Synopsis: In an outdoor courtyard in the Malian city of Bamako a court hearing is taking place listening to witnesses give evidence: the plaintiff is Africa, the accused are the IMF, the World Bank and their associates. The latter institutions are accused of causing the poverty of many African countries, through their policies. Evidence for and against their guilt is heard from a variety of witnesses, including an elderly farmer intending to make a statement, who is told to wait; and a group who describe their danger-filled experiences of attempted emigration. Meanwhile, throughout the proceedings, the inhabitants continue their daily lives walking round or through the courtroom; a wedding takes place, cloth-dyers discuss colours, children care for other children, a man lies gravely ill. Outside the courtyard walls, people discuss events, philosophise on life, and consider rumours of a lost gun, while singer Mele's relationship with her husband worsens and she leaves, taking her child. By the end of the day individual problems take centre stage resonating with the larger events discussed in the court including a violent conclusion as to the whereabouts of the gun.

> Words are something, they can seize you in your heart; it's bad if you keep them inside./ The goat has its ideas but so does the hen. When you come for something you have to do it./ My words won't remain within me.

These responses from a farmer who has come to give his evidence, but is denied permission to do so, are shown to us during the preliminaries to the trial which forms the centre of Sissako's film. His comments on the need to express your words even when space has not been made for them, placed in the earliest establishing position, before both the title and the credits, to reflect on events that follow, sets a strong opening position for this most politically committed, yet most cinematic, film. It also provides one of several circularities, which enclose and comment on the trial scenes; as, true to his intention, the farmer speaks again towards the end of the film, no longer prepared to wait for permission to give voice to his views. This takes the form of a lengthy cry and chant, in untranslated dialect, not understood by the large majority of his listeners, on screen or off, but nevertheless a highly eloquent protest and lament, a completely appropriate comment and addition to the court's deliberations.

Commentators and reviewers have stated that this film defies viewer expectations; perhaps this is because, with potent cinematic boldness, Sissako has used the fantasy potential of film to stage an impossible confrontation; no less than a symbolic trial at which the defendants are the World Bank and the IMF, accused by Africa itself, in the person of witnesses, mostly people from real life, who are cross-examined on issues of imperial exploitation, neo-colonialism and globalisation, or 'pauperization, rather than poverty', as one of them articulately insists. Equally unexpectedly, the pomp and procedure of the trial takes place in the lowly circumstances of the courtyard central to a small African community, who carry on their daily lives around and within the trial proceedings, some listening or taking part, some ignoring or taking the opportunity to make a swift profit from the participants. This remarkable form is extended further by apparent diversions; the re-enacting of a desert journey, even a film within the film, in the showing of a spoof cowboy TV programme. In addition, we observe the events of specific characters' lives, notably that of singer Mele's fracturing relationship with her husband, a man lying close to death, women dyeing cloth, and the machinations outside the courtyard wall regarding the rumoured disappearance of a gun. Sissako's skilful orchestration involves both scripted and improvised speech, producing a crammed immediacy of mise en scène, in which each element echoes and reflects on the others; a form which reflects day-to-day realities to produce a formalised politics in itself.

This is a remarkable turnaround for a filmmaker previously considered apolitical, one whose earlier films, notably that best known in the West, the influential *Waiting For Happiness*, consider themes crucial to African experience, those of exile and return, but with a reflective autobiographical slant, and a slower pacing closer to real time. Sissako's filmic background as a student for six years at the VGIK film school in the Soviet Union can be seen echoed in his use of montages of facial close-ups, the long take and highly considered arrangements of objects and framing of the shot, reminiscent of the poetics of Tarkovsky.[1] Similar effects can be discerned in *Bamako*; in the opening shots that precede the farmer incident, in which the camera follows, from behind and at a distance, a figure walking towards the horizon, as gradually the light lifts, dawn breaks and the figure reaches his destination, eventually revealed to be the mud walls of the open-air court; a quietist reflective opening in total contrast to the bustle and anger that the walls will later contain. Similarly, the camera later dwells on the still close-ups of heads of listeners, or loiterers, within and without the court, emphasising the beauty, colour and form of appearance and expressions. This attention to framing is particularly evident regarding the doorways, those leading us into the daily lives of the villagers, and particularly that which gives, or bars, entrance to the court itself. But in *Bamako* the dreamy aspect of locations and wanderings has been superseded by a more political tone: these elements have an additional function, bearing symbolic as well as real connotations regarding the opening or closing of access to power.

One further key influence can be seen in the putting together of this mix; in interview[2] Sissako draws attention to the shared experience of lack of cinematic, and political, access, for both the African nations and those of South America, situations which have given rise to the creation of Third Cinema films,[3] using the device of 'imperfect cinema', less polished or concerned with maintaining cinematic seamlessness, in which the illusion of filmic apparatus is not allowed to produce a comforting illusion, rather the process is exposed, producing a more political immediacy. To return to the opening sequence, as the figure arrives at the courtyard wall, daylight reveals he is dwarfed by the cinematic and sound apparatus being installed for relaying the court proceedings; in a later scene one of the earliest arrivals within the court is a journalist with a film camera, while the functioning or non-functioning of the technology, especially that of sound, is constantly monitored by the courtyard listeners.

Such deconstructions and distanciations of the filmic process are, of course, also loaded with other connotations; those of Western art cinema, potently influential regarding much of African cinema, due to the post-colonial continuation of a stake and of funding from the French. The problematic nature of this presence, an underlying issue for contemporary African filmmakers, has led to a concern to create other platforms.[4] In *Bamako* it is approached obliquely through Sissako's interrogation, and acknowledgement, of this past, echoing the techniques and methods of the most radically experimental and explicitly political of the French New Wave filmmakers, Jean-Luc Godard, in an appropriation of the structuring of his 1972 film, *Tout Va Bien*. Where Godard uses the symbolic structure of a two-storey factory to play out the power struggles between factory workers at ground level, and their bosses on the level above, Sissako ratchets up the irony, and the political potency of the symbolic setting, by translating this with a doubled edge; in the dual-purpose courtyard the disparities of the empowered and the powerless are twice demonstrated, in both the discourses and evidence of the court, and in the surrounding villagers whose lives reflect this state of affairs. Sissako has created a formal double jeopardy of disempowerment, building on that of Godard, while keeping the symbolism 'real', in the localised and differentiated lives on view.

Alongside these European strands there can be discerned African filmic influences: Sissako, like all contemporary African filmmakers, must negotiate the towering presence of the 'father' of committed political filmmaking in Africa, the social realist work of the late Ousmane Sembene. Diawara has pointed out[5] that in Sissako's early films, the realist strand differs from that of Sembene, being subsumed by the poetic and aesthetic effects of his cinematic techniques. There is nevertheless an element of the documentary and autobiographical: in *Bamako* an instance is the telling evidence of the desert-walkers, who recount the horrors of their attempt at emigration. But the film is not confined by a single model of what African political film should be; and in a refusal of this, typical of the New Wave of African film of which Sissako has become a standard bearer, realist techniques are not the only method used. Sissako has added an overlay of the poetic and the playful, techniques more reminiscent of a contrasting major African filmmaker, also showing European influences, Djibril Diop Mambety.[6] This is evident in the doubly symbolic world created by the court/courtyard; it can also be seen in the apparent diversions from this world, notably in the parodic referentiality of the spoof cowboy TV film. Titled 'Death in Timbuktu', this follows the comic generic exploits of a white and a black cowboy, roles taken by Danny Glover and Elia Suleiman, as they ride in to shoot up the town, with astonishing success, wiping out several innocent passers-by, concerned only with their own prowess and gain. Sissako has commented on this addition, that it provides the viewer with a break in which to assimilate more serious material, while also underlining the overall themes of violent exploitation.[7] A similar function is performed by the fictional narrative following the disintegrating relationship of Mele and her husband Chaka, which is threaded through the other events. Mele provides a further enclosing circularity; her performance as a nightclub singer serves to open the film on an upbeat note, while at its close her singing is performed through tears. While this is evidently due to her personal life, it serves equally well as a comment on the state of affairs which the film as a whole reveals; another instance of the doubly functioning technique which Sissako employs.

Some Western commentators have found Sissako's methods overly didactic and the case he presents one-sided, suggesting[8] he drowns out the very voices of those to whom he intends to give a platform and that the fictional characterisations such as Mele are underdeveloped. But this drawing together of multiple, lightly drawn elements to parallel the more intense evidences of the court gives a further dimension where fact and fiction, reality and play, act together, and in which aspects are suggestive rather than worked through. This can apply to the fictional storylines as well as to the dispersed courtyard events and the more discursive debates; as is witnessed by the distanced and ambiguous denouement of the lost gun strand. It is a technique which can provide an opaque open-endedness of outcomes. In contrast, the proceedings of the court, despite the Western set-up as a forum of impartiality, is closer to the African model of 'Truth and Reconciliation',[9] providing for acts of truth-telling and witness, intended ultimately to serve as a redress for injustice, and perhaps as a preliminary to a more positive way forward. Sissako comments[10] that a sense of universality, of the 'other' as not very different, is stronger in Africa than the West, also the sense that injustice contaminates us all. *Bamako*'s multiple stranding brings its variety of influences together in a potent mix; but ultimately the film's focus is firmly on the necessary witness of 'words that can seize you in your heart', and the prevention of their being spoken as destructive to both speaker and audience.

Notes

1. For a detailed examination of these techniques in *Waiting For Happiness*, see Manthia Diawara, *African Film: New Forms of Aesthetics and Politics*, New York, Prestel, 2010, pp. 105–12.
2. *Bamako* DVD extra, Interview.
3. Underlining this, the South American experimental filmmaker Elia Suleiman plays a cowboy in the spoof Western.
4. Sissako is a member of La Guild des Cineastes, promoting African filmmakers in Europe.
5. *African Film: New Forms of Aesthetics and Politics*, p. 100f.
6. Seen for example in Mambety's best-known film, *Touki Bouki* (1975).
7. *Bamako* DVD extra, Interview.
8. Stella Papamichael (2007) *BBC Movies*. [online] Available at www.bbc.co.uk/films/2007/02/19/bamako_2007_review.shtml (accessed 13 April 2012).
9. See also N. Frank Ukadlke, 'Calling to Account', *Sight and Sound*, February 2007.
10. *Bamako* DVD extra, Interview.

Further reading

Manthia Diawara, *African Film: New Forms of Aesthetics and Politics*, New York, Prestel, 2010.

David Murphy, *Postcolonial African Cinema: Ten Directors*, Manchester, Manchester University Press, 2008.

Lynda Townsend

El baño del papa/The Pope's Toilet (2007)

[Country: Uruguay. Production Company: Chaya Films. Directors: César Charlone, Enrique Fernández. Screenwriters: César Charlone, Enrique Fernández. Cinematographer: César Charlone. Editor: Gustavo Giani. Cast: César Troncoso (Beto); Virginia Méndez (Carmen); Mario Silva (Valvulina); Virginia Ruiz (Sylvia).]

Synopsis: A poor Uruguayan town on the Brazilian border awaits the visit of Pope John Paul II. This means pilgrims will arrive in need of food and drink, paper flags, souvenirs and commemorative medals. Brimming with anticipation, the locals hope not only for blessing but also a small share of material happiness.

Produced in 2007, *El baño del papa* takes a look back at the day on which the Pope visited the small Uruguayan border town, Melo, in 1988. This factually based event is eclipsed by the fictional, personal details of the town's inhabitants as they prepare for his arrival and the commercial opportunities the expected crowds may bring. In particular, *El baño del papa* focuses on a contraband smuggler, Beto, and his plan to obtain supplies from across the border in Brazil in order to construct a public toilet that he can charge visitors to use. Beto's smuggling activities are already complicated by his limited means of transport, his bicycle, and the film captures farcical moments as he tries to carry the construction material along bumpy dirt roads. The film's mix of humour (Beto's laughable ideas) and pathos (the failure of his plans to come to fruition) is indicative of a tendency within the Latin American region to deal with ongoing social and economic difficulties through films that are rich with colourful stories and experiences. At the same time, Beto shares screen time with a variety of carefully constructed characters that allow the particularities of their north-Uruguayan province to develop.

These particularities are supported by the poetic realist style that César Charlone (working in this case as director and cinematographer) brings to the film. On the one hand, warm hues combine with carefully chosen autumnal landscapes to create an atmospheric tone of a fading past. The film's often shallow focus draws out the expressive quality of the characters' faces and body movements while the gentle rhythms of quiet dialogue from Beto's wife Carmen, daughter Silvia and friend Valvulina are counterposed with Beto's frenzied energy, creating a dynamic tempo throughout. On the other hand, unobtrusive editing allows the action to develop within its own time and the intimacy of moments within the characters' conversations suggests the audience is eavesdropping on an existent community. This combination of expressive tendencies and realism is most apparent during the sequence subsequent to the Pope's arrival when it becomes clear that no crowds will materialise within Melo. Archive footage of the Holy Father is woven into a montage of the local citizens' doomed attempts to gather people to the food and souvenir stalls they have set up. The sequence climaxes in a slow tableau of shots that depict the excessive and simultaneous empty remains of all the products that were put on sale: sausages lie abandoned on the ground; heaps of bread rolls cover a table and spill out of large bags on the floor; plastic flags are piled haphazardly. Although the sequence could potentially terminate in stylistic abstraction, it is brought back to a humanist portrayal of the town's inhabitants through strong characterisation and attention to detail in the way the characters define themselves. In a small moment at the end of these scenes, Carmen's neighbour visits her to give her one of the Brazilian medallions that she, and others, bought on the day of the visit. It is a poignant moment as it is exactly the type of medallion that Beto told Carmen would not be popular. However, the significance is in the detail as the film replicates Carmen's close look at the medallion and then cuts to observe her quiet but pleased contemplation of the object that, rather than produce anger or frustration, solidifies her ongoing relationship with her neighbour.

This attention to the personal fabric of life in Melo is supported by the directors' decision to include a mix of professional and non-professional actors. The non-professional actors originated from the town and are able to integrate local detail and features with their performances. It is a practice that has a long history in Latin America and has been significantly highlighted in recent years through films such as *City of God* (2002) and *La Ciénaga* (2001). At a meta-textual level, this localism is further enhanced by the link the directors have to the stories they are telling. Enrique Fernández drew upon his own personal history growing up in Melo when he wrote the original script while César Charlone brought his experience as a Uruguayan domiciled in Brazil to the duo-national influences in the film. The authenticity that actors and directors lend to the film is common to productions in the region, drawing on the influence that neo-realism and post-war European auteur cinema had on Latin American directors. It ultimately helped the film gain traction in film festival and art-house circuits that support a global art cinema aesthetic based on the socio-economic and cultural background of the filmmakers.[1]

While the border crossing aspect of the film has its roots in the historical location of the plot and Charlone's desire to assimilate his transnational experience into his filmmaking, it is also symptomatic of a tendency for art cinemas to locate themselves beyond a singular national context. There is often political agency in the ability for film to remind us about the arbitrary nature of national borders. Scholars such as Hamid Naficy, Dina Iordanova and Anne Marie Stock highlight transnational filmmakers that use migrant possibilities and border crossing as a state of consciousness that transcends the limits imposed by states and government. The fluid way in which Beto and Valvulina negotiate their business deals with their Brazilian counterparts and live their lives between both countries on a daily basis confirms a state of being that exists beyond the national. At the same time, *El bañc del papa* does not leave the border behind completely and, instead, the film constantly works to rearticulate the border as site of personal and social significance. Thus, the opening shots showing the protagonists as they cycle their way past the frontier are set within wide landscapes and there is unequivocal freedom in their mobility. Yet within the same sequence, Beto and Valvulina are caught by the border guard Meleyo. He reappears throughout the film as a figure of authority that is manifest and continuously present in the characters' lives. His ability to confiscate their goods and treat them as second-class citizens reminds us of both the legal frameworks that condition where a person can and cannot work as well as the power the state exerts over ordinary citizens in this process. Although Meleyo's unfair and crooked practice represents a corruption of state power, it is clear that he is equivalent to the border in terms of the limitations to freedom that it sanctions. This is not just the restriction to travel and work but also greater freedoms such as self-determination and economic independence. Throughout the film, Melo's border status formulates much of the characters' lives. Money and resources are scarce at this outpost at the end of the country yet characters are not free to transcend the frontier in order to better their situation.

This depiction is particularly important for our current era of globalisation in which the fluidity and mobility of world citizens is celebrated. Although *El baño del papa* is set in the 1980s, and an argument could be made that the increased globalisation in the late twentieth and early twenty-first centuries represent a new world order, the challenges posed in the film remain relevant today. *El baño del papa* is part of a trend of recent films from Latin America that emphasise the difficulty of traversing national frontiers. This aspect is most often depicted in films that place characters against the US–Mexico border (*Norteado* (2009), *Sleep Dealer* (2008), *Sin nombre* (2009) but can often be found in other Latin American films (*American Visa* (2005), *Mi mejor enemigo* (2005), *Rabia* (2009) *La León* (2007).

Often these films emphasise the powerlessness that individuals feel when confronted by structures of power that are unresponsive. Meleyo is the face of unyielding border control while another one of these structures, the media, is represented by the newscaster who gives frequent updates on the preparations for the Pope's visit. Unlike Meleyo, he does not appear in the same space as the other characters but instead materialises through black and white images on various television screens. When towards the end of the film, he decrees the Pope's visit a great success and implores him to return, Beto tries to act in defiance to his ridiculous words by throwing a bottle of wine at the screen. It is telling that only the bottle smashes, and, while it drips a red wash of colour across the glass, the newscaster's image continues unrelentingly. Beto and the other characters have no ability to stop or overturn the media's misinformation and apparent lack of concern for their predicament in the same way that they have no effect on border policy and control.

As viewers, we are at a remove from this situation and we are given an overview of the events that means we do not fall into the same state of naïve optimism that infects the characters. In the first instance, the unfolding of the narrative privileges us with the ability to see that the newscaster's excited estimate of up to 200,000 attendees is a fallacy. We are also given the hindsight to understand, in a moment of bittersweet humour, the essential failure of the event. In the film's final statement the following lines appear on screen for the audience only:

> The Pope never came back. It is estimated that on May 8, 1988, fewer than 8,000 people attended the speech. Most were from Melo. 387 stands were set up. There were about 400 Brazilians and some 300 journalists.

While the position of discerning viewer invites us to laugh at Beto in the final image of the film, when we see him in his toilet hatching up a new scheme, it does not prevent identification. Instead the intimate moments that occur when the characters share conversation in the small rooms of their houses, in the basic local bar, in their small backyard and on the bumpy surfaces of the road, summon a connection with the audience that transcends the short time frame provided by the film. It is in this context that Enrique Fernández stated that 'the story finished with a broken dream but the spirit does not die'.[2] An understanding of the vital spirit and ingenuity of the characters, who in this case represent not just a fictional construct but the essence of Melo, is particularly important for global viewership of the film. At a time when the Latin American region is often constructed as backwards and incompetent, a humanist story such as *El baño del papa* makes it possible to separate the desires, hopes and energies of a people from the structures of power that define and limit their position in the global economic order.

When released, *El baño del papa* was one of only a small handful of Uruguay-based films to receive international distribution. David Martin Jones and Soledad Montañez (2007, 2009) explain the way that the film is part of an emergent new Uruguayan cinema that is influenced by the international arena yet also manages to create stories specific to contemporary Uruguayan audiences. This ability to tell a story of global significance within a deeply local context allows it to transcend the stereotypes connected with Uruguay and the greater Latin American region to show the determination of an individual community amongst national, regional and global structures.

Notes

1. See David Martin-Jones and Soledad Montañez, 2008.
2. See the film notes from Cannes Film Festival 2007: www.golem.es/elbanodelpapa/notas.php.

Further reading

Dina Iordanova, 'Shifting Politics of Place and Itinerary in International Cinema' in *Senses of Cinema*, www.sensesofcinema.com/contents/01/14/displaced.html, 2001, pp. 1–10.

David Martin-Jones and Soledad Montañez, 'Bicycle Thieves on Bicycles? El baño del papa (2007)' in *Studies in Hispanic Cinema*, 4:3, 2008, pp. 183–98.

David Martin Jones and Soledad Montañez, 'Cinema in Progress: New Uruguayan Cinema' in *Screen*, 50:3, 2009, pp. 334–44.

Hamid Naficy, *An Accented Cinema: Exilic and Diasporic Filmmaking*, Princeton: Princeton University Press, 2001.

Ann Marie Stock, 'Through Other Worlds and Other Times: Critical Praxis and Latin American Cinema' in *Framing Latin American Cinema: Contemporary Critical Perspectives*, Minneapolis, London, University of Minnesota Press, 1997, pp. xix–xxxv.

Miriam Ross

Bashu, gharibeye koochak/Bashu: The Little Stranger (1989)

[Country: Iran. Production Company: Centre for Intellectual Development of Children and Adolescents. Director: Bahram Beizai. Producer: Alireza Zarin. Screenwriter: Bahram Beizai. Cinematographer: Firooz Malekzadeh. Sound Recordists: Jahangir Mirshekari, Asghar Shahroudi, Behrooz Moavenian. Sound Mixing: Hassan Zahedi. Editor: Bahram Beizai. Cast: Soosan Taslimi (Naii), Parviz Pourhosseini (Ghesmat Shanbehsareei, Naii's husband), Adnan Afravian (Bashu), Akbar Doodkar (Marhemat), Farokhlagha Houshman (Sister-in-law), Zabihollah Salmani (Loghman), Mohtaram Khoshroo (Neighbour), Azam Rahbar (Golbesar), Mohammad Farkhah (Ooshin).]

Synopsis: The film begins in the war-torn south of Iran, and the opening sequence unfolds like an action film. Bombs hit homes and other civilian buildings, date trees disappear amidst smoke, and a woman who has been set on fire because of the explosions spins in vain to extinguish the flames. Rather incredibly, a trucker stops in the middle of falling bombs to merely check his tyres, giving a scared young boy the opportunity to take shelter in the back of the truck. The trucker, unaware of his stowaway, drives across the country. Several long shots reveal the diverse landscape of Iran. Thinking that explosions aimed at clearing the way for a tunnel are bombs, the young boy jumps out from the car when the trucker has stopped for a tea break and finds himself in the lush and unfamiliar streets of the northern province of Gilan. Wandering through rice fields, he is found by two young children and their mother. The remainder of the film captures the developing bond between the boy, Bashu, and his adoptive mother, Naii, and the challenges they face in their relationship with one another and with the intrusive people of the village.

The 1980s was not a good decade for the Iranian film industry. The 1979 Revolution, which brought the establishment of the Islamic Republic and the eight-year war with Iraq that began soon thereafter, resulted in a number of political and economic barriers for filmmakers. Nonetheless, films were produced in this period and Bahram Beizai's *Bashu, The Little Stranger* was among the handful that was critically acclaimed. Made at the height of the war, the film was completed by 1986 but did not get clearance from censors until the war's end and was not publicly screened until 1989. A stylised film revealing Beizai's identity as a playwright and a theatre director, *Bashu, The Little Stranger*, casts a critical eye on Iranian society. On one level a story of familial and national unity, it ultimately raises many questions about the structures undergirding concepts of family and nation.

Beizai tells the story of the boy's relationship to the family and his accidental new home with an often realist style that is punctuated by symbolic figures and dramatic shots. Although somewhat afraid of the boy at first, the mother takes him in, initiating clashes with nosy family and neighbours who cannot understand why she would take in a boy who looks so different and speaks a language they cannot understand. In capturing their developing relationship, the film gently raises sensitive questions about the bonds of belonging to family and nation. Similarly, it points to the asymmetrical experience of war.[1] While Naii's hardships are not wholly disconnected from the war economy, her experiences cannot compare to that of orphaned Bashu. The scars of that trauma are often represented by Bashu's deceased parents and sister, who died in the film's opening sequence, in their numerous eerie appearances on screen when Bashu is in Naii's village.

Silent and dressed in the local clothing of the Arab minority in southern Iran, they are incongruous against the backdrop of crops and dwellings characteristic of provinces in the north. They are visual reminders of how Bashu's war-torn past casts a sad shadow over him, and Bashu often covers his face and cries when he sees them. Just as Naii and the rest of the villagers cannot see the ghosts of his parents, they are blind to his suffering as an orphan of war as well. In one scene, Naii looks on, uncomprehending, as Bashu stiffens in fear at the sound of a plane overhead. Indeed, there is no apparent recognition of the war and its effects by anyone in the village.

The parents' various appearances also indicate how Naii comes to replace Bashu's biological family as his protector. As local boys pick on Bashu, a medium shot shows Bashu's mother placing her hands over her eyes; Naii slides into the frame, alert that something is awry. She then walks away, leaving the mother behind, and the next shot is of Naii waist down, wielding a stick and walking through the fields. Whereas Bashu's mother could not bear to watch her child's harassment and was in any case helpless to intervene, Naii steps in to find and scare off the kids by hitting them with a stick. At the same time, Bashu's parents also act as guardian angels of a sort. Bashu flees a number of times, sometimes for silly reasons, such as not wanting to bathe, sometimes for more serious ones, such as after reading an angry letter by Naii's husband reprimanding her for keeping a strange boy. In this latter case, Bashu's mother stands in the road, pointing out to Naii the path that Bashu has taken.

By the time we reach the film's last segments, approximately 25 minutes before its end, Bashu's parents no longer appear. The bond between Naii and Bashu has been cemented: she discards her husband's letter, determined to keep Bashu. He cares for her when she is ill, and becomes her companion and helper in all aspects of farming life. When Naii's husband arrives, he fights with his wife about keeping Bashu. But when Bashu comes to protect Naii from her husband, asking 'Who is this man?', the husband seems to have a sudden change of heart and answers, 'Your father'. This surprising, if implausible, shift in the husband's attitude eliminates the final obstacle to Bashu's integration as a full-fledged member of his adopted family. The film concludes with their first joint activity as a newly formed nuclear family: running together through the fields while making loud noises to scare off animals from eating the crops.

The heart-warming conclusion is at first glance an affirmation of family and national bonds. In spite of the prying intrusions of villagers and their objections to Naii adopting the 'charcoal black' boy, Naii's nuclear family fully embraces Bashu, and the lives of all family members are improved as a result. This familial integration can also be read as allegory for the national one: north and south come together, and the pull of belonging overcomes both superficial differences such as physical appearances as well as deeper ones such as differing languages. At the same time, the film casts light on the fragility of the ties that hold the diverse nation together, with a particular focus on Persian as the national language. Bashu can only communicate with the village children through the 'book language', poignantly evident in a scene where he starts reading 'we are all children of Iran' from a school textbook, but his accented Persian provokes laughter in the children whose own Persian bears the marks of the northern region's accent. Naii's only option for communicating with her husband when he is away is similarly restricted to Persian, though she herself cannot read or write. Persian makes communication possible but does not guarantee understanding or full participation of all involved: it is one basis for national unity but at the same time underscores differences as well. As such, Bashu's acceptance into Naii's family cannot be interpreted as a straightforward allegorical affirmation of the national bond. The story is clearly not one of a unified nation sharing the burdens of war. If that were the case, the entire village would have embraced Bashu. Instead, they shun him as racially other and show no awareness that he might be connected to the war-torn region of the south. In short, the film presents Bashu's acceptance into the family as an exceptional feat and not a given.

The film is also notable for the critical eye it casts on gender roles and the place of women. Naii is resilient, kind, and the competent head of the household in her husband's absence.[2] Whereas previous films of the 1980s had elided or downplayed women's roles, Beizai places Naii at the centre of the film.[3] Even with the restrictions on showing women without their veils, Beizai captures an active Naii who runs about the field and is shot in close-up numerous times in the film. While her husband's authority looms over decisions even in his absence, she continues to shelter Bashu despite her husband's reprimanding letter and argues with him until the very end, when he returns home.

That the film manages to raise so many pointed issues in a time of war gives some hints as to why the authorities censored the film and delayed its release. In Beizai's own words, 'At first, the censors saw no problem; then, they kept looking at the movie, and found many problems'.[4] Government censors must have eventually discerned that what at first sight may seem a simple and sentimental story is in fact a critical examination of gender and identity on the interlinked levels of nation and family.

While a significant film for all of the reasons noted above, the film nonetheless has some distracting flaws in terms of production values, pace, editing and the overall flow of the story. Shortcomings in this regard may be attributable to the lack of resources during wartime filming and the censorship to which the film was subject. Some of Beizai's directorial decisions, on the other hand, such as a tendency to emphasise the already dramatic, may be explained by his background as a playwright and theatre director. Soosan Taslimi's performance style and expressive face allow the audience to discern her conflicting and evolving emotions in relation to Bashu without her speaking. Yet in several scenes, Beizai overuses Taslimi's talents in this regard. In one of the most well-known images affiliated with the film, Naii rises into the frame when her children first alert her to Bashu's presence, and the focus remains on her for two seconds. The image is striking: in close-up, all but her eyes are covered, she is – for no apparent reason – pulling the part of her white scarf over her mouth in one direction and the segment covering her hair in the other. Later in the film, when Bashu runs away from the farmer's market and she cannot find him, Beizai shows her in a crane shot as she stands alone in the middle of the abandoned market. These dramatic moments in Beizai's cinematic direction are theatrical in their impact, piercing the otherwise realist feel of much of the film. The same is the case for his use of symbolic figures such as the ghosts of Bashu's family. Such elements give Beizai's film a distinct look and feel, distinguishing him from Iranian filmmakers who have received international attention in the late 1980s and 1990s and whose work has been described as bearing marks of neo-realism or poetic realism.

Overall, Bashu remains a seminal work in the history of post-Revolutionary Iranian cinema both because of the political context out of which it emerged and the critical issues it subtly raised in telling the story of a war orphan and his adopted family.

Notes

1. While clearly a film that addresses the war, the film is not included in the body of sanctioned war films recognised as part of the cinema of the 'Sacred Defense', as the eight-year war with Iraq is officially dubbed. In her account of this official cinema, Varzi has noted that Beizai was among a group of filmmakers who received training as part of a government-led effort to promote war films. For more information, see Roxanne Varzi, 'A Ghost in the Machine: the Cinema of the Iranian Sacred Defense', in Richard Tapper (ed.), *The New Iranian Cinema: Politics, Representation and Identity*, London, I.B. Tauris, 2002, pp. 154–66.
2. For an account of the interlinked connections among language, gender, and patriarchal authority in the film, see Nasri Rahimieh, 'Marking Gender and Difference in the Myth of a Nation: Bashu, a Post-Revolutionary Iranian Film', *Thamyris*, Vol. 3, No. 2, 1996, pp. 261–77.
3. In his assessment of Iran's post-revolution film, Hamid Naficy cites Beizai as among the exceptional filmmakers who paid serious attention to women and gender roles in the 1980s. For more details, see Hamid Naficy, 'Islamizing Film Culture in Iran: A Post-Khatami Update', in Richard Tapper (ed.), *The New Iranian Cinema:* pp. 26–65.
4. Bahman Beizai interview with the *International Herald Tribune*, 16 February 2001, as cited in Hamid Reza Sadr, *Iranian Cinema: a Political History*, London, I.B. Tauris, 2006, p. 208.

Further reading

Negar Mottahedeh, *Displaced Allegories: Post-Revolutionary Iranian Cinema*, Durham, NC, Duke University Press, 2008.

Hamid Naficy, *A Social History of Iranian Cinema: The Globalizing Era, 1984–2010*, Durham, NC, Duke University Press, 2012.

Richard Tapper (ed.), *The New Iranian Cinema: Politics, Representation and Identity*, London, I.B. Tauris, 2002.

Niki Akhavan

La battaglia di Algeri/The Battle of Algiers (1966)

[Country: Italy, Algeria. Production Company: Casbah Films, Igor Film. Director: Gillo Pontecorvo. Producers: Saadi Yacef, Antonio Musu. Screenwriters: Franco Solinas, Gillo Pontecorvo (based on an idea by Saadi Yacef). Cinematographer: Marcello Gatti. Editors: Mario Serandrei, Mario Morra. Music: Ennio Morricone, Gillo Pontecorvo. Cast: Brahim Haggjag (Ali La Pointe), Jean Martin (Colonel Mathieu), Saadi Yacef (El-hadi Jaffar), Samia Kerbash (Fatiha), Fusia El Kader (Hassiba), Ugo Paletti (The Captain), Mohammed Ben Kassen (Le Petit Omar).]

Synopsis: *Battle of Algiers* starts with Ali La Pointe's arrest in 1957, before a flashback cuts to 1954 when Ali was still a small-time thug. Radicalised in jail, he joins the National Liberation Front (FNL), becoming a key player in the battle for Algerian independence. Using Ali as a way to connect different events, the film chronicles the organisation of the FNL, as it becomes engaged in an increasingly violent urban guerrilla war with the French army, which brings in Colonel Mathieu to dismantle the FNL. While the French are successful in the short run, the film ends with its long-term inefficiency and the resurgence of disturbances in 1960, anticipating Algeria's independence in 1962.

Battle of Algiers came out of the fortuitous encounter between Italian director Gillo Pontecorvo and Algerian former FNL-leader-turned-film-producer Saadi Yacef. Chronicling and restaging a particular part of the Algerian war of independence, the film famously portrays both sides of the conflict, becoming the key film for urban guerrilla warfare, acquiring new significance in the context of twenty-first century's preoccupation with terrorism.

Battle of Algiers would be difficult to understand without a sense of its production history. After Algerian independence in 1962, Saadi Yacef, who plays himself in the film under the name of El-hadi Jaffar, founded Casbah Films and was looking for a director to transpose his story to the screen. At the same time, Gillo Pontecorvo and Franco Solinas were working on a script about a French paratrooper in the Algerian war (apparently thinking of Paul Newman as its potential star). After encountering Yacef, they entirely changed the script, working from Yacef's account of the battle, which he had written during his imprisonment, and they filmed on location with non-professional actors (except for the actor playing Colonel Mathieu), chronicling the birth of a nation, as Pontecorvo himself said (see Forgacs 2007: 356).

An Italian-Algerian co-production, *Battle of Algiers* is a surprisingly balanced film, representing more than one point of view. Early on, the film aligns us with Ali, whose face becomes the symbol for the casbah (see Mellen 1973: 40). But very quickly, the film 'attempts to distribute the emotional energy we have been encouraged to invest in Ali across the entire people of Algiers, all those figures we see in documentary-style shots, which form the visual fabric of the film' (Smith 1997: 113). Even as the FLN begins to engage in terrorist acts, the film withholds close-ups of French victims, includes shots of FLN ceremonies recognisable to a Western audience (such as the wedding scene), and above all shows Algerian victims (for instance, the worker caught in the French quarter and wrongly identified as a murderer). Smith therefore argues that the film not only produces a collective hero, but quite firmly puts our sympathies on the side of the Algerians, not on the side of an Algerian individual but of the Algerian masses.

However, the French are much more than simple opponents. Especially Colonel Mathieu, apparently a composite of several French commanders, has often been understood as being rather positively portrayed. Deeply knowledgeable and governed by a profound rationality, he may be most memorable for two scenes: once he evokes Jean-Paul Sartre (who was an outspoken opponent of the war), indirectly articulating his respect for the writer and philosopher, whom he says he would prefer not to have as his enemy; another time, he simply explains that if the French want to stay in Algeria, torture is inevitable, which has been read as shedding irony over the French colonial enterprise (Matthews 2004: 8). In addition, the milk bar sequence shows the horror of Algerian bombings in close-up: while we are in the bomber's shoes, the scene's empathy for the French is exceptional. Yacef first objected to the inclusion of the boy licking an ice cream, but Pontecorvo apparently insisted on keeping this image of an innocent French victim.

The film thus chronicles the inevitable violence in a war of liberation. In doing so, it evokes the work of Frantz Fanon, the Martinique-born writer, activist and psychiatrist, who worked at a hospital in Algeria from 1953 to 1957, and who would publish *A Dying Colonialism*, an account of the Algerian war, in 1959, and a more generalised theory of decolonisation in *The Wretched of the Earth* in 1961:

> The violence which governed the ordering of the colonial world, which tirelessly punctuated the destruction of the indigenous social fabric, and demolished unchecked the systems of reference of the country's economy, lifestyles, and modes of dress, this same violence will be vindicated and appropriated when, taking history in their own hands, the colonized swarm into the forbidden cities. Challenging the colonial world is not a rational confrontation of viewpoints. It is not a discourse on the universal, but the impassioned claim by the colonized that their world is fundamentally different.
>
> (Fanon 2004: 5–6)

We know that Pontecorvo had read *The Wretched of the Earth* (see, for instance, Criterion DVD booklet). There are certainly interesting and subtle differences between Fanon and the film, though both are works that are based on a very specific situation (the Algerian war of liberation) that has much wider application.

It is precisely this wider application that accounts for much of the film's fascination. Pontecorvo's staging of urban guerrilla warfare was informed by his own experience in the French Resistance during the Second World War. Organisations such as the Black Panthers and the Irish Republican Army (IRA) screened the film as a way of training members. Maybe most famously, in the wake of 11 September 2001, the Pentagon organised a screening for special-operations chiefs in 2003:

> How to win a battle against terrorism and lose the war of ideas. Children shoot soldiers at point blank range. Women plant bombs in cafes. Soon the entire Arab population builds to a mad fervor. Sound familiar? The French have a plan. It succeeds tactically, but fails strategically. To understand why, come to a rare showing of this film.
>
> (quoted in Reid 2005: 110)

The film thus seems to have acquired a new relevance in the twenty-first century. More recent commentators tend to single out the sequence during which the FNL embarks on a mission to clean up the casbah by purging it of drunks, prostitutes and gangsters, wondering about the 'islamic' aspect of these actions. And yet, there is no Qur'an during the wedding ceremony organised by the FNL, and religion is at best marginally present. More directly connected to twenty-first-century concerns is the chilling depiction of torture, though Matthew Evangelista reminds us that the reality was much worse: many were tortured to death by the French, or killed as traitors by the FNL. And women were equally subject to violence, including sexual violence (Evangelista 2011: 60–1).

Indeed, one of the more intriguing aspects of the film has to do with the participation of women. In the war women were unusually important: because of the repressive French policies, traditional women were suddenly freer to move in public space than men (Evangelista 2011: 54). But while some critics are intrigued by the fairly faithful depiction of women, others argue their role is underplayed. The scene in which three women transform themselves into Western-looking women and go off to plant bombs is particularly contested in this respect. Pontecorvo cut their dialogue, which works well for the atmosphere of the scene, but inadvertently removes speaking roles from women, turning them into fairly clichéd images of female impenetrability. Likewise, the film does not entirely acknowledge the role of Drif (Zohra Drif-Bitat), the woman who is being captured alongside Ali: after Yacef (Jaffer in the film) was arrested, she had assumed much of the leadership (Evangelista 2011: 49).

Much of the film's power stems from the ways in which it pretends to be a documentary and yet is not. Pontecorvo used black-and-white film stock, natural (though often filtered) light, telephoto lenses and handheld cameras, and achieved a grainy look by printing new negatives from the positive images, and then making new, rougher positive images from those. All these strategies give the film somewhat of a newsreel look, enough that the US release of the film proudly claimed that 'not even one foot of newsreel or documentary film is included in this picture' (see Harrison 2007a: 389–90). And yet, maybe more important are the ways in which the film is not a documentary. Above all, the camera can go places a newsreel camera never could: into Ali's hiding place, following the women who plant the bombs, being in the middle of shootouts. Moreover, many of the camera positions (from the bottom, from high above) are carefully set up (Harrison 2007a: 392–3). The film thus makes the experience as emotional and sensational as possible, often with the implied spectator in the middle of the action.

The film's emotional impact is significantly helped by the music composed by Ennio Morricone (maybe better known for composing the music for Sergio Leone's Spaghetti Westerns), with input from Pontecorvo himself. From Bach's *St Matthew Passion*, used in the opening sequence with the tortured man, to Bach-influenced music accompanying scenes of other victims of torture and bomb blasts, to the suspenseful action music that sets in when the French soldiers disembark in the casbah in order to arrest Ali, to local music, to powerful uses of silence, the film works on us emotionally (see Forgacs 2007: 361–2).

Stylistically, the film is thus in conversation with Italian neo-realism (maybe especially with *Paisan* (1946) and *Rome, Open City* (1945), but also with revolutionary cinema, especially the cinema of Eisenstein, where the masses likewise become the hero, and where personal psychology does not drive the plot, either. Pontecorvo is even indebted to Eisenstein's concept of graphic conflict, for instance in the prison scenes (Mellen 1973: 38). At the same time, the film is related to popular cinema, such as *Pépé le Moko* (1937), which was also set in the casbah (and in which Yacef acted as an extra). Maybe more importantly, the film became crucially important for filmmakers committed to a revolutionary, 'third cinema' aesthetic, as well as to Western filmmakers invested in political cinema, from Costa Gavras, to Oliver Stone to Ken Loach.

Battle of Algiers won the Golden Lion at the Venice Film Festival and was nominated for three Oscars. The film was a popular success in Algeria, though Yacef recounts that there were some objections to the film's action being limited to Algiers, not least since much of the war happened in the countryside (Harrison 2007b: 412). Popular mythology, perpetuated in the trailer of the film's American re-release, as well as by some of the scholarship on the film, has it that the film was banned in France. As it is, unlike other films about the Algerian war, the film was never officially censored or banned in France. The French delegation walked out of the screening at the Venice Film Festival, and criticism mostly remained negative in the 1960s (the film was not recognised as film art). But in the 1970s, many of the commentaries on the film became positive, though lobbying from groups of veterans and *pieds noirs* (former white inhabitants of Algeria repatriated to France) attempted to ban the film, making it a fulcrum for discussions about censorship practices (see Caillé 2007). Precisely because the film represents more than one point of view, because it refers both to a specific war and yet speaks to other political situations, because it presents such a powerful documentary fiction, this fortuitous collaboration is able to sustain all these debates.

Further reading

Irene Bignardi, 'The Making of the Battle of Algiers', *Cineaste*, Vol. 25, No. 2, 2000, pp. 14–22.

Patricia Caillé, 'The Illegitimate Legitimacy of *Battle of Algiers* in French Film Culture', *Interventions: International Journal of Postcolonial Studies*, Vol. 9, No. 3, 2007, pp. 371–88.

Matthew Evangelista, *Gender, Nationalism, and War: Conflict on the Movie Screen*, Cambridge: Cambridge University Press, 2011.

Frantz Fanon, *The Wretched of the Earth*, trans. Richard Philcox, with commentary by Jean-Paul Sartre and Homi K. Bhabha, New York, Grove Press, 2004.

David Forgacs, 'Italians in Algiers', *Interventions: International Journal of Postcolonial Studies*, Vol. 9, No. 3, 2007, pp. 350–64.

Nicholas Harrison, 'Pontecorvo's "Documentary" Aesthetics', *Interventions: International Journal of Postcolonial Studies*, Vol. 9, No. 3, 2007a, pp. 389–404.

Nicholas Harrison, 'An Interview with Saadi Yacef', *Interventions: International Journal of Postcolonial Studies*, Vol. 9, No. 3, 2007b, pp. 405–13.

Peter Matthews, '*The Battle of Algiers*: Bombs and Boomerangs', in booklet accompanying *The Battle of Algiers*, DVD, Criterion, 2004, pp. 6–11.

Joan Mellen, *Filmguide to The Battle of Algiers*, Bloomington, Indiana University Press, 1973.

Donald Reid, 'Re-viewing *The Battle of Algiers* with Germaine Tillion', *History Workshop Journal*, Issue 60, Autumn 2005, pp. 93–115.

Murray Smith, '*The Battle of Algiers*: Colonial Struggle and Collective Allegiance', *Iris*, Vol. 4, Fall 1997, pp. 105–24.

Sabine Haenni

Birth of a Nation (1915)

[Country: USA. Production Company: D. W. Griffith Corporation/Epoch Producing Corporation. Director: D. W. Griffith. Screenwriter: D. W. Griffith and Frank E. Woods (adapted from Thomas Dixon's *The Clansman*). Producer: D. W. Griffith. Cinematographer: G. W. Bitzer. Cast: Henry B. Walthall (Ben Cameron), Mae Marsh (Flora, the younger sister), Miriam Cooper (Margaret, the older sister), Josephine Crowell (Mrs Cameron), Spottiswoode Aitken (Dr Cameron), Lillian Gish (Elsie Stoneman), Ralph Lewis (Austin Stoneman), Elmer Clifton (Phil Stoneman), Mary Alden (Lydia Brown), George Siegmann (Silas Lynch), Walter Long (Gus).]

Synopsis: A US Civil War (1861–65) drama, *Birth of a Nation* centres on two white families, the Camerons from the South and the Stonemans from the North. Before the war, during a visit of the Stonemans to the Camerons, Ben Cameron falls in love with Elsie Stoneman, and Phil Stoneman with Margaret Cameron. The war, and politics, separates the families and the couples. Abolitionist Congressman Stoneman supports mulatto politician Silas Lynch, who after the war is elected Lieutenant Governor in the South. Meanwhile, Flora Cameron leaps to her death to escape the advances of a black man. And Ben Cameron, who was wounded during the war and pardoned by President Lincoln after a plea by Ben's mother, forms the Ku Klux Klan. The conflict comes to a climax when the Camerons hide in a cabin and Elsie Stoneman is held hostage by Lynch, who wants to marry her. The Ku Klux Klan rides to the rescue, disenfranchises blacks once again, and the film ends with the two white couples' double honeymoon.

Birth of a Nation is in all likelihood the most troublesome film in US history. Commemorating the 50-year anniversary of the end of the Civil War, the film was released as a major road show attraction. At the symbolically named Liberty Theatre on New York City's Broadway, tickets for the film cost two dollars, showing how far removed this kind of cinema was from the earlier nickelodeons and signalling film culture's aspiration to become part of high culture. *Birth of a Nation* was the first movie to be screened at the White House. Directed by D. W. Griffith, a major director of the silent era, who, contrary to popular legend rarely invented new cinematic techniques but frequently refined and combined them in ways so that they effectively became associated with his name, *Birth of a Nation* has often been hailed as a cinematic masterpiece. But from the beginning critics (often the same who praised its aesthetic) and activists denounced and protested its virulent racism. Writing in *The New Republic* in 1915, Francis Hackett argued that 'this film is aggressively vicious and defamatory. It is spiritual assassination. It degrades the censors that passed it and the white race that endures it' (Lang 1994: 163). Later, James Baldwin called it 'an elaborate justification of mass murder' and Richard Dyer a film about 'ethnic cleansing' (Baldwin 1976: 45; Dyer 1996: 169).

Released after the First World War had broken out but before the United States entered the war (a context that helps explain the references to peace), *Birth of a Nation* was the most visible and notorious Civil War film released in the teens. In 1913, an astonishing 98 Civil War films were released (Stokes 2007: 181). *Birth of a Nation* came at a time when the difference between documentary and fiction film was rather iffy, if only because the term 'documentary' was not used before 1926 (when John Grierson applied it to Robert Flaherty's *Moana*). Arguably, the line between documentary and fiction remains difficult. Time and again, the film justifies its authenticity – and authority – by inserting what it calls 'historical facsimiles' (tinted differently) and excerpts from Woodrow Wilson's *History of the American People* from 1902 (which opens Part II of the film). The status of such historical reproductions, however, is tricky, especially in scenes where the fictional characters are also present (for instance, when Mrs Cameron appeals for mercy from Lincoln, 'The Great Heart', or at Lincoln's assassination). The relationship between fiction and fact gets further complicated because Austin Stoneman was a fictionalised (and demonised) version of Thaddeus Stevens, a member of Congress from Pennsylvania who helped draft the Reconstruction Act and the 14th Amendment to the US Constitution (which helped secure rights, such as citizenship and due process, for African Americans). Despite such obvious slippages and fictionalisations, however, Griffith and others frequently defended the film on grounds of its historical accuracy. He famously claimed that:

> The time will come, and in less than ten years ... when the children in the public schools will be taught practically everything by moving pictures. Certainly they will never be obliged to read history again.
>
> Imagine a public library of the near future, for instance. There will be long rows of boxes or pillars. At each box a push button and before each box a seat .... you will merely seat yourself at a properly adjusted window, in a scientifically prepared room, press the button, and actually see what happened.
>
> There will be no opinions expressed. You will merely be present at the making of history.
>
> (quoted in Lang 1994: 4)

Given the kinds of opinions that are expressed in *Birth of a Nation*, we should be grateful that Griffith was spectacularly wrong. But we should also note that today makers of controversial films still defend themselves by insisting on a film's accuracy, a strategy that often aims at closing down discussion about a film and that disregards the fact that each film by necessity presents only a limited selection of things and cannot escape adapting a particular point of view.

Within this broader historical issue, the representation of the South (a regional identity) remains problematic. The film has often been understood as trying to valorise the South, as being nostalgic for an antebellum South, a 'Plantation Idyll'. The introduction of Dr Cameron as the 'kindly master' suggests as much, especially since the camera tilts to his feet to reveal two puppies, symbolically coloured black and white, that seem perfectly content until 'hostilities' are introduced in the form of a cat. In this vision, the South is peopled by docile and subservient blacks who do not challenge their masters, let alone ask for equality (see, for instance, the many shots in which the Camerons' Mammy – in blackface – approvingly hovers in the background). But such 'a quaintly way ... is to be no more', the intertitle introducing the 'Southland' announces. Richard Dyer has argued that even though the film privileges the South over the North by giving it much more screen time and a much more elaborate family structure, the South needs Northern whiteness, embodied by Elsie (Lillian Gish) who is lighter and more brightly lit than Margaret (Miriam Cooper), the daughter of the South.

In this context, the film can be understood as doing a form of complex cultural work: it works to give the South a new racial, cultural, and national identity at the historical moment when it was made, the teens. Michael Rogin has taken this logic further and argued that the film displaces a number of anxieties so present in US culture onto a black/white conflict. For instance, the early twentieth century saw the emergence of a 'new woman' who was no longer confined to the private sphere, but was seen in the streets, in department stores and at the movies, by herself. White slavery films from the period, such as *Traffic in Souls* (George Loane Tucker, 1913) rephrased anxieties about women's emerging public presence and (sexual) power as concerns with what might happen to unaccompanied women. By representing white women as virginal and black men as oversexualised, Rogin has argued in regard to *Birth of a Nation*, 'Griffith displaces sexuality from white men to women to blacks in order, by the subjugation and dismemberment of blacks, to reempower white men' (Lang 1994: 273). By consolidating the stereotype of the black rapist, the film also suppressed another historical truth: that especially in the antebellum South, black women were much more likely to be raped by their white masters.

By offering a sophisticated reading of the film's racism, Rogin suggests that to note the film's racism is not enough, that the more difficult task is to uncover the multiple ways in which racism can function. The turn of the twentieth century saw a decline of race relations across the board, from the systematic disenfranchisement of African Americans in Southern states to the de facto segregation and discussion of anti-miscegenation statutes, among others, in the wake of white panic about the Great Migration of African Americans to Northern cities in Northern states. *Birth of a Nation* did not only posit the antebellum plantation as an ideal, it came at a time when the Ku Klux Klan was revived (and it would be used as a propaganda and recruitment tool by the Klan). The unwillingness to hire African American actors into parts and the will to keep African American extras away from white women throughout the film speaks to the film's racism at the level of production. How African American extras experienced their jobs – and whether it was more desirable than the limited kinds of other jobs available to them at the time – is a question that would deserve much more investigation.

Racism at the level of production had complex consequences on the level of representation. There are multiple ways of signifying 'blackness' in the film. It uses stereotypically exaggerated blackface derived from the minstrelsy tradition (as in the case of the Stonemans' male servant), more 'realistic' blackface (as for instance in the case of the faithful Mammy), as well as African American extras. There is even a moment when we are supposed to be able to distinguish between white characters in blackface and black characters played by white people in blackface. Some have read this as a moment when the film's ideology undoes itself, while others argue that the multiple uses of blackface speak to the relative ease with which blacks were deemed recognisable. The film also distinguishes between 'faithful' African Americans (who essentially continue in the mode of the 'grateful slave') and rioting incendiaries (who are seen as incapable of any social or governmental organisation). But note how even 'faithful' blacks are treated differently by the camera, made to hover in the background of shots, never getting close-ups. Camera techniques, such as framing and distance, as well as performance (think of the little kids who fall off a cart at the beginning of the first Southern sequence) are thus also mobilised to dehumanise (and infantilise) all of the black characters.

It is in the recasting of history as a (family) melodrama that the film's racism becomes most apparent. Melodrama uses strongly polarised characters (villains and heroes), and thus can be used as a segregationist vehicle. It also wants to start and end in a 'space of innocence' from which the villain has to be expelled (Williams 1991: 28). *Birth of a Nation* casts Africans as villains who have intruded onto a supposedly unproblematic space – 'The bringing of the African to America planted the first seed of disunion', an early intertitle asserts (note the absence of a subject/agent in that sentence). The expulsion of African Americans from the white cabin by the Ku Klux Klan in the role of the hero completes this melodramatic narrative arc. (The rescue sequence featuring the Klan also resonates with and seeks to repress an image of another cabin – Harriet Beecher Stowe's *Uncle Tom's Cabin* (1852), which had sought to generate anti-slavery sentiment by capitalising on black domesticity.) This need to expel blacks is in tension with the film's plantation ideal, maybe a reason why we never see a deportation of blacks to Africa (though there has been some speculation among critics if there was such an alternate ending). Most fundamentally, blacks are being excluded from the family melodrama: the two white, heterosexual couples at the end span North and South – giving birth to a new, distinctly white nation. In this conflation of family, race and nation (as if these terms were interchangeable) African Americans are simultaneously deprived of family and citizenship. This use of melodrama to assert racial lines also explains that the most vilified characters in the film are mulattoes who resist the film's racially melodramatising logic.

Nonetheless, we should keep in mind that the relationship between aesthetics and politics is always complicated and never predetermined. For a long time, critics attempted to separate the film's aesthetics from its politics, which allowed them to hail the film's narrative and visual sophistication (in terms of editing, use of close-ups, economies of scale, etc.), while condemning its content. As we have seen, however, aesthetic strategies are used to make political points. What kinds of political points are being made through an aesthetic technique, however, is often quite open. Griffith himself had used crosscutting in *A Corner in Wheat* (1909) in order to argue against the US class system, thus making a progressive film, before using the same technique to racist ends in *Birth of a Nation*.

Birth of a Nation generated a flood of reactions, starting in 1915. In newspapers, Dixon and Griffith defended themselves against charges of racism; white film critics recognised the aesthetic importance of the film and seemed unable to deal with its content; Southern partisan journalists eagerly embraced the film; the NAACP (National Association for the Advancement of Colored People), founded in 1909, tried to stop the film from being screened, protesting the film's exhibition over 120 times between 1915 and 1972 (Gillespie and Hall 2006: 185). Censorship battles waged in many places; in Boston, for instance, the entire Gus sequence was cut, even tough censors often seemed more concerned about the film's ability to incite riots than about its depiction of African Americans (Gillespie and Hall 2006: 185, 191). The year of the film's release the Supreme Court ruled that movies were not protected under the First Amendment of the US Constitution, as free speech, a ruling that would be overturned only in 1952. Nonetheless, it is important to note that this ruling had less to do with discriminatory representation and much more with anxieties about, for instance, the representation of violence and sexuality on screen. The NAACP by and large lost the censorship battles, and the Production Code, which later regulated what could be shown on screen, explicitly prohibited the representation of miscegenation.

There were also a number of cinematic reactions. Griffith himself responded by making *Intolerance* (1916), which sought to respond to charges of racism but turned away from the topic of race relations. The most powerful response came from

Oscar Micheaux, a black writer and filmmaker who was a crucial director in a fledgling race film industry which in the early teens started to produce black-cast films for black audiences. In 1919, Micheaux directed *Within Our Gates*, a film that is often seen as a direct response to *Birth of a Nation*, which imagines a diasporic nation not based on race and which includes a powerful crosscutting sequence (alternating between a lynching and a near-rape) that uses this particular cinematic technique to denounce rather than add to racism.

Today, it may seem easy to dismiss *Birth of a Nation's* racism, but we should not underestimate the longevity of the film's influence or its modes of representation. In the early 1930s, a Payne Fund study found that middle and high school students' 'favourable' opinion of African Americans dropped from 7.46 to 5.93 (on a scale of 11 to 0) after watching the film, and was unlikely to come back up (Lang 1994: 199). Authorities have often remained anxious that provocative films could incite race riots (including Spike Lee's 1989 film *Do the Right Thing*). For decades, Hollywood's white male characters made it their task to be ready to kill their women before non-white men could get to them (as in John Ford's 1939 film, *Stagecoach*), to preserve them from a 'fate worse than death', suggesting just how much the film helped shape representations of white femininity. Richard Wagner's 'Ride of the Valkyries', the music which accompanies the Klan's rescue, is powerfully (and differently) used in other films, including Francis Ford Coppola's *Apocalypse Now* (1979). Structures of representation are not easy to overturn and may be unconsciously replicated. *Birth of a Nation* serves as a powerful reminder that politics cannot be disengaged from aesthetics while at the same time the relationship between politics and aesthetics remains complex and malleable.

Further reading

James Baldwin, *The Devil Finds Work*, New York, Dial Press, 1976.

Manthia Diawara, 'Black Spectatorship: Problems of Identification and Resistance', in *Black American Cinema*, New York, Routledge, 1993.

Richard Dyer, 'Into the Light: The Whiteness of the South in *Birth of a Nation*', in Richard H. King and Helen Taylor (eds), *Dixie Debates: Perspective on Popular Culture*, New York, New York University Press, 1996.

Michele K. Gillespie and Randal L. Hall (eds), *Thomas Dixon Jr and the Birth of Modern America*, Baton Rouge, Louisiana State University Press, 2006.

Robert Lang (ed.), *The Birth of a Nation*, New Brunswick, Rutgers University Press, 1994.

Melvyn Stokes, *D. W. Griffith's* Birth of a Nation: *A History of 'The Most Controversial Motion Picture of All Time'*, New York, Oxford University Press, 2007.

Linda Williams, *Playing the Race Card: Melodramas of Black and White from Uncle Tom to O.J. Simpson*, Princeton, Princeton University Press, 1991.

Sabine Haenni

Blade Runner (1982, 1992)

[Country: USA. Production Company: Ladd Company, Shaw Brothers and Warner Brothers Pictures. Director: Ridley Scott. Screenwriters: Hampton Fancher and David Peoples. Cinematographer: Jordan Cronenweth. Producer: Michael Deeley. Music: Vangelis. Cast: Harrison Ford (Rick Deckard), Sean Young (Rachael), Brion James (Leon), Rutger Hauer (Roy Batty), Joanna Cassidy (Zhora), Daryl Hannah (Pris).]

Synopsis: 2019, a chaotic, decaying Los Angeles afflicted with crime and perpetual rains brought on through climate change. Anyone who has the means has fled to off-earth settlements and space colonies. Three androids designed for strictly extra-terrestrial use have escaped and returned to LA to track down their genius inventor; they intend to have their lifespan, limited to four years, extended. Rick Deckard, a 'blade runner' or terminator of rogue replicants, is hired to find and destroy the dangerous androids.

Ridley Scott decisively changed the way we view the near future with *Alien* (1979) and *Blade Runner* (1982, 1992). Scott's films were perfectly judged for their moment. George Lucas's *Star Wars* (1977) had drawn cinema audiences back to the possibility of watching science fiction features, which by the mid-1970s had seemed like an exhausted genre. Lucas recast sci-fi as a narrative offering epic thrills accompanied by the reassuring conventions of an earlier Hollywood moment. Steven Spielberg's *Close Encounters of the Third Kind* (1979) and *E.T., the Extra Terrestrial* (1983) triumphantly combined science fantasy with the director's own family-values aesthetic. Ridley Scott's two contributions to the newly popular genre posed darker and deeper questions: What is within us that wants to lock E.T. and the Alien together in the same room, just to see what might happen?

The creation of *Blade Runner* was a fraught, highly complex process, requiring the coordination of a multitude of talents and nerves of steel. Everyone who contributed to *Blade Runner* agreed that it was the compelling commitment and vision of its director that finally brought the film to the screen. Ridley Scott was born in Tyne and Wear, England, in 1937, and was one of the first students to attend the Royal College of Art's newly established film school in the late 1950s. After a spell in New York he joined the BBC, where he worked first as a set designer, and ultimately as a director for highly successful crime series; in 1967 he moved to commercial advertising, directing over 2,000 ads, which was 'really' his 'film school' (Scott 2005: 48). Ridley Scott's first feature was *The Duellists* (1977), based on a story by Joseph Conrad. Conceived by Scott as a variant on the Western and made for a mass audience, *The Duellists*, to the director's chagrin, was restricted on release to the art-house circuit, where it achieved limited but critical success, highly praised for its 'visual flair'. Scott's breakthrough came with *Alien* (1979), which confirmed his genius for creating complex visual environments that powerfully articulate the emotional world of their inhabitants.

In each of his films Scott takes firm control of art direction to achieve a highly complex 'layering' of image; for Scott, 'a film is like a seven-hundred-layer layer cake' (Sammon 1996: 47). This visual complexity certainly contributed to *Blade Runner*'s eventual success. On release, the film fell far short of even covering its costs at the box office, and critical response was confused. But again, the moment was propitious; the increasing use of video players in the home market meant that, for the first time, viewers could pause and re-run sequences from feature films at will, and the semiotic richness of *Blade Runner* in particular invited this kind of scrutiny. When Deckard interrogates Leon's snapshot of his hotel room via Esper, the state-of-the-art police computer which, according to the film's production notes, enables 'investigators to search a room without even being there' (Sammon 1996: 146), he was anticipating our paranoid world of contemporary surveillance, and the ways in which we now interact with virtual, digitised environments. In this scene, Deckard is a metonymy for the *Blade Runner* obsessive, pausing and poring over the laden imagery of each shot in the film, if not indeed a metaphor for the avid gaze of every engaged cinema audience, which has always dreamt of truly entering the illusory world before them.

Like *The Duellists*, *Blade Runner* is that very rare film, a successful – if loose – adaptation from an existing literary property. Philip K. Dick can be accurately described as a 'visionary' SF author – he experienced intense, altered states, in one of which he was convinced that he was speaking with God. Dick's novel *Do Androids Dream of Electric Sheep?* (1968) was in part a response to the corrupting influence of the American involvement in Vietnam, then at its peak. But Philip K. Dick's radical unease with the world had older roots. While researching for his novel *The Man in the High Castle* (1962), which describes an America where National Socialist Germany and imperial Japan have won the Second World War, Dick came across the testimony of SS guards stationed at death camps in Poland. One entry described how, to their annoyance, the soldiers were 'kept awake at night by the cries of starving children' (Sammon 1996: 16). Dick became obsessed – not too strong a word – with the thought that any individual might begin to loose supposedly innate emotional responses to the point where they could not properly be described as 'human' any more. Dick explored this perception in short stories and novels over three decades, and linked it to a closely related anxiety: the possibility of creating perfect 'simulacra' through faultless replication. Where would true authenticity be located, in a world of perfectly copied objects, even persons?

The combination, in *Blade Runner*, of Philip K. Dick's existential concerns about the nature of the human essence, and Ridley Scott's complex visual intelligence, was again fortuitous (Wheale 1995: 101). The film appeared at a transitional moment in the rarefied world of academic critical theory, where structuralist preoccupations with sign theory and semiotics from the 1960s and 1970s, under critique from deconstruction and gender-based analyses, were combining with the emergent disciplines of film and cultural studies. *Blade Runner* became one of the most rewarding 'film texts' through which to negotiate the transition from semiotics, via deconstruction and gender studies, to the emerging agenda of 'the postmodern', and whatever lay beyond (Zizek 1993: 9). Scott's 'future noir' judged the mood of its time very astutely and also became a key inspiration for William Gibson's novel *Neuromancer* (1984), masterpiece of the Cyberpunk generation. Following release of the 1992 *Blade Runner: The Director's Cut*, widening interest in the film seemed to elide all distinctions between 'high' and 'mass-popular' forms of discursive attention.

One of the ways in which *Blade Runner* intrigues is its combination of a reassuringly familiar convention that is placed in an utterly new and disconcerting context. Where Lucas and Spielberg evoked the values of classical Hollywood features to engage their audiences, Scott characteristically drew on a darker heritage. Harrison Ford's Rick Deckard is immediately recognisable as a 'gumshoe', a freelance detective straight out of 1940s Hollywood. Deckard's job description, as in the film title, was found by one of the screenwriters, Hampton Fancher, in a minor work by William Burroughs, who in turn may have taken it from Victorian underworld slang. As the hired assassin of desperate and dangerous androids, Deckard is a 'blade runner' in several senses, not least that he is himself poised dangerously on a knife's edge.

The replicants that Deckard must destroy are 'intensified people', in crucial ways more human than the dull creatures of mere flesh and blood who inhabit the Los Angeles of 2019. The brevity of the androids' (four-year) life span gives them an urgency and pathos that is missing from the mundane lives of ordinary humanity. This vulnerability is quickly established with the first replicant, Leon (Brion James), constructed as no more than a brutal, low-grade operative, but he is also in search of the mother and childhood that he never experienced, as if he feels the lack of the humanity denied him through his manufacture. Roy Batty, the Blake-quoting 'Combat model' machine, has an admirable and insatiable desire for, precisely, 'more life'. Rutger Hauer, playing Roy, very acutely acted a kind of childish innocence through his role, which he described as 'this four-year-old thing' (Sammon 1996: 131).

Film theory has long recognised that female roles in cinema are constructed in significantly different ways to their male counterparts. Zhora, Pris and Rachael (Joanna Cassidy, Daryl Hannah, Sean Young), the three female-type soft machines, as 'intensified women', are supremely self-possessed and athletic, and in Rachael's case, a certain notion of femininity engineered to the extreme. Deckard's relation to the three replicant females becomes increasingly tortured as he destroys the first two and finally falls in love with the third. The manufactured perfection of these synthetic creatures seems even more thinkable now than it was in the early 1980s, given the startling twenty-first-century developments in genetic manipulation and gamete therapy.

It is entirely appropriate that there have been no less than five different theatrical, video and laser-disc releases of *Blade Runner*, all contributing to the endless play of 'undecidable' readings and response to this film text (Bukataman 1997: 82). The most widely circulated versions are the initial 1982 'International Cut' (117 minutes), and the 1992 'Director's Cut' (116 minutes), which was, in truth, yet another compromise between Scott and the studio, Warner. The two versions differ in ways that serve to cast doubt on the status of the central character (Scott 2005: 55): Is it possible that Rick Deckard is also replicant? The first version was accompanied by a dominating voice-over, narrated by Harrison Ford's Deckard, in part a tribute to the jaundiced interior commentaries of 1940s film noir, in part a response to anxieties that the film's plot was too opaque and so required explanation. This was cut in the second, 1992 release, rendering the action immediately more enigmatic. The first version's final escape sequence, in which Deckard and Rachael fly to the freedom of a far northern wilderness, and when Deckard reveals that Rachael has no 'termination date', was also removed in the later release.

The most troubling addition to the 'Director's Cut' is Deckard's enigmatic dream vision of a unicorn, which he experiences after he has analysed Leon's snap shot of his hotel room. In the closing moments of the film, Gaff, Deckard's mysterious fellow blade runner, leaves a third and final origami creature in the path of Rachael and Deckard as they are about to leave – a unicorn. By this point Gaff has come to seem more like Deckard's handler than simply another operative. Deckard picks up the foil sculpture, smiles wryly, and nods. Is he acknowledging that Gaff knows his most private thoughts and daydreams, because they too are implanted? There is an earlier, perhaps more troubling moment, when Gaff again mysteriously appears, immediately after Roy dies, and when he congratulates Deckard, saying, 'You've done a man's job, sir.' This too could be read as an 'authenticity test', in that replicant Deckard has succeeded in doing the work of 'a man'.

Here *Blade Runner* echoes Shakespeare's *King Lear,* when the villainous Edmund is seeking to have Cordelia, Lear's daughter, murdered. The otherwise anonymous individual who agrees to commit this final tragic crime of the play says simply, 'If it be man's work I'll do it' (5.3.40). He strangles the innocent daughter, proving that such atrocities are indeed the work of men. Rick Deckard is an 'undecidable' role, perhaps more, perhaps less than 'a man', but since he is the tragic hero of the movie, we have followed and identified with him as one of our own. In the final moments of the film, this serves to turn all the questions back on ourselves, as Deckard exclaimed when he discovered that Rachael is cybernetic: 'How can it not know what it is?'

Further reading

Scott Bukataman, *Blade Runner*, London, BFI Modern Classics, 1997.

Paul M. Sammon, *Future Noir. The Making of 'Blade Runner'*, London, Orion Media, 1996.

Ridley Scott, 'Directing *Alien* and *Blade Runner*: An Interview with Ridley Scott', Danny Peary, in *Ridley Scott: Interviews*, Laurence F. Knapp, Andrea F. Kulas (eds), Jackson MS, University Press of Mississippi, 2005.

Nigel Wheale, 'Recognizing a "human-Thing": Cyborgs, Robots and Replicants in Philip K. Dick's *Do Androids Dream of Electric Sheep?* and Ridley Scott's *Blade Runner*', in Nigel Wheale (ed.), *The Postmodern Arts*, London and New York, Routledge, 1995, pp. 101–14.

Slavoj Zizek, 'I or He or It (the Thing) Which Thinks', in *Tarrying with the Negative: Kant, Hegel, and the Critique of Ideology*, Durham NC, Duke University Press, 1993, pp. 9–44.

Nigel Wheale

Der blaue Engel/The Blue Angel (1930)

[Country: Germany. Production Company: Universum Film (UFA). Director: Josef von Sternberg. Producer: Erich Pommer. Screenwriters: Carl Zuckmayer, Karl Vollmöller, Robert Liebmann, Josef von Sternberg, Heinrich Mann. Cinematographers: Günter Rittau, Hans Schneeberger.

Music: Friedrich Holländer. Editors: Walter Klee, Sam Winston. Cast: Emil Jannings (Professor Immanuel Rath), Marlene Dietrich (Lola Lola), Kurt Gerron (Kiepert), Rosa Valetti (Guste), Hans Albers (Mazeppa), Reinhold Bernt (The Clown), Eduard von Winterstein (The School Director).]

Synopsis: Professor Immanuel Rath strictly enforces discipline in his high-school classroom. That is, until his curiosity leads him to his students' hangout: The Blue Angel club. There he falls in love with and sleeps with performer Lola Lola, an ordinary city girl with an extraordinary penchant for attracting men. When he returns to school, Rath is mocked by his students and later fired for his conduct. Lola nevertheless embraces him, they get married, and Rath officially joins her traveling performance troupe. Years later, the troupe returns to The Blue Angel. Lola by this point has grown bored with Rath and begins an affair with the strongman Mazeppa. Meanwhile, the professor has stooped to dressing up like a clown and crowing before an audience for a living. When Rath crows before his jeering former students, however, he is so humiliated that he flees the stage, only to stumble upon Lola in Mazeppa's arms. After feebly attempting to kill the strongman, he runs this time into the streets of his hometown and his old school. His final moments are spent in his former classroom, where he dies face down on his teacher's desk.

Film stars rise and fall, their clout waxes and wanes. Yet few tales are as apodictic or even self-reflexive with regard to this power relationship as Josef von Sternberg's *The Blue Angel*, a cautionary tale of a professor's fall from grace. Though not a vampire film, this highly refined tragedy presents one of the most symbolic vampiric acts in the history of cinema: the draining of Emil Jannings' career to feed those of Marlene Dietrich and Hans Albers. Performatively, this manifests in Dietrich consistently stealing the scene whenever she and the silent superstar Jannings appear together. Narratively, it manifests in Jannings' overdetermined decline as Dietrich's Lola Lola chooses the younger Mazeppa (Albers) over Jannings' character, who dies in the end. In this fashion, *The Blue Angel* expertly encapsulates not only this portentous passing of one actor's era, but also the latent media environment at the end of the Weimar Republic: the turbulent transition from silents to sound, the reckoning of the German film industry with Hollywood, the rise of the so-called 'new woman' and decline of male *bourgeois* respectability and wealth, as well as the triumph of mass art's exteriority and fungibility over the interiority and inertia of the *bourgeois* intelligentsia. As a 'classic', it necessarily speaks to generations beyond those of its creation, but remains also deeply entrenched within the values and debates of its time.

At the end of the 1920s, the German film industry lacked serious leverage over Hollywood on both the domestic and global markets. An international hit was needed to balance the books after UFA's recent bankruptcy. Whereas Hollywood usually wooed top talent away from Germany – Ernst Lubitsch being one famous example – veteran producer Erich Pommer moved to reverse the trend. He used Jannings, who had acting cachet in both Germany and the United States, to shoot a film in both German and English at once that would easily reach audiences across the Atlantic.[1] Two separate language films were to be filmed with the same actors on the same sets, shot for shot. For his ideal director, Jannings picked von Sternberg, an Austrian-born American who last directed him in *The Last Command* (1928) and who came a lot cheaper than Fritz Lang. But upon arrival in Berlin-Potsdam, von Sternberg balked at the prospect of shooting the Rasputin biopic Jannings had in mind. They settled instead on a script that would tap into the actor's previous masochistic roles in *The Last Laugh* (1924) and *Varieté* (1925): a heavily modified, more or less improvised version of Heinrich Mann's 1905 novel *Professor Unrat* that put its titular figure into arguably more humiliating circumstances, as well as recast the semi-innocent Rosa Fröhlich of the novel as Lola Lola, the 'heartless and immoral' *femme fatale*.[2]

To counterbalance Jannings' tempestuous personality, von Sternberg cast Lola Lola with an unknown actress from the Berlin stage whom he knew he could control: Marie Magdalene Dietrich-Sieber, aka. Marlene Dietrich. Her talent lay in her ability to manipulate her body and personality to conform to von Sternberg's highly gendered fantasies.[3] 'She became a star who *acted* stardom', writes James Naremore, or 'a hybrid figure, oscillating incessantly between voyeurism and exhibitionism', according to Elisabeth Bronfen.[4] Vastly different from the well-educated and shy actress Dietrich-Sieber under the make-up, Lola Lola convincingly seduces Rath and the audience with her working girl matter-of-factness coupled with an otherworldly performative confidence. Advertisements for the film specifically highlighted the overdetermined tensions between the two characters.[5] The combination worked: the original German and English prints of *The Blue Angel* ran to much success in international markets until the German version was banned under the Nazis in 1933 for its wilful degradation of an authority figure and the English version was heavily censored in the USA for its sexual content.[6] Audiences came to see *The Blue Angel* not only for the duel between old warhorse Jannings and the fresh-faced Dietrich, but also for the way in which the dialogue, music, sound and even silent elements innovatively served to enhance the strange new version of Mann's novel that von Sternberg was trying to tell.[7]

Patrice Petro has argued that *The Blue Angel* is an 'unstable' film poised curiously between the United States and Germany, 'among the extremely rare instances of a non-U.S. film produced with the byline of a major Hollywood director'.[8] Indeed, von Sternberg's usage of Otto Hunte's expressionist sets and Günter Rittau's foreboding shadows forms a strange admixture with the commercial melodrama of Hollywood. Lübeck, the real small town in which the film takes place, is an openly fictional locale within a dark fairy-tale Europe in which the schoolmasters are strict, the roofs dense, the streets labyrinthine, the clowns sad, and the women cold and merciless. Even the film's title, *The Blue Angel*, the club in which Jannings and Lola Lola encounter each other, recalls the romantic 'blue flowers' of Novalis, the narrative itself more resembling a surreal Tieck story than the naturalism with modernist leanings of Mann's novel. Rather than confront him with immediate privation or threatening circumstances, for example, the film initiates the plot with the death of Professor Rath's bird. And when his housekeeper simply blithely throws its corpse into the roaring stove, it serves as a precursor to Lola Lola's chilling but self-reflexive lyrics: 'Men cluster to me/Like moths around a flame/And if their wings burn/I know I'm not to blame'. Von Sternberg establishes an atmosphere of decadence and brutality that lets viewers comfortably and voyeuristically enjoy the professor's terrible decision to abandon a career over which he had little mastery (i. e. teaching) in favour of a career in which his pay is premised on his humiliation (i.e. being a clown and crowing like a rooster). No wonder Jerzy Toeplitz emphasised the film's overall 'political elasticity',[9] given its insistence on the inefficacy of the *bourgeois* educational tradition on the one hand and the brutality of the commodity-exchange-based show-biz tradition that would replace it. As a film screened during the violent and poverty-stricken years before the Nazis took power, *The Blue Angel*'s ambiguity permitted it to avoid labels from one political camp or another. The space between nations in which the film resides gives it an alibi for each and every one of the myriad of political allegories to be found within its narrative, whether they be about the corruption of the old order, the power of the symbolic over the Real, the mastery of the subject by the objects one beholds, and so forth.

When viewed today, *The Blue Angel* still resonates in surprising ways. Adolescent boys, still seen as an unruly element of society, are disciplined not so much by their teachers but by the pleasures of circulating image systems – films, comics, games – and the unwritten conformism that commodity exchange demands. The students might themselves be unwitting bearers of reactionary behaviours, as evidenced by the continuous bullying of Angst without Unrath's intervention, but they are in turn brought into the fold via the suggestive properties of the entertainment industry. Those like Professor Rath who, for whatever self-therapeutic reason, would mistake images for reality are clearly fools, but the Freudian disciplines of public relations and image control nevertheless effectively manage the public's acceptance of unpleasant facts and diffusion of blame. One cannot survive in such a libidinal economy without mastery over one's libido; nevertheless, none of us truly has survived unscathed either. The haunting image of a disgraced academic who dies clutching his desk after a disastrous mid-career change eerily invokes the personal upheavals and sacrifices necessary to exist in a neo-liberal job market, and how some simply cannot survive. Rather than interpret *The Blue Angel* along the lines of Rath and Lola's individual psychological dispositions (as well as that of von Sternberg), one might also see the film as a cautionary parable for humanity in a modern urban economy: one must learn to 'fall in love again' – to instrumentally adjust one's emotional commitments to fit unstable economic times and demeaning jobs – lest one follows one's principles to pauperdom and the grave. 'Romantic love, in other words, is an ideal that belongs to a previous stage of capitalist development, one that favored the creation of strong, altruistic family units', says Stephen Brockmann, whereas 'contemporary capitalism, in contrast, is based on selfishness rather than love'.[10] Von Sternberg's script, Dietrich's performance, Hunte's sets, and so forth may be rightfully considered products of pure artifice. Nevertheless, it is an artifice deeply entrenched in the core dilemmas of all artistic and intellectual endeavour during a selfish capitalist age.

Notes

1. Some significant debate ensued as to whether or not Jannings' English would be up for the task of shooting two language versions, as well as the costs and benefits of Janning's difficult temperament vs. his ability to pull in box office sales abroad. See Chris Wahl, 'Babel's Business – On Ufa's Multiple Language Film Versions, 1929–1933', in Christian Rogowski (ed.), *The Many Faces of Weimar Cinema*, New York, Camden House, 2010, p. 238.
2. These are Josef von Sternberg's own words. He by all rights deliberately crafted the part to be a perfectly cynical figure to 'show the downfall of an enamoured man *à la* Human Bondage'. Josef von Sternberg, *The Blue Angel*, New York, Simon & Schuster, 1968, p. 11.
3. These fantasies were partially thanks to a burgeoning romance between the two of them. Dietrich and von Sternberg became so close on the production that, upon their arrival in New York City, von Sternberg's wife filed for divorce.
4. James Naremore, 'Marlene Dietrich', in *Senses of Cinema*, 2000, http://sensesofcinema.com/2000/cteq/dietrich/; Elisabeth Bronfen, 'Seductive Departures of Marlene Dietrich: Exile and Stardom in *The Blue Angel*', in Gerd Gemünden and Mary Desjardins (eds), *Dietrich Icon*, Durham and London, Duke University Press, 2007, p. 138.
5. See for example the *Illustrierter Film-Kurier*, No. 1381, 1930.
6. Klaus Kreimeier, *The Ufa Story – A History of Germany's Greatest Film Company, 1918–1945*, Berkeley, CA, University of California Press, 1999, p. 192.
7. See Hans Wollenberg, 'Der blaue Engel', in *Lichtbild-Bühne*, No. 79. April 2, 1980.
8. Patrice Petro, 'National Cinemas/International Film Culture: *The Blue Angel* (1930) in Multiple Language Versions', in Noah Isenberg (ed.), *Weimar Cinema: An Essential Guide to Classic Films of the Era*, New York, Columbia University Press, 2009, p. 259.
9. Jerzy Toeplitz, *Geschichte des Films*, Band 2: 1928–1933, Berlin, Henschel Verlag, 1992, p. 733.
10. Stephen Brockmann, *A Critical History of German Film*, Rochester, NY, Camden House, 2010, p. 108.

Further reading

John Baxter, *The Cinema of Josef von Sternberg*, London, A.S. Barnes, 1971.

Michel Bouvier, 'Hollywood on Spree', *Ça cinéma* 18, 1978, pp. 19–35.

Gertrud Koch, 'Between Two Worlds: Von Sternberg's *The Blue Angel*', in Eric Rentschler (ed.), *German Film and Literature: Adaptations and Transformations*, New York and London, Methuen, 1986, pp. 60–72.

Barbara Kosta, *Willing Seduction: The Blue Angel, Marlene Dietrich, and Mass Culture*, New York, Berghahn Books, 2010.

Alan Lareau, 'Lavender Songs: Undermining Gender in Weimar Cabaret and Beyond', in *Popular Music and Society*, Vol. 28, No. 1, February 2005, pp. 15–33.

Heinrich Mann, *Professor Unrat, oder Das Ende eines Tyrannen*, Munich, A. Langen, 1905.

Judith Mayne, 'Marlene Dietrich, *The Blue Angel*, and Female Performance', in Dianne Hunter (ed.), *Seduction and Theory: Readings of Gender, Representation, and Rhetoric*, Urbana, IL, University of Illinois Press, 1989, pp. 28–46.

S. S. Prawer, *The Blue Angel*, London, BFI, 2002.

Andrew Sarris, *The Films of Josef von Sternberg*, New York, The Museum of Modern Art, 1966.

Gaylyn Studlar, *In the Realm of Pleasure: Von Sternberg, Dietrich, and the Masochistic Aesthetic*, Urbana, IL, University of Illinois Press, 1988.

Evan Torner

Blue Velvet (1986)

[Country: USA. Production Company: De Laurentiis Entertainment Group. Director: David Lynch. Producer: Fred Caruso. Screenwriter: David Lynch. Cinematographer: Frederick Elmes. Editor: Duwayne Dunham. Music: Angelo Badalamenti. Cast: Kyle MacLachlan (Jeffrey Beaumont), Isabella Rossellini (Dorothy Vallens), Dennis Hopper (Frank Booth), Laura Dern (Sandy Williams), Hope Lange (Mrs Williams), Priscilla Pointer (Mrs Beaumont), George Dickerson (Detective John Williams), Frances Bay (Aunt Barbara), Ken Stovitz (Mike), Brad Dourif (Raymond), Jack Nance (Paul), Dean Stockwell (Ben), J. Michael Hunter (Hunter), Jack Harvey (Tom Beaumont), Dick Green (Don Vallens), Fred Pickler (The Yellow Man), Philip Market (Dr Gynde).]

Synopsis: After finding a severed ear in a vacant lot, Jeffrey Beaumont (MacLachlan) becomes drawn into a mystery in the town of Lumberton. Jeffrey and Sandy (Dern), the daughter of the local police detective, begin investigating a woman named Dorothy Vallens (Rossellini), who is somehow connected to the case. Jeffrey soon finds himself hiding in a closet in Dorothy's apartment, watching intently while a psychopathic stranger named Frank Booth (Hopper) visits her and engages in a disturbing sexual interaction. As the story unfolds, Jeffrey becomes increasingly drawn to Dorothy and her dark sexuality, while Sandy declares her love for Jeffrey. Frank later catches Jeffrey with Dorothy, and forces them both to accompany him to the apartment of Ben (Stockwell), who is holding Dorothy's young son hostage. Frank beats Jeffrey and leaves him lying in a lumberyard. Jeffrey recovers and returns to Dorothy's apartment where he finds the aftermath of a violent confrontation, including the dead body of Dorothy's husband, he of the missing ear. Frank returns to the apartment and hunts for Jeffrey, but Jeffrey shoots him. A disturbed Jeffrey ultimately repudiates the dark world he has glimpsed, reconciling with Sandy and her hopeful worldview. Dorothy is reunited with her son.

One of the most important American films of the 1980s, *Blue Velvet* has bewildered and divided audiences since its release. A mystery film that hardly bothers to solve its crime, a teenage love story with sadomasochism, a film that completely remakes the meaning of the songs on its needle-drop soundtrack, *Blue Velvet* seemed completely original to most moviegoers when it appeared in 1986. The film proved so influential that one could say it changed the tone of a certain kind of US cinema, broadening the art film beyond the domain of European filmmakers and preparing the way for the American independent films to come in the 1990s.

At first, the film inspired either lavish praise or outrage and disgust. While some critics gushed about the film's greatness (J. Hoberman, Pauline Kael), others found its violence unredeemable (Roger Ebert). Initial theatrical audiences famously squirmed in their seats, yelled at the screen, or walked out in droves, even while others sat transfixed and dumbstruck. *Blue Velvet* is that rare thing: a film that has the genuine ability to shock and haunt the viewer. In the context of the 1980s, *Blue Velvet* stood out; its moderate success at the box office demonstrated that a segment of the commercial audience in the USA would occasionally be receptive to challenging material. In the context of the 2010s, it has become clear that this is one of the more accomplished American films of recent decades, a film that is trickier than it seems.

To the uninitiated (or analysis-averse), film criticism sometimes seems redundant, an exercise in rehashing what already appears so obvious. Lynch himself encourages this sort of untutored attitude, always attributing his method to intuition. When speaking of his films, he has said, 'I don't know what a lot of things mean. I just have the feeling that they are right or not right'.[1] However, Lynch's films are hardly naïve; in fact they virtually cry out for interpretation. While many things in *Blue Velvet* seem plain and clear, this bluntness is in fact one of Lynch's techniques and it is anything but simple. The film opens with a famous montage of happy small-town life complete with white picket fence, bright red and yellow flowers, and waving fireman, only to descend into the dirt and insects swarming underneath the neatly mown grass. Thus in the first four minutes, the film announces that it will unearth the dark underbelly of American life. In case we didn't get it, the film's protagonist Jeffrey Beaumont says later: 'I'm seeing something that was always hidden'.

This kind of symbolic obviousness is a signature Lynch trait, and once one understands that this film can and should be read flatly, what feels disquieting begins to look quite logical. Dorothy wears a wig: she is deeply uncomfortable, and wants to disguise herself. A bird holds a worm in its mouth at the film's conclusion: Sandy's sunny dream-world perspective has won out, but the dark side is still present. These heavy-handed symbols reflect Lynch's interest in banality and naïveté. But despite the obviousness, there is still that uneasy feeling, and this is the important thing: the film's affect. If 1980s audiences were already well able to interpret obvious meanings in film, today's audiences are even more suspicious of such blatant symbols. *Blue Velvet* works with its audiences' knowing gaze, enticing us in with familiar images, and then disorienting us by making those familiar images seem strange. In more ways than one, *Blue Velvet* disturbs with its peculiar explicitness.

Despite these moments of apparent transparency, and perhaps because of its powerful affect, *Blue Velvet* (like all of Lynch's work) has been subjected to many different interpretations, and a veritable cottage industry of Lynch analysis has sprung up over the decades. Depending on who one reads, *Blue Velvet* is a critique of American suburban life, or it demonstrates the Freudian concepts of the Oedipus Complex or the Primal Scene, or it enacts violence against women, or it depicts a child's eye dream of sexuality, or it is a brilliant example of postmodern cinema, replete with references to film history and popular culture – and so forth. And certainly, *Blue Velvet* is a postmodern film, filled with references to film noir (with its moodiness, crime, and a mysterious woman at the centre of the plot) and to other films (*The Wizard of Oz* (Victor Fleming, 1939), *Night of the Hunter* (Charles Laughton, 1955), and *It's a Wonderful Life* (Frank Capra, 1946)). Despite these influences, however, *Blue Velvet* manages not to feel like an empty exercise in referentiality, but instead it creates an affect that is powerful and distinct. Part of the film's singular importance is due to the way it resonates with so many cultural hot points – and yet despite all this, it still holds together as a tightly woven, formally brilliant film.

So: the film unearths the dark underbelly of small-town American life, yes, but there is more to it than that. Rather than locating its crime and horror in an outside location, the film finds the dark side at home, in Lumberton, literally in the family garden. *Blue Velvet*'s reinterpretation of familiar places (home), familiar stories (the crime film or film noir) and familiar characters (the small-town boy, the girl next door) makes banal things look perverse. As several writers have pointed out, this is precisely a dramatisation of the uncanny: making the familiar look unfamiliar. A phantasm of American family-values ideology, *Blue Velvet's* sunny small-town world has been dubbed 'Lynchtown' by critic Michel Chion, and it can also be found in several of Lynch's other works, especially his 1990–91 television program *Twin Peaks*. It is well known that the places Lynch dramatises are often amalgams of his childhood home – Spokane, Washington, in particular. But Lynchtown is more an imagined place than a real place; Lynch masterfully exploits the cinema's ability to create uncanny locales that feel one step removed from reality, and the point seems to be this: in Lynchtown, despair is all the more horrible because it is found at home. What's more, the evil in *Blue Velvet* is not merely personified by the town psychopath Frank Booth, who rapes and kills and cuts off ears; the same drives are also revealed inside Jeffrey, who, like Frank, hits Dorothy during sex. 'You're like me', Frank says to Jeffrey, and this is the truth that makes Jeffrey cry.

For years, the film was vilified by feminists for its depiction of violence against women – and from a certain perspective, rightly so, for the film does not apologise for its characterisation of Dorothy Vallens, a woman who is brutally abused, and seems to enjoy it. The film has been criticised for dramatising all the masculine biases of the Oedipal dynamic: Dorothy functions primarily as a spectacle (she performs in a nightclub, she is spied on by Jeffrey), and she embodies every cliché about mysterious, incoherent femininity. Sandy, on the other hand, may be intelligent and just as interested in solving the crime as Jeffrey, but she is so buttoned-up and square that she functions as Dorothy's opposite, the other half of the film's all too familiar binary construction of woman as either virgin or whore. On the other hand, this too can be interpreted as part of the film's encounter with the familiar – the virgin/whore dynamic is not questioned by the film, for certainly *Blue Velvet* makes no pretence at political consciousness, but rather this familiar constellation serves as the stable ground of stereotype, if you will, that allows the film to take its viewer into forbidden realms of sexual desire and dread.

The question remains, however, whether *Blue Velvet*'s use of familiar, even cliché motifs is ironic or sincere, and this point of tension is where the film most seems to confound audiences in the current moment. Many viewers today feel that the film's depiction of the sunny side of life (the neatly mowed lawns, Sandy's dream about the robins) is merely a parody, and they find the mechanical bird with the worm at the end of the film to be a mocking joke that subverts the conservatism of this robotically happy world. However, some critics have questioned this interpretation, arguing instead that while the film does contain some irony, it is mostly sincere, that Sandy's dream of robins is not a parody but a genuine alternative to the horror of Dorothy's life. At least one film scholar has perceptively tied this sincerity-in-irony tone to a post-punk aesthetic that conjoined the profane and the sincere: 'Lynch's films were among the first to move beyond postmodernism's ironic, parodic appropriation of historical genres and narrative conventions … to this day readings of Lynch as 'ironic' persist because irony has become the dominant form of reading in [our] culture'.[2] In other words, even though one can easily interpret *Blue Velvet's* happy ending as ironic, it might be more intriguing to instead consider the implications of the film's potential sincerity. Again, such a reading privileges Lynch's interest in clichés, banality and improper fantasies. As irony moved into the mainstream by the 1980s, Lynch was already way ahead of the irony game; although there is currently much disagreement on this point, it has become apparent to some viewers today that this is a film that disturbs with its sincerity.

Finally, one cannot discuss this film without mentioning its soundtrack. From the moment Jeffrey Beaumont first discovers the severed ear in a vacant lot, this film announces itself as concerned with sound. Sound effects are hugely important in this film, but even more innovative is the film's use of music. Pop music soundtracks had become increasingly common since late 1960s films such as *The Graduate* (Mike Nichols, 1967) and *Easy Rider* (Dennis Hopper, 1969) made them popular. In the 1980s, films such as *The Breakfast Club* (John Hughes, 1985) and *Pretty in Pink* (Howard Deutsch, 1986) used pop music to quickly evoke a teenage emotional landscape; in these films, the audience is moved in synch with the music. In contrast, *Blue Velvet* uses music against the grain, so to speak, evoking a familiar mood in order to reinterpret it. When Ben lip syncs 'In Dreams', for example, the wistful sadness of the melody and lyrics take on a sinister, sexually ambiguous element due to Dean Stockwell's enigmatic performance. Lynch did not invent this technique, but borrowed it from Kenneth Anger's seminal experimental film *Scorpio Rising* (1964), which had revolutionised the use of pop music in film decades earlier. *Blue Velvet* uses songs from a previous era, a practice that is much more common now than it was in the 1980s (see *The Squid and the Whale* (Noah Baumbach, 2005), or any of Wes Anderson's films). All the major songs in *Blue Velvet*, in fact, were popular in 1963 when Lynch was 17 years old, which adds to the film's strange sense of nostalgia. While most movies today still use music as an ancillary element, a backdrop that merely accompanies the visuals, *Blue Velvet's* music is anything but subordinate to the images; rather, Lynch uses music as a discrete component that is just as crucial in shaping the film's meaning as the visuals. This use of pop music as counterpoint has rarely been equalled in commercial American cinema.

Notes

1. Laurent Bouzereau, '*Blue Velvet:* An Interview with David Lynch', *Cineaste,* Vol. 15, No. 3, 1987, p. 39.
2. Nicholas Rombes, 'Blue Velvet Underground: David Lynch's Post-Punk Poetics', in Erica Sheen and Annette Davison (eds), *The Cinema of David Lynch: American Dreams, Nightmare Visions*, London, Wallflower Press, 2004, p. 72.

Further reading

Michael Atkinson, *Blue Velvet,* London, BFI, 1997.
Michel Chion, *David Lynch,* trans. Robert Julian, 2nd ed, London, BFI, 2006.
Lynne Layton, '*Blue Velvet:* A Parable of Male Development', *Screen,* Vol. 35, No. 4, Winter 1994, pp. 374–92.
David Lynch, *Lynch on Lynch,* ed. Chris Rodley, London, Faber and Faber, 1997.

Jennifer Peterson

Bob le Flambeur (1956)

[Country: France. Production Company: Organisation Générale Cinématografique, Productions Cyme, Play Art. Director: Jean-Pierre Melville. Producers: Serge Silberman, Jean-Pierre Melville. Screenwriters: Auguste Le Breton, Jean-Pierre Melville. Cinematographers: Henri Decaë, Maurice Blettery. Editor: Monique Bonnot. Music: Eddie Barclay, Jo Boyer. Cast: Roger Duchesne (Roger 'Bob' Montagné), Isabel Corey (Anne), André Garet (Roger), Daniel Cauchy (Paolo), Guy Decomble (Comissaire Ledru), Gérard Buhr (Marc), Colette Fleury (Suzanne), Simone Paris (Yvonne).]

Synopsis: Bob is an ageing, former gangster turned gambler in Montmartre (Paris), leading a pleasant if unconventional life with his friend Roger, his protégé, Paolo, and a young woman, Anne, who he has picked up on the street and who he helps out. After a spell of bad luck, he's running out of money and begins to plan one last robbery, that of a casino in Deauville. Things go badly and Bob is arrested, but not before having won a lot of money legally.

Bob le Flambeur holds a curious position within French film history. The first film that Jean-Pierre Melville made in the studio he had built in Rue Jenner in Paris, even before it was entirely finished, and yet significantly shot on location, *Bob le Flambeur* was lauded for its 'imperfect aesthetics', authorial control, cinephilia, and sense of humour. The film endeared Melville to the emerging generation of French New Wave critics (Melville would appear as Parvulesco, the writer, in Jean-Luc Godard's *Breathless* from 1960). But the affinity was short-lived, as Melville would go on to make stylised popular films. By the late 1960s, Melville was criticised for unknowingly making films imbued with the dominant ideology (Vincendeau 2003: 116, 14–16). But *Bob* remains an intriguing film, suspended between the gangster genre and a more documentary impulse.

Bob le Flambeur is a gangster film, and yet the film uses the formula surprisingly. It came out after the French critics Nino Frank, Raymonde Borde and Etienne Chaumeton had appreciatingly defined *film noir*, and after a number of successful French gangster films, or *films noirs*, such as *Touchez pas au Grisbi* (Jacques Becker, 1954) and *Rififi* (Jules Dassin, 1955) had been made. But *Bob* had lower production values, no stars and much more location shooting. Its gangster does not rise (and fall), as the US formula would have it, but had risen before the film takes place, before the Second World War. His criminal life is behind him, he even gets lifts from the police. Deeply nostalgic for the time (and the cinema) of the 1930s, the film is about the legend of gangster, rather than a contemporary gangster. 'A young old man, legend of a recent past', the voice-over, spoken by Melville himself, announces, before we see Bob through a reflecting window, in low-key lighting and on a black-and-white set. He's in a trench coat, puts on a hat, stays in the shadows and leaves a group of gamblers in a bar's backroom without saying anything. 'A real hood's face', Bob finally says as he looks at himself in a mirror. The gangster is established as a code, as style, a sign.

Bob is a survivor from a fantasised pre-War past, when hoodlums (rather than full-blown gangsters) had a moral code, even if that code was different from mainstream society's. He remembers a time when guns were not loaded, and attempts to instill the same values into the younger generation, represented by Paolo and Anne. Both Paolo and Anne fall for a very different, more malign kind of hoodlum, Marc, whom Bob refuses to help after learning that Marc had hit one of his women. A good gangster like Bob may be surprising to viewers of 1930s Hollywood gangster films, but the type can be found in pre-War French gangster films, such as *Pépé le Moko* (Julien Duvivier, 1937). *Bob le Chapeau*, a documentary included in the French DVD edition of the film, recalls how the Second World War changed the *milieu*: some gangsters joined the Resistance, others the Gestapo. These deep divisions and lack of trust among criminals remained after the war, at least in the films that imagined gangsters' lives.

Even as *Bob le Flambeur* recalls a particularly French version of the gangster film, it simultaneously needs to be understood within the context of Americanisation, in which the fascination with Hollywood participates. Generally speaking, after the Second World War France embarked on a rapid wave of modernisation, partially imposed by the United States (Forbes 1993: 47). Kristin Ross has documented the fascination with American cars in French films from the period (Ross 1995). Melville, who was born Jean-Pierre Grumbach, but adopted the American writer's name, was famous for his Stetsen, his Ray-Bans and his American cars. More specifically speaking, *Bob* was influenced by John Huston's *Asphalt Jungle* (1950). Melville said in an interview that he had written a first scenario before seeing *Asphalt Jungle*, and that after seeing the film, he realised that the preparation of a robbery could no longer be done 'dramatically or tragically' so he decided to make a more 'light-hearted' film (Nogueira 1971: 53). If *Bob* is thus a film born in transnational exchange, it is harder to say whether it admires, critiques, or is ambivalent about the United States and its cultural presence in France.

Beyond being a gangster film, *Bob le Flambeur* is also a city film invested in a 'poetry of the street' (Vincendeau 2003: 107). In an interview, Melville argued that with the arrival of the Germans during the Second World War, Paris 'ceased to be an age-old city of mystery', fondly recalling the Cité Jeanne d'Arc which he likened to a casbah, where 'no policeman ever dared set foot and where guys used to hide out when the police were after them' (Nogueira 1971: 58). Opening in the wee hours of dawn, in the first shot of *Bob* the camera pans across a dark city from a hill (Montmartre), with the voice-over announcing that the neighbourhood is 'both heaven and hell' as a funicular, underscored by music, rapidly descends the hill down to Pigalle, a neighbourhood famous for its transgressive and in this film isolated nightlife. 'People pass each other, forever strangers', the voice-over says. Here the gangster (even if he has a car) is also a pedestrian wandering around, much in the style of Baudelaire's *flâneur*. Thus, after Bob has left the club, we see him in a high-angle shot, a small person crossing an empty street, as a street-cleaning truck spraying water enters the frame, turning around in the square. Despite the poetry of the images, there is a raw quality about them, accentuated by very noticeable editing as well as by changing music and the occasional voiceover. The film's 'quality of imperfection' may have to do with its small budget, and has occasionally led to accusations of amateurism, but is also a studied refusal of seamlessness, a way of creating its rhythm (Vincendeau 2003: 104).

This opening urban scene, with small figures set against the large cityscape also helps establish loneliness and isolation as a theme. Loneliness was part of Melville's star persona, though the leap from there to his lonely characters may be a bit too tempting (Vincendeau 2003: 19). Such loneliness is deeply gendered, as Melville is known for making films about solitary, melancholy, vulnerable men (Vincendeau 2003: 21). Indeed, Bob is betrayed by two women in the film, Anne, more naïve than she knows, and Suzanne, the croupier's none too pleasant wife. And yet, the film's misogyny is complicated by Yvonne, the barmaid who offers Bob money in hopes of keeping him from robbing the casino, by Paolo who naively gives out secret information, and by Bob himself, whose code may be masculinist, but who will not tolerate violence against women and who has a complicated relationship with Anne even as he 'saves' her from the street.[1] The dominance of the film's gendered loneliness makes it a near-existential gangster film.

The chance encounters of the opening scene in the city establish chance itself as another main theme of the film. Chance, to the extent that is linked to the 'arbitrariness of existence and the futility of human endeavor', harkens back to the film's existentialism (Vincendeau 2003: 115). But it also takes on a much larger role, penetrating multiple levels of the film. Writing about gambling, Thomas Kavanagh has opposed gambling and chance to narrative logic (Kavanagh 1993: 142). Even the opening scene functions according to this logic: 'But let's come back to Bob', the narrator says, as if he had gotten distracted by the city scene. Chance unravels narrative intent, Kavanagh argues, steering a story in another direction. Bob accidentally sees Anne who will change his story. He goes to the Restaurant Le Carpeaux, even though he said he would go home. Bob accidentally wins money at the horse track, though he knows nothing about the horse he bets on. There are chance encounters and chance comes and goes. Roger accidentally hears that there are 800 million in the casino's safe. The entire second half of the film represents Bob's attempt to escape chance and gambling, and to instead impose causal logic and narrative order to insure the success of the heist. Roger 'practices' opening the safe. But in the end, chance wins: Bob forgets time and accidentally wins a lot of money. Chance and accidents can thus be good. The theme of chance also makes Bob very different from classical Hollywood characters who tend to drive the plot. Very often, Bob often does not plot, he plays, and his favourite bar is called 'Pile ou Face' (head or tails), even though we learn at the end that Bob's own coin has been doctored to avoid chance. As one critic put it, *Bob le Flambeur* follows a 'dramaturgy of distraction' (Bantcheva 2007: 115).

Chance, which is both a theme and a narrative aesthetic, can also be found in the film's music. Its use of jazz, in particular, which celebrates improvisation and the individual's assertion within the group seems well suited to the film (Schulman 2004). At the same time, a consideration of the film's music would also have to think about its mix of styles.

While *Bob le Flambeur* may have appeared at a particular historical moment, harkening back to the 1930s, anticipating both the French New Wave and Melville's own polished gangster films from later, it has also had a deep influence on more contemporary filmmakers. True, Melville's more stylised later films had more influence on the cool noir of Quentin Tarantino and John Woo, but *Bob*'s irony can also be found in Tarantino's *Pulp Fiction*. And in 2002 Neil Jordan adapted *Bob le Flambeur* into *The Good Thief*, with Nick Nolte as a modern-day incarnation of Bob.

Note

1. Vincendeau argues persuasively that Anne does not even manage to be a *femme fatale*, so that female characters remain marginalised indeed. Instead, Roger who plans everything, is Bob's partner (Vincendeau 2003: 113–14).

Further reading

Denitza Bantcheva, *Jean-Pierre Melville, de l'œuvre à l'homme,* Paris, Editions du Revif, 2007.

Jill Forbes, *The Cinema in France: After the New Wave,* Bloomington, IN, Indiana University Press, 1993.

Thomas M. Kavanagh, 'The Narrative of Chance in Pierre Melville's *Bob le Flambeur*', *Michigan Romance Studies,* Vol. 13, 1993, pp. 139–58.

Rui Nogueira (ed.), *Melville on Melville,* New York, The Viking Press, 1971.

Kristin Ross, *Fast Cars, Clean Bodies: Decolonization and the Reordering of French Culture,* Cambridge, MA, MIT Press, 1995.

Peter Schulman, 'No Room for Squares: Jean-Pierre Melville, Jazz, and the French Bachelor', *Nottingham French Studies,* Vol. 43, No. 1, Spring 2004, pp. 139–48.

Ginette Vincendeau, *Jean-Pierre Melville: 'An American in Paris',* London, British Film Institute, 2003.

Sabine Haenni

La boca del lobo/The Lion's Den (1988)

[Country: Peru, Spain. Production Company: Tornasol Films, Inca Productions. Producers: Gerardo Herrero, Benito Lizarralde, Emilio Moscoso. Director: Francisco Lombardi. Screenwriters: Giovanno Pollarollo, Augusto Cabada, Gerardo Herrero. Cinematographer: José Luis López Linares. Editor: Juan San Mateo. Music: Bernardo Bonezzi. Cast: Gustavo Bueno (Lieutenant Iván Roca), Toño Vega (Vitín Luna), José Tejada (Galardo), Gilberto Torres (Sergeant Moncado), Berta Pagaza (Julia), Antero Sánchez (Lieutenant Basulto).]

Synopsis: Vitín Luna is a young police officer who aspires to be a respected member of the armed forces. In order to achieve this promotion, he volunteers to go to Chuspi, a village in the Andes which has been badly affected by the violence of the Shining Path insurgency group. There he first encounters Lieutenant Basulto, who is assassinated by the insurgents and replaced by Roca, a much more authoritative figure. Tensions arise between the soldiers and the villagers who are all suspected of terrorism, resulting in a massacre of many innocent people. Vitín refuses to cooperate in the bloodbath, is accused of cowardice and is detained. He challenges Roca to a game of Russian roulette, and the film ends with his departure into the mountainside.

The politically motivated conflict between the Shining Path and the Peruvian state that started in 1980 and formally ended with the arrest of the insurgent group's leader in 1992, resulted in close to 70,000 victims – dead or 'disappeared' – at a time when the country was also in the throes of socio-political and economic collapse. Peru's film-makers generally avoided tackling the potentially fertile but sensitive topic of political violence during most of the 1980s, perhaps mindful of the anti-terrorism legislation restricting public debate that might be perceived as arousing sympathy for the Shining Path cause.[1] They may also have been affected by a desire to put a minimum degree of distance between past and present – between real events and their cultural representation – perhaps to give time for reflection as well as to establish the individual and collective mechanisms required to cope with such trauma (Jelin 2003: xvii).

Nevertheless, in 1988, the release of Francisco Lombardi's *La boca del lobo* brought the violence that threatened at that time to engulf the entire nation to cinema screens in the form of a fiction feature film that enjoyed critical acclaim and a warm reception from domestic and international audiences. This ground-breaking cinematic work explores the emotions and actions of soldiers sent from Lima to fight the insurgents. It draws critical attention to their encounters with the Andean inhabitants they have come to defend, as well as to the varied responses to the violence they are forced to confront. Indeed, it was the first Peruvian film to deal with one of the most serious issues faced by Peru to this day. Despite sparking controversy, it was an enormous success with audiences, and provided a benchmark for those directors in Peru who thereafter chose to offer their own cinematic responses to the worst political conflict and social crisis to affect the nation in decades.

This analysis unravels the approach of Lombardi's film to the representation of physical and psychological conflict, addressing the ways in which it explores the complex relationship between violence and national identity in Peru, including the interconnections between masculinity and institutional violence. In common with his earlier films, *La boca* explores the various effects of fear, claustrophobia and confinement on the collective and individual human psyche, and these perennial themes will be discussed with regard to the way they impact upon and interweave with the film's more topical concerns. It is likewise important to note that this was the first film made by Lombardi to be located in the Andes. Hence, it is useful to consider how the director deploys the rural landscape to emphasise the gradual subordination of a group of soldiers whose only experience is of an urban way of life and who assume a certain cultural superiority on their arrival in the village they are sent to defend. Throughout, the film highlights and critiques the dominant position of Lima (culturally, politically, socially and economically) in terms of defining and framing the image of the nation, and the subordinate position of the Andean region. It also draws attention to the misunderstandings between the soldiers and the villagers, and considers their failure to comprehend each other as at least part of the motivation for much of the violence portrayed.

In terms of what the filmmaker set out to do, he was forced to articulate this on several occasions in order to defend his work against charges of terrorist sympathies. In an interview published in 1989, Lombardi states that:

> I wanted to make others reflect upon the problem of violence that our country has suffered in recent years. As usual, I've drawn on reality in order to explore a theme that unites us all. Violence is with us every day and I think we are getting too accustomed to assimilating it more easily. The essence of the film is linked to this idea that the media, in particular the TV and the press, have led us to believe that this violence is somehow distant. I wanted to make those who live in the cities acutely aware of the violence taking place in the mountain villages that we know little about.
> (cited by Bedoya 1997)

Having debated the film before making a decision about its commercial release, the Peruvian military finally insisted only upon a slight modification to the text that is placed over the images of the prologue sequence. Hence, Lombardi was forced to remove his preferred opening title, 'Massacre at Soccos', which referred explicitly to the real attack by the military on the Andean village of Soccos in 1983, during which about 40 people – mostly innocent civilians, including women and children – were executed, without trial, on apparent suspicion of collaboration with the 'enemy'. The rest of the text remains unchanged, informing its audience that the drama is set in 1983, by which time the central Andean region of the nation had already suffered three years of violent repression. The text is fairly lengthy, mindful no doubt of the need to inform its audience of the key details of a complex conflict. It relates the main developments that led to the beginning of the so-called 'dirty war' when the military became actively involved in putting an end to the groundswell of insurgency that at first was largely dismissed by the state as the acts of mindless delinquents.

However benign it might appear, by agreeing to remove those three words that refer specifically to the real tragedy suffered by the village of Soccos, Lombardi conferred upon his film a broader metaphorical dimension that is suggestive of the brutality faced by many such communities located in remote rural areas of Peru. Rather than simply reconstruct the specific events leading up to one act of slaughter and its consequences, the film instead confronts the general terrorist phenomenon of the Shining Path. It draws attention to the intense pressure on the military to bring the escalating violence across the central sierra to a swift end, at all costs. In the event, it seems that such pressure led to a merciless campaign of repression. As a result, more inhabitants of the mountain villages were killed by both sides during 1983 and 1984 than at any other stage of the conflict as the military's strategy was based on an indiscriminate use of terror that for a while was difficult to distinguish from the tactics of the Shining Path.

The release of *La boca* coincided with a renewed period of repression, disappearances and indiscriminate executions. The community portrayed in the film had clearly already suffered at the hands of the brutal insurgents, as highlighted by images of bodies and graffiti shown in the prologue sequence as well as by the fear on the faces of those villagers who survived. The subsequent narrative depiction of rape and slaughter of villagers by the soldiers sent to defend them thus emphasises the film's apparent concern to underscore those officially sanctioned acts of violence, whether authorised by one renegade officer or by the authorities in Lima. Indeed, much of the controversy regarding portrayal of the military stems from the different character types representing different attitudes towards conflict and violence within the military itself, and more broadly from society at large.

Lieutenant Roca, for example, is the flawed father figure, a charismatic but fanatical leader. He is ruthless, authoritarian, and morally questionable, and represents the less humane approach to those innocents caught in the crossfire, prepared to deploy any means necessary to defeat subversion, even if that led to high death rates of innocent people. Roca's status as official state representative is further reinforced by images of him saluting the national flag and leading the national anthem, seen framed by a long shot remote from the crowd and almost engulfed by the church building that itself forms an oppressive centrepiece to the village. However, instead of acting with honour, he uses excessive violence, with the single aim of enforcing a brutal policy of counter-subversion.

Spectator identification with Luna as a more humane character is encouraged by depicting him as the only soldier who attempts to make an emotional connection with members of the local community. Luna stands out, for example, by showing sympathy for his comrade Gallardo's treatment of the young villager woman. Although he fails to speak out to support her, he later tries to make amends by appealing to Roca not to harm the villagers he has locked up after the raid on the wedding party. It is perhaps also significant that Luna is not involved in the second interrogation scene in the film, in which torture methods of an increasingly brutal nature are encouraged by Lieutenant Roca. A further sign of the tentative beginnings of a mutual bond of kinship comes when the villager who has acted as the regiment's mountain guide begs Luna personally to save them, as if he recognises that this young man differs from his comrades in his attitude towards the community.

The emphasis on Luna's experience as crucial to the film's overall message is further emphasised by the manner in which Roca, already depicted as crazed, hysterical and out of control, chooses to regard Luna's decision not to shoot as a sign of weakness and impotence – a crisis of masculinity. This emphasises the assumed dominance of a hard, brutal, violent form of masculinity, a machismo, that the film contests. Luna's ability to commit to the struggle is questioned, and hence also his identity as soldier. He is imprisoned as a traitor, and the physical confinement he endures is aggravated by a growing realisation that his disgust at the escalating brutality marginalises him from the rest of the group.

By challenging Roca to Russian roulette, Luna forces his superior to relive the traumatic event that triggered the psychological breakdown that he has tried to repress by consignment to oblivion. Sneered at by his comrades for his apparent weakness, Luna thereby takes control of the situation and reasserts a different kind of moral and emotional authority. In so doing, he performs his own act of rebellion against the system of patriarchy, represented by Roca, which he had admired but which has failed and oppressed him. The Russian roulette game thus serves as a dramatic device that draws the two men to a similar level by forcing each of them to confront their own mortality at the same time and within the same space. By leading the challenge with determination, Luna proves to himself and to his comrades that he is capable of facing up to his fears. In contrast, close-ups of Roca's face and hands reveal a trembling vulnerability beneath the surface of the tough image he prefers to project that is fundamental to his sense of self. As the 'game' progresses, Luna draws attention to his lack of respect for the lieutenant by addressing Roca using the informal 'tú' form, and ensures that the whole regiment observes the spectacle of Roca's degradation. While the former thus reasserts his macho masculinity before the group, the latter suffers the loss of his in the most humiliating way. In order to triumph, Luna needs to resort to the tactics of violence, but then rewrites the rules by walking away.

The film's reflective, critical approach provided an opportunity for discussion of issues that affected Peruvians in remote areas on a daily basis. Lombardi was criticised by some for creating an entertaining work in a classical style on issues of such intense and controversial concern that rejected the more overtly political aesthetics and philosophies of his 'Third Cinema' predecessors. Nevertheless, he was applauded by most for having placed a polemical fiction about contemporary Peruvian reality at the heart of public debate.

Note

1. The anti-terrorism legislation, introduced in 1981 and enhanced twice in 1987, made it much easier for the government to imprison anyone suspected of promoting a point of view that was deemed to be sympathetic towards the Shining Path cause.

Further reading

Ricardo Bedoya, *Entre Fauces y Colmillos: Las Películas de Francisco Lombardi*, Festival de Cine de Huesca, 1997.

Alberto Elena and Marina Díaz López, eds, *The Cinema of Latin America*, London, Wallflower, 2003.

Elizabeth Jelin, *State Repression and the Struggle for Memory*, London: Latin America Bureau, 2003.

John King, *Magical Reels*, London and New York, Verso, 2000.

Jeffrey Middents, *Writing National Cinema: Film Journals and Film Culture in Peru*, Lebanon, NH, University Press of New England, 2009.

Sarah Barrow

Bonnie and Clyde (1967)

[Country: USA. Production Company: Warner Brothers. Director: Arthur Penn. Screenwriters: David Newman and Robert Benton. Cinematographer: Burnett Guffey. Music: Charles Strouse. Editor: Dede Allen. Cast: Warren Beatty (Clyde Barrow), Faye Dunaway (Bonnie Parker), Michael J. Pollard (C. W. Moss), Gene Hackman (Buck Barrow), Estelle Parsons (Blanche Barrow), Denver Pyle (Sheriff Frank Hamer).]

Synopsis: A violent yet romanticised account of the career of the notorious bank-robbing couple who meet and embark on their spree amidst the poverty of the Great Depression in 1920s USA.

When first released in 1967, *Bonnie and Clyde* was a critical failure and achieved only mediocre box office sales. Even then, however, it appealed to those who embraced 1960s counter-culture in the wake of post-war social conformity and political unrest sparked by the conflict in Vietnam which cast a cloud over the entire decade. The following year, Penn's film was reassessed for its aesthetic and thematic innovations, and went on to achieve great critical acclaim and commercial success. Reappraised by most as a work of groundbreaking importance, it was also nominated for ten Academy Awards, winning for best supporting actress (Parsons as Blanche) and best cinematography for Guffey. It is now widely regarded as one of a handful of films that marked a significant turning point in US cinema's approach to form and content, at a time when the control of the Hollywood industry began to shift from producers to directors.

Working at a time of renewal in US narrative filmmaking, Penn was looked upon as one of those:

> young, wilful and maverick [US] directors having their own way and making fresh pictures that entertained millions while whispering to them about the true state of the nation.
> (David Thomson in Williams and Hammond 2006: 252)

However, while *Bonnie and Clyde* is now valued for having heralded a 'Renaissance' (King 2002: 12) period for Hollywood cinema as an art form, harking back to the pre-studio days of innovation, it struggled in its initial stages to attract funding. Indeed, Warner Brothers – perhaps recognising its potential as a gangster movie – only came on board when Warren Beatty became involved as its star and producer.[1]

The film's status as a gangster movie is worth considering as, like many belonging to that genre, it is loosely based on the true story of a villainous gang and used events of the past to set up a critique of the present. The real criminals were more brutal than their screen counterparts, but they became legendary nevertheless and much of the area where the film was shot was still known 30 years later as Barrow County. The gang became famous for rampaging through the Midwest, looting banks and causing havoc. The terrible effects of the Wall Street Crash (1929) and Great Depression that ensued were made more acute in this region by famine. Many families saw their homes and farms repossessed by banks, and the smaller banks were then forced to close. While the movie's references to the 1930s are explicitly made, an investigation of similar concerns regarding the oppression by the establishment of the poor and otherwise marginalised of the 1960s is implied. Moreover, if the protagonists are taken as representing the romantic but doomed heroes who claim to act on behalf of all society's outcasts, their tragic demise confirms the film's ideological stance, indicating 'a recognition of the dark forces that threaten the more utopian or idealistic aspirations of 1960s social movements' (King 2002: 18).

Bonnie and Clyde perplexed some and delighted others for its constantly surprising shifts of tone, from light-hearted banter, domestic squabbles and intimate moments, to shocking and apparently heartless acts of intense and aestheticised violence. It fascinated many for daring to draw inspiration as much from the stylistic experimentation of European cinema as from its own Hollywood predecessors. The influence of the Italian neo-realist movement of the late 1940s and 1950s, for example, is confirmed by the choice of 'real' locations, the use of local people as cast members, a predilection for handheld camerawork and point-of-view shots, and an overall emphasis on manufacturing an 'authentic' look via naturalistic lighting strategies. Perhaps even more obvious is the impact of the French New Wave on this film, as Penn draws upon that movement's innovations with shooting, editing and mise en scène. Indeed, an overt homage is paid early on to Jean-Paul Belmondo's iconic character, Michel, from Godard's *À Bout de Souffle* (1959) via the costume, posture and props adopted by Beatty as Clyde Barrow in his first main scene with Dunaway and Pollard at the gas station.[2]

The use of the jump cut device that was key to the New Wave style is noticeable from the very opening when Bonnie is introduced in her small and cluttered bedroom, preparing herself for yet another dull stint working as a waitress. Here, the fragmentary editing technique seems to suggest 'restlessness, edginess and a palpable sense of sexual hunger or longing' (King 2002: 12). Bonnie is clearly desperate to escape her humdrum life, and the frosted windows, bars on the bedstead, shadows across her face, all serve as symbols of the entrapment she feels.[3] Later on, in particular during the adrenaline-fuelled shoot-out sequences between the Barrow gang and the police, an even more disruptive cutting style is used that is reminiscent of the Soviet montage techniques of the 1920s. With close-up shots of blood-sullied bespectacled victims, an explicit reference is made to Eisenstein's powerful *Battleship Potemkin* (1925), another important film about resisting authoritarian oppression.

Thematically, the film offers a bold critique of the manipulation of reality by the mass media, alongside a concern for the dangers of celebrity culture. We see how the drama of their life on the run is heightened for Bonnie and Clyde by reading reports of their supposed deeds in newspapers. The pair, with their fellow misfits, are given new meaning and motivation when they see that they have been labelled the 'Barrow gang' by the press, and then feel it their duty to live up to that name. The tragedy of this situation is emphasised towards the end when Clyde shows genuine contentment after Bonnie has immortalised him through her poem about their adventures together, which is published by the papers.

Further debate was provoked by the film's vivid portrayal of apparently pointless acts of violence (at a time when sensitivities about the Vietnam War were particularly acute), and for its depiction of villains as romantic heroes to be commended for taking the side of the impoverished victims of the corporate priorities of the banking system. The film suggests that neither protagonist is really involved in armed robbery for the money itself, but that both are instead caught up in a rebellious struggle against alienation and conformity, and motivated by a desire for freedom and respect. In order to strengthen this position of sympathy, the popular Robin Hood myth is referenced by making it clear that the primary targets of their attacks are the banks that are repossessing the homes and businesses of the poor farmers and their (black) workers. Meanwhile, the irreverent depiction of the authorities (the police in particular) as incompetent and cowardly, at one point turning back from a car chase when the gang cross into another county, prevents the audience from taking their side too easily. The vengeful Sheriff Hamer, desperate to regain respect after being taunted and tortured by the gang, comes under particular attack for his obsession with status and pride.

The film highlights a concern for the complexities of identity formation in several ways. The opening scene begins with close-ups of Bonnie pouting at and preening herself in the mirror, and she quickly and carefully reinvents herself as the gangster's moll. Meanwhile, frequent references are made to the importance of photography in the modern world as a way of constructing and responding to a sense of self that is constructed largely by others. As Liora Moriel has suggested, this film is important not just for its approach to violence and society but also for its concerns with the 'fluidity of social constructions such as identity, family and race' (Friedman 2000: 148). The protagonists' shared yearning for a strong family unit of their own elicits further sympathy for their situation. This is emphasised by the brotherly bond between Clyde and Buck (more a father figure), the warmth they show towards the youngest member of their gang, C. W. Moss (as if their child), and the touching scene during which Bonnie is briefly reunited with her beloved mother.

The film uses its articulation of violence as a means to develop the identities of its main characters. It takes quite a complex approach to the relationship between violence, gender and sexuality. For example, it highlights and then distorts the meaning of the quite obvious phallic symbols (matchstick, bottle, gun) that Clyde uses to seduce Bonnie when he first meets her, confusing her shortly afterwards by declaring himself to be useless as a 'lover boy' and hinting at an ambiguous sexuality. Throughout, Clyde seems desperate to prove his status as a macho man, and uses his gun to do so, but even his efforts to become the fearless armed robber are often thwarted in almost ridiculous ways.

Bonnie is also complex as the main female character: sexually provocative and aware of her own power over men, she is at the same time vulnerable, childlike and desperate to be loved. She appears deeply hurt by Clyde's initial lack of interest in her sexually, and also by his reluctance to share any intimate moments with her. She is contrasted with Blanche, the shrill-voiced, self-righteous preacher's daughter (Clyde's sister-in-law), who is scared of everything and demands protection. Their differences are first made clear when Blanche shies away from being photographed, while Bonnie poses with excessive confidence in front of one of their stolen cars, holding a gun and pretending to smoke Clyde's cigar. By the end, however, Bonnie has largely renounced her more 'masculine' traits. In the final scene, her fascination with a delicate porcelain figure distances her from the gun-toting criminal of old and instead 'speaks to her growing domestication and desire for a new identity, one in accord with more traditional female roles' (Friedman 2000: 72).

The film of *Bonnie and Clyde* both reflected and played its part in shaping the cultural, social and political unrest of the time. It crossed boundaries and broke new ground from a stylistic and an ideological point of view, forcing its spectator to question the usual patterns of identification with its murderous (anti-)heroes. While its sexual politics may resort to a position that reifies the structures of patriarchy, it is fair to assert that this film deserves its place in cinema history for changing the shape of Hollywood forever; as Carr reminds us, 'Few movies since *Bonnie and Clyde* have had such a profound impact on [mainstream popular] culture or have generated as intense and passionate a debate' (in Friedman 2000: 72).

Notes

1. When the genre system was first established and studios began to specialise in niche areas, Warner Brothers developed its reputation as a producer of high-quality, crowd-pleasing gangster movies, such as those starring James Cagney.
2. The film was first considered by both Jean-Luc Godard and François Truffaut before being offered to Penn.
3. Geoff King does argue, however, that this is still very much a film in the Hollywood mould in which style, however innovative, is subordinate to narrative, and which draws on the old frontier mythology that was central to movies of the classical Western genre.

Further reading

Steven Alan Carr, 'From "Fucking Cops!" to "Fucking Media!": *Bonnie and Clyde* for a Sixties America', in Lester D. Friedman, ed., *Arthur Penn's Bonnie and Clyde*, Cambridge, Cambridge University Press, 2000, pp. 70–100.

Lester D. Friedman, *Bonnie and Clyde*, London, BFI, 2000.

Geoff King, *New Hollywood Cinema: An Introduction*, London and New York, I.B. Tauris, 2002.

Liora Moriel, 'Erasure and Taboo: A Queer Reading of *Bonnie and Clyde*', in Lester D. Friedman, ed., *Arthur Penn's Bonnie and Clyde*, Cambridge, Cambridge University Press, 2000, pp. 148–76.

Linda Ruth Williams and Michael Hammond, eds, *Contemporary American Cinema*, New York, McGraw-Hill, 2006.

Sarah Barrow

Das Boot (1981); *Das Boot: The Director's Cut* (1997)

[Country: West Germany (*Das Boot*), Germany, USA (*Das Boot: The Director's Cut*). Production Company: Bavaria (*Das Boot*), Bavaria, Columbia Pictures (*Das Boot: The Director's Cut*). Director: Wolfgang Petersen. Producer: Günter Rohrbach. Screenwriter: Wolfgang Petersen (based on the book by Lothar-Günther Buchheim). Cinematographer: Jost Vacano. Music: Klaus Doldinger. Editor: Johannes Nikel. Production Designer: Rolf Zehetbauer. Cast: Jürgen Prochnow (The Capitan-Lieutenant), Herbert Grönemeyer (Lieutenant Werner), Klaus Wennemann (Chief Engineer),

Hubertus Bengsch (First Officer), Martin Semmelrogge (Second Officer), Erwin Leder (Johann the Engineer).]

Synopsis: During the Second World War, *U-96*, a German submarine, ships out from its French home port on a dangerous mission to sink shipping in the Atlantic. Commanded by a still young but highly experienced captain (Prochnow), the ship also carries a journalist (Grönemeyer), sent to write a propaganda piece on the heroic crew. Over the following weeks, the ship and its young crew barely survive numerous close calls as Allied destroyers and aircraft depth-charge the vessel. A clandestine visit to a Spanish port brings only brief respite: the ship is refuelled and restocked, but sent on an even more perilous mission through the Straits of Gibraltar and into the Mediterranean. After further undersea tests of endurance, the submarine makes it back to port. But as it docks, an Allied air raid sinks the boat, killing captain and crew.

Das Boot's gripping, claustrophobic depiction of the terrors and pleasures of war under water has made it a key example of the subgenre of the submarine combat film. A German war film, telling a German war story, made with German money, it was a surprise international hit on its theatrical release in 1981. Its reputation and reach increased when it was recast as a five-part TV mini-series in 1985, and then rereleased in a much longer director's cut in 1997. Over time, it has become arguably the best-known German film overseas since *Metropolis* (1927), or perhaps *Triumph of the Will* (1935). *Das Boot* raised questions regarding the appropriate and adequate representation of German history and of the Second World War, questions that go far beyond cinema, and continue to be discussed today. But the film – and this perhaps goes some way to explaining its global success – is as much about masculinity as it is about history, as much about love as it is about the Battle of the Atlantic. It celebrates the love of sailors for their boat and the love of soldiers for each other and their unit. But above all, *Das Boot* stages and eulogises the love of *authority*, and the strong social ties that beloved leadership guarantees.

Although there had never been any shortage of films about the Second World War, the late 1970s saw an intensification of the international traffic in stories and images focusing on Germany's Nazi past. In 1978, the television mini-series *Holocaust* garnered huge audiences worldwide with its populist treatment of historical trauma, simplifying complex historical events into clear narrative lines and identificatory structures. In Germany the broadcast was a national event; it is often seen as a watershed in the treatment of the Holocaust in public life. Around the same time, for many of the auteurs of New German Cinema, the treatment of historical themes offered a way of combining a broadly critical stance with the possibility of larger audiences at home and abroad. Rainer Werner Fassbinder's *The Marriage of Maria Braun* (1979), Volker Schlöndorff's *The Tin Drum* (1979) and Helma Sanders-Brahms' *Germany Pale Mother* (1980) all succeeded at the domestic box office – always a great weak point of the New German Cinema – but also on the international art-cinema circuit. In doing so, they helped to consolidate a key element – still very much alive today – in modern German cinema's international brand: as channeller and interpreter of Germany's 'difficult and painful history'.

The team behind *Das Boot* – perhaps above all its producer Günter Rohrbach, newly arrived at the Bavaria studios, looking for a big project to consolidate his position – aimed to mine this rich seam of interest in historical themes, but on a larger scale and for a much bigger, mainstream market. The adaptation of Lothar-Günter Buchheim's autobiographical novel was planned as a big-budget contemporary entertainment film, dealing with the German past, but made in a Hollywood style and on a Hollywood scale. Moreover, the film would emulate Hollywood's latest, powerfully populist model: *Das Boot* would be a locally made *blockbuster*, its direct narration and strong identification augmented with immersive sound, corporeally involving action sequences and aggressive cross-media marketing. At the time, the film was the most expensive ever made in Germany. Deciding against Hollywood co-production, eschewing the state subsidy favoured by German art cinema, the studio gambled on lavish domestic production, raising unprecedented funds from TV stations and tax-avoiding investors.[1] Wolfgang Petersen, a shrewd populist, was engaged as director and screenwriter;

top German specialists were entrusted with a project larger than any they had worked on before. The film's look and feel owes much to their work: its immersive qualities depend on outstanding production and sound design, as well as Klaus Doldinger's music.[2] Jost Vacano's camera lent particular viscerality and intimacy: thanks to his self-built gyroscopic attachment, the camera, smaller than a Steadicam, could move exhilaratingly through the small spaces of the submarine, racing down the length of the boat, and registering the many jolts and impacts that make the film a judderingly somatic experience.

Telling a German story about the war posed questions about whose stories could be told and whose suffering and whose loss might be represented. *Das Boot* shifted the political goalposts of German cinema, implicitly discarding the critical standpoint of the New German Cinema, which, for all its complex relation to state funding, understood itself as a critical counter-cinema. Instead, *Das Boot* tapped into national myths and local identification structures in a broadly affirmative way. Questions of politics and historical responsibility were laid aside in favour of a loose notion of powerlessness. For a domestic audience, the 'us' here is not only 'we Germans', but also 'we without historical agency': the film offered the possibility of identifying with the suffering and stoicism of the ordinary German serviceman, flotsam on the blind tides of history, victim of a criminal regime and a callous high command. But there were further, more contemporary layers of national spectatorship. Given the film's relation to the blockbuster aesthetic (alluded to in direct references to Spielberg's *Jaws* (1975)), German audiences were offered not only the pathos of fatalism and victimhood, but also the complex satisfaction of seeing a local production successfully inhabiting a newly hegemonic international style.

The producers' gamble was a stunning success: the film did unexpectedly well overseas, particularly in the American mainstream market. This set up new dynamics of reception, with the interplay of the national and international giving rise to ironies and paradoxes. Overseas, a key selling point of *Das Boot* as a war film – its novelty value – was its highly atypical point of view, located firmly on the German side. To say the least, international audiences were unaccustomed to seeing German protagonists, usually simply The Enemy, as beloved figures who live, suffer and die before their eyes. Director Petersen enjoyed telling an anecdote – possibly true – which allegorises this aspect of the film's international reception. The audience at one Los Angeles test screening, he claimed, cheered the opening title telling that 75 per cent of German submariners died at sea, but the film wrenched their sympathies around, and its ending was greeted by tears and applause (Petersen and Greiwe 1997: 174). Paradoxically, this effectiveness meant that in the United States the film was to a degree denationalised, losing enough of its foreign marking to qualify as a culturally neutral, almost an American film. The triumphant proof came in six Oscar nominations, all of them for mainstream, 'domestic' awards, a different order of achievement to the vaguely condescending category of 'best foreign-language feature'.

At home, initial critical response was quite negative, largely because of the film's historical stance. The film, of course, distanced itself from the ideology of National Socialism, ridiculed in the figure of the First Officer, with his absurd self-sacrifice and his abstract musings on leadership. For critics, the problem lay rather in the film's almost total lack of historical context. In the desert of the deep, there are no civilians and few consequences, barely a glimpse of the enemy. This allowed the viewer to forget that at every moment we are asked to sympathise with the forces of the National Socialist state. Foregrounding the crew's courage and endurance occluded the boat's real function: to starve Allied populations, defeat their armies and ensure Nazi hegemony. Even the crew's hostility towards the high command and the national leadership, and their sympathy for enemy counterparts, was seen as subtly reinforcing an old, pernicious myth: that the armed forces simply did their duty, soldiering on in an insane hell, and that the real guilt lay with 'mad' leadership and with 'fanatical' units like the SS.[3]

The loyalty of the crew – and the film's invitation to audience sympathies – does not focus on the regime or the nation but on the unit and the captain. Like most combat films, *Das Boot* celebrates the profound homosocial bonding of a small group of men placed in an extreme situation.[4] In the Spielbergian phrase, the crew of *U-96* is a 'band of brothers'; women appear only in the opening scene, as singers and prostitutes, or as extras waving the boat in and out of port. But thanks to the setting, the depiction of this group is subtly different from the one in the infantry film, which, although it often uses soldiers' regional and ethnic diversity to suggest a microcosm of the nation, tends to emphasise the fate of individuals within the unit and celebrate the loyalty of the soldier to the man in the next foxhole. The focus of *Das Boot*'s representation is more abstract. The crew is a collective, and the submarine – the machine whose functioning is essential to their survival – is an enclosed lifeworld, a micro-society, a home. Throughout the film, in spite of the horrors and terrors, the boat is a *utopian* space: a world in which everyone knows his place and his job, where work is inherently and urgently meaningful, where privacy is secondary to common property and a common goal, where social bonds are unbreakable, and where authority is effective, respected and merciful.

The film is a paean to this authority, embodied in the figure of the 'Kaleun' (the 'Kapitän-Leutnant'), the submarine's captain. The captain – his aura of Good Fatherhood is unsullied by the banal specificity of a personal name – is a model of moderate masculinity, self-contained and always in control. His paternal authority does not rest on fear or coercion, but on omnicompetence and a profound understanding of his men. Several times, he describes them explicitly as 'children'; their mission is a 'childrens' crusade'. While on one level, the plot brings the ship across the Atlantic and into the Mediterranean, on another, the film stages the crew's passage to manhood – a passage indexed by beards and increasingly haggard faces – through a series of evermore profound tests of courage, in the endurance of bombardment and the prospect of inundation.[5]

The captain's authority remains unquestioned throughout. The crew responds to his leadership with trust and love, depicted as more beautiful and effective bonding agents than the abstractions of ideology, satirised in the First Officer's dogmatism. The film's incessant reiteration of good authority is above all staged visually, in the orchestration of gazes between captain and crew, and in close-ups on Prochnow's saintly face, melancholy with the weight of responsibility.[6] A key instance occurs just as the voyage begins. After the excesses of the last night on shore, the captain's benevolent regime is rewarded with professionalism: hangovers notwithstanding, the boat is ready and the crew lined up on the dockside. Standing at relaxed attention, the men gaze on the captain, their faces beaming, visibly suppressing smiles of happiness, suggesting a deep affection which sustains but overspills military protocol, necessary but inadequate in itself. No speeches required: the captain simply smiles and asks quietly, 'Na, Männer, alles klar?' ['So men, are we all set?'] As the vessel ships out, the look of love is multiplied: Thomsen, the other 'good captain', drunkard and noble cynic, comes to wave them off. In a long-lens framing, we see the *U-96* crew arranged around the conning tower, waving back towards the viewer. Cut to a close-up of Thomsen, his old alcoholic eyes filling with tears as he gazes after the departing ship.

Only once does a crack emerge, allowing the reality of power relations to appear. During yet another depth-charging, Johann the engineer breaks under pressure, abandons his station and tries to open the sea-door to escape. Faced with this one-man mutiny, the captain rushes for his revolver; but the gun is barely visible in the frame, as if, for the film, it would be obscene to depict the captain actually wielding the violent technology of ultimate authority. Minutes later, organic bonds of social order are restored. Again, this is staged through the *look*: a repentant Johann comes to beg for mercy, asking that he not be court-martialled. Huge eyes bulging in his gaunt face, he beseeches the captain, soliciting his look. At first, the captain's gaze is withheld, but eventually he turns towards the engineer. His face softens with eye contact; the desertion is quietly forgiven.

The film's largest deviation from its source material comes at the end. The real-life captain and crew of *U-96* survived the war. In fact, the real crew's first ever reunion took place during a visit to the location shoot in La Rochelle, France. But *Das Boot* turns the voyage into a tragedy. Having survived the trials of the deep, the ship is sunk in a bombing raid just as it reaches the illusory safety of the port. Crew and captain are left dead or dying on the dockside. Only the journalist, our central figure of narrative orientation, is left alive. Ultimately, he will tell the story. Before that, he – and the audience – experiences a last exchange of looks with the dying captain. In this way, the film, in its final moments, quite deliberately presents its audience with an invitation to mourn. But to mourn *what*? The answer might give us pause for thought: *Das Boot* ultimately asks the viewer to lament a lost utopian, fraternal social space, to mourn a beloved leader, and to feel, palpably, the absence of a face onto which all hopes have been projected and towards which all fears were directed.

Notes

1. Early adaptation attempts were problematic: screenplays were written and discarded, discussions with Hollywood figures (Robert Redford mooted as a star, Don Siegel as possible director) went nowhere, elaborate scale models were built, and then mothballed.
2. Sound design is crucial for the war film in general and the submarine film in particular. The repeated sonar 'ping' which plays a key role in the film is in fact a processed composite of nine separate 'pings', heavily processed to create a single rich and evocative sound (Koldau 2011: 73).
3. For an example of the critique, see Fritz J. Raddatz, 'Das Boot ist leer: Einspruch gegen ein politisch fragwürdiges Heldenepos', in Heptner and Reichmann 2006: 132–4.
4. This homosociality is usually heavily policed for suggestions of homosexuality. Among his many objections, Buchheim, the ebullient and cantankerous author, protested any hint of homoeroticism in the adaptation, as in the invented scene of cross-dressing as on-board entertainment (Buchheim 1981: 181).
5. Brad Prager, in a convincing psychoanalytic reading, sees this process as an education in continence: under constant threat of inundation, the crew must learn to be neither too dry, like the First Officer, nor too wet, like Thomsen, but just right, like the Captain (Prager 2003: 249–53).
6. The gaze towards the captain contrasts with the other main *look* in the film: the wide-eyed stare into a non-existent distance, a look without a visual object, a look of waiting and of listening, listening for sonic traces of the enemy, for the impact of a depth charge and to the ominous creaking of the hull.

Further reading

Lothar-Günther Buchheim, *Der Film* Das Boot*: ein Journal*, Munich, Goldmann, 1981.

Lothar-Günther Buchheim, *The Boat*, New York, Knopf, 1975.

Thomas Elsaesser, 'German Cinema Face to Face with Hollywood: Looking into a Two-Way Mirror', in *European Cinema: Face to Face with Hollywood*, Amsterdam, Amsterdam University Press, 2005, pp. 299–320.

Christine Haase, 'Wolfgang Petersen: Blockbuster Auteur?' in *When Heimat Meets Hollywood: German Filmmakers and America, 1985–2005*, Rochester, Camden House, 2007, pp. 63–100.

Tim Heptner and Hans-Peter Reichmann, *Das Boot: auf der Suche nach der Crew der U-96*, Frankfurt am Main, Deutsches Filmmuseum, 2006.

Linda Maria Koldau, 'Why submarines? Interdisciplinary approaches to a cultural myth of war', *Journal of War & Culture Studies*, Vol. 4, No. 1, 2011, pp. 65–78.

Wolfgang Petersen and Ulrich Greiwe, *Ich liebe die grossen Geschichten: Vom Tatort bis nach Hollywood*, Cologne, Kiepenheuer & Witsch, 1997, pp. 151–84.

Brad Prager, 'Beleaguered under the Sea: Wolfgang Petersen's *Das Boot* as a German Hollywood Film', in Randall Halle and Margaret McCarthy (eds), *Light Motives: German Popular Film in Perspective*, Detroit, Wayne State University Press, 2003, pp. 237–58.

Brían Hanrahan

Boudu sauvé des eaux/Boudu Saved from Drowning (1932)

[Country: France. Production Company: Les Établissements Jacques Haïk, Les Productions Michel Simon and Crédit Cinématographique Français (CCF). Director: Jean Renoir. Screenwriter: Renoir and Albert Valentin (uncredited, from a René Fauchois play). Music: Jean Boulze and Edouard Dumoulin. Cinematographer: Georges Asselin. Production Designer: Jean Castanyer. Editors: Marguerite Renoir and Suzanne de Troye. Cast: Michel Simon (Boudu), Charles Granval (Lestingois), Marcelle Hainia (Emma Lestingois), Sévérine Lerczinska (Anne-Marie, the maid).]

Synopsis: After losing his dog, the tramp Boudu tries to drown himself in the Seine. He is rescued by a Parisian bourgeois antiquarian bookseller, Lestingois. Insisting Lestingois is now responsible for his welfare Boudu is brought back to the Lestingois apartment. It is not long before Boudu's anarchic behaviour clashes with the prim and proper lifestyle of Mme. Lestingois. Lestingois secretly longs after his maid, Anne-Marie, but Boudu sleeps in the hallway between their rooms. Boudu visits a barber, and, complete with new appearance, seduces first Mme. Lestingois, and then Anne-Marie. After the adultery is uncovered, Boudu wins the lottery. Now rich, Anne-Marie agrees to marry Boudu. As the wedding party sail down the river, Boudu capsizes the boat. The party swim to land, but Boudu drifts downstream and disappears. He exchanges his clothes with a scarecrow, and begins his life again, happily, as a tramp.

Jean Renoir's fourth sound film, *Boudu Saved from Drowning*, is perhaps the best loved of his early career.[1] Pauline Kael described it as 'not only a lovely fable about a bourgeois attempt to reform an early hippy ... but a photographic record of an earlier France.'[2] Though its lightness sets it apart from the darker tones of *La Chienne/Isn't Life a Bitch?* (1931) and *La Nuit du Carrefour/Night at the Crossroads* (1932) and later weightier political works like *La Marseillaise* (1936) and *La Grande Illusion* (1937), *Boudu* is nonetheless an important step in Renoir's career: tonally, it explores a gracefully choreographed comedy of manners in order to satirise French middle-class values; politically, it mixes farce, slapstick comedy and social commentary to explore what Renoir sees as the fundamental irreconcilability between France's different classes.

If its central theme is a well-established trope – the comic juxtaposition of opposites (in this case, the anarchy of the free spirit set against the forces of social constraint and obligation) – it is Renoir's deployment of a range of technical innovations, and his expert marshalling of space, character and performance that mark the film as a key transitional work in early French cinema. While René Clair mixed visual humour with a dense soundscape, and Marcel Pagnol's 'Marseille trilogy' used location shooting and local patois, with *Boudu*, Renoir incorporated the new possibilities of sound cinema, biting social comment and highly theatricalised set-ups within a documentary-style rendition of Paris. *Boudu* is a *mise en abmye* of Renoir's entire oeuvre, as it introduces us to the 'Renoir style' and integrates the two key impulses of his career: 'affection for all human beings and extreme dissatisfaction with existing social orders, especially that of the French bourgeoisie'.[3]

Boudu is an adaptation of René Fauchois' 1926 play, and shows Renoir's penchant for film adaptations (which included works by Zola, Flaubert, Simenon, Maupassant, Gorki, Godden and Feydeau). Renoir remains broadly faithful to Fauchois' version (although his switch in focus from Lestingois to Boudu, and the new conclusion that saw Boudu reject the transformation from *clochard* to respected civilian did draw ire from Fauchois, and the threat of a lawsuit) and its narrative trajectory remains close to the classic French farce tradition. Renoir also added emphasis on the political implications, such as the increasing gap between rich and poor in France.

Boudu is a profoundly modern film. Its urbane structural contrasts – between interior drawing-room comedy and exterior bustle and noise of cosmopolitan Paris – showcase Renoir's appreciation of the architectural possibilities of staging in depth, and serve as a reminder of how quickly he came to terms with the exigencies of sound synchronisation. Renoir uses location shooting and deep-focus photography, and infuses the stage-bound origins of the original with a lightness of touch and an airy, fluid approach to mise en scène that refers back to the compositional complexity of Renoir's father, the Impressionist painter Pierre-Auguste Renoir. The Parisian backgrounds (streets, bridges, parks, rivers) become part of the scenery where Renoir's leisurely, semi-improvised humanistic stories unfold. His camera opens up spaces which reveal, little by little, people and events within them. Take the scene when Lestingois spies Boudu wandering the streets of Paris through his telescope – he, and we, see Michel Simon shambling along past the Left Bank *bouquinistes*, while real passers-by, unaware they are extras in a film, or who Simon is, simply carry on as normal. This is guerrilla-style filmmaking that predates the work of Godard and Truffaut by three decades, and this capturing of life 'as it is' (rather than reconstituting it in the studio, as Renoir's contemporaries Clair, Marcel Carné and Julien Duvivier would frequently resort to) allows for a far more dynamic connection between people and landscape. Boudu is one of a number of Renoir's protagonists who seem constantly in flux, literally moving in and out of focus. Precise social relationships, class hierarchies and differences, and the network of relationships that exist within communities can be embedded in tracking shots or deep-focus. Renoir's later films, most notably *The Crime of Monsieur Lange* (1936) and *La régle du jeu/The Rules of the Game* (1939), hone these choices, but *Boudu* is clearly a test case for the potential of cinema to delineate and segment space. For Renoir, using the camera to record reality in a complex and fully dimensional way was preferable to the editing and shot/counter-shot artifices of other directors.

Class injustice is never far from the surface in *Boudu*. Class division is there at the start when Boudu loses his dog, asks help from a policeman, and is chased away with the threat of prison. Moments later, an elegant bourgeois lady makes the same request, and three policemen rush to accommodate her. While this may feel like an easy punchline, it's a typical Renoir gesture – the depiction of subtle social schisms and perpetual injustice. The central premise of the film is essentially a class experiment – a Pygmalion-by-the-Seine. As Lestingois spots Boudu, he declares 'Just look at that one, he's wonderful. I've never seen such a perfect tramp.' To Lestingois, Boudu is a specimen worthy of study, and he treats him like a guinea pig, replacing his shabby appearance and social incompetence with something acceptably middle class. Yet Boudu's 'gratitude' for such a generous and benevolent act is to challenge the emptiness of the Lestingois' reforming principles and then overturn the normalising trappings of this safe, conventional, book-lined society.

Boudu is often described as the defiant triumph of anarchism over respectability. He is clearly someone marooned in the confines of the Lestingois' book-lined apartment, someone who cannot exist within the narrow spaces of domestic life. Only at the start and the end, when Boudu wanders through parks and the countryside, is he satisfied. His final embrace of the hobo lifestyle and his renouncing of his newfound wealth suggest the earthy pleasures of freedom are a worthwhile alternative to the stultifying conventions of the middle-class affluent elite. The justly celebrated scene, in which Boudu spits into Balzac's *La Physiologie du Mariage* (after being told he shouldn't spit on the floor) symbolises the stark divergence between his values and those of Lestingois.

The performance of Michel Simon as Boudu remains one of cinema's most compelling. Renoir once called the film a 'free exercise around an actor'; Simon/Boudu is the gravitational force around which the rest of the cast revolve and collide. Simon had already played Boudu on stage, and had a background as a vaudeville comedian, and so his performance appears larger than life. His gestures, tics, vocal inflections, and sheer inability to manoeuvre himself around the Lestingois apartment provide the film's comic heft. Simon's physical presence adds to this comic imbalance. He is in perpetual motion, invading personal space, banging into walls, doors and furniture, allegorising, through this sustained set of corporeal gestures, the film's culture-clash dynamic. Boudu is an alien, parachuted into the heart of culture, modernity, and sophistication – a Paris bookshop – who then proceeds to destroy the veneer of conformity and civilisation from within. Richard Boston writes that Boudu is 'a *marginal* … anarchic, chaotic, and finally, a fool … these agents of chaos act out our secret desires. If *we* see a big bum we might want to kick it: Chaplin *does* kick it … Laurel and Hardy, the Marx Brothers, Boudu, and Hulot are the enemies of conformity, of what can be regulated. They are the awkward squad.' (Boston 1992: 46).

No amount of civilising works; a trip to the barbers, or a bath, or a set of new clothes are futile gestures. A lottery win and a new bride are disposable attachments that signal conformity. Free from these artificial conventions, Boudu simply floats off, leaving as abruptly as he arrived. This mythologising of the tramp figure in 1930s French cinema was part of a conscious attempt to create an archetype separated from the world of money, social conventions and strictures, and morally dubious characters. The tramp is not just a figure of purity and innocence – his oppositional status to the bankers, financiers, and, more generally, the bourgeoisie, makes 'his conscious rejection of the capitalist world a noble and heroic act'.[4]

So, what starts as a standard class comedy – *petit bourgeois* paternalism collides with anti-social hoboism – develops into a fraught and fascinating relationship between Boudu and Lestingois. Christopher Faulkner notes Boudu 'exteriorizes something that is in Lestingois himself, that the bookseller has summoned him up from the dark reaches of the personal and social unconscious'.[5] The film's opening sequence sees Lestingois dressed as Pan, chasing the nymph Anne-Marie around an artificial forest set. As a sexual reverie, the scene indicates Lestingois's own sublimated desires to escape the shackles of desexualised social structures. Boudu's arrival – and the sexual havoc he triggers – releases Lestingois's own primal urges. In this sense, Boudu is subversive and dangerous, especially after he returns from the barber's with a new appearance. Armed with 'the manners of Caliban and the logic of Gracie Allen',[6] Boudu 'becomes' Lestingois: he looks after the bookshop in Lestingois' absence (dismissing a customer who wants a copy of Baudelaire's *Les Fleurs du mal/The Flowers of Evil* with 'This isn't a flower shop') and replaces the husband in the marital bed after his seduction of Mme. Lestingois. By marrying Lestingois' mistress, Boudu completes the ultimate displacement between the two men.

While the final sequences of *Boudu* establish 'the community of the open road as the locus of true happiness',[7] it is Lestingois who gets to hold both women under his arms, corroborating a particular kind of *ménage-à-trois*, as optimistically proposed by Renoir. Renoir, like Boudu, takes great joy in this exercise of *épater la bourgeoisie*. Like a distaff version of *El angel exterminador/The Exterminating Angel* (1962), Lestingois never seems able to make Boudu leave, and perhaps for good reason. Indeed, for all the film's opposition between bourgeois values and lower-class vulgarity, and its satirical swipes at Lestingois's *mission civilisatrice*, perhaps the real moral to this story is to be swept up by joyful amorality. Beneath the farce, lies Renoir's typical non-judgemental depiction of the human condition – Lestingois may adhere to social status, but, as Renoir's Octave reminds us in *The Rules of the Game*, 'everyone has their reasons'.

Notes

1. *Boudu Saved from Drowning* has been remade twice – in America, as *Down and Out in Beverley Hills* in 1986 by Paul Mazursky, starring Nick Nolte as Boudu, and, back in France, in 2005, with Gerard Dépardieu in the title role.
2. Pauline Kael, 'Boudu Saved from Drowning', *5001 Nights at the Movies*, New York and London, Marion Boyars, 1993, p. 72.
3. Richard Abel, 'Collapsing Columns: Mise en scène in Boudu', *Jump Cut*, 5, 1975, pp. 20–2, reprinted at www.ejumpcut.org/archive/onlinessays/JC05folder/MiseSceneBoudu.html (accessed 10 May 2012).
4. Colin Crisp, *Genre, Myth, and Convention in the French Cinema, 1929–1939*, Bloomington, IN, Indiana University Press, 2002, p. 76.
5. Christopher Faulkner, '*Boudu Saved from Drowning:* Tramping in the City', *The Criterion Collection*, www.criterion.com/current/posts/380-boudu-saved-from-drowning-tramping-in-the-city (accessed 10 May 2012).

6. Matthew Kennedy, 'Renoir on the Seine', *Bright Lights Film Journal*, www.brightlightsfilm.com/50/boudu.php (accessed 10 May 2012).
7. Crisp, p. 77.

Further reading

Richard Boston, *Boudu Saved from Drowning*, London, BFI Classics, 1992.

Christopher Faulkner, *The Social Cinema of Jean Renoir*, Princeton, NJ and Guildford, Princeton University Press, 1986.

Martin O'Shaughnessy, *Jean Renoir*, Manchester and New York, Manchester University Press, 2000.

Alexander Sesonske, *Jean Renoir: the French Films, 1924–1939*, Cambridge, MA and London, Harvard University Press, 1980.

Ben McCann

Brief Encounter (1945)

[Country: UK. Production Company: Cineguild. Director: David Lean. Screenwriters: Noel Coward, David Lean, Anthony Havelock-Allan. Cinematographer: Robert Krasker. Editor: Jack Harris. Music: Sergei Rachmaninov. Cast: Celia Johnson (Laura Jesson), Trevor Howard (Dr Alec Harvey), Joyce Carey (Myrtle Bagot), Stanley Holloway (Albert Godby), Cyril Raymond (Fred Jesson).]

Synopsis: Laura (Celia Johnson), a housewife, and Alec (Trevor Howard), a doctor, both happily married to other people, happen to fall in love with each other, quite by chance and apparently without calculation, after he removes a piece of grit from her eye. Friendship develops into romance, and the couple meet in town once a week before they finally call off their 'affair', which remains unconsummated. Their sense of duty towards their respective spouses and families, as well as their overwhelming need to behave in accordance with the accepted morality of the time, prevents them from taking their relationship any further. Instead, sexual passion is displaced by awkward conversation and furtive, loving glances at each other in the Milford Junction station tearoom or the Kardomah café.

Jeremy Paxman begins his book, *The English: A Portrait of a People*, with a detailed account of the *Brief Encounter*: a good indicator of just how far this film has become an icon not only of British cinema but also of British national identity, particularly in terms of the behaviour of its two lead characters. Raymond Durgnat proclaimed the motto of the film to be 'Make tea not love' (1971: 181). Durgnat further noted how the film that was critically lauded upon its 1945 release (even winning the Critics' Prize at the 1946 Cannes Film Festival) met with quite a different reception 20 years later, when its ethos of restraint no longer seemed quite so appealing to the exponents of sixties free love, and the most innocuous little details of the film provoked impatience and irritation in its viewers. He recalls that at one screening he attended 'Even the name of the town enraged a well-spoken young lady who finally cried out, "Where the hell is Milford Junction anyway?"' (1971: 180).

However, the suggestion that the film did not meet with antipathy until the 1960s is slightly misleading, since even in the 1940s the film had a mixed reception. When it was first test-screened in a cinema in Kent that had a working-class clientele, it was heckled and laughed at throughout because of the (much parodied) middle-class speech of its protagonists, not to mention its unimpeachably 'correct' morality. *Brief Encounter* may be a national icon but from the moment of its initial release onwards there have been any number of iconoclasts who have called into question its ability to speak for them and their national identity. Perhaps the critic Gavin Lambert was correct when he called the film a 'definitive document of middle-class repression', the last word on a particular kind of Britishness, specific to a time and a place and most crucially a *class*.[1] Even within the film, we see the operation of a slightly different moral code via the parallel relationship between Myrtle (Joyce Carey), the station tearoom manageress and Albert (Stanley Holloway), the stationmaster, who belong to a different social class from Alec and Laura, and are less inhibited about acting on their feelings for each other.[2]

Brief Encounter was the fourth and final collaboration between the celebrated playwright Noel Coward and director David Lean, who would go on to make two of the most highly regarded adaptations of Dickens novels, *Great Expectations* (1946) and *Oliver Twist* (1948) before moving into epic mode with later films such as *The Bridge on the River Kwai* (1957), *Lawrence of Arabia* (1962) and *Doctor Zhivago* (1965). Having risen to the status of the top British film editor by the end of the 1930s, Lean had been asked to co-direct the war film *In Which We Serve* (1942) with Noel Coward, providing technical expertise to complement Coward's ease with actors. The partnership proved highly successful and continued with Lean directing the family saga *This Happy Breed* (1944) and the supernatural comedy *Blithe Spirit* (1945), both adaptations of Coward's stage successes. It is a sign of Lean's growing confidence as a director that he encouraged Coward to rethink the chronological structure of his half-hour play *Still Life*, the source for *Brief Encounter*, when converting it into a screenplay. Lean told Coward that the original dramatic structure lacked intrigue and surprise. He suggested that the film version could play with audience expectation by beginning with an enigmatic scene showing the couple's final parting:

> and then you go back and explain that this is the last time they see each other. They were never going to see each other again. And you play the first scene in the picture – it made no sense to you at all and you didn't hear half the dialogue – again, and that's the end of the film.
>
> (Brownlow 1997: 194)

This strategy is highly effective, particularly as it comes at the film's most emotionally extreme moment; Laura's sudden suicidal impulse. In the first version, we remain in the tearoom with Myrtle and Laura's friend Dolly (Everley Gregg) vaguely wondering where Laura has got to, before she re-enters the room looking pale and shaky. In the second version, we go *with* Laura as she rushes out onto the platform determined to throw herself under the express train thundering past, and this time we understand the significance of the moment and know exactly why she has reached this abject state. She hesitates at the last moment and resists suicide, although as she admits in her voice-over narration (an imaginary confession to her husband, but also the key to the viewer's intimacy and empathy with the character) that this is not because of a sense of duty towards her family but because she 'wasn't brave enough' to go through with it.

Despite Lean's important contribution to the film, in 1945 the film was sold as a Noel Coward film, and Andy Medhurst has read the film as an oblique expression of Coward's homosexuality. The film's forbidden relationship is heterosexual, but its depiction of 'the pain and grief caused by having one's desires destroyed by the pressures of social convention' (1991: 204) could be understood as a coded reference to the tribulations of (then still illegal) homosexual relationships. Several decades on, Richard Kwietniowski's short film *Flames of Passion* (1990) paid homage to *Brief Encounter*'s queer subtext by offering a gay reimagining of the original film. It even takes its title from the torrid melodrama that Alec and Laura go to see at the cinema, but which they leave halfway through because they find it too silly and implausible.

Brief Encounter's 'meta-cinematic' elements (characters within the film commenting on films and the focus on aspects of 1940s cinema-going like the differently priced seats, the organist who plays beforehand, the trailers and Disney cartoon prior to the main film) are important reminders of the central role that fantasy plays in our lives; every small town has its cinema where people can spend a pleasant few hours inhabiting a cinematic dream world. However, Laura seems particularly prone to the lure of fantasy. She borrows romantic novels from the library and, as her husband Fred (Cyril Raymond) remarks, she is a 'poetry addict' able to fill in the missing word from his crossword puzzle, taken from a line from Keats ('Huge cloudy symbols of a high romance' – a phrase that could apply to Laura's own romance, punctuated by clouds of steam and smoke from passing trains). Meanwhile for down-to-earth Fred, 'romance' is just 'something in seven letters' that fits in with 'delirium' and 'Baluchistan'. Laura is the one who turns on the radio broadcast of Rachmaninov when she returns home from her final terrible meeting with Alec, and who uses the pounding dramatic Russian music as a soundtrack for her remembrance of her love affair, communicating the depth of her feelings where words fail.

Indeed, the emotive power of these elements of the film belie its reputation as a realist, restrained, repressed text, and, as Richard Dyer suggests, to see *Brief Encounter* 'as only cups of tea, banal conversation and guilt is not really to see or hear it at all' (1993: 66). Rather, it is precisely that interaction in the film between suburban mundanity – such as going to Boots to buy a toothbrush, eating a Banbury cake at a café – and overwhelming unexpected emotion – falling in love, wanting to die if one cannot be with one's lover – that makes *Brief Encounter* so resonant. At one point Laura says, 'I'm an ordinary woman – I didn't think such violent things could happen to ordinary people'; but the film never lets us forget that beneath the surface of bland normality, unsuspected flames of passion flicker away; that in the imagination of a respectable middle-class housewife, the 'pollarded willows by the canal just before the level crossing' can be magically transformed into moonlit palm trees under which she embraces her lover. The film grants us privileged access into these suppressed dreams and brings them vividly to life while also recognising the impossibility of sustaining them in reality. 'Whatever your dream was – it wasn't a very happy one, was it?' says a newly insightful Fred to Laura in the film's final moments, and on the whole he is right, for her romantic idyll causes her more pain than pleasure. And yet Laura still wants 'to remember every minute – always – always – to the end of my days'.

One final point, although it may not be immediately apparent to today's viewer, the cinema-goer of 1945 would have recognised instantly that *Brief Encounter* was not a contemporary drama but set a few years earlier, pre-war. It carefully depicts a late-1930s milieu with pointed details like Laura and Fred being able to leave their curtains open with lights blazing (no blackout), trains running on time and no coupons required to buy items like chocolate. But there is more to *Brief Encounter*'s temporal shift than simple nostalgia for the luxuries of the recent past. As Antonia Lant has argued, a 'contemporary audience member could view the film with a sense of historical superiority that appealed to his or her sense of place, knowing that the constructed epoch on the screen had a definite and catastrophic endpoint' (1991: 170). Neither Alec nor Laura seem to realise that their affair is taking place in the larger historical context of the final days before the beginning of the Second World War, and there is an irony implicit in their renunciation of each other in favour of stability and continuity ('One has one's roots after all, hasn't one?', Dolly states, a sentiment with which Laura agrees, albeit rather half-heartedly) when the world is about to change immeasurably, and roots are about to be ripped up, no matter what they choose to do.

Notes

1. Gavin Lambert in conversation with Stephen Frears and Alexander Mackendrick, during Frears's documentary *Typically British: A Personal History of British Cinema*, Channel Four/BFI, 1994.
2. It should be noted that the film's use of working-class characters as little more than comic counterpoint to the more dignified and 'important' middle-class love affair has also attracted much criticism.

Further reading

Kevin Brownlow, *David Lean*, London, Faber, 1997.

Raymond Durgnat, *A Mirror for England*, London, Faber, 1971.

Richard Dyer, *Brief Encounter*, London, BFI, 1993.
Antonia Lant, *Blackout: Reinventing Women for Wartime British Cinema*, Princeton, Princeton University Press, 1991.
Andy Medhurst, 'That Special Thrill: *Brief Encounter*, Homosexuality and Authorship', *Screen*, Vol. 32, No. 2, Summer 1991.
Jeremy Paxman, *The English: A Portrait of a People*, London, Penguin, 1999.

Melanie Williams

Die Büchse der Pandora/Pandora's Box (1929)

[Country: Germany. Production Company: Nero Film. Director: Georg Wilhelm Pabst. Screenwriter: Ladislaus Vajda. Cinematographer: Günther Kampf. Art Directors: Andrei Andreiev and Gottlieb Hesch. Cast: Louise Brooks (Lulu), Fritz Kortner (Dr Ludwig Schön), Carl Goetz (Schigolch), Francis Lederer (Alwa Schön), Krafft-Raschig (Rodrigo Quast), Michael V. Newlinsky (Marquis Casti-Piani), Gustav Diesel (Jack the Ripper), Siegfried Arno (Stage Manager), Alice Roberts (Countess Geschwitz) and Daisy D'ora (Charlotte Marie Adelaide).]

Synopsis: Lulu is a beautiful woman with a mysterious past. Raised by the drunkard Schigolch, a pimp and possibly her father, she becomes the mistress of a wealthy and respectable newspaper editor, Dr Ludwig Schön (Fritz Kortner). Schigolch introduces Lulu to Rodrigo Quast, who offers her a role in his variety show. Dr Schön gets engaged to his secretary, Charlotte. Hoping to keep Lulu despite his engagement, Dr Schön persuades his son Alwa to cast Lulu in his revue instead. Refusing to perform in front of Dr Schön's fiancée, Lulu takes him backstage and seduces him at a rehearsal. Caught in the act, Dr Schön is socially disgraced and forced to marry Lulu. The Countess Geschwitz (Alice Roberts) is also attracted to Lulu. Things get out of hand when Dr Schön 'catches' Lulu with Schigolch at their wedding reception. Mistaking them for lovers, Dr Schön asks Lulu to shoot herself but it is he who gets killed. On trial for murder, Lulu escapes with Schigolch's help, with Rodrigo Quast, Countess Geschwitz and Alwa as accomplices. The Marquis Casti-Piani recognises Lulu, on the run on a train. He blackmails and lures her into his ship, a gambling den. Alwa squanders his wealth. The Marquis shows Lulu's pictures to an Egyptian brothel-owner. Sensing a deal, Lulu tricks Geschwitz and Quast into helping her as she escapes with Schigolch and Alwa on a boat. The starving trio drift to London on Christmas Eve. Hunger drives Lulu to prostitution, leading her to Jack the Ripper, who proves to be her final undoing.

Pandora's Box gets its title from the Greek myth in which Pandora unknowingly opens a box full of evils. Frank Wedekind's two plays *Erdgeist* (The Spirit of the Earth, 1895) and *Die Büchse der Pandora* (1904) recast the mythical Pandora as Lulu, a woman who destroys men without intending to. The plays acquired enormous cultural significance as Germany struggled with rapid political, economic and social transformations during the Weimar Era (1919–33). Several theatrical and filmic adaptations of Wedekind's plays emerged soon after they were published.[1] Asta Nielsen starred in a 1923 silent version directed by Leopold Jessner, which was based on his own stage production of 1911. Such adaptations display a characteristic concern with modernity as a traumatic experience marked by a dangerous encounter with female sexuality, a key trope of Weimar cinema. Together with *Joyless Street* (1925), *Diary of Lost* Girl (1929) and *The Blue Angel* (1930), *Pandora's Box* is often cited as one of the most representative melodramas of the Weimar Era. Louise Brooks' dark bobbed hair became a superlative icon of the New Woman, earning her the soubriquet of 'the girl with the black helmet'.[2] Brooks published her recollections in several articles and interviews that revived her as a silent film star who acquired a cult following: 'There was no Dietrich, there was no Garbo, there is only Louise Brooks', remarked Henri Langlois in a comment that encapsulates her unrivalled appeal as an androgynous, sexually liberated flapper girl.[3]

However, it is important to note that such celebration did not become the norm until the late fifties. A contemporary German review wrote Brooks off rather quickly: 'Louise Brooks cannot act. She does not suffer. She does nothing'.[4] Though unflattering, this is a telling remark in that G. W. Pabst's Lulu does not apologise for her actions – she is unafraid to seek what she desires, whether it is food, sex or money. For Wedekind, Lulu represents an uninhibited, animalistic sensuousness while for G. W. Pabst, she represents evil's universal appeal. Both were drawn to Lulu precisely because she defied conventional definitions of evil: it is the reason why she is so alluring. Pabst's film was significantly different from the earlier silent version: in Brooks' words, 'Only five years earlier the famous Danish actress Asta Nielsen had condensed Wedekind's play into the moral prostitute film *Loulou*. There was no lesbianism in it, no incest. Loulou the man-eater devoured her sex victims – and then dropped dead in an acute attack of [moral] indigestion'.[5]

Pabst wastes little time to begin the film with a tableau that immediately establishes Lulu's extraordinary desirability. Lulu is the mistress of a middle-aged newspaper baron, Dr Schön. We first see her as a provocatively dressed woman who cavorts with a drunk, ageing Schigolch in a loose peignoir as he eyes her lecherously. It is clear that she has known Schigolch all her life. She sits in his lap with an easy familiarity and dances seductively in front of him as they reminisce about their past. She introduces Schigolch to the meter man outside her apartment as her 'first patron' in a turn of phrase that suggests that Schigolch is a pimp. As Dr Schön lets himself into their apartment, Lulu hides Schigolch as if he were a former lover.

The entire exchange sets Lulu up as an object accessible to a range of men, irrespective of age, class or kinship. Schigolch is her symbolic father but he tries to claim her like an incestuous lover. Dr Schön is old enough to be her father but makes love to Lulu by the end of the first sequence. Incest is again apparent in a scene at their wedding reception, where, enraged at finding Schigolch on their nuptial bed, Dr Schön ironically hands her a pistol and orders her to kill herself. In a visible loss of power, the pistol – clearly a phallic symbol – goes off in Lulu's hands, knocking Dr Schön dead. The resulting image defines Lulu as a *femme fatale* even as it positions Alwa as an infantile Oedipal son who usurps his father's place.

But Pabst does not leave it there. In a sequence that precedes the wedding, he is unabashed in his introduction of Countess Geschwitz as the woman who falls for Lulu. Geschwitz is the antithesis of Dr Schön's fiancée, Charlotte, whose wispy blond hair and faraway look mark her as a sentimental icon of femininity. Geschwitz, on the other hand, is introduced as Alwa's 'buddy'; she is unafraid of male company. Her cropped hair mimics Lulu's but the resemblance ends there. Unlike Lulu's ebony, gleaming crown of hair, hers is blond and tightly curled, while her breeches and tight jacket highlight a tightly reined in masculine personality. Transfixed by Lulu as she sets eyes on her, there is no confusion about Geschwitz's sexual desire; rather, the problem stems from her inability to express it clearly. To make matters worse, Lulu does not return her love. In Pabst's hands, this encounter is never reduced to a self-congratulatory scene of lesbianism. Instead, it reveals the complex but ambiguous nature of Lulu's sexual appeal, ironically noting Geschwitz's powerlessness. Pabst layers these sequences with shots that capture Lulu's innocence through her carefree movements and gestures; none of them openly solicit her lovers' desire. They fall for her because of her sexual magnetism.

Indeed, Pabst cast the very American Brooks in the by-then very German character of Lulu because of her candid and unaffected portrayal of sexuality. He believed that the overexposed

Marlene Dietrich would reduce Lulu's part 'to a burlesque'.[6] While he was very well respected in Germany, Pabst was not as well-known in Hollywood. Paramount immediately turned down his request to loan Brooks for *Pandora's Box* as she was still under contract. It was only when Brooks quit the studio over a salary dispute that Pabst was finally able to cast her. Disgust at the American studio system led Brooks to foreign waters – like Garbo, Brooks' gay personal life (in both senses of the word) and iconoclasm fuelled intense gossip about her bisexuality.

Brooks' collaboration with Pabst was riddled by a tense relationship that carries over into Brooks' alluring portrayal of Lulu's destructive impact on whosoever falls in love with her. In fact, Brooks claims that she never acted for the role, but just 'played herself'.[7] Trained in the Denishawn dance academy, Brooks was graceful to a fault. Pabst let her movements and her costume do the acting, a device so effective that contemporary audiences rightfully felt that she 'did nothing'.[8] Indeed, Brooks' performance of Lulu can be seen as an allegory of the film star's irresistible visual appeal. Brooks essentially plays herself when she acts as the impossibly attractive showgirl who revels in being seen. Pabst exemplifies this quality in a sequence where Lulu rehearses for Alwa's revue: everyone wants to look at her, a feature that is at the core of a cinematic image that is irrepressibly linked to feminine beauty.[9]

Above all, *Pandora's Box* documents a world thrown into sudden ideological crisis and moral flux with no secure ground to fall back on. Formally, it is dominated by indoor shots that evoke a sense of unremitting claustrophobia and entrapment, with few or almost no outdoor sequences. Interiors are bathed in high-contrast lighting that is striking in its avoidance of intimacy: close-ups conceal more than they reveal. Visually, it is pervaded by harsh, glamorous, brightly lit but cold surfaces. Exact details are generally excluded – the camera moves restlessly between disconnected objects whose meaning is not immediately apparent. Looks between Lulu and Schigolch, Lulu and Dr Schön, Lulu and Alwa, Lulu and Geschwitz rarely culminate in full eye contact, rendering cinematic meaning incomplete. The spectator is left searching for a point of contact or identification – a sequence on an open boat is shrouded in mist and fog; a scene on the train is so tightly framed that actors have barely any room to move. The camera teases by refusing to deliver what it promises: should viewers sympathise with Lulu or should they chastise her? Is Lulu responsible for her ruin?

There is no final answer: instead, Lulu and Dr Schön are often framed against mirrors or paintings that distort, dwarf or overwhelm their presence. Pabst holds an unflattering mirror to his characters, singling out the worst for biting ridicule, yet his style refuses to conform to a traditional melodramatic style that polarises good and evil. His approach cannot be reduced to a sympathetic identification with any single moral exemplar. Lulu emerges as an enigma that is simultaneously attractive and repelling. Pabst refuses to sentimentalise her – this is apparent in the final segment where she meets the fearful Jack the Ripper. The lighting is soft but unrelentingly mysterious and threatening. For the first time, Lulu openly solicits a client, saying that she 'likes him'. Instead of portraying this episode as her comeuppance, Pabst treats it as the final expression of Lulu's love, conflating death with ecstasy, fulfilment, and rest. Lulu does not suffer.

Notes

1. Thomas Elsaesser, 'Lulu and The Meter Man: Louise Brooks, G. W. Pabst and *Pandora's Box*', in *Weimar Cinema and After: Germany's Historical Imaginary*, London, Routledge, 2000, pp. 259–92, p. 264 in particular.
2. Kenneth Tynan, 'The Girl with the Black Helmet', originally published in *the New Yorker* (11 June 1979). Reprinted in a booklet included with the DVD compilation of *Pandora's Box* (Criterion, 2006), pp. 20–73.
3. Louise Brooks, 'Pabst and Lulu', originally published in *Sight and Sound* (Summer 1965). Reprinted in *Pandora's Box* (Criterion, 2006), pp. 74–93. See *Looking for Lulu* (Directed by Hugh Munro Neeley, 1988) included in *Pandora's Box* (Criterion, 2006).
4. Quoted in Tynan, 'The Girl with the Black Helmet', p. 46.
5. Brooks, 'Pabst and Lulu', p. 76.

6. Brooks, 'Pabst and Lulu', p. 78.
7. Tynan, 'The Girl with the Black Helmet', p. 32.
8. Quoted in Tynan, 'The Girl with the Black Helmet', p. 46.
9. For a detailed discussion of this point, see Mary Ann Doane, 'The Erotic Barter: *Pandora's Box* (1929)', in Eric Rentschler (ed.), *The Films of G.W. Pabst: An Extraterritorial Cinema*, New Brunswick and London, Rutgers University Press, 1990, pp. 62–79.

Further reading

Lotte H. Eisner, 'Pabst and the Miracle of Louise Brooks: *Pandora's Box, Diary of a Lost Girl*, Censorship and Pabst's Realism', in *The Haunted Screen: Expressionism in the German Cinema and the Influence of Max Reinhardt*, Berkeley and Los Angeles, University of California Press, 1956, pp. 295–308.

Amelie Hastie, 'Louise Brooks, Star Witness', *Cinema Journal*, Vol. 36, No. 3, Spring 1997, pp. 3–24.

Noah Isenberg, *Weimar Cinema: An Essential Guide to Classic Films of the Era*, New York, Columbia University Press, 2009.

Siegfried Kracauer, *From Caligari to Hitler: A Psychological History of the German Film*, Princeton, NJ, Princeton University Press, Revised edition, 2004.

Carrie J. Preston, 'Posing Modernism: Delsartism in Modern Dance and Silent Film', *Theatre Journal*, Vol. 61, No. 2, May 2009, pp. 213–33.

Anupama Kapse

Caché/Hidden (2005)

[Country: France, Austria, Germany, Italy, USA. Production Company: Les Films du Losange, Wega Film, Bavaria Film, BIM Distribuzione. Director and Screenwriter: Michael Haneke. Producer: Veit Heiduschka. Cinematographer: Christian Berger. Music: Jean Paul Bugel. Editors: Michael Hudecek, Nadine Muse. Cast: Daniel Auteuil (Georges Laurent), Juliette Binoche (Anne Laurent), Maurice Bénichou (Majid).]

Synopsis: *Hidden* is an art-house thriller which focuses on Georges Laurent, an arts journalist living in Paris, whose family comes under an unexplained threat with the arrival of several videotapes. These are anonymous surveillance tapes of the exterior of the family's apartment, an unfamiliar Paris street and the farmhouse where Georges grew up. The investigation into the meaning of the tapes evokes memories of an event from Georges' childhood in 1961. Georges' family had provided refuge for a boy, Majid, whose parents were killed in the massacre of Algerian pro-independence protesters by the French police. Jealous of his claim on the family's affections and it is implied disturbed by the otherness of the Algerian boy, Georges persuades his parents to send the boy away, betraying him and ruining his future. The anonymous tapes implicitly accuse Georges, forcing him to acknowledge the repercussions of his actions. The visual style of the videos is similar to surveillance or CCTV footage with fixed cameras, long takes and no editing. The lack of explicit resolution to the question of who is behind the camera, and who is sending the videos, confounds the expectations of classic narrative and the thriller genre conforming instead to the conventions of art cinema.

Michael Haneke is one of the most admired and controversial of contemporary directors. His work can be defined as modernist – rather than postmodernist – in his political analysis of contemporary society. His influences include the European modernist auteurs Robert Bresson and Jean Luc Godard. This is apparent in Bresson's emphasis on the materiality of the image and Godard's concept of the film as an essay which places demands on the viewer, rather than providing the pleasures of identification. Haneke's themes and style of film-making come from a desire to rupture the identification fostered by mainstream film – particularly Hollywood cinema; 'My films are intended as polemical statements against the American "barrel down" cinema and its dis-empowerment of the spectator. They are an appeal for a cinema of insistent questions instead of false (because too quick) answers, for clarifying distance in place of violating closeness, for provocation and dialogue instead of consumption and consensus' (Haneke 1992). This aim to empower the spectator lays the foundation for the dominant themes of his work, which are related to the nature of the viewing experience as well as wider social and political ideas. These include an investigation into the relationship between screen violence and spectator response, the status of images as representations of truth, and an analysis of the role class, gender and race play in constructing identity. In exploring these themes Haneke uses a distinctive film style with an emphasis on long takes and static camera, creating a slower-paced cinema with the intention of allowing the audience room to evaluate ideas, rather than being rushed into a range of emotions and responses.

Hidden personifies Haneke's concerns as a film-maker, bringing together his repeated themes and style within a genre framework. The use – and subversion – of genre conventions is typical of Haneke's work; *Funny Games* (1997) reworks the 'family under siege' thriller, *The Time of the Wolf* (2003) uses the plot of a post-apocalyptic sci-fi film. Wood (2006) has seen in the use of the thriller genre a link to Hitchcock, pointing out the similarities of the murder in *Benny's Video* (1992) to the murder of Marion Crane in *Psycho* (1960), while the mother/daughter relationship in *The Piano Teacher* (2001) evokes the similar relationship in *Marnie* (1964). '*Cache [Hidden]* is clearly linked to *Rear Window*, with "watching" replaced by "being watched", the story now told from the view point of the spied-on' (Wood 2006). (The use of solely diegetic sound in *Hidden* is also reminiscent of *Rear Window*, which is notable for its experimentation with soundtrack.) It is at the level of plot and motif that the comparison with Hitchcock can be made, in all other aspects, Wood argues, Haneke is the 'anti-Hitchcock'. While Hitchcock's oeuvre can be fundamentally defined by the use of intense identification with character, Haneke's films deliberately disallow identification, making the audience look at the characters rather than share their perspective.

The question of who is filming the Laurent's apartment and sending the tapes is part of the seemingly conventional set up of the thriller plot, teasing the audience with the promise that the enigma will be solved. The first tape is followed by a series of further clues; a child's drawing of a face covered in blood, an anonymous phone caller asking for Georges, two cards with the same sinister drawing, new tapes with new locations. The new locations allow Georges and Anne to act as detectives; deciphering the street name (Avenue Lenin); and following the trail to the flat of Majid. Majid's denial that he – or his son – is responsible for sending the tapes, despite Georges' conviction that they have, is another convention of the thriller. The figure of the hero who nobody will believe is familiar to the audience from many entries in the genre including *Rear Window* and *North by Northwest*, the denial of truth by the villains is part of the obstacle the hero has to overcome. The difference here is that the audience does not know who to believe; there is no identification with Georges and this is coupled with the increasing realisation that nothing in the film can be accepted as real. There never is any definitive resolution to the question of who sent the tapes which terrorise Georges and his family. In this *Hidden* calls to mind another Hitchcock film, *The Birds*, in which the reason for the bird attacks is left unexplained, although various rationales are put forward by a range of characters. In *Hidden* there seems to be a range of possible explanations for who has sent the tapes which work within one or more of the areas of plot, symbolism and aesthetics.

In plot terms the most likely explanation is that either Majid or his son – or the two working together – made and sent the tapes as a form of revenge for the actions taken by Georges as a boy. This is certainly the rationalisation which Georges gives and it does seem a valid one given the content of the tapes: Majid and Georges' childhood home, their current apartments, the row between the two men which was filmed in Majid's kitchen. The argument against this would be that the revenge seems implausible after such a long time, would Majid even know that his banishment was Georges' fault? And Majid and his son seem gentle, good people, not criminals. The illogicality in this explanation is negated though if Majid's revenge on Georges is read symbolically, with Majid representing the colonised and Georges the coloniser. In this reading the tapes represent the colonial and post-colonial relationship between France and Algeria (and post-colonial relationships more generally). Georges' comfortable, liberal, intellectual life masks the history of France as an oppressive regime which was guilty of torture and murder. The mise en scène of Georges' flat and workplace represent his life as walled in, protected but also isolated by shelves of books which he may not even read – the real books at home become indistinguishable from the set dressings of the studio. Georges' attempt to remain 'hidden' is what makes the surveillance videos so menacing as they show his life in plain view. In this symbolic reading Majid's revenge is to force Georges to remember and therefore acknowledge that the crimes of the past have only been hidden – their effects remain. In *Hidden* the atmosphere of dread and anxiety the characters experience comes from being forced to look and to recognise culpability. A similar feeling is constructed for the spectator by the refusal to solve the enigma of the crime drama, the central character is terrorised and guilty but there is no closure to the events of the past. In an allegorical reading of the film closure would be impossible due to the continuing iniquitous relationships of the 'post-colonial' era.[1]

An alternative interpretation of the tapes is that they are part of Haneke's exploration of the relationship between spectator and cinema, his attempt to disrupt the comfortable pleasures offered by mainstream film. From the first shot of the film the viewer is unclear as to the status of what they are seeing, which, added to the undermining of the conventional thriller plot, creates doubt and unease. This is apparent in the deliberate confusion as to what the viewer is watching; rather than making the surveillance tapes stylistically distinct they are shot on the same HD video as the rest of the film. The opening shot is a long take of a quiet suburban street, the camera is static, and there is only diegetic sound. The occasional pedestrian walks past, Anne leaves the apartment, a cyclist ride by, nothing happens. After nearly three minutes voices are heard talking over the shot, the exchange 'Well?', 'nothing' adding to the viewer's confusion. A cut changes the perspective of the scene and Georges and Anne reappear in the street and discuss where the person making the film might have stood. This revelation to the audience that they had been watching a tape with Anne and Georges rather than a conventional establishing shot of a film, is further complicated when the scene cuts back to the earlier street scene which is now being fast-forwarded. This reference to the materiality of the film itself is typical of a modernist artist reminding the viewer that the art form they're looking at is a construction with ideologies and points of view – not simply a reflection of reality. The confusion for the audience over the status of what is being seen occurs several times throughout the film. The first shot of the exterior of the son's school appears initially to be part of a surveillance tape but isn't (this throws the meaning of the final shots of the film which are also of the school further into doubt), a point of view shot from within a car driving along country roads seems to be 'real' but is abruptly fast forwarded revealing it to be a tape. A discussion which is part of Georges' arts programme is suddenly frozen; rather than viewing the live discussion the viewer is watching the editing process during post-production and here a contributor is going to be cut for becoming too theoretical.

The questioning of the status of what is being shown soon raises pertinent questions about the nature of film-making itself. To attempt to distinguish whether each scene is part of a surveillance tape or the film itself (*Hidden*) demonstrates the power images have over the audience; the easy belief that what is being shown is real, when of course both the surveillance tapes and the people who are watching them in the film are equally constructed.

Hidden constantly foregrounds the way in which society constructs images as a way of imposing ideas and values; Georges is a broadcaster transmitting a partial cultural view, censoring the guest who is – ironically – discussing the way in which Rimbaud's sister censored the poet's work after his death, Anne is a publisher, the unknown producer of the surveillance tapes is also a filmmaker, turning the scrutiny on the people who are usually in control of the image construction. These ideas lead to another hypothesis as to the maker and sender of the tapes; they are produced and sent by Haneke himself, reminding the viewer from the very first shot that cinema should be a site of discussion and argument and not a comforting representation of reality.

Note

1. In this context *Hidden* can be seen as part of a group of films which, for the first time, began to represent Algerian-French history and the war of independence: *Days of Glory* (Buchareb, 2006), *The Colonel* (Herbiet, 2006), *Intimate Enemies* (Emilio-Siri, 2007), *Outside the Law* (Bouchareb, 2010).

Further reading

Michael Haneke, 'Film als Katharsis' in Francesco Bono (ed.), *Austria (in)felix: zum österreichischem Film der 80er Jahre*, Graz, Blimp, 1992, p. 89. Cited in Mattias Frey, 'Michael Haneke' in *Great Directors*, Issue 28, *Senses of Cinema*. Available at www.sensesofcinema.com/2003/great-directors/haneke-2/ (accessed 23 November 2012).

Oliver Speck, *Funny Frames: The Filmic Concepts of Michael Haneke*, London, Continuum, 2010.

Catherine Wheatley, *Michael Haneke's Cinema: The Ethic of the Image* (Film Europa), New York, Berghahn Books, 2009.

Robin Wood, 'Hidden in Plain Sight: Micheal Haneke's Cache', *Arts Forum*, Jan 2006.

Sarah Casey Benyahia

Casablanca (1942)

[Country: USA. Production Company: Warner Brothers. Director: Michael Curtiz. Producer: Hal Wallis. Screenwriters: Julius Epstein, Philip Epstein and Howard Koch. Cinematographer: Arthur Edeson. Music: Max Steiner. Editor: Owen Marks. Cast: Humphrey Bogart (Rick Blaine), Ingrid Bergman (Ilsa Laszlo), Paul Henreid (Victor Laszlo), Claude Rains (Louis Renault), Conrad Veidt (Major Strasser), Sydney Greenstreet (Senor Ferrari), Dooley Wilson (Sam), Peter Lorre (Ugarte).]

Synopsis: Against the backdrop of refugees fleeing the German advance in Europe during the early years of the Second World War we follow three characters involved in a love triangle. Victor Laszlo (Henreid) is a Resistance leader who has escaped from a German concentration camp. Accompanied by his wife, Ilsa (Bergman), he has reached Casablanca, administered by the authorities of Vichy France. He now needs to get out of there before he is recaptured by the Germans. The only person who can help him is Rick Blaine (Bogart), who has earlier fallen in love with Ilsa in Paris at a time when she believed her husband to be dead. Rick has to choose between his love for a woman and the larger demands imposed on individuals by the war.

Casablanca is seen as a Hollywood 'classic' but how has it attained this status? Does it arise from the combination of a melodramatic love story set within a threatening world, a strong star presence enhanced by seductive cinematography, a satisfying cause-and-effect narrative that moves to an intense moment of resolution, a rhapsodic use of music reinforcing the melodrama,[1] an ironic script that counterpoints the melodrama, an exotic location enabling an escape from the everyday world, and noir lighting that reminds the spectator of the darker aspects of life that continue to exist around the fringes of this imagined space of gratification? Or is it a 'classic' created as much by marketing as through thematic content and film style? *Casablanca* was rushed through production by Warner Brothers so its release would coincide with a major Allied conference in Morocco; it was further publicised by receiving eight Oscar nominations and winning three; it became a cult film in the 1960s; and, with the advent of video and DVD, assorted anniversary box sets maintained its profile.

As a product of the Hollywood studio system, *Casablanca* could be explored as an example of the way in which inputs of studio, cast and crew come together during this period in a collaborative production process. There is a distinctive industrial-creative process at work. Ultimate corporate control is exerted by the studio, Warner Brothers, but there are also creative inputs from producer, director, stars, and other members of the cast and crew.[2] The screenplay alone involves several contributors: Howard Koch,[3] Julius and Philip Epstein[4] and Casey Robinson.[5] The music includes recurring melodies by Steiner but also the distinctive delivery of songs ('As Time Goes By' in particular) by Wilson. In performance terms, there is the star presence of Bogart and Bergman but also the character-acting of Rains, Greenstreet and Lorre. Curtiz was an experienced operator having directed over 100 films (and this was Bogart's forty-fifth Hollywood movie).[6] Overarching the whole process there is the presence of the studio dictating not only the overall 'look' of the product but also the political outlook.

The narrative shows how in wartime films Hollywood's dominant ideological concerns are altered to bring them into line with the demands of a war situation. 'Getting the girl' is not what matters in the end (such considerations are put off 'for the duration'). In the light of issues felt to be of such magnitude that they dwarfed personal relationships Hollywood emphasises self-sacrifice and duty. The final shot is of male bonding between Rick and Renault (America and Free France).

Our engagement with the melodrama can obscure the centrality of ideology to this film. Those involved were driven by a desire to address the political and (at the time) pressingly contemporary issue of German fascism. This was a fundamental concern for Warner Brothers' executives but also for liberals like Bogart, cast members like Veidt[7] and Lorre,[8] who had fled Nazi Germany, and Curtiz, who had earlier come to Hollywood from Europe. This was a 'wake-up call' for America; as Rick Blaine (Bogart) says, 'I bet they're asleep in New York. I bet they're asleep all over America.' Blaine has confronted the Italians by supplying guns to Ethiopia in 1935 and fought in Spain against the fascists in 1936; and contemporary hardships of refugees in Europe are presented in a documentary style that conflates this fictional narrative with newsreels of the period. Significantly, the film is set in December 1941, the month of Pearl Harbour. The script deals with the brutality not only of Germany but also of Marshal Petain's Vichy France administration in collaborating with the Germans against the Free French resistance. The dark presence of concentration camps in occupied Europe is behind everything we see. Often, even Rick's one-line asides carry serious bite ('What do you want for Sam?' produces 'I don't buy or sell human beings'). At the same time, despite (or because of) these intense underpinning issues, the Germans and Italians are also often presented in stereotypical comic-book fashion, and there are comic interludes as with the pickpocket and the bumbling stereotypical English couple.

The 'What do you want for Sam?' line from Greenstreet's Ferrari carries weight, beyond what Warners is likely to have intended, since Sam is African American. There are stories of audiences in all-black cinemas in America demanding the projectionist rewind Sam's parts and replay them as it was so unusual to see a black actor with anything approaching a substantial role in a Hollywood movie.[9] And yet, how we should read the presence (or present absence) of Sam within the film is a contentious issue. In theory, as Rick says, he is within the narrative free to make his own decisions but in reality Sam maintains the dutiful sense of subordinate loyalty expected in a master–servant relationship. The very notion of including a designated 'free' black man in the film within the context of an American society (and Hollywood films) founded upon segregation should not be underestimated. But, do we in fact have conservative racial politics within a film that purports to expound liberal views? At the very least it would seem a major suppression within the text to have America exalted as the bastion of democratic freedoms and cosmopolitanism (see the nationalities represented within Rick's Café Americana) while Sam is forced to passively represent millions socially and economically designated as second-class citizens in that country.[10] Just as tellingly, Moroccans are almost totally absent from the film. There is one named supposed 'Moroccan', Abdul, the doorman (Dan Seymour), and Casablanca itself as presented bears no relation to the actual place.[11]

If we are to place the film within the context the script demands we need to know about the Italian colonial enterprise in Ethiopia, the Spanish Civil War, the American debate over whether or not to become involved in the Second World War, the Vichy administration of France, the social and economic realities of racial segregation in America and the nature of the way in which North African countries and peoples were looked upon by America and other European powers. We need to be aware of the seriousness of life and death in Occupied Europe as well as some light-hearted clichéd cultural perspectives held in 1940s America.

Above all we should note how America is represented as the Promised Land for refugees, a place of safety and a guardian of freedom and democracy. This is from one perspective a factual truth of American history. Religious and political refugees (as well as economic refugees) had been amongst those crossing the Atlantic from Europe. In the 80 years or so before the Second World War, Europeans flooded in beneath the shadow of the Statue of Liberty. They formed a large percentage of both the national population and the Hollywood film-making population; as a result, there was always likely to be support for the dispossessed and oppressed of Europe. However, at the same time the United States had during the interwar years followed a strongly isolationist foreign policy, determinedly keeping out of overseas conflicts. There was, therefore, a heated debate during the late 1930s and early 1940s about whether to enter the war or not. Warner Brothers was in favour of America joining the war and *Casablanca* was part of its ongoing film-based contribution to the debate, or, if you like, propaganda for its point of view. Franklin Roosevelt had moved the country steadily nearer to war, repealing the Neutrality Act, for instance, in order to supply Britain and pushing through an act to lend or lease supplies when Britain could no longer afford to pay. But, it was not until after the Japanese bombing of Pearl Harbour on 7 December 1941 that the debate was finally clinched in favour of intervention.

If *Casablanca* is to be understood as more than a romantic wartime drama it has to be seen within a historical and political context. There is pleasure to be gained from the romance, and the suspense (as the film also operates as a thriller), but there is an additional depth of understanding that goes with grasping the contexts within which the film was made and originally shown. Imagining this being shown in the United States or Britain as the war was going on (the turning globe and narrator's voice-over at the beginning clearly suggesting this war is inescapably affecting the whole world) enables us to understand the film in a fuller, more complete way. It may also alert us to ways in which this film could be read in relation to the post-war emergence of the United States as a global imperial power.

Finally, returning to the ideological complexities of the film, if we were to consider the lead female role we might be struck by the passivity of Ilsa. She is the dutiful wife and the woman who asks her man to think for her. The film may advocate liberal values in the face of fascism but it also suppresses important issues with regard to both race and gender.

Notes

1. See Martin Marks 'The Sound of Music' in Nowell-Smith, Geoffrey (1997) *The Oxford History of World Cinema*, Oxford: Oxford University Press, p. 253.
2. This was the first project for Wallis as a unit producer at Warners. In *Round Up the Usual Suspects: the Making of 'Casablanca'*, Aljean Harmetz sees him as the key creative force, overseeing production down to details of lighting and costume.
3. Howard Koch wrote plays for Broadway in the 1920s and adapted H. G. Wells' *War of the Worlds* for Orson Welles' famous radio broadcast in 1938. He was blacklisted as a Communist sympathiser in 1951 and moved to Europe.
4. Julius and Philip Epstein worked as a writing partnership at Warners in the 1940s. Julius was investigated by the House Un-American Activities Committee, and when asked if he had belonged to any subversive organisations reportedly replied, 'Yes, Warner Brothers.'
5. Robinson is not mentioned in the credits.
6. Michael Curtiz was born in Hungary in 1886. He worked in the Hungarian film industry before making films in Austria and Germany. In 1926 Warner Brothers brought him to Hollywood. Whether the visual style of his films is attributable to him or the cinematographers and art directors he worked with has been much debated.
7. Conrad Veidt was a high-profile German actor during the 1920s and 30s, establishing his reputation as Cesare in *The Cabinet of Dr Caligari* (1919). He was a critic of Hitler in the early 30s and had eventually had to flee the country.
8. Peter Lorre acted in plays by Bertolt Brecht in the 1920s and became famous as the child-killer in Fritz Lang's *M* (1931). He was born to a German-speaking Jewish family in Hungary and fled Germany in 1933.
9. Dooley Wilson toured Europe with his band as a singer/drummer during the 1920s and worked as an actor in the 1930s before getting a contract with Paramount who also loaned him to other studios. He was an influential member of the Negro Actors' Guild of America.
10. We might also consider that Sam is (reassuringly?) desexualised.
11. See Brian T. Edwards (2003) 'Preposterous Encounters: Interrupting American Studies with the (Post)Colonial, or *Casablanca* in the American Century' *Comparative Studies of South Asia, Africa and the Middle East* 23: 1 and 2, p. 70.

Further reading

Aljean Harmetz, *Round up the Usual Suspects: The Making of Casablanca – Bogart, Bergman and World War II*, New York, Hyperion, 1992.

Clayton R. Koppes and Gregory D. Black, *Hollywood Goes to War: Patriotism, Movies and the Second*

World War from 'Ninotchka' to 'Mrs Miniver', London, I.B. Tauris, 2000.
Harlan Lebo, *Casablanca: Behind the Scenes*, New York, Simon and Schuster, 1992.
Richard Maltby, *Harmless Entertainment: Hollywood and the Ideology of Consensus*, Metuchen, NJ, Scarecrow Press, 1993.
James C. Robertson, *Casablanca Man: The Cinema of Michael Curtiz*, London, Routledge, 1993.
Thomas Schatz, *Boom and Bust: American Cinema in the 1940s*, Berkeley, University of California Press, 1999.

John White

La caza/The Hunt (1965)

[Country: Spain. Production Company: Elías Querejeta Producciones Cinematográficas. Director: Carlos Saura. Screenwriters: Angelino Pons and Carlos Saura. Producer: Elías Querejeta. Cinematographer: Luis Cuadrado. Editor: Pablo González Del Amo. Music: Luis de Pablo. Cast: Ismael Merlo (José), Alfredo Mayo (Paco), José María Prada (Luis), Emilio Gutiérrez Caba (Enrique), Fernando Sánchez Polack (Juan), Violeta García (Carmen).]

Synopsis: José, Paco and Luis – three friends who share a common history – get together for a day of rabbit hunting and invite Enrique, Paco's brother-in-law, to join. The land on which they hunt, owned by José but maintained by his tenant Juan, was the site of many deaths during the Spanish Civil War (1936–39) – a fact that gradually is revealed to both the unsuspecting Enrique and the audience. As the day's hunting events progress, tensions swell, eventually culminating in a human massacre. Of the four hunters the only one to survive is Enrique.

Heralded as one of the greatest films ever to have been made about the Spanish Civil War (1936–39) and its residual effects on a politically and culturally traumatised post-war society, Carlos Saura's third feature-length film, *La caza* (*The Hunt*, 1965), remains a triumph of modern cinema. Often characterised as a psychological thriller about fratricide, the film paints an intensely intimate, at times claustrophobic, portrait of masculinity, violence and repression, which unfolds through a starkly minimalist narrative centred on four men who spend a day together rabbit hunting on a former Civil War battlefield.

Indeed, *La caza*'s battlefield plays a crucial role in the film's visual economy, wherein it is both framed as the oppressive backdrop to the main action and foregrounded through numerous long shots and close-ups as a wounded body. A series of establishing shots (long shots and aerial views) at the film's onset show the hunters descending into the vast and hollowed subterranean valley, but the camera undercuts human presence in favour of highlighting the barren, lifeless landscape as an additional protagonist. This desert valley is, of course, reminiscent of the futuristic, post-apocalyptic descriptions in Luis's science fiction novel *El quinto planeta* ('the fifth planet'), where the post-human environment appears contaminated from a distance. These shots, in turn, are counterbalanced with medium and close-up shots that bring into sharp focus the scorched, pock-marked, almost lunar-like hunting grounds, whose holes and crevices subtly reveal bullet holes and secret bunkers – 'open wounds' leftover from the war. With the aid of Luis Cuadrado's spectacular photography, the camera captures these remnants of war not as extraterrestrial but as naturalised elements embedded in the landscape. These remains constitute spectral evidence of a collective national history that, on the one hand, the land retains and suppresses, and on the other hand, it accumulates and exposes over time. In the end, the film poignantly illustrates that the emergence of these historical traces wields a certain force or violence that haunts the present.

As the landscape gradually gains significance throughout *La caza*'s mise en scène, shifting from symbolic stage to historical site, its terrain not only embodies but also begins to exude the same tensions, anxieties, and disease that plague the protagonists. In this regard, Saura's work could be categorised as a film of and about embodiment, and specifically how place embodies time and history. In fact, one of the most unique if not radical components of the film is the way it draws on landscape not just as a reflective surface that mirrors the conditions of the post-war era, but also as a container in which the time of the present is itself conditioned, and to some degree inflicted, by other temporalities. In this regard, landscape becomes an event – a dynamic and wavering entity that settles and unsettles film subject and viewer alike, unveiling a matrix of entangled temporalities within the singular space of the film's diegesis and by extension the space of the screen. This is perhaps why a majority of *La caza*'s narrative violence emanates from the natural setting: the infernal heat and relentlessly oppressive sunlight, as well as the overall sensations of enclosure and suffocation that are evoked in the oscillation between images of the open, expansive range of the grounds and the steep, severe walls of the surrounding hillsides.

But from the 'event of landscape', the violence that manifests in *La caza* is neither depicted in a straightforward manner nor made overtly graphic until the end. Even though tensions among the hunters escalate throughout, it is not until the final scene of human massacre that the spectator is presented with the occasion to witness, as the frightened young Enrique does, an explosion of violent and fatalistic behaviour that is not only unambiguous, but also sudden and shocking. This is not to suggest that the film overall fails to treat violence as one of its central thematic concerns, which of course it does. Rather, it is important to note that while violence is central to the film – a central if silent actor – then it is neither explicit nor excessive, but instead gradually unravels through various layers of intensity.

Next to films in which violence is immediate and perhaps particularly gruesome, gory and/or bloody, such as those of American director Sam Peckinpah (1925–84), who is rumoured to have undergone a transformative experience upon viewing *La caza* that later inspired him to make *The Wild Bunch* (1969), Saura's deliberately slow-paced, methodical exploration into the evolution of violence, by contrast, is more suggestive and implicit. A good example of this is the first hunting sequence, which is performed as a routine military operation and hints at what some scholars have argued is the film's insistence on ritualised and/or fetishised forms of violence. As the four men march over the uneven terrain, weapons in hand, it is through a series of voiceovers that the spectator is given a window into their isolation, fears and internal anxieties. But what begins as seemingly innocuous observations steadily swells (José is nervous and exhausted from the sweltering heat, Paco dreads becoming 'crippled' and Enrique is troubled by the uncanny feeling of having 'been there before'). These interior monologues, though distinct in content, reach a point of convergence that anticipates the aggressive exchanges that are really taking place, and for which the rabbit hunt is merely a subtext. Underscoring this point further, once a rabbit is spotted and the shooting begins, shots of the hunters are not crosscut with images of their supposed prey, but with images of each other, creating the editing illusion of a human 'crossfire' that binds these men together in a visual display of mutual antagonism as they 'aim' at one another. Of course, the hunt sequence is only the first in a chain of actions that crescendo in anticipation of the final 'unfriendly fire' that will end in tragedy. Within this chain, Saura effectively portrays the overwhelming sense of anguish among the men, which can be seen as a kind of slow death methodically structured into every detail and made all the more palpable through the slow deterioration and alienating effects of the land, as well as by the musical score, which vacillates between silence and the funereal drum beats of a military march.

Within the spatial and temporal dynamics of what could be called *La caza*'s 'slow-moving' violence, the magnified feelings of entrapment are equally prevalent. In fact, these sensations give rise to the general tone of *dis*-ease or discomfort underlying the film's narrative. The concept of disease, along with its many allusions to contamination, quarantine, wounds, pain, and death, occupies a significant amount of screen time. For disease is closely linked not only to the heat, but also to physical ailments and mental states: José's chronic stomach pains and feelings of failure, Juan's bad leg, his bedridden mother, Paco's paranoia and regret, Luis's alcoholism, and last but not least Enrique's boyish innocence, which socially exiles him from the group. All of these examples, of course, find a narrative parallel in the myxomatosis infestation that has plagued the rabbits, a visible disease that causes death by paralysis, and which at one point Enrique describes as 'monstrous'.

To date, the allegorical readings of *La caza* are abundant. While the rabbits are often read as a metaphor for a population of sickly, devastated Spaniards, the campsite is associated with Spain, and the hunters are usually equated with the impoverishment of Franco's ultimately self-defeating legacy. From these interpretations, have risen a number of compelling readings that analyse intergenerational conflict, intragenerational difference, the theme of ageing, animalisation and dehumanisation, the role of technology and apparatuses, visibility and blindness, the relationship between censorship and self-censorship, and the notion of intertextuality.

Needless to say, scholarship on *La caza* has devoted considerable attention to the film's masterful critique of the Franco dictatorship (1939–75), a critique made all the more impressive given the strict censorship laws to which the film's production was subjected. In fact, the constraints of censorship are largely responsible for the innovative measures that Saura, along with his producer and henceforth lifetime collaborator, Elías Querejeta, had to engineer. This, in part, explains why after undergoing several script changes, not least of which included eliminating any overt national or historical references to the Civil War, the film relies so heavily on the embodied aesthetic of the landscape, as well as on framing and editing techniques that elicit a sense of confinement. From the opening credit sequence, which is a long take of agitated, caged ferrets, to the last final freeze-frame shot of Enrique running out of the desert panting for dear life, the film's visual language of imprisonment functions on multiple levels – spatial, physical, emotional and psychological – and ingeniously replicates the very circumstances under which Saura and his crew were working. Of course, the characters reproduce this logic as well, since their psychological entrapment leads to a practice of self-censoring, articulated as a symptomatic and ultimately incurable pact of silence. Thus, in order to speak about Spain's political and cultural climate of repression, Saura adopted a strategy of self-censorship, grafted onto the fiction of the text.

Worth noting is that the film was shot entirely on the location of a real former battle site outside of Madrid, a detail that has led some critics to perhaps overly emphasise the film's neo-realist aesthetic, a claim that Saura himself has repeatedly contested. But for as authentic as the geographical location and its history are, the film's mise en scène is anything but straightforwardly realist, with its high-contrast black and white generating quasi-surreal lighting extremes that oscillate between dark, impenetrable shadows and the bleached effects of underexposure, all of which are the result of the natural light of the sun. Moments of over- and under-exposure, as we have seen, occur in the narrative as well. Underneath the veneer of silence, flashes of a persistent and untimely past ignite a flame that fuels the perpetual cycle of violence.

Beyond depicting the evolution of the repetitive cycle of violence, *La caza* also examines its origins. One point of interest that curiously has been given little attention is the cadaver of the unknown solider. Often cited as an inconsequential or excessively transparent object, the cadaver, preserved and kept secret in a cave, is arguably the most important object in the film and is significantly located at the very centre of the main action. While spatially it is placed in the centre of the cave (an old bunker from the war), which is located in the centre of the hillside, temporally its 'revelation' occurs at the middle of the film's duration, indicating a decisive turning point in the narrative. Once the cadaver comes into view, what is symbolically brought to light (reiterated literally as José strikes a match in the cave to illuminate his 'secret') is the body as a site of loss.

But this body is paradoxically lost and never quite lost enough. In other words, it constitutes an absence that cannot be mourned. Similarly, the body's presence, while conjuring a common history among the men, fails to solidify their homosocial bond. It is perhaps unsurprising that the two men in the cave scene should have opposing reactions to the unveiled secret of the dead soldier's presence. This opposition underscores the fundamental tension between entering into the pact of preservation in which the lost object is guarded and shared, and wilfully casting it into oblivion, visually rendered in the film as leaving it in the dark. Between, on the one hand, the desire to witness and communicate this loss, and, on the other hand, the desire to keep it buried and thus out of sight, we begin to arrive at a deeper reading of the film: it is not simply that the hunters perpetuate a cycle of violence, but that they do so because they are unable to articulate and mourn their mutual loss.

For many critics, *La caza* stands as the neo-realist cornerstone of not only Saura's oeuvre but also New Spanish Cinema. Whether we classify the film as neo-realist or not, its cinematic invention and visual articulation of repression is nothing shy of brilliant. In weaving together a multitude of surfaces and temporalities that create new ways of seeing what could not be said, *La caza* has distinguished itself as a classic that will engage viewers for decades to come.

Further reading

Roberto Cueto, Roberto, *La Caza: 42 Años Después*, Valencia, Ediciones de la Filmoteca, 2008.

Marvin D'Lugo, *The Films of Carlos Saura: The Practice of Seeing*, Princeton, NJ, Princeton University Press, 1991.

Marvin D'Lugo, '*La caza* [*The Hunt*]', in *Guide to the Cinema of Spain*, Westport, CT, Greenwood Press, 1997, pp. 43–4.

Marvin D'Lugo, 'Landscape in Spanish Cinema', in Graeme Harper and Jonathan Rayner (eds), *Cinema and Landscape*, Bristol, Intellect, 2010, pp. 117–30.

Sally Faulkner, 'Ageing and Coming of Age in *La caza* (*The Hunt*, 1965)', in A *Cinema of Contradiction: Spanish Film in the 1960s*, Edinburgh, Edinburgh University, 2006, pp. 145–74.

Marsha Kinder, 'Carlos Saura: The Political Development of Individual Consciousness', *Film Quarterly*, Vol. 32, No. 3, 1979, pp. 14–25.

Marsha Kinder, 'Sacrifice and Massacre: On the Cultural Specificity of Violence', in *Blood Cinema: The Reconstruction of National Identity in Spain*, Berkeley, University of California Press, 1993, pp. 136–96.

Katherine S. Kovacs, 'The Plain in Spain: Geography and National Identity in Spanish Cinema', *Quarterly Review of Film and Video*, Vol. 13, No. 4, 1991, pp. 17–46.

Elena Medina de la Viña, 'Una vuelta a nuestra memoria: *La caza*, de Carlos Saura', in *Quaderns de Cine*, Vol. 3, 2008, pp. 113–19.

Antonio Monegal, 'Images of War: Hunting the Metaphor', in Jenaro Taléns and Santos Zunzunegui (eds), *Hispanic Issues. Modes of Representation in Spanish Cinema*, Vol. 16, 1998, pp. 203–15.

Felipe Aparicio Nevado, '"La Caza Del Hombre," Recreación de un motive legendario, novelesco e histórico en *La Caza* de Carlos Saura', *Arbor*, Vol. 187, No. 748, 2011, pp. 269–77.

S. García Ochoa, '"Mirarse en la pantalla": El cine de Carlos Saura', *Hispanic Research Journal*, Vol. 10, No. 4, September 2009, pp. 357–69.

Margarita Pillado-Miller, 'La República va al doctor: Síntomas de la Guerra Civil en tres películas de Carlos Saura', *Arizona Journal of Hispanic Cultural Studies*, Vol. 1, 1997, pp. 129–40.

Augustín Sanchez Vidal, *El cine de Carlos Saura*, Zaragoza, Caja de Ahorros de la Inmaculada, 1988.

Carlos Saura and Angelino Fons, *La Caza: Guión*, Madrid, S.N., 1973.

Carlos Saura and Linda M. Willem, *Carlos Saura: Interviews*, Jackson, MS, University Press of Mississippi, 2003.

Ronald Schwartz, *Spanish Film Directors (1950–1985): 21 Profiles*, Metuchen, NJ, Scarecrow Press, 1986.

John David Slocum, *Violence and American Cinema*, New York, NY, Routledge, 2001.

Guy H. Wood, '*Thomas Hobbes y Carlos Saura: Una aproximación leviatánica a* La caza', *Film Historia*, Vol. 12, Nos. 1–2, 2002, internet resource, www.publicacions.ub.es/bibliotecadigital/cinema/filmhistoria/2002/lacazahtm.

Guy H. Wood, 'Plagios, plagas y descastados en *La caza* de Carlos Saura', *Letras Peninsulares*, Vol. 16, No. 1, 2003, pp. 163–79.

Guy H. Wood, *La caza de Carlos Saura: Un Estudio*, Zaragoza, Prensas Universitarias de Zaragoza, 2010.

Patricia M. Keller

Central do Brasil/Central Station (1998)

[Country: Brazil, France. Production Company: Arthur Cohn/MACT Productions/Videofilms/Riofilme/Canal Plus. Producers: Arthur Cohn, Martine De Clermont-Tonnerre. Director: Walter Salles. Screenwriters: João Emanuel Carneiro, Marcos Bernstein (based on an original idea by Walter Salles). Cinematographer: Walter Carvalho. Editors: Isabelle Rathery, Felipe Lacerda. Cast: Fernanda Montenegro (Dora), Vinícius De Oliveira (Josué), Soia Lira (Ana), Marília Pêra (Irene).]

Synopsis: Based around the search for a father by a child who has never met him, *Central do Brasil* tells a simple story, 'yet one that is full of nuances and resonances' (Ruffinelli 2000: 690). The film relates two main quests: one by a boy, Josué, searching in the heart of Brazil for a father he longs for; and the other by a cold-hearted, emotionally deprived woman, Dora, (unconsciously) searching for her capacity for compassion. A retired teacher, Dora scrapes a living by writing letters for illiterate customers passing through Rio de Janeiro's largest train station. One day, a young mother, Ana, asks her to write a letter to the estranged father of her nine-year-old son Josué. Immediately after leaving the station, Ana is hit by a bus and dies. In an unusual act of compassion, Dora, who often destroys the letters she gets paid to mail, overcomes the initial temptation to make a profit off the boy, now a homeless orphan, by trafficking him to a corrupt couple. Eventually, she decides to take Josué to his father, who lives in Brazil's distant North-East.

As Dora and Josué traverse the country, *Central do Brasil* presents the theme of the journey as a metaphor for personal and political metamorphosis and as a national allegory. The film can therefore be read as a story about the recuperation of self-identity as well as of Brazil's national identity. Given the striking similarity in Portuguese between the words *pai* (father) and *país* (country), the search for the boy's father becomes a search for Brazil's roots. According to Walter Salles, the odyssey Dora and Josué embark on is a quest for their personal identities and is emblematic of a nation, Brazil, that is suffering a profound identity crisis at the turn of the twenty-first century and trying to redefine its future and to find its origins. Writing in 1999, Salles states that the starting point of *Central do Brasil* was the culture of 'cynicism and indifference' of the last 30 years of Brazilian political and social history. The film foregrounds the possibility of redemption for the country and, therefore, the possibility of a different future for a more compassionate and humane Brazil:

> The story came to me in a block. and the characters were already emblematic of a larger situation. Dora represents old Brazil: that culture of indifference and cynicism we had in the 1970s and 1980s, which arose from the idea that we had to become industrialised and any means were acceptable to reach specific ends. The character of the boy is exactly the opposite: he represents the possibility of certain innocence, of refusing a deterministic future and granting yourself another destiny. But he also has to do with a collective desire in Brazil today for a change.
> (cited in James 1999:14)

It could be suggested that the characters' journey, in that it is a journey towards the *sertão* (the land 'at the end of the world', heart of the most impoverished part of Brazil), also stands for the need for Salles as a Brazilian filmmaker to search for, and reunite with, his cinematic precursor – the politically motivated *Cinema Nôvo*, the avant-garde movement that revolutionised Brazilian film aesthetics in the 1960s, and in which the *sertão* came to be a privileged cinematic location. Combining national history, myth and popular culture with images of the reality of scarcity and deprivation, and the suffering and brutality experienced by the poor and dispossessed living in the interior of Brazil at the time, *Cinema Nôvo* contributed to the forging of a narrative of national belonging and a sense of shared collective experience. The movement was silenced by the early 1970s by the authoritarian government of the time, because in depicting a side of Brazil that the elite liked to ignore and made *invisible*, it was critical of the military regime that had been ruling the country since 1964 (Hayward 2000: 55–7).

Central do Brasil starts at the largest train station in Rio de Janeiro. Here we meet Dora – a callous woman who shows no sign of ethical or moral principles and is insensitive to the concerns of others. Through her we encounter a socially marginalised Brazil that could not be more distant from the image created by national television and the media in general, which have played a key role in controlling and defining Brazil's recent past (Salles 1999: vi). The young and old illiterate customers at Dora's stall represent immigrants from the impoverished North-East of Brazil. As they try to keep in touch with their relatives and friends, they also strive to maintain contact with their past and their roots. According to Stephen M. Hart, Dora's job as a letter writer (as well as her former job as a school teacher) acts as a metaphor for 'the lettered city' which exploits the provinces of Brazil. When she cynically destroys her customers' letters, Dora denies those without a voice the chance to make themselves heard. In doing so, she stands for the literate urban white elite who exert material and symbolic power over the rest of Brazil through literacy and education (2004: 184). To reinforce the impression that Dora and the Brazil she represents are trapped in a situation from which escape is impossible, the first part of the film depicts a claustrophobic world with no horizons or skies in sight. While the narrative unfolds in the monochrome urban landscape, a sense of imprisonment is created by the use of closed lenses and by the settings: the station and its constantly moving crowds, indifferent to what is happening around them; the dull façades of the external locations, such as the building where Dora lives; and Dora's cramped apartment overlooking the train tracks (Salles 1999: vii–viii).

Among those whom Dora denies the chance to be heard is Josué. His desire to find the home and the father he has never seen speaks of his willingness to challenge a predetermined destiny as a *meniño de rua*, a homeless street kid, and to take matters into his own hands, so granting himself (and, in turn, Dora) another chance. Dora's chance encounter with the symbolic figure of innocence represented by Josué – 'the moral reservoir that can still generate compassion' (Xavier, cited in Nagib 2003: xxi) – triggers her redemption and sets the journey of self-(re)discovery in motion. When on the road, Dora's horizons open up, literally and metaphorically. The further behind she leaves the gloomy monochrome of the urban landscape, the more she is changed by the places she traverses and the people she meets on the journey. This is visually reinforced by the gradual introduction of new colours. According to Lisa Shaw, the colours which become increasingly visible on the journey stand for Dora's clearer view of the world, while the blue skies of the open road, contrasting the dreary shades of the station hallway, stand for the hope that the journey brings (2003: 170). The transition between the world Dora and Josué are leaving behind and the new one they are entering is emphasised, in Salles's words, 'by the ochre hues of the drought-stricken land of the North-East' (1999: viii) – the rural scenery of the *sertão*, the other side of modern and industrial Brazil.

As Ivana Bentes (2003) has observed, if the city is a claustrophobic place of alienation with no ethical or moral values, Salles' *sertão* is presented as a friendly place where people still care for each other: an idealised, innocent, pure and benevolent place that values friendship and memory and that, although neglected by official politics and hit by poverty, is peaceful. In this respect, the film seems to depart from the depiction of the *sertão* as a violent and desperate rural area that was at the heart of the early *Cinema Nôvo* in order to suggest the idea of an 'uncorrupted' Brazil, where human values, such as dignity and solidarity, can still be found.

Central do Brasil offers the romantic *sertão*, the idealised return to the 'origins'. Its aesthetic realism, with citations of *Cinema Nôvo*, offers a utopian wager like a fable. The *sertão* emerges as a projection of lost dignity and as the promised land of a reversed exodus from the seaside to the interior, a return of the failed and disinherited who were unable to survive in the big city. It is not a desired or politicised, but an emotional return led by circumstances. Thus the *sertão* becomes a land of social reconciliation and pacification (2003: 126).

It is the *sertão* that provides the dramatic backdrop for Dora's final transformation. According to Fernão Pessoa Ramos, Dora is eventually cleansed of her moral squalor and cynicism during the procession sequence. As she physically plunges into the crowd, she also immerses herself into the popular faith in a moment of profound spiritual and cultural communion with the locals. The ecstasy she experiences during the procession is the cathartic moment of her moral redemption (2003: 68). Having completed her spiritual journey, Dora awakes in the main square of Bom Jesus, with her head on Josué's lap. The boy strokes her hair while she (self-reassuringly) pats his knees. Their initially troubled relationship has evolved towards solidarity, companionship and love as they have moved towards the rural landscape. And it is Josué who protects Dora, in a poignant image that seems to imply that 'the deep scars left by the social ills of the recent past might somehow be survived and surmounted by a creative union of the old and the new Brazils' (McCarthy 1998: 72). The image powerfully encapsulates the final message of the film regarding Brazilian identity in contemporary times. *Central do Brasil* depicts a society going through a phase of transition. Eventually facing the devastating effects of a neo-liberal culture of modernisation at all costs that has led to cynicism and indifference, alienation, and a lack of communication and integration among its different social and ethnic groups, Brazil is a country that reveals a craving for a change, an urge to overcome the mistakes of its recent past and redeem itself. The film seems to suggest that salvation is possible, and that the road to redemption passes through a rediscovery and revaluation of the importance of memory and of the country's roots, in a process that involves acknowledgment of the importance of difference and individuality, identification, solidarity and reconciliation with the 'Other within'. Dramatising the nation's contemporary reality, fears, anxieties and aspirations, the film seems to encourage different and often antagonistic groups of people within Brazilian society to see themselves as a singular body sharing common roots. In doing so, *Central do Brasil* contributes to the formation of imaginary yet strong bonds which can help hold Brazilian people together as a community.

Further reading

Ivana Bentes, 'The *Sertão* and the *Favela* in Contemporary Brazilian films', in Lúcia Nagib (ed.), *The New Brazilian Cinema*, London and New York, I.B. Tauris, 2003, pp. 121–38.

Stephanie Dennison and Lisa Shaw, *Popular Cinema in Brazil: 1930–2001*, Manchester, Manchester University Press, 2004.

Stephen M. Hart, *A Companion to Latin American Film*, Woodbridge, Tamesis, 2004.

Susan Hayward, *Cinema Studies: The Key Concepts*, London & New York, Routledge, 2000.

Nick James, 'Heartbreak and Miracles', in *Sight and Sound*, Vol. 9, No. 3, 1999, pp. 13–15.

Todd McCarthy, 'Central Station', in *Variety*, Vol. 369, No. 13, 1998, pp. 70–2.

Lúcia Nagib, *Brazil on Screen: Cinema Novo, New Cinema and Utopia*, London & New York, I.B. Tauris, 2007.

Fernão Pessoa Ramos, 'Humility, Guilt and Narcissism Turned Inside Out in Brazil's Film Revival', in Lúcia Nagib (ed.), *The New Brazilian Cinema*, London & New York, I.B. Tauris, 2003, pp. 65–84.

Jorge Ruffinelli, 'Brazil 2001 and Walter Salles: Cinema for the Global Village?' in *Portuguese Literary & Cultural Studies*, Spring/Fall 2000, pp. 681–96.

Walter Salles, 'Introduction', in Emanuel Carneiro and Marcos Bernstein, *Central Station: The Screenplay*, London, Bloomsbury, 1999.

Deborah Shaw, *Contemporary Cinema of Latin America: Ten Key Films*, New York and London, Continuum, 2003.

Ismail Xavier, 'Brazilian Cinema in the 1990s: The Unexpected Encounter and the Resentful Character', in Lúcia Nagib (ed.), *The New Brazilian Cinema*, London and New York, I.B. Tauris, 2003, pp. 39–64.

Antonella Palmieri

Chinatown (1974)

[Country: USA. Production Company: Paramount Pictures. Director: Roman Polanski. Producer: Robert Evans. Screenwriters: Robert Towne, Roman Polanski (uncredited). Cinematographer: John A. Alonzo. Editor: Sam O. Steen. Music: Jerry Goldsmith. Cast: Jack Nicholson (Jake Gittes), Faye Dunaway (Evelyn Cross Mulwray), John Huston (Noah Cross).]

Synopsis: Los Angeles, 1937: Private Detective Jake Gittes specialises in marital work. Hired to discover whether Horace Mulwray – Chief Engineer at the City's Department of Water and Power – is having an affair, Gittes finds himself enmeshed in a struggle over the future of Los Angeles. Mulwray opposes to the construction of a new dam. The local businessmen who support the dam claim the project will protect the city from drought and desert. Actually, they plan to divert the water to the San Fernando Valley, which they intend to annex, after they create an artificial drought and buy up distressed farmland from struggling citrus farmers. Their leader is Noah Cross, Mulwray's former partner and the father of Mulwray's wife. Attempting to find a murderer, foil a conspiracy, and protect two women, Gittes forgets the motto he lived by when he walked a beat in Chinatown: do 'as little as possible'. Like the mythical hard-boiled detectives on which his character is modelled, Gittes gets beaten up several times and shot at while tangling with the police and a few memorable villains, including a nose-slicer played by Roman Polanski. At the film's conclusion we finally reach Chinatown, site of Gittes's most haunting failure.

Chinatown is about corruption and greed; it's about Manifest Destiny and the control of nature; it's about voyeurism; it's about the mythology Hollywood generates about its own past; it's about enduring structures of tragedy; it's about the movies. Borrowing from *Oedipus Rex* and film noir detective thrillers from the 1940s, Chinatown mythologises critical developments in the history of Los Angeles. It has become a master text for filmmakers who want to make period movies about corruption, Los Angeles, and real estate.

Despite continued resonance and many imitations, it is hard to imagine that *Chinatown* could have been made at any period in film history other than the moment when it was made. In the late 1960s and early 1970s American filmmakers were stretching the boundaries of what could be shown or implied on screen. When the rating system went into effect in 1968, the Motion Picture Association of America (MPAA) acknowledged that the Production Code, which had policed the visual and moral universe of Classical Hollywood since 1934, had ceased to be enforceable.[1] After 1968, American filmmakers were able to tell stories about official corruption and the failure of law enforcement. They were able to represent sex and violence on-screen more explicitly. They were able to deal with taboo topics like incest.

Although it is a period thriller, *Chinatown* reflects the political concerns of the early 1970s, notably the emerging environmental movement and the protest movements for Civil Rights and against the Vietnam War. The arrival of more flexible boundaries of film narrative coincided with a cultural moment when narratives of official corruption and official conspiracy had exceptional resonance. Released less than two months before President Richard Nixon resigned, *Chinatown* was interpreted by critics of the time as an environmental movie and a conspiracy movie. The Vietnam War and Watergate had spawned a degree of mistrust for government and corporate America in particular that would have been inconceivable for middle of the road Americans during the patriotic 1940s or the conformist 1950s. The assassinations of President John F. Kennedy in 1963, Civil Rights leader Martin Luther King, Jr. in 1968 and US Senator and Presidential candidate Robert F. Kennedy in 1968 were widely interpreted as conspiracies in which powerful forces in government and the military might have participated. As Americans became aware of how the FBI meddled in protest movements, and of how the CIA meddled in affairs of other states, conspiracy theorising went mainstream.

The early 1970s was also a major auteurist period in Hollywood cinema. The French film critics associated with film journal *Cahiers du cinéma* in the 1950s invented the auteur theory to explain how directors like John Ford, Howard Hawks and Alfred Hitchcock, working within the production-line system of the Hollywood studios, managed to make genre pictures that bore the authorial stamp of their director. The concept of the auteur has also come to be associated with directors who manage to exert vertical control over their films' productions, from script to final cut.

When several of the *Cahiers* critics, including Jean-Luc Godard and François Truffaut, became the filmmakers of the French *nouvelle vague* (New Wave), they made low-budget, independent films, often inspired by Hollywood genre work. Like other French critics before them, they noticed a particular trend in American cinema from the 1940s and 50s: black and white films, often low budget, with a visual style that borrowed from German Expressionism, and a universe of moral ambiguity that was at odds with the moral clarity associated with Hollywood, which the French had dubbed *film noir*. They joined other influential European directors of the early 1960s – including Italy's Michelangelo Antonioni and Frederico Fellini and Sweden's Ingmar Bergman – in making films that embodied a directorial vision. In the 1970s, their American apostles – including Martin Scorsese, Francis Ford Coppola and Woody Allen – found themselves able to do the same thing, even when making big budget, star-driven, studio-financed productions. Roman Polanski, a filmmaker born in Paris, raised and educated in Poland, who has produced films in many countries, found this environment hospitable during his brief Hollywood career.

Chinatown was released one year before the publication of Laura Mulvey's landmark essay 'Visual Pleasure and Narrative Cinema'. Mulvey argues that the pleasures available to spectators of Hollywood narrative film are founded on voyeurism. Few movies thematise voyuerism as explicitly as *Chinatown*. Detective Jake Gittes is always peeping in a window, taking illicit photographs, ignoring signs that say 'Private' or 'No Trespassing'. At these moments the camera is often right behind Gittes's shoulder, taking us where we are not supposed to go, showing us what we are not supposed to see. Nevertheless, *Chinatown* is about the failure of vision, about Jake's failure to make sense of what he sees. In this, as in many other ways, *Chinatown* makes plain its debts to that primal detective story: *Oedipus Rex*.

After *Chinatown's* credits have finished rolling, the first thing we see is a black and white photograph of a man and woman, outdoors, mostly clothed, having sex. As the camera pulls back, we see several other stills of the same couple, in a variety of sexual poses. The only sound is a series of groans that get louder with each photo. The photos are slightly out of focus and are shuffled quickly through someone's hands. As viewers, we construct a story about sex acts captured on film, without the participants' knowledge. The camera pulls back to reveal an office filmed in colour, a man who has hired a private detective to find out if his wife is having an affair and the detective whose photographs confirm the husband's suspicions. The groans are not those of man enjoying the voyeuristic pleasure derived from homemade pornography; they are the groans of a cuckolded husband. The office furnishings, the detective's suit, the photo of Franklin Roosevelt on the table by the liquor cabinet indicate that we, as viewers, have left 1974 behind and entered the 1930s.

The black and white photographs stand in for the movie that follows. We begin in a black and white world, a world familiar to viewers of classic detective thrillers. The photographs indicate that we have entered a different visual and moral universe. This movie will show us things the 1940s movies could not even suggest; *Chinatown* repeatedly alludes to *The Big Sleep*, Hawks's 1946 adaptation of Raymond Chandler's novel. The plot of *The Big Sleep* is famously incomprehensible, in part because the Production Code made it impossible to even hint at the portions of the novel that deal with homosexuality and a lending library of pornographic books.

Gittes resembles Phillip Marlowe, the detective in the Chandler novels and the movies based on them. Like Marlowe, Gittes insults people; tangles with the police; gets beaten up; traverses the Los Angeles basin in an automobile; moves up and down the social ladder. He even uncovers some version of the truth. Gittes is different in crucial ways, however. Marlowe has a highly developed code of ethics which includes a policy against doing marital work. Marital work, which largely means providing (or manufacturing) evidence of adultery, is Gittes's 'metier'. Gittes is not above manipulating clients (or sleeping with them). Mostly, Gittes thinks he's smarter than he is. He acts like a movie detective but he turns out to be a movie detective who can't stage manage his own case well enough to protect the innocent and bring the guilty to justice.

This period thriller has two parallel plots: one about public corruption, one about private corruption. The two plots intersect in the character of Noah Cross, played by John Huston, whose performance is one of the terrifying pleasures of *Chinatown*. From the 1940s through the 1980s, Huston was one of Hollywood's most respected directors. His directorial debut, the 1941 adaptation of Dashiell Hammett's *The Maltese Falcon*, is the archetypal noir detective thriller. The plot of *The Maltese Falcon*, like the plot of *Chinatown*, is set in motion when a woman asks a detective to follow a man. In both movies, the woman is playing a part.

The events of the public corruption plot are loosely based on the machinations undertaken by politicians and businessmen in the early twentieth century to secure the water that would make it possible for Los Angeles to expand, to supplant San Francisco as the major city on the West Coast, and to make wealthy capitalists even wealthier, particularly if they invested in Southern California real estate. Horace Mulwray is loosely modelled on William Mulholland, Los Angeles's legendary superintendent of water. Mulholland became superintendent in 1887 when the city's water was managed by a private company under a lease agreement that expired in 1902. His career as an employee in the city's department of Water and Power ended in 1929, after a dam collapsed, killing over 400 people. In between, he is credited with (or blamed for) inventing modern Los Angeles. He was instrumental in securing the rights to Owens River Water in 1905. He oversaw the construction of the aqueduct which opened in 1913 and carries water 233 miles, from the Owens Valley in the foothills of the Sierra Nevada, south to Los Angeles.

Chinatown is often credited with teaching non-Californians about the history and mythology of the Los Angeles water wars. Joan Didion refers to *Chinatown* when she writes about the 'The false droughts and artful title transactions that brought Northern California water south'.[2] Very early in her biography of her grandfather, Catherine Mulholland attempts to settle scores with 'uninformed' outsiders who see 'One fictional and melodramatic movie ... as a kind of documentary work on the history of Los Angeles' or 'a clever parable on the greed and ambition of an upstart town'.[3] Abraham Hoffman begins his history of the controversy over Owen Valley Water with a presumably apocryphal anecdote about an employee at the Los Angeles Department of Water and Power who claims that the movie is 'totally inaccurate' because 'There was never any incest involved'.[4]

Incest and rape are, of course, at the centre of the private corruption plot. The horror of these crimes is revealed late in the movie, when we learn that Horace's alleged girlfriend is actually his wife's sister/daughter. Cross's rape of his daughter, and his probable future rape of his daughter/granddaughter, reads as a metaphor for other kinds of rape, particularly the rape of the land. Read through the lens of Los Angeles mythology, incest functions as a metaphor for dangerously intimate relationships between business, government, and criminal activity, relationships that make it possible for real estate development to supersede all other priorities.

Chinatown is often cited as one of the first neo-noir films: one of a series or films that translates the visual style and moral universe of 1940s *noir* to a world filmed in colour; a world where the sex, violence, and systemic corruption implicit in earlier *noir* films can be represented explicitly. Since 1974, filmmakers have repeatedly mined Robert Towne's screenplay and Polanski's film for plot and visual imagery. The most flagrant imitation is the live action meets animation thriller comedy *Who Framed Roger Rabbit* (Robert Zemeckis, 1989). In Noah Cross's place, *Roger Rabbit* gives us a cartoon villain who melts like the witch in the *Wizard of Oz*. The film ends with cloying song and dance number performed by cartoon characters. More typical is *L.A. Confidential* (Curtis Hanson, 1997), which replaces moral ambiguity with self-righteousness. *L.A. Confidential* begins with crowd pleasing violence and ends with a villain shot in the back in the name of justice. These films fail to confront audiences with the terrifying inevitabilities of a Sophoclean tragedy, or the moral emptiness of a man like Noah Cross.

If *Chinatown* could not have been made a few years earlier, it is just as difficult to imagine it being made more than a few years later. *Star Wars* (George Lucas, 1977) and Ronald Reagan reignited the market for stories that made Americans feel good about themselves. Incest lost some of its power to shock. Movie studios became less inclined to grant directorial control to filmmakers that might depress audiences, saving the big bucks for films like the first *Star Wars* trilogy and the *Indiana Jones* trilogy. Hollywood may be still haunted by *Chinatown*, but finds it preferable to market happy endings.

Notes

1. Thomas Doherty, *Pre-Code Hollywood: Sex, Immorality, and Insurrection in American Cinema 1930–1934*, New York, Columbia University Press, 1999, pp. 343–5.
2. Joan Didion, 'Times Mirror Square', in *After Henry*, New York, Simon and Shuster, 1992, pp. 222–23.
3. Catherine Mulholland, *William Mulholland and the Rise of Los Angeles*, Berkeley, University of California Press, 2000, p. 4. Catherine Mulholland's biography, which treats Mulholland as a hero, makes a point of responding to the many aspersions cast on her grandfather's life work. It is, however, the most detailed account of his life.
4. Abraham Hoffman, *Vision or Villainy Origins of the Owens Valley-Los Angeles Water Controversy*, College Station, TX, Texas A&M University Press, 1981, p. xiii. About the history of the Los Angeles Aqueduct, see also William Kahrl, *Water and Power: The Conflict over Los Angeles' Water Supply in the Owens Valley*, Berkeley, University of California Press, 1982.

Further reading

John G. Cawelti, '*Chinatown* and Generic Transformation in Recent American Film', in Barry Keith Grant (ed.), *Film Genre Reader III*, Austin, University of Texas Press, 2003, pp. 227–45.

Paul Cronin (ed.), *Roman Polanski Interviews*, Jackson, MS, University Press of Mississippi, 2005.

Mike Davis, *Ecology of Fear: Los Angeles and the Imagination of Disaster*, New York, Metropolitan Books, 1998.

James Morrison, *Roman Polanski*, Urbana, University of Illinois Press, 2007.

Laura Mulvey, 'Visual Pleasure and Narrative Cinema', in Constance Penley (ed.), *Feminism and Film Theory*, New York, Routledge, 1988, pp. 57–68.

John Orr and Elzbieta Ostrowska (eds), *The Cinema of Roman Polanski: Dark Spaces of the World*, London, Wallflower Press, 2006.

Elliot Shapiro

Chocolat (1988)

[Country: France. Production Company: TF1 Films Production, La SEPT, WDR Cologne. Director: Claire Denis. Producers: Alain Belmondo and Gérard Grosner. Screenwriters: Claire Denis and Jean-Pol Fargeau. Cinematographer: Robert Alazraki. Original Music: Abdullah Ibrahim. Editor: Claudine Merlin. Cast: Isaach de Bankolé (Protée), Giulia Boschi (Aimée Dalens), François Cluzet (Marc Dalens), Cécile Ducasse (France Dalens, as girl), Mireille Perrier (France Dalens), Emmet Judson

Williamson (William J. 'Mungo' Park), Kenneth Cranham (Jonathan Boothby), Jean-Claude Adelin (Luc), Jacques Denis (Joseph Delpich).]

Synopsis: As France, a French woman in her thirties, returns to contemporary Cameroon, she encounters an African American father and his son who think she is a tourist. She gets a ride from them, and a long flashback begins focusing on the woman's childhood in colonial Cameroon in the 1950s. France's father is the chief of a colonial administrative subdivision in the Northern outpost Mindif, while her mother runs the house. Much of the film focuses on the mother's and the child's daily interactions with the family's main servant, Protée, as well as with the locals and other white officials. A small plane has to make an emergency landing nearby bringing a motely assembly of characters to the colonial administrator's house who cause tensions as they wait for the plane to be repaired and a runway to be built. At the end of the film, the plane leaves and the narrative returns to the contemporary frame, which ends with France being at the airport with a ticket in her hand.

Chocolat, Claire Denis' widely noted first feature film, which screened at the Cannes Film Festival, was certainly inspired by her own childhood in various African places where her father was a colonial administrator, but the film remains fictional, drawing on other sources as well, for instance Ferdinand Oyono's novel, *Une vie de boy* (1956, translated as *Houseboy*), as well as African American Vietnam veterans living in Senegal, who Denis had encountered during a trip and about whom she wanted to make a documentary. She returned to fiction after being reprimanded by a local for being an insensitive tourist (Strauss 1990: 31). A meditation on French colonialism and its aftermath, *Chocolat* evokes intimate and difficult relations in the colonial order by summoning feelings, textures, bodies in moments of contact and disconnection.

Colonial politics remain on the margins of the narrative but are nonetheless complexly evoked. In once scene, we see shots of graves with German names on them and in another an inscription on the house that says 'this house is the last house on earth' – both traces of a German colonial past. We encounter a British official, and a South Asian cook more familiar with the culinary habits of British colonisers. The family's neighbours are Norwegian missionaries. And we know that the locals are meeting at night at the local school house – a hint of independence to come even though at this point there is no confrontation. As the father, Marc Dalens, says at some point, 'One day we'll get kicked out of here'.

Denis very carefully articulates point(s) of view within the film. To begin with, she 'avoided any attempt to create an African perspective or point of view in the film' (Mayne 2005: 36). In the opening scene, we see a black father and son bathe in the surf, until a 180-degree pan reveals that what we see is to a significant extent filmed from the perspective of a young French woman, France, who sits on the edge of the beach. And yet, some of the shots, especially the close-ups of father and son, cannot be from her perspective, so that as spectators we both follow her experience and yet are also displaced from it. The same is true of the story within the flashback, which focuses significantly on how the young girl experiences the colonial social order. Channelling much of our experience through the child has important consequences: the child can be somewhat more transgressive, as she is allowed to touch things (making the film's world a very tactile one), goes places where adults cannot (we often see her standing on the edges of spaces occupied by black Africans, while at the same time she also watches the white settlers from a distance). Locating point of view in a child validates a peripheral perspective and makes her a 'go-between' (Breugnet 2004: 61).

The child watches and participates in intimate colonial dynamics of power, which the characters cannot escape. France's father, Marc, is a benevolent and often self-aware colonial administrator who nonetheless does not hesitate to use his power; often absent, he is relegated to the periphery of the film, his authority decentralised. His wife, Aimée, and her relationship with the black servant, Protée, is more central to the film. Indeed, Denis has said that she was particularly interested in wives of colonial administrators, who 'found themselves in incredibly violent situations' (Strauss 1990: 32, my translation). Simultaneously dependent and authoritarian, Aimée at some point desires Protée, yet this (stereotypical) narrative is not allowed to play out: Protée refuses. While more transgressive of rules, the child also enters these dynamics of power: on the one hand she is very close to Protée, for instance able to find the answer to his riddles, or eating the ant-covered bread he prepares for her; on the other hand she easily learns to order him around (as when she orders him to return home, or when she orders him to eat her soup). He is her mentor, yet she infantilises him.

The people from the plane, stranded at the Dalens' house, may seem more problematically colonialist, yet there is a continuum between them and the Dalenses (Mayne 2005: 39). For instance Luc may want to disturb the colonial order when he works with the black men, and yet he asserts it very forcefully when he aggresses Protée verbally and physically, or when he does not respect the latter's space by using his shower. Likewise, Aimée bans Protée from the house after he rebukes her sexual advance. And Delpich hides his African mistress while engaging in some of the film's most racist behaviour.

While many black characters (and many African actors) populate the scenes and have social spaces of their own, the camera, the film and thus the spectator have less access to them. We visit some of their gathering spaces, usually following France, yet remain at a distance. We see one female servant look into the house and, together with France, make fun of Jonathan Boothby. The best-known African character is certainly house servant Protée, played by French-Ivoirien actor Isaach de Bankolé, in a crucial but, to a significant degree, silent role. Nonetheless, he gets quite a lot of reaction shots. He has the local school teacher write a letter to his parents, though he tells France that it was for his fiancée. His humiliation at the intrusion of his private space is obvious and most visible when Aimée and France almost surprise him in the servants' shower. Like other Africans, we can occasionally hear him talk in a local, untranslated language. In the film's final scene, in the framing narrative, one of the three workers at the airport is played by de Bankolé, but the film refuses to establish a clearer connection between Protée in the 1950s and the airport worker in the 1980s. It is symptomatic that Protée speaks in riddles: like African culture more generally, he remains opaque, not entirely accessible to France or the spectator. In a crucial moment, the father tells the child what the horizon is: 'the closer you get to that line, the farther it moves'. It seems an appropriate metaphor for the colonialists' as well as the spectators' encounter with Africa and Africans.

And yet, the white characters remain somewhat opaque as well, above all because Denis does not adhere to a clear-cut cause-and-effect narrative driven by character psychology. The narration is elliptical and open-ended, refusing conclusions. The relationship between the framing narrative and the flashback remains open to interpretation: to be sure, in the end we see workers load African art onto planes, suggesting that some form of neocolonialism continues. But what the relationship between colonialism and neocolonialism is, is left open. And the adult France never actually talks about her childhood (Breugnet 2004: 53). In the end, she leaves, but we do not know why or where she goes. And we know remarkably little about Marc Dalens or even his wife Aimée. The film is structured around an interruption, a plane crash. Therefore we know even less about the other characters who enter and leave on the plane. What is Boothby's story? Or even the coffee planter's? Why does Luc act the way he does? Denis has explicitly said that she prefers not to have psychological explanations (Bonvoisin and Brault-Wiart 1989: 36). As a consequence, all characters remain a bit strange, putting the spectator in a complex, open-ended relationship to them.

Instead of a cause-and-effect-driven narrative based on character motivation, the film opts for what one critic has called a 'plastic narration' (David *et al.* 2008: 61ff). *Chocolat* is driven by dynamic, quasi-embodied and carefully composed images arranged in a rhythm. Mayne has noted the importance of detail – the 'seemingly insignificant detail' – in Denis's films, and yet 'while every detail matters, it isn't always clear how' (Mayne 2005: 2). How should we in the end understand the ants on the girl's bread, the inscription on the house, the men who pee at the roadside, the chicken foot, the song Marc Dalens sings? These details evoke and provoke a feeling; they do not explain.

And these visual details are often haptical. Denis, above all, films bodies; bodies in long shots that seem frighteningly tiny in the harsh, hilly and arid landscape, bodies in close up, as in the first scene, when we see sand stick to the arm of a black boy, and sand stick to the foot of the white woman. Here, the tactility that the figure of the child introduces becomes important. The ants and the soup France eats. The body parts she touches and names (and which the boy will touch and name again). The blood Protée smears on her wrist. And, most importantly, the hand she burns when she touches a hot pipe. The tactile relationship she has with the African colony can be painful. It erases the lifelines on her hand, rendering her opaque, giving her 'no past, no future'. The film works somewhat similarly on the spectator: in the wake of a fragmented narrative with long pauses, the strange plasticity of the image imposes itself on us. Our experience of the film becomes an encounter with 'the coherent strangeness of a carnal cinema' (David *et al.* 2008: 7, my translation).

Starting with *Chocolat*, her first feature film, Claire Denis has carved herself out a space as film *auteur* with a distinct style. She herself has pointed out how Antonioni's *L'Avventura*, when she saw it as a teenager, 'plunged her into an extraordinary state of mind' (Bonvoisin and Brault-Wiart 1989: 34, my translation). Comparisons with German director Wim Wenders, for whom she worked as an assistant, could easily be made. But *Chocolat* can be put in other contexts. Stylistically, it can also be put in dialogue with films that want to touch the spectator physically (see Barker 2009). And, of course, the film is part of a larger group of films about the colonial legacy; it stands in critical relation to so-called 'heritage films' if only because it refuses any simple nostalgia (Beugnet 2004: 49–52). In doing so, it becomes part of a spate of films made by female directors that take a critical view of French colonial history (see Strauss 1990). Such a process is both laudable and not unproblematic, as one anecdote from the film's production indicates: The house in which much of the story was filmed had to be built by local villagers, into whose hands it passed after the filming, and who were thus left with a house, but also with a reconstructed colonial architecture (Bonvoisin 1989: 40).

Further reading

Jennifer M. Barker, *The Tactile Eye: Touch and the Cinematic Experience,* Berkeley, CA, University of California Press, 2009.

Martine Beugnet, *Claire Denis,* Manchester, Manchester University Press, 2004.

Samra Bonvoisin and Mary-Anne Brault-Wiart (eds), 'Claire Denis', in *L'aventure du premier film,* Paris, Editions Bernard Barrault, 1989, pp. 33–45.

Sébastien David, Rémi Fontanel, Fabrice Fuentes and Paul Givert, *Le cinéma de Claire Denis, ou l'énigme des sens,* Lyon, Aléas, 2008.

Judith Mayne, *Claire Denis,* Urbana, IL, University of Illinois Press, 2005.

Frédéric Strauss, 'Féminin colonial', *Cahiers du cinéma,* No. 434, July–August 1990, pp. 28–33.

Sabine Haenni

Chuncan/Spring Silkworms (1933)

[Country: China. Production Company: Mingxing (Star) Film Company. Director: Cheng Bugao. Screen adaptation: Xia Yan (pseud. Cai Shusheng). Original story: Mao Dun. Cinematographer: Wang Shizhen. Music: He Zhaohuang and He Zhaozhang. Cast: Xiao Ying (Old Tongbao), Yan Yuexian (A Si's Wife), Gong Jianong (A Si), Ai Xia (Lotus), Zheng Xiaoqiu (Duoduo), Gao Jingping (Sixth Treasure), Zhang Minyu (Little Bao).]

Synopsis: *Spring Silkworms* depicts the plight of Chinese silkworm farmers against the backdrop of imperialist incursion and a weakened rural economy. Living in a village in Zhejiang province, Old Tongbao and his family go into debt acquiring a large quantity of mulberry leaves to ensure the healthy growth of their silkworms. When they finally succeed in having the best cocoon harvest in the village, cheap Japanese synthetic silks flood the Chinese market, drastically driving down silk prices and throwing Old Tongbao's family further into debt.

In a 1933 symposium on the silent film adaptation of Mao Dun's celebrated short story 'Spring Silkworms' (*Chuncan*, 1932), a group of filmmakers, scriptwriters, dramatists and film critics associated with the 1930s leftist movement in Shanghai gathered to review the film and discuss its contributions to Chinese cinema. The director Cheng Bugao (1898–1966) used the term 'literature-film' (*wenxue dianying*) to refer to his work, and evoked the considerable responsibility of promoting the New Art Film (*Xin wenyi dianying*) in relation to New Literature (*Xin wenxue*).[1] The relation between literature and film is further foregrounded by Xia Yan (1900–1995), whose script for the adaptation initiates the practice of the 'cinematic literary script' (*dianying wenxue juben*), making *Spring Silkworms* (henceforth *Silkworms*) the first Chinese film to be adapted from a work of fiction and shot according to a complete shooting script. Although this seminal role is often alluded to in subsequent Chinese film history, the absence of close critical engagement with the film after the 1933 symposium remains conspicuous and problematic for understanding its formal contributions. In fact, a deeper examination of the initial reception reveals much more ambivalent attitudes toward *Silkworms*, despite the celebratory language that nominally proclaimed a victory for leftist participation in Shanghai's filmmaking industry.

Central to the debates were questions of medium specificity (literature vs. film), performance and the dramatic text, as well as the relation between the film's perceived realism and its appropriation of the 'educational' (*jiaoyu dianying*) and 'documentary' (*jilu dianying*) film genres. The ideological and rhetorical unity of cinematic 'achievement' notwithstanding, the symposium participants' detailed comments on the film are overwhelmingly critical and express markedly divergent evaluations of the successes and failures of *Silkworms*. This lack of consensus among the *Silkworms*' core group of supporters offers an important historical context for our contemporary evaluation of the film, and raises a number of interesting questions: Why did the symposium participants react so differently to the film when they were not only in agreement about the ideological significance of the original literary work, but also in their shared political agenda of transforming the film medium from mere entertainment to one that can 'educate' and 'move' the masses? Why, if all of them acknowledged the adaptation as having faithfully reproduced the powerful realism of the original short story, did they complain of its 'dull' quality and lack of emotional affect? How did a film that so unequivocally carried out its representational and didactic aims, in accordance with the aspirations of the left-wing film critics and practitioners, come under scrutiny in what ultimately amounted to a narrative of disappointment and failure?[2]

This essay will engage with the above questions by investigating *Silkworms*' treatment of the very issues that divided the symposium group – namely, the negotiation between different media, assumptions of a ubiquitous dramatic text that transcends and therefore must be captured by these mediums, and the representational logic that informs the film's documentary and pedagogical aspirations. In taking this approach, the intertitles and other verbal representations in the film will be taken as a site where issues of medium specificity, dramatic performance and representational modes converge and elucidate the sources of the reviewers' discontent. Despite being largely overlooked (the intertitles were never directly mentioned by any of the symposium participants, and only twice, indirectly, for their use of animation [*katong*]), their elaborate design and unique presentation not only destabilise the textual/visual dichotomy attributed to the mediums of fiction and film, but work to supply orality to the latter, which, in and of itself, is *silent*. In sum, the intertitles enact processes of remediation and intermediality between literature and film, in which both mediums become more than themselves and, as a result, unsettled the coherence of the leftist cinematic vision.

The 1933 silent film was produced by the Shanghai-based Star (*Mingxing*) Film Company, the earliest indigenous Chinese film company established in 1920. It was also the first film company to start collaborating with Shanghai-based leftist intellectuals in 1932, the year of the first Japanese bombing of Shanghai. The symposium on *Silkworms* took place some time between a pre-release screening, held at National Grand Theatre (*Zhongyang daxiyuan*) on 1 September, and the official opening night at Starlight Theatre (*Xinguang daxiyuan*) on 8 October. Aside from Xia Yan and Cheng Bugao, also in attendance were eight other active film writers and practitioners, such as Zheng Boqi (1895–1979), Yang Hansheng (1902–1993), A Ying (1900–1977), and others. The discussion was transcribed and published on 8 October, in a supplement to the *Morning Post* (*Chen Bao*) called 'Daily Film' (*Meiri dianying*), which was edited by Yao Sufeng (1906–1974), another participant in the symposium. The publication of the symposium transcript on the same day as the film release was obviously strategic, in terms of both advertising the film and dictating its popular reception. Although the publicity proved effective – *Silkworms* opened to a full house on 8 October, the film closed after just five days in the theatres, suggesting its failure at the box office.

During the symposium discussion, the terms 'literature-film' (*wenxue dianying*), 'educational film' (*jiaoyu dianying*), and 'documentary film' (*jilu dianying*) were evoked repeatedly in analysing *Silkworms*' merits and demerits. A brief introduction appended to the published transcript applauds the transformative impact of the film, specifically in its repudiation of theatrical (*xiju de*) exaggeration and its use of realism, consistent with Mao Dun's original work.[3] However, the comments in the transcript are far less congratulatory. In fact, Xia Yan's preservation of the elaborate procedures of silk farming in the film script, and the film's faithful reproduction of these procedures on screen became a point of critique for many symposium participants. Yang Hansheng, a politically active leftist filmmaker and author, takes issue with the heavy use of technical language for silkworm farming in the intertitles and the lengthiness of their corresponding shots. In response, Xia Yan, using the pseudonym Cai Shusheng to avoid censorship by the Kuomintang government, defends this approach by referring to Mao Dun's use of technical language and emphasising the need to employ 'documentary' filming methods in order to 'educate' the audience and retain the authenticity found in the original text. In this exchange, Xia implies that the social reality of a village industry in crisis necessitated the lengthy documentation of the labour of silkworm farming. By attributing this need to the original short story, Xia does not simply justify the use of technical language but, more importantly, establishes a link between the documentary mode of filmmaking and the discourse of national struggle. A comparison of the original short story and the script reveals that the marriage between national discourse and the pedagogical function of the documentary mode was the scriptwriter's own implement, officiated by the prelude he created for the film.

The prelude in the script sets up an opening scene in an elementary school classroom where instruction on the history of China's silk industry is taking place. A series of intertitles mimicking textbook lessons describe the recent decline of the domestic silk industry under imperialist economic incursion. The tranquil classroom quickly dissolves into a montage of newspaper headlines, economic charts, mounds of man-made silk on the docks of Huangpu River, rioting workers, foreign merchant- and warships, and other such visual cues for a silk industry in crisis. The overtly pedagogical tone of Xia's prelude is unmistakable. This pedagogy is not only occasioned by the socio-economic crisis of the Chinese silk industry, but also by the considerable distance between the environments of urban commerce (as depicted in the montage in the prelude) and rural production (the main subject matter of the original text and the film). In an article on *Silkworms* that challenges the viability of visually oriented arguments prevalent in adaptation studies, Yiman Wang argues that 'By mapping *cinema spectatorship* (where the audience is interpellated by a filmmaker's imagery and story) onto *classroom experience* (where the students are educated on China's declining silk industry by a teacher), the prelude converts the cinema into a social classroom and the elementary school students into prototypical film viewers' (original emphasis).[4] Wang's observation on cinema spectatorship is important here; what I would add to her insight is that the 'social classroom' in this instance is Shanghai, and the 'prototypical film viewers' the city's urban moviegoers. This specific demographic is crucial for understanding Xia's evocation of the documentary and educational mode because the basis for the film's instructional address is an ethnographic account of the rural silkworm farming industry, which is unfamiliar to an urban audience.

Interestingly, the prelude sequence was almost completely removed from the film after the pre-release screening; all that remains in the final-cut version on opening night was the blackboard motif used in dialogic intertitles and the shot of Mao Dun's print edition of 'Spring Silkworms', which opens the film. This is likely due to complaints by the symposium participants, who considered the prelude too lengthy. Thus, any evidence of Xia Yan's overtly pedagogical framing and ethnographic rationale was effectively removed from the final film-text.

An obvious question emerges: if the group's primary critique of the film was focused on its over-fidelity to the short story – a charge which Xia Yan concedes – then why delete the only portion of the film that marks a significant departure from the original text? In one of his responses to the other participants, Xia Yan admits, 'Bugao was too faithful to my script, and I was too faithful to the novel. As a result, this film might be too "literary" [*tai wenxue*]. Furthermore, to those who are not particularly interested in literature, I'm afraid it is of less educational value'.[5] This is only a partial concession, since the subtext of Xia's comment implies that the merits of his adaptation is understandably lost among an audience with little interest in literature – namely, leftist literature – referring, no doubt, to an uncritical, popular mass that prefers entertainment films. Thus, the practical conflict between a pedagogical cultural form that still holds mass popular appeal is left unresolved.

The issue of medium specificity also deeply troubled the reviewers of *Silkworms*. Zheng Boqi, assuming the pseudonym Xi Naifang (a transliteration of 'cinephile'), argues that the film rendition of the literary work should emphasise performance and not adhere to the original because 'every type of art has its own specific properties'.[6] For Zheng, performance is one of the essential properties specific to the film medium, and thus requires a departure from literature in the process of cinematic adaptation. Shen Xiling (1904–1940), another leftist filmmaker, echoes Zheng's iterations about performance and dramatic effect. Shen laments a lack of 'dramatic elements' (*ju de chengfen*) and suggests that the film's sense of dullness results from its misplacement of climactic tension onto the bodies of silkworms rather than the human actors.

These reactions are revealing in terms of the respondents' belief in the fundamental difference between the mediums of literature and film, and can be explained by much of the camera work used in the film. As far as Cheng Bugao and Xia Yan's faithful adaption goes, we have seen how the 'sketch'-like quality of Mao Dun's short story translated to the filmmakers' use of the documentary mode. This required painstakingly detailed filming of silkworm cultivation, in which the actors enact intricate procedures in front of the camera. Many of these sequences were captured with medium to medium-long shots, and leave little room for close-ups of the actors' expressions and body language. Instead, nearly the entire middle portion of the film documents silkworm cultivation, only depicting obstructed human bodies and the hands that labour over the silkworms. It is precisely because of these filming and editing choices, motivated by the filmmakers' aim to faithfully reproduce and represent the harsh conditions and laborious processes of growing silkworms in the documentary mode, that dramatic *human* performance was relegated to the back seat.

However, whereas the human actors do not come across as the centrepieces of dramatic performance in *Silkworms*, the intertitles of the film, through their elaborate design, layout, and even animation, consistently contribute to the dramatisation of the plot. The meticulous presentation of the intertitles delegates them into two categories: dialogic intertitles that represent the characters' speech, and descriptive intertitles that function as narration. The former use a classroom blackboard motif to present the spoken lines. The latter, often used to signal or set up scene changes, use patterned geometrical shapes in the background, which are reminiscent of avant-garde woodblock prints popularised and promoted by leftist intellectuals during the same era. All the intertitles feature enlarged key terms, skewed or arched textual alignment, and other forms of visual embellishment. These typographical strategies, in both the descriptive and dialogic intertitles in the film, constitute a kind of visual theatricality that enhances the emotive qualities of the characters and the storyline.

The film goes further than stylising textual/visual stills, and uses animation in many intertitles to enliven the text themselves. For instance, a dialogue between the main character Old Tongbao and his daughter-in-law, A Si's Wife, is rendered as follows in the film script:

> [INTERTITLE]
> A Si's Wife: 'If we hurry to buy mulberry leaves now, what do we do if, like last year, we end up with too much?'
>
> [CLOSE-UP]
> Old Tongbao heard the words 'last year' and became stern in the face.[7]

Here, the intertitle containing A Si's Wife's speech is arranged in five lines, of uneven indentation. After several seconds of display, the words 'last year', which sit in the second line, suddenly separate from the rest of the text and advance forward, while the rest recedes into the background. The words 'last year', now taking up two-thirds of the screen, remain on display for a few more seconds before the camera cuts to a close-up of Old Tongbao's angry face.

The same device is used again in a later scene, demonstrating a process in which the animated characters on screen 'act out' the description of Old Tongbao hearing the words 'last year' in the original short story as well as the film script.

This process is best explained by Jay Bolter and Richard Grusin's theory of remediation, which elucidates the twin logic of transparency and hypermediacy, whereby a new medium borrows from, and refashions older media.[8] In the animated intertitles of *Silkworms*, the process of remediation of a literary text by the silent film medium undermines the prioritisation of *human* performance articulated by Zheng Boqi and Shen Xiling. By visually representing the verbal description in the script, the text of the intertitles is made to *perform* for the audience in capturing the instantaneous moment of Old Tongbao's change of an emotional state. On the other hand, the silent film achieves the effects of orality and aurality – the selective enlargement of text as representation of an emphatic verbal statement and speech, the representation of an verbal description of the act of listening – that exceed the limitations of its own, *silent*, medium.

Thus, the intertitles of *Spring Silkworms* succeed in collapsing the boundary between its reviewers' perceived medium-specific properties, and function as a site in which issues of fidelity of adaptation, dramatic performance, and the representational mode of ethnographic documentation confront each other and reconcile through the intermediality of literature and film. Unfortunately, the potential of further experimentation with intertitles would soon be superseded by the proliferation of sound films, already underway in 1933. Nevertheless, through the framework of remediation and intermediality, the creative manipulation of intertitles by the filmmakers of *Silkworms* offer productive analytical grounds for revisiting the discursive incongruities that troubled early film adaptations in China, as well as the 1930s leftist project of promoting cultural forms capable of reconciling the intellectuals' aspirations for artistic reform with their political agenda.

Notes

1. Since the compound *wenyi* means literature and the arts, the Chinese term is also sometimes translated as 'New Literary Film'. Here, I have opted for 'New Arts Film' to retain the broader scope of the movement.
2. For more detail on this narrative of failure, see the discussion of *Silkworms*' reception in Laikwan Pang, *Building a New China in Cinema: the Chinese Left-wing Cinema Movement, 1932–1937*, Lanham, Rowman & Littlefield Publishers, 2002, pp. 46–47.
3. Chen Bo and Yi Ming (eds), *Sanshi niandai zhongguo dianying pinglun wenxuan* [A select compendium of film comments in the 1930s],

Beijing, Zhongguo dianying chubanshe, 1993, p. 250.
4. Yiman Wang, 'From Word to Word-Image: Film Translation of a "Sketchy" Chinese Short Story: Spring Silkworm', *Literature/Film Quarterly*, Vol. 33, No. 1, 2005, pp. 41–50.
5. Chen, *A Select Compendium*, p. 255.
6. Ibid., pp. 251–252.
7. See the film script for 'Spring Silkworms' in Xia Yan, *Xia Yan quanji* [The complete works of Xia Yan], Hangzhou: Zhejiang wenji chubanshe, 2005, Vol. 4, p. 27.
8. Jay David Bolter and Richard Grusin, *Remediation, Understanding New Media*, Cambridge, MA, MIT Press, 1999.

Further reading

Chris Berry, 'Chinese Left Cinema in the 1930s: Poisonous Weeds or National Treasures', *Jump Cut*, Vol. 34, 1989, pp. 87–94.

Freda Chapple and Chiel Kattenbelt (eds), *Intermediality in Theatre and Performance*, Amsterdam & New York, Rodopi, 2006.

Jubin Hu, *Projecting a Nation: Chinese National Cinema Before 1949*, Hong Kong, Hong Kong University Press, 2003.

Paul G. Pickowicz, 'Melodramatic Representation and the "May Fourth" Tradition of Chinese Cinema', in Ellen Widmer and David Der-wei Wang (eds), *From May Fourth to June Fourth: Fiction and Film in Twentieth Century China*, Cambridge, MA, Harvard University Press, 1993, pp. 295–326 and 425–8.

Vivien Shen, *The Origins of Left-wing Cinema in China, 1932–37*, New York, Routledge, 2005.

Zhang Zhen, *An Amorous History of the Silver Screen: Shanghai Cinema, 1896–1937*, Chicago, University of Chicago Press, 2005, pp. 244–97.

Myra Sun

Cidade de Deus/City of God (2002)

[Country: Brazil, France. Production Company: O2 Filmes, Globo Filmes, Wild Bunch. Directors: Fernando Meirelles and Katia Lund. Screenwriter: Braulio Mantovani. Cinematographer: Cesar Charlone. Music: Ed Cortes and Antonio Pinto. Cast: Alexandre Rodrigues (Buscape/Rocket), Leandro Firmino (Zé Pequeno/Li'l Zé), Phellipe Haagensen (Bene/Benny), Douglas Silva (Dadinho/Li'l Dice), Jonathan Haagensen (Cabeleira/Shaggy), Matheus Nachtergaele (Sandro Cenoura/Carrot), Seu Jorge (Mane Galinha/Knockout Ned).]

Synopsis: Rocket's older brother, Goose, has been part of a gang who have robbed Robin Hood style, but he has been killed by the younger, much more brutal, Li'l Dice. Li'l Dice becomes Li'l Zé, and creates a drugs empire with his childhood friend, Benny. Meanwhile, Rocket becomes part of a marijuana-smoking, hippy group and takes up photography. Benny decides he wants to leave the criminal life but at a party to mark the end of his life as a gangster is killed by someone aiming to 'take out' Li'l Zé. A turf war erupts between Li'l Zé and his rival in the drugs trade, Carrot. Finally, Li'l Zé is killed by another younger gang in revenge for his having earlier shot one of their gang, and Rocket snaps the picture of his dead body that will secure him a job at the city newspaper.

In *Drugs and Democracy in Rio de Janeiro: Trafficking, Social Networks and Public Security*, Enrique Desmond Arias says:

> Recently drug traffickers based in Rio de Janeiro's *favelas* have attacked government buildings, bombed buses, and successfully ordered widespread business closings. Over the past decade, murder rates have averaged

> 50 per 100,000, in line with the most violent U.S. cities, and overall rates may actually be even higher as a result of increasing rates of disappearances. In poor districts murder rates can exceed 150 per 100,000 inhabitants.
>
> (Arias 2006: 2)

In the *favelas*, or slums, of Rio de Janeiro, shanty towns built on the steep hillsides overlooking the city, well over a million people pursue a harsh existence.[1] Not far away, the city's wealthy middle class live in gated apartment blocks guarded by a private army of security officers in separate areas of the city such as Copacabana, Ipanema or Leblon; social conditions in these districts are at the opposite end of the spectrum of material wealth from those found in the *favelas*. In this city that is host to such extremes of wealth and poverty, the police battle to maintain the status quo by corralling and controlling the underprivileged masses living in the slums.[2] *City of God* exists as a film in some sort of complex relationship to this socio-political context. As an audience we watch a fictional narrative but we know something like what we are seeing actually exists.

Politics and the streets have long been intertwined in Rio. During the 1960s political prisoners politicised those who were in gaol alongside them so effectively that the crime organisation, Comando Vermelho, began to proclaim their enemy to be the government, big business and the middle class. In the same decade and from an only slightly different ideological perspective Roman Catholic priests began to criticise the government's failure to help the poor. Thus, the struggle between left-wing socialist/communist groups and right-wing conservative forces has a considerable history. In 1961, the president, Janio da Silva Quadros, resigned saying his attempts at reforms had been blocked by 'forces of reaction'. In 1964, the new president, Joao Bechoir Marques Goulart, attempted to nationalise the country's oil refineries and limit profits going abroad but was deposed by the army. Military rule lasted until 1985 with opposition political parties being suppressed, civil liberties curbed and strict media censorship enforced. Throughout the 1980s Brazil suffered chronic inflation while the country's foreign debt topped that of any other developing nation. During this same period the birth rate remained high and there was an economic migration of people into the city from rural areas; and these trends continued into the 1990s.

In *City of God* something that we recognise as approaching the 'real' in relation to these and other socio-political factors is constructed through the use of film techniques, narrative strategies and genre conventions. We see something we describe as 'realism' as being present in the film. And yet, in truth the only 'reality' we have before us is something constructed for us by the producers of the film. This creation of the medium is not the result of innocent aesthetic techniques but is, instead connected to a network of issues of power and knowledge. How can we read the messages and meanings of the film in relation to these dynamic, evolving and complex Brazilian contexts that are paralleled by and intimately connected to a similar series of global contexts?[3] In engaging with the framing of the world on offer in *City of God* we are engaging with reality. In offering particular representational frameworks the film is working to fix, or give value to, or stabilise the value of, 'reality' (or, a version of the world).

Our narrator, Rocket, is a young man who is exceptional in that he manages to escape the slums. As narrator he is also an observer of other people's stories, a character with a privileged position from which he is able to watch domestic, familial, communal, social and even national (with international correlative) narratives unfold. Although the film may be Rocket's story he is continually peripheral to, or on the edge of, a series of further narratives taking place around him. This status as an observer fits well with his chosen profession of photographer and further adds to our sense of an unfolding social documentation taking place.[4] Before his eyes (and therefore, before ours) human relationships involving short, energetic lives and brutal deaths are played out against an essentially unchanging social backdrop of extreme poverty. And yet, although the deprivation of the social environment remains constant, the nature of the slums is seen to change: the gang culture becomes increasingly violent as we move forward from the 1960s, the weaponry increasingly high-powered, the drugs more potent and the gang members younger. By the end of the film, the young children who are becoming gang members are not yet into their teens but are already sure of one rule, the essential thing is to kill in order to be respected. The cycle of one death (or set of deaths) leading to another is inescapable. Knockout Ned starts out from the position that motivates the classic Hollywood western hero, revenge, and he puts forward a moral outlook that centres on the naïve notion that nobody who is innocent should be killed; but, of course, he quickly becomes enmeshed in the unstoppable cycle of killings. Shaggy and later Benny both want to leave the *favelas* and escape to the idyll of a little farm in the countryside, but it is impossible. Even for the most cold-blooded of killers like Ze, there is no escaping an early violent death.

Perhaps the central relationship in the film is that between Benny and Ze. It is important to ask how these two characters are shown as being different from each other and what reasons we are given for the differences between them. We seem to know little or nothing about their backgrounds, their families, their homes, their relationships with relatives. Benny has become the leader of a brutal, drug-dealing gang controlling territory within the neighbourhood known as the Cidade de Deus while remaining a chilled, 'good' guy, while by contrast Ze has since his youngest years been a psychotic killer. (The implication during Benny's death scene is, perhaps, that this is the only person Ze has ever loved.) Both characters, it seems, are what they are because of their individual psychological make-up; essentially they have been born this way. In *City of God* the only explanation we have for Ze's nature is that he is too ugly to get a girlfriend, while there is no explanation at all as to how Benny has emerged from the cycle of violence as a free-wheeling hippy. Despite the fact that there are a series of scenes that focus either on issues of deprivation and poverty in the slums, or on the middle-class experience of life (with this second set of scenes serving only to highlight the contrast with life in the slums), no wider economic factors are addressed. The focus remains firmly on the individual and therefore on an ideology of individualism; and this is the case despite the fact that the implication of these scenes is that it is only in a collective response to these conditions that change can be achieved.

City of God shows the way in which it was only from the 1980s that cocaine came to replace marijuana as the dominant drug packaged and peddled by gangs in the slums (up until that point, cocaine had been seen as a rich person's drug of choice). It suggests that the drugs trade operates like any other business with the 'bosses' controlling certain franchises and employing managers, assembly-line workers and delivery boys. The film also exposes the involvement of arms dealers and the corruption of the police. But ultimately the film's political and social analysis of the situation is really quite thin. If the attempt is to show how each individual is a product of the social environment in which they have to live, it ultimately fails because Ze simply is an embodiment of evil.[5]

Of course, it is also true that in the process of deciding what we see as the meanings being created in any film we may be constrained by the historical moment and the culture within which we are living our lives or, indeed, by our own ideology. To see *City of God* as ultimately failing to offer a firmly grounded socio-political analysis might say as much about someone's personal ideology as it does about the film itself. As Stephen Crofts (amongst many others) has suggested, 'Not only the author and the text but, just as importantly, the reading must be seen as historically and culturally shaped' (1988: 322).[6]

Notes

1. Writing shortly after this film was made, Janice E. Perlman said: 'There are at least 752 *favelas* in Rio de Janeiro today with approximately 1.65 million inhabitants' (2005: 9). These communities are so long and well established that Perlman says: 'The only remaining distinction between *favelas* (often called *morros* or hills) and the rest of the city (commonly referred to as the *asfalto* or pavement) is the deeply rooted stigma that still attaches to them' (ibid: 10).
2. See *News from a Personal War* (Lund and Salles, *City of God* DVD extras).
3. See Barbara Mennel, *Cities and Cinema*, London and New York, Routledge, 2008, pp. 211–16.

4. The concept of 'shooting' with a camera contrasts with, and obviously demonstrates his chosen avoidance of, the more normal form of shooting favoured by his peers.
5. The filmmakers seem to suggest that as one generation has replaced another since the 1960s the political dimension to crime in the *favelas* (if it ever really existed) has now most certainly been lost so that all that is left is a 'dog-eat-dog' world. This would be in line with the reading of the situation suggested by a more recent film, *Elite Squad* (Jose Padiha, 2007). This has been described as a right-wing film that celebrates police violence, although the director, Jose Padiha, has suggested what it really shows is that the actions of individuals are determined by the system in which they find themselves.
6. See Stephen Crofts, 'Authorship and Hollywood' in John Hill and Pamela Church Gibson, *The Oxford Guide to Film Studies*, Oxford, Oxford University Press, 1988, pp. 310–26.

Further reading

Enrique Desmond Arias, *Drugs and Democracy in Rio de Janeiro: Trafficking, Social Networks and Public Security*, Chapel Hill, NC, University of North Carolina Press, 2006.

Enrique Desmond Arias and Corinne Davis Rodrigues, 'The Myth of Personal Security: Criminal Gangs, Dispute Resolution, and Identity in Rio de Janeiro's Favelas', *Latin American Politics and Society*, Volume 48, Issue 4, 2008, pp. 53–81.

Janice E. Perlman, 'The Myth of Marginality Revisited: The Case of Favelas in Rio de Janeiro, 1969–2003' in Lisa M. Hanley, Blair A. Ruble and Joseph S. Tulchin (eds), *Becoming Global and the New Poverty of Cities*, Washington DC, Woodrow Wilson International Center for Scholars, 2005, pp. 9–54.

John White

Cinema Paradiso (1989)

[Country: Italy. Production Company: Cristaldifilm. Director: Giuseppe Tornatore. Producer: Franco Cristaldi. Screenwriters: Giuseppe Tornatore and Vanna Paoli. Cinematographer: Blasco Giurato. Music: Ennio Morricone. Editor: Mario Morra. Cast: Salvatore Cascio (Totò as child), Philippe Noiret (Alfredo), Antonella Attili (younger Maria Di Vita), Leopoldo Trieste (Father Adelfio), Enzo Cannavale (Ciccio), Jacques Perrin (Totò as adult).]

Synopsis: On hearing that his old friend Alfredo has died, famous filmmaker Salvatore 'Totò' Di Vita looks back on his childhood in the fictional Sicilian town of Giancaldo. His flashback begins shortly after the Second World War when, as a small child, he fell in love with the world of movies. Alfredo, the avuncular projectionist at the local 'Cinema Paradiso', befriends and trains the boy, until a double tragedy hits: firstly, Totò learns that his father has died on the Russian Front; then, a fire destroys the cinema and blinds the old man. The movie theatre is reopened with the investment of lottery-winner Ciccio, who employs Totò as the new projectionist. As the plot jumps forward into his teenage years, Totò falls in love, gets called up for military service and has his heart broken, before leaving Giancaldo behind to pursue his dreams. Back in the present, his return after many years for Alfredo's funeral finds the cinema closed down and the town changed beyond recognition.

The intentions behind *Cinema Paradiso* are not difficult to identify. Simultaneously a nostalgic paean to a golden age of Italian film-going, and a lament at a contemporary crisis in the nation's cultural polity, Tornatore's Oscar-winning[1] sensation is a didactic, emotionally manipulative exemplar of that most marketable of European genres: the 'heritage film'.

Its evocation of a simpler time is reductively quaint in its recourse to well-worn stereotypes of the Italian South, but through its representation of the movie theatre (as both a social institution and a source of artistic output) the film offers an intriguing glimpse into the Italian experience of the late 1940s and early 1950s. The cinema, here placed at the intersection of identity and cultural memory, acts as the mediator for a post-war sensibility, and the arbiter of the nation's transition to modernity. The silver screen, indeed, provides the prism through which the film's characters view the world around them and, through alignment with the figure of the young Totò, we too are placed in the position of a child, peering in fascination and wonder at the magic of the movies.

An emblematic scene comes early on when Totò, having pilfered individual frames of celluloid from Alfredo's cutting-room floor, holds them up in turn to the flickering gas-lamp on the family dinner table. Each dusty frame provokes a brief utterance enacting a scenario lifted from Hollywood genre convention ('Shoot first, think later.'/'Hey you bastard, hands off that gold!'). This sequence captures not only the wonder, but the malleability, of the cinematic medium; the wide-eyed child is not content merely to absorb the Dream Factory's stories, but inscribes his own narratives into these tantalising fragments of filmic fantasy. Here Totò literally views his surroundings through the filter of cinema.

Such conceits permeate *Cinema Paradiso*, overtly framing each stage of Totò's coming of age as a process mediated through cinema. Kept in the same tin box as his treasured film stock, for example, are photographs of his long-lost father whose image, appropriately, is conflated with that of Clark Gable in the child's mind. Later, when the teenage Totò first sees his beloved Elena, it is through the eyepiece of a handheld cine-camera (and their first kiss takes place in the projection booth of the Cinema Paradiso). Finally, the protagonist's loss of innocence is narrated when his surrogate father Alfredo, having previously expounded words of wisdom lifted from Spencer Tracy and John Wayne, impels Totò to leave Giancaldo behind and 'discover himself'. When Totò asks if this is a line from Gary Cooper, Henry Fonda or James Stewart, the old man signs off by responding: 'No Totò. This time I'm saying it. Life is not what you see in films. Life is much harder'.

Yet *Cinema Paradiso*'s engagement with the world of movies is more complex than the central character's somewhat saccharine personal saga might suggest. Alfredo's parting admonishment is in fact a disingenuous coda for a film that, throughout, so purposefully fuses the story of Italy's post-war cinema with that of post-war Italy itself. By memorialising a specific 'moment' in the nation's cultural history, Tornatore's film offers a glimpse into the Italian experience in the years immediately following the Second World War, when a rapid transition towards a globally oriented outlook began apace. Giancaldo's movie theatre is presented as the beating heart of the community: a civic hub and forum for loud exchanges of opinion,[2] where various strata of society rub shoulders, where couples fall in love, and where the whole town congregates to laugh and cry (and, in one scene, die). More than this, though, the Cinema Paradiso acts as a facilitator, as the community negotiates a collective path through rapid changes in its cultural viewpoint: simultaneously a mirror for local identity and a window onto the outside world.

Nowhere is this more palpable than during the double bill that first introduces us to the townsfolk and their beloved cinema. The hushed solemnity that greets the preceding newsreel of Resistance veterans registers Italy's recent wartime trauma, while the immediacy of the first feature – Luchino Visconti's tale of hardship in a Sicilian fishing village, *La terra trema*/*The Earth Trembles* (1948) – is emphasised by a mirroring of film and audience (two men lament their illiteracy as they fail to understand the on-screen caption, which reads: 'The Italian language is not spoken by the poor in Sicily'). Playing alongside these artefacts of local hardship, however, are the exhilarating products of another world, offering a participatory escapism to war-weary Europeans. Firstly, the action-packed trailer for John Ford's seminal Western *Stagecoach* (1939) elicits excited Red Indian war-chants from the children in the front row. Then, the antics of Charlie Chaplin in *The Knockout* (Mack Sennett, 1914) have the whole town bursting into raucous laughter. By offering access to the allure of Americana, therefore, Giancaldo's cinema registers the changes underway in Italian consciousness in the early post-war years as the output of Hollywood gained a telling foothold.[3]

This clear sense of mounting American influence is not, however, presented as a process of domination over native customs by a hegemonic force, but one of productive cultural blending, since numerous 'classics' of Italian cinema are shown commanding audiences' attention alongside transatlantic imports (notably, *In nome della legge/In the Name of the Law* (Pietro Germi, 1949), *Riso amaro/Bitter Rice* (Giuseppe De Santis, 1949) and *I vitelloni* (Federico Fellini, 1953)); nor is the cinema itself shown to be displacing older forms of social interaction. On the contrary, *Cinema Paradiso* shows the medium seamlessly *integrating* with, and enriching, more traditional civic hubs. When a crowd is locked out of the movie theatre, Alfredo charitably turns the projector around to display the comedy film *I pompieri di Viggiu/The Firemen of Viggiu* (Mario Mattoli, 1949) on a wall of the town square. Later, fishing boats line up on the waterfront to get a makeshift view of outdoor screenings. On each occasion, a key public space of Sicilian society – the piazza, then the harbour – embraces the communal experience of cinematic spectatorship.

The South of Italy[4] has long possessed a potent mythic force in the national culture: at once a locus for Italy's past and a canvas upon which to project the fears and desires of nationhood. In turning to his childhood home, Sicilian director Tornatore consciously plugs into this pre-existing discourse to frame his tale of identity and loss. His meticulous weaving of the cinema into the fabric of this setting – in part through these literal 'projections' of fantasies and aspirations onto the spaces of the community – therefore implicates the medium as an integral agent in this memorialisation of a bygone era. While the close-knit community of the South takes on its familiar symbolic mantle as something that modern Italy has lost, the cinema comes bound up within it. The film's denouement makes this marriage of film-going and social nostalgia explicit. When the adult Totò returns to Giancaldo for Alfredo's funeral, the familiar piazza has become overrun with billboards and heavy traffic. He looks up at the old Cinema Paradiso: a derelict shell awaiting demolition to make way for a car park. Ciccio, the former proprietor, explains that 'recession, television, video' have led to its closing. Once again the message is clear: the modern world, with its fast-paced technologies, has caught up with the cinema and the town simultaneously.

This is, doubtless, a suitably elegiac ending for a film whose emotional appeal has been so carefully constructed around nostalgia, memory and loss. It is in many ways an apt document of the cultural shifts occurring in the 1980s, as the nation's cinema entered a seemingly terminal decline in the age of Berlusconi's media empire. Yet this is to oversimplify the significance of *Cinema Paradiso*. This 'heritage film' is, as the generic label suggests, espousing a consummate 'Italian-ness', but not just one of picturesque, elemental backwardness that so easily emanates from the dusty antiquity of old Sicily. The Italy memorialised in this film is also the one that underwent bewildering sociocultural change in the post-war era, and whose very identity was mediated by an increasingly cosmopolitan outlook. Within this historical context, the cinema is positioned as an integral and wholesome component in the evolution of the nation's cultural imaginary. In the film's very final sequence, Totò opens Alfredo's bequest: the countless 'kiss scenes' that had been cut out of films at the bidding of Father Adelfio to protect the town from moral degradation in the 1940s, now spliced together into one continuous reel. This symbolises more than just the wonder of the cinema. Just as Totò had reinscribed his treasured fragments of celluloid at the dinner table, so Alfredo has used the medium to engage in a creative process of experimentation. The old projectionist's parting gift is to remind Totò and the audience of the excitement, not only of spectatorship, but also of appropriation and adaptation. The cinema, finally, is not dead.

Notes

1. *Cinema Paradiso* won the Best Foreign Language Film Oscar in 1990.
2. This depiction appears to be particularly close to the actuality. Christopher Wagstaff records that the social context of *terza visione* cinema (that of 'third-run' provincial cinemas) was

one in which audience members would come and go, and talk loudly during the films, except for those parts that grabbed their attention (1992: 253).

3. In the immediate post-war years a backlog of American films was released into the Italian market and by 1946 foreign imports (most of which were American) were taking 87 per cent of the nation's box office receipts (Wagstaff 1998: 75).
4. The 'South' of Italy, known as the *Mezzogiorno*, is a conceptual entity traditionally denoting a large and diverse section of Italy comprising the mainland regions of Campania, Molise, Puglia, Basilicata and Calabria, as well as the islands of Sicily and Sardinia.

Further reading

Peter Bondanella, *A History of Italian Cinema*, London, Continuum, 2009.

Rosalind Galt, *The New European Cinema: Redrawing the Map*, New York, Columbia University Press, 2006.

William Hope, *Giuseppe Tornatore: Emotion, Cognition, Cinema*, Newcastle, Cambridge Scholars Publishing, 2008.

Millicent Marcus, *After Fellini: National Cinema in the Postmodern Age*, Baltimore, Johns Hopkins University Press, 2002.

Christopher Wagstaff, 'A forkful of Westerns: industry, audiences and the Italian Western', in Richard Dyer and Ginette Vincendeau (eds), *Popular European Cinema*, London, Routledge, 1992, pp. 245–62.

Christopher Wagstaff, 'Italian genre films in the world market', in Geoffrey Nowell-Smith and Stephen Ricci (eds), *Hollywood and Europe: Economics, Culture, National Identity 1945–95*, London, British Film Institute, 1998, pp. 74–85.

Austin Fisher

Citizen Kane (1941)

[Country: USA. Production Company: RKO Radio Productions. Director: Orson Welles. Screenwriters: Herman J. Mankiewicz and Welles. Cinematographer: Gregg Toland. Music: Bernard Herrmann. Editor: Robert Wise. Cast: Orson Welles (Charles Foster Kane), Joseph Cotton (Jedediah Leland), Everett Sloane (Bernstein), Dorothy Comingore (Susan Alexander Kane), Ray Collins (James W. Gettys), Agnes Moorehead (Mary Kane), Ruth Warrick (Emily Norton Kane), George Coulouris (Walter Parks Thatcher), Paul Stewart (Raymond).]

Synopsis: The rich, powerful media tycoon Charles Foster Kane meets a lonely demise in the vast empty rooms of his palatial home, Xanadu. A reporter sets out to uncover the meaning of his final words, interviewing people who knew him well, including his second wife and his closest business associates. Through their eyes we see episodes in Kane's life as he is rescued from childhood poverty through a chance bequest and then rises to global notoriety as his business empire grows. We see him nurture the *Enquirer*, a failing newspaper, building it into a crusading voice for the people. His campaign for high political office founders when a private scandal is made public. Both of his marriages end tragically and he gradually alienates even his closest friends. The arc of Kane's life provides a panorama of America, but there remains the mystery of his dying worlds. What was it that mattered most to the man who had everything and lost it all?

Few films have enjoyed, or been encumbered with, a reputation quite as high as that of *Citizen Kane*. In 1952 the British film periodical *Sight and Sound* asked leading film critics from around the world to choose their ten best films. *Citizen Kane* didn't feature in that first 'top ten' list but when the survey was repeated ten years later in 1962 it appeared at number one. It continued to top the poll at each ten-year interval since then. In 1992 *Sight and Sound* introduced a second poll based on the views of an international panel of film directors and again *Citizen Kane* was placed first before dropping to second in 2012.[1] Similarly, the American Film Institute's 'Top 100 Movies of All Time' in 2007 confirmed the status of *Citizen Kane* by placing it at number one.[2] Such consistent acclaim also creates its own hazards in that the film has almost become beyond criticism. Its elevated position can be daunting to any student approaching the film for the first time; can any film avoid arousing feelings of disappointment when it trails such unrivalled levels of expectation behind it.

A further obstacle to examining the film dispassionately has been the problem of disentangling *Citizen Kane* from the wider legend of its principle creator, Orson Welles. The opening of David Thomson's biography of Welles conveys something of the mythology when he writes: 'He had moved people, men and women, with anecdotes, laughter, heady company, genius, beauty, the brightest heaven of invention. He had been loved, admired, revered' (Thomson 1997: 3). Another biographer, John Russell Taylor, alerts us to Welles' own tendencies towards self-mythologising, noting that 'his favourite image for the artist in general and himself in particular was that of a stage magician, an illusionist' (Taylor 1999: vi). The legend tells us how the 'boy genius' bluffed his way into a job as an actor at Dublin's prestigious Gate Theatre when he was just 16, and how the 23-year-old Welles had convinced America that Martians were landing with his infamous radio production of *War of the Worlds*. *Citizen Kane* remains a lynchpin of the myth, the masterwork of a 26-year-old first-time director, destined to be the greatest film ever made. The myth also encompasses Welles' later decline into obesity and chat-show celebrity, a development seemingly paralleled by the 'rise and fall' plot of *Citizen Kane*. This part of the legend also includes the erroneous assumption that he was never to achieve the heights of *Citizen Kane* again; an idea belied by the vitality and artistry of subsequent films such as *The Magnificent Ambersons* (1942) and *Touch of Evil* (1958).

One straightforward way to approach *Citizen Kane* is by way of the auteur theory, seeing the film as the first cinematic expression of Welles' characteristic themes and stylistic traits. Regarding the former, Welles has often been seen as a director fascinated by the figure of the Shakespearian hero. Obvious evidence is provided for this in the form of his three film adaptations of Shakespeare – *Macbeth* (1948), *Othello* (1952) and *Chimes at Midnight* (1966) – as well as by the characters he portrays in *Mr Arkadin* (1955) and *Touch of Evil*. The narrative arc of these films presents the rise and fall of charismatic, romantic but flawed figures, brought down through their own weaknesses and by fatal over-reaching. This is certainly part of the fascination of *Citizen Kane* as we follow Charles Foster Kane from the dynamism and high-minded principles of his youth, when he turns the failing newspaper the *Inquirer* into a populist, campaigning 'voice of the people', to his final isolation and despair, imprisoned in the fantasy palace he has created at Xanadu, lonely and embittered. A much celebrated sequence which conveys this with characteristic cinematic bravura shows Kane and his first wife in a series of breakfast table encounters over the course of their marriage. A montage of shot-reverse shot combinations depicts the gradual change from intimacy to coldness as Kane's priorities shift to his political career. The final sections of the film, with the elderly Kane lumbering round the vast, empty interiors of Xanadu, contrast strikingly with the exuberance of early scenes at the *Inquirer* where an ever-smiling Kane fires up his team of young reporters with energy and idealism.

Auteurist examinations of the film have thrown up a number of other interpretations of Welles' intentions. For James Naremore, *Citizen Kane* is a fundamentally political film, offering a critique of the corruption endemic in American capitalism (Naremore 2005: 341–58). This is most apparent in the close correlation between Kane's story and that of the American media magnate William Randolph Hearst who is generally assumed to have provided the real-life model for Kane. In contrast, Laura Mulvey has read the film as both a political allegory (in which Kane's final desperate loneliness is a metaphor for America's own isolationist stance to the war in Europe) and a text that invites psychoanalytical interpretation; the latter leading her to a meticulous reading of the film's complex rendering of the inner life of its central character, as well as providing a meditation on the power of memory. Mulvey neatly summarises the rich possibilities which the film offers to those attempting auteurist textual evaluations when she argues that 'its elusiveness is one of the qualities that makes it infinitely re-viewable, re-debatable' (Mulvey 1992: 9).

Even attempting an auteur reading of the film is not without its complications. The original publication in 1971 of *The Citizen Kane Book* with its extended introductory essay, 'Raising Kane', by Pauline Kael is indicative of this (Kael *et al.*, 1974: 1–71). One of Kael's central intentions was to highlight the contribution made by the film's co-writer, Herman J. Mankiewicz, even to the extent of implying that much of the credit for the film's startling visual panache and thematic content was derived from ideas developed by Mankiewicz at the scripting stage. Welles' later apparent decline might, therefore, be at least partially attributed to the fact that Welles never worked again with the unjustly overlooked Mankiewicz. As David Thomson points out, Kael's argument was based on insecure, highly selective research (Thomson 1997: 396–8) and subsequent film historians have confirmed Welles' significant role in developing the screenplay and extending its conception in the actual filming. Kael herself subsequently publicly conceded the weaknesses of her own argument.

Another approach to the film has been to focus on it purely as a cinematic text. This has led to a good deal of work which considers the various technical innovations and manipulations of cinematic form which distinguish *Citizen Kane*. In the most reductive instances the film has almost been seen as a training manual for would-be directors, providing a catalogue of the differing effects of tone and atmosphere which cinema can achieve. In Richard Barsam's *Looking at Movies* it is the use of sound which comes under scrutiny, particularly in the party sequence at the offices of the *Inquirer* (Barsam 2007: 306–11). For Robert Kolker, it is the highly distinctive deployment of deep-focus photography in the arrangement of shot compositions which calls for close examination (Kolker 2006: 70–4). Bordwell and Thompson's now classic *Film Art: An Introduction* instead turns its attention to the narrative construction of *Citizen Kane*, systematically breaking this down into 'segments' to illustrate the complexities of its construction and the sophisticated handling of time transitions (Bordwell and Thompson 2004: 91–102).

It is certainly understandable that the film has been read as a technical tour de force. From the use of ceilinged sets and fly-away scenery, through the overlapping dialogue (which Welles had previously used as a director and actor with his Mercury Players theatre company), to the barrage of acute camera angles, swooping crane shots and startling lighting effects, the film offers a shot-by-shot repertoire of dazzling cinematic devices. This may account also for the often repeated claim that the film's principle weakness lies in the emotional coldness which arises as a consequence of Welles' fascination with surface effects. In contrast, it is precisely these qualities which account for the film's continuing fascination according to Peter Wollen. For Wollen, all other interpretations are ultimately flawed and it is only for 'its virtuosity, its variety of formal devices and technical innovations and inventions' that it can be considered a film landmark. Wollen sees it almost as a work of cinematic abstraction, whose importance lies in its 'elaboration of a formal poetic … a text which is a play with meaning rather than a vehicle for it' (Wollen 1998: 29). Wollen is dismissive of evaluations which seek to place *Citizen Kane* in any wider social or cultural context. In retrospect, his essay is symptomatic of dominant theoretical trends in film studies during the 1970s and few would be likely to support his position today. It seems eminently sensible to suggest that the film might be seen as a product of the Hollywood studio system in the classical period. Even the technical qualities which Wollen celebrates are in part a consequence of the resources which RKO put at Welles' disposal. Welles acknowledged this by giving his cinematographer, Gregg Toland, equal billing with himself on the film's end credits.

Other film historians, including Kael, have chosen to examine Welles' use of William Randolph Hearst as a source for the film's content, or considered the attempts made by Hearst to suppress the film and have Welles ostracised by Hollywood. Such approaches acknowledge the complex relationship between Welles and the studio system which both furnished him with the opportunity to create *Citizen Kane* and then set about making sure that he would never be given such a free hand again.

What this short appraisal has hopefully made abundantly clear is the extraordinary breadth of theoretical approaches which have been applied to *Citizen Kane*. In addition to those already listed, there is barely space to acknowledge Andre Bazin's immensely influential analysis of the film which held it up as an example of 'total cinema', its use of deep focus and sequence construction combining to produce what Bazin saw as a form of heightened realism.[3] Perhaps what all of these viewpoints indicate is that the real reason for the continuing fascination of *Citizen Kane* is that, rather like the Charles Foster Kane himself, the film is all things to all people; its riches lie its ambiguities and contradictions.

Notes

1. See *Sight and Sound*, Vol. 22, No. 9 (September 2012) for full details of all the polls published to date.
2. See www.afi.com for the full list.
3. See Andre Bazin, *Orson Welles: A Critical View*, New York, Harper and Row, 1979.

Further reading

James Barsam, *Looking at Movies: An Introduction to Film*, New York, W.W. Norton, 2007.

David Bordwell and Kristin Thompson, *Film Art: An Introduction*, New York, McGraw-Hill, 2004.

Pauline Kael, Herman J. Mankiewicz and Orson Welles, *The Citizen Kane Book*, St Albans, Paladin, 1974.

Robert Kolker, *Film, Form, and Culture*, New York, McGraw-Hill, 2006.

Laura Mulvey, *Citizen Kane*, London, BFI, 1992.

James Naremore, 'The Magician and the Mass Media' in Jeffrey Geiger and R. L. Rutsky (eds) *Film Analysis: A Norton Reader*, New York, W.W. Norton, 2005, pp. 340–60.

John Russell Taylor, *Orson Welles*, London, Pavilion, 1999.

David Thomson, *Rosebud: The Story of Orson Welles*, London, Abacus, 1997.

Peter Wollen, 'Introduction to *Citizen Kane*' in John Hill and Pamela Church Gibson (eds) *The Oxford Guide to Film Studies*, Oxford and New York, Oxford University Press, 1998. Originally published in *Film Reader*, No. 1, 1975, pp. 9–15.

Robert Shail

A Clockwork Orange (1971)

[Country: UK. Production Company: Warner Bros, Hawk Films. Director and Screenwriter: Stanley Kubrick. Cinematographer: John Alcott. Editor: Bill Butler. Cast: Malcolm McDowell (Alex de Large), Patrick Magee (Mr Alexander), Michael Bates (Chief Guard), Warren Clarke (Dim), Carl Duering (Dr Brodsky), Adrienne Corri (Mrs Alexander).]

Synopsis: In *A Clockwork Orange*'s Britain, the thugs who roam the streets raping, pillaging and murdering at will are at once both the savages from whom the civilised need protection, and the protectors themselves. Alex's psychotic droogs flip from outlaws to guardians of the establishment with the merest whiff of state power.

It is no surprise that the British Board of Film Classification had particular problems passing the film as it seemed a direct attack not only on the civilised values it set itself up to guard, but also on the mechanisms which purported to keep it civilised. As Janet Staiger notes, 'Since the film itself criticised government attempts to control or condition youth behaviour with the proposition that interference by authorities was more immoral than Alex's original behaviour, it might look too self-serving of the Board to question the film' (2003: 38). In the end they were saved the trouble of censoring the film by Kubrick himself who was disturbed by just how potent a cultural force the film turned out to be.

Following the film's UK release in 1971, a spate of supposedly copycat violent occurrences were reported together with a number of threats against Kubrick's own family's personal safety. As a result, Kubrick chose to withdraw the film from distribution in Britain. It remained unseen in the UK from this point until after his death in 1999. It could be that he felt the film spoke so specifically to the youth of the UK that Kubrick chose to withdraw it from this territory alone. Or it could be that he would have withdrawn it globally had he the power to do so. But the fact remains that the UK is the only country where Kubrick demanded the film be taken out of public circulation. The question is, does this say more about the nature of the film itself or British culture? Either way the two seem inextricably linked.

By the time Kubrick made the film he had long 'gone native'. Born in New York, he had moved to the UK with his family and set up permanent home far from the reaches of all but the most persistent envoys of Hollywood. Perhaps Kubrick's outsider status gave him the necessary distance to carry off such a potent critique of Britain and British cinema. *A Clockwork Orange* is the ultimate antidote to the familiar school of British Social Realism which largely dominated UK art cinema of the time. Kubrick loved to use supposedly low culture to undress high culture. Science Fiction and Horror are commonly regarded as lowbrow genres, looked down upon as 'trashy' by the literary elite. It seems a peculiarly American conceit to use a blend of these disreputable genres to dissect both British culture and the class-fixated school of Social Realism. Kubrick emerged with a visionary critique of the effects of Britain's rigid society, where everyone knows their place, the law serves the powerful and the civilised values this elite dictate form the very foundation of Britain's national identity.

If nineteenth-century Britain were to identify any single value above all others as embodying Britishness, it likely would have been a notion of being civilised. As a result, for Britons, national identity has become almost interchangeable with the idea of being civilised. If this means being considerate, educated and charitable, it also means being right, powerful and in control.

A Clockwork Orange challenges the very meaning of 'civilised' with its carefully orchestrated assault on the establishment. Kubrick has put together a checklist of characteristics of civilised Britain, placing them at the heart of the moral malaise running through his vision of a nation in decline. Classical music from Beethoven, and even more ironically, Purcell's 'Music for the Funeral of Queen Mary' become synonymous not with the genteel drawing rooms of the educated, but with the sadistic erotic fantasies of juveniles. The bowler hat and cane once associated with that bastion of Britishness, the archetypal City Gent, is now turned into a uniform of terror worn by Alex and his droogs. Science and Medicine are now to be found working for the frightened, patronising and deluded government. The British institutional construct of the State is subverted and used as a locus for power, corruption and lies. The irony of the film is that it is this very same corrupt fear which is serving to produce a nation of disaffected amoral and frustrated psychopaths. Perhaps Kubrick meant to indicate that this was also exactly the personality required for Imperial expansion and the subsequent violent 'civilising' of the world.

The striking and much mimicked uniforms of the droogs took the tropes of the City gent and rendered them into something more akin to the identifiers worn by members of any number of contemporary youth subcultures, in itself a very British idea. It comes as little surprise that so many of these subcultures were first produced by the UK. In a grey impoverished post-war Britain, the youth sought to separate themselves from their parents' 'keep calm and carry on' post-war mentality and asked: 'What has my county done for me?' The answer appeared to be 'not much'. And so the youth sought to distance themselves from their parents' lifestyles and seek out their own more colourful identities often through the rising iconography of pop music. The Teddy-boys, mods, rockers, punks, headbangers – these were all established first in Britain before being exported to the US and beyond. Watching 1960s news footage of the clashes on Brighton Beach between Mods, Rockers and police, it's easy to see where Burgess and Kubrick might have got their inspiration for Alex and his Droogs.

The disintegration of language is a further omnipresent force in the film. The so-called Received Pronunciation (RP) of the BBC news-caster and indeed virtually all public voices aired in the UK up to the 1960s is torn asunder by the Droogs' use of a slang called Nadsat. Slang is used ubiquitously by youth subcultures to differentiate themselves from the adults who control their daily lives, as a way of carving out one's own identity and presenting a challenge to social authority.

Nadsat in *A Clockwork Orange* is perhaps the most potent example of Alex's desire to live outside the state-sanctioned social system. Alex has chosen to embrace a way of speaking whose subtext is to say, 'I don't want to be a part of the society into which I'm born'. The BBC had long been seen, at home and abroad, as the voice of civilised British values in no small part because of the strongly associated intonations and accents of the dialect used by its reporters and presenters. This RP is also strongly associated with having a formal education, which in turn is often associated with being wealthy and coming from an upper-class background. Alex and his Droogs wilfully discard any aspirations to belong to the social class of the power elite by embracing their own dialect, uniform, and criminality. In the same way, Kubrick actively subverts the tropes of so-called civilised values through co-opting Purcell and the bowler hat, producing a peculiarly British critique of all that Britannia stands for. More than that, it's a call for a very British revolution.

Is this really a British film or actually a US studio film masquerading as British? After all, few of us would consider *Children of Men* (Alfonso Cuarón, 2006) a British film, even though much of it is shot on the familiar streets of London, any more than we would consider *Our Man In Havana* (Carol Reed, 1959) a Cuban film. But what is it then that makes a film belong to one culture or nation rather than another? Traditionally, because of their high production costs, films are often constructed with a cultural universality in mind. It's a rare film made outside of France, the US or Japan that can cover its production costs from within its domestic market alone. So where does this leave *A Clockwork Orange*? Is it British, American or simply the product of a global industrial process rather than the expression of any single nation's cultural identity?

A Clockwork Orange has a largely British cast, crew and setting and is adapted from a British author's novel. But it is directed by Stanley Kubrick, arguably the most significant of all American directors. Kubrick found finance for the film through Warner Brothers at the very heart of Hollywood. The US studios were actively seeking to fund their very own art-movies in order to compete with the raft of films from Europe which had lately been sweeping up awards, critical praise, and above all dollars around the globe. Using American money to fund what seems on the surface like a very British picture might have been the industrial equivalent of building a cultural Trojan Horse. Britain has long been perceived as a kind of cultural beachhead between Europe and the USA thanks largely to its common language. Warner Brothers could easily have conceived of using *A Clockwork Orange* to colonise the European art-house market from within. With their more challenging and adult approach to subject matter, films like *The Conformist* (Bernardo Bertolucci, 1970), *Alphaville* (Jean-Luc Godard, 1965) and *Belle de Jour* (Luis Buñuel, 1967) were selling tickets almost as fast as they were breaking taboos. It's likely that Hollywood wanted a piece of this action and thought that by producing something abroad, which tackled potentially controversial themes, it could beat the Europeans at their own game while keeping the international box office receipts in-country. Looking at *A Clockwork Orange*'s national identity this way opens up an intriguing argument for the film as a kind of US imperialist indoctrination of the UK in much the same manner as the film's anti-hero, Alex, finds himself brainwashed by state power. The cultural and industrial muscle of Hollywood equates easily with the financial and ethical authority of the British state as depicted in Kubrick's film.

However, *A Clockwork Orange* can hardly be labelled a US film simply because of its US director and funding. It is very hard to imagine the film functioning as successfully if located in any other country in the world besides Britain. It is this exploration of the iconography of the UK which confirms *A Clockwork Orange*'s cultural identity as truly British. There is something inherently British in the way the material addresses social flux in a timeline which could begin with a past depicted in *If...* (Lindsay Anderson, 1968), continuing through the disaffected present found in *Trainspotting* (Danny Boyle, 1995) and arriving at the dystopian future in which *A Clockwork Orange* is set. Kubrick uses an idea of Britain, a memory of Empire, casting its eye over the past of this once powerful British Imperial Civilisation and presenting us with a vision of an atrophied future where the savage and civilised have become one.

Perhaps this film is, in a perverse way, Kubrick's paean to Britain. It seems somehow a fitting tribute to the artistry of *A Clockwork Orange* that it resonated so powerfully with British youth culture while simultaneously galvanising the outraged attention of Middle England's moral Right. 'Of all the films that [Kubrick] made in Great Britain, *Barry Lyndon* and *A Clockwork Orange* are, paradoxically, the only ones whose cultural background is truly English' (Ciment 2005: 411). What other film in the history of UK cinema has been rereleased nationwide 30 years after its original debut in over 250 cinemas? If there remained any doubt over *A Clockwork Orange*'s national identity, this should triumphantly confirm its position as a key work of and for British cinema.

Further reading

Michel Ciment, '*A Clockwork Orange*', in Alison Castle (ed.) *The Stanley Kubrick Archives*, London, Taschen, 2005.

Janet Staiger, 'The Cultural Productions of *A Clockwork Orange*', in Stuart Y. McDougal, ed., *Stanley Kubrick's A Clockwork Orange*, Cambridge, Cambridge University Press, 2003, pp. 37–60.

Simon Ward

Como agua para chocolate/Like Water for Chocolate (1991)

[Country: Mexico. Production Company: Arau Films. Director and Producer: Alfonso Arau. Screenwriter: Laura Esquivel. Cinematographers: Emmanuel Lubezki and Steve Bernstein. Editors: Carlos Bolado and Francisco Chiu. Music: Leo Brower. Cast: Lumi Cavazos (Tita), Regina Torné (Mama Elena), Marco Leonardi (Pedro Muzquiz), Mario Ivan Martinez (Doctor John Brown), Ada Carrasco (Nacha), Yareli Arizmendi (Rosaura), Claudette Maillé (Gertrudis), Pilar Aranda (Chencha).]

Synopsis: The film is set in rural Mexico near the border with Texas during the Mexican Revolution of 1910–20. It is ostensibly a romance, a tale of love thwarted by rigid tradition. Tita, the youngest daughter of Mama Elena, is prevented from marrying her true love, Pedro, because it is her destiny to care for her mother in her old age. Mama Elena cruelly offers her oldest daughter, Rosaura, as an alternative match for Pedro. Pedro accepts the match, seeing it as an opportunity to be near Tita.

Like Water for Chocolate was the highest grossing Mexican film of the 1990s. In the USA it took over $21 million, more than any other foreign language film in 1993. It was widely seen as heralding a renaissance in the Mexican film industry, which had been in the doldrums since the 'golden age' of the 1930s to 1950s. The film, which cost $2 million to make, was funded by a mixture of public and private finance including from IMCINE (Instituto Mexicano de Cinematografia), Aviasco, a Mexican airline, and the Mexican Ministry of Tourism. It is a film which presents the country in a tourist-friendly manner and is packed with images of a romanticised, nostalgic Mexico which in part account for its international success.[1]

The screenplay is adapted by Laura Esquivel from her best-selling novel *Como agua para chocolate*. The novel draws on a genre of writing first popularised in Mexico in the 1850s when stories for women were published in monthly instalments intertwined with recipes, dressmaking patterns and household remedies.[2] These publications were both entertaining and instructional and were in some senses the forerunners of modern women's magazines. Esquivel's book is divided into 12 monthly chapters, each based around a recipe. The narrative is played out through the preparation and consumption of food. The film follows a similar episodic structure and retains some of the instructional elements of the book; the preparation of food is often shown in detail and in close-up. The camera lingers on mundane tasks: the grinding of corn for flour, the cracking of eggs for the wedding cake batter and the cracking of nuts for the wedding banquet. The story develops with the kitchen as its central locus and is woven through the performance of everyday domestic chores.

The film draws on a rich seam of South American magic realism, a genre which imbues 'ordinary world' situations with fantastical elements. Tita, the film's central protagonist is born in the kitchen on a tide of tears. (The salt from these tears fills a large sack and is used in the family's meals for many years.) She is brought up in the kitchen by Nacha the Indian cook and learns how to prepare traditional Mexican dishes. Her food takes on magical properties. As Nacha and Tita prepare the cake for Rosaura and Pedro's wedding banquet, Tita's tears flow into the batter and, when eaten, the cake causes an epidemic of crying and vomiting in the wedding guests. On another occasion, Tita prepares quail in rose-petal sauce, using roses that Pedro has given her. The food becomes an embodiment of her passion for Pedro and has a dramatic effect on her sister Gertrudis who develops an uncontrollable sexual desire, which she cannot quench. The heat of this desire burns down the shower house and Gertrudis, in a frenzy, runs off naked, only to be scooped up by a soldier on horseback.

The title is based on a traditional Mexican saying referring to water that is hot and bubbling like a passion or a temper. The film seethes with sensuality. The food is abundant and luscious. It ignites passion and emotion within those that consume it and we can see its effects on the faces of the diners. The food itself represents a melding of various aspects of Mexican culture, the dishes being by turn simple peasant dishes and lavish celebratory fare with expensive ingredients.

Within the film, Tita is portrayed as an idealised woman. She is talented at all domestic tasks and is beautiful and virtuous. She is the keeper of good traditions that will nourish future generations. By contrast the traditions espoused by Mama Elena are repressive and cruel. The tensions between these two traditions reflect the tensions between middle-class Hispanic values and older pre-Hispanic ways in Mexican society, which were played out in the Mexican Revolution enabling an escape from Spanish colonialism and a rediscovery of Mexican identity. As in the popular melodramas of Mexican cinema, these tensions are played out in a personal domestic setting rather than on the battlefield. In such films, the narratives contained gendered archetypes from Mexican tradition. In this film the gendered nature of these roles is destabilised. Mama Elena is the patriarch of the family. She behaves like the authoritarian father, unmoved by sentiment, disciplined and rigid in her views. Ultimately she is revealed as a hypocrite, when Tita discovers that Gertrudis is the product of her mother's affair. We are not certain whether the family traditions she cites are real or of her own making and she is selective about which traditions she chooses to honour. For example, she eschews the traditional role of nurturing mother and takes on the male role of ranch owner, but she insists that the tradition of the youngest daughter remaining unmarried to care for her mother in old age is adhered to. It is Nacha who is the traditional nurturing mother figure, a role that is bequeathed to Tita. Tita becomes the source of nourishment for all the family, including Rosaura's son whom she is able to breastfeed despite being a virgin. Rosaura, the obedient daughter who follows her mother's wishes, is incapable of nurturing her child or her husband and her failed efforts at cooking are contrasted with Tita's skill in the kitchen. Rosaura is bereft of passion, joy and imagination. She passively follows the wishes of Mama Elena and lives her life unhappily, plagued by digestive illnesses that eventually kill her. By contrast, Gertrudis, the middle daughter is a free spirit. Some commentators have suggested that her wildness is evidence of racial stereotyping within the film (Gertrudis is mixed race). However she is the character who emerges happy and fulfilled at the end of the film. She is a subversion of a key melodramatic female archetype: the whore.[3] Normally a role associated with shame and suffering, to Gertrudis it is a natural outlet for sexual passion. Later in the film she becomes a soldier, rising to the rank of general and having men under her command. Like Mama Elena she takes on a traditional male role and this gender transgression is emphasised when Tita steps out to have a serious chat to Pedro halfway through cooking fritters for Gertrudis. Rather than finish the job herself, Gertrudis employs her sergeant to complete the task.

The male characters in the film are by contrast passive: Pedro goes along with Mama Elena's rulings without question and never actively fights for Tita; Dr John Brown cares for Tita and restores her to health when she breaks down after the death of Rosaura's son but passively accepts Tita sleeping with Pedro and is still prepared to marry her despite the indiscretion. However female autonomy within the film is largely achieved by the absence of male society, politics and commerce. We have a glimpse at the male world at the start of the film when Tita's father has a heart attack in a bar and dies, having discovered that Gertrudis is not his biological daughter, but, throughout the film most of the action takes place in a matriarchal domestic setting. The revolution is used as a backdrop to the narrative rather than being a key feature and although soldiers appear from time to time, we are not told the nature of the conflict. The family themselves carry on life as normal with the fighting going on around them. Mama Elena is killed by soldiers and Chencha, the servant is raped but these events are not part of a wider narrative about the war.

There are parallels between the narrative and the traditional European folk tale of Cinderella. We can map the characters across: Tita consigned to the kitchen is Cinderella; Mama Elena, her nemesis, is the wicked stepmother who victimises Tita and treats her as a personal servant; Rosaura her eldest sister who does her mother's bidding is the ugly sister; and Nacha who supports Tita is the fairy godmother. Pedro is Prince Charming, but does not emerge as a romantic hero. He passively goes along with the rules as set down by Mama Elena and does not attempt to rescue Tita from a life of drudgery. Tita too is outwardly conformist; her rebellion is enacted through her food. Although she does not consciously control its magical effects, rather the passion just overflows from her into the food. Her cooking expresses what she herself cannot and food forms a communication between her and Pedro allowing her to 'enter his body' through the meals that she cooks him.

Tita is only free to be fully with Pedro after her mother and sister are dead. At the end of the film this complete union is both passionate and romantic. The ghost of Nacha lights a myriad of candles around the bed. Pedro and Tita are literally consumed by their passion. Pedro dies during lovemaking and Tita realises that he has 'lit all his matches' simultaneously as described by Dr John's Indian grandmother. She swallows matches to join him and the ranch is consumed in flames. Tita and Pedro walk into a tunnel of light to enjoy their happy-ever-after. This is clearly a parody of a fairy-tale ending, indicating the impossibility of eternal love and happiness. Tita succeeds in passing on a legacy to future generations in the form of her recipes and in the termination of the tradition of enslavement of the youngest daughter; the film is narrated by Tita's grand-niece as evidence of this legacy.

The message of the film is highly conservative and whereas 'domestic' feminists have praised the film for its celebration of the creativity of women and female tradition, others have noted that the film consigns Tita to success only in the private and personal realm. The public sphere of men is hidden from our view and so are the inequalities of wider society. The effect is to present domestic servitude as a natural role for women (and Indian servants), thereby ultimately reinforcing the patriarchal order.[4]

Notes

1. See Deborah Shaw's chapter, 'Seducing the public: Images of Mexico in *Like Water for Chocolate* and *Amores Perros*', in *Contemporary Cinema of Latin America: Ten key Films*, London & New York, Continuum, 2003.
2. See Maria Elena de Valdes (1995) 'Verbal and visual representation of women: *Como agua para chocolate/Like Water for Chocolate*', in *World Literature Today*, Winter 1995, Vol. 69, Issue 1, University of Oklahoma, p. 78.
3. From 'La Malinche', the Aztec princess who delivered her country to Cortez through sexual submission.
4. See Kraniauskas, J. (1993), '*Como agua para chocolate*', *Sight and Sound* Vol. 3, No. 10, pp. 42–3, BFI, London.

Further reading

L. A. Cheyne, 'Gender, Agency, Memory, and Identity in *Like Water for Chocolate*', in *Offscreen* Volume 7, Issue 4, April 2003. Available at www.horschamp.qc.ca/new_offscreen/water_-chocolate.html (accessed 14 April 2013).

C. Counihan, 'Food, Feelings and Film: Women's Power in *Like Water for Chocolate*', in *Food, Culture and Society: An International Journal of Multidisciplinary Research*, Volume 8, Number 2, Fall 2005, pp. 201–14.

J. King, A. M. Lopez and M. Alvarado (eds), *Mediating Two Worlds: Cinematic Encounters in the Americas*, London, BFI, 1993.

Janice Kearns

Un condamné à mort s'est échappé ou Le vent souffle où il veut/A Man Escaped (1956)

[Country: France. Production company: Gaumont and Nouvelles Éditions de Films (NEF). Director and Screenwriter: Robert Bresson. Cinematographer: Léonce-Henri Burel. Editor: Raymond Lamy. Cast: Francois Leterrier (Fontaine), Charles Le Clainche (Jost), Roland Monod (Le Pasteur), Maurice Beerblock (Blanchet), Jacques Ertaud (Orsini), Jean-Paul Delhumeau (Hebrard), Roger Treherne (Terry).]

Synopsis: A man involved in the French Resistance to German occupation during the Second World War, Lieutenant Fontaine, is captured and imprisoned in Fort Montluc in Lyon.[1] He carefully and meticulously plans his escape, seeing the achievement of each stage along his journey towards freedom as a personal victory. When Jost, a young teenage prisoner, arrives in his cell Fontaine is uncertain whether to trust him and take him with him as he tries to escape or to kill him in order that he cannot raise the alarm. He chooses to take him along and together they succeed in escaping.

It is often remarked that the title of this film gives the full story, and in a sense it does. It immediately takes us to the end of the film, sums up what has happened, and almost suggests the 98 minutes of screen time has essentially amounted to no more than, 'a man escaped'. As an audience our usual expectations of mainstream narrative film are, therefore, straight away challenged. And yet, when we do reach the end of the film it is not a man but in fact two men that walk away from the prison having scaled the outer wall and neither of them could have achieved this without the help of the other – 'Had I been alone I might still be there', says our central character. Cinematically, this is certainly a defiant title in that Bresson seems to eschew mystery, suspense and surprise; we know what is going to happen. However, although he does put aside a particular storytelling type of mystery, the film actually remains highly enigmatic as the French title reveals. *'Un condamné à mort s'est échappé'* suggests this is going to be a film not just about 'a man' who escapes but about 'a man condemned to death' who escapes; a man, therefore, who escapes death. Or, the French suggests, adding further mystery to enigma, we could adopt another alternative title, *'Le vent souffle où il veut/The wind bloweth where it listeth'*, which if we don't recognise it for ourselves the film will later tell us, is a quote from the Bible giving Christ's words to Nicodemus (John 3: 8), but which we might also add, sounds rather like a pretty conventional piece of proverbial folk-wisdom. And so, a little reflection on the title means things are beginning to seem rather more complex than Bresson's initial claim, given before the credits, that, 'This is a true story; I have told it as it happened, without embellishment', would seem to suggest.[2]

The opening credits to the film are presented against the background of a wall, as is apt for a film that is going to focus on the idea of a man feeling trapped and wishing to escape. During the film it is not simply that we know through spending so long with him that Fontaine is held in a small cell, individual shots are frequently composed in order to place Fontaine in an enclosed space within the frame. When he is taken to be questioned, for example, he stands facing the camera but with the blank backs of two German interrogators to either side, so that he is confined in the central section of the shot. Often we see him through the doorway of his cell so that the wall of his cell and the door take up most of the frame and he is held within a much reduced vertical space, again, centre screen. When, a third of the way through the film, he manages to get out of his cell by removing a panel in his door, we have a shot from outside the cell as his face emerges through the door but is boxed centre screen in light that casts heavy shadows on his face. When he emerges through the skylight for the first time he is similarly 'trapped' but this time in a diagonal, letterbox-like, opening across the screen. Each movement towards freedom exists within continued entrapment.

When we first see Fontaine he is in the enclosed space of the back of a car being driven to prison. Immediately the tension between being in such a space and wishing to get out of it is conveyed as he tries to escape. But before this happens at the very beginning of the film there is what seems when we first watch the film to be a strange shot that focuses on his hands. Although we only see the hands, Fontaine seems to be turning them over and inspecting them. In the film we will continually return to his hands as he works at making a chisel from a spoon, at chipping away at a door, at levering panels of wood in a door, at making rope, at shaping pieces of metal into hooks, and at other tasks he gives himself. What we are being returned to time and again by Bresson is the idea of work, of not being idle. Hubrard says later in the film, 'You must keep busy. Write to try to stay sane'.

We are immersed in Fontaine's world. Throughout the film, our focus on him is intense and unrelenting. In the car during the opening sequence there are street sounds but they are made to seem distant, as if we are in Fontaine's mind as he registers things around him and prepares to try to open the car door. Bresson allows nothing to detract from this focus on our central character. For example, the brutality of the German occupation is given but it is expressed through filmic understatement in order to ensure it does not come to occupy the foreground of the film for the viewer; the pistol-whipping Fontaine receives after attempting to escape from the car blurs into a dissolve of him getting out of the car at the prison, and later there is a brief glimpse of a guard picking up a wooden shovel handle to beat him before we cut to Fontaine being carried on a stretcher to his cell.

These sorts of brief visual glimpses not only invite the viewer to become their own storyteller, padding out the information they are being given through the use of their own imagination, but actually demand that the viewer should do so. Similarly, the dialogue is composed of short, sharp sentences that give the facts and leave room for the viewer's imagination.

> My cell barely measured three metres by two. I soon learnt to communicate with my neighbour. He was waiting to be shot any day now. He was 19 years old.

Bresson's key requirement of us is that we should imaginatively engage with Fontaine's situation. We have to remain alert to clues, as Fontaine has to remain alert to possibilities of escape. When halfway through the film we see Fontaine watching a guard winding a mechanism on a wall, for example, we have to fill in for ourselves that this mechanism is connected to a skylight and that this could form the next stage in Fontaine's escape; we have in other words to be in tune with Fontaine's thought processes.

According to Paul Schrader (1972) quoted by Joseph Cunneen in *Robert Bresson: A Spiritual Style in Film*:

> Bresson's use of the everyday is not derived from a concern for 'real-life' but from an opposition to the contrived, dramatic events which pass for real-life in movies.
>
> (in Cunneen 2003: 22)

Cunneen himself suggests Bresson's approach,

> forces the spectator to an extra alertness; it is almost as if we have to work out the specifics of the escape for ourselves, facing the same difficulties as Fontaine.
>
> (ibid: 61)

In his *Notes on Cinematography*, Bresson gives the advice that the cinematographer should,

> Accustom the public to divining the whole of which they are given only a part. Make people diviners. Make them desire it.
>
> (Bresson 1977: 54)

If the playing of the Kyrie from Mozart's *Mass in C minor* at the start of the film and the idea of an escape from death were not enough, the religious connotations of the film gradually become clearer.[3] In a sense we have an extended meditation on predestination and free will. When the Pastor says, 'Read and pray. God will save you', Fontaine's response is 'He'll only save us if we give him a hand'. This idea of man as capable of actively determining his own fate seems to be further reinforced when Fontaine discusses the position of the men in his prison block. 'We were a hundred unfortunates awaiting our fate. I was under no illusion about my own', he says. There is a slight pause and because we have come to see him as a condemned man we think we know what is coming next, we expect him to be fatalistic and accepting, but instead he surprises us concluding that his fate will be, 'to escape'. Even this though does not bring us to a conclusion in the debate on predestination: does this confidence mean he simply 'knows' he is predestined to escape, or that he is predestined to escape because he retains this determination and continues to exert his freewill in moving towards his goal? Despite at times displaying this sort of certainty, at other times he is beset by doubts.

To begin with in his relationship with the person in the neighbouring cell, Blanchet, he is the one who offers help and reassurance; although he knows this also helps him ('It's a comfort to be looking out for others', he tells Blanchet). But by the end it seems Blanchet has become the dominant party; they are in their cells next to each other, each speaking to the other without being seen by the other, and like a priest in a confessional box Blanchet says, 'Have faith in your hooks and ropes and in yourself. You have doubts?', and receives Fontaine's response, 'What's hard is taking the plunge'.

Throughout the escape itself Fontaine continues to have doubts and uncertainties. 'I had to act but I couldn't', he says at one point. The whole thing becomes a series of hesitations followed by sudden leaps of faith as he and Jost succeed in moving stage by stage towards the outer wall of the prison. Along the way Fontaine disturbingly takes on the role of a God-like arbitrator of life and death. Looking down from the height of the roof to a guard patrolling below and effectively standing between the would-be escapees and their goal, he decides, 'This man had to die'. Perhaps, therefore, in more ways than one it is fitting that the film ends with the two men walking to freedom to the sound of the opening to Mozart's *Mass*, since in the order of service the Kyrie eleison ('Lord, have mercy') follows the confession of sins.

Notes

1. Lyons, the third largest city in France, was a key centre for the French Resistance, or Maquis, within Vichy France during the Second World War.

2. The way in which Bresson's 'soundscape' embellishes the story and creates meaning would form a whole study in itself, as might elements of homage such as that to Jean Vigo's *Zero de Conduite* (1933) as Fontaine and Jost scramble across the prison roof towards the end of the film.
3. Is it too much to suggest the series of shots through the film of Fontaine looking up towards the ceiling of his cell, towards the skylight and towards Jost on the roof above him carries some reference in Bresson's mind to Psalm 121 ('I will lift up mine eyes')?

Further reading

Robert Bresson, *Notes on Cinematography*, trans. Jonathan Griffin, New York: Urizen Books, 1977.

Bert Cardullo (ed.), *The Films of Robert Bresson: A Casebook*, London: Anthem Press, 2009.

Joseph Cunneen, *Robert Bresson: A Spiritual Style in Film*, London and New York, Continuum, 2003.

Paul Schrader, *Transcendental Style in Film:* Ozu, *Bresson, Dreyer*, Berkeley, University of California Press, 1972.

Brian Price, *Neither God nor Master: Robert Bresson and Radical Politics*, Minneapolis, MN, University of Minnesota Press, 2011.

John White

Il Conformista/The Conformist (1970)

[Country: Italy, France, West Germany. Production Company: Mars Film/Marianne Productions/Maran Film. Producers: Giovanni Bertolucci, Maurizio Lodi-Fè. Director and Screenwriter: Bernardo Bertolucci. Cinematographer: Vittorio Storaro. Editor: Franco Arcalli. Cast: Jean-Louis Trintignant (Marcello Clerici), Stefania Sandrelli (Giulia Clerici), Enzo Tarascio (Professor Quadri), Dominique Sanda (Anna Quadri).]

Synopsis: Set in 1930s Fascist Italy, *Il Conformista* tells the story of Marcello Clerici's desire for conformity. Sexually repressed Marcello is tormented by the memory of a homosexual encounter during his childhood with his family's chauffeur Lino, whom he believes he killed after Lino attempted to seduce him. Having suppressed his homosexual leanings, believing them to threaten his façade of 'normality', Marcello proves his own conventionality by joining the Fascist Party and marrying a petit bourgeois woman, Giulia, whom he does not love. To show his loyalty to the regime, Marcello then volunteers his services to Benito Mussolini's secret police: during his honeymoon in Paris, Marcello will contact his former university professor of philosophy, Luca Quadri, now an anti-Fascist refugee, and will spy on him. On his way to France, Marcello learns that the counter-order from Rome is to kill Quadri.

In *Il Conformista*, the anti-Fascist professor Quadri, who lives in exile in Paris and is murdered with the complicity of his former student Marcello Clerici, is given an address and a phone number by director and scriptwriter Bernardo Bertolucci – 17, Rue St. Jacques; MED-15-37 – that belonged to French director Jean-Luc Godard, Bertolucci's cinematic mentor at the time the film was made. Moreover, Quadri's first name in the film is changed from Edmondo (Quadri's name in Alberto Moravia's novel *Il conformista*, of which Bertolucci's screenplay is an adaptation) to Luca, the Italian for Luc, as in Jean-Luc Godard. Peter Bondanella has observed that 'Marcello's assignment to murder Professor Quadri reflects not only the protagonist's Oedipal conflict but those of Bertolucci as well' (1994: 303). Meanwhile, Claretta Micheletti Tonetti has observed that by giving Godard's address, phone number and first name to Professor Quadri, Bertolucci projected 'in Marcello's killing of his intellectual father (Quadri) his own desire to suppress Godard's influence on his artistic creation' (1995: 106), in order to establish his artistic identity. As Bertolucci admitted:

> *The Conformist* is a story about me and Godard. When I gave the professor Godard's phone number and address I did it for a joke, but afterwards I said to myself, 'Well, maybe all that has some significance. I'm Marcello and I make fascist films and I want to kill Godard, who's a revolutionary, who makes revolutionary movies and who was my teacher.
>
> (Goldin 1971: 66)

The influence of paternal authority and the conflict between father and son are key themes in *Il Conformista*, and can be understood within the Freudian theory of the totemic father, whom the son must renounce to establish his male identity and symbolically enter society. In this respect, the film beautifully lends itself to a psychoanalytical reading focused on the Oedipal struggle against the father. As Christopher Wagstaff has pointed out, Bertolucci regards the Oedipal scenario as the metaphor for human existence, at the individual, sexual, social and political levels, and develops it in his films in relation to patriarchy, selfhood and repression (1996: 206). *Il conformista* was in fact shaped by Bertolucci's concomitant discovery of psychoanalysis. In an interview given to *Le Cinéma Italien* in 1978, after saying he had been under analysis since the making of *La Strategia del Ragno* in 1970, Bertolucci significantly added: 'During the time I am shooting, the film replaces analysis' (Gili 1998: 136).

Bertolucci's adaptation of Moravia's novel revolves around Marcello's quest for father figures that he feels the need to, first, please and then, in line with a classical Oedipal trajectory, rebel against and eliminate. In *Il Conformista* it is possible to identify numerous father figures: the Fascist state, which Marcello tends to perceive as 'the ultimate patriarch' (Loshitzky 1995: 65); Marcello's friend and Fascist theorist Italo Montanari; the Fascist minister, obviously presented as an authoritative father figure through the 'primal scene' Marcello witnesses in the ministry office, in which the minister embraces an uncanny double of Quadri's wife Anna; Marcello's insane father, whom Marcello sadistically torments by reminding him of his former crimes of torture and assassination as a Fascist *picchiatore* (thug); Lino the chauffeur; Alberi, Marcello's mother's chauffeur and lover, who replaces Marcello's father in the life of Marcello's mother and embodies Marcello's incestuous desire for her; the veteran agent Manganiello, who is responsible for Marcello's 'training' as a special agent of Mussolini's secret police; and then the ultimate father/teacher, Professor Quadri, whom Marcello feels he must betray and kill to establish his own identity and conform to normative masculinity. As Bondanella has observed, 'Marcello's entire existence revolves around a desire to please successive surrogate fathers, and a feeling of inadequacy brought on by a chance homosexual encounter in the distant past, which motivates his search for "normality" in the present' (1994: 303). He represses his latent homosexuality by constructing a representation of normalcy and supporting the regime, but his adult self remains obsessed by the homosexual initiation experienced in his childhood, which exists as an inerasable sin and a permanent 'fathering principle of his male identity' (Dalle Vacche 1992: 57).

With *Il Conformista*, inspired by a Freudian psychoanalytical framework, Bertolucci confronted his personal father figures: his father Attilio, an acclaimed poet, film critic and academic; famous novelist Moravia; and his cinematic mentor, Godard. Attilio Bertolucci's strong personality made a dramatic impact on his son, and Attilio was for the director the first father to 'kill'. In various interviews Bertolucci has significantly linked his love for writing poetry to a desire to emulate his father (Gili 1998: 129), while also admitting that his choice of cinema over poetry had to be attributed to a need to find a different ground on which to compete with his father (Rigoletto 2012: 124). And he certainly managed to establish his own artistic identity at a very young age. After serving as an assistant director on Pier Paolo Pasolini's *Accattone* in 1961, Bertolucci won a prestigious prize in poetry and received critical acclaim for his first film, *La commare secca*, the following year, aged just 21. Then, in

1970, came two films which secured Bertolucci international recognition and critical acclaim: *La strategia del Ragno* and *Il Conformista*.

With *Il Conformista*, Bertolucci also challenged one of the most eminent Italian novelists of the twentieth century, Moravia. According to Jefferson Kline, Bertolucci's adaptation of Moravia's novel helps us understand how the director addressed the issue of the relationship between authority and creativity, and between written text and image, for, in the film, Bertolucci 'explicitly imitated and implicitly contested' the textual authority represented by Moravia. While Kline identifies Bertolucci's refusal 'to imitate the novel's insistently systematic chronology and causality' as a most significant deviation from Moravia's novel (1987: 88), Millicent Marcus also points to the replacement of Moravia's dramatic determinism – according to which *Il conformista* is to be read as a story of inescapable fate which marks the protagonist from his childhood – with psychological determinism, with an emphasis on the force of the subconscious. Although faithful to the anecdotal level of the book, Bertolucci makes the present of his narrative Marcello's car journey from Paris to the place of the assassination. During the journey, Marcello recalls various episodes of his life leading up to his current circumstances. These memories are represented in a disorienting set of flashbacks within flashbacks that defy any linear time frame. After the murder, the film ends with a coda set on 25 July 1943, the night Mussolini was voted out of power (Marcus 1986: 287–94).

Kline has also observed that since the film is built around a series of reminiscences presented in flashbacks within flashbacks, for viewers to make sense of the plot they must read the images each scene presents associatively, rather than analytically. Therefore, association is the key to interpretation, which is possible by putting together, as an analyst does when he or she listens to a patient, the various clues that are presented (1987: 91–2). These elements and chronologies give *Il Conformista* an oneiric quality, for they operate in line with the processes of the Freudian latent dream work, which are condensation, displacement, projection, and doubling (Bondanella 1994: 301). They also imply, as Marcus argues, that Marcello's subjectivity is the source of the camera's perspective and that Bertolucci's visual style, with its surrealistic mise en scène, is to be regarded as the visual representation of Marcello's disturbed psyche (1986: 295–6).

With *Il Conformista* Bertolucci also contested Godard's anti-commercial cinema and announced the end of Godard's influence on his cinematic style. He rejected the approach to political film-making the French director had developed at the time of his most intransigent Maoism, immediately after the events of May 1968, and that was characterised by a search for more radical forms to express political ideas (Loshitzky 1995). Robin Wood has argued that, at a stylistic level, *Il Conformista*, with its elaborate tracking shots, opulent colour photography, surrealistic visual incongruities and play of light and shadow, is testament to the full blossoming of an artistic flamboyance influenced by Orson Welles, Max Ophüls and Josef von Sternberg (2000: 265). Arguably, then, the scene of the murder may be seen as the final act of Bertolucci's Oedipal journey to Paris to 'kill off' his cinematic father figure.

While Quadri is stabbed, Marcello sits and passively watches the assassination through the window of Manganiello's car. His immobile form, frozen in a dreamlike dimension, reminds us of the immobility of the cinematic spectator, of the dreamer and of the enchained people in Plato's allegory. If, as Christopher Wagstaff has pointed out, 'looking is central to the cinema, and doubly so to *Il Conformista*, where Marcello does not so much *do* things as *watch* things, and where the viewer watches Marcello watch' (1983: 68), then with this powerful scene Bertolucci urges viewers to consider the dynamics of spectatorship and our engagement with such images. When Quadri, after he and Marcello have retold the myth of Plato's cave, urges his former student not to mistake the shadows of reality for reality, the skilful lighting of the scene makes the professor look like a shadow on a wall of light, which reinforces Bertolucci's message about the illusionary nature of his art (Kline 1987: 86–7).

When viewing *Il Conformista* through an Oedipal lens, it is difficult to disagree with Kline's view that 'if it is his "destiny" to kill the father, Bertolucci succeeds where Marcello has not: he manages his murders (of Moravia and Godard) on a purely symbolic and creative level' (1987: 105). By adopting an experimental cinematic technique, Bertolucci transformed traditional narrative elements into an oneiric journey through memory and the past, making viewers aware of the very nature of the cinematic experience while urging them to reflect upon the ambiguous relationship between authority and creativity, looking and action, reality and illusion.

Further reading

Peter Bondanella, *Italian Cinema: From Neorealism to the Present*, New York, Continuum, 1994.

Angela Dalle Vacche, *The Body in the Mirror: Shapes of History in Italian Cinema*, Princeton, Princeton University Press, 1992.

Jean A. Gili, *Italian Filmmakers. Self Portraits: A Selection of Interviews*, Roma, Gremese Editore, 1998.

Marylin Goldin, 'Bertolucci on *The Conformist*', *Sight and Sound*, Vol. 40, No. 2, 1971, pp. 64–6.

Jefferson Kline, *Bertolucci's Dream Loom: A Psychoanalytic Study of Cinema*, Amherst, University of Massachusetts Press, 1987.

Josepha Loshitzky, *The Radical Faces of Godard and Bertolucci*, Detroit, Wayne State University Press, 1995.

Millicent Marcus, *Italian Film in the Light of Neorealism*, Princeton, Princeton University Press, 1986.

Claretta Micheletti Tonetti, *Bernardo Bertolucci: The Cinema of Ambiguity*, New York, Twayne Publishers, 1995.

Sergio Rigoletto, 'Contesting National Memory: Masculine Dilemmas and Oedipal Scenarios in Bernardo Bertolucci's *Strategia del ragno* and *Il Conformista*', in *Italian Studies*, Vol. 67, No. 1, February 2012, pp. 124–46.

Christopher Wagstaff, 'The Construction of Point of View in Bertolucci's *Il Conformista*', in *The Italianist*, No. 3, 1983, pp. 64–71.

Christopher Wagstaff, 'Bertolucci: An Italian Intellectual of the 1970s Looks at Italy's Fascist Past', in Graham Bartram, Maurice Slawinsky and David Steel (eds), *Reconstructing the Past: Representation of the Fascist Era in Post-War European Culture*, Keele, Keele University Press, 1996, pp. 202–13.

Robin Wood, 'Il Conformista', in Tony Pendergast and Sara Pendergast (eds), *International Dictionary of Films and Filmmakers: 1 FILMS*, Farmington Hills MI, St. James Press, 2000.

Antonella Palmieri

The Cook, The Thief, His Wife & Her Lover (1989)

[Country: UK and France. Production Company: Allarts Cook. Director and Screenwriter: Peter Greenaway. Cinematographer: Sacha Vierny. Music: Michael Nyman. Editor: John Wilson. Cast: Michael Gambon (Albert Spica), Helen Mirren (Georgina Spica), Richard Bohringer (Richard Borst), Alan Howard (Michael), Tim Roth (Mitchel), Ciaran Hands (Cory), Gary Olsen (Spangler).]

Synopsis: Albert Spica has commandeered 'La Hollandais', an exclusive restaurant where the chef, Richard Borst, creates elaborate cuisine. Albert dines there regularly with his gang of unruly associates and his wife, Georgina; he extorts protection money from Borst. During their visits to the restaurant, Georgina, bored and disgusted by her life with Spica, begins a dangerous liaison with Michael, a refined, cultivated diner. Spica takes his inevitable, bloody revenge on Michael, but Georgina triumphs by serving up her dead lover's body as a meal that he must confront and consume.

Peter Greenaway's films have always divided their audiences and critical response. But *The Cook, The*

Thief, His Wife & Her Lover is a special case because, of all his films, it seemed to capture something of its time, and even entered the broader culture, thanks to courageous performances, Michael Nyman's 'minimalist baroque' score and a very strange title. Greenaway intended *The Cook* as a savage satire, in the tradition of Jonathan Swift, 'on the current British political situation. Since this is a movie about consumer society, it's about greed – a society's, a man's' (Smith 1990: 55). Greenaway is a very literate director, and there is also a sense of medieval allegory in the way the roles of Cook, Thief, Wife and Lover seem to represent particular qualities (Wheale 1995: 180), while the cannibalistic climax of this 'contemporary melodrama' took inspiration from the excesses of Jacobean revenge drama (Greenaway 1989: 'Introduction'). As with all Greenaway films, *The Cook* is at the same time a rejection of the conventions of mass popular, feature-film cinema – 'Hollywood' – and is concocted according to its director's own distinctive recipe. This is therefore a very ambitious project: does Greenaway's highly individual aesthetic simultaneously deliver an effective social critique?

Just one year after the release of Greenaway's film, the Berlin Wall had fallen, apartheid was rapidly crumbling in South Africa, and Saddam Hussein had invaded Kuwait. Elements of the world we currently know were taking shape. Within this longer view, *The Cook* can seem like a retrospective, even claustrophobic film, addressing a domestic agenda in peculiarly British terms, in spite of its director's declared preference for European film style. The object of Greenaway's satirical attack was 'Thatcherism', or more precisely, the perceived consequences for British society of Margaret Thatcher's three Conservative administrations, first elected a decade earlier in 1979.

Thatcherism, partnered more grandly on the world stage by 'Reaganomics', broke with the post-Second World War consensus on the economic regulation of the state. The brisk new agenda demanded: privatisation of formerly state-owned industries, utilities and assets to enforce competitive efficiency; reshaping of labour markets and trade union law, again in the interests of a freer market; promotion of the entrepreneur economy in order to break the supposed 'dependency culture'; and finally, an assault on the privileges and protective practices of the established, professional classes and their institutions – legal, medical and scholastic. These radical interventions delivered greater prosperity to more than half the population, producing what the American economist, J. K. Galbraith, termed 'the culture of contentment', an unparalleled affluence for a significant proportion of the electorate, who therefore tended to become politically quiescent. However, on some calculations, at least one-third of the UK population became, in real terms, poorer than they had been in the late 1970s. The abandonment of the one-nation consensus of the post-war period therefore produced a significantly divided society, with increasing 'social exclusion' and a perception that levels of crime and disorder were inexorably rising. The impact of globalisation during the 1990s internationalised and intensified all of these trends and their consequent tensions.

The Cook strips away the armatures of society and social cohesion. The world beyond Richard Borst's restaurant is portrayed as no more than an icy blue parking lot that services a rank of restaurants and eateries; dog packs scavenge the bins. The only effective law enforcement is concerned with food hygiene, the police and officials who attempt to empty two putrefying delivery vans. One of Spica's goons, Harris, does worry about the consequences of their murder of Georgina's lover, 'the modest man' Michael: 'I'm saying the book-keeper's going to get us into trouble – and he wasn't worth it' (Greenaway 1989: 80). But crime and outrage bring no real consequences for anyone within the privileged sanctuary of the restaurant.

Greenaway is a great explicator of his own work, and is very clear about his formalist, anti-realist position as a filmmaker: 'Every time you watch a Greenaway movie, you know you are definitely and absolutely *only watching a movie*. It's not a slice of life, and not a window on the world. It's by no means an exemplum of anything "natural" or "real"' (Smith 1990: 59). Statements such as these come straight out of high Modernist, early twentieth-century aesthetics, and to that extent are perfectly traditional, in their own way. Even the title can be read as a critical perspective on mainstream cinema: just three names would read better in terms of conventional expectations: *The Thief, His Wife and Her Lover*. As an audience, we would know what to expect as we settled in our seats. But then there is also *The Cook*, a contriver of menus, surely a figure for the Director himself. The disconcerting title is an example of Greenaway working against classical film narrative expectations, and just as *A Zed and Two Noughts* (1985) and *Drowning By Numbers* (1988) were structured by the alphabet and number counts respectively, *The Cook* is zoned by colour: blue for exterior reality, green for the creative kitchen, red for the excessive eating floor, white for the restrooms.

Greenaway's alienating, formalist practice is evident right from the opening credits sequence. A steadily rising crane shot of scaffolding beneath the floor of the sound stage on which the action is being filmed demonstrates a purely Brechtian manner by 'baring the device', by foregrounding the artifice of film in general, and this film in particular. Scarlet-clad flunkies pull back curtains to reveal the theatrical mise en scène, where two delivery vans, one for meat, one for seafood, symmetrically frame the action. The opulent restaurant itself is redolent of consumer excesses of the late 80s. Two of the decade's style gurus were on hand to advise: Jean Paul Gaultier designed costumes for the waiters and waitresses, and Giorgio Locatelli of the Savoy Hotel, London, created fantasy food for display. Albert Spica's table is itself a vulgarian spectacle, dominated by a massive reproduction of Frans Hals' 'The Banquet of the Officers of the St George Civic Guard Company' (1616). Spica and his retinue are dressed in amateur-dramatic copies of the uniforms worn by Hals' officers, who were for Greenaway, 'a gang of people all dressed up with nowhere to go' (Denham 1993: 26).

The Cook, The Thief, His Wife & Her Lover began with a steadily rising crane shot, but some of its most beautiful and startling moments derive from horizontal tracking shots that run parallel to the action, or 'picture plane' of the film. The camera takes in the premodern, artisan bustle of the kitchen, and then ghosts through a wall to reveal the contemporary spectacle of the restaurant itself. Most disconcerting of all, we – courtesy of the lens – follow Georgina via a service corridor into the ladies' rest room, at which point her dress miraculously changes from scarlet to white. Is this a clinical purity that vainly hopes to disguise the messy 'end process' of all eating and drinking? The film is as much about appetite as greed, and the vulnerability of the body in desire, an ancient agenda that may finally upstage the transient politics of the 1980s. Greenaway defends his strict camera regime: 'When [my] camera moves, it moves in a very, very subjective, inorganic way. Which again is very much against the general premise of American moviemaking [which is] … psychodrama realism. … This wretched psychodrama permeates the whole of American culture' (Smith 1990: 59–60).

An obvious objection here is that Albert Spica is by any standards a pretty 'psychodramatic' creation, the figure in whom Greenaway wanted 'to create deliberately, almost in a technical way, a character of great evil, who had no redeeming features. Not like a Machiavelli or a Richard III, who have charisma, which is attractive. I had to create a man who *had* to be mediocre. And there's a way that all my heroes are mediocre people' (Smith 1990: 58). But the great paradox of Brechtian estrangement theory, in film as in theatre, is that we *must* be interested in the characters at some level, however banal, 'modest' or monstrous they are. Brecht's intention with his 'alienation-effects' was to make us interested in his characters in a *different*, more critical and reflective way. There are a number of undeniably powerful, humanly engaging performances in *The Cook*, given by actors who fully committed themselves to Greenaway's unsettling vision: Michael Gambon's Spica, Helen Mirren's Georgina, and Tim Roth's Mitchel, as well as many by the supporting cast. Greenaway has said that he would rather spend time with his cinematographer – the late, prodigiously gifted, Sacha Vierny, who had worked on Alain Renais' *Hiroshima, Mon Amour* and *Last Year at Marienbad* – than with his actors, and the actors may therefore take a kind of revenge, by delivering truly vivid performances which work against the coldness of their director's declared intentions for his vision of cinema.

The Cook, The Thief, His Wife & Her Lover is not purely European art-house cinema because it also continues the 1980s British 'gangster film' convention, which included *The Long Good Friday* (1980), *Mona Lisa* (1986) and *The Krays* (1990) (Lawrence 1997: 166). As in these films, Gambon's Spica is not a wholly repulsive villain. Is there not a kind of monstrous pathos about this thief, as when he breaks down, shouting, 'Kids, who needs kids?' His horrifying assault on young Pup shortly after is perhaps partly an attack on what he wants so badly, but cannot have; Albert had also been a choirboy, once, he says, perhaps not literally, but implying the lost innocence of his childhood (Greenaway 1989: 40). His dependence on Georgina is total, as we see in the final scene when he begs her to come back to him: 'I've – to tell the truth – been miserable' (ibid. 90). Spica is the unsocialised baby that remains within all of us. His simultaneous dependence on, and violence towards Georgina is a perfect example of the paradoxical emotions of the unconscious. There is no greater 'psychodrama' than this, one which is even more disturbingly shown by David Lynch, one of the few American directors whom Greenaway can admire, in *Blue Velvet*, made just three years earlier, where Dennis Hopper's Frank Booth makes an atrociously ambivalent assault – if there can be such a thing – on Isabella Rossellini's Dorothy Vallens.

If *The Cook, The Thief, His Wife & Her Lover* is a metaphorical film, as the director claims, what exactly could the figure of Spica stand for, in terms of an attack on the consequences of Thatcherism? Spica as a graceless monster, 'unleashed' from the working class by the new economic regime, is as much a victim of the new values as anyone else. Alan Howard's antiquarian book-dealer is a member of the cultured, professional middle class that felt itself to be increasingly marginalised in the 'new times'. The true villains of the piece are somewhere else, forever off-screen, global corporatism and transnational capital, inexorably growing in power and potential destructiveness.

Helen Mirren's Georgina surely escapes from the framework of social critique altogether and embodies, with great pathos, the consequences of sexuality and desire on the mature, vulnerable body. For Georgina's magnificent revenge, the film gleefully takes on the conventions of renaissance tragedy and clearly provided inspiration for the grotesque finale of Julie Taymor's *Titus* (1999), a vivid account of Shakespeare's long-neglected *Titus Andronicus*, an Albert Spica for even more desperate times.

Further reading

Laura Denham, *The Films of Peter Greenaway*, London, Minerva, 1993.

Peter Greenaway, *The Cook, The Thief, His Wife & Her Lover*, Paris, Dis Voir, 1989. Available at www.petergreenawayevents.com/petergreenaway.html (accessed 22 November 2012).

Amy Lawrence, *The Films of Peter Greenaway*, Cambridge, Cambridge University Press, 1997.

Gavin Smith, 'Food for Thought', interview with Peter Greenaway, *Film Comment* 26/3: 54–61, 1990.

Michael Walsh, 'Allegories of Thatcherism: the films of Peter Greenaway', pp. 255–77 in Lester Freidman (ed.) *British Cinema and Thatcherism*, London, UCL Press, 1990.

Nigel Wheale, 'Televising Hell: Tom Phillips and Peter Greenaway's *TV Dante*', pp. 163–88 in Wheale, *The Postmodern Arts*, London and New York, Routledge, 1995.

Nigel Wheale

Crna mačka, beli mačor/Black Cat, White Cat (1998)

[Country: Federal Republic of Yugoslavia, France, Germany, Austria, Greece, USA. Production Company: Ciby 2000, Pandora Film, Komuna, and France 2 Cinéma. Director: Emir Kusturica. Producer: Karl Baumgartner. Screenwriters: Emir Kusturica and Gordan Mihić. Cinematographer:

Thierry Arbogast. Music: Dr Nele Karajilić, Vojislav Aralica and Dejan Sparavalo. Editor: Svetolik Zajc. Cast: Bajram Severdžan (Matko Destanov), Florijan Ajdini (Zare Destanov), Zabit Memedov (Zarije Destanov), Sabri Sulejman (Grga Pitić), Jasar Destani (Grga Veliki), Srđan Todorović (Dadan Karambolo), Branka Katić (Ida), Salija Ibraimova (Afrodita).]

Synopsis: The shifty Matko Destanov (Bajram Severdžan) is forced to marry off his teenage son Zare (Florijan Ajdini) to the midget sister of gangster Dadan Karambolo (Srđan Todorović) in order to settle a debt, Dadan having diddled Matko on the heist of a trainload of smuggled oil. In love with waitress-cum-girl-next-door Ida (Branka Katić), Zare has other ideas, and is assisted by his seriously ill grandfather Zarije (Zabit Memedov), who decides to die on the wedding day and thus delay, if not scuttle, Matko and Dadan's down-low arrangement. Mayhem ensues: Dadan insists the wedding proceed, Zarije's corpse is 'iced' in the attic, and the unwilling bride, the horizontally challenged Aphrodita (Salija Ibraimova), elopes during the festivities. On the run and hidden under a tree stump she finds protection and unconditional love in the arms of the giant Grga Veliki (Jasar Destani), the unwed son of wizened 'boss of bosses' Grga Pitić (Sabri Sulejman), who is en route to visit the grave of his old compadre Zarije, Matko having claimed – while weaselling more sponsorship for the botched oil deal – that Zarije had died the previous year. Shots are fired, two new weddings are scheduled (Zare and Ida, Aphrodita and Grga Veliki), Grga Pitić has a heart attack and joins Zarije on ice in the attic, and by the closing credits Dadan, having fallen in the longdrop, is wiping shit from himself with one of the film's ubiquitous geese.

Bruised by criticism that his 1995 Palme d'Or winning *Underground* (*Podzemlje*) was 'hackneyed and deceitful Serb propaganda' (quoted in Iordanova 2001: 117) as French intellectual Alain Finkielkraut emblematically labelled it, in 1996, Emir Kusturica announced to a shocked cinema world that he was retiring from filmmaking at age 41. Centring on the unsettling relationship between aesthetics, ideology and cinema as national allegory, the critical division surrounding *Underground* also serves as an illuminating backdrop to the genesis of *Black Cat, White Cat*, Kusturica's 'comeback' film and direct response to the furore. Although some have dismissed the film as a minor work full of 'irrelevant diversions' (Wrathall 1999), *Black Cat, White Cat* epitomises Kusturica's 'everything plus the kitchen sink' (Gocić 2001: 1) aesthetic of excess. Featuring many of Kusturica's most beloved leitmotifs, it provokes different questions, among them, those of ethnic stereotyping and the ethics of representing subaltern groups, particularly those who in global popular culture have limited access to representing themselves.

Kusturica was born in 1954, in Sarajevo, Bosnia-Herzegovina, one of the former Yugoslavia's six constituent republics, to secular Bosnian Muslim parents. His debut feature *Do You Remember Dolly Bell?* (*Sjećaš li se Dolly Bell?*, 1981) won the Silver Lion for Best First Work at the Venice Film Festival, while his sophomore effort, *While Father Was Away on Business* (1985, *Otac na službenom putu*) gained him both his first Palme d'Or and an Academy Award nomination for Best Foreign Film. *Time of the Gypsies* (*Dom za vešanje*, 1988) further reinforced Kusturica's auteur reputation, before the relative failure of *Arizona Dream* (1992), his first foray into filmmaking in the United States.

While Kusturica had never shied away from politics in his previous films, *Underground* represented a personal and political act of caesura at a time when his fast becoming former homeland was undergoing a bloody caesura of its own. For his detractors, Kusturica's fleeting insertion of archival footage of Slovenian and Croatian crowds cheering the arrival of Nazi troops in Maribor and Zagreb (contrasted with footage of the Nazi bombing of the Serbian capital of Belgrade) was a subliminal attempt to historically justify Serbian military aggression in civil wars of the early 1990s. Perhaps given the fact that these elliptical scenes were unlikely to have been understood by most international audiences, the indictment against Kusturica was completed by aggravating off-screen factors. His disavowal of his Bosnian Muslim heritage in favour of a newly discovered Serbian one (on grounds that his ancestors were forcibly converted to Islam by the Ottoman Turks), literal and political abandonment of besieged Sarajevo for the comparative safety of Belgrade (and then Paris), and not least the revelation that *Underground* received a reported ten million US dollars of funding from Slobodan Milošević's 'rump' Yugoslav regime, all put Kusturica in the stocks as a proponent of incendiary Serbian nationalism. When his contention that *Underground* was in fact a mourning work for the death of multi-ethnic Yugoslavia failed to quell the uproar (support for Yugoslavia's territorial integrity inevitably meant support for its violent enforcement), Kusturica, at least for a short time, drew a temporary curtain on his career.

Licking his wounds, Kusturica originally conceived the film that became *Black Cat, White Cat* as a documentary on Gypsy brass bands. Looking beyond the farcical 'Rom(a)com'[1] it turned into, however, a number of critics have suggested that Kusturica's loving portrayal of freewheeling Balkan Gypsies was a 'projection of his own ostracism and homelessness.' It is a contention on which perhaps the thorniest dilemmas surrounding the film hang. Does *Black Cat, White Cat* confirm or challenge popular stereotypes about Roma/Gypsies? (Or does it manage to be simultaneously hegemonic *and* subversive?) Do we watch *Black Cat, White Cat* as a 'realistic' ethnographic document or as an autonomous act of cinematic creation by an offbeat auteur? Is the film as apolitical as commonly thought?

The carnivalesque nature of the caper keeps the all-singing, all-dancing 'poor but happy' Gypsy shtick on overdrive throughout. Snorting cocaine (kept in a crucifix vial) Dadan struts out a disco Balkan bird dance unlikely to ever have any Gangnam Style afterlife; Matko straddles a ceiling joist, Dadan and Zare swinging from his legs, screaming 'my balls are jammed'; a kleptomaniac Bulgarian customs officer is hung dead from a train crossing arm, Mary Poppins' umbrella in hand; a fat lady with a lacquered quiff sings – but it's not over until she extracts a nail from a piece of wood with her sphincter; Dadan and his mobsters 'Cossack dance' on Matko's head. Yet 'the musical Gypsy' is far from the only exaggerated stereotype Kusturica goes in for. Dadan, for example, embodies the racist folklore of the Gypsy male's alleged sexual menace towards non-Roma women, while in casting Grga Pitić as a rubbish dump magnate, Kusturica manages something of a personal trifecta: garbage disposal is a favoured enterprise of mobsters worldwide, scrapheaps are entrenched in the popular imagination as a locus of impoverished Gypsy life, and in a nod to his own oeuvre, the rubbish dump provided one of the key settings for *Time of the Gypsies*. Noted East European film scholar Dina Iordanova goes as far as to suggest that the film represents an act of 'overt exploitation or exoticisation of Gypsies' (2003: 88) which on the basis of the evidence above, is certainly a legitimate claim. But might something also be said in Kusturica's defence?

To begin with the obvious, it requires a level of disingenuousness to argue that *Black Cat, White Cat* makes the slightest attempt at verisimilitude, that is, to portray 'real existing' Roma life. Secondly, there is an underlying chauvinism in Iordanova's tone that suggests Kusturica, a non-Roma, has no right to represent Roma and that a Roma director would do things better, or at least more 'authentically'. This kind of biographical logic is foremostly a violation of artistic freedom, and then, in effect, a diktat that filmmakers only represent their own (national, ethnic, sexual, gender) communities. Thirdly, for all their madcap foibles, Kusturica's Gypsies come off very positively in a number of respects. Whether it is Matko's paternal love for his son Zare, Dadan's somewhat obsessive love for his sisters, or the warm fraternity of the two paterfamilias, the protagonists frequently display admirable solidarity and bonhomie towards one and other. Judging the film on a single axis of ethics and representation is also to ignore its significant formal properties, including the references to *Casablanca* (Curtiz, 1942),[2] Billy Wilder's *Kiss Me, Stupid* (1964), Kusturica's own body of work, not to mention its many self-referential elements, i.e. the drawing attention to its own cinematic artifice. Finally, if Kusturica really is doing his Gypsies such a disservice, where does that leave Sasha Baron Cohen's infinitely more popular *Borat* (2006)? As Eliot Borenstein reminds us, the opening scenes of Borat's home village in 'Kazakhstan' were actually shot in a Romany village in Romania, and as Borenstein notes, the villagers were oblivious to Baron Cohen's documentary ruse, their poor command of English meaning they had no idea he was presenting them as 'prostitutes, rapists, and pedophiles' (2008: 5).[3]

While the popular contention that *Black Cat, White Cat* is essentially an apolitical film is hard to dispute outright, such a reading nevertheless elides the fact that in politically turbulent times, ignoring politics is in itself a defiantly political act. If *Black Cat, White Cat* does offer political inflections, then it is the recurring image of an enormous pig munching on the plastic carcass of a Trabant – perhaps *the* emblematic symbol of Eastern Europe's failed industrial modernity – that provides best for rumination, a tragi-comic goodbye to the vanished world of European communism. Elsewhere, the smugglers who peddle dodgy oil and whiteware of dubious provenance along the Danube also have strong referents in reality. Serbia spent the 1990s under crippling economic sanctions, as western leaders tried to bring the Milošević regime, if not to its knees, then at least to heel. And in an in-joke that local (former Yugoslav) audiences would certainly not have missed, Matko first refers to Dadan being a 'war criminal', and then later, a 'businessman patriot'. Oil smuggling was the 'patriotic' business venture of choice for many an ex-Yugoslav war criminal, making Grga Pitić's counterfeit whiskey operation seem positively quaint in comparison.

Unlike *Underground*, which closed with the words 'This story has no end', its motley cast floating off to sea on a small island symbolically carved like an iceberg from a larger land mass, the fairytale of *Black Cat, White Cat* closes with an emphatic 'Happy Ending'. With Zarije's advice that 'the sun never shines here' still ringing in his ears, Zare sneakily escorts his bride aboard a German cruise ship and together they glide off down the Danube into the distance. While it is impossible to speculate on whether this kind of escapist fantasy was Kusturica's note to self, he returned from France to live more or less permanently in Serbia in the early noughties. Having apparently regained his appetite for on- and off-screen scrapping, he continues to cinematically pick over the elegiac bones of the Balkans – picking many a new fight in the process.

Notes

1. Following the sensitive and sensible lead of Nikolina Dobreva, I use the term 'Gypsies' when referring to their representation (both in the film and popular culture more generally), and the more correct 'Roma' to refer to the ethnic group itself.
2. For more on this see Francesco Caviglia's 'What is Rick Doing in the Balkans? Quotes from *Casablanca* in Kusturica's *Black Cat, White Cat* (1998)', *p.o.v.* 14 (December 2002), pp. 41–52.
3. Borenstein also suggests a number of pertinent links between *Borat* and Kusturica's 'Gypsy' film.

Further reading

Eliot Borenstein, 'Our Borats, Our Selves: Yokels and Cosmopolitans on the Global Stage', *Slavic Review* 67.1, Spring 2008, pp. 1–7.

Nikolina Dobreva, 'Constructing the "Celluloid Gypsy"', *Romani Studies* 5, 17.2, pp. 141–154.

Goran Gocić, *Notes from the Underground: The Cinema of Emir Kusturica*, London, Wallflower Press, 2001.

J. Hoberman, 'Chaos Theories', *Village Voice*, September 7, 1999. Available at: www.villagevoice.com/1999-09-07/film/chaos-theories/1/ (accessed 15 October 2012).

Sean Homer, 'Retrieving Emir Kusturica's *Underground* as a Critique of Ethnic Nationalism', *Jump Cut: A Review of Contemporary Media* 51, Spring 2009. Available at: www.ejumpcut.org/archive/jc51.2009/Kusterica/index.html (accessed 18 October 2012).

Dina Iordanova, (ed.), *Framework: The Journal of Cinema and Media* 44.2 (Special issue: Cinematic Images of Romanies), Fall 2003.

Pavle Levi, *Disintegration in Frames: Aesthetics and Ideology in the Yugoslav and Post-Yugoslav Cinema*, Stanford, CA, Stanford University Press, 2007.

John Wrathall, '*Black Cat, White Cat* – Review', *Sight and Sound*, May 1999. Available at: http://old.bfi.org.uk/sightandsound/review/97 (accessed April 15, 2013).

David Williams

Csillagosok, katonák/The Red and the White (1967)

[Country: Hungary, Russia. Production Company: Mafilm, Mosfilm. Director: Miklós Jancsó. Producers: Jenoe Goetz, András Németh, Kirill Sirjajev. Screenwriters: Gyula Hernádi, Miklós Jancsó, Luca Karall, Valeri Karen, Giorgi Mdivani. Cinematographer: Tomás Somló. Editor: Zoltán Farkas. Cast: József Madras (Hungarian Commander), Tibor Molnár (Andras), András Kozák (Laszlo), Jácint Juhász (Istvan), Anatoli Yabbarov (Captain Chelpanov), Sergey Nikonenko (Cossack Officer), Bolot Beyshenaliyev (Chingiz), Tatyana Konyukhova (Yelizaveta the Matron), Krystina Mikolajewska (Olga), Nikita Mikhalkov (White Officer).]

Synopsis: It is the year 1919. The Reds and the Whites battle in the plains of Ukraine for the victory in the Russian Civil War, which came in the wake of the October Revolution of 1917. The movie's action does not follow a main hero, or the causally connected events. Rather, viewers witness a series of happenings that take place at different locations: the monastery, the military hospital, a birch wood, and the banks of a large river. The soldiers fight a ruthless war and try to live to see another day. Atrocities are committed by both sides, and human life is not worth much. Women suffer as much as men do, and victory will be as bloody as defeat.

The Red and the White was made in 1967, on the fiftieth anniversary of the Bolshevik revolution. No doubt, it was supposed to celebrate this most important date for the Soviet Union and its allies in Eastern Europe, including Hungary. However, it was subsequently banned in the Soviet Union, revealing the complexity of cultural policies in the countries that were nominally following the same political guidelines. What bothered the Soviets? Most certainly the ambivalence with which Jancsó portrayed chaotic events of the civil war, which raged in Russia from 1918 to 1920. Neither side, the Reds or the Whites, is clearly shown to have the upper moral hand in depicted, large movements of troops and the atrocities that take place during the movie. Historical events are shown as if they constantly escaped the attempts of the people (notably the officers) to control them. There is very little glorious in warfare waged with brutality, and there is very little that can protect soldiers or civilians from the various forms of suffering inflicted upon them.

In addition to celebrating the revolution, the film was supposed to demonstrate close links between the struggle of the Reds and the Hungarians, who joined their troops. This, of course, had wider implications for the ties between the Soviet Union and Hungary at the time the film was made. The Hungarians fought with Austro-Hungarian troops against czarist Russia. They defected to the Reds after the October revolution, which came in the wake of military reversals in the First World War. The internationalist facet of the Russian revolution is evident throughout the movie. We hear Russian, Hungarian and Polish spoken during the conflict while at the end La Marseillaise is sung in Russian and Hungarian. The cause of the Hungarian revolution is intertwined with the fate of the Russian one, and the internationalist cause of the working class (temporary soldiers) is one of the most unifying aspects, holding these desperate people together in their fight.

The White officers repeatedly try to separate the non-Russian from the Russian soldiers among the captured Reds, telling the non-Russians not to fight somebody else's war, but they fail to break off the ties which bind various races and nationalities in their struggle for a better world. No doubt, this should have appealed to Soviet authorities when they were deciding whether to show the movie in the Soviet Union. But the impression that the film did not offer undivided support to the Reds held sway.

There is no principal character in the film, and the participants address each without mentioning names. It is sometimes even difficult to distinguish different sides in the conflict. Nameless groups of people move around, take various positions in relation to the opposite side in carefully staged movements. They fight and die with seeming equanimity, like pawns in a big game of politics, which they fail to influence. The fear of death and a strong desire to survive do exist, but they come to the surface on special occasions when a rare chance for escape appears. The final charge of a group of Hungarian soldiers against the much stronger enemy is futile, yet they march to death with the Marseillaise on their lips, which seems everything but glorious, although the viewers are familiar with the final victory of communism in Russia and Hungary (albeit temporary, which was not known at the time).

This narrative structure, in which there is no one character to connect the described events, and in which historical masses battle for power in society, can be compared with the Soviet montage movement of the 1920s and 1930s.[1] These films also portrayed historical events in which different classes and soldiers fought for the victory of their ideals. The difference is however striking. The unnecessary violence and cruelty in *The Red and the White* is depicted with disarming precision, which puts in doubt ideals and causes. However, the Reds show more mercy and humanity than the Whites. On both sides there are ruthless killers, but also souls able to empathise with the defeated and humiliated. Most importantly, there seems to be no justice at all. Good deeds are not rewarded, nor is evil necessarily punished. The Hungarian soldier who at the beginning refuses to shoot captured Whites is executed just a few scenes later. On the other hand, the Cossack officer who allows the rape of a civilian woman is promptly executed following the orders of the White colonel, who, as it happens, belongs to his own side. The war is shown to be merciless butchery, which seriously puts in doubt any justification of why it is fought. This might have been the ultimate reason that prompted Soviet censors to act. The revolution is not shown to be, in Lenin's words, 'the only justified war', but rather a messy affair with numerous innocent victims. This was in line with many outbursts of humanism, which characterised post-thaw art in Eastern Europe, and very much not in line with rigid prescriptions of socialist realism.

Notwithstanding its politically intriguing dynamics, the main reason why this film holds high critical status in the West is Jancsó's masterful use of the long take. The average shot length in *The Red and the White* is 52 seconds, while 68 per cent of shots have camera movement.[2] Jancsó was, in his words, deeply influenced by the work of Antonioni, whose hallmark was also the long take. But, while Antonioni dedramatised his films through, among other choices, long shots, Jancsó's film is teeming with movement, physical as well as dramatic, slow, but constant.[3]

The long take was very popular in the 1960s and later, in both Hollywood and art cinema. Dreyer, Welles, Mizoguchi, Ophüls, Tarkovsky and many others pushed acceptable boundaries of editing, and the long take became much more present in world cinema. One of the main apologists for the long take was French critic André Bazin, who demanded from film to 'bring together real time, in which things exist, along with the duration of the action, for which classical editing had insidiously substituted mental and abstract time'.[4] He praised cinema that was interested in showing the passage of time, thus grasping the existence of objects in space and in time, contrary to what he, together with Eisenstein, called a 'montage of attractions'. Indeed, Jancsó's films display deep interest in the interrelationship of objects and people in space and time, depicted within the confines of the same shot. People and horses, which are constantly present, walk, stroll, run, and gallop in and out of widescreen shots, extending off-screen space in all possible directions. Sometime shots begin with a single participant, but soon they start to incorporate many others, carefully juxtaposed in Ukraine's sprawling countryside, where the film was shot. Multiple movements prompt the viewer to carefully follow the movements of the camera, zooms, and rack focus, and connect them with the complex manoeuvring of the soldiers, officers and horses on the screen.

The action takes place in carefully chosen settings: a monastery, the banks of the river Pechetka, a military hospital, woods and eventually the banks of the Volga. Each of these is explored for its scenic potential to accommodate moving, long, widescreen takes, thus creating a magnificent setting for the staged action. This opulence runs somewhat contrary to the sombre events described in the film. Murders and fighting take place in carefully planned takes, which are aesthetically very attractive. Does this undermine the strong anti-war credentials we have described? Should war be simultaneously repulsive and pleasing? This remains the question, but it should be noted that Jancsó, except in the eerie sequence in the birch woods, strives to separate the beauty of rolling hills and rivers from the inhumane consequences of war, pointing out their sad simultaneity rather than substituting the advantages of the former for the deficiencies of the latter.

In addition to visual elements of the mise en scène, the sound plays a crucial role in creating the rhythm of the takes. Choreography of movements is achieved mostly through ordered activities of people and horses. Officers command people to walk, run, line up, move from one end of the shot to other, often stripped to the waist or completely naked. The women are ordered around as much as the men. At the same time, the movement of trotting and galloping horses is accompanied by many different sounds. Shots permeate the aural space. The symphony is complete. The long take reigns, never dull or empty. It is privileged in relation to other facets of narration, with an autonomy that is jealously protected. For example, when the communist Hungarian commander enters the church bell tower at the beginning of the movie, we see him searching for his comrades. In a long take, the camera follows him as he ascends the stairs and then walks along the tower until at one moment he turns towards the camera, staring, not revealing much emotion. He obviously sees something that viewers don't. He takes off his jacket, the hat, puts down the weapons, and begins to take off his boots, using the opportunity to throw himself off the tower, committing suicide (which we hear but do not see). Only when the two White officers enter the shot, do we see the reason for his action. Classical narration would have supplied viewers with knowledge necessary to explain his behaviour, but Jancsó refuses to do so, as it would violate the unity of space, time and action represented by the long take. Another striking instance of the autonomy of the long take in relation to the story that dominates the narration can be seen a little bit later. A high officer of the Whites enters one of the monastery's courtyards poised to show his soldiers how to treat Red prisoners. He orders them to run away, and proceeds to order the petty officers to shoot them like prey. However, the camera does not let the viewer see the results of their shots. No, it focuses on the officer and the Whites who followed his orders. Generally, the narration would inevitably show us what happened to people who tried to escape, thus completing the chain of events begun with the shooting, but Jancsó clearly breaks this 'rule' in order not to let the take be completely dominated by the demands of the story.

In the end, we should say something about the way in which Jancsó combines visual and aural elements of narration with the story constructed by viewers. His handling of the former suits the massive movements of the masses, which dominate his films. The long take provides the viewer with a vast array of elements, which can then be combined into messages, which relay the feeling of unique historical events of large proportions.

Notes

1. See Kristin Thompson and David Bordwell, *Film History: An Introduction*, New York, McGraw-Hill, 2003, p. 465.
2. See James Udden, *No Man an Island: The Cinema of Hou Hsiao-hsien*, Hong Kong, Hong Kong University Press, 2009, p.180.
3. David Bordwell has called this kind of dedramatisation 'oxymoronic'. See David Bordwell, David, *Figures Traced in Light: On Cinematic Staging*, Berkeley, CA, University of California Press, 2005, p. 157.
4. See Bazin, André Bazin, *What is Cinema? Volume I*, Berkeley, CA, University of California Press, 1967, p. 39.

Further reading

Roger Crittenden, *Fine Cuts: The Art of European Film Editing*, Oxford, Focal Press, 2006.

Peter Hames (ed.), *The Cinema of Central Europe*, London, Wallflower Press, 2004.

Anikó Imre, *East European Cinemas*, London, Routledge, 2005.

Andras Bálint Kovács, *Screening Modernism: European Art Cinema, 1950–1980*, Chicago, The University of Chicago Press, 2007.

István Nemeskürty, *Word and Image: History of the Hungarian Cinema*, Budapest, Corvina Press, 1974.

Saša Milić

Da hong denglong gaogao gua/Raise the Red Lantern (1991)

[Country: China, Hong Kong, Taiwan. Production Company: ERA International/Salon Productions/ China Film. Director: Zhang Yimou. Screenwriter: Zhen Ni (based on *Wives and Concubines* by Su Tong). Cinematographer: Zhao Fei. Music: Zhao Jiping. Cast: Gong Li (Songlian), He Caifei (Meishan), Cao Cuifen (Zhuoyun), Lin Kong (Yan'er).]

Synopsis: China in the 1920s. After her father's death, 19-year-old Songlian is forced to marry Chen Zuoqian, the 50-year-old head of a powerful family. He already has three wives, each of them living in separate houses within his compound. The competition between the wives is fierce, as their master's attention carries power, status and privilege. Each night Chen chooses the wife with whom to spend the night and a red lantern is lit in front of the house of his choice. Each wife schemes and plots to make sure she is the chosen one.

Zhang Yimou is a prominent member of the 'fifth generation' of Mainland Chinese filmmakers, the collective name given to the graduates of the Beijing Film Academy in the 1980s and the first trained after the Cultural Revolution. *Raise the Red Lantern* is the third film of Zhang's 'Red Trilogy'. The three films each star actress Gong Li and share common themes: forced marriage, oppression, rebellion crushed, self-destruction and authoritarianism. Each focuses on women battling events beyond their control in pre-revolutionary, feudal China. Equally, there are wider themes that extend across Zhang's entire body of work: the crushing of the individual as the price of community stability, Oedipal power structures and suppressed passion. *Raise the Red Lantern* also displays Zhang's signature style: balanced framing, bold use of colour and the penetrating close-up. Examined here is the presentation of spectacle and the underlying questions raised by Zhang's methods of 'looking', aspects that give the film a richness and complexity to match its content. For as the director has stated: 'When tragedy is "made aesthetic", then it is all the more overpowering' (cited by Gateward 2001: 40).

After a startling, percussive introduction, a sustained head-shot opens the film, scrutinising Songlian's responses to her unseen stepmother's instruction that she abandons her studies in order to marry. Just as we only see Songlian's half of the discussion, we are also dropped in halfway through the argument: 'stop talking, mother' she says flatly, before capitulating to unheard demands. She goes beyond submission, asking to become the concubine of a rich man, living as far away as possible. The spectator is thus positioned as her tormentor, forced to watch as this acceptance of fate overwhelms her. Fixed in the glare of the unwavering camera, she sheds a tear. This single shot anticipates the entire film in microcosm as Songlian's perverse surrender is in itself a supreme defiance, a destructive act of passive aggression that signals how she and the women she will meet are to behave towards each other.

After a further percussive outburst, a brief second scene shows Songlian staring at a passing sedan chair. Her scholarly and seemingly modern costume places her at odds with such a spectacle from the past, further emphasised by her arrival at the household. The organisation of space is striking: tight, symmetrical framing, voyeuristic high angles, intimidating low angles, rigid high walls forming a daunting grid. A handmaid washes clothes in a bucket. The transformation out of the modern world is total.

The sedan chair had been meant for Songlian. Still defiant, she refuses to allow her case to be carried but her rebellious modernism crumbles almost immediately when she meets her match in insolence: the housemaid Yan'er riles the new mistress with her sulky attitude and Songlian immediately embraces what little power her new position brings, ordering Yan'er to carry the case.

Each night, the master demonstrates his favoured concubine through a ceremonial lighting of red lanterns and Songlian is quickly seduced by the exotic ambiance, particularly the elaborate foot massage that rewards the preferred mistress and leads the women to target their destructive resentments on each other, desperate for this privilege. The film's dramatic action hinges on how the seduction of ritual and favour vies with the modernist urge to assert individuality. Songlian's modernity dooms her: comments on her education are parroted by the household almost as often as she is told, 'it's an old family custom'.

Here, as in many of Zhang's films with Gong Li, the camera uses the cinematic formula of scrutinising the female through the male gaze (Gong is coded, as feminist film theorist Laura Mulvey calls it, with 'to be looked-at-ness'). By framing all scenes involving the Master so that he is out of shot or kept at such a distance that he is unreadable, Zhang literally gives us little to look at *but* the women and their gilded prison. It is our gaze which is implicated in the act of patriarchal subjugation.

The camera continues to soak up the exoticism of the film's mise en scène. Sublime architecture is lit by a rich glow, women are draped in silk cheongsams and ceremony dictates every action. However, the women are overwhelmed by their strictly ordered, walled confines and each in some way plots against the other (the second mistress is described as having the 'face of a Buddha and the heart of a scorpion'). Both allegiances and grievances between concubines and Yan'er shift as deceptions are mutually unearthed. Ultimately, this flawed environment crumbles, resulting in the third mistress Meishan's execution and Songlian's retreat into insanity.

Madness seems inevitable: the sky, when it is glimpsed at all, is consistently restricted to a small corner of the frame, suggesting the banishment of the outside world. A single shot of the sun seen at 92 minutes in feels like a cinematic gasp of air. Thus rationed, the sky seems to offer temporary relief from oppression. The roof is the favourite location for Meishan to sing opera and also the setting where her relationship with Songlian noticeably thaws. This is extended to a thematic contrast between high-angle shots (oppression) and low-angle shots (escape). Significantly, Zhang alters the scene of execution from the source novel's well to the small structure high up in the complex, signifying that the roof as a source of freedom is a chimera.

This illusion is systematically stripped away. Songlian's initial opposition is undermined as she herself insists on abusive tradition and ritual being followed, resulting in Yan'er's death. Another roof sequence sees the focus of spectatorship briefly turned onto the Master's son, whose presence suggests to both Songlian and the audience an opportunity for romantic escape. Their second meeting, when Songlian is drunk, quickly reveals this as false as he offers her a present that she rejects with the claim that he wasn't really going to give it to her. Finally, the lanterns themselves, having become symbolic of insubstantial gain, are only permanently lit for Songlian as the backdrop to her insanity.

The film is divided into seasonal chapters, each commencing with a high-angled, voyeuristic stare down into the complex. Finally, having trapped Songlian by the gaze from the opening shot, her release only comes when the camera pointedly pulls away backwards through a series of dissolving high-angled shots as we abandon her to solitude and psychosis. Though diminished in the frame and trapped within the confines of the compound, she is back in her scholarly uniform, suggesting the absurdity of forcing a ritualised step backwards from modernity. Her defiance has been the basis of the dramatic action throughout and she has ultimately defied us: we can no longer look at her and have to skulk away.

In Zhang's earlier *Ju Dou* (1990), the gaze is overtly erotic. In a key scene, Gong's character is spied on through a hole as she bathes. She turns to her voyeur, displaying not a seductive image but a battered and dirty body. Rey Chow cites this moment as the character confronting the voyeur, attacking and making us uneasy, 'what is on display, what is being cited, is not simply the cliché of the female body but, crucially, the signs of violence it bears' (1995: 167). *Raise the Red Lantern* removes the erotic and has a more devastating effect: Songlian's self-destruction is assured from the start as she confronts the effects of unbending authority and we, like her unseen stepmother, are forced to watch how it abuses her. Defiance in the film is desperate self-destruction and challenges the spectator to confront his/her complicity. Similarly, Yan'er's refusal to apologise kills her as she is made to kneel in the snow until she capitulates. As it is Songlian's petty display of power over her maid that leads to this situation, the suggestion is that levels of oppression are relative.

As well as sumptuous visuals, the film's aural design includes the sound of the foot massages administered by rattling hammers, Meishan's singing, the oldest son's flute and the alarming sound of the lanterns being extinguished. This all presents an overtly feudalistic Chinese sheen. As a result, while the film's formal beauty is undeniable, much negative criticism has been pointed at this self-orientalising display. The spectacle of (largely invented) rituals, as well as the film's Confucian stillness, classical composition, presentation of concubinage and museum-like enactment of historical China all fetishise Chinese ethnography for Western consumption. In his critical study *Orientalism*, Edward Said defines Western approaches to thinking of the Far East as imposing a set of preconceived archetypes – literally defining the East by its differences from the West (2003). *Raise the Red Lantern* can thus be accused of Orientalist commodification – literally 'cashing in' on its 'otherness' to the Occidental spectator. Certainly, the film's Academy Award nomination raised the profile of Chinese cinema on the international market.

However, while there is optimism in the upbeat ending of Zhang's earlier *Red Sorghum* (1987), post Tiananmen Square, the outcome of Zhang's 'Red' films becomes noticeably more jaded. Far from presenting a mere spectacle of Chinese identity for commercial reasons, *Raise the Red Lantern* as a critique of inflexible rules that crush the individual (particularly the individual female) can be seen as a guarded criticism of oppressive Maoism.

In *Memoirs from the Beijing Film Academy* (2002), screenwriter Ni Zhen argues that Zhang's films offer his Chinese audience, 'cinematic representations of a "temporalised" China … they are profound diachronic descriptions and artistic expressions of the circumstances of individual Chinese people' (2003: 198). Zhang presents the oppressive nature of power and its destructive effects on people. Here, as in most of his work, authority inevitably 'triumphs' but questions are raised as to where audience sympathies lie.

The Fifth Generation's earlier work of the late eighties often situated the Confucian past as an arena for intellectual conflict. Unable to criticise openly a communist present, semi-mythologised pre-Maoist times become the environment for a dialogue about China's relationship with its past, leading to self-orientalising spectacle as a position for anti-authoritarian defiance. Criticising a Confucian other is far safer than an open assault on the Mainland government. In interviews, Zhang is understandably guarded when questioned on this.

Rey Chow also considers how the film is scrutinised by, 'the double gaze of the Chinese security state and the world's, especially the West's orientalism' (1995: 170). Zhang's self-orientalising approach challenges the voyeuristic spectator, much as Songlian and Yan'er use their powerlessness as a weapon of defiance. As tensions seethe beneath a veneer of respectability, we side with the subjugated. The feudal garlands scarcely disguise a criticism of totalitarian attitude and by peeling back the layers of tradition and exoticism, an ugly interior is revealed. Unsurprisingly, for a time it was banned in Mainland China.

Ultimately, Zhang Yimou's clearest criticism of oppression comes more from the film's form than content: it rejects the socialist realism of his predecessors. The off-screen portrayal of the master entirely prevents audience identification; he is a force of authoritarianism rendered powerful and dehumanised. Songlian's request to turn off the lights as he prepares to take her (presumed) virginity is rebuffed with the words, 'I like it bright and formal'. Songlian is subjected to the gaze throughout and, by extension, the western gaze. It is thus her struggle that drives the narrative – she is active and opposes our scrutiny, defiant in her tragedy.

Further reading

Rey Chow, *Primitive Passions: Visuality, Sexuality, Ethnography & Contemporary Chinese Cinema*, New York, Columbia University Press, 1995.

Frances Gateward (ed.), *Zhang Yimou Interviews*, Jackson, University of Mississippi Press, 2001.

Edward Said, *Orientalism: Western Conceptions of the Orient*, London, Penguin Classics, 2003.
Ni Zhen, (author) and Chris Berry (trans.), *Memoirs from the Beijing Film Academy: The Genesis of China's Fifth Generation*, Durham and London, Duke University Press, 2002.

Phil Lloyd

Dama s sobachkoi/Lady with a Lapdog (1960)

[Country: USSR. Production Company: Lenfil'm. Director: Iosif Kheifits. Screenwriters: Iosif Kheifits and Dmitrii Meskhiev. Cinematographers: Andrei Moskvin and Dmitrii Meskhiev. Music: Nadezhda Simonian. Editor: Elena Bazhenova. Cast: Aleksei Batalov (Dmitrii Gurov), Iia Savvina (Anna Sergeevna), Nina Alisova (Gurov's wife).]

Synopsis: For many viewers of this cinematic adaptation of Anton Chekhov's 1899 short story, the plot is familiar before the film begins. The middle-aged Dmitrii Gurov (Aleksei Batalov) meets the young Anna Sergeevna (Iia Savvina) while vacationing in Yalta. Their friendship quickly transitions into a romantic affair. Gurov's unconcerned snacking on watermelon following their first intimate encounter suggests his familiarity with extra-marital affairs; while Anna's profound moral distress reveals that she considers this to be her fall from innocence. Their departures from Yalta to their respective homes would seem to mark the end of their vacation tryst, but much to his own surprise, while home in Moscow, the cynical Gurov is tormented by the vapidity of his bourgeois life and, even more, by his longing for Anna. When he arrives unannounced in Anna's hometown, she, too, acknowledges her anguish, but sends him away for fear of being caught. The two resolve to meet secretly, but regularly, in Moscow, and there they begin to develop a love so profound that 'it seemed to them that Fate itself had meant them for one another, and they could not understand why he had a wife and she a husband'.[1]

In the opening episode of *Lady with a Lapdog*, director Iosif Kheifits captures the boredom endemic to Yalta, a seaside resort town located on the Black Sea. The water sonorously laps the rocky shore and sluggishly rocks a floating empty wine bottle; goats lazily graze in the low tide; and the few men populating the local café sit, nearly asleep, propping up their heads, but allowing their eyelids to droop. The men's conversation is somewhat enlivened when one of them announces the arrival of a young pretty woman vacationing alone. With a shrug of the shoulders that seems to say, 'alas, it's too bad', one gentleman acknowledges that he is accompanied on this trip by his spouse. However, Dmitrii Gurov, who sits at the neighbouring table, is in Yalta without wife or children. He, they suggest, might make the young woman's acquaintance. Without any particular response, Gurov drinks his cordial and directs his gaze out of the café onto the young woman walking her small white dog along the promenade. With every sip he takes, his hand and the wedding band on it enter the frame. The next day Gurov again sits in the café and the as-of-yet unknown woman enters. The camera focuses first on her wedding band, then on his. Following Chekhov's much-cited metaphor of the inevitability of a shot should a loaded gun be included in a play's first act, the visual linking of the two main characters via their wedding rings prepares us for a tale of infidelity.

If nineteenth-century narratives of adultery tend toward the dramatic with their forays into ecstatic highs, turbulent psychologies, social damnation and heroines' suicides (e.g. Gustave Flaubert's *Madame Bovary* (1857), Emile Zola's *Thérèse Raquin* (1867), and Leo Tolstoy's *Anna Karenina* (1877)), then this introductory episode to Kheifits's adaptation of Anton Chekhov's 'Lady with a Lapdog' (1899) marked by lackadaisical boredom presents a more reserved tenor, one devoid of public judgment and the scandals that would accompany it. Take note at how, despite being surrounded by other members of vacationing society, Anna and Gurov's introduction to one another occurs via a series of shot/countershots that frame each in the screen independently. Kheifits thus cinematically separates his protagonists from the world around them and allows their subsequent courtship to take place in isolation from potentially meddling society folk. Even the camera gives them privacy: after they first embrace and run off toward Anna's room, the camera, rather than pan along them, focuses on the dog. Furthermore, not only does the film employ specific cinematic shots to avoid showing the Yalta community judging these vacationers' tryst, but this visual theme is paired with narrative plot points: Anna's husband, who suffers from an eye ailment, summons her home, thus suggesting that he, too, is metaphorically blind to her infidelity. Kheifits couples this theme of blindness with the theme of vision to underscore the private nature of their relationship. For example, in opposition to Anna's husband's ailing eyes, Gurov sees Anna. The film opens with him looking at her walk along the Yalta promenade. After returning home to Moscow, he plays the piano while gazing at a lit candelabra and the memory of Anna's face illuminated by candlelight from the night of their first romantic encounter enters into his mind's eye. And, again, when he arrives unannounced in her hometown and attends the local theatre, certain to find her there, he spies her from a distance through his opera binoculars. Interestingly, Anna's husband, who accompanies her at the theatre, sees neither Anna nor Gurov, but directs his gaze at yet some other woman. The significance here is not that Gurov has eyes only for Anna, to use a cliché, but that their affair is entirely their own; it is private, personal, and removed from social judgment.

By 1958, when Kheifits was presented with the opportunity to shoot *Lady with a Lapdog* to commemorate the centennial of Chekhov's birth, Soviet cinema had shifted away from the demands of Stalinist culture towards a focus on the individual and on private life. Films from this period, known as the Thaw (approximately 1956–1964), tend to feature everyday people (as opposed to larger-than-life heroes), allow for realistic depictions of personal (as opposed to public) struggles, and replace the logocentricity of Stalinist cinema with evocative visual lyricism.[2] Each of these features is present in Kheifits's film and worth considering in further detail. First, neither Anna nor Gurov is constructed as an exceptional character, quite the opposite: she articulates the standard clichés of a fallen woman, and Gurov remains impervious to her barrage of banalities, having heard them all many times before. He is a usual bourgeois Muscovite, a point accentuated visually in the episode of Gurov's dinner with a friend, whom Gurov so closely resembles as to make them nearly indistinguishable. The friend is simply an older, more cynical version of Gurov. Second, while characterised as typical, Gurov's and Anna's relatable personal struggles – each married too soon and to the wrong person – make them sympathetic. This presentation of innocent infidelity also fits into Soviet cinema's cultural metamorphosis. Questions of loyalty were key to Soviet culture during the war and late Stalinism. For example, as Peter Rollberg points out, Aleksandr Stolper's Stalinist-era film *Wait for Me* (*Zhdi menia*, 1943) 'juxtapose[es] the "positive" Liza who maintains an unshakeable faith in her beloved's survival to the "negative" Sonia who gives up on her husband and enjoys the benefits of an extramarital affair'.[3] Not only did such oppositions function to teach moral behaviour, but such expressions of personal loyalty (or disloyalty) also stood for national loyalty insofar as cultural texts constructed the individual to be a representative of the state. Nothing in Kheifits's film is similarly tendentious; the viewer is neither meant to act like nor avoid acting like Anna and Gurov. Instead, *Lady with a Lapdog* implicitly rejects Stalinist mandates to showcase exemplars of right and wrong. Rather than villains, Gurov and Anna become victims of circumstance: incapable of quelling their strongest, most real feelings – their love for one another – each is forced to live a divided life. Significantly, it is their public lives, in particular their marriages, that are lies; only in their private, secret life together are they able to express their truest emotional selves.

And third, while Kheifits remains respectfully loyal to the original plot, as Soviet adaptations of literary classics tend to do, *Lady with a Lapdog* is much more than a faithful cinematic retelling. Just as Kheifits succeeds in employing Chekhov's late nineteenth-century story to capture the cinematic trends of his own contemporary moment, he also masterfully adapts the brevity of Chekhov's literary style into cinematic language. For example, in the introductory episode described above, Kheifits, in minimal time and with remarkably few shots, renders such key themes as the connection between nature and man, bourgeois ennui, and the social acceptance of men's adulterous affairs as a common diversion. Chekhov's story's notable lack of dialogue lends itself to a film built on visual subtleties. Setting, dress, coiffures, and even posture convey class affiliation more strikingly than words. The unobtrusive and restrained camera avoids rapid-fire montage and extreme high and low angles, preferring even, static medium and close-up shots that help convey objectivity. And, with the exception of the couple's reunion at the provincial theatre, which is uncharacteristically explosive, the reserved, careful pacing of the film keeps this great love story from reaching frenzied ecstasy.

Cinematically, Kheifits conveys the theme of private individualism and melancholic tone, in part, by placing he film's protagonists in natural landscapes as opposed to social settings. In an article published in the Russian film journal *The Art of Cinema* (*Iskusstvo kino*), Kheifits recalls Chekhov's own thoughts on man and nature and writes that 'between man and his environment there ought to be an inner harmony'. Thus, Kheifits goes on to argue, it is not any moral delinquency, but the unseasonably hot wind that would seem to blow in the sense of agitation that leads Anna into Gurov's embrace. Similarly, during their visit to Oreanda, Chekhov describes the monotonously breaking of the waves as supplying a constancy and 'complete indifference to the life and death of each of us'.[4] Kheifits visually repeats Chekhov's refusal to aggrandise the significance of their union by shooting the couple in plain, static medium shots and, to the contrary, the dramatic seaside mountain landscape and sunrise with emotional chiaroscuro. Their affair has minimal effect on the world around them; rather it is shown to be a passionate flame that exists only between the two of them.

Finally, Kheifits's choice of actors also helps to create the film's sympathetic portrayal of infidelity. By 1960 Batalov, who plays Gurov, was already well known to Soviet film going audiences. He had starred as the martyred revolutionary Pavel Vlasov in Mark Donskoi's adaptation of Maksim Gorky's *Mother* (*Mat'*, 1955). And in 1957 he played the young romantic, but tragic hero in Mikhail Kalatovoz's masterpiece *The Cranes are Flying* (*Letiat zhuravli*). Thus, while not precisely typecast, Soviet audiences had grown accustomed to watching him as a victim, rather than a villain. Savvina, to the contrary, debuted in *Lady with a Lapdog*. Her youth and innocence immediately endeared her to audiences; she went on to have an eminently successful acting career in both film and theatre.

Notes

1. Anton Chekhov, 'Lady with the Pet Dog', in Avrahm Yarmolinsky (ed.), *The Portable Chekhov*, New York, NY, Penguin, 1975, pp. 432–33.
2. See Josephine Woll, *Real Images: Soviet Cinema and the Thaw*, London, I. B. Tauris, 2000.
3. Peter Rollberg, 'Wait for Me' in Birgit Beumers (ed.), *Directory of World Cinema: Russia*, Bristol, Intellect Ltd, 2011.
4. Chekhov, p. 419.

Further reading

J. D. Clayton and Yana Meerzon (eds), *Adapting Chekhov: The Text and its Mutations*, New York, Routledge, 2013.

Julian Graffy. 'Literature and Film', in Evgeny Dobrenko and Marina Balina (eds), *The Cambridge Companion to Twentieth-Century Russian Literature*, Cambridge, Cambridge University Press, 2011, pp. 235–50.

Stephen Hill 'Soviet Film Today', *Film Quarterly*, Vol. 20, No. 4, 1967, pp. 33–52.

Bill Valentine, 'Nature in Chekhov's Fiction', *Russian Review*, Vol. 33, No. 2, 1974, pp. 153–66.

Dawn Seckler

Daughters of the Dust (1991)

[Country: USA. Production Company: Geechee Girls/American Playhouse. Director: Julie Dash. Producer: Julie Dash. Screenwriter: Julie Dash. Cinematographer: Arthur Jafa. Editors: Joseph Burton and Amy Carey. Music: John Barnes. Cast: Cora Lee Day (Nana Peazant), Alva Rogers (Eula Peazant), Barbara O. Jones (Yellow Mary), Trula Hoosier (Trula), Umar Abdurrahamn (Bilal Muhammad), Adisa Anderson (Eli Peazant), Kaycee Moore (Haagar Peazant), Bahni Turpin (Iona Peazant), Cheryl Lynn Bruce (Viola Peazant), Tommy Redmond Hicks (Mr Snead), Malik Farrakhan (Daddy Mack Peazant), Vertamae Grosvenor (Hair Braider).]

Synopsis: *Daughters of the Dust* is a 1991 American film written and directed by Julie Dash. Set at the turn of the twentieth century in the Gullah Sea Islands off the coast of Georgia and South Carolina, *Daughters of the Dust* is the fictional account of the Peazant family on the eve of some members' departure for the mainland and a new life. Major themes include the tension between tradition and change, family, memory, and voice. Arthur Jafa won the cinematography award at the 1991 Sundance Film Festival for his work on the film. In 2004 the Film Preservation Board honoured *Daughters of the Dust* with a place in The National Film Registry.

Daughters of the Dust, 'a lovely visual ballad about Sea Island blacks in 1902', is the first feature film by an African American woman to gain major theatrical distribution in the United States (Kauffman 1992). As an impressionistic narrative about a little-known Black linguistic community called the Gullah, *Daughters* could be seen as not merely an art film, but as a 'foreign language film' due to the characters' Gullah patois and Dash's unique film language. Dash said, 'We took an Afrocentric approach to everything: from the set design to the costumes, from the hair to the way the make-up was put on' (Boyd 1991). Further, Dash uses a style, which filmmaker Yvonne Welbon calls 'cinematic jazz'. It resonates with the fragmentary cultural forms associated with the use of collage (i.e. Romare Bearden, quilting traditions) in the African Diaspora. Such aesthetic choices typically run counter to normative American film practices, which are more likely to favour coherence and a trajectory of transformation. For example, classic Hollywood films tend to be characterised by close focus on a single leading white man, who faces clearly defined obstacles that he overcomes due to transformations in his character. By contrast, Dash uses a wide lens to capture many characters in long takes, emphasising their relationships to each other and to cinematic space rather than exclusively showing them in action. In the film, there are 'no white people – that alone can be disturbing for some' (Jones 1992). Then, *Daughters*' editing pattern is marked by simultaneity-over-continuity, which is effected through the use of scenic tableaux. They show what characters are doing in different spaces at the same time, though not necessarily with the same implications of parallel editing where two lines of action are shown together in order to create dramatic tension. Finally, 'it was shot on super 35mm film so it would look better. And of course we used Agfa-Gevaert film instead of Kodak because black people look better on Agfa' (Boyd 1991). The prestige *Daughters* has gained since its 1991 release represents a significant achievement for Dash, African American film and culture as well as American independent filmmaking in terms of both form and content.

Daughters concerns the fictional Peazant family, who are part of an actual ethnic community located among the Sea Islands, a region composed of barrier islands that extend along the Eastern coastline from South Carolina to Georgia. Most of the characters in the film are Gullah, a group that has been studied and celebrated for their unique African American culture. In terms of language, religion and cuisine, the Gullah are said to have retained a greater degree of continuity with West African cultures than did the slaves on the mainland, due to their relative geographical isolation on the islands during slavery. Thus, *Daughters* is an essential African American text about key issues of migration and cultural retention. The film seeks both historical authority and poetic expressivity on questions of identity and location within black American culture, especially where they intersect with formations of black womanhood.

The film opens on a somewhat didactic note with opening titles that introduce viewers to the Gullah. By contrast, the sequence that follows mystifies acts of ritual and religion as well as fragments of family history through disjointed tableaux in which the viewer sees an unnamed fully clothed figure bathing in an undistinguishable body of water and a pair of hands releasing dust into the air. These poetic images, which represent the Gullah's 'old ways' are later explained through dialogue but initially they lend the film an exotic and mysterious impression. Subsequent sequences focus on the domestic. For all the visual richness and emotional intensity, the actual content is simple: the extended Peazant family makes preparations for a supper to mark the eve of their migration to the mainland. On this day of both crisis and celebration, introspection and confrontation, family members of different generations question each other about what will be lost and gained personally and culturally when they leave the islands. These narrative themes are analogous to the issues of identity and location that have preoccupied African American intellectual history in works such as W. E. B. DuBois's *The Souls of Black Folk* (1903). Dash condenses these broad concerns into the intimacy of family drama. The ambivalence the Peazants feel about the old ways and what new ways await them on the mainland permeates every scene. One of the ways this tension manifests is in the presence of visual technologies in the film.

The significant and repeated appearances of three visual devices constitute a motif, which embodies the film's reflexivity: the kaleidoscope, the still camera, and the stereoscope. The fact that these devices arrive from the mainland suggest a range of possible meanings from anxieties over documenting the self, the intrusion of observing eyes outside the community and the lure of new worldly pleasures on the mainland. In the film, the kaleidoscope acts as a metonym of *Daughters*' style. Mr Snead, who is the family photographer, introduces the kaleidoscope early in the film, describing it as a blend of science and imagination. Through point of view shots, spectators see the ways in which the kaleidoscope creates abstractions of shape, colour and movement and they are aligned with the characters' delight in such formalist experimentation. These kaleidoscopic images refer to the film's impressionistic, fragmentary structure, which is composed of semi-discrete tableaux arranged in an elliptical or spiral pattern where images and themes return but not to the exact same place. These images contrast with the documentary function and style of Mr Snead's family portraits.

Meanwhile, the stereoscope, no less a device of the imagination, is used to introduce footage fragments possibly orphaned from a larger newsreel or ethnographic work. Whereas a man of science and the family documentarian introduces the kaleidoscope into the film, it is the mystical character of the Unborn Child (Kai-Lynn Warren) who uses the stereoscope. 'Sent by the ancestors to restore her father's faith in the old ways', this character is Eli and Eula's yet-to-be-born daughter, except that she appears from the future when she is about eight years old; invisible to the other characters, only Mr Snead and the spectators can see her when he looks through his camera (Jones 1992). The Unborn Child transforms the use of the stereoscope. It was a late nineteenth-century entertainment used to create the illusion of a three-dimensional image, however, in *Daughters* it is an imaginative pathway for animating postcards into motion pictures, which perhaps represent the future that awaits the family when they migrate.

Started on a budget of $200,000, Daughters took ten years to complete, and finished with $800,000. In Dash's book *Daughters of the Dust: The Making of An African American Woman's Film*, she explains that her film took so long to complete in part because its structure, themes and characters nonplussed industry representatives from whom she sought financing. Once *Daughters* was released, however, the film found its audiences and went on to receive a number of significant awards. Shot by Arthur Jafa, *Daughters* won best cinematography at the Sundance Film Festival (1991). The Black Filmmakers Hall of Fame recognised it as Best Film (1992) and that same year it received the Maya Deren Award from the American Film Institute. Dash's achievements and tenacity as independent director, writer and producer earned her The Oscar Micheaux Award from the Black Filmmakers Hall of Fame (1991). In 2004, *Daughters* was placed on the prestigious National Film Registry of the National Film Preservation Board. Defined by Dash as a black woman's film, *Daughters*' awards mark its status within intersecting independent, African American, American and female audiences and facilitates further the reaches of Dash's visionary work.

While the film's recognition is based on its uniqueness, *Daughters of the Dust* is embedded within the history of black independent films through its financing and aesthetics as well as through its casting. Many of the film's key roles are played by actors who would be familiar to audiences of black independent films: Cora Lee Day (Nana Peazant) played Oshun, a deity in Yoruba spiritual cosmology, in Larry Clark's *Passing Through* (1977) and Molly in Haile Gerima's *Bush Mama* (1979). Opposite Day in the Gerima film was Barbara O. Jones in the role of Dorothy. Jones appeared in *Child of Resistance* (1972) by Gerima, in *Diary of an African Nun* (1977) by Dash and in *A Powerful Thang* (1991) by Zeinabu irene Davis. Trula Hoosier (Trula, Yellow Mary's companion) appeared in *Sidewalk Stories* (1989) by Charles Lane, and Adisa Anderson (Eli Peazant) worked in *A Different Image* (1982) by Alile Sharon Larkin. Kaycee Moore (Haagar Peazant) appeared in Charles Burnett's *Killer of Sheep* (1977/2007) and in Billy Woodberry's *Bless Their Little Hearts* (1984), which Burnett wrote. Tommy Hicks (Mr Snead) had been seen in Spike Lee's early films *Joe's Bed-Stuy Barbershop: We Cut Heads* (1983) and *She's Gotta Have It* (1986). Significantly, these actors' prominence and the complex characters they created in *Daughters of the Dust* did not cross over to mainstream films. Their careers tend toward prominent roles in black independent films but minor roles in television or mainstream films. In using actors from the black independent film world, Dash established the film's aesthetic lineage and its target audiences outside the territory of Hollywood and dominant formations of celebrity.

Daughters is further linked with feature films by black women, which would include French director Euzahn Palcy's *Sugar Cane Alley* (1983) and American director Kathleen Collins's *Losing Ground* (1982) among others. Later films such as Cheryl Dunye's *The Watermelon Woman* (1996) and Kasi Lemmons' *Eve's Bayou* (1997) share *Daughters*' thematic concerns with memory, history, identity and visual storytelling. Further, the 1980s and 1990s saw film and literature sharing discursive concerns. Novelists such as Alice Walker (*The Color Purple*, 1983) and Toni Morrison (*Beloved*, 1987) explored black women's identity and African American memory through stories that focused on family dynamics and women's friendships. The circulation of black women's novels doubtless influenced the creation and reception of *Daughters*, which began its life as a novel, and the film helped to articulate black feminist and womanist frameworks cinematically. Dash has said that she wanted to 'make films for and about black women, to redefine African-American women' (Chan 1990). In *Making of An African American Woman's Film*, Dash gives the following hierarchy of desired or expected audiences: black women, the black community and white women. Dash hopes black women will be the film's main audience, advocates and consumers because it intervenes specifically in the history of black female invisibility and misrepresentation in the cinema.

While *Daughters* is a black woman's film it is still part of the long history of American independent and experimental filmmaking by men and white women that pushes against received traditions and industry standards. For instance, *Daughters* has much in common aesthetically with films such as Shirley Clarke's *The Cool World* (1964), John Cassevettes's *Shadows* (1959), and William Greaves's *Symbiopsychotaxiplasm* (1968). These semi-documentary and jazz-influenced films depart from dominant presentations of black identities and, each in its own way, experimented with merging film's formal, poetic expressivity and its social status as a bearer of objective visual evidence. *Cool World* and *Shadows* both depicted African American urban subcultures, teenagers and jazz musicians, respectively, while *Daughters* focused on rural communities. However, all three works avoid the black-white paradigm, in which the presentation or formation of Black identity in the film would be limited to its opposition to whiteness within adversarial American race relations – not that the effects of American racism are entirely avoided. *Daughters*, as the title of Dash's post-production book about the film indicates, was strongly motivated by the director's desire to bring African American women's stories to the screen. However, the film's aesthetics link it with significant independent films that are not explicitly concerned with black women. All these films take on broader themes of identity, location and film form.

Certainly, the success of Steven Spielberg's black-women-centred film adaptation *The Color Purple* (1985) opened up possibilities for a film like *Daughters* as it likely did for *Waiting to Exhale* (Forest Whitaker, 1995). Yet *Color* and *Waiting* followed the traditional narrative arc used in mainstream films while *Daughters* has a more languid, diffuse narrative structure. *Daughters* shares some content with *The Color Purple* or *Waiting to Exhale* but since it is done in a very different cinematic style, these films may not appeal to or reach the same audiences. *The Color Purple* was released widely and played in mainstream multiplexes while *Daughters of the Dust*'s release was limited and it counts New York City's art-house theatre Film Forum as one of its early venues. *Daughters of the Dust* and the black independent films that it references through the cast share the conundrum of reaching out to black audiences through their content but being embraced by mostly white audiences who view these films in the art-house settings to which their forms and perceptions of their inaccessibility have segregated them. Meanwhile, Dash calls for various film audiences and industry professionals to recognise the universe within black women's stories and identify with black female characters. She says, 'There's just a wide array of different characters and people and types and professions that have never before been depicted on the screen. You know, unfortunately Hollywood relies on the old standard stereotypes that are a bit worn and frayed around the edges at this point. But black women are everything and they do everything, and they have a whole lot of different concerns that are just not paying the rent, having babies, worrying about the next fix or the next john. I mean, there's a whole world in here' (Chan 1990).

Further reading

Jacqueline Bobo (ed.), *Black Women Film and Video Artists*, New York, Routledge, 1998.

Valerie Boyd, 'Daughters of the Dust', *American Visions*, February 1991, pp. 46–49.

Vera Chan, 'The Dust of History', *Mother Jones*, November/December 1990, p. 60.

Patricia Hill Collins, *Black Feminist Thought: Knowledge, Consciousness and the Politics of Empowerment*, New York, Routledge, 2000.

Julie Dash, *Daughters of the Dust: The Making of an African American Woman's Film*, New York, New Press, 1992.

Jacquie Jones, 'Film Review', *Cineaste*, December 1992, p. 68.

Stanley Kauffman, 'Films Worth Seeing', *New Republic*, 30 March 1992, p. 26.

Jacqueline Stewart, 'Negroes Laughing at Themselves? Black Spectatorship and the Performance of Urban Modernity', *Critical Inquiry*, Vol. 29, No. 4, 2003, pp. 650–77.

Winston-Dixon Wheeler and Gwendolyn Audrey Foster (eds), *Experimental Cinema: The Film Reader*, London, Routledge, 2002.

Terri Francis

Le déclin de l'empire américain/The Decline of the American Empire (1986)

[Country: Canada. Production Company: Malofilm, Image M & M, National Film Board of Canada. Director: Denys Arcand. Producers: Roger Frappier and René Malo. Screenwriter: Denys Arcand. Cinematographer: Guy Dufaux. Music: François Dompierre. Editor: Monique Fortier. Cast: Dorothy

Berryman (Louise), Pierre Curzi (Pierre), Rémy Girard (Rémy), Dominique Michel (Dominique), Yves Jacques (Claude), Louise Portal (Diane), Genevève Rioux (Danielle), Daniel Brière (Alain), Gabriel Arcand (Mario).]

Synopsis: Eight friends, four women and four men, most of them academics, spend a sunny September day chatting about culture, history, food and sex – mainly sex. The men, history professors Rémy and Pierre, their gay friend Claude, an art historian, and teaching assistant Alain, spend the afternoon in a comfortable country house by the lake preparing dinner. Meanwhile the women, history professor Dominique, contract instructor Diane, undergraduate student Danielle and Rémy's wife, Louise, are working out at the gym. As day turns into night and the friends gather at the country house, the pleasantly naughty conversation turns sour when Rémy's affair with Dominique is revealed to Louise. Tears and screams, apologies and supplications last but a few moments before civility reasserts itself. The morning after, nothing is resolved.

Denys Arcand's *Le déclin de l'empire américain* marks an important turning point in the history of Quebec cinema as its first film to have been at once an extraordinary box office hit and an international critical triumph. In 1986, it became the top-grossing film of all time within the French-speaking province, surpassing even Spielberg's *E.T.* (1982). It enjoyed a tremendous success at Cannes, and was the first Canadian film to be nominated for an Oscar in the foreign-language category (which it lost to Fons Rademakers's *The Assault*). This unprecedented feat injected great optimism in the Quebec film industry and triggered a sustained flow of successful production activity. Arcand eventually surpassed the success of *Le déclin* with its sequel, *Les invasions barbares* (2003), which exceeded the domestic and international earnings of its predecessor and finally captured the foreign-language Oscar that had eluded Arcand in 1986 and 1989 with *Jésus de Montréal.*

Le déclin's strong appeal rests in its perfect balance between bawdy entertainment, incisive social commentary and contemplative audiovisual poetry. Most of the film comprises amusing anecdotes as the characters relate various sexual experiences. While the men talk about threesomes with horny hitchhikers and fleeting but intense affairs with brilliant colleagues during academic conferences, the women reminisce about their laughable encounters with muscular men sadly endowed with tiny penises and memorable flings with passionate but hopelessly immature foreigners. Arcand often uses flashbacks to illustrate these tales, for instance, when Rémy recounts his attempt to find a prostitute for a visiting scholar from Africa, Mustafa. The prostitute he eventually approaches, a gorgeous blonde, turns out to be a man in drag. First, Rémy wittily suggests to the prostitute that having sex with his black friend would represent a gesture of generosity towards Africa comparable to singing in 'We are the World'. The punchline then follows with the surprise revelation that 'she' is a he, to which Rémy responds 'Oh boy!'

This flashback is a good example of how Arcand skilfully mixes humour with social commentary. That a white man would seek to find a white woman for a black man is, in and of itself, an intriguing variation on traditional sexual politics in North America. The more significant aspect of the scene, however, is Rémy's failure to realise that this ideal woman is in fact a man. As I have argued elsewhere,[1] that Rémy, who has slept with hundreds of women, could not tell the difference between a woman and a man dressed as one is of crucial importance. One of the central points of this film is the changing relations between men and women in the 1980s. Tellingly, when the women arrive at the country house, half-way through the film, Arcand purposefully shoots the first encounter between the two groups as a duel, opposing enemy clans visually divided along gender lines. While males and females now share positions of power – in fact, Dominique is the Chair of the History Department and as such she is the 'boss' – Rémy and Pierre still cling to an idea of women as inferior objects of pleasure. This is the subtextual purpose of the men's erotic anecdotes: a desperate attempt to hold on to fantasies of sexual dominance. Much of the film revolves around the men's inability to accept the new gender dynamics and their deep-rooted rejection of the idea of male-female equality. For 1980s men who see their patriarchal certainties challenged by feminism (with all those jokes about small penises and infantile men), women have now become too much like men; even gorgeous blondes are revealed to be men underneath their alluring outfits and make-up.

There are numerous hints peppered throughout the film that insinuate that independent 1980s women – from the point of view of declining North American patriarchy – have become men in drag. For instance, after one of Claude's stories about cruising on Mont-Royal and the scariest gay bars of St. Pauli in Hamburg, he adds disparagingly, 'Knowing I have to be home at six, 'cause the old lady has supper waiting would kill me'. Rémy interjects, 'the old lady or the old man'. To which Claude tellingly replies, 'Same thing'. Regardless of their sexual orientations, the four men all trade in traditional hegemonic masculinity, eager to maintain the feminine (whether it is embodied by women or by feminised men) in its position of subordination. In fact, Rémy all but concedes that he would prefer to dispose of women altogether and just be with men. He jokingly proposes that AIDS is the only real disadvantage to being gay; that and having to kiss a moustached mouth. Without AIDS, Rémy proclaims, 'homosexuality would be paradise on earth'. That Claude might have contracted the disease is of marginal significance within the dominant heterosexual male discourse that Arcand puts at the centre of his critical perspective.

Even the fifth man who joins the group briefly, Mario, Diane's macho working-class boyfriend whom Arcand describes as an 'unbelievable sadomasochistic rocker',[2] is implicitly presented as a reluctant heterosexual. On the surface, Mario is very different from the four intellectuals. He is tough, a genuine Québécois who speaks *joual* (French Canadian slang) rather than mid-Atlantic standard French like the professors, does not indulge in foreign foods, and prefers domestic beer over expensive imports. However, in spite of his rugged masculinity, there remain significant elements of his character that link him to the other men. First, his tough-guy persona is queered, as it were, rendered 'unbelievable', by the fact that he wears mascara. Furthermore, on the few occasions when Mario is present on screen, he is visually aligned with Claude, and there unfold peculiar games of seduction between the two men. More importantly, Mario's sexual interest in men is expressly stated by Diane. 'He's never made love to me normally', she confides in Dominique, 'always from behind, like a man'. That Arcand specifically chooses this formulation – 'like a man' – has the effect of turning Mario and Diane's S&M affair into what is essentially a relationship between two men. For the dwindling male protagonists, strong, liberated 1980s women, therefore, have become men. And as such, Arcand suggests, traditional heterosexual relationships as defined by patriarchy are now doomed to fail; as happens to Rémy and Louise's marriage at the end of the film. Arcand appears to suggest that to move forward men must fundamentally change the parameters of their interactions with women. But within the narrative limits of the film, there seems to be little hope that this will be achieved anytime soon.

Something else is doomed in *Le déclin de l'empire américain*: Quebec itself. For Arcand, Quebec is dying off. In 1980, a referendum on Quebec's separation from the rest of Canada failed to realise the nationalist dream that had ignited debates for the past 20 years (in 1995 another referendum led to the same negative result). For Arcand the failure of the referendum signified the end of Quebec history. Significantly, Quebec history stands out as a meaningfully structured absence in the film, with only one explicit reference to it: the brief appearance of Michel Brunet's book *Notre passé, le présent et nous* (1976), which Mario offers Diane as a gift.

Brunet was a celebrated Quebec historian who had been Arcand's professor during his days at the Université de Montréal in the early 1960s. He was renowned for his passionate lectures on the past, present and future of Quebec. Arcand's characters are in complete opposition to Brunet. Nowhere in the film do those historians display any of Brunet's optimistic devotion to the nation's collective destiny. When Diane shows Brunet's book to Claude, the two remain conspicuously silent. The shot of the book is held long enough to notice that the only sounds heard are those of birds, cicadas and leaves rustling in the wind. While these ambient noises have their own significance, to which I will return presently, the two characters' silence expresses their utter indifference towards Brunet. Other historians are afforded respect. European historians Fernand

Braudel and Arnold Toynbee, for instance, are cited in the film as models, whose substantial accomplishments as scholars are used precisely to counterpoint the failure of Arcand's characters as intellectuals. But when Brunet comes up, silence.

Politically, Arcand is thus undeniably cynical (he would say 'realistic') about the fate of this small island of French culture lost in the middle of a massive Anglo-American ocean. But underneath this pessimism lies a deeper layer of affect that redeems the film and renders it ironically life affirming. The birds, cicadas and rustling leaves that emphasise Diane and Claude's silence offer a hint of where salvation might reside in Arcand's world. Indeed, as laughably juvenile as the sex jokes might be and as depressingly apolitical as those pedestrian academics might appear, their beautiful natural surroundings inject a strong dose of lyricism in this otherwise sardonic narrative. While the average spectator is amused by the lecherous anecdotes, and the 'serious critic' is captivated by Arcand's caustic dissection of patriarchy and the dying nation, the cinephile finds poignant poetry in the visual and musical backdrop that sustains this comically moribund group of hopeless baby-boomers.

As the tone of the film becomes darker and increasingly cynical, the environment becomes more eerily attractive. As Dominique speaks in voice-over of the irreversible disintegration of North American civilisation in the late twentieth century, beautiful images of Lac Mephrémagog are shown as classical music and the soothing sounds of nature are heard. As the group of friends takes an after-dinner stroll in the forest by the shore, their decadent mediocrity as the useless intellectual elite of a failing society is absolved by the lake, the trees and the fog. Accompanying music plays a central role in the process, lessening the derisive tone of the dialogue. Not only does it counterpoint Dominique's doomsday lecture, it also romanticises the relationship between Diane and Mario, as brief inserts of what seems to be moments of rough intercourse are made almost tender by the soundtrack.

Music and the landscape thus work together aesthetically not to erase the melancholy of the characters, but to make their morose fate bearable, even pleasant. The filmmaker's point might ultimately be to show that, as much as resisting inevitable decline is futile, finding some happiness in appreciating nature, taking pleasure in friendship and enjoying the arts remain vital human endeavours.

Notes

1. For further elaboration of this and other themes in the film, see André Loiselle *Denys Arcand's 'Le Déclin de l'empire américain' and 'Les Invasions barbares'*, Toronto, Buffalo and London, University of Toronto Press, 2008.
2. Loiselle, p. 43.

Further reading

Michel Coulombe, *Denys Arcand : la vraie nature du cineaste*, Montréal, Boréal, 1993.

Réal La Rochelle, *Denys Arcand: A Life in Film*, Toronto, McArthur, 2005.

André Loiselle and Brian McIlroy, eds, *Auteur/Provcateur: The Films of Denys Arcand*, Westport, CT, Greenwood Press, 1995.

André Loiselle

Deewaar (1975)

[Country: India. Production Company: Trimurti Films. Director: Yash Chopra. Producer: Gulshan Rai. Screenwriters: Salim Khan and Javed Akhtar. Cinematographer: Kay Gee. Editors: T. R. Mangeshkar and Pran Mehra. Music: R. D. Burman. Cast: Amitabh Bachchan (Vijay), Shashi Kapoor

(Ravi), Nirupa Roy (Mother), Parveen Babi (Anita).]

Synopsis: *Deewaar* is the story of two brothers, Vijay and Ravi Verma, who follow widely divergent paths as adults – Vijay is a dockyard worker and later smuggler, while Ravi is the honest cop. When the management threatens to harm his family, their father an honest trade union leader is forced to sign an agreement that betrays the workers' interests. Unable to bear this disgrace, he disappears, leaving behind his wife and mother of his two children. Forced to move to the city, they try to eke out a living by day (the mother works as a low-wage coolie while Vijay works as a shoeshine boy) and sleep under the footpath by night. They both enable Ravi, the younger brother, to pursue an education. As Ravi grows up to be an honest cop he is assigned to hunt down his own brother who has by now grown into notoriety as an underworld leader. In the conflict that ensues, Vijay is killed, and the film ends with Ravi receiving an award for exemplary service.

Deewaar is an iconic, epic film in the history of Indian cinema – it is remembered as much for Indian superstar, Amitabh Bachchan's portrayal of the 'angry man'[1] as for its complex portrayal of sociological and political realities of contemporary India. The film is set in the seventies, when the 'imagined community'[2] of the nation was being threatened by a repressive state – a crisis that came to a head when Prime Minister, Indira Gandhi declared a state of Emergency in 1975. Madhava Prasad describes this moment as one of 'deep disaggregation'[3] of familiar structures resulting in the 'de-legitimization of the authority of the state'.[4] Popular Hindi cinema's response was thematised in the figure of the 'angry man' – an anti-state, if not anti-national figure, embodied in the brooding and angry screen persona of Amitabh Bachan, who became a symbol of urban working-class militancy. Rejecting the state and accumulating wealth via the underworld, Bachan's character (Vijay) in *Deewaar* is supposed to have been modelled on the real-life don, Haaji Mastaan. Mastaan's meteoric rise from a humble dockyard worker to a key player in Bombay's underworld parallels Vijay's own career in the film.[5]

As Prasad notes, the film begins as the 'unofficial memory',[6] the flashback of the Mother who receives the award for 'exemplary' performance of duty on behalf of her younger son Ravi. Thus the narrative is already dispersed in two strands as public history and private memory. Ravi is the hero of the official history, his honest actions in the service of law are rewarded by the state while the elder son, Vijay (the underworld don) is the real hero as the mother's private memory coalesces around this psychologically motivated complex figure who has to be sacrificed in order to preserve the body politic.

The flashback opens with the trade union leader, Anand Babu's (Satyen Kappu) address to the workers about a new morning that will rise when workers have access to health care, housing and education. During one such organised strike movement at the mine, the management threatens to kill his family if he did not relent to their demands. He chooses family over the community of workers – a betrayal that costs him and his family dearly. After this episode, the father never really recovers from his sense of shame and finally abandons his family to the mercy of the community. Vijay is apprehended by the workers who tattoo the young boy's arm with the words 'Mera Baap Chor Hai' ('My father is a thief') – words that are singed not only into his skin but also into his psyche, marking his destiny and his choices. They are now pushed out into the unorganised working class milieu of the city where the mother resorts to low-wage manual labour and Vijay works as a shoeshine boy, their home is a street under the bridge – the footpath. The footpath, the underside of the bridge, is the operational metaphor of the movie. It is the psychic bridge that links the two brothers, even as the bridge separates them in two moral universes, on either side of the law. If the bridge is the official site, the public monument, the footpath is the unofficial monument – the 'unintended city'.[7] It is home to millions of homeless urban poor who have been driven out in attempts at city development by the state.

Both Ravi and Vijay are framed by backstories of their childhoods that are crucial to their character formation. Vijay is the son who is 'marked'. He bears his father's shame on his tattooed arm. As a young boy he is fiercely protective of everyone he cares about and lashes out against authority and injustice. He throws a stone at the contractor who harasses his mother at the construction site where she works as a coolie. This rebellious attitude is carried into his adult life where he mobilises against the extortionists at the dockyard. Later the same fierce courage earns him both his notoriety and respect in the underworld. His sense of justice is governed by his own private morality, one that conflicts with the state.

Ravi, on the other hand, represents the perfect citizen. His childhood is framed by a sequence where he is seen running away from the footpath to watch a group of neatly dressed schoolchildren, while a song extolling the glories of the nation 'Sare jahaan se acha' plays in the background. He does well at school and Vijay makes it his life's mission to work so that his kid brother can get the education he deserves. As an educated young man growing up in the 70s, Ravi realises that degrees and certificates have become meaningless as there are no jobs for men without connections, and the nationalist song of his childhood is now rendered ironic. He is however unwavering in his commitment to law and righteousness. Through his hard work and commitment to the letter of the law, he is integrated into a respectable middle-class milieu and united with his love, Veera (Neetu Singh), who is initially separated from him by class. Vijay accuses Ravi of growing up in forgetfulness, in the famous exchange in the 'footpath scene', in sharp contrast to Vijay who constantly remembers and is reminded of his past in the ever-present tattoo on his arm. Vijay's life is a struggle to own the past by avenging it while Ravi strives to dispel it by attaching himself to an abstract citizenship realised through his ideals.

Oppositions are staged within the film's melodramatic schema: private versus public morality, community versus individual, biological versus adopted family, good versus bad woman, capital versus labour and nation versus state. These conflicts are presented through popular Hindi cinema's melodramatic device of choice – 'doubling'.[8] As Ashis Nandy points out, Vijay (underworld don) and Ravi (cop) 'are actually the same person deliberately divided and put back together again'.[9] These conflicts are ultimately resolved in the film's melodramatic ending as Vijay dies in the lap of his mother after being shot by his brother.

The film embodies a 'uterine world-view'[10] in that narrative authority is vested in the Mother (Nirupa Roy) – it is her story told to us via her flashback, she is the law and the nation, the prize and the primordial authority. The brothers vie for her affection and though she loves her elder son Vijay more, she rejects his love to stay with her righteous younger son. She even refuses to accept Vijay's gift of the high-rise apartment where she had once worked as a manual labourer and chooses instead to live with her honest cop son in a humble home. In the film's oft-cited dialogue between Vijay and Ravi under the bridge, Vijay asks: 'Mere paas bangla hai, gaadi hai, paisa hai. sab kuch hai. Tumhare paas kya hai' ('I have a bungalow, a car, money. everything. What do you have?'). Ravi answers: 'Mere paas Maa hain' ('I have mother'). This is also the film's indictment of capitalism; she the mother is the prize that money cannot buy.

The mother in *Deewaar* is 'Mother India',[11] who will sacrifice the law-breaker son for the sake of the community. In order to restore the rule of good, she, much like the epic character of the *Mahabharatha*, Kunti, pleads with her son Vijay not to harm Ravi in the inevitable clash between good and evil that will claim one of them. The invocation of the mythical story of the Indian epic *Mahabharatha* and the parallels between Vijay and the complex character of Karna[12] helps to frame the story in a moral universe familiar to an Indian audience.

While many have noted the alienated 'inner exile' of Vijay's character, Vinay Lal makes an observation about the 'impossibility of the outsider' in *Deewaar*. Vijay, at different points in his life, is bound by affect and duty to communities that he finds himself a part of. As a dockworker he takes up cudgels on behalf of the workers threatened by extortionists, and forms a close friendship with one of the workers, Rahim Chahca, whose talismanic badge he wears until the moment of his death. An alternative to the biological family is proposed in the community – the underworld boss takes the place of Vijay's father and the bar girl Anita is his lover and mother-substitute. She accepts him tattoo and all. Yet in the end it is the ties of blood that prevail – Ravi even though righteous at the end, initially cannot accept hunting down his own brother and asks to be taken off the case. Vijay, under no circumstances, will kill his own brother. Vijay is finally brought back into the fold not through an impersonal law or the rational state but through the blood family and the primordial authority of the mother in whose arms he dies at the end.

Notes

1. See Mazumdar, pp. 1–40 for a discussion of *Deewaar* and on-screen rage.
2. As Benedict Anderson famously defines it in *Imagined Communities* (1983).
3. Prasad, p. 120. See pp. 117–37, for an exegesis of this moment in India's socio-political history.
4. Ibid.
5. For more parallels with Haaji Mastaan, see Virdi, p. 6.
6. Prasad, p. 148. See detailed analysis of the film, pp. 144–53.
7. See Mazumdar, pp. 1–40, for an insightful analysis of the unintended city in the film.
8. See Pinney, p. 10.
9. Ibid.
10. K. Chandrasekhar cited in Lal's essay in Nandy, p. 246.
11. This parallel has been noted by Nandy among others. See Nandy's interview with Pinney (Pinney, p. 10).
12. See Mazumdar, pp. 1–40, Prasad, pp. 144–53, on the parallels with the *Mahabharatha* epic.

Further reading

Benedict Anderson, *Imagined Communities: Reflections on the Origin and Spread of Nationalism*, London: Verso, 1983.

Alka Anjaria, 'Relationships which have No Name: Family and Sexuality in 1970s Popular Film', *South Asian Popular Culture*, 2012, Vol. 10, No. 1, pp. 23–35.

Munni Kabir, *Talking Films: Conversation with Javed Akhtar*, Delhi: Oxford University Press, 2003.

Vinay Lal, *Deewaar: The Footpath, the City and the Angry Young Man*, Delhi: Harper Collins India, 2011.

Vinay Lal, 'The Impossibility of the Outsider' in Ashis Nandy (ed.), *The Secret Politics of Our Desires: Innocence, Culpability and Indian Popular Cinema*, Delhi: Oxford University Press, 1998, pp. 228–59.

Ranjani Mazumdar, *Bombay Cinema: An Archive of a City*, Delhi: Permanent Black, 2007.

Christopher Pinney, 'Hindi Cinema and Half-Forgotten Dialects: An Interview with Ashis Nandy', *Visual Anthropology Review*, Vol. 11, No. 2, Fall 1995.

Madhava Prasad, *Ideology of the Hindi Film: A Historical Construction*, Delhi: Oxford University Press, 1998.

Ashis Rajadhyaksha and Paul Willemen (eds), *The Encyclopedia of Indian Cinema*, London: BFI, 1994.

Jyotika Virdi, '*Deewaar*: The Fiction of Film and the Fact of Politics', *Jump Cut*, No. 38, June 1993, pp. 26–32.

Veena Hariharan

Delicatessen (1991)

[Country: France. Production Company: Constellation/UGC/Hachette Premiere. Producer: Claudie Ossard. Directors: Jean-Pierre Jeunet and Marc Caro. Screenwriter: Jean-Pierre Jeunet, Marc Caro and Gilles Adrien. Cinematographer: Darius Khondji. Editor: Herve Schneid. Music: Carlos D'Alessio. Cast: Dominique Pinon (Louison), Marie-Laure Dougnac (Julie Clapet), Jean-Claude Dreyfus (Clapet), Karin Viard (Mademoiselle Plusse), Rufus (Robert Kube), Jacques Mathou (Roger Kube), Ticky Holgado (Marcel Tapioca), Anne-Marie Pisani (Madame Tapioca), Edith Ker (Grandmother), Sylvie Languna (Aurore Interligator), Jean-François Perrier (Georges Interligator), Chick Ortega (The

Postman), Howard Vernon (Frog Man), Marc Caro (Fox).]

Synopsis: In a (probably) post-apocalyptic future, ex-clown Louison answers an advert for a handyman and arrives, pushing his taxi, at the apartment building of delicatessen owner Monsieur Clapet. Clapet sells meat for the only currency worth having in this dystopian landscape – corn. Offered a job with room and board, Louison enters the surreal world of its cannibalistic inhabitants, unaware that he is their next intended meal. Setting about his 'factor' role he encounters Clapet's myopic daughter, Julie, who falls for him as they respectively play cello and saw together. Through a combination of advice and drugging him, Julie protects him from the murderous activities of her father and the other inhabitants, who are slowly turning on each other in the quest for meat. In order to further protect Louison, Julie meets with the 'underground', a militant vegetarian resistance army known as the Troglodytes, and makes a deal with them to kidnap Louison in return for her father's corn. After one of the inhabitant families is forced to give up their grandmother to Clapet for overdue rent, and another, Aurore Interligator, fails to commit suicide despite the inhabitant's best efforts to persuade her through the 'voices' coming through the building's pipework, the Troglodytes make their move. Their kidnapping raid coincides with Clapet's and his friend The Postman's attempt on Louison's life, leading to Louison flooding the house to escape, and culminating in a dramatic (if even more surreal) rooftop battle with Clapet. Louison and Julie are left to make music together on the roof of the now peaceful and no-longer cannibalistic building.

Jean-Pierre Jeunet and Marc Caro's intricate black comedy *Delicatessen* is a film about rhythm. From the simple rhythm of chopping meat, through to the more complicated set pieces of rhythms finding their way through the house. More than that it is about the disruption to rhythm and the way that rhythm reasserts itself, weaving around the disruptive force to reinvent and re-establish in a new form. The greatest disruption is one that is never made clear to the spectator, though is hinted at through the dialogue and through the very dissolute state of the gothic location. There has been some great event that has brought society to a state where condoms are repaired, money is defunct, water pours through the roof of the building, and postmen carry guns for defence. There is reference to 'the rationing' and the landscape is permanently shrouded in an all-encompassing fog, veiling the sky and preventing the crops from growing. Whilst it is clearly set in a post-apocalyptic future there is a sense that it is rooted in the aftermath of the Second World War, and as such is an examination of the collapse of morality in the face of morality's ineffectuality in countering the brutalist logic of national capitulation with fascism. Oppression is re-versioned as cannibalism and the sense of community is overwhelmed by self-preservation and self-interest, amplified through the bizarre rationalisations of the characters and the resulting elaborate and stylised actions arising from them. Jeunet himself characterised this 'central obsession' of the film as one of 'self-sustenance and preservation from death' (Rowlands 2009: 97) and yet in its highly stylised form it becomes almost fetishistic and emblematic of how privation dehumanises even those that remain superficially civilised.

As such it shares an ultra-realist, surrealist heritage with Georges Franju (*Le Sang Des Bêtes*, 1949) and Alain Resnais (*Nuit et Brouillard*, 1955), whilst Darius Khondji's cinematography references the pre-war work of Max Ophuls, Jean Renoir, Jacques Prévert, and Marcel Carné. At the same time Khondji chose to shoot much of it using a wide-angle lens, lending the images an eerie proximity and distorting the characters' relationships with the narrative space they inhabit. It is fundamentally absurdist in nature, perhaps almost Dadaist, with a delightfully shambolic surface structure that belies its intricacy and careful, deliberate construction. Two small boys (the Tapioca children) watch events unfold through a series of vignettes 'some of which are hilarious, while others are deliberately grotesque'[1] where the film's subplots weave in and out of each other, and where the smallest of inconsequential moments (such as a ball of wool rolling down a staircase) suddenly become significant narrative devices.

However, *Delicatessen* is much more a character-driven film where, for much of the time, plot is superfluous. The house is populated by idiosyncratic tenants who all carry their own individual damage and their own particular baggage, but who also share very particular and damaged, cannibalistic relationships with each other. The house is a kingdom where there is an illusion of democracy but where it is in fact a fascist dictatorship with the butcher Monsieur Clapet at its head. Everything has become a commodity (Mademoiselle Plusse even sells herself to Clapet for meat – the obsession of everyone in the house), and even the caretakers are only there to be fattened up before being processed into food. It is into this world that the ex-circus clown Louison arrives himself already damaged by the fact that his circus partner (a chimpanzee called Livingstone) was killed and eaten. The actions of the characters are always presented as having consequences (not always the ones intended as best evidenced by the consequences arising from the repeatedly failed attempts of Madame Interligator's attempts at suicide) and Jeunet and Caro focus on the minutiae of the cause and effect relationship.

The cause and effect relationship seems at times secondary to Jeunet and Caro's use of set pieces and yet these set pieces also serve to further the cause and effect relationship. The key rhythmic sequence (one that was used as the trailer for the film) begins with the creaking bed springs as Mademoiselle Plusse pays Clapet with intercourse, and the camera follows the sound into the pipework that later becomes a vehicle for persuading Aurore Interligator that she is receiving messages from the dead. Through Herve Schneid's fluid editing the rhythm permeates the building and the collection of characters respond to it in ways that spotlight their characters. Everything is moving in relation to the rhythm and the camerawork too reflects this through constantly moving, deploying small movements through to sweeping crane and dolly shots.

In a purely comic sequence, Louison and Mademoiselle Plusse bounce gently on her bed in order for him to locate the squeaking spring and repair it. There is an old film playing on the TV in the apartment and to the strains of a 1930s tune, 'Dreams of Old Hawaii' the pair perform a synchronised piece of visual comedy that is reminiscent of the choreographed routines of Laurel and Hardy. The simplicity and beauty of this scene is amplified by the way in which the rhythm of the bedspring squeak is matched to the rhythm of the music, and by the seriousness and focus of the characters. This is later followed by the pair (again) performing the 'Tika Tika Walk' where Louison is demonstrating a routine he used to perform with his chimpanzee Livingstone and Mademoiselle Plusse joins in. A highly stylised, rhythmic set piece is observed by Julie Clapet and prompts her further into Louison's arms (though a recognition of her own jealousy) and propels the plot forward.

Transgression is at the heart of *Delicatessen*, and whilst transgression itself is transformative, Jeunet and Caro present it very much as carnivalesque.[2] Their landscape is one of disruption and one in which their characters are responding by abandoning themselves to the carnival, where social mores, moral codes, and even laws are sacrificed to misrule. The apartment building becomes a microcosm of the wider dysfunctional society, and what was once normal behaviour is reformed so that it is formerly transgressive behaviour that becomes normalised. The daily activities of the characters tend towards the bizarre: Marcel Tapioca blows up condoms in order to test his repairs on them; the Kube brothers are locked into an inefficient production line making toys that it would seem will never see a market; and in the basement a man lives in such appallingly wet conditions that he is turning himself into a frog. Inside the building it is normal to urge inhabitants towards suicide, normal to lure the elderly to their death, normal to offer a stranger a job with the sole purpose of slaughtering him for meat. Norms are reversed and these reversed norms are dressed in the trappings of the original, a transgression that is at the heart of carnival where nothing is what it seems. As the film moves towards its climax, and Louison and Julie Clapet are chased to the top of the house where he floods a bathroom in order to escape his pursuers, the carnivalesque also climaxes. The pursuers are swept away by a tidal wave inside a house; Louison is left hanging from a lavatory seat when the bathroom floor collapses with the weight of the water; and Louison fights a battle with Clapet using a television aerial as a weapon. Nothing is what it seems, the world is inverted and the surreal dominates.

Louison himself in not immune to the transformative effect of the carnival, yet his position as ex-circus clown gives him an almost privileged role within the piece. His arrival is accompanied by his having to pay for the taxi (that he has pushed to the building) with his shoes, and as the film progresses he slowly divests himself of more and more of the trappings of a 'normalised' world, taking off his braces to help him decorate a ceiling, and removing his clothes in the bathroom sequence in order to prevent water escaping. Louison is the 'hero' of the film and needs to be transformed in order to become so. In many primitive societies (and in the rituals of most modern societies) transformative rites are the method of making the 'normal' human superhuman, and Louison's victory over Clapet may be attributed to his process of transformation (one which may even include the potions of Julie Clapet as a transformative mechanism).

The transformative carnival is wrapped in a rhythmic soundtrack that is at times hypnotic and which certainly offers a backdrop to the action and which could be seen as creating a 'bubble' of sound within which the film's story is played out. Sound is heightened (from the croaking frogs, and the running water, to the squeaking of the bed springs) and as such takes on a supra-real quality. The diegetic music played by Louison and Julie Clapet (on the saw and cello respectively) simply adds to this enclosed (and enclosing) soundscape, with an almost hallucinatory effect. It is therefore fitting that when the 'bubble' rather literally bursts with the roaring deluge and the screams of the inhabitants, and the subsequent rooftop fight sequence between Louison and Clapet in the midst of a violent thunder storm, the film is brought to a conclusion with a restored norm through Louison and Julie Clapet making music together on the roof of the building in a fog-free daylight, perhaps offering a sense of hope, a sense that the madness of the carnival has purged the oppression that gripped the diegetic world.

Once again rhythm is the focus. Not the frantic, frenetic, harsh rhythms that dominate from the outset with the clanging rhythms of the refuse collectors, but rather a gentle, almost pastoral rhythm that becomes emblematic of a rebirth, a re-flowering, and of a new hope. The carnival is over and its king and queen have been crowned in order to restore order to the world and to bring blessings on the crops (in this case perhaps to work with the Troglodytes in using the proceeds of Clapet's profiteering to reseed the world). It is a restorative rhythm that leaves *Delicatessen* as a symbol of hope – a dark, surreal, hilarious, and cinematically beautiful symbol of hope.

Notes

1. Emanuel Levy, *Cinema 24/7 Film Reviews*, '*Delicatessen*'. Available at www.emanuellevy.com/review/delicatessen-1991-/ (accessed: 21 November 2012).
2. The concept of the use of carnivalesque in *Delicatessen* is explored at some length in Ester Rowlands work (see below).

Further reading

Guy Austin, *Contemporary French Cinema: An Introduction*, Manchester, Manchester University Press, 1996.

Anne Bower, *Reel Food: Essays on Food and Film*, London, Routledge, 2004.

Elizabeth Ezra, *Jean-Pierre Jeunet (Contemporary Film Directors)*, Chicago, University of Illinois, 2008.

Susan Hayward, *French National Cinema*, London, Routledge, 2005.

Remi Lanzoni, *French Cinema: From its Beginnings to the Present*, London, Continuum Books, 2004.

Ester Rowlands, *Cinematic Portraits of Evil, Christian De Chalonge's Docteur Petiot and Jean-Pierre Jeunet's Delicatessen*, New York, Cambria Press, 2009.

Freddie Gaffney

Devdas (1935)

[*Devdas* (Bengali, 1935). Country: India. Production Company: New Theatres. Director: Pramatesh Barua (P. C. Barua). Cinematographer: Nitin Bose. Music: Timir Baran. Lyrics: Bani Kumar. Cast: P. C. Barua (Devdas), Jamuna (Parvati/Paro), Chandrabati Devi (Chandramuki).]

[*Devdas* (Hindi, 1935). Country: India. Production Company: New Theatres. Director: P. C. Barua. Cinematographer: Bimal Roy. Music: Rai Chand Boral and Pankaj Mullick. Dialogue and Lyrics: Kidar Sharma. Cast: K. L. Saigal (Devdas), Jamuna (Parvati/Paro), Rajkumari (Chandramukhi).]

Synopsis: Devdas and Parvati (Paro) are childhood playmates and next-door neighbours who declare their love for each other just before Devdas leaves for Calcutta (England, in the 2002 version) for his education. On his return, Paro's family approaches Devdas to secure their daughter's marriage to him. Devdas' father however rejects this proposal on the grounds that Paro's trading family is lower in status to his own as zamindar (rich landowner). Stinging from the insult, Paro's family hastily arranges her wedding to a wealthy, elderly widower with grown children. Defying all convention, Paro comes to see Devdas in the middle of the night to plead with him to save her from a loveless marriage. Devdas, however, is unable to defy convention or his father's authority. Disappointed with himself, he seeks solace in the arms of the city and its attractions, while an old friend takes him to a brothel. There he meets Chandramukhi who falls in love with this young man who pays to see her yet never sleeps with her. From the city, Devdas writes an insincere letter to Paro: 'It never occurred to me that I desire you'. On receiving this letter, Paro now has no option but to go ahead with her marriage. She goes on to become a perfect wife and runs her husband's household and huge estate with aplomb. Never once betraying her husband in deed, in her heart she still loves only Devdas. Meanwhile, Devdas has degenerated from drink to oblivion. He is cared for by Chandramukhi who reforms herself to be with Devdas only to realise, that he can never love her as he loves only Paro. At the end of the film, Devdas after a tortuous train journey ('If it's the last thing I do, I'll come to you', he had said earlier) comes to die at the threshold of Paro's home. She runs to meet him when she is informed of a 'stranger' at her doorstep. But he dies just before she can see him even as the massive gates of her feudal home shut her inside.

The sentimental love story of the self-destructive Devdas, his childhood love Paro, and the reformed prostitute Chandramukhi, adapted from the eponymous novel by Sarat Chandra Chatterjee (1917) is Indian cinema's oft-told tale. A number of versions, adaptations, and remakes, including *Devdas* (Naresh Chandra Mitra, Bengali, 1928), *Devdas* (Bimal Roy, Hindi, 1955), *Devdas* (Sanjay Leela Bhansali, Hindi, 2002) and others, exist as testimony to the tale's magical hold over generations of Indian cine-goers.

The first popular versions of *Devdas* (1935) were made simultaneously in Hindi and Bengali, and directed by P. C. Barua for New Theatres. Barua cast himself as Devdas in the Bengali version and the legendary singing star K. L. Saigal in the Hindi one. Bimal Roy's remake,[1] starring Dilip Kumar in 1955, is perhaps the most beloved version of *Devdas*, especially amongst the post-independence generation. Sanjay Leela Bhansali's recent spectacular and operatic version (2002) starring Shah Rukh Khan, brought *Devdas* back into the collective consciousness of Indian and diasporic audiences while Anurag Kashyap's wildly divergent remake in 2006 finally broke the *Devdas* spell for a contemporary audience impatient with a maudlin, self-destructive addict, and impotent hero.

A 'mythological reference point for Hindi melodrama',[2] Chidananda Dasgupta, the pioneering film critic noted with a mixture of irritation and wonder:

> it is surprising that this immature piece of fiction[3] should have created such an archetypal hero, a romantic, self-indulgent weakling, who finds solace in drink and the bosom of a golden-hearted prostitute.[4]

Is Devdas 'only a weakling who finds solace in drink?'[5] In a passionate defence of the film,[6] Nandy attempts to restore director P. C. Barua's rightful place in the canon of Indian cinema greats. Nandy traces the biography of P. C. Barua, the handsome, charismatic and talented son of the Raja of Gauripur, and his links with the fictional Devdas, and shows Barua himself as a Saratchandra hero inhabiting a Saratchandra universe. His pathological identification with the character of Devdas, especially his alcoholism and narcissism, his failed love affairs and his longing for a maternal utopia are captured in Barua's own words: 'Devdas was in me before I was born, I created it every moment of my life much before I put it on the screen'.[7]

While critics like Kishore Valicha accused *Devdas* for being 'a love devoid of any sexual significance',[8] others like Ziauddin Sardar[9] and Poonam Arora attempt to trace the significance of his chastity. Sardar sees in Devdas not an imperfect but an unconditional love that longs not for physical but spiritual union with the lover. He reads the tortuous train journey that takes a dying Devdas to Paro, at the end of the film, as a metaphor for the spiritual union between the two.[10]

Arora,[11] in a complex reading of the film's sado-masochistic undercurrent in the relationships between men and women sees in the film's psycho-sexual dynamics a resistance to colonialist ideology. Devdas' chastity is perceived as his 'manly self-control' rather than a lack of agency. *Devdas* was the 'Bengali babu's' response to the charges of effeminacy by the colonialists. If the colonialists sought to infantilise and feminise the babu's incapacity for psychological self-determination and political self-rule, then Devdas' chastity – his manly self-control – was actually proof of his 'political and psychological coming of age' and would as such be read as agency rather than a lack of it by audiences who were perhaps constituted by a class sympathetic to the babu.

The Bengali babu's links with European aestheticism and the *Sorrows of Young Werther* have been noted, though the connection is probably superficial; the *Devdas* story is more evocative of the story of Krishna and Radha and their *viraha* (love in separation). This is made overt in Bimal Roy's film when, as Corey Creekmur points out, Paro pays a Vaishnava couple (replacing the three women in the Saratchandra novella), with three rupees she is holding for Devdas.[12] In the novel, the songs move Paro though their meaning eludes her; the film, however, draws attention to the songs, grounding the eternal love story in the mythical tradition of Krishna and Radha, familiar to an Indian audience. Their eternal yet otherworldly love is portrayed through cinematic choices that reveal extraordinary directorial vision. Both the Barua and Roy remakes are replete with such instances.

Ghatak, who was a great admirer of Barua and considered him one of the greatest directors of Indian cinema, used his films to teach cinematography to students of cinema, praising Barua's use of the 'subjective camera'.[13] It is possible that Barua was familiar with German expressionist films, as he uses parallel editing to convey telepathy between lovers, emphasising a supernatural and otherworldly connection between them. In the film's oft-cited 'telepathic' sequence – Devdas cries out in anguish on the train, the film cuts to Paro as she stumbles while carrying out her daily household duties, and then cuts back to Devdas collapsing in the train.

The relationship between Devdas and Paro is cast as one between devotee and god.[14] This is conveyed through a relay of gazes that Ravi Vasudevan defines as the 'darsanic' and which serve to 'deify the male object of desire'.[15] But the god fails and through the course of the film Devdas becomes a fallen hero who has taken the self-destructive road to his own end. However, at the end of the film, through the purity of his love and his lonely spiritual journey and death, he rises to the stature of an almost-tragic hero. His rebellion is attractive but remains so in words only, in deed he is narcissistic, masochistic and weak. Creekmur calls him a 'Hindu Hamlet'[16] and Gayatri Chatterjee places him in the genre of the 'self-destructive urban hero'.[17] His overarching emotion is self-pity rather than anger, and audiences identify with his pathology rather than emulate him as a hero.

Perhaps the greatest point of audience identification was that he was the 'first successful hero in Indian cinema who seemed to seriously negotiate the anguish of the first generation of rural elite entering the pre-war colonial city'.[18] This journey between the village and the city is emblematic of a whole generation of Indian audiences 'refashioning themselves in response to the changing demands of Indian modernization'. Devdas is portrayed as distinctly 'modern' in his education, dress, habits and opinions. When he first returns from Calcutta (England, in Bhansali's 2002 film) the novel describes his attire: 'foreign shoes, bright clothes, a walking stick, gold buttons, [and] a watch – without these accessories he felt bereft'.[19] Devdas challenges the idea of arranged marriage (at least in thought); he smokes cigarettes (in the novel, the hookah), drinks alcohol, visits the city brothels, and has cosmopolitan friends like Chunilal. However, Devdas' ambivalence toward a new urban modernity, his simultaneous alienation from tradition, and the tragic inability to reconcile the two is dramatised in his doomed love for Paro and everything she stands for.

Notes

1. Roy was Barua's cinematographer in the 1935 versions.
2. See Rajadhyaksha and Willemen, p. 244.
3. Sarat Chandra wrote the novel when he was 17!
4. Dasgupta 1991: 29, and cited by Nandy in Dwyer and Pinney 2001: 145.
5. See Nandy in Dwyer and Pinney, p. 145.
6. See Nandy's brilliant essay, in Dwyer and Pinney, pp. 139–60.
7. Cited in Poonam Arora, p. 262.
8. Kishore Valicha, *The Moving Image: A Story of Indian Cinema*, Orient Longman, 1988, p. 49.
9. See Ziauddin Sardar in Nandy (1998), pp. 31–2.
10. See Sardar in Nandy pp. 31–2.
11. See Poonam Arora (1995).
12. See Corey Creekmur (2001).
13. Cited by Nandy in Dwyer and Pinney, p 140.
14. See Sardar in Nandy, pp. 31–2.
15. See Ravi Vasudevan (2000) for a detailed analysis of the sequence from *Devdas*.
16. See Creekmur.
17. See Gayatri Chatterjee (2003).
18. See Nandy in Dwyer and Pinney, p. 146.
19. Cited in Creekmur.

Further reading

Poonam Arora, '*Devdas*: Indian Cinema's Emasculated Hero, Sado-Masochism, and Colonialism' in *The Journal of South Asian Literature*, Vol. 30, No. 1/2, Miscellany (Winter, Spring, Summer, Fall 1995), pp. 253–76.

Gayatri Chatterjee, *Awaara*, New Delhi: Wiley Eastern, 1992; rpt. New Delhi: Penguin Books India, 2003.

Corey Creekmur, 'The *Devdas* Phenomenon'. Available at: www.uiowa.edu/~incinema/index.html, 2001 (accessed: 21 November 2012).

P. K. Nair, 'The Devdas Syndrome in Indian Cinema', *Cinemaya* 56/57, Autumn–Winter 2002, pp. 82–7.

Ashis Nandy, 'Invitation to an Antique Death: The Journey of Pramathesh Barua as the Origin of the Terribly Effeminate, Maudlin, Self-Destructive Heroes of Indian Cinema' in *Pleasure and the Nation: The History, Politics, and Consumption of Public Culture in India*, Rachel Dwyer and Christopher Pinney (eds), New Delhi: Oxford University Press, 2001, pp. 139–60.

Ashish Rajadhyaksha and Paul Willemen, *The Encyclopedia of Indian Cinema*, London: BFI, 1994.

Ziauddin Sardar, 'Dilip Kumar Made Me Do It' in *The Secret Politics of Our Desires: Innocence, Culpability and Indian Popular Cinema*, Ashis Nandy (ed.), London: Zed Books, 1998, pp. 19–91.

Kishore Valicha, *The Moving Image: A Story of Indian Cinema*, Hyderabad: Orient Longman, 1988, pp. 43–60.

Ravi Vasudevan, 'The Politics of Cultural Address in a "Transitional" Cinema: A Case Study of Indian Popular Cinema' in *Reinventing Film Studies*, Christine Gledhill and Linda Williams (eds), London: Arnold, 2000, pp. 130–64.

Veena Hariharan

Días de Santiago/Days of Santiago (2004)

[Country: Peru. Production Company: Chullachaki Producciones. Producers: Tito Bonicelli, Enid Campos. Director and Screenwriter: Josué Méndez. Cinematographer: Juan Duran. Editor: Roberto Benavides Espino. Music: Manuel Larroche, Mogambo. Cast: Pietro Sibille (Santiago); Milagros Vidal (Andrea); Marisela Puicón (Elisa); Ricardo Mejía (Papa); Alheli Castillo (Mari); Ivy La Noire (Inés); Lili Urbina (Mama); Erick García (Coco).]

Synopsis: A 23-year-old Peruvian armed forces veteran struggles to reintegrate himself into society only to hit a series of roadblocks, both societal and psychological, in the feature directorial debut from Peruvian filmmaker Josué Méndez. Santiago Román (Pietro Sibille) has just returned to Lima following six years of military service. Coolly received by his parents and unable to find a stable, well-paying job, the dejected Santiago's attempt to further his education is quickly squelched when he discovers that his military pension doesn't offer the money needed to pay his way through school. Though Santiago eventually lands a low-paying job as an inner-city taxi driver, his disdain for the scum of the city finds the formerly active young soldier sinking into a deep depression. Increasingly haunted by his violent military past, he is conflicted by a desire for education and temptation to join his comrades in a decadent life of crime. The conflicted veteran must choose between an honest life of poverty and an act of desperation that could end in tragedy.

At the time of its release, *Días de Santiago* was regarded as probably the most accomplished film by a Peruvian director who was welcomed onto the domestic arena for attempting 'new narrative structures or styles that, while perhaps not innovative compared to what is happening in other cinemas around the world, brought a fresh perspective to Peruvian cinema' (Middents 2009: 191). It is notable, however, that Méndez's first film received very little financial or other support for its pre-production and production stages from conventional sources. Although the director was granted a script development award in 2000 from Conacine, the state-run operation that until 2011 administered a small pot of money in support of the development of national cinema in Peru, he financed the shoot and most of the post-production himself with a micro-budget of around $20,000. Continuing to work as an editor for national television, he shot the film on low-tech digital format over 24 days, pulling in favours from colleagues and associates. Completion was finally made possible by an award from the Hubert Bals Fund for world cinema that was established by the Rotterdam Film Festival in 1987 with the support of the Dutch Ministry of Foreign Affairs. It premiered at that festival in January 2004, and thus became the first Peruvian film to be selected for Rotterdam's official competition. The festival screenings and awards that followed made it possible for the producers to draw up and implement a comprehensive distribution plan for commercial exploitation in cinemas and on DVD. The film was finally screened in Peru, at the main festival for world cinema held in Lima, in August 2004, and thereafter enjoyed a profitable commercial run throughout the country. In fact, it remained on domestic screens in a competitive environment for an unprecedented six months from late 2004 to early 2005, and was shown in a variety of provincial cities as well as on the commercial circuit in Lima.

Días de Santiago was celebrated for taking a distinctive approach to the recurrent and familiar themes of violent conflict and national identity. Perhaps the overwhelmingly positive reception by national critics who considered it the best quality Peruvian film for several years was even more surprising than the international success it enjoyed, given the negativity that has often usually greeted a new film by a local director. The critics praised the way it took a more experimental approach to the codes of film language and adapted them to the representation of a dystopian vision of urban Peru.

Many were impressed by the director's use of a nervous, jump-cutting non-linear editing style, edgy handheld cinematography, and unpredictable switches between black and white and colour, as well as by the use of blue and orange tints to emphasise the inner turmoil of his main character. They also applauded its impressionistic approach to the use of sound: the sparing use of lamenting tones in a zither-based soundtrack, and the experimentation with everyday noises to evoke the tense, heightened reality of the moment. Moreover, credit was given for the tight composition and an intermittent voice-over which further ensure the audience is positioned to experience the world from inside the protagonist's tormented mind. Most of all, they admired Méndez's obvious passion for cinema generally, and the implicit formal references in the film to the work of internationally renowned film-makers such as Krzysztof Kieslowski and Wong Kar-Wei.

Set at the end of the 1990s, an increasingly repressive decade in political and social terms, Méndez's film follows the frustrated efforts made by Santiago, its young working-class, mixed-race protagonist, to reinsert himself into family and civilian life after several years as a marine defending the integrity of his country in the remote Amazon and Andean areas of Peru. Particular sets of enemies mentioned in the film include the Ecuadorian Army, and remnants of insurgent groups such as the Shining Path, who had by this point become linked with traffickers of cocaine. Once home, Santiago tries hard to reintegrate himself into civilian life and to fulfil the expectations of others but is blocked at every turn. His relationship with his wife crumbles, his old army comrades try to draw him into a life of crime, and he fails to develop any emotional tie with his family. His professional options are restricted, and he becomes convinced that the only way to survive in the urban jungle of Lima is by applying the tactics he learnt as a marine to everyday life. Ultimately, though, he struggles to impose strict order on his life and on those around him. When he realises that his initial strategy is failing, he tries instead to imitate the middle-class youngsters he meets who idle away their days by clubbing, drinking and shopping. Events spin wildly out of control when his violent brother's girlfriend begins to make seductive overtures and pleads with Santiago to kill her lover. In the end, Santiago cannot stop himself lashing out in frustration at those who confront and try to control him, and the narrative moves towards a disturbing and explosive ending.

Although the film focuses on the troubled inner world of one traumatised individual who cannot escape the cycle of violence in which he has become entrapped, his story may also be taken metaphorically and symbolically as a painfully realistic vision of a generation in crisis within a specific national context. It offers an effective prism through which issues of concern to young Peruvians at the turn of the twenty-first century may be understood, while at the same time it struck a chord with audiences around the world who appreciated it largely as an intricate portrayal of a young man returning from war. Santiago's story begins with his return to a place that he no longer recognises and the narrative centres on the painful process of reintegration into a society that has moved on without him. His years in the armed forces have obliged him to put certain ambitions on hold, only to have them cruelly dashed when he returns home. His world and his hopes crumble and disintegrate when he abandons the rigid structure of the armed forces; he faces an uncertain future without support and guidance from anyone who really understands what he has been through, or what he now lacks by way of psychological formation. His is an intensely personal struggle of re-assimilation into civilian life that draws attention to 'the struggle against dissolution and fragmentation' (Bauman 2004: 77).

The formal quality of Méndez's film is raw, intense, and fragmentary, reinforcing the psychological trauma of Santiago by the use of strategies of dislocation that are reminiscent of the French New Wave movement of the 1960s, revealing a little of the director's many cinematic influences. These fragmentary moments provide a discomforting viewing experience, and in so doing, they highlight the film's approach to identity as fractured, multilayered, contradictory, complex and fluid. It also focuses on the constant need to react and respond to changing social conditions and human emotions. *Santiago* strikes a far from optimistic note about humanity, contemporary Peruvian reality, and life for young people living in Lima by illustrating the tragic consequences of a society in meltdown. Moreover, although rejecting the traditional approach of flashback to depict directly Santiago's traumatic years in the jungle, the film nevertheless conveys a strong sense of an individual who cannot escape his past and who is paralysed by his own memories. As such, it deals more with the abstract concept of memory and the scars it can leave, than with individual concrete memories, offering a vivid and painful exploration of the scars left by war on human beings who return home.

Asked about where the idea for his debut feature came from, Méndez explained:

> The film is my reaction against the city. I studied in the US, came back to Lima, and I felt the city was hostile to young people. That was in 1998, when the war with Ecuador had just finished, and I started seeing all the young war veterans returning, also, to Lima. I had already started to interview war veterans when I met Santiago, who was the brother of my old nanny. The psychology of the character is completely based on this guy. So the film tells the story of the war veteran but it's also the story of all young people feeling bad in the film.
>
> (cited by Matheou 2010: 386)

Unlike the family and friends around him who remained largely oblivious to the personal impact of conflict, Santiago is unable to shake off the memories of the brutality he engaged in, and his wheelchair-bound former comrade is so consumed by the indelible psychological scars of war that for him the only way out is by committing suicide. Santiago recalls time and again the early excitement he felt at being sent out on a mission, a sentiment that was soon dashed and replaced by disillusionment sparked by the harsh treatment of recruits like him by the officers. However, even harder to confront is the rejection of his worth by civilians who have no idea what he and his comrades have been through on their behalf.

Indeed, the film is structured as a series of increasingly tense combats between Santiago and all those he encounters in civilian society, with the protagonist positioned as both victim and aggressor. As well as drawing attention to the spiralling torment he suffers, these clashes also serve to highlight further the disconnected nature of Lima society at the end of the twentieth century. The city, like so many others across the world, is presented as a complex environment that is completely divided in terms of its racial groupings. Santiago is forced to learn that the capitalist values of wealth, individual progress and private ownership are more important in this unfamiliar, uncanny world that he returns to than the socialist values that marked the country one decade before. This atmosphere of dislocation is highlighted, for example, when the intense, hyper-disciplined Santiago and his lazy, self-serving brother are forced to confront each other; when he tries to join in the social activity enjoyed by the young women in his computing class; when he makes a hesitant enquiry about his course options to the receptionist at the private college and is treated with disdain; when he is reminded of his lack of status and wealth by the department store supervisor who shows no respect for his military experience. In short, the more Santiago tries to reinstate the sense of order, discipline, camaraderie and respect that he appreciated about military life, the more he realises that his efforts to reintegrate as a civilian are doomed.

Despite resonating with such a pessimistic tone, the film was welcomed by domestic and international audiences for whom it appeared to offer a distinctive vision of everyday life in the metropolis for those who fail to conform to the expectations of consumer society. The image of a dystopian city at the turn of the century that offered nothing but isolation for a returning military man certainly struck a chord with critics and general cinemagoers alike. Moreover, it won its director a scholarship from the Cannes Film Festival that gave him the opportunity to spend six months developing his next project in Paris at *Cinéfondation*, a residency programme created in 1998 to inspire and support the next generation of international filmmakers.

Further reading

Sarah Barrow, 'Transnational Film Financing and Contemporary Peruvian Cinema: The Case of Josué Méndez', Stephanie Dennison, (ed.), *Contemporary Hispanic Cinema: Interrogating the Transnational in Spanish and Latin American Film*, Woodbridge: Tamesis, 2013, pp. 137–54.

Zygmunt Bauman, *Identity*, Cambridge: Polity, 2004.

Ricardo Bedoya, 'Peru: Films for After a War', Eduardo Angel Russo, (ed.), *The Film Edge: Contemporary Filmmaking in Latin America*, Buenos Aires: Teseo, 2010, pp. 145–59.

Demetrious Matheou, 'Peruvian Tales, *New South American Cinema*, London: Faber and Faber, 2010.

Jeffrey Middents, *Writing National Cinema: Film Journals and Film Culture in Peru*, Lebanon, NH: University Press of New England, 2009.

Sarah Barrow

Dilwale dulhania le jayenge/ The Brave-Hearted Will Take Away the Bride (1995)

[Country: India. Production Company: Yash Raj Films. Director: Aditya Chopra. Screenwriter: Aditya Chopra. Dialogue: Javed Siddiqui. Cinematographer: Manmohan Singh. Music: Jatin Pandit and Lalit Pandit. Editor: Keshav Naidu. Production Designer: Sharmistha Roy. Cast: Shahrukh Khan (Raj), Kajol (Simran), Amrish Puri (Baldev), Farida Jalal (Lajjo), Anupam Kher (Dharamvir), Satish Shah (Ajit), Parmeet Sethi (Kuljeet).]

Synopsis: *Dilwale* tells the story of Simran and Raj, both non-resident Indians (NRIs) from London, who meet each other during a European vacation in the early 1990s. While Raj comes from an upper-class family, Simran belongs to a traditional middle-class conservative family. The romance in Europe shatters everything for Simran as her enraged father, Baldev insists that the family move back to Punjab for Simran's marriage to his childhood friend's son, Kuljeet. A heartbroken Simran is left with no choice but to leave London with her family. When Raj discovers the family has left for their homeland, he is encouraged by his father to follow with a mission to get his love back. Simran's mother, Lajjo feels empathy for her daughter and at one point tells her to elope with Raj. After a series of twists, conflicts, comic moments and high drama, the couple is reunited with the blessings of both families. The last shot of the film shows the couple board a train to leave the small town of Punjab. *Dilwale* was shot in India, London and Switzerland and is one of the first films of the 1990s geared to appeal to the Indian diaspora by typically reinventing the NRI as a new figure of national identity.

Dilwale's success both outside India and in the domestic market made it a trendsetter for lavishly mounted family films of the 1990s that moved across the world. The presence of NRIs and a narrative quest to define 'Indianness' irrespective of geographical location ensured that the film received considerable scholarly and journalistic attention for the way it reframed ideas of nationhood and tradition for a globalised Indian context. Unlike earlier films where the NRI was portrayed as a debauched and decadent figure, *Dilwale* is the first of the 1990s films 'that turned Bollywood's NRI stereotype on its head' (Chopra 2002: 11–12). The typical family melodrama of an earlier period had social duties, love of nation and kinship bonds as the driving force overwhelming individual choice and desire (Thomas 1995). By contrast, the 1990s melodrama created a space for personal desires but in these films the heroine performed a symbolic function as the figure through whom the boundaries of 'Indianness' could be defined (Sharpe 2005: 64). In her reading of *Dilwale*, Patricia Uberoi has argued that 'at every turning point in the film narrative, and with every existential crisis the protagonists pause to remind themselves and each other of what it means to be Indian' (ibid: 309). *Dilwale* has also been viewed as the first film of the 1990s to set the template for the 'Bollywoodisation' of Indian cinema, a trend where a series of consumption practices began to coalesce around popular film culture, globally (Rajadhyaksha 2003). These readings are all justified and insightful but despite the conservative family values present in the film, *Dilwale* needs to be seen as an ambivalent text that struggles to come to terms with the cultural processes of globalisation by trying to maintain a balance between ideas of 'tradition', modern cosmopolitanism and a yearning for the fulfilment of individual desire.

In the various accounts of the film, few have commented on the way *Dilwale* draws its central premise from a tradition of 1960s romance films set in hill stations. Those films often saw families opposed to the romantic liaison of the protagonists; the couple had to go through intense opposition and crisis before they were legitimately accepted by both sides. Songs, travel, fashion and scenic sites were the hallmark of these 1960s films. *Dilwale* retains the core thread of these films but the location of the romance moves to Europe and the unfolding of family conflict, drama and reconciliation takes place in the North Indian State of Punjab. The train, a recurring feature in the 1960s films is replaced in *Dilwale* by the Euro-rail. It is in this careful orchestration of the films mise en scène that we see shifts in themes, art direction, costume, music and dance numbers, all geared to appeal to an Indian diaspora while at the same time also draw in an Indian audience wanting to be 'modern' and yet very 'Indian'.

Raj and Simran belong to different class backgrounds. Raj is all set to leave for a holiday in Europe with his other rich friends. Simran is keen to go with her girlfriends but knows that her father will not permit her to. In a poignant scene, Simran addresses her father and says she wants only one month's freedom and following that she will do everything that he expects of her, including an arranged marriage in Punjab with someone she has never met. Simran says she wants to experience her entire life's dreams and aspirations in that one month. The father is moved by the intensity of Simran's desire to travel with her friends and relents. It is this month-long travel across Europe that changes Simran and Raj's life.

The Europe segment of the film is a breezy collation of comic interludes, popular song sequences, and display of commodities, fashion and transportation. The landscape is picturesque. Instead of the typical hill station of 1960s cinema, we are moving across typical tourist sites of Europe by Euro-rail, expensive cars and by foot. Simran and Raj get separated from their friends and end up spending considerable time with each other. The journey from here on is centred on the development of a romance in which matters related to arranged marriages, sexual intimacy and traditional values are discussed by the two. It is in this landscape away from home that the two experience the full force and power of romantic desire. In a particular sequence, Simran gets drunk and becomes obsessed with a red dress she spots in a shop window in Switzerland. There is a sudden transition as Simran now wearing the red dress dances in the snow with Raj to a popular song. The couple is shown moving across diverse landscapes wearing different clothes. While such fantasy linked to fashion is now common in many films, *Dilwale* foregrounded the fantasy world of song sequences of the 1990s by allowing a drunken woman to experience her most immediate desires (Mazumdar 2007: 99–100). The song ends with the couple spending the night in a hotel room without having sex. Boundaries are maintained and never crossed, but there is transgression hovering just round the corner yet contained in line with the demands of a typical Hindi film.

Dilwale sets up several conversation sequences across generations and for this reason remains one of the most intuitive films about the experience of lost youth for one generation and the burning desire for fulfilment for the next. Simran's conversations with her mother both after the Europe trip and later in Punjab are loaded with sadness about the way women's desires and dreams are never fulfilled. This constant yearning and projection of individual desire at one level and the powerful presence of social norms, rituals and expectations about marriage on the other made *Dilwale* a complex narrative about the memories of a generation, desperate to reverse their own lost youth and absence of romance through their children. Yet at the heart of *Dilwale* is also a utopian desire for reconciliation and belief in the values of the Indian family. Contemporary individual subjectivities are thus drawn into the narrative and arranged for a final climax where all differences are ironed out and the 'great Indian family' lives on with its commitment to marriage, rituals and 'cultural purity' as the hallmark of their identity.

If the first half of the film is set in Europe we have a dramatic journey homeward to Punjab in the second part of the film, the entry staged via a song played over images of mustard fields. It is in this second half where preparations are on for Simran's engagement and marriage to Kuljeet that Raj enters as an outsider with a desire to claim his love. The stage is set now for a conflict but debutante director, Aditya Chopra, with the help of his dialogue writer, Javed Siddique, creates a tapestry of rich dialogues, song sequences, romantic yearning and comedy. As we move from moment to moment in the family home of Baldev, we are introduced to the joint Indian family, its rituals, its little traumas, and pleasures. It is in the second segment that Simran's mother Lajjo (Farida Jalal) emerges as a figure who has made peace with her life, but there is lack of fulfilment written in her persona, expressed in conversations with her daughter. She first tells Simran that women don't have the right to expect their dreams to come true, they don't even have the right to dream. But when Lajjo sees her daughter with Raj, she begs them to run away. Lajjo is a critical figure in the film whose world, past and values are never fully explained and yet cast a shadow on the notion of the happy family. She is a 'traditional' mother but with a difference. She tells Simran that she wants her dream to not get squashed like others.

This constant play with the reality of unfulfilled desires and yearning for fulfilment runs through *Dilwale*. Raj's father tells his son to live and enjoy his youth as much as he can since his own life was a struggle and he never had the time to experience the flush of youthful abundance. It is the structure of the narrative and its complex play with a range of characters jostling for their own voice in a world governed by social norms that makes easy ideological readings of the film difficult. This is a film of profound ambivalence, seeking a balance between tradition and modernity and creating a template for many such films in the future. What made the film unique was its clever work with the narrative and also the carefully worked out mise en scène that moved between London and Punjab.

Dilwale Dulhaniya Le Jayenge played a major role in the lives of several film professionals. It was Shahrukh Khan's major vehicle for future stardom. Khan and Kajol became one of most popular screen couples after this film and it brought to prominence the work of fashion designer, Manish Malhotra, and production designer, Sharmistha Roy. Iconic gestures identified with the film have been deployed in other blockbusters that followed. The music for the film was a huge success worldwide. For the film's publicity Aditya Chopra had for the first time created a documentary on the making of the film which was aired on television two days before the release of the film. The film's success outside India and within the domestic market reflected the changed context of globalisation and the ways in which popular film narratives actively began to cater to diasporic audiences. The use of scenic sites of Switzerland played a major role in increasing the influx of Indian tourists to the country. In 2006, the Swiss government felicitated the *Dilwale* team for its role in promoting tourism. *Dilwale* has been the longest running film in the history of Indian cinema and is still going strong at Bombay's Maratha Mandir theatre.

Further reading

Anupama Chopra, *Dilwale Dulhania Le Jayenge: The Making of a Blockbuster (The Brave Heart Will Take the Bride)*, London, British Film Institute, 2002.

Ranjani Mazumdar, *Bombay Cinema: An Archive of the City*, Minneapolis, MN and London, University of Minnesota Press, 2007.

Aswin Punathambekar, 'Bollywood in the Indian American Diaspora: Mediating a Transitive Logic of Cultural Citizenship' in *International Journal of Cultural Studies*, Vol. 8, No. 2, 2005, pp. 151–73.

Ashish Rajadhyaksha, 'The Bollywoodization of Indian Cinema: Cultural Nationalism in a Global Arena' in *Inter Asia Cultural Studies*, Vol. 4, No. 1, 2003, pp. 25–39.

Jenny Sharpe, 'Gender, Nation and Globalization in *Monsoon Wedding* and *Dilwale Dulhania Le Jayenge*' in *Meridians: Feminism, Race, Transnationalism*, Vol. 6, No. 1, 2005, pp. 58–81.

Rosie Thomas, 'Melodrama and the Negotiation of Morality in Mainstream Hindi Film' in Carol A. Breckenridge (ed.), *Consuming Modernity: Public Culture in a South Asian World*, Minneapolis, MN, University of Minnesota Press, 1995, pp. 157–82.

Patricia Uberoi, 'The Diaspora Comes Home: Disciplining Desire in *DDLJ*' in *Contributions to Indian Sociology*, Vol. 32, No. 2, November 1998, pp. 305–36.

Ranjani Mazumdar

Do The Right Thing (1989)

[Country: USA. Production Company: A Forty Acres and a Mule Filmworks Production. Director: Spike Lee. Producer: Spike Lee. Co-producer: Monty Ross. Line Producer: Jon Kilik. Screenwriter: Spike Lee. Cinematographer: Ernest Dickerson. Editor: Barry Alexander Brown. Music: Bill Lee, featuring Branford Marsalis. Cast: Danny Aiello (Sal), Ossie Davis (Da Mayor), Ruby Dee (Mother Sister), Richard Edson (Vito), Giancarlo Esposito (Buggin' Out), Spike Lee (Mookie), Bill Nunn (Radio Raheem), John Turturro (Pino), Paul Benjamin (ML), Frankie Faison (Coconut Sid), Robin Harris (Sweet Dick Willie), Joie Lee (Jade), Miguel Sandoval (Officer Ponte), Rick Aiello (Officer Long), John Savage (Clifton), Samuel L. Jackson (Mister Señor Love Daddy), Rosie Perez (Tina), Roger Guenveur Smith (Smiley), Steve White (Ahmad), Martin Lawrence (Cee), Leonard Thomas (Punchy), Christa Rivers (Ella), Frank Vincent (Charlie).]

Synopsis: Set on a city block during the hottest day of the summer in the Brooklyn neighborhood of Bedford-Stuyvesant ('Bed-Stuy'), *Do The Right Thing* follows the character of 'Mookie' (Spike Lee), a pizza delivery boy, and a day in the life of the neighborhood residents as the climate gives way to escalating encounters and disputes around culture, ethnicity and community.

Do The Right Thing was Spike Lee's third feature film following *School Daze* (1988) and *She's Gotta Have It* (1986). The film came a decade removed from the Blaxploitation film cycle and two years before the 'black film explosion' of 1991.[1] A prolific film auteur, Lee continues to challenge the idea of black film and American cinema.

The opening credits of *Do The Right Thing* open to the strains of a soprano saxophone rendition of James Weldon Johnson's 'Lift Every Voice and Sing'. The song ends screen black and the title sequence begins with Public Enemy's 'Fight The Power' and a cut to a stage. Evoking the conceit of the film musical's opening number, the montage of the sequence features the hip-hop dance of Rosie Perez in multiple costumes against a changing backdrop of Brooklyn photographs backlit by an array of colour schemes. This opening montage is cut to match the movements of Perez's dance, a dance of militancy and popping contractions with a face that never smiles. She is more than merely a woman to be leered at or reductively posed as an object of pleasure. Her dance signals a cultural politics of hip-hop and what Guthrie Ramsey notes as the mark of 'a present that has urgency, particularity, politics, *and* pleasure'.[2] With these two compositions and their distinct spatiotemporal origins, the present of *Do The Right Thing* demonstrates a century of urgency.

'Lift Every Voice and Sing' began as a poem by James Weldon Johnson that debuted in 1900. Johnson and Johnson's brother, J. Rosamond, would set the poem to music and this composition would eventually be dubbed the 'The Negro National Anthem' and adopted as the official song of the National Association for the Advancement of Colored People (NAACP). The NAACP promoted the use of the song as an anthem for the black struggle for access to freedoms and inalienable rights denied by the discriminatory and terrorist practices of white supremacy and the Racial Contract. Moreover, the use of the song during the Civil Rights Movement and its eventual retitling ('The Black National Anthem') continued the purposing of the song as black anthem of protest. As Shana Redmond points out,

> Black anthems become incubators not only for a race/sound fusion but also the merger of art and practice. The conditions that give rise to these anthems within diaspora include colonialism, Jim Crow segregation, and myriad legal and extralegal enactments of persistent inequality; therefore liberation and its pursuit are necessarily narrated and exercised in tandem with philosophies and acts of resistance.[3]

Public Enemy offers an anthem less reconciled to the Christian doctrine of social protest and nonviolence but nonetheless remains a song compelled by conditions that animate defiant verse.

While the first song offers the perseverance of faith and belief in inalienable rights, the latter demonstrates a cultural nationalist tact, a more politicised sense of culture and the black lifeworld. Cultural nationalism shifted the meaning of race from the biological to a deliberate posing of race as cultural praxis and a matter of engagement with the anti-hegemonic struggle against white supremacy as embodying features of black personhood. Moreover, the distance between the poles is made plainer with the modal of hip-hop modernism and not that of the sacred verse of gospel. As a sorrow song of what Mark Anthony Neal calls 'post-industrial soul', 'Fight The Power' offers a sobering and artful discontent from streets far removed from Birmingham, but a relation nonetheless.[4]

The depth of *Do The Right Thing* demonstrates the staging of a political art richly informed by multiple historiographies of black visual and expressive culture. The film is propelled by an intersection of history, music, cinema and blackness. This generative nexus of historical scripts encompasses such issues as gentrification, the black public sphere, police brutality, the popular, cultural and ethnic conflict, and the everyday urban. In other words, anti-realist in its stance, the film positions itself in the matrix of black representation as an interpretative echo and refabulation of race and art. The film employs a 24-hour conceit of the hottest day of the summer in the Brooklyn neighborhood of Bedford-Stuyvesant ('Bed-Stuy'). This plotting of a 'day in the life' amplifies the masterful way the film functions as a discrete representational system. The seamless accounting of the day on the block through continuity editing is facilitated by such things as Mister Señor Love Daddy's radio broadcast, colour, physical movements, emblematic framing, an intricate orchestration of ensemble casting in the depth of field, and sound bridges. With the deliberateness of the film structure, one learns to watch the film and recognise the spatiality of the setting. Eventually, one recognises that at one end of the block is Mookie and Jade's building, Mother Sister's brownstone, the Korean-run grocery, and across the street against the red wall are the corner crew (Sweet Dick Willie, ML, and Coconut Sid). At the other end of the block, starting across from the grocery is Sal's Famous Pizzeria, the stoop where the Puerto Ricans sit, the station home for 108FM 'We Love Radio', and the brownstone owned by the Celtics' fan. The film details a dynamic community of personalities and histories, a space textured by infinite encounters.

The cohesiveness of this spatial conceit does not comply with the platitudes of Our Town, USA. The film proves that the most rewarding consequence of America as 'The Melting Pot' is that the analogy has never worked. We the people are not the same: we have different cultures, belief systems, and freedom dreams. These differences represent at times collateral interests but never truly identical ones. In this way, the interethnic conflicts that circulate up and down the block are but a red herring. *Do The Right Thing* vitally avoids the classical tact of the social problem film to present the problem of differences as systemic or a result of the idea of America itself. In the social problem film, these staged eruptions of racial conflict are resolved and contained with a tacit framing of our spectatorship in terms of cinematically enacted cures.

As Michael Rogin writes, 'Hollywood, inheriting and universalizing blackface in the blackface musical, celebrated itself as the institutional locus of American identity. In the social problem film it allied itself with the therapeutic society. Generic overlap suggests institutional overlap; Hollywood was not just Hortense Powdermaker's dream factory, but also the American interpreter of dreams, employing roleplaying as national mass therapy.'[5] Social problem films with race as their object choice usually enact a limited and circumspect sense of social problem-solving. In particular, the way these films are saddled with the extra-diegetic responsibilities of reconciliation between the races promotes a dangerously ridiculous sense of film as social policy. After all, what James Baldwin called the 'price of the ticket' should mean more than matinee admission. *Do The Right Thing* poignantly demands that one's spectatorship entail a recognition of our respective subject positions and/or complicities in a productively non-patronising way.

The central conflict of *Do The Right Thing* cycles around the issue of *How come there ain't no brothas on the wall?* Outraged by the absence of black representation on the pizzeria wall, Buggin' Out (Giancarlo Esposito) organises a boycott against Sal's Pizzeria in response to the 'Wall of Fame', a collage of photographs devoted to Italian Americans. The call for economic sanctions echoes the use of these strategies throughout the twentieth century by churches, unions and civic leaders as a way of combatting the economic disenfranchisement of anti-black racism. This call for representation is emblematic of a diacritical sense of value. First, there is the value suggested by economic empowerment of a raced consumer-citizen. Second, there is the measure of culture as value. In this way, the central conflict that accrues over the course of the film becomes that of the political and cultural value of blackness.

However, the film's vessel of civil disobedience and cultural nationalism is far from sound. Buggin' Out does not articulate a clear plan of black economic development. His persona is that of empty rhetoric; more hothead than firebrand. Radio Raheem (Bill Nunn) lumbers and speaks like a heroic throwback from the mind of Jack Kirby. A laconic giant, his voice and being are embodied by 'Fight the Power', the only thing constantly blaring from his boombox. His 'Love vs. Hate' direct address constitutes the most that he ever speaks, a gesture to the absurd holy-roller ways of Robert Mitchum's itinerant honeymoon killer in *Night of the Hunter* (Charles Laughton, 1955). Yet, this *ad infinitum* struggle between good and evil, coupled with Raheem's devotion to the gospel of Public Enemy, frame him as a very textured figure. He wanders throughout Bed-Stuy spreading the word, battling any and all windmills along the way. Every interaction is a contest and exclamation of his being. Finally, closing out the rebel band is Smiley (Roger Guenveur Smith). Mentally disabled and physically spastic, Smiley's speech is as indecipherable as the irreconcilable coupling of Malcolm X and Martin Luther King Jr. in the photograph postcards he marks and peddles. Stumbling through the film, Smiley tags his cherished wares in a style imitative of Jean-Michel Basquiat.[6]

This crisis of representation emblematic of this rebel ensemble embodies the necessary tensions surrounding the political question of black representation and film as an art practice. Specifically, what is the purpose of the term 'black film'? Does it represent an entirely foreign film practice? Is it merely a reflection of black people, not art but simply black existential dictation? Like all other expressions of the idea of black film, *Do The Right Thing* should not be thought as mimetically tied to the social category of race. The 'black' of black film represents something other than merely people. Instead it must be appreciated in terms of the art of film and enactments of black visual and expressive culture. In this way, film blackness functions as a critical term for the way race is rendered and mediated by the art of film.[7]

This alienation effect of the film escalates with the final sequence of Radio Raheem's murder by the police. The broken band of rebels storm the pizzeria and what begins as canted and absurd quickly accelerates. Sal begins a litany of 'nigger' and pulls out a baseball bat. He then proceeds to destroy Raheem's boombox, silencing the roar of the Public Enemy anthem.[8] Yes, the film resonates with prejudices and interethnic conflict but it also gestures towards the idea of communities constituted by ambivalences. Regardless, the confusion of this confrontation signals a shattering break. Things have gone too far and as Radio Raheem strangles Sal, pulling him over the counter, the fight spills into the street. The fight draws a crowd and the NYPD arrive. A police hold is administered with a nightstick against Raheem's neck as he is raised and lynched until his kicks wind down. He is murdered. Radio Raheem is dead.

A void appears in the quick exit of the police with a corpse and Buggin' Out in tow. There is the mournful calm of what has happened and how it has come to this. *Mookie they killed him. They killed Radio Raheem.* A divide appears, with Mookie, Sal, Pino and Vito on one side and the witnesses from the neighbourhood frozen still, growing angrier in the street. Everyone is a stranger; everyone is revealed. *Murder. They did it again. Just like Michael Stewart. Murder. Eleanor Bumpers. Murder.*[9] The extra-diegetic victims of murder at the hands of the police (not persons unknown) now have Raheem among their ranks. Mookie walks away before returning into this breach, throwing a garbage can through the pizzerio's window. Fireman and police readied in riot gear arrive and the historical rupture is complete. Even in the absence of Birmingham's finest with German Shepherds at hand, Sweet Dick Willie makes it plain: *Yo where's Bull Connor?*[10] Smiley begins a new Wall of Fame amid the wreckage by tacking one of his postcards on the smouldering wall: finally some brothers are on the wall. But, was this really what it was all about? Smiley with his ever-delirious visage appears to be the only one to claim some semblance of a victory.

The day after brings the new normal of an awkward, yet tender, meeting between Mookie and Sal. In the end, Mister Señor Love Daddy broadcasts the only available closure – a reminder to register to vote and a mournful shout-out to Radio Raheem.[11] The film ends with scrolling citations from Martin Luther King Jr. and X before the film's final image: the King and X photograph. The offering of these two contrasting political positions – the immorality of violence and the pragmatism of self-defence – is one of the major reasons that the film continues to haunt, inspire, and provoke. For only there on the screen does their proximity hint at some kind of dialectical resolve or compatibility. *Do The Right Thing* orchestrates the tensions and distinctions between social categories of racial being and the art of film. The film is a question masquerading in the form of a call to action. In other words, the film functions in a way too irresolute to be thought of as merely provocative protest. If the film is troubling, so be it. Killing the messenger has always been convenient, but it never truly disavows that a message has been sent. *Always do the right thing. That's it? That's it. I got it. I'm gone.*

Notes

1. For more on the history of the Blaxploitation cycle and the significance of 1991, see Ed Guerrero, *Framing Blackness*, Philadelphia, PA, Temple University Press, 1993.
2. Guthrie Ramsey, *Race Music: Black Cultures from Be Bop to Hip-Hop*, Berkeley, CA, University of California Press, 2003, p. 178.
3. Shana L. Redmond, 'Citizens of Sound: Negotiations of Race and Diaspora in the Anthems of the UNIA and NAACP', *African and Black Diaspora: An International Journal*, Vol. 4, No. 1, 2011, p. 22.
4. See Mark Anthony Neal, *What The Music Said: Black Popular Music and Black Public Culture*, London and New York, Routledge, 1999, pp. 125–57.
5. Michael Rogin, *Blackface, White Noise: Jewish Immigrants in the Hollywood Melting Pot*, Berkeley, CA, University of California Press, 1998, p. 221.
6. The photograph was taken on March 26, 1964, in the halls of the United States Capitol Building during Senate debates on the Civil Rights Bill. It documents the only meeting between the two men and lasted only a few minutes.

7. For more on 'film blackness', see Michael B. Gillespie, 'Reckless Eyeballing: *Coonskin*, Film Blackness, and the Racial Grotesque', in Mia Mask (ed.), *Contemporary Black American Cinema: Race, Gender and Sexuality at the Movies*, New York, Routledge, 2012. Also, see the press conference (May 1989) that followed the premiere screening of *Do The Right Thing* at the Cannes Film Festival. (Available on the Criterion Collection and 20th Anniversary Edition DVD releases of the film.) The insistence by much of the audience on reading *Do The Right Thing* in social reflectionist terms glaringly illustrates the need to distinguish between black people and black film.
8. The baseball bat references Howard Beach and the death of Michael Griffith. On the evening of 19 December 1986, a group of black men entered a pizzeria in the Queens neighbourhood of Howard Beach seeking help after their car broke down a few miles away. Upon leaving, the men were confronted by a group of Italian Americans from the neighbourhood armed with baseball bats. Attempting to escape from a continued beating by the mob, Griffith was struck and killed by a car on the highway.
9. Michael Stewart was a New York City graffiti artist killed while in the custody of New York Transit Police (1983). Eleanor Bumpers was a mentally ill, African American senior citizen killed by NYPD officers during the eviction from her home (1984).
10. Eugene 'Bull' Connor served as Public Safety Commissioner of Birmingham, Alabama (1957–1963). A rabid white supremacist, Connor was responsible for the brutal and violent responses (the use of police dogs and fire hoses against protestors) to the desegregation campaigns spearheaded by the Southern Christian Leadership Conference.
11. This call to vote was part of Lee's endorsement of David Dinkins' mayoral run. Dinkins would be elected New York City's first African American mayor the following year.

Further reading

Darby English, *How to See a Work of Art in Total Darkness*, Boston, MIT Press, 2007.

Ed Guerrero, *Do The Right Thing*, London, BFI Publishing, 2001.

Stuart Hall, 'What is this "black" in black popular culture?' and 'New Ethnicities' in David Morely and Kuan-Hsing Chen (eds), *Stuart Hall: Critical Dialogues in Cultural Studies*, New York, Routledge, 1996, pp. 468–78.

Spike Lee with Lisa Jones, *Do the Right Thing*, New York, Fireside, 1989.

Mia Mask (ed.), *Contemporary Black American Cinema: Race, Gender and Sexuality at the Movies*, New York, Routledge, 2012.

Paula J. Massood (ed.), *The Spike Lee Reader*, Philadelphia, PA, Temple University Press, 2007.

W. J. T. Mitchell, 'The Violence of Public Art: Do the Right Thing', *Critical Inquiry*, Vol. 16, No. 4, Summer, 1990, pp. 880–99.

Michael B. Gillespie

Double Indemnity (1944)

[Country: USA. Production Company: Paramount Pictures. Director: Billy Wilder. Producer: Joseph Sistrom. Screenwriters: Billy Wilder and Raymond Chander (based on the novella by James M. Cain). Cinematographer: John F. Seitz. Editor: Doane Harrison. Music: Miklos Rozsa. Cast: Fred MacMurray (Walter Neff), Barbara Stanwyck (Phyllis Dietrichson), Edward G. Robinson (Barton Keyes), Porter Hall (Mr Jackson), Jean Heather (Lola Dietrichson), Tom Powers (Mr Dietrichson),

Byron Barr (Nino Zachetti), Richard Gaines (Mr Norton).]

Synopsis: Framed as an episodic flashback narrated by insurance agent Walter Neff (Fred MacMurray), the story begins with an encounter between Neff and housewife Phyllis Dietrichson (Barbara Stanwyck) during a sales call. She incites him to dream up a plot to murder her husband in order to collect a 'double indemnity' insurance policy. Initially, the pair commit the crime without being detected, but an investigation by Barton Keyes (Edgar G. Robinson), a claims adjuster who is also Neff's good friend at the company, slowly reveals the deception. Adapted from a James M. Cain novella, *Double Indemnity* is recognised as one of the signal achievements of film noir, a type of film that forms a dark countercurrent to Hollywood's tendency toward positive characters and happy endings.

Increasingly critics and scholars have ranked *Double Indemnity* as one of the greatest films noir, describing it as 'the gold standard of 40s noir' or 'archetypical noir'.[1] But what is film noir? One answer to this question points to specific aspects of the film, such as Barbara Stanwyck's performance as a femme fatale, the film's fatalism, its first-person approach that emphasises psychological interiority, John Seitz's low-key cinematography, etc. A more general definition might say that *Double Indemnity* is a film noir because it inverts certain Hollywood conventions, such as a happy ending where the protagonist triumphs over the forces that oppose him. Instead, this film tells a story that is a dark reflection of the conventional Hollywood narrative; we can sum it up in an oft-quoted bit of Walter's dialogue, 'I didn't get the money and I didn't get the woman. Pretty, isn't it?'

Defining noir is tricky, however; it has been called 'one of the most amorphous categories in film history' (Naremore 1998: 11). So while it is impossible today not to celebrate *Double Indemnity* as a quintessential film noir, this designation should only be a first step in approaching the film and not a destination. After all, none of the people who worked on *Double Indemnity* would have had any idea what film noir meant. Bosley Crowther in his review for the *New York Times*, for instance, called the film a 'tough melodrama'. Unlike 'western' or 'historical drama', noir was not a term that filmmakers of the 1940s would have used; rather, it emerged retroactively from the vocabulary of critics.[2] So while some writing on *Double Indemnity* concentrates on identifying how the film fits into a predetermined category of noir, this essay will present readings that enrich that concept by complicating and expanding our understanding of it.

One prominent method of approaching the film uses the insights of feminist psychoanalysis. Claire Johnston emphasises how a male point of view tends to dominate the film, making the woman into an object of the masculine gaze. The way that Walter's voice-over narration structures the story, providing his perspective on the events, is a good example of this tendency. The repeated close-ups from Walter's point of view of Phyllis's ankle as she descends the stairs in her house are another way the film emphasises the male position. In both instances, there is a marked disparity in power – it is the man who speaks/looks, and the woman who is the object of the story/look.

Johnston's point is not simply that the film is sexist, however. Instead, she argues that the film 'traces the precariousness of the patriarchal order and its internal contradictions' (1978: 103). By 'contradictions' she refers to the notion that the woman occupies a peculiar position in a patriarchal (i.e. male-dominated) society. In such a system, the woman signifies lack; she is without the phallus, without power, which makes her both fascinating and terrifying.

According to the psychoanalytic view, *Double Indemnity* enacts the fundamental scenario of Oedipal struggle. Walter wants to beat the system, which is another way of saying that he wants to test the authority of the Law, as symbolised by Keyes. Phyllis represents a way to achieve that desire; she embodies a kind of desire that exists outside of the sanctioned order, outside of the bounds of the family and the patriarchal law that designates woman as (sexual) property. The film attempts to contain the dangerous desire and to restore the status quo, both by introducing another, 'good' woman (Lola) and by (somewhat implausibly) dispatching the 'bad' woman (Phyllis). The question remains open, however, whether this attempted containment actually eradicates the interesting possibilities raised by the dangerous woman.

Another insight offered by a psychoanalytic approach to the film concerns the relationship between Walter and Keyes. Johnston raises the point, which other writers have pursued as well, that although Keyes may represent the Law of patriarchy, he also harbours a maternal side ('a heart as big as a house'). The upshot of this observation is to prompt us to think about the relationship between Walter and Keyes as harbouring the possibility of an alternative affective bond, which finds expression in the ritualised exchange of matches and the film's final line, 'I love you, too'. Whether this bond between Walter and Keyes can be characterised as homosexual in a contemporary sense is debatable. Some people insist that the relationship is a paternal one, but we can ask whether such an emphasis rules out the possibility of an erotic dimension.[3]

Psychoanalytic readings tend to construe films as closed systems, resulting in readings that rarely pursue questions related to the film's cultural contexts. Many readings, however, do consider how the world outside of the film has shaped what appears on the screen. The examples of a contextual approach that we will consider here focus on the film's relation to its source materials.

There are two accounts of the inspiration for the James M. Cain novella on which the film was based that can serve as entry points for contextual readings. When asked about the genesis of the story for *Double Indemnity*, Cain mentioned an anecdote he heard from H. L. Mencken about a newspaper typesetter who, after years of faithful service, purposely let a dirty typo in a headline slip through. The outline of this situation, where a faithful employee runs amok, is present in the film in a somewhat modified form when in Walter's voice-over narration he talks about 'the guy behind the roulette-wheel'. Regardless of the specific form this common thread takes, the basic germ of the story concerns someone trying to beat a system.

James Naremore picks up on this aspect of the film, arguing that a modernist critique of mass culture undergirds the film. He points out that a significant similarity in temperament that unites the three major creative contributors – Cain, Chandler and Wilder – is an outsider's mentality (Cain came from the East Coast and Wilder from Austria and Berlin, Chandler grew up in England). This outsider's mentality manifests itself in a critique of life in an age of industrial capitalism that is encapsulated in the phrase 'straight down the line'. This phrase first occurs during Walter's initial sales patter, then gets picked up by Walter and Phyllis, who use it as a way to refer to their commitment to one another, and finally gets used by Keyes, who turns it into an image of a trolley ride whose final stop is the cemetery.

This metaphor signals a critique of what Naremore calls, referencing a Weimar intellectual tradition, 'Fordist Amerika', a view of American society that sees an assembly-line logic having permeated all aspects of material and mental life, turning people into alienated, robotic slaves, *à la Metropolis*. This line of argument leads to Naremore's provocative claim that the ending that Wilder originally envisioned for the film – a long, predominately silent sequence in which Walter is executed in the San Quentin gas chamber with Keyes as a witness – represents a better version of the film. This argument reverses the conventional wisdom about the gas chamber ending, which critics, following Wilder's own statements, have discounted as excessive and unnecessary. For Naremore, the gas chamber ending is the necessarily grim culmination of the film's engagement with the logic of 'straight down the line'.

Another contextual reading relies on the more frequently identified source for *Double Indemnity*, the trial of Ruth Snyder and Judd Gray. Snyder, a Long Island housewife, and Gray, a corset salesman who became Snyder's lover, murdered Snyder's husband. The trial was a major media event from March 1927 to January 1928. James M. Cain, whom critic Edmund Wilson called one of the 'poets of the tabloid murder', was working for *The New York World* during the trial and certainly would have been immersed in the coverage.

Penelope Pelizzon and Nancy West connect the coverage of the case in prominent New York City tabloids to its echoes first in the Cain novella and then in the film. This context allows Pelizzon and West to propose different readings of such textual features as the 'straight down the line' metaphor. They read this motif as Cain's adaptation of an insight in H. L. Mencken's review of Judd Gray's confession/book, where Mencken analyses Gray's thinking as an example of the notion of Presbyterian predetermination, which stipulates that some people are predestined to be sinners. This reading provides an interesting colouring to observations about this film's 'fatalism'.

A detail of the film's mise en scène that the Snyder–Gray context also illuminates is Barbara Stanwyck's blonde wig. This costume choice often has been seen as anomalous or dissident; it was famously singled out for ridicule at the time of production when Paramount production head Buddy De Sylva reportedly commented, 'We hire Barbara Stanwyck, and here we get George Washington'. Wilder claimed that he realised the wig was a mistake after it was too late to make a change, but he also justified his choice by saying that he wanted Phyllis to have a 'sleazy' look. This adjective suggests how the wig can be connected to the Snyder–Gray trial; the tabloids frequently commented on Ruth Snyder's hairstyle, dubbing her 'the burning blonde' or 'the synthetic blonde murderess'.

The tabloid context also places the gas chamber ending in a different light. One of the most famous moments in the Snyder–Gray media coverage occurred during the executions when Thomas Howard, an enterprising photojournalist for the *New York Daily News*, strapped a miniature camera to his ankle and took a photograph at the moment the executioner threw the switch on Ruth Snyder. This sensational photograph took up the entire front page underneath the gigantic headline 'DEAD!' Pelizzon and West suggest that the cut ending, for which Wilder had an exact replica of the San Quentin gas chamber built, registers the power of the execution snapshot, 'those familiar with the photo might be tempted to see it as a palimpsest beneath Wilder's death chamber, as if the latter image were superimposed onto the earlier one' (2005: 212).

The connotations of tabloid journalism provide an important context for the film's initial reception as well. When *Double Indemnity* premiered, it was seen as 'provocative', which is to say sordid and trashy. Wilder's usual screenwriting partner, the urbane Charles Brackett, refused to participate in the project, which he considered in bad taste. Wilder, who consistently pushed the boundaries of censorship, tested the Hayes code with *Double Indemnity* by taking on a literary property that was supposedly unfilmable; at the time of its making he described *Double Indemnity* as a film 'to set Hollywood back on its heels'.[4]

When Walter drives away from the Dietrichson household, he muses in voice-over, 'How could I have known that murder can sometimes smell like honeysuckle?' This striking juxtaposition of the foul and the sweet is not a bad emblem for noir more generally. Even though noir is difficult to define precisely, we could do worse than to call it a beautiful mode of filmmaking about ugliness, an aesthetic approach to darkness, violence, and corruption, of which *Double Indemnity* is an extraordinary example.

Notes

1. Capsule review of *Double Indemnity* in *Time Out London*, issue 1838, 9–16 November 2005 (accessed 19 June 2008) at www.timeout.com/film/reviews/65700/double_indemnity.html; and Philip Kemp, 'Billy Wilder', in Sara Pendergast and Tom Pendergast (eds), *The International Dictionary of Films and Filmmakers*, Vol. 2, 'Directors', 4th ed., Detroit, St. James Press, 2001, p. 1079, accessed via the Gale Virtual Reference Library.
2. For an excellent genealogy of the concept of film noir, see James Naremore, 'The History of an Idea' in *More than Night: Film Noir in Its Contexts* (pp. 9–39).
3. For a theorisation of how homosocial desire operates at the expense of women, see Eve Sedgwick, *Between Men: English Literature and Homosocial Desire*, New York, Columbia University Press, 1985.
4. Wilder in the *L. A. Times*, quoted in Sikov 1998: 194. For a perceptive chapter on *Double Indemnity* that, among other things, builds on Naremore's insights and pursues Wilder's connections to the field of journalism, see Gerd Gemünden, 'The Insurance Man Always Rings Twice: *Double Indemnity*', chapter two of *A Foreign Affair: Billy Wilder's American Films*.

Further reading

James M. Cain, *Double Indemnity* (1936), New York, Knopf/Everyman's Library, 2003.

Gerd Gemünden, *A Foreign Affair: Billy Wilder's American Films*, New York, Berghahn Books, 2008.

Claire Johnston, '*Double Indemnity*', in E. Ann Kaplan (ed.), *Women in Film Noir*, London, BFI, 1978, pp. 100–11.

James Naremore, *More than Night: Film Noir in Its Contexts*, Los Angeles, University of California Press, 1998.

V. Penelope Pelizzon and Nancy M. West, 'Multiple Indemnity: Film Noir, James M. Cain, and Adaptations of a Tabloid Case', *Narrative*, Vol. 13, No. 3, October 2005, pp. 211–37.

Ed Sikov, *On Sunset Boulevard: The Life and Times of Billy Wilder*, New York, Hyperion, 1998.

Neil Sinyard and Adrian Turner, *Journey down Sunset Boulevard: The Films of Billy Wilder*, Ryde, Isle of Wight, BCW Publishing, 1979.

Billy Wilder, with Cameron Crowe, *Conversations with Wilder*, New York, Random House, 1999.

Billy Wilder and Raymond Chandler, *Double Indemnity* (1944), Berkeley, University of California Press, 2000.

Oliver Gaycken

Elena (2011)

[Country: Russia. Production Company: Non-stop Productions. Director: Andrei Zvyagintsev. Producer: Aleksandr Rodnyanskiy. Screenwriters: Oleg Negin, Andrei Zvyagintsev. Cinematographer: Mikhail Krichman. Pre-existing music: Philip Glass. Editor: Anna Mass. Cast: Nadezhda Markina (Elena), Andrei Smirnov (Vladimir), Elena Lyadova (Katerina), Aleksei Rozin (Sergey), Evgeniya Konushkina (Tatyana), Igor Ogurtsov (Aleksandr).]

Synopsis: Elena is married to Vladimir, her former patient, a wealthy Russian businessman. They both have children from previous marriages: Elena a lazy, slovenly son, and Vladimir a wayward, estranged daughter. Elena financially supports her unemployed son and his family, sometimes secretly with Vladimir's money. Vladimir suffers a heart attack at the same time as Elena's grandson needs Vladimir's help to avoid serving the compulsory military service. Vladimir refuses his support, and declares to Elena that his daughter will be his only heiress. Backed into a corner, Elena unwillingly comes up with the solution that would solve her son's family's predicament: murder Vladimir and inherit half of his wealth.

Elena is the third feature directed by Andrei Zvyagintsev, and the third film on which he worked with the director of photography Mikhail Krichman. Collaboration between these two filmmakers is, according to Zvyagintsev himself, of crucial importance for the way in which the shots are structured, and for the final outcome facing the viewer.[1] In film history there are a significant number of important films which were made in such collaboration, and we need to bear this in mind when discussing Zvyagintsev's films.

Their first two films, *The Return* (*Vozvrashchenie*, 2004) and *Banishment* (*Izgnanie*, 2007), stirred a lot of excitement when they appeared. In particular, *The Return* caused a stir among critics at the festival in Venice, where it received the Golden Lion. These two films are alike in many ways, the relation between the beautiful image and ambiguous narrative works along similar lines, harking back to Antonioni, one of Zvyagintsev's heroes. The tribute paid to Tarkovsky was so evident that many saw Zvyagintsev as the heir to the famed director, and called him the most significant figure to appear in Russian cinema since Tarkovsky.[2] These films have resisted precise interpretation, while creating a rich associational field of not clearly defined messages. The audience was attracted to the visual power of individual shots, and saw the allusions to the Old and New Testaments as the films' decisive advantages.

When *Elena* appeared the obvious innovations struck the observers. With their cryptic structures, *The Return* and *Banishment* left room for flights of critical imagination, while *Elena* was more clearly structured, following a seemingly simple and easily understandable plot. The image was still impressively well designed, although lush exteriors have given way to urban settings, mostly interiors. The explanatory coherence was almost completely fulfilled, and individual events were not left unexplained or enigmatic. *Elena* has a balanced structure and can be described as a seemingly perfect film of a moral dilemma.

The main character, Elena, is torn between two characters who cannot get along. On one side is her husband, a rich Russian businessman, and, on the other, her lazy and poor son Sergey and his family. Their abodes clearly define their social positions: Elena and her husband reside in an exquisite apartment in a posh part of Moscow, while the son's family lives in a communal building in one of the poor suburbs. The luxurious apartment is the setting for most of the film, and plays a very important role. For Zvyagintsev the link between the characters and their setting is always essential, and it is here as well. The apartment is furnished in a minimalistic fashion, which enables Zvyagintsev and Krichman to capture the freedom with which characters move around, as well as to compose the shots which impress with their clear, easily apprehended layout of the objects they comprise, contrary to the crammed, claustrophobic shots of Elena's son's apartment. Judging by this, it is certainly worthwhile for Sergey's family to strive for change; at the end of the film they move into Vladimir's place. What they make out of it is a different matter.

Elena tries to make both sides happy. She takes her pension and regularly hands it over to her son, while at the same time she defends Vladimir and his reluctance to financially help Sergey. This strategy seems to work until Sasha, Sergey's son, grows old enough to serve in Russia's compulsory military. Sasha's parents are worried because of the army's poor reputation and want to avoid his departure. One way to do so is to enrol Sasha in college, but they need money to do so. And they can get enough money only from Vladimir. Here the plot thickens, and Elena must sail the rough waters to solve this problem. Incidentally, Vladimir has a heart attack just when the money is needed, making him totally dependent on Elena's help and care. Elena talks to Vladimir's estranged daughter, Katrina, asking her to visit her ill father in the hospital. Surprisingly, father and daughter make amends, and Vladimir decides to leave practically all his wealth to his daughter, probably and rightly afraid that Elena would use his money to support the lazy habits of her son and his equally unimpressive family. Elena sees that she will not be able to help her grandson, and she decides to kill Vladimir by giving him an extra strong dose of Viagra.

From the beginning, the path for the viewer is to identify with Elena's predicament. She, like a proper mother and wife, tries to reconcile opposing ends. When she discusses problems with Vladimir, she defends Sergey, and when Sergey verbally attacks Vladimir, she defends him. She even tells Sergey that 'there is truth in his [Vladimir's] words'. When the decisive moments come, the viewer has to decide between motherly love, loyalty to the husband and society's moral code. It is necessary and obvious that Elena is on edge. When Vladimir tells her about his future will, she is irritated, of course, but what interests her is Vladimir's decision about money for Sasha. Does it mean that she would not kill Vladimir were he to provide for Sasha's safe future? It seems so. Thus Vladimir signs his own death warrant by being relentlessly hostile to Elena's family. She seems compulsorily drawn to immediate danger, to Sasha, rather than driven by an elaborate plan from the very beginning of her marriage to Vladimir, as Katya tells her she is. After Vladimir's heart attack she goes to church to genuinely pray for his well-being, but she is also able to coldly lie about the money in the safe when Katya asks her about it at the meeting with Vladimir's lawyer. So, the moral dilemma persists from the beginning of the film all the way to the end. But, we can rightly ask, is this what Zvyagintsev really wanted us to think? In one of his interviews he claims that he wanted to portray conundrums and difficult moral choices that contemporary Russian society forces upon its members.[3]

The BBC has concluded that this film goes against the tradition of Tolstoy and Dostoevsky who saw ordinary members of Russian society as the basis of morality, incapable of evil.[4] If we agree that Elena's decision is premeditated evil, then not much of a dilemma is present. In this case, what we see is a matter-of-fact report about a murder, in which the victim and the culprit are clearly identified. But it is not so. As we have seen, Elena goes through real emotional turmoil, and we see that the family finally takes precedence in this carefully balanced plot. Her decision clearly breaks the moral rules on which society is based, but there seems to be enough room for sympathy for her and her behaviour. One of the last images is a high-angle shot of Elena's little grandchild sleeping and waking up on Vladimir's bed. The change has been completed: new life has taken the place of an old one. The force of nature overrules the laws of society with the help of some of society's seemingly most loyal agents.

Such a view of Elena is enabled by a complex relation between the space of a shot and the narrative woven by the viewer. We have already mentioned the importance of setting and characters. This is only one aspect of the mutual relationship of objects in the film. The main details are not immediately clearly outlined for the viewer; rather, they all seem to be placed at an equidistance from the camera and from the narrative. This creates temporary ambiguity which allows the viewer more autonomy in creating the story. She is led to a prolonged process of judgement, which allows her to feel that she has well understood

Elena's dilemma. Thus, the narrative process is varied and well developed on the level of the shots, which, at first sight, serve more descriptive rather than narrative purposes. Sound also plays a very important role in this. In such a loose structure it leads the viewer's attention across the images and off-screen; and enmeshed with visual cues it brings the viewer to certain conclusions about the story. We often hear sounds from TV sets without seeing the image. While Vladimir watches sports, Elena is interested in talk shows. It underlines his competitiveness and her domesticity.

Despite the plot's seeming simplicity, the shots are not easily interpreted. Zvyagintsev uses long takes in this film, as he did in previous ones. Repeatedly, some takes last longer than necessary for the viewer to apprehend spatial parameters, objects, their initial interrelationships, as well as their narrative importance. That is why they cause difficulties in interpretation. We may ask: What is it that the director tries to say? Why are these takes so long? And on a theoretical level, what is it that causes boredom in some viewers, while others feel an intensified presence of reality? This is an old question in film theory, which goes back at least as far as Italian Neorealism. One answer is that strength of attention matters. The great majority of contemporary viewers are accustomed to quick cutting, one scan of the situation, then we move to something else, and then perhaps we return to the initial setting, but again in a short take. When the takes get longer, our attention tends to weaken, which leads to boredom. Zvyagintsev repeatedly tests the viewers regarding this matter. It seems that in his long takes not much happens, but, especially as the plot develops, he allows the viewers to infuse the shot with more complex meaning than short, clear takes would allow. Often, very small changes allow for new interpretations of a situation. This has two consequences. On one hand, there is an intense feeling of the solidity of objects, their autonomy in relation to the viewer and in relation to the narrative. On the other, there is also the impression of the richness of the text, of the complexity of its meaning. Of course, none of this would be the case if the narrative were to be weak and non-engaging, if it did not allow the viewer to employ this (newly) found potential of objects.

Meaning and rhythm in cinema are closely connected. Sometimes this has been perceived as the closeness of cinema and music. But here, the rhythm of the film stands opposed to the rhythm of the viewer's mental processes. In other words, in order to achieve a certain meaning, the film has to agree with the viewer's abilities to rhythmically perceive the same. If the rhythmic component falls flat, the meaning may not be fully apprehended, and the message fails, communication has not been fully established. Philip Glass's music infuses this carefully paced film with tension as well as rhythm that reminds us of Hitchcock's use of Bernard Herrmann's music.

Notes

1. Interview with Zvyagintsev, Serbian Television, Friday, 18 May 2012, 10:30 pm.
2. Available at: http://observer.com/2004/02/oedipal-drama-russian-style-zvyagintsevs-the-return.
3. Available at www.1tv.ru/sprojects_edition/si5756/fi9186.
4. Available at www.1tv.ru/sprojects_edition/si5756/fi9186.

Further reading

Birgit Beumers, (ed.), *Russia on Reels: The Russian Idea in Post-Soviet Cinema*, London, I. B. Tauris, 1999.

Birgit Beumers, (ed.), *The Cinema of Russia and the Former Soviet Union*, London, Wallflower Press, 2007.

Nancy Condee, *The Imperial Trace: Recent Russian Cinema*, Oxford, Oxford University Press, 2009.

http://az-film.com/en/Publications/?type=2& movie = 6& p = 1.

http://depesha.com/arts/andrey-zvyagintsevs-elena.

http://kinoart.ru/journal/elena.html.

Saša Milić

Les enfants du paradis/Children of Paradise (1945)

[Country: France. Production Company: Pathé. Director: Marcel Carné. Screenwriter: Jacques Prévert. Producer: Raymond Borderie. Music: Maurice Thiriet. Cinematography: Marc Fossard and Roger Hubert. Production Designer: Alexandre Trauner. Editors: Henri Rust and Madeleine Bonin. Cast: Garance (Arletty), Baptiste Debureau (Jean-Louis Barrault), Frédérick Lemaître (Pierre Brasseur), Lacenaire (Marcel Herrand), Louis Salou (Édouard, Count de Montray)].

Synopsis: The film, which takes place in 1840s Paris, is divided into two parts. In the first, Garance (Arletty) is unhappy in her relationship with Lacenaire (Herrand), a dandified thief. She attracts the attention of Baptiste (Barrault), a mime artist at the Funambules Theatre. Baptiste has a rival for his affections in aspiring actor Frédérick Lemaître (Brasseur). The wealthy Count de Montray (Salou) declares his love for Garance. She initially displays no interest, but when the police accuse her of being implicated in an attempted murder carried out by Lacenaire, she turns to the Count for protection. The second part starts a few years later. Baptiste is married and has a son. Garance, who has been travelling abroad with the Count, has returned to Paris. She visits the Funambules and realises she has only ever loved Baptiste; but she leaves him and flees into the mass of carnival-goers on the Boulevard du Crime. Baptiste, pursuing her, is swallowed up by the crowd.

Les enfants du paradis remains Marcel Carné's most accomplished film; a French super-production that is as ambitious as anything von Stroheim, Ophuls or Lean ever attempted. Clocking in at over three hours, it remains a canonical work in world cinema. Carné received a special César award in 1979 to honour 'the best French film in the history of talking pictures', and few would disagree.

From the moment a stage curtain rises to show the full extent of the clutter, chaos, and confusion of nineteenth-century Paris, the reciprocity between art and life for Carné is clear. Its enduring appeal resides less in individual talents and personalities (although Arletty, Jean-Louis Barrault and Pierre Brasseur were never better) than in the intense ethos of invention, Carné's poised compositional sense, and, above all, the film's recurring register of warmth and kindness. Essentially a film about actors acting, Carné's theatricalised melodramatic world combines different performance modes – tragedy, Shakespeare, pantomime – inflected with pessimism and romanticism. This is, as Pauline Kael recognised, a film poem 'on the nature and varieties of love – sacred and profane, selfless and possessive.' [1]

By 1939, Marcel Carné had become the leading standard bearer of French 'Poetic Realism', a film style that combined romantic-fatalist narratives with claustrophobic milieus and an accentuated mise en scène.[2] The German Occupation of France in 1940, however, meant the imposition of a different kind of cinema. Realism – poetic, social, magical or otherwise – was out. Carné's two wartime films thus opted for historical recreation. *The Devil's Envoys* (1942) was a fairy-tale romance set in the Middle Ages, while *Les enfants du paradis* took place in an 1840s Paris populated by real characters of the time.

When Carné first heard the news of the Allied landings in Normandy in spring 1944, he deliberately slowed down the post-production process. He instinctively realised that rather than being the last film of the Occupation, *Les Enfants du paradis* could be the first film of the Liberation. For a film that expressed the freedom of the individual faced with social restrictions, such a strategy was apposite: when the film was released in March 1945, it became a huge commercial success, screening in Paris for over a year and grossing 41 million francs. If *Les enfants du paradis* was an explicit attempt to revitalise the post-Liberation film industry, it was also a veiled attempt to use film as a means of facing up to the realities of the Occupation. It exemplifies a form of 'symbolic resistance'; the recuperation of the self-respect of an occupied population through uplifting displays of national narcissism and self-esteem (Forbes 1997). Indeed, what is especially fascinating is how Carné and Prévert were able to pull off a thinly disguised allegory of French resistance under German rule.

This is a film about seeing and being seen in a world where the differences between street life and the theatre, audience and actor, reality and illusion intertwine as each is appropriated, inverted or compounded by the other. Certainly, the film has provided the template for many recent historical recreations, literary adaptations and big-budget melodramas in French cinema – films like *Cyrano de Bergerac* (Jean-Paul Rappeneau, 1990), *The Lovers of Pont-Neuf* (Léos Carax, 1991) and *Queen Margot* (Patrice Chéreau, 1994) share numerous thematic and visual sensibilities with *Les enfants du paradis*. However, there is something deeply old-fashioned about the film. It accomplishes its beauty and power through an austere compositional formalism and a striving for stylistic perfection within existing conventions. Carné's editing is generally unobtrusive, with his camera often holding on faces or incidents before cutting or wiping, and apart from the remarkable opening scene the camera is rarely mobile. His self-effacing directorial style is exemplified in the scene when Lacenaire murders the Count: the act is presented through Avril's voyeuristic reactions rather than focusing on the crime.

Les enfants du paradis is concerned above all with the theatre. At the beginning and end of both parts a curtain rises and falls, situating the narrative as a theatrical spectacle. Throughout, opposing theatrical forms are at play – mime, pantomime, melodrama and tragedy – which highlight the redeeming power of the theatrical mode. Carné also pays homage to 'backstage' activity, where performers at the Funambules are fined for making noise in the wings, and rival theatre companies fight on and off stage. The fragile sensitivity of Baptiste forms a strong counterpoint to the blustery Frédérick. For the latter, not being able to speak is 'agony when I have an entire orchestra inside me'. He admires Baptiste as he 'speaks with his legs, replies with his hands, with a look, with a shrug'. It is this set-up between the loquaciousness of Frédérick and the silent dignity of Baptiste that suggests the film is profoundly nostalgic for the freedom of silent cinema, extolling the aesthetics of mime, gesture and dance.

The opening scene is an effective mirror of the film's theme. Just as the theatre companies lining the Boulevard offer brief outdoor shows before beginning the main attraction inside, so too does Carné's expository panorama display, in visual shorthand, the substance of the plot to come. After the curtain rises, Carné's tracking camera functions as an omniscient third-person narrator, drawing the audience's attention to a tightrope walker, Jéricho, horse-drawn carriages, a weightlifter, a monkey on stilts, a merry-go-round, the booth advertising truth in the well and the stage door to the Funambules. The initial impact of these images may be wholly pictorial, but as the film advances, it transforms these compact figures of meaning into extended narrative functions. Immediately, the film's ongoing dialogue with theatre, performance, and truth has been introduced.

Throughout the film, this indiscernible membrane between theatre and life is successively ruptured. When Frédérick ridicules the melodrama he acts in, he discards his lines, begins improvising and turns the play into a farce. When Baptiste runs into the blind beggar and befriends him, he discovers when they arrive at a tavern that the man has been 'acting' blind. In all of these explorations, Carné and Prévert anticipate the mid-1950s theatre-as-life-as-theatre of Jean Renoir, as exemplified in *The Golden Coach* (1953) and *French Can-Can* (1955) and Max Ophuls's *The Fall of Lola Montès* (1955).

The primacy of theatre in *Les enfants du paradis* elevates the narrative to the level of allegory. The theatre audience (periodically captured in a wide-angle reverse shot) may be regarded as a metaphor for the suffering French who sought relief throughout the Occupation by going to theatre and cinema. In this respect, the film proposes a dynamic agenda for retaining dignity in the face of defeat; the collective spirit produced by the theatre seemed to reflect France's unassailable confidence in her own historical and artistic status, which in turn served as a wider metaphor for her indomitability. Indeed, the theatrical mode is not just a means of exploring the lives and loves of the main characters, but the political dimension of

Les Enfants du paradis resides in Carné's view of the theatre as a privileged site of collective redemption.

Commentators have sought to compare the film to *Gone With The Wind* (Victor Fleming and George Cukor, 1939); both films were national projects, both had epic status, and both were set at time of civil upheaval. As a character notes in *Army of Shadows* (Jean-Pierre Melville, 1969), France will not be free until its inhabitants can watch *Gone With The Wind*. *Children of Paradise* can be compared to its Hollywood counterpart, but that would fit too easily into the melodrama genre that the latter conforms to. *Gone With The Wind* is a 'woman's film' of the kind David O. Selznick excelled at, but *Les enfants du paradis* is arguably a 'man's film'. It is Baptiste whom we feel sorry for at the end, and throughout the film, it is a melodrama about men. For Forbes, what we might expect of Hollywood melodrama has been turned on its head. However, the 'male melodrama' is inextricably bound up in the character of Garance, in many ways the cornerstone of the film. As played by Arletty – the closest the French ever got to creating their own Marlene Dietrich – Garance seems less like a real character than an icon or symbol. She provides the film with a basic structure – four men fall in love with her and then lose her – and in her first incarnation, as 'truth' in the well, she sets the tone for the rest of the film. According to Turk, Carné had a tendency 'to reduce [women] to banal sweethearts or mythologise them into awesome sorceresses' (Turk 1989: 51). The latter is undeniably true of Garance. Her ambiguity is one of the most beguiling elements of the film; she invites Frédérick into her bed moments after Baptiste professes deep love for her, and grows perceptibly colder as the film develops, unable to say 'I love you' to the Count. Perhaps the film's most poignant line belongs to her: 'I'm not sad, but not cheerful either. A little spring has broken in the music box. The music is the same but the tone is different'. Her capricious nature may bring her a succession of moments filled with pleasure, yet the comfort of love evades her.

Truffaut said of this film: 'I have made twenty-three films. Well, I would swap them all for the chance to have made *Les enfants du paradis*'.[3] The film cast a shadow over the careers of all those involved in it – like Carné, few of its personnel ever reached such pinnacles again. Yet its bold exploration of sexuality, its radical cultural strategy and its proto-postmodernist fusion of high and low art merits its place in cinema's pantheon. If Dickens, Tolstoy or Balzac ever made a film, it would probably look, sound and feel like this one.

Notes

1. Pauline Kael, 'Children of Paradise', *5001 Nights at the Movies*, New York and London, Marion Boyars, 1993, p. 133.
2. For more on the French Poetic Realist tradition and Carné's contribution to it, see Dudley Andrew, *Mists of Regret: Culture and Sensibility in Classic French Film*, Princeton, NJ, Princeton University Press, 1995.
3. Truffaut had earlier denounced Carné's work from the 1950s as exemplifying the conservative, so-called retrograde *cinéma de papa* that had emerged in post-war France. This recuperation at the hands of one of his chief tormenters was greeted with a certain degree of irony by Carné. See Carné's autobiography, *La vie à belles dents*, Paris, Belfond, 1989.

Further reading

Jill Forbes, *Les Enfants du paradis*, London, BFI, 1997.

Jean-Pierre Jeancolas, 'Beneath the Despair, the Show goes on: Marcel Carné's *Les Enfants du paradis* (1943–5)', in Susan Hayward and Ginette Vincendeau (eds), *French Film: Texts and Contexts*, London and New York, Routledge, 2000, pp. 78–88.

Ben McCann, 'Marcel Carné', *Senses of Cinema*, Vol. 58, 2011. Available at www.sensesofcinema.com/2011/great-directors/marcel-carne (accessed 29 November 2012).

Edward Baron Turk, *Child of Paradise: Marcel Carné and the Golden Age of French Cinema*, Cambridge, MA, and London, Harvard University Press, 1989.

Ben McCann

El espíritu de la colmena/The Spirit of the Beehive (1973)

[Country: Spain. Production Company: Elías Querejeta Producciones Cinematográficas, Jacel Desposito. Director: Víctor Erice. Screenwriters: Ángel Fernández-Santos and Víctor Erice. Producer: Elías Querejeta. Cinematographer: Luis Cuadrado. Editor: Pablo González Del Amo. Music: Luis de Pablo. Cast: Ana Torrent (Ana), Isabel Tellería (Isabel), Fernando Fernán Gómez (Fernando), Teresa Gimpera (Teresa), Milagros (Queti de la Cámara), José Villasante (Frankenstein's monster), Juan Margallo (the fugitive).]

Synopsis: Set in 1940s post-war Spain, Ana and her sister Isabel go to the movies one evening to see a screening of *Frankenstein*. Afterward, Ana becomes fascinated with the story and nature of Dr Frankenstein's creation – the monster. As she seeks out ways to explore her fascination, she retreats from her family life, which is portrayed as isolated, disconnected and laden with a terrible sadness. One night Ana runs away from home and, as if in a fantasy, encounters the monster. The next day she is brought back home by her father but that same night she calls to the monster again by announcing her presence before its mystical power, closing the film with the simple words: 'Soy yo, Ana' (It's me, Ana).

'Is he a ghost?'

This is the question that the young, wide-eyed Ana (Ana Torrent) asks her sister Isabel (Isabel Tellería) in a memorable scene from Víctor Erice's *The Spirit of the Beehive*, where the two girls, late one night, discuss the identity of the monster in the movie they have just seen. That movie, the most prominent example of intertextuality in Erice's film, is of course none other than James Whale's 1931 'original horror show', *Frankenstein*. Isabel's answer is at once simple and evocative. 'No, he's a spirit', she tells Ana. Since the release of *The Spirit of the Beehive*, critics have debated the significance of the film's poetic but in many ways enigmatic title, focusing largely on the numerous allusions to insularity and hierarchy implied by the word 'beehive', and which are closely associated with the authoritative father (Fernando Fernán Gómez), who himself is a beekeeper. It has been suggested that the figure of the beehive is also a metaphor for the isolation of war-torn Spain, depicted in the film through the melancholic and remote village 'somewhere on the Castilian plain' and visually reinforced with images of the dark, cloistered interior of the family house, the honeycomb-shaped windows of which diffuse a diaphanous yellow light. But the meaning of 'spirit' in the film's title is far less easily discernible. The word itself denotes a non-material presence or the affect of an invisible entity. In fact, when Ana inquires why they killed the monster, Isabel unhesitatingly explains that he could not have been killed since she has seen him alive and since 'spirits do not have bodies' anyway.

Indeed, the question of 'spirit' – its location, visualisation, embodiment and feeling – governs not only the film's visual aesthetic but also its narrative. In the same scene, Isabel also cautions her sister not to believe everything she sees 'Because everything in the movies is fake. It's all a trick'. Earlier, this same idea is voiced in the presenter's preliminary announcement to the screening of *Frankenstein*: 'It's one of the strangest stories ever told', he warns the audience. 'It's about the great mysteries of creation: life and death. Prepare yourselves. You may be shocked, or even horrified! Few films have had greater impact all over the world. But I would advise you not to take it too seriously'.

That the movies stir emotions and yet are not to be believed, or at least not believed too much, is certainly not a new concept, but its double inclusion here leads us to wonder if at the heart of Erice's film lies a deep interest in the 'spirit of cinema'. Erice himself has written extensively about the medium as an artistic language able to conjure ghosts and bring back the past. In many ways, and much like his two later feature-length films, *El sur* (*The South*, 1983) and *El sol del membrillo* (*Dream of Light*, 1992), Erice's critically acclaimed and internationally celebrated 1973 debut masterpiece ruminates on the 'mysteries of creation'.

Aside from the monster's spirit, which fascinates and troubles the protagonist, other mysteries are cultivated as well through the film's mise en scène which channels the vitality of place: the desolate but captivating landscape on the outskirts of Hoyuelos, the ruinous charm of an abandoned barn and adjacent well, the enchanted forest where the girls pick mushrooms with their father. A shot from the forest of the neighbouring hillsides, bucolic and shrouded in a dense fog, implies that they too are a secret hiding place, perhaps a reference to the *maquis*, an anti-Francoist resistance movement; the father also alludes to a supernatural element, commenting that the best mushrooms are 'over there' and that he will take the girls one day if they promise not to say anything to their mother. Even the family house seems to possess a certain vibrancy that emits an attractive yet mystifying energy. Though these places appear largely uninhabitable, they nevertheless absorb the subject who enters into them.

We could say that *The Spirit of the Beehive* contains the kernel of what will become the main subject of the auteur's later projects: the mystery of cinema. By equal measure, the film is also invested in the experience and power of cinematic revelation – a point underscored in the documentary-style 'movie theatre' sequence, where the camera captures the audience's spontaneous reactions to what ostensibly is their first time viewing of the film within the film. This is perhaps also why Erice's visual compositions so often contain few establishing shots and use a transition style that frequently displaces the viewer, allowing our awareness of shifts in point of view, setting and narrative time to unfold in a gradual, reflective process.

In this regard, we might note the film's strong resemblance to painting. Given the steady, hypnotic pace of long takes and delicate composition of cinematic images that arrestingly move into stillness, Erice's cinematography has been likened to tableaux. His images seem to meditate on the quality and duration of light, perhaps delving into yet another mystery wherein each shot strives to make the invisible visible. One can recall any number of examples of visual ellipses where the time of the shot lingers beyond narrative time to measure the way light sways, or the way it is cast onto objects and flickers in the dark (of course, the study of light and its relationship to painting will become the primary focus of *Dream of Light* or *The Quince Tree Sun*, filmed nearly two decades after *The Spirit of the Beehive*).

But it is not only light that fascinates Erice. The experiential quality of time is a point of intrigue in his work as well. This is what Erice's contemporary, the much-admired Russian filmmaker Andrei Tarkovsky, might have called 'sculpting time'. The acute attention given to the symbiotic relationship between time and light is a particular element that marks Erice's work not just as 'painterly', but also as intensely photographic. One interesting moment where time, light and space converge is with the extraordinary and now iconic image of Ana and Isabel waiting on the railroad tracks. As the tracks bisect the frame, vanishing into the horizon, the girls listen attentively, ears pressed firmly to the metal frame of the rails in an effort to feel the pulse of the train arriving, which after several minutes rhythmically charges through the landscape, bringing a rush of movement to this otherwise static place. In a sense, the train measures time, but what the shot (and Luis Cuadrado's exquisite photography) remarkably reproduce is the time of waiting – first for the train's arrival, then for its passage – as an extremely sensorial experience. A haptic cinema in which the screen fills with feeling and time seems tangible.

In *The Spirit of the Beehive*, the time of dreams and play, as well as cinematic time and the time of the past all constitute alternate temporalities that traverse the time of the present – 1940, as the intertitle at the beginning of the film indicates. We should not forget however that the film opens yet another window onto the temporal possibility of mythic time. A preceding intertitle, which reads 'once upon a time', introduces the larger framework of fairytale that brackets the 'real time' of narrative action. Luis del Pablo's sound motifs further underscore these temporal distinctions, oscillating between ethereal flute music that recalls children's songs and the harsh reality of the train whistle. As one critic has observed, Erice's cinema might best be characterised as 'frames within frames', which could refer just as much to physical structures that give the film its architectural look (doors, windows, façades and especially thresholds, a key image with which the film concludes), as to temporal configurations that anchor and un-anchor time.

Of course, the main characters are drawn into this entanglement of real and imaginary time on a diegetic level as well: whereas the mother writes about time, the father keeps time with his pocket-watch (in a curious voiceover, he reads a passage from his diary that describes a glass beehive as the 'movement ... of a clock'). The girls also gauge time through a series of daily rituals (going to school, frequenting the train tracks, visiting the tattered barn). And the fugitive whom Ana befriends, presumably a republican soldier in exile, is inserted back into time after accidentally having been gifted the father's pocket-watch. As a marginal but no less crucial character in the film, the fugitive embodies temporality in many intriguing ways. Unlike the monster, who is never really killed, the fugitive is executed one night in a scene that is literally shot in the dark. Through death he is reinstated back into not only the present time of our viewing, but also the immortal time of cinema. His body is displayed directly beneath the film screen in the town hall, which previously doubled as the town's improvised movie theatre.

Not coincidentally, just as the fugitive's body enters into the space of cinema, which is portrayed as the domain of the law, the monster's body materialises outside the theatre, 'appearing' to Ana in the middle of the night shortly after she has run away from home.

Here, the reference to horror implied by *Frankenstein*, but ultimately never screened, is remapped onto the figure of the outlaw, whose body and the traces of violence inflicted upon it are shown. Some critics have compared the two – monster and fugitive – as embodiments of 'otherness'. But perhaps more accurately, we should note their difference: whereas one exemplifies a fictional invention that comes to life, the other represents the living dead that can only be revived once subsumed by a space of fiction. Thus, to equate Ana with 'otherness' since she pursues both figures, at times literally following in their footsteps, may be too simple. Like the film, she is never completely within or outside of the boundary between reality and fiction, but rather stands as an intermediary who connects to both simultaneously.

A haunting visual achievement, *The Spirit of the Beehive* could easily be categorised as a film about film – that is, about how film not only creates multiple planes of time but also seduces the viewing subject into the powerful world of fantasy that it projects. But it is equally a work about childhood. In fact the themes of childhood innocence and loss permeate the film from the opening credit sequence comprised of children's drawings (apparently real drawings done by the two lead child actresses) to the very last shot of Ana, bathed in moonlight as she stands in the threshold of the house after having summoned the spirit outside.

What the film portrays is the child's unique ability to perceive horror in a new light. This ability, and in Ana's case this desire to see and understand something rendered horrifying, is a point that visually resonates with different references to sight (the school anatomy lesson with don José, the film screening) and close-up shots of eyes, those organs of asking, as poet and critic John Berger calls them. But Ana's willingness to seek out the spirit sets her apart. That the film relies so heavily on the presence of – and anticipated encounter with – this mysterious spirit, is a fact that invites further reflection. As tempting as it may be to ascribe an allegorical meaning wherein the spirit becomes a metaphor for Spanish history, we might learn more by considering its non-allegorical implications.

For spirits are things that return from a time and space beyond the present moment, making that moment strangely out of touch with itself. But, this return also signals a way in which we can be affected by other senses and experiences of time. This is, after all, perhaps the most compelling definition of cinematic experience. For Erice, widely considered to be a visionary, the cinema is nothing if not a way of coming into contact with what has been lost, a way of 'bringing back what was once seen'.

But whether this means invoking the ghosts of history, or experiencing cinema's ghosts, remains open to interpretation. Either way, the beauty with which Erice's *The Spirit of the Beehive* poses this question to us will endure for ages to come.

Further reading

Jans Baetens, '"Transmedial Aesthetics is Ordinary": Some Remarks on Víctor Erice's *The Spirit of the Beehive*', *Kritika Kultura*, Vol. 1, 2011, pp. 57–69.

Adrian Danks, 'Víctor Erice', *Senses of Cinema*, 21 March 2003, Internet Resource, http://sensesofcinema.com/2003/great-directors/erice.

Chris Darke, '"Les enfants et les Cinèphiles": The Moment of Epiphany in *The Spirit of the Beehive*', *Cinema Journal*, Vol. 49, No. 2, 2010, pp. 152–8.

Celestino Deleyto, 'Women and Other Monsters: Frankenstein and the Role of the Mother in *El espíritu de la colmena*', *Bulletin of Hispanic Studies*, Vol. 76, No. 1, 1999, pp. 39–51.

Marvin D'Lugo, 'Landscape in Spanish Cinema', in Graeme Harper and Jonathan Rayner (eds), *Cinema and Landscape*, Bristol, Intellect, 2010, pp. 119–29.

Marvin D'Lugo, '*El espíritu de la colmena [Spirit of the Beehive]*', in *Guide to the Cinema of Spain*, Westport, CT, Greenwood Press, 1997, pp. 56–7.

Juan F. Egea, 'El monstruo metafórico en *El espíritu de la colmena*', *Revista de Estudios Hispánicos*, Vol. 36, 2002, pp. 523–43.

Linda C. Ehrlichn (ed.), *An Open Window: The Cinema of Víctor Erice*, Lanham, MD, Scarecrow Press, 2000.

Alberto Elena, 'Dream of Light: Erice, Kiarostami and the History of Cinema', *Studies in Hispanic Cinemas*, Vol. 6, No. 2, 2009, pp. 99–110.

Víctor Erice, 'Writing Cinema, Thinking Cinema', in Linda C. Ehrlich (ed.), *An Open Window*, 2000.

Peter Evans, '*El espíritu de la colmena:* the monster, the place of the father, and growing up in the dictatorship', *Vida Hispánica*, Vol. 31, No. 1, 1982, pp. 13–17.

Marsha Kinder, 'Breaking New Ground in *Los golfos, El cochecito,* and *El espíritu de la colmena*', in *Blood Cinema: The Reconstruction of National Identity in Spain*, Berkeley, University of California Press, 1993, pp. 87–133.

Jo Labanyi, 'History or Hauntology; or, What Does One Do with the Ghosts of the Past? Reflections on Spanish Film and Fiction of the Post-Franco Period', in Joan Ramon Resina (ed.), *Dis-remembering the Dictatorship: The Politics of Memory in the Spanish Transition to Democracy*, Amsterdam, Rodopi, 2000, pp. 65–82.

Luis Moreno-Caballud, 'La Ceguera De Cronos. Historia y tiempo en el cine de Víctor Erice', *Revista Hispánica Moderna: Boletín Del Instituto De Las Españas*, Vol. 62, No. 2, 2009, pp. 197–212.

Tony Patridge and María Diaz-Caneja, 'Art as revelation: Andrei Tarkovsky's films and the insights of Víctor Erice', *Journal of European Studies*, Vol. 41, No. 1, 2011, pp. 23–43.

Chris Perriam, '*El espíritu de la colmena*: Memory, Nostalgia, Trauma (Víctor Erice, 1973)', in Joan Ramon Resina (ed.), *Burning Darkness: A Half Century of Spanish Cinema*, Albany, NY, SUNY Press, 2008, pp. 61–81.

Yvonne Gavela Ramos, 'El acto colectivo de recordar: Historia y fantasía en *El espíritu de la colmena* y *El laberinto del fauno*', *Bulletin of Hispanic Studies*, Vol. 88, No. 2, 2011, pp. 179–96.

Xon de Ros, 'El Espíritu De La colmena/Spirit of the Beehive', in Alberto Mira (ed.), *The Cinema of Spain and Portugal*, London, Wallflower, 2005, pp. 139–47.

Xon de Ros, 'Innocence Lost: Sound and Silence in *El espíritu de la colmena*', *Bulletin of Hispanic Studies*, Vol. 76, No. 1, 1999, pp. 27–37.

Xon de Ros, 'Víctor Erice's "Voluntad de estilo" in *El espíritu de la colmena* (1973)', *Forum for Modern Language Studies, Vol. 31, No. 1, 1995, pp. 74–83.*

Paul Julian Smith, 'Between Metaphysics and Scientism: Rehistoricizing Víctor Erice', in *The Moderns: Time, Space, and Subjectivity in Contemporary Spanish Culture*, Oxford, Oxford University Press, 2000, pp. 23–41.

Paul Julian Smith, 'Between Metaphysics and Scientism: Rehistoricizing Víctor Erice's *El espíritu de la* colmena (1973)', in Peter Evans (ed.), *Spanish Cinema: The Auteurist Tradition*, Oxford, Oxford University Press, 1999, pp. 93–114.

Santos Zunzunegui 'Between History and Dream: Víctor Erice's *El espíritu de la colmena*', in Jenaro Talens and Santos Zunzunegui (eds), *Modes of Representation in Spanish Cinema*, Minneapolis, MN, University of Minnesota Press, 1998, pp. 128–54.

Patricia M. Keller

Europa Europa (1990)

[Country: Germany, France, Poland. Production Company: Central Cinema Company Film (CCC)/ Les Films du Losange. Director: Agnieszka Holland. Producers: Artur Brauner, Margaret Ménégoz. Screenwriter: Agnieszka Holland (based on Solomon Perel's book). Cinematographer: Jacek Petrycki. Music: Zbigniew Preisner. Editors: Isabelle Lorente, Ewa Smal. Cast: Marco Hofschneider (Solomon Perel/Josef Peters), Julie Delpy (Leni), René Hofschneider (Isaak Perel), Piotr Kozlowski (David Perel), André Wilms (Soldier Robert Kellerman), Ashley Wanninger (Gerd), Halina Labonarska (Leni's Mother), Klaus Abramowsky (Solomon's Father), Michele Gleizer (Solomon's Mother), Marta Sandrowicz (Bertha Perel).]

Synopsis: *Europa Europa* offers a picaresque tale of the childhood and adolescence of the German Jewish Solomon 'Solly' Perel during the Nazi regime, the Holocaust, and the Second World War. Solly lives happily with his family in Peine, Germany, but, when the persecution of Jews commences, they flee eastward, where he eventually becomes separated from his family. After a stint in a Soviet school, that is subsequently attacked, Solly uses his perfect German to join a German army unit as its Russian interpreter. His life takes another surprising turn when his Wehrmacht commanding officer decides to adopt Solly and send him to an elite Hitler Youth boarding school, where he both excels (not least with an 'Aryan' young woman Leni) but also has to conceal his identity from even more people. When mobilised along with other Hitler Youth in the last stages of the war, Solly finds he cannot bring himself to fire on Soviet soldiers and instead surrenders to them. Confused by his German uniform but perfect Russian, his erstwhile comrades are about to shoot him when his brother recognises him. The film ends with the voice-over that he emigrated to (then) Palestine, having decided to be openly Jewish after these many years and narrative twists of hiding his born and childhood identity.

Europa Europa (1990; released as *Hitlerjunge Salomon* in Germany in 1991) won the Golden Globe in 1992 for Best Foreign Language Film; it is still the veteran director Agnieszka Holland's best-known film; and it is regarded by many as having kicked off the wave of 1990s and early 2000s Holocaust feature films, including Spielberg's *Schindler's List* (1994) as well as the later *Life is Beautiful* (Roberto Benigni, 1998) and *The Pianist* (Steven Spielberg, 2002).[1] Notably, however, it was not submitted for the Oscar for Best Foreign Language Film – its Golden Globe win was seen as a belated, diminished recognition – because its own origins could not be easily traced to any single country. A Polish-directed, German–French financed coproduction in which Polish, Russian and German are all spoken, it did not obviously qualify as a candidate from any particular nation. This underscores how *Europa Europa* manifests a very particular moment not only in the collective (mediated) memory of the Holocaust but also in European history, when the system in which Holland had grown up (and that she had deliberately departed shortly before) was falling apart. The sudden porousness of borders, unexpected vagaries of identity, and the contradictions of places and people are themes of both the film and the historical moment that produced it.

It is especially remarkable, but also telling, that the film did not end up Germany's nominee for the foreign language Oscar, as one German committee did not deem the film 'German' enough for the nomination while another emphatically rejected it (both Holland and her father are Jewish, and the film's prominent, German Jewish producer Artur Brauner, pointed out this irony of not being ruled German enough).[2] The decision against Holland's film reflects how complex and challenging the film remains about a topic, the Holocaust, about which clear moral legibility would seem most requisite, particularly for German audiences, sensitised and sensitive as they are about Germany's crimes during the Holocaust. In terms of expected moral clarity, the film does, indeed, lead viewers to empathise with its Jewish protagonist, Solomon Perel (usually called by his nickname Solly), and certainly derides its many convinced and crude

Nazis, ranging from Hitler Youth teachers all the way 'up' to Hitler. But both the narrative trajectory and the aesthetic register in which Holland traces Solly's unlikely arc challenges, even defies, any Manichean good versus evil logic. Although the film can be seen to have initiated the wave of high-profile Holocaust films of the 1990s and 2000s, it is a good deal more aesthetically ambitious and ambiguous than those better-known works.

The key confusions and challenges to facile moral clarity seem to be two: on the one hand, the uncanny ability of Solly to assume and navigate completely, even shockingly, contradictory identities (German and Polish, committedly communist and then fervently Nazi, but ultimately Jewish); and, on the other, the repeated foregrounding, as well as overt eroticisation, of his adolescent body and even genitalia. Tellingly, key events of the Holocaust (1930s Nazi pogroms, 1939 invasion of Poland, 1941 invasion of Soviet Union, 1940s ghettoisation) intersect Solly's familiar teenage struggles with inchoate identity and sexual awakening. The film's first extended sequence foregrounds these interwoven processes of personal and sexual identity and the body in which they are housed when viewers watch, from the point of view of children peering through a window, Solly's circumcision, which he claims to remember as an adult (the first of a number of unlikely claims made by the protagonist/periodic voice-over narrator, to add to the representational complexity). This circumcision and its role in identity is immediately thematised in the very next sequence, 13 years later, in which Solly is naked to bathe before his bar mitzvah. Subsequently, throughout the film, he assumes different identities, left nonetheless to struggle with this corporeal mark and marker of his identity.

These struggles with identity and the body on which it is indelibly written hit new heights, or lows, when, late in the film and an unlikely pupil at a Hitler Youth boarding school, Solly decides he has to reclaim his foreskin by thread and needle rather than continue to conceal his Jewish origins to Nazi friends and superiors who know him as Josef 'Jupp' Peters. A series of uncomfortable scenes – Solly/Jupp has to continue the school's rigorous athletic programme despite his urological auto-surgery – reinforces the film's exploration of the body and obsessions with it as key to the Nazi's emphatically biopolitical project. As Janet Lungstrum convincingly argues, the film's fetishism of Solly's body and its circumcision in particular both mimics and critiques the regime's obsession with the Jewish body, with foreskin as marker of indelible difference and fascination that so impressed and obsessed the Nazi state.[3] For Lungstrum, there is a revealing parallel between the Jewish male, on the one side, and cinema's female characters more generally, on the other: both Solly and women characters become the obsessive target of the fetishising gaze and both have to renounce their own desires in a disavowal of lack of those endowed with the gaze.[4]

This indelible mark on and of the body of the Nazis' paradigmatic victim is, however, only one side of a contradiction that obtains throughout the film because, of course, Solly is able to become both the perfect Soviet Communist and Aryan Nazi at various times.[5] Central to the film is the fundamental and constitutive performativity of identity and subsequent mutability of person, great Brechtian themes that Solomon's autobiography seems unwittingly to convey. In this sense, the lines offered to Solly by '[his] only friend' at the time he has joined the Wehrmacht, soldier Robert, seem perhaps the best maxim for the entire film. When Solly/Josef is taking a bath in a barn – another fateful bathing episode foregrounding his naked body – Robert sneaks up behind him, makes a pass and comes close to discovering his secret until Solly/Josef (once again) leaps from the tub and dances elusively away. But the young, naked hero finally breaks down and reveals to the closeted gay soldier that he is Jewish. One of only two (Gentile) Germans to learn that Solly/Josef is Jewish, Robert answers Solly/Josef's question 'Isn't it hard always playing someone else?' with the resonant 'It's easier than playing yourself'. It is notable that another sequence, one of two dream sequences, also has Solly/Josef in the closet, though he is sent out by the similarly crotch-covering and cowering Hitler (his likewise dreamt sister whispers that the Führer is also Jewish). Robert's resonant recognition of the performances of identity, however, still presumes a core self the film seems (also in a Brechtian mode) at times to obliterate – it is often not clear, to viewers or Solly, who or what his self is. Holland mentioned being struck by how the contradictory selves Solly assumed each left its mark on him, as when Robert asks whether he prays and he answers with the Marxist dictum 'religion is the opiate of the masses', even though by that point he is comfortably in a Wehrmacht uniform.

When Solly/Jupp initially confesses his Jewishness to Robert, Robert assures him that 'there are other Germans', presumably those who will not murder him for the identity his body still dictates. Among these 'other Germans' is the mother of Solly/Jupp's later girlfriend Leni, whom he meets at the elite Hitler Youth near Brunswick (Braunschweig). Solly/Jupp lands at the school when he is adopted from his Wehrmacht unit by its commanding officer, an aristocratic captain who tells him he needs schooling, not more time in the army. He chooses for his charge one of the Hitler Youth's schools dotting Germany at the time, where Solly/Jupp shines in the school's sports competitions (swimming in full military kit) as well as in burgeoning sexual identity (a paradigmatic BDM member, Leni is lusted after by many of the school's boys). The irony of Solly/Jupp's success amidst the most convinced anti-Semites underscores the film's generally picaresque approach, in which Solly/Jupp, a teenager without qualities, lands in the unlikeliest of contrasting situations.[6] One critic has pointed to the film's 'deconstructive humor' in these sequences' depictions of buffoonish Nazis, perhaps most entertainingly represented in another of Solly's dreams, in which Hitler dances with Stalin.[7]

As the war and film draw to their ends and the Hitler Youth are thrown to the front, Solly/Jupp finds that he cannot fire on his former Soviet comrades and flees his Hitler Youth schoolmates, who shoot at him as a parting gesture. He throws himself at the mercy of the Soviets, who do not know what to make of his perfect Russian but Nazi uniform; when he explains that he was hiding himself among Nazis elites because he is Jewish, they decide to let Jewish camp inmates decide what to do with him. At the moment an inmate raises the Soviet pistol to shoot him, he hears 'Solek' from off-screen by his long-lost brother Isaak (played by the actor's actual brother, René Hofschneider). Their reunion is a revealing long-take embrace of laughing and crying, limning and blurring the two as the entire film has. The film concludes with voiceover by Solly that he decided to be openly Jewish from then on, to emigrate to Palestine, and segues to a shot of the actual, now old Solomon Perel singing the song offered by his mother just before the opening circumcision. Singing, he walks off in to a verdant landscape, a seeming citation of the similarly singing-and-landscaped opening sequence of Claude Lanzmann's magisterial 1984/85 *Shoah*.

This sudden happy end, with brother Isaak ex machina, was one of the most notable liberties taken by the film with the source text. As the epilogue emphasises, *Europa Europa* is based on Perel's autobiography, with a number of details changed (perhaps the most important other instance, the abrupt and powerful opening, with the 1930s murder of his sister, was an invention of the script; Bertha was, in fact, murdered late in the war on a death march from one concentration camp to another). In his autobiography, Solly/Jupp's service to the Reich ended not when he wilfully fled the Hitler Youth for the Soviets; rather he was taken prisoner, along with some other Hilter Youth, by US soldiers, stripped of Nazi regalia, and then released. Subsequently searching for news of his family in both his old (German) hometown of Peine as well as Bergen Belsen (the first British liberated camp), he received information about them from some Jews who recognised him from his time in Lodz. Perhaps most surprisingly given the film's arc, Solly also worked in this period for the Soviet occupational authorities as an interpreter, although he did later decline to extend his work with Soviet forces. Eventually, through information gained from friends in Peine, he did make his way to his brother Isaak, then living in Munich after being liberated form Dachau, and then finally, as the film indicates, to Palestine and his brother David.

As noted above, *Europa Europa* helped initiate the 1990s and 2000s wave of Europe-set blockbuster Holocaust films, with most assuming the generic contours of historical drama. In fact, many scenes and scenarios of *Europa Europa* reappear in these films. For instance, the non-linear beginning and end appear in *Schindler's List*, which, like *Europa*

Europa, commences with a Jewish religious ceremony and ends by departing its fictional diegesis for shots of the people on whom the film has based its fictionalised account (of Solomon Perel in *Europa Europa* and of the various 'Schindler Jews' as well as Schindler's wife in *Schindler's List*, though, notably, Holland has said she dislikes the ending of *Schindler's List*). Like the *Pianist*, *Europa Europa* wraps its Jewish protagonist in a Nazi jacket for ironic warmth and protection. *Life is Beautiful* revisits the memorable scene in which its protagonist is displayed before schoolchildren to illustrate how one can easily identify the Aryan body by its markers and measurements, when, in fact, the body used in the pedantically racist demonstration is actually Jewish. In none of those later and subsequently better-known films, however, is the line between victim and perpetrator as deliberately blurred and then satirically exploited, to such disquieting and devastating effect, as in *Europa Europa*.

Notes

1. Hansen, '*Schindler's* List is not *Shoah*', pp. 292–3.
2. Lungstrum, 'Foreskin Fetishism', p. 54.
3. Ibid., p. 58ff.
4. Ibid., p. 61.
5. Holland named Woody Allen's *Zelig* as an inspiration; see Rosenbaum, 'What is a Jew?'.
6. Perel mentioned Voltaire's *Candide* as a model for his autobiography; see Lungstrum, 'Foreskin Fetishims', p. 55.
7. Linville, 'Agniezska Holland's *Europa, Europa*'.

Further reading

Omer Bartov, *The Jews in Cinema: From the* Golem *to* Don't Touch My Holocaust, Bloomington, Indiana University Press, 2005.

David Bathrick, Brad Prager and Michael Richardson (eds), *Visualizing the Holocaust: Documents, Aesthetics, Memory*, Rochester, NY, Camden House, 2008.

Susan Bernofsky, 'Restaging the Past: *Hitlerjunge Salomon* and its reception in Germany', *faultline*, No. 1,1992, pp. 11–20.

Miriam Hansen, '*Schindler's List* is not *Shoah*: The Second Commandment, Popular Modernism, and Public Memory', *Critical Inquiry*, Vol. 22, No. 2, Winter 1996, pp. 292–312.

Annette Insdorf, *Indelible Shadows: Film and the Holocaust*, Cambridge, Cambridge University Press, 1983, 2003.

Susan E. Linville, 'Agniezska Holland's *Europa, Europa*: deconstructive humor in a Holocaust film', *Film Criticism*, Vol. 19, No. 3, 1995, pp. 44–53.

Janet Lungstrum, 'Foreskin Fetishism: Jewish Male Difference in *Europa, Europa*', *Screen*, Vol. 39, No. 1, Spring 1998, pp. 53–66.

Solomon Perel, *Europa Europa*, New York, Wiley, 1999.

Jonathan Rosenbaum, 'What is a Jew?' *Chicago Reader*, November 8, 1991. Available at www.jonathanrosenbaum.com/?p=7287

Jaimey Fisher

Fanny och Alexander/Fanny and Alexander (1982)

[Country: Sweden, France and West Germany. Production Company: Gaumont. Director: Ingmar Bergman. Producer: Jörn Donner. Screenwriter: Ingmar Bergman. Cinematographer: Sven Nykvist. Music: Daniel Bell. Editor: Sylvia Ingemarsson. Art Director: Anna Asp. Cast: Pernilla Allwin (Fanny Ekdahl), Bertil Guve (Alexander Ekdahl), Ewa Fröling (Emilie Ekdahl), Allan Edwall (Oscar Ekdahl), Jan Malmjsö (Bishop Edvard Vergérus), Erland Josephson (Isak Jacobi).]

Synopsis: *Fanny and Alexander* is set in the Swedish town of Uppsala in the early 1900s and depicts the complex web of relationships connecting members of the wealthy Ekdahl family. Oscar Ekdahl is a theatre director, happily married to Emilie. The narrative is largely seen through the eyes of their two young children, Fanny and Alexander. Home life is warm and creative, until the idyll is shattered by Oscar's death following a stroke. Emilie remarries to a widower, Bishop Vergérus, and moves with the children into his house. The contrast with their former life could hardly be starker, as the Bishop is puritanical, repressive and unbendingly severe. His relationship with Alexander develops into a battle of wills as the Bishop tries to crush the boy's resistance. With help from a Jewish antiques dealer and friend of the family, Isak Jacobi, the children, and then their mother, are magically freed from the Bishop's grasp and restored to the loving bosom of the ever-growing Ekdahl clan. However, the ghostly legacy of the Bishop is not so easily left behind.

Few national cinemas have been as dominated by a single filmmaker as Sweden's has by Ingmar Bergman. He bestrides Swedish cinema, and European art cinema for that matter, like a creative colossus. His preoccupations with death, loss of religious faith, psychological and sexual breakdown, and fractured relationships, combined with the melancholy nature of many of his film narratives, and a famously austere visual style, have become synonymous with the popular image of his country. As Brian McIlroy put it, among all Swedish directors 'if anyone is well known for his work outside of Sweden, it is Ingmar Bergman' (McIlroy 1986: 44). One might also suggest that Bergman's work has provided one of the mainstays for the whole tradition of film as art in Europe.

Ingmar Bergman was born on 14 July 1918 in Uppsala. Home life was shaped by two dominant influences which were to affect him long into his adult life, both of which are evident in *Fanny and Alexander*. The first was his relationship with his father, a severe Lutheran minister whose religious convictions created an atmosphere of fear and oppression. The second was his immediate love for the life of the imagination, expressed through a fascination with toys such as a magic lantern, a Chinese shadow theatre or the cinematograph. In his autobiography he describes the excitement of first making the cinematograph work: '*Then I turned the handle!* It is impossible to describe this. I can't find words to express my excitement' (Bergman 1989: 16). At university in Stockholm he was involved in theatrical productions, as well as devouring films. They became his twin passions and he moved between the two throughout his subsequent career, making more than 60 films for cinema release or television, as well directing as over 170 theatre productions.

Bergman's early work from the late 1940s through to the mid-1950s is varied in approach, though often incorporates both realism and melodrama. A frankness in his handling of sexuality is already apparent in *Summer with Monika* (1953) and *Smiles of a Summer Night* (1955), but it was *The Seventh Seal* (1957) that brought him to international prominence. With its unforgettable images and story of a medieval knight (Max von Sydow) delaying his inevitable demise by playing a protracted game of chess with the cloaked figure of Death (Bengt Ekerot), the film gave full voice to the director's own crisis of faith. The knight isn't afraid of dying but wants to be sure of God's existence beforehand, something he has come to doubt as he experiences the pain and cruelty of human existence. But the film provides no answers and eventually Death leads him away in a sequence which would later be borrowed by one of Bergman's many admirers, Woody Allen. The starkness of the visual style, as realised in Gunnar Fischer's luminous black and white cinematography, and pessimistic themes were continued and intensified in *Through a Glass Darkly* (1961), *Winter Light* (1962) and *The Silence* (1963), which formed a loose trilogy and further cemented his critical reputation.

Bergman developed a repertory company of actors, many of them female, who worked with him repeatedly through the 1960s and 1970s including Bibi Andersson, Erland Josephson, Ingrid Thulin and Liv Ullman (who appeared in nine of his films). He adopted an increasingly improvisational technique with his actors and shifted his concerns somewhat from the spiritual to the inner emotional and psychological lives of his characters. This is especially evident in *Persona* (1966), which is probably his most formally experimental work, as well as in *Cries and Whispers* (1973), which also returns to themes of mortality and faith. Following his arrest for tax evasion (the charges were eventually dropped) in 1976 he went into self-imposed exile, making a number of films as international co-productions. *Fanny and Alexander* marked his return to Sweden for what he intended to be his cinematic swansong, although he went on to write a number of screenplays after this and directed films for television. He finally retired from filmmaking in 2003.

One of the most striking aspects of *Fanny and Alexander* is its strongly autobiographical flavour. Alongside its position in Bergman's canon as a kind of coda, this aspect gives the film the status of a summation of his concerns as a filmmaker, as well as expressing his feelings as he came towards the twilight of his creative life. In his memoirs Bergman wrote movingly of the pleasure the film afforded him: 'Sometimes there is a special happiness in being a film director. A rehearsed expression is born, just like that, and the camera registers it' (Bergman 1989: 66). This is probably embodied most in the depiction of the film's two fathers. The first, Oscar Ekdahl, becomes the idealised symbol for a life steeped in creativity and familial concerns, while the Bishop seems closer to the reality of Bergman's own relationship with his father. The film's tangle of romantic and sexual relationships can also be read as a reflection of Bergman's own personal life (five marriages, nine children, and several very public relationships with his leading actresses), as well as a plea for reconciliation. The director's abiding obsessions with the lasting power of childhood, the shadow of death, and the presence (or absence) of God are embedded throughout the narrative of the film.

The story divides classically into three distinct sections. The first is a celebration of love, home and the imagination, as we see the wide circle of the Ekdahl family and their friends preparing for Christmas. The family home is warm and cosseted, but these qualities are also repeated among Oscar's second 'family' at the theatre where he works as managing director. Bergman draws a direct link between the two worlds, cutting between them and mirroring the decor of the theatre with the theatricality of the Ekdahls' Christmas celebrations. Fanny and Alexander soak up these influences and then express them through their own play with a model theatre and a magic lantern. The relationships within the family span the generations from the children to their grandmother, Helena, the matriarch of the clan, and takes in Oscar's brothers and their wives and mistresses. Infidelity and sex are depicted with an air of indulgent acceptance, as all the relationships are underpinned by love, tenderness and tolerance. Both of Oscar's 'homes' are depicted through a colour palette of reds and golds, created by cinematographer Sven Nykvist and designer Anna Asp, which has them appear bathed in warm light. Although Alexander's world is not without its sexual tensions, the abiding impression is of security and love.

The film's second section provides a total contrast. It begins when Oscar suffers a stroke during a production of *Hamlet* and subsequently passes away at the family home. The driving force which shapes this section is the introduction of Bishop Edvard Vergérus whom Oscar's widow, Emilie, meets and subsequently marries, taking the children to live in his residence and breaking the family's links both with the theatre and the wider Ekdahl family circle.

The film makes it plain that the Bishop has preyed on Emilie's vulnerable emotional state; his religiosity is often a mask for blatant self-interest in his motivations. The world of the Bishop's residence is evoked by an entirely contrasting range of colours, through grey, blue and black, to evoke a cold, forbidding environment. His Lutheranism is equated with meanness of spirit and a denial of pleasure that is the absolute antithesis of the film's first section where the joy of existence is always paramount. For the Bishop, pleasure is equated with sin, God is a severe judge rather than an indulgent father, and children are dangerous, anarchic forces which need to be kept tightly controlled. Increasingly Alexander becomes the focus of resistance to his stepfather, eventually drawing his mother back onto his side and through her reaching out to the distant Ekdahl family, and especially to Helena, for rescue from their virtual imprisonment.

This conflict between opposing forces is resolved in a most startling manner in the film's final third as the children are able to flee from the Bishop's home with the help of a Isak, a Jewish friend of the family, who seems to literally 'magic' them from the Bishop's grasp. The film evokes the powers of a world beyond our own as Alexander sees his father's ghost and then has a premonition of his stepfather's death in a fire. These 'visions' can be given rational explanation as the subjective thoughts, or even wishes of Alexander. In this respect, the film's blurring of reality and subjectivity echoes concerns previously examined by Bergman in films such as *Persona*. However, it is hard here to avoid the thought that Bergman's work has come full circle, so that having abandoned the religious impulse of his early work for a doomy existentialism, he finally returns to a form of mysticism. An alternative dimension seems to exist here alongside the material world and some powerful, external forces are at work. As Egil Törnqvist observes, one of the more unusual aspects of the film is that this mysticism has a decidedly non-Christian dimension to it: 'The Christian dualism of grace and punishment, heaven and hell, gives way to a Jewish, pantheistic monism, a belief that "everything is alive, everything is God and the thought of God, not only the good but also the cruellest things"' (Törnqvist 1995: 177).

Fanny and Alexander was released in two versions. The full edition, running more than five hours, was initially screened on television in four episodes. A three-hour edit was screened theatrically to considerable acclaim, winning the Academy Award as Best Foreign Language film, although for connoisseurs the full-length version is definitive. The final scenes, with a double celebration for the birth of Emilie's and Edvard's child and of the child of Uncle Gustav Adolf and the family maid, Maj (happily accepted into the Ekdahl family by all) balanced by the chilling reappearance of Edvard's malevolent ghost, brings to a memorable conclusion the twin streams running through this and all Bergman's work. *Fanny and Alexander* is, as Peter Cowie suggests, 'a kind of climax to Bergman's career', and a very fitting one (Cowie 1985: 335).

Further reading

Ingmar Bergman, (1989) *The Magic Lantern: An Autobiography*, trans. Joan Tate, London: Penguin.

Peter Cowie, (1982) *Ingmar Bergman: A Critical Biography*, London: Secker and Warburg.

Peter Cowie, (1985) *Swedish Cinema, From Ingeborg Holm to Fanny and Alexander*, Stockholm: Swedish Institute.

Brian McIlroy, (1986) *World Cinema 2: Sweden*, London: Flicks Books.

Noel Simsolo, (2011) *Masters of Cinema: Ingmar Bergman*, Paris: Cahier du Cinema.

Egil Törnqvist, (1995) *Between Stage and Screen: Ingmar Bergman Directs*, Amsterdam: Amsterdam University Press.

Robert Shail

Festen/The Celebration (1998)

[Country: Denmark. Production Company: Nimbus Film. Director: Thomas Vinterberg. Cinematographer: Anthony Dod Mantle. Original Music: Lars Bo Jensen. Producer: Brigitte Hald. Editor: Valdis Oskarsdottìr. Cast: Ulrich Thomsen (Christian), Henning Moritzen (Helge, father), Paprika Steen (Helene), Thomas Bo Larsen (Michael), Birthe Neumann (Else, mother).]

Synopsis: A father's sixtieth birthday is a cause for family celebration but as the extended relatives gather to rejoice a cloud hangs over them. Helge, the father, hopes his close family will support the festivities but eldest son Christian has something he wants to share with his family and will do so via a speech at the birthday dinner, a speech of truth. Christian is reunited with his siblings, Helene and Michael, but the three are still mourning the death of his twin Linda, who committed suicide the year before. There is tension surrounding the family and questions unanswered over the death of Linda, but Christian sets out to challenge his patriarchal father and answer everyone's questions.

Despite his relatively short career, *Festen* being only his third full-length feature, Vinterberg used his film to push the boundaries of his work. The young director from Denmark presented this film as the first to come from the 'Dogme 95 Manifesto'. Conceived by Vinterberg and Lars Von Trier, a more established director at the time, Dogme 95 was seen as a rejection of Hollywood cinema. The pair believed that the illusion of Hollywood was too much; to pretend that something was real with all the technical input that went into it was false. And so they aimed to strip filmmaking back; Dogme 95's 'Vow of Chastity' contained a set of rules that these innovative directors believed would bring film-making closer to their goal of authenticity. The 'Vow' consisted of ten rules such as, the camera must be handheld, there must be no optical effects and no post-recorded sounds, props cannot be brought to a location but can only be used if found there.

It is a challenge to say that Vinterberg should be commended for the success of this filming style as Dogme 95 rules state that a director should not be credited; indeed, the members express no belief in the 'Auteur'. However, despite this, Vinterberg received great critical acclaim for his family-centred vision and the film was a global success. Having received a Jury Prize at Cannes (joint with *La Classe de Neige,* a film of the same taboo topic), *Festen* was later screened in just short of 600,000 cinemas in France and achieved distribution in the US market. This was a great feat for a Danish film of a small production. The film's success is pinned not simply to its unconventional style but also to its theme. Set against a backdrop of Danish tradition, the celebration of father Helge is a universal story. The main subject of the film is one of taboo, child abuse; however the cinematic audience was becoming more open. It is a subject that has impact and should be addressed globally. Vinterberg was also clever with his depiction of a family reunion as again all audience members can relate to the feeling of meeting relatives that haven't been seen for years, rivalry between siblings and he even adds in a senile Grandpa to provide a comic relief from the intensity of Christian's revelations.

Festen critiques the hierarchy of the family; Christian arrives at the celebration to expose the truth about his father's abuse towards himself and his twin. But the film also comments on the hierarchy of society. The original title was *Blood of the Bourgeoisie*; however, it was felt that this was too similar to titles used by Buñuel and so it was changed to *Festen.* The original title would have been fitting as we see lower-status characters such as the chef and waitresses aid Christian in his speech. The waitresses hide the car keys of the guests so that they cannot leave and are forced to hear Christian completely. Kim is the chef; he is a childhood friend of Christian's who encourages him not to give up and to force the truth upon his family. These lower-status characters are rebelling against those in power, they want to bring the bourgeoisie down to the level of the proletariat. This could be considered reflective of Vinterberg's rejection of Hollywood and desire to produce his film differently.

This hierarchy is also evident in the levels of the siblings. Michael is the youngest, the tearaway character, he lacks control of his anger. Helene is free-spirited and independent and Christian is a success in his work. Each character is so different that the viewer may be able to recognise themselves in at least one of them; they are stereotypical and relatable. Linda is the sibling we do not see; her funeral has occurred a year before the narrative but she is discussed several times in the dialogue between the other three. At times the camerawork makes the viewer feel as though we may be observing through Linda's eyes. As the camera is handheld there is often a sense of point-of-view shots as though Linda is watching. The cinematography is by Anthony Dod Mantle, who since has worked on many of Von Trier's films. Mantle filmed with three cameras giving a feeling that the mansion is being recorded with CCTV. This 'Big Brother' style of filming makes the viewer feel as though they are intruding on private events. Often during Christian's revealing speech the camera hovers behind him, it gives the impression of a live audience, like we are witnessing a reality television show and being asked to pass judgement on the characters. Owing to the use of three cameras there is more shot choice for the editor and so the narrative is always continuous. The cameras capture the reactions of Christian's audience when he exposes the sexual abuse his father dealt him as a child. In formal style his parents and siblings are spread around the dinner table so they can each act as host to a smaller section of the guests, the editing juxtaposes close-ups of his family's reaction, which does not fit the information they have received. The underwhelming reaction is conventional of the bourgeoisie, similar to Buñuel's characters in *The Discreet Charm of the Bourgeoisie*, Vinterberg's characters act initially as if nothing has been said, the atmosphere of farcical celebration is upheld.

The handheld camera is also used to an advantage when Michael tries to remove Christian from the party. The fighting acts as a commotion that almost justifies chaotic camera work. Owing to the documentary feel the audience don't expect to be able to see all that is going on. As a character that has been unable to control himself throughout; losing his temper with the hotel manager, his wife and the maid with whom he had an affair, Michael acts in the only way he knows. Trying to please his father he lashes out at Christian. In earlier conversation further links were made to bourgeoisie lifestyle as Helge offers Michael a place in the Freemasons. Despite the fact that the offer is undermined as he is second choice due to Christian's refusal, Michael is overjoyed and seizes the opportunity to take part in something with his father. It is apparent that Michael was not victim to his father's abuse but has instead received other negative attention. He is in strong contradiction to Christian who is at all times the calm voice of reason despite the hardships he has faced.

Christian's calmness is also portrayed in the scene where we are first introduced to Helge. He emerges from the dark and asks to talk to Christian, the pair shake hands as they greet each other and take a seat in a room with low-key lighting. Christian continually rubs his hand, as if he is trying to remove the trace of his father's handshake. This action combined with the fact that his father's face is never fully lit, as he hides in the shadows, act as signifiers to the audience that he is shameful and a dark twist may occur. However, the conversation between the pair does not reveal much as Christian remains reserved. The focus of the film's narrative is very much on the family's dark secret; this means the viewer is constantly focussed on finding out the truth about the family. The only sign of a life outside of the mansion is when Helene's new boyfriend, Gbatokai arrives. Even then there is no extension of the characters. Gbatokai is a victim of racism from Michael who refers to him as 'Charlie Brown' and from Helene's mother who presumes this is the same black man that her daughter has brought home before and refuses to make any attempt to pronounce his name accurately. Even with this slight development in Helene's character, no resolution is provided for the audience, as the racism remains unsettled.

As well as raising issues of racism, the character of Else (the mother) also calls into question the guilt of those who do nothing to prevent abuse. In a speech of her own Else compliments her husband Helge for his commitment to her. Discussing each of her children it is clear that her praise is laced with criticism. The only thing she praises Michael for are the grandchildren he provides, and whilst complimenting Helge's independence she criticises her choice of studies and career path. In reference to Christian she implies that he has fabricated his father's abuse similar to the way he would fabricate his imaginary friend as a child, stating 'I think Snoot has been with you today'. She undermines him and through this suggests to her guests that Christian has lost his mind. The handheld camera is fixed on Else's face and switches to Christian. Similarly to during Christian's speech, Else's face continues to give nothing away. There is no shock, implying that she was aware of what her husband had done but didn't act, instead choosing to hide it. Birthe Neumann, who plays Else, states it is the vilest character she has ever played. This calls into question some of the practices of filming claimed by the Dogme 95 rules. As Marie-Lise Betemps argues 'How can Dogme 95 praise the refusal of illusion and at the same time praise the presence of actors and emphasise their work to such a tremendous extent?' (2002: 16). Cinematographer, Mantle, agrees with this stating, in *The Making of Festen* (2005), that the actors have more freedom due to the fluidity of the cameras. As they did not have to wait for lighting to be set up or cameras to be put into position the actors were able to complete scenes more quickly allowing for more creativity.

Once Christian has completed his speech his calmness remains. Exposed and ashamed his father simply retires to his room. He is no longer in the strong patriarchal position, yet bourgeois tendencies remain. The awkward atmosphere is evident yet there is little acknowledgement of the revelations. Else continues to converse as if nothing has happened, the elephant remains in the room.

Vinterberg's *Festen* was the first of the Dogme 95 films. He achieved his goal of creating a piece of cinema that didn't rely on façade. As John Rockwell argues in his discussion of Trier's film *The Idiots*, 'Low-budget European movies look technically raw, and Dogma just pushes that extreme further. They concentrate on close-ups and conversation rather than polished craft' (2003: 9). This is most definitely the tone that Vinterberg's feature set. It is interesting to note that Trier's career has been successful whilst shrouded in controversy, whereas Vinterberg has received more limited critical praise since. Although Dogme rules state that a filmmaker should only create one Dogme piece, perhaps this is where Vinterberg's talents lie.

Further reading

Marie-Lise Bétemps, 'Dogmatic Festen: How a viewer could not escape Thomas Vinterberg's *Festen*'. *Norden 1*: *Europa*, 2002, pp. 14–21.

Danny Leigh, 'The Salutary Tale of Thomas Vinterberg, Ghost of Filmic Failure Past'. Available at: www.guardian.co.uk/film/filmblog/2011/may/27/thomas-vinterberg-lars-von-trier-film, 2011 (accessed 12 February 2012).

Peter Matthews, 'Festen Review'. Available at www.bfi.org.uk/sightandsound/review/49, 1998 (accessed 12 February 2012).

John Rockwell, *The Idiots*, London, BFI, 2003.

Eric Lennart Peterson, *The Making of Festen*, exclusive to the tenth anniversary edition of Festen. Electric Parc Aps, 2005.

Holly Taylor

Freaks (1932)

[Country: USA. Production Company: Metro-Goldwyn-Mayer. Director: Tod Browning. Producers: Tod Browning, Irving Thalberg (uncredited). Screenwriters: Willis Goldbeck and Leon Gordon (uncredited). Suggested by Tod Robbins' story 'Spurs'. Cinematographer: Merritt B. Gerstad (uncredited). Editor: Basil Wrangell (uncredited). Cast: Wallace Ford (Phroso), Leila Hyams (Venus),

Olga Baclanova (Cleopatra), Rosco Ates (Roscoe), Henry Victor (Hercules), Harry Earles (Hans), Daisy Earles (Frieda), Rose Dione (Madame Tetrallini), Daisy Hilton (Daisy the Siamese Twin), Violet Hilton (Violet the Siamese Twin), Schlitze (as himself, The Pinhead Girl), Josephine Joseph (Half Woman-Half Man), Johnny Eck (Johnny the Half Boy), Frances O'Connor (The Armless Girl), Peter Robinson (The Human Skeleton), Olga Roderick (The Bearded Lady), Koo Koo (The Bird Girl), Prince Randian (The Living Torso), Martha Morris (The Armless Girl), Elvira Snow (Zip the Pinhead), Jenny Lee Snow (Pip the Pinhead), Elizabeth Green (The Bird Girl), Angelo Rossitto (Angelino), Edward Brophy (Rollo Brother), Mat McHugh (Rollo Brother).]

Synopsis: Circus dwarves Hans and Frieda (Harry and Daisy Earles) are engaged to be married. They work in a tight-knit community of 'freaks' that includes a 'human torso', a pair of conjoined twins, a 'half boy' and assorted other characters. The conniving trapeze artist Cleopatra (Baclanova), a 'normal', learns that Hans has an inheritance, and she seduces him for his money. At the wedding feast after they marry, Cleopatra is offered a loving cup as part of her initiation into the freaks' community. However, at this point she heartlessly rejects the freaks and turns against Hans. Soon after, the freaks learn that Cleopatra and her boyfriend, the strongman Hercules (Victor), have begun poisoning Hans. In retaliation for this attempted murder, the freaks attack Cleopatra and Hercules in a climactic rainstorm chase scene. At the film's conclusion, Cleopatra is revealed as now transformed into a legless, quacking 'human duck'.

Scorned in its own time, Tod Browning's *Freaks* eventually became one of the most important American cult films. First released in 1932, this film starring little-known actors and circus sideshow performers was an anomaly in the production roster of Metro-Goldwyn-Mayer, the studio renowned for its high production values and its slogan: 'More stars than there are in heaven'. This is a film that critiques the star system, both in its casting and in its narrative; indeed, it can be interpreted as a denunciation of our culture's obsession with appearances. The differently abled bodies of the freaks who star in the film – armless, legless, small or exceptionally thin – serve to undermine the typical ideology of beauty promulgated by other Hollywood films. (I use the term freak without quotation marks in the spirit of defiance with which the term has been reclaimed by some in the disability community, much like the word queer has been reappropriated.) The film's very plot involves unmasking a beautiful circus star – Cleopatra, the trapeze artist and 'peacock of the air' – as a greedy, repugnant character whose exterior attractiveness is ultimately destroyed at the end, when she is turned into a 'human duck' and becomes a sideshow spectacle herself.

Director Tod Browning is renowned for his films about outsiders. Browning himself had a background in circuses, having travelled with a number of carnivals and sideshows in his youth. *Freaks* is Browning's most well-known picture due to its status as a cult film, along with the early sound version of *Dracula* (1931) he made for Universal, which stars Bela Lugosi. Browning also made a number of important silent-era features with actor Lon Chaney, the legendary 'Man of a Thousand Faces', in particular *The Unholy Three* (1925) and *The Unknown* (1927). *The Unknown*, considered by many today to be Browning's masterpiece, tells the story of a circus performer (Chaney) who has his arms cut off to please the woman he loves (she fears the embrace of men), only to discover she has fallen for a strongman.

Freaks has been controversial since its release. Initially produced as a horror film, the picture was made at a time when disabled bodies were becoming viewed less as curiosities, as they had been in the old freak show tradition, and more as medical anomalies that could be 'fixed' by modern science. Freak shows had come to be looked down upon as low entertainment, and disabled people were now subjected to pity rather than gawking. Needless to say, neither approach allows the disabled person the dignity of his or her difference. What's more, despite the changing attitudes about disability in the 1930s, the film still encourages an openly voyeuristic gaze. This seemingly anachronistic gaping, coupled with the film's emphasis on the sexual desire of the freaks (Hans the circus dwarf explains that 'I am a man, with the same feelings [other men] have!'), evidently made the film distasteful for 1932 audiences. Even after substantial re-editing by the studio, the film was a commercial flop, and it was quickly pulled from distribution by MGM.

Freaks then disappeared until 1947, when infamous B-picture director Dwain Esper purchased the film's distribution rights and placed it on the exploitation circuit. Esper added a lengthy prologue, which reads in part:

> Before proceeding with the showing of the following HIGHLY UNUSUAL ATTRACTION, a few words should be said about the amazing subject matter. BELIEVE IT OR NOT —— STRANGE AS IT SEEMS. In ancient times anything that deviated from the normal was considered an omen of ill luck or representative of evil. For the love of beauty is a deep seated urge which dates back to the beginning of civilization. The revulsion with which we view the abnormal, the malformed and the mutilated is the result of long conditioning by or forefathers. The majority of freaks, themselves, are endowed with normal thoughts and emotions. Their lot is truly a heart-breaking one. Never again will such a story be filmed, as modern science and teratology is rapidly eliminating such blunders of nature from the world. With humility for the many injustices done to such people (they have no power to control their lot) we present the most startling horror story of the ABNORMAL and THE UNWANTED.

This prologue, accompanied by documentary-style orchestral music, regularly appears as part of the film today, but it must be understood as something that was added later for the film's exhibition as an exploitation feature; it was never part of Browning's original film. The prologue also highlights the film's two opposing themes: the humanisation of freaks (who are 'endowed with normal thoughts and emotions') and the exploitation of freaks (who are 'blunders of nature').

After its initial commercial failure, *Freaks* was rediscovered as a cult film in the 1960s. The film's successful reissue began at the 1962 Cannes Festival Repertory, where it appeared as the official horror film entry. The film soon gained newly appreciative audiences in Europe and the USA, who interpreted it quite differently than previous generations. In a new era, when the meaning of the term 'freak' had changed, audience members were more inclined to proudly fly their freak flag high. Instead of pitying the freaks or wondering how they might be fixed, these spectators were more likely to identify with their struggle against the cruel and conventional world of the 'normals'. The film played regularly in late-night movie theatres for years in the late 1960s and early 70s, making it 'possibly the oldest of all midnight attractions'.[1]

Freaks has thus been received in widely varying reception contexts, and as such, it demonstrates the importance of audiences in shaping film meaning. From horror film flop in 1932 to cult film hit in the 1960s and after, this film has meant quite different things to different spectators in different historical moments. *Freaks* continues to inspire a wide range of responses in viewers today, from amazement to outrage. Such divergent responses are produced not only by different reception contexts outside the film, but also by the film's own inner textual ambivalence: the first two-thirds of the film work to humanise the film's freaks, but the concluding section reinscribes them as classic horror-genre monsters. The question surrounding this film today has become: is it humanising, or is it exploitative?

For many viewers, the story of Hans's doomed love for Cleopatra pales in comparison with the film's portrayal of everyday circus life. The first section of the film introduces the viewer to a cast of sideshow characters, many of whom were circus performers of some renown. Many of the actors had worked for Ringling Bros. and Barnum & Bailey Circuses, or on Coney Island. One of the most memorable performers in the film, Prince Randian 'The Human Torso', began his long career working for P. T. Barnum in 1889, and was still working in a freak show on Times Square at the time of his death in 1934 at age 63; the film features part of his cigarette-rolling and lighting act. Perhaps the most famous of the film's sideshow performers, Daisy and Violet Hilton, were conjoined twins who had toured Europe and the USA as a Siamese Twin act from the age of three, playing music and dancing on vaudeville. Harry and Daisy Earles, who played Hans and Frieda, were brother and sister who comprised part of a four-sibling little people act called 'the Dancing Dolls'. (Harry Earles had already starred in Browning's film *The Unholy Three* and would later appear as one of the 'Lollipop Kids' in *The Wizard of Oz* (Victor Fleming, 1939).) Johnny Eck, 'The Half Boy', had long performed a sawing-in-half magic act with his full-bodied twin brother. Angelo Rossitto, memorable as the dwarf who passes the loving cup around the table at the wedding feast, parlayed his experience as a sideshow performer into a highly successful career in cinema, working in numerous films and television programs; he eventually became one of the founders of Little People of America. As this brief account of just some of the cast of *Freaks* begins to indicate, part of the film's appeal is the sense of realism achieved by the casting of real actors with disabilities. This realism, however, is counterbalanced by a strong dose of fantasy, as the performers' everyday life is fictionalised into a horror story.

In its opening scene, the film encourages its audience to identify with the freaks. 'But for the accident of birth, you might be even as they are', a carny talker says to the audience-within-the-film. The film's first half then contains a long sequence that serves to normalise the freaks. We see them going about their everyday business: working, playing, and, in keeping with the film's salacious tone, reproducing: 'The bearded lady's baby is born!' Much of the sequence is accompanied by swirling Calliope music on the soundtrack, which sets it apart from the rest of the film.

Once this circus music background finally stops, the narrative of doomed love begins to dominate the film. The film's tone becomes progressively more carnivalesque, building up to a sensational wedding banquet scene which is preceded by the film's only intertitle, which reads, 'The Wedding Feast'. In this scene, Hans has just married Cleopatra, and the freaks decide to initiate her into their group. They begin to chant: 'Gooble gobble, gooble gobble! We accept her, we accept her! Gooble gobble, gooble gobble! One of us, one of us!' This chant filled with nonsense words sounds like a different language, and the scene has been criticised for making the freaks seem inscrutable and alien. At the same time, however, the crazy babbling quality of the chant has surprised and delighted audiences for decades, and it has become a kind of initiatory battle cry for the film's cult audience. (The Ramones' punk rock slogan 'Gabba Gabba Hey', featured in their song 'Pinhead', was famously inspired by this chant.) Despite their offer of a loving cup, Cleopatra brutally rejects the freaks' allegiance, and proceeds to humiliate Hans by dancing around with him on her shoulders. After that, she tries to murder him. If one has been siding with the freaks, the revenge that follows seems well deserved.

The macabre revenge sequence that finally comes, however, does indeed turn the freaks into monsters, undoing the humanising work of the first portion of the film. Johnny Eck, Angelino, Schlitze, and others – even Prince Randian, carrying a knife in his mouth – march and slither through a rainstorm in the mud to attack Cleopatra and her 'normal' boyfriend, Hercules the strongman. While audiences may cheer their cause, the characters who generated so much empathy earlier have now been rendered devilish mutants, after the manner of classic horror villains. The film's humanising has been neutralised in a blaze of sensationalism, and the film's conclusion raises the tone of voyeuristic fantasy even higher with the shocking image of Cleopatra, legless and quacking like a duck after having been deformed by her assailants. *Freaks* may be far more acceptable now than when it was first released, but it is a product of the 1930s with a sensibility that could not be reproduced today.

Note

1. J. Hoberman and Jonathan Rosenbaum, *Midnight Movies*, New York, Harper and Row, 1983, p. 295.

Further reading

Rachel Adams, *Sideshow U.S.A.: Freaks and the American Cultural Imagination*, Chicago, University of Chicago Press, 2001.

Sally Chivers, 'The Horror of Becoming "One of Us": Tod Browning's *Freaks* and Disability', in Christopher R. Smit and Anthony Enns (eds),

Screening Disability: Essays on Cinema and Disability, Lanham, University Press of America, 2001, pp. 57–64.

Oliver Gaycken, 'Tod Browning and the Monstrosity of Hollywood Style', in Christopher R. Smit and Anthony Enns (eds), *Screening Disability: Essays on Cinema and Disability*, Lanham, University Press of America, 2001, pp. 73–85.

Robin Larsen and Beth A. Haller, 'The Case of *Freaks:* Public Reception of Real Disability', *Journal of Popular Film and Television*, Vol. 29, No. 4, Winter 2002, pp. 164–72.

David Skal and Elias Savada, *Dark Carnival: The Secret World of Tod Browning, Master of the Macabre*, New York, Anchor Books, 1995.

Jennifer Peterson

Gavaznha/The Deer (1976)

[Country: Iran. Production Company: Maysaghieh Studios. Director: Masoud Kimiai. Producer: Mehdi Maysaghieh. Screenwriter: Masoud Kimiai. Cinematographer: Nemat Haghighi. Music: Esfandiar Monfared-Zadeh and Farhad Mehrdad. Editor: Abbas Ganjavi. Cast: Behrouz Vossoughi (Seyyed), Faramarz Gharibian (Ghodrat), Nosrat Partovi (Fati), Garshasb Raufi (Asghar), Enayat Bakhhi (Ali Agha), Parviz Fanizadeh (Mohammad).]

Synopsis: Bleeding slowly from a bullet wound and carrying a suitcase full of stolen bank money, Ghodrat (Gharibian) searches for his high school best friend, Seyyed (Vossoughi), to give him shelter. When he finally locates Seyyed, instead of the imposing school legend renowned for his toughness and valour, Ghodrat finds a burned-out heroin addict who is barely hanging on to his current job as a barker for a lowly variety theatre. Despite an initial memory lapse, Seyyed eventually remembers his old friend and happily takes Ghodrat to his small and humble rental room in a large house with several other poor and down-on-their-luck neighbours, which he shares with his girlfriend, Fati (Partovi), an actress in the same theatre. Ghodrat gradually reminds Seyyed of his past glory and encourages him to stand up for himself. Seyyed's reawakening leads to a number of violent confrontations, which include him beating his despotic landlord, and stabbing to death his main drug supplier, Asghar (Raoufi). Ghodrat, who now thinks that Seyyed has regained his honour, asks his old friend Fati to deliver the stolen money to another trusted friend. Upon their return, they find the house surrounded by an army of policemen who are after Ghodrat. Seyyed convinces the police chief to allow him to negotiate a peaceful surrender with Ghodrat. But when he runs toward the house, he is shot and wounded. He survives to join Ghodrat for one last heroic stand. In the end, the building where Seyyed and Ghodrat are barricading themselves is subjected to a hail of bullets and is blown to bits by heavy explosives.

By the time *The Deer* was released in 1976, 35-year-old Massoud Kimiai, with films such as *Gheysar* (1969), *Reza, the Cyclist* (1970) and *Dash Akol* (1971), was already established as one of the leading directors of Iran's New Wave Cinema of the 1970s.[1] His visual style and thematic consistency had also solidified his reputation as an auteur par excellence. Starting with *Gheysar*, his second film (and one of the possible starting points of the New Wave), a documentary-like approach, real location shooting, kinetic and restless camera-style, and fast-paced editing based on constantly changing camera angles marked all of Kimiai's films. Accordingly, he regularly worked with certain actors (including Vossoughi and Gharibian who play the two protagonists in *The Deer*) and production crew members (including cinematographer Haghighi). He also consistently collaborated with the famed composer Esfandiar Monfared-Zadeh and counterculture singer-songwriter Farhad Mehrdad in most of his pre-Revolutionary films. Together Monfared-Zadeh and Farhad (as he was known by his first name only) not only composed memorable music for Kimiai's films, but the pair also created the soundtrack of Iran's disaffected urban youth of the 70s, thus associating Kimiai's films with that generation's angst and dissatisfaction with social and cultural norms.

However visually and aurally consistent Kimiai's films were, his auteurial signature and presence was most significantly recognised in terms of the thematic and narrative coherence of his cinema. Again, starting with *Gheysar*, themes of *refaghat* (male friendship and loyalty), *gheyrat* (the traditional masculine code of honour and pride), *namous* (another masculine code of honour concerned with the protection of women's virtue) and vigilante justice almost always structured Kimiai's dominantly revenge narratives. Kimiai's stories were also populated with the lower middle class and/or working-class characters, who embodied many of the above-mentioned traditional values. He often wrote his own screenplays, but even when he adapted well-known literary works such as Sadegh Hedayat's (Iran's most celebrated twentieth-century writer) *Dash Akol*, the same themes were central in the film adaptation.

It was precisely this apparent cultural traditionalism that put many modernist intellectuals and artists in adversarial position toward Kimiai and his films. Traditionalism was also one major factor contributing to a lack of acceptance and cultural translation of Kimiai outside Iran's borders. Even when occasionally shown at film festivals, his films were judged to be too parochial for a Western audience. He never attained the same degree of post-Revolutionary international success that many colleagues of his generation, such as Abbas Kiarostami, Bahram Beyzai and Amir Naderi, enjoyed. The unease that many Iranian intellectuals felt toward Kimiai was definitely not an isolated case, but symbolised a certain social tension between two possible paths for Iran's future (both critical of the Shah's despotic regime) that manifested itself in the cinematic sphere. Regardless, Kimiai always enjoyed domestic popularity and success.

While *The Deer* displays many of the same formal and thematic aspects of Kimiai's previous films, it also marks a number of shifts. Firstly, gone is the gross misogyny of *Ghazal* (1975), in which two brothers kill the woman they both love in order to resolve their sibling rivalry. The main female protagonist of *The Deer*, Fati, is a strong, outspoken and financially independent woman, who takes care of Seyyed. Now this does not mean a feminist turn in Kimiai at all; masculine codes of honour, *gheyrat* and *namous*, still play a significant role in the film. Fati expects Seyyed to protect her against the sexual advances of her co-actors and is disappointed when he does not confront them. Seyyed's indifference toward defending Fati's honour has downgraded their sexual relationship to a platonic one. The first sign of Seyyed's reawakening after Ghodrat's arrival is punching the male lead of the play for pinching Fati, a seemingly chivalrous act that reignites Fati's romantic feelings for Seyyed.

While friendship (*refaghat*) is one the film's main themes, it is presented not as a given and fixed entity (as it had been in Kimiai's previous films), but as a complicated and layered relationship that needs to be constantly renegotiated and reconstructed. Ghodrat and Seyyed's exchange of disbelieving gazes and the failure to remember old friends create a heartbreaking moment signifying disillusionment and shattered dreams. The enigmatic title of the film, *Gavaznha* (*The Deer*, plural) itself is a euphemism for wasted potentials and a fall from grace. Hamid Naficy quotes Kimiai recalling a childhood memory: 'He remembers as a schoolchild his teacher telling the class that deer have ugly legs, but beautiful horns, and that what saves them in a tight spot is their speed, thanks to their ugly scrawny legs, while that which snares them is their long pretty horns. The reverse is true of the film's main character: two close friends with a vast potential for social good fall victim to vice – one to heroin addiction, the other to robbery' (2012: 383–4). And like deer locking horns, it is only through brutal honesty and confrontation that Ghodrat and Seyyed are able to remember and reconnect as friends and eventually as allies. However, it would have been easily decipherable for Iranian audiences in the 70s that Ghodrat and Seyyed's characters are heavily encoded by Kimiai as allegorical constructions of social forces: their complicated relationship certainly conveys social and political significance that goes beyond a simple friendship.

One may justifiably argue that *The Deer* is Kimiai's first explicitly political film. The questions of class and social (in)justice that had always been bubbling under the surface in the previous films, here emerge as central themes. The figure of Ghodrat (literally meaning power), a moustachioed bank thief wearing glasses (iconic visual signs of Iran's leftist intellectuals in the 70s) and speaking the leftist rhetoric of revolutionary resistance, ambiguously represents the first cinematic acknowledgement of that era's urban guerrilla warfare.[2] Vossoughi's tour-de-force performance as Seyyed becomes a thinly veiled allegory for the traditional lower classes, easily recognised and decoded by the literate urban spectators. Seyyed needs to be reminded and reawakened by Ghodrat's persistent questions about his honourable past identity and his present passive and parasitic existence, a dialogue that was at the core of the urban guerrilla warfare meant to shock and mobilise the passive populace. Although Seyyed's decline is largely attributed to his drug addiction, his current position as a theatre barker is not accidental. By linking mass entertainment, drug addiction, indifference and passivity to class oppression and by delineating an integrated network of social relations, *The Deer* constructs a social map of 70s Iran. The violent explosion in the final act seems to foreshadow the political upheaval a few years later.

The question of violence, in previous films always framed in ritualistic terms of codes of honour (*gheyrat* and *namous*), is now reframed in *The Deer* as the oppressor's brutality versus the righteous self-defence of the oppressed. In one key scene, in response to Seyyed's observation that despite their different paths in life, they have both ended in the same place – Ghodrat with a bullet wound in his stomach and a briefcase full of bank money, and Seyyed a drug addict and a former petty pusher – Ghodrat patiently but resolutely rejects any similarities between their positions. He explains the difference between the drug business's devastating effect on the youth of the nation and his own justified bank robbery that redistributes the wealth, feeds the poor or provides shelter for the homeless. This discussion seems to be the catalyst for Seyyed's righteous acts of violence that ensue shortly. The difference between Ghodrat and Seyyed in terms of violence is also shown in their choice of weapons. The traditional Seyyed uses a switchblade to kill Asghar, while Ghodrat uses an automatic handgun in his confrontation with the police. Ultimately, both weapons seem inadequate in confrontation with the overwhelming military might of the state in the final scene. While the film depicts the heroic stand as tragic and futile, once the hail of bullets starts, the camera never goes back inside Seyyed's room and never shows the comrades dying or dead. In a way, the denouement acknowledges the social potential of such isolated moments of resistance, as the final shot and freeze-frame shows the building after the explosion with smoke rising from it, perhaps a foreshadowing of the social upheaval to come.

Regardless of all the film's formal and narrative qualities, *The Deer* has become a quintessential film in Iranian film history for three main reasons. First, it was the movie in which Vossoughi transcended his popular image as a superstar and matinee idol and became universally hailed as a skilled actor for his complex and layered portrayal of Seyyed: a conflicting combination of an addict's desperation for the next fix and selfness sacrifice for an old friend. Although the Iranian Revolution disrupted Vossoughi's career, he is still respected as one the best actors in the history of Iranian cinema. Undoubtedly, his Seyyed in *The Deer* is one of the most highly regarded performances of his career. The visual transformation of Vossoughi from a dashing action and romantic hero into a hunched-over, burned out, drug addict was a remarkable crossover success that also marked the merging of popular and art cinemas, at least in certain moments.

Second, the unambiguous and explicit depictions of violence and poverty, veiled references to urban guerrilla warfare, and most importantly, the enthusiastic public reaction to the film brought the censors' wrath upon *The Deer*. The synopsis that was presented in the beginning of this piece describes the first version of the film that was screened for the first time in the third International Tehran Film Festival and that was immediately banned. According to Ahmad Amini, 'in various circulating synopses of the film and even in a conversation with Kimiai in the festival's bulletin, Ghodrat is unconvincingly and repeatedly characterised as an ordinary burglar. [H]owever, the film's audacity was intolerable and it was confiscated.' (1993: 226).[3] Vossoughi was interrogated by SAVAK (the state's secret police) several times and was threatened with death, even though he had won the festival's best actor's award and was present at a screening in the royal palace with the Shah's sister, Ashraf Pahlavi (Naficy 2012: 385–6). Kimiai and the producers were asked to make certain alterations in order to get the permission for public screening including 'altering some of the dialogue and reshooting and reediting parts of it with fewer police in the final shootout' (Naficy 2012: 386). There were at least two alternative endings in the altered versions. In one ending, Ghodrat shoots Seyyed, and in another 'Ghodrat was re-fashioned into an ordinary burglar and deserts Seyyed to surrender to the police' (Amini 1993: 228).

Despite the censors' attempts to transform Ghodrat's personality, even to this day, in its heavily censored available version, the dominant reading of *The Deer* is that of an allegory of urban guerrilla warfare and heroic resistance against the police and the government. The attempt to erase Ghodrat's political character backfired precisely because inconsistencies between the narrative's ostensible portrayal of him as a burglar and his other attributes as a redeeming and provocative agent opens holes, i.e. interpretive possibilities that run counter to the censors' intentions. It was exactly *because of* and not *in spite of* censorship that the public always remembered the original version and tried to reinterpret the altered versions to insert what they imagined had been erased from these versions.

Notes

1. *The Deer* is forever linked in the public imagination with the Cinema Rex fire where 470 spectators perished in an arson set at a screening of the film by the extremist Islamists in the Southern city of Abadan on 19 August 1978. Even though the causes of the event and the public trials related to the fire are very significant in relation to Iranian cinema and the Iranian Revolution of 1978–79, they are not directly related to Kimiai's film, therefore, they will not be part of this essay's discussion. For an illuminating discussion of the significance of the Cinema Rex tragedy see Hamid Naficy's *A Social History of Iranian Cinema*, Volume 3, Durham, NC, Duke University, 2012.
2. Historically, the start of urban guerrilla warfare in the late 60s and early 70s by *The Organization of the People's Fedayeen's Guerrillas of Iran*'s (OPFGI) and *The Mujahedden-e Khalgh* (*The People's Mujahedeen* or MEK) was a startling event in Iran's desolate political landscape. Regardless of the successes and failures of this strategy against a highly organised and well-financed military machinery and secret police, the presence of these active and unpredictable young intellectual urban guerrillas marked the public imagination and social consciousness in profound ways.
3. English translations from Farsi are by me.

Further reading

Ahmad Amini, *Sad Film-eh Tareekh-eh Cinema-eh Iran* (*One Hundred Films of The Iranian Cinema*), Tehran, Shaida Cultural Institute, 1993.

Hamid Naficy, *A Social History of Iranian Cinema*, Volume 2, Durham and London, Duke University Press, 2012.

Hossein Khosrowjah

Gegen die Wand/Head-On (2004)

[Country: Germany. Production Company: Wüste Filmproduktion, Corazón International, NDR, Arte. Director: Fatih Akin. Producers: Ralph Schwingel, Stefan Schubert. Screenwriter: Fatih Akin. Cinematographer: Rainer Klausmann. Music: Alexander Hacke, Maxeo Parker. Editor: Andrew Bird. Cast: Sibel Kekilli (Sibel), Birol Ünel (Cahit), Catrin Stirebeck (Maren), Güven Kiraç (Seref), Hermann Lause (Dr Schiller), Demir Gökgöl (Yunus Güner, father), Cem Akin (Yilmaz Güner, brother), Aysel Iscan (Birsen Güner, mother), Meltem Cumbul (Selma).]

Synopsis: Cahit and Sibel, two Germans of Turkish origin, encounter each other in a psychiatric hospital after having made separate suicide attempts. Trying to escape the restrictions of her conservative family home, Sibel spontaneously proposes a marriage of convenience to Cahit, which gives her the (above all sexual) freedom she so desperately desires. But Cahit slowly falls in love with her, and kills one of her lovers in a fit of jealousy. Sibel becomes aware of her own feelings for him, and while he is in jail, moves to Istanbul, first waiting then beginning to make a new life. After

Cahit gets out of jail, they meet one more time, with an uncertain outcome.

The first German film to win the Golden Bear at the Berlin Film Festival in 18 years, and recipient of many other awards, *Head-On* put Turkish German film director Fatih Akin on the map. Conceived as a love story, but more often read as an intercultural film, *Head-On* takes place in a 'no man's land of cultural identification' (Lebow 2005: 60), where second-generation Germans of Turkish origin attempt to (re)make their lives. Not confined to social realism, this 'filmic spectacle of auto-destruction' (Fachinger 2007: 257) features an accessible and visually compelling story with its share of sex and violence, and Turkish and punk rock rhythms, while at the same time producing a nuanced image of Turkish life in Germany. Director Fatih Akin himself said that he tried to take into account Turkish, Turkish German and German audiences, even as he did not manage to escape controversy.

Head-On must be understood in the context of Turkish migration to Germany, and the cultural production that followed from it. In the 1960s, a large number of so-called Turkish 'guest workers' arrived in Germany, very often from rural (and thus fairly traditional) parts of Turkey. While the initial thought was that these workers would not stay, by the 1970s, they were allowed to bring their families; after 1989 (the date of the German reunification), and even more so after the Islamic terrorist attacks of 9/11, the debate on citizenship accelerated and intensified. Within mainstream German media, stereotypes of oppressed Muslim women and criminal males developed, as did stories of honour killings and accounts of a 'parallel' (i.e. non-integrated) society, a term first introduced by German sociologist Wilhelm Heitmeyer in the early 1990s (see Ewing 2006).

What role films play in this – whether they complicate, combat or buttress such media discourses – can be debated. For sure, however, Turks in Germany became an object of cinematic representation at the very latest in the 1970s. Most critics agree that films of the 1970s and 1980s mostly concerned themselves with the depiction of guest workers' problems and anxieties in a social realist vein, even as they single out Fassbinder's *Ali: Fear Eats the Soul* (originally titled *All Turks are called Ali*). By the 1990s, a new generation of Turkish German filmmakers who had grown up in Germany became a vital force in German cinema, appropriating generic conventions, and by the twenty-first century, making more critically engaged films (see Göktürk 2002; Hake and Mennel 2012: 1–8). In the book that accompanies the film, Akin includes an excerpt from Maxim Biller's 'Dritte Ethnie' (Third Ethnicity), which celebrates the second generation's creative energy, as well as Georg Diez's essay on how the Turkish German second generation's energy will save German culture (Akin 2004: 267–8 and 253–8; see also Fachinger 2007: 243–4).

Within these contexts, *Head-On* has been understood both as a film that continues to draw on traditional concepts of culture and as a film that overturns stereotypes. While Sibel's parents are certainly traditional, small details are important: the father listens to and accepts Sibel's choice despite obvious misgivings about the husband; the mother dyes her hair, smokes, tries to rescue a photograph of Sibel and secretly says goodbye to her daughter, which has led some to argue that she has learned how to negotiate a system. Maybe more importantly, *Head-On* depicts a wide range, and very different kinds of Turkish characters, dispelling any sense of a homogeneous society.

The two main characters, Sibel and Cahit, often seem to be determined more by their individual idiosyncrasies than by collective cultural habits, so that one could argue that conflict is as much generational and psychological as it is cultural. But even as the film refuses to wrap up its storylines neatly, some commentators have understood it as a 'conservative cautionary tale' and a 'back to the roots' fantasy, as Sibel becomes the mother in a bourgeois family and Cahit visits his Turkish home town (Lebow 2005: 61).

These arguments suggest the ambivalence and complexity of the two main characters, Sibel and Cahit. Early on in the film, ironically named Dr Schiller cites a song, 'If you can't change the world, change your world', and tells Cahit 'if you want to terminate your life, then terminate your life, but you don't have to die to do so'. As they progress from suicide attempts to new lives, Sibel and Cahit seem to take this initially paradoxical and thus comical comment to heart. Before doing so, however, both of these characters run against walls, both literally (in the case of Cahit) and metaphorically. The literal translation of the film's German title is 'Against the Wall' – an appropriate governing metaphor for much of the film. Especially Cahit seems enclosed in claustrophobic spaces, for example his apartment (Fachinger 2007: 258).

We should not forget how dissimilar the two are. Sibel is hungry for life, and longs to transgress Turkish and middle-class conventions, but refuses to leave Hamburg because of her bond with her mother. She often consciously works her own hybridity in order to negotiate her own position. The cafeteria sequence early in the film subtly illustrates how Sibel's body language changes when talking to the men of the family, or when talking to her mother, while also establishing a degree of complicity between the women. Later on, she claims to be a Turkish wife in order to get rid of an unwanted lover, while transforming herself with fashionable and sexy clothes, a belly button ring and a tattoo. She alternately performs 'virtuous daughter, untouchable, Gucci bride', and those performances do not lessen after she moves to Turkey (Lornsen 2007: 20).

Sibel's 'intentional' hybridity is countered by Cahit's 'organic' hybridity that comes unconsciously rather than consciously (Lornsen 2007: 17). Unlike Sibel, Cahit seems to have little to no family, and while he was born in Turkey, he 'threw his Turkish away', as he explains to Yilmaz, Sibel's brother. He is worried that Sibel's cousin from Istanbul will bring a 'suitcase full of Turks' and calls the guys who beat him up 'Scheiss-Kanaken' (fucking Kanaks).[1] And yet, his self-hatred changes over the course of the film, while he comes to stand for an alternative model of Turkish German manhood, a topic that is being prepared fairly early on when he visits Yilmaz and his friends. Invited to come along to a brothel, he asks why they don't fuck their own wives. Yilmaz's friend explodes, chillingly not because of the question, but because Cahit used the word 'fuck' in relationship to Turkish wives. Akin himself has expressed his admiration for a character who has the courage to disregard tradition and who in the process destroys himself, likening the type to James Dean. A complex and contradictory character, Cahit tries to find an adequate male identity in the absence of any suitable role models (Fincham 2008: 61).

The complexity of characters is mirrored in the complexity of locations. *Head-On* mostly takes place in Hamburg and Istanbul. There is no easy juxtaposition of these two cities, even though Akin has opened himself up to charges of orientalising Istanbul, maybe not least because Sibel ends up smoking opium there (Lebow 2005: 61). Nonetheless, within the film Istanbul is also the location where Sibel dons tomboyish attire, watches European Champion Turkish female weightlifter Sibel Şimşek, and experiences capitalism. (Selma's fancy hotel contrasts with the working-class lives of her relatives in Germany). Above all Istanbul is contradictory: 'much more vibrant' than Hamburg and yet also 'harsher' and 'seedier' (Fachinger 2007: 254; Lebow 2005: 61). Akin's ability to produce local specificity and accents may be particularly striking as at the same time he also produces patterns of global migration and capital. In this sense it is typical that in Istanbul Cahit (whose Turkish is still partial) and Selma (who does not speak German) end up speaking English with each other. It nonetheless comes as a surprise to the spectator – a moment that rips us out of the texture of the localities in which the film immerses us, yet another moment that takes us out of the action of the film, like the performances of the folk song that punctures the plot.

Indeed, no discussion of *Head-On* would be complete without a discussion of its aesthetic structure and style. Akin himself has said that he did not want a classical narrative arc, Hollywood style, in the course of which characters encounter and overcome obstacles (Akin 2004: 236). Comedy and tragedy are close to each other. Maybe most strikingly, the use of folk songs, performed by Selim Sesler and Orchestra (Idil Üner singing), with the Suleymaniye Mosque across the Golden Horn in the background, divides the film into five acts. Akin himself has commented on the postcard-like effect of this device, which makes the spectators aware that the film is a film, pulling them out of the action, keeping them simultaneously emotionally involved yet critically distanced (Fachinger 2007: 258–9). After the first performance of the musical group, the film abruptly cuts to a low-angle shot of a glaring overhead light, and we find ourselves in the post-concert rubble of Die Fabrik (The Factory), a cultural centre in Altona (Hamburg), where Cahit collects bottles and drinks leftover beer. Akin's editing does often not conform to continuity style; instead he uses visible editing and radically different camera positions, along with music (both musical bridges and abrupt cuts) to give the film varying, sometimes calming, sometimes pulsating rhythms.

The film's success was not without controversy. The German tabloid *Bild* quickly found out that Sibel Kekilli had previously appeared in porn films, and exploited the story with relish right after the film had won the Golden Bear. The story may have contributed to a particular conflation of fiction and reality within both the Turkish and German press. In Germany, the conservative press missed the nuances of the film, reading it as a commentary on the oppression of Muslim women, while others understood it as rejuvenating German film culture (see Machtans 2012: 153–6). Likewise Turkish television interviewed Kekilli's parents who talked about their shame, while at the same time the national media criticised but also took pride in the film, conveniently ignoring the production of porn in Turkey, which had flourished especially 1974–80 (see Arslan 2008).

Like its characters refusing any easy categorisation, this multilingual film clearly belongs to an increasingly transnational film production that has recently become a main focus of film studies (see Ezra and Rowden 2006; Durovicová and Newman 2009). At the same time, the Turkish German film movement can also be compared to similar ethnically accented film movements in other countries. Akin likes to compare himself with Italian American filmmakers in the United States in the 1970s who would quickly move to the centre of American cinema, noting in particular Martin Scorsese's *Mean Streets* (1973). A more contemporary comparison may be made with the North African ('*beur*') film movement in France and directors such as Abdellatif Kechiche who have successfully moved out of narrowly conceived ethnic subject matter. Within Germany, this kind of cinema is seen as distinct from the immediate post-Wall cinema, which is regarded as a cinema of consensus (Fachinger 2007: 259).

Note

1. Kanake is a derogatory term for people from Southern countries, which occasionally also gets co-opted by Turks as a self-designation.

Further reading

Fatih Akin, *Gegen die Wand, das Buch zum Film: Drehbuch/Materialien/Interviews*, Cologne, Kiepenheuer & Witsch, 2004.

Savaş Arslan, 'Head-On, Head-Off: How the Media Covered a Former Porn Actress's Rise to Stardom', *Film International*, Vol. 6, No. 6, 2008, pp. 62–71.

Natasa Durovicová and Kathleen E. Newman (eds), *World Cinemas, Transnational Perspectives*, London, Routledge, 2009.

Katherine Pratt Ewing, 'Between Cinema and Social Work: Diasporic Turkish Women and the (Dis)Pleasures of Hybridity', *Cultural Anthropology*, Vol. 21, No. 2, May 2006, pp. 265–94.

Elizabeth Ezra and Terry Rowden (eds), *Transnational Cinema, the Film Reader*, London, Routledge, 2006.

Petra Fachinger, 'A New Kind of Creative Energy: Yadé Kara's *Selam Berlin* and Fatih Akin's *Kurz und schmerzlos* and *Gegen die Wand*', *German Life and Letters*, Vol. 60, No. 2, April 2007, pp. 243–60.

Victoria Fincham, 'Violence, Sexuality and the Family: Identity "Within and Beyond Turkish-German Parameters" in Fatih Akin's *Gegen die Wand*, Kutluğ Ataman's *Lola + Bilidikind* and Anno Saul's *Kebab Connection*', *GFL: German as a Foreign Language*, No. 1, 2008, pp. 39–72.

Deniz Göktürk, 'Beyond Paternalism: Turkish German Traffic in Cinema', in Tim Bergfelder, Erica Carter and Deniz Göktürk (eds), *The German Cinema Book*, London, BFI, 2002, pp. 248–56.

Sabine Hake and Barbara Mennel (eds), *Turkish German Cinema in the New Millennium: Sites, Sounds and Screens*, New York, Oxford, Berghahn Books, 2012.

Alisa Lebow, 'Head-On', *Cineaste*, Vol. 30, No. 3, Summer 2005, pp. 60–1.

Karin Lornsen, 'Where Have All the Guest Workers Gone? Transcultural Role-Play and Performative Identities in Fatih Akin's *Gegen die Wand* (2004)', in Robert Schechtman and Suin Roberts (eds), *Finding the Foreign*, Newcastle, Cambridge Scholars Publishing, 2007, pp. 13–31.

Karolin Machtans, 'The Perception and Marketing of Fatih Akin in the German Press' in Sabine Hake and Barbara Mennel (eds), *Turkish German Cinema in the New Millennium: Sites, Sounds and Screens*, New York, Oxford, Berghahn Books, 2012: 149–60.

Sabine Haenni

The Godfather (1972)

[Country: USA. Production Company: Paramount Pictures. Director: Francis Ford Coppola. Screenplay: Mario Puzo and Francis Ford Coppola, based on the novel by Mario Puzo. Producer: Albert S. Ruddy. Cinematographer: Gordon Willis. Editors: William Reynolds, Peter Zinner. Music: Nino Rota. Cast: Marlon Brando (Don Vito Corleone), Al Pacino (Michael Corleone), James Caan (Santino 'Sonny' Corleone), Robert Duvall (Tom Hagen), Diane Keaton (Kay Adams), Talia Shire (Connie Corleone Rizzi), Gianni Russo (Carlo Rizzi), John Cazale (Fredo Corleone), Simonetta Stefanelli (Appollina Vitelli Corleone), Lenny Montana (Luca Brasi), Richard Castellano (Peter Clemanza), Richard Conte (Emilio Barzini), Tony Giorgio (Bruno Tattaglia), Al Lettieri (Virgil 'the Turk' Sollozzo), Salvatore Corsitto (Bonasera), Al Martino (Johnny Fontane), Alex Rocco (Moe Greene).]

Synopsis: At the height of his power, the Godfather, Don Corleone, grants wishes to people he protects during his daughter's wedding ceremony. Thus, he sends Tom Hagen to Hollywood to intimidate a studio head so that he gives his godson a movie role. But when Don Corleone is sceptical about participating in the emerging drug traffic, his rivals attempt to assassinate him. The eldest son, Sonny, takes command. His youngest son, Michael, first prevents a second assassination attempt on Don Corleone, then kills a drug baron and a corrupt police officer, and takes refuge in Sicily where he marries Appollina, who will, alas, get killed. After Sonny is killed on the way to protecting his sister from her husband's abuses, Don Corleone stops opposing the drug trade, which allows Michael to return. He marries Kay, takes over the family business, and promises to make it legitimate, but gets drawn more deeply into the feuds, finally orchestrating the deaths of his rivals, his traitor and his brother-in-law while standing godfather to his nephew and becoming the new Don.

'I believe in America', the opening line of the first *Godfather* film famously goes. Released in 1972, when Hollywood was barely coming out of a big financial crisis, directed by a mostly unknown Francis Ford Coppola, *The Godfather* became one of the highest grossing films of its time. It also became a social phenomenon, often quoted and referred to in casual interactions, spawning two sequels (*The Godfather, Part II* was released in 1974 and *The Godfather, Part III* in 1990) and a TV miniseries that combined the first two films in chronological order (1977). It is said to have altered the self-image of the Mafia. And it became a crucial film for scholars to think about the function and effects of mass culture in general.

Despite the success of such late-sixties films as *Bonnie and Clyde* (Arthur Penn, 1967) and *Easy Rider* (Dennis Hopper, 1969), which included an unprecedented amount of violence and sexuality, tapped into the counter-cultural movement, and showed Hollywood how to live through a major cultural revolution, by the early 1970s the industry was still going through a major box office crisis. Unemployment reached an all-time high in March 1970, a staggering 42.8 per cent.[1] *The Godfather* signalled the beginning of Hollywood's emergence out of this crisis. In many ways the film is part of a number of socially progressive films from the late 1960s and early 1970s, when a desperate Hollywood gave more flexibility to directors who promised to tap into the mood of the time and especially into the new youth market (Hollywood's redefined audience). Ironically, however, *The Godfather* also signalled the beginning of a new era in Hollywood marketing, fully achieved with cinema events such as *Jaws* (Stephen Spielberg, 1975) and *Star Wars* (George Lucas, 1977), 'calculated blockbusters [that] are massive advertisements for their product lines' (Schatz 1993: 32) and that appeal to a wide mass audience. It may be because it is suspended between these two poles – a critical cinema of the late 1960s and early 1970s and the mainstream blockbuster – that *The Godfather* remains so universally popular.

While *The Godfather* is an aesthetically much more conventional film than *The Godfather, Part II,* it nonetheless can be understood as a combination of European art film and American commercial cinema. At the very least, the film is characterised by a very careful aesthetic style. Many have called Coppola's aesthetic theatrical, as defined by mise en scène – a subtle adaptation of theatrical features into cinematic language that allows actors to showcase their talent. Who could forget, for instance, the look on Kay's (Diane Keaton's) face in the very last shot of the film, as the door closes on her in medium close-up? Or the close-up of Bonasera (Salvatore Corsitto) in the very first shot of the film, as he pronounces his faith in America, before the camera begins to zoom out to reveal the back of Don Vito Corleone (Marlon Brando)? Or the magisterial handling of the bright, outdoor space of the wedding and the dark, indoor office in the opening sequence, that establishes Don Corleone's power over both, while also revealing the tension between a joyous social group and a secretive individualism?

Beyond working with actors and mise en scène, Coppola also manipulates conventional narrative. The sensational effect of Jack Woltz, the studio head, discovering his priced racehorse's head in his bed, is achieved through both mise en scène (the incongruity/surprise of a horse's head in a bed) and narrative. The entire sequence in Hollywood is marked by narrative ellipses that leave out crucial information – that Jack Woltz changed his mind after checking out Tom Hagen and invited him to his mansion, that Tom Hagen dropped his pleasant behaviour and had the horse killed. William Simon has argued that these missing turns in plot increase the surprise, and make us into active spectators. One editor, who would be fired from the film and who may have been motivated by selfish reasons, complained that Coppola had 'no idea what continuity means' (Browne 2000: 30). Such editing that tweaks classical continuity is also audible in the film's soundtrack, worked on by Walter Murch, who would go on to create the field of sound design, using multi-channel sound tracks for the first time in *Apocalypse Now* (Coppola, 1979). When Michael (Al Pacino) shoots Sollozzo at Louis' Italian-American Restaurant, for instance, the noise of the elevated train is less realistic and more an indication of Michael's state of mind, an effect that disassociates him from his surroundings (see Jarrett and Murch 2000).

At the same time, *The Godfather's* thrust is not only aesthetic but also social. Like other films from the period, it is critical of America, especially American politics and American capitalism. In a *Playboy* interview conducted after *The Godfather, Part II* came out, Coppola declared, 'Like America, Michael began as a clean, brilliant young man with incredible resources and believing in a humanistic idealism. Like America, Michael was the child of an older system, a child of Europe. Like America, Michael was an innocent who had tried to correct the ills and injustices of his progenitors. But then he got blood on his hands'. Coppola then went on to suggest that the main characters 'could have been the Kennedys'. In this sense, *The Godfather* becomes a 'horror-story statement' about where American politics and American capitalism could go (Browne 2000: 181).

It is no coincidence that *The Godfather* revised the gangster genre, for the original gangster films from the 1930s (such as *Scarface* (1932)), being produced at the height of the Great Depression, were likewise understood as allegorical treatments – and indictments – of the excesses of American capitalism, with the gangster cast as a capitalist gone bad. In this context, it is good to remember that even the early gangster films' attitude toward the gangster were ambivalent – both critiquing and glorifying him. Nonetheless, one of the biggest differences between the early gangster films and the Mafia films starting in the 1970s has to do with the fact that the descendants of immigrants were now directing the films. Unlike *Scarface*, *The Godfather* often gives us Michael's point of view (as in the restaurant shooting). And the family, dysfunctional at best in *Scarface*, now assumes a crucial function, so that the gangster film has effectively been fused with the family melodrama. And the family, we should note, is not only defined by blood, but can be asserted via adoption, marriage or employment.

The influential cultural critic Fredric Jameson has taken *The Godfather's* mixing of the crime film with the family melodrama as a starting point to reflect on the function of mass culture more generally. According to Jameson, mass culture simultaneously serves two functions, appealing to a utopian wish fulfilment while also performing an ideological operation. *The Godfather*, on the one hand, contains a pointed critique of American capitalism, uncovering the violence and deterioration of family and social life attending its development: 'I wanted to destroy Michael' (and by extension capitalism), Coppola said of the final image of Michael Corleone in *The Godfather, Part II*, which shows a successful Michael sitting utterly alone, abandoned by everybody (Browne 2000: 181). On the other hand, the substitution of the Mafia and the extended Sicilian-American family for big business allows the film to fantasise about a utopian, social collectivity – the possibility of the survival of a complex familial organisation. This utopia becomes most apparent in the brightly lit Sicilian sequences and the operatically staged family rituals that take place in the USA. Nonetheless, a closer examination of these sequences also reveals more complexity. For one thing, the repetition of family rituals invites us to compare them with each other, possibly asking us to diagnose a decline – or at least a transformation.[2] For another, as Thomas Ferraro has argued, family, violence and business are so intricately linked that they cannot be disassociated from each other. The Americanisation of the strong-willed Appollina (the first wife), and her eventual demise, as well as the crosscutting between the baptism of Connie's son and a series of killings in *The Godfather's* climactic scene make this abundantly clear. Family business is bloody business.

One of the more troubling effects of mid-century family life has to do with the ways in which it mobilises (consciously or unconsciously) a gender politics that already seemed outdated at the time of the film's release. We have already mentioned the film's ending with the exclusion of the wife from the male sphere of decision. Kay, of course, is Michael's non-ethnic wife, who sometimes asks a few questions too many, especially about Michael's business. Intriguingly, Appollina may be the most interesting female character, while Connie often seems all too masochistic. We would do well to remember that *The Godfather* was released during the height of second-wave feminism. It is thus hard not to understand *The Godfather* as a reaction to – and negotiation of – the women's movement. In fact, something similar could be said about the film's ethnic politics. In the wake of the Civil Rights movement, Malcolm X and the Black Panthers, in the wake of race riots in American cities, *The Godfather* almost seems to embody 'the wish for an all-white militant group'.[3] An all-white male militant group.

The Godfather had all kinds of (sometimes strange) effects. For one thing, it is said to have captured the *myth* of the Mafia exceptionally well. As Alessandro Camon has pointed out, the Mafia itself based its image on a myth. Its advocacy of a mysterious masculinity, a paradigm of 'power balanced by fairness, virtue, and control', seemed to dovetail well with efforts in the 1970s to construct an alternate masculine image (Browne 2000: 63). But the film itself changed the Mafia, which became much more media-conscious with dons transforming themselves from inconspicuous characters to celebrities, locking themselves into a cycle in which media and crime feed each other. (By the early twenty-first century, media-conscious terrorists often replaced the media-conscious mafiosi.) On the level of the film industry, *The Godfather* showed the way to a different future: by the late 1970s, Hollywood would be dominated by well-calculated blockbusters that advertised a series of related products and that appealed to as wide an audience as possible. The financial success of *The Godfather* paved the way for this development, although it was not entirely in this paradigm yet. (That *The Black Godfather* – a lowly blaxploitation precursor to *American Gangster* (2007) – was produced in 1974 suggests that film entrepreneurs were still thinking in terms of niche marketing as a way out of the economic slump.) Coppola himself went a somewhat different path: the 1974 sequel to *The Godfather*, more resolutely innovative in style, is often called an art film, not least because of how it messes with chronological storytelling. While less extremely successful at the box office than *The Godfather*, the sequel cemented Coppola's reputation as a director – and the emergence of the director as a star – to which we owe today's reverence for directors as well as the fascination with the 'director's cut' and directorial DVD commentary.

Notes

1. Jon Lewis, 'If History Has Taught Us Anything. Francis Coppola, Paramount Studios, and *The Godfather, Parts I, II* and *III*', in Browne 2000: 23.
2. Naomi Greene, 'Family Ceremonies: or, Opera in *The Godfather* Trilogy', in Browne 2000: 138.
3. Vera Dik, 'The Representation of Ethnicity in *The Godfather*', in Browne 2000: 96.

Further reading

Nick Browne (ed.), *Francis Ford Coppola's* The Godfather *Trilogy*, Cambridge, Cambridge University Press, 2000.

John G. Cawelti, 'Myths of Violence in American Popular Culture' (1975), in *Mystery, Violence and Popular Culture*, Madison, University of Wisconsin Press, 2004, pp. 152–72.

Thomas J. Ferraro, 'Blood in the Marketplace: The Business of Family in *The Godfather* Narratives', in *Ethnic Passages: Literary Immigrants in Twentieth-Century America*, Chicago, University of Chicago Press, 1993, pp. 18–52.

Fredric Jameson, 'Reification and Utopia in Mass Culture', in *Signatures of the Visible*, New York, Routledge, 1992, pp. 9–34.

Michael Jarrett and Walter Murch, 'Sound Doctrine: An Interview with Walter Murch', *Film Quarterly*, Vol. 53, No. 3, Spring 2000, pp. 2–11.

Thomas Schatz, 'The New Hollywood', in Jim Collins, Hilary Radner, and Ava Preacher Collins (eds), *Film Theory Goes to the Movies*, New York, Routledge, 1993, pp. 8–36.

William Simon, 'An Analysis of the Structure of *The Godfather, Part One*', *Studies in the Literary Imagination*, Vol. 16, No. 1, Spring 1983, pp. 75–89.

Sabine Haenni

Gone with the Wind (1939)

[Country: USA. Production Company: MGM. Producer: David Selznick. Directors: Victor Fleming, George Cukor and Sam Wood. Screenwriters: Sidney Howard, Oliver Garrett, Ben Hecht and Jo Swerling. Cinematographer: Ernest Haller. Music: Max Steiner. Cast: Clark Gable (Rhett Butler), Vivien Leigh (Scarlett O'Hara), Leslie Howard (Ashley Wilkes), Olivia de Haviland (Melanie Hamilton), Hattie McDaniel (Mammy).]

Synopsis: The film is a saga of destruction and reconstruction during and after the American Civil War. Against this background of an aristocratic society collapsing then struggling to adjust to harsh new commercial and social realities, the love affair between Rhett and Scarlett flickers, then flames into passion, but then burns out, leaving only ashes. Rhett consigns Scarlett to damnation at the very moment she recognises her long infatuation with

Ashley Wilkes (Leslie Howard), who has encouraged her feelings whilst having no intention of leaving his devoted wife Melanie (Olivia de Haviland), has been a false romantic illusion. When Melanie dies and Ashley cocoons himself in egoistic self-pity, she realises her mistake, but it is too late. 'What's to become of me?' she cries, to which Rhett delivers the immortal reply: 'Frankly, my dear, I don't give a damn'. It was an expensive reply, too. Such profanity was forbidden under the Production Code and Selznick had to pay $5,000 to the Motion Picture Producers and Distributors of America for permission to use that line, the shock effect being slightly diluted by Gable's delivery, where he shrewdly places emphasis on the word 'give' rather than 'damn'.

If one were to put a date on the moment that indelibly marked the high point of Hollywood in its heyday, one might suggest 15 December 1939. This was the date of the premiere of *Gone with the Wind* in Atlanta, Georgia, an event attended by over 50 film stars and nearly 2,000 dignitaries and regarded as so special that the Governor had declared a state holiday. Nothing was more remarkable about the film than the fact that it lived up to its own publicity. It was to win ten Oscars and to be a colossal box office success, being seen at that time by more people than any other motion picture in history (a record, many say, that still holds). It was a fittingly spectacular end to the year of 1939, which has since often been looked on as a golden year for Hollywood film production; and indeed in some ways it is the culmination of Hollywood's dominance of the 1930s as the Mecca of mass entertainment and appeal.

The driving force behind all this was the producer, David Selznick, son-in-law of the head of MGM, Louis B. Mayer, but a fiercely independent spirit who was determined with this project to top all his previous successes. The story behind the film (and no film has inspired so many books about its making) was to be as dramatic as the film itself. On acquiring the rights to Margaret Mitchell's novel, Selznick rapidly became aware that he was not just adapting a text but a literary phenomenon with a fanatical following. Within six months of its publication, the publishers had been obliged to publish nearly half a million copies to keep pace with demand; and with that came a loyal readership holding strong views about what the film should be like and who should play the leading roles, demands that Selznick would have to satisfy.

No effort or expense was spared in the endeavour to bring to the screen a cinematic realisation that did justice to the novel. The bulk of the screenplay was written by Sidney Howard, a respected dramatist and adaptor of others' material, particularly admired for his play and then screenplay based on Sinclair Lewis's novel, *Dodsworth* (filmed by William Wyler in 1936): sadly, Howard was to die before the film opened. Nevertheless, no fewer than 16 other writers worked on it at different stages, including such eminent figures as Scott Fitzgerald and Ben Hecht. Although in the end the direction was credited solely to Victor Fleming (who had come onto the film after directing most of another enduring classic of that year, *The Wizard of Oz*), the first director on the film was George Cukor, who had done a year's preparation on it but who, after three weeks of filming and to the distress of his leading actresses, was fired because of what were called 'creative differences' with the producer. Director Sam Wood was also called in to help out towards the end of the picture when Fleming had a nervous collapse after yet another blazing row with his leading actress, which had left him, he was to say later, with the urge to drive off the nearest cliff. Meanwhile Selznick's indefatigable chief publicist, Russell Birdwell, was devising ever more ingenious strategies to keep the film in the public eye, even to the extent of sending the press foreign-made typewriters with the initials of the film highlighted by coloured keys.

The main publicity inevitably centred on the casting of the two central roles, the tempestuous lovers at the heart of the drama, Rhett Butler and Scarlett O'Hara. The public had already made up its mind about who must play Rhett: the leading heart-throb of the day, Clark Gable. Selznick had to pay a high price to persuade his father-in-law to release Gable from his MGM contact for the film; and, indeed, by providing half the film's financing in return for world distribution rights and half the profits, MGM did very well out of the deal. But the real teaser, which Selznick exploited to the full for publicity purposes, centred on the question of who was to play Scarlett O'Hara. Thirty-two actresses were tested and a decision had still not been made when the film began shooting with the famous burning of Atlanta sequence, which had to be shot first to make room for the other sets. Legend has it (and it has never been contradicted by anything as mundane as the truth) that Selznick's younger brother, Myron, a top Hollywood agent, was visiting the set at that time in the company of Laurence Olivier and Vivien Leigh, who were lovers and shortly to be married. 'Hey, genius', Myron called out to his brother, 'meet your Scarlett O'Hara!' David turned round, took one look at Vivien Leigh against the background of the flames, and realised his search for Scarlett was at an end.

The phrase 'gone with the wind' comes from a love poem 'Cynara' by the nineteenth-century poet Ernest Dowson, and its famous refrain 'I have been faithful to thee, Cynara, in my fashion' might have suggested to Margaret Mitchell something of the tempestuous on-off romance of her two strong-willed leading characters. In the context of the film, however, as an opening title penned by Ben Hecht reveals, 'gone with the wind' refers to the world and values of the American South blown away by the forces of war and change. As Butler, a pragmatic realist who sees the writing on the wall before his Southern friends and adjusts his life and expectations accordingly, Gable's performance cannot be faulted: it has all the romantic charisma the part requires, but he seasons it with a wicked wit, never more so than in his dealings with Scarlett, whose selfish deceptions attract as much as appal him because he recognises something of a kindred spirit. 'We're alike', he tells her at one stage, 'selfish and shrewd, but able to look things in the eye and call them by their right name'. As Scarlett, Vivien Leigh seems at first all feminine caprice, which must later turn to ruthless self-preservation, but she also always conveys underneath the frivolous surface the character's sharp intelligence that is to captivate Rhett. She is a character with dynamism in a society that does not value or encourage such qualities in a woman, so that much of her energy and potential, one feels, become warped by the delusion that love should be the consuming goal of her life. In this respect, it is a performance that anticipates her definitive portrayal of another Southern belle of later vintage, also clinging to her romantic illusions as her body and her property are threatened by violation, Blanche du Bois in *A Streetcar Named Desire* (1951), which, like *Gone with the Wind*, also won her an Academy Award.

The film is an awesome spectacle that even today would be hard to match: perhaps a reason that thus far it has never been remade. The burning of Atlanta remains an exciting set piece. Some of the individual shots are breathtaking, none more so than the moment when the camera cranes away from Scarlett as she searches for a doctor at the Atlanta depot to reveal hundreds of wounded soldiers lying in the street awaiting treatment: a masterful visual exposition of an individual's plight being subsumed and overwhelmed by national tragedy. At moments like this, one is reminded that, for all Selznick's desire to please the public, he was not afraid to take risks. There are no battle scenes to add spurious excitement; there are moments of striking brutality (an amputation suggested by shadow, Scarlett's shooting of a Yankee deserter at point-blank range in the face); and, of course, an open rather than happy ending.

It is inevitable that the film would have dated in some respects, though even that is interesting in the sense that it tells you something about the tastes and values of the time. Historically, it has little to say about the causes of the War. The black characters now look either patronised or caricatured, though Hattie McDaniel succeeds in creating a strong and admirable character out of Scarlett's maid, Mammy, and also created history by being the first black performer to win an Oscar. The sexual politics look dubious now, and a feminist writer, Angela Carter, has expressed outrage at the notorious and, for its time, daring 'marital rape' scene, when a drunken Rhett carries Scarlett to bed; particularly when it is implied that Scarlett appears to have enjoyed the experience. On the other hand, it must be pointed out that other audiences have seen Scarlett as a precursor of feminism in her bravery, business acumen, determination and resilience. Certainly, one of the great moments of the film occurs when, half starving amidst the fields of her beloved home Tara that has been ravaged by war, she rails at the heavens. 'If I have to lie, steal, cheat, kill', she cries, 'as God is my witness, I'll never be hungry again!'

Gone with the Wind remains a monument to Hollywood craftsmanship and is the ultimate Hollywood film of the 1930s in terms of style and conception. It is big, brash and romantic, all this heavily underlined by the soaring music of Hollywood's top composer of the age, Max Steiner. It is star-studded and confident of its appeal, which is more emotional than intellectual, directed more at the heart than at the mind. It has colossal narrative authority and, even allowing for Selznick's overarching control, it is essentially a triumph of corporate more than personal filmmaking. Dozens upon dozens of supreme professionals have combined their talents on a project which, as de Haviland suggested at the time, they seemed to sense was not only something special but even promised immortality. The theme of a society suffering and then surviving a terrible war undoubtedly struck a chord at the end of that difficult and tormented decade. More than that, though, in its lament for a vanishing world, it contained its own implicit forecast and comment on the film capital itself. After *Gone with the Wind*, Hollywood was never to look quite so self-confident again.

Further reading

Sidney Howard, '*Gone with the Wind*' *Screenplay*, edited and with an introduction by Richard Harwell, London, Lorrimer, 1981, republished Faber, 1990.

Ted Sennett, *Hollywood's Golden Year 1939*, New York, St Martin's Press, 1989.

Helen Taylor, *Scarlett's Women: 'Gone With the Wind' and its Female Fans*, London, Virago, 1989.

David Thomson, *Showman: The Life of David Selznick*, New York, Knopf, 1992.

Neil Sinyard

La Haine/Hatred (1995)

[Country: France. Production Company: Canal+, Cofinergie 6, and Egg Pictures. Director and Screenwriter: Mathieu Kassovitz. Cinematographer: Pierre Aim. Music: Assassin. Cast: Vincent Cassel (Vinz), Hubert Kounde (Hubert), Said Taghmaoui (Said).]

Synopsis: Three friends from different ethnic backgrounds experience the prejudices of French society in the 24 hours after a 'race' riot. Vinz has found a handgun and seems crazy enough to use it. Hubert, searching for ways to create something positive from his life, is more thoughtful and seems more balanced. Said observes, watching events develop around him and treading the difficult middle ground between his two friends. They journey into the centre of Paris and then back out to the working-class satellite town where they live, and as they do so they are confronted firstly by the well-to-do middle class, then by racist elements in the police force, and finally by right-wing skinheads. Back on their home turf, Vinz is accidentally killed by plain-clothes police and Hubert points a gun at the officer responsible for the death. We hear a shot but are left uncertain who may now have been killed.

As he set out to make this film, Mathieu Kassovitz's spiritual mentor could well have been Roland Barthes. Kassovitz's intellectual starting point is the insight Barthes gives us as he famously sits down at the barber's shop and picks up a copy of *Paris Match* with an image on the front cover of a young black boy in uniform, looking up and saluting the French flag. 'I see very well what it signifies,' says Barthes, 'that France is a great Empire, that all her sons, without colour discrimination, faithfully serve under the flag, and that there is no better answer to the detractors of an alleged colonialism than the zeal shown by this Negro in serving his so-called oppressors' (1972: 125–6). Kassovitz begins a metaphorical search behind that front cover, an exploration of the attitudes, values and politics of late twentieth-century multicultural French society. He is guided by an underpinning realisation of the inescapable presence of the past within the present and an awareness of any society's inability to deal with its current manifestation of itself without both knowledge and acknowledgment of its past.

The ethnic origins of our three central characters, Said, Vinz and Hubert, are made clear from the outset: Said is Arab African–French (Beur), Vinz has a Jewish background and Hubert is black African–French. To them, drawn together by a shared youth culture, these differences seem unimportant; but at the same time each of them is very aware of the ways in which others in France might look at their ethnicity. Because he is 'white' it is Vinz, for example, who is given the task of attempting to gain entry to a middle-class block of flats in central Paris.[1]

But, of course, Kassovitz is also producing an engaging narrative that will sit comfortably and entertainingly within the sphere of popular cinema and so the characters are carefully delineated. Through a series of scenes, for example, Vinz is associated with the key prop of the handgun: the object that is dangerous in that it is likely to 'go off' with deadly consequences. He is linked to this object, not only physically in that he possesses it but also emotionally in that he displays himself as something of a 'loose cannon', someone who could explode into violence.[2] Hubert is the most carefully outlined character: we see him alone in his bedroom and at home with his mother, for instance, in scenes that do not move the plot forward but which increase our understanding of his character and intensify our sense of empathy with him. (That Hubert is more politically aware is signalled, for instance, by the pictures on his bedroom wall.) Said watches events unfold, seeing the story of his two friends play itself out before his eyes with a fatal inevitability within the context of the wider social narrative. After the opening documentary footage of riots, the film begins with Said contemplating the presence of the police on the streets and we end the film in a somewhat similar manner.

The first scenes are played out to the sound of 'Burnin' and Lootin'' by Bob Marley and the Wailers, suggesting for the audience a particular way of seeing the documentary footage and positioning the filmmakers ideologically. Marley was associated with radical black politics and a willingness to confront state authorities that are seen as repressive.

La Haine was to some extent based on an actual event: the death of an 18-year-old black youth shot dead during interrogation by police in 1992. But the riots and the violent confrontation between the police and young people is placed within a much longer socio-historical context. The posters on the wall in Hubert's bedroom, for example, show, first, Muhammad Ali, a black boxer who famously refused to fight in Vietnam, and, second, the 'black power' salute given by African American sprinters Tommie Smith and John Carlos at the 1968 Mexico Olympics. Within contemporary French society we are taken into a youth culture of music, dance and language ('verlan', street talk) that is seen to exist as a vibrant hybrid cultural fusion.[3]

And, alongside the politics of race, Kassovitz presents us with the politics of class. A strong sense of the nature of the working-class experience is given through location shooting amongst the bleak, stark walls and tower blocks of the estate where the central characters live and this is reinforced by the deliberate choice of black and white film stock. Later, by transporting the friends into central Paris the contrast between their experience of life and the middle-class experience is made clear. (This also, incidentally, places the problem firmly within the heart of French society rather than leaving it as a peripheral issue out in the satellite towns, or 'projects', of Paris.)

The 'projects', or les banlieues, where the central characters live are satellite 'new towns' up to 20 miles out of Paris that almost seem designed to keep the poor out of the middle-class centre of the city. These areas are stereotyped in the media as places of urban deprivation, crime and drug use. In the film, we see a TV crew staying within the 'safety' of their car while attempting to interview Said, Vinz and Hubert about the previous night's riot. They are positioned in such a way as to literally 'look down on' the three friends in a space that resembles a bear pit or zoo enclosure.

Youth unemployment is a constant feature of the social 'backdrop': neither Said, nor Vinz, nor Hubert has a job. Police brutality is clearly an issue, though the role of Samir and the presence of black police officers within the mise en scène of several scenes, suggests this is not a simple and clear-cut matter. Racism is displayed, most obviously in the scene with the skinhead gang. The social exclusion experienced by some young people, as shown for example by the scenes on a tower block rooftop, in an art gallery and in an empty high-tech shopping mall, is seen to have created an 'underclass'. And, an inevitable product of this would seem to be rebellion and social conflict.

In another scene the three main characters are placed in a children's play area in such a way as to convey the sense of utter boredom being experienced. A single static shot of them sitting equidistant from each other in a bleak, empty space is held for some time and then an edit 'jumps' us forward to a shot of the same three characters in the same space but occupying slightly different positions within the frame. Because they have moved marginally we experience the cut as a jolt. The combination of holding the initial shot for longer than we might normally expect and then using a distinctive edit ensures the tedium of their lives is conveyed clearly but succinctly to the viewer. As a purposeful contrast to this, a scene of a DJ using his decks to blast out an anti-police message from his flat above the street is filmed and edited to convey an experience of momentary freedom, escape and release for the young people of the community, with the camera eventually moving out across the rooftops.

Techniques such as these are employed to give a rounded picture of the life of marginalised young people in Paris, and yet at the same time to create a film that sits relatively comfortably within the context of popular cinema. In a scene in which two experienced plain clothes policemen 'question' Said and Hubert in an interrogation cell while a younger trainee officer looks on, a static camera is used, refusing us any respite from viewing the racial abuse and beating that is taking place. We are denied the potential relief of looking away and yet by refusing this possibility the filmmakers in fact only highlight for us just how much we would like to turn our heads. Intercut shots of the trainee watching the performance display his distaste for what is happening and demonstrate how careful Kassovitz is to avoid being seen as simply adopting an anti-police stance. The rookie officer's silence, his inability to speak out, is given a particular eloquence through the editing.[4]

At the end of *La Haine* we are given the basic outcome of the day's events for our three central characters, but the wider issues raised by the film are clearly unresolved. We have been presented with a whole set of possible reasons for the state of society and a further set of potential outcomes that might result from this, but nothing within this wider social context has been resolved; what might happen here is left open although the spectre of fascism has been raised by the confrontation of the three friends with a skinhead gang.[5]

Notes

1. As a major colonial power in the nineteenth and twentieth centuries, France had colonies in Africa, the Caribbean and South-East Asia. In some of these places, such as Algeria (which gained independence in 1962) and Vietnam (where the French were defeated at Dien Bien Phu in 1954), the struggle for independence was particularly bitter. Some colonies, like Martinique, remain and are able to send representatives to the French Assembly. Other former colonies, like Senegal, remain closely linked to France and French culture. French policy towards non-white ethnic groups has always been one of 'assimilation' with people being expected to take on French cultural norms and values. North Africans (Algerians, Moroccans and Tunisians), who began to come to France for work during the 1960s, have to some extent resisted this policy.
2. The gun is symbolically handed over to Hubert by Vinz towards the end of the film in acknowledgment of the fact that he has learnt something both about himself and about the reality of gunplay, thereby making the final scene all the more poignant. The prop takes on a role and significance within the film over and above its mere presence as a material object.
3. Verlan, or 'backslang', began around Paris in the 1980s amongst second-generation ethnic minority young people who saw themselves as positioned somewhere between their parents' culture and French culture.
4. The film has been attacked as having an anti-police 'message': whether this is true or not would depend on how we interpreted scenes such as this within the film and how we understood the filmmakers to be using film construction techniques to emphasise and elevate certain perspectives above others. It might also, of course, depend on our own personal views on 'the police' and our background within any particular community, culture, or subculture.
5. Right-wing politicians in France (as in other European countries) have since at least the 1980s consistently raised immigration as a key issue. In 2012, Marine Le Pen, the National Front presidential candidate, received 18 per cent of the first round votes.

Further reading

Roland Barthes, *Mythologies*, London, Cape, 1972.

Alain Gabon, 'The Transformation of French Identity in Mathieu Kassovitz's Films *Metisse* (1993) and *La Haine* (1995)' in Hafid Gafaiti, Patricia M. E. Lorcin and David G. Troyansky (eds), *Transnational Spaces and Identities in the Francophone World*, Lincoln, NE, University of Nebraska, 2009, pp. 115–48.

Yosefa Loshitzky, *Screening Strangers: Migration and Diaspora in Contemporary European Cinema*, Bloomington, IN, Indiana University Press, 2010.

Ginette Vincendeau, *La Haine*, London, I.B.Tauris, 2005.

John White

Hiroshima mon amour (1959)

[Country: France and Japan. Production Company: Argos Films, Como Films, Daiei Studios and Pathé Entertainment. Director: Alain Resnais. Screenwriter: Marguerite Duras. Cinematographers: Sacha Vierny and Takahashi Michio. Music: Georges Delerue and Giovanni Fusco. Cast: Emmanuelle Riva (Woman/French actor/'Nevers'), Eiji Okada (Man/Japanese architect/'Hiroshima').]

Synopsis: A Japanese man and a French woman meet and become lovers in Hiroshima in 1959. The woman is in Japan to act in a film aimed at promoting peace. The intensity of this brief love affair allows her to revisit the trauma of her first love at the age of 18 with an occupying German soldier in Nevers in France during the Second World War. Everything that happens occurs explicitly against the backdrop of the dropping of the atomic bomb on Hiroshima in 1945 and implicitly against the tension of the Cold War arms race of the 1950s.

In July 1945 scientists in the United States tested the first atomic bomb in New Mexico. On 6 August, as part of the endgame of the Second World War and with Germany defeated, an atom bomb was dropped on Hiroshima in Japan. The bomb levelled the city and caused around 80,000 immediate deaths. Three days later a second atom bomb was dropped, this time on Nagasaki, causing 40,000 deaths. On 14 August Japan surrendered. In 1952 the United States tested its first hydrogen bomb. Less than a year later, the Soviet Union tested its first hydrogen bomb. The Cold War was fully underway. *Hiroshima mon amour* has to be seen against the historical background offered by the Second World War and the Cold War, and more specifically against the backdrop of the emergence of thermonuclear warfare.

The film is both an exploration of the nature of human society and in investigation of individual human experience. At the beginning of the film the central female character tells her Japanese lover she has paid four visits to the Hiroshima Peace Memorial Museum.[1] Her recall of this place along with her testimony to the impact it has had on her enables the filmmakers to take us on a virtual tour of the museum. The full horror of the brutality of war is brought home to the viewer.[2] Over a shot of exhibits in glass jars such as might be seen in a laboratory, her voiceover records, 'Human skin, floating loose, still bearing the fresh bloom of suffering'. The poetry of Duras's language (here centred in the tension created between the idea of 'fresh bloom' set against the dreadfulness of the rest of the sentence) continually forces us to reflect longer and harder on a subject we might already find distressing enough.

But we might also note the strength of political conviction inherent in the words and images we are shown. When, for example, over shots of Japanese protests and demonstrations against nuclear weapons,[3] the woman tells us, 'Anger stirred whole towns', Duras goes on via her character to tell us who these people were angry with.

> They were angered whether they knew it or not by the fundamental inequality imposed by some nations on others, by the fundamental inequality imposed by some races on others, by the fundamental inequality imposed by some classes on others.

If this is the voice of the woman, it is also the polemical stance of Duras. *Hiroshima mon amour* exists within a strong socio-political context; in part the motivation behind the film is the straightforward desire to document within a forceful fictional narrative the obscenity of a thermonuclear attack.

However, Resnais and Duras have chosen not to use the documentary form but to frame documentary aspects within a tragic love story. They are aware of the problems inherent in making a film about 'Hiroshima': how could a film crew from the West, fly to Japan for a few weeks or months and hope to create a record of such an experience?[4] In their film the woman asks at one point: 'What can a tourist do other than weep?' And this highlights the problem; when all is said and done, they are 'tourists'.[5]

At the same time, the film that is eventually created also clearly demonstrates the awareness of

Resnais and Duras that neither 'documenting' nor 'fictionalising' human experience is in any way 'straightforward'. How can the experience of Hiroshima on August 6th 1945 be 'experienced' after and beyond the event itself? Even exhibits in the museum cannot move beyond being 'reconstructions' as the woman frequently acknowledges.

Despite her attempt to recount precisely all she has seen in Hiroshima relating to the bombing, the woman's Japanese lover repeatedly tells her, 'You saw nothing in Hiroshima'. The first time he says this, she responds, 'I saw everything; everything'.[6] There is, of course, a sense in which she did see 'everything'; she did see some sort of record of all that wo/man is capable of inflicting on fellow human beings, and she did, therefore, 'see' in a way some sort of definitive statement of all that there is to be said about wo/man. In another sense she saw 'nothing' of the real horror of the actual experience of the bomb and its immediate aftermath. And yet, in the deeper, more profound, sense in which the word 'nothing' has often been used in literature, she did see the emptiness, the hollowness, the 'nothingness' of human life and the individual human experience.

In an effort to counter his repeated pronouncement in the first few minutes of the film that she saw nothing she has her own mantra-like, repeated phrase. 'Four visits to the museum in Hiroshima', she recites, as if the precision of her documentation ('four times') and the sheer number of visits must mean she has acquired some type of solid, factual knowledge.

Echoing the man's use of 'nothing', the woman sums up her problem, that is also the problem for Resnais and Duras, and the problem for us both as viewers of the film and as people looking back on the dropping of the atom bomb:

> I saw people walking round. People walking pensively past photographs, reconstructions: since there is nothing else. Photographs, photographs, reconstructions: since there is nothing else. Descriptions, since there is nothing else.

And yet, she clings to the attempt to use language and memory and her own 'reconstructions' of events in order to hold on to something rather than nothing. The repetition in the language use here is part of the effort to attempt to provide some sort of solidity and certainty; and it echoes the way in which we repeat remembered narratives of the past in an attempt to hold on to something of the past.

What quickly becomes clear is that beyond the socio-political macro world, the filmmakers are intensely interested in the individual human experience. The long opening sequence juxtaposes the naked bodies of the lovers in all their vulnerability with footage of the aftermath of the atomic attack. The whole film might be seen as an examination of the human ability for love and tenderness, set against the equally powerful human ability for hatred and destruction. Time and again, we cut back to the lovers either from some image of physically scarred and maimed bodies or from the traumatised stare of a victim. The juxtaposing of images, and the setting of words against contrasting images, forms a key part of the film technique. As the voiceover describes flowers 'springing reborn from the ashes', we see images of doctors and nurses working on the burns of adults and children.

From the first images, when we see only entwined parts of the bodies of the lovers and are denied an establishing shot, the viewer is constantly challenged to make sense of what she is seeing. If meaning exists, it is to be found somewhere within the complexity and the contradictions.

The story of the woman's experiences in Hiroshima is interrupted by flashbacks, which are used to intensify the sense of the character's mental state; and yet, we are never entirely certain if any of this is fantasy rather than memory. 'When you talk, I don't know if you are lying or telling the truth', says the man. To which he receives the enigmatic response, 'I lie. And I tell the truth'. Of course, for Resnais and Duras, if what constitutes 'knowledge' is problematic and 'memory' is highly questionable, then the whole nature of 'truth' is, to say the least, rather tricky.

Furthermore, the uncertainties attaching to communication mean there is always distance between people however close their bodies may be as lovers. Next morning he is asleep and she is up and on the balcony. She has a brief flashback, a memory of a dead man on the ground, her German lover in the war. She re-enters the room, her Japanese lover wakes, and instantly she asks, 'Coffee?' What is captured is how much both our memories and our minds are our own, and how they operate in parallel with and often dislocated from our day-to-day functioning selves.

The greatest terror for our central female character is the way in which human beings inevitably forget. The immediate pain fades and we forget, both as individuals and collectively as societies. However intense the experience our memories always fade. 'Like you', says the woman, 'I am endowed with memory. I know what it is to forget.' The two aspects of human experience, 'memory' and 'forgetting', are yoked together so strongly that they are the same thing: memory is forgetfulness, to remember is to forget. The man's response is, 'No, you are not endowed with memory'. And, of course, he is right. Human beings do not have the ability to remember, they have the talent to forget. Interestingly, she is not really disagreeing with him. Like characters in a Samuel Beckett play they are coming at the same question from different angles, batting it back and forth between them.[7] 'Listen, I know', she says, 'I know everything; life went on'. And this is the point, she suggests, however horrific the experience may be, however traumatising, life will go on. The concept of 'I know' is usually highly problematic in that philosophically we might say it is impossible to 'know' anything; but, on all the evidence, this is one thing we can 'know' she goes on to suggest. It should not be possible after the death of a lover for life to go on, but it does; equally, it should not be possible after Hiroshima for another such event to take place, but it will.

> Listen to me. I know this too: it will happen again.

Notes

1. This was opened in the Peace Memorial Park with its Memorial Cenotaph just four years before *Hiroshima mon amour* was filmed.
2. 'Awakening in the morning, the women found their hair had fallen out', says the woman in voiceover, and the mere mention of 'hair' alongside images of women with apparently shaven heads creates an intertextual reference not only to newsreel footage of Holocaust death camps but also to Resnais's earlier film, *Nuit et Brouillard/Night and Fog* (1956).
3. In 1954, the United States exploded a 15-megaton (one megaton is an explosion equivalent to one million tons of TNT) nuclear bomb in the Marshall Islands. The radioactive fallout from this weapon was immense and dusted a Japanese boat, the *Lucky Dragon*, tuna-fishing 160 km from the test site.
4. 'The power relationships in the film are complex, since the narrative is centred in a Western character visiting Japan, yet that character is a woman, inverting a gendered hierarchy of unequal cultural relationships.' (Scott Nygren, *Time Frames: Japanese Cinema and the Unfolding of History*, Minneapolis, MN, University of Minnesota Press, 2007, p. 187.)
5. This is a particularly intense example of the problem with all forms of knowledge and the whole idea of what it means to 'know'. When the man says he cannot imagine Nevers, she responds, 'Nevers. 40,000 inhabitants. Built as a country seat', as if encyclopaedic knowledge really helps someone to 'know' something.
6. Her response is given over a black screen.
7. 'One must avoid thinking of the difficulties this world presents, otherwise it would be unbearable', for example, could come straight from any dramatist working within what Martin Esslin classified as Theatre of the Absurd.

Further reading

Kyo Maclear, 'The Limits of Vision: *Hiroshima Mon Amour* and the Subversion of Representation' in Ana Douglass (ed.), *Witness and Memory: The Discourse of Trauma*, New York and London, Routledge, 2003, pp. 233–48.

Emma Wilson, *Alain Resnais*, Manchester, Manchester University Press, 2006.

John White

His Girl Friday (1940)

[Country: USA. Production Company: Columbia Pictures Corporation. Director: Howard Hawks. Screenwriter: Charles Lederer (based on the play 'The Front Page' by Ben Hecht and Charles MacArthur). Cinematographer: Joseph Walker. Editor: Gene Havlick. Cast: Cary Grant (Walter Burns), Rosalind Russell (Hildy Johnson), Ralph Bellamy (Bruce Baldwin), Gene Lockhart (Sheriff Peter Hartwell), Frank Orth (Duffy), John Qualen (Earl Williams), Helen Mack (Mollie Malone), Billy Gilbert (Joe Pettibone), Edwin Maxwell (Dr Max J. Eggelhoffer).]

Synopsis: Ace reporter Hildy Johnson returns to *The Morning Post* to notify Walter Burns – the *Post*'s Managing Editor and Hildy's ex-husband – that she plans to quit the paper, move to Albany, and marry insurance salesman Bruce Baldwin. Burns exhibits few scruples as he attempts to disrupt this plan. While breaking up Hildy's engagement and remarrying her himself is a secondary goal, Burns is more immediately concerned with convincing Hildy to interview condemned murderer Earl Williams; write a front page story sympathetic to Williams; get Williams reprieved; and get the sheriff and mayor (running for re-election on a law-and-order ticket) kicked out of office. In service of these ambitions, Burns deploys (among other dirty tricks) a pickpocket, a vamp, and $450 in counterfeit money. Most of the movie takes place in the press room of the criminal courts building, the sole location used in *The Front Page*, the stage play on which the film is based. Each plot twist introduces new members of a skilled ensemble of character actors. The last character, an incorruptible buffoon of a *deus ex machina* named Pettibone, turns out to be the 'unseen power' that watches over Hildy, Walter, and *The Morning Post*.

A popular joke about Hollywood in the 1930s has it that, once the movies learned to talk, they wouldn't shut up. Hollywood produced hundreds of movies in the 1930s that are not fast-talking comedies. But the fast-talking comedies from the 1930s and early 40s – from the reality-bending productions of the Marx Brothers, to the heteronormative screwball romances that brought together skilled actors including William Powell and Myrna Loy, Clark Gable and Claudette Colbert, and Cary Grant and a string of leading ladies – are among the most satisfying products of an extremely satisfying decade in American cinema. At decade's end, *His Girl Friday* (1940) stands out as one of the fastest – and funniest – films of all time.

Films from the 1930s are unmatched not just for the speed of the dialogue but for their wit thanks to the journalists, playwrights, short-story writers, satirists and novelists hired by the studios after sound film became the central product of the Hollywood system. Viewed in retrospect it is striking, and anomalous, that in these films the women got lines as good as the men's. The most prominent comedians of the silent film era were men: Charlie Chaplin, Buster Keaton, Harold Lloyd. So were most of the comedians who made the transition from Broadway, vaudeville, or silent film to the talkies: the Marx Brothers, Laurel and Hardy, W. C. Fields, Bob Hope. Mae West, performer and playwright, was a notable exception. But the enforcement of the Production Code beginning in 1934 more or less put West out of business. From the 1970s through the first decade of the twenty-first century, when US comedies have been vehicles for male comedians who made their names in stand-up comedy or on Saturday Night Live, women have existed mostly to look pretty. In the early twenty-first century, David Denby has identified a genre of comedies that he terms 'slacker-striver romance[s]'. Of the typical heroine in these pictures, Denby writes, 'she doesn't have an idea in her head, and she's not the one who makes the jokes'.

Comedies of the 1930s and 40s feature actresses like Loy, Colbert, Carole Lombard, Irene Dunne, Katherine Hepburn, and *His Girl Friday's* Rosalind Russell – actresses who get terrific dialogue and the opportunity to demonstrate that they are terrific comic actresses. Even when they are enmeshed in plots that fail to imagine roles for women much beyond the roles available to Jane Austen heroines, their verbal acuity gives them a kind of presence that is rare in Hollywood pictures of any era. As in Austen's novels, even when the plot moves women inexorably towards marriage, a sense of possibility accompanies the sheer pleasure of seeing (or reading about) women who are as smart as men and are not afraid to show it.

Even in this group, *His Girl Friday* is unusual. The film's female lead is not a society girl choosing between two potential husbands, as in *It Happened One Night* (Frank Capra, 1934) or *The Philadelphia Story* (George Cukor, 1940), or a charming sparring partner for her detective husband, as in the *Thin Man* movies. Hildy Johnson is a working woman, an ace reporter, the best writer on the criminal justice beat in some big city. The script for *His Girl Friday* is based on *The Front Page*, a stage play written by Ben Hecht and Charles MacArthur. (The play was adapted for the screen under its own name in 1931 and again in 1974). While audiences who saw *The Front Page* on stage in New York or London missed most of the local references, they knew the play took place in Chicago. When the play moved to the screen, the local references disappeared – the script is careful to indicate that the film does not take place in Chicago, New York, Baltimore or any recognisable city. The Production Code, enforced most rigorously between 1934 and 1941, included the following clauses, 'the presentation must not throw sympathy with the criminal as against the law. The *courts* of the land should not be presented as *unjust*' (Doherty 1999: 351). If Joseph Breen, the man in charge of administering the Production Code, saw the film as an indictment of contemporary politicians, he could have halted production. *His Girl Friday* takes place in a generic city and features generic yellow journalists. In case we miss the point, the opening disclaimer announces, 'you will see in this picture no resemblance to the men and women of the press today'.

This 1940 adaptation of *The Front Page* is built around one radical decision: in the play Hildy Johnson – protégé of Walter Burns, reporter for the *Chicago Herald and Examiner* – is a man. He has chosen to leave the newspaper business, marry Peggy Grant, move to New York, and work in an advertising firm owned by his fiancée's uncle. In *His Girl Friday*, Hildy is a woman and Burns's ex-wife. Peggy Grant becomes Bruce Baldwin, an insurance salesman from Albany, who apparently resembles movie actor Ralph Bellamy. Burns is less a Mephistophelean, thoroughly unscrupulous manipulator than a charming rogue. Choosing between Burns and Baldwin, Hildy is given the same choice, and the same stacked deck, given to Irene Dunne's character in *The Awful Truth* (Leo McCarey, 1937). Who would choose Ralph Bellamy over Cary Grant?

A good deal of mythology surrounds the decision to turn Hildy into a woman. Howard Hawks tells a story in which he reads the play out loud with a female employee reading the reporter's part. When he heard the lines read by a woman, he decided it sounded better that way (Breivold 2006: 26, 142). Whether this story is true, it says a great deal about Hawks's control over the production process during his long and productive career. He began as a screenwriter during the silent era, directed his first film in 1926, his first sound film in 1930, and his forty-fifth and final picture in 1970. From 1932 on he produced his own films. Never tied to a particular studio, Hawks produced and directed films for all eight of Hollywood's major studios. He is recognised as a director who managed to produce outstanding films across a range of genres. He directed films still considered among Hollywood's finest examples of the gangster film, the adventure film, film noir, western and comedy.

Hawks's early adventure films are stunningly male-oriented (and strikingly homosocial). By the late 1930s, Hawks proved himself exceptionally good at romantic comedies. In some of his most successful movies, notably *To Have and Have Not* (1944), he combined genres, bringing adventure and flirtation together in a single confection. Despite this extraordinary range, Hawks films have recognizable characteristics. But it took the French film critics of *Cahiers du cinéma*, inventors of the idea of the *auteur*, and auteurist critics, such as Robin Wood and Peter Bogdanovich, to articulate the signatures of a Hawks film. The time span represented in the diegesis tends to be limited to a few days or even hours. The action is linear, presented without flashbacks, parallel action or technical wizardry. The pace is snappy. The mastery of continuity and invisible editing is unmatched. The camera is positioned at eye level. Camera position and shot duration tend to show multiple characters in space, allowing the actors to move around and interact with each other. Less frequently noted is the fact that the films almost always feature musical performance, although they are rarely musicals (*His Girl Friday* is an exception). Most of all, the films are fun to watch, no matter what the genre.

The scene in Walter Burns's office, at the beginning of *His Girl Friday*, illustrates these qualities as well as any Hawks-directed scene. The scene lasts more than ten minutes and takes place entirely in a small office. For more than nine of those minutes, the only characters in the room are Hildy and Walter, except for a brief cut to the *Morning Post's* city editor, and a foiled attempt by the same editor to enter the office. Hildy and Walter spend those nine minutes talking to each other. Stage business is limited to answering a phone, standing up and sitting down, taking a glove off and putting it back on, lighting a cigarette, putting a carnation into a lapel. But nothing about this scene feels confining. There are a few brief close-ups, and a few brief shot/reverse shot sequences, but most of the time both characters are in the shot, usually in medium shots that show head, shoulders and torso.

These characteristics carry through to the rest of the film. While the play takes place entirely in the press room in the criminal courts building, the film adds almost 25 minutes in other settings to the beginning of the film. Once Hildy arrives at the press room, we are there for most of the rest of the film. This confinement doesn't feel stagey. Nor does the speed of the dialogue wear on viewers. For this, it's hard not to give Hawks credit. Hawks is a master of pace, using silence as effectively as dialogue. Mollie Malloy's speech to the newsmen shames them into silence. Her exit is followed by almost 20 seconds in which no one speaks, and then only to answer a phone. Twenty seconds of silence is deafening in a film that talks as fast as this one.

As a film about a career woman, *His Girl Friday* anticipates the movement of women into the workforce during the 1940s in numbers that would not be matched for 30 years. During the Second World War, male military conscription, and the expanding wartime economy, made women's employment an economic necessity and a patriotic duty. The Second World War movies feature women who work. After the war, when an ideology of domesticity pushed women back into the home, domestic melodramas feature women who must choose between career and family. Women who try to have both, such as the title character in *Mildred Pierce* (Michael Curtiz, 1945), are punished. Hildy Johnson has the remarkable opportunity to choose both marriage and career.

Two of the films cited in Laura Mulvey's landmark essay in feminist film criticism 'Visual Pleasure and Narrative Cinema' are Howard Hawks films: *Only Angels Have Wings* (1939) and *To Have and Have Not* (1944). Both screenplays are credited in whole or part to Jules Furthman, one of Hawks's frequent collaborators. Furthman also wrote *Morocco* (Josef von Sternberg, 1930), Marlene Dietrich's Hollywood debut, and another film discussed in Mulvey's essay. All three films feature women who work at the morally questionable profession of stage performer. All three films dramatise the sacrifices women must make to demonstrate the devotion that will make them worthy of the leading man's attention. While Johnson gets to choose husband *and* career (thus avoiding the sacrificial trap in which the heroines of melodramas are routinely placed) the movie dramatises a shift in the balance of power between Hildy and Walter. At the movie's outset, she has left him for a life of respectability. He spends the film in pursuit. By the end, she is prepared to return to her earlier life, apparently on terms identical to those she rejected before.

Robin Wood describes Hawks films as products of and celebrations of collaboration (2006: xvii). He gives Hawks credit for exerting exceptional control over his productions. We must give Hawks similarly paradoxical credit for creating female characters like Hildy Johnson – smart, confident, self-assured – and then for placing them in movies in which they must learn to submit to their men.

Further reading

Scott Breivold (ed.), *Howard Hawks Interviews*, Jackson, University of Mississippi Press, 2006.

David Denby, 'A Fine Romance', *The New Yorker*, 23 July 2007, pp. 58–65.

Thomas Doherty, *Pre-Code Hollywood: Sex, Immorality, and Insurrection in American Cinema 1930–1934*, New York, Columbia University Press, 1999.
Ben Hecht and Charles MacArthur, *The Front Page: From Theater to Reality*, edited by George W. Hilton, Hanover, Smith and Kraus, 2002.
Gerald Mast, 'From Howard Hawks, Storyteller', in Gerald Mast and Marshall Cohen (eds), *Film Theory and Criticism*, third edition, New York, Oxford University Press, 1985, pp. 563–71.
Laura Mulvey, 'Visual Pleasure and Narrative Cinema', in Constance Penley (ed.), *Feminism and Film Theory*, New York, Routledge, 1988, pp. 57–68.
Peter Wollen, 'The Auteur Theory', in *Signs and Meaning in the Cinema* (1969), Bloomington, IN, Indiana University Press, 1972, pp. 74–115.
Robin Wood, *Howard Hawks* (1968), Detroit, Wayne State University Press, 2006.

Elliot Shapiro

Hua yang nian hua/In the Mood for Love (2000)

[Country: Hong Kong, France. Production Companies: Block 2 Pictures, Jet Tone and Paradis Films. Director and Screenwriter: Wong Kar Wai. Cast: Maggie Cheung Man-yuk (Su Li-zhen), Tony Leung Chiu-wai (Chow Mo-wan).]

Synopsis: In Hong Kong, 1962, Su Li-zhen, Chow Mo-wan and their respective partners rent rooms in adjacent flats. The two gradually become aware that Li-zhen's husband is having an affair with Mo-wan's wife and begin to seek solace in each other's company. They work through their shared pain by role-playing scenarios, such as imagining how the affair began or confronting the unfaithful other half. Mo-wan eventually declares his growing love for Li-zhen but the terrifying prospect of gossip splits the two, with Mo-wan leaving for a new life in Singapore.

Obsessed with passing time and infused with a romantic vision of a vanished past, *In the Mood for Love* is a typical Wong Kar Wai film. However, by dispensing with the hitherto characteristic use of voiceover narration, Wong instead finds alternate routes into his characters' inner lives that widen the potential of cinema to investigate memory, perspective and emotion.

Early on, as the new pairs of neighbours move in on the same day, removal men inadvertently mix up their property. This proves prophetic as their space, relationships and identities will all eventually become intertwined. Later, it is the doubling of the unfaithful spouses' handbags and ties that alerts Li-zhen and Mo-wan to the affair. Significantly, Li-zhen's husband and Mo-wan's wife are never shown face on to the camera, but are usually presented via telephone, separated from sight by door frames or reversed in mirrors. This has the effect of presenting the pair as 'other' – outside of the film's main narrative thrust and deliberately distanced from the spectator. Wong suggests that through this device we see 'both relationships – the adulterous affair and the repressed friendship – in the one couple' (Rayns 2000). This absence also elides a structural distraction: if we cannot see them, then we judge them not as individuals but as catalysts for our protagonists' emotional experience. Wong also circumscribes the issue of presenting a couple who can reject characters played by Cheung and Leung, two of Hong Kong cinema's most glamorous actors.

We are nevertheless given glimpses into the ordeal of the absent pair. The suffocating, cramped environment and lack of privacy from gossiping neighbours and colleagues that wound Li-zhen and Mo-wan's relationship must affect them too. Wong allows us a brief insight into their difficulty through a thorny shared phone call shortly before they disappear from the film altogether. This mirrors the silent call between Li-zhen and Mo-wan near the end. We are also teased with a fleeting shot of Mrs Chow weeping in the bath. This too is later echoed when Li-zhen allows herself a brief cry after a lecture from her landlady. In both scenes, the edit prevents the moment from lingering, tightly reining in the screen time allotted to the women's parallel outpouring of emotion. The crucial difference is that Li-zhen's anguish is based on what she desires, rather than has acted upon. She experiences a simulacrum of the other woman's experience, resulting in genuine grief.

Equally, after Mo-wan and Li-zhen have mutually confirmed their knowledge of their partners' affair, we watch them walking down the street, flirting with one another. Genre and narrative expectations lead us to suppose that their own amour has been stirred but Li-zhen suddenly stops. She criticises Mo-wan's portrayal of her husband. The scene begins again as before but with minor differences. We now realise that they are pretending to be the adulterous couple initiating their affair, the result of a seemingly throwaway question from the prior scene as to how the relationship began. This sequence operates both diegetically (the couple have a second go at their role play) and non-diegetically as the cut and recommencement also stirs us to become aware of film as a medium: it appears as if two slightly different takes have been left in the final edit.

A corresponding sequence occurs later when they imagine Li-zhen confronting her husband with her suspicions. This time Mo-wan disapproves of Li-zhen's performance and the scene begins afresh until Li-zhen breaks down in tears at the pain this has caused her to feel. Perhaps bookending the sequence where the affair starts, this game suggests a scene where the affair may end. Later, she and Mo-wan rehearse their own imminent break-up (on-screen) before it actually happens (off-screen). Now typically, the imitation informs genuine emotion and replaces the actual event.

Throughout, the couple are terrified of the gossip their seemingly chaste relationship will stir, though their genuinely adulterous spouses appear largely to avoid this. Likewise, Li-zhen's employer's own affair is ironically organised through Li-zhen's helpful diarising, acquisition of gifts, and advice on ties. Meanwhile, Mo-wan's boorish friend Ah Ping is unashamed of openly discussing his bad debts and visits to a brothel. Much of the disapproval Li-zhen and Mo-wan fear comes from within, further internalising the repression and anxiety of what others *might* say, rather than what they do say.

Public and private space within the film is carefully constructed to reflect its central characters' emotions. Wong conveys an overcrowded Hong Kong through cinematography and set design that cramps (however elegantly) the characters, trapping them in doorways or pressed against furniture. Maggie Cheung is squeezed into 22 different ornate cheongsams to play Li-zhen, lending her the air of a work of art: sculpted, desirable, unobtainable.

Cui Mengyang has noted the importance of costume in the shot where Li-zhen briefly faces her love rival seen arriving from behind for a game of mah-jong. Li-zhen's characteristic, high-neckline cheongsam contrasts with Mrs Chow's Westernised, low-cut dress. Li-zhen's elaborate, untouchable hair diverges from the other woman's fashionable 1960s flips. Mrs Chow also arrives with a seductive wiggle in contrast to the elegance and poise that Maggie Cheung brings to her role. This fleeting sequence, states Cui, verifies Wong's method of 'expressing certain meanings or feelings by veiling them and showing them also partially' (2007: 44). One could add that this is exactly the function of Cheung's elaborate dress in itself.

Wong also uses those cheongsams to steer the narrative through some editing that seems designed to misdirect the spectator. The usual rules of shot-reverse-shot are uprooted when what seems to be a continuous scene is revealed as taking place over different times, signified only by a sudden change of dress, perhaps suggesting how repetition and ritual dominates the Li-zhen/Mo-wan relationship.

Similarly ambiguous, the film's final intertitle meditates on the distance between the past, memories and the present:

He remembers those vanished years.
As though looking through a dusty window pane
The past is something he could see but not touch.
And everything he sees is blurred and indistinct.

Have we then been privy to Mo-wan's perspective? This presents us with a conundrum: the couple miss each other during the penultimate sequence of Mo-wan's return in 1966. He fails to learn of Li-zhen's separation from her husband and motherhood to a child which we could reasonably (though not certainly) surmise is his. How could this be taken from Mo-wan's perspective? Wong has wrong-footed us with ambiguity and 'blurred and indistinct' feeling over narrative logic.

Further levels of perspective/playfulness also invite us to question, yet buy into, the unreality. Li-zhen's ascent of the stairs to Mo-wan's hotel room, a venue for the possible consummation of their relationship, is shot from multiple angles that contradict a sense of continuous direction. Logically, she is travelling toward her destination but the editing gives the impression of her hesitation and internal moral conflict. Mo-wan's closing of the door on her departure also brazenly signals the number 2046, alerting the spectator to the date of Hong Kong's absorption into Mainland China, a *verfremdungseffekt* that sits oddly in such a film steeped in emotion, stepping beyond the narrative to point forward to a key date in a future reality, rather than a nostalgic past. A domestic audience would certainly note the significance. While Mo-wan is a native of Hong Kong, Li-zhen is an immigrant from Shanghai, an aspect that hints at a reading of the film made in the context of the period of handover to the Chinese mainland. It is therefore perhaps significant that it is Mo-wan who becomes displaced and leaves Hong Kong to live abroad.

2046 (2005) is also the title of Wong's sequel to *In the Mood for Love*, which contrarily avoids continuation of narrative, genre, style and characterisation. Mo-wan's character is wholly inconsistent with Leung's portrayal of him in *In the Mood for Love*. He is effectively an entirely different man, indistinct, albeit with the same name and memories. Looking backwards, Maggie Cheung's character is also a supposedly 10-years-older version of her role in *Days of Being Wild* (1990). As that film is set only two years earlier, the logical impossibility again reinforces Wong's 'blurred' portrayal of remembrance.

Chris Berry and Mary Farquhar suggest that *In the Mood for Love* is 'not exactly about a lost love but, more precisely, about an obsession with what might have been. [Combining] allegorical potential with nostalgia and the desire for different futures' (2006: 43). This implies that from the English title, it is the act of *being in the mood* that takes precedent over the love itself. Another untrustworthy aspect of the film's approach to memory, nostalgia and an imagined past comes in its Bangkok location shoot, which evidently seems to have better resembled a bygone Hong Kong than Hong Kong itself.

Whether concerning changing cultural identity or an individual (and therefore perhaps more universal), wider sense of a lost past, the film wallows in its carefully constructed sense of nostalgia through lavish visual presentation, casting of beautiful actors, dreamy construction and lingering soundtrack. The overall effect suggests a feeling of what Pam Cook calls 'prosthetic memory' (2005: 4), a deliberately nostalgic evocation of an idealised past that requires suspended disbelief, 'predicated on a dialectic between longing for something idealised that has been lost, and an acknowledgement that this idealised something can never be retrieved in actuality, and can only be accessed through images' (ibid). *In the Mood for Love* goes further by being a film that is not only conscious of this but at pains to signal it to the spectator, national and international, becoming consciously self-reflective. 'The obsessive desire to recapture the past, accompanied by the knowledge that it cannot be retrieved, is at the heart of Wong's evocation of the diasporic experience of the displaced Chinese communities' (2005: 9).

Further complicating our reading of the imaginary space of *In the Mood for Love* is the inclusion of deleted scenes placed outside of the body of the film on the DVD release. Their presence questions the nature of authenticity in cinematic narrative: should we watch these scenes as 'missing episodes' from 'what really happened' – most importantly, the consummation of the Mo-wan/Li-zhen relationship that the stand-alone film leaves ambiguous? Or are these to be purely read as rejected ideas that exist wholly outside of the narrative? In the current era of the commercialisation of the director's cut, these questions are arguably facile but perhaps worth considering in the context of a film so steeped in the values of subjectivity.

Maggie Cheung Man-yuk and Tony Leung Chiu-Wai as the role-playing Li-zhen and Mo-wan become performers commenting on performance in a highly stylised, romanticised past. These two fine actors convey the complex emotions of the characters with absolute conviction, making them highly artificial yet utterly believable. *In the Mood for Love* stokes the intellect whilst pulling at the heartstrings. The unveiling of subjectivity in cinematic narrative has never been so sumptuously presented.

Further reading

Chris Berry and Mary Farquhar, *China on Screen*, New York, Columbia University Press, 2006.

Peter Brunette, *Wong Kar Wai*, Chicago, University of Illinois Press, 2005.

Pam Cook, *Screening the Past Memory and Nostalgia in Cinema*, London & New York, Routledge, 2005.

Mengyang Cui, *The Cinema of Wong Kar Wai: Chinese and Western Culture Differences in Narrative Cinemas*, Florida, Universal Publishers, 2007.

Tony Rayns, 'In the Mood for Edinburgh', *Sight and Sound*, August, 2000. Available at: http://old. bfi. org.uk/sightandsound/feature/55 (accessed 29 June 2013).

Phil Lloyd

Idioterne/The Idiots (1998)

[Country: Denmark, Spain, Sweden, France, Netherlands and Italy. Production Company: Zentropa Entertainments. Director: Lars von Trier. Producer: Peter Aalbæk Jensen. Screenwriter: Lars von Trier. Cinematographer: Lars von Trier. Music: Kim Kristensen. Editor: Molly Marlene Stensgaard. Cast: Bodil Jørgensen (Karen), Jens Albinus (Stoffer), Anne Louise Hassing (Susanne).]

Synopsis: Following a chance encounter in a local restaurant, a lonely woman named Karen (Jørgensen) meets a group of people known as the 'idiots', a collective whose aim is to challenge bourgeois social norms and to expose middle-class pretensions and hypocrisies. The group members undergo a procedure known as 'spassing' – in which they mimic the behaviour of mentally disabled people – in order to make contact with their 'inner idiot'. Although initially resistant to their methods, Karen is increasingly drawn into the idiots' community, and begins to find an unexpected sense of peace through 'spassing'. Cracks eventually appear within the group, and several members leave the community after its self-appointed leader Stoffer (Albinus) urges them to take their 'spassing' to ever greater extremes. The film's unsettling ending sheds new light on Karen's emotional trajectory and brings into focus the distinction between empty posturing and authentically provocative action.

The Idiots is a film that has shocked and polarised audiences ever since its premiere at the Cannes film festival in 1998. From the film's amateurish camcorder aesthetic and 'politically incorrect' premise to director Lars von Trier's courting of controversy through inflammatory public pronouncements and other publicity stunts, *The Idiots* embodies the spirit of wilful provocation that has since become synonymous with von Trier's authorial persona. But the film is also significant for its relation to several other contexts and debates: as the second film to be released with the Dogma 95 certificate, *The Idiots* reflects on the status of global art cinema at the end of the twentieth century, and opens up new perspectives on debates about cinematic realism. As one of a growing number of art-house films to feature graphic, unsimulated sex, the film is significant for its relation to debates about censorship, and for the issues it raises regarding the ethics of spectatorship in contemporary cinema. In this respect, the film anticipates the trend towards a 'new extremism' in European filmmaking, and finds affinities with the work of a range of contemporary European directors, including Michael Haneke, Ulrich Seidl and Catherine Breillat.[1] Finally, like the other films in the 'Gold Heart' trilogy of which it forms a part, *The Idiots* also raises important questions about gender representation.

The Idiots has garnered a reputation as one of the most provocative films in recent cinema history. Given the film's boundary-pushing premise, it is not difficult to see why it should have achieved this status. However, it is equally important to understand how the context of the film's release contributed to its notoriety. In 1995, von Trier came into prominence as the author of the polemic Dogma 95 manifesto: a provocative series of statements and decrees whose 'supreme goal' was to 'counter the film of illusion' and to 'force the truth out of characters and settings'.[2] Dogma directors would submit to a strict 'Vow of Chastity': ten rules about how films should be made, with an emphasis on authenticity and aesthetic 'purity' over the 'trickery' and 'superficial action' of popular effects-driven cinema.[3] As the second film to be released with a Dogma 95 certificate, *The Idiots* attracted a great deal of early attention as an example of the movement's aims and aesthetics. For instance, in keeping with Dogma rules, *The Idiots* uses location settings and is filmed using handheld cameras; it largely eschews the use of props, sets, and special lighting, and the director remains uncredited. *The Idiots* also ups the ante by including 'real' blood, 'real' sex, and 'real' tears, thus heightening the film's claims to authenticity, and contributing to the film's notoriety.[4] *The Idiots* was one of the first mainstream, art-house films to feature unsimulated sex on-screen, anticipating a wave of similarly graphic films by directors such as Catherine Breillat,

Patrice Chéreau and Christophe Honoré.[5] The inclusion of 'real' sex in *The Idiots* became the subject of much controversy at the Cannes premiere, when British critic Mark Kermode was ejected from the screening after shouting derogatory remarks during the now-infamous 'gang-bang' sequence, in which the idiots 'spass' while having group sex.[6] Despite the inclusion of brief shots of unsimulated sex in this sequence, the film was passed uncut for theatrical release in a number of countries, including the UK, Norway, Sweden and Denmark, and was released with censorship bars over body parts in the USA.[7] The combined allure of the recently launched Dogma 95 movement, together with the scandal created by the inclusion of graphic sex, helped to establish the film's reputation as a genuinely provocative viewing experience. However, it is important to note that while *The Idiots* adheres to some of the Dogma rules, it flagrantly flouts others, such as the use of porn actor stand-ins for the sex scene, and the use of filters in post-production.[8] As many commentators have noted, *The Idiots* should not be seen as a direct embodiment of Dogma rules, so much as a parallel exploration of questions about the 'inter-relationship of truth, reality and fiction'.[9] According to Caroline Bainbridge, this dialectic between 'authenticity and artifice' is at the heart of nearly all of von Trier's films, which are frequently fuelled by an uneasy tension between heavily ironic game playing, on the one hand, and a quest for unbridled emotional truth on the other.[10]

These tensions are distilled in a particularly complex fashion in *The Idiots*, and make for an intensely unsettling viewing experience. On an immediate narrative level, the film calls attention to the uneasy division between sardonic role-playing and authentically provocative action through the device of 'spassing'. 'Spassing' initially appears as an elaborate prank, intended to mock social pretences and to expose hidden prejudices of unwitting members of the public. In early scenes, the fly-on-the-wall style camera observes as group members 'spass' in various public locations, including a factory, a swimming pool, and a local bar. These sequences are highly ambiguous, mining a deep sense of discomfort from the situation, whilst generating a dark humour from the complicity between the idiots' antics and the film's audience. It is important that at this point in the film, we as spectators are 'let in' on the joke; this allows us to laugh along with the idiots, and to find safety in our position as distant observers. However, by the end of the film, the meaning of 'spassing' undergoes a transformation, as Karen responds to Stoffer's challenge to bring 'spassing' into her everyday life. While other members of the group fail to live up to this challenge, Karen's 'spassing' becomes a genuine vehicle for provocation when she uses it to confront her family with the pain and alienation that she has been experiencing since the death of her son. In the film's shocking climax the camera focuses intently as Karen quietly 'spasses' in her family's sitting room, dribbling half-eaten cake and coffee out of the side of her mouth, and arcing her head back slightly. In response, her husband suddenly strikes her across the face. Many critics have commented on the intensity of this sequence and its importance for the film's project of forcing the truth out of the situation.[11] In this scene, Karen brings the shared emotions that her family has tried to suppress to the surface, shattering their reserve, and viscerally rejecting their need for social conformity. This scene also enacts a crucial shift in terms of the way that spectators are positioned. Asbjørn Grønstad notes that one of the reasons why this scene feels so unsettling is 'its subversive intimacy – the sense that we as spectators have been allowed in, as if by mistake, to see something that we were not supposed to see'.[12] In contrast to the black humour of the earlier 'spassing' sequences, the intensity of this scene takes us by surprise, and solicits a very different type of emotional response, in which the safety of our position as distant onlookers is turned against us. Although some viewers accused von Trier of using sadistic tactics – of 'kicking the audience in the face'[13] – several critics have insisted on the deeply ethical aspect of the film's finale. *The Idiots* has played a major role in recent scholarly debates about ethics and film spectatorship.[14] From this point of view, it is important to understand the way that the film stages a series of moral questions for the spectator: How should we react when confronted with difference or disability? Is it ever acceptable to hide behind social scripts and conventions? How should we respond to the suffering of others? How does a society negotiate moral limits concerning depictions of sexuality? Some scholars have argued for the ethical merit of *The Idiots* because of the way that it refrains from supplying easy answers to such questions, insisting that it is up to spectators to chart these muddy waters for ourselves. Michele Aaron argues that *The Idiots* is a deeply ethical film because it actively stages 'the dilemma of implication, and the discomfort of those looking on'.[15]

Finally, *The Idiots* is also noteworthy for its relation to feminist debates in film studies. It is the second film in von Trier's 'Gold Heart' trilogy, which includes *Breaking the Waves* (1996) and *Dancer in the Dark* (2000). With its emphasis on female suffering and sacrifice, this trilogy has fostered much debate around the question of gender representation. Many critics have suggested that the trilogy's association of femininity with suffering, goodness, and transcendence is highly problematic for feminism, because it reinforces stereotypes of female victimisation and male dominance.[16] Others, however, have noted that in evoking such stereotyped images von Trier is drawing attention to, and potentially unmasking, dominant perceptions of femininity in a patriarchal society. Bainbridge notes that the 'Gold Heart' trilogy can hence 'be seen to draw attention to the way femininity often exceeds the boundaries imposed on it by patriarchal systems'.[17] In *The Idiots*, Karen plays this dual role. On the one hand, her fragility and emotional openness, along with her victimisation, can be seen to shore up ideas about feminine passivity and weakness. Karen also follows Stoffer's orders, submitting herself to him as the group's ultimate authority figure. However, her capacity for empathy and her ability to confront her family in such a raw and profound way clearly moves beyond the hollow version of masculine provocation embodied by Stoffer. In this sense, while the film clearly raises problematic issues around gender representation, it can also be read as a critique of the role of women in patriarchal society.[18]

Notes

1. Tanya Horeck and Tina Kendall, 'Introduction' in *The New Extremism in Cinema: From France to Europe*, Edinburgh, Edinburgh University Press, 2011, pp. 1–17.
2. Lars von Trier in John Rockwell, *The Idiots*, London, BFI Publishing, 2003, pp. 81–4.
3. Ibid.
4. Jack Stevenson, *The Idiots*, London, BFI Publishing, 2002, pp. 121–2.
5. Daniel Hickin in Tanya Horeck and Tina Kendall (eds) *The New Extremism in Cinema: From France to Europe*, Edinburgh, Edinburgh University Press, p. 117.
6. Mark Kermode, 'Has Porn Entered Mainstream Cinema for Good?' *The Observer*, 4 June 2006. Available at www.guardian.co.uk/film/2006/jun/04/features.review (accessed 22 June 2012).
7. Stevenson, p. 131.
8. Ibid., pp. 132–4.
9. Caroline Bainbridge, *The Cinema of Lars von Trier: Authenticity and Artifice*, London, Wallflower Press, 2007, p. 93.
10. Ibid., p. 87.
11. See Stevenson 2002, Rockwell 2003, Bainbridge 2007, Aaron 2007, and Grønstad 2012.
12. Asbjørn Grønstad, *Screening the Unwatchable: Spaces of Negation in Post-Millennial Art Cinema*, Basingstoke, Palgrave Macmillan, 2012, p. 17.
13. Stevenson, p. 131.
14. See especially Michele Aaron 2007, Caroline Bainbridge 2007, and Horeck and Kendall 2011.
15. Michele Aaron, *Spectatorship: The Power of Looking On*, London, Wallflower, 2007, p. 104.
16. Linda Badley, *Lars von Trier*, Chicago: University of Illinois Press, 2010, p. 70.
17. Bainbridge, p. 138.
18. Badley, p. 69.

Further reading

Stig Björkman (ed.), *Trier on von Trier*, London, Faber and Faber, 2003.

Tina Kendall

If... (1968)

[Country: UK. Production Company: Memorial Enterprises. Director: Lindsay Anderson. Screenwriters: David Sherwin and Anderson from script 'Crusaders' by Sherwin and John Howlett. Cinematographer: Miroslav Ondricek. Music: Marc Wilkinson. Editor: David Gladwell. Cast: Malcolm McDowell (Mick Travis), David Wood (Johnny Knightly), Richard Warwick (Wallace), Christine Noonan (The Girl), Rupert Webster (Bobby Phillips), Robert Swann (Rowntree), Hugh Thomas (Denson), Peter Jeffrey (Headmaster), Arthur Lowe (Mr Kemp), Mary MacLeod (Mrs Kemp).]

Synopsis: Travis, Knightly and Wallace routinely defy the traditions and Establishment values of their public school. In an attempt to bring them into line, they are beaten viciously by head prefect, Rowntree. This triggers an increasingly surreal series of episodes culminating in an attack from the rooftops with automatic weapons on parents, dignitaries, and boys gathered for the annual Founder's Day service.

Being firmly located within the public school environment *If...* announces itself clearly as a British film and yet the use of this quintessentially national institution as a metaphor for society means the film has much wider resonance. The school system has a clear hierarchy of power and authority maintained by ritual and physical discipline. New boys, like Jute, are indoctrinated into this quasi-society with frightening aggression by those just above them in the pecking order, who are themselves cowed into compliance by the threat of physical violence. Nonconformists, like Travis, Knightly and Wallace, who question the values of the current social order, receive brutal, often sadistic, treatment.

The striking use of images of revolution helps to place this film within the context of a period of intense social upheaval. The boys' common-room walls have pictures of Che Guevara and Geronimo in direct opposition to the paintings of traditionalists, past headmasters or benefactors, looking down on the boys from the dining hall walls. A magazine photograph of a black freedom fighter on Travis's wall is referred to by him as 'magnificent' and the images of lions asleep in a tree may well reference Percy Shelley's 'The Mask of Anarchy':[1]

> Rise like lions after slumber
> In unvanquishable number –
> Shake your chains to earth like dew
> Which in sleep have fallen on you –
> Ye are many – they are few.

The year the film was released saw the youth-led drive towards social change[2] which was such a feature of the early 1960s in the West, culminate in riots in Paris that threatened the future of the de Gaulle government. This is a film that has at its heart contemporary student concerns from the period such as the threat of a nuclear holocaust ('The whole world will end very soon – black brittle bones peeling into ash'[3]) and Third World poverty and inequality in the distribution of wealth ('In Calcutta somebody dies of starvation every eight minutes').

Anderson was a key figure in the Free Cinema documentary movement and is often associated with the early 1960s British New Wave; but this film actually sits a little uneasily in relation to the focus on working-class life found in much New Wave filmmaking. Free Cinema did focus on ordinary people and everyday life, and as a result did in some sense point towards the social realism, but it also emphasised the importance of personal film statements and artistic freedom. This was Anderson's focus, highlighting directors as artists, or auteurs, who were bringing their own distinctive visions to the screen. At the heart of Free Cinema for Anderson was a belief in filmmaking as an art that centred on personal expression and rejected commercial values.

If... is clearly of its time and yet also distinctively different from other British films of the period. Both its form and its content, expressed in the radical attitudes and actions of the central characters, made it challenging to the conservative mainstream. These characteristics link it to an earlier film, *The Loneliness of the Long Distance Runner* (Richardson, 1962); and these two films, one based firmly within an upper-middle-class experience and the other within the working class, suggest the widespread nature of the challenge to the old order in the 60s.[4] And yet, Anderson had his own view on the extent to which *If...* could be said to advocate revolutionary change since he saw the right to challenge authority as central to the British tradition:

> You could say the boys in *If...* were traditionalists. They are part of the tradition of independence, the rights of the individual, the right to question authority, and to behave freely. When traditions have become fossilized, and instances of reaction as well, then they have to be rebelled against. That act in itself is a tradition.
>
> (Friedman and Stewart 1994: 167)

> Anarchy is a social and political philosophy which puts the highest possible values on responsibility. The film is not about responsibility against irresponsibility. It is about rival notions of responsibility and consequently well within a strong Puritan tradition.
>
> (Aldgate and Richards 2002: 209)

Coming from a theatre background, Anderson was interested in exploring the use of Brecht's 'alienation effect'[5] within film. This film offered him the opportunity of bringing to a wider commercial audience the sort of challenging material theatre audiences were becoming used to seeing in the 60s. The film is divided into eight chapters much as a novel might be with chapter headings appearing on screen as intertitles. On the stage Brecht used text in a similar way; in *Mother Courage and Her Children*, for example, a summary of what is about to happen is displayed before each scene. This is an anti-illusionistic technique designed to prevent the audience becoming passive watchers and encourage them to become actively engaged in thinking about what is being presented on stage or screen. The act of reading breaks the illusion of reality that film (and drama) has conventionally been so interested in attempting to achieve, forcing the reader to see the work as a construct that demands to be thought about in an active way. Theoretically, this enables what is shown to be considered in relation to the way in which the viewer can see society as operating outside of the cinema (or theatre). It was a technique employed in theatre in Britain in the period; for example in John Arden's *Serjeant Musgrave's Dance* directed by Anderson at the Royal Court when it was first staged in 1959.[6] This play which according to Arden does not 'advocate bloody revolution' contains a third act in which a group of army deserters train a Gatling gun on a group of townspeople and threaten to open fire.

Anderson also uses the device of changing from colour to black and white film stock to further prevent the audience becoming engaged with the film as a realist text. These changes occur between scenes but also within sequences, and indeed as has been noted seem to obey no particular logic.

> Anderson's use of colour and black and white seems to obey a not always comprehensible logic.
>
> (Murphy 1992: 158)

In Brechtian terms this lack of clear patterning within the choice is part and parcel of the process of disrupting the audience's viewing of the film. The process of film construction is again foregrounded in such a way that the audience is unable to forget they are watching a film that has been put together or constructed. The aim is again to encourage them to think about what is being presented. Usually mainstream film (certainly prior to 1960) would do everything possible to suggest what was on offer was a realistic slice of life. Anderson works to bring this reality status into question, to make the nature of film and the audience experience of it problematic and open to reflection and intellectual consideration. The supposed and usually taken for granted 'truth' of film is brought into question and our position as readers who need to make sense of the text is emphasised. The status of the classic realist narrative (in this particular film but also in all other films claiming that status) is undermined and brought into question.

The third key method used by Anderson to disrupt the viewing process is the movement between fantasy and realism, and indeed making the viewer unsure as to whether what he or she is watching is fantasy or realism. In his book on the director John Ford, Anderson quotes the scriptwriter Dudley Nichols saying Hollywood had been half destroyed by its efforts to achieve 'realism': 'making everything appear exactly as it does to the average man, or to a goat, instead of sifting it through the feelings of an artist' (Anderson 1981: 86).

Unlike Sillitoe, the author of the original short story and scriptwriter for *The Loneliness of the Long Distance Runner*, Anderson and those involved in writing the script for *If...* are from the Oxbridge middle classes and their connection with the working class can never be more than that of privileged outsiders. *Every Day Except Christmas* (1957), one of Anderson's key contributions to Free Cinema was supposed to make ordinary people 'feel their dignity and their importance' (Armes 1978: 266) but in fact comes across as patronising. With the subject matter of *If...* Anderson is able to work from material comfortably within his own experience and create a film that can be seen to stand as a metaphor for society as a whole.

Notes

1. And perhaps points towards the final scenes although it is noticeable that the boys do not rise in 'unvanquishable' numbers with most of them continuing to align themselves with the current order.
2. In Britain, through popular music and fashion, and in their lifestyle choices, young people were challenging tradition values. In America, in cities such as Los Angeles and Detroit, there were black uprisings and increasing identification with the revolutionary aims of the Black Panthers. In 1968 there were student demonstrations and occupations of university buildings across the United States and Europe. The most dramatic events occurred in France where on the 'Night of the Barricades' (May 10) the police were driven from the Left Bank in Paris by students and there followed two weeks of strikes and factory occupations as workers joined the protests.
3. In 1962 the Cuban Missile Crisis had brought the world to the edge of nuclear war.
4. At times *If...* seems to directly parallel *The Loneliness of the Long Distance Runner*. In the final scenes of both, for example, representatives of the various elements of the upper/ruling classes gather to witness the final act of rebellion. But Anderson's film should also be seen alongside Jean Vigo's *Zero de Conduite* (1933) not only in terms of storyline and themes but also in relation to notions of the auteur and the challenge to mainstream society.
5. Brecht's idea was that the audience needed to be 'alienated' from what they were seeing, distanced from what they were watching in order to be able to maintain the position of thoughtful, detached observers. His effort was to break the illusion of reality and prevent that identification with characters he saw other dramatists as attempting to create.
6. Arden described this as 'a realistic play, but not a naturalistic play' and this is very much in line with Anderson's thoughts on *If....*

Further reading

Anthony Aldgate and Jeffrey Richards, *Best of British: Cinema and Society from 1930 to the Present*, London and New York, I.B.Tauris, 2002.

Lindsay Anderson, *About John Ford*, London, Plexus, 1981.

Roy Armes, *A Critical History of British Cinema*, London, Secker and Warburg, 1978.

Ali Catterall and Simon Wells, *Your Face Here: British Cult Movies Since the Sixties*, London, Fourth Estate, 2002.

Lester Friedman and Scott Stewart, 'The Tradition of Independence: An Interview with Lindsay Anderson' in Wheeler Winston Dixon (ed.), *Re-Viewing British Cinema, 1900–1992*, New York, State University of New York, 1994, pp. 165–76.

Jonathan Hacker and David Price, *Take 10: Contemporary British Film Directors*, New York, Oxford University Press, 1991.

Erik Hedling, *Lindsay Anderson: Maverick Film-Maker*, London and New York, Cassell, 1998.

Gavin Lambert, *Mainly About Lindsay Anderson*, London, Faber, 2000.

Robert Murphy, *Sixties British Cinema*, London, BFI, 1992.

John White

Im Lauf der Zeit/Kings of the Road (1976)

[Country: West Germany. Production Company: Wim Wenders Produktion. Director and Screenwriter: Wim Wenders. Cinematographer: Robbie Müller and Martin Schäfer. Music: Axel Linstädt. Editor: Peter Przygodda. Cast: Rüdier Vogeler (Bruno Winter), Hanns Zischler (Robert Lander), Lisa Kreuzer (Cashier) Rudolf Schündler (Robert's father), Marquard Böhm (Man who has lost his wife), Dieter Traier (Garage owner), Franziska Stömmer (Cinema-owner), Patrick Kreuzer (Little boy).]

Synopsis: In a pre-title conversation between Bruno, a travelling film projector engineer, and the elderly de-Nazified owner of cinema, the film cuts to Robert, a newly separated depressed paediatric psychologist, who is driving his iconic Volkswagen Beetle at high speed into a West German border lake. Surviving the half-hearted suicide attempt he hitches a lift with Bruno, who is heading from Hof to Luneburg through the *Zonenrandgebiet* area along the border with East Germany. Following the border, they encounter a recognizably seedier side of life with derelict cinemas and morally derelict characters, overshadowed and overwhelmed by the post-war German history. The two men separate at an abandoned Border post, when Robert departs while Bruno sleeps. At a nearby railway station Robert meets a small boy who is writing a notebook of everything he sees. Robert swaps his sunglasses and his suitcase for the notebook, and boards a train. The ending echoes the beginning, with Bruno conversing with the female owner of a mothballed cinema.

There was once an open wound in Germany, a seeping scar that ran its length and separated East from West, dividing families, and provoking a national psychosis that only began to be healed with the fall of the Berlin Wall in 1989. The duality of a divided Germany was amplified through the massive influence that America had on the West, and that the Soviet Union had on the East, with each half increasingly removed, yet remorselessly connected. It was against this background that Wim Wenders presented *Im Lauf der Zeit/Kings of the Road* in 1976, as the final part of his 'road movie' trilogy; the other parts being *Alice in den Städten/Alice in the Cities* (1974) and *Falshe Bewegung/Wrong Move* (1975).

Its opening of 'Kamikazi' (Robert) driving his VW Beetle into a lake, only to find that it is not deep enough to submerge the car is analogous to the situation of West Germany during the 1970s. The post-war generation, now adults, were facing the challenges of a divided Germany; challenges that led to psychological crisis. Bruno speaks with an elderly cinema owner at the start of the film with little understanding of his Nazi past. The impotence of this generation, cut off from their roots, meant that they too were suffering a deep psychological tear, mirroring the wound slicing their country in half. They were living in an Americanised version of Germany, where American rock 'n' roll filled the air, and American movies filled the screens, and where the country was still occupied by an American Army that had been there since 1945. Yet they still felt German, still were German, and not a sectionalised, divided, occupied and crippled by history German, but a modern, productive German at the heart of a new European sensibility.

Director Wim Wenders was not unaffected by this schism, placing it at the heart of *Kings of the Road*, both in subject matter and in form. Wenders borrows the quintessential American form, the road movie, to explore the snaking border line, where so many roads were now truncated by the barbed wire and no man's land of the Iron Curtain. The road that Robert drives wildly down ends in a lake, one created as part of the border. The point where their journey ends is an abandoned American border post, graffiti covered, derelict, and watching over a border that the west seems no longer to care about and yet which looms silently over the German people, holding them in stasis. Indeed the very end of the film has a mothballed cinema central to the action; a metaphor for the youth of Germany, or possibly a comment from Wenders about the older generation, still quietly holding onto their past and hoping for a reunited Germany that will rise once again. As Wenders himself, put it:

> it has something to do with being born in post-war Germany in a land that tried to forget about its own history, tried to forget about its own myths, that tried to adapt to anything, especially American culture.[1]

Wenders' sense of the rambling road movie is central to an understanding of the lingering, often empty, feeling of *Kings of the Road*. Shot in much the same way as the Hollywood westerns he grew up with, Wenders offers the landscape of the border as a character itself, with Robbie Muller's photography emphasising its interplay with the principal characters. Part of the film has an intensity created through close up shot-reverse-shot sequences necessitated by the settings of travelling in Bruno's van or of the confined spaces in the projection booths. This proximity to the central characters is mitigated however by other exterior scenes where the characters and their situations are dominated by an empty and often barren landscape of the border that serves to amplify their alienation and their rudderless, drift towards an uncertain future. Wenders had taken the model of the American road movie and filled it with European angst, replacing the optimism of a savage land facing civilisation, with the pessimistic remnants of a destroyed civilisation facing an aching emptiness. He combined the road movie with the western, reinventing them, inculcating a new sensibility and in doing so capturing the zeitgeist.

Whilst not formally connected to the founders of the *neue deutsche Kino* (New German Cinema), Wenders certainly fulfils their aims whilst rejecting their uncompromising nature through embracing American cinema and making it his own. Their Oberhausen Manifesto stated, among other things:

> The collapse of the conventional German film finally removes the economic basis for a mode of film-making whose attitude and practice we reject. the future of the German film lies in the hands of those who have proven that they speak a new film language.
>
> This new film needs new freedoms: freedom from the conventions of the established industry; freedom from the outside influence of commercial partners; freedom from the control of special-interest groups. The old film is dead. We believe in the new one.[2]

Kings of the Road can well be seen as a meditation on the Oberhausen Manifesto from a new generation of filmmakers, but it can also be seen as a living embodiment of the manifesto; filmmaking by those who speak a new film language, and who are operating outside of the old commercial parameters.

The film is dominated by Wenders' predilection towards long takes of seemingly inconsequential matter, making the ordinary supra-ordinary, where the events of six and a half days are translated into just over three hours' screen time. As such it captures a realistic sense of male companionship, where irrelevance and separation dominate, and the two men find it easier to bond through singing along to American rock 'n' roll, than through connecting over issues of substance. There is a palpable absence of women in the film (they are present but have no significant role and no significant connection to the male characters), echoing the divided Germany. Bruno and Robert cannot raise themselves from their own disfunctionality, cannot make themselves 'whole' in the absence of women, in the same way that West Germany cannot become 'whole' without embracing its dislocated other half. In capturing this dislocation, this disaffection, Wenders chooses to avoid many of the standard techniques of the Hollywood mainstream – the camera lingers on actions that are usually conventionally excised (Bruno's lengthy walk from projection booth to his van), whilst the editing avoids the conventional cut to a reaction shot, favouring instead a cut to just after a reaction. This absents the conventional signposting and leaves the audience to capture significance from the events seen and engaged with, or not. It is the emotion sitting underneath the seeming emptiness, the moments of quiet, of hesitance between the lines of dialogue that are so affecting. Whilst Wenders cites American filmmakers John Ford, Nicholas Ray and

Sam Fuller as key influences on his understanding of landscape and character, it was Japanese director Yasujiro Ozu whose approach to filmmaking seemed to confirm so much of what Wenders had begun experimenting with. The decentred narrative of *Kings of the Road*, and its ability to deliver narrative without the imposition of storyline[3] are central techniques that Wenders shares with Ozu, and this stripped-down approach is echoed in the foregrounding of elements of both style and content.

The film is shot in black and white (using a mix of 35mm and 16mm stock), flagged to the audience in the title sequence, alerting them to an immediate sense of the alternative to American and European film's concentration on stylised colour palettes. It was a decision that betrays a longing for a past form that was less superficial, or that perhaps presages a distantiation device that he was later to use in *Der Himmel über Berlin/Wings of Desire* (1987). This choice also serves to add a resonance to the desolate landscape, with compositions that deliberately echo the photographs of America taken during the Great Depression by Walker Evan. This particularly stark aesthetic with its socio-political-historical connotations brings a particular depth to Robert's statement that 'The Americans have colonised our subconscious.' It is not simply that the West Germans have been Americanised as the dress codes, the cultural reference points, and even the soundtrack of the film would suggest, but that they have been assimilated into a particular form of American duality – the consumerist and the victim of unrelenting capitalism.

While there is a sense of an empty Americana spilling out from the interaction of the two leads and the treatment of the creative elements surrounding them, there is a distinctly anti-American, or anti-decadent critique present in the film. This is most obviously manifested in the sequence where Bruno enters a cinema that is showing a porn film, where (like all good cinephiles) he finds himself unhappy with the quality of the image and goes to complain. In the projectionist booth the projectionist is caught masturbating and exits rapidly. Alone, Bruno cuts together a sequence of film into a loop of breasts, a burning house, and a woman being raped – a clear criticism of the influence of American cinema at this time. Less obvious but more powerful, is the sequence where Bruno walks to the foreground of a landscape shot, crouches, and defecates. This ultra-realism, this brutal acknowledgement of what it is to be human is defiant in the face of the exploitative fare of mainstream cinema, and also perhaps serves to answer a question posed by Wenders – How should one live?[4] Morally reduced by conventions that barely relate to a national context, or free, even if within the confines of a no-man's land of truncated roads and ambitions?

The film bears all of the motifs that dominate Wenders' subsequent works, roads, railway lines, trackways, and indeed the ever-present separation – the border with its warnings, its watchtowers and its barbed wire. These form the backdrop against which the two central characters discover and restore themselves, and in doing so embody a nation discovering a past not talked of and thereby redeeming itself. Yet with this metaphor it is the border that still restricts redemption as it literally truncates the paths and symbolically truncates all journeys. Wenders concludes the film with the titular track 'King of the Road', a song of the rootless wanderer, and so grants Bruno and Robert their apposite title of 'Kings', though painfully of a divided and psychologically arrested kingdom.

Notes

1. Wim Wenders quoted in Sean Axmaker, 'Road Movie to the Soul: The Cinematic Journeys of Wim Wenders' (27 September 2010), on the Parallax View Blog. Available at: http://parallax-view.org/2010/09/27/road-movie-to-the-soul-the-cinematic-journeys-of-wim-wenders/ (accessed 27 November 2012).
2. Oberhausen Manifesto translation quoted in Nick Roddick, 'The Road Goes on Forever' in *Sight and Sound* (Jan, 2008).
3. Paraphrased from Wenders' own description of what he learned about his own work from watching the films of Ozu in Wim Wenders, *The Act of Seeing: Essays and Conversations*, London, Faber and Faber, 1997.
4. Quoted in Glenn Kenny, Tuesday Morning Foreign Region DVD Report (20th July 2010).

Available at http://mubi.com/notebook/posts/tuesday-morning-foreign-region-dvd-report-kings-of-the-road-in-the-course-of-time-wim-wenders-1976 (accessed 27 November 2012).

Further reading

Timothy Corrigan, *New German Cinema: The Displaced Image*, Bloomington and Indianapolis, Indiana University Press, 1994.
Thomas Elsaesser, *New German Cinema: A History*, London, Palgrave, 1989.
Kathe Geist, *The Cinema of Wim Wenders: From Paris, France, to Paris, Texas*, Ann Arbor, Michigan, University of Michigan, 1988.
Sheila Johnston, *Wim Wenders*, London, BFI, 1981.
Robert Kolker and Peter Beicken, *The Films of Wim Wenders: Cinema as Vision and Desire*, Cambridge and New York, Cambridge University Press, 1993.
John Sandford, *The New German Cinema*, New Jersey, Barnes & Noble, 1980.
Wim Wenders, *Emotion Pictures: Reflections on Cinema*, London, Faber & Faber, 1989.
Wim Wenders, *The Logic of Images*, London, Faber & Faber, 1992.
Wim Wenders, *The Act of Seeing: Essays and Conversations*, London, Faber & Faber, 1997.

Freddie Gaffney

Invasion of the Body Snatchers (1956)

[Country: USA. Production Company: Walter Wanger Productions. Director: Don Siegel. Screenwriters: Jacky Finney, Daniel Mainwaring and Richard Collins. Cinematographer: Ellsworth Fredericks. Music: Carmen Dragon. Editor: Robert Eisen. Cast: Kevin McCarthy (Dr Miles J. Bennell), Dana Wynter (Becky Driscoll), Larry Gates (Dr Danny Kaufman), King Donovan (Jack Belicec), Carolyn Jones (Theodora 'Teddy' Belicec), Jean Willes (Nurse Sally Withers).]

Synopsis: A small-town doctor learns that the population of his community is being replaced by emotionless alien duplicates. As both a tale concerning invading alien pods and a stark critique of small-town America, *Invasion of the Body Snatchers* stands as a significant US film; whether it is considered merely a low-budget science fiction B-movie, a fantastic story that serves as an allegorical warning or an accurate portrayal of suburban life in the 1950s, the film continues to challenge modern audiences.[1] This is a taut mixture of conspiracy narrative and contemporary fears; a film noir tale (Booker 2006: 59), as told by its main protagonist, Dr Miles Bennell, of the 'outsider' as threat to a supposed tranquil American idyll. David Seed rightly places the film within its cultural contexts, stating that

> A cluster of films from the mid-fifties demonstrates a consistent paradigm of such invasion-as-conspiracy where the battle for the nation's mind is played out in Smalltown USA.

In *Invasion* and these other contemporary films,

> The instrumentality of threat comes from outside (creatures from Mars or Venus, pods from outer space) but the real power of these films is carried by their transformation of humans rather than the crude 'monstrous' devices, their fracturing of the nuclear family or local community.
>
> (Seed 1999: 132–3)

The last point is crucial, since the family and community were seen by many politicians, including those involved with the Communist witch-hunts of Senator Joseph McCarthy and the House Un-American Activities Committee (HUAC), as important weapons in the fight against Communism and the socialist threat to American capitalism. *Invasion*'s significance partly lies in its role as a social barometer for America in the 1950s but also in the fact that it dared to compare the imaginary invading 'other' with the then largely unrecognised danger posed by America's consumerist ideology.

Mark Jancovich (1996: 15) points out that most critics of the decade's invasion narratives see them as being inextricably linked to Cold War ideology. American films of the decade, this critical orthodoxy claims, demonised both the Soviet Union and any resistance to the status quo, ensuring that the institutions and authorities of the country were protected from the so-called 'red menace' that was seen as permeating the nation. Americans were given two choices, either support America or be seen as a Communist sympathiser – in *Invasion* this distinction is clearly represented between Miles and the residents of Santa Mira as they try to persuade him to become a pod person. This distinction meant that there was a clear line between right and wrong, America and the alien 'other'. However, Jancovich contends American culture was itself going through a sort of identity crisis as men returned from war to face changes in the work and domestic spheres. The so-called 'suburban dream' was little more than a cover for a loss of individual identity, the threat posed by the Communist as 'alien' was not as pressing as the threat posed by the push to conform: men having to go to work in the city dressed in grey flannel suits and return home to idealised, yet all too similar, modern suburban homes. The technological advancement of consumer culture that had promised so much was instead stifling Americans' own self-worth:

> It has often been pointed out that the qualities that identify the aliens with the Soviet Union are their lack of feelings and the absence of individual characteristics. It was certainly the case that during the 1950s many American critics claimed that in the Soviet Union people were all the same; that they were forced to deny personal feeling and characteristics, and to become functionaries of the social whole. It should also be noted, however, that. it was common in the 1950s for Americans to claim that the effects of scientific-technical rationality upon their own society was producing the same features within America itself.
>
> (Jancovich 1996: 26)

Despite the contradictory reasons for America's feeling of vulnerability in the 1950s, the fact remains that the alien, its desire to conquer Earth and technological pre-eminence, were common themes in films of that decade. Along with *Invasion of the Body Snatchers* films such as *The Day the Earth Stood Still* (1951), *War of the Worlds* (1953), and *Invaders From Mars* (1953) presented America and the world in the grip of emergencies – emergencies 'that jeopardized the future of the race; they were not national, nor even international, but planetary' (Biskind 2000: 102). *Invasion* took that external threat and made it a discernibly internal one by focusing on the invasion of the human body by an alien force (Hendershot 1998: 26). Yet, what makes this film stand out is its constant ability to contradict itself, to offer the audience competing definitions of what might be the most attractive lifestyle to have.

In Miles the audience has an ideal role model, a successful professional man loved by the local community. His race to prevent the pods from spreading to the rest of the west coast and perhaps the entire country is a heroic representation of American masculinity. At that time, such masculinity was valorised as part of the nation's Communist containment strategy:

> the decade's focus on rigid gender roles, respect for authority, patriotism, and hygiene was part of a larger fear that [America] might unravel from within.
>
> (Caputi 2005: 142)

For Elaine Tyler May (1999), the Communist threat could be contained by a return to the family values of a pre-Second World War America where men went to work and women stayed at home. However, with the disruption that the war brought, husbands were displaced in both the home and at work by their wives; this led to a sense of masculinity in crisis as the traditional male breadwinning role became increasingly obsolete. Thus, like the male protagonists of popular books such as Sloan Wilson's *The Man in the Gray Flannel Suit* (1955) and

William Whyte's *The Organization Man* (1956), Miles is a man caught in a suburban nightmare, unable to escape the encroaching conformity symbolised by the white picket fences and mundane daily routine of work and family responsibility. The kiss between Miles and Becky Driscoll towards the end of the film, and his revulsion as he realises she has become a pod person, has been read as an indicator of emasculating femininity and symbolic of Miles' latent homosexuality – a common theme in science fiction films of this period (Benshoff 1997). Christine Cornea, for example, links the role of women in the film to the then contemporary theory that domineering mothers who smothered their teenage male offspring posed a threat to the patriarchal status quo (2007: 43–4). However, what really appears to be at stake here is the notion that America's changing society is the threat to Miles; neither the pods as Communism nor Becky as the feminine are as critical as the choice he has to make between becoming a pod person or continually running from the conformity that a pod society ultimately represents.

When Miles and Becky are confronted by the pod versions of Jack Belicec and Dan Kaufman they are offered the choice to become pod people. The complicated emotions of modern life such as 'love, desire, ambition, faith' would be destroyed and life simplified; and since the pod people have no need for these 'human' traits their society would be one without conflict and pain – Miles and Becky would be 'reborn into an untroubled world'. This scene is an important signifier of the social contradictions at the heart of 1950s America, conformity to the status quo would offer a safe society in which to bring up the nuclear family – free from a Communist threat and wealthy enough to participate in a consumer lifestyle; yet conformity also signals an end to the individualist ethos of American culture – the business ethos of the period was creating a society of 'clones' with no individual creativity. What is truly horrific and unnerving in this exchange and underlies the tensions beneath the film's narrative is that both choices are attractive:

> Amid all this critical activity, one might also note that there is a definite emotional appeal to the idea of being 'taken over' which goes beyond the inherent attractions presented by the pod-psychiatrist in *Invasion of the Body Snatchers*. That added emotional attraction is 'no more responsibility'. Being 'taken over' can be likened to being drafted, to having to follow orders. 'Taken over', we cannot be held accountable for our crimes – passionate or passionless.
>
> (Sobchack 1998: 123)

It is the mundane appeal of conformity, the normality and familiarity of small-town life, which the film makes out to be threatening. The look and feel of the film underscores the contradictions in individual identity; the audience becomes vigilant in watching for anything that looks out of the ordinary. The low-budget mise en scène, black and white colourisation, and flat characterisation contribute to painting a picture of domestic drudgery that was both desired and despised:

> What is visually fascinating and disturbing ... is the way in which the secure and familiar are twisted into something subtly dangerous and slyly perverted.
>
> (Sobchack 1998: 124)

Humans in this film are dehumanised in such a way that we can neither tell them apart nor perhaps want to differ from them.

Note

1. Produced on a shoe-string budget, *Invasion of the Body Snatchers* continues to stand the test of time both visually and in terms of narrative. Contesting accounts of the production budget put the film's price tag as low as $382,000 (LaValley 1989: 3), dead on $400,000 (Booker 2006: 64) and as high as $417,000 (Cornea 2007: 71). In an interview by Stuart Kaminsky (1976: 77), Don Siegel specifies $15,000 went on the special effects that produced the transforming pods and replica corpses. Although these figures appear insignificant compared to other more special-effects-orientated science fiction films of the decade they do draw attention to the understated nature of the film's production and the important role this

plays in the construction of a believable and, at first glance, normal small-town setting.

Further reading

Harry M. Benshoff, *Monsters in the Closet: Homosexuality and the Horror Film*, Manchester, Manchester University Press, 1997.

Peter Biskind, *Seeing is Believing: How Hollywood Taught Us to Stop Worrying and Love the Fifties*, London, Bloomsbury, 2000.

M. Keith Booker, *Alternate Americas: Science Fiction Film and American Culture*, Westport, Praeger, 2006.

Mary Caputi, *A Kinder, Gentler America: Melancholia and the Mythical 1950s*, Minneapolis, University of Minnesota Press, 2005.

David Castronovo, *Beyond the Gray Flannel Suit: Books from the 1950s that Made American Culture*, New York, Continuum, 2004.

Christine Cornea, *Science Fiction Cinema: Between Fantasy and Reality*, Edinburgh, Edinburgh University Press, 2007.

Barry Keith Grant, 'Movies and the Crack of Doom' in Murray Pomerance (ed.), *American Cinema of the 1950s: Themes and Variations*, New Brunswick, Rutgers University Press, 2005, pp. 155–76.

Cyndy Hendershot, 'The Invaded Body: Paranoia and Radiation Anxiety in *Invaders from Mars*, *It Came from Outer Space*, and *Invasion of the Body Snatchers*', *Extrapolation*, Vol. 39, No. 1, 1998, pp. 26–39.

Mark Jancovich, *Rational Fears: American Horror in the 1950s*, Manchester, Manchester University Press, 1996.

Stuart M. Kaminsky, 'Don Siegel on the Pod Society' in Thomas R. Atkins (ed.), *Science Fiction Films*, New York, Monarch Press, 1976, pp. 73–83.

Al LaValley (ed.), *Invasion of the Body Snatchers: Don Siegel, Director*, New Brunswick, Rutgers University Press, 1989.

Elaine Tyler May, *Homeward Bound: American Families in the Cold War Era* (revised edition), New York, Basic Books, 1999.

David Riesman, *The Lonely Crowd*, New Haven, Yale University Press, 1950.

David Seed, *American Science Fiction and the Cold War: Literature and Film*, Edinburgh, Edinburgh University Press, 1999.

Vivian Sobchack, *Screening Space: The American Science Fiction Film*, New Brunswick, Rutgers University Press, 1998.

J. P. Telotte, *Science Fiction Film*, Cambridge, Cambridge University Press, 2001.

Lincoln Geraghty

It Happened One Night (1934)

[Country: USA. Production Company: Columbia Pictures. Director: Frank Capra. Screenwriter: Robert Riskin. Cinematographer: Joseph Walker. Music: Howard Jackson and Louis Silvers. Editor: Gene Havlick. Cast: Clark Gable (Peter Warne), Claudette Colbert (Ellie Andrews), Walter Connolly (Alexander Andrews), Jameson Thomas (King Westley), Roscoe Karns (Oscar Shapeley), Alan Hale (Danker).]

Synopsis: In his book about Hollywood screenwriters, *Talking Pictures* (1975), the critic Richard Corliss suggested you could summarise the plot of this film in a single headline couched in the style of its reporter-hero: 'Star Reporter Trails and Nails Heiress – for Life'. On the run from her wealthy father (Walter Connolly) who disapproves of her marrying a playboy aviator, King Westley (Jameson Thomas), Ellie Andrews (Claudette Colbert) has hopped on a bus to New York to be united with King, but, in so doing, she inadvertently occupies the seat of a brash reporter, Peter Warne (Clark Gable), who has just been fired from his job. Warne quickly sizes up her situation, but promises to help her if he can report her story exclusively and win himself back into his editor's favours. As the journey proceeds, they fall in love.

If the plot is slight, the film, thanks to the inventiveness of Capra and Riskin, teems with memorable bits of comic business. The antagonistic interplay between Gable and Colbert is incessant, ranging from the best way to dunk a doughnut, in which he mocks her refined habits, to the best way to hitch a lift, where she undercuts his arrogance by demonstrating that the display of a shapely leg is more effective than the waving of a thumb. Most famous of all perhaps is the blanket Gable drapes across the middle of their shared motel room – the so-called 'Wall of Jericho' – that decorously separates their living space and which might be Capra's and Riskin's joke at the expense of the new Production Code which was tightening up on Hollywood's depiction of sexual morality. When Gable's character reveals during this section that he wears nothing under his shirt, movie legend has it that the revelation led to a 40 per cent reduction in the sale of men's vests: evidence of Hollywood's influence on the fashions of the time!

It Happened One Night was a runaway hit about a runaway heiress. Opening modestly in New York to respectful rather than rave reviews, it began to gather word-of-mouth recommendation amongst audiences in second-run theatres in the United States and by the end of the year had become one of 1934's most successful films. It then proceeded to win all the major awards at the Hollywood Oscars in 1935 – best film, best actor, best actress, best director, best screenplay – a feat that was not to be equalled until *One Flew Over the Cuckoo's Nest* (1975) 40 years later.

The popularity of the film had taken Hollywood by surprise. It was a modest subject without lavish production values, and was produced by Columbia Pictures which at that time was a minor studio without previous Oscar success. (It was essentially this film that put Columbia 'on the map'.) The original material, a short story called 'Night Bus' by Samuel Hopkins Adams, had been bought for little money and there was comparatively little enthusiasm for the project when it looked like proving difficult to sell as a movie. Two 'bus movies' – MGM's *Fugitive Lovers* (1933) and Universal's *Cross Country Cruise* (1933) – had failed with the public the previous year and there was little expectation that this new vehicle would fare any differently.

Casting also proved a major headache. In his autobiography, *The Name above the Title* (1971), director Frank Capra recalled that several actresses (including Miriam Hopkins, Myrna Loy, Margaret Sullavan and Constance Bennett) turned it down before Claudette Colbert accepted it, although only on condition it would be finished in five weeks so that she could go on holiday and that she would receive twice her usual salary. She still seemed unconvinced the film was anything exceptional, even when it proved popular and garnered Oscar nominations; she had booked a journey to New York on the night of the awards and had to be driven hastily to the ceremony with a motorcycle escort. On loan from MGM, Clark Gable was only cast for the leading role when Robert Montgomery turned it down (on the grounds that he did not want to do another bus movie). With the possible exception of *Casablanca* (1942), it is hard to think of another classic film that had such an unpromising preparation and launch.

Capra was later to claim that a key turning point came with the intervention of the studio's story editor, Myles Connolly, who identified the weaknesses of the original script. Make the heroine not just an heiress but a reluctant heiress, Connolly argued: this will make her more sympathetic to a general audience. Also, if you change the hero from an artist to a working man – a journalist, say – he too becomes a character with whom a popular audience can more readily identify. The plot – a familiar standby about a couple whose initial antagonism on meeting turns to love as they share various adventures – was essentially a modern variation on *The Taming of the Shrew* and that has invariably proved a winning formula. Capra's regular screenwriter at this time, Robert Riskin, got to work on this new concept with his customary intelligence and imagination and the material suddenly seemed to jell.

The spark that ignited all these ingredients was Capra himself, who was just entering the most creative phase of his career and about to become arguably the major Hollywood director of the decade: he was to follow this film with best directing Oscars for *Mr Deeds Goes to Town* (1936) and *You*

Can't Take It With You (1938) as well as making classics like *Lost Horizon* (1937) and *Mr Smith Goes to Washington* (1939). Comedy had always been Capra's particular forte. He had begun his film career in the silent era as a gag-man for the legendary Mack Sennett and then written and directed the early hit comedies of Harry Langdon, *Tramp, Tramp, Tramp* (1926), *The Strong Man* (1926) and *Long Pants* (1927), which had briefly put Langdon on a par in terms of popularity with Charlie Chaplin, Buster Keaton and Harold Lloyd. Always ferociously ambitious in reaction against his impoverished childhood, Capra had moved to Columbia Pictures and had rapidly become their star director. He had made a bold and stylish film about racial prejudice and misunderstanding, *The Bitter Tea of General Yen* (1933); and then been nominated for an Oscar for *Lady for a Day* (1933), being left to squirm with embarrassment when, responding to the call of the presenter Will Rogers, 'Come and get it, Frank!', he realised halfway to the podium that Rogers was actually summoning another nominee, Frank Lloyd to collect the award for *Cavalcade* (1933). This only made Capra more determined to win, and although *It Happened One Night* might not have seemed immediately to be the kind of property that would bring this about, it did have all the components that played to Capra's comic strengths: pace, situations that were funny but also believable, and, above all, a strong and sympathetic sense of humanity across a broad social spectrum. Capra's best films were always to be optimistic fanfares to the common man.

Like Dickens, Capra also always gave as much life to his minor characters as his major ones, knowing that they too had a story to tell, a history and a mystery about them. Roscoe Karnes has an excellent cameo as a salesman on the bus who tries to ingratiate himself with Ellen and then uncovers her identity, only to be frightened off by Peter who pretends to be an armed gangster and that Ellen is part of his kidnapping plot. (It was daring of Capra and Riskin to make a joke about kidnapping so soon after the notorious kidnapping of the child of Charles Lindbergh and its tragic outcome.) Alan Hale storms into the picture when he offers the couple a ride, cannot stop singing in the car, but is revealed to be a small-time thief when he attempts to run off with their things. (Peter somehow manages to overtake his speeding car on foot: by this time, the film is obeying its own comic logic.) There is an especially happy sequence that seems spontaneous and semi-improvised when the passengers on the bus take turns in singing a verse of 'That Daring Young Man on the Flying Trapeze' and where even the driver, hitherto a peripheral and rather gloomy figure, is so caught up in the joyful spirits that he joins in. It is a scene with the kind of vigour and generosity of spirit that is quintessential Capra. Hitchcock used to say that if you have four good scenes, you have got a picture; *It Happened One Night* was taking no chances – it has close on a dozen that live in the memory.

The film has been seen as a trailblazer in being the first successful example of a new genre – the so-called 'screwball comedy'. The term 'screwball' derived from baseball, describing a pitch with a wicked and unexpected curve on it, and also tied in with the English expression of 'having a screw loose' to suggest someone behaving in a lunatic manner. Generally speaking, screwball comedy was noted for its verbal witticism, frantic pace and slapstick craziness, with a particular emphasis on an evenly balanced battle of the sexes and also often a class conflict with a significant wealth divide between the two antagonists that love reconciles. Both *Twentieth Century* and *The Thin Man* had opened in the same year as *It Happened One Night* with some of these characteristics, but the former lacked the sympathetic characterisation of the Capra and the latter allied (and diluted) the sizzling verbal wit exchanged between husband and wife, Nick and Nora Charles (William Powell and Myrna Loy) with a murder mystery plot. Screwball comedy was to achieve its most complete expression in classics such as Leo McCarey's *The Awful Truth* (1937), Howard Hawks's *Bringing up Baby* (1938) and Preston Sturges's *Palm Beach Story* (1942).

Much has been written about *It Happened One Night* in the context of the screwball genre: how characteristic it is and whether it can truly be claimed to be the originator. How far is the film a sophisticated striking back at the Production Code, appearing to adhere to its rules (even down to its 'Wall of Jericho') whilst actually circumventing them? No one could miss the sexual elements in the film even though no intimacy is shown. The film's sexual politics has also generated a lot of discussion over the years. Beneath the wit and the supposed equality of the characterisation, is the film still reinforcing the values of patriarchy, as a rebellious young woman is brought to heel by a man who can control her; or is it alternatively showing a new kind of heroine prepared to sacrifice wealth and position for the freedom to make her own moral, material and marital choices? Whatever one concludes, there is no doubt that *It Happened One Night* was one of those rare screen comedies, like *The Graduate* (1967) in the 1960s, like *Annie Hall* (1977) in the 1970s, that caught the mood of the time, answering an audience's need for romantic escapism and its hope for a harmony between wealth and worth. Capra himself had the simplest explanation for the film's popularity and it may in the end be the most plausible: 'It succeeded because it was pure entertainment, well done entertainment, believable entertainment, and unfettered with any ideas, any big moral precepts, or anything else. Just sheer entertainment, fun'.

Further reading

Frank Capra, *The Name Above the Title*, London, Macmillan, 1971.

Richard Corliss, *Talking Pictures*, Newton Abbot, David & Charles, 1975.

Richard Maltby, '*It Happened One Night*' in *Film Analysis: A Norton Reader*, Jeffrey Geiger and R. L. Rutsky (eds), New York, W.W.Norton, 2005, pp. 216–37.

Ed Sikov, *Screwball: Hollywood's Madcap Romantic Comedies*, New York, Crown, 1989.

Neil Sinyard

Jamón, Jamón (1992)

[Country: Spain. Production Company: Lola Films, Ovídeo TV S.A., Sogepaq. Director: Bigas Luna. Screenwriters: Bigas Luna and Cuca Canals. Cinematographer: José Luis Alcaine. Music: Nicola Piovani. Editor: Teresa Font. Cast: Penélope Cruz (Silvia), Stefania Sandrelli (Conchita), Anna Galiena (Carmen), Javier Bardem (Raúl), Jordi Mollà (José Luis), Juan Diego (Miguel).]

Synopsis: José Luis is an executive at his parents' underwear factory where his girlfriend Silvia works on the shop floor. When Silvia falls pregnant, José Luis promises her that he will marry her, most likely against the wishes of his parents. His mother is determined to break her son's engagement to a girl from a lower-class family, and hires Raúl, a would-be bullfighter to seduce Sylvia.

Early on in Pedro Almodóvar's 1995 film *The Flower of My Secret*, a melodramatic novel by the film's main character is thrown away in disgust. Surprisingly for the author, it turns up later in the film: as the screenplay for a much later work by José Juan Bigas Luna, director of *Jamón, Jamón*. Is this a knowing joke by a filmmaker well known for his tendency to recycle old movies and stories, including his own?[1] Or is it a bitchy suggestion that Bigas Luna's films steal their best ideas, making them little more than trash: the lowest of the low?

A less debatable point regarding Almodóvar's reference is that our familiarity with the late Bigas Luna's films, for audiences outside Spain at least, is a by-product of his fellow director's renown. Peter William Evans suggests that the international success of Almodóvar's late 1980s output, especially the international success of *Women on the Verge of a Nervous Breakdown* (1988), changed the direction of Spanish cinema and facilitated its wider distribution (2004: 22); and it is notable that Bigas Luna had made seven films already prior to his international breakthrough with *Jamón, Jamón*. However, while the distinctive Almodóvar blend of low- and high-cultural reference is very much present in Bigas Luna's film, the tendency to cluster it within largely unspecific conceptions of national or 'Almodóvarian' cinema does not quite do justice to *Jamón, Jamón*'s peculiar vision. Derivative it may be: trash it definitely isn't.

Subject as audiences are to the fads and reductive generalisations of world cinema distribution, reading beyond Anglophone clichés that buzz around *Jamón, Jamón* – 'A wild Spanish paella' that is 'Hot, sexy and outrageous', according to the Tartan Video DVD – is necessary but tricky. This is because the film is largely about such clichés, the problem of acting according to them, and the possibility or otherwise of escaping them. This is emphasised by the way Bigas Luna, along with co-writer Cuca Canals, bind their interrelated characters after the fashion of classical tragedy – or maybe, given the film's incredible convolutions, tragicomedy – where conflicting desires lead inevitably toward disaster.

The film, consequently, is a web of irreconcilable, incestuous passions: Conchita, the wife of a successful underwear magnate, Miguel, loves her spoiled son José Luis, who plans to marry his pregnant seamstress girlfriend, Silvia, but who in reality is devoted to Silvia's mother, Carmen: a sometime prostitute (and sometime lover of Miguel) who runs the local brothel. Conchita hires ham delivery-driver and underwear model Raúl to seduce Silvia, to eventual good effect; in the process, though, Conchita falls in love with Raúl (and, metonymically, the garlic cloves he chews for enhanced sexual performance), while the latter falls for both Silvia *and* Conchita. The denouement of this tragic knot has José Luis, already enraged by Raúl's seduction of Silvia, discovering Raúl and Conchita together in a ham storage warehouse. This primal scene prompts José Luis to attack Raúl with a leg of ham, only for Raúl to kill his rival in like fashion. Too late, José Luis's death brings about a rapprochement amongst the cast of characters, frozen in a classical tableau of grief as a flock of sheep – previously heard in the film's opening – sweep across the scene, returning its doomed players to the dust.

Yet *Jamón, Jamón* exceeds the hyperbole of its plotting, and its possible reduction to farce, firstly in the way its network of impossible desires is used to explore gender performance and sexual politics. Bigas Luna's notorious fixation with breasts, less as objects of erotic fixation than as objects of consumption – both José Luis and Raúl are obsessed with the way Silvia's breasts taste of ham and *tortilla* – emphasises the way the female body signifies dually within normative heterosexuality: at once the possession of the female by the male, but also a possession of the male by the (maternal) female. Notably, the soft-core explicitness of the film, and its possible objectification of the female body (especially that of the then teenage Penélope Cruz) are offset by an emphasis on the male's supine dependency on the breast (especially in the case of the spoiled José Luis), effectively infantilising them and, by implication, the titillated heterosexual male viewer. As the first part in what Bigas Luna called his 'Iberian Trilogy' (*trilogía ibérica*), continuing with *Golden Balls* (1993) and *The Tit and the Moon* (1994), the Catalan-born director is here looking to deconstruct Castilian archetypes and myths: here, that of the mother as giver of milk and object of devotion, but also the sublimated figure of sexual desire. This explains Bigas Luna's decision, in the final credits, to list Conchita and Carmen respectively as *la madre puta* (literally, the mother whore) and *la puta madre* (the whore mother). As John Hooper has pointed out (1995: 166), *de puta madre* – a slang phrase which loosely translates as 'great' – sums up the paradoxes and perversity of this dual image within the Spanish imaginary.

As this outline suggests, though, *Jamón, Jamón* treads a fine line between exploitation and criticism. The opening sequence, with its shot of Bardem's Raúl practising bullfighting, an erection visible through his tight shorts, establishes the film's uneasy tone. Yet this ambiguous approach makes sense in terms of the melodramatic schema Bigas Luna devises for his protagonists, none of whom escape their own subjection to the deep-rooted, gendered national archetypes that deny the possibility of an 'authentic subjectivity' (Evans 2004: 31). The fact that Raúl, for instance, constantly needs an audience for this bullfighting prowess – which in the film, pointedly, is another man, with whom he later practices in the nude – suggests that this *macho* ideal traps him in a narcissistic (and also homoerotic) self-reflection.

Jamón, Jamón in this sense shares aesthetic sensibilities with the Hollywood melodramas of Douglas Sirk (themselves a sizeable influence on Almodóvar's films), in the way an excessive figuration of mise en scène, colour, music and action makes visible to the viewer that which the protagonists themselves fail to see. The film consequently takes place in a kind of mythical desert (Los Monegros, a barren region in northwest Spain), whose enveloping red hue pre-determines the film's violent conclusion. This movement toward bloodshed, fuelled by machismo, is marked by the sign of Taurus: not here the constellation, but the huge two-dimensional bull (formerly advertising placards for Osborne brandy, and still familiar roadside figures throughout Spain) from beneath which the opening camera shot pans down, and under which many of the film's fateful couplings take place. The melodramatic effect – the sense of social actors blind to their own fates, which we can nevertheless foresee – is produced in this gap between protagonist and viewer perception: in the process this becomes the interpretive space for ideological critique.

The key distinction here between tragedy and tragicomedy, or even between early and later (postmodern) melodrama, is the way that the melodramatic gesture – in classical melodrama, a sign of the character's entrapment or oppression by society (see Brooks 1995) – becomes an object of derision, or even kitsch, such is the character's enslavement to now overfamiliar cultural archetypes. Discovering he has been cuckolded by Raúl, José Luis bashes the already-cracked giant testicle of the Osborne bull, until it breaks off and drops; a figure for the emasculation he must endure without resolution until his inevitable death. Similarly, after killing José Luis, and in a clear graphic allusion to the earlier scene, Raúl reaches for the upright circular badge on the front of Miguel's Mercedes (the make of car promised him by Conchita for seducing Silvia and remaining her lover): the badge snaps off in his hand before he falls to the ground, still clutching the symbol of his desire. This last image brings into focus the film's concern with consumerism, representative of Spain's delayed modernisation (see below), which is here wrapped up with other forms of Iberian consumption, sexual and culinary. This connection between all symbolic aspects in *Jamón, Jamón* turns its apparent clichés into coherent narrative images; as in the moment, for example, when Raúl and Silvia noisily consummate their courtship against a cafeteria slot machine, which promptly starts to ejaculate *pesetas*.

These aspects of *Jamón, Jamón* seem like surrealist pastiche, especially as the film makes obvious allusion to the kind of imagery familiar from the films of Luis Buñuel: a dream sequence of a bull's horn being sawn off; a fly noisily crawling over a lover's face; or the incongruous flock of sheep, a direct quote from the end of Buñuel's *El Ángel Exterminador* (1962). It should be clear that such a view underestimates *Jamón, Jamón*'s more critical dimensions; but we should also stress that the film's aesthetic heritage is not so much surrealism, but the less travelled and less translatable quality of *esperpento*. Synonymous with the theatrical work of Ramón de Valle-Inclán, and with its roots in the grotesque realism of Francisco Goya and Miguel de Cervantes, *esperpento* is best defined (in Valle-Inclán's play *Luces de Bohemia* (1920)) as a 'systematically deformed aesthetic': an inverted world whose heroes are represented as if through a concave mirror. In Spanish cinema, this aesthetic finds its most coherent expression in a form of social realist black comedy, in films such as *El Cochecito* (Marco Ferreri, 1960), *El Verdugo* (Luis García Berlanga, 1963) and Almodóvar's *What Have I Done to Deserve This?* (1984).

In these films, made during the period of modernisation within Franco's Spain, the desire for often paltry material goods is juxtaposed with the horrific acts of violence undertaken to procure them: hence in *El Cochecito*, an old man kills his family in order to buy a motorised wheelchair; while in *El Verdugo*, a young father becomes a state executioner in order to secure a new apartment for his family (see Hopewell 1986: 59–63; Kinder 1993: 111–16). As in *Jamón, Jamón*, this is not just a grotesque parody of consumerism, but a parody of Spain itself as (to again quote Valle-Inclán) a 'grotesque deformation of European civilisation'. The national specificity of this aesthetic comes from the violent clash between imagination and brute fact; what John Hopewell calls 'the anomalous abyss between Spain's sublime tradition and ... dismal reality' (1986: 59). In the later *Jamón, Jamón*, then, the discrepancy is between archetypal identification with premodern Iberian traditions, and Spain's entry into the soon-to-be European Union, with its transnational flows of imports and exports (notably, the film's elliptical cutaway shots are dominated by the movement of container-lorries hurtling towards the border, while all the film's cars are German makes).

Seen in this light, the film's moments of incongruity take on a critical but also poignant aspect. The graphic juxtaposition in the film's opening, between the *toreador*'s sword and cape wielded by Raúl, and the chain mail glove, sewing-machine needle and fabric wielded by Silvia, brilliantly evokes this transition from the imaginary to the real; just as the debris of consumption – José Luis proposes to Silvia using the ring-pull from a coke can – drag the film's mythic setting into a disposable consumerist world. The fatal duel with hambones, meanwhile, is not cut-price surrealism, but a parodic visual allusion to Goya's *Duel With Cudgels* (Kinder 1993: 157): a final underscoring of the way this film's characters are bound by iconography and archetypes which impede their psychological progression.[2] But it is also a pointed comment on the way such violent imagery – part of what Marsha Kinder calls Spain's 'black legend' – circulates around Spanish culture, and a reminder of its disturbing appeal.

Notes

1. The plot of Leo's novel in fact forms the basis for Almodóvar's 2006 film *Volver*.
2. Kinder describes the earlier, much less ironic reference to Goya's painting in Carlos Saura's *Llanto por un bandido* (1963).

Further reading

Peter Brooks, *The Melodramatic Imagination: Balzac, Henry James, Melodrama, and the Mode of Excess*, New Haven and London, Yale University Press, 1995.

Peter William Evans, *Jamón, Jamón*, Barcelona, Paidós, 2004.

John Hooper, *The New Spaniards*, revised edition, Harmondsworth, Penguin, 1995.

John Hopewell, *Out of the Past: Spanish Cinema after Franco*, London, BFI, 1986.

Marsha Kinder, *Blood Cinema: The Reconstruction of National Identity in Spain*, Berkeley, Los Angeles, University of California Press, 1993.

Neil Archer

Das Kabinett des Dr Caligari/ The Cabinet of Dr Caligari (1919)

[Country: Germany. Production Company: Decla-Bioscop AG. Director: Robert Wiene (and Friedrich Feher). Screenwriters: Hans Janowitz and Carl Meyer. Art designers: Hermann Warm, Walter Rohrig and Walter Reimann. Cinematography: Willy Hameister. Cast: Werner Krauss (Caligari), Conrad Veidt (Cesare), Lil Dagover (Jane), Feher (Francis), Hans Heinrich von Twardowski (Alan).]

Synopsis: Francis tells in flashback the story of how he and his friend, Alan, had competed for the love of Jane. He recounts the way in which he and Alan saw Dr Caligari and the somnambulist, Cesare, at a carnival in Holstenwall and how Cesare accurately predicted Alan's brutal death. In the story Francis tells, we then see Cesare being sent by Caligari to kill Jane. But Cesare is overcome by her beauty and carries her off pursued by the people of the town. Still in flashback, at a nearby asylum Francis finds that the doctor in charge is none other than Caligari, who has been responsible for a series of murders. Finally, in a twist, the extended flashback ends and we find Francis is a patient in an asylum run by a doctor who looks like Caligari.

Watching *The Cabinet of Dr Caligari* the audience, confined in the world of someone classified as insane, sees what the madman sees: distorted perspectives, eerie lights and shadows, an angular world of fears and apprehension. Expressionist sets are employed in order to convey the asylum patient's thoughts, intensify the emotions of the characters, and emphasise potential psychological depths behind the action. Holstenwall is a bizarre, nightmare-like place, filled with jagged roads, buildings with pointed rooftops, misshapen windows and doors, and drapes that appear to hang above characters as barely concealed threats. The whole town seems about to fall in on itself and engulf the residents.[1]

Made at an early point in film history *Caligari* can be seen as an attempt to release mainstream cinema from any need to be involved in the straightforward recreation of reality. In its use of staged settings and in the performance of the actors this film purposely tries to present a look that is alien and unreal, to create a psychological state rather than a physical reality and, perhaps, in doing so to suggest that the 'real' underlying nature of the world is just such a place of fear and dark forces. The filmmakers are, therefore, both questioning the nature of reality and through example suggesting film is a medium that can do things other than simply offering the photographic representation of life. In doing this they raise the issue of what film should be used for, and contribute towards extending the scope of filmic possibilities.

The fact that the film was stylistically 'different' may have helped it to receive a distribution outside of Germany, and in the process may have assisted other German films from the period to access outside markets. In 1919 German filmmakers were inevitably finding it difficult to arrange distribution of their films in some European markets; the First World War had only just ended and both French and British exhibitors were refusing to show German films. However, French film enthusiasts, intrigued by its challenging style and content, acquired prints of *Caligari* and held their own screenings. Eventually, demand for the film was such that the French government lifted its ban and *Caligari* opened in France in 1922.

Some of its appeal may have been in the fact that it was one of the first horror films. As such it set some of the plot conventions that would be used and reused in coming decades: the evil doctor, or mad scientist, who commits murder through a 'monster' who he controls; the mysterious carnival with freakish, peep-show characters that comes to a town bringing terror; the monster who falls in love with a beautiful, innocent young girl; and angry townspeople who chase the monster out of their community. Of course, in a wider cultural context each of these features of the story is nothing new, having deep roots in the oral tradition of folk tales found across Europe.

The original script from Hans Janowitz and Carl Mayer, without the framing device of Francis telling the story as an inmate of an asylum, amounted to a bleak, pessimistic view of post-war German society. Caligari was evil incarnate and authority was duplicitous, manipulative and, ultimately, murderous. It was their suggestion that settings for the film should be created from bizarrely painted canvases, and the production company then hired Expressionist designers Hermann Warm, Walter Rohrig and Walter Reimann to create the sets.

Twisted shapes, sharp angles, and a conscious avoiding of verticals and horizontals characterise both the exterior and interior sets. But it is not just the sets that are painted in the fantastical style of Expressionism, the costumes, furniture, and even the performances of the actors are integrated into the whole. Both Werner Krauss (Caligari) and Conrad Veidt (Cesare) move in distinctive ways, suggesting they are part of this strange world. Veidt has a tall, thin, angular body and moves slowly, almost gliding along the walls, while Krauss is hunched and moves in short, sharp steps accentuated by the use of a cane. Repeated use is also made of the penetrating, staring eyes of both actors. Heavy make-up, in particular on Veidt's face, emphasises the eyes and creates the appearance of something like a mask.

It may be that the framing story, that makes the whole story seem to emerge out of the mind of a patient in an asylum, was only added when the film was in production.[2] This makes the film 'safe'. The audience is allowed to escape the film's insane world because in the end it turns out to be the harmless vision of someone who is mad, and not a nightmarish reality. And as a result, the filmmakers are able to position themselves so that they are not quite so directly and obviously critical of German society. From this perspective the sets are simply used to convey the thoughts of Francis and to lay bare this character's emotions. The framing of the central story by the episodes in the asylum becomes reassuring; order has been restored in the sense that the murders and the accompanying evil were all simply figments of the imagination of a madman. Yet, the film does still manage to end on a disturbing note: the final shot of Krauss's face is ambiguous and open to interpretation, perhaps Francis was right all along and the doctor is Caligari.

It would be possible to put forward a scenario suggesting that not only those who are murdered, but also Cesare and Francis himself, are victims of Caligari. From this perspective Caligari is seen first, as manipulating Cesare to carry out his wishes[3] and then, second, in his role as director of the asylum, as having Francis totally within his power at the end. Frustratingly for Francis, if we take this viewpoint he alone knows who is responsible for the murders taking place in the world but is powerless to expose the villain; and, disturbingly for us as an audience, the character with the role of hero is unable to defeat evil and restore order. If we do take Francis as the hero and see the close-up of the director's face towards the end as the triumph of evil, then the film as a story has not performed its ritualistic taming of the horrors of the world, the restoration of the world as a place of safety has not been achieved.

In this reading, Caligari becomes an embodiment of evil and the film takes on added symbolic power in its ability to talk about the nature of evil within the wider world. In *From Caligari to Hitler*, the film critic Siegfried Kracauer[4] suggested films from this period had been able to project forward from the contemporary state of Germany in the 1920s to foretell something of the monstrous nature of events that would unfold in the 1930s and early 1940s. Perhaps more obviously, it is important to remember that when *The Cabinet of Dr Caligari* was made the First World War, and the horror of the trenches on the Western Front and starvation at home, had only just ended; and in a powerfully real sense this recent past was still visibly present on an everyday basis in the shape of the physically and psychologically maimed casualties to be found on the streets of German towns and cities. Asylums were full of people who continued to 'live' the full horrors of what human beings were able to inflict on each other.

Undeniably, ideas of death and the bringing of death are at the heart of this film as they are at the centre of other films from the period in Germany, such as *Nosferatu – Eine Symphonie des Grauens/Nosferatu, the Vampire* (F. W. Murnau, 1922). Once we have taken in the dark aspects of *Caligari* we can no longer avoid seeing the simple 'cabinet' of the title as in fact a threatening, if not frightening, image of a coffin, and this may be particularly so if we are aware of the way in which this same image is also used and re-used in *Nosferatu.*[5]

Logically, with an entranced Jane wandering through the opening scene in *Caligari* and Cesare standing in the asylum at the end, the main story has to be seen as arising from within Francis's crazed imagination. Such aspects of the film are clearly a difficulty for any reading that tends towards attaching insanity to the character of Caligari rather than Francis; and yet, it is not always the most reasoned account of events that we take away with us from a film. The power of some of the central images involving Caligari and Cesare as a fairground attraction (along with already mentioned the final image of Caligari looking into the camera in close-up in his role as director of the asylum) live on in our minds in such a way as to imaginatively carry forward the original concept of the writers, Janowitz and Mayer, to present an examination of all-powerful authority as essentially evil.

Interestingly, the stylistic use of visual distortions continues into the final scenes within the asylum. And this clearly raises further questions about how we should interpret the whole film since, even as we realise we have been hearing the story of a (supposed?) madman, we are still being presented with a vision of the world, and therefore seeing the world, as a nightmarish reality. Furthermore, we are also implicated in the labyrinth of possibilities at an additional level. Because of the way in which if we identify ourselves with the listener in the opening scene, by the end we find we have been identifying with a person who is insane. We too are in the asylum where we have been listening to a story told by an inmate. Does that mean we too are an inmate of this madhouse? Does this mean we too are insane or, worse, sane but trapped within the insanity of the asylum? And does the asylum then become a metaphor for the world at large?

Notes

1. The Expressionist movement had an impact in particular on art and the theatre in Europe and perhaps especially in Germany during the early twentieth century. Expressionism aimed to give a subjective view of the world, expressing emotions and feelings rather than presenting an objective view of reality. In theatre, the effort was to use stylised staging and symbolic lighting effects to increase the emotional impact of the work on the audience. The dark cynicism of the new phase of German Expressionism in art that began after the First World War, *Die Neue Sachlichkeit* (*The New Objectivity*), and can be seen in the work of Otto Dix and George Grosz, might also be relevant here. In the work of these artists the subject is often rendered as a distorted caricature.
2. We open with Francis about to tell his story to an inmate in an asylum and close with him still confined within the asylum surrounded by characters resembling figures from his dark imaginings.
3. Cesare, we might note, is not only put into a state where he will not question orders but is also trained to kill to order.
4. Siegfried Kracauer, *From Caligari to Hitler: A Psychological History of the German Film*, Princeton, NJ, Princeton University Press, 2004.
5. There is, for example, an image of Orlok (Max Schreck) entering Hutter's (Gustav von Wangenheim) room in the middle of the night in which the door opens like the lid of a coffin.

Further reading

Stephen Brockman, *A Critical History of German Film*, Rochester, NY, Camden House, 2010, pp. 59–69.

Uli Jung and Walter Schatzberg, *Beyond Caligari: the Films of Robert Wiene*, New York, Berghahn Books, 1999.

Anton Kaes, '*The Cabinet of Dr Caligari*: Expressionism and Cinema' in Ted Perry (ed.), *Masterpieces of Modernist Cinema*, Bloomington, IN, Indiana University Press, 2006, pp. 41–59.

David Robinson, *Das Cabinet des Dr Caligari*, London, BFI, 1997.

John White

Kolya (originally released as *Kolja*) (1996)

[Country: Czech Republic. Production Company: Space Films, Portobello Pictures, Česká Televize and CinemArt. Director: Jan Svěrák. Producers: Eric Abraham and Jan Svěrák. Screenwriter: Zdeněk Svěrák (story: Pavel Taussig). Cinematographer: Vladimír Smutný. Music: Ondřej Soukup. Editor: Alois Fišárek. Cast: Zdeněk Svěrák (Louka), Andrej Chalimon (Kolja), Libuše Šafránková (Klára), Ondřej Vetchý (Brož), Stella Zázvorková (Maminka/Mother), Ladislav Smoljak (Houdek), Irina Bezrukova (as Irina Livanova) (Naděžda), Silvia Šuvadová (Blanka), Liliana Malkina (Tamara).]

Synopsis: In the summer months before the Czechoslovak Velvet Revolution of 1989, the 60-something František Louka (Svěrák) augments his meagre income as a politically suspect cellist in a funeral ensemble by touching up the gold leaf lettering on Prague gravestones. He begins an affair with the singer Klára (Šafránková) and also agrees to marry a Russian woman, Naděžda (Livanova), so that she and her five-year-old son, Kolja (Chalimon), can come and live with her aunt in Prague. He agrees to the sham marriage for a fee that allows him to buy a car and settle some of his debts. Naděžda absconds to West Germany and her aunt is soon hospitalised, leaving Kolja in the crotchety Louka's care. The confirmed bachelor and the young boy struggle to understand each other at first but eventually develop a strong friendship despite police attention and disrupted seductions. The Velvet Revolution comes, Naděžda returns for Kolja, Louka is reinstated in the Czech Philharmonic and Klára is pregnant.

Kolya is perhaps best known as the first film from the former Eastern bloc to win an Academy Award (for best foreign language film) since the fall of the Berlin Wall in 1989. Jan Svěrák's first feature, *The Elementary School* (*Obecnáškola,* 1991), also scripted by Zdeněk Svěrák, was nominated in the same category five years earlier and Svěrák's short student film, *Oil Gobblers* (*Ropáci,* 1988) also won a number of film festival awards from around the world. The father and son team have won a number of Czech Lions, the country's Oscar equivalent, with Svěrák junior winning best director for *Kolya*, *Tmavomodrýsvět* (*Dark Blue World,* 2001) and *Vratné lahve* (*Empties,* 2007) while Zdeněk Svěrák's screenplays for the first two films were also winners.

There are a number of clear themes that run through *Kolya*. Most obvious perhaps is the importance of freedom, both personal and political. Louka is relatively free in the sense that he has no family ties and, at 60, is still living the life of a seducing bachelor with no particular dependents, apart from his mother for whom he has already provided. *Kolya* is the middle film in the Svěráks' 'maturation' trilogy, beginning with childhood (*The Elementary School*), moving onto middle age in *Kolya* and then finally ending with retirement in *Empties*.[1] Thus, *Kolya* shows the gradual change from carefree youth to responsible adulthood, even though Louka is perhaps a little late in coming to this stage. It is only when unexpected fatherhood is thrust upon him that Louka learns to care for someone other than himself and so gives up certain freedoms in favour of the other great theme of the film, love.

While his initial freedom is based on selfishness, to find true love Louka must give up his self-interest and embrace the needs of others. Kolja is the initial catalyst but soon Louka begins to engage and empathise with others, particularly his soon-to-be pregnant lover, Klára. His move to monogamy is heralded by the *deus ex machina* of the Velvet Revolution, to use Jan Čulik's formulation. Just as he, and the country he represents, gains political freedom so he gives up the fleeting and lonely pleasures of bachelorhood.

The third theme of the film is death. Represented most obviously by the funerals at which he plays cello and by the gravestones that he restores. Čulik sees this as an 'apposite metaphor for life in communist society during normalisation' where life has been all but extinguished and 'limited to the minimal necessities of existence' (Čulik 2007: 88).

Thus, while Louka goes through the motions of life he is figuratively dead and is only brought back to life through his relationship with Kolja, whose naive drawings, linked to Louka's own gold leaf lettering, feature crematoria and corpses.

There are number of symbolic objects and other motifs that occur in the film and it is their materiality that seems to be central to the thinking of *Kolya*. Firstly, touch itself is foregrounded. The first shot of the film during the opening credits is of clouds, which we quickly realise are seen from an aeroplane as a young boy's hand presses against the aircraft window leaving a misty print. This is our first introduction to Kolja and, of course, it is his touch that will change Louka's life. We are introduced to Louka himself in the next scene where we see his fingers playing the cello before we see Svěrák's well-known face. His cello playing is quickly sexualised when he uses the bow to lift Klára's skirt to expose the back of her legs as she sings a piece from Antonín Dvořák's biblical songs. This ironic juxtaposition of high seriousness and good-natured bawdiness is echoed in the contrast between the grand locale of the funeral and Louka's threadbare socks – he takes his shoes off to play in comfort – and homely soup flask. Shortly afterwards Louka and Klára touch each other in a post-coital game instigated by her hiccups which, she says, always come on 'after it'. Louka's cello is further associated with sex when his young Slovak pupil, Blanka (Šuvadová), visits him in his picturesque tower flat and grips the cello between her legs suggestively. Louka's seduction however is interrupted by a phone call announcing Naděžda's defection to West Germany and this will inevitably lead to Kolja's arrival at his flat. At first Kolja rejects Louka's touch, flinching when he tries to comfort the weeping boy and refusing to take Louka's hand as they cross a busy street.

As the pair become more used to each other, we gradually see more intimate moments of touch especially at bath time until, as they leave the hospital where Kolja's grandmother has just died, he looks up at a typical Czech pedestrian crossing sign which shows an adult man in an anachronistic hat holding the hand of young child, and Kolja takes Louka's hand. From this moment on their relationship strengthens and they are often shown physically close. At the end of the film Kolja rides on Louka's shoulders as they join the protest crowds in Wenceslas Square and also when they go to Prague airport to meet his mother. In an image familiar from the film's poster, Kolja playfully places his hands over Louka's eyes indicating the level of trust between man and child. As Kolja finally embraces his mother and both fly to the West we see a repeat of the first image of clouds with the boy's hand pressed against the window, once again leaving an outlined handprint on it. The first time we see this image it is Kolja's farewell to Russia, now it is a goodbye to Louka. Kolja's life had been dominated by women and he now leaves a new father for an even newer one in the West. Louka plays his cello in his reinstated position in the Czech Philharmonic, intercut with documentary sequences from the actual concert conducted by Rafael Kubelík performing Bedřich Smetana's *Mávlast* (*My Country*). Klára touches her pregnant stomach as she looks on from the gathered crowd. All the connections have been made and the Russian Kolja conveniently flies off elsewhere once his magic spell has been cast and Louka has learned to touch.

The language clash between Louka and Kolja, the Czech and the Russian, is central to the comedy of the film. While every Czech was supposed to have learned Russian at school, Louka proudly displays his ignorance of the language as one of his many petty rebellions. They communicate mainly through gesture and Slavic similarity and this leads to one of the important moments of comic misunderstanding when Louka is forced to display the Czech and Soviet flags in his flat window to demonstrate Czech-Soviet friendship. Kolja points to the flags and says, in Russian, 'Ours is red', which confuses Louka as the Russian красный (red), sounds exactly the same as the Czech 'krasný' meaning 'beautiful'. 'What's so beautiful about it?' he wonders.

It is the women in Louka's life who are able to speak to Kolja in Russian. Blanka greets him enthusiastically in Russian while one of Louka's mistresses, a schoolteacher, reads Kolja a fairytale over the telephone. Earlier, in one of the film's more touching scenes Kolja tells his dead grandmother that he misses her, using the shower attachment in the bath as a spectral telephone.

Kolja's understanding of Czech quickly improves and even Louka manages to dredge up some Russian vocabulary. The most significant word he uses is the heavily accented 'Čemodan', a word meaningless in Czech, for Kolja's small, battered suitcase. It is this suitcase that heralds Kolja's arrival and departure and Louka's use of the Russian word for it emphasises its role as a literal transitional object.

Before making the decision to marry Naděžda, Louka visits his mother's village and while clearing out her gutters finds a jewellery pendant which initially looks as if it might solve her money worries, but turns out to be worthless. The pendant reappears a number of times during the film and there is speculation that it may have been thrown into the gutter during a lovers' tiff. A more sensible explanation is offered by Klára who suggests that it would probably have been dropped by a magpie or jackdaw. She says, 'It's still beautiful, even if it's worthless'. Louka's actions are initially motivated by money but at the end of the film he realises that it is those things that cannot be bought – love, friendship, trust – that define what it means to be truly human. Ironically, of course, the freedom that is about to arrive will be one in which the human is even more brutally reduced to monetary worth.

The 1968 Soviet invasion and occupation of Czechoslovakia is central to *Kolya*, as is the Czech loathing of Russians. Louka helps Kolja's mother leave Russia, admittedly out of self-interest, and is then suddenly landed with the unwelcome guest. Kolja is the metaphorical invader who stands in for the two major Soviet arrivals into Czechoslovakia: liberation from Nazi rule in 1945 and the imposition of normalisation in 1968. However, as Dina Iordanova points out, Kolja is not so much a threat to Louka as a nuisance.[2] In fact, Kolja's presence makes it easier for Louka to pretend that his sham marriage was indeed genuine: why else would he take charge of a five-year-old child? For Iordanova, Louka's relationship with Kolja is an ironic post-colonial rereading of the Soviet subjugation of Czech freedom as Louka's literal subservience, as he kneels to put on Kolja's slippers, becomes the sign of a Czech acceptance of Russian humanity.

While Louka is initially inconvenienced by Kolja's presence, the boy's absolute vulnerability and dependence allows Louka to feel sympathy for the young Russian and by extension for all the Soviet occupiers who have always been treated by the Czechs as usurpers. The Russian family we meet at the wedding ceremony are friendly and the two soldiers who Kolja befriends outside Louka's mother's house are shown sympathetically. When they ask to wash their oil-stained hands, they politely accept Louka's obvious lie that the water has been cut off. Louka is clearly uncomfortable with his own mother's absolute antipathy to both the Russian soldiers and to Kolja. The film argues that the Soviets are now weak and therefore should be treated with compassion and should ultimately be forgiven for past transgressions because, like the child Kolja, they have had no real choice in their actions. Sympathy for the foreign occupier and for their Czech collaborators is the central message of the film. The Svěráks make a plea for forgiveness and an understanding of mutual humanity which echoes the broadly humanist politics of both Václav Havel and T. G. Masaryk, respectively the late playwright-turned-president of post-communist Czechoslovakia and the philosopher-president of the first democratic Czechoslovak Republic between the two world wars.

Kolya's lush photography, back-lit mise en scène, sentimental humanism and gentle irony combine to make a film that, despite its broad appeal, manages to negotiate the tricky terrain between the harshness of political history and individual desire in a way that betrays neither.

Notes

1. See Eddie Cockrell, Review of *Empties* (*Vratne lahve*). *Variety*, 407, 2007, p. 29.
2. See Dina Iordanova (2008) Kolya (1996) Jan Svérák. [online] Dina View. Available at: www.dinaview.com/?p=194 (accessed 30 May 2012).

Further reading

Jan Čulik, *Česká společnost v hraném filmu devadesátých a nultých let* [What We Are Like: Czech Society in

Feature Films of the 1990s and 2000s], Host, Brno, 2007.
Peter Hames, 'The Ironies of History: The Czech Experience', in Aniko Imre (ed.), *East European Cinemas*, New York and London, Routledge, 2005, pp. 135–50.
Peter Hames, *The Czechoslovak New Wave* (2nd ed.), London, Wallflower Press, 2005.
Peter Hames, *Czech and Slovak Cinema: Theme and Tradition*, Edinburgh, Edinburgh University Press, 2010.

David Sorfa

Kukuli (1961)

[Country: Peru. Production Company: Kero Films. Producers: Luis Arnillas, Enrique Meier, Enrique Vallve. Directors: Luis Figueroa, Eulogio Nishiyama, César Villanueva. Screenwriters: Hernán Velarde (Quechua dialogue), Luis Figueroa, César Villanueva, Sebastián Salazar Bondy. Editor: Ricardo Rodríguez Nistal. Music: Armando Guevara Ochoa. Cast: Judith Figueroa (Kukuli), Victor Chambi (Alaku), Lizardo Pérez (Ukuku), Emilio Galli (Cura/Priest), Felix Valeriano (Machula/Grandpa), Martina Mamani (Mamala/Grandma), Simón Champi (Brujo), Mercedes Yupa (Mercedescha), Eduardo Navarro (Narrator).]

Synopsis: Kukuli, a young llama herder lives a simple life with her grandparents high in the Andean mountains of Paucartambo, in the countryside of Cuzco. She leaves to attend the annual Feast of Mamacha Carmen in the town of Paucartambo. On the way she meets Alaku, a mestizo who has lost his land. He seduces her, and they enter into servinakuy (trial marriage). Continuing their journey to Paucartambo, they consult a sorcerer with a llama skeleton hung outside his house. Reading the coca leaves, the sorcerer notes Alaku's lack of a home and declares that death accompanies them. Fleeing in fear, the couple reach Paucartambo where, during the fiesta Alaku is killed by the Ukuku, a legendary figure, half man, half bear, who also abducts Kukuli. In death, the lovers are transformed into llamas: one white and one black; and they fall in love again.

Kukuli is one of Peru's rarest feature fiction films. It was the world's first 35mm film to use the Quechua language, and is considered by many film historians to be central to the birth of a distinctive national cinema for Peru.[1] It was nominated for international awards at the time of its release, such as for the 'Grand Prix' for the trio of directors from the second Moscow International Film Festival, 1961, and is considered a landmark for contributing to the portrayal of the ancient cultures of South America and Peru.

Dedicated to 'the Indians of Peru', *Kukuli* was the first fiction film produced by the *Cienma School of Cuzco*, an important movement that began as an influential screening club and which later also supported the production of documentary and feature films. These films were made in and around the ancient Andean city of Cuzco between 1955 and 1966 by indigenous filmmakers, and drew on local customs, rituals and legends for their inspiration. The two main objectives of this School were to promote the production of local films, and to exhibit non-commercial domestic and foreign films with the aim of contributing to the development of local culture. They also organised events, such as seasons of European cinema, that helped to raise funds that would support local filmmaking. Even when they stopped working as a collective, the independent filmmakers continued to have the Andean world as their core theme, and placed emphasis on giving a voice to the indigenous world of rural Peru. The Cuzco School is considered to be one of the inspirations for the indigenous film movements of today, united by a desire to use cinema to tell stories and express culture themselves rather than finding themselves portrayed as the 'Other' by filmmakers from elsewhere.[2]

Filmed on location in the communities of Paucartambo and Mollomarca, *Kukuli* is essentially a work that seeks to integrate authentic representation with imaginative form. Adapted from a local myth, it presents a hallucinogenic mix of love story and animistic Peruvian mythology. Regarded by many as a piece of cinematic poetry, it recounts the legend of the seduction of Kukuli, a shepherdess, by Alaku, and her subsequent kidnap by the beast of the mountains, the *Ukuku*. The apparent narrative simplicity provides the framework for the exploration of the symbolic significance of the dances, festivals, customs, everyday rituals and beliefs of the indigenous people of rural Peru. As such it is also a provocative political statement that sets out to reclaim a stake in the discourse of national identity that was dominated by the coastal, mestizo culture of Lima and the conservative regime of President Manuel Prado, who was against the depiction of indigenous Peruvians and their culture on screen. The film's soundtrack recorded in China using the Peking Symphonia, a fact that had to be hidden for a long time since travel to socialist countries was strictly forbidden by the right-wing regime of the time. Moreover, its blend of the material and the supernatural, with exquisite work on colour and sound and a deliberately lyrical script, demonstrates the influence of the European surrealists whom Figueroa met while in Paris in the 1950s, and with whom he discussed the potential of magical realism as an effective and valid aesthetic approach for politically committed cinema.

Despite concerns about its politics and its rather esoteric aesthetic approach to style, the film was enthusiastically received by domestic audiences. One of the first reviews following its premiere in Lima described it thus:

> *Kukuli* narrates an Andean legend in colourful images; this is a love story that highlights the desperate isolation of the young couple, the purity of feeling that unites them, the guilty indifference of other men. Everything plays out with unforgettable serenity along the path that destiny seems to have assigned to the people of the mountains.
>
> (Claudio Capasso, *El Comercio*, July 1961)

European critics were likewise full of admiration at what the filmmakers had achieved with such meagre resources, and regarded it as a key work in the development of a distinctive Latin American cinema that eschewed Hollywood styles and drew instead on such movements as Italian neo-realism and surrealism:

> *Kukuli* is an inspiration for Latin American film-makers, expressing with images the soul of the mountain villages, very profoundly, in a bid to react against cultural colonisation, particularly through the art of cinema.
>
> (Julián Garavito, *Europe*, July–August 1966, Paris)

Moreover, the themes dealt with by this landmark film are of enormous relevance to its context, covering class, gender, social and race relations. The marginalisation of the two young protagonists when they arrive in Paucartambo from the mountains, for example, is crucial to an understanding of how difference was viewed as something dangerous and to be feared. Their failure to understand the local rituals and symbols is in part responsible for their deaths. Horror and beauty are intermingled through character, landscape and narrative, and through the juxtaposition of images of extreme poverty with those of great harmony.

There are several ways of interpreting the figure of the Bear (Ukuku) and the myth from which this film has been adapted: some have argued that it is an allegory for the first sexual experiences of young indigenous people, while others, notably filmmaker/academic Gabriela Martínez (2006), have suggested that the Bear instead represents the colonial 'Conquistadors' and their descendants who have not only exploited the land but have also abused the local young women. Martínez also proposes that the scene when Kukuli first encounters Alaku is not one of horrific violation (as it certainly appears if one reads the young woman's face as an expression of fear) but of playful seduction, drawing on the local Quechua notion of the *pukllay* (literally means 'game' or 'playful' but in the context of male-female relationships means reciprocal 'courtship' which might lead to sexual relations and an agreed quasi-marital arrangement called *sirvinakuy*). For renowned critic-author Ricardo Bedoya, the film's meaning is very clear:

> It is a journey of initiation through the most characteristic spaces and myths of Andean culture. She experiences sex, desire, and the mythological violence embodied by the 'Ukuku', the bear who steals little girls. Kukuli is the embodiment of an image of the Andes as legendary and outside of time.
>
> (2010: 155)

Screenings of *Kukuli* were until very recently extremely rare mainly due to the loss of the negative during a fire at the processing lab in Buenos Aires in 1970. However, it was recently restored by German film conservationists, and is now selected quite regularly for screening at significant events celebrating Peruvian culture around the world.[3] Moreover the use of a female protagonist, one of very few representations of Andean women in Peruvian fiction cinema, has been influential on contemporary filmmakers such as Claudia Llosa, whose second feature, *Milk of Sorrow*, is discussed on p. 518.[4] Perhaps even more significant in terms of the legacy left by this film, and the Cuzco School more generally, is the impact made on inspiring subsequent generations of filmmakers based outside the capital of Peru to continue to use cinema as a means of exploring and expressing their own lives, communities, identities and ambitions on screen. Names such as Flaviano Quispe, Omar Ferero, Mélinton Eusebio and Daniel Nuñez are all now familiar and respected amongst the Peruvian filmmaking world, and several are well known internationally via festival appearances, and via the many more opportunities to generate awareness of their work that is afforded by social media networks.

Notes

1. The film's dialogue is entirely in Quechua, a bold but important decision given the stigma against the regional language at the time, when Castellano (Spanish) was the only official language of Peru, even though around 40 per cent of Peruvians spoke the indigenous language.
2. See Edward Said's work on the 'Other' in *Orientalism*, first published in 1978 and reprinted as a 25th anniversary edition in 2003. Although Said's focus was on the 'East', his understanding of the way the West has developed romantic and exotic pictures of Oriental cultures, and may be viewed as a reflection of European imperialism and racism is in many ways relevant to depictions of and relations with cultures from more remote parts of Latin America. This notion was also set out by the 'indigenista' movement, whose main proponent was the Peruvian intellectual and author José Carlos Mariátegui (1894–1930).
3. The newly restored print was shown at a screening in London 2011 as part of the season of events celebrating Latinos in London.
4. Llosa's debut feature *Madeinusa* (2006) offers an updated view of life for young women in the Andes, drawing also on the dialogue between horror and beauty that dominates the landscape, and upsets any preconception of peaceful coexistence.

Further reading

Marc Becker and Harry E. Vanden, *José Carlos Mariátegui: An Anthology*, New York, Monthly Review Press, 2011.

Ricardo Bedoya, 'Peru: Films for After a War', Eduardo Angel Russo, ed., *The Film Edge: Contemporary Filmmaking in Latin America*, Buenos Aires, Teseo, 2010, pp. 145–58.

John King, *Magical Reels*, London and New York, Verso, 2000.

Gabriela Martínez, 'Kukuli and the Cuzco School of Cinema', *Cronicas Urbanas*, No. 11. Editorial Guamán Poma de Ayala, Cusco, Peru, 2006.

Edward Said, *Orientalism, 25th anniversary edition*, London, Penguin, 2003.

Cine Andino de Luis Figueroa Yábar, http://luifigueroa.blogspot.com/, 2007

www.youtube.com/watch?v=MJEJCjDsv-c (clip of *Kukuli*)

www.youtube.com/watch?v=kTasAshilWo& feature = related (clip of film about Figueroa)

Sarah Barrow

Kurutta ichipeiji; sometimes *Kurutta ippeiji/A Page of Madness* (1926)

[Country: Japan. Production Company: Shinkankakuha Eiga Renmei and Nashonaru Āto Firumusha. Director: Teinosuke Kinugasa. Story: Yasunari Kawabata. Screenwriters: Yasunari Kawabata, Minoru Inuzuka, Bankō Sawada, Teinosuke Kinugasa. Cinematographer: Kōhei Sugiyama. Art directors: Kasaku Hiyashi, Chiba Ozaki. Lighting: Masao Uchida. Editor: Umeko Numazaki. Music (1971): Modern Bamboo Flute Ensemble. Composer: Minoru Muraoka. Arrangement: Yo Kurishima. Cast: Masao Inoue (The Janitor), Yoshie Makagawa (His Wife), Ayako Iijima (Their Daughter), Misao Seki (The Chief Doctor), Eiko Minami (The Dancer), Kyōsuke Takamatsu (The Bearded Patient/ Patient B), Shintarō Takiguchi (The Gateman's Son) (Western style – family names last).]

Synopsis: A woman is committed to a mental institution after her baby drowns while her sailor husband is away. He is now a janitor at the asylum. Their adult daughter is about to marry but is worried about her fiancé's reaction to her mother's madness. She visits the asylum and is surprised to find her father working there. A bearded patient attacks her in the gardens but the daughter runs away. One of the inmates dances and rouses the asylum into a frenzied riot during which the wife is thrown to the ground by the same bearded patient. The janitor attacks him and is reprimanded by the asylum director. Back in his room, the janitor dreams of winning a lottery prize that he can give to his daughter as a wedding gift. He tries to persuade his wife to escape the asylum but she is afraid to leave. He dreams that in the escape he kills the director and that his daughter marries the bearded patient. The next day he imagines that he gives all the patients folk masks and dons one himself. Later he mops the floor of the asylum as the bearded patient bows to him.

Teinosuke Kinugasa (1896–1982) began his career in film as an *onnagata*, acting female roles, before becoming a director in the early 1920s. *A Page of Madness*, inspired partly by Kinugasa's visit to Tokyo's Matsuzawa mental hospital, was his first real success and was supported by a number of influential figures. Yasunari Kawabata, who would go on to win the Nobel Prize for Literature in 1968, was commissioned to write a 'good, artistic film' and the celebrated actor Masao Inoue starred as the janitor. The film, while produced independently, was supported by the major film studio Shōchiku and a managing director, Shirai Shintarō, offered Kinugasa the use of an abandoned studio in Kyoto free of charge. Shōchiku also invested in the film which eventually cost around 20,000 yen, more than most high-budget studio productions of the time (Gerow 2008: 22–7). The film was first screened publicly in Tokyo on 10 July 1926 and received mixed reviews which saw the film as, either bravely experimental, elitist, or even highly accessible and realistic (see Gerow 2008: 56–64). The film disappeared soon afterwards and Kinugasa assumed that the print had been destroyed in a fire at the Shōchiku studios. In 1971, however, the director found two prints concealed in rice cans in his old house and the film was restored with an added soundtrack and rereleased in 1975.

The film was associated with the Shinkankaku (new impressionist) school of avant-garde and modernist literature, not least since Kawabata and a number of the other writers associated with the film[1] were allied with the Shinkankaku. This movement acknowledged the influence of cubism, futurism and surrealism and therefore it is not surprising that traces of these are often discerned in *A Page of Madness*. More radically, Shinkankaku rejected traditional literary and other artistic forms as 'yesterday's shit' (Peterson 1989: 38), and the film has been read as an oppositional political tract. Gerow is careful to position Kinugasa within the existing Japanese avant-garde and within independent and experimental cinema of the time, particularly the Pure Film Movement, in contrast to the sense in the 1980s that Kinugasa arrived at the making of the film *ex nihilo* with 'no cinematic training, with no overpowering influences. a completely personal poetic statement in cinema' (Richie quoted in Gerow 2008: 20).

A Page of Madness has no intertitles and was designed to be projected without the usual accompanying commentary of a *benshi* actor. Kinugasa particularly cites the importance of F. W. Murnau's *The Last Laugh* (*Der letzte Mann*, Germany, 1924), another attempt to dispense with intertitles, to this approach. The film attempts to present the subjective mental experience of many of its characters while still maintaining a surprisingly straightforward sense of narrative. The film experiments with cinematography to present the personal viewpoints of various characters and Peterson identifies a number of innovative technical devices that occur throughout the film: superimpositions, distortion of the image with a curved mirror, whip pans, spot lighting, split screens, upside-down footage and soft focus (Peterson 1989: 42). The editing structure of the film often confuses the reality of the mental asylum with recollections, hallucinations and characters' subjective perception of themselves. This last feature is perhaps the most sophisticated and Gerow comments that 'subjective depictions were prominent in Shinkankaku writing but less in order to authenticate the perceiving subject than to explore how immediate subjective impressions could complicate subjective unity' (Gerow 2008: 14). *A Page of Madness* quite radically undermines the stability of not only what we see but who the characters in the film really are. For Gerow, the film tries to show subjective states through the manipulation of cinematography and editing rather than through mise en scène like *The Cabinet of Dr. Caligari* (Gerow 2008: 80).

The most obvious understanding of the film is that it is told mainly and fairly reliably from the point of view of the janitor with frequent switches to the subjective mental states of other characters, most notably his wife, who recalls the circumstances of her baby's drowning, and the dancing woman. The dancer's representation appears to be her own imagining of herself as a Kabuki performer in front of a striped, revolving ball. This creates a moiré pattern that is echoed in frequent images of cell bars but also in the button that the wife frequently uses to facilitate her hallucinations. What is striking about the dancer's vision of herself is that her fellow inmates seem to be able to see it as well. The film argues that there is no particular distinction between subjective and objective realities, and that personal subjective states are available to others within the diegesis just as they are available to the cinematic spectator. Gerow explores the porous nature of borders within the film in some detail and argues that the circular motif (balls, wheels, dots) represents the unstable division between sanity and madness 'which underlines fears regarding the fate of repetition (for example, the fear that the insane [the mother] will breed the insane [the daughter])' (Gerow 2008: 87). The fear that madness is always about to engulf sanity is particularly played out in the figure of the janitor who, while ostensibly sane, occupies a rather ambiguous position in the asylum and there is a suggestion – although this is never concretised – that he is either not there (he sometimes appears as a transparent ghost), or that he is himself insane and therefore his vision, which is the film we see, is entirely untrustworthy.

This is perhaps most clearly expressed in the final sequence where the janitor imagines himself distributing masks to all the inmates. Kawabata in a later autobiographical story about the making of the film, *The Man Who Did Not Smile*, writes: 'I shall make the last scene a daydream. Gentle smiling masks will appear all over the screen. Since I could not hope to show a bright smile at the end of this dark story, at least I could wrap reality in a beautiful, smiling mask' (1929/2006: 139). The film scene begins with a long montage reminiscent of Ozu and then we see the janitor handing out Noh masks to the agitated inmates who, on donning them, immediately begin to act normally. The janitor himself finally puts on the mask of an old man, nods happily and is joined by his wife and a gaggle of Noh daughters. While this is clearly marked as happening in his imagination, the following sequence in which the janitor returns to mopping the floor disturbs the apparent simple delineation between illusion and reality. As he mops, the bearded patient is led past and bows deferentially to the janitor as if he were the real power behind the institution. The asylum is the janitor's creation. Gerow eloquently describes the ambiguous nature of the film: 'The vectors of transgression are multiple as outside invades the inside and vice versa. At the same time that the camera first breaks into the asylum, the psychology of the disturbed begins to prompt an invasion of the subjective/unreal into the objective/real' (2008: 88–9).

A Page of Madness is a tour de force of experimental film design as well as a sophisticated exploration of the possibility of representing not only insanity, but subjectivity as such, on screen. The film finally refuses to indicate who is sane and who is not and in doing so also refutes the easy psychology of attributing mental illness to a single traumatic event.[2] The film has been read as a political comment on 'state repression' as well as a mise-en-abyme treatise on the role of the artist in contemporary society (Gerow 2008: 84). Kinugasa himself suggests that the film was inspired by a sighting of Emperor Yoshihito (1879–1926), famously troubled by neurological disorders, and that, as Gerow and others point out, the film comes out of a world 'that masked its own contradictions and delusions in social propriety, national ideology, and abstract order' (2008: 84).

Notes

1. The authorship of the screenplay has been much discussed and Gerow identifies no less than four authors (Yasunari Kawabata, Minoru Inuzuka, Bankō Sawada and Kinugasa himself) and a further four important contributors (Richii Yokomitsu, Kunio Kishida, Teppei Kataoka, Shinzaburō Iketani). See Gerow's chapter 'The Screenplay' for a full discussion (2008: 26–33).
2. Sigmund Freud and Joseph Breuer's *Studies in Hysteria* (1895) succinctly – and perhaps rather naïvely – describes the aetiology of hysteria as being a simple, originary and traumatic event which, if uncovered, quickly leads to a complete cure. They write: 'We found, at first to our great surprise, that the individual hysterical symptoms disappeared immediately and did not recur if we succeeded in wakening the memory of the precipitating event with complete clarity, arousing with it the accompanying affect, and if the patient then depicted the event in the greatest possible detail and put words to the affect' (p. 10).

Further reading

Noël Burch, *To The Distant Observer: Form and Meaning in the Japanese Cinema*, Annette Michelson (ed.), Berkeley and Los Angeles, University of California Press, 1979, pp. 126–39.

Eric Cazdyn, *The Flash of Capital: Film and Geopolitics in Japan*, Durham, NC, Duke University Press, 2002.

William O. Gardner, 'New Perceptions: Kinugasa Teinosuke's Films and Japanese Modernism', *Cinema Journal*, 43 (3), pp. 59–78, 2004.

Aaron Gerow, *A Page of Madness: Cinema and Modernity in 1920s Japan*, Ann Arbor, Center for Japanese Studies, The University of Michigan, 2008.

Yasunari Kawabata, 'The Man Who Did Not Smile' in *Palm-of-the-Hand Stories*, trans. Lane Dunlop and J. Martin Holman, New York, Farrar, Strauss and Giroux, 1929/2006.

Yasunari Kawabata, 'Page of Madness' in *Modanizumu: Modernist Fiction from Japan, 1913–1938*, William Jefferson Tyler (ed.), Honolulu, University of Hawaii Press, pp. 92–104, 1926/2008.

James Peterson, 'A War of Utter Rebellion: Kinugasa's "Page of Madness" and the Japanese Avant-Garde of the 1920s', *Cinema Journal*, 29 (1), pp. 36–53, 1989.

Vlada Petrić, '*Page of Madness*: Neglected Masterpiece of the Silent Cinema', *Film Criticism*, 8 (1), pp. 86–107, 1983.

Jasper Sharp, *A Page of Madness* (1927), *Midnight Eye*, 2002. Available at: www.midnighteye.com/features/silentfilm_pt1.shtml (accessed 26 July 2012).

David Sorfa

Ladri di biciclette/Bicycle Thieves (1948)

[Country: Italy. Production Company: Produzioni De Sica. Producer: Giuseppe Amato and Vittorio De Sica. Director: Vittorio De Sica. Screenwriters: Cesare Zavattini, Suso Cecchi D'Amico, Vittorio De Sica, Oreste Biancoli, Adolfo Franci and Gerardo Guerrieri. Cinematographer: Carlo Montuori. Music: Alessandro Cicognini. Editor: Eraldo Da Roma. Cast: Lamberto Maggiorani (Antonio Ricci), Enzo Staiola (Bruno Ricci), Lianella Carell (Maria Ricci), Gino Saltamerenda (Baiocco), Vittorio Antonucci (the bicycle thief), Giulio Chiari (the beggar).]

Synopsis: In the economic depression of post-Second World War Italy, unemployed Antonio Ricci finally finds some work to support his wife and two children. The condition of the job as a poster hanger is that he needs to have a bicycle, but in order to feed his family Antonio had already pawned his bicycle. Facing this crisis, his wife Maria takes the family bedsheets to the pawnbroker to raise the money to redeem the bicycle so he will be able to take the job and bring in an income. With the remaining money she visits a fortune teller, anxious for some positive prospects. Antonio mocks her gullibility in believing in the occult. After starting the job he has his bicycle stolen and, finding the police see this as a relatively insignificant crime, he takes to the streets with his son Bruno and his friend Baiocco and tries to track down the thief. His actions progressively become more desperate and he even visits the fortune-teller, giving her his last remaining money but receiving only the same platitudes that she gives to all her clients. By chance he later discovers the thief who feigns a seizure when the police are called. The thief's neighbours give him an alibi and the police refuse to act on only Antonio's word. Despairing, Antonio succumbs himself and steals a bicycle, only to be caught and humiliated in front of his disillusioned son. Antonio is released and he walks off with his son, now a bicycle thief.

The Italian Neo-Realist movement spawned some films that are rightly seen as masterpieces of cinema, but none are as brutally realistic and ultimately as fatalistic as Vittorio De Sica's *Bicycle Thieves*. Shot on the streets of Rome amid the bombed out ruins of the immediate aftermath of the Second World War and the defeat of Mussolini's Fascists, the desaturated palette offers a bleak realism that lends the simple story a real resonance with anyone who has faced ruin. Poverty seeps from every frame with Antonio and his family forced to sell their property to survive, and the real threat of starvation facing them if he fails them. The pawnbroker's is overflowing with goods, the soup kitchens are filled with the poor seeking a hot meal, and those who have nothing turn to superstition in the hope it will prove their salvation. Its backdrop of utter privation and immeasurable poverty lends the film a visual style at once both realist and allegorical.

Italy at the end of the Second World War was a broken, occupied country with mass unemployment and unfettered corruption (much of which stemmed from the now defunct Black Shirts, or from the Christian Democrats, or the Communist Party, with each group giving preference its own interests and promoting its members or associates over others). Facing a crisis both politically and socially, poor Italians suffered their society falling apart whilst the rich seemed to continue their lives oblivious to this fact. The poor were faced with the same choice Antonio faces – live a moral life permanently hobbled by extreme poverty, or step into immorality and illegality to avoid starvation.

National Catholic Register reviewer Steven Greydanus states that 'the heart of this story's power is not in the style of the telling, but in the power of the situation it describes'[1] and it is the understanding of the situation beneath the story that makes this film so powerful, and indeed led the playwright Arthur Miller to describe the film as being 'as though the soul of man had been filmed'.[2] In stating this Miller is leaning towards the suggestion that whilst the Neo-Realist movement as a whole gives realism primacy, *Bicycle Thieves* does so from a humanist perspective. Miller noted that 'The film is unafraid to examine, openly, straightforwardly, the terrible, distorted, destructive world which man has made for himself. It has a point of view. It is genuinely angry, in fact, ferocious.'[3] The film has at its centre an examination of the inhumanity of the human condition and as such stands out clearly from other Neo-Realist works (other than perhaps De Sica's later work *Miraculo a Milano/Miracle in Milan* (1951), which offers a more hopeful if surreal perspective). Fellow Neo-Realist Rossellini's work is pivotal in its realist agenda, yet because of its observational nature it often feels detached, whereas De Sica takes the camera into the soup kitchen, and into the emotions of the characters, acknowledging that the emotional drama of life is as realist as the actuality of the events.

Miller acknowledges the unrelenting despair of the film – something many spectators find difficulty with, whilst others celebrate as an antidote to the implausibility of mainstream (often American) narrative. Antonio has problem heaped upon problem, reaches despair and then is broken. De Sica chooses not to leave the pain at this point, but rather focuses on the despair of Antonio's son Bruno who not only sees his father in trouble having stolen a bicycle, but also recognises that his father has betrayed himself in an act of desperation. In this moment the audience also recall Antonio's earlier revelation to his son that if they do not recover the bicycle he will not have a job, and with nothing else left to sell they are doomed to starvation. Bruno's tears mark the premature end of his childhood, the point where he not only recognises the fallibility of his father but also the nature of the terrible world lying ahead of him. De Sica has been accused of maudlin sentimentality for focusing on Bruno's anguish, yet of course the demands of true realism should expect nothing less as realism is feeling as well as seeing. The lyricism of *Bicycle Thieves* is something that could also be seen as counter to realism. One implies subjectivity and the other objectivity, and they are often seen as mutually exclusive sets. However, it is entirely possible to reconcile the two in the admission that an intense personal expression of feeling can be framed by a realist milieu, though not just as a backdrop but as an integral part of constructing the personalised expression.

De Sica chose to use non-actors and real locations to express the feeling of poverty and desperation. In doing so he avoids the emotional inflation trained actors bring, and restricts the construction of the mise en scène by ensuring the 'reality' of the location frames and structures any additional set dressing. The (non-)actors bring a sense of realism born out of their own desperate post-war experiences and accordingly an emotional intensity De Sica chooses to prioritise. Whilst other directors may have chosen perhaps to focus their energies more on sequences of the flea market where thousands of stolen bicycles are sold on or dismantled and sold as parts, emphasising the socio-economic situation, De Sica focuses on the realism of Antonio's inner journey. His internal crisis as he moves from hope to despair, from responsibility to a desperate act of criminality, is as 'real' a story as any external narrative. De Sica's ability to connect with the realism of human failing is all too evident in his focus on Antonio's wife Maria and the duality of her faith in religion and in the occult. Her minor subplot could so easily have been either cut or used simply as a transitional device, and yet it is testament to the power of De Sica as director and to Cesare Zavattini as writer that the desperation of her story, both echoes and mirrors Antonio's. She is shamed in her primitive beliefs by Antonio, who is himself shamed by his fall into criminality and his own replication of the act (the theft of a bicycle) that has brought him so low. De Sica here captures not only the realism of gender politics but also the simple realism of interpersonal relationships. It is De Sica's simple aesthetic realism that allows the tale of a man who spends a whole day looking for his stolen bicycle to become such an emblematic and powerful film, one where the banality of the commonplace is recognised as the true drama of life. A man denied the tools of his livelihood, is a man denied his livelihood: there need be no greater drama added than this.

Andre Bazin described *Bicycle Thieves* as the 'only valid Communist film of the whole decade'[4] and goes on to state that:

> Its social message is not detached, it remains immanent in the event, but it is so clear that nobody can overlook it, still less take exception

> to it, since it is never made explicitly a message. The thesis implied is wondrously and outrageously simple: in the world where this workman lives, the poor must steal from each other in order to survive.[5]

It is this simple idea, of the poor stealing from each other to survive, which is central to the film's impact on its audience. There is no sense of exterior forces here – even superstitions are shown to be impotent in the face of the dereliction of humanity – there are only the poor, bonding and disseminating. De Sica even manufactures an opportunity for Christianity to assist the plight of Antonio and his son when a group of Austrian clerics shelter in a porch with them, and yet fail to notice their distress and so fail to help them. In De Sica's reality there is no God to lift the troubled out of their travails, there is just humankind. It is the true crime of humanity that it betrays itself, and De Sica shows this both through the criminal society that protects the thief, but also through Antonio's own descent into criminality. He does not show the future of Antonio, and does not comment on the further choices available to him, instead offering realism within the confines of the event. It is the fact that De Sica respects these confines that allows this film to be something more than a vehicle for a social message, with its sense of realism rising to the fore so that the message becomes part of the realist schema as opposed to the realism serving the message.

A pivotal moment in Antonio's descent arrives when he comes to the decision to steal the bicycle. His shame is to the fore and so he sends his son to wait at the tram stop, and Bruno is shown in distress not at being sent away but in the recognition of what his father is about to do. Antonio's crime is then witnessed by his son which only serves to amplify his pain, but De Sica does not depict it thus out of sentimentality, but rather does so to show that these events are witnessed by children and that pain accompanies this.

Similarly, the final moments of the scene where Antonio and Bruno walk off together is ripe for an assault on the audience's emotions, and indeed the moment where Bruno slips his hand into Antonio's is often seen as a slip into sentimentalism. However, this is perhaps an over-simplistic view of the end of the film and one that does not do justice to its genius. In one simple gesture De Sica captured not a sentimental moment, but rather a moment of change in a familial relationship. The moment where the roles reverse, the son realises his father is not superhuman, and the father realises he can no longer command the respect of his son, but rather has to earn it. This ending is not a dramatised event but is the capturing of an event that goes unnoticed in relationships, and in doing so completes the film by focusing not on the grand narrative but rather on the minutia, the everyday detail that is realism.

Notes

1. Steven Greydanus (2010) '*The Bicycle Thief (Bicycle Thieves)* (1948)' at Decent Films Guide. Available at www.decentfilms.com/reviews/bicyclethief (accessed 23 November 2012).
2. Arthur Miller, 'Italians' Secret: Humanity', *New York Times*, 8 January 8 1950.
3. Ibid.
4. Andre Bazin, 'Neorealism and Pure Cinema: *The Bicycle Thief*,' *Cahiers du cinéma* (1948). Available at http://kit.kein.org/node/366 (accessed 23 November 2012).
5. Ibid.

Further reading

Andre Bazin, *What is Cinema? Volume 2*, Berkley, CA, University of California Press, 2004.
Robert Gordon, *Bicycle Thieves*, BFI, London, 2008.
Mira Liehm, *Passion and Defiance: Film in Italy from 1942 to the Present*, Berkley, CA, University of California, 1986.
Milicent Marcus, *Italian Film in the Light of Neorealism*, Princeton, NJ, Princeton University Press, 1986.
Stephen Snyder and Howard Curle, *Vittorio De Sica: Contemporary Perspectives*, Toronto, University of Toronto Press, 2000.

Freddie Gaffney

The Ladykillers (1955)

[Country: UK. Production Company: Ealing Studios. Director: Alexander Mackendrick. Screenwriter: William Rose. Cinematographer: Otto Heller. Music: Tristram Cary. Editor: Jack Harris. Cast: Katie Johnson (Mrs Wilberforce), Alec Guinness (Professor Marcus), Cecil Parker (Major Courtney), Herbert Lom (Louis), Peter Sellers (Harry), Danny Green (One-Round).]

Synopsis: The eccentric, old-fashioned home of Mrs Wilberforce, in a quiet London cul-de-sac, provides the unlikely venue for the planning of an audacious train robbery. The sinister figure of Professor Marcus takes a lodging room with the seemingly gentle old lady and holds regular musical soirees there with his friends, forming a string quintet. These meetings are actually a cover for the criminal gang's planning sessions, the music provided by a gramophone record! All goes well until Mrs Wilberforce discovers the robbers with their ill-gotten loot in her beloved home. While she decides on a course of action, they decide to draw lots to select someone to bump 'Mrs Lopsided' off! However, she proves to be a much more resilient individual than they imagined. Despite being outnumbered, she soon has the advantage as the house and the neighbouring railway yard become the setting for a darkly comic game of cat and mouse.

The Ladykillers is widely recognised as the last of the major Ealing comedies and thereby acts as coda for this sequence of films. *Hue and Cry* (1947) is usually taken as the starting point and the other substantial landmarks include *Passport to Pimlico* (1949), *Whiskey Galore* (1949), *Kind Hearts and Coronets* (1949), *The Lavender Hill Mob* (1951) and *The Man in the White Suit* (1951). Along with several minor films, they form a body of work which has retained its popular appeal and become synonymous with a particular vein in British film comedy. In *The Encyclopedia of British Film*, Charles Barr describes them as 'gentle, cosy, whimsical' (McFarlane 2003: 193). They typically celebrate the British love of eccentricity and side with the uncommon individual against larger corporate or state institutions. In doing so, there is often a fascination with the minutiae of British life, from schoolboy comics to those endless cups of tea. Individuals or whole communities frequently find themselves having to rebel or even turn to crime to protect themselves against bureaucracy or big business. Despite the potential seriousness of this as a topic, the handling is consistently light and warmly sympathetic.

Much of the responsibility for the company's ethos can be attributed to its head of production, Michael Balcon. Although Balcon often takes the producer credit on Ealing's films (including *The Ladykillers*), the job of producing individual films was usually in the hands of an associate producer (in this case, Seth Holt). Nonetheless, Balcon's influence was writ large throughout the company. Ealing adopted the slogan, 'The Studio with the Team Spirit', and its symbol 'became the Round Table at which, every week, producers, writers and directors consulted freely together' (Barr 1977: 6). Balcon seems to have viewed the studio as a family unit, with himself cast in the role of the firm, but kindly father (Balcon 1969: 138). A communal spirit was both part of the company's production ethic and also reflected in the films they made. By the late 1940s Ealing had established a reputation for both populist comedies (with a strong appeal to working-class audiences) and for documentary-realism (as seen in the propagandist films they produced during the Second World War). Elements of both approaches are apparent in the Ealing comedies. Realism is evident in the use of location shooting, the strong sense of place and the focus on ordinary citizens, although this realism is often overlaid by fantasy and visual stylisation, as is the case with *The Ladykillers*.

Balcon was also concerned that Ealing's films should reflect the intrinsic nature of Britain and then project this image out to a wider world. When the studio was sold in 1955 he provided the wording for a commemorative plaque: 'Here during a quarter of a century were made many films projecting Britain and the British character.' As a result, Ealing's films often reflect in a direct way on the contemporary condition of Britain. The political landscape of the immediate post-war period was radically shaped by the election of Clement Atlee's Labour government in 1945. Atlee's administration set about realising the socialist dream of a welfare state which would offer its citizens care and opportunity 'from the cradle to the grave', whatever their individual social background.[1] This was a social experiment which Balcon broadly supported, although not without a sense of ambivalence:

> Though we were radical in our points of view, we did not want to tear down institutions. We were people of the immediate post-war generation and we voted Labour for the first time after the war: this was our mild revolution.
>
> (Ellis 1975: 119)

However, by 1951 the Conservatives were back in office, where they were to remain for the next 13 years. The forces of reaction had seemingly prevailed over Labour's short-lived 'mild revolution'. It is against this context that *The Ladykillers* needs to be read.

Another factor in assessing the film is the position within Ealing of its director and its writer, Alexander Mackendrick and William Rose. Rose was an American, whilst Mackendrick was born in Boston and brought up in Scotland. Although it's easy to over-interpret the importance of their backgrounds, at Ealing, the most English of studios, they seem to have shared a sense of distance from the prevailing ethos which Balcon fostered. Roy Armes suggests that Mackendrick's work 'transcends the self-imposed limitations of the Ealing style' (Armes 1978: 190). Similarly, in his study of Mackendrick, Philip Kemp suggests that 'by disdaining the bland, conciliatory endings that Ealing favoured, he constantly questions the studio's assumptions even while ostensibly operating within them' (Kemp, 1991: 135). Mackendrick was frequently at odds with Balcon and *The Ladykillers* has the air of a final declaration of intent before his departure for America.

At first sight, the film has many characteristics which position it firmly within the canon of Ealing comedies. It sympathetically portrays a criminal gang and its action is rooted in a strong sense of place, with the central robbery taking place at Kings Cross Station and several sequences shot in nearby streets. The minutiae of English life are recreated with Ealing's typical attention to mundane detail, from the rank of shops near Mrs Wilberforce's home to the cluttered interior of her house. The love of eccentricity is embodied in the all the characterisations and encapsulated by the attitude of the local police superintendent (Jack Warner) towards Mrs Wilberforce; we are first introduced to her when she makes one of her regular visits to the police station to explain that her friend Amelia's sighting of a spaceship was actually just a dream. The police treat her with characteristic kindness and indulgence. The film even offers a little gentle knockabout humour in the sequence following the robbery when Mrs Wilberforce manages to inadvertently cause a street brawl between a barrow boy and a cab driver, played by the two popular comics Frankie Howerd and Kenneth Connor.

However, the film is more remarkable for the ways in which it deviates from the Ealing norm. From its opening, when the sinister, grotesque Professor Marcus (Alec Guinness) arrives to rent the spare room in Mrs Wilberforce's house, the film abandons Ealing's usual reliance on surface realism and adopts a stylisation which borders on the Gothic. This stylisation is apparent in the depiction of the interior of Mrs Wilberforce's house, with its mountains of bric-a-brac, caged birds and heavy drapery. The house itself is 'lopsided' from subsidence caused by wartime bombing and the plumbing can only be persuaded to work if the pipes are pounded with a wooden mallet. The cramped interior creates a feeling of claustrophobia, rather than the cosy comfort one might expect in an Ealing comedy, and Otto Heller's colour cinematography, with its palette of garish greens and yellows, gives the film an ambience of decay. The underlying menace comes to the surface in the second half of the film as the humour gradually drains out of Rose's script and we are faced with a modern morality play, as the criminal gang destroy themselves, leaving the scene scattered with bodies in the manner of a Jacobean revenge tragedy.

At the core of the film's approach is the ambiguous presentation of Mrs Wilberforce herself.

In more conventional Ealing fare she would simply be a loveable old lady, but she proves to be rather more formidable and destructive than might be expected. After all, she sees off a hardened gang of train robbers and ends up with the loot herself. At the film's conclusion, the increasingly deranged Professor Marcus is forced to conclude that she is too strong for them; even with a hundred men they wouldn't have been able to beat her. Her chosen weapons are the endless cups of tea with which she attacks the gang, but they prove more potent than Louis's (Herbert Lom) gun. For Philip Kemp, Mrs Wilberforce is a representation of traditional England: 'what she patently symbolises, besides innocence, is the past in which England is mired' (Kemp 1991: 120). The film presents Mrs Wilberforce, and her house, as a metaphor for post-war Britain, a place crippled by inertia, clinging to the past and blindly ignoring the fact that the whole construction is falling to bits. Mrs Wilberforce, and all her friends, dress in Edwardian clothes and have names like Constance and Lettice; they seem to have been preserved from an era before the First World War. This world certainly has its appeal; it is genteel, polite and ordered, but it also doesn't work properly (the plumbing) and has no room at all for the modern. Mrs Wilberforce's victory over the gang is a clear indication of the real power of 'old England' to maintain the status quo.

Aldgate and Richards suggest that the film provides an oblique commentary on the nature of 1950s Britain, or 'cul-de-sac England' as their essay is called. They interpret the gang as representatives of the social forces (youth, the working class, intellectuals) which would soon come to the fore and radically alter British society during the 1960s. Their defeat by the forces of repression and reaction (Mrs Wilberforce) encapsulates a key historical moment, as '1955 is almost the last year in which these dissident elements can be contained, for they are about to burst forth in all directions' (Aldgate and Richards 1999: 163). This is most perfectly captured in the scene when the gang are forced to join the tea party which Mrs Wilberforce throws for her friends. Charles Barr, slightly playfully, pushes this reading even further by suggesting that the gang actually represent Atlee's post-war Labour government (Barr 1977: 171–2). They take over 'the house' (parliament), with plans to redistribute wealth (the robbery), but find themselves unable to surmount the forces of conservatism which eventually defeat them (the Tories election victory of 1951). Barr offers this reading in a tongue-in-cheek manner, but nonetheless argues that the film illustrates 'the absorption of the dynamic by the static, of change by tradition, of the new by the old, which is the essential pattern of post-war British history' (Barr 1977: 172).

A further fascinating level of metaphor, which is picked up by Aldgate and Richards, is that the film's allegory is a critique of both post-war Britain and Ealing itself (Aldgate and Richards 1999: 159). Mrs Wilberforce stands for Balcon, the eternal nanny, benevolently overseeing her slightly wayward young men and trying to keep them on the right path. It's hardly surprising that Mackendrick left for America after making the film. The remarkable achievement of *The Ladykillers* lies in its ability to move beyond the familiar comforts provided by the secure world of the Ealing comedy and provide instead a mischievous portrait of a country caught on the brink of change. With a foot in both camps, it offers us a picture of traditional English values in the form of Mrs Wilberforce, a figure as likely to induce alarm as affection.

Note

1. See 'That Topic All-Absorbing: Class' and 'The Welfare State' in Arthur Marwick, *British Society Since 1945*, London, Penguin, 1986.

Further reading

Anthony Aldgate and Jeffrey Richards, *Best of British: Cinema and Society from 1930 to the Present*, London, I.B. Tauris, 1999.

Roy Armes, *A Critical History of British Cinema*, London, Secker and Warburg, 1978.

Michael Balcon, *A Lifetime of Films*, London, Hutchinson, 1969.

Charles Barr, *Ealing Studios*, New York, The Overlook Press, 1977.

John Ellis, 'Made in Ealing' in *Screen*, 16 (1), Spring 1975.

Philip Kemp, *Lethal Innocence: The Cinema of Alexander Mackendrick*, London, Methuen, 1991.
Brian McFarlane, *The Encyclopedia of British Film*, London, Methuen, 2003.
Robert Murphy, *Realism and Tinsel: Cinema and Society in Britain, 1939–1949*, London, Routledge, 1989.
Tim Pulleine, 'A Song and Dance at the Local: Thoughts on Ealing' in Robert Murphy (ed.) *The British Cinema Book*, London, BFI, 2001, pp. 79–84.

Robert Shail

The Last Wave (1977)

[Country: Australia. Production Company: Australian Film Commission, Ayer Productions, Derek Power. Director: Peter Weir. Producers: Hal McElroy and James McElroy. Screenwriters: Peter Weir, Tony Morphett and Petru Popescu. Cinematographer: Russell Boyd. Music: Charles Wain. Editor: Max Lemon. Production Designer: Goran Warff. Cast: Richard Chamberlain (David Burton), Olivia Hamnett (Annie Burton), David Gulpilil (Chris Lee), Nandjiwarra Amagula (Charlie), Frederick Parslow (Reverend Burton).]

Synopsis: David Burton (Richard Chamberlain) is a corporate tax lawyer living in middle-class comfort in Sydney, Australia with his wife and two young daughters. His life is turned upside-down when he agrees to defend a group of young aboriginal men who have been accused of murder. He quickly becomes convinced that the motive is 'tribal' and wants to use this as the basis of his defence case; it would lead to a more lenient sentence under Australian law. However, the aborigines refuse to cooperate, preferring long prison terms to revealing their secrets. David becomes friendly with Chris (David Gulpilil), the most forthcoming of the group, who introduces him to Charlie (Nadjiwarra Amagula), an old man who seems to have supernatural powers. David, who is troubled by recurring dreams, discovers that he may be a 'mulkurul', the name given by aborigines to the descendants of South American settlers, who share their mystical abilities. The trial is a disaster for David, and his wife leaves with their children for her mother's home as his behaviour becomes increasingly unpredictable. Led by Chris, David finds a sacred mulkurul site in the Sydney sewers and is finally confronted by an apocalyptic vision.

Peter Weir emerged in the 1970s as one of the leading figures in the new Australian cinema. Although filmmaking in Australia can be traced right back to the late nineteenth century, and Australia can lay claim to having made the first feature length narrative film (*The Story of the Kelly Gang*) in 1906, it was only in the 1970s that it burst on to the world stage with a distinctive voice of its own, shaking off years of economic instability and cinematic domination by the United States and Great Britain. This transformation was largely as the result of deliberate intervention by government at both national and regional level. Characteristically, the funding for *The Last Wave* was substantially bolstered by support from the Australian Film Commission and the South Australian Film Corporation. Successive governments during the 1970s invested heavily in Australian films, so that between 1970 and 1974 the Australian Film Development Corporation was responsible for the financing of more than 50 feature films (Shirley and Adams 1989: 221). The motivations were both economic and cultural, pragmatically combining a desire for international financial success with an aspiration to lift up and project Australian national culture.

The cinema which emerged in the 1970s developed a repertoire of genres, some of which were Australian hybrids of American originals, while others seemed more purely Australian in character. A brief look at the content and structure of a number of recent academic studies of Australian cinema tends to confirm this, with Jonathan Rayner's *Contemporary Australian Cinema* divided into chapters on 'Australian Gothic', 'The period film' and 'The male ensemble film'. Moran Vieth's *Film in Australia* lists 13 separate genres which include Hollywood staples such as the Musical or the Teenpic, as well as others like the Adventure Film which have a decidedly different connotation within the Australian production context.

In addition, key thematic groupings tend to emerge. There are films such as *Breaker Morant* (Beresford, 1980) and *Gallipoli* (Weir, 1981) which deal explicitly with the impact of British colonial rule. Another group of films focus on the feelings of disquiet apparently experienced by descendants of the original white European settlers as they contend with the 'otherness' of their new homeland. Films in this category include Weir's own *Picnic at Hanging Rock* (1975) and the same thematic undercurrent is even manifest in the sense of anxiety underlying the fantasy world of George Miller's Mad Max trilogy. A further extension of this theme can be found in films which deal more directly with the relationship between those Australians of European descent and the indigenous aboriginal population, as evidenced by Fred Schepisi's powerful *The Chant of Jimmie Blacksmith* (1978).

Peter Weir's work of the 1970s and early 1980s intersects with a number of these themes and genres. His debut as feature director, *The Cars That Ate Paris* (1974), takes fears over the possible moral inadequacies of Australia's majority population and turns it into a grotesque horror comic. If *Picnic at Hanging Rock* deals with not dissimilar feelings in a totally different way, then it also belongs to the genre of Australian Gothic, as well as to the Period Film. *Gallipoli* is both a Period Film and a not always subtle attack on the alleged maltreatment of Australian troops at the hands of British commanders during the First World War, which attracted controversy for its historical inaccuracies. Interestingly, as Serena Formica's monograph on Weir suggests, these themes have continued into his American films. Work as diverse as *Witness* (1985), *Dead Poets Society* (1989), *Green Card* (1990) and *The Truman Show* (1998) all concern themselves with individuals who are alienated from their social setting in one form or another, and although they tend more to melodrama than the Gothic there is still a focus on the search for identity, with often tragic repercussions. Whilst Formica's study asserts that while Weir had to 'adapt his way of working' to find success in Hollywood, there is nonetheless 'a common thematic element' in his work which centres on the 'struggle of the individual against the social environment in which he lives' (Formica 2012: 164–7).

If *The Last Wave* does not directly address the theme of Australia's relationship with Britain, it does embody both the tensions between the majority population and indigenous Australians, and the sense of displacement experienced by the descendants of European settlers. It also incorporates the Australian Gothic style established by films like *Picnic at Hanging Rock*; the film plays out, at least in part, as an atmospheric suspense film and was marketed along these lines. Further generic elements are apparent in the elements of courtroom melodrama and murder mystery which provide the film with a recognisable narrative structure. The feeling that Australia is a 'strange' place is evoked in one the first scenes where we witness bizarre weather as a rural school is beset by a sudden storm arriving out of a clear blue sky and pelting the children with fist-sized hailstones. In the city, David drives home in a monsoon and arrives to find that it is 'raining' inside his own house. He is plagued by nightmares which are made more disturbing in the film's diegesis by the fact that they are not always signalled as dreams until he eventually wakes. Rainstorms punctuate the film and take on biblical dimensions as frogs drop from the sky and the rain turns black. Later David dreams of an apocalypse in which the city has been drowned by a massive wave. The aborigines, Chris and Charlie, are explicitly linked to this 'strangeness' as they appear in David's dreams, or suddenly materialise in the street outside of his house. As they explain to him, the reality he perceives is only one level of experience; beyond it lies the 'dreamtime', an alternative dimension which is trying to speak to him through his dreams.

Assailed by these unsettling developments, David becomes increasingly sensitive to the inadequacies in his own value system. As a work colleague points out to him, he is just another white middle-class liberal who makes a living helping rich people avoid paying tax. His home life is certainly comfortable but oddly bland, a world of tennis and dinner parties. Its values are easily undermined as David becomes obsessed by the idea that he may have a form of aboriginal ancestry of his own as he is descended from South American settlers who had lived in close harmony with the aborigines. This seems to give him access to 'powers' which other Australians do not possess but which the aborigines immediately recognise in him. When his wife leaves, taking the children, she tells him that she doesn't know who he is any more. At one point, he tells Charlie that he believes he is no longer a man but a spirit. As McFarlane and Mayer suggest, Weir's work is often marked by a fascination with 'such polarities as guilt and innocence, innocence and corruption, the ordinary and the bizarre', expressing this through imagery as much as plotting (McFarlane and Mayer 1992: 224). Here, in the final third of the film, the focus of the narrative moves decisively away from the murder mystery towards David's own quest to find out more about his own identity, with the prospect that he may be able to connect to a more ancient and meaningful value system. This proves more enticing than the comforts of conventional domesticity and work.

One of the more contentious aspects of the renaissance in Australian cinema in the 1970s was the image it often presented of aboriginal culture. The dangers of slipping into a romanticised view, built on feelings of collective guilt, have been well documented. The film is certainly open to this critique. One scene shows a conversation between David and his step-father, who is a Christian priest. David accuses him of having always tried to explain away the mystery of human experience. He says, 'We have lost our dreams. They come back and we don't know what they mean.' This is in stark contrast to the representation of the aborigines David has met, who are clearly in touch with this other, higher dimension of life.

In an interview with Peter Weir released on the Criterion DVD edition of *The Last Wave*, the director is keen to emphasise that the film is his own story, told from a Western point of view. He talks eloquently about how David's life in the film was a reflection of his own upbringing, and of his own growing awareness of living in a land that was in some fundamental sense not his own, but that belonged to others who had been there for much longer. This led in turn to two of the film's key visual metaphors: the repeated images of water washing away at contemporary Australia; and the placing of the aboriginal shrines in the tunnel network of sewers under Sydney. Aboriginal culture becomes a secret, hidden world sitting next to, or underneath, the culture built by the descendants of the European settlers. This provides a way of reading the film which avoids anthropological stereotypes of indigenous people; the film is not really about them at all but instead expresses the anxieties of the urban majority, whose outward confidence and economic prosperity is depicted here as curiously fragile.

This is given its fullest expression in the film's final sequences when David abandons his house and follows Chris into the labyrinth under Sydney, discovering a subterranean world of paintings, icons and sculptures. Here he finds his own death mask, symbolising the demise of his old identity; meanwhile, Chris heads back into the dreamtime. For a moment David finds he cannot return to the world above, but eventually he makes his way through the tunnels emerging into a timeless landscape of the beach and sea. His final vision, and that of the film, is of a vast primeval wave heading in the direction of modern Australia to sweep it away.

Further reading

Michael Bliss, *Dreams within a Dream: The Films of Peter Weir*, Carbondale, Southern Illinois University Press, 2000.

Serena Formica, *Peter Weir: A Creative Journey from Australia to Hollywood*, Bristol and Chicago, Intellect, 2012.

Brian McFarlane and Geoff Mayer, *New Australian Cinema: Sources and Parallels in American and British Film*, Cambridge, Cambridge University Press, 1992.

Albert Moran and Errol Vieth, *Film in Australia: An Introduction*, Cambridge, Cambridge University Press, 2006.

Jonathan Rayner, *Contemporary Australian Cinema*, Manchester and New York, Manchester University Press, 2000.

Graham Shirley and Brian Adams, *Australian Cinema: The First Eighty Years*, Sydney, Currency Press, 1989.

Robert Shail

Låt den rätte komma in/Let the Right One in (2009)

[Country: Sweden. Production Company: EFTI, Sandrew Metronome, Filmpool Nord, Sveriges Television, WAG. Director: Thomas Alfredson. Screenwriter: John Ajvide Lindqvist (adapted from his novel). Cinematographer: Hoyte Van Hoytema. Sound Design: Per Sundstrom. Cast: Kare Hedebrant (Oskar), Lina Leandersson (Eli), Per Ragnar (Hakan), Peter Carlberg (Lacke), Ika Nord (Virginia).]

Synopsis: Twelve-year-old Oscar (Kare Hedebron), bullied at school, lonely and silently revengeful, befriends his new neighbour, palely androgynous Eli (Lina Leandersson) also twelve. She encourages him to fight back against his schoolboy tormentors, and gradually they realise their love for each other. But her arrival coincides with a series of bloody attacks and murders, and she displays strange characteristics which cause Oscar to realise she is a vampire. Local suspicion of the girl grows, and she prepares to run, seemingly abandoning Oscar as he prepares to face up to the bullies' leader. The climax, involves a grisly outcome in the local swimming baths, and a brief suggestion of a fantasy world constructed from unhappiness and an empty apartment next door, before it ends with questions raised regarding the possibility of a life together for the strange couple, whether they can escape the consequences of Elie's nature, and the price that Oscar will pay.

Former Swedish TV director Tomas Alfredson's first feature film mixes the teen fantasy vampire genre with a realist strand of teenage romance, and one of school bullying, and turns these apparent mismatches into an unexpectedly visual, emotive and affecting version of the horror genre. The chill beauty of the location and cinematography acts metaphorically for the theme and dialogue, producing a remarkable original take on the vampiric norms, by a director who claims no previous knowledge or interest in the genre yet has skilfully reinvented its use of iconography, for a twist on audience expectations.

Alfredson's wry description of his film as '*Romeo and Juliet*, written by Strindberg'[1] neatly combines two key aspects of the focus put on this adaptation of John Ajvide Lindqvist's novel and screenplay. Alfredson places the emphasis firmly on the developing pre-teen love story between the meekly pale and lonely Oskar, and his strange, equally pale, new neighbour Eli, his mirror image,[2] dark, active and strong. But there, despite the romance focus, the 'Twilight-esque' comparisons end, since Eli's undead status is more Swedish than Hollywood vampire-light; a coolly semi-realist depiction of the fantasy myth.

Critic, Philip French, points out[3] that the vampire pervades Swedish art, from Edvard Munch's 'Vampire', through to numerous Strindberg heroines, indeed the remix in this version links back to Dreyer's *Vampyr*[4] with its strangely androgynous, yet female-named, undead one, here reworked in the ambiguous sexuality of Eli, whose appearance seems to belie her declaration that, 'I am not a girl'; one of many moments left open for viewer interpretation of unresolved verbal or visual hints.[5]

Alfredson's re-Vamp of the genre turns on this light establishing of the factual or fantasy status of events. The combination of the horror myth with the well-trodden themes of coming of age narratives, make both new. To this end, Oskar's state as a passively bullied 12-year-old is placed at the centre of his characterisation; opening scenes depicting his violent knifing of a tree and his collection of newspaper cuttings of murderers and suicides making clear his revengeful powerlessness.

The location is detailed through the cold barriers and concrete structures of suburban Stockholm; ostensibly the Blackeberg housing estate of the novel, but mostly filmed further north, in Leth, to increase the metaphoric and the actual, coldness of the urban snowscapes. The realist stylistics can be discerned in a narrative centred on domestic and school settings, and played out in the various parental failures surrounding the young couple, from Oskar's non-communicating divorcing parents to the elderly man Hakan, who cares for Eli, and who later proves to be another area of unexplained ambiguity, perhaps a former lover. Yet, even these day-to-day elements are imbued with a Gothic air, from the horror techniques used in the shooting of some of the school corridor scenes, to the betrayal through casual neglect of Oskar's visits to his father. They are more explicit in Hakan's grim though inexpert blood-gathering excursions, yet conversely the filming remains observationally matter-of-fact. The objects and locations, 1980s blocks of flats, the playground where Oskar and Eli meet, and the Rubik's cube which he presents to her, increase this realist air, seen too in the naturalistic dialogue of the young people's developing relationship: their exchanges as Oscar slowly takes in the uncanny aspects of his companion, notably seen in the scene where, lying side by side in bed, they discuss, without resolution, the nature of Eli's life, her age, and questions over her gender and humanity.

The horror aspects of the stylistics, though given less prominence than the genre might suggest, are none the less highly effective when they occur. Hakan's failed blood gathering in the forest is paralleled by Eli's own bloodletting, narratively minimised through emphasis on its necessity due to Hakan's ineptitude; when it comes, it is surprisingly graphic, animalistic and shocking – a jump onto her prey from the bridge of an underpass with the location carefully chosen for the greatest effect of height.[6] A school skating trip combines the icy stillness of location with the generic expectation of frozen corpse discovery, set up through Hakan's disposal of victims, and skilfully combined with an early incident of Oskar's revenge on his persecutors; both a neat dovetailing of narrative strands and a precursor of the anticipated but withheld final bloodbath – aptly continuing the low-key re-inventions of genre in its placement in the municipal swimming pool.

These generic set pieces serve as a contrast to the downplayed hints of Eli's vampiric nature, only gradually revealed, to the audience as to Oskar; her incapacity to feel cold, 'I've forgotten how –', added to her inability to match Oskar's precise statement of his age, in years and days. To visit Hakan in hospital we glimpse her scaling the walls like a veteran of the Murnau *Nosferatu* tradition.[7] But some aspects of mythic convention receive further twists, as when we see a glimpse of her lapping blood on the ground to avoid giving Oscar the vampiric bite, while the titular necessary invitation to enter receives full focus as vampire lore, in Eli's demonstration of the consequence of entering without invitation, shown in an affecting scene as her eyes stream with tears of blood, described by critic Peter Bradshaw as 'a haemophilia of rejection'.[8]

Perhaps the most graphic of the horror moments is connected only indirectly to the main couple through their older counterparts, the local Lacke and his love Virginia. She provides the most direct evidence of Eli's gruesome effect, detailed for us at her vampiric transformation after being bitten and in her choice of death by sunlight. Lacke's later attempts at revenge, in his pursuit of Eli and Hakan, ultimately drives Eli to flee: 'I must go and live, or stay and die'.

The haunting quality of the cinematography is the result of a design which enhances the mixing of the generic horror conventions with the realist. Some of its shots are rooted in the minimalist filmic interventions favoured by the Scandinavian Dogme group of filmmakers – highly influential in Scandi film largely due to the Trollenberg location of von Trier's studios.[9] When Oskar runs out on his disastrous visit to his father, and decides to hitchhike home at night, the scene is made more affecting by being lit only by the headlights of passing cars. Similarly, the highly effective, and critically acclaimed, sound design is based on real sound, even when later given some digital enhancement; biting into sausages becomes the sound of the vampiric bite, emphasising Alfredson's intention to bring out the animalistic in human nature.[10] This is ratcheted up a level in the cat attack scenes; even here real cats are used in the mix with stuffed and CGI ones. The lighting again epitomises the effect as cinematographer Van Hoytema invented a technique they called 'flat light' to spread and dull rather than to pick out features;[11] this is enhanced by the process of using mostly fixed camerawork, and minimal editing, to produce a pervading effect of frozen stillness.

For the most part, the filmic point of view remains determinedly mid-level, observational, and distanced. This is enhanced by Alfredson's emphasis on eyes, their level and focus. He has commented[12] on the influence of portraits by Holbein, where the eye direction is slightly out of the frame. In his own use of this technique the focus is initially at some distance, coming into close up as the film progresses. This can be seen to great effect in a culminating moment, the scene of Oskar and Eli's first kiss, which is deliberately held back by the director for fullest impact.[13] Significantly, this is the moment when Oskar decides for Eli, and against humanity, despite her necessarily murderous lifestyle, having just witnessed her dispatching of the vengeful Lacke. Consequently, the kiss takes place with the blood of the kill still on her lips; the eye level is over the shoulders of both, rather than locking, yet the effect, if coolly depicted, is full of pathos, suggesting loss as well as gain.

Critic Peter Bradshaw has commented that perhaps the film concentrates on horror effects to the detriment of its generic narrative suspense.[14] Yet, the determined ambiguity creates its own suspense, through the gaps and questions left; those regarding Eli's long undead life, occasionally brought home through hints such as her production of a Faberge egg, and especially in the gradual realisation of the likely outcome of pursuing the relationship for Oskar. Most strikingly, a narratively playful 'false ending' scene precedes the final outcome: Oskar is apparently left alone, as Eli prepares to run for her life, and the possibility of her as an entirely imagined solution, situated in the empty apartment next door, is briefly presented to us, only to be subsumed by events.

A shot described by the director as 'Hitchcockian' presents a bird's eye view which alerts the viewer to a presaging of a bloody outcome,[15] as the culmination of both the mismatched love plot and the bullying theme takes place in a nail-biting bathing scene, when Oskar is lured by one of the bully gang, for a head-on underwater challenge. The scene does not disappoint, presenting a stunning underwater view of the dismembered results of Eli's eventual keeping of her earlier promise 'be stronger than you dare – and I will help you' – disturbing close-ups of Oskar's head held under widen out to reveal the consequences of Eli's superhuman nature; much as the narrative of the film as a whole has done.

In a switch of mood back to the more continuous low-key atmosphere, the lovers are reunited in a setting reminiscent of the pursuit in the nineteenth-century version of the myth in Bram Stoker's novel,[16] as a train journey effects the couple's removal from the bloodletting, reinstating the emphasis on the lovers. It also adds to the effect of ambiguity, in both the generic suspense generated through waiting to reveal the next location to be infected, and the emotive suspense of Oskar's hurtling, perhaps knowingly, towards a Hakanesque future. The vampiric icon of the coffin is cleverly reworked as a trunk onto which Oskar makes use of the Morse code previously used to communicate through the barriers of walls between their neighbouring apartments. Now, from the protection of the trunk the encoffined Eli taps 'kiss', to which Oskar's tapped reply is 'small kiss'. The force of genre has overridden our briefly encouraged suspension of belief, while the ambiguity of the situation enhances rather than lessens its emotive effect, in the viewer's knowledge that Eli's decision to 'leave and live' may well be self-destructive for Oskar.

Notes

1. *Let the Right One In*, DVD Extra: Director's Notes.
2. Ibid.

3. Philip French '*Let the Right One In*'. *The Observer*, 12 April, 2009.
4. *Vampyr*, Carl Theodor Dreyer, 1932.
5. A glimpse of scarred genitals hints at the novel's back story, of Eli's past as a castrated boy.
6. DVD Extra – Director's Notes.
7. *Nosferatu*, F. W. Murnau, 1921.
8. Peter Bradshaw '*Let the Right One In*'. *The Guardian*, 10 April, 2009.
9. The Dogme 'Brotherhood' of filmmakers initiated by Lars von Trier in 1995.
10. DVD Extra – Director's Notes.
11. Ibid.
12. Susan King, 'Tomas Alfredson: Taking A Deep Look At Horror', *Los Angeles Times*, 19 October, 2008.
13. In the novel this key moment occurs much earlier.
14. Peter Bradshaw (2009) '*Let the Right One In*'. *The Guardian*, 10 April.
15. DVD Extra – Director's Notes.
16. Bram Stoker, *Dracula*, 1897.

Further reading

Mariah Larsson and Anders Marklund, *Swedish Film: An Introduction and Reader*, Lund: Nordic Academic Press, 2010.

Elizabeth Miller and Dacre Stoker, eds, *The Lost Journal of Bram Stoker*, London: Robson Press, 2012.

Lynda Townsend

The Lodger (1926)

[Country: UK. Production Company: Piccadilly Productions. Director: Alfred Hitchcock. Screenwriter: Elliot Stannard. Cinematographer: Gaetano di Ventimiglia. Editor: Ivor Montagu. Cast: Marie Ault (Mrs Bunting), Arthur Chesny (Mr Bunting), June (Daisy Bunting), Malcolm Keen (Joe Betts), Ivor Novello (The Lodger).]

Synopsis: Adapted from a successful novel by Marie Belloc, the film reinterprets and offers a solution to the story of infamous serial killer Jack the Ripper and reimagines the seedier parts of London in the nineteenth century.[1] After an initial sequence that makes clear that the killer known by his calling card as 'The Avenger' has just committed another murder, and that his victims are all blonde young women, the film then introduces the working-class Bunting family who run a typical lodging house in a grimy impoverished part of the city. This family centres round Mr and Mrs Bunting (Arthur Chesny and Marie Ault), the elderly and devoted parents of aspiring model Daisy (played by an actress known only as 'June'), but also includes Daisy's would-be suitor, police detective Joe Betts (Malcolm Keen). A little later, the detectives who have been assigned to work on the notorious case deduce that the pattern of murders appears to be moving towards the very same lodging house; and the mysterious lodger (Ivor Novello), who arrived there a day after the seventh murder and who was absent from the house at exactly the time the eighth was committed nearby, is held under suspicion. Meanwhile, Daisy and The Lodger fall in love, much to the concern of her parents and the great discontent of Joe, who then turns the murder case into a personal vendetta and a quest to reclaim his damaged masculine pride.

Although officially Hitchcock's third feature, the director himself preferred to refer to The Lodger as his first proper film. Indeed, it was his first suspense thriller, a genre he went on to make his own with more world-famous films such as *Vertigo* (1958 USA) and *Psycho* (1960 USA). It also stands out as the film that drew attention to him as a prominent filmmaker whose approach was for a long time difficult to categorise. In fact, with films like *The Lodger*, Hitchcock began to shape new categories and drew on a wide range of cinematic and broader cultural influences, from German expressionism to the psychoanalytical work of Sigmund Freud. Moreover, *The Lodger* was responsible for introducing a range of what were quickly to become classic Hitchcockian themes, for as Robert Murphy has pointed out: 'What makes the film so fascinating is the way it dissolves into pre-echoes of Hitchcock's later work' (in Pym 2003: 691). Issues of gender struggle and questions about guilt, suspicion and redemption are all wrapped up in an engrossing yarn that encompasses violence, romance, chase scenes and moments of raw emotional intimacy.

The compelling story of *The Lodger* benefits from a carefully crafted plot, in which twists and turns keep audiences guessing about the identity and motivation of the protagonist until the very end. It does so with very few intertitles, relying deliberately instead on the power of the cinematic image and the melodramatic performance style of its actors.[2] Such suspicion of dialogue (intertitled or otherwise) was part of a general concern Hitchcock shared with filmmakers like F. W. Murnau and Fritz Lang around the introduction of synchronised sound to what had until then primarily been a visual medium. There was a logic to their resistance to change in that they, like Chaplin and Eisenstein, feared that sound would adversely affect the possibilities of filmmaking and make audiences lazier in their consumption of films. As Duguid notes, 'the limitations of silent cinema meant that directors were forced to be imaginative in using images to convey dialogue and effects',[3] and many were afraid that such creativity would be lost if the addition of sound were made possible.

In any case, *The Lodger* shows Hitchcock's mastery of (silent) film technique in his use of a wide variety of camera techniques and props to communicate the emotions of the various characters. He also deploys a frugal yet strategic placement of intertitles to announce characters, break up the narrative, and to add to the sense of mystery. Perhaps an even greater sign of cinematic sophistication is the staging of much of the plot in the narrow, multilevel boarding house which allows characters on different storeys to be seen interacting with the plot simultaneously. On a narrative level, the film is also quite complex. It moves towards a memorable finale, in which quick cuts between frames from different angles follow The Lodger as he is chased by a bloodthirsty mob. Just before this, a short but effective flashback sequence from The Lodger's tragic past allows Daisy and the audience privileged access to the motivation for his strange behaviour and his air of melancholy.

The opening sequence, using an almost expressionistic style with quirky tilt angles and shadows, sets the mood of a city terrorised by a mysterious killer. Indeed, as Geoffrey Macnab points out, 'the pleasure of the film lies less in its being about a serial killer per se than in its manipulation of audiences' expectations and its evocation of mist-shrouded London streets' (2007: 11). This section incorporates frantic scenes in a newspaper office, printing office, and out on the streets as people clamour with a mix of fear and anticipation to read about the latest murder in their neighbourhood. Such images are intercut with others featuring catwalk models preparing themselves for work, and the transition from one activity to another is set up by the delivery of a note from the killer to the show that states he is on the lookout for a girl with golden curls. At first all seem to be blonde and hence all ideal targets for the killer, but as their peroxide wigs are removed, it is quickly revealed that only very few possess the features that might attract The Avenger.

Such features, the 'golden' hair and translucent fair skin in particular, are exactly those that are on display again three decades later via *Rear Window*'s Lisa (Grace Kelly, 1954), *Vertigo*'s Madeleine/Judy (Kim Novak, 1958), *Psycho*'s Marion (Janet Leigh, 1960) and *The Birds*' Melanie (Tippi Hedren, 1963). In fact, the idea of a constructed and idealised, yet threatening female identity that is so clearly explored by those later films is pre-echoed in *The Lodger* by the reference to wigs, make-up and costume, the display of young models, and the playful use of fake dark hair by one of the fair-haired girls to try to outwit the killer. Indeed, while critics continue to debate whether Hitchcock was uncomfortable with and hostile to women, or whether he admired them, it is clear that, as Mark Duguid points out, 'Hitchcock saw female sexual vulnerability as a powerful dramatic device, which he exploited ruthlessly'.[4]

The supposed villain of the piece is portrayed with some ambivalence: the initial careful framing of The Lodger's face makes him appear menacing and mysterious, while later on he looks vulnerable and victimised. The direct, frontal angle which shows only part of his head as the rest is sheltered from the cold by a thick scarf, adds to the piercing and mesmeric nature of his eyes, his ghostly, translucent skin and sharply contrasting dark hair, all of which make him appear quite monstrous at first. Moreover, his unexpected arrival at the Buntings' lodging house is prefigured by a flickering and inexplicable extinction of the kitchen gas lamp, and a frenzied malfunction of the family's cuckoo clock. As Mrs Bunting opens the door, The Lodger seems to appear from the fog itself, creating a memorably chilling moment that sets the tone for the assumptions that are made about this tragic stranger, until it is almost too late. In fact, The Lodger's eccentric appearance and behaviour have more to do with his upper-class background, but are misunderstood by the Buntings and Joe as evidence of his deviance.

All this helps generate the tone of suspense by which Hitchcock's work was later defined. The sinister way in which The Lodger turns round all the paintings of women on the walls of his room and then insists that they are removed sets up questions about who he is, where he has come from and what his intentions might be which are left unanswered for the majority of the film. The shaking of the kitchen lamp as he paces above and the use of a transparent ceiling/floor to allow the audience to see his feet as they walk up and down, heighten the effect of anxiety. Moreover, the very timing of his arrival to coincide with the hysterical reporting of the seventh murder and his absence from the boarding house while the eighth is committed only deepens the effect of suspicion within the diegesis and for the audience. Could this man really be The Avenger lurking within their very midst? And yet, his tenderness towards Daisy and her absolute faith in his integrity leads to further uncertainty.

On another level, this is also a film about patriarchy and Joe's assumed ownership of Daisy as his fiancée-to-be. While he appears to assume a right to become her husband, he also seems to realise that he needs to prove himself to her. She seems less than impressed by his early attempts to woo her, and downright insulted when he sadistically handcuffs her to the staircase while The Lodger watches. He appears to have the approval of Daisy's parents but has not won her heart. Will his attempts to apprehend the Avenger impress her sufficiently? Her rebuttal of his advances and rejection of his proposal send him into a jealous rage, especially when he catches her playing chess with The Lodger in his room, and later finds them locked in amorous embrace. His determination to win her back becomes entangled with a parallel obsessive quest to capture the murderer and to remove or destroy the threat to his macho sense of self.

All the classic Hitchcockian issues of gender and class difference, fetishistic sexuality, misunderstanding and mistaken identity surface in this gripping silent drama that shows a maturity of style and tone. It oscillates between suspense and humour, fear and tenderness, and demonstrates the young director's growing confidence in using cinema to connect emotionally with an audience. At this stage, however, Hitchcock did not have as much control over his work as he would later enjoy. It has been reported that he would have preferred to construct a more ambiguous ending to *The Lodger*'s narrative, but the British studio involved wouldn't allow the suggestion that The Lodger might actually be the murderer to be confirmed.[5] Nevertheless, the film, like its originating story, caught the public imagination and marked the start of the career of one of the British film industry's greatest directors.

Notes

1. The film was also known as *The Case of Jonathon Drew and The Lodger: A Story of the London Fog.* It was supposedly based on an anecdote told by a landlady who was sure that one of her tenants had been Jack the Ripper.
2. Even the intertitles are visually attractive with their 'explicitly graphic quality' (Sergeant 2005: 89) thanks to the deco-style designs of McKnight Kauffer.
3. Mark Duguid, 'Hitchock's Style', 2003–06. Available at www.screenonline.org.uk/tours/hitch/tour3.html (accessed 14 July 2006).

4. Ibid.
5. Novello (1893–1951) was a box office draw in the 1920s: he was praised for his acting ability as well as his good looks.

Further reading

Geoffrey Macnab, 'Still making a killing', *Independent,* 4 May 2007, pp. 10–11.

Robert Murphy, 'The Lodger', in John Pym, *Time Out Film Guide* 2004, London, Penguin, 2003, p. 691.

Amy Sergeant, *British Cinema: A Critical History,* London, BFI, 2005.

François Truffaut, *Hitchcock,* London, Simon & Schuster, 1985.

Sarah Barrow

Lola rennt/Run Lola Run (1998)

[Country: Germany. Production Company: X-Filme Creative Pool, Westdeutscher Rundfunk (WDR), Arte. Producer: Stefan Arndt. Director and Screenwriter: Tom Tykwer. Cinematographer: Frank Grieber. Original Sound: Frank Behnke. Editor: Mathilde Bonnefoy. Cast: Franka Potente (Lola), Moritz Bleibtreu (Manni), Herbert Knaup (Vater), Nina Petri (Jutter Hansen), Ludgar Pistor (Herr Meier).]

Synopsis: Lola receives a phone call from Manni asking for her help to replace 100,000 Marks that he has misplaced on the subway. The money is for his gangster boss, who is certain to kill Manni if he doesn't receive it. Lola has 20 minutes to find the cash and reach Manni before he resorts to robbing a supermarket. The film portrays three varying narrative timelines of events where small choices made by Lola impact not only on Manni's own fate but also all on those with whom she comes into contact.

Tykwer's fourth feature was a huge success in Germany and sparked what was considered to be a new era of German cinema. Functioning at an extremely high pace, the film reflects restlessness in a German society that had been through enormous change and that was preparing to embark on a new century. Heavily influenced by American and British genre cinema, Tykwer set out to create a film that presented national themes in an international way. As discussed by David Clarke, with the innovative look to his films, Tykwer was soon considered to be an auteur by critics, with a clear focus on action throughout and themes about questioning the natural elements of life such as relationships and the future. This essay discusses how the unusual filmic style and signature themes of Tykwer situate him as an easily recognisable auteur.

The film begins with a blurred vision of a crowd and a voiceover questioning the purpose of life. This voiceover comes from Hans Paetsch (1939–2002), Germany's most popular fairy-tale narrator. Faces are picked out from the crowd; the audience doesn't know it yet but these are the people that Lola will interact with and whose lives she will affect. One man in the crowd looks into the camera and says, 'the ball is round, the game is 90 minutes, everything else is just theory'. This is in fact a quote from the football coach, Sepp Herberger, who brought the German football team to victory in the 1954 World Cup. The use of Paetsch and Herberger in this opening sequence provided instantly recognisable reference points for the contemporary national audience of this film, but also for those familiar with German culture generally.

The film's heroine, Lola, is quickly introduced. She is on the phone to her boyfriend, Manni, and a series of flashbacks play out in black and white, explaining what had occurred in the hour before. This black and white style clearly signifies the past, as by contrast, both characters are surrounded by bold colours in the present time scenes. Lola has bright red hair and Manni appears in the bright yellow phone booth; both are colours that Tykwer uses to signify the danger that the characters are in. Both characters are heard repeating the mantra '100,000 Marks' from many different camera angles. The repetition of this action from different perspectives links in with the different angles that Lola's life will take depending on the choices she makes hereon in. This is also evident in the television programme that Lola has playing in the background, as it shows one domino fall into another, the consequence being that all the others fall. The 'domino effect' is repeated several times in the film; for instance in one scenario Lola causes a car accident, delaying Manni's gangster boss from reaching him on time, but in the other scenario the car crash is avoided and so Manni has no respite from his violent boss.

The familiarity that is used to draw in the national audience is echoed throughout the film, as familiarity is a driving force of Tykwer's work. As the film has three alternative narratives set in the same locations, we become extremely familiar with Lola's surroundings. We are introduced to Lola in her bedroom in her parent's apartment. The room is dingy and a 360-degree track shot shows us that each wall is painted a different colour; it is messy and fits in with her scruffy appearance. On first impressions it could be that this dark room is part of a bedsit or small flat; however, when Lola emerges we enter the rest of the luxurious apartment and it is bright and fresh in stark contrast to Lola's room. The apartment and appearance of her mother on the telephone is reminiscent of the bourgeois portrayals of earlier German cinema. Lola appears as a rebellious nonconformist young woman. This is supported by the soundtrack that accompanies Lola as she runs: techno music plays and footage is edited on the beat, switching from long shots to close-ups. As Lola runs down the street, frames are removed making it appear that she is advancing faster. This filming style appears similar to that of music videos, perhaps trying to appeal to the MTV generation of the late 1990s, as reflected by the character Lola herself. In these opening minutes Lola is presented as outgoing and confident, not afraid to express herself or break the rules.

The filming style of Tykwer is a key component in engaging the audience. The 20 minutes of Lola's run are played out three times, heightening the suspense as the resolution is delayed. Each time Tykwer presents the first segment of Lola's run in an animated style. Combined with the fast-paced music the scene has the look of a video game; each time the sequence is slightly different – the first time Lola is scared of a dog in the hallway, the second time she is tripped up by its owner, but the third time she jumps over them. This reinforces the video game style as Lola has learnt from her mistake and improves the first section of her run, just as the player would learn how to complete a level of a videogame after a few attempts. The camera spirals the staircase each time echoing the camera work from an earlier auteur, Alfred Hitchcock in masterpiece films such as *Vertigo* (1958).

As Lola continues to run, parallel editing is used to cut to her father working at the bank. He is having an affair with his colleague, Jutta, and she is questioning his love for her. He is a successful man with a family, and to outsiders he appears content with hit lot, but his life is full of cracks and deceit. These scenes are not shot with the same crispness as the outdoor scenes of Lola running. The footage is grainy and the handheld camera is deliberately distracting for the audience. This serves to distance us from these characters and causes our empathy to remain with the vibrant Lola. She interrupts the lovers' conversation and asks her father to give her the 100,000 Marks that Manni needs, but as he doesn't know who Manni is, he refuses. Escorting her off the premises he tells her he is not her father and won't be returning to the family home. This bizarre and blunt exchange occurs so quickly that it is almost dreamlike.

The hazy red bedroom scenes that occur in between the second and third timescales prompt the concept that the film's three narrative scenarios are dreams. Lola and Manni lie in bed sharing their thoughts with each other. Lola asks Manni if he loves her and questions how he can be sure, and then the second scenario begins. This is the scene that we go back to, reinforcing the central importance of their relationship. Manni asks Lola, what would she do if he were to die? She responds saying she wouldn't let him and so the last scenario begins. It could be argued that the narratives that follow are dreamlike sequences where Lola is playing out the questions they have posed to each other. Would she be able to save him? How would she do it? Do they love each other enough to risk everything? In each scenario obstacles get in her way and a second's difference in her actions or a slight change in her decisions alter the story that follows greatly. It becomes intriguing to the audience that familiar surroundings, characters and conversations do not become predictable, as each narrative differs.

The filming style constantly provides the viewer with the unexpected. In the first order of events a split screen is used to show in one half Lola running to Manni and in the other half him waiting for her. The clock then appears at the bottom of the screen highlighting her race against it. An audience influenced by Hollywood cinema may expect Lola to reach Manni just in time, akin to the action films where the hero is in a race against the clock to disarm a bomb. However, expectations are not met as the clock reaches 12 and Manni enters the supermarket to rob it. As the couple flee the supermarket 'What A Diff'rence A Day Makes' sung by Dinah Washington is the accompanying track. This recognisable voice and recognisable lyrics enables an international audience to relate to the song, expanding the film's familiarity from the national appeal of the opening scene.

Unconventional turns in the narrative continue as the police arrive and Lola is shot. This is a shock as we expect the heroine to escape the ordeal. As Lola falls to the ground the audience may well question where the director will take the characters now, as we are only 20 minutes in. This results in a lack of satisfaction; the death of the heroine is not the conventional resolution. Luckily for an audience requiring a more 'Hollywood' conclusion Tykwer quickly provides an alternative ending. Tykwer often employs a graphic match to change narrative direction, between locations or time frames and here he does so again. The red bag containing the stolen money spins into the air and is interchanged with the spinning red phone, which Lola uses to communicate with Manni at the start of the narrative. The graphic match takes us back to the beginning, signifying that Lola has another chance to make things work.

Throughout her run Lola comes into contact with several strangers; as we see them three times during the film, these characters become recognisable to us. Each time she sees them Lola has a slightly different impact upon their lives. This theme of consequence runs through the 81 minutes of the narrative as it is presented. Her inability to pick up Manni in the first instance is the trigger for the entire film. Lola's behaviour also affects the way she is treated; for example, as each sequence passes she becomes more erratic and violent. Thus the security guard at the bank shows less and less empathy towards her each time. Lola comes into contact with the homeless man who has Manni's money in all three sequences but there is a few seconds' difference in timing. First she runs past him but the next time she runs into him; Manni has told her that a homeless man has the money but she is so focussed on her goal that she doesn't see the person she has collided with. It could be argued that Tykwer is demonstrating how in society we are in close proximity with each other but we do not pay attention to what surrounds us; we are in fact individuals only focussed on ourselves not community.

Tykwer's cinematic style is exhilarating to watch, his narrative contains mainstream conventions put together in an unconventional way. The ambiguity of the film is eventually concluded as Lola succeeds in her quest in the last sequence, and so Tykwer's action-packed style conforms finally to the Hollywood endings that had inspired his generation of filmmakers and which has global appeal.

Further reading

David Clarke, 'Welcome to Tykwer-World: Tom Tykwer as Auteur', in *GFL*. Available at www.gfl-journal.de/3-2006/clarke.pdf (accessed: 12 February 2012).

Richard Falcon, 'Review: *Run Lola Run*', in *Sight and Sound*, 1999. Available at www.bfi.org.uk/sightandsound/review/245 (accessed: 14 February 2012).

Thom Holbrook, 'Good God Run Lola Run', in *Thom Holbrook's Hollywood Homepage*. Available at http://home.earthlink.net/~jinxo/lola.html (accessed: 14 February 2012).

Annegret Mahler-Bungers, 'A Post-Postmodern Walkyrie: Psychoanalytic Considerations on Tom Tykwer's *Run, Lola, Run* (1998)', in Andrea Sabbadini (ed.), *The Couch and the Silver Screen: Psychoanalytic Reflections on European Cinema*, London, Routledge, 2003, pp. 82–93.

Barrie Wilson, 'What's It About? Reflections on Tom Tykwer's *Run Lola Run*'. Available at www.barriewilson.com/pdf/Reflections-on-Run-Lola-Run.pdf (accessed: 12 February 2012).

Holly Taylor

M (1931)

[Country: Germany. Production Company: Nero-Film AG. Director: Fritz Lang. Screenwriters: Thea von Harbou and Lang. Cinematographer: Fritz Arno Wagner. Cast: Peter Lorre (Hans Beckert), Otto Wernicke (Inspector Karl Lohmann), Gustaf Grundgens (Der Schranker), Ellen Widmann (Frau Beckmann), Inge Landgut (Elsie Beckmann), Theodor Loos (Inspector Groeber), Friedrich Gnass (Franz, the burglar).]

Synopsis: With a child-murderer in their midst the people of a German city are gripped by fear. The police crack down on known criminals in an effort to find the killer. This disrupts crime in the city, and so, the criminal fraternity set out to find the offender themselves. They track him down and the police arrive just in time to save him from death at the hands of a kangaroo court.

M is an extended meditation on evil and its presence within society. It is also an exploration of the reactions of society to this presence. Human beings are shown as being fascinated by evil. Lang points to the vicarious pleasure we gain from reading about it: newspaper sales, for example, take off in this city with a child murderer on the loose. The magazine salesman who comes to Elsie's mother's door functions within the plot as a means of increasing suspense during the tense opening minutes of the film, but is also very deliberately seen to be offering the public something 'suspenseful, captivating, sensational'. These words could also be used to describe both the product Lang is putting before his audience, and what we are looking for as we very deliberately and intentionally sit down to 'enjoy' the film.[1]

Lang portrays a society that is very willing to condemn evil (in others), and to call for the death penalty to be carried out; screaming faces cry 'Kill the murderer', and 'Put this animal to death' at the climax to the scene in which Hans Beckert (Peter Lorre) finds himself before the 'court' organised by the criminals. It is also a society in which the public can quickly become a mob; an elderly man helping a young girl is quickly surrounded by a crowd, and a pickpocket who is being arrested is mistaken for the murderer and attacked. The public at the 'trial' sit as might an audience for a play starring Lorre, a well-known theatre actor, but continually teeter on the brink of giving way to their pack instinct. They are controlled by the mock form and order given to the event by the leader of the criminals, Schranker (Gustaf Grundgens). But they are also stirred to a pitch of intensity by this same man, who like a Fascist orator can become passionately animated. 'A man who claims about himself that it was forced upon him to destroy lives: that man must be extinguished like a bonfire! That man must be obliterated: wiped out!' he rages at one point.[2]

Germany in 1931 is a country quickly moving towards being taken over by Adolf Hitler's National Socialist Party. After the humiliation of the peace conditions imposed on the country at the end of the First World War, a proportion of the population had been willing to entertain the extreme right-wing politics of this party. Now, after the full impact of the global economic depression that started in 1929 has begun to bite, and with millions unemployed, the audience for their ideas has grown considerably.[3] The Nazi Party's brown-shirted militaristic wing, the Sturmabteilungen (SA), has begun to openly attack Jews, Communists, trade unionists and others in the streets. As an artist, it is becoming increasingly difficult, not to say, dangerous, to include even liberal democratic social sentiments in your work.

When, in the film, we see the authorities deciding what is to be done about finding the serial killer, we realise it is not just Schranker who employs terminology that sounds as if it is moving us towards a totalitarian state. The solution from one is: 'Increase ID checks, systematic searches of the whole city, and raids.' From another: 'Every home-owner, landlord, everyone owning property must be forced to consent to detailed searches.' And when we move to the criminals discussing the same situation the cry from one of them is: 'We need more informers!' These elements of the dialogue effectively sum up the increasing difficulties felt by those of a liberal persuasion living in Germany.

In the end, Beckert is shown as having a greater capacity for self-reflection than Schranker. He knows where the evil resides, that it is within himself. As he describes it: 'Always I have to roam the streets and I always sense that someone is following me. It is me! And I shadow myself! Sometimes I feel like I'm hunting myself down. I want to run – run away from me! But I can't! I can't flee from myself!' Beckert knows the dark heart, the alter ego, is always there. Schranker, on the other hand, has no awareness of the irony of forcefully advocating a drive to 'extinguish', to 'obliterate', to 'wipe out' even as he condemns somebody else for their drive to 'destroy lives'.

One artist who did consistently produce work of social protest in the period that was directed especially against the brutality done to the young by war was Kathe Kollwitz. In black and white drawings and prints she depicted grieving mothers and women with their arms wrapped protectively around their children. The final frames of Lang's film show three women in black at the end of Beckert's proper trial. The one at the centre is the mother of Elsie Beckmann, the child killed at the start of *M*, and she addresses us directly. 'This will not bring our children back', she says. 'One has to take more care of them.' The shot then fades to black before her final word comes across the screen in a gentle pleading voice, 'You!' Lang's final sentiment[4] echoes Kollwitz, and the connection makes it clear that he is attempting to talk about more than just serial killers in this film.

Kollwitz was also an artist who depicted poverty and working-class life with compassion. And again, Lang does the same. At the beginning of the film, the domestic routine of the women in the tenement where Elsie lives is portrayed with tenderness and attention to detail. Later, the police investigation allows for a documentary-style shot inside a hostel for homeless men; two long rows of men, described as 'the vagrant population', are tightly packed on camp-beds. Within the narrative we have a city in which the streets are so alive with beggars that the criminals can easily organise them as spies to look for the murderer without suspicions being raised; and, on the back of this, Lang (himself invalided out of the army during the war) can use shots of a legless man and another with one leg, begging.

Lang, however, is aware that situations are complex rather than simple. And so, he presents an understanding of the position of the poor and the economic context of the time,[5] but also voices more critical perspectives on the public in general. 'Most of the public still think, "What's in it for me?" It never occurs to the masses that what happens to even the poorest or most unknown child on the street is a matter for everyone's conscience', says one official. Similarly, lest we should think Karl Lohmann (Otto Wernicke) is simply the voice of common sense, Lang gives a shot of him from a very low angle beneath his desk that presents him as a rather fat slob with a cigar who quite enjoys questioning suspects. Most importantly of all, he makes sure we see exactly how brutal the members of the crime world are in reality when they question a night-watchman at the factory where Beckert is hiding.[6]

Finally though, it is worth remembering that as we are watching this film all of the attention so far offered here to contexts needs to be placed alongside an awareness of Lang's artistry. If we just take the opening to the film, for example, we find that without any graphic images we are moved quickly and frighteningly towards the first murder within just eight minutes of the film starting. Interestingly, despite the speed with which this takes place in overall screen-time, the audience is made to feel every second that passes. The clock on the wall ticks; Elsie bounces her ball to the rhythm of a ticking clock; her mother moves with slow, heavy steps; the camera holds shots for longer than is necessary; and the editing cuts backwards and forwards, backwards and forwards. There is much more that could be said about the meticulous detail of the construction, but as one more example consider the shots of empty spaces with which we are confronted in this opening. The shot of Elsie's ball rolling into an empty patch of wasteground signals her death, but see how we have been prepared for this. We have had shots of an empty landing, an empty stairwell, an implied empty street (as Elsie's mother leans from the window to call her name), back to the empty stairwell, an empty loft-space, an empty chair, and only then, the empty patch of wasteland. The ball rolls into shot from right to left, against the more normal movement of left to right across the screen, and in the same direction as the balloon moves as it is taken out of the telegraph wires by the wind in the next shot.[7]

Lang's dramatic use of sound is also often commented on.[8] Beckert, for instance, hauntingly whistles the most famous few bars from 'In the Hall of the Mountain King', part of Edvard Greig's music to Henrick Ibsen's play, *Peer Gynt*. That the pace of the music becomes faster and more insistent as he is driven towards committing murder is entirely appropriate, but the work is also thematically relevant. This is a play set in the Land of the Trolls who are used by Ibsen as a symbol of evil. The trolls were originally the implacable enemy of man and would eat unwary travellers who strayed into their land after dark. In the end it is difficult to pin down simple, straight correspondences between events and characters in *M* and Germany as an emerging totalitarian state, and in the end the film is much richer because of this. However, there are sufficient oblique thematic links like this to push an audience towards these sorts of reflections; and there were enough perceived connections to mean the film was banned in Germany in 1934 when the Nazis came to be fully in command of the country.

Notes

1. The nursery rhyme the children sing at the beginning of the film about the 'bogeyman' coming to get them quickly and efficiently reminds us of the crucial role given to evil in popular/folk culture.
2. This is not a one-off moment of ranting from Schranker. When we first see him he enters a room in his black leather coat and within a few minutes is clenching his fists and proclaiming: 'This monster has no right to survive. It must disappear, be eliminated; exterminated without mercy or scruples'.
3. In the elections of 1930 the National Socialists gained around 6.5 million votes compared to well under a million in 1928. They became the second largest party in the Reichstag with 107 seats. In 1932 the Party polled almost 14 million votes and won 230 seats.
4. And he has recorded how important Thea von Harbou's contribution was to this. See Gero Gandert, 'Fritz Lang on *M*: An Interview' in Barry Keith Grant (ed.), *Fritz Lang: Interviews*, Jackson, MS, University Press of Mississippi, 2003, pp. 33–7.
5. With carefully chosen dialogue we learn, for example, that Beckert has been taken to an old distillery that 'folded in the Depression' and since then has been 'abandoned and nobody gives a damn about it'.
6. Earlier a camera has travelled along the haul the police have made from their raids on criminal haunts and revealed in amongst the burglary tools and stolen goods, knives, pistols and vicious-looking knuckle-dusters.
7. When Elsie comes out of school a few minutes earlier she tries to cross the road from right to left back across the shot and is almost run over by a passing car. (We have also, incidentally, been prepared for these wires, scored violently across the screen, by earlier shots of washing lines.)
8. See, for example, '*M* (1931) or Sound and Terror' in Stephen Brockman, *A Critical History of German Film*, Rochester, NY, Camden House, 2010, pp. 113–27. Also Todd Herzog, 'Fritz Lang's *M* (1931): An Open Case' in Noah Isenberg (ed.), *Weimar Cinema: An Essential Guide to Classic Films of the Era*, Columbia University Press, 2009, pp. 291–310.

Further reading

Anton Kaes, *M*, London, BFI, 2000.

John White

Machuca (2004)

[Country: Chile, Spain, UK, France. Production Company: Wood Producciones. Director: Andrés Wood. Producers: Mamoun Hassan, Andrés Wood and Gerardo Herrero. Screenwriters: Roberto Brodsky, Mamoun Hassan and Andrés Wood. Editors: Fernando Pado, Soledad Salfate. Cinematographer: Miguel Ioann Littin Menz. Music: Miguel Miranda, José Miguel Tobar. Cast: Matias Quer (Gonzalo Infante), Ariel Mateluna (Pedro Machuca), Manuela Martelli (Silvana), Ernesto Malbran (Father McEnroe), Federico Luppi (Roberto Ochagavía).]

Synopsis: Set in the turbulent months leading up General Augusto Pinochet's violent coup on 11 September 1973, the film's historical events are witnessed by child protagonists, Gonzalo, Pedro and Silvana. Specifically, the film follows Gonzalo as his loyalty is caught between his middle-class, and mostly right-wing family, and his two new friends, Pedro and Silvana, who come from a newly erected slum in the capital city Santiago. Their meeting is the outcome of a socialist programme within Gonzalo's private school that offers scholarships to students from poor backgrounds yet much of the film plays out amongst their families and the urban districts of Santiago. At the same time that Gonzalo's father sweeps confidently through the black markets and his mother conducts a clandestine affair with a wealthy Argentine benefactor, Pedro and Silvana join their uncle making small change from selling memorabilia to the opposing political factions demonstrating on the streets. The friendship and the conflict around them change their lives and their country forever.

When Andrés Wood's *Machuca* opened to nationwide box office success and critical acclaim in Chile during 2004, it placed itself within a twenty-first-century generation of bold and provocative Latin American films and proved that after almost 30 years without any significant film industry, Chilean cinema was able to return to the world stage. It was all the more remarkable for its sensitive treatment of Chile's political history at a time when discussion of the country's military dictatorship (1973–1990) remained taboo.

Machuca's examination of class, social structures and the state is part of a lengthy political filmmaking tradition in Chile yet one that was interrupted and sent overseas for an extended period. Although Chilean filmmakers such as Miguel Littin, Raúl Ruiz and Helvio Soto were at the forefront of an expansion of radical cinema across the continent in the 1960s and 1970s (the New Latin American Cinema movement), their work was curtailed by a military regime that not only exiled and executed left-leaning filmmakers but also removed historical memory of the nation's cinema through the destruction of important archives. Peter B. Schumman points to the extraordinary situation in the late 1970s whereby, for the first time in cinema's history 'a national cinema has been forced to try to continue its life internationally because almost everyone working in film has been driven into exile' (1979: 13). Patricio Guzman, Raoul Ruiz, Miguel Littin, Helvio Soto and other directors continued to provide critical analysis of their home country, often touching on the same time period as *Machuca*, but their locations overseas necessitated reflective, often introverted, consideration of their new position as an exile caught between past and present, home and afar. *Machuca* was the first major release emanating from within Chile's national borders to explore the military coup and to suggest how a national public sphere may see itself and its past. This is not an unproblematic task and, as Luis Martín-Cabrera and Daniel Noemi Voionmaa (2007) have discussed, *Machuca* provoked fierce public and critical debate about the relevance the problems depicted in the film have for contemporary Chilean society. They suggest that the film itself is conscious of society's difficulty of 'seeing' the events of the coup and understanding how they continue to have an impact on the present.

On the one hand, *Machuca* is able to address these issues due to the authenticity and weight that it given by the well-known factual basis of events within the film. Although Wood has stated emphatically that the film is not autobiographical, his film draws on moments that did occur. Wood was of a similar age to Gonzalo during 1973 and his school participated in the experiment whereby the catholic priests decided to mix their students with boys from the lower classes. The true-life nature of events and the trauma that ultimately unfolds means that comparisons can be drawn between *Machuca* and the testimonial literature that emerged in the wake of repressive military regimes across Latin America in the twentieth century. Each fictional account bears witness to painful situations that might otherwise be forgotten or overlooked. Within *Machuca*, the attention to detail in the audio and visual recreation of 1970s Chile – from the careful reproduction of costume, props and music as well as graffiti on walls, newspaper headlines and political slogans on placards – means that this testimony is recreated in vivid detail. Although many of the successful political films of the New Latin American Cinema movement, such as *La Hora de los Hornos/The Hour of the Furnaces* (Octavio Getino and Fernando Solanas, 1968), *Deus e o Diabo na Terra do Sol/Black God, White Devil* (Glauber Rocha, 1964) and *Memorias del subdesarollo/Memories of Underdevelopment* (Tomás Gutiérrez Alea, 1968), experimented with film style and narrative tendencies, *Machuca* returns to more conventional storytelling techniques (a linear narrative, continuity editing and lucid characterisation) in order to show its events in a coherent manner.

At the same time, *Machuca* purposefully eschews objectivity by filtering events through the eyes of children in a way that reminds us of the instability of obtaining a clear view. Within *Machuca*, the child's gaze is the mechanism for positing the problem of 'seeing' events and so the scope of the film is continuously limited to the direct experience of the children. This use of the child's view continues a trend within Latin American filmmaking that uses children as central characters to explore wider social and political issues. Following films such as Leonardo Favio's *Crónica de un Niño Solo/Chronicle of a Boy Alone* (1964), Hector Babenco's *Pixote* (1981) and Fernando Meirelles and Katie Lund's *Cidade de Deus/City of God* (2002), the children's innocence and youth is juxtaposed with the role of the adult oppressor and the abuse of power. When the coup does take place, these characters have no overview of the political mechanisms that are taking place at a national, regional and global level (the US support for the new regime for example). They are unaware of how their country is dramatically changing but instead experience highly personal moments such as the entry of soldiers into the school; the poignant moment during which Padre McEnroe denounces the new regime by devouring the sacred host and declaring god is no longer there; and the harrowing moment when Silvana is shot dead. Although highly traumatic, these events should not necessarily be read as a micro-representation of the situation as a whole. Instead, they point to the fragmented and destabilised situation that negated any possibility of a rational or balanced understanding of what occurred.

Frequently in Latin American films with child protagonists, marginalised children become a symbol of a society in which it is impossible to grow. This factor becomes all the more important at the end of *Machuca* when Gonzalo retreats into his comfortable middle-class world and Pedro and Silvana have exited the screen. Martín-Cabrera and Voionmaa rightly note that by the end of the film, Gonzalo has become a witness to state-sponsored violence and that the football field that he looks out onto in the final sequence is haunted by the ghosts of Chile's violent past. Nonetheless his small, diminutive figure within the scene makes it clear that it will take time before he is old enough to understand what it is that he has witnessed.

The film premiered at a time (14 years after the end of the dictatorship) when Gonzalo would have reached adulthood and been at a suitable age to undertake this understanding; thus the reflective, looking back nature of *Machuca*. However, Woods evades any sense of presenting black and white facts and has stated in interview that 'it's a partial history, subjective, and it doesn't pretend to be the official story' (cited in Esther, 2005: 67). There is a constant use of nostalgic moments (Pedro and Gonzalo sharing a bike, reading comic books in bed, attending the birthday party of Gonzalo's sister) and objects (lollipops, Adidas sneakers, black and white television sets) that present the familiar and remembered past in a way that calls for an emotional relationship with the film's content.

Gonzalo and Pedro's loving consumption of the Lone Ranger comic books, their greedy scoffing of condensed milk cans, and dancing to the vibrant pop music of the time means that the chaos and suffering around them are mitigated and complicated by genuine enjoyment of their childhood state. In turn, the audience is asked to share in these mixed feelings and produce an emotional as much as an analytical reflection on the past. It is this quality that prevents any potential for a didactic political message within the film's content.

Nonetheless, critical questions are raised. While Pedro's racial heritage is not explicitly referred to within the film, his dark features were picked up by various Spanish language reviewers who described him as Indio (Indian/Indigenous). This aspect allowed them to make a comparison between the young friends and the conflicted but often reconciliatory relationship between cowboys and Indians in the comic books that the young boys adore. This in turn points to the uneasy relationship between not only left- and right-wing political factions in Chile at this time but also the hierarchies of class, race and family heritage left over from the country's colonial era. It is telling that Gonzalo is given the most screen time within the film, and it very much appears to be his story, but it is Pedro, whose surname is Machuca, who becomes the namesake for the film. In this way, *Machuca* doesn't completely avoid the tendency for Chilean culture to ignore its racially inscribed subjects, but does find a way to refocus attention on those who might otherwise go 'unseen.'

The ongoing traces of these issues in contemporary society made the film particularly potent on its release, provoking much debate within cinemas and across Chile's various press and other media. While the debates provoked by *Machuca's* treatment of Chile's past will never be conclusively resolved, the national and international presence of the film has allowed it to introduce an audiovisual reflection on a difficult period in history that demands audience engagement which is active and involved.

Further reading

Julianne Burton, 'The Camera as "Gun": Two Decades of Culture and Resistance in Latin America', *Latin American Perspectives*, 5:1, 1978, pp. 49–76.

John Esther, 'Chile in the Time of the Generals: An interview with Andrés Wood', *Cineaste*, Summer, 2005, p. 67.

John King, 'Chilean Cinema in Revolution and Exile', Michael T. Martin (ed.), *New Latin American Cinema, Volume Two*, Detroit, Wayne State University Press, 1997, pp. 397–419.

John King, *Magical Reels: A History of Cinema in Latin America*, London, Verso, 2000.

Luis Martín-Cabrera and Daniel Noemi Voionmaa, 'Class conflict, state of exception and radical justice in *Machuca* by Andrés Wood', *Journal of Latin American Cultural Studies*, 16:1, 2007, pp. 63–80.

Zuzana M. Pick, 'Chilean Cinema in Exile, 1973–1986' Michael T. Martin (ed.) *New Latin American Cinema, Volume Two*, Detroit, Wayne State University Press, 1997, pp. 423–40.

Peter B. Schumann, 'The Chilean Cinema in Exile', *Framework*, 10, 1979, pp. 13–14.

Miriam Ross

Mad Max (1979)

[Country: Australia. Production Company: Crossroads. Director: George Miller. Producer: Byron Kennedy. Scriptwriters: James McCausland, George Miller and Byron Kennedy. Cinematographer: David Eggby. Music: Brian May. Cast: Mel Gibson (Max Rockatansky), Joanne Samuel (Jessie Rockatansky), Hugh Keays-Byrne (Toe-cutter), Steve Bisley (Jim Goose), Vince Gill (Nightrider),

Tim Burns (Johnny the Boy), Roger Ward (Fifi Macaffee), Geoff Parry (Bubba Zanetti), Sheila Florance (May Swaisey).]

Synopsis: Set in a future time 'a few years from now' *Mad Max* tells the story of a battle between nomad bikers who are running rampant on the roads, and the policemen who are chasing them, trying to curb their anarchic behaviour. Max Rockatansky, played by a youthful Mel Gibson in a role that launched his career, is one of the policemen working for the law enforcement group, Main Force Patrol (MFP). Max divides his time between his commitment to his family, his wife Jessie (Joanne Samuel) and son Sprog (Brendan Heath), and the dangerous demands of his job. After a series of tragic events, an increasingly solitary Max finds himself doomed to a life on the road, and the film becomes a fully-fledged revenge narrative.

> No other Australian films have influenced world cinema and popular cinema as widely and lastingly as George Miller's *Mad Max* movies – *Mad Max*, *Mad Max 2* (US title, *The Road Warrior*) and *Mad Max Beyond Thunderdome*.[1]

Mad Max is a landmark film in Australian cinema history. While it started out as a small, independently funded production, it went on to achieve phenomenal national and international success, and spawned two sequels, *Mad Max 2: The Road Warrior* (1981) and *Mad Max 3: Beyond Thunderdome* (1985). Film scholar Adrian Martin has persuasively argued that no other Australian films have had such a profound or extensive influence on world cinema as this trilogy of films.[2] So, how did this important film get to be made, and what was it about *Mad Max* that created such global interest, leading to several sequels?

The origins of *Mad Max* began with the fateful meeting of George Miller and Byron Kennedy at a film seminar in Melbourne in 1971. Both Miller and Kennedy had already made short films before, but it was here that they decided to join forces and make films together. Their first film was the short, *Violence in the Cinema, Part 1*, a playful engagement with debates about screen violence that were provoked by films like *A Clockwork Orange* (1971) and *Straw Dogs* (1971). This film found an audience and was distributed commercially and sold overseas.[3] In 1975 the Kennedy-Miller team turned their attention to their first feature film, *Mad Max*. Miller co-wrote the screenplay with journalist James McCausland, and assumed the directorial role. Kennedy produced the film, but was also creatively involved in some filming and post-production work. *Mad Max* was independently financed with a budget of around $380,000, and while there was a time towards the end of post-production where they literally ran out of money, it went on to make over $100 million worldwide.

In the late 1970s the Australian film industry was dominated by two types, or models, of film-making. These were the disreputable 'ocker comedy' (*The Adventures of Barry McKenzie* (Bruce Beresford, 1972) and *Alvin Purple* (Tim Burstall, 1973)) and the 'well-made' quality film (*Picnic at Hanging Rock* (Peter Weir, 1975) and *The Getting of Wisdom* (Beresford, 1977)). Australian cinema historian Tom O'Regan, says that *Mad Max*'s arrival onto cinema screens 'rudely shook up' the film industry in a number of ways. First, it was a genre film, which up until then was uncommon in Australian filmmaking. Second, it was independently funded, in an industry that relied largely on funding from government sources. Third, its international success was more the result of a growing cult status rather than a launch at a film festival such as Cannes. And, fourth, it proposed very different ideas of what was meant by 'Australianness'. So, as O'Regan explains, *Mad Max* challenged a litany of conventional practices, and it did this in a highly visible way on a national and international stage.[4]

Further evidence of the film's provocation can be found in reviews written at the time. Most critics acknowledged its technical virtuosity, but were concerned about its violence. O'Regan himself said that when he first saw the film he 'remembers saying aloud to no one in particular in the theatre, "This film is evil"'.[5] Producer and writer Philip Adams shared some of O'Regan's anxiety and said that while 'Dr. Miller has … revived a geriatric genre …. [his] epic has all the moral uplift of Mein Kampf'.[6] Adams even suggested the film should be banned. Film reviewer Martha Du Bose, expressed a point of view that was widely shared, and that was that the film was 'extremely violent [and] patently lacking in redeeming social value'.[7]

When asked, in an interview for *Cinema Papers*, where the idea of *Mad Max* came from, George Miller spoke about the 'car culture' that he saw when he was growing up in regional Queensland, and that he continued to witness when he worked as a doctor in a casualty department in a city hospital.

> Every year, in an entirely predictable fashion, about a thousand people die on Victorian roads. In spite of our efforts we are not able to modify those numbers significantly. The statistics are so consistent; it is as though we are operating under some immutable law of nature. We make funny noises, but none of us really understands what's happening. The USA has its gun culture, we have our car culture.[8]

And yet, while the story of *Mad Max* may have initially been motivated by real-life 'car culture' and the trauma of car accidents, the film's depiction of stylised cars and spectacular car crashes is as far away from documentary realism as you could imagine. Instead, the 'car culture' of the film is one that replays different elements of cinematic genres such as the western, the road movie and the action film, underlining the fact that the greatest source of inspiration for *Mad Max* is the cinema.

In his *Mad Max Movies* book Adrian Martin elaborates on the centrality of the cinema to *Mad Max*. He begins by declaring that George Miller is 'Australia's most completely cinematic filmmaker'[9] and that his passion for the cinema is evident in every aspect of the film's formal construction: in its audiovisual palette and its montage construction, as well as in its many references to other films. Martin goes on to cite the many ways in which Miller is inspired by some quite classical filmmakers such as Fritz Lang, Orson Welles, Alfred Hitchcock and Robert Aldrich.[10] But, while Martin acknowledges the classical cinematic lineage that Miller's film draws on, he also argues that:

> *Mad Max* is Australia's greatest B movie. That it is not often acknowledged as such is due to several extenuating factors, such as its huge box office success and the retroactive gloss cast by its much more expensive sequels.[11]

In making this claim about *Mad Max*, Martin both celebrates and takes pleasure in some of the film's more expressive formal strategies such as 'multiplying the cuts and insert shots' and 'boosting the musical score with a large orchestra at full throttle'.[12] These B movie features are part of Miller's playful, experimental, and sometimes outlandish, choreography of images, sounds and montage that immerse us in a world of car chases, motorcycle rides, collisions and angry confrontations, with cars framed low to the road, the road unfurling in front of us, and a series of ricocheting point of view shots that take us inside and outside of cars.

But Miller also uses these editing strategies to pose questions that are at the heart of many crime stories. The very first shot of the film is of a building called The Halls of Justice, and this dissolves into a view of a road, then a skull and a road sign pointing to Anarchie Road. From an imposing image of justice to an image of anarchy and lawlessness, this juxtaposition of images invites us to question what form justice will take in this film. These questions continue when we are introduced to a man who is viewing two people making love through a gun's telescopic sight. This voyeur turns out to be a policeman called Roop and his surveillance operation is interrupted with a call on CB radio directing him and his fellow policeman The Big Bopper to chase a 'cop killer'. Such questions about whether there is any difference between the policeman and the cop killer continue to be asked throughout the film.

Mad Max has gone on to be regarded as a key film in Australian cinema history and has been the subject of many erudite and scholarly analyses such as those by Ross Gibson and Meaghan Morris who have examined different ideas of 'Australianness' that the film explores. For example, in a close reading of the third film in the trilogy *Beyond Thunderdome*, Gibson discusses the landscape and suggests that the trilogy can be read as 'a chronicle of the collective loss of faith in the drive to conquer the environment'.[13] In an article called 'White Panic, or *Mad Max* and the Sublime' Morris provides a particularly insightful analysis of *Mad Max* where she asks how a 'national' cinema like Australia's has dealt with 'the psycho *dynamics* of whiteness'.[14] These issues of the landscape, whiteness, indigenous relations, and invasion tap into larger questions about what it means to live in Australia.

Thirty years after its release, *Mad Max* continues to exert an ongoing influence on all forms of cultural production. At the 2009 Venice Biennale the artist Shaun Gladwell exhibited 'MADDESTMAX-IMVS' which was inspired by *Mad Max* in a number of ways, from the video that features a black-helmeted motorcycle rider in a hostile landscape to the fully functioning 'sculptural' replica of Max's V8 Interceptor car that was part of the installation. The remix artists Soda_Jerk have also drawn on *Mad Max* in their trilogy of video works titled, *Terror Nullius*, where they explore cinematic representations of Australia and their connections to histories of invasion. One of the pieces in the trilogy, titled 'Picnic at Wolf Creek', features a plot that includes 'the girls from Hanging Rock', 'the psycho from Wolf Creek' and a 'rescue attempt by Mad Max and Skippy', combining several mythic characters and narratives from Australian cinema.[15]

In addition to these ongoing influences, the Mad Max trilogy is about to become a quartet. In 1999, on the anniversary of the first *Mad Max* film, George Miller announced that there would be a *Mad Max 4*. Out of the many possible reasons to make a fourth *Mad Max* film, Miller has spoken about CGI and the way in which these technical developments would make the *Mad Max* films 'a whole new ball game'.[16] However, just as there were obstacles and problems encountered with the production of the first film, so there appear to have been many more with this latest instalment. In early 2012, ten years after the initial announcement, *Mad Max 4: Fury Road* is listed as currently in production and the road warrior's journey is set to continue.

Notes

1. Adrian Martin, *The Mad Max Movies*, Sydney, Currency Press and Screen Sound Australia, 2003, p. 1.
2. Adrian Martin, *The Mad Max Movies*, p. 1.
3. '*Mad Max*', *Cinema Papers*, April 1979, pp. 43–9.
4. Tom O'Regan, 'The Enchantment with Cinema: Film in the 1980s' in Albert Moran and Tom O'Regan (eds), *The Australian Screen*, London, Penguin, 1989, p. 126.
5. Ibid, p. 126.
6. Phillip Adams, 'The Dangerous Pornography of Death', *Bulletin*, 1 May, 1979, pp. 38–41.
7. Martha Dubose, 'Violent, Lacking in Social Value', *Sydney Morning Herald*, 7 July 1979, p. 21.
8. George Miller interview, *Cinema Papers*, April 1979, p. 47.
9. Martin, p. 12.
10. Martin, p. 26.
11. Martin, p. 14.
12. Martin, p. 14.
13. Ross Gibson, 'Yondering: A Reading of *Mad Max Beyond Thunderdome*' in *South of the West: Postcolonialism and the Narrative Construction of Australia*, Bloomington, IN, Indiana University Press, 1992, p. 174.
14. Meaghan Morris, 'White panic or *Mad Max* and the sublime' in Kua-Hsing Chen (ed.), *Trajectories: Inter-Asia Cultural Studies*, London and New York, Routledge, 1998, p. 240.
15. 'Pixel Pirate 11 & Soda_Jerk Interview', *AE. Reblog*. Available at www.artificialeyes.tv/reblog/2007/02/pixel_pirates_ii_soda_jerk_int.html (accessed 29 June 2012).
16. Noel King, 'Things that Move Fast Through the Landscape: An Interview with George Miller', *Metro Magazine*, No. 123, p. 28.

Anna Dzenis

Malu tianshi/Street Angel (1937)

[Country: China. Production Company: Ming Xing. Director: Yuan Muzhi. Screenwriter: Yuan Muzhi. Cinematographer: Wu Yinxian. Music: Tian Han. Cast: Zhou Xuan (Xiao Hong), Zhao Dan (Xiao Chen), Zhao Huishen (Xiao Yun), Wei Heling (Lao Wang).]

Synopsis: Orphan sisters Xiao Yun and Xiao Hong from war-plagued northeast China live under the exploitation of their adoptive parents in Shanghai 1935. Xiao Hong, forced to work as a teahouse singer, falls in love with her neighbour Xiao Chen, whose room window faces hers. Her elder sister, the silent and gloomy Xiao Yun, has been subjugated to prostitution already and suppressed her desire for Xiao Chen. When Xiao Hong discovers that her adoptive parents plan to sell her off to the coveting local despot, Xiao Chen and his friends do all they can to stop it while dealing with their equivocating moral judgment on Xiao Yun, who, at the end, sacrifices herself to save her sister.

Produced by the Ming Xing Company[1] with a strong cast[2] and long-lasting melodies,[3] *Street Angel* is one of the most beloved left-wing films made in 1930s semi-feudal, semi-colonial China.[4] As the cultural milieu in Shanghai was informed by both Western entertainment forms and a nationalistic urge for survival, the imported medium of film quickly adapted to the local situation. *Street Angel* by director Yuan Muzhi is representative of such an effort: allegedly a remake of a Hollywood film of the same title, Yuan's *Street Angel* has a new story, unique aesthetic and compelling social message.[5]

The film exemplifies the kind of Chinese left-wing filmmaking of the 1930s that is characterised by its active commitment to class contradiction, nation-building agenda and tremendous mass appeal in terms of entertainment and sentimentalism.[6] Studies mostly take note of these films' hybrid nature in narratological and stylistic terms, but their complex hybridity unsettles Western theoretical frameworks and calls for re-evaluations from cultural and historical perspectives (see Berry 2006: 77–82; Ma 2002: 107–8). In his cultural reading of 30s left-wing cinema, Ning Ma offers a set of useful parameters:

> Narration in leftist films … deviates from [the melodramatic narrative] norm in its construction of a *social allegory* that frames the melodramatic narrative of the text. The presence of a[n] … ethico-political scheme, made possible by blending different artistic modes through various *extradiegetic* intrusions and explicit social references, *socializes* the diegetic time and space of the melodramatic narrative.
>
> (Ma 2002: 102, my emphasis)

Ma's emphasis on the process of 'socializing' postulates the interactivity between the film text, the audience and the social milieu through (1) the construction of the social allegory and (2) the introduction of an extradiegetic social presence. *Street Angel*, in this sense, serves as an interesting case study, as the film poses questions on how 'the social' makes its presence felt under melodramatic and realist rubrics: it has dual female characters embodying two melodramatic plots showing a difference between social and personal moral legibility. The incoherencies, though, ultimately authenticate an individual perception of social victimhood.

While the female body is often the object of competition between patriarchal and imperialist forces, in *Street Angel*, it is more than evident that Xiao Hong and Xiao Yun, two sisters dislocated from the then Japanese-occupied Manchuria to the highly Westernised Shanghai, are metaphors for the then divided nation (see Berry 2006). The characters' 'retrieval and staging of innocence', the core of melodrama, is applicable to the nation (Williams 1998: 42). However, the female body is dangling between the role as object of desire for the male and that as an allegorised collective. In *Street Angel*, the melodrama is not only personal, but also serves as a social allegory.

At first glance the two female bodies fit in what Linda Williams describes as 'a dialectic of pathos and action' (Williams 1998: 42). Xiao Hong, a naive sing-song girl, is fully dynamic and expressive. In contrast, her big sister Xiao Yun is a silent and jaded prostitute. The sisters have both undergone a melodramatic revelation of virtues: Xiao Hong is seen 'dating' a local despot, but later clears her name in a tearful fight with Chen, with whom she is in love. Xiao Yun dies because she helps her younger sister escape from the arranged marriage with the despot. In a tableau shot at the end – a convention symbolic of the public recognition of their virtues (Williams 1998: 52) – Xiao Yun is surrounded by her semi-family members, including her now brother-in-law Chen, who once despised her because she attempted to seduce him, but who finally apologises. Rejected, sacrificed and physically injured, Xiao Yun's body is doubly victimised by the unjust class stratification and the patriarchal judgment within the lower class. It is on her deathbed that she finally ascends to a position of legible morality: 'We are equally unfortunate. There's nothing to forgive'.

However, although both Xiao Hong and Xiao Yun's wronged virtues are recouped in the end, Xiao Yun's moral legibility is only recognised when it is aligned with the victimhood of the lower class. Chen reluctantly begins to accept Xiao Yun when she becomes his family member – a patriarchal alliance indeed. On the level of audience engagement, the narrative does not allow the audience to take an omniscient vantage point to survey the moral situation (Williams 1998: 49); Xiao Yun gets less screen time, fewer shots and fewer lines, so that her passivity – her passive subjectivity – goes underexplored. In front of the camera, Xiao Yun's observation, persuasion and protection of Xiao Hong all take on an enigmatic veneer: after a shot of her figure or face to indicate her presence, there are usually few reverse shots to allot her an equal portion of attention, and even fewer eyeline match reverse shots to suture the audience into her point of view. There are shots that reveal Xiao Yun's secret feelings towards Chen. But without any consistent focalisation on Xiao Yun and her motivation, Xiao Yun's action is not adequately explained. And her personal moral conflict is not so much resolved as relinquished to the social conflict. It is reasonable to ask: do the affects for the character strictly correspond to those for the social issues? In other words, is the latter predicated on the former? Are there possibly other emotional sources?

In purely cinematic terms, Linda Williams has discussed the relation of realism to melodrama, suggesting that melodrama is an operative mode and realist effects are make-believe functions in the service of affect (Williams 1998: 42). Laikwan Pang coins the term 'engaging realism' to foreground the functional aspect of realism in Chinese leftist films (see Chapter 8 in Pang, 2002). She notes that realism was introduced to China as a political/philosophical notion for a purportedly objective and challenging representation of the status quo. In practice it effectively conveys the social message and engages the audience. As we can see in *Street Angel*, the cinematic style forms a signification process that seeks to activate the viewer's association of the narrative with their social experience off-screen. The realist registers here are not ambience-building effects (Williams 1998: 74), but a direct address reaching beyond the diegetic space and time to speak to the culturally informed viewer.

In *Street Angel*, as in many other Chinese leftist films, social references are often inserted via newspaper headlines. Ning Ma thoroughly analyses how such 'journalist discourse' contradicts or agrees with 'populist discourse', such as wordplay, mime and singing. In terms of cinematic technique, the 'open POV structure' (i.e. an establishing shot plus a shot on the characters in the scene, who are rendered as 'lookers without a vision') used in the opening wedding procession, is a device that allows the viewer to experience changing looking positions in order to critically assess the grotesque social conditions (Ma 2002: 107). Moreover, the visual motif of the newspaper-walled room expressionistically frames the contradiction between headlines and the characters' social experience; as a realist mise en scène *per se*, the walls covered with newspapers invite the audience to relive these contradictions.

A more sophisticated admixture of image, sound and discourse takes place in the sequence of Xiao Hong's singing of the *Song of the Four Seasons*. While singing is usually regarded as an extra-diegetic spectacle, it is more productive to recognise it here as a populist element lodged in Chinese print culture for its lack of bodily performance, which is very different from musicals full of dance (see Lee 1999: 91). When singing, Xiao Hong's subjectivity recedes: within the diegetic space, the camera stays at an objective view point, showing only Xiao Hong's and the local despot's actions; but there are additional images placed in the sequence that directly correlate with the lyrics – among the more noticeable are war images alluding to the Japanese aggression on Chinese territory. These images thus bypass both the diegetic space and the literal meaning of the lyrics ('lovers are parted by the ruthless violence') and create 'a new hermeneutic space' (Pang 2002: 217). Given the rising patriotism among the audience and censorship of the images of Japanese aggression (Yeh 2002: 88), this montage is not so much to alienate or educate the audience as to unannouncedly evoke the viewer's emotional response.

By the same token, we may conclude that for the purpose of evoking authentic affects in response to social realities, the construction of the allegory modifies Xiao Yun's personal, 'significant and interpretable' struggle to fit the social terms.[7] When Chen disagrees with Lao Wang on whether Xiao Yun deserves to be saved, the close-up of a picture of Chen and Co is inserted to mark the change of Chen's attitude. It shows the viewer the phrase written on the side of the picture: 'To share the joy and shoulder the adversity together', bestowing collectivity on the plot that follows. There are two flashbacks in the final scene that feed into the omniscient survey of the viewer: when Xiao Yun awakes she finds herself in the arms of Chen – in the reverse shot, Chen's face is blurred to suggest Xiao Yun's point of view. In the reaction close shot, Xiao Yun is given water to drink. A flashback shows Chen's rejection of Xiao Yun in a pervious scene, when he threw her glass of water to the ground. Xiao Yun closes her eyes in humiliation. What follows is a stationary, relatively long take (and also a long shot) that frames Xiao Yun, Chen and Xiao Hong and that shows Xiao Yun stroking Chen's collar. Another flashback to a previous scene is inserted: in the dark alley Xiao Yun does the same thing, which causes Chen's hostile reaction. Compared with the first flashback sutured in the close point-of-view shots, the second flashback shows less Xiao Yun or Chen's subjectivity with regards to the love triangle that also involves Xiao Hong. Rather, it is an objective presentation of the two temporally juxtaposed spaces in order to arouse the pathos of the audience vis-à-vis the concept of misunderstanding. This transition transposes the audience's expectation into something less personal and less focalised. Afterward, we hear Xiao Yun's comments on Lao Wang's kindness as a friend (rather than his love for her), on her fear of the police (i.e. the regulatory powers of a capitalist society) and on the ants-like meagre lives of the poor. Thus the moral struggle on the personal level is not so much solved as it is eclipsed by the emphasis on the irresolvable social conflict.[8] Finally, pans from the dark alleys of underground Shanghai to the inaccessible, overpowering skyscrapers. The ant-like individuals, despite the intricate power relationship among themselves, are levelled and suppressed at last.

Notes

1. The Ming Xing Company was one of the first film production companies that recruited leftist filmmakers in response to the rising leftist sensibilities among the audience. For details see Pang 2002, Chapter 2.
2. Nicknamed 'the Golden Voice', Zhou Xuan (1918 or 1920–1957) was a popular singer and actress in the 1930s and 40s with about two hundred songs and 42 films under her belt. Zhao Dan (1915–1980) was one of the most popular and important leftist film stars in the history of Chinese cinema.
3. *Song of Four Seasons* (siji ge) and *The Wandering Singsteress* (tianya genu) were composed by He Luting and the lyrics were written by Tian Han. Both songs have enjoyed long-lasting popularity. Music is indeed crucial to the understanding of the film's production and the filmmakers' choice of drawing from cinematic languages in the sinification process. For an insightful analysis, see Yeh (2002).
4. In the official Communist historiography, the signing of the Treaty of Nanking in 1841 marked the reduction of China to a 'semi-colonial and semi-feudal' status, referring to the state of the nation with residual local feudal economic and political relations

and the Western encroachment on Chinese sovereignty.

5. *Street Angel* (1928), directed by Frank Borzage, is a silent film produced by the Fox Film Corporation.
6. As a corrective to the state-approved ideological reading of the film as critical realism with solely proletarian interests, scholars overseas have explored the melodramatic elements of these films for their mass appeal.
7. Peter Brooks states that everyday reality is made 'significant and interpretable' in melodrama. See Brooks (1976: 200).
8. In his reading of the finale, Chris Berry thinks the moral conflict is resolved while the social conflict is not. Although I agree with his method of separating the two realms, I think this statement needs a clearer distinction between a solution in the plot and the viewer's satisfaction provided by storytelling. See Berry (2006: 87).

Further reading

Chris Berry, 'Chapter 4 Realist Modes: Melodrama, Modernity, and Home', in Chris Berry and Mary Farquhar (eds), *China on Screen: Cinema and Nation*, New York, Columbia University Press, 2006, pp. 75–107.

Peter Brooks, *The Melodramatic Imagination: Balzac, Henry James, Melodrama and the Mode of Excess*, New Haven, Yale University Press, 1976.

Leo Ou-fan Lee, 'The Urban Milieu of Shanghai Cinema, 1930–40: Some Explorations of Film Audience, Film Culture, and Narrative Conventions', in Yingjin Zhang (ed.), *Cinema and Urban Culture in Shanghai, 1922–1943*, Stanford, Stanford University Press, 1999, pp. 74–98.

Ning Ma, 'The Textual and Critical Difference of Being Radical: Reconstructing Chinese Leftist Films of the 1930s' in Harry H. Kuoshu (ed.), *Celluloid China: Cinematic Encounters with Culture and Society*, Carbondale and Edwardswille, Southern Illinois University Press, 2002, pp. 93–109.

Laikwan Pang, *Building a New China in Cinema: The Chinese Left-wing Cinema Movement, 1932–1937*, Lanham, Rowman & Littlefield Publishers, 2002.

Linda Williams, 'Melodrama Revised', in Nick Browne (ed.), *Refiguring American Film Genres*, Berkeley and Los Angeles, University of California Press, 1998, pp. 42–88.

Yueh-yu Yeh, 'Historiography and sinification: Music in Chinese cinema of the 1930s', *Cinema Journal*, Vol. 41, No. 3, Spring 2002, pp. 79–97.

Yiping Qin

Maynila, sa mga kuko ng liwanag/ Manila, In the Claws of Neon (1975)

[Country: Philippines. Production Company: Cinema Artists Philippines. Director: Lino Brocka. Producers: Miguel de Leon, Severino Manotoc, Jr. Screenwriter: Clodualdo del Mundo, Jr. Cinematographer: Miguel de Leon. Music: Max Jocson. Editors: Ike Jarlego, Jr, and Edgardo Jarlego. Cast: Rafael Roco, Jr (Julio Madiaga), Hilda Koronel (Ligaya Paraiso), Tommy Abuel (Pol), Lou Salvador, Jr (Atong), Tommy Yap (Ah Tek), Lily Gamboa-Mendoza (Perla).]

Synopsis: Based on a 1967 novel by Edgardo M. Reyes, *Manila* tells the simple tale of a country lad named Julio who ventures to the big city in search of his girlfriend, Ligaya.[1] The latter goes missing shortly after being recruited to work as a housemaid. Between back-breaking jobs at a construction site and a brief stint as a call boy, Julio prowls Manila's brothel-ridden Chinatown for any signs of Ligaya. Months later, he runs into her outside church. An ex-prostitute, Ligaya now lives as the kept woman of a Chinese shopkeeper named Ah Tek and as mother to Ah Tek's baby. Julio convinces her to follow an ill-conceived escape plan. Ligaya does not show up at the appointed time, and dies under mysterious circumstances that same night. After her burial, Julio exacts revenge on Ah Tek by stabbing him with an ice pick. Fleeing the murder scene, Julio attracts a mob that corners him in an alley and lynches him.

Manila, in the Claws of Neon is a beautiful, devastating film about working-class life in the third world metropolis. It is widely regarded as Lino Brocka's magnum opus and one of the finest works of Philippine cinema.[2] Apart from tracking Julio's quest for Ligaya, the film touches on three problems affecting the working class. These problems, which Brocka treats in overlapping episodes, concern unjust conditions at the workplace, unequal property relations, and human trafficking and prostitution.

The exploitation of labourers takes many forms in both film and novel (which was based on the author's experiences as a peon). The scenes at the construction site detail the schemes used by the foreman, Mr Balajadia, to cheat labourers of their pay. These schemes include an almost 30 per cent salary cut and a kind of high-interest payday loan called 'taiwan'. Brocka portrays the hellish working conditions through a combination of over-modulated construction sounds, off-kilter shots conveying the immensity of structures being built, and the alternation of quick editing and repetitious actions emphasising the pace and tedium of their work.

The problem of unequal property relations is examined through the story of Julio's fellow construction worker Atong. Midway through the film Atong takes Julio in for a few days when the latter is kicked out of the construction site. Atong resides in a vast squatter's area surrounded by factories and a polluted canal. The slum is called Sunog-Apog (burnt-lime), evoking the contrasting hues of the tar-black sludge of the canal and the light shades of unburned garbage. Atong, his sister Perla, and their mute and paralyzed father end up in Sunog-Apog after being kicked out of their homestead by a land grabber. Months later, after Atong is beaten to death in jail, the shanties catch fire. His father is engulfed by the flames while his sister, who was away during the fire, ends up in the streets, and later, in the brothel. The total dispossession and ruin of Atong's family prefigures Julio and Ligaya's fates. It also portrays Manila as a proletarian inferno, one whose circles of despair go deeper than Julio can fathom.

Brocka portrays the third problem, human trafficking and prostitution, as both real and symbolic conditions. The system of trafficking is laid out as a puzzle. Julio, uneducated and new to the city, must rely on the help of his friends to search for Ligaya based on information contained in the only letter she sent him. Julio's buddies figure out that Ligaya's recruiter, Mrs Cruz, used a false name and sold off Ligaya as a sex slave instead of a servant because of her good looks. Being sold to Ah Tek, Ligaya believes, spared her from the worst of the flesh trade – heroin injections, group sex. To Julio, however, she seems to have lost everything in spite of having fled the world of prostitution. Her gaze is empty, and her spirit, broken. It was Brocka's idea to put both his hero and heroine through the horrors of Manila's flesh trade. (Julio's night at the male brothel was grafted on the screenplay only upon the director's request.) In Brocka's portrayal of a dog-eat-dog world, not only the mighty exploit Manila's poor. Marginal figures, such as Chinese émigrés and homosexuals, also prey on them. The film's central motif of fatal brightness appears in scenes of the hero and heroine's sexual exploitation. Depicting Ligaya's confinement in Ah Tek's house, Brocka frames Ligaya as a silhouette enclosed in a flash of light seeping through translucent window panes. Likewise, when Julio enters the flesh trade, neon signs burn, looming over the park where a call boy recruits him. The motif recurs when Julio sets foot in a male brothel ablaze with tacky lighting.

While there are no reliable box office records to prove it, *Manila* opened successfully.[3] At the 1975 Filipino Academy of Movie Arts and Sciences (FAMAS) Awards, Brocka's entry bagged most of the trophies. Reviews were mixed. Some griped that the film was unfaithful to the novel; others complained it was derivative. There were critics who charged Brocka of anti-Chinese racism, and those who felt squeamish about the film's gay scenes. But many hailed *Manila* as a triumph.[4] Positive reviews described it as 'bold and daring', 'an uncompromisingly great film', and 'the best thing to happen to the film industry in a long time'.[5]

In praising the film, critics noted the elements that departed from mainstream conventions: 'no big-name stars, a prestigious source material, new heights of realism'.[6] They admired the 'natural' acting, the cinematographer's 'visual stunners', and the musical score that 'puts to shame all others in the field'.[7] Many of these elements were neither unique to *Manila* nor first observed in that film. They would be identified later by critics as the hallmarks of a large body of accomplished filmmaking during the 1970s and 1980s called the New Philippine Cinema.[8]

What might account, then, for the film's exceptional claim to greatness in Philippine cinema? The critic Noel Vera offers this insight: '*Maynila* isn't much more than an excellently made melodrama; what makes the film great is finally its skin'. Vera here is referring to *Manila's* 'marvellous visual texture', 'voluptuous' images that are 'raw and honest', and the 'immediacy' that makes for Brocka's 'melodramatic energy'.[9] This explanation, given in 2002, echoes the assessment of critics who have written about *Manila* since its release. A kind of tension informs the language critics use to characterise the film. Vera describes the film's imagery, for instance, as 'raw and honest' (terms associated with documentary and realism) but also as 'voluptuous' and 'melodramatic' (words linked to beauty and artifice, respectively). Similarly, a review from 1975 ascribed 'harsh poetry' to the film's 'squalid, sordid settings'.[10]

Indeed, these terms used by critics aptly describe *Manila.* They identify tensions felt on a number of levels. The tension within the work's representational mode also extends to its genre identity. The contrast between realistic and beautified images is related to the tension between the work's identities as social exposé and as parable. In both film and novel, *Manila* comes across as reportage (of the underclass at a particular place and time) and also as a universal tale of life and death in the modern city. *Manila* juxtaposes the language of peons as well as vivid portrayals of their routines with lyrical montage sequences and allegorical names (for example, the heroine Ligaya Paraiso's name translates as 'joyful paradise').[11] Brocka's addition of 'Manila' to the novel's title heightens this productive tension. The reference to the Philippine capital specifies the socio-historical setting where the parable of moths drawn to the flame is enacted. Brocka's title reinforces the film's variable identity as exposé and parable. This versatility may have been one of the factors that spared the film from the strict censorship policies of President Ferdinand Marcos's authoritarian regime.

Vera's notion that the film could be 'nothing more than excellently made melodrama' is worth pondering. The statement appears to imply the tension between the film's superior craftsmanship and its less-than-prestigious categorisation as melodrama. It may well be that *Manila's* designation as melodrama is key to its top spot in Philippine cinema. While many critics dismiss melodrama's 'low' cultural value, others believe that melodrama enjoys a unique status as Philippine cinema's traditional mode of expression.[12] Apart from satisfying this criterion of cultural authenticity, *Manila* enjoys the advantage of being associated with an acclaimed literary work and a great director.[13]

Other writings on *Manila* discuss the movie in light of Brocka's art and politics, the representations of sexuality and gender in his films, and filmmaking in the third world and in autocratic regimes.[14]

The World Cinema Foundation, chaired by Martin Scorsese, sponsored the film's digital restoration. That version screened at the Cannes Film Festival in 2013.

Notes

1. The literal translation of the novel's title, 'Sa mga Kuko ng Liwanag' is 'In the Claws of Light'. The title has been translated in several different ways, but the recurrence of 'neon' in the novel justifies its use in the widely preferred translation.
2. See Joel David, *Fields of Vision: Critical Applications in Recent Philippine Cinema*, Manila, Ateneo de Manila University Press, 1995, pp. 125–36; and Stephen Locke, '*Maynila*: In the Claws of

Neon' in Frank Magill (ed.), *Magill's Survey of Cinema*, Vol. 4, Englewood Cliffs, NJ, Salem Press, 1985, pp. 1991–5.

3. Box office data for old films is hard to find in the Philippines. *Manila's* screenwriter, Clodualdo del Mundo, Jr. recalls in an e-mail correspondence that he saw many theatres filled to capacity during the film's opening.
4. Criticism of the film's deviations from the novel appear in many of the Philippine-published works cited here. Favourable comments on the 'gay sequence' appear in Culture Staff, 'Many Facets of a Film', *Philippine Collegian*, 30 July 1975, p. 7.
5. Mario Hernando, '*Maynila*: Brocka's Best' in Nicanor Tiongson (ed.), *The Urian Anthology 1970–1979*, Manila, M. L. Morato, 1983, pp. 210–13; and Cristina Pantoja-Hidalgo, 'Pros and cons on the best local film,' *The Times Journal*, 21 July 1971, p. 15.
6. Justino Dormiendo, 'Mula sa Eskapismo Tungo sa Realismo' ('From Escapism Toward Realism'), *Sagisag*, August 1975, pp. 51–5.
7. Hernando, '*Maynila*', pp. 210–13.
8. See David, *Fields of Vision*, p. 9.
9. Noel Vera, *Critic After Dark: A Review of Philippine Cinema*, Singapore, BigO Books, 2005, p. 180.
10. Though its publication details are missing, I found this review insightful: Roque, Ma. Socorro Garcia (n.d.) 'Goodbye to Fantasyland', Lino Brocka 1977 Scrapbook, Lino Brocka Collection, Cultural Center of the Philippines.
11. Similarly, Julio's last name, Madiaga, is eponymous. It sounds like 'matiyaga', the Filipino word for patience.
12. The critic Bienvenido Lumbera, Jr defines the 'traditional Filipino movie' as being 'plot-oriented and dramatic' – in short, melodramatic – and attributes Brocka's mass appeal to his grasp of this mode. See 'Kasaysayan at Tunguhin ng Pelikulang Pilipino' ('The History and Prospects of the Filipino Film') in Tiongson (ed.), *Urian Anthology*, p. 43. The notion that some national cinemas have a dominant mode is asserted by Linda Williams, who writes that 'melodrama is the fundamental mode of American popular motion pictures'. See 'Melodrama Revisited' in Nick Brown, *Refiguring American Film Genres: History and Theory*, Berkeley, CA, University of California Press, 1998, p. 42.
13. On the other hand, Armes finds Brocka's use of realism (a 'cleaned–up version of poverty') and knack for the 'straitjacket of melodrama' problematic. See Roy Armes, *Third World Film Making and the West*, Berkeley, CA, University of California Press, 1987, p. 153.
14. See Gina Marchetti, 'Four Hundred Years in a Convent, Fifty in Hollywood: Sexual Identity and Dissent in Contemporary Philippine Cinema', *East-West Film Journal*, Vol. 2, No. 2, June 1988, pp. 32–4. Patrick Flores, 'The Slum and the Town: Reassessing the Brocka Paradigm in Philippine Progressive Cinema', *Diliman Review*, 1992, Vol. 39, No. 4, pp. 45–52.

Further reading

Mario Hernando, *Lino Brocka: The Artist and His Times*, Manila, Cultural Center of the Philippines, 1993.

Charles Tesson, 'The Cult of the Image in Lino Brocka', in Rafael Ma. Guerrero (ed.), *Readings in Philippine Cinema*, Manila, Experimental Cinema of the Philippines, 1983, pp. 236–8.

Rolando Tolentino, 'Cityscape: The Capital Infrastructuring and Technologization of Manila', in Mark Shiel and Tony Fitzmaurice (eds), *Cinema and the City: Film and Urban Societies in a Global Context*, Oxford, Blackwell, 2001, pp. 158–70.

José B. Capino

Meghe dhaka tara/The Cloud-Capped Star (1960)

[Country: India. Production Company: Chitrakalpa. Director: Ritwick Ghatak. Producer: Chitrakalpa. Screenwriter: Ritwick Ghatak. Cinematographer: Dinen Gupta. Editor: Ramesh Joshi. Music: Jyotirindra Moitra, Ustad Bahadur Khan. Cast: Supriya Choudhury (Nita), Anil Chatterjee (Shankar), Niranjan Ray (Sanat), Gita Ghatak (Gita), Bijon Bhattacharya (Father), Gita Dey (Mother).]

Synopsis: *Meghe dhaka tara* tells the story of Nita who takes on the role of breadwinner for a refugee family struggling to retain its middle-class status. When the movie opens Nita seems to be moving towards a relatively happy future, despite the self-destructive generosity with which she responds to the demands made on her by members of her family. Through the course of the film, though, Nita loses the man she loves to her attractive and worldly sister, is forced to give up her studies for a full-time job and, in an incredibly sad final sequence, is left to die of TB in a sanatorium. On the other hand, every member of Nita's family, even her beloved and other-worldly older brother, become engrossed in their now financially secure family life, suppressing the memory not just of Nita, but also of the parasitic and cynical path that led to their status as properly middle-class folk.

An early sequence in *Meghe dhaka tara* points to a dynamic that continues to operate powerfully through the rest of the movie. Nita, the self-sacrificing heroine of the film, returns home with the money she's earned from tuitions. Instantly, she's surrounded by members of her family who stake their claim on the money. Gita, her younger sister, wants a sari because she finds it intolerable to go to college in her old one, and her brawny younger brother wants a pair of football boots. Even her unworldly older brother, Shankar, demands a rupee for the razor blade he needs to get rid of week's growth facial hair. And cutting through the cacophony of these demands is her mother's bitter complaint that Nita thinks of everything and everyone except the household expenses.

Nita's brother gets his football boots and her sister a sari, and both use gifts like these to push their way out of the economy of scarcity in which the family has been trapped ever since their migration from Bangladesh to a refugee colony in Calcutta. Even Shankar – Nita's hopeless older brother – finds fame and fortune as a singer, and it is he who takes her to that sojourn in the hills they had longed for throughout their lives. The irony is Nita is already terminally ill with tuberculosis and the clean and hygienic sanatorium where she is deposited has no answer to her anguished cry: 'Brother, I've wanted to live'.

Nita's early death is the inevitable termination of a life lacerated at every point by family members adept at normalising their many acts of brutal exploitation as the claims they naturally have on a daughter's, or sister's, love. Through the course of the movie, Nita is obliged to give up her studies for a full-time job, defer her marriage to the brilliant Sanat before losing him to her sister, and refuse an X-ray for an early diagnosis of what will turn out to be a terminal illness, because the family cannot run without the income she regularly brings in.

For Ghatak, Nita's family is a microcosm of the world outside. Gita smiles when she announces that Sanat has decided to marry her (and not Nita), not only because she experiences little personal guilt but also because she is sure her decision will bring no social opprobrium. Gita's willingness to lure away a man who she has always known to have been in love with her sister will, thus, prove to be the basis of a stable, financially secure family and, in this sense, of her status as a well-adjusted middle-class woman. The nexus, embodied in Gita's behaviour between, on the one hand, those great objects of middle-class desire – domestic stability, financial security and upward mobility – and, on the other, venality, treachery and compromise provides the key to an understanding of *Meghe dhaka tara*. It is not only replicated thematically in Sanat's abdication of research for a secure income and domestic stability, and in the worldliness that even Shankar acquires once he becomes a commercially successful vocalist. More important is that Ghatak's tragic sense of the tension between the expansive possibilities of poetry, music or the most selfless forms of human behaviour, and the banal demands of security and success, is made to unfold through a set of cinematic innovations unprecedented in Indian cinema in their originality, power and precision.

The opening scene of *Meghe dhaka tara* ties the tragic and inextricable knot between its celebration of unconstrained spaces always capable of sustaining creativity, freedom and happiness and those dark dingy interiors saturated in meanness, exploitation and bitterness. The film opens with a tracking shot of the tiny approaching figure of Nita, as she passes beneath a spreading gulmohor tree. The first real look we get at Nita is through a close-up of her sideways-turned face. She smiles with benign pride as she watches Shankar, unshaven but utterly absorbed in the early morning raga he is practicing. The gentle stretch of an adjoining lake and the unfolding length of a train as it slides slowly along the tracks beyond the lake, only extend our sense of an expansive and accommodative landscape. But it is precisely at this point, so full of possibilities, that Ghatak introduces a sharp cut to move the action to the cramped local marketplace. Here Nita is rudely confronted by the grocery store owner who demands payment for purchases made by her family over several weeks.

The opening scene, in fact, puts on full display two outstanding features of Ritwick Ghatak's film-making: on the one hand, the extremely original ways in which his films deploy music and, more generally, sound and, on the other, his ability (inherited, undoubtedly, from his hero Sergei Eisenstein) to intertwine lines of action in ways that will always keep in active play the tragic tension at the heart of his greatest films.

Meghe dhaka tara is an unforgettable experience for anyone with some knowledge of the musical traditions of Ghatak's home state, Bengal. The film is saturated in the classical music which Shankar practices, but it also achieves some very powerful effects with its use of Baul folk songs and of a well-known musical composition by Bengal's greatest poet Rabindranath Tagore. The Rabindrasangeet and the Baulgeeti in *Meghe dhaka tara* are of the highest musical quality but they are not brought into play in and for themselves, or even as resources to deepen some local effect. Rather, music in a Ghatak film is part of a larger soundscape where elements develop independently, and in relation to each other to articulate, for example, the whole burden of pain that may have accumulated over many tiny events in the past, or to express an anxiety that will drive a new destructive course of action. For example, the cruel swish of whiplashes that Ghatak plays on the soundtrack when Nita first discovers Sanat's infidelity is amplified and superimposed later on the Tagore song that Nita and Shankar sing together. The song – 'Je Rat e Mor Dooar Guli' ("That Night when the Storm broke down my Door') – is an immediate sequel to the scene where Shankar confronts Nita, for the first time, with the full extent of the betrayal she has suffered. As the song nears the end Ghatak's camera slowly shifts from Shankar to Nita, and lingers on a close-up of Nita's upturned face while the fading song gives way to the amplified sound of whiplashes. This cinematic configuration – produced by the masterly use of camera angles and light as well as a soundtrack where a deeply moving song is overlaid with the harsh sounds of whiplashes – has become, in Bengal, an iconic image of the suffering that underlies the silence of a self-sacrificing woman.

But the soundtrack not only works to give depth and meaning to what has already happened, it also initiates new tensions. For example, towards the middle of the film, Ghatak picks on an utterly familiar sound from everyday life and transforms it into a dynamo that will drive much of the subsequent action. This is the sound of boiling rice and, in Ghatak's film it is inseparable from the open, central courtyard of Nita's makeshift house in the refugee colony. Nita's mother often sits in this courtyard, over a primitive and smoky oven on which the family's meals are cooked. It is from this controlling location, which produces the family's subsistence and, at the same time, gives Nita's mother visual access to the rooms around, that she monitors the unfolding of Nita's relationship with Sanat. The destructive impulse encoded in her look of anxiety when she realises Sanat might marry Nita and take away her income from the family is intensified many fold by the amplified sound that drowns everything else: the gurgle and hiss of boiling rice. Ghatak, thus, finds in the sound of boiling the means of raising to an unspeakable, 'scalding' level of intensity the tension that will drive Nita's mother to deflect Sanat's affection, through a series of subtle barely understood manoeuvres, from Nita to her younger sister.

The unfathomable depths of cynicism that underlies human behaviour in *Meghe dhaka tara* may elude the comprehension of the characters who practice it, but the consequence of every act of selfishness or cynicism is inexorably registered in the world of Ghatak's film.

Meghe dhaka tara, it bears reiteration, in the light of the popular perception of Ghatak as a brilliant but chaotic filmmaker, is a complex but perfectly structured film. It unfolds predominantly through the intercutting of sequences underpinned by selfishness, exploitation and greed that are normalised as the imperatives of everyday life and the far more vulnerable lines of action driven by a generous belief in people and their ability to rise to their full potential. Typical of the film's structure is a sequence where Ghatak intercuts a very moving Baul song and the gentle and expansive mood that it introduces with the sordid emotional transactions – a parasitic father's anxiety about losing status and a nasty, embittered mother's litany of unfair complaints – that are played out in the dingy interior of Nita's home.

The deeply pessimistic trajectory along which *Meghe dhaka tara* is driven from the beginning may be encapsulated in two scenes that appear at the beginning and towards the end of the film. In the first, Shankar catches Nita reading a letter from Sanat who is, at that point, deeply in love with her and who compares the many great qualities that lurk behind her self-effacing personality to the brilliance of stars obscured temporarily by a bank of clouds. It is a letter that looks forward with great hope to their life together. Towards the end of the film, a now successful Shankar returns home after several years only to encounter Nita in a familiar position, crouching over something she appears to read. Shankar lunges at her alleging, playfully, she is reading another love letter. What he comes up with is a handkerchief spattered with the blood that Nita has brought up from her tubercular lungs.

Ghatak's own life was not all that different from Nita's. Despite the adulation of a fanatically devoted band of younger filmmakers who were deeply influenced by his work, he never received any real recognition during his life. The photographs of him taken through the two or three years before his premature death at 50, show a shrunken, unshaven face with a crop of dishevelled hair – a face that might have belonged to beggar, if it had not been for those piercing eyes behind the thick black-rimmed spectacles. For the typical Bengali, whose commitment to respectability only slightly exceeds his respect for artistic talent, Ghatak is the classic embodiment of genius whose self-destructive traits, particularly his reckless abuse of alcohol debarred him for the recognition he might have achieved. Yet to describe Ghatak as an alcoholic is seriously reductive. He consumed huge quantities of rough, country liquor not because he was passively dependent on that nasty stuff, but because it was one of his means of staving off the success that pulls so many of his characters into compromise, insensitivity and ultimately degradation.

Further reading

Haimanti Banerjee, *Ritwik Kumar Ghatak*, Pune, National Film Archives of India, 1985.

Shampa Banerjee (ed.), *Ritwik Ghatak*, New Dehli, Directorate of Film Festivals of India, 1981.

Megan Carrigy, 'Ritwick Ghatak', *Senses of Cinema*. Available at http://sensesofcinema.com/2003/great-directors/ghatak/ (accessed 29 November 2012).

Sibaditya Dasgupta and Sandipan Bhattacharya (eds), *Ritwik Ghatak: Face to Face: Conversations with the Master 1962–1977*, trans. Chilka Ghosh, Kolkata, Cine Central, 2003.

Ritwick Ghatak, *Cinema and I*, Calcutta, Ritwik Memorial Trust, 1987.
Ritwick Ghatak, *Rows and Rows of Fences*, Calcutta, Seagull Books, 2000.
Ashish Rajadhyaksha, *A Return to the Epic*, Mumbai, Screen Unit, 1982.
Ashish Rajadhyaksha and Paul Willemen (eds), *Encyclopedia of Indian Cinema*, London, BFI & Oxford University Press, 1994.
Jonathan Rosenbaum, 'Ritwick Ghatak', *Rouge* 9, 2006.
Paul Willemen and Behroze Gandhy, *Indian Cinema*, London, BFI Dossier No. 5, 1982.

Sambudha Sen

Mies vailla menneisyyttä/Man without a Past (2002)

[Country: Germany, France, Finland. Production Company: Sputnik, Pyramide Productions, Pandora Filmproduktion, Bavaria Film, YLE-TV. Director: Aki Kaurismäki. Producers: Aki Kaurismäki, Ella Werning. Screenwriter: Aki Kaurismäki. Cinematographer: Timo Salminen. Music: Olli Kykkänen. Editor: Timo Linnasalo. Cast: Markku Peltola (M), Kati Outinen (Irma), Juhani Niemelä (Nieminen), Kaija Pakarinen (Kaisa Nieminen), Annikki Tähti (Manager of Flea Market), Sakari Kuosmanen (Anttila), Esko Nikkari (Bank Robber), Aino Seppo (Ex-wife).]

Synopsis: *Man without a Past* follows the noirish travails of its protagonist M, who, in the film's first sequence, arrives in the city on the train with a modest suitcase in tow, only to be mugged and beaten in a city park. Having sustained a gruesome head injury, M suffers from amnesia that has him forgetting both his personal identity and profession. He is taken in by a community of unemployed and underemployed container-dwellers near the city's harbour, highlighting the film's economic themes. With a budding relationship with the deadpan Irma and his career finally remembered, he happens to witness a bank robbery, which belatedly interests the police in his curious case. When they run his picture in the newspaper asking if anyone can identify him, his estranged/now ex-wife reveals he headed to the city after they had separated. A potential reconciliation with her funnily falls flat, and he opts for Irma and the harbour community. A climactic confrontation has that community overcoming the thugs who had mugged M and commenced his struggles. Much music and harbour-side merriment follows.

Man without a Past is the probably most acclaimed Finnish film of all time, made by Finland's most famous director, Aki Kaurismäki. Aki and his brother Mika are both prolific filmmakers and together have been responsible for about one-fifth of the total output of the Finnish film industry since the early 1980s. It is Aki's films, however, that have broken through to international notoriety: like his fellow small-country Scandinavians Ingmar Bergman and Lars von Trier – though with a thoroughly different sensibility – Kaurismäki has managed to put his nation's minor cinema on the global art-cinema map. *Man without a Past* won the Grand Prix at the 2002 Cannes Film Festival (usually seen as the second prize, behind Polanski's controversial win with *The Pianist* and ahead of a strong field that also included Michael Hanekc and Abbas Kiarostami); *Man without a Past* also won the Cannes Prize of the Ecumenical Jury as well as a surprise acting prize for Kaurismäki regular Kati Outinen. *Man without a Past*, Kaurismäki's most famous film to date, was also, in 2003, Finland's first ever finalist for the foreign language Oscar. Despite this critical acclaim and Academy honour, Kaurismäki notoriously refused to attend the ceremony because he said he was, as he put it, 'not in a party mood' due to the (second) US–Iraq war, which had begun just days before Hollywood feted itself.[1] Such deliberate, even cultivated, ambivalence toward Hollywood and the USA is a leitmotif running throughout Kaurismäki's films. European art cinema often holds itself at arm's length from classical and blockbuster Hollywood but rarely does it reach the ironic, even sardonic, heights of Kaurismäki's cinema in general and *Man without a Past* in particular.

This fundamentally ambivalent posture toward Hollywood is manifest in the film's memorable opening. Like many a classic noir – cf. *Strangers on a Train* – the camera first finds its protagonist, dubbed simply M, on a train, arriving from a place unknown in the big city (in Finland's biggest city of Helsinki, which figures in many of Kaurismäki's films). From there, toting a suitcase, M (Markku Peltola) proceeds to a park where he is summarily and brutally attacked, robbed, and left for dead by a trio of younger thugs. A drifter discovering violence in the big-city park away from the moneyed, urban masses recalls other noirs as well, like Welles's similarly stylised opening in *Lady from Shanghai*, as does the unusual long take, point-of-view tracking shot of M's wounded stumbling for help, invoking the consistently heightened subjectivity of noir (cf. *Lady in the Lake*).

Yet, even while invoking these venerable noir traditions, Kaurismäki is quick to simultaneously, and ironically, distance himself from them. Kaurismäki has emphasised in interviews how uncomfortable he was with the violence in *Man without a Past*'s memorable and effective opening, offering that he wanted to make this violence 'honest', because, 'if people want to see violence looking good, there is something wrong with their heads. So I make it look as it really is, fast and ugly'.[2] The adjective 'ugly' characterising his stylised version of violence recurs as well in his self-conscious contrast of his casting to Hollywood's, with his preference clearly for 'ugly' characters and actors.[3] Even while the plot parameters draw close to noirish syntax, his style pulls in another direction, away from the Hollywood mantle he simultaneously foregrounds and rejects.

Man without a Past belongs to a trio of films usually known as the 'loser trilogy' (sometimes, more precisely, termed the 'second loser trilogy' or the 'Finland trilogy'), with which Kaurismäki greeted the severe financial crisis that hit Finland in the 1990s.[4] At that point, the break-up of the eastern bloc reverberated throughout the small country (the USSR was a main trading partner, positioned as Finland is between east and west). Trilogies, of course, lend any group of films a certain marketable coherence and useful auteurist imprimatur, although Kaurismäki also cites his lack of motivation to justify organising his work this way: 'I'm so bloody lazy that I have to tell everybody I make trilogies. If I didn't, I wouldn't do anything but play cards'.[5] Kaurismäki has, with the 2011 *Le Havre,* since commenced a yet another trilogy, lending a certain symmetry to his now over 22 features, which also include his breakthrough road movie *Leningrad Cowboys Go America* (which he rates as 'the worst film in the history of cinema, unless you count Sylvester Stallone films'[6]) as well as literary adaptations (*Crime and Punishment* or *Hamlet Goes Business*), that likewise underscore his art-satirical approach to the sort of high-cultural products often featured in European art cinema.

In the Finnish financial crisis inspiring the late 1990s–early 2000s trilogy, unemployment hit 16 per cent in some corners of the country, and there was a general concern with retooling the nation's identity, certainly a key theme in *Man without a Past,* in which the main protagonist is compelled to completely reinvent himself, leaving an ineluctably lost past behind. Kaurismäki said he felt compelled to make films about unemployment at that point.[7] But he also noted that he had long been inclined to focus on the Finnish working class, because he prefers the 'people who are hidden' (Leigh 2003) to the upper classes, in which he is simply not interested: 'I don't know how to write dialogue for them, I don't know how they talk'.[8] This perhaps owes in part to Kaurismäki's own financial struggles at early moments in his career (he was, among other things, a dishwasher and postman) – he says there were 'some years when I only had a sleeping bag. So I like losers. I am a loser myself'.[9] Even though *Man without a Past* bears clearly stylised genre markings as well as an ironically dreamlike atmosphere, it was largely shot on location in shipping containers in a harbour shanty town and many of the film's extras were actually homeless. Such location shooting and nonprofessional actors underscore the film's clear links to neorealist aesthetics, a tradition invoked but also overturned by the film's sardonic tone and self-reflexive stylisation.

Memory-loss films are almost always about identity, both its inherited and performative aspects, but *Man without a Past* tends to generalise M's personal identity in a number of spare sequences that collectivise its protagonist's rather fragmentary, episodic experiences. For example, per Kaurismäki's assiduous criticisms of the Finnish state, the police only get involved in M's case (after having ignored his severe beating) when it intersects with a bank robbery that he coincidentally witnessed. M happens to be in the bank for the robbery because he has gone there to try to open an account: wandering around the harbour, he suddenly realises he was an industrial welder in his past life (skills to which the audience was cued when his muggers played with his welding helmet and placed it over his face as a premature death mask). Restored to his old and forgotten vocation, he is informed that there is plenty of work at the shipyard for a skilled welder, but that he will need a bank account to be paid. When at the bank trying to open an account – difficult without a name – a jowly and dour middle-aged man comes in with a shotgun and demands a withdrawal from his own business's account, which the bank has punitively (and self-servingly) frozen. The clearly inexperienced robber, however, is insisting on the money not for himself, but to pay his workers who have been denied their wages for work done. These details – and the distrust of banks, at the heart of Finland's 1990s crisis – underscore the trilogy's economic concerns as well as the solution that Kaurismäki seems to long for in an ethics of simple and abiding solidarity between small-business bosses and workers, pitted as they are against the larger institutional bureaucracies of corrupt banks and apathetic police.

The key to Kaurismäki's work with genre, both noir and melodrama, is his consistent de-dramatisation of charged and even climactic moments, tipping tense scenes over into deadpan irony. The police consider M an accessory to the bank robbery since he will/cannot give his name, and the film reaches its de-dramatised high point when the police run M's photo in the paper asking if anyone knows this man. M's long-lost wife surprisingly comes forth, her never reporting him as missing explained away with her unhappiness at his gambling and at their impending divorce. When he meets her to learn about his former self, the encounter unfolds in the affectively flat style of all of Kaurismäki's scenes, any histrionic sentiment drained from this arch melodramatic moment. Similarly, his wife's new lover, hovering protectively nearby, asks M to step outside, ready to fight him on the doorstep of the house that once belonged to our protagonist. M asks why they should bother and offers instead to have a cigarette with him, defusing the conflict that one would expect at the heart of a memory-loss plot and the sundry genre forms with which Kaurismäki is playing. Gratefully liberated from the (conventional) past about which he just learns, M chooses his homeless friends and container life instead. He returns to the harbour and his newfound lover Irma, though the three thugs from the beginning return to greet him back to the big city. This time M braces for a fight, but again, the duel is defused when an army of homeless people, who have been harassed by these youths, appear to back M, sending the thugs running.

This sort of consistent, ironic de-dramatisation throughout the film is augmented by Kaurismäki's signature still camera, his stilted blocking, and especially by the performances of the actors, who almost all recur from film to film. The Brechtian overtones of the beggar's army seem confirmed in the modernist acting style Kaurismäki deploys, one he shares with major influences like Robert Bresson and Yasujiro Ozu, both of whom would rehearse actors to remove what they regarded as excess, and useless, affect from performances. Whereas both Bresson and Ozu would have actors rehearse lines until they had drained them of superfluous emotion, Kaurismäki allegedly gives actors the relevant bits of script right before shooting, so the lines are unfamiliar and their performances subsequently defamiliarising. He allows the actors minimal rehearsals and takes, so they cannot limn the line for emotional subtly. Such flat and vaguely surprised performances tend to augment the overarching deadpan humour.

The lines that the actors end up delivering typically mix very formal, often somewhat antiquated speaking styles with humble surroundings and a working-class milieu. For example, Irma remains coldly formal with M throughout their relationship, even as we realise that M will help her realise the fantasy and longing she manifests in her surprising, secret listening to songs like 'Do the Shake' before going to bed at night. As with Irma's musical tastes, Kaurismäki has alternated throughout his career between classical and (often) popular forms, especially of early rock 'n' roll and rockabilly of the sort M comes to coax out of the Salvation Army band he then manages to local and lucrative success. Such constant alternation of high and low corresponds to one of Kaurismäki's trademark visual strategies, again influenced by Ozu, namely, the placing of a noticeable streak of bright red in almost every image of this dreary world. Like his use of seemingly out-of-context, upbeat music, these curious and surprising splashes of colour illuminate and even enchant Kaurismäki's engagement with a modest, downtrodden world from which many films simply avert their gaze.

Notes

1. Krohn and Kaurismäki, 'Interview'.
2. Leigh, 'I am a lousy filmmaker'.
3. Ibid.
4. Van Bagh, 'Aki Kaurismäki'.
5. Krohn and Kaurismäki, 'Interview'.
6. Coslovich, 'The Finnish Touch'.
7. 'I couldn't bear to look at myself in the mirror until I made a film about unemployment'. Van Bagh, 'Aki Kaurismäki'.
8. Leigh, 'I am a lousy filmmaker'.
9. Coslovich, 'The Finnish Touch'.

Further reading

Peter van Bagh, 'Aki Kaurismäki: The Uncut Interview', *Film Comment*, 2011. Available at www.filmcomment.com/article/aki-kaurismaki/.

Gabriella Coslovich, 'The Finnish Touch', *Euroscreenwriters*, March 14, 2003. Available at http://zakka.dk/euroscreenwriters/interviews/aki_kaurismaki.htm.

Peter Cowie, *Finnish Cinema*, London, The Tantivy Press, 1976.

Aki Kaurismäki, 'Robert Bresson – a Wolf', in James Quandt (ed.), *Robert Bresson*, Toronto, Cinematheque Ontario, 1998, pp. 561–62.

Eric Krohn and Aki Kaurismäki, 'Interview: I am not interested in the upper classes', *IndieWire*, 20 October 2011. Available at www.indiewire.com/article/interview_le_havre_director_aki_kaurismaeki_im_not_interested_in_the_upper_.

Danny Leigh, 'I am lousy filmmaker', *Guardian*, January 16, 2003. Available at www.guardian.co.uk/culture/2003/jan/17/artsfeatures1.

Andrew Nestingen, 'Why Nation? Globalization and National Culture in Finland, 1980–2001', PhD, University of Washington, 2001.

Lana Wilson, 'Great Directors: Aki Kaurismäki', *Senses of Cinema*, July 09, 2009. Available at http://sensesofcinema.com/2009/great-directors/aki-kaurismaki/.

Jaimey Fisher

Memorias del subdesarrollo/ Memories of Underdevelopment (1968)

[Country: Cuba. Production Company: Cuban State Film and Instituto Cubano del Arte e Industrias Cinematograficos. Director: Tomás Gutiérrez Alea. Screenwriters: Tomás Gutiérrez Alea and Edmund Desnoes. Producer: Miguel Mendoza. Cinematographer: Ramón F. Suárez. Music: Leo Bouwer. Editor: Nelson Rodriguez. Production Design: Julio Matilla. Cast: Sergio Corrieri (Sergio

Carmona Mendoyo), Daisy Granados (Elena), Eslinda Núñez (Noemi), Omar Valdés (Pablo), René de la Cruz (Elena's brother).]

Synopsis: Tomás Gutiérrez Alea's masterpiece, *Memories of Underdevelopment* is based on a novel by Edmundo Desnoes released three years before the film. The film focuses on Sergio, a bourgeois intellectual and a landlord whose family including his wife has left for Miami. Sergio decides to stay in Cuba and dreams and fantasises about women in the midst of the transformations taking place all around him. He is bored even as the country is busy and excited about change. And yet Sergio is unable to slip away from this as he confronts his psychic and physical isolation. The film moves between the Bay of Pigs invasion of 1961 and the Cuban Missile crisis of 1962. Despite staying, Sergio constantly refers to the country as 'underdeveloped'. Sergio's encounter with himself, with others and with a society experiencing change forms the main thread in this unusual, complex and aesthetically innovative portrait of the Cuban revolution.

Memories is Alea's fifth and perhaps most well-known film and continues to resonate even today for its sheer craft, novelty in style and its deployment of boredom and interior monologue to penetrate the aftermath of the revolution. There is a casual episodic quality to the narrative as banal ordinary incidents are juxtaposed with events of great historical importance, in the process carving out a powerful reflection on the nature of historical consciousness. Sergio's meanderings through the city of Havana, his modernist apartment, official spaces, and his own memories are put together in the form of a collage. Here objects, photographs, documentaries, posters, billboards, books, clothing and filmic waste jostle for coherence in what is a treatise on historical subjectivity. Rather than use the point of view of a figure from the midst of the revolutionary process, Alea chooses to enter this world from the point of view of someone who is on the margins. In doing this, *Memories* displays a superbly confident disposition while at the same time offering a complex account of the relationship between memory, history and cinema.

The film opens with a carnival dance charged with energy which then cuts to the Jose Marti Airport in Havana where Cubans who want to leave after the revolution have congregated. Fidel Castro has given his countrymen one final chance to leave if they wished to. It is here at the airport that Sergio makes his break with his family. He returns home to his very stylish apartment sculpted by the camera to reveal its décor, objects, furniture and clothing. Sergio begins to type out his monologue – a diary of sorts that will contain his experiences and memories. Sergio wanders through the apartment, makes a snack for himself and then views the city through a telescope on his balcony. His voice externalises his internal monologue, as he comments on the change Cuba is going through. The film's formal structure moves with this interaction between voice-over and an impressionistic collage of images. Sergio is free of his family but isolated and alienated from the Cuban Revolution. As boredom takes over, Sergio fiddles around with his wife's clothing, listens to a recorded argument between them, and covers his face with her stockings. The voice reveals his views on women, commodities, life, Cuba and isolation and opens out a narrative of tremendous philosophical and formal power for the viewer.

We continue to journey through this episodic structure that introduces us to different characters. But each of these episodes moves between the characters, impressions of everyday life, and a constant engagement with the moment of historical transformation relayed through documentary images. Thus the banality of Sergio's present stands alongside the public unfolding of revolutionary change and for this Alea creates a labyrinthine structure that is at once dissonant, poetic and lyrical. The episodic structure introduces us to characters such as Sergio's friend Pablo, Elena, the girl with whom he has an erotic liaison, Hannah, a girlfriend from the past, Laura, the estranged wife, and the maid. Through each of these characters the film conducts a sort of spatial and temporal travel that is almost epic in its sweep. Documentary footage of the Bay of Pigs invasion, international statistics and images of poverty in Latin America, anti-race riots in the USA, a public seminar on literature and underdevelopment, footage of the Cuban Missile Crisis, etc. are drawn into the film's collage structure. Sergio moves through this maze reflecting on his own self, on the state of the world and on the people he encounters. Like diary jottings these reflections spill out of the film, making us aware of the emptiness of his life. This is the psychic landscape of a member of the wealthy educated class of a once colonised nation. Sergio is neither able to identify with the revolution nor with those who have left Cuba. Caught in between in a time warp, he remains an intellectual who is gradually enveloped by his own irrelevance even as he is an unusual witness to the spiral of history in the making.

Elena is the most important character Sergio encounters and this relationship forms the centrepiece of the film. She is as an 'underdeveloped' girl who in Sergio's words is 'inconsistent'. She does not share his interest in art, literature, and music. She is culturally alien to him while he himself is far too Europeanised to identify with the reality around him. What begins as a sexual encounter slowly turns into a burden as Sergio finds himself increasingly bored with Elena. The journey of this relationship and its afterlife is structured around a series of little sequences to highlight the incongruity and disconnect between the characters. The couple visit Ernest Hemingway's house, now turned into a museum. Sergio's intellectual pretensions and Elena's lack of interest collide in the space of the museum. In this remarkable scene, Alea engages in multiple critiques – of Hemingway, Sergio and Elena. Hemingway's servant who he picked up from the streets of San Francisco now works at the museum as a guide. Sergio reflects on this relationship between the master and the slave, referring to Hemingway as 'unbearable' even as he himself is consumed by a desire to be European and not Cuban. Sergio tries to mould Elena to be 'cultured' like him, introducing her to Hemingway's collection of memorabilia but Elena has no time for this. She wanders aimlessly through the museum, bored and disinterested.

The Hemingway Museum sequence is the turning point after which Sergio begins to avoid Elena. She then accuses him of rape and Alea creates a vivid sequence to present the encounter between Sergio, Elena's belligerent and extremely traditional family and a court trial. Sergio is visibly distressed and scared and does not expect justice in a system that now identifies with the 'people'. Elena's mother is constantly erupting with angry remarks like 'Girls must go to the altar as virgins. That is their greatest treasure'. The family demands that Sergio marry Elena. A trial follows and the judgment comes as a surprise to Sergio when he is acquitted for lack of evidence. In this encounter between Sergio's upper-class liberal views, Elena's family's conservative values and a fair trial verdict, Alea again displays his ability to navigate multiple layers of critique – of Sergio's own class position and attitude to women, and of Elena's family's manipulative style. The verdict is a surprise to both parties. Alea's complex relationship and ultimately his support for the revolution is present through the entire narrative but not without nuance. There is no abstract celebration of the 'people' in *Memories* but a series of encounters that foreground the interior life of political transformation.

Sergio's relationships with the other women are woven into the film in the form of memories and dreams. The flashback to his German Jewish girlfriend, Hanna, is structured in the form of a personal album of memories as Sergio reflects on that time. Flashbacks in the film are impressionistic allusions and include explosive moments of his difficult relationship with his wife Laura, his acquiring of a furniture store, and his encounter with prostitutes in his teens. The maid appears in his erotic fantasies as projections. All these very personal accounts unfold alongside newsreel and documentary images. This constant play with personal and public pasts, private and public time, and public spaces and private abodes is the highlight of the film. Depending entirely on a cinematic rather than a literary model, Alea uses all forms of media material in the film – radio, television, photographs, tape recorder, newspapers and celluloid. The result of this combination is a rich tapestry that philosophically reflects on the nature of historical time and individual consciousness. Alea deliberately rejects a straightforward narrative in favour of a non-linear structure. Some have referred to the film as an 'unusual provocation'[1] that is in dialogue with the best traditions of European Art Cinema techniques.

In a wonderfully reflexive sequence of the film, Sergio and Elena visit the office of ICAIC. Alea along with Sergio, Elena and other functionaries of the Institute are shown viewing film rushes of pornographic material censored by the previous regime. In the conversation that follows, Alea says he wants to use the footage in a collage-like film about everything. This is a direct reference to the structure of *Memories*, reflexively alluded to by the director himself. The self-reflexive technique here is clearly in line with the work of filmmakers like Luis Bunuel and Jean Luc Godard. Alea's aesthetic strategy in the film was clearly experimental with a desire to bring to the fore a form that would capture the complexities of a political phenomenon from a deliberately distanced point of view. It is this ironic and distanced disposition that has allowed *Memories* to retain its aura of artistic value and political relevance more than 50 years since its release.

Note

1. Michael Chanan, 'Interior Dialogue in the Work of T. G. Alea', *Framework: The Journal of Cinema and Media*, Vol. 44, No. 1, Latin American Film and Media (Spring 2003), pp. 11–21.

Further reading

Tomás Gutiérrez Alea, 'I Wasn't Always a Filmmaker', *Cinéaste* Vol. 14, No. 1, 1985, pp. 36–8.

Tomás Gutiérrez Alea, *The Viewer's Dialectic*, Editorial, Habana, Jose Marti Press, 1988.

Tomás Gutiérrez Alea, *Memories of Underdevelopment*, New Brunswick, New Jersey: Rutgers University Press, 1990.

Julianne Burton, 'Individual Fulfillment and Collective Achievement: An Interview with Tomás Gutierrez Alea', *Cinéaste*, Vol. 8, No. 1, Summer 1977, pp. 8–15, 59.

Julianne Burton, 'Memories of Underdevelopment in the Land of Overdevelopment', *Cinéaste*, Vol. 8, No. 1, Summer 1977, pp. 16–21, 58.

Henry Fernandez, D. I. Grossvogel, Emir Rodriguez Monegal and Isabel C. Gómez, '3/on 2 Desnoes Gutiérrez Alea', *Diacritics*, Vol. 4, No. 4, Winter, 1974, pp. 51–64.

Margot Kernan, 'Cuban Cinema: Tomas Guiterrez Alea', *Film Quarterly*, Vol. 29, No. 2, Winter 1975–1976, pp. 45–52.

Paul B. Miller, Sergio Corrieri and Dennis West, '*Memories of Underdevelopment*, Thirty Years Later: An Interview with Sergio Corrieri', *Cinéaste*, Vol. 25, No. 1, 1999, pp. 20–3.

Mercedes Santos Moray, 'The Creative Work of Two Cuban Filmmakers: Tomás Gutiérrez Alea and Fernando Pérez', *Le Mouvement Social*, No. 219/220, Apr–Jun., 2007, pp. 57–64.

Ranjani Mazumdar

Mildred Pierce (1945)

[Country: USA. Production Company: Warner Brothers Pictures. Director: Michael Curtiz. Screenwriter: Ranald MacDougall. Cinematographer: Ernest Haller. Music: Max Steiner. Editor: David Weisbart. Art director: Anton Grot. Cast: Joan Crawford (Mildred Pierce), Jack Carson (Wally Fay), Zachary Scott (Monte Beragon), Eve Arden (Ida Corwin), Ann Blyth (Veda), Bruce Bennett (Bert), Jo Ann Marlowe (Kay), Butterfly McQueen (Lottie).]

Synopsis: In contrast to the novel on which it is based, the film is structured as a fragmented flashback which gradually unravels the story of a murder. The deliberate omission of a standard reverse shot that would have clarified the situation, tricks the viewer into thinking there is no ambiguity regarding the identity of the murderer, but questions are raised and complexities gradually woven into the story as it progresses. Throughout, Mildred maintains her devotion to her daughters, especially the spiteful, hard-nosed Veda. When her neglected husband turns to another woman for attention and solace, Mildred asks him to leave and decides to fend for herself financially. Much to Veda's disgust, she finds work as a waitress; later, she summons all her powers of persuasion to buy a restaurant which she develops into a successful business. Still her daughter is resentful and her selfishness gets dangerously out of control, until eventually both mother and daughter must confront tragic consequences.

Mildred Pierce was a huge hit when it was first released in 1945 and remains a favourite to this day. As the first film she made with Warner Brothers after her contract with MGM came to an end, it was responsible for revitalising the flagging career of classical Hollywood icon Joan Crawford.[1] It was nominated for six Academy Awards in 1946, with Crawford winning Best Actress Oscar for her performance as the self-sacrificing heroine.[2] Based on a novel by James M. Cain, known for hard-boiled noir fictions, the screenplay reworks his plot, cutting characters and reorganising the structure, but retains the sharp edge of the original.

Taking a hybrid approach that was relatively unusual for its time, the film embraces many key generic features of both noir *and* melodrama, setting itself up as a site of struggle and uncertainty in structural terms that is reflected by the emotional conflict between its main characters. Thus, the moody low-key lighting and disruptive shadows of noir are set against the cluttered sets and emotive score that are more familiar to viewers of melodrama. Themes of love, betrayal and revenge, suffering and torment, mother/father-daughter relationships, female solidarity and the burden of family duty are amongst those articulated in this complex tale.

Historically, the context of *Mildred Pierce* is the austere yet uncertain 1940s post-war era of social and economic transition. While this is not strictly a period piece in that it does not explicitly deal with a specific moment of history, the film nevertheless responds to key concerns of the time. As Corrigan and White have argued, *Mildred Pierce* 'visibly embraces a crisis in the public narrative of America' (2004: 252) with its heart-rending portrayal of the collapse of the nuclear family at a time when many women resisted attempts to force them back into the home. As a fictional story of intimate, personal experiences, it nevertheless resonated so intensely in large part because many women of the day could identify with Mildred's plight.

An intermittent voice-over narration delivered by Mildred confirms this as a story that privileges her point of view; it also acts as the principle device to establish identification between the spectator and the protagonist, thereby securing initial support for her position. This approach to storytelling, with its apparent focus on the female perspective, was very much at odds with the anti-feminist slant of most noir films. However, any tension provoked by this ambiguity is eventually relieved when Mildred's version of events is called into question by the detective who has spent all night listening to her only to reveal that he knows full well she is hiding the truth. The binding structure of sympathy that had been developed is abruptly ruptured, and an alternative view of Mildred as social menace is offered. She is finally punished for threatening patriarchy by causing the downfall of the three men in her life, and the representative of the Law is able finally to restore order and stability.

Partly because of its ambivalent relation to the genre system, *Mildred Pierce* is complex in terms of its articulation of gender issues, and attempts to interpret these have drawn on Marxist and psychoanalytic approaches to film theory. As part-melodrama, it is bound to give greater attention to its female characters than most other classic genres, while melodrama is also 'one of the few generic areas in Hollywood in which masculinity in general, and "virile" masculinity in particular, has been constantly qualified, questioned, impaired or castrated' (Neale 2000: 186). Indeed, in *Mildred*, the protagonist's own husband has his masculinity called into question by her supposed neglect of his emotional and sexual needs and his lack of employment. Meanwhile, suitor Wally Fay constantly sees his advances rejected and second husband Monte, who comes to rely financially on his wife, is punished for his deception and betrayal of her with the loss of his life.

In film noir, as E. Ann Kaplan points out, 'women are central to the intrigue' (1980: 2).

Nevertheless, given that this is noir, the strong women portrayed must never be allowed to rise far above their station and patriarchy must triumph in the end. Independent women such as Mildred who abandon the home, seek solace in female friendship and reject male comfort are regarded as a social menace, a threat to the order which upholds those capitalist values upon which western society rests. Mildred is a particularly complex character as she assumes both archetypal female roles of noir: the nurturing figure *and* the 'spider woman' described by Janey Place as the 'evil seductress who tempts man and brings about his destruction' (1980: 35). She becomes a 'tycoon' restaurateur, owning a chain of quite glamorous establishments; she lures Wally Fay into a trap that threatens his freedom by framing him as a murderer; yet she also remains a self-sacrificing mother, risking everything she owns for the sake of her daughters. Even more dangerously for patriarchy, she takes on the conventional father's role of providing for her daughters when Bert is no longer able to do so, denying him a social role (and effectively erasing him from most of the rest of the narrative).

Noir films often also include corrupt, duplicitous children, especially daughters, who have to be punished just as their mothers are. Here the excessive Veda, only around 14 at the start of the story, gradually steals the role of treacherous *femme fatale* from her more sexually uncertain mother. Since Veda is the source of most of the marital tension between her parents, she and Mildred have to be separated in order that husband and wife might resume their 'normal' relationship.[3] Even more shocking perhaps, as Pam Cook explains, is the way in which Monte and Veda's relationship verges on 'transgression of the ultimate taboo: that against father incest' (1980: 75).

As Corrigan and White point out, *Mildred Pierce* is so compelling partly because its narrative structure oscillates tantalisingly 'between the classical and alternative narrative traditions' (2004: 252), both deploying and deliberately tampering with the conventions of cinema storytelling. The extended flashback (lasting four years) proceeds in a linear fashion, pausing only a few times to return to the 'present' of her so-called confession before the detectives (lasting one night). This 'present' is where most of the noir conventions of the film are to be found and where, ultimately, its ideological force resides. However, this interpretation is complicated by a retelling of the past from Mildred's point of view which more clearly draws on the features of melodrama, during which the increasingly elaborate costumes and sets reflect, at a glance, Mildred's changing social status and developing sexual allure. The multi-layered approach is reinforced by the use of noir lighting conventions that draw attention to shadows that suggest that all may not be revealed while by contrast, the more even, high-key lighting used in the sections recalled by Mildred gives the impression of plenitude and truth. That the latter eventually gives way to the former indicates that Mildred's account of events might be dubious, even before the detective confirms this suspicion.

In the end, despite all its complexities and transgressions, *Mildred Pierce* offers a 'reassuringly' conservative and conformist resolution. Mildred is forced to recognise the error of her independent ways, and returns to her ex-husband. Her 'confession', a strategy for maintaining control, is finally rebuffed. In effect, 'the temporal and linear progressions in Mildred's material life are … ironically offset by her loss. of emotional and spiritual life' (Corrigan and White 2004: 252) throughout the film. Her 'dangerous' sexuality has already been punished, for example, with the sudden death of her younger daughter, Kay, after her one night of illicit passion with Monte. While it is clear from the outset that Mildred wants to be found guilty of an actual crime of murder, according to the conventions of noir, she is *also* considered guilty of an offence against patriarchy: for having abandoned her marital vows and her domestic duties, albeit for the sake of her children.

In the film's final shot, the reunited couple leaves the police station together and walks away from the institution that represents national law and order. As they become engulfed by the modern building's enormous structures and exit through the perfectly framed archway, the silhouette of the Empire State Building, absolute symbol of western capitalism, is clearly visible in the background. Meanwhile in the foreground, two women can be seen scrubbing the steps, on their knees, as a reminder of the inextricable link between domesticated repression and patriarchy.

After all, part of the project of *Mildred Pierce* was to highlight the need to restore clear gender-based boundaries, and to encourage 'acceptance of the repression which the establishment of such an order entails' (Cook in Kaplan, 1980: 63). Thus, finally, after the struggle, torment, loss and self-sacrifice, Mildred reluctantly acknowledges that it is her social duty to return to the family home and support her (ex) husband. Her adventures as an independent career woman are over. Moreover, the ambiguity and blurred boundaries of generic hybridity are also finally resolved as the rational logic and cool intellect of noir overcome the emotional excess of melodrama.

Notes

1. Crawford later claimed she 'found' the part of Mildred, which had already been turned down by arch rivals Bette Davis and Rosalind Russell. Jack Warner was sceptical about casting Crawford in this more mature role, but was rewarded with a hit that marked a change of direction in the star's career.
2. Nominations for Best Actress in a Supporting Role also went to Ann Blyth as Veda and Eve Arden as feisty restaurant manager, Ida. According to her daughter, Crawford desperately wanted to win the Oscar but was so nervous about attending the ceremony that she took to her bed with 'pneumonia', from which she miraculously recovered in time for the celebratory press photographs. See *Joan Crawford: The Ultimate Movie Star* (DVD Special Feature, 2002).
3. In feminist discourse, this enforced separation is described as a form of 'castration' in that the beloved child, in Freudian terms, is considered to be the extension of the female body, the phallus she refuses to let go.

Further reading

John Belton, *American Cinema, American Culture*, New York, McGraw-Hill, 2005.

Pam Cook, 'Duplicity in *Mildred Pierce*', in E. Ann Kaplan (ed.) *Women in Film Noir*, London, BFI, 1980, pp. 68–82.

Timothy Corrigan and Patricia White, 'Narrative Value in *Mildred Pierce* (1945) and *Daughters of the Dust* (1991)', in *The Film Experience*, Boston, Bedford/St Martins, 2004, pp. 252–4.

E. Ann Kaplan (ed.) *Women in Film Noir*, London, BFI, 1980.

Steve Neale, *Genre and Hollywood*, London and New York, Routledge, 2000.

Janey Place, 'Women in *film noir*', in E. Ann Kaplan, *Women in Film Noir*, London, BFI, 1980, pp. 35–54.

Sarah Barrow

The Misfits (1961)

[Country: USA. Production Company: Seven Arts Productions. Director: John Huston. Screenwriter: Arthur Miller. Cinematographer: Russell Metty. Music: Alex North. Editor: George Tomasini. Cast: Clark Gable (Gay Langland), Marilyn Monroe (Roslyn Taber), Montgomery Clift (Perce Howland), Thelma Ritter (Isabelle Steers), Eli Wallach (Guido), Kevin McCarthy (Raymond Taber).]

Synopsis: Roslyn, a former burlesque dancer, has travelled to Reno, Nevada, to obtain a 'quickie' divorce. She takes up with Gay, an elderly cowboy, who persuades Perce, a struggling rodeo rider, to join him in rounding up some of the last feral mustangs of the region. Assisted by Guido, a freebooting pilot, they manage to capture a small family group of the horses, but Roslyn is appalled when she is told that they will be slaughtered for pet food. A struggle follows to release the mustangs, and the hunt has irrevocably changed her feelings for Gay.

The Misfits may be the most compellingly flawed film discussed in this collection. It fascinates as a symptomatic work, in the way that some films seem to show more than they intend, gathering together their times and displaying them in ways that writer, director and actors could never have foreseen. This film is also revealing about the nature of acting for cinema, just at the moment when the medium was falling from grace with its audience. *The Misfits* plays with its starring cast in a very knowing way, using the politics of charisma with remorseless cruelty. Of all the elements that contribute to a successful film, the work of the actors is rarely given enough attention in critical writing, and this film seems to show what acting for the screen truly is, even if it fails to convince as film fiction.

The Misfits in part represents the studio majors at a loss, increasingly unsure of their audience. It is a product of that moment when, no longer capable of staging great emotions through the convention of the world's most successful mass-audience entertainment, 'American cinema shrank into seriousness. History may show that the feature form was exhausted by 1960, waiting to be transformed by diversity and experiment' (Thomson 2003: 342, 743). As a decayed Western, *The Misfits* is a cruel parody of the formulae of a major Hollywood genre that could no longer work on its old terms. Yet there is no nostalgia for 'the lost West', only unflinching realism about what life in that territory has become, when Nevada is the 'Leave It' state, a dumping ground for everything from former wives to atom bombs. There are scenes and shots suffused with a peculiarly American bleakness, on the cusp between two very different decades. *The Misfits* seems to face in opposed directions: the ethos of the 1950s is acted and filmed in a way that anticipates the raw cinema of the 'Nouvelle Vague', John Huston directing with a casual, brutal truthfulness of the kind Jean Luc Godard so admired in American cinema. Godard's *Pierrot Le Fou* (1965) could be the French New Wave's remake of *The Misfits*.

Huston was the difficult, seasoned director of highly successful features, including his first film *The Maltese Falcon* (1941), *The Treasure of the Sierra Madre* (1947) and *The African Queen* (1952). He relished the high-risk element of making movies for Hollywood, and could treat actors with calculated sadism. While shooting *Moby Dick* (1956) he almost drowned Gregory Peck, who, as Captain Ahab in his death throes, was strapped to a two-ton rubber whale that pitched uncontrollably in gale force winds generated by the special effects team. Huston felt a need to adapt respected writers for the screen, from Herman Melville and Tennessee Williams to Flannery O'Connor and James Joyce; Arthur Miller's drama clearly appealed to him in this way. But he also rapidly lost interest in films that were not going well, and he routinely gave little explicit direction to actors, depending on the chemistry of the shoot to create drama in front of his cameras. All of this can be sensed in the risk-laden direction and acting in *The Misfits*. What is also extraordinary is that this creator of rugged, male-centred action films chose to put Marilyn Monroe's Roslyn at the nominal centre of his film. Huston was the director least likely to understand this role, or to bring out the best in his by now fragile and deeply vulnerable female lead.

Miller had been working on the screenplay since 1957, but it was still unfinished when shooting began in 1960 in the July heat of the Nevada desert. Four years earlier, he had met an eccentric pair of cowhands in Nevada, who hunted down some of the remaining wild mustangs for sale to the slaughterhouse. The dramatist was struck by these men and their degraded work, and drew on them for his screenplay, which was to reveal 'our lives' meaninglessness and maybe how we got to where we are' (Spoto 1993: 477). Fatally, Miller had a low opinion of writing for movies, and his commitment to *The Misfits* was in fact a desperate personal gamble; he was intending to create the perfect vehicle for his then wife, Marilyn Monroe, as a way of regaining her affection and perhaps salvaging their marriage.

Miller's screenplay is frankly pretentious and disjointed, drawing heavily on the cult of a vulgarised psychoanalysis that pervaded American culture in the late 1950s. The modern tragedy of broken marriages, failed family life and solitude is painfully established in the opening sequences, as in

Roslyn's poignant tautology before she goes to the divorce court – 'If I'm goin' to be alone I want to be by myself'. Mothers recur throughout as figures of loss, rejection and death, fathers as desperate and utterly deluded about their children. The only functioning 'family unit' is the group of mustangs that the cowboys finally isolate, a stallion, four mares and a colt, and which is destined for a pet-food plant. All of this would be too close to heavily symbolic melodrama, were it not for the desperate intensities with which the cast perform their roles. Inseparable from this is the moviegoer's compelling fascination with the lives of stars. *The Misfits* can be such an involving film because it incorporates this compulsion as an inescapable part of the attention we bring to the screen.

The Misfits was an ambitious risk with a budget of three and a half million dollars, which it overshot by another half million. The making of the film was hauntingly captured by nine Magnum photojournalists, including Eve Arnold, Henri-Cartier Bresson and Elliott Erwitt, for promotional purposes (Toubiana 2011). Huston wrote, 'The cast alone made *The Misfits* the most expensive black and white film – above the line – which had been made until then' (Leonard 1997: 239). The director could hardly have chosen a more unstable and demanding trio for the central roles than Monroe, Clark Gable and Montgomery Clift – and both director and his leads were in the grip of serious addictions that came near to destroying the entire production. Clift was intimidated by Gable but could not respect his acting, which he considered limited. Gable had no time for Clift as a product of the 'Method' school, yet he came to admire the younger actor's willingness to perform his own stunts. Despite being heavily dependent on drugs and alcohol, Clift was highly professional on set. Against Clift's 'Method' training, Gable simply said, 'I gather up everything I was, everything I am and hope to be. That's about it' (Leonard 1997: 241). Monroe's technique, paradoxically, was nearer to that of Gable than Clift, calling on her own innate abilities and troubled history while relying heavily for support on her drama coach, Paula Strasberg. What her husband's screenplay could never allow her to display was her essential genius for comedy and the free spirit that the film had been intended to celebrate. Clift and Monroe, recognising each other as lost souls, rapidly came to trust and depend on one another.

For Monroe, the experience of making *The Misfits*, her twenty-eighth and last completed film, could not have been more painful. Miller's script, begun as a celebration of her qualities, now catalogued the tragic failures in her life. The scene introducing Roslyn Tabor shows Monroe struggling to learn lines before her appearance in the divorce court, and immediately frames her as little more than an inept burlesque performer. She is being coached by Isabelle (Thelma Ritter), and the scene reproduces details and even lines from Monroe's own divorce case. She was persistently late on set, though often with genuine justification, as Miller would pass rewritten scenes to her at the last possible moment.

Miller chose Gable as his wife's romantic lead because he was the actor she had idolised 'as my father' since she was a child. Gable did become a paternal figure, patiently reassuring her even as he became exasperated with her erratic behaviour. She was, in her turn, frustrated by the role her husband was creating for her, which she knew to be poorly conceived. At the dramatic climax of the mustang round-up, rather than arguing with the cowboys about what they have in mind for the horses, Roslyn is shown simply screaming hysterically.

> I guess they thought I was too dumb to explain anything, so I have a fit – a screaming, crazy fit. I mean nuts. And to think, Arthur did this to me.
>
> (Spoto 1993: 482)

Yet at a very painful level, the role of Roslyn is profoundly accurate as the representation of a compelling female icon, misrecognised for what she is by the competing males who circle around her. As Monroe said,

> Everyone was always pulling at me, tugging at me, as if they wanted a piece of me. God, I've tried to stay intact, whole.
>
> (Ibid: 483)

Here too *The Misfits* anticipates Godard, in his critique of screen femininity and the gender politics of its time.

On its release, *The Misfits* divided audiences, as well it might, but was praised by some of the critics: 'The theme with its implications of an essentially male savagery suits Mr Huston, and he has drawn extraordinary qualities from all his chief players' (Dilys Powell, *Sunday Times*[1]). Other, more puzzled responses described the film, not inaccurately, as a cowboy story for an art-house theatre, or as an 'eastern western'. Others complained that nothing really happens in the film, but it is precisely the unmotivated series of random events where everything depends on the ordinariness of experience that brings the narrative close to French New Wave narration. As Roslyn remarks to Perce behind the saloon, 'Maybe all there is, is just the next thing'.

When Roslyn, Gay and Guido first dance in the unfinished house, a desperate intensity develops between them, because so much seems at stake. Roslyn is worshipped by the pair as the only person who uniquely has 'the gift for life', but she is stricken by the tragedy of what unfolds around her: 'We're all dying aren't we, all the husbands and all the wives.' At the end of the drunken evening, Roslyn goes outside and dances alone, while the other three look on. Monroe wrote to her analyst from a sanatorium shortly after the film was released, and commented movingly on this scene: 'Did you see *The Misfits* yet? In one sequence you can perhaps see how bare and strange a tree can be for me' (Spoto 1993: 509).

Each of the characters is vulnerable in their own, painful way, and none of them acts their true age. Gay is at the point of turning into an old man, while Roslyn behaves with a girlish naivety. This is what becomes so painful about Isabelle's witless repetition of 'Dear girl' to Roslyn, and it is also what gives such poignancy to the only child who appears in the film, the boy-cowboy with the strangely blank gaze, perched on the bar during a bat-and-ball wager. When Perce is thrown from his horse at the rodeo, Clift conveys an absurd vulnerability that suddenly becomes an image for the madness of cherished American aspirations, as 'Old Glory' streams in the background and a clown-faced cowboy hovers around him. *The Misfits* has failings, but also the power to haunt, as in the ominous final shot, when Roslyn and Gay drive into the night. She asks him, 'How do you find your way back in the dark?' He replies, 'Just head for that big star straight on. The highway's under it – it'll take us right home.' Miller's screenplay adds, 'They both keep their eyes on the star that shines above and beyond – the bright star of hope. FADE OUT.' But now the ending is inseparable from the fate of its two stars, and the fiction of the movie is co-opted by the mythic truth of the screen god and goddess, both shortly to die.

Note

1. Available at http://www.movie-film-review.com/devfilm.asp?rtype=1&id=7533 (accessed 16 June 2014)

Further reading

Maurice Leonard, *Montgomery Clift*, London, Hodder and Stoughton, 1997.

Donald Spoto, *Marilyn Monroe: The Biography*, London, Chatto and Windus, 1993.

David Thomson, *The New Biographical Dictionary of Film*, London, Little Brown, 2003.

Serge Toubiana, *The Misfits: Story of a Shoot*, London, Phaidon, 2011.

Nigel Wheale

Modern Times (1936)

[Country: USA. Production Company: Charles Chaplin Productions. Director: Charles Chaplin. Producer: Charles Chaplin. Original Music: Charles Chaplin. Editor: Willard Nico. Cinematographers: Ira Morgan, Roland Totheroh. Cast: Charles Chaplin (a factory worker), Paulette Goddard (a gamin).]

Synopsis: The Little Tramp's final film strings together Depression-era vignettes. In an 83-minute film, the Tramp is arrested five times and works at four different jobs. He begins the film as an assembly line worker but a nervous breakdown sends him to the hospital. After his release, he is arrested and imprisoned for allegedly leading a communist protest, then pardoned and released for foiling a jail break. A job at a shipyard lasts for a few minutes. Hoping to return to prison, he gets himself arrested, then escapes with a homeless teenaged girl (the Gamine). He is employed as a night-watchman for one night, then arrested again. When he returns from prison, he and the Gamine set up house in a shack. He gets work at his old factory and is arrested for the fifth time after accidentally throwing a brick at a police officer during a strike. The Gamine gets work as a dancer in a night club and the Tramp is hired as a singing waiter. But, when the police show up to arrest the Gamine the two hit the road. They walk off into the dawn and the curtain falls on cinema's most recognizable character.

Entering the critical discussion about the work of Charles Spencer Chaplin and his long-time alter ego – The Little Tramp – means engaging with a discourse of hero worship that the most ardent Judy Garland fan would find a little embarrassing. What makes Chaplin's apotheosis particularly striking is that the worshipful language emerges from the pens and word processors of film critics, who are, as a group, critical. In a canonical paean to silent comedy, published in 1949, James Agee writes:

> Of all comedians [Chaplin] worked most deeply and most shrewdly within a realization of what a human being is, and is up against. The Tramp is as centrally representative of humanity, as many-sided and as mysterious, as Hamlet, and it seems unlikely that any dancer or actor can ever have excelled him in eloquence, variety or poignancy of motion. The finest pantomime, the deepest emotion, the richest and most poignant poetry were in Chaplin's work.
>
> (Agee 2000: 488, 490).

In his massive 1998 book *'You Ain't Heard Nothin' Yet': The American Talking Film, History and Memory 1927–1949*, Andrew Sarris includes essays about a number of directors of silents, including Chaplin. The Chaplin essay begins, 'Charles Chaplin is arguably the single most important artist produced by the cinema, certainly its most extraordinary performer and probably still its most universal icon' (Sarris 1998: 139). David Robinson, a Chaplin biographer, whose recorded introductions are included in the Chaplin DVD releases, describes the Tramp as 'the most universally recognized representation of a human being in the history of mankind' (Robinson 1985: xiii).

While silent films may seem remote in ways that even early sound films may not, Chaplin films have lost neither their charm nor their power to invoke laughter. Because silent film depended not on dialogue but on pantomime, the silents crossed language barriers in ways that sound film never will. Chaplin was one of the first international film stars, and remained the most international of film stars through the end of his career as a director and star of silent films. The Little Tramp was most recognizable film character in the world from the mid-teens until his final screen appearance in *Modern Times.*

Chaplin was the most rigorous of perfectionists: he rehearsed, shot and reshot until he was thoroughly satisfied. His unmatched popularity, feverish work ethic, and shrewd business sense made him one of the most independent filmmakers in the history of Hollywood. One can graph the astonishing rise in his popularity, the expanding market for film entertainment (and Chaplin's aggressive negotiating tactics) through his contracts. Chaplin had grown up in London slums and had appeared on stage since he was a child. His first film contract, with Keystone studios, signed in December 1913, guaranteed Chaplin $150 a week, good money in 1913. Signing this contract meant retiring from his career in a touring musical comedy company and joining the troupe, supervised by Mack Sennett, that produced three comic pictures per week, each 10 to 30 minutes long. After a year in which he appeared in 33 Keystone films, several of which he also directed, Chaplin signed a contract with Essanay in November of 1914. The new contract guaranteed $1,250 per week, with a $10,000 signing bonus. Chaplin directed and appeared in 11 Essanay films, then signed with Mutual in February, 1916. The legendary Mutual contract guaranteed Chaplin $10,000 per week, with a signing bonus of $150,000. After directing and starring in several of his most acclaimed short films, Chaplin moved to First National in 1917, where he signed a contract with an annual salary of $1,075,000. By January of 1918 he was working in the studio he had built. In 1919, Chaplin joined with the period's other big stars, Douglas Fairbanks and Mary Pickford, and director D. W. Griffith to form United Artists. He had just turned 30.

Two months after the 1927 premiere of *The Jazz Singer* – the mostly silent film which marked the beginning of the end of silent cinema as a viable commercial enterprise – Chaplin began work on *City Lights*. *City Lights* took more than four years to complete, premiering in high style in February 1931. By this time the transition to sound film, the most wrenching artistic and economic storm to hit Hollywood, exacerbated by the onset of the Great Depression, was more or less complete. The careers of some of the most famous silent film stars and directors were over. New actors and comedians had already begun to take their places. *City Lights* included a few sound effects, and a score composed by Chaplin, but no dialogue. It is recognizably a silent film. And yet it was one of the year's most successful films, critically and commercially (Doherty 1999: 370–1).

The most astonishing fact about *Modern Times* is its release date – 1936 – almost nine years after the release of *The Jazz Singer*. To put this date in perspective, it's worth considering how far into the sound era Hollywood had travelled by 1936. After a careful build-up, silent film star Greta Garbo had spoken in *Anna Christie* (1930). In an attempt to maintain Garbo's international appeal, this film was released in English, German, and Swedish versions. German cabaret performer and film star Marlene Dietrich had made nine English language films, including an English language version of *The Blue Angel* made simultaneously with the German version. The Marx Brothers had made their most memorable films. Fred Astaire and Ginger Rodgers had danced together in four films.

Glancing through films represented in this volume, we see that, by the time *Modern Times* was released, Frank Capra had directed *It Happened One Night* (1934), one of the first and finest of screwball comedies, a genre that depends – more than almost any other – on dialogue.

Technically, *Modern Times* is not a silent film. It has a recorded soundtrack, but the soundtrack contains only sound effects, a musical score (composed by Chaplin), and some recorded speech, none of it dialogue. Most of the speech is mediated by technology. Speech is transmitted through a PA system, a videoscreen, a record, or a radio. *Modern Times* does contain the first and only film sequence in which The Tramp opens his mouth and words come out. In the film's final minutes, while working as a singing waiter, he is compelled to perform a song. He writes the lyrics on his (detachable) shirt cuff but, during his opening dance, he flings off his cuffs and is forced to improvise. The words that come out of his mouth sound vaguely Italian, perhaps with some French inflection, but they are entirely gibberish. Most of the conversation between characters is communicated either through pantomime or via a handful of intertitles, which had otherwise vanished from the screen. The Tramp still communicates through Chaplin's extraordinary control of his body and extraordinarily expressive face.

Chaplin was generally seen as left leaning, with his films as evidence, and was considered politically suspect enough to be a subject of FBI interest from 1922 until his death in 1977. Certainly his films provide plenty of evidence that Chaplin sympathised with the poor. Chaplin spent 18 months travelling after the release of *City Lights*. During this time he developed an economic theory intended to lessen the consequences of the Depression. This interest emerged in part from visiting European countries that were suffering the economic consequences of depression, consequences that were already having a political impact. *Modern Times* in particular is legible as a critique of the dehumanising power of technology and, by extension, of industrial capitalism.

The opening factory scenes in *Modern Times* owe a great deal to Fritz Lang's *Metropolis* (1927). *Metropolis* makes melodrama out of the achingly repetitive work of assembly line workers and of the dangerous gulf separating the capitalists from the labourers on whose work they depend. In *Modern Times*, the critique of the assembly line is played for comedy. Chaplin's film spends much less screen time on the capitalists. This time is efficiently damning however: the factory owner monitors his workers through video screens, and pushes them to work harder and faster. Apart from doing surveillance, he sits at his desk doing jigsaw puzzles. The critique of technology is also legible as a critique of sound cinema. The harsh recorded voices contrast with the lyrical elegance of Chaplin's dancing comedy. The amazingly funny sequence in which the Tramp tests out the eating machine cast suspicion on the idea that technology can improve any experience: technology is just as likely to destroy the pleasure of a sensual experience.

When the film leaves the factory the focus on technology disappears. The concern for the poor does not. The Tramp was always an economically marginal figure and usually an urban one. Chaplin films routinely make comedy out of the Tramp's pretence to respectability despite his poverty. *Modern Times* was the first Chaplin movie conceived during the Great Depression. *Modern Times* is concerned with widespread poverty, not just with the marginality of a particular poor character or a particular region of a city.

At the same time, *Modern Times* contains Chaplin's most astute, and funniest, comment on how his fame makes his politics visible and suspicious. This anticipates his banishment from the USA two decades later. In the second of the film's four acts, Chaplin sees a flag fall off the back of a truck (even in black and white, we know the flag is red). Chaplin picks up the flag and chases after the truck, waving the flag as he does so. A march of unhappy workers appears behind him. Waving the red flag, Chaplin accidentally finds himself leader of a movement.

Modern Times is read as one of Chaplin's most overtly political films, along with *The Great Dictator* (1940), the distinctly weird parody of Adolf Hitler, which trades on the striking resemblance between two of the most famous men in the world, born four days apart in 1889. Chaplin plays both, Adenoid Hynkel, Dictator of Tomania, and a Jewish barber, one of the persecuted residents of Tomania's ghetto. The barber resembles the Tramp, but he speaks. The character plays on the widespread suspicion that Chaplin was a Jew, something he refused to deny, although he was not. He was happy to be considered Jewish, especially during the Nazi period, when he saw it as an expression of solidarity with European Jews (Robinson 1985: 154–5). It almost goes without saying that neither *Modern Times* nor *The Great Dictator* was released in Germany. West German audiences had to wait until 1956 to see the Little Tramp as factory worker, until 1958 to see Chaplin as Hynkel; East Germans had to wait until reunification.

During the McCarthy era, Chaplin was a prime target for anti-communist witch hunters. Puritanical ideas about sex were as apt to cause suspicion as were leftist politics. Chaplin's marital history – four marriages, all to much younger women, plus a paternity suit which found him guilty of fathering a child out of wedlock, despite a blood test which proved he could not have been the child's father – did not help his cause. Despite his decades of work in the US he never took US citizenship. In 1952, Chaplin set sail for Europe and his re-entry visa was revoked. He spent the rest of his long life living in Switzerland, and did not return to the USA until 1972, when he received a series of honours, including a special Academy Award.

In recent years cineastes have been apt to compare Chaplin to Buster Keaton, another one-time Keystone comedian who struck out on his own as director and star in the 1920s. Keaton never had the control over his productions that Chaplin had, and his character did not survive the earthquake of sound, although he continued to appear in movies and on television until his death in 1966. Keaton now looks like a more innovative filmmaker, more apt to experiment with film technology and movie magic. But discussion as to who one should rate more highly seems a little silly. As viewers, we are a lucky that these two men made brilliantly funny silent films, and that so much of their work has survived.

Further reading

James Agee, 'Comedy's Greatest Era', in *Agee on Film: Criticism and Comment on the Movies*, New York, Random House, 2000, pp. 391–412.

Thomas Doherty, *Pre-Code Hollywood: Sex, Immorality, and Insurrection in American Cinema 1930–1934*, New York, Columbia University Press, 1999.

Charles J. Maland, *Chaplin and American Culture: The Evolution of a Star Image*, Princeton, Princeton University Press, 1989.

David Robinson, *Chaplin: His Life and Art*, New York, McGraw Hill, 1985.

Andrew Sarris, *'You Ain't Heard Nothin' Yet': The American Talking Film, History and Memory 1927–1949*, New York, Oxford University Press, 1998.

Elliot Shapiro

Mon oncle/My Uncle (1958)

[Country: France and Italy. Production Company: Gaumont. Director: Jacques Tati. Screenwriters: Jacques Tati and Jacques Lagrange. Producers: Jacques Tati and Louis Dolivet. Music: Franck Barcellini and Alain Romans. Cinematographer: Jean Bourgoin. Production Designer: Henry Schmitt. Editor: Suzanne Baron. Cast: Jacques Tati (Monsieur Hulot), Jean-Pierre Zola (Charles Arpel), Adreinne Servantie (Madame Arpel), Alain Bécourt (Gérard), Adelaide Danieli (Madame Pichard).]

Synopsis: The young Gérard Arpel (Bécourt) lives with his mother and father in their ultra-modern villa on the edge of Paris. Gerard finds it hard to adapt to the monotony and regimented routine of this life. The father (Zola) works for a large plastic pipe factory, while his mother (Servantie) cleans the house all day – she is particularly fond of turning on and off a fish-shaped fountain in the front yard for admiring guests. Her brother, Monsieur Hulot (Tati) visits them at the villa for a garden party, and then his brother-in-law at the factory. He brings disaster with him.

For David Thomson, Jacques Tati's elaborate talent for refined visual comedy was expressed with the consistency and neatness of a great miniaturist.[1] Among French cinema's most inventive comics, Tati is fondly remembered by audiences and critics alike for his near flawless body of work. He was a silent film star in a post-silent world, and is remembered as one of the great screen comedians – perhaps the greatest – of the sound era, up there with Buster Keaton, Chaplin, and Leslie Nielsen. With little or no dialogue in his films, Tati employed tightly choreographed slapstick action and innovative, often unsettling sound designs to move the story forward. His precise films (he was a notorious perfectionist, ranked with Robert Bresson for the total control he exerted on set) were made to look breezy and effortless, and given a greater depth by successfully merging farce, visual comedy, and social commentary on issues such as materialism, class relationships, and the increasingly impersonal nature of modernisation. *Mon oncle*, like Tati's other films, is remarkable for its symbolic colour schemes, its dense use of sound effects, its love-hate relationship to American culture, and its 'economy of style and apposite gesturality'.[2]

Tati once described Hulot as 'a character with a complete sense of independence, utterly unselfish, whose distraction, which is his main flaw, make him – in our functional times – a misfit'.[3] He was an apolitical Everyman, a perplexed figure marooned in a fast-changing France, a silent witness to a new vogue in efficiency and urban renewal. His absent-mindedness seemed the counterbalance the vacuousness of the new glass and steel constructions; Hulot is a 'distracted spectator', not so much cynical of modern urban life as totally bemused by its encroaching workings and practices. Tati used Hulot in four films – from *Les vacances de M. Hulot/Monsieur Hulot's Holiday* (1953), via *Mon oncle* and *Playtime* (1967), to *Trafic* (1971) – and gradually became less ridiculous, less farcical, and less obtrusive, part of Tati's tactic to de-emphasise his main character and make the audience focus more on other characters and actions. Hulot was not a comedian in the sense of being the source and focus of the humour; rather, he was 'an attitude, a signpost, a perspective that reveals the humour in the world around him'.[4]

It is not surprising that *Mon oncle* is burdened with so strong a spirit of ambivalence towards modernity and progress. Tati was one of the few French film-makers of the 1950s and 1960s to engage in a critical dialogue with the modernising and emergent mass consumerist aspect of French society. His work is notable for its engagement with 'new and disquieting forces infiltrating the sphere of the quotidian in post-WWII France'.[5] These forces might be expressed as the effects of technology, mechanisation, urban planning and design, and modernity at the level of human behaviour – a period, in the words of Kristin Ross – of 'fast cars and clean bodies'. Tati's two previous films, *Jour de fête/The Big Day* (1949) and *Monsieur Hulot's Holiday*, as well as the later *Playtime* all, to a greater or lesser degree, problematise the notion that technological progress is to be embraced and automatically succumbed to. *Mon Oncle* is often regarded as a paean to a bygone France that has gradually been usurped by the grand architectural renovations taking place in French urban areas throughout the 1950s and casts a satirical eye on the so-called benefits of modern design and technology. *Jour de fête* had already used the postman's bicycle as an emblem of tradition that is being replaced by the mechanised systems installed by American postal companies. By the time of *Mon oncle*, Tati was creating dramatic tension through the clash of cultures between old and new France, allegorised in the Arpel's new modern villa built on the outskirts of Paris.

The Arpel home, all white walls and sleek furnishing, looks deliberately ridiculous, bereft of function and domesticity. Despite the aesthetic quality of the house and its proportional and linear harmony, it is clearly a space that has not improved the lifestyle of its end users. The fashionable notion – forwarded by Le Corbusier – that modern architecture could provide an ideal form of utopian self-improvement is contested throughout Tati's work and reaches a critical juncture in *Mon oncle*. The villa is a clear link back to Le Corbusier's concept of housing as 'machines for living in' (complete with whirring gadgets, sparse decor, and ergonomically suspect sofas) and highlights Tati's ambivalence towards the wholesale embrace of modern architecture. This new model for living entrenches gender roles and places conspicuous consumption and the acquisition of possessions as the *sine qua non* for happiness. In fact, it does the opposite – Gerard is an unhappy child, unloved and isolated. As Tati was fond of saying, 'modern architecture does not produce amiable inhabitants'.

Tati began filming *Mon oncle* in autumn 1956 and completed principal photography in early 1957. It would take another year in the editing room for Tati to master the dubbing process and sound effects that would become so critical to the aural complexity of the finished work. In keeping with Tati's own background as a mime artist, his films are 'silent' – dialogue is muffled or incomprehensible, train station announcements are garbled, and doors open and close to the sound of twanging elastic bands. Such techniques are used in *Mon oncle* – the gimmicks and gadgets in the villa and the factory are accompanied by clicks, buzzing, squeaks, screeches and whistles – the soundscape becomes deafening, and suggests that the human voice is also under threat in this new mania for mechanisation.

Like Clair and Chaplin before him, Tati's representation of the modern workforce in *Mon oncle* is defined by a series of obligatory rituals. He shows how Taylorism has moved beyond the modes of production, and now obliges its inhabitants to work and live in particular ways, 'with all their movements synchronized with their intended desires or objectives'.[6] Mrs Arpel carries out her housekeeping duties with exaggerated accents on her motions, as if acting out her role in the household though no one is there to watch her performance. None of the workers in Arpel's factory actually 'work'; instead, they sit quietly, disengaged, and only rouse themselves when Arpel passes by.

While the Arpel villa remains a justly celebrated example of production design, Hulot's own garret room, at the apex of rickety old building that takes him a eternity to reach, is indicative of an old France resistant to wholesale change. Far from a site of blank functionalism and automated gates, his living space retains a nostalgic charm. Hulot uses a mirror to shine sunlight onto a bird to start it singing – not only is this another opportunity for Tati to use sound in an amusing, childlike way, but also indicates the sustainability of old-style values and a cherished engagement with activities that are not battery-operated. Despite the ramshackle nature of the town square, it remains a dynamic site of community interaction, complete with market-sellers, playing children, and people unfazed by the pressures of modernity. Unlike the Arpels, who bring their ultra-modern chairs out of the house, and carefully position them on the patio to sit and watch the television from further away, Hulot's world involves face-to-face communication. The irony is that this old *quartier* is exactly the sort of urban space that would be flattened in the 1950s and 1960s as France relocated its working-class masses from inner-city tumbledown housing to high-rise suburban apartments. For Tati, this type of city living is destined to rapidly disappear.

Despite the attendant promises of precision and certainty posited by the Arpel villa, such sureness is radically undermined. The brave new world of architectural modernity is not a space of expanding imagination but rather a confusing and unstable one. Tati subverts the supposedly ideal futurist dream as represented in modernist architecture, and recasts it as a space in which modes of behaviour have eroded to robotic gestures and automated responses.

Tati's camerawork creates a distancing effect between the spectator and the on-screen events. There are very few close-ups, or even shot-reverse shots, in *Mon oncle* – the majority of scenes in the 'modern' world are filmed from a distance, in long-shot. The extended garden party sequence exemplifies this approach. It's a 20-minute tour de force of choreography, sight gags, and comic tension that invite us to watch from a distance. Such a 'democratic'[7] approach to comedy (so many 'bits of business' are happening in these long-shot frames that we are unsure where to look or focus our attention next, for fear of missing an equally exquisite sight gag happening simultaneously) typified Tati's visual and sonic aesthetic.

Mon oncle is Tati's warmest film, despite its cool, detached style, and despair of the soulnessness of modern life. It's there in the title – a story about family bonds that ends happily. As Hulot leaves for a job in the provinces, Gerard connects with his father when a whistle goes wrong. Hulot, despite his bumbling demeanour and being an agent for chaos, is a catalyst for Gerard to find an inkling of boyish adventure in his father, and the two form a long overdue connection.

The message of *Mon oncle* is 'not a defence of tradition' but instead a 'clear indictment of progress at any price'.[8] In the near-decade interim before *Playtime* France would demonstrably change, and the Arpel villa that so baffles Hulot would become the default design aesthetic for urban planners. The France of the 1960s was changing, and the uncertainties that Hulot may once have overcome through sheer bumbling endeavour transformed exponentially in *Playtime* into dilemmas that would leave him 'shaken and discomfited by the shifting sands of a Paris in the throes of metamorphosis'.[9] *Mon oncle* won the Academy Award for the Best Foreign Film of 1958, and when he arrived in Hollywood for the ceremony, the Academy asked Tati if there was anywhere he would like go. Tati asked that he be allowed to visit the nursing homes where Buster Keaton, Stan Laurel, and Mack Sennett then lived.

Notes

1. David Thomson, *The New Biographical Dictionary of Film*, 4th ed., London, Little Brown, 2003, p. 862.
2. Susan Hayward, *French National Cinema*, 2nd ed., London and New York, Routledge, p. 189.
3. See Cauliez, pp. 80–107.
4. Bert Cardullo, 'An Interview with Jacques Tati by André Bazin, with the Participation of François Truffaut', *Quarterly Review of Film and Video*, 19:4, 2002, p. 286.

5. Lee Hilliker, 'Hulot vs. the 1950s: Tati, Technology and Mediation', *The Journal of Popular Culture*, 32:2, 1998, p. 59.
6. Nezar AlSayyad, 'Cynical Modernity, or the Modernity of Cynicism', in *Cinematic Urbanism: A History of the Modern from Reel to Real*, London and New York, Routledge, 2006, p. 101.
7. See Jonathan Rosenbaum, 'Tati's Democracy', *Film Comment*, May–June, 1973, pp. 37–40.
8. See Hayward, p. 190.
9. Lee Hilliker, 'In The Modernist Mirror: Jacques Tati and the Parisian Landscape', *French Review*, 76:2, 2002, p. 321.

Further reading

David Bellos, *Jacques Tati*, London, The Harvill Press, 1999.

Armand J. Cauliez, *Jacques Tati*, Paris, Seghers, 1968.

Michel Chion, *The Films of Jacques Tati*, trans. Antonio D'Alfonso, Toronto, Guernica Editions, 2003.

Brent Maddock, *The Films of Jacques Tati*, Metuchen, NJ, and London, Scarecrow Press, 1977.

Jonathan Rosenbaum, 'Tati's Democracy', *Film Comment*, May–June, 1973, pp. 37–40.

Ben McCann

Mother India (1957)

[Country: India. Production Company: Mehboob Studios. Director: Mehboob Khan. Producer: Mehboob Khan. Dialogue: Wajahat Mirza and S. Ali Raza. Cinematographer: Faredoon Irani. Music: Naushad. Lyrics: Shakeel Badayuni. Editor: Shamsudin Kadri. Dance Director: Chiman Sethi. Costumes: Fazal Din. Cast: Nargis (Radha), Raaj Kumar (Shyamu), Sunil Dutt (Birju), Rajendra Kumar (Ramu), Kanhaiya Lal (Sukhi Lala), Master Sajid (young Birju), Jiloo (mother-in-law), Chanchal (Rupa).]

Synopsis: Set in rural India in the years surrounding India's independence (1947), *Mother India* tells the story of Radha, a poor, illiterate villager who struggles to care for her family. Radha's husband Shyamu is forced to pawn the gold bangles which come in her dowry (known as *stree dhan* or the woman's wealth), their land, their cows and ancestral brassware to pay their usurious debt to the village moneylender Sukhi Lala. Floods strike, destroying Radha's home and killing two of her four children. Seeing an opportunity, Sukhi Lala offers Radha money in exchange for sexual favours after Shyamu abandons her. Refusing to relent, Radha raises her two surviving children single-handedly. Her enormous strength and willpower enable her to succeed where Shyamu fails. Radha's accomplishments earn her the title of the mother of the entire village, which becomes a symbol for the nation as a whole: hence the iconic title *Mother India*.

Mother India was a remake of Mehboob's own hit talkie *Aurat* (*Woman*, 1939), inspired by the Hollywood film *The Good Earth* (1937). *Aurat's* success helped Mehboob to set up his own studio, which featured a hammer and a sickle in its logo.[1] Although it is often taken to be a sign of communist propaganda, Mehboob's use of the hammer and sickle is better understood as a strong evocation of his humble origins as a farmer and his love of peasant life.[2] *Aurat* was one of the earliest talkies to be set in rural India. While *Aurat* is a gritty tale of female suffering and sacrifice that ends in the death of a heartbroken mother, Mehboob elevates *Mother India* to a national scale by drawing on the twin experiences of independence and partition. This is evident not only from the change in the title but also in various stylistic augmentations, made possible by the then new technology of Gevacolor.[3] Mehboob and his cameraman

Faredoon Irani shot on location using synch sound in his native Gujarat, bringing a heightened, spectacular realism that was new to Bombay cinema. The new version included actual footage from a flood which was matched with carefully constructed studio shots.

Mother India combines a striking use of red earth tones with sensational scenes of rural festivity, deploying them to create a glamorous family drama that unfolds in the unlikely setting of the village. The film opens with Soviet-style imagery of tractors that till a verdant, thriving land set against the backdrop of a newly constructed dam. Asked to inaugurate the dam, an old Radha, seen in extreme close-up, shakes her severely lined, worn face in disbelief. Contemporary audiences would have immediately recognised the tractor and dam as potent signifiers of the Nehruvian ideal of socialist progress. As villagers urge her to perform the prestigious task, memories of Radha's traumatic past break through the dam's floodgates. This provocative segue sets up a point of view that is distinctly marked as one that belongs to Radha, leading to a flashback that reveals a competing, untold story. We then see Radha as a young, stunningly beautiful bride who unselfishly removes her bridal finery to throw herself into the task of nurturing her home. The paying off of the debt tells only one part of this story. Shyamu loses both his arms (and his masculinity) in a horrific accident that reduces him into another mouth to be fed. Radha is harassed by Sukhi Lala at every opportunity; in a significant downturn, her younger son Birju betrays her trust by turning into a *ganja* (marijuana)-smoking bandit. As if this is not enough, Birju kidnaps Sukhi Lala's daughter Rupa from her wedding altar. Although Birju is driven by a desire to avenge his mother's mistreatment, in doing so he jeopardises Radha's painstakingly earned goodwill and *izzat*, a word that connotes chastity as well as respectability. Radha implores Birju to give Rupa up and not harm her *izzat*: by now, *izzat* encompasses the chastity and respectability of *both* women. When Birju refuses, Radha threatens to kill him, a move that signifies her greater commitment to the village. In a shocking and unprecedented move, Radha shoots her beloved son in one single, spectacularly fatal shot. No other Indian film has portrayed motherhood so graphically, showing Radha's awesome beauty at one moment while telescoping her brutal loss in the other.

The fall-out between son and mother embodies all the key struggles that structure *Mother India*: money against honour, debt against self-reliance, subjugation versus independence, individual identity against the collective Good, traditional family loyalty against the modern State, and finally, male inadequacy against female power. While *Mother India* begs to be considered as an Oedipal drama, it also disrupts any straightforward Freudian reading by depicting a son who, within the world of the film, cannot have the mother: instead, the mother kills the son. Radha herself embodies an intense maternal love that turns against itself in the explosive climax.

Indeed, *Mother India*'s universe is one that threatens to fall apart constantly. Its polarisation of personal love and national commitment is extreme. The two can be reconciled only in the affective realm of the personal but not in the material, social world of the film. Only Birju's spectacular death can leave his memory intact. The event allows *Mother India* to register the volatility of a transformation that turns the nostalgic, idyllic space of the village into a unit reorganised along the lines of a modern nation state that provides partial and insufficient justice. Equally, the film also celebrates Radha's herculean effort in a haunting frame that depicts a human map of undivided India against the lush, lyrical background of fields swelling with grain; a shot that wishfully erases painful memories of the Partition. This shot is followed by an iconic tableau that rejoices in a Christ-like Radha, harnessed to a plough that eventually becomes her cross as she heaves herself unknowingly into a traumatic future.

Scenes like this translate the trauma of colonialism and Partition into a recognizable psychic register organised according to love between mother and son who are sundered apart. So profound was *Mother India's* dramatic impact that it may well be characterised as the mother of melodrama in Bombay cinema. Central here is the problem of allegiance to the new nation, which demands a rapid overhaul of older loyalties, forms of kinship and their attendant moral values: Birju sacrifices his life for his mother's honour while Radha sacrifices Birju for the future of her land. Radha's torn state of mind is illustrated in a key sequence that occurs during *Holi*, a festival that celebrates the spring harvest. Sukhi Lala's daughter Rupa dances seductively at the festival, wearing Radha's bangles to seduce Birju. The audience knows that Sukhi Lala has wrongfully appropriated jewellery from Radha's dowry. Thus Rupa's expression of sexual desire is perverse and sadistic; moreover, she berates Birju for coveting the bangles instead of her. Incensed, Birju tries to yank his mother's bangles from Rupa's wrists. Afraid of Birju's intensifying rebellion, Sukhi Lala accuses him of molesting his daughter. This sets off an angry mob, which ties Birju to a stake and smokes him out of haystacks when he tries to hide, injuring him with a bullet. Red hues from Birju's blood, Radha's sari and the rising flames bleed into each other in quick swish pans that evoke a sense of hysteria and panic. This is a make or break moment of truth: Radha must choose between love for her son or uphold her respect and duty toward the land. Colour orchestrates the effects that express Radha's abiding love for Birju while her chilling screams reverberate across a land from which she is suddenly alienated. Memories of this impossible choice pervade the concluding sequence, where blood washes across the scene as Radha reluctantly unlocks the dam's floodgates, releasing red water. Blood ties finally triumph over the memory of Radha's public quelling of Birju, making room for a recollection that at last acknowledges his psychic motivations: he dies in her arms, clutching her blood-soaked bangles. This telling image is superimposed over images of a past that appear heroic to others but are now suffused with recognition of Radha's colossal sacrifice.

Mother India remains significant for a number of other reasons as well, particularly because it marks a major shift in its lead actress Nargis's career. In her previous collaborations with co-star and director Raj Kapoor, Nargis often appeared as an urban, seductive heroine. In Mehboob's *Andaz* (1949), she appeared as a spoiled, rich city girl. Other examples include *Awara* (1951) and *Shree 420* (1955), which feature variations of an urban star persona epitomised by her short, bobbed hair, westernised attire and frank sexuality. Together, Nargis and Raj Kapoor stood for sexual boldness because of their much-publicised affair. However, Kapoor was already married and apparently refused to marry her.[4] Nargis had become so involved with Raj Kapoor that she neglected her original mentor Mehboob until disenchantment with her current relationship with Kapoor pushed her into taking *Mother India* on. Given this history, Nargis's portrayal of Radha remained highly sexualised – in another famous sequence, she offers herself to Sukhi Lala in a decision that says 'anything to feed my hungry children'. Divine intervention helps Radha to find the strength to fight Sukhi Lala but her willingness to risk her reputation pushes the limits of what screen mothers can and cannot do, in a film where female honour is at an absolute premium. What's more, Nargis would bid a permanent goodbye to Kapoor and soon marry her co-star Sunil Dutt. Ironically, Dutt played Birju in *Mother India*. In the climactic fire sequence discussed above, rising flames threatened to kill both actors but Dutt saved Nargis in a brave, selfless act that has now become a legendary story about abiding love.[5] In his career, though, Dutt was a beginner. His Birju came across as an uncouth, attractive youth with a raw machismo. The performance worked and won the audience over as it responded to Birju's iconoclastic vigilantism. Nargis was clearly the bigger star here but her marriage to an unknown actor provided even more grist to the gossip mills, adding to *Mother India's* wild popularity. Ultimately, Nargis came to be remembered most for her performance as the rustic, fiercely independent Radha and as the wife of Sunil Dutt. Though Mehboob tried to suppress news of the so-called 'mother-son' marriage, it spread like wildfire, doing little damage to the film's success: in *Kala Bazaar* (*The Black Market*, 1960), *Mother India* appears as a film so popular that it launched a thriving black market in Bombay cinemas. In fact, the scandal structured one more melodramatic coup d'état that allowed the son to 'get' the mother although she had destroyed him on screen.[6]

Indeed, *Mother India* inspired dozens of other films, notably *Gunga Jumna* (1961) and *Deewar* (The Wall, 1975).[7] The print was carefully guarded to prevent duplication, ensuring that it ran continuously in theatres until the 1980s, a period that saw major transformations in post-independence

Bombay cinema. Like Birju, *Deewar*'s protagonist Vijay dies in a lover-like embrace in his mother's arms. Politicians like Indira Gandhi drew significantly on Nargis as Mother of the Nation during election campaigns, replacing older iconographies with a cinematically inflected political reappraisal.[8] *Mother India*'s long afterlife offers further testimony of its searing melodramatic intensity. More recently, the fire sequence reappears in Farah Khan's *Om Shanti Om* (2007) as an example of a struggling actor's undying love for the film's leading female star. Whatever the emphasis, *Mother India* plays out on a monumental scale that remains unsurpassed in Bombay cinema.

Notes

1. *Aurat* was produced by National Studios. Ashish Rajadhyaksha and Paul Willemen note that Mehboob started out as an actor in the silent era, gradually working his way up to direct films for some of the most important studios of the late silent and early sound era, including Imperial and Sagar movietone. See *Encyclopaedia of Indian Cinema*, London, British Film Institute, 1999, p. 145.
2. Mehboob explains in an article published in *Filmfare*, 1957, 'I took the hammer and sickle as our symbol, because we considered ourselves workers and not just producers, directors and stars. I am not communist' (quoted in Chatterjee, 2002: 72).
3. The film was shot in Gevacolor and printed in Technicolor. See Chatterjee, 2002: 20–1.
4. For a detailed discussion of Nargis's pre-*Mother India* star persona, see Majumdar, 2009: 153–5. See also Thomas, 1989: 23.
5. Sunil Dutt recounts this moment in the documentary *Nargis Dutt*, dir. Priya Dutt, Films Division, 1992.
6. See Thomas, 1989: 27: 'the son [finally] "got" the mother'. This marriage shocked viewers because Nargis came from a Muslim family while Dutt was a Hindu. Nargis's mother was a poet, scriptwriter and filmmaker during the silent era at a time when any association with cinema tarnished the woman's reputation. Nargis, on the other hand, was brought up in Bombay and had had a privileged, Westernised education. Mehboob persuaded her to star in his *Taqdeer/Fate* (1943), where she played her first lead role, at the age of 14. Her subsequent affair with Kapoor fuelled speculations about her loose character, which came to be associated with her mother's disrepute. Her appearance in *Mother India* and her marriage to Sunil Dutt had a defining effect on Nargis's final public persona, that of a social activist and champion of India's social upliftment.
7. Other films that ran continuously for long periods of time include *Sholay* (1975), *Hum Apke Hain Kaun* (1992) and *Dilwale Dulhaniya Le Jayenge* (1996).
8. As a newly elected Member of Parliament at the Rajya Sabha, Nargis attacked Satyajit Ray's *Pather Panchali* (1955) for catering to Western audiences by foregrounding India's poverty, rather than its success as a nation. See Parama Roy, *Indian Traffic: Identities in Question in Colonial and Postcolonial India*, Berkeley, University of California Press, 1988, pp. 168–73; also Thomas, 1989: 29 for an insightful discussion of how Indira Gandhi appropriated captions like 'Mother India needs you' in the 1980 electoral campaign.

Further reading

Sumita S. Chakravarty, *National Identity in Indian Popular Cinema 1947–1987*, Austin, University of Texas Press, 1993.

Gayatri Chatterjee, *Mother India*, New Delhi, Penguin, 2002.

Neepa Majumdar, *Wanted Cultural Ladies Only!* Chicago, Illinois University Press, 2009.

Rosie Thomas, 'Sanctity and Scanda: The Mythologization of *Mother India*', *Quarterly Review of Film and Video*, Vol. 11, No. 3, 1989, pp. 11–29.

Anupama Kapse

Moulin Rouge! (2001)

[Country: USA, Australia. Production Company: 20th Century Fox Film Corporation, Bazmark Films. Director: Baz Luhrmann. Producers: Fred Baron, Martin Brown, Baz Luhrmann. Screenwriters: Baz Luhrmann, Craig Pearce. Cinematographer: Donald McAlpine. Editor: Jill Bilcock. Original Music: Craig Armstrong. Sound Director: Marius de Vries. Choreographer: John O'Donnell. Cast: Nicole Kidman (Satine), Ewan McGregor (Christian), John Leguizamo (Toulouse-Lautrec), Jim Broadbent (Harold Zidler), Richard Roxburgh (English Duke).]

Synopsis: The plot follows naïve, penniless English writer Christian in bohemian Paris, falling for beautiful courtesan, Satine. Glittering star of the low-life Moulin Rouge, Satine is dying of consumption. Manager, Harold Zidler, desperate to save his theatre, trades her sexual favours to a wealthy English Duke. Forced to choose between love and poverty with Christian, or musical career for sexuality to the Duke to save the cast, Satine rejects Christian to protect his life. When Christian angrily invades the spectacular stage show, she declares her love. As they sing a duet, the cast overthrow the Duke's gun intended for Christian's death, and virtuous love triumphs over villainy in seemingly glorious Technicolor.

A conductor stands before Disney-style *Fantasia* stage curtains, dramatically opening to the iconic tune of 20th Century Fox. Traditional can-can music announces an intertitle – *Paris 1900*: silent sepia images flicker on-screen and Toulouse Lautrec's singing sweeps us into highly theatricalised black and white sets and digital 3D reconstructions of turn-of-the-century Montmartre. The camera alternates between bleached low-lit or black-and-white shots, and flashes of brilliant colour, as it zooms into the garret of a bereft writer, and we enter *Moulin Rouge*, Baz Luhrmann's third in a trilogy of what Bell (in Mayer and Beatti 2007: 203) defines as his 'red curtain' cinema, after *Strictly Ballroom* (1992) and *Romeo and Juliet* (1996).

This musical extravaganza is a cinematic homage to melodrama, opera, silent cinema, Hollywood musicals and 1980s' music video as, with characteristic verve, Luhrmann fuses post-modern technology with moving-image history. If Stanley Donen's 1956 MGM musical *Singin' in the Rain* celebrates film's transition to sound, *Moulin Rouge* adopts silent film conventions from 1895 onwards in the self-conscious flickering sepia credits, the swooping Abel Gance-like shots of Montmartre characters, and the animated moon comically mirroring Melies' *Trip to the Moon* (1904). The faded sequences of Christian typing his story '*of love*', suggests also documentary-style veracity and 1930s Depression-era colour-cinematography. This contrast, with the artifice of garish sets and costumes of the Moulin Rouge, offers a cinematic essay on the conflict between innocent love and the seduction of showmanship, sexual exploitation and wealth.

In the Hollywood musicals, colour served the luxury dream palaces to provide cinematic relief from the Depression, the Second World War and post-war austerity, giving rise to the notion of the musical as escapist. The colour cinematography in *Moulin Rouge* initially functions playfully, like the Technicolor excess of a musical, reiterating Christian's naïve optimism. But the colour also highlights the façade of the theatre. Like Dorothy in the *Wizard of Oz* (Victor Fleming, 1939), who found '*there's no place like home*' in sepia-coloured Kansas, Satine and Christian in *Moulin Rouge* find '*true love*' in his low-lit and impoverished garret, or in the contrast of his modest clothes against the glitter of the show costumes.

Indeed, reframed for contemporary audiences *Moulin Rouge's* spectacular musical numbers, high-angled singing/dancing shots, heightened colour and costumes, are consciously styled as Hollywood musicals and MGM Broadway Melodies, recalling e.g. RKO's *Top Hat* (1935), MGM's *Singin' in the Rain* (1952) and *Gentlemen Prefer Blondes* (1953). This parody of classic cinema confirms Feuer's notion of contemporary redefining of the musical as nostalgic in its ironic conservatism (Altman 1986: 173).

Luhrmann also integrates iconic musical numbers to move the narrative forward. For example, as Christian first enters the Moulin Rouge, rapid editing cuts to the music in highly choreographed shots of the visual excesses of the dancers and costumes. In contrast, the sound fades and Satine descends like a 'sparkling diamond'. In top hat, red lipstick and glittering diamante costume she sings, *Diamonds are a Girl's Best Friend,* in direct homage to Marilyn Monroe and Jane Russell, mirroring the themes of gender exploitation in both films. Christian's simultaneous voice-over, progresses this theme further as he narrates falling in love with Satine at the same moment as his rival, The Duke, Zidler's rich investor.

In this coming-of-age, paper-thin plot, the aesthetic conventions of the Hollywood musical's two character opposites merge, with Satine and Christian diametrically opposed, the fallen courtesan and bourgeois artist finally sharing their love through song and dance (Altman 1986: 200).

But this oppositional structuring also derives from theatrical melodrama. A product of the Theatre Licensing Act banning the spoken word in popular theatres (Gledhill, 1987), the melodrama, from the Greek *melos* (melody) and French *drame,* developed in the eighteenth century as theatre accompanied by music. With its strong emotionalism, moral polarisation, dark plottings and overt villainy (Brooks 1995: 11–12) melodrama's emblematised characters were not psychologically motivated but rather personified the clash of good and evil as in a medieval morality play.

In *Moulin Rouge* we thus identify the helpless heroine Satine victimised by the Duke's villainy but saved by the innocent hero Christian, as implied in his name, and virtuous love triumphs over financial and sexual exploitation.

The stagey cinematic style of *Moulin Rouge* also draws on both the musical and the melodramatic aesthetic for, what Luhrmann defined as, 'theatricalised cinema' achieving 'a cinematic form … where the audience participate' (DVD commentary). Audiences are encouraged to recognise reframed lyrics, classical films and musical numbers as well as songs from 1980–90s music video culture such as Madonna's *Like A Virgin,* Elton John's *Now You're in the World.* The lyrics propel the plot onwards in a simultaneously representational and ironic way engaging the audiences' participation.

Furthermore, audience participation is inscribed through the process of producing a show. As Christian works on the show with Toulouse Lautrec's team, the generic lexicon of backstage theatre traditions, as well as lyrics from *The Sound of Music,* draw attention to its artifice. This cinematically inscribes spectators as theatre audiences to reiterate their participation and the illusion of community engagement in what Jane Feuer identifies as the folk art legacy of the musical, which foregrounds the celebratory spirit of the backstage tradition of the 'show within a show' (Altman 1986: 168).

But the staged settings, audience participation and inscribing of cinema spectators at proscenium distance, also reiterate melodrama's lack of invisible fourth wall on stage where actors faced towards the audience in direct address, like the traditional '*He's behind you!*' of pantomime. Likewise, the performers in film musicals address the inscribed spectators/diegetic audiences directly through the song and choreographed dance routines and this artifice breaks the realism and dialogue-led, linear narrative flow (Altman 1986: 168–71). Audiences engage in this for the pleasure of song and dance. Mayer and Day-Mayer (2001) argue that this function derives from the American stage melodramas and silent cinema such as the conventions of inserting musical interludes/dances in *The Great Train Robbery* and *Uncle Tom's Cabin.* But the musical numbers also shift focus from the forward linearity of the classical plot to the verticality of emotions underlying the dialogue. Altman defines this dual focus as the structuring principle for the plot rather than the singularly linear classical narrative. Hence, as in melodrama, the heightened excess of dance, movement, music and lyrics conveys non-dialogue-led expressions of emotional truth and dramatic conflicts.

One of the finest examples of both a pleasurable and thematically effective choreographed sequence in *Moulin Rouge* is the scene in which Satine visits the jealous Duke to ensure he finances the show. As they wait, the cast perform a dance, which mirrors the main plot while functioning as a self-contained piece of entertainment. In creating this evocative and layered song and dance scenario, sound director Marius de Vries juxtaposed an Argentinian tango for choreographer John O'Donnell's emotionally charged dance sequence, with the principal dancer narrating the story. In a synchronised collage of words, song, dance and music, it tells of a man who, falling in love with a prostitute, is consumed with jealousy betrayal and rage as she tangos erotically with the clients.

The soundtrack is overlaid with the narrator singing Sting's *Roxanne* intercut with shots of Satine visiting the Duke. A further tension intersects this as Christian sings of his jealousy, providing a third musical and visual layer and building the tension to an emotional and visual crescendo. As the Duke imprisons Satine in a diamond necklace, she cannot reciprocate his love so he attempts to sexually force her. She flees to Christian and the heightened musical resolution descends to dialogue as they optimistically pronounce their love. This scene thus progresses the narrative while functioning independently to deepen the emotional range beyond dialogue.

Feuer notes that Hollywood comedy musicals, in developing from traditions of vaudeville and stage musicals, led to generic expectations of spontaneity, celebratory spirit and heightened optimism (Altman 1986: 162). But while *Moulin Rouge's* resolution celebrates the lovers' union, it is also a story of tragic 'love' following conventions of nineteenth-century melodramatic novels, plays, operas, such as *Trilby, Les Dame aux Camelia, La Traviata* and *La Boheme* (an opera Luhrmann had produced). And in the final scenes, Satine, behind the stage façade, melodramatically collapses with tuberculosis, coughing blood.

Melodrama in its heightened intensity and pathos, functions as a cultural myth in apprehending spiritual truth or emotional desire that lie beyond words and the ordinary in which 'the true subject is hidden and masked' (Brooks 1995: 5). The shots backstage of Christian holding the dying Satine, are intercut by stills of the cast removing their masks or exposing the artifice of their stage paint, streaked by tears. And as words become inadequate Christian's cry can only allude to his grief and loss, as we witness a melodramatic tableau of Satine's death.

The melodramatic pathos of Satine's death however does raise feminist questions about *Moulin Rouge*'s polarised positioning of women: the Madonna/whore dichotomy which meant that, within nineteenth-century conventions, a courtesan or fallen woman like Satine, unsuitable for a bourgeois hero, has to die. Reading Sally Potter's avant-garde film *Thriller,* which deconstructs the objectivity/subjectivity of young seamstress Mimi in *La Boheme*, E. Ann Kaplan concludes that Mimi had to die because 'an old seamstress would not be considered the proper subject of a love story' (Kaplan 1990: 160). Like *Moulin Rouge*'s backstage seamstresses, old age is an anathema to romance. Satine in *Moulin Rouge,* like Mimi, is sacrificed for the life of the male artist. And while Luhrmann's postmodern resolution exposes these contradictions through irony and excess, it offers a less satisfactory modernist reading than, for example, Jane Campion's *The Piano* (1993), which reframes Victorian codes more sympathetically for Ada, her nineteenth-century protagonist, who lives to survive her fall from grace.

However, *Moulin Rouge*'s concern with the commodification of culture and sexuality, does offer a postmodern challenge to traditional repressions. Luhrmann's ironic musical reframing of *Like a Virgin*, for example, references Madonna as a powerful signifier for reclaiming historicised female passivity in her reconstructing the prostitute's clothing for acceptable mainstream fashion and ironically links Satine to this rebellion. Furthermore, Pam Cook's progressive readings of Gainsborough costume melodramas, demonstrate that female audiences also identify pleasurably with fallen women, such as Margaret Lockwood in *The Wicked Lady* (1945), who although dies at the end, maintains pleasurable subjectivity through rebellion (1996: 59). The melodramatic excesses of female deviant behaviour and the punishing endings expose the contradictions of the classical narrative and exceed the patriarchal ideological status quo. Hence in *Moulin Rouge* we could sympathise with Satine's rebellion of her prescribed position rather than see her as punished as a fallen woman.

Audiences from this perspective can engage both with the traditional pathos of Satines' death, classically presented in the extreme close-up on Christian holding her as she whispers to him to write a story, while also maintaining a modern ironic distance, visualised in the extreme long shots which track back to his garret for 'the end' of the story.

Further reading

Rick Altman, 'The American Film Musical: Paradigmatic Structure and Mediatory Function', in *Genre: The Musical*, London & New York, Routledge, 1986, pp. 197–207.

Philip Bell, 'Moulin Rouge', in Geoff Mayer and Keith Beatty (eds), *The Cinema of Australia and New Zealand*, London, Wallflower Press, 2007, pp. 203–11.

Peter Brooks, *The Melodramatic Imagination: Balzac, Henry James, Melodrama and the Mode of Excess*, New Haven, Yale University Press, 1995.

Pam Cook, 'Neither here Nor There: National Identity in Gainsborough Costume Drama', in Andrew Higson (ed.), *Dissolving Views: Key Writings on British Cinema*, London, Cassell, 1996, pp. 51–65.

Jane Feuer, 'The Self-Reflexive Musical and the Myth of Entertainment', in Rick Altman (ed.), *Genre: The Musical*, New York & London, Routledge, 1986, pp. 159–74.

Christine Gledhill (ed.), *Home is Where the Heart Is: Studies in Melodrama and the Woman's Film*, BFI, London, 1987.

E. Ann Kaplan, *Women and Film: Both Sides of the Camera*, New York and London, Routledge, 1990, pp. 154–61.

David Mayer and Helen Day-Mayer, 'A "Secondary Action" or Musical Highlight? Melodic Interludes in Early Film Melodrama Reconsidered', in Richard Abel and Rick Altman (eds), *The Sounds of Early Cinema*, Bloomington, Indiana University Press, 2001, pp. 220–31.

Trish Sheil

La mujer sin cabeza/The Headless Woman (2008)

[Country: Argentina, Spain, Italy, France. Production Company: Aquafilms, El Deseo S.A., R&C Produzioni, Slot Machine, Teodora Film. Director and Screenwriter: Lucrecia Martel. Producer: Pedro Almodóvar. Executive Producer: Verónica Cura. Cinematographer: Bárbara Álvarez. Art Director: María Eugenia Sueiro. Editor: Miguel Schverdfinger. Sound Director: Guido Beremblun. Cast: María Onetto (Verónica), Claudia Cantero (Josefina), César Bordón (Marcos), Daniel Genoud (Juan Manuel), Guillermo Arengo (Marcelo), Inés Efrón (Candita, Vero's niece), Alicia María Vaner (Aunt Lala).]

Synopsis: While Verónica, a white, provincial middle-class dentist, is driving along a rural road, she hits something or someone, a dog or a dark-skinned child – neither she nor the viewer can be sure – but doesn't stop to find out what it is. In the days following the accident, she is confused and emotionally disconnected from the people and events in her life. She becomes obsessed with the possibility that she may have killed someone. Although the police confirm that there were no accidents reported in the area, a drowned child is found in a roadside canal. Her middle-class family conceals any evidence of her possible guilt and everything returns to normal.

Lucrecia Martel is one of the key contributors to the rebirth of independent Argentine cinema known as the *Nuevo Cine Argentino*, first with the 1995 short *Rey muerto*, then the 2001 opera prima *La ciénaga (The Swamp)*, and the 2004 *La niña santa (The Holy Girl)*.[1] Not surprisingly, like the director's previous pieces, *La mujer sin cabeza* (2008, distributed in the United States as *The Headless Woman*) is located in Salta, Martel's home province in the north of Argentina. There are also stylistic and thematic affinities with her previous features, primarily in the representation of class and gender tensions of bourgeois families, the force fields of desire that ignore all norms, and the formal virtuosity that foregrounds the intrusive presence of the unknown over the known. But *The Headless Woman* is perhaps the most disconcerting of Martel's films because perception – and its distortions – are at the centre of the story. The film is subjectively narrated to the extent that the information given is restricted to that known to the protagonist, a woman who had an accident and is in a state of shock.

The plot of the film is simple. A mobile phone sounds in the middle of a deserted provincial road. The driver, Verónica or Vero, a bourgeois blonde (María Onetto), tries to find the vibrating object within her bag, a slightly careless search, and then a brutal crash. An anonymous corpse lies on the road. Apparently it is a dog but there will never be enough hints to know. The power of this decisive moment is strengthened by the suspense built up by the film's opening sequence: shot predominantly in shallow focus extreme close-ups, the crosscutting between a group of young boys (dark-skinned and poor) playing on the side of the road with their dog and Vero nearby gossiping with friends (light-skinned and privileged), and later driving in a distracted state, makes us feel the impending accident. When it happens, the blonde woman trembles. She is in state of shock. Eventually she puts on her sunglasses and leaves the scene. After a while she stops at another location. Martel holds an extended shot as a powerful rainstorm arrives. Visibly disoriented, Vero gets out of the car and walks in circles under the rain. The camera has not moved and her head is cut off because of the framing. Only then do we get the film's opening titles: *The Headless Woman*. After the accident, Vero has 'lost her head'.

As in the opening sequence, the entire film's narrative is designed for the viewers to explore an individual subjectivity. This immersion in the mind of the character dictates the filmmaker's stylistic decisions. While we get to scrutinise the protagonist from the outside, Martel withholds point of view shots from her perspective and transmits the disoriented gaze of Vero through experimentation with framing, shallow focus, and off-screen spaces.

More than in previous films, in *The Headless Woman* sensorial uncertainty is a mode of narrative organisation. Following the accident, Vero lapses into a state of shock, nearly unable to talk and moving like a sleepwalker unaware of her surroundings. During the health check-up at the hospital she is not capable of remembering her name or phone number. The next day, when a cab drives her to her workplace, a dental surgery office, she proceeds to sit in the waiting room, flicking through a magazine instead of taking care of her patients' dental needs.

Vero's enigmatic breakdown implies emotional detachment as well. The sense of disconnection in relation to family bonds – so characteristic of Martel's films – is embodied by this blonde creature who wanders through her routines with an odd smile. Tensions within her family, including her affair with a cousin, an aunt's growing dementia, and a niece's crush on her, became merely background noise. After the accident, former familiar ties have become senseless. In many scenes she struggles to recognise her relatives among the confusing faces that pass in front of her eyes and this atmosphere of alienation is reinforced through shots that use shallow focus and leave her head outside the frame.

Shallow focus and off-screen spaces play a crucial role not only in the narrative, but also on the mise en scène. Martel uses a widescreen image, often divided by precise framing and a shallow focus to leave parts of the image illegible, and fleshed out by disconcerting sounds, often unidentifiable, that come from illegible or off-screen spaces. These sound-images invite the viewer to participate in Vero's disorientation. As in previous Martel films, in *The Headless Woman* there is the constant appearance of presences, of which, as aunt Lala says from her bed, it is 'better not to talk' but to 'forget about'. While Vero tries to forget about the accident, strange facts keep unfolding off screen: there is something weird buried in her garden and dead animals have drowned in the new swimming pool of the village. There is another marginal area from which Vero cannot escape: little poor children, like the one she might have killed, come knocking on the door asking for food, but lighting and shallow focus confines them to the less visible space of the screen.

When it is clear that everything is beyond her control, Vero confesses to her husband that she killed someone on the road. That night they return to the highway, the crime scene, and he convinces her that she has only hit a dog. Later, when a boy's body is found in the canal, Vero's relatives seem determined to 'protect' her by hiding the truth and shielding her from the consequences of her actions. They erase all traces of the accident: the car is repaired; her X-rays are removed from the hospital, the records of her stay at a hotel, post-accident, mysteriously disappear.

From this point on we can witness Vero's process of re-apprehending the world. After her male relatives take care of the situation, she goes back to work and dyes her hair dark. This action – the only action she has the ability to decide for herself – can be interpreted as an attempt to be less visible, in a situation that requires keeping a low profile, but simultaneously changing her hair colour is a way to 'move on'. And the closing sequence of the film suggests that she is successful at it. Vero joins a bourgeois party at the hotel where she stayed the night of the accident. The camera stays behind a glass door and captures Vero as she retreats into the comfort of family and friends suggesting that in this provincial wealthy society nothing has happened.

In *The Headless Woman*, Lucrecia Martel is primarily interested in making us inhabit her character's sealed world. The close framing and shallow focus, the absence of expository dialogue, all deprive the viewer of context, and together mimic the situation of a dazed Verónica. But the film is a rich character study that explores the personal repercussions of an immoral act. While Verónica's mental anguish is difficult to witness, what is especially upsetting about *The Headless Woman* are the social mechanisms of denial and forgetting at play.

Vero and her bourgeois family conceal evidence of her possible guilt in what could be a hit-and-run accident. Taking us inside the psyche of a character for whom trauma and denial are two sides of the same coin, *The Headless Woman* puts ethics at its centre. In interviews Lucrecia Martel has described the film as a reference to the class disparity between Argentina's middle and lower class.[2] The use of shallow focus and lighting in the scenes of blonde and light-skinned Vero interacting with darker-skinned servants and children suggest that they are mostly invisible to her. The film explores both class and gender differences, but it also heightens the impact of these disparities by aligning them with Argentina's public memory. The minimalist, intimate style of most of Lucrecia Martel's films can appear resistant to political analyses, but, in the way Vero's family promotes a culture of forgetting, *The Headless Woman* can be read as a political parable, where Vero's denial of guilt may be symbolic of the former dictatorial regime's silence about 'the disappeared'.[3] In this way, interpreting the movie as mediation on Argentina's historical memory, *The Headless Woman* suggests an ethical key to future possibilities.

Notes

1. It is important to place Martel's work in the context of the New Argentine Cinema, alongside filmmakers such as Martín Rejtman, Adrián Caetano, Pablo Trapero and Lisandro Alonso. The fervour of filmmaking that renewed Argentine cinema was less a movement than a generational shift facilitated by a boom of new film schools, the passing of the 'Cinema law', as well as the rebirth of film journals. The trait that binds the directors of New Argentine Cinema into this 'movement' is neither a shared aesthetic nor pedagogical program, but rather a commitment to break away from a certain style of Argentine cinema of the previous decade that they regarded as clichéd (see Aguilar 2008: 7–17).
2. In an interview with Amy Taubin, Lucrecia Martel said: 'In Argentina, my country, I see people that still carry the weight of the really bad stuff that they did not denounce back when it happened under the dictatorship. A lot of people decided they didn't want to see, they didn't want to know what was happening. And now the same process is occurring, but it's in relation to poverty. A lot of people

pretend they do not see that a huge part of the country is becoming poorer and poorer and is undergoing great suffering. The same mechanism that we used in the past to ignore the suffering of others is still very present today. That's why in the film, I use music from the Seventies at the same time that people use mobile phones and drive contemporary cars. What I wanted to stress with these elements is that the same mechanism that started back then is continuing. So I use anachronisms to create that continuity' (Lucrecia Martel, 'Shadow of a Doubt: Lucrecia Martel Interviewed by Amy Taubin', *filmcomment.com*, 2008, Internet).

3. According to Cecilia Sosa, by presenting the existentialist drama of an upper-class woman involved in a seemingly minor car accident, the film manages to stage a counter-narrative of the traumatic past that affected the whole of society beyond obvious sites of suffering. In Martel's film each viewer becomes a survivor and a witness and is thereby subtlely compelled to respond. See Cecilia Sosa, 'A Counter-Narrative of Argentine Mourning'. *Theory, Culture and Society*, Vol. 26, 2009, pp. 7–8.

Further reading

Gonzalo Aguilar, *Other Worlds: New Argentine Cinema*, New York, Palgrave Macmillan, 2008.

Jens Andermann, 'Accidents and Miracles: Film and the Experience of History', in *New Argentine Cinema*, London: I.B. Tauris, 2012, pp. 155–75.

Oscar Jubis, *The Films of Lucrecia Martel: The Salta Trilogy*, Saarbrücken, Germany: VDM Verlag, Dr. Müller Aktiengesellschaft & Co, 2010.

Joanna Page, 'The Politics of Private Space', in *Crisis and Capitalism in Contemporary Argentine Cinemam*, Durham, NC, Duke University Press, 2009, pp. 180–95.

Irene Depetris Chauvin

My Life Without Me (2003)

[Country: Spain and Canada. Production Company: El Deseo and Milestone Productions. Director: Isabel Coixet. Producers: Esther García and Gordon McLennan. Screenwriter: Isabel Coixet (based on the story 'Pretending the Bed is a Raft' by Nanci Kincaid). Cinematographer: Jean-Claude Larrieu. Art Director: Shelley Bolton. Music: Alfonso Vilallonga. Editor: Lisa Jane Robison. Cast: Sarah Polley (Ann), Leonor Watling (Ann, the neighbour), Deborah Harry (Ann's mother), Amanda Plummer (Laurie), Scott Speedman (Don), Mark Ruffalo (Lee), Maria de Medeiros (the hairdresser).]

Synopsis: In *My Life Without Me*, Catalan director Isabel Coixet offers the story of a young woman's diagnosis of terminal cancer. Ann (Polley) spares her family and friends the knowledge of her illness. As she is dying, she experiences a sensual awakening and transforms the lives of those around her.

My Life Without Me, a Spanish film made with Canadian and American actors and filmed in English belongs to a spate of recent films from Spain that have offered representations of angelic mothers. Critics have argued that these films respond to a complex history of representing women in Spain as symbols of the state in which, in the Franco and post-Franco eras, mothers were alternately glorified and punished.[1] Currently, a 'pro-natalist' discourse has again arisen in Spanish culture that is reacting to the previous generation's attacks on motherhood by investing in a project of redeeming the family in the service of a new picture of the nation.[2]

Coixet's film reclaims motherhood by self-consciously engaging with the classic Hollywood maternal melodrama and its particular modes of addressing gender, culture, and class. Like Pedro Almodóvar, who produced the film, Isabel Coixet finds in melodrama a cinematic form that constructs highly emotionally charged scenarios that speak critically of the social and psychological condition of women under dominant ideologies and offer a fantasy resolution to the problem of their suffering.

At one level, the film presents itself as pointed social commentary, and appears to invite a materialist understanding of the relationship between women's economic conditions and suffering through its secondary characters and subplots. Filmed in a restricted chromatic palette of blues, whites, and greys under harsh electric lights that evoke a documentary realist style, a cast of female secondary characters who represent the working class are shown to be alienated from their labour, from themselves, and from other human beings, trapped in vicious circles of self-abnegation. The film suggests that they suffer from a range of hysterical afflictions ranging from depression to bulimia to body dysmorphic disorder to transvestism because of this alienation. Through its examination of their condition, the film creates a space for critique of the social abandonment and economic marginalisation of women.

Yet in its primary plot line, the film uses conventions of the melodramatic genre to recast female victimhood as a matter of individual choice. The protagonist Ann (Polley) seems to consider women's suffering to be a cultural rather than an economic or social problem. Her mother (Harry) tearfully watches weepies like *Mildred Pierce* (1945) and even narrates *Stella Dallas* (1937) to her granddaughters as a bedtime story in lieu of Cinderella. For her mother, the maternal melodrama most accurately reflects the cyclical experience of female abjection. Ann, however, is angered by the genre's depictions of 'mothers making dumb-assed sacrifices' and at the prospect of these narratives of martyrdom being passed down to her daughters. She seems to suggest that women's experience of alienation relates more to a *cultural* system of myths and ideas coded in and reproduced by genres of women's stories that interpellate women into subject positions defined by misery. At stake in the film then are two possibilities for understanding women's lives; the first is that women suffer because of their material conditions while the second is that women suffer because they opt into a myth of their own powerlessness that condemns them to repeat dysfunctional patterns.

On the surface, Ann's own story reads like pure melodrama. Born into poverty in a broken family, she becomes pregnant at 16. Her husband has not held a job in years and she lives in a trailer in her unhappy mother's backyard. She develops a fatal disease and experiences her illness alone and in silence. She falls in love with another man, but must leave him for the sake of her family. And she selflessly procures a new mother for her children and wife for her husband before she dies.

And yet, by refusing to suffer, Ann refuses the interpretive lens of melodrama that would frame her life as tragic and resists identifying with a culture of victimhood. Instead, she proceeds to model a mode of feminine resistance based on personal autonomy rather than collective social action, and on the pursuit of pleasure in everyday life. The visual elements of the film that encourage a historical materialist reading of female suffering are harshly lit, monochromatic and thus coded as realist, while those associated with Ann's more individualistic mode of resistance to suffering are naturally lit and often dreamlike, drawn out in vivid slow-motion sequences that seem to prolong this dying woman's experience of the richness of the present. Throughout *My Life Without Me,* Ann and her daughters are associated with bright colours, especially oranges, blues, and pinks. While, in classic melodramas like Douglas Sirk's technicolored palettes signified entrapment, claustrophobia and hysteria, here they signify aliveness. Adorned with sparkling curtains of pink beads, the trailer's interior represents a magical place of familial intimacy – a world that Ann has built from nothing – and stands as an emblem of the film's wish that whatever the terms of their material conditions, individual women *can* resist becoming subjected to ideology and live a life of emotional wealth if they choose to follow a different cultural script or system of representations.

How different is this script really? The inherent contradictions between the film's historical-materialist and the cultural-ideological propositions about the causes of gendered suffering are resolved, though perhaps not in a recognizably Marxist or feminist way, by the film's position on family. The film proposes a certain kind of motherhood as a solution to the social and personal problem of women's abjection. We can call it 'new motherhood' because it is the antithesis of the suffering motherhood that Ann's own mother offers. In *My Life Without Me*, being a good mother who lovingly chooses to give and take pleasure is what offers the path towards personal autonomy, the building of community, and the continuity of the family. More importantly, 'new motherhood' is also what resolves the challenges of class inequality that the film's attention to social and economic issues exposes.

Ann's solution to the film's titular problem – of her 'life without me' – is to provide her family a surrogate 'new' mother, a double of herself who is also named Ann (Watling). Yet the substitution is also an improvement; life for the family without Ann will do more than just go on because Ann, the neighbour, is a nurse and thus a healer. Moreover, as a member of a professional class, she is educated and owns a house; the family will move up in the world with her at its head. After Ann (Polley) dies, we see her family going to the beach with Ann the neighbour – something that the dying mother had fantasised about doing before she died but did not manage to do. The scene nostalgically symbolises the bourgeois life of *leisure* that only the 'new mother' can provide.

The resolution of the film demands to be read in the context of the classic maternal melodramas that make Ann's mother weep and Ann get angry. In *Stella Dallas*, Stella (Barbara Stanwyck) abandons her daughter to a better – that is an upper-class – mother in order to facilitate her daughter's marriage to a wealthy boy. Having condemned the melodramatic genre's construction of mothers' sacrifices for their children and their suffering because of them, Ann essentially ends up acting out the script of motherhood from *Stella Dallas*. However, she updates it by excising its motif of suffering. She transforms the genre's typical presentation of masochistic fantasies, that family is the reward for being a good woman but also its punishment, into a presentation of a different mode of wish fulfilment, suggesting that a special kind of motherhood is equally rewarding for mother and family. That the 'new mother' is happy can be seen as transforming the implicit rules of melodrama because female pleasure is a new development in a genre that does not usually allow for such things. Yet that Ann is replaceable and life goes on without her instrumentalises motherhood just as classic melodrama does, rendering it as a narrow slot to be filled in the service of social interests external to women.

Melodrama must be seen as a contradictory nexus in which social, psychical, and artistic determinations are brought together in an aestheticised form, but in which the problems they represent cannot be successfully resolved.[3] This is melodrama's strength as well as its weakness; the genre can expose the contradictions inherent in social life as much as it reinforces structures of gender, culture, and class. *My Life Without Me* is no different. There are contradictions between its social commentary on the economic conditions and dominant ideologies that women face on the one hand and its seamless presentation of a fantasy 'new mother' on the other.

Critics have unanimously perceived the film's ending as happy, a reading which would seem to embrace the film's reactionary celebration of the role of the good 'new mother' and its attendant instrumentalising understanding of women. It is possible, however, to argue that the contradictory visual motifs of the film – its juxtaposition of the dark palette with harsh light and the bright colours – permit a reading of the film's nostalgia-imbued ending as unhappy. In this reading, Ann's story – her refusal to play out a cultural script of victimhood, her disavowal of her own social and material determinants, and her successful elevation of her family's economic status upon her death – is, in cinematic language, hyperreal, that is to say not real. Compared to the more gritty realistic depictions of the condition of women's suffering and its many social material determinants, Ann's life both with and without her can be argued to represent the film's wishful fantasies about female resistance which only manage to colour over the grim life of women around her.

Notes

1. See Andres Zamora, 'A Vindication of the Spanish Mother: Maternal Images in the Filmic Make-Over of the Nation', *Studies in 20th and 21st Century Literature (ST&TCL)*, 33: 2, Summer 2009, pp. 354–74.
2. See Barbara Zecchi, 'All About Mothers: Pronatalist Discourse in Contemporary Spanish Cinema', *College Literature* 32: 1, Winter 2005, pp. 146–65.
3. See Geoffrey Nowell-Smith, 'Minnelli and Melodrama', *Screen* 18: 2, 1977, pp. 113–18.

Further reading

Mary Ann Doane, *The Desire to Desire: The Woman's Film of the 1940s*, Bloomington, Indiana University Press, 1987.

Christine Gledhill (ed.), *Home is Where the Heart is: Studies in Melodrama and the Woman's Film*, London, BFI, 2002.

Annette Kuhn and Ann Marie Wolpe (eds), *Feminism and Materialism: Women and Modes of Production*, New York, Routledge and Kegan Paul, 1978.

Annette Kuhn, *Women's Pictures: Feminism and Cinema*, London, Verso, 1982.

Julie Levinson, 'Genre and Gender: The Subversive Potential' in Natalie Harris Bluestone (ed.), *Double Vision: Perspectives on Gender and the Visual Arts*, New Jersey, Associated University Presses, 1995, pp. 138–52.

Tatjana Pavlović, Inmaculada Alvarez, Rosana Blanco-Cano, Anitra Grisales, Alejandra Osorio, Alejandra Sánchez (eds), *100 Years of Spanish Cinema*, Malden: Wiley-Blackwell, 2009.

Linda Williams, 'Melodrama Revisited', in Nick Browne (ed.), *Refiguring American Film Genres: History and Theory*, Berkeley, University of California Press, 1998, pp. 42–88.

Monique Tschofen

Night of the Living Dead (1968)

[Country: USA. Production Company: Image Ten. Director: George A. Romero. Producers: Russell W. Streiner and Karl Hardman. Screenwriters: George A. Romero and John Russo. Cinematographer: George A. Romero. Editor: George A. Romero. Music: Stock music from the Capitol Hi-Q music library. Make-Up: Hardman Associates, Inc. Special Effects: Regis Survinski and Tony Pantanello. Cast: Duane Jones (Ben), Judith O'Dea (Barbara), Karl Hardman (Harry Cooper), Russell Streiner (Johnny), Marilyn Eastman (Helen Cooper), Keith Wayne (Tom), Judith Ridley (Judy), Kyra Schon (Karen Cooper).]

Synopsis: When the recently deceased begin to rise from the dead to feast upon the flesh of the living, a small group of embattled survivors attempt to stave off destruction by taking refuge in an abandoned western Pennsylvania farmhouse. They face the ghoulish threat of the living dead from without, but also increasing tension from within as they argue over who is in charge and what course of action they should follow. Infighting, botched plans, and the relentless assault of the living dead eventually claim everyone with the exception of Ben (Jones). But when a posse of militiamen come to his rescue, they mistake him for a walking corpse and kill him as well.

Here's how the important American film industry periodical *Variety* greeted *Night of the Living Dead* upon its original release in 1968: 'Until the Supreme Court establishes clearcut guidelines for the pornography of violence, *Night of the Living Dead* will serve nicely as an outer-limit definition by example … [the film] casts serious aspersions on the integrity and social responsibility of its Pittsburgh-based makers, distrib Walter Reade, the film industry as a whole and exhibs who book the pic, as well as raising doubts about … the moral health of filmgoers who cheerfully opt for this unrelieved orgy of sadism' (quoted in Lowenstein 2005: 154). And yet by 1970, *Night of the Living Dead*'s director, George A. Romero, was traveling from Pittsburgh to New York to host a screening of his film at one of America's most prestigious temples of high culture, the Museum of Modern Art. This extraordinary transformation from 'orgy of sadism' to modern art only begins to hint at the power of *Night of the Living Dead*: it is not just one of the most successful and influential horror films ever made, but one of the most significant independent American films of any kind.

From today's vantage point, it is easy to see the evidence of *Night*'s success and influence. How many films, let alone films produced on a shoestring budget (reportedly $114,000) far from Hollywood without any recognizable names in its cast or crew, can claim the kind of legacy that belongs to *Night* in the international realm of popular culture? This legacy includes Romero's own increasingly ambitious and sophisticated series of sequels (*Dawn of the Dead* (1979), *Day of the Dead* (1985), *Land of the Dead* (2005), *Diary of the Dead* (2007), and *Survival of the Dead* (2009) thus far), the remakes of *Night of the Living Dead* (Tom Savini, 1990), *Dawn of the Dead* (Zack Snyder, 2004), and *Day of the Dead* (Steve Miner, 2008), the campy variation *The Return of the Living Dead* (Dan O'Bannon, 1985) and its own sequels, numerous homages and offshoots that range from the suspenseful *28 Days Later* (Danny Boyle, 2002) to the hilarious *Shaun of the Dead* (Edgar Wright, 2004) to Sam Raimi's wonderfully berserk series begun with *The Evil Dead* (1981), an entire subgenre of gruesome Italian cannibal/zombie films like *Cannibal Holocaust* (Ruggero Deodato, 1980) and *City of the Living Dead* (Lucio Fulci, 1980), the smash hit television series *The Walking Dead* (Frank Darabont, 2010 to present), books such as John Skipp and Craig Spector's horror anthology *Book of the Dead* (1989), video games like *Resident Evil* (Capcom, 1996) that have become the basis for comic books and films in their own right, and even the long-form music video for Michael Jackson's 'Thriller' (John Landis, 1983).

The matter of *Night*'s status as a landmark in independent American cinema is a more complicated subject, but finally just as undeniable. Hollywood's success has always been rooted in the skilful manipulation of familiar genres and stars to deliver what has been broadly construed as 'entertainment' to as wide a public as possible. Films that depart from this mission of entertainment, opting instead for art or politics or education, have usually been relegated to the ranks of foreign, documentary, exploitation, avant-garde, or independent cinema. What *Night* accomplished so successfully that it can be considered a precedent for many films that followed was its melding of a popular genre (a marker of entertainment) onto a set of independent, anti-establishment aesthetics and politics (a marker of art). Of course, this is not to say that *Night* was the first or the only American independent film to accomplish this feat, but in the post-classical era of American film dating roughly from 1960, its model has been a particularly forceful one.

A number of social, historical, and industrial factors contributed to *Night*'s phenomenal success. Part of the aforementioned transformation in the film's reception as sadistic in 1968 and artistic in 1970 has to do with the fact that these years were some of the most turbulent in American history. The space between 1968 and 1970 exposed the American public to such traumatic events as the My Lai massacre in Vietnam, the assassination of Martin Luther King, Jr., and the killings of anti-war student demonstrators at Kent State University by the Ohio National Guard. Shattering events like these crystallised the national turmoil surrounding the Vietnam War and drove home a sense of America in deep crisis, perhaps even on the verge of self-destruction. In this chaotic social climate, what once looked like pornographic violence in *Night* now seemed closer to political commentary. For example, the American critic Elliott Stein, in his 1970 review of *Night* published in the British film journal *Sight and Sound*, suggested the film's possibilities for political allegory when he compared the film's walking corpses who crave the flesh of the living to President Richard Nixon's 'silent majority' (quoted in Lowenstein 2005: 154). If America was eating itself alive metaphorically during the Vietnam era, then *Night* made that metaphor literal. In one of the nation's darkest moments, *Night* showed America to itself in ways few other films dared.

Among the daring aspects of *Night* is its casting of Duane Jones, an African American actor, in the lead role of Ben. Ben is the film's central protagonist, the leader inside a country farmhouse where a group of seven people struggle to survive an onslaught by 'ghouls' that have risen from the dead to eat the living ('zombie' is not a term used within the film, but it has become attached to *Night* subsequently). The strength, courage, intelligence, and resolve displayed by Ben is something rare to find in lead film roles for blacks even today, never mind in 1968. Indeed, the fact that *Night*'s critical redemption followed the film's pairing on a double bill with a slavery drama (*Slaves* (Herbert J. Biberman, 1969)) suggests that *Night*'s racial subtexts were crucial for its reception as 'art'. Romero completed the film prior to King's assassination, but *Night* did not reach audiences until afterwards. So Ben's demise at the end of the film, when he is shot by a posse of white militiamen who 'mistake' him for a zombie, inevitably evokes for viewers the often violent resistance faced by the civil rights movement, including lynchings and of course, assassination.

Ben's murder concludes *Night* on a truly devastating note. For Ben, a character that we have rooted for throughout, to survive the awful ordeal of the zombies only to be shot by his 'saviours', is the final blow in the film's steady assault on our desires for reassurance that things are going to be OK. This grim sense of a world so damaged and dangerous that the only destiny imaginable for its 'heroes' ends with an early, violent death is a sentiment shared by a number of American films during the Vietnam era that proved particularly resonant with younger audiences identifying with the counterculture. In this light, *Night*'s kindred spirits are films such as *Bonnie and Clyde* (Arthur Penn, 1967), *Easy Rider* (Dennis Hopper, 1969), and *Joe* (John G. Avildsen, 1970). All of these films capture the counterculture's belief that the establishment is not just something to rebel against, but something bent on destroying them – a belief substantiated all too vividly in Vietnam and at Kent State. So it is not surprising that *Night* became a sensation as a 'midnight movie', a film watched by younger audiences at times and places bound to foster a sense of countercultural community, even 'cult' adoration. In New York, for instance, *Night* played at midnight continuously (with the exception of several weeks) 'for over two years, from May 1971 through mid-July 1973' (Hoberman and Rosenbaum 1983: 126).

Surely part of *Night*'s cult appeal had to do with its notorious presentation of graphic gore. But the film's most graphic scenes, when the zombies feast hungrily on human intestines and assorted body parts, are relatively brief and few. There are other disturbing images (including a rotting corpse and a mother stabbed to death by her zombie daughter), but given the disturbing, sometimes bloody news footage from Vietnam reaching American living rooms through television as well as the garish colour spectacles of graphic violence pioneered in earlier exploitation films such as *Blood Feast* (Herschell Gordon Lewis, 1963) and taken to operatic heights in contemporary mainstream hits like *Bonnie and Clyde* and *The Wild Bunch* (Sam Peckinpah, 1969), *Night*'s shock value can hardly be attributed to the sight of gore alone. What distinguishes *Night*'s graphic violence and sets it apart as particularly upsetting is that it is embedded so matter-of-factly within a low-key, low-budget, black-and-white, nondescript, western Pennsylvanian reality that refuses to surrender to flights of fancy. Certainly the film's premise about a mysterious plague that reanimates the recently deceased, possibly instigated by radiation from a space probe returned from Venus, participates in the typically fantastic hallmarks of the horror and science fiction genres (Romero was especially inspired by Richard Matheson's classic SF novel *I Am Legend* (1954)), but *Night*'s dogged preference for the ordinary over the extraordinary is not very typical at all.

In fact, one of the most striking aspects of *Night*'s ordinariness is its investment in the unspoken and the unacknowledged. Barbara (Judith O'Dea), the first character we meet during the film's opening in a graveyard, is so traumatised by an encounter with a zombie who attacks both her and her brother that she spends the rest of the film nearly comatose, speaking only in rare outbursts. Ben's race is never referred to by anyone, even though the steadily escalating disputes between Ben and the shifty white father/husband Harry Cooper (Karl Hardman) are shot through with unspoken racial tensions. But even Harry, easily the film's most irritating and exasperating character, clearly suffers from his own unarticulated fears: that his daughter will die from wounds inflicted by a zombie, that he will fail as a father and a husband in the eyes of his wife. Tom (Keith Wayne) and Judy (Judith Ridley), the film's young lovers, are barely granted a brief, exceedingly awkward moment of romantic confession before they burn alive together in a botched escape attempt. The ways that Judy and Helen Cooper (Marilyn Eastman) tend to the incapacitated Barbara and Karen Cooper (Kyra Schon) suggest the tentative outlines of a female community, perhaps even the stirrings of limited feminist identifications, but again, these connections remain almost entirely implicit.

Finally, the film's concluding scenes transpire as a series of bitter, unspoken ironies. Ben, the last survivor, must finally seek refuge from the zombies by barricading himself in a basement, the very act he condemned repeatedly as suicidal when Harry advocated it during their earlier arguments over plans of action. And of course, Ben's death at the hands of his would-be rescuers, his fate as a corpse indistinguishable from the zombies he battled against so strenuously, leaves the audience shell-shocked over the greatest silence of all: none of the characters whose struggles we have just witnessed has lived to tell the tale. In this way, as in so many others, *Night of the Living Dead* refuses to allow the daylight comforts of normality to return. This may well be a nightmare from which we cannot awaken, or perhaps no nightmare at all – the film's 'living dead' might be understood ultimately as 'living history'.

Further reading

Paul R. Gagne, *The Zombies That Ate Pittsburgh: The Films of George A. Romero*, New York, Dodd Mead, 1987.

Ben Hervey, *Night of the Living Dead*, New York, Palgrave Macmillan, 2008.

J. Hoberman and Jonathan Rosenbaum, *Midnight Movies*, New York, Harper and Row, 1983.

Adam Lowenstein, *Shocking Representation: Historical Trauma, National Cinema, and the Modern Horror Film*, New York, Columbia University Press, 2005.
Tony Williams, *The Cinema of George A. Romero: Knight of the Living Dead*, London, Wallflower Press, 2003.
Robin Wood, *Hollywood from Vietnam to Reagan ... and Beyond*, New York, Columbia University Press, 2003.

Adam Lowenstein

Nippon konchūki/The Insect Woman (1963)

[Country: Japan. Production Company: Nikkatsu. Director: Shōhei Imamura. Producers: Kano Ôtsuka and Jirô Tomoda. Screenwriters: Keiji Hasebe and Shōhei Imamura. Cinematographer: Shinsaku Himeda. Music: Toshirō Mayuzumi. Editor: Mutsuo Tanji. Cast: Sachiko Hidari (Tome), Kazuo Kitamura (Chūji), Sumie Sasaki (En), Jitsuko Yoshimura (Nobuko), Tanie Kitabayashi (Madam), Seizaburô Kawazu (Karasawa), Masumi Harukawa (Midori).]

Synopsis: Born in 1918, Tome is the daughter of an economically poor, dysfunctional family in early twentieth-century rural Japan. While working as a servant to the owners of the land her family tends, Tome is raped by the landlord's son and falls pregnant. After the war has ended, leaving the child behind in the care of her mentally unstable father, she flees to Tokyo in search of riches and soon begins to work in a brothel. Learning her trade from an experienced madam, Tome ruthlessly climbs up the ranks of the sex trade and, with the support of her lover Karasawa, eventually becomes the owner of a successful call-girl business.

The relationship between cinema and external context is often slippery and difficult to define. This is particularly true of the narrative feature film, which historically has been primarily concerned with the linear progression of story and the logical development of character. Although there are exceptions, such as films which take a given historical moment as the material for a character-driven story (e.g. *Schindler's List* (Steven Spielberg, 1993) and *Good Bye Lenin!* (Wolfgang Becker, 2003)), the content of the average narrative feature film tends not to be primarily defined by social, political and economic contexts. Instead, it is reliant on generic archetypes (crude examples of which would include the love story, the police procedural film or the action film) and as such, any links to a given external context are often either circumstantial aids to verisimilitude or purely metaphorical. Because of this, analyses which base their approach on intrinsic, defining connections between a narrative feature film and an external context must tread carefully to avoid charges of over-interpretation, of either seeing things which may or nor be there or assigning too much relevance to innocuous details.

Such risks are not a factor when considering Shōhei Imamura's *The Insect Woman*, a film so firmly and obviously rooted in the socio-political and industrial contexts of its time of production that any critical reading of the film which did not consider the environment of 1960s Japan would be a naïve one. Alongside filmmakers such as Nagisa Ôshima (*Cruel Story of Youth*, 1960), Masahiro Shinoda (*Pale Flower*, 1964) and Seijun Suzuki (*Gate of Flesh*, 1964), Imamura was a key figure in the Japanese New Wave, a group of young filmmakers who sought to use their formally inventive work to directly and brusquely challenge what they saw as the inequities and injustices of contemporary Japanese society. Of course, the name, ideological nature and timing of the Japanese New Wave all bring about inevitable comparisons to the French New Wave, something reflected in the fact that the popular Japanese term for the movement was and remains *nūberu bāgu*, a phonetic translation of the French *nouvelle vague*. However, while there is some broad legitimacy in these claims, the industrial origins and social concerns of the Japanese New Wave give it a distinct identity of its own.

Many of the filmmakers involved in the Japanese New Wave began their careers in the film industry by working as assistants to established directors during the 'golden' age of Japanese studio production. In the 1950s, filmmakers such as Yasujirō Ozu (*Tokyo Story*, 1953), Mikio Naruse (*Late Chrysanthemums*, 1954) and Kenji Mizoguchi (*Street of Shame*, 1956) produced films which are still today regarded as the abiding classics of Japanese cinema, especially by Western audiences. Imamura's own apprenticeship was exemplary of this model, serving under the master practitioner Ozu on several films including one of the most celebrated pieces of cinema to ever emerge out of Japan, *Tokyo Story*. Rather than being inspired by his time working alongside the widely respected Ozu, Imamura found that his ideas on cinema greatly differed from those held by his senior. Finding the rigidity of Ozu's filmmaking style, particularly the strict and inflexible instructions given to actors, to be 'repugnant' (Bock 1978: 289), Imamura would later comment that the great director's influence on his career was a significant one, but only because it was an education in the type of films which he *did not* want to make.[1]

Given that many, if not all, of Imamura's New Wave peers shared a similar disdain for the cinematic practices and ethical positions of the previous generation of Japanese filmmakers, it is understandably tempting to label the movement as being simply a reaction against the industrial conditions in which they were attempting to operate. However, as David Desser, in his groundbreaking study of the Japanese New Wave, stresses, such analyses completely preclude the socio-political environment of 1960s Japan and do 'not suffice to explain the rigorous, insightful, insistent, and often angry challenges the best of the New Wave films and filmmakers issued to Japanese society' (Desser 1998: 2). As opposed to the thematic and political cautiousness which arguably characterised much of pre-1960s Japanese cinema, New Wave filmmakers were not afraid to take an anti-authoritarian position by associating with radical left-wing political movements and unblinkingly addressing contentious subjects such as racism and sexual violence. While there was a degree of variety in the narrative and formal preferences of individual New Wave filmmakers, overall they were driven by a desire to present non-sugar-coated depictions of a Japan where the social, political and psychological effects of the war and subsequent American Occupation still loomed large.

Audie Bock states that Imamura and others 'turned their backs on what now seemed to be the naïve universal humanism of the past and searched for the essence of Japaneseness' (1978: 14). Indeed, the work of Shōhei Imamura, particularly during the 1960s, is primarily concerned with the cinematic representation of the real Japan. What the 'real' means for Imamura is an unromantic depiction of the lower-class segments of society which were perhaps under-represented in the classical Japanese cinema of the 1950s. The focus of *The Insect Woman* is typical of this approach. Imamura centres the narrative around Tome, a woman from a rural community in Northern Japan, a region which had not been subject to much attention from a previous generation of filmmakers who had largely chosen to myopically concentrate on the nation's larger cities. Given that the narrative of the film begins in 1918 and stretches through five decades, it is fair to say that the film's subject matter, at least on the surface, is the historical position of Japanese women. But there is a wider focus and many of the issues approached in *The Insect Woman* are applicable to Japanese society at large. It could therefore be argued that women are merely the vessel Imamura uses to convey more macrocosmic social concerns; according to the film's star Sachiko Hidari, 'if you want to say something about Japan, you have to focus on women', and critic Tadao Sato argues that, for Imamura, the status of the typical Japanese woman 'realistically mirrored the conditions of the masses since they seldom rose to positions of leadership or became members of the ruling class'.[2] In *The Insect Woman*, Tome rises from simple prostitute to pimp, but her position is an ultimately insecure one as she is completely reliant on her male lover Karasawa, who financially and logistically enables the enterprise. Accordingly, when his support comes to an abrupt end, Tome is immediately returned to the lower economic classes from whence she emerged. By exposing the shallow foundations of Tome's new wealth, Imamura could just as easily be said to be commenting on the superficiality of the economic 'miracle', which from the mid-1950s brought about an extended period of prosperity in Japan, as he is making a salient point about the continued inability of Japanese women to prosper in society without male patronage.

Nevertheless, there is a significant amount of material in the film which exclusively refers to the status of the Japanese woman. The poor treatment of Tome by her rural family speaks to the historical subjugation of Japanese women under *ie* (literally, 'household'), a system of extended family, which saw women at the foot of a strictly organised patriarchal hierarchy headed by the eldest male of working age. While living in the countryside Tome, like most women under *ie*, has no practical or economic independence of her own and her survival is wholly contingent on those above her in the familial hierarchy. However, the version of *ie* in *The Insect Woman* is a distorted one, with the man who would normally head the family, Tome's father Chūji (who is, in fact, not her biological parent), being mentally incompetent and thus unable to do so.

The time span of the film's narrative corresponds with the gradual dissolution of *ie* which occurred in the first half of the twentieth century. Tome initially leaves the *ie* by going to work in a silk factory before relocating to Tokyo, where she eventually becomes involved in prostitution. The trajectory of Tome's life therefore references two of the most historically significant developments for women during this period; the increased, if not complete, independence which came for young women with the collapse of *ie*, and the rise and fall of urban prostitution. The two events are indirectly connected. There were various factors leading to the sharp rise in the smaller, nuclear-style *katei* ('family') units which replaced *ie* as the dominant mode of cohabitation, not least of which was the demographic shift from country to city which occurred amongst the younger generation as a result of an explosion of white-collar industry in Japan. The growth of these industries demanded a large workforce, who in turn had expendable income to spend on entertainment. Given that the office workers with the highest salaries were exclusively male, the early twentieth century saw an increased demand for female courtesans in Japan's larger urban settings, particularly Osaka and Tokyo. Prostitution in Japan was far from a new phenomenon and had always been subject to a degree of official approval. In the early part of the twentieth century, this support reached unprecedented levels in the evergrowing urban expanses with the establishment of the 'licensed quarters', geographically defined areas where brothels operated with the full approval and protection of the police. Unsurprisingly, the immediate post-war years saw a change in the status of the sex industry in Japan, with licensed quarters being rapidly outlawed by the American Occupation and the nation's first-ever crop of elected female politicians leading a gradual change in public opinion, with the eventual result being the criminalisation of prostitution in 1956. In *The Insect Woman*, the brothel which employs her as a prostitute is closed by the police and her own initially flourishing call-girl business eventually falls foul of the law, at which point she is left on the verge of destitution; a situation also faced by the thousands of women who were employed in brothels prior to 1956.

As well as directly referencing socio-political events (documentary footage of student protests is also shown in the film, as is Tome's flirtation with trade unionism during her time working in the silk factory), Imamura's inclusion of taboo themes in *The Insect Woman* similarly tallies with the Japanese New Wave's commitment to presenting the realities of Japan. Violence by men towards women is given particular emphasis through the depiction of Tome's rape – an incident which causes her to give birth to a child out of wedlock – and the beating which Chūji inflicts on his wife, who is herself characterised as deeply promiscuous. Yet the most shocking element of the film, thematically and visually, is the incestuous relationship between Tome and Chūji. In a particularly striking scene, Imamura shows Chūji suckling on Tome's breasts in a graphic fashion, which would simply not have been seen in previous decades. The direct handling of taboo themes and the visceral style of this scene in particular are symptomatic of the willingness of a younger generation of filmmakers to exploit the 1960s Japanese film industry's more relaxed approach to censorship, which had been fervent during the war and Occupation years, to enhance the poignancy of their work.

Given the various injustices committed on Tome and that *The Insect Woman* is essentially the story of her life, it might seem natural to assume that the viewer is encouraged to sympathise with her plight throughout. This is not the case, and Imamura employs several techniques in an attempt at objectivity. First, Tome is not presented as a character with the imperious moral code that a 'hero' might be expected to have. In fact, during the second half of the film she becomes a character who could best be described as callous of mind and mean of spirit. Although we can rationally posit that this transformation is the end product of the endemic abuse during her adolescence and young adulthood, it remains difficult to favourably identify with a character who financially exploits her call-girl employees and even physically assaults a girl who she suspects of disloyalty. Whatever the viewers may think of Tome, they are given equal opportunity to both sympathise with and be repulsed by her. At the conclusion of the film, there is no closure or resolution for Tome (and only a limited amount for her daughter Nobuko), further underlining Imamura's refusal to spoon-feed his audience.

As well as coming up with dynamic approaches to narrative and character, the Japanese New Wave was also notable for experimentation with film form. In *The Insect Woman*, this stylistic innovation contributes to the final sense of emotional detachment from the events and characters of the film. The use of anti-realist devices such as the freeze-frame and accompanying voiceover prevent viewers from becoming fully submerged in the world of the film and gives opportunity to reflect on the wider implications of the on-screen content. Imamura himself stated that he made his films in such a way to encourage viewers to adopt a critical rather passive position; in other words, to think (Bock 1978: 293). Assaulting narrative, thematic and formal conventions, *The Insect Woman* is a vibrant example of Japanese New Wave cinema.

Notes

1. See Chuck Stephens, 'The Lower Depths', *Film Comment*, Vol. 42, No. 4, 2006, p. 11.
2. See Joan Mellen, *Voices from the Japanese Cinema*, New York: Liverlight, 1975, p. 201, quoted in Desser 1988:108; Tadao Sato, *Currents in Japanese Cinema*, Tokyo, Kodansha, 1982, p. 76, quoted in Desser 1988: 122.

Further reading

Audie Bock, *Japanese Film Directors*, Tokyo, Kodansha, 1978.

David Desser, *Eros plus Massacre: An Introduction to the Japanese New Wave Cinema*, Indiana, Indiana University Press, 1988.

Michael Smith

La Noire de … /Black Girl (1966)

[Country: Senegal, France. Production Company: Filmi Domirev. Director: Sembène Ousmane. Producer: André Zwoboda. Screenwriter: Sembène Ousmane (based on his short story). Cinematographer: Christian Lacoste. Music: No Credit. Editor: André Gaudier. Cast: Mbissine Thérèse Diop (The Maid/Diouana), Anne-Marie Jelinek (Madame), Robert Fontaine (Monsieur), Momar Nar Sene (The Young Man), Ibrahima Boy (Boy with Mask).]

Synopsis: A young black woman in newly independent Senegal accompanies her employers to France to work as a governess. She imagines she will enjoy the comforts of bourgeois French society. Instead, she discovers her second-class status as an exotic outsider, leading to a crisis of identity and, ultimately, suicide.

Black Girl (*La Noire de ...*), the first feature film of Senegalese novelist and director Ousmane Sembène, may be rightly credited with helping to put African cinema – a cinema 'that stars [black] Africans, is cinematographed, written, directed, etc., by blacks' – onto the world stage.[1] Released in 1966, it won the Prix Jean Vigo, which previously been awarded to such filmmakers as Jean-Luc Godard for *Breathless* (*À bout de souffle*), Alain Resnais for *Night and Fog* (*Nuit et brouillard*) and Chris Marker *Statues Also Die* (*Les Statues meurent aussi*). Similar to *Statues*, *Black Girl* is concerned with the after-effects of colonialism, but rather than seeing African art compromised by being decontextualised in French museums, Sembène's film tells the story of a young African woman taken from Dakar to the French Riviera to be a nanny, but treated as a maid and *objet d'art* for other white French people. *Black Girl*'s iconic status may be attributed to its relatively straightforward narrative style, Christian Lacoste's striking black and white cinematography, and its strong anti-colonial themes.

The first feature film by an African director was almost not made at all. Because of the relative scarcity of avenues for independent film production and distribution, the *Consortium Audiovisuel International* (CAI) and *Bureau de Cinéma* (Film Bureau), under the auspices of the post-independence French Ministry of Cooperation could exert influence over the ideological content of the films by refusing to assist filmmakers with whose politics it did not agree or to produce films whose subject matter it did not approve.[2] Though the Bureau would eventually buy the distribution rights, it rejected the script to *Black Girl*, leaving Sembène to produce the film independently with the aid of André Zwobada, who also gave Sembène access to editing equipment.[3]

The frustrations of the filmmaking process, and patronising attitudes of the former French colonial rulers continuing to exercise a pseudo-colonial control over the recently independent Senegal, which gained its independence in 1960, inform the film's themes. *Black Girl* opens with a boat coming to harbour that contains the titular 'black girl', who, as in the more ambiguous French title (*La Noire de ...*), is caught between one world – Africa – and another – Europe – without belonging fully in either. Fittingly, she wonders whether anyone will be waiting for her after she disembarks from the ship. Credited as 'The Maid', she is the only character in the film with a name – Diouana. She has come to the French Riviera to work for an unnamed white couple, referred to only as 'Madame' and 'Monsieur'. She was given the impression that her time in France would be devoted to tending the children and exploring France. She does not imagine herself an equal, but underestimates the degree of her subjugation as a cheap African labour.

Early shots of her mopping while wearing high heels and earrings underscore the contrast between what she believed she had come to France for – to attend the family's children and explore France as a modern space of commercial possibility – and her function once she arrives: a maid, or as she later understands herself, a paid slave. While she longs for status items (i.e. pretty dresses, shoes, silk lingerie, and pretty wigs that she imagines will make her friends, relatives and acquaintances back in Dakar jealous) it begins to dawn on her that she is a status symbol for her white patrons – a sign of their sojourn in Senegal and a reminder of the recent colonial past – who show her off to their guests and insist that she cook 'native' Senegalese food for them. During the lunch, she is humiliated when one of their guests accosts her for the pleasure of kissing a 'Negress' for the first time. When she is visibly upset, they complain that independence has made the Africans 'less natural'. Her frustration builds throughout her time in France until she refuses to work or eat, finally committing suicide, pledging 'never, ever will I ever be anybody's slave again'. Recalling the tone of the short story upon which the film is based, her suicide is recounted in the newspaper's *faits divers* – a section devoted to brief sensational or lurid stories thought to be of little consequence. Monsieur returns her effects to her mother who, like Diouana, refuses his money.

One of the most striking stylistic features of the film is its distant tone. The story achieves its tone through an objective, wry, journalistic prose style, beginning by declaiming, 'It was the morning of June 23, the year of our Lord nineteen hundred and fifty-eight. On the Croisette, neither the destiny of the French Republic, the future of Algeria, and even less those territories under the boot of the colonisers, worried those who swarmed the beaches of Antibes'.[4] The film adopts a graver, more subjective point of view, presenting viewers with a steady stream of extra-diegetic monologue (the voice of Haitian actress Toto Bissainthe) and close-ups of Diouana's expressive face and gestures. To the extent that the other characters notice she does not speak, they attribute her silence to a poor grasp of French rather than a refusal to speak, though her silence could also be attributed to technical difficulties.[5] A third reading would link the two, and see the contrast between her inner monologue and outward muteness, even among friends, as Sembène's wry meta-commentary on the conditions under which the film was made. The tight ideological control over the content of films produced under the supervision of the Bureau made it such that, like Diouana in *Black Girl*, the filmmakers could just be status symbols, shown off to other Europeans as a sign of cultural advancement and sophistication. Diouana's expressive but, to the white characters within the film, inscrutable face and motives makes her analogous to the 'indigenous' mask she first gives as a gift to Madame, who collects them.

Whereas her silent inscrutability gives her power, her inability to communicate in her own voice is also disabling. Diouana receives a letter from her mother in the course of the film, chastising her for not sending money home. Unable to read it, Monsieur reads it to her, then offers to write a response. When she does not dictate the letter to him, he writes it anyway, instructing her to stop him if he says anything false. She tears up the letter from her mother – no doubt written by someone else on her behalf – and leaves the room. In the circumstances where one's speech is so carefully curtailed and allowed within such a narrow range of predictable responses, the film seems to ask, why speak at all? How can one? It is fitting, then, that a boy from Diouana's neighbourhood uses the mask, which Monsieur returns to Diouana's mother, as an ambiguous sign that Monsieur correctly takes as a threat, but one that remains ambiguous.

Themes of alienation, displacement and disappointment in post-independence Senegal recur in Sembène's films, often with a politically tough, but ultimately warm, humanism. In *Mandabi* (1968), his second feature film, a money order from France slowly reveals itself as curse rather than blessing for a Wolof-speaking man who, unable to navigate an official bureaucracy conducted in French, falls prey to a family member. *Xala* (1975), the story of a corrupt politician who believes himself under the spell of a curse (*xala*) of impotence, ends with his ritual humiliation/cleansing by those members of the underclass whose interests he has neglected. Though one can read Sembène's films in terms of native–foreigner, coloniser–colonised, traditional–modern dichotomies, doing so misses the ways his films implicate each pole in the other, and display people who struggle to anchor their traditions and hopes in a world that has little place for them (the characters or the traditions).

Black Girl differs from his later features in that it features a young, female protagonist, someone whose status is relatively uncertain in traditional society, and thus someone set up for both a greater expectation and a greater disappointment. Reading it strictly in terms of the recent independence that so dominates the subtext of the film misses its deeper engagement with history, as when Diouana declares 'Never ever will I be anybody's slave again'. In that line, as in all of the moments where she understands herself as a slave rather than employee – that is, understands herself to be fundamentally without the right to control her labour in any meaningful sense – it is hard not to hear resonance with the transatlantic slave trade. Asked about it, Sembène said, 'We [Africans, Senegalese] were the first slavers ... We even hunted down slaves so that they could be deported. We should be courageous enough to say it'.[6] He tells the story of the transformation of traditional slavery as a social status related to war to the slave trade. In this brief anecdote, his commitment to history, and the obligations to history, is clear, and links the domestic and the slave as an historical rather than a sentimental connection.

The white French couple, however, is also depicted as unmoored, bereft of the traditions that had previously given their lives meaning. Though Madame is powerful in Dakar and can have her pick of maids from women who go every day and wait to be selected, in France she is bored, ill-equipped for or uninterested in caring for her own children, anxious about her status and her husband who, like Diouana, is practically mute. Colonialism, the source of their prior power, is gone, leaving in its wake uncertainty and turmoil. They cannot understand why Diouana would be unhappy, why she would wish to die. They cannot understand why she would take back the mask she initially gives to Madame as a token of friendship (though they already have several masks), or why she would refuse payment. It is a cinema geared towards catching a historical shift in progress.

In the final scene in Dakar, having failed to resolve things with Diouana's family or community, Monsieur finds himself the object rather than the subject of the look. The entire town stares at him with open contempt once they learn his identity. The Boy with Mask holds the mask over his own and follows Monsieur to the edge of town. Monsieur's spell, like the allure France had held for Diouana has been broken, but there is still power in that mask, in the presentation of Africa in the present. Beyond that, it makes the Africans themselves subjects rather than passive objects of looking and of narrative. Monsieur can never know what has been said about him, if anything, and an ironic twist that we can only refer to him by a formal title objectifies him, denying him back story and imaginable future while the people of Dakar, especially the Boy with Mask whose gaze off is the last image of the film, is the one whose future viewers are invested in. If not free, he is independent from France, and the decontextualisations of the museum.

Notes

1. From French film historian Georges Sadoul, *Histoire du cinéma mondial*, Paris, Flammarion, 1973, p. 499. Quoted in Manthia Diawara, *African Cinema: Politics and Culture*. Bloomington, Indiana University Press, 1992, p. 24. Though *Black Girl* is a French language film, later films would use Wolof more extensively.
2. Claire Andrade-Watkins, 'Film Production in Francophone Africa 1961–1977: Ousmane Sembène – An Exception', *Contributions in Black Studies*, Vol. 11, 1993, pp. 26–32, and Diawara, *African Cinema*, pp. 23–8.
3. Andrade-Watkins, 'Film Production in Francophone Africa', p. 30.
4. Sembène, 'La Noire de … ', *Voltaïque*, Paris, Présence Africaine, 1962, p. 157.
5. The principal characters are all voiced by actors other than those who appear on-screen, and rarely is sound synced to source.
6. 'An Interview with Ousmane Sembène by Sada Niang', *Contributions in Black Studies*, Vol. 11, 1993, pp. 89–90.

Further reading

David Murphy, *Sembène: Imagining Alternatives in Film and Fiction*, Oxford and Trenton, NJ, Africa World Press, 2000.

David Murphy, 'An African Brecht: The Cinema of Ousmane Sembène', *New Left Review*, Vol. 16, July–August 2002, pp. 115–29.

Francoise Pfaff, *The Cinema of Ousmane Sembène*, Westport, CT, Greenwood Press, 1984.

Kamal Salhi, ed., *Francophone Post-Colonial Cultures: Critical Essays*, Oxford, Lexington Books, 2003.

Anthony Reed

Nosferatu, eine Symphonie des Grauens/Nosferatu, A Symphony of Horrors (1922)

[Country: Germany. Production Company: Prana Film. Director: F. W. Murnau. Screenwriter: Henrik Galeen. Cinematographers: Fritz Arno Wagner and Günther Krampf. Cast: Max Schreck (Count Orlok), Gustav von Wangenheim (Hutter), Greta Schröder (Ellen), Alexander Granach (Knock).]

Synopsis: In the town of Wisborg, a demented estate agent called Knock sends his employee Hutter to a remote Balkan castle on a mission to sell a vacant property opposite Hutter's house to the mysterious Count Orlok. In an inn, a book titled *Nosferatu* that warns of supernatural perils is left for Hutter by an unrevealed benefactor. The sceptical Hutter takes the book but ignores the advice. Orlok's vampire nature soon becomes apparent, traumatising Hutter and unleashing terror upon Wisborg, much to Knock's delight. Hutter's wife Ellen discovers the abandoned book and learns that she must sacrifice herself to end the terror.

The most haunting of the iconic images from the brief, brilliant era of Weimar cinema is that of the freakish vampire shadow scuttling up a staircase like a spider. His elongated, ghastly claw curls first around the door handle before inching towards his terrified victim's heart. In 1922, *Nosferatu* established much of the mythos of the screen vampire, particularly the deadly effects of sunlight, and is still perhaps the best of its genre. Throughout, the mechanics of cinema are interwoven with narrative and thematic concerns. Also, while the tale itself is timeless, the film is immersed in the thinking of its unstable interwar context.

The plot is clearly derived from that of Bram Stoker's *Dracula* but with the crucial omission of a perceptive Van Helsing to take charge of the hunt for the vampire.[1] This leaves the main characters strangely adrift, with Hutter particularly slipping away from his perceived function as protagonist in the final quarter of the film. Similarly, the secondary characters Bulver, Sievers and Harding (all recognisable as equivalents of figures from the novel), serially blunder and make grave misjudgements. Each in different ways represents 'authority' through age, experience or social position, signalling a total breakdown of traditional social hierarchy and descent into chaos.

Conversely Orlok is the spirit of anarchy, all impulse and gratification with no real logic to his actions, while the crazed Knock barely contains a state of near-ecstasy throughout. Compared to the Hutters' affectionate but seemingly passionless marriage, the film draws heavily on the opposing forces of staid comfort versus rapture. For an undead creature, Orlock is greedily full of primal life, memorably performed by Max Schreck with evident relish.[2] As with any decent vampire, what has actually died is the creature's self-restraint.

Weimar cinema is well recognised for its use of elaborate mise en scène, performance style and lighting. All Murnau's films are in this respect certainly noteworthy, despite Gustav von Wangenheim's hammy Hutter. *Nosferatu*'s famous shadow on the staircase is one of many examples of dramatically precise staging. Throughout, movement on stairs, through archways or across bridges is used to suggest psychological and atmospheric shifts.

Much else is remarkable. Unlike the majority of German films made in the 1920s, which were largely based within the studio in order to fully control the mise en scène, *Nosferatu* utilises extensive location shooting as well as artificial sets. At times, an unexpected documentary air is implied through wildlife footage of 'werewolves' (actually hyenas), spiders, a Venus flytrap and microscopic images of polyps. All posit the predatory count as a force of nature.

Contrastingly, the early scenes in Wisborg are particularly picaresque, purposefully evoking a gemütlich, pre-war past. Murnau then entwines this fairy-tale fiction and documentary realism with visions of the wild-looking Balkan Mountains. Less reliant on the overt expressionism of many of his peers, Murnau draws on images of a feral wilderness or portentous cloud formations to recall the romantic paintings of Caspar David Friedrich. Consequently, the idyllic Wisborg's disintegration into pandemonium becomes more dreadful.

The sublime evocation of nature gives way to the openly gothic via the medium of 1920s cinematic modernity as Hutter steps foot in the Count's domain. Stop-motion cinematography presents the vampire's phantom carriage its unnatural speed; double exposure allows him to pass through brick walls or suddenly materialise; extreme high and low angles suggest unnatural domination; most memorably, the use of negative footage of the carriage racing through the forest transports the hapless Hutter from the real world into the 'land of ghosts'. The climactic sequence of Orlok feeding off Ellen is another example of a painterly influence on *Nosferatu's* composition, evoking Henry Fusili's *The Nightmare*, again making plain the Gothic/Romantic inspiration.

In the 1960s, Lotte Eisner claimed that in Murnau's films, 'cinematic composition was never a mere attempt at decorative stylisation. He created the most overwhelming and poignant images in the whole German cinema' (1969: 97). Murnau championed the use of the 'unchained camera', taking every opportunity to employ dynamic motion to his cinematography.[3] Examples here include the sweeping seascapes of the doomed ship, *The Empusa*, parallel cut with panoramic landscapes, contrasting Orlok and Hutter's separate journeys to Wisborg. Compare this to the stiff, studio-bound contemporary *The Cabinet of Dr Caligari* and the two films seem to be from wholly different eras.

Nosferatu also uses editing to create an undercurrent of psychological unease: at no point in the film do characters mention loss of self-control or psychic connections – both key themes of expressionist cinema – yet throughout, intuitive links are made clear by the use of creative cross-cutting. This deliberately undermines the townsfolk's hapless assumptions and protestations. The connection between Orlok and Knock is explicit, yet there are evident ties that bind the trio of Hutter, Ellen and Orlok, suggesting that the underlying passion that seems missing from the Hutters' rather stiff relationship feeds the uninhibited Count as much as blood.

The scene where a somnambulistic Ellen communes with the vampire attacking her husband thousands of miles away takes its logic from the shot-to-shot relation of the corresponding scenes. No exposition explains this. Ellen passionately calls out to Hutter but it is Orlok who responds through a false eyeline match across the separate shots of the two. Later, during the respective journeys of Orlok and Hutter, Ellen sits on a beach (portentously surrounded by graves) waiting for her 'beloved'. Hutter had set off on horseback; it is Orlok who is coming to her by sea.

The female in Weimar expressionism tends to be reduced to the roles of damsel or whore but Ellen is a far more complex character, being married but seemingly virginal. The contradiction is evident in the final sequence where she gives herself to Orlok. The sexual metaphor of the vampire feeding is obvious, but it's never been as complex as here. As with many other German films of the period, *Nosferatu* deals with the fear of loss of control, but in this sequence, who controls whom? Who leads whom to their death? Ellen is remarkably both 'innocent maiden' and 'femme fatale'; faithful to her husband by giving herself to another; damsel in distress and saviour. Orlok is both victim and predator.

The film's refusal to explain its subtextual oddities gives it the logic of a dream that slips into nightmare. Eisner suggest that the attraction/repulsion nature of the Ellen/Orlok relationship evokes a feeling of, 'the impress of (Murnau's) inner complexity, of the struggle he waged within himself against a world in which he remained despairingly alien' (1969: 98), namely the director's homosexuality and the morality of German society at the time. Possibly, there is some validity in this, though it is striking that the image of the vampire, unlike the majority of its screen successors, is utterly hideous, rather than seductive. Orlok's erect, thin body, oversized bald head and sharp teeth have been often likened to the image of the toothed phallus, emphasising the repulsion aspect of predatory, invasive and aggressive male sexuality. Ellen's sacrifice thus becomes loaded with both abandon and revulsion as she lures the primal creature to their mutual destruction. Orlok is attractive perhaps because he is *so* repulsive: a figure of wild, destructive abandon and sexual horror. In this respect, perhaps Orlok's true screen successor is less the generic vampire and more Ridley Scott's *Alien* (1979).

However, there are darker issues that should be considered when placing the film into its context beyond debatable speculation about its director's psychology. First, the influenza pandemic that trailed the war took twice as many casualties as those killed in action. *Nosferatu*'s parade of coffins and frequent references to plague are references a 1922 audience would have found chillingly familiar. Second, is the vampire here an anti-Semitic image? After the Balkan invasion of Transylvania in 1916, there were numbers of Eastern European Jews migrating to Germany at a time when the right-wing press were looking for scapegoats for the increasingly disastrous events of the war. There are unmistakable parallels between the monsters depicted in the films of this time and some of the anti-Semitic propaganda from the later Nazi period.[4] Vicious rumours of Jews as plague spreaders had been used to justify their continuous wholesale persecution and murder since the Middle Ages and the word 'nosferatu' means not 'undead' but 'plague carrier'.

We should be cautious though. Murnau himself does not appear to have espoused anti-Semitism, leaving the increasingly fascist-leaning Germany for America in the mid-1920s. It is unclear whether Murnau was conscious of any implications in the images he was creating and it could also be argued that the cruel images of the 1930s drew on pictures of recent screen villains for inspiration, rather than the other way round.

In his analysis of Weimar cinema, Anton Kaes takes a radical look at the film and sees an allegory of the recent German war experience, revealing a wounded nation expressing the post-traumatic shock of a devastating defeat through cinema. The argument is convincing: Hutter journeys as an unprepared young man into a death zone and Knock even points out Hutter's destination on a map as the central Balkans, where the war began. Hutter encounters horrors such as the face of Orlok peering up through the dirt between the broken planks of his coffin, clearly a grisly image based on those experienced in the trenches. The returning Hutter is stricken with symptoms of shell shock and apparent impotence. The formerly cosy Wisborg is transformed into a town ravaged by mass death, trauma and hysteria (Kaes 2009: 87–127). The breakdown in social order through the incompetence (Bulver, etc.) or madness (Knock) of authority is certainly an apt metaphor for the German war experience.

Ellen, in this reading becomes the model wife left at the home front as her husband goes off to 'war', yet the shell of the man who returns is incapable of resuming their innocent former relationship. The overwhelming external force drives her into an act of self-sacrificing abasement, recasting defeat as tragic victory. Thus, Ellen becomes an embodiment of Weimar Germany itself: unstable, beset by forces of anarchy and doomed.

Writing in the late 1940s, Siegfried Kracauer famously and contentiously considered that the monsters of Weimar cinema represented a nation's collective premonition of the totalitarianism that would dominate the thirties. Kracauer branded Orlok a 'tyrant figure' (1947: 79) but a tyrant suggests some form of order, however terrible. Orlok is not that; he is a figure of anarchy, horror, madness and destruction let loose by the blinkered and the deluded. For a wounded nation flirting with chaos, he personified both the recently ruinous war and an inadvertent – yet fitting – premonition of Hitler.

Notes

1. In 1922, the novel was still in copyright, resulting in legal problems that affected the film's circulation for decades.
2. A contemporary photograph of Schreck on set in full costume is especially sinister.
3. The technique culminates in the brilliant *Sunrise* (1927).
4. See Kaes, 2009, pp. 109–13.

Further reading

Lotte Eisner, *The Haunted Screen*, Berkeley, University of California Press, 1969.

Anton Kaes, *Shell Shock Cinema: Weimar Culture and the Wounds of War*, Princeton, Princeton University Press, 2009.

Siegfried Kracauer, *From Caligari to Hitler*, Princeton, Princeton University Press, 1947.

Phil Lloyd

Nran guyne/The Colour of Pomegranates (1969)

[Country: USSR. Production Company: Armenfilm. Director: Sergo Paradjanov. Screenwriter: Sergo Paradjanov. Cinematographer: Suren Shakhbazian. Music: Tigran Mansurian, Sergo Paradjanov. Editors: Sergo Paradjanov, M. Ponomarenko, Sergei Iutkevich. Cast: Sofiko Chiaureli (Poet as a Youth, Anna, the nun, Angel of Resurrection, the pantomime actress, the pantomime actor, Poet's muse), Melkon Meliakain (Poet as a child), Medeia Dzhaparidze (Poet's mother), Spartak Bagashvili (Poet's father), Avet Avetisian (Avet-aga) Hovhannes Minasian (Prince), Onik Minasian (Prince).]

Synopsis: At the narrative centre of Paradjanov's *The Colour of Pomegranates* is a biography of the Armenian poet-troubadour Arutin Sayadan (1712–1795), known as Sayat-Nova, or The King of Song. The film traces different events in Arutin's life, from earlier years till his death. Paradjanov structures his film as a set of narrative tableaux that correspond to the childhood, youth, and adulthood of the famous Armenian poet. Paradjanov dedicates the first tableaux to Arutin's life with his parents and his education at the monastery. In the next set of narrative episodes, Paradjanov depicts Arutin's maturation, his service as a poet and musician at the court of Iraklii II of Georgia, and his unhappy love affair with Princess Anna. The final events in the poet's life take place at the Haghpat monastery, in which he lives as a monk until his death at the hands of the Persian army.

Paradjanov's films, including his 1969 *The Colour of Pomegranates*, fit well with the overall atmosphere in Soviet cinematography of the 1960s through the 1970s. Soviet cinema of the 1950s through the first half of the 1960s experienced a period of aesthetical and ideological liberation – the Thaw under Nikita Khrushchev's government (1953–1964) – the influence of which could still be detected in the late 1960s. At that time, many filmmakers, such as Andrei Tarkovskii, Iurii Il′enko, Leonid Osyka, Tengiz Abuladze, Artavaz Peleshian and Otar Iosseliani, were developing various methods and techniques that allowed them to create their films in the tradition of poetic cinema.[1] Iu. Z. Morozov argues that Paradjanov already, in his 1964 film *Shadows of Forgotten Ancestors* (*Tini zabutykh predkiv*), had touched upon the theme of poetic worldview, represented in the main protagonist Ivanko, 'who had a poetic perception of the world, but who was not a poet by his occupation and his public and social status' (1991: 149). Later, in *The Colour of Pomegranates*, Paradjanov shifts this topic of the poet and his search for beauty and truth into the centre of his creative and aesthetic practices. In his films, Paradjanov is a poet who operates not only with words, but also with sounds and images. In this respect, *The Colour of Pomegranates* is a somewhat autobiographical film, and Sayat-Nova is an embodiment of Paradjanov's spiritual, artistic, and emotional search.

With the removal of Khrushchev from the position of the First Secretary of the Communist Party in 1964, the second half of the 1960s marked the period of increased censorship and intensified state control over cultural production in the Soviet Union. Therefore, Paradjanov's innovative, poetic cinematic language was restrained by the state. As many other Soviet directors with innovative, unorthodox cinematic vision, such as Tarkovskii, Kira Muratova, Andrei Konchalovskii and Aleksandr Askol′dov, Paradjanov became the victim of this rigid system with its attempts to renew and reinforce socialist realist principles. Before directing *The Colour of Pomegranates*, Paradjanov had an opportunity to experiment with narrative, visual, and aural forms in *Shadows of Forgotten Ancestors*, *Kiev Frescoes* (*Kievski freski*, 1966) and *Hakop Hovnatanian* (1967) – the films in which he already deviated from socialist realist aesthetics and methods. All these films also represent a struggle between the cultural producer and the state and either were censored and shelved or severely edited and reached only a limited audience.[2]

Partially because of the intensified state control over cultural production during the Leonid Brezhnev administration (1964–1982), but mainly because of Paradjanov's love for stylistic and visual experimentation, the cinematic language of *The Colour of Pomegranates* is highly metaphorical, even allegorical. Paradjanov warns his viewers about the allegorical nature of his film already in the opening scene for 'the film uses the symbolism and allegories specific to the tradition of Medieval Armenian poet-troubadours (Ashougs)'.[3] Even though Paradjanov structures the events in the poet's life in chronological order, it may be difficult for viewers to follow the story, because the traditional linear narrative is constantly interrupted by symbolic imagery and intertitles with Sayat-Nova's poetry. The deciphering of allegorical meanings is also complicated by the fact that the original version of *The Colour of Pomegranates* was censored by the state, and another Soviet director, Sergei Iutkevich, revised and reorganised Paradjanov's film, as instructed by the film studio administration.[4]

Paradjanov leads his viewers to allegories by skilfully weaving various metaphors, symbols, repetitions, and allusions into the narrative, visual, and aural texture of the film. The multilayered quality of *The Colour of Pomegranates* creates additional complexity of meaning. Paradjanov juxtaposes shots of Armenian homes, monasteries, and the royal court with images of open books, paintings, Orthodox icons, animals, pomegranates, dying fish, seashells, laces, bread, soil, and a traditional Armenian music instrument – the kamancha. He creates a cinematic poem by adding the rhythmic, repetitive sounds of church bells, rain, grape stomping, and pieces of mother-of-pearl falling on the poet's kamancha, and continuous, sometimes monotonous, prayers, songs, and poems. Complimented by diegetic and non-diegetic sound and music, the setting and the objects on the screen function as a meter and a rhythm and build a chain of meanings, at the centre of which is the process of the poet's self-realisation, his awakening as a sexual being, the discovery and shaping of his artistic and spiritual identity.

In addition to the sound and the setting, colour plays an essential role in Paradjanov's film and becomes an independent character both of narrative and visual structures of *The Colour of Pomegranates*. Three colours – red, black, and white – dominate the screen and function as signifiers for a number of concepts, important for Paradjanov. The film studio administrators' choice to rename Paradjanov's film from *Sayat-Nova* to *The Colour of Pomegranates* was dictated by their inability to understand the director's stylistic approach to creating a biopic, but, at the same time, was not entirely accidental and inaccurate.[5] Paradjanov emphasises the importance of the colour red and already introduces it in the opening scene: the shots of red pomegranates and a knife with blood, juxtaposed in a rhythmic montage with an open book of Sayat-Nova's poetry, point to the special connection between these images. They represent the poet's emotional and spiritual sufferings as a part of the creative process and his special status as a martyr. The intertitles with his poems support this statement: 'I am the man whose life and soul are tortured'. The red colour returns as a leitmotif of Sayat-Nova's life and art throughout the rest of the film. It recurs as the colour of Armenian national rugs, in the clothes of little Arutin, in nuns' clothes, as the blood of sacrificed roosters, and as red laces on the young lovers' faces. The colour red, on the one hand, symbolises life and libidinal energy; on the other hand, it functions as a signifier of blood, pain, and suffering. Paradjanov uses the beginning of Sayat-Nova's life as a little boy as a starting point of his narrative and ends *The Colour of Pomegranates* with the poet's death. Everything else – the spiritual, physical, and sexual maturation of the main protagonist – happens between these two main points of Sayat-Nova's hagiography. Paradjanov uses the white and the black colours as a contrast to the colour red and as markers of transformation. The poet and his beloved Princess Anna exchange a white flower and white laces as a symbol of their innocent love. After the lovers from two different social strata transgress and their pure, platonic relationship turns into a passionate, physical attraction without any future, the objects and settings around them turn red. After overcoming his secular desires and lust, and dedicating his life to poetry, music, and later to God, Sayat-Nova wears the black robe of the monk and obtains the status of martyr for refusing to renounce his

Christian faith. As other symbols of pure faith in the film – white boy-angels and a white nun, uncorrupted by mundane passions – the poet dies in white clothes.

Paradjanov made *The Colour of Pomegranates* in his home country – Armenia – after the Soviet government forbade his film *Kiev Frescos*, which he was making at the Dovzhenko film studio in Kiev. After a decade of making films in Ukraine, Paradjanov finally had an opportunity to go back to his ethnic roots and scrutinise his parents' culture. Therefore, *The Colour of Pomegranates* combines the individual and the national; on the one hand, it thoroughly explores the psychological, emotional, and spiritual maturation of Sayat-Nova and, on the other, it offers a detailed ethnographic examination of the everyday life in rural Armenia. Similarly to *Shadows of Forgotten Ancestors* that explores Hutsul traditions in the Carpathian Mountains, their language, and commonplace culture, *The Colour of Pomegranates* focuses on the mundane part of Armenian life in the eighteenth century, such as cooking, doing laundry, taking baths, and doing house chores. Paradjanov's ethnographic study also includes old Armenian traditions and rituals, such as weddings, baptisms, funerals, national costumes, architecture, music, and poetry. Through a rhythmic montage, a contrast of colours, a juxtaposition of light and shadows, he poeticises and stylises the routine aspects of Armenian everyday culture, thus, transmuting them into magical, almost fairytale-like narratives.

However, it is difficult to assign Paradjanov to one specific national film tradition – he rather belongs to the group of cultural producers who supersede the boundaries of national cinema and create transnational cinematic texts. Paradjanov's own transnational background helped him to easily cross the borders between different national traditions: he was born in Georgia to Armenian parents, studied in Moscow at the All-Union State Institute of Cinematography, and made his films in Ukraine and Armenia. Prior to and after *The Colour of Pomegranates*, Paradjanov made a number of films, in which he created a detailed study of various ethnic cultures: Moldovan culture in *Andriesh* (1955),[6] the Hutsul groups in *Shadows of Forgotten Ancestors*, Armenian art in *Hakop Hovnatanian*, Georgian folk legends in *The Legend of Suram Fortress* (*Ambavi suramis tsikhisa*, 1984) and Azerbaijan folklore in *Ashik Kerib* (1988).[7] Even the choice of the protagonist for *The Colour of Pomegranates* – a poet who wrote his poetry in Armenian, Georgian, and Azerbaijani – once again emphasises the transnational, or even universal, status of an artist. This film, as many other Paradjanov's films, glorifies the creative power of art through allegorical imagery and national music, architecture, and poetry. In an interview, Paradjanov explains the main idea of the film: 'And then I tried to depict the art in life, and not life in the art. Conversely, I wanted that the art was reflected in the life' (Fomin 2006: 149). As suggested by *The Colour of Pomegranates*, any art, whether it is literary, visual, or performing, should serve as a spiritual path to the transcendental in every human's life.

Notes

1. Poetic cinema was not a new phenomenon during the Khrushchev years, but was rather a return to the early Soviet cinema of the 1920s–1930s, exemplified by Aleksandr Dovzhenko's films.
2. The administration of the Dovzhenko film studio stopped the pre-production process of *Kiev Frescos*, and only about 15 minutes are available for viewing nowadays.
3. After the first review of the film, the studio administration requested that Paradjanov add some explanatory intertitles. Later, Iutkevich cut the original version into pieces, restructured them, and added intertitles before each narrative vignette. For more details on Iutkevich's revisions of Paradjanov's film, see Fomin 2006: 153–61.
4. The original version – the 'director's cut' – was lost, and the pre-production materials were discovered in a very poor condition in the 1990s. This version of *The Colour of Pomegranates* was initially completed by Paradjanov in 1969 and was shown to a limited audience at the film studio, before Iutkevich's drastic editing.
5. For the official film studio recommendations on changing Paradjanov's film, see Valerii

Fomin (ed.), *'Polka': Dokumenty. Svidetel'stva. Kommentarii*, pp. 133–61.

6. He co-directed this film with a Ukrainian filmmaker, Iakov Bazel'ian.
7. *Ashik Kerib* is based on the poetry of famous Russian poet and writer, Mikhail Lermontov, which adds another transnational layer to Paradjanov's cinematic inheritance.

Further reading

Levon Hm. Abrahamian, 'Towards a Poetics of Parajanov's Cinema', *Armenian Review*, Vols. 47.3–4/48.1–2, 2001–2002, pp. 67–91.

Valerii Fomin, 'Tsvet granata', in *'Polka': Dokument, svidetel'stva, kommentarii*, Issue 3, ed. Valerii Fomin, Moscow, Materik, 2006, pp. 132–61.

Geiorgi Gvakharia, 'Sergei Parajanov's Ecumenical Vision', *Armenian Review*, Vols. 47.3–4/48.1–2, 2001–2002, pp. 93–104.

Iu. Z. Morozov, 'Plastika – iazyk kinopoezii' in *Kinovedcheskie zapiski*, Vol. 11, 1991, pp. 149–56.

Karla Oeler, 'Nran Guyne/The Colour of Pomegranates', in Birgit Beumers (ed.), *The Cinema of Russia and the Former Soviet Union*, London and New York, Wallflower Press, 2007, pp. 139–50.

James Steffen, 'From *Sayat Nova* to *The Color of Pomegranates*: notes on the production and censorship of Parajanov's film', *Armenian Review*, Vols. 47.3–4/48.1–2, 2001–2002, pp. 105–47.

James Steffen (ed.), *Sergei Parajanov*, special edition of *Armenian Review*, Vols. 47.3–4/48.1–2, 2001–2002.

James Steffen, 'Parajanov's Playful Poetics: On the "Director's Cut" of *The Color of Pomegranates*', *Journal of Film and Video*, Vol. 47, No. 4, Winter 1995–96, pp. 17–32.

Olga Klimova

Oldboy (2003)

[Country: South Korea. Production Company: Egg Films, Show East. Producer: Dong-joo Kim. Director: Chan-Wook Park. Screenwriters: Garon Tsuchiya, Nobuki Minegishi. Cinematographer: Chung-hoon Chung. Editor: Sang-beom Kim. Cast: Min-sik Choi (Oh Dae-Su); Ji-tae Yu (Woo-jin Lee); Hye-jeong Kang (Mido); Dae-hanji (No Joo-hwan); Byeong-ok Kim (Mr Han).]

Synopsis: The protagonist, Oh Dae-Su is imprisoned in a cell with only a television for company. He doesn't know why he has been held captive or by whom. After 15 years, Oh Dae-Su escapes, but it soon becomes clear that his efforts were all part of his captors plan as he is given five days to discover the reasons behind his imprisonment. What starts out as his quest for the truth quickly turns into a journey of revenge for the 15 years stolen from him.

Chan-Wook Park's *Oldboy* (2003) was the second instalment of his *Vengeance Trilogy*. Whilst the first instalment asks its audience to have sympathy for the character of Mr Vengeance, the second film takes a more distanced approach. Although sympathy is not initially evoked, the cinematic style implicates viewers in the violence, a long shot from the static camera during fight scenes allows for the audience to interpret all of the action. During scenes where Chan-Wook Park chooses to employ close-ups, such as in the scene where Oh Dae-Su cuts off his tongue, the viewer is taken so close to the action that it cannot be escaped. The violent action is mixed with visceral sound which acts as an assault on our senses; we not only see but hear the violence causing it to have a greater impact. Chan-Wook Park's choice of music remains upbeat and as such contrasts with the dark mise en scène. Criticism has been directed towards much of the violence used within films coming from East Asia as it is thought that its purpose is simply designed to shock. However, Chan-Wook Park's violence is not only eye-catching but it also gives a heightened sense of the characters emotions. By giving life to these emotions, the violence is no longer purposeless as it delivers a message to the audience.

The messages delivered through the violence in *Oldboy* can be seen as a critique of Korean society. South Korea has suffered a very turbulent, if short, cinematic history. Under government control films were highly restricted. It was not until 1992 when, as Liese Spencer discusses in *Sight and Sound*, censorship ended and films were no longer banned but instead given labels as a warning to audiences of their explicit content (2004: 18–20). At first filmmakers remained afraid to create progressive cinema but this soon changed as directors such as Chan-Wook Park began to make challenging and complex work that broke the boundaries of previous political constraints. Considered commercial cinema as they recoup their budget, films such as *Oldboy* helped transform and strengthen the South Korean film industry allowing directors the confidence to experiment and to expand into uncharted territory.

Many South Korean films, including *Oldboy*, explore Korea's struggle for identity. The North and South of the country were divided by political values and Korea struggled to find one joint voice; the cinema produced at this time aimed to reflect the confusion and social crisis caused by this divide. The interest in re-examining the past and rediscovering identity is apparent in *Oldboy* as the protagonist's quest to find the truth runs parallel to his quest to explore his own identity, and as such may be read as a broader exploration of identities in crisis. Upon his escape he begins a relationship with a young girl called Mido. When Oh Dae-Su discovers his true identity and the identity of Mido he rejects that identity, and undergoes hypnosis in order to forget his discovery. This rejection of his past mirrors the way South Korean cinema had been forced by censorship to reject the past.

Oldboy follows the tradition of focussing on individual characters, rather than looking at collective class issues as is the case for the cinema of North Korea. South Korean cinema frequently portrays problems as private, not communal, which is evident in *Oldboy* as Oh Dae-Su relies on just one old school friend and shares his worries with Mido alone. This in turn reflects the social structure in some Asian societies where many subjects are considered private, and is in keeping with the concept of 'saving face' whereby giving the impression of being in control is essential for South Korean society: giving an aura of success and calm, while behind closed doors the truth reveals a struggle with inner turmoil, attempting to find their future paths and identity.

In *New Korean Cinema* (2005), Chi-Yun Shin and Julian Stringer suggest that this similarity of cultural values throughout the rest of Asia may account for the success and appeal of South Korean films outside the domestic market. The similarities allow for a wider audience to relate to the themes and characters within films such as *Oldboy* and so the messages of political and social struggle within the film have further reach. *Oldboy* also critiques the cultural expectations of mainstream society; this is evident in the female characters of the *Vengeance trilogy* who are often shown as a hindrance to the male characters rather than providing support or an emotional partner. In *Sympathy for Mr Vengeance* (2002), for example, Ryu's sister commits suicide leaving him alone and guilt-ridden, causing him to commit several murders. In *Oldboy*, Mido aids Oh Dae-Su on his journey eventually sleeping with him; however, in a final twist she turns out to be his daughter and this incest drives Oh Dae-Su to erase all memory of the relationship. Then in the final instalment of the trilogy *Sympathy for Lady Vengeance* (2005) Lee Geum-ja uses several men to exact her revenge on the male responsible for her incarceration. None of the leading women in the *Vengeance trilogy* are married and whilst the films show an increasing tolerance towards sexual expression they still give the message that marriage is the only way for women to secure dignity in modern Korean society.

Oldboy draws attention to several other issues thought to be at the heart of South Korean society, including desensitisation towards media violence, and lack of communication within communities. Shin and Stringer argue that desensitisation might be seen as a result of the conflicting media profile that Korea has received in recent history. Having been highly influenced by American import movies at a time when domestic films were struggling, South Koreans had become used to American tastes. When combined with the experimentation that domestic directors preferred, this resulted in a very provocative cinema containing images of extreme violence and sexual relations. As society has become saturated with these images they no longer hold a high degree of shock value and, therefore, no longer generate such strong reactions from their audiences. This is reflected in Chan-Wook Park's characters. For example, upon his escape Oh Dae-Su comes across a man attempting to commit suicide; as this is the first human he has seen for 15 years, Oh Dae-Su wishes to tell the man his story. On completion, the man asks Oh Dae-Su if he will listen in return but Oh Dae-Su leaves the man uninterested and so the man commits suicide. After 15 years with only a television for company Oh Dae-Su has become desensitised by the violent images it continually reveals. He is not shocked by the man's desire to kill himself, nor does he care. Not only has the television caused him to become disconnected from the real world but it has become his companion and educator. Oh Dae-Su watches the television endlessly, learning new knowledge and skills that he puts into practice when released. The notion that the media desensitises us and disconnects us from others, via the violent images we constantly consume without thought, is also evident in *Sympathy for Mr Vengeance*. The character Tong-jin attends the autopsy of Ryu's sister: again, something that should disturb fails to move Tong-jin, and he becomes bored, yawning throughout.

The themes explored in Chan-Wook Park's trilogy are not only accessible within the domestic market but also prove to have global reach. Whilst the films manage to convey social themes that are specific to a certain part of the world, they do so via entertaining portrayals of exciting, fascinating and oddly sympathetic characters that may be appreciated by global audiences. Moreover, Park uses techniques that may attract an international audience such as the incorporation of real footage of significant events into his films. For example, he shows the marriage of Prince Charles and Princess Diana and then coverage of her death, the events of 9/11 and changes in political regimes. These references to the passing of time and change in world policy and economy are accessible to a socially aware audience around the globe.

Park's pioneering films highlight socio-political concerns of the modern society in which he lives, whilst incorporating timeless storylines. As Spencer's article reveals, Park chooses to cover what he believes to be the most dramatic subject in the world, revenge. Part of the appeal for domestic audiences is that his films act out violent fantasies that were impossible under the old censorship laws. Park's films follow the trend of South Korean cinema to mix comic elements with graphic violence. Here, however, the mix serves a serious purpose. Whilst we laugh at one scene, we may be shocked by the next and so the film has the effect of making us question why the violence, like the comedy, is entertaining. It causes the audiences to wonder what purpose the violence has, asking us to question what the characters are achieving through theses acts. Park's violence is brutal yet it quickly becomes repetitive, illustrating how we as the audience are soon bored by these images. This emphasises his belief that violence within society is often meaningless and so he uses his film to make us consider the effects it has both on the victim and the perpetrator.

Because of the questions his films raise, Chan-Wook Park's violence cannot be considered irresponsible, as many have claimed, but in fact the opposite. The violence in his films is not packaged as mere entertainment but instead as a way of causing the audience to question what they consume. His films are unique as they manage to pose philosophical questions to a global audience, in an entertaining and challenging way.

Further reading

Chi-Yun Shin and Julian Stringer, *New Korean Cinema*, Edinburgh, Edinburgh University Press, 2005.

Wimal Dissanayake, *Melodrama and Asian Cinema*, Cambridge, Cambridge University Press, 1993.

Maarit Khan, 'Asian Films in Britain', *Vertigo*, 1 (6) 36–8, 1996.

Hyangjin Lee, *Contemporary Korean Cinema: Culture, Identity and Politics*, Manchester, Manchester University Press, 2001.

Liese Spencer, 'Revengers Tragedy', *Sight and Sound*, 14 (10) 18–20, 2004.

Holly Taylor

Om Shanti Om (2007)

[Country: India. Production Company: Red Chillies Entertainment. Director: Farah Khan. Producers: Gauri Khan, Shahrukh Khan, Sanjiv Chawla and Anil Sable. Screenwriters: Farah Khan and Mushtaq Shaikh. Dialogue: Mayur Puri. Cinematographer: V. Manikanandan. Music: Vishal Shekhar. Editor: Shirish Kunder. Production Design: Sabu Cyril. Cast: Shahrukh Khan (Om Prakash Makhija/Om Kapoor), Deepika Padukone (Shanti Priya/Sandy), Arjun Rampal (Mukesh 'Mike' Mehra), Shreyas Talpade (Pappu Master), Kiron Kher (Bela Makhija).]

Synopsis: *Om Shanti Om* tells the story of Om, a junior artist in the Bombay film industry of the 1970s, and Shanti Priya, a big star in a secret marriage with a film producer, Mike. Om is in love with Shanti. Om witnesses the brutal murder of Shanti by Mike because he wants to marry an industrialist's daughter. The murder takes place at a palatial set that is burnt down by Mike leaving Shanti locked inside. Om is a helpless witness to this and is finally killed in an accident when he tries to get help. This story is largely set in the period of the late 1970s and early 1980s. We then move to the present and the story of reincarnation. Om is now a young man and a big star known as Om Kapoor (O.K.). In the second half of the film O.K. recalls his previous birth in flashes. The climax of the film is staged in the same palatial set with Mike, now a major Hollywood producer who has returned to India to resume business. A lookalike of Shanti becomes the bait through whom O.K. takes his revenge, killing Mike at the same site where Shanti was murdered.

Om Shanti Om was released amidst much fanfare. The film takes a popular reincarnation story to splinter the film industry into two moments of the present and the recent past. A junior artist's relationship to the film industry, his murder, rebirth and act of revenge forms the narrative thread of the film. In taking Hindi cinema's biggest star, Shahrukh Khan to play the lead, *Om Shanti Om* also displays an affectionate disposition for the cultures associated with popular stardom. Farah Khan's portrait of the industry takes the spectators through a journey of film memory, insider knowledge and genre mythologies. Some have referred to Farah Khan as a historian of popular culture who brought to life an imagination of cinema set in the quintessential 1970s and early 1980s, particularly as some of the insider stories go back further to the 1950s.[1] In an early part of the film, Om saves Shanti on a set that catches fire. This scene clearly cites a well-known accident on the sets of Mehboob Khan's *Mother India* where the actor Sunil Dutt saved Nargis from a similar accident.

The film references the history of popular cinema through gestures, iconic moments, posters and narrative style. The title of the film comes from a film *Karz/Debt* (Subhash Ghai, 1983) with Rishi Kapoor in the lead. A moderate hit in the 1980s, *Karz* presented a revenge narrative based on the theme of reincarnation. Reincarnation was deployed earlier in 1958 by Bimal Roy in his film *Madhumati* but *Karz* had a different story and as the director Subhash Ghai himself has acknowledged, it was inspired by the Hollywood film *The Reincarnation of Peter Proud* (J. Lee Thompson, 1975). Farah Khan's *Om Shanti Om* borrows its title from a popular song from *Karz*. Paying tribute to Ghai's film, the director begins her narrative with the original sequence of the song which has Rishi Kapoor dancing to it on stage. The difference is that Shahrukh Khan, as Om, the hero of her film is standing and cheering with a crowd of junior artists. While the title *Om Shanti Om* is borrowed from *Karz*, the mise en scène draws a lot from Roy's *Madhumati*.

Om Shanti Om is an ironic film that affectionately carves out a world of the film industry. But the film also presents a space of work that is not usually visible in a star-studded cinema. Thus throughout the narrative we are made to see the role of stunt artists, music directors, junior artists, set designers and various other kinds of work. Khan manages to use the two different periods of the film to showcase the changing landscape of cinema, stardom and other working practices of the industry. Thus in the first part, posters, costumes, gestures and dialogues evoke the high melodrama associated with the 1970s. Bela Makhija (Kiron Kher) as Om's mother is a caricature of the mother phenomenon popular in the cinema of the 1970s. But behind this performance is the fact of identity, that of junior artists who live and work on the periphery of the industry. The film is clearly interested in foregrounding this world of work that exists beyond stardom, even if it is in the form of a feel-good fairy tale and revenge narrative.

Om Shanti Om lampoons the overall film culture associated with popular cinema and offers a fairly astute account of its functioning. This is most significantly developed in the comic interludes, the lavish costumes, and the award ceremonies. The typical and most recognizable gestures of well-known stars such as Rajnikant are paraded in a series of comic sequences. The film's desire to dialogue between two moments gives it a retro aesthetic. Retro as has been argued is a culture of revival, an imaginative phenomenon that can be tracked across different kinds of media. A retro past is also implicitly linked to either playful nostalgia or a loss of faith in the future. There is a desire to memorialise the utopian values associated with an earlier time and retro tends to embody a collective visual memory of the recent past.[2] But how does one recreate this memory imaginatively on screen? This is where the role of production and costume design is so critical. It wouldn't be wrong to suggest that Sabu Cyril as the production designer of the film performs the role of a playful historian of design, architecture and objects. The recreation of a material world temporally distanced from our present was staged in *Om Shanti Om* with an explicit desire for fantasy and irony, never to attempt realistic verisimilitude.

The role of sets is something the film highlights throughout. We are taken through these artificially constructed structures in Film City and the frames are busy with people moving objects and wood panels.[3] The set becomes the temporal connection between the past and the present and is the place of memory and recall. The set is in fact created, burnt down, and then recreated for the final climax. The staircase, high ceilings, the chandelier, and the dazzling light draw on the space of the typical Hindi film living-room. In the studio we move through a maze of make-up rooms, editing rooms and projection rooms, drawing us into an invisible world of film production. Sabu Cyril created an ensemble of surfaces to mark the 1970s – from billboards advertising products such as Exide batteries to Ovaltine placed next to a banner of *Sholay* (Ramesh Sippy, 1975), a major blockbuster of the 1970s. Cyril's detailing of the set was geared to enhance the director's mobilisation of film culture as the backdrop for the story. For instance, the *Sholay* billboard says at the bottom – 'still running' – marking the film's temporal world a few weeks or months after the release of the film in 1975. Cyril also presented a series of vignettes such as the art deco facades that dot Bombay's urban scape. As someone who has one of the largest collections of design books, Cyril did extensive research to present the audience with the texture and identification marks of well-known Bombay buildings but combined this with his knowledge of Miami deco. Bombay deco's original inspiration was always the Miami form and in combining building facades from both cities to create a hybrid texture, Cyril evoked a fantastical art deco architectural imagination for *Om Shanti Om.*[4] The theatre where Shanti Priya's film is premiered is sculpted by the camera to highlight its art deco ceilings, its facades and the single screen experience.

The first part of *Om Shanti Om* has a fairytale form that turns awry. In the second half we are introduced to film culture associated with the contemporary especially via song sequences. In a comic sequence, Om Kapoor, now a superstar arrives with great pomp to the studio. The crew has been waiting for a while. As soon as the star arrives he is told by the director that he has to perform grief as the woman he loves is being married off to someone else. Om is informed by the director that he is playing the role of a deaf, dumb and blind person with amputated arms! Om reacts to this and says the film will flop with such a handicapped hero. He then suggests that an item number be introduced (a typical song and dance performance commonly deployed as an attraction in mainstream Indian cinema). Though item numbers have traditionally been associated with women, in *Om Shanti Om*, Shahrukh Khan as the star performs the dance in a dream sequence. It was for this item number that the star worked on his body for over six months something that was released as information during the publicity campaign of the film. The very popular song 'Darde Disco' ('The disco of heartache') was used for the performance and became one of the high points of the film. This comic moment presented spectators with a bizarre set of mannerisms where the narcissistic hero demands an item song to which he would dance with a bevy of item girls. This sequence in a sense also establishes the two different moments of filmmaking staged in the film. The circulation of information about Shahrukh Khan working to build his body for the song generated a lot of discussion clearly showcasing the centrality of stardom and star discourses in the making of *Om Shanti Om's* song sequences.

This fascination for star power is also visible in the other popular song of the film, 'All cool boys come on make some noise'. Here the director draws on iconography associated with the spectacle of star-studded live stage shows performed across the world. These live performances by Bombay's film stars have catered primarily to Indian diasporic audiences. Tickets for these shows sell on an average from around US$35 to US$500 and every show is almost always sold out. The shows are shot on video, generally using a 14-camera set-up, and rights for the telecast of these shows are sold to television channels like Zee, Sahara, Colours and Sony.[5] The stage shows are lavishly mounted extravaganzas of stars, dance, fashion, music, brand advertising and technological wizardry – an event choreographed and laid out for an enthusiastic and highly receptive audience. The power of the live show and its attendant mise en scène is now a significant part of television iconography and not surprisingly the concept makes its way into *Om Shanti Om* when with the extremely popular song 'All cool boys and girls' we see the coming together of 31 stars for the first time in Hindi cinema. Performed like a little show within a film about film, the sequence foregrounds star spectacle as an important marketing device. Noone recognises the power of the live show more than Shahrukh Khan. Khan's 2004 concert, *Temptation*, was produced by his own company, Red Chillies Entertainment. *Temptation* became a legendary tour of 27 cities around the world which was then organisationally managed and shot on video for telecast on television. It was *Temptation*'s success, captured on video along with the presence of wild and enthusiastically cheering crowds that made Khan realise just how popular he had become over the years.[6] In *Om Shanti Om*, Khan's own stature and position is displayed through his ability to bring together so many big stars. At the same time the star retains an upper hand working his way through the song's aesthetic of 'liveness'.

At the time of its release, *Om Shanti Om* was the highest grossing Hindi film ever. Its combination of ironic storytelling, nostalgia and exhibition of film culture via sets, costumes and songs was unique for its time. It also joins a number of films about the film industry made by directors with insider knowledge. As a film text about film culture, *Om Shanti Om* temporally marks a certain historical moment of industrial transformation and for this reason alone will continue to fascinate historians of cinema in the years to come.

Notes

1. Interview with director Anurag Kashyap, Bombay, January 2008.
2. Elizabeth E. Guffey, *Retro: The Culture of Revival*, London, Reaktion Books, 2006.
3. Film City in Bombay is an integrated studio set up built by the Mharshatra State Government to help the film industry. The space is landscaped and has lakes, rivers, grounds, mansions, recording spaces and many other facilities.
4. Interview with Sabu Cyril, January 2012. See also Mushtaq Shiekh, *The Making of Om Shanti Om*, New Delhi, Om Books International, 2008.
5. Interview with Mohammed Morani of *Cineyug*, Bombay, January 2005.
6. Mohammad Morani and Ali Morani of *Cineyug* recall how they were completely taken aback by the extent of Shahrukh's popularity during the tour. (Interview, Bombay January 2005.) Nasreen Munni Kabir who travelled with the tour, had the same observation. (Interview, London, June 2009.)

Further reading

Charles Affron and Mirella Jona Affron, *Sets in Motion: Art Direction and Film Narrative*, New Brunswick, NJ, Rutgers University Press, 1995.

Ranjani Mazumdar, 'Film Stardom After Liveness', *Continuum: Journal of Media and Cultural Studies*, Vol. 26, No. 6, December 2012, pp. 833–44.

Ranjani Mazumdar

On The Waterfront (1954)

[Country: USA. Production Company: Columbia Pictures and Horison Pictures. Director: Elia Kazan. Producer: Sam Spiegel. Screenwriter: Budd Schulberg. Cinematographer: Boris Kaufman. Music: Leonard Bernstein. Cast: Marlon Brando (Terry Malloy), Lee J. Cobb (Johnny Friendly), Rod Steiger (Charley), Eva Marie Saint (Edie Doyle), Karl Malden (Father Barry), Pat Henning ('Kayo' Dougan).]

Synopsis: After he is used to unwittingly set up Edie Doyle's brother to be murdered, Terry Malloy begins to see those who run the longshoremen's trade union for the thugs they have always been. He falls in love with Edie, and through her and Father Barry has his eyes opened to the injustices of life in the docklands. He stands up to the union leader, and despite receiving a physical beating his actions give the local working men the strength to unite and stand up for themselves.

This film has always been mired in controversy because of its intimate connections to the post-war Communist witch-hunt in the United States. Three of the key creative personnel, who had been in the Communist Party (Kazan, Schulberg and Cobb), went before the House Un-American Activities Committee that was investigating communism in Hollywood and named others they knew to be party members. (Cobb testified before the Committee just the year before *On the Waterfront* was made.) Not only were they then able to continue working in the film industry while others were blacklisted as a result of their testimony but they then made a film about giving evidence to a crime commission in order to break a mob's grip on a community. Former Communist Party members who refused to 'name names' were, in the terms of this film, acting as if 'D and D' (deaf and dumb) in support of a corrupt organisation. Brando for one was not keen to work with Kazan because he had testified and was even less enthusiastic about the project when he realised he also had to work with Schulberg and Cobb.

The film itself provides the audience with a classic Hollywood-style narrative in which a downtrodden community gains the self-confidence to fight back as a result of the actions of one heroic character. In effect it is a Western played out in the New York docklands, or as Kazan called it an 'eastern'. Criticism of the upper echelons of society is paired down to the absolute minimum, effectively amounting to one cutaway shot to the home of a rich businessman within the courtroom scene as the central character, Terry Malloy (Brando), gives evidence against the union boss, Johnny Friendly (Cobb). The anonymous businessman's comments make his involvement in the corruption clear, and since he is essentially faceless it is implied that he represents a whole group or class. However, the focus of the film is not on the privileged capitalist elite but on the union as a brutal organisation that rules through terror. There is no real analysis of how extreme poverty and hardship has become a feature of the lives of those living in the docklands, although there is genuine sympathy for the community being portrayed expressed through the documentary realism employed.

For many the most striking thing about *On the Waterfront* is the performance of Brando[1] as the docker who journeys towards an understanding of the corruption with which he is surrounded and an awareness of the need to stand against it not only because it is morally right to do so but also in order to achieve some restored sense of self-worth. Kazan spoke of 'the contrast of the tough-guy front and the extreme delicacy and gentle cast of his behaviour' and of 'the depth of guilt as well as tenderness' he felt Brando managed to achieve in his performance (Bruccoli 1991: xxxi–xxxii). As far as Kazan was concerned, 'If there's a better performance by a man in the history of film in America, I don't know what it is'. The *New York Times* review from 1954 described Brando's presentation of Terry as 'a shatteringly poignant portrayal of an amoral, confused, illiterate citizen of the lower depths' (Rapf 2003: 153). A full investigation of Brando's performance would need to consider the body language (the walk and the gestures used, for example), the facial expressions (the movements of the eyes and direction of the gaze, for instance) and the delivery of lines (including crucially, pauses, mumblings and silences). When Edie confronts him with the simple notion of certain actions being right and others wrong because they either amount to treating others with decency or a lack of decency Terry's verbal response is simply: 'You're such a fruitcake'. However, Brando's facial and bodily response totally contradict the dismissive nature of these words, revealing the intense awkwardness he feels when in effect being confronted by his conscience. He shifts uneasily and looks down, anywhere but at Edie. He knows the harsh reality of the world of the docks doesn't naturally provide a space for Edie's humanity but equally he has a side to his character, exemplified by the gentleness with which he cares for his pigeons, that recognises what Edie says. Brando may not have got on with either of them but the performances of Lee Cobb (Johnny Friendly) and Rod Steiger (Charley) match his own. Cobb's speech, 'My mother brought us up on a stinking watchman's pension … ' jolts the viewer into a realisation of the depth of these characters; it is not just the character of Terry that has been formed by his experience of life. Steiger's facial expression of the turmoil of emotions he is experiencing as he finally decides to sacrifice himself for his brother is at least as good as anything Brando does and seems to have been given in defiance of Brando who had left him to complete the scene on his own. Maybe it was the tensions between the actors and between Brando and the director that brought out these performances, the determination to show the others what you could do.

According to Schulberg (!), Kazan described this as one of the best three scripts he had ever received; the other two being Arthur Miller's *Death of a Salesman* and Tennessee Williams's *A Streetcar Named Desire*. What is clear is that Schulberg had real empathy for the community he was attempting to portray. He describes time spent researching the material in the waterfront districts of New York, drinking in local bars listening to the stories that were told and sitting in the kitchen of the man who was showing him around writing down 'lines I could never make up' (Broccoli 1991: xi). As a result there is a documentary dimension that attaches to the writing; the script, to some extent at least, grows out of the everyday experiences and language use of longshoremen, their families and others living in the docklands community during the particular historical moment of the late 1940s and early 1950s.[2] Schulberg also points out that while they were in Hollywood attempting to get a studio to back the project Kazan was heavily involved in rewriting parts of the script. But a further contribution to the script also apparently came from the producer, Sam Spiegel, who forced rewrite after rewrite. 'He thought it was over length and sometimes discursive. Lots of times he was right.' says Schulberg (Bruccoli 1991: xvii).[3] The re-writes meant Kazan and the cast had an already tight script with which to work, the only remaining perhaps overly didactic section being Father Barry's speech in the ship's hold after the death of 'Kayo' Dougan. In an article from 1954, Schulberg said after initially becoming involved in trying to write a script based on dockland corruption, it was 'four years and at least eight full scripts later' before the film reached the screen (Rapf 2003: 151).

Further reinforcing the social realist style embodied in the documentary aspects of Schulberg's approach to the script was Kazan's decision to shoot on location in Hoboken, New Jersey during harsh, winter conditions of 1953–54. Although the famous 'I coulda been a contender' scene between Brando and Steiger playing Terry's brother Charley (the mob's lawyer) was a studio rig-up little else seems to have been. Schulberg says the film was made 'without a single set being built' (Rapf 2003: xvi) by using the piers, bars, rooftops and coldwater flats of the Hoboken district. The dialogue, derived from close observation of the community, and the location filming, work together to create a social realism somewhat at odds with Hollywood norms. If we consider any single location, however – outside of the church where the railings seem to pen Terry in and where the swing helps to connote the childlike aspect to his character, for example – it is clear that the selection of place has been a carefully considered aspect of film construction. Similarly with sound – if we move slightly beyond the environs of the church we see Terry and Edie in a scene played out on wasteland at the edge of the water where a siren is realistically but also symbolically able to tear through their conversation. The symbolism is on occasion too obvious – the pigeons that are clearly indicative of a softer side to Terry's nature are contrasted with the hawks who prey upon them, and the coat is passed as the mantle of truth from Edie's brother to 'Kayo' Dougan and eventually to Terry – but it also has an integral role to play in the construction of meaning.

At one level the film is as an investigation of human potential thwarted by social environment. Terry is consistently referred to as 'slow', but Edie recognises his potential. Asked by Terry how she would have got a better response from him at school Edie says through showing him kindness. And, of course, although the Golden Warriors gang strand of the narrative doesn't ring true in some places, the boys relate to Terry because he gives them time and attention. What Terry has (and we are constantly reminded of this) is a conscience. After Charley is killed, Terry to some extent becomes the traditional male hero, especially in leading the men back to work in the final scene; but unconventionally he defeats Johnny Friendly through the courts and is actually physically beaten at the end (although morally triumphant). As we see Terry rejecting his old way of life Edie's keynote lines become increasingly significant: 'Shouldn't everybody care about everybody else: isn't everybody a part of everybody else?'

Kazan had been a Communist for two years (1934–36) but testified before the Un-American Activities Committee in 1952. He continues to put forward socialist views in this film (although couched in strongly Christian terms) while attacking corruption amongst trade unions. Many scenes fleshing out the extent of that corruption were apparently cut as the script was honed to a tight essentially Hollywood structure.

> In truth, I had started with a broader canvas, wanting to tell not only Terry Malloy's personal story, but the waterfront priest's, and to set it all in social perspective. I wanted to define the pecking order, right up to the Mayor and the 'Mr Big' who owned him.
>
> (Schulberg in Rapf 2003: xvi)

When Father Barry is speaking in the hold of the ship after the murder of Dougan, if we take away the dog collar we have a straight didactic speech on socialism. Even those who are corrupt are shown to have their corruption founded upon the hardship of their upbringing (*Johnny Friendly*: My mother brought up ten of us on a stinking watchman's pension.). Terry needs the active agency of Edie (and to some extent Father Barry) to be 'saved' from his harsh experiences as a child and young man, but the film also shows honest, hard-working people like Edie's father defying all the odds to maintain their integrity.

Notes

1. Frank Sinatra was initially lined up for the part of Terry but was passed over when it became clear Brando could be brought on board (Schickel 1991: 88).
2. Schulberg based the idea for the screenplay on articles written by Malcolm Johnson for the New York *Sun*, in which he exposed the bribery, 'payoffs' and extortion that went on in the docks.
3. 'He did have an instinctive story sense; he knew it had to be unrelenting as it unfolded, and it should never let up tension and always aim for the end,' says Kazan (Bruccoli 1991: xxi).

Further reading

William Baer, *Elia Kazan: Interviews*, Jackson, Mississippi, University Press of Mississippi, 2000.

Leo Braudy, *On the Waterfront*, London, BFI, 2005.

Matthew J. Bruccoli (ed.), *On the Waterfront: Budd Schulberg*, London, Faber and Faber, 1991.

Elia Kazan, *Kazan on Kazan*, London, Faber and Faber, 2000.

Darwin Porter, *Brando Unzipped*, New York, Blood Moon Publications, 2005.

Joanna E. Rapf, *On the Waterfront*, Cambridge and New York, Cambridge University Press, 2003.

Richard Schickel, *Brando: A Life in Our Times*, London, Pavilion Books, 1991.

John White

Once Were Warriors (1994)

[Country: New Zealand. Production Company: Communicado Productions, New Zealand Film Commission, New Zealand On Air. Director: Lee Tamahori. Screenwriter: Riwia Brown (based on the novel by Alan Duff). Cinematographer: Stuart Dryburgh. Music: Murray Grindlay and Murray McNabb. Cast: Rena Owen (Beth Heke), Temuera Morrison (Jake Heke), Mamaengaroa Kerr-Bell (Grace), Julian Arahanga (Nig), Taungaroa Emileb (Boogie), Cliff Curtis (Bully), Pete Smith (Dooley), George Henare (Bennett), Mere Boynton (Mavis), Shannon Williams (Toot).]

Synopsis: Jake is an alpha male in a man's world who engages in domestic violence as easily as he does a pub brawl. By reconnecting with her Maori roots his wife, Beth, finds the strength to break out from the cycle of violence and take her children away from Jake, but not before their teenage daughter, Grace, has taken her own life after being raped by one of Jake's drinking mates.

In the British Museum in London there is a tall, glass display cabinet that is big enough to walk around and view from both sides. It is filled with artefacts, images and snippets of information, each of which give some additional, sometimes slight, sometimes larger, insight into Maori culture. It is not necessary to have seen this display before viewing *Once Were Warriors*, but, if you do, your appreciation of the film will have been altered in some way or other. But how much knowledge should a spectator expect to have to bring to a film like this that so clearly focuses on a minority culture about which most of us will have little understanding? How important is it, for example, that we should know that the family name, Heke, has a series of potential meanings that might in some way add to our understanding of the film?[1]

The ending suggests no matter who we are and where we are coming from, however much or little knowledge we have of Maori culture, there is only one way to interpret this film: this is the story of a woman in an abusive relationship who finds the strength to stand up to a violent man. Beth moves from domestic servitude (the first time we see her she is not only enclosed within wire-mesh fencing but also pushing a supermarket trolley) to the person who asserts as she leaves her husband, 'From now on I make the decisions for my family'.[2] But should we be more sympathetic, or at least empathetic, towards her husband, Jake. It is, after all, his story that highlights the plight of a certain proportion of Maori males.

There are more than half a million Maori living in New Zealand, more than 80 per cent in urban areas, and most in Auckland and the East Cape. They have become an urbanised minority group, detached from their tribal roots, alienated from mainstream culture and having low economic expectations. Beth accuses Jake of being a 'slave' to his fists, to alcohol, and to himself; and, indeed, a higher percentage of the Maori male population than the European male population is in prison, unemployed, drug and alcohol dependent, and/or involved in domestic and street violence. When Jake comes home at the start of the film he has just been made redundant. 'I got lucky: I got laid off', he says. 'I signed up for the dole – it's only 17 bucks less a week than my wages.' Toot is a very different character to Jake, a gentle, underage, homeless boy living in an old car, but again the height of his aspiration is to be able to sign on for the dole. (Of course, in the film he has the fairy-tale ending of becoming Beth's surrogate son, but that only happens in movies.) And, Jake has had an additional handicap: he comes from a long line of slaves.[3] The Maori culture that the film suggests 'saves' Beth and gives new meaning to life for her son, Boogie, according to Jake, views him as an 'old black-ass' and not good enough for Beth, who by contrast was 'the pride of the tribe'. What the film seems, ultimately, to suggest is something along the lines of 'once a slave, always a slave'; that Jake's slave blood will out in just the same way Beth's chieftain lineage will at some point assert itself.

Theorists from a cultural studies background employ a few key concepts when theorising about texts. First, they suggest texts such as films are part of a complex process of hegemony by which the dominant class gains the consent of everyone else for things to remain as they are in society. Second, they suggest some readers can reject what is on offer as the preferred reading embedded in a text and instead come up with a negotiated reading, or even an oppositional reading. Third, they suggest the meaning of any text is never simple or singular but that every text is polysemic, or open to a range of interpretations. So, what exactly would be the preferred meaning of this text (that is, not necessarily the consciously intended meaning of the author but the meaning in keeping with the current status quo in this society)? In addition to the idea of 'you are what is in your blood', would it be that things are changing for Maoris, that men like Jake are being consigned to the past, that women within the Maori community are taking charge of their destiny, that young Maori men like Boogie are reconnecting with their ethnic past, that concepts such as whanau (the extended family) and mana (pride and dignity) are being rediscovered, and that there is, therefore, no need to campaign for further change because the system as it stands, the status quo, is already dealing with the problems? Certainly, it could be argued,

Maori land claims have been taken more seriously in the past 30 years, the Maori presence in Parliament has increased, and the importance of rediscovering the Maori language has been accepted. But maybe we would want to negotiate our relationship with the text more carefully. Perhaps, we would wish to accept some elements, such as the importance of the role of women, while rejecting others, such as the concept that a slave past determines the nature of a Maori male's present. Or, perhaps, we would wish to produce an oppositional reading, to reject this text entirely, seeing it as attempting to lay the blame for social ills with the individual rather than social institutions.[4]

Because texts are open to a range of interpretations there are still many further possibilities for what readers may get from watching *Once Were Warriors*. Reception studies often reveal that the viewers of films can take away interpretations theorists might not have immediately thought possible. Jake is shown violently beating his wife and brutally raping her. Later, he stands over his daughter snarling in anger in a posture that echoes the low-angle shot of the dogs to which we cut as he rapes Beth. All of his strength is defeated as he attacks with an axe the tree from which Grace hung herself;[5] and he becomes a small figure in the frame as Beth rings her family and says she wants to bring Grace 'home' for the funeral, and is similarly diminutive (with his voice correspondingly weak) as Beth walks away from him to a new life. Yet, despite all of this, I suspect, some readers will take away most strongly an image of Jake's 'cool' violence, an endorsement of macho values.

Because we can only make vast generalisations about the divisions within an audience for any film, we can never account for all of the available interpretations. What we can say is that any interpretation will exist in relation to the composite background of the person who brings it into being. The national audience[6] for this film might be thought to divide most strongly between those of European/British ethnicity and those from a Maori background; yet, clearly, there is not *a* white interpretation and *a* Maori interpretation. Worryingly, identifying such a division in the first place in the audience would seem to accept some implied concept of ethnic purity. And even if we do establish such broad ethnic origins for our audience, how will this affect any individual viewer's attitude to the film? If, like Beth, you are Maori and are able to trace your ancestry back through tribal chiefs, that is one thing; but what if, like Jake, you know you come from that 'long line of slaves'? Perhaps, the issue of interpretation should be seen to revolve around cultural identification on the part of the individual rather than actual ancestral lineage. And yet, the very essence of the difficulty for urban Maoris has been seen to be a lack of any solid cultural identification; hence, Nig's efforts to achieve a 'patch', find a new 'family', and attain (sub-)cultural identity.

The reality of the Maori experience, that *Once Were Warriors* because it is a film is able to transcend with its fantasy ending, is the death of Grace. As things stand there is no escape, nothing can come of Grace's fantasising, like Ophelia in Shakespeare's *Hamlet* she has to die. As Nig tells her: 'You'll have plenty of time to clear up after drunken parties when you get married ... It's just the way things are ... It's just a matter of time.'

Notes

1. (1) Hone Heke was a chief of the Ngapuhi who famously defiantly chopped down the flagpole flying the Union Jack at Kororareka four times in the mid-1840s. (2) The heke (or rafters) in the whare (or Maori house) are not only seen as the ribs of the body of the house which is literally seen to be a living being, but also as the representation of the lines of descent from the ancestors. (3) Heke can also mean a migration or journey (and may recall a heke such as that the Ngati Toa chief, Te Rauparaha, took his tribe on in the early 1820s).
2. Female Maori artists have in recent years been keen to depict the strength of women in their work, identifying with a concept of mana wahine, or women's dignity.
3. Maori culture is built around three social groupings (the iwi, or tribe; the hapu, or sub-tribe; and the whanau, or extended family) and three classes (the chieftain class, commoners and slaves).
4. This reading would suggest not only that the film sees Jake as the problem rather than poverty and unemployment, but also that all it

takes for a solution to be found is for Beth to change – that is, that once again the problem is the individual rather than anything else. (Clearly, in one sense seeing an abused woman stand up and embody mana, taking it into herself as her son draws it down into himself while performing his haka, is empowering, but in another it is very Hollywood-like in its unrealistic creation of a fairy-tale resolution.)

5. Unlike Hone Heke (see note 1), Jake is unable to chop down the 'flagpole' (like a flagpole, the tree is bare and seemingly unable to bring forth life) from which the metaphorical flag of colonialism has hung. Like the Maori people (and Hone Heke, because the flagpole he attacked was simply put up again and more heavily defended every time he chopped it down), Jake has been defeated by colonialism.
6. The potentially vast international audience would encompass viewers from all sorts of backgrounds and dispositions who for all sorts of reasons might identify with an array of different facets of the film. Beth's experience of domestic violence, or Jake's slave background, might echo aspects of a viewer's own past or might be things about which the viewer would have only second-hand knowledge.

Further reading

Emiel Martens, *Once Were Warriors: the Aftermath – the Controversy of OWW in Aotearoa, New Zealand*, Amsterdam, Aksant Academic Publishers, 2007.

Jane Smith, 'Knocked around in New Zealand: Postcolonialism Goes to the Movies' in Christopher Sharrett (ed.), *Mythologies of Violence in Postmodern Media*, Detroit, MI, Wayne State University Press, 1999, pp. 381–96.

John White

Onna ga kaidan o agaru toku/When a Woman Ascends the Stairs (1960)

[Country: Japan. Production Company: Toho Company. Director: Mikio Naruse. Screenwriter: Ryūzō Kikushima, Cinematographer: Masao Tamai. Music: Toshiro Mayuzumi. Cast: Hideko Takamine (Keiko Yahiro), Masayuki Mori (Nobuhiko Fujjasaki), Reiko Dan (Junko Inchihashi), Tatsuya Nakadai (Kenichi Komatsu), Ganjirō Nakamura (Goda), Daisuke Katō (Matsukichi Sekine), Eitarō Ozawa (Minobe), Keiko Awaji (Yuri).]

Synopsis: *When a Woman Ascends the Stairs* is a careful character study of Keiko, a widowed bar hostess in Tokyo's fashionable Ginza neighbourhood. At age 30, Keiko faces three life choices: to remarry before her society regards her as too old to do so, to become a kept woman of a wealthy business owner, or to open her own bar, for which she will need financial assistance from men. She realises the dangers of all three options and fears losing her independence and dignity.

When a Woman Ascends the Stairs is a poignant portrait of Keiko, a widowed 30-year-old bar hostess whom everyone respectfully calls 'Mama', as she works in Tokyo's Ginza, the entertainment district associated with high fashion and luxury. Played by the glamorous Takamine Hideko (1924–2010), Keiko is older and wiser than her peers and is most desired by male customers. In her adherence to dignity above all, Keiko contrasts with the characters around her, including her former rival Yuri who commits suicide, the young hostess Junko who tries to turn difficulties of the job to her advantage, her male manager Komatsu who is in love with her but exploits other women, and her mother and brother in the countryside who scorn her profession yet need her financial support. Keiko suffers from debts, customers' demands, stress ulcers, internal dilemmas, and betrayals by the people she had trusted, all of which she expresses to the film audience through voiceovers. Although dark, this elegant film is an enlightening view into the lives of bar hostesses, who rarely wrote or filmed their own stories, and the poverty behind Ginza's opulent image. Director Naruse Mikio (1905–1969), famous for his pessimism toward human nature and Tokyo society, uses an all-star cast, elaborate stage sets, and simple camerawork to offer a parable of survival.

Naruse, who produced around 89 films in his career that spanned 1930 to 1967, has been praised for his empathetic portrayals of the daily lives of working women from the lower middle classes. Naruse's films feature female protagonists who are more honourable and determined than their peers and family members, with whom they often fight, and are constricted by their economic situations, domestic responsibilities, and by their inabilities to advance in the larger patriarchal society around them. Keiko is a prime example of how Naruse's women strive to improve their lives by taking the initiative in their families or in the service industries where they work, while realising they are most likely doomed to fail. As Naruse said of his characters, 'If they move even a little, they quickly hit the wall'.[1] Film critic Donald Richie observed, 'Tragedy is constantly hanging over Naruse's characters, and they are never more vulnerable than when they for once decide upon a personal choice of action'.[2] Naruse often cast Hideko Takamine as his female lead, especially after he divorced actress Chiba Sachiko who had starred in his *Wife! Be Like a Rose* (*Tsuma yo bara no yo ni*, 1935). The collaboration between Naruse and Takamine began with *Hideko the Bus Conductress* (*Hideko no shashō-san*, 1941), which he had named after her. Takamine designed the costumes for *When a Woman Ascends the Stairs*. Naruse adapted literature, including Nobel Laureate Kawabata Yasunari's novel *Sound of the Mountain* (*Yama no oto*, 1954) and six stories by Hayashi Fumiko, known for her depictions of women who persevere in the face of hardship, including *Lightning* (*Inazuma*, 1952), *Late Chrysanthemum* (*Bangiku*, 1954), and *Floating Clouds* (*Ukigumo*, 1955).[3] *When a Woman Ascends the* Stairs, however, is based on an original script by Kikushima Ryūzō who also wrote for Kurosawa Akira.

Naruse uses Ginza, Tokyo's most affluent commercial district, to convey the importance of money, a theme of the film. Ginza was constructed as a showpiece of Japanese urban modernisation in the late nineteenth century and became known for lavish cafés, bars, and department stores in the 1920s. The 1950s Ginza was the site of expensive hostess bars, where women served and flirted with men as café waitresses had in the 1920s. Scenes of Ginza streets frame the beginning and end of *When a Woman Ascends the Stairs*. In her opening voiceover, Keiko explains that Ginza bars during the day are like 'women without makeup', indicating to the film audience that she will reveal what these places of labour are truly like beneath their veneer. Naruse set most scenes inside bars and other spaces considered modern at the time, including high-rent Western-style apartments where most people could not afford to live. The jazzy xylophone film score by Mayuzumi Toshiro furthers this stylish atmosphere, inspired by American fashions. The destruction of Tokyo during the Second World War and its recovery and growth after is alluded to in other ways. Ginza hostesses joke about foreigners (implied Americans) who kiss and drink cocktails mixed with juice. Bars are stocked with supplies obtained from middlemen who go to the black markets, although not directly referred to as such. Strategically placed daytime scenes of Keiko's hometown in an outlying province and of Tokyo suburban streets where children play form visual contrasts to Ginza.

Through voiceovers and conversations with other characters, Keiko explains the business of running a bar in Ginza and aspects of her job that the film audience presumably does not know. Bar hostesses differ from geisha, who were paid entertainers trained in classical Japanese arts, and from the various kinds of sex workers in immediate post-war Tokyo. Although Keiko is visually distinguished from the other bar hostesses by wearing kimono instead of dresses and by plainly tying her hair, she does not symbolise a woman of a past era. Instead, she is grounded in the circumstances of 1950s

Tokyo. Keiko represents the large number of women who came to Tokyo from the countryside seeking employment in the rapidly developing city – part of the 'urban poor', as the bar hostesses remark. Hostesses know that the ability to handle men is the key to their survival. Keiko finds ways to subtly refuse the advances of the men she serves, but she is not immune to falling in love with them. In a voiceover, she comments that Ginza's 16,000 hostesses head home between 11:30 pm and 1:00 am, the best leaving by taxi, the middle tier by train, and the worst going home with their customers. Keiko explains that if hostesses did not wear expensive clothing and perfume, take taxies, and live in apartments, male customers would lose interest in them. She is shown performing degrading tasks, such as visiting her customers' offices to try to collect the money to pay their tabs. During a fight with her mother, Keiko most ardently states her disgust with her lifestyle of drinking too much, being the plaything of men, and going into debt in order to maintain a fashionable appearance in Tokyo and send an allowance to her family. In reality, there would have been other choices, albeit few, for a woman like Keiko. Most female office workers quit while in their twenties or after they had married, and factory labour was arduous and with low pay. Keiko's family did not own a farm or business. The film implies that Keiko and her peers chose to be hostesses because of the glamorous image and potential for higher salaries than other occupations. None of the hostesses in the film quits and finds a different profession; instead the hostesses reiterate their goal of opening their own bars. Keiko does not want to return to the tedium of countryside life and enjoys living apart from her mother and brother and the financial problems they face.

The wealthy men who frequent the bars where Keiko works represent jobs profitable and powerful at the time, especially owners of the large factories that were propelling Japan's economy premised on manufacturing. Most are middle-aged and married. The theme of married men chasing other women is present in other Naruse films, including *Wife! Be Like a Rose* about a man with two wives. Arguably, the trio of main male characters who pursue Keiko represent her three general choices: the manager who is in love with her and would like to marry her, Sekine who proposes marriage but has a wife, Fujisawa who offers money to help her establish her own bar.

A very short sequence of Keiko's lower legs, clad in kimono, and feet in elegant *geta* sandals ascending the stairs to the bars where she works is used as a visual motif and plot device and is accompanied by Keiko's voiceovers. In the beginning of the film, Keiko tells the film audience that climbing these stairs is what she hates most in life, but once she had ascended them, she 'took everyday as it came'. As she left one bar to work in another, the staircase changed. Importantly, Keiko is only shown ascending and not descending stairs. Her struggle to elevate her financial position and find a sense of security is an upward climb; the steps symbolise the series of disappointments, disillusionments, and bad decisions she endures. Yet she does not submit to any kind of downfall. In the beginning of the film, this sequence is followed by a close-up of Keiko's face as she feigns a smile at her male customers, which fades after they leave. In general, Naruse shows his characters in continual motion, walking Tokyo streets, riding in buses and cars, and working while on their feet. This action can be read allegorically as their quest for social and economic mobility.

When a Woman Ascends the Stairs does not idealise the bar hostess, moralise about her, or provide her with a sense of redemption. The final image of Ginza is associated with strength and perseverance but not with hope. Naruse provides his female characters with more agency to determine their life courses than his contemporary Mizoguchi Kenji (1898–1956) did in his films of women who had fallen into compromising positions, such as his 1936 *Osaka Elegy* (*Naniwa ereji*) and 1956 *Street of Shame* (*Akasen chitai*) set in a Tokyo brothel. A more optimistic portrait of hostesses is presented in author Ariyoshi Sawako's 1961 'The Tomoshibi', a charming story about women who find confidence through the positive atmosphere at the Ginza bar where they work. As remarked by film critic Phillip Lopate, 'One of the charms of Naruse's art is its earned pessimism. It takes for granted that life is unhappy; therefore, we can relax in the possession of sadness, acquiesce from the start to a fated disenchantment, the only suspense being how he will bring it about this time'.[4] *When a Woman Ascends the*

Stairs was adapted into a six-episode television drama, starring Ogawa Mayumi, which aired on the Nihon Terebi commercial network from January 5 to February 9, 1970.

Notes

1. Lopate, *When a Woman Ascends the Stairs*.
2. Richie, *One Hundred Years of Japanese Film*, p. 127.
3. See Russell, 'From Women's Writing to Women's Films in 1950s Japan'.
4. Lopate, 'A Taste for Naruse', p. 12.

Further reading

Sawako Ariyoshi, 'The Tomoshibi', trans. Keiko Nakamura, in Makoto Ueda (ed.), *The Mother of Dreams and Other Stories: Portraits of Women in Modern Japanese Fiction*, Tokyo, Kodansha International, 1986, pp. 240–57.

Phillip Lopate, 'A Taste for Naruse', *Film Quarterly*, Vol. 34, No. 4, 1986, pp. 11–21.

Phillip Lopate, *When a Woman Ascends the Stairs: They Endure*, The Criterion Collection, February 19, 2007. Available at www.criterion.com/current/posts/471-when-a-woman-ascendsthe-stairs-they-endure (accessed 27 August 2012).

Donald Richie, *One Hundred Years Of Japanese Film*, Tokyo, Kodansha International, 2001.

Catherine Russell, Catherine, 'From Women's Writing to Women's Films in 1950s Japan: Hayashi Fumiko and Naruse Mikio', *Asian Journal of Communication*, Vol. 11, No. 2, 2009, pp. 101–20.

Alisa Freedman

Ossessione/Obsession (1942)

[Country: Italy. Production Company: Industrie Cinematografiche Italiane. Producer: Libero Solaroli. Director: Luchino Visconti. Screenwriters: Mario Alicata, Gianni Puccini, Giuseppe De Santis, Luchino Visconti. Cinematographers: Aldo Tonti, Domenico Scala. Editor: Mario Serandrei. Cast: Clara Calamai (Giovanna); Massimo Girotti (Gino); Juan de Landa (Bragana); Elio Marcuzzo (Lo Spagnuolo/The Spaniard).]

Synopsis: Set in the Po Delta, *Ossessione* tells the doomed love story of a handsome vagabond and a frustrated wife. When Gino stops in Bragana's roadside gas-station restaurant for a meal, he meets the owner's young spouse, Giovanna. Inescapably attracted to each other, they soon begin a passionate affair, and eventually Gino agrees to help Giovanna kill Bragana in a staged car accident. After the murder, distrust and resentment grow between guilt-stricken Gino and his lover, but when she tells him of her pregnancy, they reconcile and decide to start life together afresh. However, as they drive away, eager to evade arrest, their truck skids off the road. Giovanna dies instantly and Gino is apprehended.

Luchino Visconti's directorial debut *Ossessione* stands as an aesthetic and thematic watershed in the history of Italian cinema. Made during the Second World War in 1942, the last year of Benito Mussolini's Fascist government, the film broke with the traditional canons of the entertaining and spectacular cinema of the regime, based on a sanitised version of reality, studio artifice, plot contrivance, and the pompous nationalistic rhetoric of Fascism. Mira Liehm has observed that while only a minority of the films made during Mussolini's regime promoted Fascism openly, most productions were sentimental comedies and romantic melodramas – known as 'white telephone films' (in reference to the iconography of American high-society comedies) – that were intended to have little in common with everyday life (1984: 21). At a time when Italian cinema was focusing on tales of the rich and beautiful, *Ossessione* brought to the screen an image of provincial Italy never shown before.

Centred on the gritty daily lives of those at the margins of society, *Ossessione* anticipated some of the themes and styles that were to become characteristic of Italian Neorealism – the distinctive and influential approach to fictional filmmaking that would blossom in post-Second World War Italy – in its use of professional and non-professional actors, its preference for location filming, its attention to incidental characters and small details of places and people, its empathy for the disenfranchised and its strong emphasis on the link between narrative, characters and landscape. Visconti's cinematic style was first significantly influenced by Jean Renoir, who Visconti credited with helping him not only develop his interest in cinema, but also raise his political consciousness as he got close to the Popular Front (Tonetti 1983: 20–1). In 1940 Visconti assisted Renoir with a film version of Giacomo Puccini's opera *La Tosca*. The collaboration introduced Visconti to the Italian film world and, in particular, to a group of anti-fascist critics and filmmakers who gathered around the journal *Cinema*. The editors of *Cinema*, who loved American fiction and held in high esteem the works of the French Popular Front, Soviet directors and the Sicilian late nineteenth-century *veristic* writer Giovanni Verga, argued that Italian films should be inspired by *verism*, a literary movement that emphasised the importance of depicting objectively the lives of the disenfranchised and that had a profound impact on Italian culture, fostering a new interest in realism among filmmakers (Bacon 1998: 9–13). Arguably 'the boldest representation of the realistic trend' in the early 1940s (Thompson and Bordwell 2003: 280) was *Ossessione*, the result of Visconti's collaboration with *Cinema* contributors Giuseppe De Santis, Mario Alicata and Gianni Puccini.

Ossessione has been widely credited as a major precursor of Neorealist filmmaking, although it neither denounced the horror of the Second World War nor celebrated the heroism of the Resistance fighters during the Nazi occupation of Italy. Nor did it deal with themes central to Italian post-war reconstruction such as unemployment, shortage of housing, and social strife, which are among the thematic concerns traditionally associated with Italian Neorealism. One of the features of *Ossessione* that has contributed to its characterisation as a forerunner of a new filmic style (or even as the first manifestation of a new filmic style) is its attention to incidental characters and incidental details of places and people. An example comes immediately after the opening credits have rolled in a scene shot on location, as two truck drivers, played by non-professional actors, arrive at Bragana's roadside service station to fill up their lorry. While their role in the plot is simply to get the story started (unbeknownst to them, Gino has travelled on the back of the truck), their clothes, faces and gestures as they get off the vehicle, take a quick swig of water from a *fiasco* and then wipe the sweat from their faces, all function to give a sense of 'real people' in a 'real place'. Furthermore, as the camera follows one of the drivers as he crosses the road, calling Bragana's name to attract his attention, we can see in the background another incidental detail – a man riding his bicycle. In his work on Visconti Henry Bacon has suggested that the director 'took as his starting point the ability of the film to create an illusion of a fictional world' but also emphasised narrative structure and verisimilitude in acting and mise en scène to make a 'statement about reality' (1998: 13).

This approach is evident for instance in the scene that introduces Gino as he enters the restaurant. He briefly stops on the doorstep, and as he puts his hand in his pocket to check how much money he has got, we are offered a glimpse of his quite ragged clothes. The interior of the restaurant is meticulously detailed, offering further elements of social realism, from the elderly punters sitting at a table playing a hand game to the hunter standing by the piano and the dogs sniffing Gino's sockless feet and worn-out shoes. Throughout the film, incidental actions carried out in the background of the dramatic action – people riding bicycles, a hotel guest brushing her hair by a window – are common. Meanwhile, the film carefully avoids any picturesque use of the landscape. Rather, as would become typical of Neorealist films, in *Ossessione* 'landscapes are not a simple backdrop … they are used to embody meanings, orchestrate formal themes, demonstrate or refer by analogy to other spheres of reality,' (Sorlin 1996: 94). This is, for instance, exemplified by the juxtaposition of the dark and claustrophobic interiors of the restaurant and of Bragana's home with the scenes shot on location in Ancona. While the former act as a metaphor for Giovanna's suffocating situation and, later, Gino's guilt and sense of entrapment after the murder, the latter, by emphasising the size of the city and the fact that it is a seaport, function to powerfully associate Gino and Lo Spagnuolo with an idea of existential freedom, as in the scene where the two characters sit contently on the wall of the Piazzale of San Ciriaco smoking cigarettes, their legs swinging as they take in the view of the Adriatic sea in front of them.

Ossessione's social realism offered an unflattering portrait of everyday life in Fascist Italy that was in stark opposition to the regime's optimistic social self-image. Set against a backdrop of rundown bars, dirty buildings and potholed roads, *Ossessione* challenged ideological aspects typical of the established social order of the time, from the sanctity of marriage and family values, to oppressive social conformity, and in particular the enforced claustrophobia of domesticity, to money as a determining factor in human relationships. As Marcia Landy has argued, 'the film dissects the social and sexual relations that underpin idealised fantasies of heterosexual romance leading to marriage, probing the craving for financial security and social conformity that are identified with violence and loss of freedom' (2000: 214). Both Gino and Giovanna are socially marginal characters. To escape a life of prostitution after losing her job as a seasonal worker, Giovanna has married an older man she cannot bear. Her longing for 'respectability' and financial security has come at a huge cost, as she is now trapped in a loveless, mediocre life, slaving in the kitchen and waiting on her vile and tyrannical husband hand and foot. The fortuitous encounter with young and virile Gino seems to offer her passion and liberation. For his part, Gino is a drifter with no stable occupation who does not care for financial security and does not want to 'settle down'. The way out Gino offers, to a life of wandering from place to place, is too financially uncertain for Giovanna to accept. She cannot renounce financial security but wants out nonetheless – on her own terms. Her plan is to replace Bragana with Gino and invest the life insurance money in expanding the family business and improving their lifestyle. But the comfortable life she is desperate to enjoy with her lover no matter the cost only makes Gino feel like a caged animal. And yet, while the young Gino despises the petty bourgeois values Giovanna is enslaved to, he is unable to curb his passion and relinquish the woman who has become his obsession.

In that it attacked established social conventions, and in particular the morality and sanctity of marriage, procreation and family life, values strongly upheld by the Fascist government, *Ossessione* is certainly a film critical of Fascism. As such, although it never made overt reference to politics or the war, it has been credited as an anti-fascist film, particularly because of the character of Lo Spagnuolo (The Spaniard). A young man who travels from town to town, performing, and who Gino encounters during his wanderings, Lo Spagnuolo has no counterpart in Cain's novel. Created by the writers of *Ossessione*, he was originally conceived as 'a proletariat who returned to Italy, becoming a vagabond in order to disseminate propagandistic ideas about socialism, antifascism, and communism' (Van Watson 2002: 188), although, in order to pass censorship, the writers made sure to avoid any direct references to a socialist alternative to Fascism. According to Liehm, Lo Spagnuolo is the embodiment 'of a state of mind and attitudes towards human problems carrying in themselves the possibility of antifascism' (1984: 55). Indeed, as he offers Gino his companionship as an alternative to the destructive attraction he feels for Giovanna, Lo Spagnuolo prompts Gino to break free from oppressive social and sexual conventions, encouraging in him an urge for freedom. It is significant that Lo Spagnuolo's association with nonconformity and a freer life do not translate into selfish individualism. When we are first introduced to him, his sense of comradeship is apparent in his claim that 'we need to help one another' (he offers to pay penniless Gino's train fare). Later, his anticapitalist views can be read between the lines of a speech imbued with a sense of humanitarian socialism, as he tells Gino that money should be redistributed: 'You see Gino, money has legs and should always be on the move … if it stays in the pockets it gets mouldy. You take a bite and then you pass it on to someone else who also can live.'

A powerful tale of the destructive power of obsessive passions, *Ossessione* challenged the regime's ideas of artistic, moral and social propriety as it narrated in realistic terms the immorality and squalor of everyday life in provincial Italy in the last months of the Fascist government. In so doing, *Ossessione*'s realism came as an aesthetic and intellectual revelation that marked the end of an era and the beginning of a new one in the history of Italian cinema.

Further reading

Henry Bacon, *Visconti: Explorations of Beauty and Decay*, Cambridge, Cambridge University Press, 1998.
Peter Bondanella, *Italian Cinema from Neorealism to the Present*, New York and London, Continuum, 2004.
Marcia Landy, *Fascism in Film: The Italian Commercial Cinema, 1931–1943*, Princeton, New Jersey, Princeton University Press, 1986.
Marcia Landy, *Italian Film*, Cambridge, Cambridge University Press, 2000.
Mira Liehm, *Passion and Defiance: Film in Italy from 1942 to the Present*, Berkeley, Los Angeles, and London, University of California Press, 1984.
Geoffrey Nowell-Smith, *Luchino Visconti*, London, British Film Institute, 2003.
Pierre Sorlin, *Italian National Cinema 1896–1996*, London and New York, Routledge, 1996.
Kristin Thompson and David Bordwell, *Film History: An Introduction*, New York, McGraw-Hill, 2003.
Claretta Micheletti Tonetti, *Luchino Visconti*, Boston, Twayne Publishers, 1983.
William Van Watson, 'Luchino Visconti's (Homosexual) *Ossessione*', in Jacqueline Reich and Piero Garofalo (eds), *Re-viewing Fascism: Italian Cinema 1922–1943*, Bloomington and Indianapolis, Indiana University Press, 2002, pp. 172–93.

Antonella Palmieri

Ostře sledované vlaky/Closely Observed Trains (1966)

[Country: Czechoslovakia. Production Company: Filmové studio Barrandov. Director: Jiří Menzel. Production Manager: Jaroslav Wagner. Story: Bohumil Hrabal. Screenwriters: Jiří Menzel and Bohumil Hrabal. Cinematographer: Jaromír Šofr. Music: Jiří Sust. Editor: Jiřina Lukešova. Sound: Jiří Pavlik. Cast: Václav Neckář (Miloš Hrma), Jitka Bendová (Maša), Vladimír Valenta (Stationmaster), Josef Somr (Hubička), Jitka Zelenhorská (Zdenička Svatá), Nada Urbánková (Viktoria Freie), Květa Fialová (The Countess), Vlastimil Brodsk (Zedníček).]

Synopsis: Miloš Hrma, the youngest in a long line of layabouts, starts his first job as a trainee signalman at Kostomlaty train station a few kilometres outside of Prague during the Nazi occupation of Czechoslovakia in the early 1940s. The isolated station is headed by an inept and frustrated stationmaster who is more interested in caring for his doves and the station is actually overseen by the lecherous but good natured Hubička who takes Miloš's education, both rail-related and sexual, in hand. While Miloš and Maša, a train conductor, flirt with each other, Hubička seduces the station telegraphist and stamps her thighs and behind with indelible 'Pelican company' ink. Miloš is unable to consummate his first night alone with Maša and checks into a hotel where he slits his wrists in the bath but survives. Back at the station, a German munitions train is to come through and Hubička is asked by the resistance to bomb it as it passes. The agent (code-named Viktoria Freie) who gives them the bomb also successfully initiates Miloš into sexual life. Hubička is unable to bomb the train as his stamp-related disciplinary hearing is called for the same time and Miloš decides to act instead. Full of confidence he arranges another meeting with Maša before dropping the bomb on the passing train. He is, however, shot by a soldier on the train, falls onto one of the carriages and is blown up along with the train.

Jiří Menzel, like so many Czech film directors, studied at FAMU, the Prague Film School (Akademie múzickch umění Filmová a televizni fakulta). He first worked on Věra Chytilová's student film *The Ceiling* (*Strop*, 1962) as both assistant director and actor. Menzel's subsequent films are exclusively adaptations of literary sources, most significantly the stories and novels of the avant-garde writer, Bohumil Hrabal (1914–1997). After a few student experiments, his first film, *The Death of Mr Balthazar* (*Smrt pana Baltaraza*, 1965), was part of an anthology film made with his fellow students based on stories by Hrabal, while his second, included in the portmanteau film *Crime in the Girls School* (*Zločin v dívčí škole*, 1965), is based on the detective stories of Josef Škvoreck who would himself go on to write the first history of the Czech New Wave while in exile in Canada in the early 1970s. In 1966, in collaboration with Hrabal, Menzel wrote the screenplay and directed *Closely Observed Trains* (*Ostře sledované vlaky*) which won the Academy Award for Best Foreign Film in that year. These films are all marked by a gentle, absurdist humour with an emphasis on human frailty and desire. It is perhaps no surprise that Menzel cites Jean Renoir's sensual *Partie de campagne* (1936) as his most formative film.

Closely Observed Trains is a *bildungsroman* and takes as its central development the movement from childhood to adulthood (see Čulik 2012: 35). This is mapped onto a theme of innocence and experience. However, Miloš's progress from self-absorption to an understanding of the importance of community and his own place within that society does not necessarily imply a loss of innocence since experience in the film does not result in a cynical abjuration of integrity. Miloš's predecessors had chosen to withdraw from everyday toil and indulge in fanciful pursuits. His father had retired at 48 since, as an engine driver, he was able to accrue double-time while working, while his grandfather Vilem performed as a hypnotist and had attempted to stop invading German tanks by standing in their way and using the power of his mind alone. His quixotic gesture however only resulted in his decapitation. There is therefore a clear link, as Čulik argues, between 'reaching adulthood and death' (2012: 35). The risk of taking action at all, necessarily involves the risk of annihilation and Hrabal 'presents an insoluble dilemma' (Čulik 2012: 36) which Menzel attempts to solve through humour.

Miloš describes his family background in a deadpan voice-over at the beginning of the film as he prepares for his first day of work as a trainee signalman at Kostomlaty station (the film was actually shot at Loděnice about the same distance from Prague but to the west). He says that the 'whole town knows that I went on the course because I don't want to do anything but stand on a platform with a signal disc and avoid any hard work, while others work and work and work'. It is important that Miloš here does not describe himself directly in this way, but rather presents himself as seen through the eyes of others. At the beginning, Miloš has no individual agency even from his own perspective and the film charts his shift from this initial passivity to action. His family background, however, demonstrates only either withdrawal or spectacularly ill-judged and ill-fated intervention.

The station at Kostomlaty is also staffed by characters who have withdrawn from life in general. The stationmaster is more interested in looking after his livestock than in overseeing the station, but even his animal husbandry is rather useless as he cannot even bring himself to kill one of his rabbits and this task is given over to his wife. Women in this world are more able to act than men and often take the lead, especially in sexual situations. Hubička, the de facto station supervisor, devotes most of his energies to seducing various female employees but is also active in the resistance.[1] Thus, his sexual prowess is linked to an ability to take action both on the stationmaster's couch and in the moral universe of history. Ironically, of course, Hubička's sexual proclivities deny him the opportunity to bomb the German train himself. Paradoxically, that which marks him as a person of action (his sexual experience) allows him to engage in the world at large but is also that which prevents him from doing so. Once again, Hrabal and Menzel present an insoluble dilemma. It is Miloš who provides the answer to this particular logical knot.

Miloš is an introverted character who seems to have no inner life of his own and, as Girelli points out, the world of *Closely Observed Trains* is one where there is very little space for privacy and every action is observed in one way or another. She writes that the film,

> is virtually all set in public spaces: the protagonists' lives unfold in a situation of almost constant exposure, as even the rare scenes set in private homes see them being policed by intrusive parents or relatives. Miloš's suicide attempt takes place in a brothel, and his rescue is due to a workman who, having made a hole through the wall, is able to check what is happening in the room where Miloš has just cut his wrists.
>
> (2011: 55)

Miloš's suicide attempt comes after his failed attempt at sexual intercourse with Maša in the back room of her lecherous uncle's photography studio. At the hospital the kindly Dr Brabec (played by Menzel himself) explains his dysfunction with a clinical diagnosis of *ejaculatio praecox,* premature ejaculation, but Miloš describes the problem elsewhere as him becoming 'as limp as a lily' or, as he explains unselfconsciously to the stationmaster's wife, 'Look, I am a man, but when I try to prove it that I am a man, then I no longer am'. The wife listens expressionlessly as she vigorously massages a goose's phallic neck. Miloš adds, 'At this moment, I am a man'. The problem, then, is not one of acting too quickly but of not being able to act at all. When it comes to the crucial moment, Miloš is impotent. There are however three moments at which Miloš does act.

The first of these is the suicide itself. The scene is short but extremely brutal and very out of character with the style of the rest of the film which adds to its impact. Menzel recalls being admonished by Jiří Weiss, a respected film director, that he should not film scenes that will make more noble members of the audience faint. After his failed seduction, Miloš checks into the hourly rate hotel, runs a bath and, after he gets in, prepares two straight razors. One he fixes, blade upright, in a crack in a wooden bathroom table and slits his left wrist with the other. He then brings down his right wrist onto the waiting blade with a loud bang. While both these actions happen off-screen their impact is visceral and it is Miloš's careful, ritualistic and unemotional preparation and execution which precludes any sentimental pathos. The character has no complicated internal psychology: Miloš merely wishes to die. It is this pure act, thwarted by an external rather than internal agent that precipitates his transformation into an adult in the world.

His second act is his sexual encounter with the resistance agent, Vikoria Freie, following which we see him in exactly the same post-coital presentation as Hubička earlier in the film, a medium shot from behind stretching and whistling on the station platform. It is this newfound confidence and structural position that enables Miloš to take the bombing of the German munitions train into his own hands while Hubička is detained by his misconduct hearing. Miloš is now fully able to take action and while making his way to the position from which he will drop the bomb he also makes a date with Maša. However, of course, he is killed in the course of the bombing; but the film ends, not with his death as such, but with the laughter of the station employees as they are buffeted by the wind of the explosion. Menzel had in fact shot an alternative ending in which Miloš improbably survived the detonation and is seen hanging in the branches of a tree. He chose not to use this cartoonish ending, relying on the celebration of his act of resistance to provide an upbeat conclusion to the dilemma of participation. The argument of *Closely Observed Trains* may be summarised as: one may die if one acts, but if one does not act then there can never be true joy.

Notes

1. Jonathan Owen has criticised Menzel's presentation of women in this film and in his other Hrabal adaptations for showing 'an all too conventional erotic admiration for lithe, nubile youth' (2009: 510) and for demonstrating a

more conservative attitude 'towards women and sexual politics' (2009: 497) than Hrabal himself. Owen argues that Menzel simplifies Hrabal's women and 'overemphasises the subversive power of sex' (2009: 510).

Further reading

Jan Čulík, 'Jiří Menzel and the construction of historical experience in his films dealing with traumatic 20th century events' in J. von Puttkamer and W, Borodziej (eds) *Europa und sein Osten. Geschichtskulturelle Herausfoderungen* (Europas Osten im 20. Jahrhundert. Schriften des Imre Kertész Kollegs Bd.1), Munich: Oldenbourg Verlag, 2012, pp. 25–46.

Elizabeth Girelli, 'Subverting Space: private, public and power in three Czechoslovak films from the 1960s and 70s', *Studies in Eastern European Cinema*, Vol. 2, No. 1, 2011, pp. 49–59.

Peter Hames, *Czech and Slovak Cinema: Theme and Tradition*. Edinburgh: Edinburgh University Press, 2009.

Peter Harmes, *The Czechoslovak New Wave*, 2nd ed., London: Wallflower Press, 2005.

Antonín J. Liehm, *Closely Watched Films: The Czechoslovak Film Experience*, New York: International Arts and Sciences Press, 1974.

Jonathan L. Owen, 'Closely Observed Bodies: Corporeality, Totalitarianism and Subversion' in 'Jirí Menzel's 1960s Adaptations of Bohumil Hrabal', *Canadian Slavonic Papers*, Vol. 51, No. 4, pp. 495–511, 2009.

Josef Škvoreck, *All The Bright Young Men and Women: A Personal History of the Czech Cinema*, trans. Michael Schonberg, Toronto: Take One/Peter Martin, 1971.

David Sorfa

Pan's Labyrinth (2006)

[Country: Spain, Mexico, USA. Production Company: Estudios Picasso. Writer, Director, Producer: Guillermo del Toro. Producers: Bertha Navarro, Alfonso Cuaron, Frida Torresblanco, Alvaro Augustin. Cinematographer: Guillermo Navarro. Production Designer: Eugenio Caballero. Original Music: Javier Navarrete. Editor: Bernat Vilaplana. Special Effects Supervisor: David Marti. Cast: Ivana Baquero (Ofelia), Sergi Lopez (Vidal), Maribel Verdú (Mercedes), Ariadna Gil (Carmen), Doug Jones (Faun/Pale Man).]

Synopsis: It is 1944. Ofelia is uprooted and sent with her mother to a Fascist military outpost run by her stepfather, Vidal. Ofelia's mother is pregnant with Ofelia's brother, but the pregnancy is not going smoothly and Ofelia's mother is sick en route. In order to cope with the loneliness, isolation and fear that characterise Ofelia's new home, she absorbs herself in a rich fantasy world. In this world she is given three tasks. Being successful at these tasks will mean that Ofelia can be restored to her rightful place as a Princess in another world. Despite support from Vidal's servant, Mercedes, and the rising strength of the resistance movement, Ofelia's end is tragic.

Guillermo del Toro's *Pan's Labyrinth*, is a powerful piece of cinema that offers a range of experiences to the viewer. It provides stunningly realised visuals and a beautifully haunting score. It has an ideological, as well as emotional impetus. It merges fantasy and reality to such powerful effect. It offers a fascinating study of what happens to childhood when forced to confront the horrors created within the adult world. Above all, it is a challenging piece of cinema that contains a rich discourse that seeks to engage, shock, move and trouble audiences.

One of the first images the audience sees is Ofelia dying. This image predicts that the narrative will be a retelling of what led to this tragedy. The centrality of this character and the subjective nature of the viewer's future narrative journey are then confirmed with a zoom into Ofelia's eye. We are encouraged to enter her subjectivity and the story is refracted through the consciousness of the child. The narrative structure subverts the audience's expectations of Todorov's three-stage structure. The equilibrium stage is generally assumed to be chronologically first and evident within a film text. Ofelia's equilibrium is revealed only when the viewer learns about her life with her mother and father (a tailor). The majority of the film is spent in a situation of dis-equilibrium with the Fascists (and even the fawn) as agents of disruption. The mill and its surrounding area are the arena of conflict. Of course, there are two realities in this film and Ofelia's quests also exist within the disequilibrium. As indicated at the beginning of the film, Ofelia's story in the real world ends with her death. Although the end of this narrative also sees the resistance succeed in their defeat of Vidal and a re-appropriation of land by its rightful inhabitants, the death of a child is a brutal narrative conclusion. The subsequent fantasy resolution, in which Ofelia is reunited with her family and reinstated on the throne, does seek to offer some solace to the viewer, but in the real world of the story, if there is a new equilibrium, it is hard won and deeply shocking.

Del Toro's film is a heady mix of fantasy and reality, with the 'real' parts of the film still touched by elements of the fictional. From 1936 to 1939, Spain experienced a Civil War. This was an incredibly complicated and turbulent period within Spanish history, which saw right-wing generals attempt to overthrow the newly democratically elected leftist government. These rebel Nationalists were headed by Francisco Franco and were supported by the Catholic Church and Spain's landowning elite. With significant aid and armed support from both Mussolini in Italy and Hitler in Germany, the right was eventually successful and General Franco controlled Spain until his death in 1975. It was the stories of and from Spanish exiles, who came to Mexico after Franco's takeover, and the impact that these individuals had on Mexican culture, that helped spark del Toro's interest in the period. Del Toro's film ends with the Fascists defeated and the rightful heirs to the Mill (and therefore,

Spain) victorious. However, these small victories did nothing to stop Franco and the Fascist party.[1]

Del Toro has stated that: '*Pan's Labyrinth* uses fantasy and the supernatural to confront the malevolence and violence of the real world (Spain under Franco)', (www.panslabyrinth.com). Fantasy and fairy tale are filters through which del Toro can articulate the horrors experienced by both Ofelia and Spain. The striking visuals of the dark fairytale worlds of storytellers like the Brothers Grimm and the fact that these stories focus on moral questions, are elements that are clearly evident in *Pan's Labyrinth*. Ofelia is obsessed with Fairy Stories. They are her escape before she even arrives at the Mill. The Russian Formalist Vladimir Propp's character roles, derived from the study of Fairy Stories, can be productively applied to *Pan's Labyrinth*: the Faun as the 'donor'/'helper', Ofelia as the 'Princess'/'Heroine', etc. Creatures in classic tales include goblins, elves, trolls, animals and talking animals. *Pan's Labyrinth* has the Faun, the Toad, the Pale Man and the Mandrake baby. The classic fairytale quest has three tasks, as does Ofelia. There are three fairies and Ofelia must choose to unlock one of three doors in the Pale Man's Lair.

Fairy tales provide a perfect context for the most challenging and powerful of messages. They contain moral ambiguity and thus challenge the viewer to reflect on their own moral choices. The Faun is a morally ambiguous character. He is enigmatic, the holder of secrets, cruel at times and then comforting. He helps Ofelia in her quests, but by doing this then propels her towards her death. Fairy stories are about 'rites of passage'. Often a nearly pubescent girl is challenged to a series of quests in order to prepare her for her future. Ofelia fits this 'type' and experiences all of the hurdles and hardships that any fairy story character would in her quest for truth and adulthood. Fairy stories merge fantasy and reality in order to pitch the child up against the horrors of the adult world. By creating worlds in which fantasy and reality coexist, the monstrousness of adult action can take on a monster's form and be battled by the child.

In terms of its genre credentials, *Pan's Labyrinth* draws from two main generic sources. Del Toro clearly cites the horror genre as one of his influences:

> there is certainly a re-assurance to our well-being to be able to vicariously see the misfortune of someone else .... The other power of the genre is that there is no other that generates images that stay embedded in your mind so strongly.
>
> (in Wood 2006: 29).

He was always interested in the fantasy and horror genres, and as a child his three favourite actors were Boris Karloff, Vincent Price and Peter Cushing. *Pan's Labyrinth*'s horror credentials are clear. Ofelia encounters monsters: the fantasy versions and the Fascist Vidal, who is far more frightening. The site of horror in classic horror films is an isolated place in which humanity is devalued and threat abounds. The Mill is a place of summary judgement, torture and death. Early German Expressionist horror films, such as Robert Wiene's *Das Cabinet des Dr Caligari* (1920) and F. W. Murnau's *Nosferatu* (1922), presented light and dark in conflict and tension with each other. The real and fantasy worlds within *Pan's Labyrinth* also present a collision between light and dark. The shadows and dark corners of the Mill provide a stark contrast to the light-saturated court of the fantasy ending. As with these early examples, *Pan's Labyrinth* also presents a contrast between what is ideologically light and dark. *Pan's Labyrinth* also includes both the internalised and the externalised forms of the monstrous found in Horror films. The fantasy monsters represent externalised forms of monstrosity, but can they ever be less threatening than the monstrous psychopathology of Vidal?

The fantasy elements of *Pan's Labyrinth* have already been discussed in terms of narrative, but are, of course, crucial to the generic tone of the film, too. Fantasy films are designed to engage the viewer through striking visuals. The sumptuous horror of the Pale Man's lair is one of the many striking elements. Within classic conventions, the arena of fantasy in a film is one where the rational has been rejected and the subconscious is made visually manifest. As Ofelia retreats more and more into the 'safety' of the fantasy world, the two worlds become more intertwined. Fantasy films use the supernatural, myth and legend to draw on for both characters and storylines. *Pan's Labyrinth* is no different. Daedalus created the labyrinth at Knossos for King Minos of Crete. Its function was to hold the Minotaur (half-man, half-bull), which was eventually killed by the Athenian, Theseus. The only way that Theseus could then escape from the labyrinth was with the help of Ariadne, who gave him a ball of string to tie at the start of the labyrinth, unravel as he went in and thus secure a path out. The Faun aids Ofelia in her journey, as she seeks to escape her earthbound context and rejoin her fantasy family. Fauns exist within Roman mythology as spirits of the woodland. They have the body of a man, but the horns, tail, ears and legs of a goat. Del Toro's faun is formed from trees, leaves and wood. He is half-man, half-goat, sharing the explicit connection to nature of the Roman original.

Representation of the family is a significant element within the messages and values of *Pan's Labyrinth*. The family is restorative and restored in this film, but only within the fantasy narrative. When Ofelia enters the light-soaked fairy kingdom, she sees her family restored. They are not only alive again, but are royal and adored by their many subjects. Ofelia's quest has ended and she has been reunited with her family, as well as reinstated to her birthright. The mise-en-scène and cinematography of this scene both point to its credentials as a resolution. In the real world, however, families are destroyed and lost. The family unit is utterly vulnerable and its sanctuary cannot be guaranteed. As a support for individuals when facing oppression, the family does not always overcome. It is significant, for example, that the rabbit poachers are father and son, and that the father is forced to watch the brutalising of the son by Vidal. Ofelia's mother is no armour for her against Vidal and neither is Mercedes, who becomes Ofelia's surrogate mother. In the case of Mercedes and her brother, however, the strength of the family does eventually save the day, but this difference is consistent with the way in which the film codes the resistance as having a real future.

In terms of the representation of the female gender in *Pan's Labyrinth*, the three main female characters present very different discussions. Ofelia resists oppression. She is transgressive and fights for what she believes to be true. Ofelia does not have Mercedes's capacity for violence, but then she is still a child. She is also far more vulnerable than Mercedes and is eventually crushed by Vidal. Carmen is represented as subject and subjugated. She is a passive character, who needs Vidal in order to define and financially support her. For Carmen, her emotional and financial position would be untenable without male support. She gives up her freedom and potentially that of her daughter in order to secure that support. Carmen's function for Vidal (and within the story) is to produce a child and once she has done this, she is no longer needed (and dies). Mercedes, in contrast, resists. She is active in the resistance movement and smuggles supplies to them. Mercedes represents a female spirit that is far more indomitable than Carmen's. She is courageous and can inflict great violence on her oppressors; the half-smile that she carves into Vidal's face is brutal and grotesque.

Vidal is, of course, the main male character and true monster of the film. His masculinity is cold, brutal and demanding of acknowledgement. Vidal's sense of himself as a potent male is so strong that he refuses even to believe that his baby will be anything other than male. For Vidal, his sense of himself as one in a long line of men is essential. He wants his legacy to live on through his son, but thankfully the viewer knows that this will not happen. Vidal is Fascism distilled; he is also the monster that lurks at the back of every child's psyche. Unlike the men of the Resistance or Dr Ferreiro, Vidal has no sense of empathy or sympathy for other individuals. He is the juggernaut of Fascism personified.

As physical manifestations of primal fears, the creatures do not need to be gender identified. They are greed, brutality, death, disease and age. They represent humankind's worst fears for themselves, but they also contribute to the ideological debate through their need to control and destroy. Both the Pale Man and the Faun can be read as representing a masculinity that is in conflict with femininity, rather in harmony with it and, thus, they share the threatening masculinity that is evident in Vidal. The Pale Man is relentless in his attempt to capture Ofelia. His violence is sudden and horrific when his environment is under threat. Vidal shares both of these characteristics. The Faun is controlling, ambiguous and even cruel.

In 2006, Del Toro described a labyrinth as: 'A maze is a place where you get lost .... But a labyrinth is essentially a place of transit, an ethical, moral transit to an inevitable centre' (cited by Kermode 2006, podcast). *Pan's Labyrinth* presents the journey of a child and that of a country. Both journeys are painful and tragic, with problematic resolutions, but both journeys are also powerfully and beautifully evoked.

Notes

1. For further detail on Spanish cinema's response to the Civil War and Franco, see John Hopewell's *Out of the Past: Spanish Cinema after Franco*, London, BFI, 1986.

Further reading

Mark Kermode, 'Review: *Pans Labyrinth*', *Guardian*, 2006.

Vladimir Propp, *Morphology of the Folk Tale*, Bloomington: Indiana University Press, 1958.

Tzvetan Todorov and A. Weinstein, 'Structural analysis of Narrative Author(s)', in *NOVEL: A Forum on Fiction*, Vol. 3, pp. 70–6, Durham, Duke University Press, 1969.

Jason Wood, *Talking Movies: Contemporary World Film Makers in Interview*, London, Wallflower Press, 2006.

Tanya Jones

La passion de Jeanne d'Arc/The Passion of Joan of Arc (1928)

[Country: France. Production company: Société Générale de Films. Director: Carl Theodor Dreyer. Screenwriters: Carl Theodor Dreyer and Joseph Delteil. Cinematographer: Rudolph Maté. Art Directors: Hermann Warm and Jean Hugo. Cast: Reneé Falconetti (Joan), Eugène Silvain (Cauchon), Antonin Artaud (Massieu).]

Synopsis: A chronicle of the trial of Jeanne d'Arc on charges of heresy, and the efforts of her ecclesiastical jurists to force Jeanne to recant her claims of holy visions.

The poet and proto-feminist 'H.D.' (Hilda Doolittle) wrote about her experience of watching this film in 1928. She describes feeling nervous to the point where her hands became raw and bleeding: 'Bare walls, the four scenes of the trial, the torture room, the cell and the outdoors about the pyre, are all calculated to drive in the pitiable truth like the very nails on the spread hands of the Christ' (quoted in Lopate 2006: 42). More disturbingly, reports allege that, in 1929, two New Yorkers died of shock during a screening. Meanwhile, considering that Joan's canonisation had only recently taken place in 1920, the Catholic Church demanded that scenes be excised (Wahl 2012: 2).

The Passion of Joan of Arc opens with the turning of pages from the historical record, thus making great play of its authenticity. Otherwise, Dreyer assumes the audience will be familiar with the background as to why and by whom Joan is put on trial: in 1431, the defeated French Catholic heroine of the Hundred Years War is being tried by a court sympathetic to the English. The accusers attempt to make Joan rescind her claim to divine communion through various means including trickery and threat of torture. The exhausted Joan relents to save herself from the stake but quickly withdraws her confession, embracing her martyrdom.

Seemingly perverse in using such dialogue-heavy source material, the film fits both in and wholly apart from its context of the late silent era. The actors recite lines direct from the trial records while intertitles greatly abbreviate their exchanges. In a film made with a pan-European crew, elements of the best of 1920s European cinematic innovation are to be found: a touch of German-style expressionism in design, French impressionistic cinematography and Soviet-style montage editing are all detectable but filtered through the austere, minimalist sensibilities of its director. *The Passion* is therefore precise in its adherence to historical truth and naturalism of performance, while simultaneously utilising a modernist cinematic method that self-consciously draws attention to itself.

A young woman's face is probed by a camera positioned so closely that we are compelled to study her tiny frown lines and freckles. Suddenly, the image zooms alarmingly towards the stern face of an unyielding accuser, every mole, wart, pore gaping open for our scrutiny. Abruptly, a tracking shot drags us inexorably along a line of smirking, whispering clergy. *The Passion of Joan of Arc* presents a vivid inspection of the human face. Indeed, the film is often described as being entirely constructed through the use of close-ups. Though this is not entirely accurate, a disturbing proximity dominates. Throughout, the counterintuitive cinematography seems to revel in the contradiction between elaborate, often dizzying, movement and a remorseless, dogmatic approach to framing that is still startling nearly a century later. As Joan, Renée Falconetti's face dominates, but a balance results from the contrast between her near-perpetual tears with the domineering judges, particularly the bloated countenance of Eugène Silvain's Cauchon and the pained earnestness of Antonin Artaud's Massieu. Given the film's curious construction, it is the close-up that secures a coherent viewing experience while editing and shot selection are the crucial elements in signalling the emotional impact.

When the tiniest flickering of eyelids is magnified on screen, credible performance becomes essential and the 35-year-old Falconetti is utterly compelling as the beleaguered 19-year-old Joan. Without her intense portrayal of heightened emotion through the tiniest kinetic detail, the film would utterly fail to convince. Nevertheless, Falconetti's screen presence should be considered in the light of Dreyer's legendarily harsh direction. He demanded endless retakes in order to select the exact nuance from each shot, effectively exhausting the actress into an extreme state resulting in Falconetti becoming hysterical on set when shooting the scene where her hair is clipped (Wahl 2012: 5). However, if the film's reputation rested on performance alone, then it would be merely powerful, rather than canonical.

In 1945, Béla Balázs named the reading of this penetrating and revealing shot of the human face in cinema 'microphysiognomy'. He characterises *The Passion* as a series of 'dangerous duels' played out across the characters' features, where 'we see every thrust and every parried blow, every feint, every rapier lunge of the mind,' (2010: 102). However, it is problematic to suggest that Joan applies any sort of tactics, when it is her refusal to engage with any guile that makes her exposed and vulnerable. Only her accusers present a range of deliberate manoeuvres. Joan's real 'battle' comes not through some theological jousting but from her moment of weakness where she temporarily capitulates to the demand for confession.

Less contentiously, Balázs asserts that the close-up scrutinises '*beneath the play of expressions*', so that 'real expression is created in the barely perceptible movements of the tiniest parts of the face' (ibid: 104). Therefore, the scrutiny to which Joan is put by the camera deliberately mimics her interrogation.

In 1975, the feminist film theorist Laura Mulvey identified the image of the female on screen as an arena for power play. She asserted that in the classic Hollywood-dominated cinema, women were 'simultaneously looked at and displayed, with their appearance coded for strong visual and erotic impact so that they can be said to connote to-be-looked-at-ness' (in Penley 1988: 62). It is tempting to consider the fetishisation of ecstatic religious martyrdom by taking the connotations of the film's title literally. However, if Falconetti is not really gazed at for openly erotic purposes, then she is persistently scrutinised from a position that looks down on her. This contrasts to the generally low-angled shots that emphasis her tormentors' dominance. The result is the male bullying of a possibly disturbed young woman, rather than an ideological interrogation, and we are positioned along with the interrogators. It is this aspect, the grilling of Joan through the film's form as well as through its subject matter, which seems to be at the root of why the film may have upset the Catholic Church, unnerved H.D., and suggests the necessity for an accompanying health warning.

However, in 1989, clearly citing Mulvey, Raymond Carney considered that, 'The instability of Dreyer's photographic practice puts us in a very different imaginative relationship to the image than does the standard glamour close-up' (1989: 200). Carney argues that the infatuating gaze that we might normally associate with the objectification of the female on screen is prevented by the consistently shifting camera position and its disorientating movement. Figuratively, Joan won't be brought into focus, which prevents her from being simplistically understood: 'We look at her from different positions; we see her from various sides and angles; but we can never quite grasp her. She remains almost as far beyond a viewer as she stays beyond her judges and accusers' (ibid: 200). Ultimately, as with her judges, our scrutiny of Joan proves unenlightening. She stays remote from our Earthly concern.

Furthermore, the film's construction through editing seems to defy almost every rule of the classic Hollywood style, which had been set as international standard for the preceding 14 years. Eyeline matches do not maintain a comforting consistency; spatial depth is near-impossible to gauge for much of the time; the convention of shot reverse-shot proves unreliable and establishing shots are infrequent. For example, one of Joan's key 'crimes' is her adoption of men's clothing but Dreyer so rarely shows her in other than a facial close-up that the charge perhaps surprises us. Closely examining the film's deliberately disjointed diegesis, David Bordwell's 1981 study of Dreyer succinctly sums up what makes the film so 'strange': 'if *every* cut violated the 180° rule, that violation would quickly become contextually intelligible. The dynamism and uncertainty of the editing stem from the constant play between embedded norm and violations of it' (1981: 80).

Dreyer's canted angles are supported by a set that is just as challenging. Windows are slanted into perspective-defying shapes. Foregrounds and backgrounds seem to shift optically as shots change, rendering the space of each sequence impossible to orientate. The stark whiteness that characterises almost every shot of the film was actually a shade of pink chosen to have that very effect when exposed onto the monochrome film stock. Echoing his work on the famous expressionistic set for *The Cabinet of Dr Caligari* (Robert Weine, 1919), art co-designer Hermann Warm's set is crucial in developing the film's singular look.

Crucially, the peculiarities of cinematography, editing and set do not seem intended to be read as subjective. The set does not seem to present a point of view linked to Joan's, as the perspective of insanity justifies the strangeness of *Caligari*; nor does *The Passion*'s eccentric cinematography seem to suggest an impressionistic perspective on her behalf. Bordwell suggests that: 'Dreyer's film puts the intelligibility of subjectivity into question' (ibid: 84). To re-emphasise: we are made to look at Joan, to witness her ardour but we are not really asked to understand her – that seems to be a matter between her and her God.

Conversely, though their faces become starkly known to us in minute detail, the intertitles leave unnamed all characters but Joan. Only through the end credits might we identify their names, if we happen to be familiar with particular actors or (even less likely) the trial record so Dreyer hardly allows them our empathy. Instead, he employs an unflattering method that simultaneously attracts and repels character identification: the technicalities of the film leave us proximately close to, yet involuntarily detached from, its deglamorised subjects.

Perhaps we should reconsider the role played by Artaud. If Joan herself is too fixed as the object of the camera's gaze, it is his Massieu onto whom we may latch for our perspective, particularly in his anxious warnings to her for giving 'dangerous' responses. Handsome and more sympathetically portrayed than the other accusers, he is concerned with saving a young, misguided woman's life rather than the abstract concept of her soul through her burning. Here is perhaps the conduit of the (masculine) twentieth-century perspective. Arguably, as spectators we are desperate to find the sense in this, identifying ourselves with an accuser who reflects our concerns, doubts and compassion.

Considering how Dreyer disrupts the rationality of diegesis and narrative, it is surprising how coherent the film appears. If not actually comprising the entirety of the film's shots, then the structure of *The Passion* is held together by the close-up. The minute changes of Falconetti's face rebuild the fragmented space established by the cinematography, mise en scène and editing (ibid: 85). Just as the action of the film revolves around the oppressive interrogation of a young woman who is potentially either divine or foolish, the cinematic style forces a dual scrutiny of both Joan (character) and Falconetti (performer). Our gaze becomes similarly penetrative and exhaustive, yet conflicted and disrupted. We stare hard at Joan/Falconetti fascinated, fixed, appalled and confused. We wish to save her, though we know she is doomed. She defies us, refusing our desire to connect. She is elsewhere, detached: with God, possibly, but terribly removed from us by the distance of time and the mechanical detachment of silent cinema.

Further reading

Béla Balázs and Erica Carter, *Balázs' Early Film Theory: Visible Man and The Spirit of Film*, Oxford & New York, Berghahn Books, 2011.

David Bordwell, *The Films of Carl Theodor Dreyer*, Berkeley, University of California Press, 1981.

Raymond Carney, *Speaking the Language of Desire: The Films of Carl Dreyer*, Cambridge, Cambridge University Press, 1989.

Hilda Doolittle, 'The Passion of Joan of Arc', in Phillip Lopate, (ed.), *American Movie Critics*, Des Moines, The Library of America, 2006.

Laura Mulvey, 'Visual Pleasure and Narrative Cinema', in Constance Penley, (ed.), *Feminism and Film Theory,* London & New York, Routledge, 1988, pp. 57–68.

Jan Wahl, *Carl Theodor Dreyer and Ordet: My Summer with the Danish Filmmaker*, Kentucky, University Press of Kentucky, 2012.

Phil Lloyd

Pather Panchali/Song of the Little Road (1955)

[Country: India. Production Company: The Government of West Bengal. Director: Satyajit Ray. Producer: The Government of West Bengal. Screenwriter: Satyajit Ray (based on the novel by Bibhutibhushan Bandopadhyay). Cinematographer: Subrata Mitra. Music: Ravi Shankar. Editor: Dulal Dutta. Cast: Kanu Bannerjee (Harihar Ray), Karuna Bannerjee (Sarbojya Ray), Subir Bannerjee (Apu), Uma Das Gupta (Durga), Chunibala Devi (Indir Thakuran).]

Synopsis: In the lush Bengali countryside the struggles of everyday life for the Ray family unfold through the stories of its members. The long-suffering mother, Sarbojya, is subjected to the ignominies of life so common to the poor, while her daughter Durga, a clever, often naughty girl who is tragically bereft of horizons, languishes under her mother's stern discipline, but remains co-conspirator and friend of elderly Aunt Inder. Little Apu is the pride and hope of his family, and he carries great expectations on his tiny shoulders, especially when his father, Harihar sets off on a long and difficult journey to find work. Struggle and ultimately tragedy ensue, and Harihar's return, and all of the hope and potential it held is sundered by Durga's untimely death.

Pather Panchali is often cited as the film that put India on the cinematic map, but this view takes only one side of the relationship of recognition into account. While it is certainly the case that Satyajit Ray's (pronounced Sho-tyo-jit Rye) early masterpiece brought Indian cinema into wider critical and popular consciousness in the West, the domestic film industry in India had been thriving since long before Ray's arrival on that scene. Indeed, Ray himself frequently commented on the state of Indian cinema(s), and what he saw as the comparative lack of sophistication evident in so many of the products of his homeland, particularly when viewed against the films of several European directors with whose work Ray had become quite impressed during his period of residency in London. In a telling recollection of that period, written in 1948 and titled 'What Is Wrong with Indian Films?' Ray is characteristically engaged on several fronts, simultaneously critical of much of Hollywood's production, correcting the widely held misperception that cinema was a late arrival in India, and also addressing himself thoroughly to the titular question. He observes that there are problems from the practical (e.g. poor planning, hasty production, budgeting difficulties), to the thematic (e.g. the undue influence of Hollywood, a penchant toward the fantastical), to the technical (e.g. poorly executed scripts, cinematography, and editing) that plagued Indian film in the period from its inception through the late 1940s, and closes with an exhortation that would guide his own practice throughout his career: 'The raw material of the cinema is life itself. It is incredible that a country which has inspired so much painting and music and poetry should fail to move the filmmaker. He has only to keep his eyes open, and his ears. Let him do so'.[1]

Throughout his career, and indeed in much of the critical uptake of his work, Ray was and still is often slung between India and the West, a sort of uneasy go-between, pioneering a new style in the Indian context (referred to by turns as 'Indian New Wave', 'Parallel Cinema', or 'Indian Art Cinema'), but often reductively viewed through his affection for De Sica, Renoir, Ford, Kurosawa and Chaplin, among others, as not entirely 'of' India either at home or abroad. Ray's films often struggled at the box office both in and outside of India, despite his status as a favourite of the international film festival circuit, and he himself said that his films were not generally intended for a mass audience. The problem lies less with who Ray was, or where he belonged, than with the fact that his cinema contains within it the capacity to transcend the local, the specific, rendering the ineffability of the human condition universally legible, transparent beyond the boundaries of culture and idiom (though certainly never abandoning it either), visible, and made so through the apparatus of camera and projector.[2]

Pather Panchali owes a debt to Di Sica whose *Ladri di Biciclette (Bicycle Thieves)* had an immediate and significant impact on the young Ray. In the introduction to a volume of his collected writing on cinema, Ray offers this recollection: 'Within three days of arriving in London I saw *Bicycle Thieves*. I knew immediately that if I ever made *Pather Panchali* – and the idea had been at the back of my mind for some time – I would make it in the same way, using natural locations and unknown actors' (Ray 1976: 9). But even though the marks of Italian Neo-Realism are in evidence throughout the film, Ray employs a far more lyrical style, and, for example, his use of exquisitely shot musical montage sequences to denote the passage of time, setting images of Bengal's pastoral beauty to Ravi Shankar's evocative and magnificent soundtrack, marks a distinctly different aesthetic imperative that is at work in Ray's film.

A side-by-side comparison of *Pather Panchali* and *Ladri di Biciclette* yields both great affinities and notable differences. Ray's use of non-professional actors, shooting on location, and eschewing complexity in the plot in favour of highlighting the mundane struggles of regular people, all speak to this affinity. However, Ray's aesthetic and narrative choices yield a very different feeling and form of intervention into modernity than is to be found in *Ladri di Biciclette*. Ray's extensive use of Ravi Shankar's brilliant soundtrack, the greater artistry with which shots are composed, his aforementioned juxtaposition of Bengal's pastoral beauty with the gritty realities of life for its rural poor, and the choice to invert Di Sica's focus on Antonio Ricci's struggles outside the domestic context, staying instead in the home and the village rather than following Harihar on his journey to find work all speak to ways in which Ray expands on the potent Neorealist model, bringing it into contact with an interventionist, avant-garde sensibility. As Ray scholar Keya Ganguly has written:

> [Ray's] avant-garde impulse [is] a specific mediation of realism, not only given the constitutive place of the technology of film (which is both modern and modernist) but also because it is fundamentally untenable to equate humanism with liberal reformism .... For Ray, as is evident from his cinematic practice as well as his journalistic and creative writings, cinema was not only an 'art', but a mode of intervening in politics and philosophy. It is in this specific sense that he was an avant-garde director. Like the European avant-gardes of the early twentieth century, his effort was not only to disrupt accepted ways of making films, but also to question the very institutions of art and political practice in their relations to other sociocultural realities. However, unlike the European avant-garde artists ... Ray's historical location as well as his personal convictions took him out of a purely intellectual engagement with the visual image into a questioning of the historical and social contradictions that govern the production of art .... It was a conceptualization of the world, rather than a representational reaction to it.
>
> (2002)

In marking the distinction between Ray's cinematic practice and the variants of realism more typical in Western cinemas, Ganguly frees Ray from the shackles of being seen as merely an Indian exponent of a European tradition in film, exposing instead an artist with a unique practice, directly engaging the sociocultural issues of his day and questioning the conventions of cinema, particularly Indian popular cinema, in the process.

If Ray is most often seen as a critic of class and feudal hierarchy, and modernity more broadly, it is important to draw attention to another of his frequent critiques of the sociocultural milieu that is in evidence in *Pather Panchali*, namely, the position of women in Indian society. The film follows the mother and daughter of the family, Sarbojya and Durga, most closely, and though much of the dramatic tension is provided through the father/husband Harihar's departure from the village in search of work, he is not a primary driver of the plot except by his absence. Indeed, the majority of male characters in the film occupy positions of nominal authority, but seem largely impotent, as it is the women in the film who are shown doing all of the various work necessary to survival. Sarbojya clearly runs her household, and her husband's ineffectiveness as the family's income generator is a constant threat to their well-being. Further, in scenes of both innocence and familial love, Durga and Sarbojya are seen feeding the younger male child Apu by hand, despite the boy's clear ability to feed himself. In addition, Harihar is routinely shown as dependent on Sarbojya for the fulfilment of his needs, from the bodily to the professional/spiritual, from the coals for his hookah to his need for her to accompany him in taking part in a religious ritual for which his services have been retained. The male characters are sent outside the home, Harihar for work, Apu for school, but the site of the majority of the film's action occurs within its intimate confines, a space in which the women work and provide for the maintenance of the men, and one can hardly miss the point that Apu, the family's hope for the future, and Harihar, the family's ostensible provider, are both essentially dependent on the women in their lives.

Bishnupriya Ghosh has commented on Ray's attentiveness to articulating the female subject, viewing his work as an opportunity to construct 'a third-world feminist critique' (1992).[3] It is imperative that in addition to reading Ray's work in terms of a feminist critique, the additional contextualisation of its being 'third-world' be taken into account. According to Ghosh, 'Firstly, [Ray] attempts to construct a female subject through the use of space, and, secondly he critiques modes of representation through self-reflexive image-making .... His depictions of gender are, inevitably, inscribed within the specific cultural practices of Bengal which cannot be explained through ahistorically situated psychoanalytic paradigms' (1992: 171). The cultural specificity of the various practices to which the audience is witness in *Pather Panchali* and Ray's other films (not all of which are set in Bengal, nor in the contemporary era) provide an opportunity for feminist critics outside the West to, as Ghosh describes, 'theorize the non-western elements of our experience, the elements that acquire their meaning in the context of specific cultural practices .... [To undertake] a construction of female identity, in order to conceptualize differences in western and third-world cinematic hermeneutics' (1992: 165).

Pather Panchali is a document of its time and place; India had not yet been independent for a full decade, and the transition from colonial state to world's largest democracy was juttering forward with both great expectations and the more-than-occasional misstep. Ray would come to be criticised in later years as a Europeanised aesthete by many in the very cinema culture he was instrumental in expanding, if not creating, in his homeland.[4] But its lasting resonance, from its continued inclusion on myriad top film lists, to the seemingly constant Ray retrospectives being held somewhere at any given time, to its common appearance on film studies syllabi around the world, stems from Ray's ability to capture the humanity of his characters in its stark beauty, its many difficulties, and its total, universal lucidity.

Notes

1. Many of Ray's writings on cinema, both on his own films and the works of others, as well as several manifesto-like short pieces on cinema as art and as social engagement, are collected in a short but extremely provocative and insightful volume. See Ray (1976).
2. For an extended exegesis of cinema as it relates to universality, as well as Ray's avant-gardism, and its differences with realism, see Ganguly 2002. Although she is dealing with another film from Ray's *Apu Trilogy*, Ganguly's commentary is as relevant to the majority of Ray's other works as it is to *Apur Sansar* itself.
3. Ghosh is primarily concerned with Ray's 1960 film *Devi (The Goddess)*, but her interest in potentially reading Ray as mounting a feminist critique maps as easily onto *Pather Panchali* as it does on this later work, despite this line of critique being more pronounced, and the critique itself more trenchant in *Devi*. While Ray is more often read as a critic of class and feudal social hierarchies, the theme of women and their exploitation and subjugation is at least as prominent a theme that resonates throughout his oeuvre, particularly *Devi, Mahanagar (The Big City) Charulata (The Lonely Wife)* and *Ghare Baire (The Home and the World)*.
4. For an extensive and fascinating study of the Film Societies of India, see Rochona Majumdar's essay 'Debating Radical Cinema: A History of the Film Society Movement in India', *Modern Asian Studies*, Vol. 46, pp. 731–67, 2012, in which she charts the origins and development of film societies across the country, including their evolving definition of 'good films', from aesthetic considerations to more politically driven criteria. She does so in the context of wider debates in late-colonial India in what she calls 'left-oriented cultural movements', which, in addition to many of these societies, included the Progressive Writers Association and the Indian People's Theatre Association.

Further reading

Shyam Benegal, *Benegal on Ray: Satyajit Ray, a Film*, Calcutta, Seagull Books, 1988.

Darius Cooper, *The Cinema of Satyajit Ray: Between Tradition and Modernity*, Cambridge, UK, Cambridge University Press, 2000.

Keya Ganguly, *Cinema, Emergence, and the Films of Satyajit Ray*, Berkeley, University of California Press, 2011.

Keya Ganguly, 'Cinema and Universality: Satyajit Ray's *Apur Sansar*', *Race and Class*, Vol. 44, No. 2, pp. 57–70, 2002.

Suranjan Ganguly, *Satyajit Ray: In Search of the Modern*, New York, Penguin Books, 2000.

Bishnupriya Ghosh, 'Satyajit Ray's *Devi*: Constructing a Third-World Feminist Critique', *Screen*, Vol. 33, No. 2, Summer 1992, pp. 165–73, 1992.

Rochona Majumdar, 'Debating Radical Cinema: A History of the Film Society Movement in India', *Modern Asian Studies*, Vol. 46, No. 3, pp. 731–67, 2012.

Satyajit Ray, *Our Films, Their Films*, Hyderabad, Orient Longman, 1976.

Andrew Robinson, *Satyajit Ray: The Inner Eye*, Berkeley, University of California Press, 1989.

Robin Wood, *The Apu Trilogy*, New York, Prager, 1971.

Gabriel Shapiro

Pépé le Moko (1937)

[Country: France. Production Company: Paris Film. Director: Julien Duvivier. Scenario: Henri La Barthe and Julien Duvivier. Cinematographers: Jules Kruger and Marc Fossard. Music: Vincent Scotto and Mohamed Ygerbuchen. Cast: Jean Gabin (Pépé Le Moko), Lucas Gridoux (Inspector Slimane), Mireille Balin (Gaby), Line Noro (Inès), Fernand Charpin (Regis).]

Synopsis: Directed by the prolific Julien Duvivier, *Pépé le Moko* is based on a pulp crime novel written by Détective Ashelbé, a pseudonym for Henri La Barthe. It tells the story of a charismatic and glamorous master thief Pépé le Moko, played by Jean Gabin in one of his iconic roles, who has fled from his native Paris after a robbery and has been hiding out in the Casbah in French colonial Algiers. Pépé appears to live a charmed life inside the mysterious and exotic Casbah. He is the boss of a loyal crew, maintains an amicable relationship with the Algerian police inspector Slimane, and is loved and revered by the Casbah's diverse inhabitants who go out of their way to support and protect him. He is romantically involved with the gypsy Inès, and lives with her, although he has a reputation as a ladies' man, with Slimane snidely observing that there will be '3000 women at his funeral'. However, the protection of the Casbah is also a prison for Pépé, and a fateful meeting with the Parisian tourist Gaby stirs romantic feelings and also reactivates his desire for Paris, which leads to tragic outcomes.

Pépé le Moko is a fascinating and challenging film that is riddled with contradictions. On the one hand it has been celebrated as a 'classic' French film of the 1930s, a crystal-like culmination of the developing formal style of post-sound French cinema. On the other hand it has been criticised as a film replete with colonialist and racist ideas and values. So what is it about this film that mesmerically draws us into its world, enchants us, and invites us to care about its characters, but also confronts us with troubling questions about its politics?

There are several obvious reasons why *Pépé Le Moko* has been elevated to the status of a cinema 'classic'. In the first instance, it is a frequently cited example of poetic realism, a film movement that emerged in France around the mid-1930s. Poetic realism was seen to combine documentary realism and a poetic stylisation, and featured stories about working-class characters and difficult loves. It has also been described as an early example of film noir, in part because of its story of criminal masterminds, fatal women and the expressive use of light and shadows. In addition to being recognised as an early example of these film movements, it has also been recognised for its accomplished formalism. In her great BFI book on the film, Ginette Vincendeau says that *Pépé le Moko* does in fact offer 'an anthology of camera angles and movements, editing, lighting and music then in use in the best of the French cinema, as well as of Duvivier's virtuosity'.[1] Further testament to Duvivier's virtuosity comes from the great filmmaker Jean Renoir himself, who said that 'If I were an architect and I had to build a monument to the cinema, I would place a statue of [Julien] Duvivier above the entrance .... This great technician, this rigorist, was a poet.'[2]

As well as these formal qualities there is the compelling performance of the actor Jean Gabin, one of the preeminent actors in French cinema during the 1930s. Gabin starred in some of the most celebrated films that were made in this period, including Duvivier's *La belle équipe* (1936), Renoir's *La grande Illusion* (1937) and *La béte humaine* (1938), and Carne's *Le quai des Brumes* (1938) and *Le jour se léve* (1939). David Thomson describes the Gabin of the late 1930s as 'the perfect expression of a working-class figure hating his squalid environment – in factory or lodgings – but drawn towards a dangerously innocent woman and consequent fatal violence as the only means to dignity'.[3] Thomson's description of the Gabin character is certainly true of *Pépé* who tries very hard to transcend his working-class background, but still finds himself destined to replay a fatally violent ending.

While it can successfully be argued that *Pépé le Moko* is a pivotal film in film history because of its stylishness and the presence and performance of Jean Gabin, the film's setting in, and its fascination with, the Casbah inevitably raise questions about colonialism and the fraught relationship between France and Algiers. Vincendeau tells us that in 1931 in Paris a key cultural event that took place was the *Exposition Coloniale*. She describes this as an exhibition that 'reconstructed habitats, and displayed folkloric dances, artefacts and merchandise, from North and West Africa, Indochina, and other far-flung colonies'.[4] While Vincendeau acknowledges that *Pépé le Moko* does not 'depict or advocate territorial conquest'[5] she does say that it is a film that is 'steeped in colonialist culture and ideology'.[6] Much of this arguably arises from the way the setting and the culture and people of Algiers are viewed as exotic and 'other'.

This depiction of the Casbah as a place of mystery and 'difference' is evident from the opening sequence of the film which takes place in an Algerian police station in the European quarter. The Algerian police are sitting around, fanning themselves in the oppressive heat, and they are trying to explain to the visiting Parisian police inspector why they haven't been able to catch Pépé le Moko for two long years. The reason that is given is the place, the Casbah. One of the policemen goes to a map on the wall and this image of the map dissolves into a documentary-style montage sequence of the Casbah, through which we are given an overview of the place. As a camera pans across rooftops, followed by closer views of labyrinthine alleyways, closed doors, disappearing stairwells and streets with strange names, the policeman's narration describes 'dark winding streets like so many pitfalls', 'slimy porticos' and a 'population of 40,000 people where there is room only for 10,000'. We are shown a melting pot of races, nations, religions and types, including women of 'all shapes and sizes'. This documentary-style survey of the Casbah functions as a visual explanation for why the police have been unable to capture Pépé but it also addresses us as tourists who might be fascinated by this teeming, mysterious place.

Arriving late to this meeting about Pépé le Moko is Inspector Slimane. Slimane is the chameleon who has the special ability to straddle the two worlds, being that of a police inspector who has a job to do, and also someone who walks the streets of the Casbah and has friendly conversations with Pépé and his crew. His relationship with Pépé is reminiscent of the relationship between Lt. Vincent Hanna (Al Pacino) and Neil McCauley (Robert De Niro) in another great crime story *Heat* (Mann, 1995) with their mutually respectful but inevitably conflicted relationship. And just as Vincent tells Neil, in the famous coffee shop meeting, that he will eventually 'take him down', so Slimane sets out to trap and capture Pépé, and finds a way of doing this by tempting him with the Parisian tourist Gaby.

The attraction between Gaby and Pépé is at the centre of the film and the motivation for Pépé's final fateful decision. There is a key scene that takes place inside the Ali Baba café where their flirtation is played out in terms of the two places – distant Paris and the ever-present Algerian Casbah. This scene further underlines the extent to which the film is both enchanting but also, as Vincendeau tells us 'steeped in colonialist culture and ideology'. Slimane has brought Gaby to Pépé – delivered her, as if she is a lure, in some kind of game of chess. The scene begins with Pépé's girlfriend Inès outside the café, looking through the window at Pépé talking to a group of people that includes Gaby and the other couple who have travelled to Algiers with her, Mlle Berthier and Gravère. Pépé reaches out to hold Gaby's hand and outside Inès watches, a cross-like shadow covering her face, reminiscent of a film noir victim as she sees her lover fall for another woman. Gravère flippantly says that he always imagines he is somewhere else, rather than the place he is in, giving voice to his touristic inattentiveness. Mlle Berthier notices the phonograph and says that they should put some music on. She picks up a record and says, with insensitive indifference, 'Cheka Tema – it must be native music', playing it for a short time before she chooses a more familiar jazz-styled song, which is part of Vincent Sotto's soundtrack. So, in this brief exchange, Gravère and Mlle Berthier show contempt for the local culture, and this is the immediate context for the flirtatious exchange between Gaby and Pépé in which they also express a longing to be somewhere else.

Gaby is luminous, wearing a white satin top that literally gleams, framed by diamond earrings and bracelets. She is like a shining beacon – literally – and her whiteness is quite a contrast to the darkness of Inès. Pépé is intoxicated, both by her appearance and possibly by the value of her diamonds. She asks Pépé if he knows Paris and they recall different places in some kind of nostalgic game of one-upmanship, reanimating the memories of being in Paris: Rue Saint-Martin, Gare du Nord, The Opera, The Boulevards, Barbès la Chapelle, Rue Montmartre, Boulevard de Rochechouart, Rue Fontaine. And just as if they were in a screwball comedy they both say 'Place Blanche' at the same time and look at each other. The connection between the two of them is confirmed by their shared memories of Place Blanche. But this nostalgic evocation does more than suggest that their attraction is a matter of destiny. Paris and Gaby come to stand for everything good and desirable in Pépé's mind and heart; and Inès and the Casbah becomes a trap, a prison, an oppressive place to escape from. This also appears to be a view that the film shares. The story makes it clear that Gaby is a tourist and Pépé is an escaped criminal, and that they are both enjoying the colour, the energy, the diverse inhabitants, the comforts and the protection of the Casbah. However, in spite of the evidence that their presence in this place is exploitative and temporary, their doomed affair is still enchanting, and as they dance in this café, it is difficult not to be charmed by the way that they occupy this contradictory space.

Pépé le Moko proved to be an influential film and evidence of this can be found in the fact that it has been remade many times. In 1938 it was remade as *Algiers*, starring Hedy Lamarr and Charles Boyer. It was also remade in 1948 as *Casbah*, a musical starring Tony Martin, Märta Torén, Yvonne de Carlo and Peter Lorre. It is said to have been a key influence on *Casablanca* (1943), particularly in the way that an impossible romance is played out against a colonial outpost. In 1951 there was even an Italian version titled *Totò le Moko* which was a playful parody. And perhaps the most playful homage of all is to be found in Chuck Jones' creation of the skunk Pepe le Pew.[7] In the episode *The Cats Bah* (1954) Pepe le Pew has a domicile next to Pépé le Moko and emanates a charm that we have come to expect from no one else but Pépé le Moko himself.

Notes

1. Ginette Vincendeau, *Pépé le Moko*, London, BFI, 1998, p. 11.
2. Jean Renoir cited in catalogue – Museum of Modern Art, Julien Duvivier retrospective, May 1–28, 2009.
3. David Thomson, *The New Biographical Dictionary of Film*, 5th ed., New York, Knopf Doubleday, 2010, p. 35.
4. G. Vincendeau, *Pépé le Moko*, p. 7.
5. G. Vincendeau, *Pépé le Moko*, p. 55.
6. G. Vincendeau, *Pépé le Moko*, p. 56.
7. There were 16 Pepe Le Pew cartoons in total, starting with *Odor-able Kitty* (1945) and ending with *Louvre Come Back to Me* (1962). Chuck Jones, the Warner Bros. creative animator responsible for Daffy Duck, Bugs Bunny, Wile E. Coyote and the Roader Runner, directed 14 of the Pepe Le Pew cartoons.

Further reading

Henry A. Garrity, 'Narrative Space in Julien Duvivier's *Pépé le Moko*', *The French Review*, Vol. 65, No. 4, March 1992, pp. 623–8.

Peter Limbrick, '(De)Colonising the Casbah: Masculinity and the Colonialist Imaginary in Pepe le Moko', *New Literatures Review* 30, winter 1995, pp. 17–29.

Janice Morgan, 'In the Labyrinth: Masculine Subjectivity, Expatriation, and Colonialism in *Pépé le Moko*', *The French Review*, Vol. 67, No. 4, March 1994, pp. 637–47.

Martin O'Shaughnessy, '*Pépé le Moko* or the impossibility of being French in the 1930s', *French Cultural Studies*, Vol. 7, No. 21, October 1996, p. 247.

Ginette Vincendeau, *Pépé le Moko*, London, BFI, 1998.

Anna Dzenis

Persepolis (2007)

[Country: France. Production Company: 2.4.7 Films, France 3 Cinema, The Kennedy/Marshall Company, French Connection Animations, Diaphana Films, Celluloid Dreams, Sony Pictures Classics. Directors: Vincent Paronnaud and Marjane Satrapi. Producers: Remi Burah, Tara Grace, Marc Jousset, Kathleen Kennedy, Xavier Rigault, Marc-Antoine Robert, and Vitaliy Versace. Music: Olivier Bernet. Editor: Stephane Roche. Art Department: Marc Jousset and Thierry Million. Cast: Chiara Mastroianni (Marji as teenager and woman), Catherine Deneuve (Mrs Satrapi), Danielle Darrieux (Marji's grandmother), Simon Akbarian (Mr Satrapi), Gabrielle Lopes Benites (Marji as child), Francois Jerome (Uncle Anouche), Amethyste Frezignac (Marji as child – English version), Sean Penn (Mr Satrapi – English version), Iggy Pop (Uncle Anouche – English version), Gena Rowlands (Marji's grandmother – English version).]

Synopsis: An animated feature film based on Marjane Satrapi's autobiographical comics about her coming of age in revolutionary Iran. The film begins just before the 1979 revolution in Iran, and unfolds from the perspective of Marji, a precocious 10-year-old girl from an upper-class, Marxist intellectual family. The story follows Marji from childhood to early adolescence in the Islamic Republic of Iran at which point her parents send her abroad to Vienna. In Vienna, we follow her story as she struggles with the travails of life in exile and her guilt about living in the security of Europe while her family and friends in Iran suffer through the 8-year-long Iran-Iraq war. Four years after her arrival in Europe, and following a failed love affair, a nervous breakdown, a period of homelessness and serious illness, Marji returns to Iran. There she has difficulty re-adapting to her old home. Eventually, she gets married and divorced, and then leaves Iran again – this time for good.

Persepolis is a critically acclaimed film that was nominated for and won several prestigious international film awards. Most notably, it won the Jury Prize at the 2007 Cannes Film Festival, and received an Oscar nomination for Best Animated Film, losing the award to *Ratatouille*. The film, however, is as reviled by Muslim state officials as it is celebrated by critics in the West. The Islamic Republic of Iran's Farabi Cinema Foundation issued a letter to organisers of the Cannes Film Festival condemning their inclusion of *Persepolis* in the festival. Their complaint was that the film misrepresents 'the glorious' aspects of the Islamic Revolution; thus the principal issue, for the Iranian government, was the film's interpretation of Iranian history. Although the Cannes Festival ignored the requests of the Farabi Foundation to bar the film from screening, the Bangkok International Film Festival succumbed to the pressure imposed by the Iranian Embassy in Thailand and pulled the film from its festival. In May 2012, Nabil Karoui, owner of the Nessma TV network, was fined for screening *Persepolis* on Tunisian television. He was charged with disrupting 'public morals' and triggering social disorder. Amnesty International issued a statement condemning the charges against Karoui, stating that the legal charges against him presage a darkening of the future of Tunisian democracy.

The film, therefore, has generated strong reactions from totalitarian regimes; a likely reason being that both the graphic novel and the film illustrate the dynamic nature of memory in reconstructions of the past. In other words, the single narrative about a triumphant Islamic Republic and the benefits of the 1979 revolution for all 'the people' as expounded by the Iranian state is brought into question in the autobiographical retelling of Marjis's childhood during Iran's revolutionary years. As both comic book and animated film, *Persepolis* places the concepts of traumatic memory and of revolutionary history at the heart of its narrative. However, the remediation of Satrapi's comics into an animated feature film has entailed some modifications to the comics' version of the narrative, and these changes are expressed through the film's use of framing devices. The filmic narrative unfolds almost entirely through the technique of the flashback. The flashback marks a distinction between the present time in which the story is told and the narrative reconstruction of the past; the concepts of memory, history, and nostalgia are thus integral to this technique.[1] The filmic version of *Persepolis*, through flashback, exemplifies Svetlana Boym's analysis of nostalgia: as a longing for not just another place, but for another time imagined as somehow better than the present.[2] In this case, the flashback scenes of Marji's childhood and adolescence – which include traumatic moments of revolution, war, and exile – repeatedly interrupt Marji's existence in the temporal present, visually pushing her to one side of the screen, rendering her a passive observer of her own life. Despite the painfulness of some of her recollections, the relationship between her memories of the past and her location in the present is weighted by nostalgia.

The use of the flashback in *Persepolis* accentuates the ways in which the present moment is always imbricated with the past, stressing one of the features of traumatic memory: that the traumatic past repeatedly encroaches upon the present.[3] Reflections on the past also work through the prism of nostalgia, as past and present collapse into each other but always with an awareness of futurity. The four brief scenes depicting Marji in Paris' Orly airport, filmed in the present time and in colour, exist in the shadow of her narrative of the past. In classic flashback shots, the screen fades or dissolves to reveal the past in memory, but the use of the flashback technique in *Persepolis* is significantly different: the principal narrative unfolds almost entirely through flashback with the present time emerging in the form of staccato articulations through the narrative retelling of the past. In this film, scenes of the past provide not only context for the narrative in the present, but the past literally intrudes on the present; for example, the first transition to the flashback mode in the film begins with Marji's 10-year-old self bounding into the frame occupied by an adult Marji in Orly.

This first flashback segment concludes in the Tehran airport with a 14-year-old Marji saying goodbye to her parents as she leaves for a new life in Austria. Her parents embrace her and smile reassuringly, but Marji makes the mistake of turning back for a final look only to see her mother collapse into her father's arms. The image of her distraught parents is swallowed into the darkness of the screen. The backwards glance, then, is a dangerous one: the nostalgic person who looks back and becomes mired in the past risks not moving forward. James Olney has described memory as 'both recollective and anticipatory';[4] in other words, our present moment is always inflected by the ways in which we remember the past and how we anticipate our future selves. Similarly, Boym describes nostalgia as both retrospective and prospective. But in *Persepolis,* Marji's nostalgic look at the past threatens her ability to move forward. Situated in the ephemeral and transitional space of the airport lounge, she becomes a spectator of her past, watching impassively as images of her past dominate the screen. Throughout the film, the Marji of the past succeeds in taking over the Marji of the present, shown in various places in the airport, looking defeated and overwhelmed.

In media interviews about the film, Satrapi has repeatedly stressed the universal elements of the film. Claiming that her's is a universal story about the destructiveness of oppressive and dictatorial systems, Satrapi has stated that she deliberately chose to make an animated feature film precisely because of what she understands to be its universal appeal. But the film's animated depictions of Marji's family members and friends undercut Satrapi's claim about the so-called 'universal' appeal of animation. Marji's Iranian family, for instance, is represented as a European (specifically, French) family. Indeed, her family and friends are all portrayed through a very European aesthetic. The deliberate imitation of French culture signals a very specific cultural and economic class in Iran: historically, the Iranian aristocracy has performed their class status through an emulation of French tastes and cultural practices. And, this recognizable 'type' of Europeanised Iranian is evoked in Satrapi's filmic depiction of her family and friends.[5] Representatives of the revolutionary regime, on the other hand, are more noticeably racialised with thick black eyebrows, dark beards, and violent expressions. In fact, as animated film, *Persepolis* succeeds in particularising representations of Iranians as both menacing and racialised – thus affirming mainstream Western media representations of Muslims as fanatical and threatening. While the comics' version also reproduces racialised representations of supporters of the Islamic regime, *Persepolis I*, in particular, makes efforts to acknowledge political, cultural, and social differences amongst Iranians.

The film version of *Persepolis* thus indulges a nostalgic longing for a very particular, pre-revolutionary past. The sense of total loss and deep longing for a past, pre-revolutionary Iran alongside the rejection (and even derision) of present-day Iran fuels the nostalgic impulse in the film. The audience is left to mourn what is irretrievably lost: a refined, 'civilised' and very European world belonging to Marji's parents. Infused with nostalgic desire for another, better time, the film has difficulty escaping its own flashback-based structure of nostalgia and longing. The film's final scene in which Marji is finally able to move forward by leaving the airport and returning to her diasporic life in Paris necessitates a breaking away from the flashback mode in which longing for the past becomes a form of pathology. Thus, while the bulk of the film struggles with the paralytic effects of nostalgic desire, it ends with a more productive interpretation of nostalgia which understands the backwards glance as inflected with a healthy awareness of the present and the future.

Notes

1. See Maureen Turim's detailed study of the use of the flashback technique and its relationship to memory in cinema in *Flashbacks in Film: Memory and History*, New York, Routledge, 1989.
2. See Svetlana Boym's 'Off-Modern Homecoming in Art and Theory' in Marianne Hirsch and Nancy K. Miller (eds), *Rites of Return: Diaspora Poetics and the Politics of Memory*, New York, Columbia University Press, 2011, pp. 151–65.
3. In her landmark study on trauma, Cathy Caruth describes how traumatic memories continue to haunt the suffering subject. She argues that traumatic events cannot be processed in the moment of their happening; the memory of the trauma is always belated and recurs throughout a person's life. See Caruth's 'Introduction: The Wound and the Voice' in *Unclaimed Experience: Trauma, Narrative, and History*, Baltimore, Johns Hopkins University Press, 1996.
4. James Olney, *Memory and Narrative: The Weave of Life-Writing*, Chicago, University of Chicago Press, 1998, p. 343.
5. Interestingly, Satrapi's second feature film, *Chicken with Plums*, based on her graphic novel of the same name, is a live action feature that evokes a French cultural context aesthetic rather than an Iranian one, and has a cast that includes only one Iranian actor, Golshifteh Farahani.

Further reading

Hilary Chute, 'Graphic Narrative as Witness: Marjane Satrapi and the Texture of Retracing' in *Graphic Women: Life Narrative & Contemporary Comics*, New York, Columbia University Press, 2010, pp. 135–73.

Manuela Constantino, 'Marji: Popular Commix Heroine Breathing Life into the Writing of History' in *Canadian Review of American Studies*, Vol. 38, No. 3, 2008, pp. 429–47.

Babak Elahi, 'Frames and Mirrors in Marjane Satrapi's *Persepolis*' in *Symploke*, Vol. 15, No. 1–2, 2007, pp. 312–25.

Typhaine Leservot, 'Occidentalism: Rewriting the West in Marjane Satrapi's *Persepolis*' in *French Forum*, Vol. 36, No. 1, Winter 2011, pp. 115–30.

Amy Malek, 'Memoir as Iranian Exile Production: A Case Study of Marjane Satrapi's *Persepolis* series' in *Iranian Studies: Journal of the International Society for Iranian Studies*, Vol. 39, No. 3, September 2006, pp. 353–80.

Nancy K. Miller, 'Out of the Family: Generations of Women in Feminism. The Case of Marjane Satrapi's *Persepolis*' in Giorgio Adalgisa and Julia Waters (eds), *Women's Writing in Western Europe: Gender, Generation and Legacy*, Newcastle upon Tyne, England, Cambridge Scholars, 2007, pp. 22–37.

Nima Naghibi, 'A Story Told in Flashback: Remediating Marjane Satrapi's *Persepolis*' in Michael A. Chaney (ed.), *Graphic Subjects: Critical Essays on Autobiography and Graphic Novels*, Madison,

Wisconsin, University of Wisconsin Press, 2011, pp. 164–77.
Nima Naghibi and Andrew O'Malley, 'Estranging the Familiar: "East" and "West" in Satrapi's *Persepolis*' in *English Studies in Canada*, Vol. 31, No. 2–3, 2005, pp. 233–47.
Marjane Satrapi, *The Complete Persepolis*, New York, Pantheon Books, 2007.
Kimberly Wedeven Segall, 'Melancholy Ties: Intergenerational Loss and Exile in *Persepolis*' in *Comparative Studies of South Asia, Africa and the Middle East*, Vol. 28, No. 1, 2008, pp. 38–49.
Gillian Whitlock, 'Autographics: The Seeing "I" of the Comics' in *Modern Fiction Studies*, Vol. 52, No. 4, 2006, pp. 965–79.

Nima Naghibi

The Piano (1993)

[Country: Australia, New Zealand, France. Production Company: Australian Film Commission, CiBy 2000, Jan Chapman Productions. Director and Screenwriter: Jane Campion. Music: Michael Nyman. Cinematographer: Stuart Dryburgh. Editor: Veronica Jenet. Cast: Holly Hunter (Ada), Harvey Keitel (Baines), Sam Neill (Stewart), Anna Paquin (Flora).]

Synopsis: It is the mid-nineteenth century. Ada is a mute who has a young daughter, Flora. In an arranged marriage she leaves her native Scotland accompanied by her daughter and her beloved piano. Life in the rugged forests of New Zealand's South Island is not all she may have imagined and nor is her relationship with her new husband Stewart. She suffers torment and loss when Stewart sells her piano to a neighbour, George. Ada learns from George that she may earn back her piano by giving him piano lessons, but only with certain other conditions attached. At first Ada despises George but slowly their relationship is transformed and this propels them into a dire situation.

The Piano is a Gothic costume-romance about the language of love, desire and the paradox of self-determining female agency. At a time when women's positions in society were defined by patriarchal repression, the arranged marriage of Ada (Holly Hunter) to the middle-class Stewart (Sam Neill) who is colonising the unrelenting New Zealand bush, offers her and her daughter Flora (Anna Paquin) little choice over their future. Ada's voice-over is a Scottish child's – maybe Flora's – narrating her apprehension over the forthcoming journey. However, visually we discover her self-appointed autonomy and resistance to female positions through her defiant muteness from the age of six, via her gestures, sign language, written notes and translations through her daughter. Ada's expressions of emotion and desire are also articulated through music as we see her lost in the ecstasy of playing her piano. It is a rare moment of unselfconscious joy in the film, halted by an intrusive servant.

Cinematically framed to mirror and conspire with each other, Ada and Flora, in their restrictive dark Victorian bonnets and hooped skirts, struggle to negotiate the landing, the boat and the ruthless waves when they arrive in New Zealand, as rough sailors deliver them unceremoniously onto an empty, white and hostile beach. All the trappings of Victorian Scotland, symbolised by Ada's household items of luggage, lie like abandoned anomalies on an ancient shore. But even more difficult is the unloading of Ada's prized possession – the piano; symbol of Western civilisation in an uncultivated land, it stands in its wooden crating against the oncoming tide, waiting like Ada, to be unpacked, touched and resound with its own emotional tones.

Michael Nyman's music in *The Piano* very much defines Ada's character. Impressed with Nyman's minimalist scores for Peter Greenaway's films,

Campion had requested a romantic, lyrical, poetic and conservative piece of expressive music for her film. Nyman was inspired by nineteenth-century Scottish ballads and Mendelsohn's songs without words and composed ahead of shooting, in collaboration with Campion's script, unlike contemporary scores which are added in post-production. When Holly Hunter was finally cast, Nyman then levelled his score to match her highly competent musical ability. This allowed Holly Hunter to invest Ada, as a nineteenth-century composer, with her own emotional commitment through the music, and intervene further in the character creation.

Claudia Gorbman notes that the 'authenticity gained in this process' (in Margolis 2000: 47) owes much to this personalised approach as, rather than presenting Ada as just a skilful or professional player of a nineteenth-century musical repertoire, Ada produces the music from her own being as a composer and female artist with an inner language beyond the spoken word. This allows the music to move beyond its usual illustrative function in classical cinema, to express her more ambiguous subjectivity and emotional language, as seen in her playing of her piano in the film, although this goes unrecognised by her new husband Alasdair Stewart.

So in a muddied, restrictive suit, formal top hat and showing Victorian discomfort at finding Ada and Flora sheltering under the hoops of women's undergarments on the New Zealand beach, when her husband meets them, he pragmatically decides to leave the piano behind, and unwittingly rejects his new wife's voice and emotional connection. It is rather Baines (Harvey Keitel), more emotionally attuned and liberated by Maori culture, who she stubbornly persuades to take her back to the beach. Her expressive and intimate playing of the piano, with Flora dancing and cartwheeling exuberantly across the sand, then entrances Baines who has clearly never seen women behave with such wild abandon.

He thus begins the erotically charged negotiations for the piano and Ada; he offers 80 acres of land to Stewart for the piano and then he and the Maori's transport it through the all-consuming mud and bush to his house. Ignoring again Ada's ownership of the piano, Stewart insists Ada gives Baines lessons. But in reality Baines only wants to listen and touch Ada, and in private negotiates with her to remove items of her clothes and permission for him to touch her, in exchange for the piano.

It's a fragile bargain which ostensibly positions Ada as passive victim of male power, prostituting herself for the sale of individual keys. But Jane Campion inverts the liaison to reveal more subtle tones of female/male desire. Ada's rejection of Baines' advances – halting the music in protest of his physical invasions of her personal space, reluctantly removing her clothes, lying rigidly on the bed with him – demonstrate female resistance to patriarchal control even as he takes advantage of her position.

These scenes also simultaneously unfold a reluctant awakening of Ada's sensual desire, reiterated in the mise en scéne and the cinematography. The building up of the rare soft-focus amber glow, a palette specifically reserved for intimate moments in the film, contrasts with the predominantly suffocating sea tones of the inhospitable bush in which 'The air seems green as at the bottom of a deep sea' (Campion 1993: 17). The framing, positioning and cutting between Ada and Baines, also offers both the male and female perspectives of erotic desire, resulting in a levelling of gender power.

In *Visual Pleasure and the Cinema*, Mulvey demonstrated that the look of the camera in classical Hollywood cinema privileges a voyeuristic gaze positioning the woman as object of male desire. But Stella Bruzzi, in *Desire and the Costume Film*, demonstrates Campion's progressive, feminist inversion of Mulvey's theory. While costume can function as a fetish for male desire, Baines' removal of his clothes alongside Ada's is a vestimentary performance of parity, and a cinematic offer of sensual pleasure in the male/female body. And while the scene of Baines naked and alone as he dusts and caresses the piano, could be seen as perversely festishistic, it reveals unusually, under Campion's sensitive direction and softened amber lighting, a sensual vulnerability through the eroticising of the male protagonist for a female spectator. Like Marvell's poem of courtship in *To His Coy Mistress*, in the conclusion of this cinematic ritual, Campion awards the final decision to the woman. So when Baines believes the desire is non-mutual he releases

Ada and gives her the piano unconditionally. Once given true free will over her sexuality, Ada returns inexorably to Baines to consummate the relationship.

Peter Brooks notes that nineteenth-century melodrama is defined by its polarised moral codes in which good and evil battle against each other for the ultimate triumph of virtue. Its conflict is symptomatic of a spiritual demise in nineteenth-century culture and the imposing of moral meaning on a familial structure. Hence women, wives, mothers were idealised as the moral locus of the family, the angels in the house who function as integers of stability in an ever-changing society of industrial progress and shifting demographics. Fiction, theatre and paintings emblematised this struggle for spiritual and mythical meaning, or what Brooks defines as the moral occult, through the representation of recognisably evil villains, worthy heroes and innocent heroines in distress, with a clear-cut resolution of upholding moral virtue or being punished for deviance.

Within these conventions of Victorian morality Ada must also pay a price for her adultery. Infused by Bronte's wild landscape of *Wuthering Heights*, Campion films in a Gothic, moody, ruthless atmosphere as the plot reaches terrifying and mythological proportions. Ada slips away through the unforgiving mud to meet Baines, and we witness the terrible consequences of female deviance in nineteenth-century culture when Stewart, who has spied on Ada and Baines making love, blocks her way and brutally attempts to rape her. Ironically in her struggle to escape, it is Ada's hooped petticoats, so representative of Victorian restriction, which protect her, as well as the arrival of Flora on the scene. But in the final outcome, when Ada sends her daughter to give Baines a piano key inscribed with her love, Flora betrays her to Stewart. Ominous as a wood-chopper in a Brothers Grimm tale, Stewart wielding his axe, drags Ada from the house, holds her hand onto the woodblock and brutally chops off her finger. In shock she staggers away, sinks slowly into the mud, her ballooning skirt holding her up like fragile doll.

In this violent scene, Stewart is represented as the Bluebeard villain, the oppressive patriarch who owns his wife as property. But, this melodramatic villainy is also tempered for a more contemporary audience. Campion represents him also as a victim of his cultural and class limitations, the outsider, the voyeur, unable to relate to the feminine world of his strange wife and as Campion comments in interview, 'his shell, his place, his future have been broken by her' (1994: 72).

But Campion's feminist plot ultimately reframes nineteenth-century female restrictions to favour Ada's personal fulfilment, so ultimately, once Ada recovers, Stewart releases her. As Baines, Ada and Flora leave the settlement to sail to Wellington, the camera finally reveals glimpses of hopeful blue sky through the mangled tree-scape. But, in a final challenge to her obdurate willpower, once on the boat Ada rejects the coffin-like piano and putting her foot in the uncoiling rope hauling her piano into the ocean, she is pulled overboard. She sinks down into the blue ocean and wonders, in the dreamy voice-over, whether through her silence it is death she is, and has been, choosing, now and throughout her life – a symbolic drowning reiterated in the suffocating and sea-saturated tones of the cinematography throughout the film. But finally, in the deep underwater quiet, she resists, struggles out of her boot and rises, much to her own surprise, towards the light to start a new life with Baines.

It is an innocent, romantic love that Campion presents as idealised in a mythical fairy-tale sense. Ada, in choosing the love which has woken her like a princess from her deep sleep, voyages from six-year muteness towards a consenting adult relationship, finally articulated in her motivation to reject silence for speech. In Brooks' terms her text of muteness has finally brought redemption for her

But Ada's muteness is also unusual given the predominance of spoken dialogue in films since 1927. Michael Nyman noted one function of his score was to replace dialogue and in this the music, alongside the gestural performance codes, functions like the international language of the silent film era where translated intertitles moved the narrative forward. In *The Piano*, the subtitles also subtly link transnational cultures of Maori speech and Ada's sign-language although politically this is precariously close to reiterating colonial and gender hierarchies. But on a commercial level this silent film aesthetic cleverly integrates international cultural boundaries for export of a crossover Art cinema/mainstream title in the world market. Margolis notes that, produced in Australia with French/US funding and Hollywood stars, *The Piano* succeeds in promoting New Zealand national identity through location choices and the use of Maori and *pakeha* (white New Zealand) culture, managing the 'conflicting demands between the culturally specific and the internationally acceptable' (2000: 5).

Ultimately the Piano was an award-winning, critical and popular success and while marking a shift in Campion's work from the challenging plot construction of *Sweetie* (1989) to the more coherent classical narrative costume drama of *Portrait of a Lady* (1996), *The Piano* also reiterates Campion's thematic concerns with cultural and historical shifts in male/female relationships, power, autonomy and the eroticising of female desire through a feminist cinematic lexicon, to articulate female narratives which have traditionally been silenced.

Further reading

Peter Brooks, *The Melodramatic Imagination: Balzac, Henry James, Melodrama and the Mode of Excess*, New Haven and London, Yale University Press, 1995.

Stella Bruzzi, *Undressing the Cinema: Clothing and Identity in the Movies*, London and New York, Routledge, 1997.

Stella Bruzzi, 'Jane Campion: Costume Drama and Reclaiming Women's Past', in Pam Cook and Philip Dodd (eds), *Women and Film: A Sight and Sound Reader*, London, Scarlet Press, 1993, pp. 232–42.

Jane Campion, *The Piano*, London, Bloomsbury, 1993.

Jane Campion and Kate Pullinger, *The Piano: A Novel*, London, Bloomsbury, 1994.

Claudia Gorbman, 'Music in the Piano', in Harriet Margolis, ed., *Jane Campion's The Piano*, Cambridge University Press, Cambridge, 2000, pp. 42–58.

Misha Kavka, Jennifer Lawn, Mary Paul, eds, *Gothic NZ: The Darker Side of Kiwi Culture*, Otago University Press, Dunedin, New Zealand, 2006.

Harriet Margolis, ed., *Jane Campion's The Piano*, Cambridge, Cambridge University Press, 2000.

Trish Sheil

Popiół i diament/Ashes and Diamonds (1958)

[Country: Poland. Production Company: Zespól Felmowy KADR. Director: Andrzej Wajda. Screenwriters: Jerzy Andrzejewski and Andrzej Wajda (from the novel by Andrzejewski). Cinematographer: Jerzy Wójcik. Music: Filip Nowak. Editor: Halina Nawrocka. Production Designer: Roman Mann. Cast: Zbigniew Cybulski (Maciek), Adam Pawlikowski (Andrzej), Ewa Krzyzewska (Krystyna), Waclaw Zastrzezynski (Szczuka), Bogumil Kobiela (Drewnowski), Jan Ciecierski (Old Porter).]

Synopsis: The action of *Ashes and Diamonds* takes place over the course of a single day: the 8th of May 1945, the final day of the Second World War. However, for Andrzej (Adam Pawlikowski) and Maciek (Zbigniew Cybulski), two soldiers in the outlawed Polish Home Army, the hostilities are not over. The pair has been ordered to assassinate a leading Communist official, Szczuka (Waclaw Zastrzezynski). When their first attempt fails and results in the deaths of two innocent factory workers, they retire to a busy hotel to wait for a second opportunity. While there, the men drink and remember their fallen comrades. Maciek, who has seen too much killing, first flirts with and later falls for the hotel's beautiful young barmaid, Krystyna

(Ewa Krzyzewska), and begins to long for a normal life. Andrzej, however, reminds his young friend of his duty and warns him that failure to execute his orders would be tantamount to desertion. Meanwhile, Szczuka arrives at the hotel and attempts to locate his son, who also fought for the Polish Home Army and is now a prisoner of the Communists. As people gather to celebrate the end of the war, Maciek overhears Szczuka's plans to walk across town to visit his son in prison. The assassin follows his target and shoots him on a deserted street. The next morning, as drunken revellers dance a Polonaise in the hotel bar, Andrzej drives away and Maciek heads to the train station, however, when he tries to avoid an ambitious, self-serving informant, Drewnowski (Bogumil Kobiela), he bumps into a patrol of Polish soldiers who shoot and mortally wound him when he attempts to run. Maciek continues running but dies, writhing in agony, alone on a scrapheap.

Ashes and Diamonds was the concluding part in director Andrzej Wajda's so-called 'War Trilogy'. The series, which chronicled the tragic experiences of ordinary Poles during the Second World War, began with Wajda's debut feature, *A Generation* (1955), which centred on a group of students who join the anti-Nazi resistance. This was followed by the Cannes prize-winning *Kanal* (1956), a harrowing depiction of the Warsaw uprisings. *Ashes and Diamonds*, however, is the most accomplished and complex of the three. It established its director as a key exponent of the Polish Film School, an informal movement which emerged during the political 'thaw' of the late 1950s and early 1960s and included the work of filmmakers such as Andrzej Munk and Jerzy Kawalerowicz. More than this, however, it has come to be hailed as both the finest achievement of Wajda's six-decade career and perhaps of Polish cinema in general.

Played by the brilliant 30-year-old actor, Zbigniew Cybulski, Poland's answer to Marlon Brando and James Dean, Maciek is one of the great anti-heroes in post-war European cinema; a figure who spoke to both the generation of Poles who fought and died during the war and the nation's increasingly rebellious youth in the late 1950s, when the film was released. (Cybulski became an iconic figure in Polish culture, and his premature death – perhaps an accident, or perhaps suicide – formed the basis for Wajda's deeply self-reflexive, *Everything for Sale*, in 1968).

Maciek does not conform to the simple proletarian heroes typical of Eastern Block Socialist Realist cinema, who obediently sacrifice themselves to the cause. Not only does he fight against the Communist Party, he is also an intelligent, even rebellious figure, who comes to question his mission. This newfound complexity in the characterisations is representative of the so-called 'thaw', the period of de-Stalinisation which took effect in the late 1950s, and similarly conflicted, human characters can be seen in contemporary Soviet films of the time, such as Mikhail Kalatozov's *The Cranes are Flying* (1957) and Grigoriy Chukhray's *Ballad of a Soldier* (1959).

Ashes and Diamonds is also a remarkably complex portrait of a country divided against itself and Wajda extends an equal compassion to Szczuka, the target of the assassination attempt. He is a decent, sympathetic man; a veteran of two wars who wishes only to be reunited with his son. Indeed, a kind of surrogate father-son relationship develops between Maciek and Szczuka which comes to a tragic end when the older man dies in his killer's arms, the sound of gunfire drowned out by the fireworks set off to mark the official beginning of peace. This seemingly even-handed treatment did not, however, meet with official approval. Szczuka, not Maciek, had been the central character in Andrzejewski's original novel, and the decision to shift the focus to the subordinate character proved controversial with hard-line critics and the authorities, who thought, not incorrectly, that Wajda romanticised a protagonist who was a member of a renegade, anti-Communist organisation, while making the Communist official a dignified, if somewhat ineffectual character. As a result, the state refused to allow the film to compete at the 1958 Cannes Film Festival and did not allow Wajda to attend the out-of-competition premiere that the Festival organised. Moreover, the director remembers that the film was only given a limited release in its native Poland.

Despite such run-ins with the censors, which have been a far from uncommon occurrence in

Wajda's career, he has, unlike several younger Polish directors, such as Roman Polanksi (whom Wajda mentored) and Jerzy Skolimowsky, elected to remain in his native country, regardless of the problems inherent in making films under a Communist regime. Indeed, he has maintained that the 'censorship of money', which dominates commercial film industries such as Hollywood, is far harder to circumvent than the political censorship he has laboured under.

Wajda has also noted that state censors are often very literal in their thinking and that they have a tendency to censor words and to overlook the visual subtext of a film. For example, he has argued that it was 'impossible to censor the acting of Zbigniew Cybulski' and that his remarkably physical performance contained a certain something 'between sound and picture that constitutes the soul of [the] film' and that 'it was his way of dealing with people which [...] was politically unacceptable' (Falkowska 2006: 51). Additionally, the censors were not quick to pick up on the rich and potentially subversive visual symbolism that permeates many scenes.

Oddly, many critics in the West also failed to notice some of the film's symbolic resonance and accused Wajda of indulging in visuals which have been described as baroque or even excessive. While it is unquestionably more stylised than the comparatively conventional *A Generation*, and the austere look of *Kanal*, the elaborate mise en scène can neither be dismissed as mere window dressing nor simply as another move away from Socialist Realism. Indeed, just as Maciek's reason for never removing his dark glasses is revealed not to be a stylish affectation, but rather the result of having spent too much time in the sewers during the Warsaw uprising, one must look beyond the surface of the visuals to the more profound meaning underneath.

For example, the notable sequence in which Krystyna and Maciek talk amongst the ruins of a bombed-out crypt and then read the poem by the Polish Romantic poet and ardent nationalist, Cyprian Norwid, which gives the film its title, is richly symbolic. Norwid's poem asks if the flames of martyrdom for the national cause will bring only chaos, or if its ashes also 'hold the glory of a star-like diamond'. This work, which Maciek knows by heart, therefore expresses the young man's doubts about the sacrifice he may be required to make for his country, but it also alludes to his doomed Romanticism, and his determination to make that sacrifice. The poem's reference to flames is also significant, and the film is full of recurring images of fire, from the glasses of vodka Maciek lights in memory of his dead friends, to the flames that burst out of the bullet wound of one of the men killed in the first botched assassination attempt, to the fireworks that explode as Szczuka is killed. Immediately after this poem is recited, Wajda conjures up one of the most striking images in the film: as the pair enters the crypt, the camera tilts down and in the foreground of the shot, bisecting the frame and dividing the two lovers is a large upside-down crucifix, with the face of Christ illuminated by a shaft of light. The downward movement mirrors the film's opening shot, where the camera cranes down from a cross on top of a church (a metaphorical fall). However, the inverted cross symbolises a world in turmoil and dramatically underscores the protagonist's loss of spiritual faith as well as his loss of faith in the cause he is fighting for, while the gentle swaying of the cross, like a pendulum, also reminds the audience that time is running out for the two lovers.

Although it would be wrong to view the film as being either unoriginal or less than authentically Polish, and the film's romantic pessimism is certainly characteristic of the Polish Film School in which Wajda played an central part, *Ashes and Diamonds* also betrays a complex and eclectic array of influences. On the one hand, the rubble, bombed-out buildings, and ruined churches that characterise the film's exteriors are reminiscent of Italian Neorealism (perhaps the key inspiration on the Polish Film School). Yet there are also moments of almost Buñuelian surrealism, such as the sight of the white horse trotting down the street past Maciek. The lighting is highly stylised and Expressionistic, and betrays the influence of Hollywood *film noir*. For example, Maciek's death on a deserted rubbish heap, which is certainly amongst the most affecting and memorable in European cinema, recalls Sterling Hayden's death throes in John Huston's *The Asphalt Jungle* (1950). However, perhaps the key American influence is *Citizen Kane* (1941). Inspired by the numerous low-angle shots in Orson Welles' film, Wajda had his production designer, Roman Mann, include ceilings in all of the interior sets. Wajda's compositions, with their considerable depth of field, similarly bring to mind Gregg Toland's work on the earlier film.

Aside from the visual kinship, it is not too grand to make comparisons between Wajda's film and Welles's. Just as *Citizen Kane* changed the direction of American cinema, *Ashes and Diamonds*, both politically and aesthetically, was instrumental in helping to foster a new Polish cinema free from the constraints of Stalinism and (at least temporarily) from the doctrine of Socialist Realism. Also, more than any other Polish filmmaker, Wajda has probed into the national myths surrounding the Second World War and its aftermath. However, despite major works such as *A Generation*, *Kanal*, *Lotna* (1959), *Samson* (1961), *Landscape After Battle* (1970), *Korczak* (1990), *The Ring With the Crowned Eagle* (1993) and, more recently, *Katyn* (2007), *Ashes and Diamonds* remains his most significant, complex and moving depiction of his nation's tragic involvement in this conflict.

Further reading

Janina Falkowska, *Andrzej Wajda: History, Politics and Nostalgia in Polish Cinema*, New York, Berghahn Books, 2006.

John Orr and Elzbieta Ostrowska (eds), *The Cinema of Andrzej Wajda: The Art of Irony and Defiance*, New York, Columbia University Press, 2003.

Andrzej Wajda, *Wajda on Film: A Master's Notes*, London, Acrobat Books, 1991.

Brian Hoyle

Il Postino/The Postman (1994)

[Country: Italy, France. Production Company: Cecchi Gori Pictures, Pentafilm, Esterno Mediterraneo Film, Blue Dahlia Productions, Le Studio Canal. Director: Michael Radford.[1] Producers: Mario and Vittorio Cecchi Gori and Gaetano Daniele. Screenwriters: Anna Pavignano and Furio Scapelli (based on the novel *Ardiente Paciencia* by Antonio Skármeta). Cinematographer: Franco di Giacomo. Music: Luis Bacalov. Editor: Roberto Perpignani. Cast: Massimo Troisi[2] (Mario Ruoppolo), Philippe Noiret[3] ('Don' Pablo Neruda), Maria Grazia Cucinotta[4] (Beatrice Russo), Renato Scarpa (Telegrapher), Mariano Rigillo (Di Cosimo), Anna Bonaiuto (Matilde), Linda Moretti (Donna Rosa).]

> I've ranged the far-famed seas,
> the nuptial stamen of each island,
> I'm a great paper seafarer,
> and I ran, ran, ran,
> to the uttermost foam
>
> Pablo Neruda, *El Canto General* (1950)

Synopsis: In the 1950s, in a fishing port on a small Italian island in the Mediterranean Sea, Mario, illiterate and unemployed, dreams of a more attractive elsewhere (The New World, America). At the local cinema, he watches newsreels and hears of the impending arrival in the village[5] of the great exiled poet from Chile, Pablo Neruda, which leads to his employment as postman charged with bringing Neruda his daily mail.

The daily encounters between the two men, one illiterate the other a future Nobel Prize-winning writer, slowly transform into a friendship. Under the benevolent authority of the *maestro*, Mario is slowly initiated into the mysteries of poetry. His vision of the world, of human beings and of things is slowly being transformed and he begins to write poetically himself, bold enough to imitate, even copy, Don Pablo himself.

He falls in love with Beatrice, the waitress in the village restaurant, carefully watched over by her sour-tempered aunt, Donna Rosa. Carried away by the power of brand-new words that move him deeply, and assisted by Neruda, he conquers and marries her, or rather she allows herself to be conquered. His mentor leaves, leaving him alone with his illusions, corresponding only occasionally and inconsistently. His disappointment is big: 'He treated me like a friend, like a brother'. He becomes radicalised politically, identifying with the communist cause. He opposes the corrupt official who in order to get elected promises to bring running water to the village, he defends exploited fishermen and finally dies during a turbulent demonstration against the social democrats' election victory. When Don Pablo returns to the village, he simultaneously learns about Mario's death and the birth of Mario's son, Pablito.

As a novel and film about apprenticeship, *Il Postino* can be considered on three interconnected levels that suggest the hero's progressive maturation in terms of his intellectual ability, love life and political consciousness.

Poetry, arguably literature's most accomplished form, represents something like magic for Mario. It awakens his dormant sensibilities; it allows him to name things; and to name what is beyond things. He, whose father is illiterate like the other fishermen, begins to realise that the physical world is legible, decipherable, and that he did not know anything about it. Having a novice's innocence, he asks the question that recurs throughout the film: what is a metaphor? This figure of speech, which enriches thought by hiding a first meaning in favour of a hidden meaning, is thus a form of creation. Mario breathes the air of gods, he is transfigured. He will invent images without even knowing it. Don Pablo confesses that poetry cannot be explained, it is felt. 'It is only with the heart that one can see rightly', Saint-Exupéry said in *The Little Prince*. In the film, Neruda says: 'Better than any explanation is the experience of feelings that poetry can reveal to a nature open enough to understand it'. Mario is open and ready.

Because of the letters Don Pablo receives, Mario believes with a touching naiveté that poets are loved by women. It gives him the strength to approach voluptuous Beatrice, whom he calls 'one of the wonders of the island' and who speaks to him primarily through her body. To describe her, Mario finds new words like new-laid eggs – 'Your smile spreads like a butterfly' – while throughout the film a deeply symbolic table football suggests how the line – immobile and flat – transforms into the three-dimensional roundness of the earth and the stars. Mario discovers nature, which the director wanted to look 'oppressive and beautiful' – a volcano towers over the landscape – he is transported, ennobled, grows.

Through poetry, the man who, borrowing Don Pablo's words, said that he was 'tired of being a man' obtains a sort of superhumanity and, like Rimbaud's poet, *sees* what human beings only imagined they saw. Words and their sonorous flesh invade him, the rhythm of a sentence dances as if tossed on a boat. However, words are not innocent; if we believe Donna Rosa they carry tensions and threats, in love as well as in politics. Words are 'loaded guns' (Brice Parain).

But for Mario everything acquires a poetic dimension, the real is transposed: the beauty of women, the sky, the sea, the sound of waves, the belly of a pregnant woman, all things that he records with the tape recorder that Pablo leaves him, so as to lose nothing of the vibrations of the World and the Universe. Mario, the character and Massimo, the actor with a suffering body – do they realise that the end is close?

This island fable is historically based on the communist poet's Italian sojourn. After the Communist Party was banned, Neruda went into hiding, and in 1949, into exile.[6] It benefits from the discrete music dominated by a tango leitmotiv, 'as if it came out of Neruda's soul, took the little postman and makes him into an accomplished human being' (L. Bacalov). The rich chromatic palette (the ocre of the house, the Mediterranean vegetation, and the warm and intense blue of the sea) provide a setting favourable to a spiritual odyssey.

The film was successful in both Europe and the United States, where it played in 270 cinemas, an exceptional number for a foreign film. It received multiple awards, including an Oscar for Best Dramatic Score (and four other nominations) and three BAFTA awards. This success was to some extent connected to Massimo Troisi's tragic death a few days after the end of shooting. Suffering from a cardiac malformation, he had been advised against making the film and told to wait for a heart transplant. He decided otherwise, but could stay on his feet for only a few moments, and was doubled in many scenes.[7]

A gaunt body marked by illness, looking a bit like Pasolini, a nasal Neapolitan voice, facial expressions, expressive gestures and eloquent hands also evoke the tragedy of existence for a Mediterranean soul like Mario. With this film, we are at the source of the history of the Mediterranean (*mare nostrum*) which worships the word, the verb, exhaling as if with the promise of a great spiritual civilisation to come. 'The honor of mankind, sacred SPEECH', (Paul Valéry).

In Mario's destiny and in the film itself, there is both the sun of Eros and the shadow of Thanatos.

> And it was at that age ... Poetry arrived
> in search of me. I don't know, I don't know where
> it came from, from winter or a river.
> I don't know, how or when,
> no, they were not voices, they were not words, nor silence,
> but from a street I was summoned,
> from the branches of night
> abruptly from the others,
> among violent fires
> or returning alone,
> there I was without a face
> and it touched me.
>
> Pablo Neruda[8]

Notes

1. Michael Radford, a British filmmaker born in India (New Delhi) has made 13 films as director and 8 films as screenwriter. *Il Postino* is his sixth film.
2. Massimo Troisi (1953–1994) was born in Campania, in the Province of Naples, appeared as actor in seven film comedies, and as actor-director in six other films.
3. Philipee Noiret, born in 1925 in Paris, has acted in more than 200 films and has directed 5.
4. Maria Grazia Cucinotta was born in Messina, Sicily, in 1960. *Il Postino* was her fifth film.
5. The village in ruins was reconstructed by the filmmaker.
6. He would receive the Nobel Prize in Literature in 1971.
7. His double is Gerardo, who resembled Troisi so much that at Troisi's funeral, people thought he was Troisi's ghost.
8. This text appears at the end of the film, before the final credits. Paul Valéry, 'The Pythoness' in *Charms*, trans. James L. Brown, Chico, CA, Forsan Books, 1983, p. 69.

Further reading

Ann Ryan, *Il Postino, Study Guide*, Irish Film Institute. Available at www.irishfilm.ie/downloads/il_postino.pdf.

Marie-Pierre Zoui, *Il Postino. Un film de Michael Radford*, Dossier pédagogique, Les Grignoux, Liège, 1997.

Daniel Armogathe (translated by Sabine Haenni)

Psycho (1960)

[Country: USA. Production Company: Shamley Productions. Director: Alfred Hitchcock. Screenwriter: Joseph Stefano (from a novel by Robert Bloch). Music: Bernard Hermann. Cinematographer: John L. Russell. Editor: George Tomasini. Cast: Anthony Perkins (Norman Bates), Janet Leigh

(Marion Crane), Vera Miles (Lila Crane), John Gavin (Sam Loomis), Martin Balsam (Arbogast).]

Synopsis: After stealing money from her boss, Marion Crane drives out of town and stops at a motel off of the main freeway. There she meets Norman Bates, the young owner of the motel. Marion decides to return the money but is murdered before she can do so and Norman disposes of her body. Marion's sister, Lila, and her lover, Sam, come looking for her along with a private detective, and together they uncover Norman's intense relationship with his mother.

As with several Hitchcock films, *Psycho* has at the heart of its plot the violent abuse of a woman by a man and could be read as a misogynistic text. Through both the central character of Marion Crane and Norman Bates' mother, women are represented as deceptive, manipulative, controlling and, from a male perspective, unfailingly unpredictable. The key passage in the film that has become one of the most famous scenes in the history of cinema – the shower scene – focuses in intimate detail on the brutal murder of a vulnerable woman. In a film often seen as the original 'slasher' movie this is the central action towards which everything prior to this leads and from which everything after it follows. The scene is graphic for the period – only being passed for viewing after well-documented tactical exchanges with the censors (and retaining one frame in which the knife penetrates flesh) (Rebello 1998: 145–6). Marion is 'raped' via Norman's preceding voyeuristic act as well as through the use of the phallic dagger.

Adding to the disturbing nature of the attack is the fact that as a result of the preceding voyeuristic observation of the 'prey' the violence is clearly presented as sexually motivated. As an infant who the domineering mother has not allowed to develop into adulthood the discovery of a woman who rouses the sexual adult can lead it seems to only one outcome. Furthermore, from a 'male' perspective, as viewers we could be said to be implicated in the voyeurism, not only by sharing Norman's view of Marion through the peephole in the previous scene but also as a result of any pleasure we may gain from viewing Janet Leigh as Marion in all her naked vulnerability in the shower prior to the attack.

On a first viewing the spectator would not be expected to see the attacker as Norman (although this would depend upon how much prior knowledge of the storyline has been gained from friends or background reading before coming to the film). On subsequent viewings the spectator's involvement in the scene will essentially shift from the shock or surprise created as a result of the original restricted perspective on events to a sense of expectation attaching to our now omniscient knowledge of the narrative. Our identification with Marion (and hence our sympathy for her) should never be in doubt since it has been her and the events that have happened to her that we have followed from the beginning of the film. In the parlour we have heard her announce her intention to return to Phoenix to seek redemption and in the shower we have seen her symbolically washing away her guilt (so that she goes to her death with a restored sense of innocence). But, still, we do spy on her from Norman's perspective, we do observe her in her nakedness beneath the shower, and we do experience the knife attack from the attacker's perspective. The positioning of the viewer, whether male or female, via film construction, and more importantly the way in which that position is accessed and activated by the viewer, becomes critical for the individual's reading of the shower scene moment.

If we move beyond the issue of whether or not this scene and this film might be said to be misogynistic, *Psycho* offers the possibility of an even more disturbing overall perspective. If the central image of woman is of someone at the mercy of voyeurism and physical abuse, the image of man in the form of Norman is of a creature at once vulnerable and weak while also being predatory and brutal. This is not presented as an unsympathetic portrait of a serial-killer; Norman is not seen simply and comfortingly as a monstrous aberration, on the contrary, in both his importance to the narrative and the achieved emotional impact upon the viewer his presence completely overpowers the role of Sam as the conventional heroic Hollywood male. John Gavin (Sam) has a cardboard cut-out of a part that reflects not just Hitchcock's lack of interest in (and therefore, weak focus upon) this aspect of the narrative but more fundamentally the shift of attitudes within society away from confident idolisation of the 'good guy' hero towards an almost mesmeric fascination with the darkness existing just beneath the veneer of civilisation. This may be too simplistic in that films and filmmakers have always shown an interest in darker characters but to see *Psycho* within the context of a loss of faith in John Wayne-style heroes at least moves us towards considering this film within a wider social context rather than as a simple expression of the vision of Hitchcock the auteur.[1]

Furthermore, if the image of man that is presented could be said to be as bleak as that of the brutalised woman, the image of male-female relationships hardly reinforces the concept of the 'American Dream'. The opening scene makes the bitter failure of Sam's first marriage clear; and in the next scene the best Cassidy can do for his daughter, even with all of his money, is to buy off unhappiness. Moments of pleasure, like that of Sam and Marion in the hotel room, it seems have necessarily to be obtained surreptitiously and against society's wishes. The social institutions of marriage and the family are placed under intense scrutiny. In the opening scene, despite the context of the illicit hotel rendezvous, Marion actually demonstrates her allegiance to an idealised notion of marriage that she aspires to attain seemingly at any cost. Ironically, the moment at which she realises that the false allure of this socially constructed norm can lead you into a trap is the point at which, because of her innocent openness towards another being, her fate is sealed. The central theme of life as a process that constantly ensnares people into traps from which (it seems) they find it impossible to extricate themselves is made clear in this scene in the parlour between Norman and Marion. Norman's entrapment and its origin within a 'family' comprising an absent father and domineering mother is given powerful visual representation in the final haunting superimposition of the mother's face over his.

Depending on your perspective *Psycho* (as with Hitchcock's wider body of work) can be seen to be underpinned by either a murky, unforgiving view of life or an entirely realistic view of humanity. It seems as if everybody has guilty secrets; even Caroline (Pat Hitchcock) in the early office scene, hemmed in by a husband and a mother who continually check-up on her (effectively at the mercy of family and marriage) has a secret supply of tranquilisers that help to make her life bearable. Each character is motivated by self-interest or uncontrollable desires, or a combination of the two. Civilised behaviour is no more than skin deep. The killer is in our midst but cannot be easily detected. In a parody of the supposed best aspects of a civilised society Norman offers hospitality and friendship but this it seems is a cover for the savagery that is just below the surface, a savagery nurtured within the most cherished institution of Western civilisation. The psychiatrist may offer the conventional comforts of the Hollywood resolution that has an authoritative male figure demonstrating a reassuringly controlled understanding of events, but we do not end on this note, we end with not only the image but the haunting words of the absent presence of Hitchcock's caricature of cherry-pie 'mom'.

From the beginning the examination of contemporary US society has been clear. We open with Marion and Sam taking part in an extramarital relationship in a cheap downtown hotel that rents rooms by the hour during the middle of the day. This might focus on individuals but it is about the condition of a whole society. Sam feels trapped by his life as Marion does by hers. The temptation to transgress social boundaries of acceptable behaviour is present for each character. And we are not left out of the equation; we have our position as voyeurs very clearly marked out us from the outset by the elaborate opening camera movement that slips us in through the partially open hotel window to view a couple's intimate behaviour and listen in on the personal details of their lives. From scanning the city skyline we are taken in beneath the surface of society to view just one example of the lives being played out everywhere.

When Norman leads Marion into his parlour behind the reception area of the Bates Motel editing emphasises the stuffed birds. There is the predatory owl in mid-swoop followed by the ominously sharp-beaked shadow of a crow, a harbinger of death (or perhaps a raven even more strongly associated with the gallows in English folklore). Owls are clearly associated with hunting and the eating of flesh: crows (and even more so ravens) with being meat-eating scavengers but also as capable of dispatching defenceless, unsuspecting prey. The pheasant positioned behind Norman symbolises a species bred purely for the purpose of being ritually slaughtered. Meanwhile Marion nibbles thoughtfully on bread and milk, a nurturing food associated with mothering and helping the young and otherwise weak. Nor should we miss the paintings of classical nudes on the walls: the female body displayed in all its naked vulnerability before the essentially male gaze. Norman wrings his hands, lurches between one position and another ('I say I don't mind, but I do'), leans forward to seemingly take Marion into his confidence, leans back as she retreats from his position of confidentiality, and finally moves from nervous smile to aggressive confrontation. Marion perches on the edge of her chair, her body posture and arms in a tight defensive position as she weighs her words thoughtfully. What is said makes it clear that Norman's and Marion's positions are effectively metaphors for the general state of being experienced by us all.

Note

1. Writing about *Notorious* Chopra-Gant suggests that when considering Hitchcock's work it is important to consider the ways in which 'the films register contemporaneous discourses that articulate key social anxieties of their historical moment' (Chopra-Gant 2005: 361). His point in relation to *Notorious* is that moral decline is being linked to the absence of parental authority during the early post-war period and maternal domination, or 'momism', to the infantilisation of men.

Further reading

Charlotte Chandler, *It's Only a Movie: Alfred Hitchcock, a personal biography*, London, Simon and Schuster, 2005.

Mike Chopra-Gant, 'Absent fathers and 'moms', delinquent daughters and mummy's boys: envisioning the postwar American family in Hitchcock's *Notorious*', *Comparative American Studies* Vol. 3, No. 3, 2005, pp. 361–75.

Raymond Durgnat, *A Long Hard Look at Psycho*, London, BFI, 2002.

Janet Leigh and Christopher Nickens, *Psycho: Behind the Scenes of the Classic Thriller*, New York, Wings, 2005.

Patrick McGilligan, *Alfred Hitchcock: A Life in Darkness and Light*, Chichester, Wiley, 2003.

Stephen Rebello, *Alfred Hitchcock and the Making of Psycho*, London and New York, Marion Boyars, 1998.

Donald Spoto, *The Dark Side of Genius: The Life of Alfred Hitchcock*, London, Plexus, 1983.

John White

Pulp Fiction (1994)

[Country: USA. Production Company: A Band Apart and Miramax Films. Director: Quentin Tarantino. Screenwriter: Quentin Tarantino (stories: Tarantino and Roger Avery). Cinematographer: Andzrej Sekula. Editor: Sally Menke. Cast: John Travolta (Vincent Vega), Samuel L. Jackson (Jules Winnfield), Uma Thurman (Mia Wallace), Ving Rhames (Marsellus Wallace), Bruce Willis (Butch Coolidge), Tim Roth (Pumpkin), Amanda Plummer (Honey Bunny), Quentin Tarrantino (Jimmie).]

Synopsis: *Pulp Fiction* is structured around three interlinking story segments which are told in non-chronological order. Vincent and Jules, two hitmen working for the gangster Marsellus, retrieve a briefcase of money belonging to their boss which had been stolen by a group of minor drug dealers. While carrying out this job they accidently shoot one of the dealers and have to hide the body at their friend Jimmie's house. Marcellus has paid Butch, an ageing boxer, to throw a fight but Butch, prompted by the memory of his dead father, decides he can't do it. During his attempt to escape after the match, Butch shoots Vincent but then literally runs into Marsellus. Before Marcellus is able to kill Butch they are kidnapped, in a random sequence of events, by the owner of a pawn shop and his cousin who rape and torture Marsellus, Butch escapes but decides to return and rescue Marcellus, by doing so he cancels his debt and is free to leave with his fiancé.

It is difficult to think of another contemporary film which has created a similar impact to *Pulp Fiction.* Others have been as controversial (e.g. *The Last Temptation of Christ* (Martin Scorsese, 1988), *Natural Born Killers* (Oliver Stone, 1994)) but *Pulp Fiction* is different in the way that its reception affected not only the industry and audiences but also pressure groups and academics, resulting in arguments about the morality of the film and the future of filmmaking. *Pulp Fiction* was an event film in the context of mid-1990s postmodern culture and the cinematic trend of 'cool violence', already linked with Quentin Tarantino's previous film *Reservoir Dogs* (1992). Tarantino himself became a star and selling point for the film. The divided reactions to *Pulp Fiction* have to be read through the debate around postmodernism itself as being either a mainstream or an oppositional mode. In other words, is it a stylish but superficial imitation of existing texts, or a reinterpretation and reassessment of cultural forms?

The success of *Pulp Fiction* challenged (particularly in the US) the boundaries between art-house, independent and mainstream cinema. *Pulp Fiction* was the first fully formed incarnation of the 'independent major'; an increasingly pejorative term for a film which has conventions associated with independent cinema (i.e. unconventional style and structure, character rather than action led) but which is coded to appeal to a more mainstream audience because of demands on the producer/distributor as an affiliate of a media conglomerate. This style of filmmaking was embodied – perhaps invented – by Miramax in the mid-to-late 1990s. The Hollywood agent Rick Hess described the way *Pulp Fiction* amalgamated art-house and Hollywood styles: 'Yes it had an unusual timeline totally non-linear in every way, but it had sex and drugs and rock 'n' roll, and violence, and that's something that every studio would have gone for' (Biskind 2004: 169). Miramax, although owned by Disney in 1994, had developed a marketing brand as an independent, small-scale producer battling against the power of Hollywood (a narrative repeated in the persona of Tarantino as the outsider). They had had a relatively successful period distributing independent American and European films before the incredible commercial success of *Pulp Fiction.* The estimated budget for the film was $8.5m which represented minimal risk to Miramax as they had sold the worldwide rights for $11m before filming began. The film went on to gross over $100m at the US box office – the first time an independent film had achieved this. The effect of this success on the independent film sector is debatable. For some filmmakers *Pulp Fiction* created economic opportunities and an interest in new filmmakers which hadn't existed before. Others were concerned about the phenomenon of 'indiewood' – independent films now carried the kind of financial expectations more usually associated with Hollywood films.

The mixing of Hollywood genres and European cinema styles which made this film so appealing to the emerging independent majors can be also read as an example of postmodernism (which continues to be evident Tarantino's more recent work, *Kill Bill* (2003) and *Grindhouse* (2007)). The discussion of postmodernism as an aesthetic is itself controversial with some critics arguing the postmodern is a period rather than a style (Jameson 1983). However, there are characteristics which have become accepted as signifying a postmodern text – and which are particularly applicable to film. This categorisation relies on the interrelated concepts of simulation, bricolage and intertextuality. All these concepts emphasise the 'ready made' nature of postmodern culture – the assembly of new texts from existing ones. It is this stylistic tendency which has led to readings of postmodernism as ahistorical.

This interpretation argues that the lack of any history or context beyond the reference to other texts in the postmodern aesthetic results in a loss of meaning and analytical possibilities.

Postmodern characteristics are apparent in *Pulp Fiction* in the acknowledgement of film history through references to and recycling of genres, narratives and visual styles. Intertextuality is evident in the construction of the plot, where narrative 'old chestnuts' (gang member takes out the boss's wife and must not fall for her, a boxer past his best is bribed to throw a fight, hitmen on a mission) of b-movie history are retold. Genre iconography from the 1940s – guns, black suits, briefcases, cigarette smoke, crimson red lipstick and nail polish – appear throughout the film but don't signify that the film belongs to a specific genre. The concept of recycling is also evident in the use of stars; specifically John Travolta whose back catalogue (*Saturday Night Fever* (1977) rather than *Look Who's Talking* (1989)) allows his turn on the dance floor to be read as iconic (rather than merely nostalgic or poignant).

Individual characters are also linked to a specific genre or film style, even though the rest of the cast may not coexist within it. Mia (the wife of the boss, Marsellus Wallace) is introduced as a femme fatale, her entrance imitating Barbara Stanwyck's in *Double Indemnity* (1947). She is represented in black and white fragments – black hair, trouser legs, ankles, mouth – we don't see her face until the car pulls up at Jack Rabbit Slims. Her role as the untouchable but irresistible wife also echoes the triangular set up of 1940s film noir. Mia is a failed TV actress whose cancelled pilot *Fox Force Five* is an example of Tarantino's references to invented cultural signs (Jack Rabbit Slims, the Big Kahuna Burger) which are intertwined with examples of real popular culture and people (*Modesty Blaize*, Douglas Sirk). Mia's ability to affect the film stock itself – she draws a square on the screen to illustrate 'Don't be a square' – points to the increasingly slippery distinctions between reality and representation highlighted by postmodernism. Mia is a character constructed from the fragments of other imaginary characters whose back story is an invented (but real in the film) TV pilot for a series which never existed (in any context). These levels of referencing and quotation within a single character are reminiscent of *À bout de souffle* (Jean-Luc Godard, 1959) and the way in which Godard constructs the character of Michel Poiccard (Jean Paul Belmondo) as a 'would-be gangster' who imitates Humphrey Bogart.

The difficulty of defining postmodern style is evident in the differing claims for it as either oppositional to or part of mainstream culture; parody or pastiche. The mainstream tendency is pastiche – a visually exciting imitation of existing styles which remains superficial because it is divorced from wider contexts (often dismissed as form over content). The oppositional mode – parody – is also imitative but aims to evaluate and subvert the original codes or meanings associated with the imitated form. The oppositional tendency questions and challenges, attempting to construct new meaning through placing existing cultural styles and movements in new contexts. In postmodern cinema this could refer to the way the intertextual mixing of genres (e.g. blaxploitation, gangster and musical) changes the meaning of the original representations (e.g. race and gender). The mainstream mode is merely an imitation or copy with nothing new to say. Whether a text is parody or pastiche it will share characteristics of style, form and content but it will operate within either the oppositional or mainstream mode. Predictably, the categorisation of texts in these terms is open to debate.

This debate is particularly pertinent to the main areas of controversy around *Pulp Fiction*; the representation of violence and race. The sudden shifts and contrasts in tone which continually move from suspense and violence to comedy and the banal is another important borrowing from Godard and the French New Wave. In 'The Bonnie Situation' Vincent accidentally shoots Marvin, the student who he and Jules specifically did not kill in interrogating Brad and his partners. The impact of the violence is undercut by humour – the gun unexpectedly goes off – and irony, as at that moment Vincent is asking Marvin whether he believes that God controls peoples' actions. After the death in the car, Jules is more upset about the ensuing mess created in Jimmie's bathroom, more fearful about his reaction than the death of a young man. The most sustained period of suspense, verging on horror, is during 'The Gold Watch' when Butch and

Marsellus are tortured in a pawn shop basement by the owner and a corrupt sheriff – both of whom are drawn as stereotypical hillbillies reminiscent of *Deliverance* (1972). Even when the two men are gagged, bound, covered in petrol and blood, and while the threat of rape is clear but unspoken, the use of film language provokes comedy. This is achieved through the long takes – so long that they have the effect of the uncomfortable silence referred to earlier by Mia – someone in the audience will have to break it, quite likely through nervous laughter. As the sheriff plays 'Eenie Meenie' between the two men to select his victim the camera remains on their faces capturing their intense concentration on the game and the moment of hope in Marcellus' eyes when he thinks he isn't 'it'. The contrast between the children's game – and the gravity given to it – and the grown, sadistic men becomes absurd and is part of the representation of masculinity in the film; the men are often childlike and bewildered. It is characteristic of Tarantino's style of this period that the actual violence takes place off screen; behind closed doors or just out of frame. This technique allows greater manipulation of the audience whether through the anticipation created in the period before the violence or through the unguarded reaction (often laughter) to the unpredictable. It is in this context that the violence initially made the film so controversial and led to calls for censorship. This tone is not new in American cinema – *Bonnie and Clyde* (1967) also deliberately copied this technique from European films – but in *Pulp Fiction* it is allied to an explicitness that was not previously possible.

Perhaps the more lasting and divisive controversy of the film though is that of the representation of race, particularly in the use of racially taboo words. The effect on the audience is similar to the effect of the unexpected violence – shock and laughter. That it is the director himself speaking the words (as Jimmie) means an aura of 'cool', of being daring and transgressive, is also attached. For some critics (see Hill 1998) the use of postmodern style in Hollywood films operates at a conservative level, smuggling in traditional ideologies (of, for example, race and gender) beneath the experimental style and references to culture beyond the mainstream (blaxploitation, b-movies, French New Wave, etc.). Controversy over the use of the term 'nigger' is increased by the suggestion that it is being 'legitimised' by the homage to blaxploitation, the character of Jules, and that Bonnie (Jimmie's wife) is a black woman.

The use of such a taboo word, in the context of a white American speaking it to an African American, illustrates why postmodernism is such a divisive concept. *Pulp Fiction* shifts the status of black popular culture by reclaiming marginalised forms and to do this it cuts them off from their original time and place. The shock of the use of racial terms in the film shows how strong the hold of historical and social meaning is – not all signs are easily removed from their context.

Further reading

Peter Biskind, *Down and Dirty Pictures: Miramax, Sundance and the Rise of Independent Film*, New York and London, Bloomsbury, 2004.

Warren Buckland, 'Narrative Chronology in Pulp Fiction' in his *Understand Film Studies*, London, Hodder Education, 2010, pp. 56–60.

John Hill, 'Film and Postmodernism', in John Hill and Pamela Church Gibson (eds), *The Oxford Guide to Film Studies*, Oxford, Oxford University Press, 1998.

Fredric Jameson, *Postmodernism*, London, Verso, 1983.

Sharon Willis, 'Style, posture, and idiom: Tarantino's figures of masculinity', in Christine Gledhill and Linda Williams (eds), *Reinventing Film Studies*, London, Arnold, 2000.

Sarah Casey Benyahia

Les quatre cents coups/The 400 Blows (1959)

[Country: France. Production Company: Les Films du Carrosse and Sédif Productions. Director: François Truffaut. Producer: François Truffaut. Screenwriters: François Truffaut and Marcel Moussy. Cinematographer: Henri Decaë. Music: Jean Constantin. Editor: Marie-Josèphe Yoyotte. Cast: Jean-Pierre Léaud (Antoine Doinel), Patrick Auffay (René), Claire Maurier (Gilberte Doinel – Antoine's mother), Albert Rémy (Julien Doinel – Antoine's father), Guy Decomble ('Petite Feuille' – The French teacher).]

Synopsis: The narrative of *The 400 Blows* condenses events drawn from several years of Truffaut's own childhood into what appear to be a few weeks or months in the life of Antoine Doinel. Antoine's world revolves around three locations: the cramped apartment he shares with his mother (Claire Maurier) and adoptive father (Albert Rémy); the school classroom where he clashes daily with the ill-tempered schoolmaster (Guy Decomble); and the Paris streets into which he escapes with his best friend, René (Patrick Auffay). At school, Antoine is bored and inattentive, and frequently finds himself in trouble. At home, things are little better. He seems to be used as a skivvy by his parents and there is little warmth or joy or their relationship. His discovery that his mother is having an affair simply adds to tensions in the household. His one escape is out into the streets, cafés, fairgrounds, and cinemas of Paris; despite the seemingly constant rain, the film is a love letter to the city, right from the opening montage of tracking shots down avenues that take us closer and closer to the Eiffel Tower. As the story progresses, Antoine finds himself in escalating trouble. After a brief period of peace at home, Antoine and René are suspended from school and Antoine takes to living surreptitiously in René's house (his parents are even more neglectful than Antoine's but have more money). An abortive attempt to raise funds by stealing a typewriter from his father's office ends with Antoine's arrest and removal to an 'observation centre', as well as to his parents virtually disowning him. A final break for freedom leads to one of the most memorable and heart-stopping final shots in all cinema.

By 1959 François Truffaut was established as a key figure within the emergent French New Wave. The origins of the movement lay with the group of young film enthusiasts writing for *Cahier du cinéma*, the magazine co-founded by theorist Andre Bazin; Bazin became a father figure for Truffaut who dedicated his first feature film, *The 400 Blows* (1959), to his late mentor's memory. Along with Truffaut, the group included Jean-Luc Godard, Jacques Rivette, Claude Chabrol and Eric Rohmer, all of whom would move from film criticism to directing. Reacting against the 'quality' tradition of safe, studio-bound productions which dominated French cinema in the 1950s (critiqued by Truffaut in his article 'Une certaine tendance du cinema Français'), and inspired by Alexandre Astruc's call for cinema to have an equal artistic status with more established forms such as the novel, the *Cahiers* critics championed films which reflected the individual vision of their maker, assumed to be the director. Appropriately, Truffaut opens his book *The Films in my Life* with a quote from Orson Welles: 'I believe a work is good to the degree that it expresses the man who created it' (Truffaut 1980: 1). The *Cahier* critics identified such film-makers via their own excited responses to that personal vision producing an eclectic list of approved auteurs, as evidenced by the range of work Truffaut chose to highlight in his book, from the more obvious John Ford, Mizoguchi or Bergman, to the idiosyncratic with Mervyn LeRoy or Anatole Litvak.

It was logical enough for the group to move from polemics to film-making themselves, even if the means was not always easy to secure. The young directors quickly realised that low budgets were the path to freedom of expression. Michel Marie charts this development back to Jean-Pierre Melville's *Silence of the Sun* (1947) and Agnes Varda's *La Pointe*

Courte (1954) (Marie 2003: 48–52). The latter was produced by Ciné Tamaris who were able to cut costs by acting as a co-operative, a model adopted by the New Wave directors who often pooled their talents to reduce overheads and improve the chance of obtaining funding. Increasing criticism of policies pursued by the Centre National de la Cinématographie (CNC) led to a change in strategy with financial subsidies directed away from mainstream, large-scale productions towards cheaply made independents such as Claude Chabrol's debut, *Le beau Serge* (1958), often credited as the real beginning of the New Wave. Truffaut's own path into features lay courtesy of more providential funding: his father-in-law, Ignace Morgenstern, being a leading film distributor. It was he who provided the backing for *The 400 Blows* through Truffaut's own production company Films du Carrosse. The film's impressive box office performance, along with a positive critical reception, was followed by similar responses to Chabrol's *The Cousins* (1959) and Godard's *Breathless* (1960). Together these films announced the arrival of the New Wave (Marie 2003: 66).

The seeds of *The 400 Blows* lay in Truffaut's earlier short film, *Les mistons/The Mischief-Makers* (1957), which had drawn on memories of his own childhood. From this he began to develop ideas for a screenplay which would use a number of interlocking stories on the subject of childhood (Baecque and Toubiana 2000: 126–7). One of these episodes, 'La Fugue d'Antoine (Antoine's Flight)', was based directly on an incident in Truffaut's youth when he had tried to cover his truancy by telling his school teachers that his mother had died, resulting in his father slapping his face in front of the class. This story eventually formed one of the key sequences in *The 400 Blows*, with the film itself growing out of an accumulation of childhood stories, some of them Truffaut's own and others drawn from friends and collaborators, which became the tale of a single character, Antoine Doinel (Jean-Pierre Léaud). To develop these anecdotal moments into a coherent whole Truffaut worked with the novelist and screenwriter Marcel Moussy. Nonetheless, many scenes and details in the film belong specifically to Truffaut's own memories, including his stay at the Villejuif Observation Centre for Minors and the fact that, like the film's protagonist, Truffaut was born out of wedlock, passed around various family members including his grandmother, and then adopted by his mother's new husband. So closely did Truffaut identify with his alter ego that he subsequently brought him back to the screen on four further occasions, with Léaud aging each time in parallel to the director.

If personal commitment to a project was an essential of the New Wave's creed, this is apparent in more than just the autobiographical elements of *The 400 Blows*. The film was shot on location around parts of Paris which Truffaut had frequented as a boy, even down to the cinemas he used to play truant to from school: 'I saw my first two hundred films on the sly, playing hooky and slipping into the movie house without paying' (Truffaut 1980: 3). Films and film-going are an important part of Antoine's growing up; his happiest time with his parents comes on an evening out to see a film (curiously entitled *Paris nous appartient*, the name of the film then being made by Truffaut's friend, Jacques Rivette which was not completed until 1960). The films is also filled with cameo appearances from Truffaut's friends in the New Wave, from fellow directors Philippe de Broca and Jacques Demy, to the actors Jean-Claude Brialy and Jeanne Moreau, and even Truffaut himself who can be seen briefly in the funfair sequence. One of Antoine's friends at school is even called Chabrol.

In a manner typical of much early New Wave cinema, and of virtually all Truffaut's work, the film is constructed as a series of self-contained vignettes. At home we see Antoine taking out the rubbish or laying the table. He sits at his mother's dressing table, his face caught in a profusion of mirrors. We witness Antoine's fascination with the writer Balzac which leads to his constructing a shrine to the father of French realism, only for this to inadvertently catch fire resulting in another fight with his father. At school, he is initially punished for looking at a girly magazine in class, then for writing graffiti on the wall, and finally for his drastic lie about his mother's death (although this is a last resort brought about by sustained bullying from the schoolmaster). Out in the streets, he sees his mother with another man and spends a night scavenging for food and a bed. He also visits the cinema, a funfair, and a children's puppet show. In themselves, these scenes appear minor but they gradually, almost casually build the impression of Antoine's life; of boredom and bullying at school, of neglect and indifference at home, with only the streets and his friendship with René providing relief. Tellingly, the original French title, *Les quatre cent coups*, translates more accurately as 'raising hell', indicating defiance rather than the melancholy of *The 400 Blows*.

The film's power derives as much from its technique as its narrative. The overriding mode is of realist social observation, with evocative use of location and natural light to build a feeling of place and space. A number of scenes have the feel of documentary, including the kids playing in the school yard or the small children observed in the audience of the puppet show. This is emphasised further by Henri Decaë's camerawork. For the sequences at home and at school the camera is often static or tracks slowly back and forth across the confined space, while in the streets, and especially during Antoine's concluding run towards freedom, the camera is either highly mobile or is set in extreme wide shot or at a high angle emphasising the space around Antoine. As Anne Gillain suggests, 'these alternations give the film its powerful rhythm of tension and release' (Gillain 2000: 144). Selective use of close-up brings us near to Antoine at moments of emotion, while the subtle mise en scène frequently reminds of the degree to which he is imprisoned, with recurring motifs of bars or lattices in front of his face. Antoine's subjective experience of events is suggested by point-of-view shots, including an elaborate upside-down image when he is on a ride at the fair.

These techniques also place us firmly inside Antoine's perception, so that we empathise completely with him. The adult world as seen through his eyes is cold and phoney. His mother only becomes interested in him when there is a threat that he might tell her husband about her affair. When the truth comes out anyway, she wrongly blames Antoine and abandons him to his fate. He is beaten at home, at school, and at the reformatory to which he is sent. As in Dickens' novels, the maltreatment of children is seen as symptomatic of a rotten society. The only warmth he experiences is from his friend René who, with characteristic irony, is not permitted to visit him in the reformatory while his mother is allowed in, if only to reject him. This is a world where young and old are utterly at odds. In the end, there is no escape. Even out in the open, Antoine is hemmed in by sea and sky. Realising this, he turns accusingly to face us.

Further reading

Antoine de Baecque and Serge Toubiana, *Truffaut: A Biography*, Berkeley and Los Angeles: University of California Press, 2000. Originally published as *François Truffaut* (1996). English translation by Catherine Temerson.

Anne Gillain, 'The script of delinquency: François Truffaut's *Les 400 coups* (1959)' in Susan Hayward and Ginette Vincendeau (eds), *French Film: Texts and Contexts*, Oxford and New York: Routledge, 2000, pp. 142–57.

Michel Marie, *The French New Wave: An Artistic School*, Oxford: Blackwell, 2003. Originally published as *La Nouvelle Vague: Une école artistique* (1997). English translation by Richard Neupert.

Phil Powrie and Keith Reader, *French Cinema: A Student's Guide*, London and New York: Bloomsbury, 2011.

François Truffaut, *The Films in my Life*, London: Allen Lane, 1980. Originally published as *Les Films de ma Vie* (1975). English translation by Leonard Mayhew.

Robert Shail

Rabbit-Proof Fence (2002)

[Country: Australia. Production Company: Rumbalara Films and Olsen Levy. Director: Phillip Noyce. Screenwriter: Christine Olsen. Cinematographer: Christopher Doyle. Editors: John Scott and Veronika Jenet. Music: Peter Gabriel. Cast: Everlyn Sampi (Molly), Tianna Sainsbury (Daisy), Laura Monaghan (Gracie), Kenneth Branagh (A. O. Neville), David Gulpilil (Moodoo).]

Synopsis: In 1931, three aboriginal girls escape after being plucked from their homes to be trained as domestic staff and set off on a trek across the Australian Outback.

Rabbit-Proof Fence takes as its subject the forced removal and 're-education' of mixed-race Aboriginal children in early twentieth-century Australia. Given this backdrop, we might expect the film's title to be metaphorical, and indeed it is – though not necessarily in the way we might expect. Dividing the whole of Western Australia, the fence was put up in the early 1900s to separate the state's infamous plague of rabbits from arable land. In *Rabbit-Proof Fence*, though, the man-made barrier does not divide race from race, or even person from person, but rather provides the route map for a journey home. In the case of Philip Noyce's film, itself a homecoming of sorts for the Australian director based throughout the 1990s in Hollywood, the fence helps lead three young girls – Daisy, Gracie and the surrogate parent Molly – back to their northwestern home after escaping from the Moor River settlement in which they had been interned: a journey, on foot, of 1,500 miles. This is no mere poetic conceit on the part of the film's makers: this trip, remarkably, did take place, and is the basis of Doris Pilkington's 1996 book *Follow the Rabbit-Proof Fence.* Yet the film's central route provides a suitable image for the children's perspective on the world, and above all, a resistance to the spatially and racially informed segregation policies of the period.

The epic canvas of the film, which begins with striking overhead shots of the Australian outback as a kind of scorched abstract painting, is the location for a relatively short (90 minutes) and in structural terms very simple story. At the film's opening, the young girls are marked for removal and future integration into 'civilised' white society by A.O. Neville, the 'Chief Protector of Aborigines' (a post the real-life Neville held from 1915 to his retirement in 1940). Once established at the settlement, where they are forced to abandon their mother tongue in favour of English language and etiquette, the three children manage to make a break for freedom and begin the long walk home. Along their trip – for which the fence, thousands of miles along the way, provides the link – they must outwit not only the increasingly reluctant police staff under the orders of Neville, but also the sharper and more effective senses of Moodoo: an Aborginal 'tracker' whose main task is to hunt down and return escapees.[1] Essentially a tale of endurance and will under the most extreme of conditions and circumstances – Noyce, along with his director of photography Christopher Doyle, take pains to evoke the parched and shelterless terrain through which the girls walk – the film, sold and distributed internationally by the American company Miramax and veteran British producer Jeremy Thomas, struck a chord with filmgoers beyond its country of origin.

If international audiences warmed to its story of courage and resilience, in Australia the film's production and release was not without controversy. Funded by the Australian Film Finance Corporation, *Rabbit-Proof Fence* was made in the wake of the 1997 Royal Commission for the investigation of, amongst other things, the 'stolen generations' described in the film, and was in tune with the popular message of historical revision and apology central to the 2000 Sydney Olympics opening ceremony (the games at which Aborignal athlete Cathy Freeman lit the Olympic torch, and later became the first athlete of Aboriginal descent to win an individual gold medal). Because of its overt condemnation of a government policy enacted as late as 1971, and its implicit attack on decades of historical whitewashing, the film became the subject of conservative and extremist criticism both during its production and on its subsequent release (Petzke 2007: 235–6). Such negative publicity made *Rabbit-Proof Fence* a subject of national discussion, and may have helped it become – almost without precedent for a film on this subject – the second most popular domestic film of the year.

That the success of *Rabbit-Proof Fence* makes it something of a phenomenon only reflects, of course, the limited nature of such representations within the longer history of Australian cinema. The high-profile status (amongst critics, if not necessarily for paying audiences at the time of release) of films such as *Walkabout* (1971) or *The Chant of Jimmie Blacksmith* (1978), both of which feature Aborigines as key protagonists, only emphasises their relatively unusual subject matter. In her 1993 report on Aboriginal representation in cinema (actually written at the request of the Australian Film Commission), Marcia Langton argues that the narrow range of available imagery in the mainstream gives rise to a vicious circle of incomprehension. As she writes: 'Critics find it difficult to discuss Aboriginal works because of an almost complete absence of critical theory, knowledge of, and sensibility towards Aboriginal film and video production'; and yet it is precisely from '[f]ilm, video and television … that most Australians "know" about Aboriginal people' (Langton 1993: 23, 33). Films such as *The Chant of Jimmie Blacksmith*, then, about a young Aborigine driven to mass murder by systematic injustice, may merely have confirmed prevalent racist conceptions of 'beserk boongs hacking to death white ladies' (Colin Johnson, quoted in O'Regan 1996: 59), notwithstanding the film's subsequent critical recuperation. Yet Langton also makes the interesting point that 'correct' representations, and in particular the conviction that only Aboriginals can create 'right' or 'true' representations of Aboriginal life, itself carries racist assumptions about the Aboriginal people's mutual similarity and collective otherness to the foreign observer (1993: 27).

From this perspective, the marriage of *Rabbit-Proof Fence*'s story with a white male Hollywood director is informed not just by commercial pragmatism, but also by a desire to move beyond the closed circle of 'correct' representation. Peter Gabriel's score, for example, in the same vein as his various 'world music' collaborations throughout the 1990s, fuses indigenous motifs into an epic, globally resonant soundscape. This effort to make the universal out of the particular (a key to success in global cinema markets) characterises the whole film. As their journey is readable within familiar generic frameworks, especially that of the road movie or the prison-break drama, the girls' typicality, not their difference, is accentuated. But also, despite its apparent aim of representing the hidden side of Australian history, the story of *Rabbit-Proof Fence* is actually at one with the very Australian cultural myth of the underdog: what Ingo Petzke calls the 'little Aussie battler', exemplified amongst other figures by the outlaw Ned Kelly (2007: 239).

Combined with the fact that the film draws on a fascination with the wilderness, and in particular with a form of wandering – concepts which, Petske suggests, are 'deeply enshrined in the Australian psyche', from the song *Waltzing Matilda* to the *Mad Max* films (ibid.) – *Rabbit-Proof Fence* is not so much an 'unofficial' representation as an archetypical piece of Australian national cinema. Or more accurately, it is national cinema in the sense that national cinemas do not represent the nation as such, but rather contribute to an imaginary construction of the nation through and as myth; narrative forms which, to follow the anthropologist Claude Lévi-Strauss (1968), provide imaginary solutions to social contradictions. Like the Hollywood Western for an increasingly urban and later suburban American population, the Australian outback film has clearly been a powerful object of romantic identification or phantasmic projection for a largely coastal (and globally diasporic) metropolitan population. Similarly, heroic underdogs on the wrong side of authority's mistreatment have typically provided a powerful imaginary outlet for anti-Imperialist sentiment; be it the human cannon fodder ordered over the top by British officers in Peter Weir's 1981 film *Gallipoli*, or the honest Aussie cricketers battered and bruised by the unsporting tactics of the English captain in the TV miniseries *Bodyline* (1984). This is a practice described by Tom O'Regan as the cinematic 'dedominionizing' of Australia (1996: 67–8).

Rabbit-Proof Fence's screenwriter Christine Olsen has claimed her determination to bring Phillip Noyce on board (going so far as to track down the director's private Hollywood telephone number) was influenced by the way his films offer an unbiased and human view of all protagonists.[2] This is a fine intention, though it is arguably not so obvious in this particular work. British actor Kenneth Branagh brings his customary subtlety and intelligence to the role of Neville: a man who, as Branagh portrays him, was driven by an apparently well-meaning colonialist conviction that civilisation through ethnic 'whitening' was a good thing for all concerned. A possible shortcoming of the film, though, is that it does not provide the space for a more detailed portrait, in the way a documentary or a longer television series based on the events might have been able to do. As a result, Neville inevitably comes across as a sort of sophisticated child catcher, albeit a fairly articulate one; a view encouraged by the way he is frequently filmed through tilted camera angles, expressionistically offsetting the perpendicular lines of his monochromatic office. The effect of this, in distinct contrast to the fluid, luminous images of the three girls' world, is to evoke Neville's British bureaucratic mindset as a kind of derangement, a world apart from the 'natural' landscape inhabited by Daisy, Grace and Molly.

This decision to film the two respective worlds in different modes nevertheless generates what are, in terms of the history and politics of representation, very appropriate visual effects. The separation of the Aborigine's and the coloniser's space – on the one side, warm elemental tones of earth, sky and flora, on the other, the cold geometry of white civilisation – is also a distinction between ways of seeing. While our first glimpse of the three girls sees them clambering and climbing via close, floating camera movements, the first view from 'outside' is a long shot from the perspective of the police constable who will later take them away. This shot therefore establishes a detached, clinical and above all 'ethnographic' point of view: the sort of 'othering' vision that underpinned much of the colonial project, and which is most obviously represented in this film by Neville, who at one point provides a photographic slide show for the educational benefit of middle-class metropolitan ladies.

Significantly, then, the world from the three girls' viewpoint is not so much represented by a photographic vision – symptomatic of the technology of Empire – but by an idea of non-visual sensory connectivity underscored by Gabriel's music, but most pointedly represented by the sense of touch. When at one point the girls grasp the wire of the rabbit-proof fence, a reverse shot shows Molly's mother doing the same thing, as if the gesture physically bypasses and transcends distance and authority. As film theorists such as Laura Marks (2000) have discussed, the emphasis in film on touch and tactility has a political potential, especially in the representation of marginality or exile, partly in its resistance to objectifying visual regimes. In this instance, it is especially significant that the physical, tactile object connecting the girls from their home was a government-sanctioned divide, drawn on a map: that most clinical embodiment of man's (*sic*) desire to visually order and master the world. It is also notable that, the one and only time that Molly and Neville actually meet (during the girls' brief residence at Moor River), Neville is seen in a direct point-of-view shot from Molly's perspective: a distorting, fish-eye image that makes him look like an alien species, accentuating what to Molly (and by implication, us) must be the strange and unfathomable mystery of his being.

Notes

1. Moodoo is played by David Gulpilil, Australia's most well-known Aborigine actor. Gulpilil brings a familiarity and humanity to his performance that accentuates Moodoo's own ambivalence towards his (enforced) profession.
2. As described on the audio commentary track for the UK DVD.

Further reading

Marcia Langton, *'Well, I heard it on the radio and saw it on the television … '*, Sydney, Australian Film Commission, 1993.

Laura U. Marks, *The Skin of the Film: Intercultural Cinema, Embodiment and the Senses*, Durham NC and London, Duke University Press, 2000.

Tom O'Regan, *Australian National Cinema*, London and New York, Routledge, 1996.
Ingo Petzke, 'Rabbit-Proof Fence', in Geoff Mayer and Keith Beattie (eds), *The Cinema of Australia and New Zealand*, London: Wallflower, 2007, pp. 233–9.
Dora Pilkington, *Follow the Rabbit-Proof Fence*, Brisbane, University of Queensland Press, 1998.
Claude Lévi-Strauss, *Structural Anthropology*, London: Penguin, 1968.

Neil Archer

Rebel without a Cause (1955)

[Country: USA. Production Company: Warner Bros. Pictures. Director: Nicholas Ray. Screenwriter: Stewart Stern. Producer: David Weisbart. Music: Leonard Rosenman. Cinematographer: Ernest Haller. Editor: William H. Ziegler. Cast: James Dean (Jim Stark), Natalie Wood (Judy), Sal Mineo (John 'Plato' Crawford), Corey Allen (Buzz Gunderson), Edward Platt (Ray Fremick), Jim Backus (Frank Stark), Ann Doran (Carol Stark), William Hopper (Judy's Father), Rochelle Hudson (Judy's Mother), Virginia Brissac (Jim's Grandmother), Marietta Canty (Crawford's Maid), Dennis Hopper (Goon), Jimmy Baird (Beau).]

Synopsis: Set in suburban Los Angeles, *Rebel without a Cause* tells the story of an affluent family and their troubled son, Jim, who makes friends at the local high school with equally troubled teenagers, Judy and Plato. Jim is teased by a group of high school students, particularly their leader Buzz, and in order to prove his manhood agrees to race stolen cars to an abyss, a competition during with Buzz gets killed. Jim and Judy escape to an abandoned mansion, where Plato joins them. When they are found, Plato starts shooting randomly, escapes and hides in the Griffith Observatory where it comes to the final standoff.

Rebel without a Cause was symptomatic of the fifties as a transitional era. A WarnerColor Cinemascope production starring James Dean and Natalie Wood, borrowing its title from a 1944 non-fiction book, the film was part of a larger shift in Hollywood towards addressing a teenage audience, at a time when teenagers started to be seen as a distinct subculture in marketing terms. The film tapped into some of the era's pertinent social issues: teenage angst and delinquency, family conflicts in white middle-class suburbia, social conformity, changing gender norms among both the parental generation and their children, the nuclear holocaust, and the violence all these tensions in social relations so easily engendered. In doing so, it anticipated the larger cultural revolution that was to rock society and Hollywood cinema in the 60s.

Not least because it was seen as targeting a teenage audience, the Production Code Administration (PCA), which enforced the Production Code, a lengthy document outlining what could not be shown on screen, adopted by the film industry in the thirties, voiced concerns about *Rebel without a Cause.* Juvenile delinquency especially was a hotly debated topic – *The Saturday Evening Post* had run a series on the subject under the title 'The Shame of America' (Simmons 1995: 58). Other films, such as *The Wild One* (László Benedek, 1953) and *Blackboard Jungle* (Richard Brooks, 1955) tackled similar themes, the former starring Marlon Brando as a biker, the latter Sidney Poitier as a teen in a racially troubled high school. Not least because the state of America's youth was a hot-button topic, and because opinion as to the causes of juvenile delinquency was divided, the PCA objected to any 'derisive gesture' toward police officers, to what they (erroneously) took be the smoking of marijuana, to the implications of incest, to teenage sexuality, and to violence (the film originally started with Buzz's gang senselessly assaulting and beating a young man at night). These concerns were partially voiced from the increasingly important foreign market. The British Board of Film Censors (BBFC), which had banned both *The Wild One* and *Blackboard Jungle*, ordered cuts in *Rebel without a Cause* and limited its exhibition to those over 15 years old (Simmons 1995).

The tensions and contradictions that caused censorship concern were made visible on the level of acting – specifically James Dean's method acting – which exemplified 'a daily psychic tug of war between personal identity and social identity, or, ... individualism and conformity, alienation and patriotism' (Braudy, 1996: 193). Going back to the Group Theatre in New York City in the 1930s, and developed by Lee Strasberg at the Actor's Studio in the 1940s and 1950s, Method acting was an 'art based on the armature of the body', producing 'models of being' and 'models of social behaviour in postwar America' (Braudy 1996: 196, 195). In that sense it was part of a larger discourse about the performance of the body, which can also be found, for instance, in the fiction of Jack Kerouac or the poetry of Allen Ginsberg (Braudy 1996: 194). Such acting produced a 'layered self', depths of feeling in which the repressed became visible. Its ascendancy coincided with the rise of rebellious new male stars – Montgomery Clift, Marlon Brando, James Dean (Braudy 1996: 191–204).

Jim's anxiety has everything to do with the troubled nature of the postwar, white, suburban family. The film gestures towards postwar affluence – 'Don't I buy you everything you want?' Jim's father asks, and Plato's dad's contact with his son consists of his generous alimony checks. But money and consumerism cannot sustain families. Moreover, Jim's family is torn by gender conflicts, many of which centre on the father's emasculation. After having seen his father wearing a flowery apron over his grey-flannel suit, Jim becomes increasingly disillusioned about the possibility of getting help from his father, and assertively kicks in his mother's portrait when he storms out of the house after an argument in a later scene. *Rebel without a Cause* can thus easily be called a paternal melodrama – where what is at stake is the ability of fathers to become role models. And we might add that the context of and anxieties about the Cold War does not help stabilise paternal authority. 'It's just the age', Judy's mother says; 'the atomic age', Judy's little brother exclaims and shoots his toy rifle at the dinner table. Likewise, the otherwise so cockily performing teenagers look up in fascination and terror as they witness a cosmic explosion and the end of Earth at the Planetarium (the Griffith Park Observatory in Los Angeles): 'Man, existing alone, seems himself an episode of little consequence. That's all', the lecturer finishes. No wonder that the film perceives the authority of the father and the post-war patriarchal family structures as being besieged on all fronts. It mourns the loss of fatherly authority while simultaneously criticising its continued existence, most notably in the case of Judy's stern father.

The film's concern about the contradictions within the nuclear family was part of a larger post-war discourse about the effects of suburbanisation. In 1950 sociologist David Riesman published *The Lonely Crowd*, in which he suggested that the suburbs changed people's psychic life: equipped with internal 'radar', they constantly scan those around them and adjust their behaviour accordingly, thus becoming 'other-directed'. Riesman's work was part of a larger interest in – and anxiety about – how the post-war suburban economy affected especially male psyches. In 1955, the same year *Rebel without a Cause* came out, *The Man in the Gray Flannel Suit* was published, Sloan Wilson's novel about a Second World War veteran with domestic troubles working for an oppressive and conformist mental-health network. The following year, *The Man in the Gray Flannel Suit* was made into a film, and William Whyte's bestselling book, *The Organization Man*, was published, suggesting that corporate planning affected employees' inner lives, and ending with a chapter on suburbia – the 'organization man at home'. In these contexts, suburban men are successful, but other-directed businessmen who struggle with conformity, oppression and emasculation. Above all, more valiant forms of masculinity, more likely to be found outdoors (or in Western films) than in the suburbs, no longer seemed possible. The suit under Jim's father's apron did not suggest a masculine alternative.

Rebel without a Cause's trouble, however, extends beyond the family and beyond the suburbs. Already the PCA was concerned with the implications of a homosexual relationship between Jim and Plato, though it remained unable to determine what part of the script contained that inference, so that they dropped the issue (Simmons 1995: 59). From the opening scene at the police station, Jim is drawn in two different directions: Judy and Plato. The latter keeps a picture of actor Alan Ladd in his school locker, and competes with Judy for Jim's love and attention. Not unimportantly, in line with Hollywood's homophobia, Plato is also marked as the most disturbed character; and his potential queerness is deflated by an effort to stage the scene at the abandoned mansion – quite possibly the most utopian moment in the film – as a possible alternative nuclear family, with Jim as father, Judy as mother, and Plato as son. 'If only you could have been my father', Plato says to Jim.

Nonetheless, the film's gender and sexual politics are ambiguous and contradictory enough to be read in multiple ways. Judy longs for Jim's 'different' and 'sincere' masculinity: 'a man who can be gentle and sweet, like you are', she tells Jim. Of course, this longing itself may speak to changing notions of masculinity in the post-war era. But critics have also read it differently, as suggesting, for instance, Jim's 'butch' identity. In this context, *Rebel without a Cause* becomes a film about ambiguous gender identity, a film that can be read in lesbian terms, with Jim in the role of the butch and Judy in the role of the femme. As Kelly Hankin has wittily observed, Jim 'suffers from bathroom trouble', walking towards the women's bathroom in his new high school (1998: 7). Ray had directed gender-troubled films before, maybe most famously *Johnny Guitar* (1954), a Western where the final shootout occurs between two women. Dean's ambivalent sexuality – he appears to have had relationships with both men and women – also facilitates such a reading through extratexual knowledge about the film's star. Of course, a queer reading of *Rebel without a Cause* has become easier in subsequent decades, not least because in 1955 homosexuality was illegal, classified as a mental disease, so that lesbians made up part of the incarcerated or institutionalised youth (Cartier 2003: 447).

Rebel without a Cause is remarkable for how it mobilises cinematic style to emphasise and draw out the instability of gender and social conventions. Filmed in widescreen and brilliant colour, *Rebel without a Cause* was one of these films Hollywood thought could compete with television, which had emerged as a major force in entertainment, but which still remained constrained in terms of its aspect ratio and black and white image. In *Rebel without a Cause*, Ray uses the widescreen format effectively in terms of suggesting the tensions among the characters. In the early scene at the police station, for instance, he first films Jim, his father mother and grandmother in one frame, with the two women standing between the two men (literally and figuratively), and then follows up with a shot-reverse-shot pattern between Jim on the one hand and his father, mother and grandmother on the other. The three adults share the frame, with the grandmother intervening between the parents, in a way that suggests both their conflicts as well as their combined overpowering force. Another memorable scene occurs later in the film, when Ray films a conflict between Jim and his parents on the stairs in their suburban home, making use of the wide frame, the mise en scène (particularly the difference in height due to the stairs) as well as lighting. The film's conflicts, that is, are very much worked out and suggested on the stylistic level.

As a film that addressed both social problems and a teenage audience, *Rebel without a Cause* can be placed within a larger group of widely diverging films, ranging from George Lucas' *American Graffiti* (1973), to the teen comedies of John Hughes, and the more politically charged *Boys Don't Cry* (Kimberly Peirce, 1999), based on the actual murder of a transgender man in Nebraska. That *Rebel without a Cause* is connected to such widely different films suggests how it can be read in different ways, how, in the guise of popular entertainment, it lay bare the contradictions within American social conventions.

Further reading

Leo Braudy, '"No Body's Perfect": Method Acting and 50s Culture', *Michigan Quarterly Review*, Vol. 35, No. 1, Winter 1996, pp. 191–215.

Marie Cartier, 'The Butch Woman Inside James Dean or "What Kind of *Person* Do You Think a Girl Wants?"' *Sexualities*, Vol. 6, No. 3–4, 2003, pp. 443–58.

Thomas Doherty, *Teenagers and Teenpics: The Juvenilization of American Movies in the 1950s*, revised and expanded edition, Philadelphia, Temple University Press, 2002.
Kelly Hankin, 'A Rebel without a Choice?: Femme Spectatorship in Hollywood Cinema', *The Velvet Light Trap*, Vol. 41, Spring 1998, pp. 3–18.
David Riesman, *The Lonely Crowd: A Study of the Changing American Character*, New Haven, Yale University Press, 1950.
Jerold Simmons, 'The Censoring of *Rebel without a Cause*', *Journal of Popular Film*, Vol. 23, No. 2, pp. 56–63.
J. David Slocum (ed.), *Rebel Without a Cause: Approaches to a Maverick Masterwork*, Albany, State University of New York Press, 2005.
Sloan Wilson, *The Man in the Gray Flannel Suit*, New York, Simon and Schuster, 1955.
William H. Whyte, *The Organization Man*, New York, Simon and Schuster, 1956.

Sabine Haenni

The Red Shoes (1948)

[Country: UK. Production Company: The Archers. Directors and Screenwriters: Michael Powell and Emeric Pressburger. Cinematographer: Jack Cardiff. Editor: Reginald Mills. Music: Brian Easdale. Cast: Moira Shearer (Vicky Page), Anton Walbrook (Boris Lermontov), Marius Goring (Julian Craster), Leonide Massine (Grischa Ljubov).]

Synopsis: Based on Hans Christian Andersen's folk tale, the plot follows the career of Vicky Page (Moira Shearer) who rises to fame to dance the ballet of The Red Shoes. She falls in love with conductor Julian Craster (Marius Goring), but impresario Boris Lermontov (Anton Walbrook), fiercely protective of Vicky's career, forces Julian to resign. Vicky follows him in loyalty but marriage fails to fulfil her. While holidaying in Monte Carlo, she agrees once more to dance The Red Shoes ballet, but Julian arrives to persuade Vicky not to dance, making her choose between ambition and love. Lermontov dismisses Vicky: 'Go with him, be a faithful housewife, a crowd of screaming children and finish the dancing forever!' But as she tells Julian that she does love him, the camera cuts to her red shoes. His realisation that she loves dancing more than him precipitates his departure. Lermontov raises his arms in a gesture of triumph but, as Vicky heads towards the stage, the shoes impel her to her death.

The Red Shoes is a significant British film in terms of both its melodramatic aesthetic and its representation of shifting gender roles in a post-war economy. While today we may wonder at the extremity of Vicky's choice, it was very pertinent to British women in the late 1940s who had been mobilised for work for the duration of the Second World War. In the post-war period, official advice for a returning serviceman was that he should resume his rightful place as breadwinner of the household and the Treasury halved its subsidies for nurseries after 1945. However, the baby boom from 1947–1951, the establishment of a National Heath Service and the changes in welfare and education services, created new jobs for women in administration, nursing and teaching which contradicted the official message, reinforced by film-makers, that the real role for women still lay in 'home-making' (Braybon and Summerfield 1987: 259–77; Curran and Porter 1983: 291).

The Red Shoes explores these issues in terms of Vicky's conflict between career and domesticity. Narrative closure offers only death but her strength of will and artistic aspirations are celebrated in the film through an extravagance of spectacle, colour and glamour. J.B. Mayer's 1948 survey of Forties' audiences showed that women enjoyed the colour, romance and exoticism of the melodrama films of that time.[1] Powell and Pressburger's *The Red Shoes* thus provided the pleasure of a sparkling romance for a strong-willed heroine set for the most part in the sunshine of glamorous Monte Carlo.

Furthermore, as rationing still continued after the war, women began to resist government-imposed utility fashion designs, and there was a hunger for romantic dressing. Christian Dior's 1947 New Look design of wasp waists and longer, fuller skirts satisfied this war-weary desire for romanticism and in *The Red Shoes* the modern and stylish costumes designed by French couturier Jacques Fath for Moira Shearer followed this romantic trend. As Powell recalls:

> In 1948 England was still on rationing. Austerity was the cry. We had won the war. We had lost the Empire. Now we must tighten our belts and save Europe […] But not the Archers. We thought the best way to save Europe was to make extravagant, romantic British films.
>
> (1992: 23)

Powell's insistence on extravagance may have been influenced by the Rank Organisation's aspirations since 1945 to emulate Hollywood production values and fund 'prestige' rather than 'quality' British films, for export to the US market (Murphy in Barr 1986: 60–1). But in 1946, Powell also stated that he was searching for a new form of storytelling. He wanted an aesthetic that required 'visual wit, movement, pantomime, comedy, eked out with music, songs and dialogue … only when it was needed' (in Baxter *et al.* 1946: 109). This led him to draw inspiration instead from melodrama and silent cinema and to prioritise image over the dialogue, claiming that: 'In my films, images are everything; words are used like music to distil emotion' (Powell 1992: 168).

Powell's first experiences of silent cinema in the Nice studios of Metro Goldwyn Mayer working on Rex Ingram's 1925 silent film *Mare Nostrum* informed this aesthetic: 'This was pretty heady stuff for a first picture, and looking back I am not surprised that I never had much taste for kitchen-sink drama' (1992: 128). As in silent films, Powell wanted music, rather than dialogue, to be the master. He experimented with the composed shot in which acting is choreographed and edited to a previously composed musical score; for *Black Narcissus* (1947) he produced a 5-minute composed sequence and for *The Red Shoes*, a 17-minute composed ballet. 'For me, film-making was never the same after this experience' (1992: 583).

In *The Red Shoes*' ballet, Brian Easdale's Oscar-winning soundtrack leads the choreography of movement to music, allowing Powell and Pressburger to explore highly codified gestural language rather than dialogue, for the tension between dancing and love, ambition and domesticity and the expression of female desire. A shoemaker (Leonide Massine) presents a pair of red ballet shoes to a young girl who leaves her lover to dance downstage; in a magical jump-cut the scarlet ribbons wrap around her ankles and she is suddenly dancing in the red shoes. Her lover gradually recedes and from hereon we, like the girl, are caught in a spell of fantastical extravagance as we follow her balletic journey through Bauhaus-trained production designer Hein Heckroth's painterly and expressionist sets and compellingly grotesque masks, heightened by Jack Cardiff's Technicolor lighting. Vicky is driven relentlessly by the red shoes as she exhausts her dancing partners to the lonely heights and depths of fame. Forever lurking in shadows, dancing around her, is Massine as the tireless shoemaker. 'Intensely musical, a superb mime and a good actor' is how Powell recalls the great Russian performer (1992: 642).

Powell acknowledged that the ballet in *The Red Shoes* was a significant attempt on his part to 'lift storytelling onto a different level and leave naturalism behind' (1992: 652), and the theatrical gestural codes of the ballet draw on melodramatic practices to infuse the young woman's struggle with a poignant dimension of pathos as, in the finale, she gestures to the preacher to remove the shoes and dies exhausted in his arms.

Drawing on exaggerated, mimetic acting codes and music, the subjective realm of dance and inner desire in *The Red Shoes* articulates the dancer's aspirations beyond language into a life/death struggle. As Gledhill notes, melodramatic characters do not function in the interests of psychological interiority but as anthropomorphised, emblematic signs of social forces, personifying good, evil, virtue, vice, through exaggerated performance codes (in Gaines 1992: 139). And the young dancer in The Red Shoes ballet could emblematise Gledhill's 'victim of persecuted innocence' (Gledhill 1987: 32) through the sacred/secular struggle of the demonic shoemaker, the lover, and the preacher outside the church.

In the main narrative we see Vicky Page lured to career heights by the nineteenth-century Svengali-like figure of Lermontov, but prevented by patriarchal domesticity and the love of her husband. We can also identify a virtuous/fallen woman ideology in the mise en scène and camera angles as Vicky's ambition and success are cinematically inscribed in terms of a melodramatic rise and fall. At one point, she climbs the steps to a villa: 'a simple flight of steps up the mountain, but it has one hundred, two hundred, what do I know, maybe three hundred steps going heavenward, with no villa in sight' (Powell 1992: 638). And on reaching the fairy-tale heights of her career, she is told she will be the principal dancer. But this success becomes spatially demonised through her histrionic fall in the film's closure as her unadulterated artistic pleasure is morally punished.

Once Vicky has chosen dancing over marriage, and the red shoes impel her to her doom, the frame privileges a cast-iron spiral staircase. In extreme close-up the red shoes are followed running down the stairs, delineating the melodramatic fallen woman. Technically, this was a difficult sequence to shoot. In order to keep ahead of her shoes, the film-makers first tried putting the camera on an elevator, but so as to see more of her feet they used a spiral staircase on a turntable which rotated slowly as Moira Shearer ran down. By adjusting its speed to hers they kept her continually in view. They cut two takes of the same shot and edited them together to extend it to five seconds and thus draw out the suspense (Powell 1992: 652). The fall is further exaggerated as she throws herself over the edge of a balcony, her arms histrionically gesturing towards unspeakable desires which can find no place in her social framework. This image in itself thus becomes suggestive of the price the woman must pay for her deviance from patriarchal norms.

Vicky's death, as in the dramatic plunging to death of the heroine in both *Black Narcissus* and *Gone to Earth* (1950), shows that the dizzying heights that women aspire to in Powell and Pressburger's films also provide the locus for their fall. Hence, the Archers' post-war films have been read by some as belonging to a trend of films that aim to bring strong women down to size (Aspinall in Curran and Porter 1983: 284–5). But the energy and daring of their heroines create an excess of pleasure for female audiences that runs the risk of diminishing the punishing endings, and scholars such as Harper have warned against an overarching feminist analysis: 'For Powell and Pressburger, females were not passive bearers of tradition but key speakers of it. Nor were they sacrificial victims of it' (in Higson 1996: 110). In this sense, *The Red Shoes* conforms more to the spirit of Gainsborough melodramas, such as *Madonna of the Seven Moons* (Crabtree, 1943) and *The Wicked Lady* (Arliss, 1945), which 'were popular with wartime female audiences, not because good triumphs over evil, but because the case for pleasure is made so convincingly,' (Aspinall in Curran and Porter 1983: 276). Hence, while the all-important tension between Vicky's career and home life is melodramatically realised through the extremity of the punishing closure that confirms the status quo and the prevailing ideology of femininity as homemaker, the melodramatic conventions of excess offer a more open reading of female resistance which allow us to sympathise with the pleasure of Vicky's artistic aspirations and the unfairness of her social position indicating a tension very pertinent to post-war British women.

Note

1. J. B. Mayer, *British Cinemas and Their Audiences: Sociological Studies*, London, Dennis Dobson, 1948, p. 107.

Further reading

Sue Aspinall, 'Women, Realism and Reality in British Films, 1943–53', in James Curran and Vincent Porter (eds) *British Cinema History*, London, Weidenfeld & Nicholson, 1983, pp. 272–93.

Gail Braybon and Penny Summerfield, *Out of the Cage: Women's Experiences in Two World Wars*, London, Pandora Press, 1987.
Christine Gledhill (ed.) *Home is Where the Heart Is: Studies in Melodrama and the Woman's Film*, London, BFI, 1987.
Christine Gledhill, 'Between Melodrama and Realism: Anthony Asquith's *Underground* and King Vidor's *The Crowd*', in Jane Gaines (ed.) *Classical Hollywood Narrative: The Paradigm Wars*, Durham/London, Duke University Press, 1992, pp. 129–67.
Claudia Gorbman, *Unheard Melodies: Narrative Film Music*, London, BFI, 1987.
Sue Harper, '*Madonna of the Seven Moons*', *History Today*, Vol. 45, No. 8, August 1995.
Sue Harper, 'From Holiday Camp to High Camp', in Andrew Higson (ed.) *Dissolving Views: Key Writings on British Cinema*, London, Cassell, 1996, pp. 94–116.
Robert Murphy, 'Under the Shadow of Hollywood', in Charles Barr (ed.) *All Our Yesterdays: 90 Years of British Cinema*, London, BFI, 1986, pp. 47–54.
Michael Powell, 'Your Questions Answered', in R. K. Nielson Baxter, Roger Manvell and H. H. Wollenberg (eds), *The Penguin Film Review*, London, Penguin, 1946.
Michael Powell, *A Life in Movies: An Autobiography*, London: Mandarin Paperbacks, 1992.

Trish Sheil

Redupers: die allseitig reduzierte Persönlichkeit/Redupers: the All-Round Reduced Personality (1977)

[Country: West Germany. Production Company: Basis-Film, ZDF. Director: Helke Sander. Producer: Clara Burckner. Screenwriter: Helke Sander. Cinematographer: Katia Forbert. Music: Ludwig van Beethoven, Walter Kollo, Lothar Elias. Editor: Ursula Höf. Cast: Helke Sander (Edda Chiemnyjewski), Joachim Baumann (*Stern* reporter), Andrea Malkowsky (Dorothea Chiemnyjewski), Ronny Tanner (Werner), Gesine Strempel (photographer), Gislind Nabakowski (photographer), Gisela Zies (photographer), Helga Storck (photographer).]

Synopsis: Edda Chiemnyjewski is a freelance photographer and single mother in late 1970s West Berlin, struggling to make a living from small commissions to photograph public events. Alongside her professional work, she has her own artistic projects – both individual and as part of a women's photography collective – which try to capture the reality of the city in less hackneyed ways. Winning a commission from the city government, the women experiment with site-specific installations, with mixed results. Edda and her collaborators continually come up against obstacles, including entrenched sexist attitudes, condescending and dismissive. But Berlin itself, although battered and divided, remains a space of social possibility and aesthetic inspiration.

In West Germany, the political and cultural upheavals of the late 1960s gave new impetus to political cinema, and ushered in a new feminist film culture, vigorous and inventive, if always embattled. In both contexts, Helke Sander was a key figure, as filmmaker, writer, editor and organiser. Her films are not easily defined, perhaps most easily summed up with reference to Jean-Luc Godard's distinction between *making political films and making films politically*: in other words 'correct' political content should align with a commitment to formal innovation and, where possible, to changing the circumstances and conditions of film production and reception.[1] As a subtle and complex artwork, and a document and artefact of a broader movement, Sanders' *Redupers: The All-Round Reduced Personality* has often been singled out in overviews of West German feminist filmmaking. There are risks in focusing on one film and one director in this way: the risk of elevating one figure among many to *auteur* status, abstracting a film away from its context, mummifying its political content by film-historical canonisation.

Bearing those caveats in mind, the film is well worth the attention it has sustained. Its knot of thematic preoccupations connects the politics of everyday life, the particular experience of women and mothers, the political life of images, the ideological formation of social life, and the inseparability of – the false distinction between – public and private spheres. Generically hybrid, *Redupers* essays new modes of narrative form and political expression, combining fiction and documentary elements, overlaying its action with commentary and interspersing it with self-reflexive moments and occasional avant-garde visual devices. Gaps and discontinuities are included, and commented on. However, the experiments are not in the service of obscurantism, aestheticism or cleverness. Rather, they are an attempt to find adequate expression for social form, and an invitation to the viewer to reflect on the circumstances of her own life. Finally, the film is one of few West German films that address the Cold War division of Berlin and of the country, a striking blind spot in cultural production.[2] The many car-borne traveling shots, probably *Redupers*' most memorable visual motif, document late 1970s West Berlin in stark black and white, preserving the streetscapes of that vanished urban exclave, simultaneously 'capitalism's shop window' and home to a thriving counter-culture.

At its simplest, *Redupers* is an analytic portrait of a woman (Edda Chiemnyjewski, played by Sander herself) over a few days in the spring of 1977. Sketching the circumstances of her life, the film traces connections and reveals tensions between her work as a freelance press photographer, her life as a single mother, and her political activities in a women's photography collective. In part through Sander's voice-over – hovering between authorial voice and the character's diary-like commentary on her life – we gain access to Edda's thoughts, hopes, dreams and frustrations. But the private is not merely personal; it is inseparable from the structures and strictures of the society in which she lives. These determinants are concretised in the built environment, dominated by the Wall, whose political and military architecture demarcates Edda's neighbourhood, literally at the end of the street. They are also carried in the flow of images and discourses which suffuse public and private space, heard in ubiquitous radio broadcasts from West and East, seen in street-level advertising billboards, sensed in the clichés and used-up images which Edda's oppositional politics must both contest and avoid replicating.

From her earliest cinematic work, Sander had engaged with questions of mass media and the public sphere. One of just two female directors in the first cohort of the Berlin film school in 1967, her first film was typical of that highly politicised milieu, if perhaps unusual in its formal panache.[3] *Brecht die Macht der Manipulateure* (*Break the Power of the Manipulators*, 1968) was a document of the campaign against the right-wing Springer press group, and an activist film within the movement. Inspired with the revolutionary hopes of the time, the film was experimental and insistently pedagogical, deploying Brechtian aesthetics – instructional sketches, intertitles and diagrams, juxtapositional montage, authorial reflections to camera – to bring audiences to think as well as feel, reflect as well as see, and ultimately to act.

Even at this point Sander's radicalism was profoundly feminist. In a historic 1968 speech, she denounced the patriarchal culture of the student movement, demanding that women's issues be recognised and addressed, not disingenuously postponed until after a notional revolutionary transformation.[4] Her work in the following decade, the time between *Brecht die Macht* and *Redupers*, helped establish new spaces and ideas for feminist practice, both general and film-cultural: this included television documentaries on childcare and contraception, and the organisation of exhibitions of women's films. Just as significantly, in 1974, she was a founding editor of the journal *frauen und film* [*women and film*], for which she also wrote, her interventions marked by a careful, sceptical materialism, insistent on the need for experiment and rigor (see, for instance, Sander 1988: 75–81).

Thus while *Redupers* – her first full-length film, containing autobiographical elements – reflects on the politics of images, the question of representation is not separate from the practical difficulties of working, of raising money, of finding time for other commitments (above all, the question of childcare). Going beyond cinema and beyond any narrow definition of 'women's issues', the film offers a resolutely materialist analysis of media production, asking where images come from, how they are produced and what they might be used for. Through Edda's struggle to earn a living as a freelance photographer, the audience sees the labour involved in producing images that circulate in the public sphere, learns the cost of materials and the monetary worth of a photograph. We become witnesses to the physical work of photo development, the time wasted, the theft of images, the dim hopes of a scoop. In short: refusing notions of the image as a transcendental glimpse of freedom and authenticity, the film highlights the work of production usually concealed in the frantic consumption of images.[5]

Edda does much of her work at home or from home, her professional and personal life coexisting uneasily in domestic space. Likewise, it is from 'private' spaces that the photography collective prepares its interventions in the public sphere – the progress of these efforts at alternative production and exhibition constitutes the film's thin narrative thread. Eschewing the 'women's issues' which their funders expect, the group focuses on the Wall, the world-historical object in the neighbourhood, which – aside from political graffiti – seems to have become almost invisible, the division of the city normalised. In a variety of projects, the women look to make the fact of division visible, while questioning its absolute nature. One intervention builds a viewing platform to look over the Wall to the East: using curtains to create a 'window' view, they simultaneously defamiliarise the scene and render it visible. Enlarging photos of the Wall, they make portable billboards to display in locations around the city.

None of these interventions are entirely successful; in situ, the blown-up images are less impressive than hoped, the audience on the viewing platform is more inclined to gawk than think. On one level, this relative failure constitutes a disappointing learning process. But the work is performed not only as a critical practice, but also as a social one, a way of being and working together, bringing with it frustration, but also moments of happiness and solidarity between the women. On another level, the Wall functions as a kind of meta-symbol – all the more abstract for its literally concrete reality – for divisions of all kinds including gender division. Thus, insisting on the permeability of supposedly impassable barriers, Edda photographs the mundane media connecting East and West: sewers and airborne pollution, the economy of garbage disposal, the old women who cross the border as tolerated traffickers of goods.

Of course, as well as thematising images, the film is itself made of images. Sander's status as a modernist filmmaker, committed to undermining the deceptions and illusions of conventional stories and images, has sometimes led to an underestimation of her particular visual style. In *Redupers*, individual shots and sequences are frequently both beautiful and clearly legible. But visual pleasure is not an end in itself, and neither is legibility reducible to a single bullet point of meaning. Early in the film, for example, we see Edda in her apartment's narrow hallway, leaving for an assignment. Her young daughter cries and clings desperately, hanging onto her mother's long scarf. On one level, the image presents the contrary pull of motherhood and professional obligation, but it transcends the simple enactment of an intellectual point – the constricted space and the passion and grace of the figures' movements lend the scene something pressing, urgent and laden with emotion. Immediately afterwards, an extreme long shot shows Edda's white Volkswagen driving in front of the crumbling Reichstag, scene and site of so much twentieth-century history. A readable juxtaposition: History, in ruins, looms over the tiny vehicle bearing Edda, her business and her thoughts. But the wryness and delicacy of the image – the brute old building veiled in late winter mist, the Beetle very *beetle*-like – qualifies and shades schematic readings, haunting them with the ghost of the concrete.

The main factor uniting the film's disparate elements is not visual but acoustic. The critic B. Ruby Rich, in an astute and influential reading, argued that Sander's voice-over is key to her specifically feminist modernism, which used unconventional form not to establish authority (she suggests Alexander Kluge as counter-example), but to make an intricate connection between author, characters and spectators, a bond no less substantial for being complex and reflexive (Rich 1998: 238–52).[6] Recalling the tradition of women's letter writing, Rich reads the film as 'cinema of correspondence', fostering communication and solidarity without reneging on intellectual rigor. Sander's vocal performance, her citation of women writers, and her 'shifts between interior and exterior discourse' thus contribute to the 'collective enterprise of fashioning a feminist voice' (Rich 1998: 251). This *correspondence* is highlighted in one much-cited image: in a generous gesture of inclusion, the screen divides into four quadrants, each showing another feminist film – including Yvonne Rainer's *Film About a Woman Who* (1974) and Valie Export's *Invisible Adversaries* (1977) – while Sander's voice reads from a letter from Edda's elderly female relative.

The film's early reception was dominated by affirmative readings, emphasising its feminist poetics. What went less emphasised were the film's darker moods: the 'reduction' – as the title suggests – of the personality by the incessant demands of everyday life, its vulnerability in the face of economic and ideological forces. As well as a work of feminist seeing-anew, the film can also be read as a document of the waning hopes of the 1970s German left, bearing the traces of exhaustion and political disappointment. As European political cinema, the film is a product of an epoch of the hollowing out of historical 'grand narratives', with their sense of direction and of historical agency. Politics turns, if not inwards, then downwards, as mass organisation gives way to micro-political action, and utopian hopes survive mostly in small surpluses of interpersonal warmth. Even Edda, worn out by demands, grows dispirited at times with the meagreness of her and her friends' activism. As if the Grand Dialectic – progress and reaction, labour and capital – is here replaced by a much smaller dialectic, the push and pull of exhaustion and hope.

Perhaps *resolve* is a better word than hope. In the film's final sequence, a satellite view of the city gives way to a final street scene, with mother and daughter meeting outdoors, apparently by chance, the archetypal private relation restaged in a public place. A long shot shows a brief tender conversation, then they go their separate ways, Edda walking down the street, away from camera, into a vertiginously deep space that contrasts with the shallow planes dominant in most of the film. The voice-over quotes Christa Wolf, an East Berlin author – 'and so we go on, piecemeal, in little steps ... feet on the ground, head in the clouds' – and recalls the limits and gaps of diary form, reminding us of all it leaves untold. An appropriately dense conclusion: a moment of grace in ordinary social life, a deconstruction of heroic-bombastic notions of Progress, and a reflexive nod – almost a smile – to the audience; as if to say 'to be continued', not in a sequel, but in the continuity of the film with the life that goes on beyond it.

Notes

1. Jean-Luc Godard, 'What Is to Be Done?' *Afterimage*, No. 1, April 1970, pp. 10–16.
2. Wim Wenders' *Kings of the Road* (1976) and *Wings of Desire* (1986) are rare exceptions.
3. Other students in the group included the essay-filmmaker Harun Farocki, Wolfgang Petersen, director of *Das Boot*, and Holger Meins, later to join the Red Army Faction and die on prison hunger strike. On 1968 and film school culture, see Volker Pantenburg, 'Die Rote Fahne. Deutsche Film- und Fernsehakademie, 1966–1968' in Martin Klimke and Joachim Scharloth (eds), *1968. Handbuch zur Kultur- und Mediengeschichte der Studentenbewegung*, Stuttgart, Metzler, 2007, pp. 199–206.
4. Helke Sander, 'Rede des Aktionsrates zur Befreiung der Frauen, gehalten bei der 23. Delegiertenkonferenz des SDS im September 1968 in Frankfurt', in Ann Anders (ed.), *Autonome Frauen. Schlüsseltexte der Neuen Frauenbewegung seit 1968*, Frankfurt, Athenäum, 1988, pp. 39–47.
5. Compare, for example, the function of images in Wim Wenders' *Alice in the Cities* (1974).

6. On voice-over, see also Kaja Silverman 1983. For Sander's own criticism of Kluge, see Sander, 1974: 16–22.

Further reading

Thomas Elsaesser, *New German Cinema: a History*, New Brunswick, NJ, Rutgers University Press, 1989.

Miriam Hansen, 'Messages in a Bottle: 'Frauen und Film', Women's Cinema and Feminist Film Theory in West Germany', *Screen*, Vol. 28, No. 4, 1987, pp. 30–9.

Julia Knight, *Women and the New German Cinema*, London: Verso, 1992.

Judith Mayne, 'Female Narration, Women's Cinema: Helke Sander's *The All-Round Reduced Personality/Redupers*', *New German Critique*, Vol. 25, 1982, pp. 155–71.

Renate Möhrmann, *Die Frau mit der Kamera: Filmemacherinnen in der Bundesrepublik, Deutschland*, Munich, Hanser, 1980.

B. Ruby Rich, 'She Says, He Says: The Power of the Narrator in Modernist Film Politics' [1983], in *Chick Flicks: Theories and Memories of the Feminist Film Movement*, Durham, Duke University Press, 1998, pp. 238–52.

Helke Sander, 'Feminism and Film' [1977], in Eric Rentschler (ed.), *West German Filmmakers on Film: Visions and Voices*, New York, NY, Holmes & Meier, 1988, pp. 75–81.

Helke Sander, 'zu kluges gelegenheitsarbeit einer sklavin', *frauen und film*, Vol. 3, 1974, pp. 16–22.

Kaja Silverman, 'Helke Sander and the Will to Change', *Discourse*, Vol. 6, 1983, pp. 10–30.

Brían Hanrahan

Roma, città aperta/Rome, Open City (1945)

[Country: Italy. Production Company: Excelsa Film. Director: Roberto Rossellini. Producer: Giuseppe Amato. Screenwriters: Sergio Amidei and Federico Fellini. Cinematographer: Ubaldo Arata. Music: Renzo Rossellini. Editor: Eraldo Da Roma. Cast: Aldo Fabrizi (Don Pietro), Anna Magnani (Pina), Marcello Pagliero (Giorgio Manfredi), Harry Feist (Major Bergmann), Francesco Grandjacquet (Francesco), Vito Annichiarico (Marcello).]

Synopsis: In Nazi-occupied Rome, the Gestapo is hunting the ringleaders of the local Resistance movement, Manfredi and Francesco. The pursued men are hidden and assisted by the local people, including the local priest Don Pietro and Francesco's fiancée, Pina, while the diabolical Major Bergmann tracks them down from the comfort of his office. Francesco is captured and driven away, and Pina killed by German troops in the ensuing chaos, only for partisans to liberate Francesco once again. Eventually, Don Pietro and Manfredi are betrayed, arrested and questioned by Bergmann. Manfredi is tortured to death by the Gestapo, but does not betray his comrades. In the final scene, Don Pietro is executed as a band of child partisans (including Pina's son, Marcello) look on, ready to continue the struggle.

Roma città aperta/Rome, Open City occupies such a canonical position in film history that detaching oneself from received wisdom or preconception can require an effort of will. In the months following the Nazi withdrawal from Rome in June 1944, with the city's film studios out of action, Roberto Rossellini took to the ruined streets with salvaged film stock to capture the recent traumas of occupation in their harrowing immediacy. By entwining itself within the events' authentic urban spaces to register real-life experiences of everyday Italians, the film resisted Hollywood's impending hegemony and offered a pole of identity for a renewed 'national' cinema. So goes the legend.

None of the above is false. As a record of fact, it tells a compelling and valuable story, whose significance for national culture and subsequent filmmaking should not be underplayed. With Italy on its knees, its nationhood shamed in the wake of Fascism, the Allies who took control of Rome unapologetically sought to overpower what was left of a local film industry with the politically 'safe' products of American cinema.[1] By turning so directly to the Italian experience of war, Rossellini's film therefore raised the possibility of an alternative, inward-looking trajectory: a social and national orientation that would become the touchstone for Italian cinema's global redemption and make *Roma città aperta* the exalted founding text of the 'neorealist' aesthetic. Such a binary reading of Italy's cinematic culture in the post-war years, however, conceals the complexities that surrounded this film's emergence. The neorealist trend, for example, was not simply a parochial reaction to the approaching transatlantic behemoth, but a filmmaking style with roots in the Fascist era (Luchino Visconti's *Ossessione/ Obsession* (1943) is commonly located as the movement's alternative starting point), and one which frequently borrowed from American narrative formats.[2] Moreover, despite its 'documentary' stylistics (soon afterwards to be identified as one of the hallmarks of neorealist cinema), *Roma città aperta* is by no means an objective record of the Italian experience in these years. The film is in fact a meticulously constructed intervention in the national discourse.

This dramatic construction is most apparent when Rossellini deploys episodes of melodramatic or comic amplification, which are woven into the narrative structure for maximum impact. Much of the first half of the film is taken up by detailed character establishment, which introduces and polarises caricatured villains and fallible, sympathetic protagonists. Francesco and Pina share an intimate moment in the tenement stairwell, reminiscing about the past and expressing hopes and fears for the future. Francesco's rousing words to her – 'We're fighting for something that must come true. It may be long and difficult, but there will be a better world for all our children: Marcello, and the one we are expecting' – both emphasise the fact that she is pregnant with his child and link this fact to a brighter future free of tyranny. By so investing our hope in Pina as an emblem of regeneration, however, the filmmakers are setting up a cruel irony. The traumatic scene for which *Roma città aperta* is most commonly remembered comes barely halfway through the film, and enacts a dramatic turning point as character-based drama gives way to untrammelled brutality. Pina, the world-weary, salt-of-the-earth Italian (played by much-loved local film star Anna Magnani) is senselessly gunned down by an off-screen (and therefore faceless) Nazi gunman. In stark contrast to her powerlessness to alter the events around her, Major Bergmann exudes sinister omniscience, his antennae seeming to reach into each alleyway as he declares: 'Every night I "stroll" through Rome without ever leaving this office'.

Bergmann's role is however more complex than Harry Feist's somewhat vaudevillian portrayal suggests. The film's most significant element, from a cultural-political perspective, is its preoccupation with the contested memory of the Resistance. As an ideological counterpoint, the character of Bergmann operates as an important vehicle for this undertaking. When Manfredi's prolonged ordeal at the hands of the Gestapo at last leads to his demise, Bergmann instructs his clerk to record the cause of death as a heart attack, and the deceased's name as 'Giovanni Episcopo' (the alias Manfredi used when he was in hiding), so as not to give the Resistance another martyr. The film, of course, undercuts the Nazi's words even as they leave his mouth, by openly showing both the cruelty of the torturers and the dignity of the victim. The cinematic techniques further enhance this sense that the film is bearing solemn testimony to this sacrifice. As the torture scene begins, the bound Manfredi and his interrogators are seen through a doorway, pointedly left open to force Don Pietro to watch the brutality. The positioning of the camera outside the torture chamber, only briefly at first registering the horror of what is to come before the shot cuts to the priest's reactions, suggests an accidental glimpse and positions the viewer as an inadvertent witness to events intended to be hidden from public view. The process we see being enacted here is one with considerable significance for post-war Italy. By framing the very memory of Resistance sacrifice as an epistemological battleground, both Bergmann's attempt to doctor the official record and Rossellini's stylistic undermining of that attempt attest to the symbolic potency of the struggle against Nazism, and of its memorialisation.

In the immediate post-war period, the harrowing events of 1943–1945 offered Italians a compelling myth of national solidarity against a common enemy. *Roma città aperta* must be considered in this context, as a purposeful mediation of these events in the very moment at which they are passing into the realm of 'history' and attaining their singular discursive force. In this film, the 'Popular Front' against Fascism that briefly united Communists and Catholics, factory workers and middle classes, is deployed dramatically to stand in for the fortitude and dignity of the Italian people. Don Pietro exploits the fact that priests are granted right of passage during curfew to operate as a channel of communication between the insurgent cells, enmeshing the Church within the rebellion. Meanwhile, Major Bergmann disdainfully flicks through a pile of confiscated publications comprising the newspapers of each of Italy's main political parties, aptly symbolising their burial of differences in opposition to his ilk: *L'unità* (Communists), *Avanti* (Socialists), *Risorgimento liberale* (Liberals), *Il popolo* (Christian Democrats) and *L'italia libera* (Action Party).

Even while the film methodically weaves this narrative of national unity, however, it betrays unease for Italy's future. In an attempt to make his victims betray their pact, Bergmann hisses words of discord to each in turn. Don Pietro is told of Manfredi: 'He's a subversive and an atheist: your enemy!' Manfredi is then told: 'You're a Communist. Your party has signed a treaty with reactionary forces. You're marching together against us. But tomorrow, when you occupy Rome … will these monarchic officials stick by you?' Doubtless, these lines serve the diegetic purpose of further emphasising the fortitude of the Italian spirit. Manfredi's response is to spit in the Nazi's face, and immediately afterwards his martyrdom is completed as he is trussed up in a Christ-like pose to be tortured to death. Yet Bergmann's words are not simply diabolical Nazi propaganda; they also bespeak neuroses that Italy would soon be split down the middle. In this subtext lies a significant prescience.

Roma città aperta's fusion of Catholic and Communist sentiment represents a concerted effort to bestride a chasm that would soon engulf Italian political life once Fascism had been defeated. The increasingly bitter ideological battle between the Italian Communist Party (PCI) and the Christian Democrats (DC) in the lead-up to the 1948 General Election would have a considerable influence upon how the memory of the war would be assimilated into the new Italy's political landscape. As the events passed into memory, it was the Left above all political persuasions for whom the Resistance and its memorialisation would become a pole of identity and pride, but also a reminder of betrayal by erstwhile allies. It is partly for this reason, and despite the fact that the film actually downplays the Communists' central role in the Resistance, that *Roma città aperta* became exalted in the annals of the political Left as much as in those of cinephilia. It simultaneously captures the heady promise of renewal and consensus fostered by the fragile alliance, while registering widespread fears amongst the Left that these hopes would be shattered once the DC, supported by America, assumed power. By the late 1940s, cinema had itself become one of Italy's key political battlegrounds, as the socially progressive neorealist trend was championed by the PCI and condemned by the DC in equal measure. The legacy of *Roma città aperta* would be a controversial one.

In hindsight, Rossellini's seminal film serves to render conceptions of 'national cinema' problematic. Insofar as it seeks to define 'the nation' at a moment of crisis, *Roma città aperta* certainly offers a valuable insight into Italy's attempts to emerge from the Fascist era, and to tread a path out of the rubble of warfare and occupation. Despite its celebrated status as a panacea for the local industry, however, it was proposing just one among many visions of national reconstruction: one that, by advocating a 'Popular Front' consensus, would soon be swimming against the tide of history. The framing of the recent past was, at this pivotal moment in the negotiation of Italian national identity, an unavoidably divisive process. The film's opening caption claiming that 'any resemblance to actual persons is coincidental' is therefore somewhat extraneous. Its relationship to the historical 'reality' of the events is much less important than its mode of representation: one of political memory being played out, and co-opted in the service of the present. Internationally, however, *Roma città aperta* was lauded as a trailblazer for a new realism, and there can be no doubting this film's importance to subsequent cinema. Jean-Luc Godard, whose own early filmmaking practice owed much to the experimental approach of neorealism, put a seal on this legacy by declaring: 'All roads lead to *Rome, Open City*' (Brunetta 2009: 117).

Notes

1. Admiral Stone, the head of the Allied Military Government's Film Board, publicly announced: 'The so-called Italian cinema industry was invented by the fascists. Therefore it must be suppressed, as must be the instruments that incorporated this invention' (Wagstaff 1995: 93).
2. Neorealism's debt to transatlantic popular formats is most evident in the melodramatic emotional appeal of such 'classics' as *I ladri di biciclette/The Bicycle Thieves* (Vittorio de Sica, 1948) and *Riso amaro/Bitter Rice* (Giuseppe de Santis, 1949).

Further reading

Peter Bondanella, *A History of Italian Cinema*, London, Continuum, 2009.
Gian Piero Brunetta, *The History of Italian Cinema*, Princeton, Princeton University Press, 2009.
David Forgacs, *Rome, Open City (Roma città aperta)*, London, British Film Institute, 2000.
Sidney Gottlieb (ed.), *Roberto Rossellini's* Rome Open City, Cambridge, Cambridge University Press, 2004.
Christopher Wagstaff, 'Italy in the Post-War International Cinema Market', in *Italy in the Cold War: Politics, Culture and Society 1948–1958*, Christopher Duggan and Christopher Wagstaff (eds), Oxford, Berg, 1995, pp. 89–115.

Austin Fisher

La Roue/The Wheel (1923)

[Country: France. Production Company: Films Abel Gance. Producers: Abel Gance and Charles Pathé. Director: Abel Gance. Screenwriter: Abel Gance. Assistant: Blaise Cendrars. Cinematographers: Gaston Brun, Léonce-Henri Burel, Marc Bujard and Maurice Duverger. Editors: Abel Gance and Marguerite Beaugé. Original Music: Arthur Honegger. Cast: Séverin-Mars (Sisif), Ivy Close (Norma), Gabriel de Gravone (Elie), Pierre Magnie (Jacques de Hersan).]

Synopsis: A railroad operator, Sisif, saves a young child, Norma, from the wreckage of a train crash. He raises the orphan girl alongside his biological son, Elie. The children grow up believing that they are related by blood. Both Sisif and Elie fall in love with Norma. Sisif reveals his feelings for Norma and the secret of her provenance to Monsieur de Hersan, a wealthy company engineer. Hersan blackmails Sisif in exchange for Norma's hand in marriage. Norma marries Hersan and Sisif tries to kill himself. After an accident that leaves him partially blind, Sisif moves from Nice to Mont Blanc where he operates the funicular railway. Hersan and Elie fight for Norma and both men die. Norma moves in with Sisif and he dies peacefully at home.

The mythology of Abel Gance's epic film, *La Roue* (The Wheel), includes a short declaration from Jean Cocteau: 'There is cinema before and after *La Roue*, as there is painting before and after Picasso'. This claim has been read, almost without exception, as an affirmation of Gance's unique film and cinematic talent (Abel 1983; Brownlow 1992; Cuff 2011). The comparison of Gance with Picasso also underscores the modernist, mechanical style that characterises the film. Indeed, *La Roue* depicts multiple train crashes and domestic conflicts through cinematographic collisions and visual ruptures. Gance tears both a family and a film apart, cobbling them back together in motley, unfamiliar ways. But critics have overlooked the joke in Cocteau's judgment, the double meaning drawn from the symbol at the centre of Gance's film: the wheel of life and modernity that turns, thoughtlessly, relentlessly, crushing any individuals in its path. In this reading of Cocteau (and Gance), there is cinema before and after *La Roue*, but the film does not make any difference. Cinema continues to turn, with or without it, before and after it. One cannot say whether Cocteau intended his assessment of Gance to be so playfully ambiguous, though the avant-garde experimented with word games, slips of the tongue, and uncanny doublings in the 1910s and 20s. One can, however, make the case for both readings of *La Roue*.

By nearly every measure, *La Roue* is an extraordinary cinematic work, visually and narratively divided into two expansive halves: 'the symphony in black', shot on location along the railroads of Nice, and 'the symphony in white', shot amid the spectacular snow-capped peaks of Mont Blanc. A melodramatic plot joins these distinct geographic sites together and guides its protagonist, Sisif (Séverin-Mars), from a life of drudgery, despair, and incestuous desire to (Oedipal) blindness, salvation, and, at last, his peaceful death 14,000 feet above the life he used to know. Despite the film's attention to the industrial and transport technologies that rationalised and accelerated the rhythms of labour and leisure in the late nineteenth and early twentieth centuries, *La Roue* is a film that stretches out and takes its time, that wanders and seemingly gets lost in a string of improbable tragedies. Indeed, the film meanders unpredictably and inefficiently between Nice and Mont Blanc, gathering multiple train crashes, suicide attempts, fantasies, and deaths (by gunshot and mountain's edge) along the way.

Production of *La Roue* lasted more than two years and far exceeded the limits of Gance's original contract with Pathé (Cuff 2011: 224). The film premiered in Paris in 1922 with a running time of almost nine hours. It took three days to screen the entire film. It was projected on consecutive Thursdays at the Gaumont Palace theatre to a sold-out audience of 6,000 spectators (Abel 1983: 26). The colossal size of Gance's film owes, in part, to his theory of cinema. In a 1912 essay, 'The Sixth Art', Gance defines cinema as a combinatory practice, a synthesis of the arts that surpasses them all:

> Let the cinema be naturally grandiose and human […]. Let it not be theatrical, especially, but allegorical, symbolic. To plumb the depths of each civilization and construct the glorious scenario that sums it up, embracing all the cycles of all the epochs […] – that is one of my highest dreams.
>
> (Gance 1983: 66–7)

One can detect this dream in the unusual shape and structure of *La Roue*. The film brings together a dense network of mythological, religious, poetic, literary, and visual signs, many of which enter the film by way of direct quotation. The film opens with an epigraph from Victor Hugo – 'Creation is a great wheel which cannot move without crushing someone!' – and intersperses reflections on the nature of life, loss, and mortality from a diverse set of sources: Sophocles, Pascal, Chamfort, Baudelaire, Kipling, Zola, Cendrars. The list goes on. Each voice interrupts the narrative, what Gance might describe as the 'theatrical' layer, and reminds spectators of the larger allegorical stakes of these lives spent along the railway.

The unwieldy, fragmentary quality of *La Roue* can also be read against the personal melodramas that circumscribed the film's production. Gance wrote and revised the script as he went, and as the health of his fiancée, Ida Danis, demanded. Danis was diagnosed with tuberculosis shortly before filming began. The abrupt narrative shift from black to white, from Nice to Mont Blanc, was born out of an abrupt shift in Danis's health. Gance moved production (and the narrative) to help her ailing lungs. Production time expanded as Gance's attention drifted elsewhere. Danis died on the very last day of shooting, April 9, 1921, and Gance dedicated the film to her memory. The lead actor, Séverin-Mars, also died of illness shortly after completing the film. These twin tragedies offer an alternative framework for understanding the film's sprawling narrative structure, as well as its allegorical engagement with cycles of shadow and light, death and resurrection. That is, the narrative took on the shape of *actual* tragedies unfolding beyond the frame and its allegory of the unforgiving wheel is shot through with the specificity of real, individual loss.

For Gance, the distinct power of cinema lies not only in its ability to bring together diverse creative practices, but also to set them in motion. On the cinematic screen, 'characters descend from their frames' and 'the wings of the Victory of Samothrace actually quiver' (Gance 1983: 66). Almost all forms of cinema mobilise characters and objects that the literary and plastic arts once petrified. However, *La Roue* exceeds this order of mobility. Gance layers movement upon movement within each shot and experiments with the rhythms constructed out of the spaces between them. The film assembles an incredible range of techniques – mobile cinematography, multiple superimpositions, rapid montage, textual animations, and special effects – each of which contributes to a kind of hyperactive visual dynamism. In one of the film's first scenes, the camera captures a single line of track from the back of a moving locomotive. The track splits and diverges, curves and eventually returns to the form of a single iron rail. This image is a very literal representation of the railroad, of its speeding trains and tracks. But it is also a figure for speed itself, for the (cinematic and industrial) machines that produce new ways of moving and seeing. The mountains of Mont Blanc are similarly abstracted, transformed from the crystalline shapes of on-location shooting to a blur of white, a figure of emptiness or renewal. One finds here, too, a counterbalance to the theatrical and referential tendencies of the 'sixth art'. The movements of *La Roue* momentarily transform the diegetic world beyond all recognition.

More than a collage of artistic practices, *La Roue* is a great, tottering paean to the European avant-garde of the 1920s and 30s. The film's oscillations between theatrical and allegorical expressions, between narrativity and abstraction, and between the patterns of human existence and the movements of machines betray a disparate set of cinematic impulses and influences. Indeed, French film scholar Richard Abel argues that *La Roue* is a 'paradoxical' film, torn between 'several competing theories of film then emerging in France' (Abel 1983: 29). For Abel, Gance inherits his commitment to on-location shooting from a school of realism developed by Louis Delluc and André Antoine; he develops his graphic and rhythmic sensibilities alongside 'pure' film theorists like Fernand Léger; and he constructs his story within the paradigms of French social realism (29–30). But one must also look beyond the boundaries of France to see the breadth of Gance's aesthetic genealogy. *La Roue* borrows from the formal experiments with line, shape, and movement that define the cinema of Walter Ruttman, Hans Richter, and Viking Eggeling (among others). The film's montage sequences, as well as its obsessive return to the wheels of modern life and the cycles of twentieth-century labour echo Dziga Vertov's 1922 *Kino-Pravda* series. One can also trace a line from *La Roue* to the burgeoning 'city symphony' genre and, in particular, Paul Strand and Charles Sheeler's *Manhatta* (1921). The latter premiered during the production of *La Roue* and, not unlike Gance's film, interspersed its images with the words of Walt Whitman.

The promiscuity and proportions that made *La Roue* such an exceptional cinematic event equally made it an unreproducible (and perhaps undesirable) production model, a nearly unexportable product, and a very difficult film to both restore and study. Three months after the film's premiere in Paris, Gance began tinkering with the size and shape of *La Roue* for its general release. Multiple iterations of the film followed, each with a slightly different length, combination of shots, and plot structure. Gance routinely remade his films in post-production. Both *J'accuse* (1919) and *Napoleon* (1927) underwent a similar set of reductions and re-releases. According to Paul Cuff, who inventories the many versions of *La Roue* in his history of the film's restoration:

> The premiere version was 10,730 metres long, approaching nine hours in length, and divided into a prologue and six 'chapters'. The six-chapter version was subsequently distributed in many provincial areas, but Gance created a slightly shortened version [9,200m] for the Parisian general release in February 1923. [...] Gance planned that the six-part version would be the standard edition shown within France and that a shorter [4,200m] version would be the standard export version. In fact, the 9,200m version was to be more widely seen in metropolitan France than the premiere version, and most foreign countries didn't even receive the two-part, 4,200m version. The film never achieved an American release.
>
> (2011: 224)

These various iterations of *La Roue* circulated throughout the 1920s; some versions were still in theatres when Gance's next film, *Napoleon*, premiered (Cuff, 225). The 'original' film, however, has not survived and the version available to contemporary scholars (without access to archival prints) represents just one of the many 'copies' that circulated after its première and, of course, just one of the many possible restoration projects. Lobster Films completed the restoration work of this particular version in 2008. The film's running time is just four and a half hours.

In Walter Benjamin's canonical essay, 'The Work of Art in the Age of Its Technological Reproducibility', he refers to both Abel Gance and Séverin-Mars and dismisses their views of cinema as 'insensitive' and 'forced'. Benjamin argues that both figures mistake film for the kind of artistic practices that the moving image forcefully opposes, if it does not completely annihilate them. He writes:

> It is instructive to note how their [Gance and Séverin-Mars] desire to class the film among the 'arts' forces these theoreticians to read ritual elements into it – with a striking lack of discretion. Yet when these speculations were published, films like *L'Opinion publique* and *The Gold Rush* had already appeared. This, however, did not keep Abel Gance from adducing hieroglyphs for purposes of comparison, nor Séverin-Mars from speaking of the film as one might speak of paintings by Fra Angelico.
>
> (Benjamin 2003: 258–9)

For Benjamin, cinema does not extend or compound the auratic qualities of art. It diminishes the singularity of the original work in an endless and indistinguishable set of copies produced automatically by machines. As a film object, however, *La Roue* troubles the model of mass reproduction that Benjamin has in mind. It also, remarkably, opposes the very images of modern, industrial labour (gears turning, trains colliding, bodies suffering, etc.) that dominate the film's diegesis. *La Roue* is a staggeringly excessive, personal, and manifold film. In other words: it is much closer to the autographic arts than Benjamin allows. The title refers not to an original and its copies, but to multiple originals, each one as idiosyncratic as the next. Returning to the claim from Cocteau with which this essay began, there is no 'before and after' *La Roue*, because there is no one version of the film, no single moment that marks its history. *La Roue* also fails to change the course of the cinematic arts precisely because it deviates so considerably from them. Instead, the wheels of cinema continued to turn and rolled right past *La Roue.*

Further reading

Richard Abel, 'Abel Gance's Other Neglected Masterwork: *La Roue*', *Cinema Journal*, Vol. 22, No. 2, 1983, pp. 26–41.

Walter Benjamin, 'The Work of Art in the Age of Its Technological Reproducibility', in Howard Eiland and Michael Jennings (eds), *Selected Writings: Volume 4, 1938–1940*, Cambridge, MA, Harvard University Press, 2003, pp. 251–83.

Kevin Brownlow, 'Abel Gance', in *The Parade's Gone By*, Berkeley, University of California Press, 1992.

Paul Cuff, 'Interpretation and Restoration: Abel Gance's *La Roue*', *Film History*, Vol. 23, No. 2, 2011, pp. 223–41.

Abel Gance, 'The Era of the Image Has Arrived!' in Mary Lea Bandy (ed.), *Rediscovering French Cinema*, New York, Museum of Modern Art, 1983 [1927], pp. 53–4.

Abel Gance, 'A Sixth Art', in Richard Abel (ed.), *French Film Theory and Criticism: A History/Anthology, 1907–1939*, volume I, Princeton, NJ, Princeton University Press, 1988 [1912], pp. 66–7.

Lynne Kirby, *Parallel Tracks: The Railroad and Silent Cinema*, Durham, NC, Duke University Press, 1997.

Katherine Groo

Samt el qusur/Silences of the Palace (1994)

[Country: Tunisia. Production Company: Canal Horizons, Cinétéléfilms, Mat Films. Director: Moufida Tlatli. Screenwriters: Nourid Bouzid and Moufida Tlatli. Cinematographer: Youssef Ben Youssef. Editors: Camille Cotte, Karim Hammouda and Mouifda Tlatli. Music: Anouar Brahem. Cast: Hend Sabri (Alia age 15), Ghalia Lacroix (Alia age 25), Amel Hedhili (Khedija), Kamel Fazaa (Sidi Ali), Sonia Meddeb (La J'neina).]

Synopsis: Alia is the illegitimate daughter of Khedija, a servant in an old Ottoman royal palace, Tunis. Her presumed father is Prince Sidi Ali, one of the last beys (Turkish governors), now a puppet of French colonial rule during the mid-1950s, when the movement for independence is growing violent. Khedija is beautiful, she works in the kitchens and serves as waitress, but she is also a singer and dancer, entertaining the bey, his brother and their families. Sidi Ali's wife, La J'neina, 'was betrayed by her womb' and they remain childless; the bey cannot openly acknowledge Alia as his daughter, though he deeply loves both her and her mother. The narrative unfolds in flashbacks from the day of Sidi Ali's death. Alia is now a young woman, a 'failed singer' like her mother, living with Lotfi, a teacher and former political agitator. She is to endure yet another abortion the following day, and is profoundly unhappy. She returns to her father's palace, where she relives her tormented adolescence.

Moufida Tlatli was born in 1947 near Tunis, one of a generation that produced several significant Tunisian directors, including Férid Boughedir and Nourid Bouzid. Tlatli's fascination with cinema was encouraged by a French schoolteacher of philosophy who organised one of the many *ciné clubs* that thrived in the Francophone culture of Tunisia, and she absorbed the work of the European *auteur* directors. During the 1960s Tlatli studied editing at the Institute des Hautes Etudes Cinématographiques in Paris, attended by many North African directors, and worked in French television. She returned to Tunisia in 1972, where she collaborated on some of the most significant films of the '*Cinema Jedid*' (New Cinema) movement.

Silences of the Palace has been described as 'the finest of all Maghreb fictional films by a woman director' (Armes 2005: 73), winning several international festival awards, and even making a modest profit; distribution was however confined to Tunisia and Europe, probably because the content was deemed offensive. *Silences of the Palace* also demonstrates the paradoxes and contradictions that confronted post-colonial cinemas during the decades following independence. The credits sequence to the film acknowledges funding and support from the leading European cultural agencies and media channels, and its audience was restricted to art-house and international festival circuits: how far might the content and preoccupations of the film be conditioned by the taste and priorities of this mainly European patronage? What kind of new cinema could win the attention of mass popular audiences beyond Europe?

The post-colonial cinema of Tunisia had focused from its beginning on the role and experience of women within the culture, giving rise to a characteristic *cinéma du femme*, according to Férid Boughedir (Shafik 2007: 148). This was due to the relatively liberal conditions established in the country – it is significant that the events of the 2011 'Arab Spring' were provoked by unrest that began in Tunisia. *Silences of the Palace* combined radically different kinds of cinematic conventions precisely in an attempt to reach beyond its immediate constituency among European and North African *cinéastes*, and to appeal to a broader audience. Crucial moments in plotting and narrative rely on the popular, non-naturalistic conventions of melodrama, a genre that has been defined in part by its appeal to female audiences. Among other devices, melodrama heightens narrative tension through the use of improbable coincidence: Alia is born within minutes of the birth of Sarra, the daughter of Si Bechir (Sidi Ali's brother) and his wife. The girls grow up together within the confines of the palace, and become virtually inseparable; as children they are able to cross the boundary between kitchen servant quarters and 'upstairs' – a word which carries exactly the same connotations for the Tunisian royal palace as for *Gosford Park* or *Downton Abbey*.

Sidi Ali and his family appear to be thoroughly 'Europeanised', they wear Western clothing and drive around in noisy black cadillacs; Si Bechir reads French poetry aloud as he walks in the gardens, and each brother has taken only one wife. But older elements of Ottoman culture persist: Sidi Ali is particularly fond of Apple, a female 'dwarf' servant. The brothers' father wears traditional high-status dress and reads the Koran; for Sarra's engagement all the men adopt the fez and djellabah to play at cards, though the wives and daughters display modish evening gowns (not a single veil or burqa is worn throughout the film). Tradition inevitably bears down most heavily on the women and men working 'below stairs' in the premodern kitchens, and most damagingly of all on Khedija as Sidi Ali's mistress. Their relationship appears to be genuinely loving and passionate, but it will destroy her. In one scene she is summoned to wash Sidi Ali's feet in rose water, and as they begin to embrace, their hands clasp and re-clasp as each attempts to gain final control, hand over hand; the hand of the bey triumphs.

Khedija dances for one of the beys' parties, performing the *raqssharqi* ('belly dance') backed by an eclectic ensemble of Arabic and Western instruments. The dance is simultaneously an erotic spectacle for the male and female audience and also a virtuoso performance of female autonomy and self-possession, with nothing of the Western flagrancy of lap dancing. Yet the figure of the female singer and dancer is inevitably also a person vulnerable to exploitation. Although Khedija has forbidden Alia from attending the party, she and Sarra look on in fascination. Alia becomes possessed by the idea of her mother's performance, and steals away to her father's marital bedroom. She selects one of La J'neina's gowns, experiments with her make-up, and begins tentatively to dance to an old record. Unable to mime her mother's mature adult performance, she gives up, and whirls childishly about, falling on the bed in a self-induced swoon. La J'neina enters and in cold fury exclaims, 'Like mother, like daughter! Born to sin. Get out!'

The paradoxical nature of woman's dance within this culture intensifies when Alia notices her father, during daytime, entering the rooms she occupies with her mother, and locking the door. Alia by now knows very well that this is an assignation, and she runs distractedly through the grounds of the palace, pausing in front of a collection of caged birds. She runs on to open grass, where she races in a tight circle and faints. Si Bechir discovers her, begins to caress her, and then carries her, unconscious, back to her bed. Khedija enters, concerned, and finds Si Bechir gazing at the sleeping Alia. He violently assaults and rapes Khedija, overheard by Alia, now frozen in horror. The girl's whirling dance is her desperate attempt to escape from the confines of the palace and the encroaching attentions of men, which may destroy her as surely as they will destroy her mother.

The most intense sequence drawing on melodramatic convention is the final, climactic event when Alia sings for the celebration of Sarra's engagement, at her own father's request. Simultaneously, Khedija is undergoing an abortion, the consequence of Si Bechir's rape – or perhaps her assignations with Sidi Ali. The men are in a separate room, gambling and smoking, while the women are seated for Alia's performance. She begins by flaunting the power of her singer's art, 'I'll sing tunes to intoxicate my listeners. Song is the life of the soul. Song can mend the broken hearts that doctors cannot cure.' Gradually she captures all attention: her father leaves the gaming table to hear her, Lotfi gazes from a doorway, La J'neina stares fixatedly. Then, in pure defiance, Alia without warning launches into the inflammatory anthem of the insurrection beyond the walls, which Si Bechir had attempted to ban from the palace: 'Green Tunisia seems in a daze, its sorrow erupts in flashes that shake the sky and extinguish the stars.' The orchestra falls silent behind her, and the audience begins to leave, mutely and without protest, the men return to their cards. At this precise moment the film cuts to Khedija in terrible induced labour pains, she screams and haemorrhages, from which she will die.

So many elements of this powerful sequence are non-naturalistic, and some may be even frankly symbolic: what will the Tunisian revolution bring to birth? Analogies of this kind also apply to Alia herself, as her painful development and disappointed early adulthood seem to parallel the larger, national experience beyond the gates of the palace: 'The heroine of my story is a woman, the type that in our countries is sometimes said to be "colonised by the colonised", a woman inferior by birth, a woman born to serve man' (Murphy and Williams 2007: 170). This parallel between Alia's development and the Tunisian independence movement is made explicit by Lotfi, a political agitator taking refuge within the palace. Alia is immediately attracted to the young man, who offers to teach her to write. He attempts to embrace her, and she shrinks away; he reproves her, saying 'You are as indecisive as our country. One word thrills you, another word scares you. Things are going to change. A new future awaits us. You will be a great singer. Your voice will enchant everyone.' Alia listens to and performs the songs of Umm Kulthum, the legendary Egyptian singer whose recitals were followed throughout the Arab world (Lohman 2010). But when Alia sings such well-loved classics as Abdal Wahab's '*Amal-hayati*', 'Hope of My Life', in the opening sequence of the film, the lyrics only serve to drive home the degree of her vulnerability and hopelessness.

Sidi Ali in fact is sympathetic to the insurrection, and has covert meetings with some reformers. He asks Alia to tell the cooks to prepare fava bean stew, the food of the poor, and La J'neina is witheringly scornful: 'You're attached to them. You've sunk so low.' When Alia conveys his wishes to the kitchen staff, they too are sceptical, and laugh: 'We don't envy their wealth, but they envy our poverty.' The servants who work 'below-stairs' in the traditional kitchens of the palace are a compelling ensemble. Many of the film's most eloquent images are of these kitchen women, with moving performances by Fatima Ben Saïdane as the vulnerable Mroubia and Najia Ouerghi as Khedija's protector, Khalti Hadda.

Moufida Tlatli argues that Arabic and Islamic society is profoundly allusive, an intrinsically poetic culture that constructs meaning through metonymy and indirection. She also argues that the formal devices of cinema rely on exactly these strategies, which are fundamental to *Samt el qusur* (Gauch 2007: 19). Silence pervades the film, speech is subordinated to exchange of significant looks and meaningful gaze, but silence is also continually displaced by eloquent song and the sound of the oud, thanks to the voices of the kitchen women and Anouar Brahem's beautiful music track. It is exactly this allusiveness of the silent image, compelling performance and the culture's lyric genius that puts into question the legitimacy of presiding regimes, Ottoman and French colonial, and whatever may succeed. *Samt el qusur* is dedicated to the director's mother.

Note

With grateful thanks to Dr Walid Abdul-Hamid for material and advice.

Further reading

Leila Ahmed, *Women and Gender in Islam*, New Haven, CT, Yale University Press, 1992.

Roy Armes, *Postcolonial Images: Studies in North African Film*, Bloomington, IN, Indiana University Press, 2005.

Suzanne Gauch, 'Silent Reflections' in *Liberating Shahrazad: Feminism, Postcolonialism, and Islam*, Minneapolis, University of Minnesota Press, 2007, pp. 13–34.

Laura Lohman, *Umm Kulthum: Artistic Agency and the Shaping of an Arab Legend, 1967–2007*, Middletown, CT, Wesleyan University Press, 2010.

David Murphy and Patrick Williams, *Postcolonial Cinema: Ten Directors* Manchester: Manchester University Press, 2007.

Viola Shafik, '*Samt al-Qusur* (*Silences of the Palace*), MoufidaTlatli, Tunisia/France, 1994', in Gönül Dönmez-Colin (ed.), *The Cinema of North Africa and The Middle East*, London, Wallflower Press, 2007, pp. 145–56.

Nigel Wheale

Sankofa (1993)

[Country: USA, Ghana, Burkina Faso, Germany, UK. Production Company: Mypheduh Films (Co-production with the Ghana National Commission on Culture, Diproci of Burkina Faso, NDR/WDR Television and Channel 4). Director: Haile Gerima. Producers: Shirikiana Aina and Haile Gerima. Screenwriter: Haile Gerima. Cinematographer: Augustin Cubano. Editors: Haile Gerima and Shirikiana Aina. Music: David J. White. Cast: Oyafunmike Ogunlano (Mona/Shola), Alexandra Duah (Nunu), Nick Medley (Joe), Mutabaruka (Shango), Afemo Omilami (Noble Ali), Reginald Carter (Father Raphael), Kofi Ghanaba (Sankofa, the Divine Drummer), Hasinatou Camara (Juma).]

Synopsis: While on a photo shoot in the site of a former slave castle, a self-absorbed African American model is magically transported back to a Jamaican plantation where she experiences the realities of slavery first-hand. Having experienced a slave revolt and joining a maroon colony, she returns to her present-day life with a deepened connection to her past, and a renewed sense of racial solidarity.

Sankofa (1993), like its Ethiopian-born filmmaker Haile Gerima, is important both in African and African American cinema history. One of the few internationally known Anglophone African filmmakers,[1] Gerima was a member of the Los Angeles School of Black Filmmakers (also known as the L.A. Rebellion Film Movement) along with Charles Burnett, Larry Clark, Julie Dash, and others.[2] The movement, which emerged from UCLA in the 1960s–1980s, is characterised by the filmmakers' loosely shared set of pan-African political commitments and by their shared desire to create cinema outside the conventions and influence of classical Hollywood cinema, and without using the Hollywood studio for financing. In Gerima's case, this has often meant serving as producer, writer, director and editor of his own films. Though their political commitments and filmmaking styles are diverse, so much so that any summary is necessarily also a distortion and partial misrepresentation, The Los Angeles School of Black Filmmakers emerged at the heady moment when the mainstream US Black Power movement had become broadly internationalist and anti-colonial.

Reflecting these internationalist politics and a desire to forge common links between Africans and African Americans, *Sankofa* is, on one level, a period piece, filmed primarily in Jamaica and Ghana, that depicts US slavery. This film represents Gerima's efforts to use 'cinema's devastating capacity to colonise … in a way that projects one's own human story – without apologies'.[3] The film opens with an African American model, Mona, being photographed on location at a Cape Coast slave castle in Ghana, one of the sites through which Africans who had been captured or sold passed before being enslaved in the New World. Because Mona clearly does not appreciate the significance of this site, Sankofa, the Divine Drummer, confronts her with the need to respect the sacred site of the slave castle. Abruptly, she is soon thereafter transported back in time. The castle fills with chained Africans who look directly at Mona and, through her point of view, the audience. She is transported back across the Atlantic Ocean and through centuries into the past where she is enslaved by whites who no longer recognise her as American and who rename her Shola. Most of the film details the process by which her understanding evolves and she begins working toward freedom.

The bulk of the film takes place in the past, and it is to a large extent a recognizable cinematic representation of slavery. *Sankofa* is distinct, however, insofar as it focuses on the experience and point of view of the African rather than salvation – religious salvation for the whites who repent their ways and physical salvation for the slave delivered from slavery,[4] or other concerns that minimise slavery.[5] It is also unique insofar as it focuses on the daily life of slavery, and the ways the enslaved understood their own condition. The film depicts rape during the middle passage and in the present, and offers an unflinching view of the forms of psychological and physical discipline deployed, as when slaves are murdered or made to flog each other under the threat of death. Unlike other films about slavery, individuals are not redeemed through their individual acts of heroism, but collective acts of resistance. The triumph at the end of the film is Mona/Shola's becoming a rebel leader in her own right, then returning through the 'Door of No Return' in Cape Coast castle, finally recognising herself as part of a broader community of people in the African diaspora. Using a contemporary African American woman as the focus of its story, the film's power comes in the present transformation of this ordinary woman through the power of storytelling so visceral it becomes an experience in its own right.

Though the film features an unsuccessful slave revolt, it has less in common with blaxploitation-era's revenge fantasies[6] than with such Cinema Novo films as Carlos Diegues' *Quilobmbo (*1986), which similarly seeks to excite present audiences to reconsider their historical connections. Though the film is set in the southern USA, one of the rebellion leaders, Shango, is from the Caribbean. His name, which he shares with the god of fire, lightning and thunder in the West African Yorùbá pantheon and with Xangó in Caribbean and Latin American pantheons, itself symbolises the preservation of African heritage that survived or was reconstituted in the New World. The emphasis on the autonomous community, African retentions, and Mona's revised understanding of herself as belonging to a larger pan-African community are the film's ultimate theme, related to the L.A. Rebellion Film Movement's desire to create new, 'decolonised' images of black life.

In simplest terms, the film targets audience members of African descent who, having known nothing else, accept their present living conditions and misconceptions. Even within the film's diegesis, having been born a slave makes it easier to accept being a slave. But the aim of the film is not just information, but witnessing slavery and its effects, and establishing a kind of communion with the dead. Witness, however, is not just visual. The first word spoken diegetically is 'listen', and characters throughout insist on the incantatory power of the word, and of storytelling. The word *'sankofa'* itself is an Akan concept: 'We must go back and reclaim our past so we can move forward; so we understand why and how we came to be who we are today'. Without that practice, which in the film is fundamentally ethical, we are bound to repeat that history in the specific sense of those filmmakers Gerima criticises for remaking films without even realising their films are remakes.[7] Thus, the project of *Sankofa* is not so much an adequate representation of slavery than the ethical responsibility to remain aware of slavery – to bear witness to slavery – and to reconstitute the lines of commonality among people of the African diaspora.

Though the ostensible topic is slavery, the film doubles as a broad allegory of the process of decolonisation as in part a process of recovering one's lost heritage. The film is one of the few to depict not only the immediate terror of slavery, but the long consequences of slavery's brutality, especially rape. Joe, the child born of Nunu's rape on the slave ship by a white man, is the male counterpart to Mona within the film. However, whereas she is unaware of her African heritage, Joe actively rejects it in the hopes of gaining favour from the whites who have enslaved him. He is the embodied spirit of the Middle Passage's physical and epistemological violence: a Christian who sees his suffering as a guarantee of future salvation, a slave struggling to be perceived as a man rather than a beast, a man not sure whether he is a child of God or a 'heathen Guinea woman', Nunu. He cuts himself off from the traditions that sustain the other slaves by his racial difference and by his desire to appease whites and assimilate into white culture, though even he eventually falls out of favour.

Read uncharitably, Joe's character is not only at fault for failing to recognise his heritage, but also for his racial impurity. He knows where his ancestors are from, but rejects Africa in favour of Christianity, and the respectability and personal salvation it promises. While viewers are clearly supposed to identify with Mona, the rebellious Shango and the saintly Nunu, Joe is irredeemable. He eventually kills both his mother and Father Raphael in a church, ensuring that he has no descendants. His plot line is the most complex and ambiguous in the film: Joe is as much an embodiment of the Middle Passage as Mona. Through those characters, the film tacitly suggests that all descendants of slavery are the descendants of rape, but only the female characters are able to overcome that legacy and locate themselves within a larger African diaspora community.

Joe's character may be read as an example of the psychological strain of oppression and cultural assimilation, a figure that tries to navigate two worlds and ultimately chooses the oppressors, in contrast with Mona/Shola who ultimately chooses the oppressed. This choice is the key. Through it, *Sankofa* is unlike other films about slavery. The resolution is not the individual's freedom or integration into society, nor is it the martyrdom of the rebellious slaves. The film ends with Mona having come back through the Door of No Return, facing an uncertain future alongside other Africans on the beach. One might here detect in this film the influence of revolutionary Martinican psychologist Frantz Fanon who (along with Guinea-Bissauean leader Amilcar Cabral) was a key intellectual figure for the L.A. Rebellion Filmmakers. For Fanon, the roots to oppression lie partially in the psyches of the oppressed who mistake historical relationships for natural ones. Decolonisation for Fanon, and Gerima, lies in more than the end of formal colonial relations, but in removing mental colonisation as well. For *Sankofa* suggests, decolonisation is an ongoing process that must first begin with recognising that one is colonised.

Notes

1. Manthia Diawara makes this claim in *African Cinema: Politics and Culture*, Bloomington, Indiana University Press, 1992. The emergence of Nigerian 'Nollywood' films – films primarily produced using digital cameras and distributed either direct-to-video or electronically primarily to Nigerian and Nigerian diaspora audiences, complicates his claim. Nollywood extends the independent ethos of filmmakers like Gerima without imagining the theatre as the ideal screening site. Still, though Nollywood has come to name the third largest national film industry in the world (behind the US and India), consumers tend to become more invested in serialised stories than individual filmmakers.
2. Ntongela Masilela provides an in-depth analysis of the ways the filmmakers sought to 'find a film form unique to their historical situation and cultural experience, a form that could not be appropriated by Hollywood', and helpfully locates the movement within a milieu informed by the Black Arts Movement, the Black Panther Party, African Marxism, politically engaged European cinema and Third World Cinema. See his essay 'The Los Angeles School of Black Filmmakers', in Manthia Diawara (ed.), *Black American Cinema*, New York and London, Routledge, 1993, pp. 107–17.
3. John L. Jackson, Jr., 'Decolonizing the Filmic Mind: An Interview with Haile Gerima', *Callaloo*, Vol. 33, No. 1, Winter 2010, pp. 25–36.
4. One might think here of contemporary films such as Stephen Somers' *The Adventures of Huck Finn* (1993) and other films such as *The Adventures of August King* (1995), *Amistad* (1997), or Michael Apted's *Amazing Grace* (2007), where slavery provides a litmus test – or occasion – for white characters' moral development.
5. For example, films like James Ivory's *Jefferson in Paris* (1995), Ang Lee's *Ride with the Devil* (1997), Anthony Minghella's *Cold Mountain* (2003), or Lars von Trier's *Manderlay* (2005) use slavery either as an occasion to reflect upon US history and ideology, or as an incidental backdrop to a love story.
6. I.e. Richard Fleisscher's *Mandingo* (1975), which depends on its representation of interracial desire more than anything, its sequel *Drum* (Steve Carver, 1976), or the Mondo Cane film *Addio Zio Tom* (Jacopetti and Prosperi, 1971), a 'mockumentary' that links slavery's graphic violence and exploitation to Black Power ideology and urban rebellions.
7. Jackson, 'Decolonizing the Filmic Mind', p. 31. To counteract this tendency, and other unconscious effects of colonialism, Gerima translates English sources into Amharic then back, bringing the film closer to an oral, decolonised perspective.

Further reading

Sylvie Kandé, 'Look Homeward, Angel: Maroons and Mulattos in Haile Gerima's *Sankofa*', trans. Joe Karagnis, *Research in African Literatures*, Vol. 29, No. 2, Summer 1998, pp. 128–46.

Kara Keeling, *The Witch's Flight: The Cinematic, the Black Femme, and the Image of Common Sense*, Durham, Duke University Press, 2007.

Mark A. Reid, *Black Lenses, Black Voices: African American Film Now*, Oxford, Rowan & Littlefield, 2005.

Anthony Reed

Sátántangó/Satan's Tango (1991–1994)

[Country: Hungary, Germany, Switzerland. Production Company: MAFILM, Mozgókép Innovációs Társulás-Von Vietinghoff Filmproduktion, Merlin-Vega Film AG. Director: Béla Tarr. Screenwriters: László Krasznahorkai, Béla Tarr (adopted from László Krasznahorkai's novel with the same title, based on Mihály Víg, Péter Dobai, and Barna Mihók's texts). Cinematographer: Gábor Medvigy. Editor: Ágnes Hranitzky. Music: Mihály Víg. Cast: Mihály Víg (Irimías), Dr Putyi Horváth (Petrina), Erika Bók (Estike), Peter Berling (Orvos), Miklós Székely B (Futaki), László feLugossy (Schmidt), Éva Almási Albert (Schmidtné), Alfréd Járai (Halics), Erzsi Gaál (Halicsné), János Derzsi (Kráner), Irén Szajki (Kránerné), Barna Mihók (Kerekes), István Juhász (Kelemen), Zoltán Kamondi (Kocsmáros), Péter Dobai (Százados), András Bodnár (Horgos Sanyi), Ica Bojár (Horgosné), Mihály Rádai (narrator).]

Synopsis: The film takes place in the isolated and dilapidated Hungarian countryside sometime at the end of communism. The locals spend their days drinking, dancing, and quarrelling with each other, or just sitting around doing nothing. A few of them decide to steal whatever little money the community has left and leave the village forever. However, their plans are crossed by the much-admired and feared crook, Irimiás and his friend, Petrina, who make a surprising return after being gone for years. The two dupe and threaten the villagers once again; they cheat them out of the money by falsely promising lucrative jobs in the city.

Béla Tarr's movie, *Sátántangó* has excited and fascinated film fans since its first release in 1994. The same year the film received the 'Caligari' award at the Berlin International Film Festival and the 'Age d'Or' prize at the Brussels International Film Festival. Bloggers, film critics, and academics continue to attend special screenings and to write extensively about this epic movie. Their dedication is remarkable for such a low-budget, Hungarian film that is black and white and over seven hours long, has very little in terms of plot, and progresses at an excruciatingly slow pace. In what follows, I discuss some important aspects of why *Sátántangó* has become a cult classic in a newly emerging global art cinema scene.

Since the French New Wave and New German Cinema's relative popularity in the 1960s and 1970s, critics have been talking about the slow erosion of avant-garde cinema in Europe. *Sátántangó* not only brought Hungarian filmmaking back from the fringes of contemporary international cinema, but it also provided proof against such negative prognosis for art movies all around the world. Tarr's film is often considered a prime example of the revival of European modernist cinema in the 1990s. Called a 'radical modernist', Tarr's style lines up closely with the cinemas of Reiner Werner Fassbinder, Andrey Tarkovskij, Yasujirō Ozu, Michelangelo Antonioni and Jim Jarmusch.[1] Indeed, starting with *Damnation* (1988), Tarr's films showcase all major aesthetic and narrative characteristics of modernist cinema: monochrome film stock, extremely long shots, carefully choreographed camera movement, and the use of amateur instead of professional actors. The tension between the characters' social and economic position and their elaborate, sermon-like, poetic speech, also common in avant-garde cinema, is especially striking in *Sátántangó*.

One can argue that *Sátántangó* pushes the above-described elements of modernist cinema to the limits. The film is so radical and so extreme in its style that, as some critics have suggested, it dissolves its own boundaries and questions the very definition of cinema. Probably the best example of Tarr's radicalism is the film's marathon length. Besides the obvious difficulties of commercial distribution, watching the screen for seven and a half hours requires an enormous effort and investment from the audience. Such viewing experience goes directly against the logic of comfortable entertainment in mainstream commercial cinema. *Sátántangó*, in all its aspects, is a self-proclaimed, extreme counterpoint to contemporary fast-paced, action-oriented, heavily digitised and overacted Hollywood films. The film was more than a simple experiment in style and narration for Tarr; it was a real gamble – but one that has clearly paid off.

Nevertheless, it would be a mistake to understand *Sátántangó* as only a gesture of provocation. The film's aesthetic elements are integral to its internal logic, the archaic and mythical nature of its fictional world. The extremely long takes (the average shot length is 2 minutes 33 seconds) and very slow pace create an overall sense of prolongation and suspense that is not self-absorbing, but that achieves the desired visual affect of endless monotony and repetition. Suspending temporal progression instils a mythical circularity in the narrative and lends it a sense of inevitability and intransience. In other words, the length and particular cinematographic style of *Sátántangó* are not simply matters of aesthetic radicalism: they become the film's main theme as well.

Like most of Tarr's movies, *Sátántangó* is the filmic adaptation of a well-known Hungarian novel with the same title by contemporary author, László Krasznahorkai. Therefore, the issue of intermediality – the complex relationship between words and images – is central in understanding the aesthetic as well as narrative elements in the film. Praised for its extraordinary faithfulness to the novel, *Sátántangó* follows similar, circular temporal structure, slow pace, fragmented narration and dark imagery.[2] The sentences that stretch over several pages in the book become very long takes while the long internal monologues are replaced by sustained silence. Repetition, circularity and complicated sentence structure in the novel find their visual counterparts in form of black and white film stock, slowly panning camera, and a limited number of shots with the goal to create the same sense of stationary, monotonous and desolate reality.

There are two aspects of intermediality worth investigating further: the structuring of time and the question of the narrator. First, the film and the novel both alter the viewer's experience of time as structured and material to replace it with mythical, 'thick' time through length, slow pace, and monotony. Further, temporal overlaps and simultaneity (witnessing the same event from different angles) are equally present in the novel and the film. For instance, in the first scene when Futaki, having spent the night with Schmidt's wife, hides from the returning husband, we watch the action from two different angles. At the beginning, we see the events from inside the house and then again from outside, behind a neighbouring barn. In the novel, events are re-told by different narrators. 'Satan's tango', the central scene of the movie, is a case in point: we see the events first from the point of view of Esztike who is standing outside the pub in the rain looking at the drunk, partying crowd; and then from inside the pub. But, while in the novel such simultaneity has the effect of undermining narrative coherence, in the film it actually achieves the opposite effect. Repetition becomes a force of cohesion and reinforcement due to the concreteness of the image.[3] Second, the specificity of the medium used (written versus visual language) also impacts narrative stability. The novel destabilises the narrative voice: virtually all characters function as narrators and, at the very end we arrive back to the beginning as the Doctor starts writing the first few lines of *Sátántangó*. The film, however, creates a much more coherent, strong, principle narrator, who is invisible and omnipotent. The Doctor is only one of many characters with a clearly subjective point of view on the events. The temporal and narrative structuring in the film is therefore heavily impacted by the medium in which it operates.

Beyond such formalist analyses, *Sátántangó* is also an interesting commentary on Hungary's politico-economic reality in the late 1980s. When Krasznahorkai's novel was first published in 1985, Tarr immediately contacted him to work together on a film adaptation. However, he did not receive sufficient funds to start the production because the communist political censorship at the time was not ready to allow for such a bleak and critical depiction of Eastern European late-socialist reality. Indeed, the characters' inability to assume control over their lives, to escape their disintegrating world, as well as the fatalism that determines their actions reflect a sense of futility, paralysis, and uncertainty that Eastern Europeans faced in their everyday life. Desperate for change, Esztike, Futaki, Schmidt, Kráner, Halics and the rest are all waiting for a 'saviour' to come. However, the land of promise never arrives. Instead Irimiás, the false prophet appears, whose sophisticated language and phony proposal about a model farm that will save the deteriorating community is symbolic of the contemporary political regime's attempt to maintain its hegemony through corruption, exploitation and deception.[4]

Sadly, the total failure of the communist utopia did not result from the people's disinterest, ignorance or laziness. Instead, long hours of hard labour that consumed the lives of millions over 50 years of communism bore no other fruit but poverty, bankruptcy, and desolation. The images of decay, ruin, and barrenness are visual metaphors for the futile human sacrifice required from all Eastern Europeans by the Communist Party. Their humiliation, powerlessness, and exploitation force the characters into self-destructive, immoral, and irrational behaviour in a way that is dramatic and astounding, yet without clichés.[5] What makes the film particularly successful today is the way it elevates the historically specific critique of the late-socialist surveillance state (e.g. Irimiás' cobweb metaphor) to a philosophically relevant argument about humanity's misfortune and fallibility.

Some critics have read Tarr's film through the lens of postcolonialism. Such analyses usually interpret *Sátántangó*'s dilapidated world as a self-exoticising gesture for Western audiences. In a postcolonial reading, the viewers are drawn to the movie because of a mixed sense of repulsion and fascination with the backwards and archaic Hungarian countryside. *Sátántangó*, it has been postulated, presents Eastern Europe in a one-dimensional and ahistorical way, not as a real place with its complexities, but rather as an abstraction, a space where all material decay and human misery come to the surface. Ultimately, the film sets up an uneven power relation between the viewer and the viewed, making the cinematic gaze into a tool of colonisation for Western audiences.

Tarr's mastery is in seamlessly intersecting the politically poignant critique of Hungary's late socialist reality with an existentialist meditation over human imperfection. The film oscillates between two interpretative dimensions: between the universal and the material, between the abstract and the concrete, the historically specific and the atemporal, mythical. The harsh landscape of the Hungarian countryside anchors the characters' lives in a highly material way. The crumbling walls, relentless rain, and flat, dreary landscape could not be more concrete and tangible. Yet, the overwhelming images of decay are also symbolic of the transience and eternal passing of everything man-made. The same is true for the film's characters. Irimiás, for instance, is undoubtedly a thief and a crook. At the same time, he embodies a fundamental materialism that, in Tarr's dark vision, drives all human behaviour. Esztike, on the other hand, can be seen as a sacrificial lamb, whose body after her death transforms into a spirit. Yet, she is very much the victim of the community's economic and social misery, of human negligence and abuse. The banal and wretched material existence of these characters thus transforms into a vision of universal human drama. However, *Sátántangó* denies the possibility that transcendental forces would control human behaviour. Every time the universal and mythical comes close to the metaphysical (Petrina's prayer, Irimiás' hallucination), the film circles back to an inescapable materiality disallowing any sense of mysticism. Despite the Biblical references (Irimiás, the prophet, the sacrifice of the lamb, apocalypses, etc.), God is clearly absent from this world.

Sátántangó has clearly benefited from a newly emerging, global art cinema subculture that is more democratic, but also more private and individualised.[6] Because of the recent revolution in film and communication technology as well as in contemporary viewing practices, the relationship between national, regional and global cinema has undergone a fundamental transformation. On the one hand, high-speed internet and social media facilitate the dissemination of films as well as their criticism quickly and widely within the global cinephile community. On the other hand, individual members of this subculture do not necessarily share values or lifestyles except for an appreciation for the film's radical aesthetics. The rapidly growing interest in transnational and global cinema trends makes individual films relevant only in so far as they resonate with audiences all over the world. *Sátántangó* has achieved a cult status on the global art cinema scene exactly because a wide variety of viewers from all over the world find themselves invested in the movie. First of all, there is a draw to the myth that surrounds the film's making.[7] Second, its extraordinary length and slow pace requires an enormous investment on part of each viewer. Third, film fans seem to appreciate *Sátántangó*'s radical modernist style that is an open provocation to the ever more consumption-oriented Hollywood cinema culture. Most importantly however, Tarr's apocalyptic vision resonates with all who, in a way or other, have experienced 'universal moral degradation' and misery that is tragic, yet inescapable and utterly human.[8]

Notes

1. See András Bálin Kovács, 'The World According to Béla Tarr', *Kinokultura*, Special Issue 7, February 2008.
2. For a detailed analysis on the issue of film adaptation, see István Margocsy, 'Kinek a szemével?', *Filmvilág* 1994/6.
3. See Gábor Gelencsér, 'Késő vagy után? A *Sátántangó* modernsége', *Filmszem*, Vol. 1, No. 3, August 2011, pp. 23–33.
4. See Hajnal Király, 'Making Meaning in Béla Tarr's Adaptation of *Satan Tango*', in Ágnes Pethö, *Words and Images on the Screen: Language, Literature, Moving Pictures*, New Castle upon Tyne, Cambridge Scholars Publishing, 2008, p. 82.
5. A feeling of disillusionment and anger is expressed in statements such as, 'is it possible that they show up from nowhere and take everything away? There shall be order here again, my friend, in this country, there shall be order again!' (the tapster) or the schoolmaster as he offers Schmidt's wife to take her away to the city when finally 'those who are deserving will be in power'.
6. See András Bálint Kovács, 'A negyedik dimenzió', *Filmvilág*, 2009/02, pp. 4–5.
7. Although he had been planning to make *Sátántangó* since 1984, Tarr could not find funding for it until after 1989, the fall of the socialist political regimes in Eastern Europe. When finally he gathered the necessary financial support, it took over three years to shoot and edit it (from 1991 until 1994), making not only the length of the movie epic but also the length it took to actually realise it.
8. See András Bálint Kovács, 'Sátántangó', in Peter Hames and István Szabó (eds), *The Cinema of Central Europe*, London, Wallflower Press, 2004, p. 237.

Further reading

Hajnal Király, 'Making Meaning in Béla Tarr's Adaptation of *Satan Tango*' in Ágnes Pethö (ed.), *Words and Images on the Screen: Language, Literature, Moving Pictures*, Newcastle-upon-Tyne, Cambridge Scholars Publishing, 2008, 76–87.

András Bálint Kovács, 'Sátántangó', in Peter Hames and István Szabo (eds), *The Cinema of Central Europe*, London, Wallflower Press, 2004, pp. 237–43.

Lilla Tőke

Saturday Night and Sunday Morning (1960)

[Country: UK. Production Company: Woodfall Film Productions. Director: Karel Reisz. Screenwriter: Alan Sillitoe. Cinematographer: Freddie Francis. Editor: Seth Hilton. Cast: Albert Finney (Arthur Seaton), Shirley Anne Field (Doreen), Rachel Roberts (Brenda), Hylda Baker (Aunt Ada), Norman Rossington (Bert).]

Synopsis: A rebellious, hard-living factory worker juggles relationships with two women, one of whom is married to another man but pregnant with his child.

Released in 1960, *Saturday Night and Sunday Morning* is rooted in the new cinematic and literary movements of its day. Its screenplay, written by so-called 'angry young man' Alan Sillitoe, was based on his novel of the same name, and its director Karel Reisz was involved in the Free Cinema movement of the late 1950s. This, Reisz's first fiction feature, was at the forefront of the short-lived 'British New Wave' (1959–1963). With its working-class protagonists, focus on controversial yet ordinary issues, and a commitment to represent working-class life, this groundbreaking movement included films that took a resolutely humanistic, poetic and non-commercial approach to cinema. They were also collectively known as 'kitchen sink' films.[1]

The 1960s saw the rise of the independent film company as a significant force in British cinema and Woodfall was a prestigious example. Formed by another of the 'angries', John Osborne, in partnership with Tony Richardson, it was financed by the proceeds of Osborne's stage success, *Look Back in Anger*. Woodfall's aim, according to Richardson, was 'to get into British film the same sort of impact and sense of life that the Angry Young Man cult has had in the theatre and literary worlds' (in Hill 1986: 40).

Independent production gave directors the freedom to represent their society in original ways and tackle issues previously considered taboo. They were helped in this by the new 'X' certificate, introduced by the BBFC in 1951 and granted to all the 'new wave' films apart from *Billy Liar* (John Schlesinger, 1963). This allowed them to be more daring in content, albeit within reason: for example, Arthur (Finney) was allowed the contentious use of the word 'bloody', but 'bugger' was too much and had to be changed to 'beggar'; likewise, a reference to the gin and hot bath abortion had to be cut.[2] Nevertheless, the frank presentation of Arthur's sexual attitudes, Brenda's (Roberts) adultery, and the unwanted pregnancy seemed adult and contemporary next to Hollywood films still labouring under a draconian Production Code.

It is unsurprising therefore that *Saturday Night and Sunday Morning*, like *Room at the Top* (Jack Clayton, 1959) before it, hit a nerve with the cinema audience. Despite a small publicity budget, it was the third most successful film at the box office in 1961, won the BAFTA for Best Film and was the first film to take £100,000 in the three weeks of its London run alone. This film reflected the political and social changes shaping British society at this time. It was released in the middle of the prosperous consumer boom of the 1950s, but before the 'swinging sixties'. Considered daring on its release for its representation of sexuality and working-class youth, its moral values look old-fashioned even compared to *Georgy Girl* (Silvio Narizzano, 1966) and *Alfie* (Lewis Gilbert, 1966), let alone *Blow Up* (Michelangelo Anonioni, 1966) and *Performance* (Donald Cammell and Nicolas Roeg, 1970). By 1963, gritty realism and working-class angst were no longer box office draws.

Nevertheless, the fact that radical representations of working-class life were at the heart of these new literary and cinematic movements is explained by contemporary changes in society. The economic boom of the 1950s had brought unprecedented prosperity to a class used to defining itself in terms of the battle for a living wage. This led to new tensions around class identity and working-class masculinity in particular, defined as it was in its opposition to oppression in the workplace. After the 'hungry thirties' and the austerity of the war years, the 1950s were the 'never had it so good' Macmillan years. Wages doubled between 1951 and 1959, inflation and bank rates were low. Between 1957 and 1959, television ownership went up by 32 per cent; between 1952 and 59 ownership of cars doubled. Advertising investment increased fourfold between 1947 and 1960. In 1959 alone 200,000 motorbike licences were issued (Sandbrook 2006: 97).

Jack's (Bryan Pringle) motorbike and sidecar and his promise to buy Brenda a television; Robbo's (Robert Cawdron) outrage at Arthur's pay packet of over £14; Doreen's (Shirley Anne Field) comments about Arthur's suits – 'Are all these clothes your'n? They must have cost you a pretty penny.' – are all precise contemporary details. A class that had previously defined itself as producers now had to redefine itself as consumers. Increased wealth plus access to university education offered greater class mobility than ever before, but also challenged established ideas of what it meant to be working class. From the perspective of 1960, it seemed conceivable that the working class as it had been was an endangered species, and *Saturday Night and Sunday Morning* reflects these feelings of uncertainty, confusion and social paranoia.

The seminal text setting the agenda for intellectual debate about working-class identity was Hoggart's *Uses of Literacy* (1957). Hoggart contrasts the 'good' authentic working-class culture of the past with the 'shiny barbarism' of the modern consumer culture he sees as destroying it. Most of the 'new wave' films produce representations of working-class life premised on this binary opposition. Sillitoe read Hoggart after writing *Saturday Night and Sunday Morning*, but agreed that his novel 'pointed out more or less the same thing' (in Hill 1986: 203). The opening shot frames Arthur as traditionally working class, shirt sleeves rolled up and working at his lathe, voicing his combative attitude to authority and his determination not to be ground down. Doreen's new council house, with its modern furnishings, is seen as an unfriendly and repressive place set against the homely welcome of Arthur's traditional terraced home, reflecting the distrust of middle-class aspirations. Arthur's scathing comment that television produces people who are 'dead from the neck down' is a recurring motif found in most of the 'new wave' films.

Saturday Night and Sunday Morning pushes beyond this fixed ideological model to present a more ambivalent view. Jack, staid on his motorbike, seems more old-fashioned than Arthur on his pushbike; in the club, the younger generation listens to their pop music and the older generation enjoy their sing-song: neither group is held up as more desirable than the other. This is different from the clear privileging of the rich brass band concert over the television quiz show in *A Kind of Loving* (John Schlesinger, 1962). Even the final sequence, where Arthur throws a stone at the modern housing development and expresses his preference for an older house, finishes with a resigned acceptance that he and Doreen may live there. Moreover, several times in the film, Arthur himself expresses disdain for 'the good old days'. While this is framed within an awareness of how hard those times were, there is no nostalgic admiration for the people who lived through them.

Most of the 'new wave' films sidestep uncomfortable exploration of class identity by projecting all the problems onto the female characters, who become embodiments of the threats posed to traditional working-class culture. A stereotype of the new wave is the woman obsessed with consumer goods and middle-class aspirations. This neat containment of the debate lets the men off the hook; demonising the women prevents further uncomfortable debate over class identity. *Saturday Night and Sunday Morning* shares this misogynistic tendency, but, whereas in other new wave films, the male view is privileged, this one is more ambivalent in its audience positioning. Effective examples include the sequence where Arthur deliberately tips a pint of beer over the woman in the club, the sequence where he puts a dead rat on the bench of a female worker and the sequence where he shoots Mrs Bull (Edna Morris). In the first two incidents there is a lack of clear motivation, while in the third we are encouraged to assume it is a payback for Mrs Bull helping to bring about the arrest of the man who threw the brick through the shop window. Reaction shots of Arthur laughing after each incident suggest this is part of Arthur's rebellious streak, or his addiction to 'having a good time', but in neither sequence are Arthur's values prioritised as superior. The messages regarding class and gender remain quite ambivalent.

The extremity of Bert and Arthur's hatred for Mrs Bull is disturbing. They call her 'a bitch and a whore', 'rat face', 'old bag' and suggest she 'wants poleaxing'. Because this hatred cannot be masked by the more acceptable guise of class resentment, it can be seen as straightforward antagonism towards women. It is tempting therefore to read the film as emphatically sexist. The sexually attractive 'good girl' gets her man, while the transgressive woman is punished for her deviance.

Doreen seems to fit this first stereotype, described by some as 'a smashing bit of stuff', but 'first kiss and she'll expect a ring'. When Arthur does agree to marry Doreen, despite the film's analogies between marriage and fishing, the film is ambivalent about their relationship. Has Arthur's rebellious masculinity been tamed like Jack's before him (as suggested by the shot of the brick-throwing man being restrained by a group of threatening women), or does his relationship signal a more adult recognition of who he is? In the final sequence his comment that it will not be the last stone he throws, and the mildness of Doreen's rebuke, further resist misogynistic readings about the female emasculation of the male.

Similarly, while Brenda's agency in the narrative (adulterous wife who is punished for her transgression) seems unambiguous, the representation of her is more complex. For example, in the 'Sunday morning' sequence we see her in three conflicting stereotypical roles: in bed with Arthur confirming her pleasure with their sexual relationship; serving him breakfast in a way which recalls the servile role of Mrs Seaton; and, finally, hugging her child. Her ease and confidence in all these roles of lover, wife and mother constructs a representation at odds with the more misogynistic elements of the film. Her courage in deciding to go ahead with the pregnancy and 'face whatever comes of it', her speech about what it means to be a mother, and the final shot we see of her in the film, trapped in the spotlight with a crowd of hostile spectators around her just after she has been publicly slapped by Jack, invite the audience to sympathise with her. Meanwhile, in the penultimate sequence of the film where Arthur consummates his relationship with Doreen after their engagement, the camera privileges Doreen's unease. This, combined with the sequences involving Brenda, give a complex and empathetic look at the female experience of sexuality and marriage in the late 1950s, before the contraceptive pill and the abortion law started to have a real effect on women's lives.

Saturday Night and Sunday Morning is unusual in its implicit criticism of the ways in which challenges to working-class male identity manifest themselves. Like the 'angry young men' of the time, Arthur's anger is real but its focus remains unclear. The film gives a real sense of Arthur's unhappiness with his situation but is less clear about why he feels like this or what the solution may be. Arthur articulates this crisis of identity in juxtaposition with searching shots of his face in the mirror: 'I'm me and nobody else. Whatever people say I am that's what I'm not. God knows what I am'. To this extent the film is a more provocative and searching exploration of its time than some of the other 'kitchen sink' films which present a more apparently coherent picture of what 'working class' might mean.

Notes

1. Susan Hayward, 'Free Cinema', in *Cinema Studies: The Key Concepts*, London & New York, Routledge, 1996, pp. 132–5.
2. Tom Dewe Mathews, *Censored*, London, Chatto and Windus, 1994, pp. 151–2.

Further reading

John Hill, *Sex, Class and Realism*, London: BFI, 1986.

Richard Hoggart, *Uses of Literacy: Aspects of Working Class Life*, London: Chatto & Windus, 1957.

Dominic Sandbrook, *Never Had it So Good: A History of Britain from Suez to the Beatles*, Oxford: Abacus, 2006.

Jean Welsh

The Searchers (1956)

[Country: USA. Production Company: C.V. Whitney Pictures. Director: John Ford. Screenwriter: Frank Nugent. Cinematographer: Winton Hoch. Music: Max Steiner. Editor: Jack Murray. Cast: John Wayne (Ethan Edwards), Jeffrey Hunter (Martin Pawley), Natalie Wood (Debbie Edwards), Vera Miles (Laurie Jorgensen), Ward Bond (Reverend Captain Samuel Clayton), Henry Brandon (Scar), Hank Worden (Mose Harper).]

Synopsis: Ethan Edwards's brother, his sister-in-law and their young son, are killed in a Comanche attack on their homestead. Two of his nieces are carried off by the Indians. One is quickly killed, but Ethan and Martin Pawley, who as an orphan was adopted by Ethan's brother, continue to search for the other girl, Debbie. Eventually, they find her and free her and take her home, in the process killing the Comanche chief, Scar.

With 'Red Indians' set against homesteaders and John Wayne playing the strong, silent hero the basic elements to plot of *The Searchers* might suggest the film is likely to present simplistic interpretations of both the history of the American West and the nature of human psychology. What emerges though is something that is much more complex and resistant to easy analysis. The film moves towards a re-evaluation of Hollywood's version of 'Wild West' history within the changing post-war world.[1]

Initially the representation of Native Americans is as the threatening brutal savage set against the home-making, peace-loving white folk, in other words as part of the classic anticipated binary opposition of Westerns. However, although Ethan Edwards (Wayne) and the Comanche chief, Scar, are constructed as diametrically opposed foes the strong similarity between them is at least as important to the dynamics of the film. The Native American has literally been scarred by his experience of the clash of civilisations that has occurred and in this he is clearly presented as a parallel to Ethan (and possibly his alter ego, a self that is able to play out the full extent of Ethan's restrained savagery). Together they represent a past that needs to be purged so that the future can be shaped by a new generation.

The way in which Martin and the homesteaders need Ethan as a protector has often been commented upon but it is the younger man who actually rescues his adopted sister and kills Scar, leaving Ethan with only the opportunity to re-emphasise his repressed brutality by scalping Scar. Martin displays the same tenacity in trying to find his sister as his uncle but with the difference that he is driven by the motivation to save life rather than to take life. Ford denies both us and Ethan (the old-style hero) the classic final 'shoot-out'. The emerging new liberal hero, Martin, kills not within the context of glorifying ritual spectacle but simply, off-screen and of forced necessity. He rejects the racism not only of Ethan but of his fiancée, Laurie, who demonstrates the deeply ingrained nature of prejudice; and he reacts with simple compassionate humanity both to the plight of white women driven insane by their experiences at the hands of 'Indians' and to the massacre of women and children by the 7th Cavalry.

By contrast, Ford steadily exposes the reality of the nature of Ethan, the old order hero. In blind hatred, for example, he shoots out the eyes of a dead Comanche in order that his soul should not enter the spirit world and slaughters bison in manic fashion in order that the tribes should not be able to feed themselves. The viewer, certainly in 1956 when Wayne was at the height of his popularity, is placed in the potentially uncomfortable position of having to reject the values embodied in the character played by the iconic star.

On the other hand, it is also true that Ethan's motivations are more complex than is often allowed. To see him simply as seeking revenge is to neglect the extent to which he is also driven by guilt. He is the Indian-hater who knows his adversary's ways better than others, and yet he allows himself to be drawn away from the home, allowing the massacre of his brother's family and the woman he loves.

Ethan is full of the contradictions Ford seemed to see in contemporary United States. He is the brutal man who scalps Scar and then lifts Debbie to the sky with such compassion. Wayne's character in many senses remains the traditional hero: he knows what to do in any situation, can deal with any foe, and is never scared even in the face of his own death. Yet, he is also a frightening man with dark corners to his personality – in many ways an anti-hero. Frequently Ford uses careful direction and shot composition as well as dialogue and action to show us this complex man; but when Wayne, the jocular hero of so many Westerns, shifts suddenly to the dark anti-hero the dislocation is stark. The viewer is disorientated and faces the central flaw in the film – the way in which it uncomfortably straddles the divide between an older Hollywood version of 'how the West was won' and a new emerging perspective on history and nationhood.

If Ethan's similarities with Scar are at least as important as their opposition the same is also true of his relationship with Martin. Old and young, avenger and saviour, traditional hero and new emerging hero they might be, but at the same time Martin is Ethan's natural heir and the one who is able to carry Ethan's inheritance into the future. Like Ethan, Martin's natural element is the outdoors; he arrives in the film bare-chested and riding bareback suggesting his mixed blood but also the way in which he is at home in the landscape. He has Ethan's determination but shaped by a new outlook. Their interaction throughout the film has all the tensions of a father-son relationship.

The Searchers is set in the past and yet in many ways mirrors the tensions and fears of late 1950s America. Reactionary forces are perceiving the uncertain loyalties of some as a threat while at the same time new understandings of old conflicts are attempting to shape a new world. The civil rights movement is underway and the strongly perceived external and internal threat posed by the Soviet Union and communism hangs over every political decision. From our vantage point *The Searchers* can be seen as a politically flawed product of the 1950s, a strongly situated historical construct revealing the cultural perspectives of the period in which it was made. The issue of racism is at the heart of both the film and the central character. The civil rights movement has made the question of race unavoidable and this film reflects that contemporary reality. From the start, despite being part Native American, Martin is welcomed into the family by Ethan's brother and his wife. Ethan, the racist, respects the domestic sphere but the performance clearly shows us he only grudgingly accepts Martin's presence at the dinner table. Both Martin and Debbie are orphaned by the violence of the past and are seen by Ethan as in different ways tainted by their contact with the formerly excluded Native American 'Other'; but both are welcomed back into the community.

The film is set in Texas in 1868. This is a crucial period in the history of the United States: massive westward expansion is underway and this brings with it the inevitability of clashes with the Indian nations. The Cheyenne–Arapaho wars (1861–64) and the Sioux wars (1862–67) have only just ended and more are to follow. In addition, the American Civil War (1861–65) has only just finished and slavery has only just been abolished (1866). The Jorgensens with their East European/Scandinavian background contribute towards showing the United States as an ethnic melting pot. Martin is eighth Cherokee, with the rest Welsh and English. The film it seems aims to include references to almost every aspect of conflict embodied in the American 'invasion' of the West.

Yet, despite all that has been said here regarding the seriousness of the issues at stake humour is often used: do these scenes act effectively as comic relief, or do they flaw the whole concept? The episodes involving 'Look' who is later slaughtered by the cavalry embody the most simplistic stereotyping imaginable of both women and the Native American 'Other'. On the other hand it is also a woman, Mrs Jorgensen, who often puts the events of the film into some perspective acting as a voice of reason. She fully recognises that it is the harsh nature of the pioneering experience that lies at the heart of the hardship suffered ('It's this country killed my boy.') and begs for something better for the next generation beyond that which she fears Ethan offers, 'Don't let the boys waste their lives in vengeance.'

Ford's direction means as much is revealed through facial expression, physical stance and subtle gesture as through dialogue. Insights into characters are conveyed by body language and looks that carry implied meaning, for example Wayne's unspoken love for Martha and Aaron's uncertainty about Ethan. The cinematography clearly contrasts the inner spaces of the homesteads with the vast open tracts of landscape outdoors but again how this should be interpreted is not so easy to decide. Martha and Aaron's home is solid, homely and warm but it is also overbearing and claustrophobic (see the low-angle shots revealing the heavy, low ceiling). It is clearly designed and shot as a place of safety and refuge but proves to offer no security. Outside the vast panoramas offer a sense of both beauty and freedom but it is a harsh beauty and the apparent emptiness of the space harbours the unseen threatening savagery.

Ultimately, the film is filled with contradictions. As both minister and soldier, the concept of the character of Clayton embodies the moral dilemmas of frontier life. Both Indians and whites are capable of alternating compassion and brutality. There are no easy answers, nothing as simple as good versus evil; unless that is we look for both good and evil within each character. The cavalry massacres men, women and children at the settlement and Scar has had two sons killed by white men.

It is the importance of the future that is consistently emphasised. Martin represents that future and Ethan recognises this when he leaves him everything in his will. Debbie is perhaps symbolically even more a representation of the future than Martin and Laurie (see how many ethnic groups come together in their union). Debbie is that which is being searched for, she is hope, she is reconciliation, she has lived in both cultures and in that sense is the future.

Note

1. This is particularly the case when the film is read alongside its contrasting but in many ways companion volume from a few years later, *The Man Who Shot Liberty Valance* (Ford, 1962). In this film Ranse Stoddard (James Stewart) embodies democratic values – education for all, a free press, law and order. The very ordinary people who come to the school he establishes are given a sense of ownership; it is pointedly 'our' country, and a republic we are told is a state in which the people are 'the bosses'. Pompey (significantly as the African American) recites from the Declaration of Independence, 'We hold these truths self-evident that all men are created equal'. Yet, in the end even Stoddard has to admit, 'When force threatens talk's no good anymore'. Ultimately, he needs Tom Doniphon (Wayne, again) to defeat the baddie, the ironically named Liberty Valance. This it seems is the ultimate belief upon which Ford's type of democracy is built, that in the end you sometimes have to defend democracy and the rights it brings.

Further reading

Lindsay Anderson, *About John Ford*, London, Plexus, 1981.

Ian Cameron and Douglas Pye, *The Movie Book of the Western*, London, Studio Vista, 1996.

Arthur M. Eckstein, 'Darkening Ethan: John Ford's *The Searchers* from Novel to Screenplay to Screen' in *Cinema Journal* Vol. 38, No. 1, 1998, pp. 3–24.

Arthur M. Eckstein and Peter Lehman, *The Searchers: Essays and Reflections on John Ford's Classic Western*, Detroit, Wayne State University Press, 2004.

Scott Eyman and Paul Duncan, *John Ford: The Complete Films*, London, Taschen, 2004.

Julia Leyda, 'Home on the Range: Space, Nation and Mobility in John Ford's *The Searchers*' in *The Japanese Journal of American Studies* No 13, 2002, pp. 83–106.

Armando Jose Prats, *Invisible Natives: Myth and Identity in the American Western*, Ithaca and London, Cornell University Press, 2002.

Gaylyn Studlar and Matthew Bernstein, *John Ford Made Westerns: Filming the Legend in the Sound Era*, Bloomington, Indiana University Press, 2001.

John White

Shennu/The Goddess (1934)

[Country: China. Production Company: Lianhua Film Company. Director and Scenarist: Wu Yonggang. Cast: Ruan Ling-yu (the mother), Zhang Zhizhi (the Boss), Li Keng (the son), Li Junpan (the headmaster).]

Synopsis: A devoted mother supports her child through prostitution. Despite being domineered by a gangster called 'the Boss', she squirrels away part of her earnings in order to give her young son an education. Gossip about the mother's profession soon begins to spread around and, despite the kindly headmaster's protests, leads the school board to expel the boy. Distraught and finding her savings stolen and gambled away, the mother kills the Boss in a fury. Imprisoned for murder, the mother is partly consoled as the headmaster promises to take the boy under his wing.

When the 24-year-old actress Ruan Ling-yu was buried in 1935, the funeral procession stretched for five kilometres around Shanghai. Several female fans reportedly followed her in suicide, one leaving a note that read: 'If Ruan Ling-yu is dead, what else is there to live for?' (cited in Meyer 2005: 163). The legacy of Ruan's powerful screen presence is symbolic of the social and political struggles of its era. Partly, this is down to the roles: a parade of tragic females, trapped by circumstance into self-destruction, unhappiness and often suicide. Partly it is that these roles closely mirrored the actress' own chaotic life. Partly it is the staggering scale of her fame and fan devotion. The rest is down to her undeniable skill as an actress.

Much discussion of Ruan tends to dwell on the biographical: a disadvantaged background in a rapidly changing China, a victim of abusive relationships, celebrated by adoring fans and the target for salacious press gossip. Her popularity and early suicide on International Women's Day compounds the tragedy, adding an additional poignancy to her screen roles. That Ruan's life experience mirrors her celebrated roles is a terrible irony, though often a distraction from her achievements as a performer. Moreover, comparisons with Stanley Kwan's 1991 palimpsest film *Center Stage*, starring Maggie Cheung as Ruan, further complicate a modern reading of *The Goddess*. Here, we shall step back from the biography to analyse the film's ideological legacy and how this is embodied in Ruan's performance.

Shanghai in the early 1930s was a hub of opposing social forces: feudalistic tradition remained stubborn in a period of enforced modernisation and upheaval. Western influence made the city the so-called Paris of Asia while Japanese invasion had already been attempted and would soon recommence. Governance of the city came from the ruling nationalists (the KMT) whose main endeavour was to crush the influence of the growing Communist Party, largely through the aid of criminal gangs. Shanghai was therefore a metropolis of extremes: the glamour of decadent capitalism, the high life and movie stars rubbed up against violent criminality, corruption at high levels and appalling poverty.

Perhaps in keeping with these contradictions, the Lianhua Film Company was founded in 1930 by Luo Mingyou, a nationalist supporter who employed left-wing directors and writers. The result was a series of roles for Lianhua's star actress that alternate between conservative and anti-traditional principles, with *The Goddess* a clear example of the latter.

The left was particularly influenced by the May Fourth Movement, the revolutionary group that rebelled against feudalistic Confucianism and called for a modern nation that would break from tradition and engage with Western ideas. The emancipation of Chinese women was a priority. As a still young and hugely popular medium, cinema was an ideal form to express radical ideologies. The KMT ban on representations of the Communist Party on screen led to Ruan's directors 'disguising the political nature of the plots and presenting them as melodramatic soap operas. The messages were clear, but the endings usually hued to the KMT party line' (Meyer 2005: 41). Thus, while *The Goddess* has a perhaps narratively convenient ending, there is much that suggests its Marxist intention, most prominently the absence of character names.

In her analysis of gender representation in pre-Maoist Chinese film, Shuqin Cui asserts:

> The image of 'modern woman' as an embodiment of national enlightenment implies rejection of sociocultural tradition and acceptance of the advent of modernity. The modern woman as a self, however, is torn between the given identity and a problematic reality. In chaotic circumstances, when the nation undergoes international humiliation and domestic turmoil, the metaphor of nation-as-woman signifies a homeland under the pressure of foreign violation or civil division.
>
> (2003: xiii)

Thus, *The Goddess* operates on both a literal level, as a Chinese woman trapped by an oppressive society who seeks emancipation through education (a May Fourth ideal), and on a wider symbolic level, as contemporary China itself. This dichotomous self-image of the nation as prostitute and devoted mother sits at the heart of the film's complex ideology.

The 'Goddess' of the title signifies the duality of both a celebration of motherhood (an ironically Confucian ideal) and a Chinese euphemism for a sex worker. The opening image is of a sculpture of a nursing woman and child, followed by a still of the beaming mother and son, which leads into a shot of Shanghai's flashing neon lights. Further parallels are drawn explicitly throughout by the intertitles, while the mise en scène juxtaposes exteriors and interiors where the streets represent the prostitute and the home the mother. The spatial shift also signifies both modernity and tradition. Prostitution was indeed rife during the period, though the film conspicuously offers no sense of this as degrading, but as a necessary evil in order for the mother to ensure a better future for her son. Crucially, for the social concept to work, *The Goddess* avoids analysis of how the mother's situation has come about and never judges her. Instead, the spectator is asked to condemn the different social classes that have together cornered her into this lifestyle: the Boss' feckless, destructive and parasitical attitudes and the neighbours' sanctimonious disapproval.

William Rothman's analysis of the film suggests that the selfless values endorsed by the headmaster are already perfectly articulated by the mother: 'she is not on a quest of a self because she does not doubt that she already has or is a self' (Rothman 2004: 63). It is the male characters who have an ideological development to make in order to reach narrative fulfilment, not the mother. It can perhaps be added that the use of the form of melodrama would have targeted any ideological message at a largely female audience.

As a reductive portrayal of female duality, a mother/whore depiction is of itself nothing new but *The Goddess* takes the archetypes usually portrayed as opposites and blends them into a sympathetic and believable whole. The film successfully depicts the mother's lifestyle that avoids erotic cliché. Selling herself is a chore, with the camera lingering over shots of feet, to emphasise the laborious aspect of streetwalking. Her weariness on her return home is evident.

Rothman contrasts Wu's presentation of Ruan on-screen with much of classic Hollywood's portrayal of the female and suggests that the film is refreshingly free of an eroticised presentation of the main character, considering the mother's profession. He cites the sequence where she makes up in preparation to walk the streets, noting the absence of a typical point of view shot that would allow us to linger over the star's reflected image as she looks provocatively into the camera. The effect mocks 'our guilty wish to reduce her to an object' (2004: 60).

Only the headmaster ever reaches out to touch her in a way that Rothman reads as potentially erotic (2004: 67). This is arguably a stretch, as he seems to represent less a patriarchal than a developing moral authority; the embodiment of a modern, educated society that recognises its responsibility to its disadvantaged. He notably wears a Western suit in contrast to the rest of the school board when he resists their calls to expel the boy to save their reputation. Conversely, the traditionally dressed Boss' relationship with the mother seems oddly free of lust. He demands her obedience and is unconcerned at the misery this brings her but their relationship seems oddly chaste, as if he is a demanding, overgrown baby placing himself as a cuckoo in her nest. The mother (and by extension through her other surviving screen roles, Ruan) can be read as an early twentieth-century feminist icon.

However, challenging *The Goddess'* proto-feminist credentials, Cui notes a male hand at work: writers and directors reinforcing the traditional uneven gender divide by depicting an 'enlightened saviour stooping to help an unawakened female figure' (2003: 13). Indeed, the mother is caught between three male figures: the unenlightened boss, the principled headmaster and the boy she hopes to advance.

Similarly, Rey Chow observes that many Chinese male authors of the period looked to the suffering woman as symbolic of their nation as 'feminized because weak, passive, invaded and tragic' (in Berry and Farquar 2006: 121). The camera may discretely avoid fetishising her but 'the overall male narrative point of view is clear' (ibid: 122). Perhaps then, the political impetus undermines the enunciation of a truly female perspective.

Nonetheless, Berry and Farquhar highlight the film's use of female subjectivity to articulate a vision of a possible future, concluding that, 'if Ruan herself embodies a China that cannot act now, she also acts as a channel for the expression and articulation of hopes for future agency' (ibid: 124).

Overall, whether a Marxist or feminist paradigm, the film's success as both metaphor and melodrama hinges on the tremendous subtleties of Ruan's performance, of which there are numerous examples. For instance, when the Boss imposes his 'protection', her whole body stiffens in fear. A fleeting, hysterical laugh is quickly choked down and Ruan looks like a caged animal.

Later, at the school performance, sat next to the mother, the censorious neighbour scowls and begins to gossip. Awareness creeps in and the mother's face clouds as delight shifts to fear. During the headmaster's visit, subjective shots are exchanged and he notes the truth in the gossip as to her income from the cheongsams hanging up on the wall. Ruan's face crumples. Her protest at his declaration that the boy must leave is passionate and forceful, making believable the headmaster's change of heart.

Finally, when confronting the Boss with his theft, Ruan explodes with all the primal force of a furious mother whose child is in danger. Having dominated her throughout with his size and aggression (sometimes aided by memorable cinematography such as the shot of the cowering mother framed between his legs), he now seems genuinely alarmed at her passion. Illustrating his perspective, she approaches the camera with a bottle in hand, subjecting the spectator to the intensity of her rage.

Rendering shame, joy, despair, wrath or resignation, Ruan Ling-yu's screen roles are reflective of the period's crucible of contradictions: an era so unbalanced that it could not last. Full Japanese invasion was imminent, and the upheavals of the Mao era would soon follow. The final image of *The Goddess* is of the mother locked away surrounded by darkness, smiling beatifically at the superimposed image of her son. She rejects the possibility of ever seeing him again, but at least hopes that he will have a better future. The scene is not a happy ending and would be difficult for any actress to carry off. If a melodrama can be said to possess restraint and subtlety, it is to be found here.

Further reading

Chris Berry and Mary Farquhar, *China on Screen*, Columbia University Press, 2006.

Rey Chow, *Primitive Passions: Visuality, Sexuality, Ethnography & Contemporary Chinese Cinema*, New York, Columbia University Press, 1995.

Shuqin Cui, *Women Through the Lens*, Honolulu, University of Hawaii Press, 2003.

Jonathan Fenby, *The Penguin History of Modern China*, Penguin, London, 2008.

Richard J. Meyer, *Ruan Ling-Yu: The Goddess of Shanghai*, Hong Kong University Press, Hong Kong, 2005.

William Rothman, *The 'I' of the Camera: Essays in Film Criticism, History, and Aesthetics*, Cambridge, Cambridge University Press, 2004.

Phil Lloyd

Shi mian mai fu/House of Flying Daggers (2004)

[Country: China. Production Company: Beijing New Picture Film Co, China Film Co-production Corporation, Edko Film, Elite Group Enterprises and Zhang Yimou Studio. Director: Zhang Yimou. Editor: Cheng Long. Screenwriters: Bin Wang, Feng Li and Zhang Yimou. Cinematographer: Zhao Xiaoding. Cast: Andy Lau (Leo), Takeshi Kaneshino (Jin), Ziyi Zhang (Mei).]

Synopsis: China 859 AD, the mysterious House of Flying Daggers leads a rebellion against a corrupt government. News reaches military captain Leo that one of the members of the House can be found in a local brothel. Hatching a plan to capture the rebel, Leo sends one his men, Jin, to the establishment. This leads to the imprisonment of the beautiful blind girl Mei. Aided by Jin, Mei escapes and they embark on a perilous journey across the region in the hope of locating the rebel base. Meanwhile Captain Leo and his soldiers pursue the pair.

The most prolific of the fifth generation of Chinese film-makers,[1] Zhang Yimou garnered acclaim in the West as Chinese film began to become famous outwith its own borders during the late 1980s. His early strand of cinema such as *Red Sorghum* (1987) was notable for combining overt political criticism through easily read allegorisation married to bold aesthetics. During this period, his films were well received in domestic arenas and by overseas 'art-house' audiences. Contrastingly, *House of Flying Daggers* facilitated a shift to mainstream appreciation for the director in the West while disappointing ticket sales within mainland China indicated that local audiences had grown weary of Zhang's newfound enthusiasm for refashioning the Wuxia epic.[2] In addition, many Chinese critics harshly judged the film as a calculated addition to the post millennium trend for revitalising traditional forms for Western consumption: filled with exoticist thematics and orientalist imagery that hoped to opportunistically facsimile the global success of Ang Lee's *Crouching Tiger, Hidden Dragon* (2000).[3]

Such accusations are problematic. From the silent era, the Wuxia film has been exotic by its nature and has always attracted local audiences with an overt attention to the aesthetically ambitious, sensational and epic married to technological advances (Szeto 2011: 21). Zhang earnestly pays heed to this mindset with beautifully choreographed action scenes situated in lavishly saturated set-pieces that maintain an impetus on the attraction of the fantastic. The dynamic nature of the many combat scenes that litter the narrative concede to an eclectic mix of indigenous and transnational forms: an amalgamation that typifies his enthusiasm for a cosmopolitan approach to film-making. For instance, the extravagant displays of fighting styles find their roots in Chinese operatic forms in which spectacle and body performance enchanted audiences through dance-like combat.[4] This is adroitly aligned with Hollywood computer graphics technology and a kinteticism typical of Japanese 'beat-em-up' video games.

When analysing the text there is a danger of unwittingly permitting the film's inherent grandiose qualities to overshadow interpretation. If we are to understand the film more fully we need to investigate the economic and political motivations behind the content. In effect, we need to intertwine aesthetic qualities with an examination of China's eagerness for post-socialist market-orientated cultural and economic reform: a financially dictated ethos accentuated by entry into the World Trade Organization in 2001. In doing so we can view the film as symptomatic of a national film industry propped up by the state that actualises a model that both mimics and resists the Hollywood blockbuster.

In a state-backed drive to emulate the recent 'soft' cultural power of other East-Asian territories[5] and to regain moviegoers at home lost to the increasing influx of Hollywood cinema, the Chinese film industry has negotiated rather than resisted the American blockbuster. With an emphasis on gaining audiences through the fantastic and lavish set-pieces, the Wuxia film arguably already shared some of the characteristics intrinsic to the Hollywood blockbuster. As such, the genre easily moulds itself to an excessive faith in a big-budget and high-concept mentality.

In this ongoing process of 'contested transaction' (Berry and Farquar 2006: 208), the 'Diapan'/ Chinese blockbuster has become a lucrative export. Despite disappointing audience figures at home and censure from Chinese critics such as Yingjin Zhang who condemns the Diapan picture as characterised by 'largely shallow content behind their alluring façade of audiovisual treats' (Yingjin 2010: 177) this increasingly internationalised model of film-making has risen to become the most popular foreign national cinema in the West (Rosen 2010: 42).

As the Diapan picture continues to demonstrate an eagerness for international influences, defining national cinema requires elasticity beyond the limits of geographically bound demarcations. Although the production companies were based in China, *House of Flying Daggers* was partly filmed in the Ukraine, had international production and artistic staff and benefited from global distribution from major Hollywood studios. A more appropriate definition of this work might be found in one that acknowledges local and transnational influences in both the production process and final text while interrelating the unmistakable ambition of the Chinese film industry to compete with Hollywood product. Perhaps Klein's favoured term, 'global Chinese-language film' (2007: 189) makes the most viable attempt to summarise the text as exemplar of the recent radicalisation of the Chinese cultural economy.

Distinguished from the Martial-Arts and Kung-Fu film by its pronounced use of the fantastic, particular historical settings, swordplay, and chivalrous characters, the Wuxia genre has maintained its popularity by adapting itself to pronounced social and political allegorisation as fits the time period. The text continues this route but mischievously deviates from generic frameworks so as to offer up some novel approaches that are indicative of a willingness to open up the genre to global audiences. Although this is symptomatic of the economically motivated sanctions endorsed by the ethics of the new model of global Chinese-language film, we have to merge these with directorial initiative to gain a more rounded understanding. Zhang is adept at breaking through the rigidity of commercial genre structure to focus on humanist perspectives and personal emotional conflict. For instance, *Shanghai Triad* (1995) pertains to be just another violent mobster movie but beneath a curtain of generic expectations lies a gracious parable on the cyclical nature of cruelty. As he has claimed of *House of Flying Daggers*, 'I don't want to make an ordinary martial arts film. I want to talk about passion, interesting characters ... my own style of Wuxia film' (2003: 9).

The smog of civil unrest and discord surrounds the tale and the first act promises a predominately political construct. This is a promise unfulfilled. We find out that the underground alliance is rebelling but we never get to learn what against: details of corrupt government deeds are enduringly inconspicuous and factions remain largely unheeded by political leaders. In substitution, Western style romance becomes an ever-prominent motif as the narrative progresses.

The inclusion of the 'swords-woman' hero is not unique to the text and traditionally romantic relationships have simply served as a conduit for larger overarching themes such as the political and economic (Gomes 2010: 171). Revisioning accustomed forms, the text finds parallels with the recent glut of post-millennium Wuxia[6] by dramatically foregrounding this Western-style romance (albeit one marred by deceit and deception). Accentuating this inclusion has softened the masculinist overtones previously typical of the genre and ousted spectatorship from the enclaves of cult appreciation in the West outward to a multiplicity of audiences.

Centralising on the love triangle enacted by Mei, Jin and Captain Leo at the expensive of political detail also facilitates a contemporary allegorical reading. Rather than remaining apolitical, the text actually forges meaning from absence. Through the narrative personal lives entwine and ideals of commitment to revolution and political power structures are lost to the pursuit of individual happiness. As China continues a consumer-based post-socialist modernisation process with the personal increasingly replacing the political perhaps Zhang has cynically fashioned a text that mirrors shifting values within modern Chinese society.

As subterfuge and heightened emotion become ever prominent themes within the narrative, nature and landscape become of vital importance when reading the film in the context of Zhang's authorial signature and the influence of classical Chinese arts. Possibly the most constant factor in his oeuvre, Zhang's work has always opened itself up to easily read metaphorical interpretation. Continuing this leitmotif, emotions are externalised through barren woodlands and flowering pastures and melancholy concludes with meadows blanketed by snow that engulf the lovers' final confrontation. These broad strokes run the risk of seeming crude but the sparse constitution of the script favours space for laden symbolism.

Elsewhere Zhang spotlights nature and landscape as devices for respite from the perils that plague the journey to the *House of Flying Daggers*' headquarters. With Leo and his soldiers in close pursuit of Mei and Jin these are only fleeting moments soon to be punctured by conflict from the outside world. Elsewhere, bird's-eye shots of grand vistas that diminish characters punctuate the narrative. Such compositions extend local cultural patterns familiar to the mediums of early poetry and painting and continue Daoist beliefs in nature as a place of solace and harmony with humans as just one element in the grander scheme of life.[7]

Zhang's liberal use of these classical techniques is noteworthy: these devices confirm both a return to the quintessential visual style of his early cinema and further a fondness for local forms within his work. As he has said, 'If in twenty years, after I've made a lot more films, they write one more sentence about me in a textbook, I'd be satisfied if they said: "Zhang Yimou's cinematic style is strongly visual in a distinctly Chinese fashion"' (2008: 148). This claim may seem at odds in a text so beholden to transnational influences and global spectatorship. But it is this synergy of the local and international that makes *House of Flying Daggers* such a fascinating text.

Notes

1. These include Chen Kaige, Hu Mei, Tia Zhuangzhuang, Wu Ziniu, Zhang Juazhao, Zhang Yimou and Zhou Xiaoien.
2. See Braester, Yomi (2005) 'Chinese Cinema in The Age of Advertisement: the Filmmaker as a Cultural Broker', *The China Quarterly*, 183, pp. 549–64.
3. Zhang claims that he had prepared both *Hero* and *House of The Flying Daggers* before the release of *Crouching Tiger, Hidden Dragon* in 2000.
4. See the discussion of this aspect of the film in Chris Berry and Mary Ann Farquhar's *China on Screen*, pp. 47–74.
5. In particular, the recent global popularity of South Korean entertainment often termed as the 'Hanryu'.
6. Alongside Zhang's work these include *The Banquet* (Xiaogong Feng, 2006), *The Promise* (Kaige Chen, 2005) and *Seven Swords* (Hark, Tsui, 2005).
7. See the chapter by Woo Cho Yi-Yu, Catherine, in Chris Berry (ed.) *Perspectives on Chinese Cinema*, pp. 197– 1.

Further reading

Chris Berry and Mary Ann Farquhar, *China on Screen*, New York, Columbia University Press, 2006.

Catherine Gomes, 'Lost in Translation: American Critical Audience and the Transnational Chinese Swordswoman', in Dong, Lan (ed.), *Transnationalism and The Asian-American Heroine. Essays on Literature, Film Myth and Media*, North Carolina, McFarland, 2010, pp. 168–86.

Christina Klein, 'Kung Fu Hustle: Transnational production and the global Chinese-language film', *Journal of Chinese Cinemas*, 1: 3, 2007, pp. 189–208.

Lo Kwai-Cheung, *Excess and Masculinity in Asian Cultural Productions*, Albany, SUNY Press, 2010.

Stanley Rosen, 'Chinese Cinema's International Market', in S. Rosen and Ying Zhu, (eds), *Art, Politics and Commerce in Chinese Cinema*, Hong Kong, Hong Kong University Press, 2010, pp. 35–54.

Kin-Yun Szeto, *The Martial Arts Cinema of Chinese Diaspora: Ang Lee, John Woo and Jackie Chan in Hollywood*, Illinois, Southern Illinois University Press, 2011.
Stephen Teo, *Chinese Martial Arts Cinema: The Wuxia Tradition*, Edinburgh, Edinburgh University Press, 2009.
Catherine Woo Cho Yi-Yu, 'The Chinese Montage: From Poetry and Painting to the Silver Screen', in Chris Berry (ed.), *Perspectives on Chinese Cinema*, London, BFI, 1991, pp. 21–9.
Zhang Yimou, 'Beyond the Fifth Generation: An Interview with Zhang Yimou', Cardullo, Bert, *Out of Asia: Essays and Interviews*, Newcastle-upon-Tyne, Cambridge Scholars Publishing, 2008, pp. 127–50.
Zhang Yimou, *Sony Classics: House of Flying Daggers press kit*, 2003. Available at http://sonyclassics.com/houseofflyingdaggers/_media/presskit.pdf (accessed 20 July 2012).
Yingjin Zhang, *Cinema, Space and Polylocality in a Globalizing China*, Honolulu, University of Hawaii Press, 2010.

Dave McCaig

Shichinin no samurai/Seven Samurai (1953)

[Country: Japan. Production Company: Toho. Director: Akira Kurosawa. Screenwriters: Akira Kurosawa, Shinobu Hashimoto and Hideo Uguni. Cinematographer: Asakazu Nakai. Music: Fumio Hayasaka. Editor: Akira Kurosawa. Cast: Takashi Shimura (Kambei Shimada), Toshiro Mifune (Kikuchiyo), Isao Kimura (Katsushirō Okamoto), Yoshino Inaba (Gorōbei Katayama), Daisuke Kato (Shichirōji), Minoru Chinaki (Heihachi Hayashida), Seiji Miyaguchi (Kyuzo).]

Synopsis: Japan 1587, during a period of chaotic civil war, a group of marauding bandits makes plans to rob an isolated village as soon as the harvest is in. One villager, hiding on a woodpile, overhears them and the farmers go to their elder for advice. As they have nothing to offer but food, he tells them to hire 'hungry samurai' to help defend their village. Four men travel to the nearest town where every samurai they approach rejects their offer. However, after they witness an experienced samurai, Kambei (Takashi Shimura), perform an act of bravery and kindness they approach him and he agrees to fight for their cause. Two younger samurai, Katsushirō (Isao Kimura), and the almost feral, Kikuchiyo (Toshiro Mifune), who also witnessed the older samurai's actions, ask to join the cause and follow him. He accepts the former as an equal but rejects the brash Kikuchiyo. After several days, Kambei and the farmers manage to recruit four more Ronin: Gorobei Katayama (Yoshino Inaba), who becomes Kambei's lieutenant; the good-humoured Heihachi (Minoru Chinaki); Shichirōji (Daisuke Kato), Kambei's old friend; and Kyūzō (Seiji Miyaguchi), an almost silent master swordsman. They travel to the village, pursued by Kikuchiyo, who they reluctantly take along. Realising that there are more than 40 bandits, the samurai begin to prepare a defensive strategy, building fortifications around the village and training the villagers to fight with bamboo sticks and spears. The samurai and the villagers eventually warm to one another, even though the former discover that the villagers have killed wandering samurai in the past and have hidden the young women in the forest for fear that they would be raped. Kikuchiyo, who reveals himself to be a farmer's son, tells the samurai that their treatment of the lower classes is also to blame for such actions. As the harvest approaches, the attack finally comes. Kambei gives orders to let the bandits through a gap in the fortifications one at a time, so that they can be picked off. This largely succeeds, although a few villagers are killed. Over the course of several skirmishes Heihachi and Gorobei are killed. On the third night the men prepare for one final attack. Katsushirō makes love to one of the farmer's daughters, who he has fallen in love with. In the ensuing battle the samurai kill most of the remaining bandits. However, Kyuzo is shot by one of the bandit chiefs. Kikuchiyo attacks and kills the chief but is mortally wounded in the process. The next day, Katsushirō watches the villagers harvest and contemplates staying behind. However, as Kambei and his old friend, Shichirōji, observe that the samurai have lost and that the 'winners are those farmers … not us,' the young samurai realises that the gulf between him and his lover is too wide.

Although Kurosawa has come to be closely associated with the Japanese genre of the historical film, the *jidai-geki*, with the exception of a handful of works, most notably his international breakthrough, *Rashomon* (1950), the director had previously worked primarily in the *gendai mono* genre, making films about contemporary life in Japan. With *Seven Samurai* however, he fulfilled his ambition to make a serious contribution both to the *jidai-geki* and the subgenre of the *chambara*, the sword fight movie, which Kurosawa thought rarely lived up to its full potential.

The production of *Seven Samurai* was perhaps the most elaborate of any Japanese film up to that time. Kurosawa, in his relentless pursuit of authenticity, refused to use a studio set and instead had an entire village built on the Izu Peninsula. Filming lasted almost 150 days, around four times more than the allotted time, and the shooting schedule was finally spread out over an entire year. The budget also escalated to around $500,000, making the film the most expensive ever made in Japan (a record Kurosawa would go on to break more than once). The director found himself vilified in the press for his overspending, tardiness and perfectionism. And while these criticisms were in part justified, there were also matters that were beyond Kurosawa's control, and the shoot was beset with logistical problems, including bad weather and a shortage of extras and horses. The lengthy schedule was also the result of the studio, Toho, shutting down the production on two occasions due to lack of funds. Kurosawa, who had never made an unprofitable film, was justifiably confident that they would always find the money to restart the production.

The final cut, which Donald Richie has called 'the best Japanese film ever made' (Richie 1998: 108), was personally edited by the director and lasted three and a half hours. It also went on to break box office records in its native country. However, regardless of its domestic success, Toho did not feel confident that the film would play well to Western audiences and the version released in America and the United Kingdom was reduced by almost an hour, ridding the film of a good deal of complex characterisation. (Subsequently, the full-length version has been restored and released internationally.)

Yet despite its length, *Seven Samurai*, is a film of great economy in which all extemporaneous information is elided. For example, the central conflict between the villagers and the bandits is established in the film's opening two minutes; the journey of four of the villagers to recruit samurai in the nearest town is not shown at all, while their return to the village, with the six warriors and Kikuchiyo following them, takes only three minutes. Conversely, the fortification of the village and the preparation for the ensuing battles are lovingly detailed, with Kurosawa's camera lingering on Kambei's tactical map of the village, thus allowing the audience to gain an understanding of the heroes' strategy.

The film's scope and length also allows Kurosawa to develop the characters of all seven samurai, and several of the villagers, in far greater depth than one usually expects in a genre film. Of these major characters, the most complex are Kambei, the pragmatic leader of the group, played by Takashi Shimura, a veteran character actor who appeared in over 20 of the director's films; and Kikuchiyo played by Kurosawa's favourite leading man, Toshiro Mifune. The latter character is the film's wild card. A late addition to the screenplay, Kikuchiyo is a farmer's son who poses as a samurai. His recklessness and lack of discipline is however offset by his ferocity and bravery as a fighter. The character's dual nature therefore allows Kurosawa to explore the divide between the warriors and the farmers and to puncture the myth that being a samurai is merely a question of birth and class.

It is also worth noting that the four samurai who die are all shot, not killed with swords. This prefigures Kurosawa's later period masterpiece, *Kagemusha* (1980), in which the he dramatises the fatal cavalry charge of the Takeda clan at the Battle of Nagashino, arguably the first modern battle in Japanese history, in which the gun began to supersede the sword. Both films therefore depict the end of an historical era, and perhaps an age of chivalry. In this respect, *Seven Samurai* shares a kinship with films such as John Ford's *The Man who Shot Liberty Valance* (1962) or Sam Peckinpah's *The Wild Bunch* (1969) as a film about a group of men who have outlived their time.

The film's thematic similarity to American Westerns is indeed apparent, and it is perhaps for this reason that its story could be so easily transposed to a Mexican setting in John Sturges' 1960 remake, *The Magnificent Seven*. However, just as one should be cautious of seeing Kurosawa as the most American-friendly Japanese filmmaker, one should also be careful not to view *Seven Samurai* as merely an 'Eastern Western'. Rather, it is more accurate to see this film as drawing on a series of universal archetypes as well as some concerns that are also uniquely Japanese. Indeed, the film's complex examination of feudal hierarchies may initially be lost on Western viewers, as might some allegorical comments on Japanese militarism and the post-war American occupation, which only officially ended in 1952, not quite two years before its release.

While an understanding of such contextual matters can greatly enhance one's appreciation of the film, *Seven Samurai* remains remarkably accessible, not least because of its pacing and superbly executed action sequences. As Donald Richie notes, the film's key quality is its sense of motion. On the one hand, narrative momentum is maintained throughout; the story is never allowed to sprawl or give way to unnecessary subplots. On the other, the film is defined by its sense of movement. Whether it is the camera or an actor, or the two moving in tandem, the film never ceases to *move*. At times, Kurosawa employs slow motion to elongate an action, underscoring its dramatic impact. However, more often than not, these movements are remarkably kinetic, as in the scene where Kikuchiyo raises the alarm to make a point to the ungrateful villagers. His six comrades all spring into action. Kurosawa films each one of the samurai in a medium close-up, the camera tracking in step alongside them as they sprint. When these six shots are cut together it gives the impression of a single motion, with the samurai united in a common goal.

The final sortie between the samurai and the bandits, which takes place during a torrential rainstorm, is a particular *tour de force*. As a montage sequence, it has often been compared to the climactic battle in Sergei Eisenstein's *Alexander Nevsky* (1938), and the sequence is indeed notable for the rapidity and skill of its editing. However, the impression of chaos was only achieved through meticulous planning and an innovative shooting style (despite his reputation as something of rearguard filmmaker, Kurosawa never stopped experimenting with new techniques). In order to maintain perfect continuity, the director employed three cameras, often equipped with telephoto lenses which allowed him to keep them at a distance while also covering the action with startling intimacy. Kurosawa would become so fond of this technique that he would begin employing it in many of his subsequent feature films and not only in action sequences.

With its rapidly cut, but still coherent battle scenes, and its use of slow motion, *Seven Samurai* has arguably become the most influential action film ever made. Not only has it spawned one direct remake (which itself spawned three sequels), it can also be seen as a key inspiration for films such as Robert Aldrich's *The Dirty Dozen* (1967), John T. Murakami's *Battle Beyond the Stars* (1980), John McTiernan's *The Thirteenth Warrior* (1999), Tsui Hark's *Seven Swords* (2005) and Takashi Miike's *Thirteen Assassins* (2010) among many others. However, few if any films genre films can lay claim to the same combination of technical virtuosity, deft characterisations and thematic complexity.

Further reading

James Goodwin, *Akira Kurosawa and Intertextual Cinema*, Baltimore, The Johns Hopkins University Press, 1993.
Joan Mellen, *Seven Samurai*, London, BFI, 2002.
Stephen Prince, *The Warrior's Camera: The Cinema of Akira Kurosawa*, Princeton, Princeton University Press, 1999.
Donald Richie, *The Cinema of Akira Kurosawa*, Berkeley, University of California Press, 1998.

Brian Hoyle

Singin' in the Rain (1952)

[Country: USA. Production Company: Metro-Goldwyn-Mayer. Directors: Stanley Donen, Gene Kelly. Producer: Arthur Freed. Cinematographer: Harold Rosson. Editor: Adrienne Fazan. Art Directors: Randall Duell, Cedric Gibbons. Set Decoration: Jacques Mapes, Edwin B. Willis. Costume Design: Walter Plunkett. Cast: Gene Kelly (Don Lockwood), Donald O'Connor (Cosmo Brown), Debbie Reynolds (Kathy Selden), Jean Hagen (Lina Lamont).]

Synopsis: *Singin' in the Rain* opens at the 1927 premiere of *The Royal Rascal*, a costume drama starring above-the-credit silent film stars Don Lockwood and Lina Lamont. On the red carpet, Don tells the adoring crowds about his training in the arts of high culture, framed by the motto, 'Always dignity'. A montage shows us the real story: pool hall dancer; beer hall fiddle player; performer in low-rent vaudeville houses; a film career that began when Don replaced a stunt man injured on the job. We also learn why Don despises his co-star, Lina Lamont. After the premiere, Don meets and falls for Kathy Selden, a nightclub performer and aspiring actress. Stunned by the monumental success of *The Jazz Singer*, Monumental Pictures bets that Lockwood and Lamont can make the transition to sound. When their first effort, *The Duelling Cavalier*, flops, Don, Kathy, and Don's sidekick Cosmo Brown decide to remake *The Duelling Cavalier* as a musical, with Kathy acting as a vocal double for Lina Lamont. *Singin' in the Rain* closes at the opening of *The Dancing Cavalier*. A coda reveals a billboard advertising Monumental Pictures' next blockbuster, a Lockwood/Selden musical called *Singin' in the Rain*.

Singin' in the Rain holds a privileged place in the canon of American movies, comparable to the places held in the rock and roll canon by Elvis Presley and the Beatles. Among the various top-10, -25, -100 lists on which this 1952 nostalgia fest has appeared the most emblematic (and most frequently cited) may be *Sight & Sound's* 1982 poll of critics for the 10 best movies of all time: *Singin'* came in fourth; no other musicals made the list. Indeed, while musicals were among the most popular forms of Hollywood entertainment during the 1930s, 40s and 50s, and the genre remains beloved among devoted cinephiles, musicals tend to be marginal in film surveys. Dramas, melodramas, and comedies dominate this and most comparable lists, along with representative thrillers and Westerns and the occasional science fiction or horror film. Musicals are often cloying; their plots challenge even the most devoted viewer's capacity to suspend disbelief; the music doesn't always age well. What makes *Singin' in the Rain* different?

To address this question, it's worth asking another question: what is a musical? A few American films offer points of comparison. *Casablanca* (1942), many people's favourite movie, includes a good deal of diegetic music; five different songs are performed in their entirety within the imaginary world of the film.

'As Time Goes By' and '*La Marseillaise*' provide crucial thematic structure. But most people would not call *Casablanca* a musical.

One cannot define musicals as movies in which characters sing and/or dance without any plot motivation. The question of the relationship between musical numbers and the surrounding plot (if there is any) is often complex. In 'integrated' musicals songs advance plot or develop a character in various degrees, while revues hardly have a plot. But distinctions are often not that clear. Backstage musicals, such as *Gold Diggers of 1933*, deal with the problem of characters spontaneously breaking into song or dance by locating their plot in the entertainment world. Nor can we limit the definition to movies, like *West Side Story*, which feature original music (original, in this case, to the stage show on which the film is based). Of the 12 songs performed in *Singin' in the Rain*, 9 appeared in earlier MGM musicals. Only two – 'Moses Supposes' and 'Make 'em Laugh' – were written for *Singin'*. (Even this is a stretch. 'Make 'em Laugh' has virtually the same musical structure as Cole Porter's 'Be a Clown', the finale of *The Pirate* (Vincente Minnelli, 1948).)

Singin' is the last, and best, of a post-Second World War sequence of what are now called juke-box musicals. Warner Brothers started the trend with *Night and Day* (1946), a sanitised and fictionalised version of the life of Cole Porter. *An American in Paris* (1951) and *Singin' in the Rain*, both produced by the Arthur Freed unit, both starring Gene Kelly, represent the most successful examples of the MGM jukebox musical. *American* is built around a catalogue of songs composed by George Gershwin with lyrics by Ira Gershwin. *Singin'* is built around songs composed by Herb Nacio Brown, with lyrics by Arthur Freed. While neither is a biopic of the *Night and Day* genre, *Singin'* glorifies producer Freed – who began his MGM career as a lyricist – and Kelly – whose name appears in the credits three times: as above-the-credits star, as choreographer (with Stanley Donen), and as co-director (also with Donen).

Of course, this movie does more than glorify its creative team. *Singin' in the Rain* is about movie magic. Set in the historical moment when sound film threatened the supremacy of silent film, this movie mythologises the development of the movie musical, and presents movie magic as evidence of film's superiority to the cinema's new, terrifying, and never-mentioned competitor: television.

Singin' in the Rain's intertextual relationship to *Babes in Arms* (1939), the first musical produced by Freed, is particularly noteworthy. *Babes* is the prototypical 'let's put on a show in the barn' movie. Mickey Rooney and Judy Garland play children of vaudeville performers whose livelihood disappeared when sound film killed vaudeville. In *Babes* the vaudevillians' children put on a musical show to forestall their parents' insolvency.

In *Singin'*, three characters hatch a plan to put on a musical movie and save a studio. The film dramatises the transition from vaudeville to the movies twice: in the opening sequence, when Don Lockwood moves from vaudevillian to stuntman to star, and again in the 'Broadway Ballet' sequence, which dramatises the ascent of a Lockwood-like character from no-name to Broadway star. Although this number glorifies The Great White Way, everything about it reinforces its cinematic qualities. The number demonstrates that the movies can encompass all other performing arts – song, music, dance – and offer them all up in a glossy package.

As a film, *Singin'* is structured by musical spectacle, nostalgia and creative anachronism. Musical spectacle dominates the diegesis from the film's opening moments to its closing. The credits feature a very wet performance of the film's title song by the film's three stars: Kelly, Donald O'Connor and Debbie Reynolds. The film's closing moments feature a duet of Kelly and Reynolds singing 'You are my Lucky Star', a number finished by an invisible choir as Kelly/Don Lockwood and Reynolds/Kathy Selden are transformed into billboard images advertising a film called *Singin' in the Rain.* While this film qualifies as a backstage (or backlot) musical, and the plot motivates the performance of some musical numbers as entertainment or as components of a film within the film, other numbers, which express character moods, exist mostly as spectacle.

After the opening credits, the film locates us firmly in a nostalgia-inflected past. A billboard at the centre of the frame advertises the premiere of 'The Biggest Picture of 1927' at Grauman's Chinese Theatre in Hollywood. We settle in for the pleasures of a nostalgia film: we'll appreciate the retro costumes and antique cars, and smirk at the characters' inability to foresee a future that is already past. Viewers with any knowledge of film history will immediately note the significance of 1927, the year *The Jazz Singer* was released, which along with other films signalled the beginning of the end of the silent film era. When studio chief R. F. Simpson (Millard Mitchell) shows a talking picture at the post-premiere party, his guests pronounce it: 'a toy', 'a scream' and 'vulgar'. A director intones, 'It'll never amount to a thing'. Cosmo Brown (Donald O'Connor) appears to be the only one with any foresight when he says, 'That's what they said about the horseless carriage'.

In the next scene, on the front lot at fictional studio Monumental Pictures, Cosmo reads a headline from *Variety* about *The Jazz Singer's* smashing success in its first week. An extra looks up from his coffee to opine that it will be flop in the second. This kind of dramatic irony is frequently used by Hollywood to offer viewers a position of superior knowledge: in films made about the 1920s, characters fail to anticipate the stock market crash. In films set in 1941, characters don't know Pearl Harbor is about to be attacked. In fact, experiments with sychronised sound go back virtually as far as experiments with film technology. Sound shorts were far from unknown before the release of *The Jazz Singer*. However, Warner Brothers was willing to bet the studio on a film starring Al Jolson, the most popular performing celebrity of the day, and were able to convince enough theatre owners to rewire their houses for sound. A successful earlier short featuring Jolson convinced the Warners to build their gamble around him. Nonetheless, the transition to sound film did not happen overnight. It took three years for sound film to fully replace silents as the dominant product of the Hollywood system.

Some of the pleasures of *Singin'* come from the film's willingness to both grant us positions of superior knowledge and give us backlot passes. We see silent film production, and then see the new technologies of sound film on display. We are granted the illusion that we are seeing how movies are really made. Just as we are privy to the artifice through which movies are created, we are privy to the artifice through which stars are created. As Kelly/Lockwood narrates the publicity department version of his career, we see images of the 'real' history: the education of a third-rate vaudevillian who started his movie career as an on-set musician and got a break as a stuntman. Of course, the 'real' story is as staged as anything else in the movie. Since we know we are watching a fictional film, we are in on the joke. The interplay between artifice and 'reality' continues throughout the film, from the invented romance between Don Lockwood and Lina Lamont through the dubbing which substitutes Kathy's voice for Lina's in the musical version of *The Dancing Cavalier*.

As with any film, artifice made visible to the audience masks other kinds of artifice. In *Singin'* the most mind-boggling joke played on us concerns vocal dubbing. While Reynolds sings for herself in 'All I do is Dream of You' and 'Good Mornin'', other voices are dubbed over Reynolds' when Reynolds/Kathy is shown dubbing in her voice for Lina Lamont's. Betty Noyes actually sings the song recorded for *The Dancing Cavalier*, while Jean Hagen, the actress who plays Lina, speaks the dubbed dialogue attributed to Selden.

The film creates a similar illusion about film history, compressing years of history into weeks or minutes. Even as we swallow the fictionalised version of film history we are struck by a raft of anachronisms, many apparent even to casual moviegoers. The most significant anachronism is the use of dubbing technology to dub Kathy's voice over Lina's. Even if casual viewers were not aware that this technology was not available to the filmmakers of 1927, when synchronised sound was a technology in progress, they might notice the discrepancy between the 'Beautiful Girls' number and the later love scene from *The Dueling Cavalier*. When filming *The Dueling Cavalier*, the camera is placed inside a soundproof booth (an actual booth used in early sound pictures). The Monumental Pictures crew goes to great lengths to ensure that Lockwood and Lamont's voices get recorded without extraneous noise such as a thrown cane or the beating of Lina's heart.

Showing this rocky transition to sound, the film represents some real bumps on the road to sound film. However, when filming 'Beautiful Girls', not only is the camera freed from its booth, while sound is recorded through an overhead microphone, but R. F. Simpson manages to carry on a conversation with the director without interfering with the filming. The number concludes with an overhead camera shot of dancers forming kaleidoscopic patterns, a technique of choreographing and filming dance numbers pioneered by Busby Berkeley in the early 1930s, years after *Singin'* takes place. In the earliest film musicals the camera films head-on while simultaneously recording the sound. The sound quality was often poor and the camera was mostly immobile.

More than most (or perhaps any) musicals from the period, *Singin' in the Rain* never feels wholly dated. The pace, the production values, and the quality of the performances are crucial. The interplay between artifice and greater artifice flatters viewers. The film can acknowledge the artifice of movie magic and still use movie magic to seduce its audience, which is fine with us – we would not be watching if we did not want to be seduced. Steven Cohan makes this point succinctly in his argument about and *Singin'*s status as 'the first camp picture'. He writes: '*Singin' in the Rain* stands out as "the ultimate MGM musical" because it can simultaneously be appreciated as one of the best films ever made *and* as feel-good escapism from a bygone era that still works its movie magic' (2005: 202–3).

Produced when Hollywood was panicked about a new competitor – television – this glorification of movie magic, and of the all-encompassing capacity of the musical, reminds viewers to remember the silver screen. That tiny black and white TV set might help you keep up on old movies, but nothing can match the glorious feeling you get from the big screen, technicolor, star-studded, MGM musical.

Further reading

Rick Altman, *The American Film Musical*, Bloomington, Indiana University Press, 1989.

Steven Cohan, *Incongruous Entertainment: Camp, Cultural Value, and the MGM Musical*, Durham, Duke University Press, 2005.

Scoto Eyman, *The Speed of Sound: Hollywood and the Talking Revolution*, New York, Simon & Schuster, 1997.

Jane Feuer, *The Hollywood Musical*, 2nd ed., Bloomington, Indiana University Press, 1993.

Elliot Shapiro

Stachka/Strike (1925)

[Country: USSR. Production Company: Goskino. Director: Sergei Eisenstein. Screenwriters: Grigori Aleksandrov, Ilya Kravchunovsky, Valeryan Pletnyov and Eisenstein. Cinematographers: Edouard Tisse and Vassili Khvatov. Cast: Ivan Klyukvin (activist), Alexander Antonov (member of strike committee), Grigori Alexandrov (factory foreman), Mikhail Gomorov (worker), Maxim Strauch (police spy), I. Ivanov (chief of police).]

Synopsis: *Strike* is set in Russia in the years before the 1917 Revolution. A factory worker pushed to the edge by management hangs himself and this is seen as the final straw by his fellow workers who go on strike. At first there is joy as they are able to experience the pleasure of being with their families but then the hardship of having no income begins to bite. Meanwhile, the factory owners, well dressed and fat, continue to enjoy the good life. Agent provocateurs are used by the authorities and they set fire to a building. Rather than tackling the blaze, the firemen are ordered to turn their hoses on the demonstrating workers. Next, the army is called in. They attack the strikers and many are killed. The film ends by reminding the audience in the new communist Russia not to forget this and other similar brutalities in Tsarist times.

This film gives an account of a strike by factory workers in Tsarist Russia that is defeated by the scheming of the factory bosses, the underhand tactics of the secret police and the brutality of the army. It is made to support the Bolshevik government in power in Russia after the 1917 Revolution and unapologetically puts forward a strongly defined political position.

Eisenstein uses a series of approaches to film construction which challenge the expectations of anybody more used to a standard Hollywood format.[1] Because of their own very particular ideological perspective, Hollywood movies have traditionally focused attention on the individual, creating heroes who resolve problematic situations in such a way as to restore order out of chaos. In particular, the audience is encouraged to identify with these individual heroes by the amount of time that is spent following their trials and tribulations. Eisenstein, by contrast, emphasises the movement of social forces rather than the psychological make-up of individual characters. His film is built around the struggle between the workers and the forces of capitalism. The cast is listed not by named character but by generic role: police spy, factory foreman, worker, chief of police, queen of thieves, etc. Individual personalities are not emphasised but instead the whole social group of the workers is presented as a collective hero while the capitalists en masse are seen as the villain within the narrative structure. Individual characters are not named on intertitles as they would be in a Hollywood production, nor are they focused on in such a way as to enable the audience to identify with a particular protagonist and his or her struggle. Instead, actors portray what are suggested to be typical representatives of particular social classes; e.g. the rich, fat factory owners being waited on in palatial surroundings, enjoying bizarrely indulgent (if not debauched) tastes, or the defiant worker who despite recognising what the consequences will be for himself refuses to betray his comrades.

In places the film feels like a naturalistic documentary but at other points individual shots are intensely constructed as single photographic images.[2] When we are offered glimpses of day-to-day domestic life in the homes of the striking factory workers as they revel in the experience of having time to play with their children, we are given a feeling of the 'fly-on-the-wall' observation that we associate with the documentary. Since we do not have a main character with whom we strongly identify reminding us by their presence of the centrality of the narrative thrust and of the need to be alert to the twists and turns of a plot, and because, as a result, we are able to relax away from this type of narrative engagement, we are easily able to feel we have an unobtrusive camera simply documenting everyday life in the homes of workers. However, the political is never far away. If we are to fully appreciate sequences like these in the homes of workers we have not only to respond emotionally to the depth of the pleasure of these moments of parenthood but also to intellectually understand the oppressive nature of a system that never allows what would now be called 'quality time' as a possibility for workers.

Alongside scenes that might be said to document events, Eisenstein uses visual metaphors that immediately destroy any 'illusion of reality'. Shots of police spies are intercut, for example, with images of animals such as an owl and a fox that it is visually suggested they resemble. Most famously, the final massacre of the surrounded workers by armed troops, shown as dramatic and chaotic action, is paralleled by shots of the slaughter of a cow in an abattoir, shown in full (if quickly edited) throat-cutting and blood-letting detail. The first set of animal images mentioned here is used for comic effect in direct contrast to the seriousness of the abattoir footage, but in both cases what we are being shown is clearly anti-naturalistic in that these animals are not to be found within the imagined scene itself but are inserted as a form of commentary on the action by the filmmakers. They break us out of the apparently 'real' scene and force us to think about what they might imply. These sorts of shots used by Eisenstein have no place within any realistic representation of either the police spies or the violent onslaught on the strikers but work to create meaning above and beyond realism. At the same time, as suggested above, the effect of these two examples is very different: the first (showing the spies as various animals) works at the level of humour and ridicule, the second functions at the pitch of Shakespearean tragedy. It might be argued Eisenstein ends up with rather a hotchpotch of different filmic effects, or it might be suggested he has the confidence that an audience can move backwards and forwards between a range of emotional and intellectual responses and a belief that film is about more than just photographic realism.[3]

Filmmaking techniques that are carefully manipulative of audience response are used all the time here but always in the service not simply of generating response but of creating meaning for the spectator. Conveying clearly the unfair, unjust, not to say brutal, nature of the Tsarist regime is the overriding aim at all times. Editing is seen as a major means of organising the form of the film and generating meaning, and not simply as a technique that is there to serve narrative progression. Eisenstein is not interested in maintaining the illusion of reality, which might be seen to be the major concern dominating the thinking of filmmakers attempting to create the standard Hollywood product. Instead, he wants to actively seek out ways of creating the maximum collision from shot to shot and sequence to sequence. The whole film is constructed around the juxtaposition of shots that comment on each other. His interest to a large extent centres on his concept of montage: that is the arrangement of shots in such a way that the clash between them creates a new enhanced meaning. The chosen style could be seen as an attempt to dogmatically force certain perspectives on the spectator, or more positively as an effort to make the spectator active rather than passive in terms of intellectual engagement.

Clearly, this film is made as propaganda for the new regime in Russia and puts forward a strongly Marxist message. Apart from the more obvious brutalities brought down on the strikers and their families by the factory owners and the authorities in the main narrative, simple aspects of mise en scène such as the wealth, space and grandeur that surrounds the industrialists, compared with the poverty, confined space and basic furnishing to be found in the workers' homes, work to drive home Eisenstein's key point. *Strike* looks back to what it portrays as the brutality of pre-Revolution days when any attempt by workers to defend the simplest of rights for themselves was violently put down and says, in consigning all of that to the past, those days must not be forgotten. The substance of what Eisenstein is dealing with is non-fictional in that it is based on historical events, but he is presenting his chosen material in a very particular way. The message is given at every point along the way in the final, constructed fiction that is brought to the screen.

The most shocking scene for many viewers might be that in which a small child is held aloft by a soldier on horseback and then dropped from a high walkway between the tenement buildings on to the ground below. This is made all the more effective by the fact that we have been made to focus on the innocence of children both earlier in the film in the home of a striking worker and also just a few shots previously as young children play while the chaos of their parents' struggle with the soldiers goes on around them, and a few scenes previously when a child has wandered off and sat in amongst the hooves of the Cossacks' horses.[4] The choreographed busyness of the scene in the tenement block – where carefully chosen angles of shot create a range of angular boxed spaces at different depths of field within which people, men, women, children and soldiers on horseback move in different directions adding to a complex of lines and movement and spaces so that the eye is unable to settle, is unable to take everything in, but is forced to flit in desperation – is at least as powerful as the more famous Odessa Steps sequence in *Battleship Potemkin* which was made in the same year.

Most powerfully, in propaganda terms, the title of this film in itself announced a particularly worrying form of worker action for those who had financial stakes in industrial concerns across Europe during the 1920s. The concept of 'striking' is put forward as an imperative and would have been certain to antagonise capitalist governments in Europe faced with the possibility that the Russian Revolution might prove to be a catalyst for further revolts by workers in other countries.[5] So, for example, in Britain this film and others from the Soviet Union were not shown for years, other than in film societies with private (middle-class) memberships.[6]

Notes

1. Eisenstein recognises filmmaking as a political act that involves using cinematic techniques to represent the world (and, therefore, inevitably your understanding of the world) to an audience.
2. Some of the shots early in the film with workers standing in front of, or behind, the turning flywheels of industrial machinery could exist as part of a modernist film essay, a paean to heavy industry.
3. More prosaically, it may have been that there was an awareness that the working-class target audience was likely to be used to more piecemeal forms of entertainment such as that offered by cabaret, or the circus. And, at the same time, in this his first feature film and as part of a collective group making the film, Eisenstein is learning and debating with others about how best to use film in a revolutionary context.
4. This thematic concern with children and the use of their innocence and vulnerability in order to emphasise the brutality of the Tsarist regime is something that is also famously taken up in *Battleship Potemkin* (1925) in the famous Odessa Steps sequence.
5. In Britain in the years immediately before the First World War, for example, there had already been a series of strikes by miners, dockers and transport workers that had moved the country to a point some believed to be close to revolution. In Germany in 1919, the Communist Party organised an uprising in Berlin that had to be violently suppressed with key revolutionaries, Rosa Luxemburg and Karl Leibknecht, being arrested and summarily executed by government troops.
6. Arthur Marwick, *War and Change in Twentieth Century Europe*, Maidenhead, Open University Press, 1990, p. 146.

Further reading

David Bordwell, *The Cinema of Eisenstein*, London, Routledge, 2005.

Ian Christie and Richard Taylor, *Eisenstein Rediscovered*, London, Routledge, 1993.

James Goodwin, *Eisenstein, Cinema and History*, Champaign, IL, University of Illinois Press, 1993.

John White

Star Wars (1977), aka *Star Wars, Episode IV: A New Hope*[1]

[Country: USA. Production Company: Lucasfilm/ 20th Century Fox. Director: George Lucas. Screenwriter: George Lucas. Cinematographer: Gilbert Taylor. Sound Designer: Ben Burtt. Music: John Williams. Editors: Richard Chew, Paul Hirsch, Marcia Lucas, T. M. Christopher (special edition). Production Sound Mixer: Derek Ball. Dolby Stereo Sound Consultant: Stephen Katz. Cast: Mark Hamill (Luke Skywalker), Harrison Ford (Han Solo), Carrie Fisher (Princess Leia Organa), Peter Cushing (Grand Moff Tarkin), Alec Guinness (Obi-Wan 'Ben' Kenobi), Anthony Daniels (C-3PO), Kenny Baker (R2-D2), Peter Mayhew (Chewbacca), David Prowse (Darth

Vader), James Earl Jones (Darth Vader, voice), Phil Brown (Uncle Owen), Shelagh Fraser (Aunt Beru).]

Synopsis: Princess Leia Organa, a member of the Rebel Alliance, steals the plans for the Death Star, an Imperial space station. She is captured by Darth Vader, the Galactic Empire's deadliest enforcer, but not before programming the plans into the 'droid R2-D2. R2 and C3PO escape to the planet Tatooine to deliver Leia's plans to former Jedi knight Obi-Wan Kenobi. A young romantic named Luke Skywalker falls in love with Leia when he sees R2's recording of her message. When he finds that Imperial forces killed his uncle and aunt while pursuing the 'droids, Luke helps Obi-Wan hire Han Solo and his partner Chewbacca to fly them to the rebel base on Alderaan, only to find the planet was destroyed by the Death Star. After the Death Star captures Solo's ship, Luke and Solo rescue Leia while Ben arranges for their escape. Vader, once Obi-Wan's pupil in the ways of a mystical religion called the Force, challenges his former mentor to a lightsabre duel. Vader apparently kills Obi-Wan, but his friends escape to deliver the plans to the rebels, who discover the Death Star's weak point: an exhaust shaft leading to the core reactor. As the voice of Ben/Obi-Wan urges him to trust the Force, Luke closes his eyes and fires a torpedo from his star fighter that ends the Death Star's deadly career.

When you've been in the business of studying films for a few years, you take your duties for granted as you would in any other job – until new acquaintances ask you about it. When people ask exactly what it is that I do, their next question inevitably takes one of two forms: *What made you decide to do that?* Or, *What's your favourite film?* These are reasonable questions, but they startle me because no particular film or viewing experience sent me marching to the graduate school catalogues to seek my fortune. I chose this profession because it seemed a natural extension of my interests in literary interpretation and in the histories of such mass cultural media as comic books, movies, television, and video games, not because the profession chose me.

Yeah, right. That's what I've been telling myself for a long time, but at last I see that I've been repressing the true answer. After mumbling responses about post-war French cinema and Hollywood film noir and Gloria Grahame and Luis Buñuel for years, I've finally come to terms with my professional primal scene: My epiphany happened in 1977 when I was nine years old, watching a summer blockbuster that my small-town single-screen theatre screened one season late because it had held over *Smokey and the Bandit* for 20 weeks. That blockbuster was *Star Wars*, and it is my favourite film of all time.

Why did it take me so long to admit this to myself? The best reason I can come up with is that the original *Star Wars* is a world-class guilty pleasure for a serious film scholar. For one thing, it's not as original as we imagined it was three decades ago. There isn't much new about the story or the presentation of Luke Skywalker's development from whiny farm boy into galactic freedom fighter. The plot cobbles together – some would say plagiarises – snippets from sources as diverse as Tolkien's swords-and-sorcery epic *The Lord of the Rings*; Frank Herbert's science fiction classic *Dune* with its desert-bound moisture farmers (Tatooine, anyone?) and spice-trade intrigue; and even Joseph Campbell's nonfiction book *The Hero With a Thousand Faces* (1949), a work of comparative mythology inflected by Carl Jung's theory that all cultures cast human maturation as a mythical journey from antisocial naïveté to public heroism. For influences on the visual style of *Star Wars*, one needs look no further than Stanley Kubrick's *2001: A Space Odyssey* (1968) with its massive but plausible-looking space stations, courtesy of Douglas Trumbull's detailed plastic miniatures and groundbreaking process photography.

But writer and director George Lucas cast his genre-poacher's net wider than fantasy, myth, and science fiction. He showed his effects team aerial combat sequences from Hollywood war movies to demonstrate the shot setups and pacing he wanted for the Millennium Falcon's battle with imperial TIE fighters. Thematically, Lucas drew upon the obsession with honour, duty, and the spoils of loyalty and betrayal found in post-war Japanese *chanbara* (swordplay) films, especially the epics directed by Akira Kurosawa. Lucas's eclecticism was hardly unique. His generation of 'movie-brat' directors, which included his friends Francis Ford Coppola, Brian De Palma, and future *Raiders of the Lost Ark* collaborator Steven Spielberg, learned their trade not by the traditional means of Hollywood apprenticeship, but by becoming movie omnivores. They grew up watching classic films on late-night television and in big-city art-house theatres, and wound up attending film schools like Lucas's own University of Southern California that offered courses on global film history as well as on production. The references *Star Wars* sweeps together probably seemed as natural to Lucas and his cohort as they seemed incoherent and unprofitable, at first, to the executives at 20th Century Fox. If not for Fox executive Alan Ladd Jr's faith in Lucas's 'kiddie film', the studio would have abandoned this expensive, uncategorisable project without looking back.

Before you start berating those industry stuffed-shirts for their lack of vision, please bear in mind that the 'old' Hollywood generation had been burned by big ideas too many times not to play it safe. As witnesses to expensive flops in the recent past (such as *Dr. Doolittle*, *Darling Lili*, and *Cleopatra*, the epic that nearly sank Fox in the early 1960s), studio chiefs took note of the surprise success of the no-frills countercultural film *Easy Rider* in 1967 and placed smaller piles of their investors' chips on personal films about anti-heroes dealing with everyday obstacles. Once Coppola's *Godfather* films (1972 and 1974) and Spielberg's horror-thriller *Jaws* (1975) became mega-hits, Hollywood seemed to be turning another corner, back toward the straightforward, goal-oriented plots and more formulaic filmmaking procedures of its past, but no studio felt compelled to rush to the blockbuster model just because a couple of extraordinary films had done extraordinary business. Rather, *Star Wars* earned its position in Hollywood history by demonstrating the earning potential of a new kind of formula film, the 'high-concept' blockbuster. Its success helped convince studio executives that they had to reorganise their business model if they hoped to reap the unparalleled profits generated by the blockbuster phenomenon.

Though it differed in obvious ways from its immediate predecessors in blockbusterdom, *Star Wars* also incorporated key elements from *The Godfather* and *Jaws*: the epic sweep of history-making conflict and the changes it wreaks, the American family as a locus of this conflict, and suspense and surprise techniques borrowed from crime movies, Hitchcock's suspense thrillers, and horror films. Lucas was as familiar with the theme of intergenerational discord as he was with science fiction. His USC thesis film, a sci-fi short titled *THX-1138* (reshot as a feature-length film in 1971), chronicles a man's attempt to escape a post-apocalyptic society that dehumanises its citizens. In Lucas's breakthrough film, *American Graffiti* (1973), two guys from the high school class of 1962 spend a final night drag racing through their hometown and wrestling with doubts about their departure for college the next day. Frustrated by the cuts that MCA/Universal forced him to make to *American Graffiti*, Lucas demanded final cut rights on *Star Wars* and has gotten, or taken, those rights ever since. His legendary commitment to overseeing his projects at every stage already showed through in his establishment of Lucasfilm LTD to produce *Star Wars* (the Fox studio merely fronted production money and distributed the film), and Industrial Light and Magic (ILM), the in-house special effects unit which founding head John Dykstra quickly made the most sought-after effects company in Hollywood.

What no one predicted was that Lucas's reboot of the science fiction genre, a film so disrespectful of the genre's conventions that its first title screen sets the scene not in the future but '[a] long time ago, in a galaxy far, far away', would garner such critical admiration and viewer fanaticism that it would gross more than one hundred million American dollars (1977 dollars, mind you) by the end of the summer – before the Burt-Reynolds-drunk Majestic Theater in Centerville, Iowa, had even bothered to bring the movie to my attention. However unoriginal its plot and premise, however unintentionally awkward its dialogue, the film succeeded then (and still grips viewers now) because it simultaneously surprised us with its unexpected juxtapositions of diverse elements and bathed us in the aura of straightforward, plot-driven filmmaking – something most viewers had not experienced in a new-release movie house, to paraphrase Ben Kenobi, for a long, long time. That mixture of the familiar and the unfamiliar certainly caught the attention of my father, whose interest was piqued largely by John Williams's orchestral score. A life-long opera buff who spent a winter's worth of Saturday afternoons taping radio broadcasts of Wagner's Ring Cycle with his reel-to-reel, my dad was smitten with Williams's use of musical leitmotifs to emphasise the entrances of characters like Luke and Leia and to reflect plot turns and mood shifts by modulating these themes as necessary. The classical score, inspired by Kubrick's use of classical masterworks in *2001*, instantly turned Williams into an industry star himself. It's difficult now to watch starships on a movie screen without hearing the sweep of strings or the hammer-blasts of trombones, even if only in our imaginations.

I couldn't have put any of that into words in 1977, of course. I had no idea that Hollywood had ever experienced a business-model crisis, or that Lucas's dialogue made his actors want to throttle him, or that practically the only things that distinguished *Star Wars* from Kurosawa's *The Hidden Fortress* (1958) were, first, that the central comic duo consisted of androids R2-D2 and C-3PO instead of Japanese peasants, and second, that Lucas was not able to convince *Fortress* star Toshiro Mifune to play Obi-Wan. What captivated me about the film back then was its level of *definition*. No movie I had seen outside a Disney feature presented such clear and vivid heroes – young, attractive, squabbling idealists accompanied by the grandfatherly Kenobi (an unselfconsciously noble Alec Guinness) – and grotesque villains with names like Darth Vader and Grand Moff Tarkin (played by British B-movie vampire killer Peter Cushing) who spouted bwa-ha-ha bad guy lines like 'There'll be no escaping us this time' as slimily as did Ming the Merciless in the old *Flash Gordon* serials (from which *Star Wars* also borrows). It kept up an unrelenting level of tension as Luke, Princess Leia, and Han improvised their way out of the Death Star space station and then returned to destroy it. It developed a world, a galaxy rather, in which smart-mouthed 'droids and humongous starships looked so grungy and were treated with such nonchalance that they seemed as plausible as my dad's Impala station wagon. Speaking for the kid I was, who dreamed of being either a cartoonist or a superhero in a town where neither aspiration meant much to anybody else, a story about a frustrated kid who dreamed as fervently of escape from being misunderstood as he did of escaping to the stars seemed the height of verisimilitude.

Star Wars's low-tech high-tech aesthetic may in fact be its key innovation. Scuttling the *science* of science fiction and permitting the fantasy elements to dominate allows the film's special effects to thrill and convince us more completely than they could have if Lucas had stuck to the gospel of 'hard' science fiction preached by fiction writer Larry Niven in the 1970s. Dykstra constructed his starships out of spare parts from hundreds of model cars and planes, aged them artificially with grease, grime, and dents, and filmed them using an electronically timed motion-control system that he and ILM essentially invented for the movie. By synchronising the models' movements exactly to the background shots into which they would later be matted, Dykstra imbued 'ships' no larger than a foot or two in length with a solidity and kineticism more convincing than any computer-generated starship I have seen since. This aesthetic makes *Star Wars* an important bridge between the warts-and-all realism of seventies Hollywood and the future-grunge look of the action-blockbuster era, especially visible in such films as *Alien* and *Aliens*, *Blade Runner*, the *Terminator* films, *Total Recall*, and *The Matrix*. Lucas's technologised galaxy seemed to reflect American culture's alternating smugness and anxiety about its scientific achievements. Machines could draw moisture from the sands of Tatooine and cool a movie theatre on a summer afternoon, but they could also destroy a planet at a whim, a worry as close to Americans' minds as the Cold War and its hottest hotspot, the recently abandoned Vietnam conflict.

Indeed, Lucas's mass-culture obsessions led him to make a personal film that coincidentally appealed to the growing conservatism of post-Vietnam political culture in the US. *Star Wars* changed the industry by making book on spectacle and simplicity while echoing the political means by which conservative politicians tried to 'heal' the wounds of an ambiguous and humbling war: a hard turn to the political right, to an ideology that divided the planet into the light and dark sides of the Force as definitively as Lucas divided up the galaxy. When US president Ronald Reagan called the Soviet Union an 'evil empire' and dubbed his administration's never-realised nuclear deterrent blueprint 'Star Wars', no one who paid close attention to the film's simplistic image of political conflict should have been surprised.

Lucas's fortune-making decision to retain the rights to all *Star Wars* marketing, including everything from action figures to pyjamas, strikes me now as a crass betrayal of the idealist ethos he represented for me as soon as I knew his name. And I get angry along with scholar Will Brooker when he chastises Lucas for banishing the original release versions of *Star Wars* and its first two sequels, *The Empire Strikes Back* (1980) and *Return of the Jedi* (1983), by refusing to rerelease them to theatres or the home market since he foisted digitally 'enhanced' Special Edition versions of the films on the public in the late 1990s. Sure, Lucas invented these characters and concepts and stories, but what gives him the right to change or efface the labour of the actors and crew who helped craft the film into the hit it became, or to ride herd over the historical importance of how these films initially looked and sounded? (To be fair, I must note that Lucas eventually capitulated to fan pressure and appended the original versions to the most recent Special Edition DVD sets.) In the late seventies, however, whatever monies Lucas collected from the mounds of toys that Kenner produced for Lucasfilm seemed to me more than his just desserts. I wasn't even envious of his own intergalactic empire, built on billions of bits of painted plastic doomed to be dropped from car windows or lost in furniture cushions forever; the original *Star Wars* action figures weren't things I *wanted* so much as *necessities* akin to Nacho Cheese Doritos or my bicycle. Without plastic effigies of Luke, Leia, Vader, and the 'droids near me as totems, my frustrated dream of proving myself a deep, sensitive hero would have become unbearable. Like most proper nerds, I suspect, but unlike the majority of *Star Wars* fans, I completely identified with Luke, shunned bad-boy Han Solo for his similarities to the anti-intellectual bullies I encountered in middle school, and wanted Princess Leia for my very own with all the proto-erotic, preadolescent angst that a nine-year-old hetero boy could muster, no matter how closely her hairdo resembled twin cheese Danishes.

That's my confession, dear reader. But tell on me at a cocktail party and I'll deny everything, shriek something about the glories of *Citizen Kane* or Antonioni, and accuse you of remaining a closet Wachowski Brothers fan even after *Speed Racer* crashed and burned. Please, then, let this be our secret, OK? I'll keep mum if you will.

Note

1. Katherine Fusco provided invaluable research assistance for this essay.

Further reading

'"Star Wars": The Year's Best Movie', *Time,* 30 May 1977, pp. 54–6ff.

Gary Arnold, '"Star Wars": A Spectacular Intergalactic Joyride', *Washington Post,* 25 May 1977, p. B1.

Peter Biskind, *Easy Riders, Raging Bulls: How the Sex-Drugs-and-Rock-'N'-Roll Generation Saved Hollywood,* New York, Simon and Schuster, 1998.

Will Brooker, *Using the Force: Creativity, Community, and 'Star Wars' Fans,* London, Continuum, 2002.

Owen Gleiberman, 'Empire of Fun [review of "special edition" re-release of *Star Wars*]', *Entertainment Weekly,* 31 January 1997, pp. 32–3.

Matt Hills, '*Star Wars* in Fandom, Film Theory, and the Museum: The Cultural Status of the Cult Blockbuster', in Julian Stringer (ed.), *Movie Blockbusters,* London, Routledge, 2003, pp. 178–89.

Derek Johnson, '*Star Wars* Fans, DVD, and Cultural Ownership: An Interview with Will Brooker', *Velvet Light Trap,* Vol. 56, Fall 2005, pp. 36–44.

David A. Kaplan, with Adam Rogers and Yahlin Chang, 'The Force is Still With Us [report on "special edition" re-release of *Star Wars*]', *Newsweek,* 20 January 1997, p. 52.

Jack Kroll, 'Fun in Space', *Newsweek,* 30 May 1977, p. 60.

'Murf', 'Star Wars', *Variety,* 25 May 1977, n. p.

Justin Wyatt, *High Concept: Movies and Marketing in Hollywood,* Austin, University of Texas Press, 1994.

Paul Young

Sunrise (1927)

[Country: USA. Production Company: Fox Film Corporation. Director: F. W. Murnau. Scenario: Carl Mayer (based on the story 'Die Reise nach Tilsit' by Hermann Sudermann). Producer: William Fox. Titles: Katherine Hilliker, H. H. Caldwell. Cinematographer: Charles Rosher, Karl Struss. Special Effects: Frank D. Williams. Editor: Harold Schuster. Art Director: Rochus Gliese. Art Department: Gordon Wiles. Musical Score: Hugo Riesenfeld. Cast: George O'Brien (the man), Janet Gaynor (the wife), Margaret Livingstone (the woman from the city).]

Synopsis: A nameless woman of the city vacations in the countryside, seducing a man, a simple farmer with a wife and a child. She convinces him to drown his wife, but at the last moment, he cannot bring himself to do it. After the wife escapes to the city and the man follows her, they witness a wedding, which makes them reconcile and enjoy the city. They return to the farm, but a thunderstorm capsizes their boat and the wife barely survives. After this final ordeal, the couple is back together while the woman leaves.

William Fox's production of *Sunrise*, directed by German émigré Friedrich Wilhelm Murnau, was a bid for status and power. In the mid-twenties, Fox's studio was not as prestigious as Paramount or MGM. Fox therefore launched an expansion plan that included issuing common stock; the acquisition of the Roxy, the most famous picture palace on New York City's Broadway; an interest in sound technology; and the hiring of Murnau whose German film, *The Last Laugh* (1924), had been a great critical success. Fox granted Murnau great 'financial and artistic freedom' to make a 'highly artistic picture' (Allen 1977: 335). Such a bid for artistry was not only in Fox's but also in the industry's interest, not least because it had been rocked by a number of moral scandals (such as the murder of Thomas Ince and the indictment of 'Fatty' Arbuckle). Even though Fox made a number of 'strategic errors' (Lipkin 1977: 339) in marketing the film, even though it did not do that well at the box office and got mixed reactions, it received the Academy Award for 'Unique and Artistic Picture' during the first year of the Academy Awards' existence (the first and only time this category existed as distinct from 'Outstanding Picture').

Because *Sunrise* was a product of the influx of foreign talent into Hollywood, the film remains hybrid – suspended among a variety of influences. One might easily call it a 'Euro-American art film', a term coined by Peter Lev for much later films (such as Michelangelo Antonioni's *The Passenger* (1975) or Wim Wenders' *Paris, Texas* (1984)).[1] Part of this hybridity is stylistic. Critics have commented on the film's borrowing from German expressionism – a cinematic style maybe most famously associated with *The Cabinet of Dr. Caligari* (Robert Wiene, 1920), where, for instance, characters' inner feelings are projected onto the set, so that the distorted landscape comes to reflect the characters' inner turmoil. In *Sunrise* it may be above all the figure of the husband who expresses expressionism's inner conflict. Not exclusively, but especially during the marsh sequence, George O'Brien's acting expresses his tormented psychology, a feat aided by the lead weights that the director asked him to carry in his shoes, and enhanced by eerie lighting, the tracking camera and the sinister music. As Dudley Andrew has put it, the illicit encounter with the city woman in the marsh as well as the two trips across the lake simultaneously borrow from the 'aesthetic of the horror tale, the mystery novel, the gothic romance' (1984: 33).

Another way of describing these competing aesthetic influences has been to point out the film's borrowing from both the cinema of Georges Méliès, the early French film pioneer famous for his investment in cinematic tricks and magic, and of the Lumière brothers, better known for their investment in recording external reality. In this context, the scene in the marsh and the visions of the city can be understood as being invested in the fantastic, while moments like the couple's exiting the church derive from an aesthetic of realism. This conflict between the fantastic and the realistic can also be understood as a conflict between transgressive desire and social order. Robin Wood, who first pointed out this tension within the film, argues that the magic is being connected with an 'untrammelled libido' while realism stands for 'order' (1976: 11).

In this sense, the film's conflicting visual styles also stand for conflicting thematic and contextual issues, and the most prominent among those must be that of the tension between the country and the city. Film has often been aligned with the urban experience, as editing and superimpositions so easily turn urban dwellers into 'kaleidoscope[s] gifted with consciousness,' as poets like Charles Baudelaire and writers like Walter Benjamin wrote.[2] Especially in the 1920s, so-called 'city symphonies' – films like *Man with a Movie Camera* (Dziga Vertov, 1929) and *Berlin, Symphony of a Great City* (Walter Ruttmann, 1927) – used cinematic techniques to create varied, but dazzling concepts of urban consciousness. The woman's vision of the city, characterised by lights, rapid traffic, jazz, and a body consumed in out-of-control dance movements, which are created by camera movement, editing, and superimpositions, exemplifies the erotic allure of the city.

The division between the country and the city is thus deeply gendered: the city woman is a vamp – a pleasure-loving 'vampire' bent on exploiting and destroying men – while the country girl is Madonna-like, connected to child-rearing and domesticity. The city woman enjoys being in public, and evokes not only the vamp, but also the 'flapper', a female urban type of the Jazz Age. Flappers – most famously embodied by Clara Bow in *It* (1927) – cut their hair into bobs, wore short, boxy dresses and often smoked or drank alcohol. They tapped into the revolution in leisure in the early twentieth century, in which the movies participated. While in the nineteenth century a woman alone in the streets was easily understood as a 'streetwalker', women now had increasing access to public space. The years after the First World War also saw a sexual revolution and new styles of dancing – in short, new ways of understanding and relating to one's body. Despite the film's demonisation of the city woman, in the end the country girl also enjoys a good time in the city.

The film thus chronicles how the frequently gendered difference between country and city is increasingly difficult to sustain. The montage about summer vacations, which brings urban dwellers to the countryside, the easy transportation to the city, and the city's infatuation with the peasant dance and the pig suggest a traffic between country and the city that has the potential the erode the presumed differences between these locations. Even the rural couple needs the city and its pleasures to find happiness. At the photographer's studio, for instance, modern technology allows them to be pictured before the background that they dreamed about. This easy traffic between city and country is in tension with the film's argument about the 'carefree and happy' country life, as suggested in an intertitle.

It is one of *Sunrise's* distinguishing marks that these thematic tensions are always elaborated in terms of cinematic aesthetics, for instance in terms of the conflict between silence and sound. To be sure, the film features no synchronous sound. (When it was first exhibited at the Times Square Theatre in New York City, in late September 1927, it was preceded by a Movietone newsreel of Benito Mussolini and the Vatican Choir; just days later, the premiere of *The Jazz Singer* followed, a film featuring sequences of synchronised sound narrative.) Coming at the cusp of the film industry's transition into the sound era, the film has been called a 'technological hybrid' (Allen, 1977: 327), a silent film that works hard to integrate camera and sound. Noteworthy moments on the soundtrack include 'the foreboding, repetitive theme (consisting largely of two alternating, ominous notes) that accompanies The Man's walk through the marshes to meet his lover; the raucous jazz motif… that conjoins the city sequence; the rippling melody (with wind sounds) that marks the episode of the couple's sail home in a storm; the church bells that ring at the exact moment The Man decides to spare his wife … [the] plaintive series of notes on the French horn that approximate [The Man's] cry' (Fischer 1998: 31). Very often, these sound effects help elaborate thematic issues. For instance, after witnessing a wedding ceremony that renews their trust in each other, the couple exit the church. They obliviously walk through city traffic, imagining themselves in a rural, picturesque environment, when they are suddenly awakened by the onslaught of urban traffic. The romantic soundtrack, associated with the rural fantasy, is pushed into the background by an explosion of urban sound effects, though the romantic music never entirely disappears and picks up again once the couple has safely reached the sidewalk. The soundtrack thus aurally stages the complex interaction between the urban and the rural.

Such aural tensions are amplified visually. In the same urban sequence, a simulated tracking shot of the couple walking in front of a projected screen displaying a rural space – a simulation indicating the dreamlike nature of the couple's projection – is followed by a quick montage of urban shots. Tensions within the story are thus also worked out in terms of camera work and editing. Critics have noted Murnau's masterful use of the tracking shot – for instance the shot tracking the man through the marsh, or the shot following the trolley – a mastery for which he was well known by the time he made *Sunrise,* since the same technique already distinguished *The Last Laugh* (1924), the German film that brought Murnau to Hollywood in the first place. The fluid tracking shot can easily be associated with late silent cinema, which had developed fairly complex camera movements, while the quick montage may be associated with early sound film, if only it provided a way out of the conundrum that early sound cameras were less mobile than late silent models. Nonetheless, the montage had also been very much present in silent cinema, among other things because it was associated with the urban environment, maybe most famously in *The Man with a Movie Camera.* Quickly edited shots seemed a particularly apt vehicle to convey the intensity of kaleidoscopic urban stimuli and impressions. At the same time, Murnau also uses other methods to convey the frenzy of the city. For instance, at the beginning of the amusement park sequence, a quickly spinning, lit wheel visually represents urban stimulation. Elements of mise en scène – such as the complex movements of the rides in the amusement park – and photographic effects – such as superimpositions – also help stage the city. Importantly, the tracking shot is by no means absent in the city. For instance, in the amusement park sequence, a slow tracking shot brings us inside the space of amusement itself. Urbanity is thus expressed by multiple stylistic means, and a particular use of a stylistic element does not always indicate the same kind of social commentary. As in the case of the soundtrack, the interpenetration of the tracking shot and the montage in the city helps complicate – on the stylistic level – any simple opposition between the rural and the urban.

Sunrise gives us insight into such topics as individualised psychology and desire, the lure of the new (urban) leisure economy, gender regimes, the conflict between the rural and the urban, and the transition to sound cinema. In the end, the film does not merely stage conflicting views, but also complicates any simple opposition between European and American cinema, expressionism and realism, silence and sound, the country and the city, etc. Maybe most importantly, it explores a number of cinematic devices for social commentary while never assuming that a stylistic element always has the same social or cultural significance.

Notes

1. Peter Lev, *The Euro-American Cinema*, Austin, University of Texas Press, 1993.
2. Charles Baudelaire, *The Painter of Modern Life and Other Essays*, trans. and ed. Jonathan Mayne, New York, Phaidon, 1964, p. 9; Walter Benjamin, 'Paris, Capital of the Nineteenth Century', in *Reflections*, ed. and intro. Peter Demetz, trans. Edmund Jephcott, New York, Harcourt, Brace, Jovanovich, 1978, pp. 146–62.

Further reading

Robert C. Allen, 'William Fox Presents "Sunrise"', *Quarterly Review of Film Studies*, Vol. 2, No. 3, August 1977, pp. 327–38.

Dudley Andrew, 'The Turn and Return of *Sunrise*', *Film in the Aura of Art*, Princeton, Princeton University Press, 1984.

Lucy Fischer, *Sunrise: A Song of Two Humans*, London, BFI, 1998.

Sumiko Higashi, *Virgins, Vamps, and Flappers: The American Silent Movie Heroine*, Albans, Eden Press Womens' Publications, 1978.
Steven N. Lipkin, '"Sunrise": A Film Meets Its Public', *Quarterly Review of Film Studies*, Vol. 2, No. 3, August 1977, pp. 339–55.
Robin Wood, 'Murnau's Midnight and Sunrise', *Film Comment*, Vol. 12, No. 3, May–June, 1976, pp. 4–19.

Sabine Haenni

The Sweet Hereafter (1997)

[Country: Canada. Production Company: Alliance Communications and Ego Film Arts. Director: Atom Egoyan. Producers: Robert Lantos, András Hámori, David Webb, Camelia Friedberg, Atom Egoyan, Sandra Cunningham. Screenwriter: Atom Eogyan (based on the novel by Russell Banks). Cinematographer: Paul Sarossy. Art Director: Kathleen Climie. Music: Mychael Danna. Cast: Ian Holm (Mitchell Stevens), Sarah Polley (Nicole Burnell), Tom McCamus (Sam Burnell), Gabrielle Rose (Dolores Driscoll), Bruce Greenwood (Billy Ansel), Alberta Watson (Risa), Maury Chaykin (Wendell), Arsinée Khanjian (Wanda), Earl Pastko (Hartley), David Hemblem (Abott), Caerthan Banks (Zoe Stevens).]

Synopsis: *The Sweet Hereafter* is a film about trauma. After a fatal bus crash that kills almost all of a town's children, a lawyer tries to rouse some of the victims' families to pursue a class action suit. The young girl, who is the sole child to survive the crash, and also a survivor of incest, tells a lie at the deposition that puts an end to the town's greed and punishes her father for his crimes.

Atom Egoyan's adaptation of Russell Banks' *The Sweet Hereafter* treats two tragedies: a bus crash in which all but one of a community's school-age children plunge to their deaths in icy water, and incest. In North American cinema, films about trauma tend to make a spectacle of suffering through a focus on the immediacy of individual pain and loss. Egoyan's understated film avoids spectacle and zooms out to look instead at how the *representation* of trauma shapes communities' experiences of it over time. Focusing on the mediation of trauma (including its own), the film explores the unstable nature of truth and knowledge and the continuities and discontinuities of traumatic memory through a disorienting multi-perspective narrative structure that moves back and forth through over 20 different time frames. This structure juxtaposes different kinds of remembering and forgetting to lay bare their deeper ideological investments. As a whole, the film's structure models a way of representing traumatic history that allows a plurality of voices to be heard, the inconsistencies in their perspectives to be acknowledged, and above all, a means of articulating deeper truths than those of history's referential recordings through art's modes of memorialising.

In the storyline of the bus crash, Mitchell Stephens (Ian Holm) is a silver-tongued lawyer who coaxes the bereaved parents into letting him 'represent' them in a class action lawsuit. Legal discourse is premised on the notion that it is possible to make truth claims about the past by linking a chain of events to outside causes in order to assign culpability, even when events might have no discernible cause and defy rational comprehension. Mitchell's seemingly objective rationalism has another component though; he offers carefully selected parents the prospect of being compensated for loss through a cold calculus that weighs their social worth against the degree of their suffering. As a mode of representation, his legal depositions appear to be committed to the documentation of an event into public memory, making it available to reflection and scrutiny. However, the film represents this as a trap. By instrumentalising individual suffering, Mitchell's approach to trauma narrative severs the bonds that link families and communities. By dwelling on the moment of the accident, it congeals the past at the expense of cultivating a way of living in the 'hereafter.' And by linking facts to finance, it encourages distortions and untruths.

The storyline about incest offers another perspective on representation, this time in relation to the visual rather than the verbal. Nicole (Sarah Polley), the only child to survive the bus crash, is also a survivor of incest. At the outset of the film, Nicole is a performer, onstage before a doubled photograph of herself to emphasise both that she is a split subject and that she is always measured against a fantasy image of herself. In this early scene, she is cast as the object of a gaze which conflates her father's incestuous one with the camera's and thus the film's viewers'. Nicole thus lays bare the problem that the cinema is a machine designed for (illicit) pleasure; trauma narrative seems to run contrary to its nature because we find victims appealing. At the same time, though, the film suggests that the cinema's way of seeing creates its victims. Nicole is shown to be strongly interpellated by the image of the beautiful rock star her father constructs of her, and becomes an active agent in her own seduction when she moves from rehearsing to actually playing what Laura Mulvey calls her 'to-be-looked-at-ness,' dressing up for her father, lying on top of him, pressing him into her embrace.[1] That she is not the passive victim of her trauma makes the truth of this trauma muddy and the assignation of blame very complicated.

Yet, Nicole is not only an object of representation. At her deposition, Nicole goes from being silent, an object of sight, to a speaking subject. The detailed answers she gives about her remembrance of the bus crash – all lies – subordinate her father's and Mitchell's representational systems to succinctly put an end to their instrumental ways of approaching her. Her deposition of a false memory seems starkly factual, but its facts are not the ones she claims to be offering; when she says things were 'going too fast' and that she was 'scared' while intensely gazing at her father who now is the uneasy object of sight, she is in fact speaking about his seduction. Through an act of rhetorical displacement she finds a way to speak publically about something that has been unspeakable. Still, she represses the affective dimensions of her twinned traumas, which remain secreted.

Nicole's terse false testimony contrasts sharply with the discourse developed in a third narrative line through the testimony of Dolores Driscoll, the school bus driver (Gabrielle Rose). Dolores movingly memorialises each and every child who died in the crash as the camera slowly pans over a wall of photographs she has kept as though the children were her own family. Dolores offers a verbal and visual history of the community's children from the perspective of someone who cares deeply about them, and bears witness to the town's loss with empathy and compassion.

In a fourth narrative thread that weaves the incest and crash stories together, Nicole's voice offers the perspective of art on the representation of trauma. Early in the narrative, she recites Robert Browning's poem *The Pied Piper* to the children she babysits, and this recitation becomes an extra-diegetic voice-over that haunts the rest of the film. The poem illuminates significant moments in both the incest and the bus-crash narratives obliquely, neither summarising nor commenting on nor explicitly memorialising them. Like a musical motif that weaves in and out of the main song lines, it brings a greater resonance to the notes that are played.

Browning's poem is about a man who, angry at townspeople who refuse to pay him for ridding them of rats, coaxes all of their children to follow him into a mountainside never to be seen again. It is, as Nicole tells the children, a story about anger and so connects thematically to both Mitchell's rage and her vengeance. It is also a poem about seduction. Browning's children are seduced by the piper's promises of wondrous things, just as in *The Sweet Hereafter* the townspeople are seduced by Mitchell's promise of wealth, and just as Nicole is seduced by her father's fetishistic constructions of her. And it is a poem about lost children. Nicole is connected to the children who are promised impossible joys and consequently engulfed in a mountainside, as well as to the poem's one lame child left behind.

Twice in the film Nicole reads a portion of the poem about the lame boy – once in the incest scene, and once at the deposition: 'And in after years, if you would blame / His sadness, he was used to say, – / "It's dull in our town since my playmates left! / I cannot forget that I'm bereft / Of all the pleasant sights they see, / Which the Piper also promised me."' These short lines written by someone else offer Nicole a language to acknowledge her own pain and its future legacy of sadness. They articulate the ways she assumes she would be 'blamed' for the incest because of her willing compliance. They represent her feelings about the loss of the other children, and they describe the allure of her father's seductive promises. Without being documentary in the way that Mitchell's discourse is, and without imposing the weight of the silence Nicole's father's gaze begets, the poem draws its threads from the fabric of cultural memory to speak a more profound and universal kind of truth. It is important that Nicole recites the poem *over* rather than merely *within* the narrative because this lends her voice authority over the film's other discourses. It is also important that this discourse's authority is not authoritarian. Rather, her poetic discourse is associative, fluid, open-ended, and non-instrumental insofar as it has no material effect on the action of the narrative. Through it, she represents both the communal and private dimensions of trauma and mourning and so complements Dolores Driscoll's art of memory.

While many critics have signalled that the differences between Mitchell and Nicole's father (Tom McCamus)'s controlling and manipulative narrative strategies on the one hand and Dolores and Nicole's subtly resistant ones on the other are offering a critique of patriarchal power, the film's critique also extends to our dominant epistemological models that offer purportedly neutral, objective and disembodied knowledge in the service of other kinds of unequal power relations such as between law and community, the able-bodied and disabled, and adults and children.

The Sweet Hereafter thus offers a kind of study in the relationship between trauma and representation. By laying out multiple storylines, the film signals the impossibility of an authoritative perspective on trauma. By thematically and formally presenting different modes of visual and verbal representation to expose their underlying assumptions and blind spots as well as their stakes, the film shows the frames through which knowledge is mediated. By developing a narrative solution to the challenge of revealing complex relationships between the past, present, and future tenses of memory, the film avoids presenting history as a strict series of causes and effects. Most importantly, the film makes an argument for the powers of art's aleatory and associative ways of thinking, its ability to convey cultural and not just personal memory, and its ability to reach across time.

Note

1. See Laura Mulvey, 'Visual Pleasure and Narrative Cinema', *Screen* 16.3, 1975, pp. 6–18.

Further reading

Melanie Boyd, 'To Blame Her Sadness: Representing Incest in Atom Egoyan's *The Sweet Hereafter*' in Monique Tschofen and Jennifer Burwell (eds), *Image and Territory: Essays on Atom Egoyan*, Waterloo, ON, Wilfrid Laurier University Press, 2007, pp. 275–95.

Patricia Gruben, 'Look but Don't Touch: Visual and Tactile Desire in *Exotica*, *The Sweet Hereafter*, and *Felicia's Journey*' in Monique Tschofen and Jennifer Burwell (eds), *Image and Territory: Essays on Atom Egoyan*, Waterloo, ON, Wilfrid Laurier University Press, 2007, pp. 249–74.

Vivian M. May and Beth A. Ferri, 'I'm a Wheelchair Girl Now' in *Women's Studies Quarterly* 30: 2, 2002, pp. 131–50.

Jonathan Romney, *Atom Egoyan*, London, British Film Institute, 2003.

Katherine Weese, 'Family Stories: Gender and Discourse in Atom Egoyan's *The Sweet Hereafter*' in *Narrative*, 10: 1, 2002, pp. 68–90.

Emma Wilson, *Atom Egoyan*, Urbana, IL, University of Illinois Press, 2009.

Monique Tschofen

Sweet Sweetback's Baadasssss Song (1971)

[Country: USA. Production Company: Yeah. Director: Melvin Van Peebles. Producers: Jerry Gross and Melvin Van Peebles. Screenwriter: Melvin Van Peebles. Cinematographer: Robert Maxwell. Music: Earth, Wind & Fire and Melvin Van Peebles. Cast: Simon Chuckster (Beetle), Melvin Van Peebles (Sweetback), Hubert Scales (Mu-Mu), Mario Van Peebles (Young Sweetback), John Amos (Biker).]

Synopsis: Following an unfortunate run-in with the LAPD, resulting in the injury of two police officers, our eponymous hero (Van Peebles), a sex-worker-turned-revolutionary, flees Los Angeles and makes his way to Mexico. Along Sweetback's journey, we encounter a cross section of the city's citizens, from storefront preachers to prostitutes and hippies. Lauded as the inspiration for blaxploitation films from the early seventies, *Sweetback* is responsible for introducing many conventions of the genre, including an empowered African American anti-hero, villainous white characters, urban settings, contemporary soundtracks, and a proactive stance on institutionalised racism. While the film's many imitators would follow fairly conventional narrative structure, Sweetback's experiences often take the form of a fever dream, as our hero makes his way across the city accompanied by self-conscious editing, handheld camera work, and a funky soundtrack by then-unknown Earth, Wind & Fire. In the end, and despite these avant-garde flourishes, *Sweetback* is a classic American story of a lone hero fighting against unfair power structures, all played against a backdrop of renewed African American political protest and urban unrest.

'A Baad Asssss Nigger is Coming Back to Collect Some Dues' With these provocative words, Melvin Van Peebles ended his third feature film, *Sweet Sweetback's Baadasssss Song*. This somewhat tongue-in-cheek coda, equal parts political and aesthetic threat, became the defining moment for African American cinema during the 1970s. Most often considered the model for 'blaxploitiation', or Hollywood's attempt to capitalise on the popularity of narrative focusing on African American gangsters, pimps, and drug dealers, *Sweetback* was a trendsetter as well as a product of larger national and international filmmaking trends itself; its style and subject matter as much indebted to the French New Wave as it was to the Black Arts Movement. The film also was the product of Van Peebles' experiences and vision, and in order to gauge its place in cinema history it's important to understand how creator, aesthetics, and politics combined for box office success.

Melvin Van Peebles began making films in France during the 1960s. After a stint in the Air Force and assorted jobs in San Francisco, Van Peebles moved to Amsterdam in 1959, where he enrolled in the University of Amsterdam. It was at this point that Melvin Peebles became Melvin 'Van' Peebles. During the 1960s, Van Peebles moved to France, where he supported himself by writing novels and performing (singing, dancing, acting). His debut in filmmaking came when he adapted one of his novels, *La Permission*, for the screen with the help of a grant from the French government. The resulting film, *Story of a Three-Day Pass*, tells of an African American soldier stationed in France who meets a white Frenchwoman during a three-day furlough. The affair is soon discovered by white members of the soldier's unit, and his future in the military is jeopardised as a result. While the film's story verged on the conventionally melodramatic, its style evidenced influences from the French New Wave and Italian Neorealism. Shot on location with a handheld camera, *Story of a Three-Day Pass* featured jump cuts, direct address, and fantasy sequences disrupting the linear flow of the narrative. In story and structure it was a product of its time and place as well as a precursor of what would come.

Van Peebles returned to the United States in 1967 when *Story of a Three-Day Pass* was screened as part of the San Francisco Film Festival. Based on success of this film, the director was contracted to work with Columbia Pictures (legend has it that Columbia executives were initially unaware that he was African American), where he directed and scored *Watermelon Man* (1970), a satire about a white advertising executive who wakes up one day to discover that he has become a black man. While the film's subject matter was timely – American viewers were familiar with Civil Rights struggles and Black Power rhetoric – the film earned only a modest return in its first year, making approximately $1.5 million dollars on a budget of $1 million. One possible reason for the film's disappointing box office might be due to *Watermelon Man*'s experimentation with style, including jump cuts and the use of colour filters for symbolic impact, which was still relatively innovative for American mainstream cinema. Perhaps more important, however, was that *Watermelon Man* required that viewers take the point of view of an African American man – albeit a successful middle-class businessman – a narrative shift that was almost unheard of at this point in American film despite Sidney Poitier's efforts to change the face of American film heroes.

Next came *Sweet Sweetback's Baadasssss Song*. Van Peebles' third film was a hybrid; the product of the director's experiences with and exposure to innovative and self-conscious European Art Cinema and the more conventional Hollywood mainstream. Most directly influenced by the director's experimentation with form and narrative structure, the film also was enabled by his involvement with Columbia Pictures: Van Peebles used his salary from *Watermelon Man* to fund his next project. The film is at one and the same time an experimental independent feature with massive box office appeal.

Sweetback is legendary for its innovative approach to production and marketing – it was produced, directed, edited, and scored by Van Peebles, who also performed in the lead role. The film was made on a budget of approximately $500,000, from a combination of sources, including Van Peebles' personal funds and last-minute investments from African American celebrities like Bill Cosby. Production costs were kept to a minimum by using nonprofessional actors (most notoriously the director's son, Mario, as the young Sweetback who is initiated sexually by an adult prostitute) and a non-union crew masquerading as a porn production. Once released, the film received an 'X' rating, which Van Peebles used to buoy the box office through clever marketing (claiming on posters, for example, that the rating was given by an 'all white jury'). Rental income was supplemented by the sale of a companion soundtrack album and 'making-of' book. Made on a tiny budget, *Sweetback* became one of the highest grossing films of the year, with most sources estimating a box office of $5–15 million.[1]

The film's plot is fairly simple. Unofficially adopted by prostitutes as a child, Sweetback (Van Peebles) grows up performing odd jobs and sex acts in a Watts brothel. When the LAPD is in need of somebody for a police line up, Sweetback is 'volunteered' by his boss after he's coerced into doing so by police detectives. On the way to the precinct, the police pick up Mu-Mu, a young black revolutionary, whom they beat (initially while he's still attached to Sweetback with handcuffs). During Mu-Mu's thrashing, Sweetback turns on the cops, beating both unconscious. This moment is presented as Sweetback's political awakening. It is also the beginning of Sweetback's flight from the police – action that consumes the remainder of the narrative, puts Sweetback in touch with other residents of the black community, and maps out certain areas of urban and rural Southern California. During his flight, Sweetback sleeps with a number of women, beats two more cops, and leaves the city, famously promising to come back to collect some dues.

While the plot is relatively straightforward, the film's form is more experimental, the product of budgetary constraints and Van Peebles' continuing interest in cinematic reflexivity. The film's narrative structure provides the first indication that *Sweetback* was breaking new ground (at least in the United States). The narrative is elliptical, following Sweetback's flight through the city and its surroundings. While Sweetback spends the majority of the film running from the law, he doesn't seem to get anywhere, and the film's repetition of shots of Sweetback in flight supports this interpretation. Moreover, the film's famous coda leaves the narrative unresolved, a rarity at this point in Hollywood filmmaking, which tended to provide audiences with films with straightforward and satisfying endings. Like his earlier films, Van Peebles used a combination of direct address, jump cuts, montage sequences, superimpositions, and colour filters as a self-conscious means of creating a reaction in spectators. The soundtrack, an often asynchronous combination of music by Van Peebles and the then-unknown Earth, Wind & Fire, acted as an aural counterpoint to the film's visuals, and often functioned in a similar manner as montage sequences, providing audiences with an Eisenstein-like collision of sound and image.

The film was shot on location in and around the Watts section of Los Angeles and this, in combination with the use of handheld camera and non-professional actors, supported *Sweetback*'s claim (in its opening shots) that it starred the community. More important, community support for Sweetback in the film sent a message of solidarity to its audiences. Sweetback, in the tradition of a Staggerlee, was the people's hero: he fought back in the face of skewed justice, and the community came to his aide with food, shelter, and transport out of the city. *Sweetback*'s experimental moments actually served to forward this message. Late in the film, for example, there appears a montage sequence of different people answering whether they know Sweetback's whereabouts. In each instance, the answer is no, but the overall effect suggests unity.

Not surprisingly, *Sweetback* sparked heated debate upon its release. For viewers still reeling from the assassinations of John F. Kennedy, Martin Luther King, Jr., Malcolm X, and Robert Kennedy, and the violent urban insurrections that followed in cities like Los Angeles, Detroit, and Newark, New Jersey, the film directly embodied (and in some scenes, visually echoed) the frustration, pain, and fear of American race politics. But unlike more mainstream – or politically neutered – Hollywood products about race inequities (such as the 'message movies' of the previous decade), *Sweetback* offered a more assertive alternative in its characterisation of its eponymous hero: Sweetback fought back, the first time an African American character did so in a film with nationwide release.

The debate over *Sweetback* normally fell between two poles. Identified as 'revolutionary' filmmaking by Van Peebles, an attempt to 'de-colonise' his audience's minds, the director argued that Sweetback's mythic qualities, sexual virility, and political agency empowered African American audiences.[2] This view was supported by Huey Newton of the Black Panthers.[3] An equally common viewpoint, often voiced by the black middle class (in the pages of *Ebony*, for example), criticised that very same violence, sexism, and the film's insinuation that a revolution could succeed through sexual dexterity and violent action.[4] Here, the film's echoing of the images of recent urban insurrections (burning cruisers, for example) was seen as counter to Civil Rights advocacy.

While these debates continued over the next few years, their focus shifted to what would be *Sweetback*'s more immediate legacy: its influence on Hollywood's investment in blaxploitation film. During the late 1960s the film industry was financially struggling, the result of a number of factors, including lagging attendance as people moved to the suburbs, the increasing popularity of television, and a rising youth audience hungry for more unconventional (less staid) film fare. After a number of costly flops, such as Robert Wise's *Star!* (1968), industry executives were looking for projects that offered high returns for little risk.[5] Additionally, the industry was coming under fire from African American groups, primarily the Hollywood branch of the NAACP, for its dismal hiring record for African American personnel. *Sweetback* offered the perfect model for Hollywood; a low-risk, high-gain, and easily repeated formula. Moreover, the film's box office suggested the profitability of previously underexplored target audiences, particularly African American urban youth audiences.[6] Starting with *Shaft* (Gordon Parks, Sr., 1971), an action film featuring Richard Roundtree as Private Detective John Shaft, the industry began releasing films featuring African American (mostly) male outsiders – pimps, drug dealers, and a few private detectives – 'sticking it to the man'. The blaxploitation cycle lasted roughly until 1975, when Hollywood, sparked by Steven Spielberg's *Jaws*, moved onto other models of profitable filmmaking. For a few years, however, *Sweetback* existed in blaxploitation.

Sweetback's immediate legacy may have been one of controversy and co-optation, but its reputation as one of the most important American films of the 1970s still stands. The film is a clear example of American, and African American, film narrative and style in transition. Breaking away from political and aesthetic conventions, the film provided a blueprint for socially and politically committed filmmaking that was also profitable. By drawing upon international filmmaking movements, not the least of which was the French New Wave and Italian Neorealism, Van Peebles provided a workable approach to low-budget filmmaking; a model that was used by Hollywood in the 1970s, but which was resurrected to much longer-lasting effect in the 1980s when a younger generation of African American filmmakers, Spike Lee and Robert Townsend, for example, used Van Peebles' approach to 'guerrilla' filmmaking as inspiration for their own independent features. Furthermore, *Sweetback*'s unconventional narrative structure, cinematography, and editing proved that American audiences were ready for more demanding, more self-conscious filmmaking. In all these ways, Sweetback continues to collect his dues.

Notes

1. Actual box office figures vary. *Variety* lists the first year's gross at approximately $5 million, while www.imdb.com suggests a figure closer to $15 million. Van Peebles, in various interviews, has estimated that the film earned $10 million. See also 'Big Rental Films of 1971', *Variety*, 5 Jan. 1972, p. 9.
2. Quoted in James P. Murray, 'Running With *Sweetback*', *Black Creation*, Vol. 3, No. 1, Fall 1971, p. 10.
3. See Newton's commentary on the film in *The Black Panther* 6, 19 June 1971.
4. Lerone Bennett and Don L. Lee, 'The Emancipation Orgasm: Sweetback in Wonderland', *Ebony*, September 1971, p. 108. For a detailed overview of the critical responses to the film see Jon Hartmann's 'The Trope of Blaxploitation in Critical Responses to *Sweetback*', *Film History*, Vol. 6, No. 3, 1994, pp. 382–404.
5. *Star!* was made for $14 million. The film earned a mere $4 million during its first year of release, suggesting that audiences were no longer interested in big-budget musicals.
6. American independent cinema began exploiting target markets in the 1950s, especially teens with expendable income (a result of post-war affluence). While studios were aware of the African American segment of the box office since the 1920s, it did not actively seek to capitalise black audiences until the 1970s. For more on early exploitation practices, see Thomas Doherty, *Teenagers and Teenpics: The Juvenization of American Movies in the 1950s*, Philadelphia, Temple University Press, rev. 2002, and Eric Shaefer, *Bold! Daring! Shocking! True: A History of Exploitation Films, 1919–1959*, Durham, Duke University Press, 1999.

Further reading

Manthia Diawara (ed.), *Black American Cinema*, New York, Routledge, 1993.

Ed Guerrero, *Framing Blackness: The African American Image in Film*, Philadelphia, Temple University Press, 1993.

Paula J. Massood, *Black City Cinema: African American Urban Experiences in Film*, Philadelphia, Temple University Press, 2003.

Mark Anthony Neal, *Soul Babies: Black Popular Culture and the Post-Soul Aesthetic*, New York, Routledge, 2002.

Paula J. Massood

Tasogare Seibei/Twilight Samurai (2002)

[Country: Japan. Production Company: Shochiku Company. Director: Yōji Yamada. Screenwriters: Yōji Yamada and Yoshitaka Asama. Cinematographer: Mutsuo Naganuma. Music: Isao Tomita. Cast: Hiroyuki Sanada (Seibei Iguchi), Rie Miyazawa (Tomoe Iinuma), Nenji Kobayashi (Chōbei Kusaka), Ren Osugi (Toyotarō Kōda), Miki Itō (Kayano Iguchi), Min Tanaka (Zenemon Yogo), Hiroshi Kanbe (Naota), Erina Hashiguchi (Ito Iguchi), Mitsuru Fukikoshi (Michinojo Iinuma), Kanako Fukaura (Yae Iinuma).]

Synopsis: In the nineteenth century at the end of Japan's feudal age, widowed, low-ranking samurai Seibei Iguchi is an accountant at his regional lord's storehouse, where he has been nicknamed 'Twilight' (Tasogare) because he refuses to socialise after working hours. Instead, he rushes home to care for his two daughters, Kayano (age ten) and Ito (age five), and his senile mother and to farm and do piecemeal jobs to pay debts. The sudden reappearance of Seibei's childhood crush Tomoe, who has returned to her brother Iinuma Michinojo's house to escape an abusive marriage, offers the potential for a love story. Seibei faces two obstacles: first, he challenges Tomoe's alcoholic ex-husband, Toyotarō Kōda, to a duel, but uses a wooden practice sword to knock Kōda unconscious rather than kill him. After winning respect for the swordsmanship he had tried to keep hidden, Seibei is ordered to assassinate an elderly samurai Zenemon Yogo who has sided with a losing political faction and whose family situation resembles his own. Seibei knows that he must uphold the samurai code of honour and his own ethics and that either he or Yogo must die.

Twilight Samurai (*Tasogare Seibei*) exemplifies Yamada Yōji's (1931–) character-driven films, the likable, unpretentious protagonists of which, no matter if they are of the past or present, face problems in their families and jobs and suffer from decisions made by their political leaders, just as their Japanese film audiences do. One of Japan's most prolific directors, Yamada created 81 films between 1961 and 2012. He was responsible for the longest-running series in world cinema history: *It is Tough Being a Man (Otoko wa tsurai yo)*, 48 films over 25 years (1969–1995), which ended with the death of its leading actor Atsumi Kiyoshi (1928–1996). The series, more sentimental and less meditative than *Twilight Samurai*, was extremely popular in Japan but received little international attention, in part because its humour premised on Japanese daily life and current events was difficult to translate. Its main character Tora-san – an itinerant salesman, who, in each film, falls in love, travels Japan to help the woman he desires, but never wins her love – became a folk hero. Yamada won best film honours at the Japanese Academy Awards four times: *The Yellow Handkerchief* (*Shiawase no kiiroi hankachi*, 1977), *My Sons* (*Musuko*, 1991), *A Class to Remember* (*Gakko*, 1993) and *Twilight Samurai* (2002). *Twilight Samurai* earned 11 additional Japanese Academy Awards, including best director, actor, actress, supporting actor, cinematography, screenplay, and soundtrack, and was nominated for Best Foreign Film at the 2002 American Academy Awards. This big-budget blockbuster with global theatrical release was the first of Yamada's trilogy based on novels by Fujisawa Shūhei (1927–1997), one of Japan's most famous writers of samurai fiction, and was followed by *Hidden Blade: Oni's Claw* (*Kakushi ken oni no tsume*, 2004) and *Love and Honor* (*Bushi no ichibun*, 2006); the three films had different all-star casts.[1] Like such other Yamada films as *Our Mother* (*Kabei*, 2008) set during the Second World War and *About Her Brother* (*Ototo*, 2010), about family care, *Twilight Samurai* is sincere with occasional humour, historical yet contemporary, understated but intense, and rich with local details. The story unfolds at a slow, steady pace, allowing emotions to heighten and end in tears. As stated by film critic Mark Schilling, 'Yamada keeps the schmaltz content low and the pathos on high'.[2] He respects his audiences' intelligence and earns their emotional responses.[3]

Seibei Iguchi (played by leading actor and karate expert Sanada Hiroyuki) is a low-ranking samurai who works as an accountant at his regional lord's grain storehouse, the 'office' which has a hierarchical spatial arrangement similar to twentieth-century corporations. With no wars to fight and under the tightly regulated social order imposed by Tokugawa Shogunate, the hereditary position of samurai meant being a bureaucrat rather than a warrior, and salaries were given in the form of stipends depending on the size of the family's estate. Samurai were permitted to carry two swords, one long and the other short, an honour not allowed to farmers and merchants, who were lower in the social hierarchy, and they were often trained in martial arts, which they did not use in battle. Seibei's fellow samurai coworkers nickname him 'Twilight' (*Tasogare*) because he refuses to join them at drinking establishments after working hours, a form of socialising also required of modern businessmen. Seibei has no time to take care of himself, and his regional lord reprimands him for his torn clothes and body odour. His wife died from tuberculosis caused in part by their poor living conditions for which Seibei feels guilty. Despite his difficulties, Seibei is content with his modest life and does not desire to advance his position or to remarry. A theme of *Twilight Samurai* is that people should be judged by their honourable deeds and sense of honour rather than their social and economic status. Throughout the film, voiceover narrations by now elderly Ito, grateful for her father's care, adds another layer of empathy for the plight of Seibei and Tomoe.

The story unfolds through small moments of family intimacy, and serious topics – death, childcare, aging parents, divorce, workplace stress, debt, political strife, and murder – are handled with emotional restraint. In arguably the most poignant scene, Seibei asks Tomoe to help him properly dress and perform rituals for his duel with Yogo. This implies that Tomoe would be the last of Seibei's close friends and family he would see if he dies. He humbly admits his feelings for Tomoe, who regretfully states that she has already accepted a marriage proposal, adding further suspense about what might happen if Seibei lives. The sparing dialogue is accompanied by the gentle soundtrack by established composer Tomita Isao, noises of village daily life, and well-placed silence. The characters are filmed from varying angles, including from behind as if seen from a doorway, in medium and close-up shots to wordlessly convey their emotional states and to make the film audience feel privy to a private moment. After Seibei leaves for Yogo's house, the audience is finally permitted catharsis in Tomoe's tears as she sobs when Seibei's senile mother asks who she is, a refrain in the film.

Yamada both works within and subverts the genre of '*jidai geki*' and masterfully uses Japanese history as a means of subtle critique. *Jidai geki* are period films, television programs, and stage plays set mostly during the Edo period and often featuring sword fighting (*chambara*) and stories of samurai revenge.[4] (Films set in modern times can be categorised as '*gendai geki*'.) *Twilight Samurai* differs from many other *jidai geki* through its focus on a samurai's routine domestic life rather than his quest for glory. (Humanistic director Kore'eda Hirokazu was perhaps inspired by this approach in his 2006 film *Hana* (*Hana yori mo naho*).) On the one hand, Seibei represents the way of the ideal samurai (*bushidō*) – to be self-sacrificing, honourable, resourceful, talented in military arts, among other qualities, and to be loyal to the clan above all. In the Edo period, this behaviour was more prevalent in literature and theatre than in reality. *Twilight Samurai* dramatises the crisis of needing to choose 'duty' (*giri*) over 'passion' (*ninjō*), a common theme of Edo-period popular culture. On the other hand, Yamada shows the suffering of Japan's last generation of samurai in the 'twilight' of their period of dominance, facing financial hardships and reduced to bureaucrats in an outdated political order. Seibei and his cohorts are strikingly different from Edward Zwick's 2003 Hollywood film *Last Samurai* that was shown in theatres in the United States around the same time. Yamada also alludes to the fact that these men were no better off after the system of military rule was abolished in the dawn of the Meiji Period (1868–1912). Sword fights are skilfully performed without special effects, at a time when computer graphics were plentiful in *jidai geki*, and are not pleasurable to watch. This underscores Yamada's strong message about the inanity of fighting to the death, a theme Kurosawa Akira had emphasised in his samurai films. Yamada also visualises differences between the rich and poor. Many scenes of *Twilight Samurai* are shot inside samurai houses in various levels of upkeep and decay, and Yamagata village life provides a backdrop. (Yamagata is used as a metonymy for the Japanese countryside in such other recent films as *Departures* (*Okuribito*, 2008), which was chosen over Yamada's *Kabei* for best film in the Japanese Academy Awards.)

While depicting the decline of samurai men, Yamada presents advancements of samurai women. Tomoe is progressive, outspoken and determined, and, with the help of her brother, she is granted a divorce and is permitted agency in choosing her next husband. Tomoe works within the system and uses her abilities to do housework and raise children to better the lives of people around her. She decides on her own volition to help in Seibei despite reprimands that women should not visit men. She teaches Seibei's daughters Kayano and Ito needlework and other skills they will use as future wives and mothers. She takes them to village festivals run by peasants that were officially forbidden to samurai, showing the closing gaps between the social castes. Kayano and Ito attend a neighbourhood school for girls where they study books that were mostly taught to only boys so that they will learn to be better thinkers. Their practice recitations of Confucian precepts are an aural refrain in the film.

In general, Yamada's films, both *jidai geki* and *gendai geki*, reaffirm the importance of the family. Yamada's protagonists are various kinds of renegades and tramps who do not fit seamlessly into their social milieus. They are not ostracised but instead choose to be detached because they are cognizant of their own faults and the contradictions in their societies. These men find meaning by being accepted by their families, and if they wander, like Tora-san, they always return home. Yamada directly states this message in the tearjerker endings of several of his films. In her closing voiceover in *Twilight Samurai*, Ito reiterates that Seibei had not been poor and unlucky, as his fellow samurai had assumed; instead her father had enjoyed the great fortune of loving his family and being loved by them.

Notes

1. *Twilight Samurai* was adapted from three Fujisawa novels: *Tasogare Seibei*, *Chikkō shiatsu*, and *Iwaibito sukehachi*.
2. Schilling, 'A Feast for Film Buffs'.
3. Bourne, 'Japan Cuts 2010 Review'.
4. *About Her Brother* (*Ototo*, 2010), Yamada's eighty-first film, was his first *gendai geki* in ten years.

Further reading

Christopher Bourne, 'Japan Cuts 2010 Review: Yoji Yamada's About Her Brother', *The Bourne Cinema Conspiracy*, July 16, 2010. Available at http://chrisbourne.blogspot.com/2010/07/japan-cuts-2010-review-yoji-yamadas.html (accessed 9 September 2012).

Mark Schilling, 'A Feast for Film Buffs: Japan Offers Formidable Alternatives to Hollywood Fare in 2010', *Japan Times*, January 8, 2010. Available at http://search.japantimes.co.jp/cgi-bin/ff20100108r1.html (accessed 9 September 2012).

Alisa Freedman

Taxi Driver (1976)

[Country: USA. Production Company: Bill/Phillips, Columbia Pictures and Italo/Judeo Productions. Director: Martin Scorsese. Screenwriter: Paul Schrader. Cinematographer: Michael Chapman. Music: Bernard Herrmann. Editors: Tom Rolf and Melvin Shapiro. Cast: Robert De Niro (Travis

Bickle), Cybill Shepherd (Betsy), Jodie Foster (Iris) and Harvey Keitel ('Sport').]

Synopsis: Travis Bickle, seemingly a Vietnam War veteran, gets a job working as a taxi driver in New York City. As he drives around the city he increasingly feels himself to be surrounded by the worst of humanity but manages to find some sort of hope in Betsy, a worker for presidential hopeful, Senator Palatine. He becomes obsessed with her and tries to establish a relationship. When this doesn't work out he seems to be tipped over the edge of sanity. He arms himself and sets out to assassinate Palatine. Thwarted in this, he then commits himself to 'saving' Iris, a child prostitute. He attacks the brothel where she 'works', killing three men in a brutal bloodbath. We move forward in time and find Travis has become a newspaper hero and has a letter from Iris's parents thanking him for saving their daughter.

This film offers an intense portrayal of a man on the edge who spends more and more time detached from the world in the borderlands between sanity and madness before becoming, in his own words, 'a man who could not, a man would not take it any more'. Often the locations in which we find Travis Bickle mirror his alienated psychological state. Enclosed within his taxi he cruises a dark, noir-like urban realm of dirt and squalor, cut off from that world, observing it in a disengaged, distant fashion. In his bleak, grey flat, again eschewing contact with human society, he exists with few comforts, observing life on a TV screen, unable to sleep and therefore unable to gain any respite. When he is with his fellow drivers he remains disconnected and removed, existing within his thoughts and, ironically, wary of all those who might be seen as outsiders.

We follow Travis constantly, spending much more time with him than any character in the film would ever wish to, and because of this (fulfilling our role as audience) we attempt to identify with him; but the activities he engages in are often alienating, the things he says ominous and doom-laden ('Some day a real rain will come and wash all this scum off the streets.'), and his looks to camera scary, so that we find it impossible to empathise with him. His presence within the film has been compared to that of the brooding Ethan Edwards in *The Searchers* (Ford, 1956), a man who lives on the margins of society and yet feels he has a responsibility as a moral guardian for that society. Like Ethan, Travis has returned home as a defeated war veteran: both have taken part in a war that has split the United States into two diametrically opposed camps.[1]

Our relationship with Travis at the screen interface demonstrates exactly why he is such a loner. He is not easy to be with; monosyllabic and frequently rather embarrassing, we wish to turn away from him as almost everybody else in the film seems to, and yet we cannot because we are held in position as a viewer growing increasingly uncomfortable but also as a voyeur aware that Travis' repressed anger is certain to erupt at some point. The camera allows us to look away as he phones Betsy, moving to the emptiness of the dull corridor, but still we cannot escape. Our embarrassment in listening to his painfully stilted words becomes if anything more intense since with little of visual note in the screen and with our attention drawn to the words by the obvious camera movement we concentrate on them even more. The glance away that we have been permitted only serves to intensify the extent to which we wish to escape his claustrophobic world. The most intense relationship in the film is thus successfully constructed as being between the main character and the viewer.

This is an examination of an altogether darker mind than that of Charlie (Harvey Keitel), the central character in Scorsese's *Mean Streets* (1973), but the focus on a single male character and his search for redemption remains. Here the cross (of the crucifix) which is such a recurring image in that earlier film is etched into the end of bullets by Travis. There is also the same symbolic use of mirrors as a looking into the self but on an altogether more frightening level. Most disturbingly, at one point Travis appears to talk directly to us when supposedly addressing himself in a mirror, positioning us as the outsider who he sees as a moral threat and wishes to violently confront. We are both his mirror image or other self, drawn on with him towards the denouement we know is surely coming, implicated in his actions and unable to escape being part of what is to happen, and also the enemy within himself and the world around him that he is (and we know he is) preparing to exorcise. Steadily he cuts himself off from the world and his psychological deterioration is paralleled in the deteriorating state of his room until he symbolically kicks over the television, both his last line of communication with the outside world and the epitome of the cold, faceless world of the city (and of Western society).

For Travis the urban life of New York is a vision of hell; vibrant reds, oranges and yellows flash across the predominant darkness of the screen like the glow from some subterranean inferno. To him the people who live here, the 'pimps', the 'whores' and all the others, are 'scum'. The 'garbage and trash of the sidewalks' is literally there but this is also his metaphorical summation of the inhabitants of this netherworld. At a further level it is like a jungle: 'All the animals come out at night', he tells us. The device of the diary enables him to talk directly to us, further drawing us into his inner world as a confidante, and further reinforcing what the camera has already been telling us that the key relationship in this film is going to be between us and this increasingly deranged character that nobody (and certainly not us) is able to help.

The climax carries extreme violence and much of the negative critical reaction to the film focused on Scorsese's moral stance toward this bloodbath, claiming it was portrayed as a positive, cleansing ritual that redeemed Travis' character. Indeed, within the context of the narrative the bloodletting does seem to be in some way to be therapeutic. But *Taxi Driver* is more complex than such a simplistic interpretation would suggest. De Niro appears in nearly every scene and we see nearly everything through his character's skewed vision, but this does not mean we can necessarily identify Travis's views and perspectives on life with those of Scorsese or anybody else involved in the filmmaking process.

Public concern with the shock of this powerful visual representation of violence, ironically, gives expression to the confused morals in modern life to which the film draws our attention. The real shock should not be that someone with such a fragile grip on sanity would tip over the edge but that he should then become a hero, heralded in the newspapers for his stand as a vigilante. This is the ultimate expression of the degradation of the society portrayed in the film. The failure to be shocked by this truly disturbing aspect of the narrative while vehemently condemning the visual representation of what is merely an inevitable outcome within such a world crystallises the misguided value system of the society receiving the film.

The power of our experience throughout is produced from the coming together of script, camerawork and performance. For example, the scene that involves Scorsese's cameo performance as 'Man Watching Silhouette' is one in which we seem to be offered a momentary escape from our close confinement with Travis; and yet we find ourselves thrown into an altogether darker perspective on the world than even that offered by the central character. Dressed in black and with black hair and beard, Scorsese offers us a portrait of a human being embodying the cold distance of absolute satanic evil. We are once again trapped within the claustrophobic space of the taxi, as camerawork, performance and dialogue harmonise to create a less than harmonious vision of society. The utter viciousness of Scorsese's cameo role as the husband who is being cheated on but who is about to exact a terrible vengeance is actually, as a result of its use of a male linguistic code of misogyny, more brutal than the climactic bloodbath involving Travis.

For Travis women are either blonde and beautiful and to be set upon a pedestal as with Betsy (Cybill Shepherd) or delicate and vulnerable and therefore to be protected as with Iris (Jodie Foster). Like Charlie in *Mean Streets*, Travis has difficulty understanding women but where Charlie dances in his imagination with the black stripper Travis takes the idealised female with him to watch the male fantasy of woman in a porn movie thereby associating himself with the very aspects of the street he claims to despise and emphasising the male confusion. Betsy, he says, 'appeared like an angel out of this filthy mess', but by the end of their relationship he states, 'I realised now how she was like all the rest, cold and distant – women for sure'. The difficulties men find in understanding women is a theme for Scorsese, as it is throughout Western (male-dominated) culture: women are either beautiful goddesses to be worshipped or vulnerable prizes to be protected, and ultimately usually deceptively cold and deadly. Scorsese's cameo role in this movie highlights this same theme. But perhaps the most worrying aspect of this strand of the narrative comes at the end of the film when Betsy appears to get into Travis's cab and is seemingly attracted to this man who has become a hero.

The ending in fact resolves nothing but, with Travis once more cruising the streets, potentially leaves the whole scenario to be played out again in a never-ending loop. Once more, as in *Mean Streets* but to a greater degree, the final sequences leave us with unanswered questions. In a way there is a classic resolution with the hero winning the day, and yet what sort of hero is this? And what sort of society can create a hero of such a person? The nature of both the city and society would seem to be unchanged. Did Travis lose his sanity and has it now been restored? What is certain is that the film refuses easy answers? In that sense it is true to the noir tradition; this remains a dark world without traditional values that cannot be changed and within which men and women are destined to play out the same scenarios in an unending cycle.

Note

1. 'Both Ethan Edwards and Travis Bickle have returned from war, having fought on the losing or retreating side. For both of them the dividing line between war and peace is a wavering line.' Lesley Stern, *The Scorsese Connection*, Bloomington, IN, Indiana University Press, 1995, p. 57.

Further reading

Peter Brunette (ed.), *Martin Scorsese: Interviews*, Jackson, University Press of Mississippi, 1999.

Pete Fraser, *Taxi Driver*, London, York Press, 2000.

Ben Nyce, *Scorsese Up Close: A Study of Films*, Lanham, MD, Scarecrow Press, 2004.

Paul Schrader, *Taxi Driver: Screenplay*, London, Faber and Faber, 2000.

Amy Taubin, *Taxi Driver*, London, BFI, 1998.

John White

Tesis/Thesis (1996)

[Country: Spain. Production Company: Las Producciones del Escorpión and SOGEPAQ. Director: Alejandro Amenábar. Executive producers: José Luis Cuerda and Emiliano Otegui. Screenwriters: Alejandro Amenábar and Mateo Gil. Cinematographer: Hans Burmann. Music: Alejandro Amenábar and Mariano Marín. Editor: María Elena Sáinz de Rozas. Cast: Ana Torrent (Ángela), Fele Martínez (Chema), Eduardo Noriega (Bosco Herranz), Xabier Elorriaga (Castro), Miguel Picazo (Figueroa), Nieves Herranz (Sena), Rosa Campillo (Yolanda).]

Synopsis: Film student Ángela is writing her thesis on violence in audiovisual media. At the university, she discovers the body of her thesis director, Prof. Figueroa, who died while watching a video that turns out to be a snuff film. The plot of this psychological thriller unfolds through Ángela's research on the disappearance of a former classmate, tortured and murdered on tape. Unsure about whom to trust, Ángela is targeted as the next victim as she draws closer to exposing an underground ring of snuff films produced by a fellow student and professor. Set in the 1990s, the film engages a critique of violence in television and film, market forces producing audiovisual media, and voyeuristic desires of audiences, as well as the burgeoning practices of security camera vigilance in public spaces.

Amenábar's feature-length debut, a psychological thriller of the intrigue genre about 'snuff' film, is in many ways an exploration into the darkest underside of the demand for spectacle in which visual media are produced, whether for television or film. As the film student Ángela pursues research for her thesis on audiovisual violence ('a daily occurrence in film and television'), her desire to view footage all too graphic to appear in the media is eclipsed by the dangers of exposing an underground ring of snuff films produced in the university. It is this turn from Ángela's interest in viewing graphic violence to the threat that she herself could become the next victim of a snuff film which structures the narrative for viewers, similarly to the genre of a detective thriller whodunit, in which all relationships outside the family are suspect. The ensuing intrigue confronts viewers with complex questions about spectatorship itself in which the morbid interest in seeing tortured and mutilated bodies censored from the public eye is satisfied by an underground market that must 'give the audience what it wants to see', as Professor Castro (one author of the snuff ring) lectures to his film students. In this sense, the notion of desire constructed in the film is understood as a complex, intersecting terrain of psychological, market-driven, and sociocultural factors which generate, at once, the spectator's libidinal desire to consume censored images, an underground market of snuff film produced in response to the demand for violence, and the gendered roles of the characters as either objects or perpetrators of this violence, among others. The demand for morbid images, in other words, exists within a market economy inseparable from the characters' fascination with and horror for 'real' explicit visual material that is censored or in the case of Ángela's research subject, conspicuous in the media.

Notably, it is only once Ángela perceives that she is being pursued as the next victim of the snuff ring, as the very object of filmed violence which both terrifies and intrigues her, that her desire to view graphic images begins to wane, leading her to abandon her research altogether by the end of the film. Nevertheless, Ángela's ambiguous transformation from a subject who desires to see recorded violence to become herself a target of 'real' violence is not entirely clear given that Amenábar constructs desire for his audience in less simplistic terms.[1] Viewers are shown images of Ángela peeking through her fingers to catch a glimpse of the filmed horror that so fascinates her, an ambivalence which is evidently more complex in her character's psychological portrait. For, Ángela also fantasises about a sexual encounter with the suspect Bosco in a disturbing dream sequence which oscillates between Ángela's terrified resistance to her aggressor, who subdues her in bed with a suggestive phallic switchblade, and her erotic attempt held at knifepoint to seduce Bosco, which could be read as a survival tactic were it not for the director's choice to portray this scene disturbingly with evident lust. To her horror, a dreaming Ángela realises that she is being filmed during the sex act, as an object of desire targeted for annihilation, which draws a clear parallel for the film's viewers between woman as object in pornography and the brutal victimisation of the innocent in snuff. This parallel is furthermore reinforced by an earlier shot of the university film catalogue in which hardcore 'pornography and other films' (snuff) are categorised and archived together. The dream sequence, along with the late revelation that Ángela has been filmed secretly at home by her co-researcher Chema – a recording in which she caresses and kisses the image of Bosco displayed on the television screen – emphasises the perverse trappings of a desire through which Ángela's character, unknown to the film's audience, had demonstrated a conscious, invested sexual interest in the suspect Bosco, caught on tape. The voyeuristic recording likewise exposes her projected desire for simulacrum in the form of images (in film, television), a scene with greater social implications than Ángela's character portrait alone. Sexual desire is played out similarly in displaced ways among other characters, in Bosco's attempt to seduce Ángela's unsuspecting younger sister, in Ángela's 'feigned' kiss with Bosco in order to distance her sister from the suspected assassin, in the alleged jealousy of Bosco's girlfriend towards Ángela, in Chema's voyeuristic recording of Ángela, and even between men in Bosco and Chema's former friendship which remained a secret to Ángela, a suspicious matter when this bond was revealed to her by Bosco's girlfriend.

In this sense, Ángela's confession earlier in the film 'I don't like to be recorded' echoes Amenábar's recurrent questioning of camera vigilance and its blurred distinction between the public eye and private intimacy, whether subjects are deliberately filmed, as in these scenes, or passively recorded by the university's security cameras which provide evidence to incriminate Ángela in the discovery of Professor Figueroa's dead body in the auditorium. Viewers might draw an immediate comparison between the growing presence of security cameras in public space at the time of the film's release and Amenábar's critique of camera vigilance, both public and private. Moving beyond this initial assessment, the film also suggests that even when institutional vigilance is justified under the guise of security (i.e., mandated by the university or state), and thereby presumably void of subjective interest, a voyeuristic desire indeed underpins authority and serves to both conserve and usurp it; as viewers will remember, the closed circuit cameras incriminate Ángela, but also film Professor Castro's suspicious lurking presence in the university film archive before Figueroa's death.

In its increasingly muddied distinction between the public and private, intimacy and vigilance, the film also problematises the strict separation between access to mediated (recorded or simulated) violence in the form of images and 'real violence' experienced in the first person.[2] Viewers are reminded throughout the film that any absolute distinction between the 'mediated' and the 'real' – whether desire, violent images, or otherwise – is ultimately ungrounded. Ángela asks Chema if he has ever seen a real dead body, which gives way to two interpretations: Chema asserts that he has, in the explicit video recordings he watches with Ángela, and yet to the contrary, for Ángela audiovisual violence is not 'real' per se (she argues, 'not on television, but a real dead body'). From the film's opening sequence in a train station, in which Ángela approaches the train tracks desiring to view a 'body split in two' that is never actually seen (through the camera that occupies her first-person gaze), Amenábar structures the film's imagery, and at times Ángela's sight, through similar camerawork that seldom shows significant footage of gore, if at all.[3] Instead, the characters' horror is transmitted to the audience through shots of their expressions when viewing the snuff film and, most importantly, through the viewer's psychological response when imagining violent images through the use of diegetic and non-diegetic sound, particularly in the victim's chilling screams for help as she is being tortured. In fact, Amenábar's choice not to show viewers significant violence or gore, but rather to play on the viewer's horror by imagining this violence through sound, is perhaps most noteworthy for film students interested in Amenábar's use of diegetic and non-diegetic sound in conjunction with the full omission of visual information (i.e. established as a motif in the opening sequence with a recorded voice-off which fades to the first frame).[4] Chema and Ángela's tense adventure into the cellar of the university archives, equipped with only a box of matches that must be lit consecutively, also plays with the audience's ability to see only the duration of each lighted match, interspersed with shots of complete darkness which play upon the viewer's expectations of surprise in the thriller genre. Such is the nature of Ángela's psychological, imaginative horror when she chooses not to view the snuff film, at first, but darkens her television screen through the contrast function so that only the audio recording can be heard, which proves disturbing for her character in later scenes, as she listens obsessively to the film's audio recording on her portable tape recorder.

Nevertheless, it should be noted that when violent images are shown to the film's viewers, Amenábar often chooses to demonstrate the characters' ability to analyse them critically. For, the rapid advances in digital camera technology at the time are what lead Chema and Ángela to deduce the brand of camera used to record the snuff film, through a close analysis of the recording's image quality, as well as the camera's date of release and purchase, which would serve as vital information to track down Professor Castro and Bosco as leaders of the snuff ring. Chema and Ángela furthermore provide a 'close visual reading' of the quick jump cuts in post-production editing, which aim to delete the victim's mention of her torturer's name, allowing them to conclude that the victim knows her murderer. It could be argued that these two fundamental pieces of information, used to crack the case, are derived from the protagonists' critical analysis of graphic images, providing a similar key to Amenábar's proposal for his viewers to deconstruct their own relationship to violence with critical reflection.

One should note that the word *morbo* used to describe Ángela's 'morbid' desire to view extreme, violent images, is defined in Spanish as both 'an unhealthy interest in persons or things' and 'an attraction to unpleasant events'. In this sense, the film's dark reflection on spectatorship and the morbid fascination with explicit images in the media may be traced to the film's release, contemporary to the upsurge in violence in Spanish cinema at the time, noted by Jordan and Morgan-Tamosunas, Klodt, Moreiras-Menor and Tierney, among others, as well as the flourishing of the first private television networks in Spain in the 1990s. Summarised in the market-driven maxim of Professor Castro on the film industry, to provide viewers literally with what they most desire to see, programming in commercial television is largely dependent upon the number of viewers in a given audience share, supported by advertising spots (see Maxwell 1995). It is no surprise that Amenábar closes the film, then, with a sequence of images from a fictitious sensationalist news show, *Justice and Law*, whose anchor summarises the 'unbelievable' and 'macabre' story of gruesome murders of disappeared girls found on tape. Framing for her audience that it is 'not easy for us to show these images,' the anchor both conditions the viewer's expectations before seeing the footage ('and now, the images you've been waiting for') and justifies the broadcast as 'a document by itself', unmediated and lacking critical analysis. In this final sequence, the camera shows Chema and Ángela walking through the hallway of a hospital, interspersed with images of patients fixated on the same television broadcast, a suggestive critique of a greater social desire to view violence in televised media, which is not altogether unique to Spain.[5] Keeping in mind the film's potential to question intimacy, vigilance, and the increasingly blurry distinction between the public and private – a more subtle gesture than the explicit nature of extreme violence in the film's exploration of snuff – one could conclude in this final scene that Amenábar proposes a greater social critique of the production of and desire to consume images in a market-driven economy that jettisons ethical considerations in favour of audience share or box office revenue. In other words, the viewing audience most desires to consume, with morbid fascination, not only violence but voyeurism in which private matters are made public – the form of television programming that defines sensationalist news media and the gossip varieties of popular talk shows that turn the intimate details of private lives into spectacle-driven commodities for mass consumption. After all, perhaps summarised most disturbingly for the film's viewers, when Ángela kisses the television screen, her secret desire for the assassin is only made public, terrifyingly and intriguingly so for the viewing audience, when caught on tape.

Notes

1. As Cristina Moreiras-Menor argues, 'Lejos … de ser una película que trabaja exclusivamente en torno a la mirada fascinada del sujeto contemporáneo hacia la violencia, *Tesis* va más allá al exponer tanto su razón, la espectacularización masiva e indiferencia de la realidad, como su origen, la formación del sujeto y la manipulación de su mirada a la realidad a partir de procesos simbólicos de educación asentados fundamentalmente en estructuras de poder (institucionalizadas) que privilegian la espectacularización consumista del lado más sórdido de la naturaleza humana y social' [Far … from being a film that works exclusively around the fascinated gaze of the contemporary subject towards violence, *Tesis* goes beyond this to expose both its raison d'être, mass spectacularization and indifference towards reality, and its origin, the formation of the subject and manipulation of the subject's view of reality from symbolic processes of education seated fundamentally in (institutionalized) structures of power that privilege consumerist spectacularization of human and social nature's most sordid side.] (Moreiras-Menor 2002: 260).
2. See Dolores Tierney, 'The Appeal of the Real in Snuff: Alejandro Amenábar's *Tesis* ("Thesis")', *Spectator – The University of Southern California Journal of Film and Television*, Vol. 22, No. 2, Fall 2002, pp. 45–55.

3. As Amenábar notes, 'opté por el camino opuesto, mirando hacia el otro lado, a la cara de los actores, jugando con la proyección psicológica del espectador, con lo que no está viendo, con lo que se está imaginando' [I chose the opposite route, looking the other way, at the actors' faces, playing with the psychological projection of the viewer, with what one is not seeing, with what one is imagining.] (Marchante 2002: 59).
4. See Dominique Russell, 'Sounds like Horror: Alejandro Amenábar's Thesis on Audio-Visual Violence', *Canadian Journal of Film Studies*, Vol. 15, No. 2, Fall 2006, pp. 81–95.
5. See Jason E. Klodt, '*En el fondo te gusta*: Titillation, Desire, and the Spectator's Gaze in Alejandro Amenábar's *Tesis*', *Studies in Hispanic Cinemas*, Vol. 4, No. 1, 2007, pp. 3–17.

Further reading

Barry Jordan and Rikki Morgan-Tamosunas, *Contemporary Spanish Cinema*, Manchester University Press, Manchester and New York, 1998.

Oti Rodríguez Marchante, *Amenábar, vocación de intriga*, Madrid, Páginas de Espuma, 2002.

Steven Marsh and Parvati Nair (eds), *Gender and Spanish Cinema*, Oxford and New York, Berg, 2004.

Rosanna Maule, 'Cultural Specificity and Transnational Address in the New Generation of Spanish Film Authors: The Case of Alejandro Amenábar', in Cristina Sánchez-Conejero (ed.), *Spanishness in the Spanish Novel and Cinema of the 20th-21st Century*, Newcastle, Cambridge Scholars, 2007, pp. 107–20.

Richard Maxwell, *The Spectacle of Democracy: Spanish Television, Nationalism, and Political Transition*, Minneapolis, MN, University of Minneapolis Press, 1995.

Cristina Moreiras-Menor, *Cultura herida: Literatura y cine en la España democrática*, Madrid, Ediciones Libertarias, 2002.

Joan Ramon Resina (ed.), *Burning Darkness: A Half Century of Spanish Cinema*, Albany, NY, State University of New York Press, 2008.

Paul Julian Smith, *Television in Spain, from Franco to Almodóvar*, Woodbridge, UK and Rochester, New York, Tamesis, 2006.

Jon Snyder

La teta asustada/Milk of Sorrow (2009)

[Country: Peru. Production company: Wanda Visión. Producers: José María Morales, Antonio Chavarrías, Claudia Llosa. Director and Screenwriter: Claudia Llosa. Cinematographer: Natasha Braier. Editor: Frank Gutiérrez. Music: Selma Mutal. Cast: Magaly Solier (Fausta), Susi Sánchez (Aída), Efraín Solís (Noé), Bárbara Lazón (Perpetua), Delci Heredia (Carmela).]

Synopsis: The film portrays the life of Fausta (Magaly Solier), a young woman whose family has moved from the Andes to Manchay, one of the *pueblos jovenes* or shantytowns which has emerged on the outskirts of Lima. Fausta grieves for the loss of her mother, Perpetua (Bárbara Lazón), who dies in the story's opening sequences. But Fausta is already grief-stricken before this loss, her emotions paralysed and her interest in life diminished as a result of being born during the turmoil which saw conflict between the Peruvian military and the terrorist group Shining Path. The film's Spanish title refers to a syndrome in which Andean mothers who suffered from physical violation during the unrest gave birth to children believed to be without a soul. The syndrome suggests that the horror of rape and torture was conveyed to foetuses in the womb and then to infants through mother's milk contaminated by trauma and shock. Thus, Fausta, whose father was executed and mother was raped, lives as a young adult with the consequences of the violence enacted on her parents.

La teta asustada was the second feature from Peruvian director Claudia Llosa. An international co-production with Spain, set in and around Lima, the drama made worldwide headlines in February 2009 when the film won the prestigious Golden Bear award at the Berlin Film Festival. Despite this award and other recognition across the festival circuit, the film failed to win the main prize at the Lima Latin American Film Festival giving rise to speculation about responses from the home audience which were more likely to be offended by the portrayal of the Quechua culture on-screen.

The director has suggested that the film isn't so much about politics as it is about the legacy and collective trauma of the civil war experienced in Peru, which still is spoken about only very rarely and yet which permeates all levels of society. Here she uses the young woman's body as a site for articulating that trauma. In his thoughtful analysis, Ryan Prout suggests that the film extends 'ideas about the body and its ailments to determine two categories of people and to locate them on either side of a boundary defined by attitudes to knowledge rendered adversarial and incompatible: behind the desk is the doctor and all that he represents – progress, modernity, empirical science – while Fausta and her uncle, on the other side, are made coterminous with superstition, atavism, and old wives' tales' (2009).

Shutting herself off from society, Fausta's isolation is emphasised by a family business focused on matrimonial conjugation. Fausta is pictured at her cousin's wedding, a lonely figure before the artificial backdrop provided by the photographer. It is her immediate grief for her mother which forces her along a path which will ultimately lead to her overcoming that other more deep-seated sorrow of collective trauma. Determined to repatriate her mother's body to her native province, Fausta takes a job as a servant with Aida who promises her maid a pearl each time she agrees to repeat for her the lullaby-like song which she sings to herself. Eventually, Fausta accepts help for her physical condition and only then is she able to take her mother's body to be laid to rest.

The release of Llosa's film provoked controversy and revealed deep-rooted tensions between the different parts of Peruvian society and culture. Although its international acclaim was a source of considerable national pride, for some viewers, the film's focus on issues of migration and racial difference were unsettling in their apparent perpetuation of old stereotypes of underdevelopment and barbarism. Many Peruvian spectators were angry that a Hispanic director of a privileged background would dare to portray a sensitive aspect of their culture in such a bold way, and yet others suggest that a more liberating feminist reading is possible. For the film concludes with Fausta, an indigenous woman, having made the decision to overcome her difficulties and having taken the responsibility to take care of her mother's body herself. She lifts herself out of her state of passivity, and seems at peace with herself in the final scene.

As a talented storyteller, Llosa uses symbols in ways that defy easy interpretation. The potato, for example, is at first a self-inflicted reminder of the oppression and violence inflicted on her parents, but also a sign of communication and recovery as the narrative progresses and characters interact. It is Noé, Aida's gardener who tells Fausta that 'The potato doesn't flower very much.' And yet it flowers at the end, once removed from her body.

Llosa's film has been highly praised for its aesthetic qualities for picking out the beauty of the everyday activities of Fausta's family as well as the stereotypical landscape views. Often the beauty of the cinematography jars with the downbeat nature of the narrative, and yet the film seems strengthened by such an approach. Fausta's exhausting daily struggle becomes embedded into panoramic views that appear to force the spectator to question the way they look at such landscapes.

In addition to its success on the international festival circuit, *La teta asustada* was a box office smash hit in Peru on its release, beating *Slumdog Millionaire* in ticket sales during its first week in Lima. It was also shown, with Llosa in attendance, in several rural areas of Peru where its open-air community screenings became the sites and occasions of significant celebration. However, from the recordings of these events on the DVD special features, it is clear that such celebration focused on the very existence of an award-winning film, rather than on the subject matter that proved controversial and uncomfortable for many indigenous viewers. To highlight this further, it should be noted that the film was not shown via the new network of micro-cinemas that has been developed by the Chaski Group to allow for cinema viewing and engagement throughout the Andes. According to its coordinator, Stefan Kaspar, this was for three reasons:

> Claudia was not able to convince the commercial distributor to allow it; later she was not able to convince the Spanish producer to allow it several months after its commercial release; and third but not least and most decisive: because the popular spectators who attend the micro-cinemas did not like the film.
>
> (Kaspar 2013)

Meanwhile the 'festival' critics were largely impressed with the film's aesthetic qualities as well as its approach to the portrayal of complex themes, focusing on its handling of trauma at an individual level and the degree to which this translated effectively for an international audience. Although Nick James, the editor of *Sight and Sound*, made only the briefest reference to Llosa's winning film in his article on the Berlin festival in April 2009 as he had left the event before her film was screened, 18 months later she was named (and pictured) as one of the 'Nine Kings and Queens' of contemporary Latin American cinema in an article by Argentine critic and festival director Sergio Wolf in the September 2010 edition of the same publication. Meanwhile, French critic Charles-Stéphane Roy praised the strength of her image-making and referred to her film as 'the bright hope of Peruvian cinema' in his review for *Séquences*, 2009.

Overall, *La teta asustada* seems to have pleased the festival viewers and critics more than audiences across Peru. And yet its impact on Peruvian cinema should not be underplayed, for it served to place a spotlight on the possibility for creating of high-quality cinema in a country that has hitherto dismissed its capacity to do so. Controversially, it reminds its viewers of the tensions and terror that resulted from two decades of political conflict in Peru.

Further reading

Ricardo Bedoya, 'Peru: Films for after a war', in Eduardo Angel Russo (ed.), *The Film Edge: Contemporary Filmmaking in Latin America*, Buenos Aires: Teseo, 2010, pp. 145–58.

Maria Chiara D'Argenio, 'A contemporary Andean type: The representation of the indigenous world in Claudia Llosa's films', *Latin American and Caribbean Ethnic Studies*, 8: 1, 2013, pp. 20–42.

Stefan Kaspar, Interview (email), 15–19 August 2013.

Rebeca Maseda, 'Songs of pain: Female active survivors in Claudia Llosa's *The Milk of Sorrow*', *Violence Probing the Boundaries*, Prague, Czech Republic, 9–11 May 2013.

Demetrious Matheou, 'Peruvian tales', *New South American Cinema*, London: Faber and Faber, 2010, pp. 371–90.

Diana Palaversich, 'Cultural dyslexia and the politics of cross cultural excursion in Claudia Llosa's *Madeinusa*', *Bulletin of Hispanic Studies*, 90: 40, 2013, pp. 489–503.

Ryan Prout, 'Golden Bears, Amulets, and Old Wives' Tales?' *JGCinema.com*, www.jgcinema.com/single.php?sl=Per%F9-terrorism-gender-trauma-pain-class-Sendero-luminoso-rape, 2009 (accessed July 2013).

Charles-Stéphane Roy, 'Berlin – Claudia Llosa: l'espoir d'un cinéma péruvien', *Séquences: la revue de cinéma*, 260, 2009, p. 12.

Sarah Barrow

Thelma and Louise (1991)

[Country: USA. Production Company: Metro-Goldwyn-Mayer. Director: Ridley Scott. Screenwriter: Callie Khouri. Cinematographer: Adrian Biddle. Music: Hans Zimmer. Editor: Thom Noble. Cast: Susan Sarandon (Louise Elizabeth Sawyer), Geena Davis (Thelma Yvonne Dickinson), Harvey Keitel (Hal Slocumb), Brad Pitt (J.D.), Timothy Carhart (Harlan).]

Synopsis: Thelma is a neglected housewife who ditches her bullying husband to spend a weekend fishing with her friend Louise, a hashhouse waitress who drives an impeccably maintained 1966 Thunderbird convertible. A quick stop at a bar leads to trouble when Thelma is accosted by a local man. Louise shoots the guy. The two women flee, believing that Thelma's drunken behaviour on the dance floor will make their sexual assault claim untenable. The rest of the films follows their panicked dash across the backroads of the southwest attempting to flee law, order and patriarchy.

Released in 1991, *Thelma and Louise* cost MGM a modest $16.5 million and was a rather unlikely bet for a mainstream Hollywood film. Callie Khouri's first screenplay was prompted by dissatisfaction with the way women were portrayed in Hollywood film:

> I wanted to write about two normal women .... I wanted to write something with strong women in it .... that's another one of the things I've never seen dealt with in a film, the anger women feel about the way they're talked to.[1]

and inspired by an incident which resonates within the film's narrative:

> I was walking down the street, when this old guy in a car starts talking to me. I'm ignoring him, which is what you're supposed to do in that situation. Then he said, 'I'd like to see you suck my dick', and I just lost it for a second. I walked over to the car and said, 'I'd like to shoot you in the fucking face'.[2]

In the pragmatic business world of Hollywood the script stood no chance without an accredited director behind it. Ridley Scott had power in Hollywood due to the success of *Alien* (1979) and *Blade Runner* (1982) and his decision to direct the film made it a viable proposition. He recalls that 'the script. had floated around for ages and fallen through the net .... You'd be amazed how many directors turned it down'.[3] Two strong female leads, an array of unattractive male characters, a generic mix of Western and road movie which were generally considered 'male' genres and were not in fashion, plus a downbeat ending – certainly not reassuring ingredients for box office success. Scott was aware the subject matter needed careful handling if it was to succeed with a mainstream audience: 'I thought it should be really humorous and then you didn't ostracize two thirds of the audience'.[4] While this suggests Scott 'watered down' the script's feminist credentials to secure a mainstream audience Khouri herself has commented that, if anything, he made the male characters less sympathetic than her originals:

> When you read the script you'll see that in *Thelma and Louise*, the male characters were portrayed in a way that was more caricatured on the screen than on the page. And that was a decision made by the male director and the male actors who played them.[5]

She is also ambivalent about the film's status as a feminist text: 'the issues surrounding the film are feminist. But the film itself is not'.[6]

Considering all these factors, the film's reception was surprising. An immediate hit with audiences, it made $45 million in the US and £4 million in the UK. Critical acclaim followed with an Oscar and a Golden Globe for the screenplay, and three further Oscar nominations.[7] The American popular press were equally fascinated by the film: *Time* magazine carried the headline, 'Why *Thelma and Louise* strikes a nerve'.[8] Subsequent critical debate even found its genre contentious: road movie, buddy movie, screwball comedy, rape-revenge narrative, Western? This strange generic mix, the unlikely pairing of Khouri and Scott, and the 'feminist' issues mapped onto a mainstream Hollywood film, provide a framework for understanding the paradoxical and controversial response to the film.

The opening shot of the desert road stretching ahead to the hills is iconic of both the road movie and the Western and encourages particular generic expectations. It connotes not just the wide open spaces of the American West, but the freedom and self-determination coded into the myth of 'the West' and popularised by Hollywood. The first sequence (Thelma being bullied by Darryl in her dimly lit kitchen, and Louise waiting tables in a diner) resonates with ideas of entrapment because of its juxtaposition with the opening shot. The sense of forbidden territory is increased by the fact that to an audience familiar with Hollywood films such spaces are gendered: in both the road movie and the Western this is a predominately 'male' space.

Encounters along the road with a series of men are used to explore, as Hal Slocumb trenchantly puts it, all the ways women can be 'fucked over'. The road movie and the Western are genres which explore the relationship between the individual and society, and related issues of freedom and justice. Here this is inflected specifically towards issues of power and gender. Each incident shows how men exert power over women: with brute physical force (Harlan), bullying and belittling (Darryl), emotional abuse (Jimmy), financial exploitation (JD), sexual harassment (the truck driver) and, in a more complex way, under the guise of fatherly protection (Hal, who betrays them to the FBI). The laws of society are portrayed as 'some tricky shit' and do not protect the women from abuse.

So far, so radical; but also present in the opening sequence are comic elements creating audience expectations which temper the seriousness of this message. The narrative structure and iconography of the road movie (long shots of the road, shots of the road through the rearview mirror, the 'T-bird') mixed with Western (mesas, desert scenery, the flight to Mexico, outlaws, Stetsons, bandanas, guns, the law) is undercut by the element of 'feminine' screwball comedy, evidenced by the appearance of the two women at the beginning of the film (Thelma's incompetent packing, their names, their witty badinage). This mix of genres complicates the ways in which we read the film. The very image of Thelma and Louise against the typical scenery of the Western constantly reminds audiences that they are out of place, and the dialogue underlines this. The 'feminine' nature of their discourse juxtaposed against the setting and 'masculine' narrative in which they find themselves produces humour: comments such as 'Thelma, don't you litter!' and 'Would you do that to your mother or your sister?' are staples of motherly discourse but their displacement onto the narrative of the Western/road movie (shootings, flight from the law, hold-ups) make them comically ludicrous, and paradoxically remind us these women are not *really* the outlaws the narrative seems to make them. This makes the female representations oxymoronic in ways which may reflect more truly the ambivalent position of women in society.

Scott's decision to emphasise the humour, pushing the male characters further towards caricature, is another way in which meanings are destabilised. The sharpness of the critique of male power is lessened and the audience can react to the encounters along the road with enjoyment, untroubled by the depressing lack of power which got the women into these situations or the dubious morality of their responses. Darryl stepping into his pizza, his exaggerated comic gestures on the phone to Thelma, the traffic cop's finger wiggling impotently through the bullet hole in his car, and the truck driver shaking his fists against the backdrop of his exploded vehicle ensure humour predominates and the very male power the narrative is criticising is stripped of threat. The strongly cathartic element in some of the incidents: the shooting of Harlan, the blowing up of the tanker and the 'Nazi' traffic cop reduced to an impotently weeping shadow of his former self, invert the usual power balance. This has an obvious appeal to women all too familiar with the status quo but the element of comedy enables the appeal to transcend gender. This combination of elements makes the film a heady and exhilarating mix: a powerful evocation of 'busting out of your life'.[9]

The attempted rape at the Silver Bullet is the only sequence devoid of a comic element. Here the film's exploration of gender and power is at its most bleak and literal. Positioned to share Thelma's distress, the powerlessness of women is at its most apparent. The appearance of the gun, as if by magic in the top right-hand side of the frame, stops the attack. Much controversy was aroused by the women's appropriation of that quintessentially male symbol, but this is the only point where the gun is used to kill. A symbol of power in the film, it is used primarily to question just how much power it bestows. Here it can stop the rape but it cannot change the attitude that led to it. Some critics felt that for women to use the gun to exert power was a pyrrhic victory for feminism, but the meanings which cluster around the image of the gun are more complex.

Although the attempted rape and the unspoken story of what happened to Louise in Texas are used to highlight the injustice of the law, it is what happens after the attack which really interests Khouri: even armed with a gun Louise is not taken seriously by Harlan and he continues to insult her. She shoots him because of this contempt ('I should have gone ahead and fucked her') and her final comment ('You watch your mouth, buddy') reflects this. This becomes a central and contradictory metaphor in the film: women may appropriate all the trappings of male power but they will never overturn the power balance. Part of the force of the film can be explained by the complexity of this one moment: it is at one and the same time a depressing acceptance of powerlessness, a fairy-tale ending to an ugly all too common female experience, the start of an adventure which makes Thelma and Louise unlikely outlaws, and the beginning of Thelma's growth to self-knowledge, discovering 'her calling' and feeling more 'wide awake' then she ever has in her life.

Subsequent encounters along the road can be read as comic replays of the rape sequence. Each balances a recapturing of the 'feel-good' element with restating the stark fact that women have no real power. Thelma and Louise's attempt to get an apology from the male characters – the word echoes through the film, starting with Harlan ('You say you're sorry, or I'm going to make you sorry.') and ending with the truck driver ('We think you should apologise') – reasserts their femininity; they remain essentially 'nice' women, feminine in their demeanour, apologising profusely as they go. They are parody mothers, on a mission to improve the manners of the men ('We think you have really bad manners'), but the fact is they have no power to make any of the men apologise, not even at gunpoint.

This makes their choice at the end a fitting conclusion: there is no place for them in this society. The law, represented by the hyperbolic display of male power facing them on the edge of the Grand Canyon, is uninterested in justice. However, to anyone who has seen the film this potentially depressing reading doesn't ring true to the experience of *watching* the film. The ambivalence of the ending with its tension between the essentially depressing representation of female powerlessness and its fairy-tale happy ending where the women 'just keep going' (emphasised by the use of the freeze-frame and the reprise of shots from earlier in the film) are in keeping with the rest of the film. The slow motion image of Hal, arm outstretched, forever trying to catch the women and forever doomed to fail, underlines their ultimate escape from male power and allows the audience to leave the cinema feeling uplifted rather than outraged. A great part of this film's power is to achieve the seemingly incompatible aims of both presenting a stark reality and providing an enjoyable escape from it.

Notes

1. Callie Khouri interviewed by David Konow. Available at www.creativescreenwriting.com (accessed 2 February 2007).
2. 'The Art of Visual Storytelling: Callie Khouri on creating character in *Thelma and Louise*'. Available at www.sydfield.com (accessed 2 February 2007).
3. 'Ridley Scott Uncut', *Times Online*. Available at timesonline.co.uk (accessed 2 February 2007).
4. Ibid.
5. Marita Sturken, *Thelma and Louise*, London, BFI, 2000, p. 20.
6. Ibid, p. 8.
7. Data from the Internet Movie Database (IMDb) (accessed 9 May 2007).
8. Sturken, 2000, p. 20.
9. Ibid, p. 16.

Jean Welsh

The Third Man (1949)

[Country: UK. Production Company: London Film Production. Director: Carol Reed. Screenwriter: Graham Greene. Cinematographer: Robert Krasker. Editor: Oswald Hafenrichter. Music: Anton Karas. Cast: Joseph Cotton (Holly Martins), Orson Welles (Harry Lime), Alida Valli (Anna Schmidt), Trevor Howard (Major Calloway).]

Synopsis: Based on a story by Graham Greene, it charts the post-Second World War moral and material decay of Western Europe via the adventures of a naive American writer, Holly Martins, who goes to Vienna in search of his old friend Harry Lime (Orson Welles on magnificent form). At first told that he is dead, Martins is then disturbed to discover that Lime is alive and stands accused of being involved in black market drug-dealing, indirectly causing the death and suffering of hundreds of people, and hiding out in the Russian sector of the rubble-strewn city. Eventually Martins finds him but the story does not end easily for any of the characters involved. Such a simple tale and yet somehow *The Third Man* has succeeded in becoming one of the greatest British films of all time, with one of the most famous and memorable scenes in all cinema.

The Third Man has become an indisputable classic of British cinema, a mystery thriller with a wonderful twist, drawing on *noir* techniques, themes, characters, and moods. However, before unravelling this film's apparent 'greatness', it is worth pondering its status as a 'British' film. Well before critics and academics began debating the complexities of 'transnational' cinema, along came a feature that posed a challenge to most of the traditional ways of deciding the national identity of a film. But surely *The Third Man*'s credentials as a British film cannot be called into question? The film's iconic pre-titles image of Big Ben and accompanying text clearly establish its production 'home' as London, its celebrated director and writer were both British, and it was one of the first films to benefit from a new grants scheme set up to boost national cinema production.[1] And yet, before either Carol Reed or Graham Greene's names appear on screen, the spectator is informed that the film is 'presented by' Alexander Korda and David O. Selznick. Korda was the Hungarian-born founder of London Film Production, whose Austrian-held account was called upon while filming in Vienna, while Selznick was already widely considered as one of the most influential Hollywood producers of all time.[2] Furthermore, *The Third Man* tells the story of one American character (Harry Lime) from the point of view of another (Holly Martins), while the British actors Trevor Howard and Bernard Lee play only supporting roles. As Rob White points out, it would be 'misleading to call it simply a British film, given the central involvement of Selznick, Cotton and Welles' (2003: 9). Notwithstanding, while its national identity remains ambiguous, its status in British film culture is indisputable: in 2000, it came top of a poll of industry representatives designed to identify the best British films of the twentieth century, fighting off at least eight others made during the immediate post-war period when British cinema suddenly flourished.[3] Moreover, it led to its director being considered one of the greatest British film-makers of all time.

Perhaps its anomalous national status is part of what makes *The Third Man* so distinctive, especially since ambiguity is at the core of the film's thematic preoccupations. But of course the reasons for its longevity must extend far beyond its complicated production context which is already long forgotten. We need also to look at the way in which it draws so deftly on a range of cinematic influences, and crafts a story and characters of such interest as to create a work of overwhelming magnetism. Techniques of German expressionism, conventions of film noir and tricks of the thriller genre are all used to set up an engaging and unique portrayal of a post-war context that was steeped not in the more conservative ideals of conformity and unity, but in complex questions about the value of human life. Moral ambiguity is inscribed in its main characters, and the whiff of corruption, deception and betrayal pervades a city depicted as ravaged by conflict and ripped into four occupied zones along nationalist lines (British, American, French and Russian). In fact, the film foregrounds a constant blurring of physical, social, political and moral boundaries. Vienna is portrayed as a place of deep mistrust and a ubiquitous spy culture. Having suffered extensive damage from bomb attacks, its citizens are forced to survive despite relentless food and power shortages by relying on a thriving black market. The film's shifting mood, from bleak cynicism to dark humour, is deftly achieved as national stereotypes are set up and then torn apart, preventing us from ever being really sure when to take things seriously. Much of what is regarded as important by the authorities – passports, border patrols – is ridiculed by the lack of respect paid to such conventions by most of the film's main characters.

It is important also to emphasise the distinctive formal components of this magnificently composed film, since it is only through a thorough understanding of them that we can begin to comprehend the complexities of the chaotic situation it seeks to express. As Phillips has observed, '*The Third Man* is an accomplished example of the ways that mise en scène, cinematography, editing and sound can help reveal and support a film's settings, subjects, moods, and meanings' (2002: 179). While its cyclical narrative structure, starting and ending with the funerals (one a part of the deception, the other all too real) of one of its main characters is quite simple, what gives this film its classic status is its inventive cinematography and uncertain atmosphere. Robert Murphy describes it as a philosophical thriller, with just the right blend of: 'realistic locations + slanting shadow throws + deeply diagonal night-streets. + strong, insolent, secretive faces + charged acting + zithery-slithery vibrations tangling and unwinding our nerves, teasing and haunting us like a ghostly gurdy-hurdy' (2001: 144). Robert Krasker's Oscar-winning monochrome camera work accentuates the baroque contours of this once magnificent city, reminding the viewer of its high-culture status (statues and spires reaching up above the rubble) that has been largely deposed by a seedy underworld of criminality and deception.

The film's opening moments are particularly remarkable for the neat and concise way in which so much information is quickly conveyed. The image over which the titles appear is almost abstract with its extreme close-up of the moving strings and sound-hole of a zither, the music from which establishes the film's uncertain tone, jaunty and sinister at the same time as if concealing a sense of unease amidst its irritatingly upbeat chords. As Amy Sargeant points out, 'the Anton Karas score pervades the film, endorsing both its location. and its mood: the famous Harry Lime theme is woven is woven into an almost continuous warp' (2005: 167). The director himself then anonymously provides a brisk and ironic voice-over commentary as a swift montage of images gives further warning of the tone and concerns of the piece: street racketeers shiftily reveal cheap, fake watches hidden in suitcases, a dead body floats along the Danube, soldiers march up and down under instruction to defend artificial borders that mark the beginning of Cold War frontlines; classical buildings lie in ruins or cluttered by rubble.[4]

Amidst this rubble, Reed's emotionally complex characters struggle with questions of loyalty and morality. Which is worse – betrayal of love, or deception and crimes against humanity? The answer should be clear but the beauty of *The Third Man* is that nothing is ever clear. Harry Lime may be morally repugnant, but he is charming and charismatic nevertheless. He doesn't even appear until just over halfway through the film and yet – thanks to that zither – his presence is felt throughout. Even after his death, his influence is such that his girlfriend will not acknowledge the 'friend' who finally betrayed him, despite his offer of help. Meanwhile, this friend, Holly Martins, who should be the hero of the piece, is constantly found wanting. He has only come to Vienna because Harry has promised him a job, and then tries to steal his girlfriend's affections. This girlfriend, Anna, is herself the embodiment of masquerade: as a comedy stage actress, she is used to performing for the sake of others and her grief at losing Harry is revealed only in her most private moments.[5] As the object of the male gaze and passive until the final moments of the film (to Holly's great disappointment), she operates in a kind of limbo throughout in terms of her own moral authority. Found guilty of identity fraud, she refuses to strike a deal with the authorities, but in taking that decision she becomes complicit in Harry's crimes and thus the whole notion of loyalty is called into question. And so, it is left to Major Calloway, supported by his sidekick Sergeant Paine, to provide the moral backbone of the film, somehow bringing order to the chaos around him, sweeping up the mess and offering the voice of common sense. Perhaps this is what really confirms the film's national allegiance: its apparent alliance of the qualities of decency and valour with Britishness, and those of treachery, malevolence and violence with the Americans, the Czechs, the Hungarians and the Russians. Anyone but the British.

The ending of *The Third Man* was the subject of a major dispute between Reed and Greene, the latter unconvinced that audiences would tolerate anything other than a happy conclusion with Anna and Holly leaving together. The choice of closing image is even more striking for its bold use of a long-held deep-focus shot that allows Anna to walk towards and then past the camera, as the Harry Lime theme plays out. It worried Selznick also for expecting audiences to wait until the end (he shortened it), but its mixture of suspense and defiance works a treat. As Murphy suggests, 'like the strings pulling up the sails in a bottle it jerks everything into place' (2000: 198). In the end, questions have been answered and order is restored as Calloway drives off to resume service.

Notes

1. This scheme was administered by the newly established Film Finance Corporation, and Korda was successful in winning a grant of £1.2 million to support the making of *The Third Man*.
2. Selznick provided substantial funding although this came at a price. As Rob White explains, the formidable producer ordered controversial cuts in the American version (removing unsubtitled German speech and shortening the ending), and it was 50 years before the British version of the film was properly released in the US (2003: 9).
3. The US version was included in a poll of 100 Greatest American Films. The UK version fought off such classics as *Brief Encounter*, *The Red Shoes* and *A Matter of Life and Death* to come top of the British poll in 2000.
4. In all, 28 shots are shown in just 66 seconds of film during the montage sequence that opens the film.
5. Alida Valli (Anna) was already reasonably well known in Britain for her roles in Italian neo-realist films.

Further reading

Robert Murphy, *British Cinema and the Second World War*, London and New York, Continuum, 2000.

Robert Murphy, *The British Cinema Book*, 2nd edition, London, BFI, 2001.

W. H. Phillips, 'Expressive Film Techniques in *The Third Man*', in *Film: An Introduction*, London, Palgrave, 2002, pp. 35–43.

Amy Sargeant, *British Cinema: A Critical History*, London, BFI, 2005.

Rob White, *The Third Man*, London, BFI, 2003.

Sarah Barrow

Tianming/Daybreak (1933)

[Country: China. Production Company: Lian Hua. Director: Sun Yu. Producer: Lu Hanzhang. Screenwriter: Sun Yu. Cinematographer: Zhou Ke. Art: Fang Peilin. Cast: Li Lili (Lingling), Gao

Zhanfei (Zhang Jin), Ye Juanjuan (Lingling's Cousin), Yuan Congmei (the Young Boss).]

Synopsis: Unable to pay the local taxes imposed by the warlord, Lingling and her fiancé, Zhang Jin, leave their hometown, a fishing village, for the big city Shanghai, where their cousin and her husband live. The four of them work at the same factory. Unfortunately, Zhang is soon fired and has to start to work on the sea. Meanwhile, Lingling is raped at a dinner party hosted by her young boss at the factory. When the girl pointlessly wanders around afterwards, she gets abducted and ends up being sold to a brothel. Two years later, having endured the painful life of prostitution, Lingling turns into a skillful and street-smart social flower. Zhang returns back to Shanghai as a revolutionary. The two meet at Lingling's apartment, without knowing that a secret agent chasing Zhang has followed them there. In order to help Zhang escape, Lingling gets arrested and is sentenced to death. When they are about to execute her at daybreak, the girl keeps smiling at gunpoint.

The early 30s of the last century saw the 'golden age' of Shanghai cinema. Film companies financed and run by Chinese nationals had been developing for a decade in Shanghai and cultivated loyal moviegoers, who craved endlessly for new films in the two most popular locally grown genres – family melodrama and martial arts-magic spirit films. At this moment, on the one hand, imperial Japan invaded the northeastern region of China. Territorial crisis stirred up a surge of nationalism among Chinese elites as well as raised their desire to wake up people's consciousness through cultural means. Cinema's propaganda function thus loomed larger for certain left-leaning intellectuals. On the other hand, as a semi-colonial port city, Shanghai remained out of the reach of direct warfare; therefore, the film industry there was able to keep thriving as a profit-catering business and to continue offering entertainment. As one of the masterpieces representative of the aesthetics and ethos of Shanghai cinema's Golden Age, *Daybreak* (1933) embodies the contradictory and competing thoughts and sentiments that were tiding at once in this cosmopolitan city, at a time of political chaos and military tension.

The film visualises a piece of Chinese folk wisdom through a sad urban tale: always the darkest before daybreak. The clearly demarcated two parts of the film constitute a symmetric structure – echoing the female protagonist Lingling's fall and redemption. It also corresponds to a binarism between the industrialised, evil-inducing city and the natural, romantic countryside that is central to the narrative. Repetition and contrast are heavily used to highlight the film's thematic concern – the recurrence of young migrant women's ill fate in the city. The film opens with a montage depicting a busy body of migrant peasant-workers at a local dock, lining up and waiting to board their ferry to Shanghai. It then cuts to an old man staring at them, whining with angst, 'To the city! ... Same thing every day! ... Every year! ...'. A point of view shot follows, where Lingling smiles innocently, consoling a bunch of little kids. Another sequence almost identical to this one appears at the beginning of part two, whereas this time Lingling is dressed rather flamboyantly and flirts freely with several men. One of the film's most important symbolic props is a water chestnut necklace Zhang makes for Lingling, whose name literally means 'water chestnut' in Chinese (the fruit is a signifier of purity, because it has a dark and hard shell yet white pulp underneath). The necklace serves the girl as a medium of certain sympathetic magic which 'transports' her back to the genuine happy moments in the village. Whenever she touches the necklace, the film cuts to a high-key lighted and romanticised sequence where she and Zhang, wearing shorts and bare-footed, run, jump along the river bank or boat on the lake. When she falls into the murky den of the red light district, she also loses hold of her necklace and appears instead with either an oversized flower or some lavish jewellery on her chest. In addition, the film sets Lingling's apartment in Shanghai on the top of a residential building, so that when she stands there at night against the city's skyline, which is decorated with myriads of neon lights, it is as if her tiny body is overwhelmed by a giant, glittering yet suffocating diamond necklace.

Narratives about the hardship women have to encounter and endure in Chinese cinema were not simply meant to tell a cautionary tale for young urban women about the potential danger and punishment in heterosocial relationships. Binarisms of innocent and fallen women, evil city and genuine countryside, abound in early cinemas around the world (America, France, Germany, Russia and elsewhere). They served as the tropes of popular culture's conscious critique of modernity: 'the contradictions of modernity are enacted through the figure of the woman, very often, literally, across the body of the woman who tries to live them but more often than not fails .... [W]omen function as metonymies ... of urban modernity, figuring the city in its allure, instability, anonymity, and illegibility' (Hansen 2000: 15). Women are usually victimised in this narrative tradition and die in the end, since 'rape, thwarted romantic love, rejection, sacrifice, prostitution function as metaphors of a civilization in crisis' (Hansen 2000: 15). In addition, in the context of Chinese modernisation, many scholars point out that, repressed by colonial power and local political corruption, male intellectuals in the early twentieth century (including the filmmakers of early cinema in Shanghai) frequently betrayed a 'masochist identification with (oppressed) women' in their writings and artistic works (Zhang 2005: 29). Indeed, many Chinese filmmakers in the 1930s chose to represent women characters with a certain level of agency. As Miriam Hansen observes, the 'social flower' persona sometimes serves as a device of masquerade or performance for women characters that are potentially transformable and revolutionary, as shown in *Daybreak.* In the scene where Lingling undergoes interrogation by two secret agents in her apartment, in order to win some time for Zhang to escape, she brings her charm and 'professional' tactics into play, revealing her legs seductively. When she insists on posing optimistically in front of the guns as if she was in front of a camera (which she is indeed, extradiegetically), her brave and sexy smile leads to the revolt of several soldiers, who end up dying with her at the foot of their 'fellow citizens'. Read in this way, Lingling's fall becomes a subliminal passage, culminating in her death – a sacrifice, through which she achieves certain transcendence. Though quoted from von Sternberg's *Dishonored*, this last scene makes Lingling able to realise 'the sacrificial-redemptive pathos that the Dietrich figure in *Dishonored* is denied' (Hansen 2000: 19).

In general, the fallen women characters in Chinese cinema in the 1930s were sometimes coded with more complicated meanings, compared to their counterparts in Western traditions of the same period. They became embodiments of utopian and progressive ideals, amalgamating self-devoted spirit with unwitting physical sexiness. This kind of new treatment was owed to the rise of a cluster of intervolving modern thoughts in society that reshaped the body politics concerning women at that time. Most eminent among them was the change happening to some of the entrepreneurs and talents within the film industry, who gradually became left-leaning and started to cooperate with leftist writers and artists, therefore bringing modern girls and revolutionary boys onto screen to replace the previously dominant figures of romantic intellectuals, sentimental ladies, or action heroes/heroines. Appreciation of modern, athletic beauty was also encouraged by the Republican government, which in the late 1920s started to revitalise Confucianism and promote a healthy life style. In the arena of literature and art, the female body had been made a legitimate aesthetic object, therefore films and fanzines also became filled with the so-called 'soft elements' – i.e. shots or illustrations of naked body parts and excessive sensual plots. On the one hand, nudity and Hollywood style athletic beauty became the metonymies of 'modernity'; on the other, sports and fitness were realised as the means to save the country – by remoulding its citizens' bodies. For example, Sun Yu, the left-leaning filmmaker who wrote and directed *Daybreak*, used to claim that, once 'we all acquired well-built bodies, we ought to be able to change it [the social condition which was in mire]' (Li and Hu 1996: 330). These new emerging discourses helped bring the athletic body and optimistic images of Li Lili and her kind of star persona into the focus of public attention and onto the silver screen.

It is not hard to observe that *Daybreak* is clearly marked with traces indicative of Sun Yu's authorial control. Having studied film in the US in the 1920s, Sun Yu was one of the Shanghai filmmakers with a most unique personal style. Versed in both modern Western and traditional Chinese artistic languages, Sun was able to cook his work into a mixed stew of progressive messages as well as 'softening' elements – making up his own cinematic 'chop-suey' soup (Zhang 2005: 364–76). Moreover, Sun was known for his nuanced cinematic treatments. His works are usually touched up with realistic and symbolically charged details. The water chestnut necklace mentioned above is one instance; moreover, when Lingling's cousin is introduced in the film, several small plots are constructed to lead our attention to her makeup, her pneumonic coughs, and the jewellery she wears, which are all excessive or abjective body extensions symbolising the vanity and morbidity of urban working girls. However, Sun's realism frequently diverted from the kind of critical realism applauded by the leftist critics, betraying the director's pursuit of a more utopian and poetic quality. Flashbacks of Lingling and Zhang's country life are the most telling scenes of this kind, especially the one in which they pick up water chestnuts on a lake covered with lotus blossoms. The mise en scène delivers an outlandish beauty of the rural life, which Sun Yu's critics deemed unreal and inappropriate for a proletarian aesthetics. Until recently, many of Sun Yu's early works such as *Daybreak*, *Wild Flowers* (1930), and *the Big Road* (1934) were still defined by film history texts in China as defective leftist experimentations and were criticised for their idealistic treatments.[1] However, it was indeed Sun's insistence on poetic representations that made these films one of a kind.

In *Daybreak*, we can also perceive the amount of 'authorial' influence on the film text a rising female star like Li Lili was able to exert in the 1930s, by mediating her healthy, modern star persona into the tragic heroine in the story. Li started her performing career in her early teens, when she played a sidekick part in her father's film and then entered the 'Bright Moonlight Song and Dance Troupe' established by Li Mingwei. When she cooperated with Sun Yu and became one of the new generation of film stars along with Wang Renmei and Jin Yan in the early 1930s, her previous experiences of singing and dancing soon helped shape her star persona into of a new type of 'modern girl' – who is at once young, energetic, healthy, and sporty. In a sense, *Daybreak*, *Queen of Sport* (1934), *Blood of the Passion on the Volcano* (1932), and *the Big Road* can be said to be the star vehicles Sun created for her. At that time, Li and others alike, 'despite their on-screen images as oppressed peasants or workers, were marketed for their Hollywood-style physiques and athleticism' (Zhang 2005: 279–80). Off screen, in all kinds of fanzines, newspapers and other media, Li was a spokesperson for toothpaste, swimming suits, and healthy life. She revealed her daily life to the readers in an issue of *Film Life* (1935, No.6): 'every Wednesday and Saturday I practice the dancing routines I am unfamiliar with. Tuesday and Friday I practice singing; Thursday, I plan to watch a film; Monday, I was done with some private teaching already … then I would have time to go for a hike outside the city on Sunday with some friends'. Such an image of exuberantly optimistic and comedic quality cannot be removed from her on-screen characters, even in a sad story like *Daybreak*. There are always some shots of her wearing 'hot pants' or 'mini skirts', moving her trademark legs in her films. Close-ups of her shining teeth, bright smile, curvy lower body, short wavy hair, and muscular legs construct her image as a girl who would 'go for it aggressively', which transcends the limit of the particular diegesis of one film and travels intertextually. Attractive as this type of 'new women' was to the audiences of the 1930s, it soon faded out of Chinese cinema. For various reasons, Sun Yu and Li Lili stopped making films soon after the People's Republic of China was established. Li turned to teaching at Beijing Film Academy in 1953, while Sun's ambitious project *The Life of Wu Xun* (1950) unfortunately became the first target of a large-scale governmental interference into the arena of film, indeed, culture in general.

Note

1. For an example of such recent critique of *Daybreak*, see Li and Hu, 1996: 332–3.

Further reading

Miriam B. Hansen, 'Fallen Women, Rising Stars, New Horizons: Shanghai Silent Film as

Vernacular Modernism', *Film Quarterly*, Vol. 54, No. 1, 2000, pp. 10–22.
Sean Macdonald, 'Li Lili: Acting a Lively Jianmei Type', in Mary Farquhar and Yingjin Zhang (eds), *Chinese Film Stars*, London and New York, Routledge, 2010, pp. 50–66.
Laikwan Pang, *Building a New China in Cinema: the Chinese Left-wing Cinema Movement 1932–1937*, Lanham, Rowman & Littlefield, 2002.
Suyuan Li and Jubin Hu, *History of Chinese Silent Film*, Beijing, China Film Press, 1996.
Zhen Zhang, 'Fighting over the Modern Girl: Hard and Soft Films', in *An Amorous History of the Silver Screen: Shanghai Cinema, 1896–1937*, Chicago: the University of Chicago Press, 2005.

Dan Gao

Tilaï (1990)

[Country: Burkina Faso. Production Company: Les Films de L'Avenir. Director: Idrissa Ouedraogo. Screenwriter: Idrissa Ouedraogo. Producers: Béatrice Korc, Idrissa Ouedraogo. Cinematographers: Jean Monsigny, Pierre Laurent Chenieux. Music: Abdullah Ibrahim. Editor: Luc Barnier. Cast: Rasmane Ouedraogo (Saga), Ina Cissé (Nogma), Roukietou Barry (Kuilga), Assane Ouedraogo (Kougri), Sibidou Sidibe (Poko), Moumouni Ouedraogo (Tenga), Mariam Barry (Bore), Seydou Ouedraogo (Nomenaba), Mariam Ouedraogo (Koudpoko).]

Synopsis: In *Tilaï*, Saga returns to his village after a protracted absence, to learn from his brother, Kougri, that their father, Nomenaba, has taken Saga's betrothed, Nogma, as his wife, making her their stepmother. Indignant, Saga settles in a hut on the outskirts but begins trysts with Nogma, with the connivance of the latter's feisty, prepubescent, sister, Kuilga. The lovers' relationship is discovered and deemed a crime, adultery, incest and, crucially, violation of *tilaï* (the law), which must be redressed by Saga's execution. Nogma's father, Tenga, commits suicide to redeem the family honour just as Nogma's mother, Poko, disowns her. When the community draws straws to assign an executioner, it fatefully falls on Kougri. Tormented, Kougri fakes Saga's death, and aids his escape on condition that he never returns. Later, Kougri confides in their mother, Koudpoko, and Nogma. Saga finds refuge in his Aunt Bore's distant village, and is joined by Nogma. Nogma becomes pregnant, but with news that Koudpoko is seriously ill, Saga dashes off to his natal home only to meet her funeral procession, where he is momentarily mistaken for a ghost. Banished by Nomenaba for failing to execute Saga, Kougri grabs his brother's gun and shoots him dead. As the film ends, Kougri walks off in silence, into the distance, past Nogma and Bore still on Saga's trail.

Tilaï was nominated for the Palme d'Or at the Cannes film festival in 1990, but won the Grand Jury Prize; the following year, at FESPACO, African cinema's premiere film festival, it snagged the coveted top prize, Etalon de Yennega. Notwithstanding critical acclaim in international cinema circuits, the film has often been located within the depreciatory ambits of 'Calabash cinema', a reductive system of representation in which a timeless, ornamental Africa, imbued with exoticism and spectacle, indulges Western ethnographic fantasies and desires. As will be shown, however, the film's slow pace, episodic narrative dynamics and minimalist aesthetics belie its narrative complexity and, remarkably, invite the spectator to contemplate the interplay between surface and depth, as nuances of action, character and setting are used to explore social paradoxes. Arguably, the film's ostensible simplicity is part of a larger project through which Ouedraogo contends that the Africans' appropriation of cinema as a tool for social critique necessarily invites eclectic aesthetic practices rather than mere thematic diversity or, for that matter, uniformity.

The film's understated aesthetic brings to the fore how editing is used to manipulate narrative space. Using long shots, deep focus, wide angles, on-location shooting, scant dialogue, silence, ellipses, evocative musical scores, nonprofessional cast, rudimentary costumes, and primarily natural lighting, Ouedraogo unfolds the narrative rather unhurriedly in ways that suggest an observational film style. Whereas the film, especially its sweeping, quasi-mythical vista, may suggest a folkloric reverie, Ouedraogo is not concerned with novelty, enchantment, the ephemeral or sentimental. Through emphasis on subtleties, the film's unpretentious aesthetics, ordinary characters, narrative rhythm and structure create points of identification that advocate sensitivity to its cultural world, at least, in ways that do not engender voyeurism and fetishism. Here, style goes beyond mere concern with aesthetics, mood, atmosphere and contributes immensely to the social, gender and cultural dynamics of the narrative. In linking style firmly to the circulation of meanings, issues of self-definition and expression, the conceptual vision that emerges from this visual framework and narrative elements is earnest. Arguably, Ouedraogo's spare direction mimics the austere setting and, crucially, reconfigures it as a cultural crucible.

Given the centrality of culture and 'tradition' in African nationalist discourses, especially maintaining its distinctiveness and sacrosanctness, a key element of the film, remarkably, is how unquestioning allegiance to 'tradition' can hinder prospects of nascent subjectivities. Disclosing, in an interview, that aspects of 'tradition' which anchor the drama and dilemmas were his own inventions,[1] Ouedraogo's imaginative leaps position the ostensible immutability of 'tradition', in a reflexive manner, with an instance of its invention and representation. Neither cynical nor satirical, Ouedraogo's is a cautionary, even radical tale about social and communal catastrophes as well as the enduring essence often imputed to 'tradition'. Significantly, 'tradition', usually valorised, is here tainted with violence and tragedy. Hence, rather than romanticise 'tradition', say, by assigning it a glib reassuring function, Ouedraogo explores its principles, values, discrepancies, with particular respect to love, family and honour.

At its simplest, *Tilaï* is a narrative about love and loyalties. However, it is not a romantic fantasy: neither is Saga a folkloric Prince Charming nor do the lovers live happily ever after. Even after finding refuge in Aunt Bore's village, the lovers still occupy a charged space between autonomy and ostracism. Through Saga, insofar as he is opposed to two recalcitrant patriarchal figures, Nomenaba and Tenga, Ouedraogo proposes a progressive notion of masculinity. Similarly, Nogma is neither naive nor passive. Assertive and strong-willed, she contravenes 'traditional' ideals or stereotypes, particularly as she enters the relationship on her own terms and volition. So, at a more profound level, it is a humanist narrative that dramatises an epoch and its predicaments. Here, Ouedraogo invests 'tradition', its established orders and social relations, with nuances, ambiguities, tensions and, crucially, capacities for transformation. Seen this way, Saga's relationship with Nogma, configured and inextricably linked to the pursuit of their own destinies, becomes a mode of resistance. Notably, Ouedraogo eschews a 'return to order' in the form of a reassertion of patriarchal power and privilege or a trite reintegration of the couple into the folds of family and community. This not only implicates certain social and cultural systems; importantly, it underscores the need for their critical reappraisal.

Remarkably, it is through the lure of 'tradition' and allure of honour that the film's figures of patriarchal power and repression, Nomenaba and Tenga, are cast and, eventually, undone. Tenga's suicide is significant, especially as through it, the charm or lure of 'honour' is assigned a problematic link to patriarchy. At issue here is the role of 'tradition' in the construction of gender identities and reinforcement of patriarchal codes. In this, particularly as 'honour' rests on the permissible use of suicide as a redemptive gesture, are conflicting issues of morality and culpability as well as 'tradition' and community. This ambiguity accentuates the film's critical exploration of the relationship between self, society and gendered codes of conduct that entrap or leave little room for negotiation. So, while he sacrifices self for 'honour' and 'duty', he does not come across as heroic; more so, Tenga's quest for 'honour' rests on the interplay between problematic gender dynamics, hubris and a desire for vindication. As such, Ouedraogo calls for closer examination of the defining elements of 'honour' and dangers of reading such as uncomplicated.

Similarly, Nomenaba's claim on Nogma, however 'lawful' under the culture, may not be so dutiful, insofar as it is bound up with issues of power, authority, lust, anxiety about emasculation, and reassertion of his waning or questionable virility. Also, with Nomenaba, we see how patriarchal privilege implicates individual desires and, crucially, social relations *engendered* by the 'law'. Notably, here 'tradition', its vaunted timelessness, constitutive elements, paradoxes and the patterns of social relations it elicits, leads to an impasse. In juxtaposing 'tradition' with crisis, through drawing attention to the problematic mythic codes on which it rests, Ouedraogo is not calling for a descent into anarchy. Given the narrative's ruminative verve and reformist spirit, he is suggesting, particularly in making the 'law' a locus of contestations, that cultures and societies evolve through negotiations not, literally and figuratively, through the repression of dissent.

Positioned at the intersections of family, passions, power and culture, the film is immersed deeply in the community's gender politics, and illuminates the dynamics through which male anxieties, privileges, and social expectations work to subjugate women. Here, in contesting patriarchal prescriptions of subservience and domesticity, the women, with the exception of Poko, pose a collective threat to the structures of patriarchal authority. In showing African women of different generations in sororal solidarity, Ouedraogo consolidates forms of oppositional consciousness, which foreground their resilience and ongoing interrogations of the social order. Together they enact shifts from 'tradition' as the staple and stable site for self-definition to those of contestations and negotiations. Hence, their relation to the film's narrative core, particularly the quest for autonomy, signals the search for alternatives to problematic cultural tenets.

Set in opposition to the patriarchs, Koudpoko's self-effacing demeanour, as confidante and dutiful mother, belies her involvement in the lovers' quest. Very maternal and independently minded, she belies the frail matriarchal stereotype and is shown, for instance, offering discerning advice and encouragement to her beleaguered offsprings, and feeding a constrained Nogma. The difficult social terrain Koudpoko negotiates, as a figure of transformation, balancing her own needs, family obligations and cultural expectations, speaks to the relationship between patriarchy and women's circumscriptions. Notably, her death is not an ideological subterfuge to contain female agency, or reassert patriarchy; in concert with Saga's tragic return, it invites contemplation of maternal and devotional bonds, and is strategic to the various questions the film raises around 'the law' and 'honour'. So, while the film's setting may have drawn apprehensions, its narrative trajectories are progressive and function, largely, to undo the matrix of elements that limit women's agency.

Opposed to Tenga and Nomenanba, Saga projects a tempered notion of masculinity. Sober, sensitive and pragmatic, he not only rejects offers for an alternate bride, as a way out of the impasse; he forgives Nogma's infidelity with a stranger, thereby abdicating the 'virtuous woman' ideal. Taken together, both actions urge the reappraisal of patriarchal codes. Set against prohibitions of incest, adultery, the law and patriarchal power, their relationship constitutes much of the dramatic tension, especially as it was adjudged to transgress moral and familial orders. While ruptures around the nuclear family and codes of kinship are central to the narrative, and a cursory reading of Saga's affinity for Nogma may elicit vestiges of an Oedipal relationship, not far off the mark is the Phaedra Complex, insofar as Saga, according to the 'law', is Nogma's stepson. Even then, Ouedraogo is careful not to make Nogma a mere object of desire or contention between father and son.

African filmmakers had, generally, favoured a cinema of functional value, and, until lately, been antipathetic or dismissive of romance narratives, which were seen as trivial or escapist fantasies.

With *Tilaï*, however, the trials-and-tribulations framework of love stories is lodged in the crisis of 'tradition' and, by extension, patriarchy, thereby reaffirming the primacy of critical engagement with social issues in African cinema. In the film, 'the law' does not provide security but conundrums, nor is 'tradition', often idealised as a repository of communal values, transcendent identities and defining qualities, congruent with stability. Instead, 'law' and 'tradition' are charged with disintegrative elements. Appropriately, Ouedraogo's quest for a dynamic cultural space is anchored in articulating alternatives and representing a society on the verge of transition. The narrative's lack of a cathartic closure, arguably, is a warning sign and needful starting point for reflection. So, while it may be difficult, given the ending, to predict what further directions the shift in 'tradition' may take, the film's critical trajectories are significant in ways that advocate social emancipation.

Note

1. Leahy, James. *Senses of Cinema*, Issue 28, October 2003; 14 June 2013. www. sensesofcinema.com/ 2003/cteq/tilai).

Further reading

Roy Armes, *African Filmmaking: North and South of the Sahara*, Bloomington, IN, Indiana University Press, 2006.

Olivier Barlet, *African Cinemas: Decolonizing the Gaze*, London, Zed Books, 2000.

Manthia Diawara, *African Cinema: Politics & Culture*, Bloomington, IN, Indiana University Press, 1992.

David Murphy and Patrick Williams, *Postcolonial African Cinema: Ten Directors*, Manchester and New York, Manchester University Press, 2007.

Alexie Tcheuyap, *Postnationalist Cinemas*, Manchester and New York, Manchester University Press, 2011.

N. Frank Ukadike, *Black African Cinema*, Berkeley, CA, University of California Press, 1994.

Jude G. Akudinobi

Todo sobre mi madre/All About My Mother (1999)

[Country: Spain, France. Production Company: El Deseo, Renn Productions, and France 2 Cinéma. Director: Pedro Almodóvar. Producer: Augustin Almodóvar. Screenwriter: Pedro Almodóvar. Cinematographer: Alfonso Beato. Music: Alberto Iglesias. Editor: Jose Salcedo. Cast: Cecilia Roth (Manuela), Marisa Paredes (Huma Rojo), Antonia San Juan (Agrado), Penélope Cruz (Hermana Rosa).]

Synopsis: Manuela, a single mother living in Madrid sees her only son, Esteban, die in a car crash as he runs to request an autograph from Huma, a theatre actress he idolises. In her grief, Manuela travels to Barcelona to find Esteban's father, a transvestite named Lola who does not know that they had a child. In Barcelona, Manuela is reunited with her friend, Agrado, and meets a young nun, Rosa, who is pregnant with Lola's child. Manuela gets a job as an assistant to Huma, the actress her son admired. When Rosa discovers she is HIV positive Manuela gives up her job to nurse her and on Rosa's death adopts her son.

At Rosa's funeral Manuela meets Lola and introduces him to his second son, also named Esteban. Despite contracting HIV at birth Esteban Jr. is free from the virus at the end of the film.

All About My Mother is an Almodóvar film. This is not simply a director's credit indicating a technical role but signifies; 'ways of being, ways of looking and certain types of movies' (Arroyo 2011: 7). Paul Julian Smith (2000: 2) has argued that to understand this particular sensibility and style it is vital to recognise the three fundamental issues central to Almodóvar's work; 'gender, nationality and homosexuality' to which Arroyo has added cinema itself. These ways of being are explored through a series of paradoxes and conflicts within the construction of visual style, characterisation, genre and plot. The paradox as a concept and motif becomes central to understanding the Almodóvar world view. This is a world where the mise en scène and narrative foregrounds artifice but the characterisation rests on emotional authenticity and a real relationship with the spectator. This paradoxical framework of Almodóvar's films has led to a range of positive and negative critical responses. Epps (2009: 1) summarises this characteristic in considering the reception of Almodóvar's films in academic, critical and popular contexts, where they have been described as both 'serious and superficial, political and apolitical, moral and immoral, feminist and misogynist, experimental and sentimental, universal and provincial.' The disagreement and conflicting value judgements in response to Almodóvar's work may in part be provoked by the seeming ambiguity of the postmodern aesthetic. In an Almodóvar film though this aesthetic functions to subvert traditional representations of ways of being and behaving, seen most explicitly in representations of gender, sexuality and the family. It is this which provokes the controversy often attached to Almodóvar's films where the audience is frequently expected to align with characters who are amoral and their behaviour shocking.

All About My Mother is the epitome of an Almodóvar film. It is a genre film and an auteur, art-house film. It is a film about authenticity and artifice, told through wild and exaggerated stories about unbelievable people which is entirely convincing. The success of the film relies on the bonds of identification between spectator and character, producing a strong emotional response. The film is typical of Almodóvar's style in its use of melodrama, the references to cinema history, the theatre and popular culture and in its exploration of themes of performance linked to gender identity.

Melodrama is the ideal form for exploring the themes which concern Almodóvar. Traditionally the form has been referred to pejoratively in comparison with drama; in part due to its close association with female stars and female audiences. The form of melodrama is itself paradoxical. Its use of extreme events and coincidences renders it unbelievable at one level but it can only function successfully by creating a powerful emotional response in the audience; something which might be assumed to be impossible due to the distancing effect of the incredible events. The artifice – but affective – style of the melodramatic plot foregrounds the constructed nature of narrative. This provides a formal reflection for Almodóvar's worldview; that the most authentic people are the people who construct their own lives and identities, rather than accepting their 'natural' and inevitable place in life. The only relatively unsympathetic characters in the film, Nina (an actress Huma is in love with) and Rosa's mother, are implicitly condemned for their lack of authenticity. Nina rejects acting and her relationship with Huma to return to the suburbs, marry and have a child; her traditional choices are signalled as a form of cowardice and subterfuge in comparison to the characters that are on the margins of society. Rosa's mother is ashamed by her daughter's behaviour, letting Manuela replace her in her role as mother. In an explicit judgement on her lack of authenticity, Rosa's mother works as a forger, creating copies of paintings by famous artists.

All About My Mother is an example of reflexive cinema in that it draws the audience's attention to its status as a work of art, as a construction with a particular point of view – rather than a form of realism. This reflexivity is apparent in the emphasis on the theatre with its inherent qualities of staging and acting. The theatrical aesthetic is central to the mise en scène and mise en shot and has become a recognizable Almodóvar signature in his mature films. The predominant style is the use of a medium two-shot with the actors placed next to each other on the horizontal axis, like actors on a stage. The composition is balanced, nearly symmetrical to the extent that a line could be drawn down the middle of the screen, creating a mirror image of the two sides. The style is characterised by a narrow plane of depth; flat blocks of colour provide a backdrop for the action. The compositional symmetry and simplicity of the shots create meaning in itself; the pure focus on people is typical of Almodóvar's humanist concerns, but also through contrast when broken. Manuela and her son Esteban are repeatedly framed together at the beginning of the film. Sitting on the sofa together watching *All About Eve*, the framing is relatively tight in medium close-up creating even greater emphasis on their togetherness. Behind them the wall and framed prints creates a flat backdrop emphasised by the use of colour in the shot; Esteban and Manuela are dressed in blue and orange, the same colour as their surroundings. The camera is static, the scene captured in a long take, reminiscent of early tableau cinema. On the night of Esteban's death, they are framed in a similar way as part of the theatre audience, side by side. After his death Manuela goes to the same performance in Barcelona (an example of repetition and return which becomes a theme of the film) once again she is on the left of the frame; the emptiness of the space next to her symbolises her grief.

The reflexive nature of the film is evident in the many different examples of storytelling in the film; Estoban is writing a book titled 'All About My Mother', it isn't clear if this is a journal, a biography of his mother or the screenplay of the film we're about to watch. The title is a play on the film title he and Manuela have just watched, *All About Eve*, a Hollywood film about the obsession of a fan for a famous actress. The plot line of that film is partially repeated in the plot of *All About My Mother*, a homage which serves to draw attention to film as a construction. Estoban's notebook is also presented in an unconventional shot – where the camera seems to cross over to the 'wrong' side of the screen creating a point of view shot for the spectator from inside his writing, perhaps foregrounding Almodóvar's presence as the author of all these different narratives.

It is soon apparent that all the characters in the film are performers in different ways – some more explicitly than others. Manuela at first appears to be a conventional character fulfilling typical gender expectations; she is a nurse, has a loving relationship with her son and is introduced in a traditional, domestic environment – preparing a family dinner. As the film progresses Manuela is also shown to be a performer of roles. As the head nurse of an organ transplant unit she acts in a training film. This is a simulation to help doctors discuss organ donation with the bereaved relative, Manuela plays the role of the wife who cannot accept that her husband is dead, a very similar situation to the one she later plays for 'real'. (The scenes in the transplant unit are also familiar from very similar scenes in Almodóvar's previous film, *The Flower of my Secret*.) She tells Esteban about her days as a student actor when she played Stella in *A Streetcar Named Desire* ('the play marked my life', she says), the narrative and themes of the play echoing the developments in *All About My Mother*. Manuela also understudies for Nina and once again plays Stella – a character who is pregnant. This emphasis on the different roles Manuela plays is a way of questioning the role which society often claims is the most natural for a woman, that of mother. At the end of the film when Manuela is a mother again she is the non-biological mother of a child whose parents are a nun and a transsexual. Like many of the characters in the film, the role she has chosen for herself is the most authentic one.

In *All About My Mother* this idea of authenticity through selection finds its personification in Agrado, Manuela's friend who was born biologically male but has constructed a new identity, one which refuses easy biological distinctions. Agrado outlines the changes and modifications made to her body in a scene which brings together many signature Almodóvar techniques at the level of plot, visual style and cultural references. One night at the theatre when Huma's play has to be cancelled, Agrado takes to the stage to provide an 'alternative production'. Rather than seeing manipulation and construction in the creation of identity as false, Agrado explains that 'you are more authentic the more you resemble what you've dreamed you are'. This concept is illustrated through the monologue in which Agrado lists her operations and cost for each procedure done; cheeks, hair, breasts, etc.

During the monologue Agrado states, 'I'm very authentic, all made to measure' and earlier explains to Manuela that 'All I have that's real are my feelings – and the silicone'. The meaning of Agrado's persona is also produced through the mise en scène and framing of the sequence. Agrado stands alone on the theatre stage in front of the grand, velvet curtain (itself a motif repeated in Almodóvar's films, it appears as the backdrop to the credit sequence in *Talk to Her*) to perform the story of her life, a narrative which Agrado has constructed with great ingenuity and wit. Theatre – and performance – plays a central role in *All About my Mother*, it is a place where people can be transformed into their real selves.

These performances are also part of the motif of repetition which has become recognisable within and across his films. The most explicit exploration of this theme is found in the idea that 'life imitates art imitates life'. For Epps (2009) the theme of repetition is linked to the structuring authorial theme of return; *All About my Mother* is about the need to return to find resolution and the possibility of renewal. Manuela's return to Barcelona is represented as an emotionally draining, cathartic experience through a visual metaphor for rebirth as Manuela travels through the train tunnel and into the lights of Barcelona. This experience is further emphasised by the musical soundtrack which soars over the swooping shots of Barcelona at night. To 'return' has a political resonance in a country which had agreed to the 'pact of forgetting' in the aftermath of Franco's dictatorship (symbolised perhaps by the character of Rosa's father suffering from dementia and memory loss) but where in 2006 'The Law of Historical Memory' was passed which recognised the need to return psychologically and literally (those who were exiles under Franco were given 'the right to return') to the era of dictatorship. In returning to Barcelona, Manuela fulfils Esteban's wish to know all about his father, she acknowledges the secrets of the past and in doing so recreates her own life.

Further reading

Jose Arroyo, 'Pedro Almodóvar', in Yvonne Tasker (ed.), *Fifty Contemporary Film Directors*, 2nd edn., London and New York, Routledge, 2011, pp. 6–17.

Bradley S. Epps, 'Approaching Almodóvar: Thirty Years of Revolution', in Bradley S. Epps (eds), *All About Almodóvar: A Passion for Cinema*, Minneapolis, MN, University of Minnesota Press, 2009, pp. 1–34.

Paul Julian Smith, *Desire Unlimited: the Cinema of Pedro Almodóvar*, London, Verso, 2000.

Sarah Casey Benyahia

Tokyo monogatari/Tokyo Story (1953)

[Country: Japan. Production Company: Shochiku Eiga. Director: Ozu Yasujiro. Screenwriters: Noda Kogo and Ozu Yasujiro. Cinematographer: Atsuta Yuhara. Cast: Hara Setsuko (Noriko), Ryu Chishu (Shukichi), Higashiyama Chieko (Tomi).]

Synopsis: The elderly Shukichi and Tomi Hiroyama leave their youngest daughter Kyoko in Onomichi to visit their other grown-up children in Tokyo. Mild disappointment dogs the whole enterprise as their presence is clearly considered burdensome. Only their widowed daughter-in-law Noriko shows genuine warmth and welcome. Returning home, Tomi falls ill and dies. The family expresses regret but only Noriko and Kyoko show more than superficial duty. Shukichi urges Noriko to remarry and move on while he contemplates his own lonely future.

Tokyo Story's plot is simple. However, 'explaining' *Tokyo Story* is like trying to have the last word on *Citizen Kane*. Its director, Ozu Yasujiro has been considered both modernist and traditionalist; his work Zen-like while wryly urbane; his themes specific to their context, yet universal. Ozu's films were not seen outside of Japan until after his death in 1963 because domestic critics considered that, 'the West couldn't possibly appreciate anything so "truly Japanese"' (Mars-Jones, 2011: 5).

Though universal acclaim met their international release, what strikes the first-time viewer is the unfamiliarity of Ozu's technique. Its antithesis to Hollywood style prompted David Bordwell to outline a formalist analysis that links Ozu's stylistic 'self-imposed constraints' to the rigid codes of Japanese poetic tradition (1988: 144).

Additionally, Western analysis of Ozu's work is dominated by identification of his apparent Zen aesthetic, characterised in 1972 by Marvin Zeman as 'the immediate and therefore inexpressible individual experience whose aim is inner enlightenment' (1976: 17) – essentially a mastery of technique presented as simplicity, harmonising form and content without irrelevant details. This approach describes *Tokyo Story* well, but so does Mark Cousins' description of Ozu's films as 'classical' as the term is applied to European art (2004: 129); though different in culture, the appreciative outcome is the same: form and subject are harmoniously balanced. Thus, we could conclude that Ozu's mature films are simultaneously radical in their deviation from (relatively recently established) cinematic tradition, while conservative in general aesthetic.

Seasonal moods are said to be central Zen tenets. Most closely cited in reference to Ozu is 'mono-no-aware', a melancholic, autumnal awareness of impermanence. His films are characteristically concerned with stillness and contemplation and his composition compares to classical Japanese art. Conversely, this stillness has led some critics to note similarities with European near contemporaries such as Michelangelo Antonioni (Desser 1997: 3). The stylistic similarities may be superficial but as far as cinematic aesthetics go, to label Ozu as uniquely Japanese is arguably reductive.

Similarly, while his titles have an air of haiku (e.g. *An Autumn Afternoon*, *Early Summer*, *Equinox Flower*), the Japanese critic Hasumi Shigehiko questions the Orientalist stereotyping, noting that the seasonal titles divert attention from the characteristic weather in the Ozu film: a dry heat more reminiscent of Californian Hollywood than subtropical Japan (in Desser 1997: 119). A typical Ozu scene usually disrupts character stillness with the persistent wafting of fans.

David Desser convincingly argues that *Tokyo Story* is 'paradoxically, both insular and immensely universal. Is it about the breakup of the traditional Japanese family in the light of post-war changes ...? Or is it about the inevitabilities of life: children ... leaving their ageing parents behind?' (ibid: 4). Uniqueness of style and universality of theme both suggest why Ozu's films and *Tokyo Story* in particular hold such international acclaim and affection.

Central to the emotional weight of *Tokyo Story* are the performances of Ryu Chishu and Hara Setsuko as Shukichi and Noriko respectively. Ryu recalled endless retakes as Ozu harmonised even the smallest movement by actors within his compositions but it is these two performers upon whom Ozu's calm cinematic rhythms depend for the full dramatic effect of both *Tokyo Story* and Ozu's other masterpiece, *Late Spring* (Zeman 1976: 26).

For example, Ryu utilises a non-verbal purring noise ('hmmm') to express a huge array of complex emotion and meaning. Whilst fanning the ailing Tomi, his calm assurance that she will soon recover is belied by a look of awful panic that briefly clouds his face. Later, he conveys the full devastation of Shukichi's loss when told Tomi will be dead by sunrise through the barest of physical movement.

Matching the complexity of Ryu's minimalistic purr is the much-discussed Hara smile. This seems to convey everything from unguarded joy to a polite veneer masking devastation, disgust or fury. When Noriko brings her parents-in-law home, she pops to her neighbour to borrow sake. She returns to find the Hirayamas admiring a photograph of her dead husband. Her smile rises in polite response but realisation that she also needs to borrow cups gives her reason to momentarily excuse herself. Their backs turned, the smile lightly crumples. It is the gentlest of scenes in this unwaveringly gentle film that transcends context, culture, formalist debate and ideology. When Noriko receives news of Tomi's critical illness over the phone, at last she has a moment alone to let the public face drop. Her reply to Kyoko's blunt, 'Isn't life disappointing' is a beaming, Beckettian 'yes it is'. In this, the film's most famous exchange, every possible emotional interpretation can be found – the crystallisation of Ozu's cinema in two lines of dialogue.

A particularly noted Ozu technique is the 'pillow shot'; not a term used by Ozu himself, but a way of defining his singular method of moving from scene to scene. Breaking with conventional dissolves or establishing shots, Ozu generally offers a cluster of exterior views using straight cuts between key scenes. Debate clusters around whether these provide the same function as a theatrical curtain, as a brief respite from the 'action' of scenes or an embodiment of Zen aesthetics. Interpretation can run wild but it is worth noting that in *Tokyo Story* these shots often suggest thematic links to the characters' living circumstances and, by extension, personalities. Onomichi (and thus the Hiroyama elders) is signified by gently chugging tugboats, temples and open landscapes.

Conversely, Ozu largely ignores any Tokyo landmarks except for a few cursory tourist shots on the Hiroyama's bus ride, preferring images of smoke-spurting chimneys – suggestive of their children's urban lives and personalities. Noriko lives in the same city but Ozu signifies her key scenes with images of washing (purity or duty, perhaps). These sequences are generally considered to operate outside of the narrative, which is what differentiates them from straightforward establishing shots, but occasionally over-interpretation misses the point when Ozu actually *is* giving us an establishing shot. The Hiroyamas' unanticipated stopover at Osaka is signified by Osaka Castle, for example.

Tokyo Story is typical of Ozu's narrative structure, which deliberately omits the events one would anticipate as the most dramatic. Thus, the most seemingly substantial scene occurs off screen: the collapse and illness of Tomi. Counter-intuitively, we are instead shown Keizo, a son mentioned but until here unseen, discussing the incident with a work colleague. This approach asks the audience to fill in the gaps, trusting the spectator to do some dramatic work and respect the characters' dignity. It also maintains the consistently moderate pace of the film and mirrors the realities of our participation in the action. As in life, we hear of crucial events related second-hand.

Instead, Ozu's scenes often commence with an empty space into which characters enter. He then either refrains from cutting for several seconds after characters exit or lingers on them after conversation has ended. Thus, the silences and empty moments become the lyrical points of signified meaning far more than the deliberately understated dialogue.

Typically, interiors are largely shot from an unusually low camera height of two feet, just below head-height when the characters adopt the traditional kneeling position for socialising. More extraordinary is Ozu's unique approach to cinematic space. Almost all filmmakers obey the 180° rule, where an invisible line is never crossed for fear of breaking the directional continuity. Ozu operates within a 360° space, with the result that characters suddenly appear to be facing screen left when in the previous shot they had faced screen right. An example of this can be seen when Keizu approaches his office late in the film. He is shot outside entering a door screen right but the following shot shows him enter the room also from screen right, not the customary left. He appears to have turned back on himself. This would normally be considered cinematically 'wrong'.

While many viewers may not notice this oddity at all, what is unmistakable is the framing of dialogue. Ozu positions the spectator literally at alternate perspectives in a conversation so actors often speak facing the camera. This again can be unsettling at first but perhaps allows an unusual intimacy with the characters. Conversely, Ozu never milks emotion through an overemphasising close-up, instead typically holding fast to the medium or even long shot. His camera may loiter for longer than comfortable but never 'cheats' by intruding on heightened emotion, evoking perhaps a sense of polite awkwardness.

While the overall theme is certainly accessible, some context does prove useful in engaging with *Tokyo Story*. As with all of Ozu's mature films, it is an example of the shomin-geki genre. This typically focuses on the lives of the contemporary Japanese middle class, though logically its characters (most clearly the war-widow Noriko) are still reeling from post-war defeat, devastation and humiliation. 1953 saw the end of a period of allied occupation and cinema censorship. Thus, the inter-generation fissure between the traditions of the elders and the Westernised attitudes of the younger generation takes on a far more dynamic resonance than might at first appear, notable for instance, when Shukichi's friend Hattori complains about his young lodger's attitude and addiction to pinball. Subsequently, while out drinking, an off-screen, very Western big band tune diegetically intrudes on the elders' reflections on their past.

In his critical study *Noriko Smiling*, Adam Mars-Jones takes Ozu critics to task for 'extreme readings': 'the history of his films' reception in the West has been a tug-of-war between the Zen transcendentals, with Paul Schrader at their head, and neo-formalists like (Kristin) Thompson and her husband David Bordwell. For both camps the films are apolitical, indifferent to history except as it impinges on family relations' (2011: 34). Mars-Jones instead considers the context of a nation adjusting to the aftermath of being the losing side of a devastating war and 'the recent replacement of a theocratic militarism by a democracy that no-one had voted for' (2011: 141) as vital in reading Ozu.

However approached, *Tokyo Story* boasts dozens of beautiful and striking moments. Space allows three examples. The heads of the passengers gently bobbing about in comical unison during the Hiroyama's bus tour is a droll sight gag straight out of a Harold Lloyd film. In contrast, as the couple prepare to leave Tokyo, gently joking that they are 'homeless', Ozu allows his camera to perform its rarest of functions in his films: it moves. A brief tracking shot reveals them sat isolated on the grass and ends with a second, following them up the road. Their remoteness from their disappointing family and the loss this implies is severe.

Lastly, while fondly watching her grandchild, Tomi shifts from doting to sudden awareness of her mortality. The boy is oblivious to this moment of terrified insight and blithely picks flowers. There are many scenes in this beautiful film that suggest not so much a Zen-like wisdom nor an approach to cinema art that is predominantly Japanese or formalistically different. It is universal and in touch with human frailty. There is more, of course. There is no last word on *Tokyo Story*.

Further reading

David Bordwell, *Ozu and the Poetics of Cinema*, Princeton, Princeton University Press, 1988.

Mark Cousins, *The Story of Film*, London, Pavillion, 2004.

David Desser, (ed.), *Introduction to Ozu's Tokyo Story*, Cambridge, Cambridge University Press, 1997.

Adam Mars-Jones, *Noriko Smiling*, London, Notting Hill Editions, 2011.

Marvin Zeman, 'The Zen Artistry of Yasujiro Ozu', in John Gillet and David Wilson (eds), *Ozu*, London, BFI, 1976.

Phil Lloyd

Touki-Bouki/The Journey of the Hyena (1973)

[Country: Senegal. Production Company: Cinegrit and Studio Kankourama. Director, Producer, Screenwriter: Djibril Diop Mambéty. Cinematographer: Georges Bracher. Art director: Aziz Diop Mambéty. Editor: Siro Asteni. Cast: Mareme Niang (Anta), Magaye Niang (Mory), Ousseynou Diop (Charlie), Aminata Fall (Oumi).]

Synopsis: Mory and Anta are young lovers who dream of escaping from the slums of Dakar,

Senegal to the city of their dreams, Paris, capital of the former colonial power. Anta attempts to study at university, Mory rides around town on his motorbike decorated with zebu horns on the handlebar and an elaborate Dogon fetish as a backrest. They choose to wear ragged, filthy clothes, Anta dressed as a youth with her hair cropped short, while their contemporaries sport the latest 1970s striped flares and cool shades. Through a series of bizarre incidents and adventures they contrive to steal money, clothes and a chauffeured car. Anta leaves for France, but Mory is unable to board ship, left behind to a dubious fate in Dakar.

Djibril Diop Mambéty (1945–1998) was born to a Wolof family in Colobane, a small town on the fringes of Dakar; his father was an imam – 'all these films are immersed within an Islamic context and affirm the importance of this influence in the daily lives of their characters' (Niang 2002: 120). Mambéty trained as a stage actor, but was expelled from the National Theatre, Dakar, because he chose to spend more time working in *café-théâtres* and for Italian film projects. Senegal was entering a relatively self-confident period in the late 1960s during the presidency of the poet, Léopold Senghor; the first World Festival of Black Arts convened in Dakar in 1966, launching the careers of a number of Senegalese filmmakers. At the age of 24, after experimenting as a composer and with no experience of filmmaking, Mambéty made his first short, *Contras' City* (*City of Contrasts*, 17 minutes), followed by *Badou Boy* (60 minutes), which won the Silver Tanit Award in 1970 at the Carthage Film Festival. *Touki-Bouki*, Mambéty's first full-length feature, appeared in 1973, winning the International Critics' Prize at Cannes and the Special Jury Award at the Moscow Film Festival; the budget for *Touki-Bouki* was $30,000, partly funded by the Senegalese state, but the film was, perhaps unsurprisingly, received critically in Dakar.

Mambéty made only one more feature, *Hyènes* (*Hyenas*, 1992), a continuation of *Touki-Bouki* in the sense that it showed the return of Linguère Ramatou, a woman like Anta, now 'as rich as the World Bank', to her home town in Senegal where she pursues a vendetta against the Mory figure, Draman Drameh: 'The world made me a whore: I want to make the world a brothel' (Speciale 1998: 54). Mambéty intended to complete a trilogy exploring the ravages of power and insanity with a third film, *Malaika*, which was not made. A second trilogy of short films, *Contes des Petites Gens* (*Tales of Ordinary People*), and intended as a parallel to the first group, featured poor, struggling individuals and is highly regarded, but was also incomplete at Mambéty's death from lung cancer in 1998.

Mambéty said that *Touki-Bouki* was created out of anger: 'Perhaps I could no longer stand the physiognomy of African cinema, which exasperated me, it was too superficial. Not on the ideological level, but on the level of form. It never pushed any further, nothing is ever shaken. This rage in a minor key gave birth to *Touki-Bouki*' (Speciale 1998: 52); Mambéty was reacting against the example of more established Senegalese directors such as Paulin Soumanou Vieyra, who had made the first Francophone African film, *Afrique sur Seine* in 1955, and the socialist realism of Ousmane Sembène, then the most celebrated Senegalese novelist and director, whose *Emitai* was banned in 1973 because of its anticolonialist content. The theme of escape to the promise of the good life in France was also the subject of Sembène's *La Noire de ...* (*The Black Girl*, 1966), but *Touki-Bouki* offers a radically different critique of the false dream because it is 'the first African film that wore on its sleeve a postcolonial concern with how representation works' (Oloruntoba 2008: 119).

Following this deconstructive vision, the opening sequence of *Touki-Bouki* is deceptive, in several ways, since it appears to meet audience expectations for a generic 'African film' of the early 1970s: a languorous pastoral shot, with 'traditional' flute music playing, and a large herd of zebu long-horn cattle being led towards the camera by a young boy, astride a cow. It is precisely these conventional expectations that Mambéty critiques and contradicts in the film that follows. Some viewers have also inferred that the child leading the herd is Mory himself, but this is not necessarily the case; the status of chronology, truth and reality are always at issue throughout Mambéty's film owing to the critique of representation and cinematic form that he was compelled to follow.

The second sequence shows the fate of the zebu when the animals are unceremoniously slaughtered in filthy conditions. We then see the herdboy slowly returning, now without the cattle, and the sound of a motorbike displaces the African pastoral soundtrack. In the next, frantic sequence, the bike weaves dangerously close to shops and people, in an over-the-shoulder shot, Nouvelle Vague style, taken between the zebu horns. Mory had been a cowherd, like the child in the pre-credits sequence, but his innocence was lost in the slaughterhouse and now he struggles to survive in the slum districts of Dakar, and most significant of all, in an utterly different cinematic genre.

Mory comes off his bike trying to avoid a smart red jeep full of trendy young 'political' students. They accuse Mory of distracting Anta from their meetings and political work, and appear to begin to lynch him. Scenes of Mory being paraded, Christ-like, on the back of the jeep, a rope around his throat, his face covered in dust, are intercut with images of the slaughter of a goat; this shot recurs through the following sequence. We see Anta desperately seeking Mory, a search culminating in their meeting and lovemaking on a clifftop next to the ocean – a daring scene for African cinema of the early 1970s. As their passion moves to its climax, we see metaphorical shots, of breaking waves and Anta's hand grasping the Dogon fetish that serves as a backrest on Mory's bike. This elaborate cross is a sacred symbol of fertility among the nomadic herders whom Mory has abandoned for life in the city. Chronology and causality are manipulated to an extreme degree here. The same scene returns as the penultimate image of the film: was Mory in fact killed by the students? Was Anta remembering their happiest, most intimate moment, when he first talked of escaping to France in order to make their fortune so that they could return as a Wolof prince and princess? Is all the intervening action nothing but their shared fantasy? Some commentators have even located the entire action as a dream of the young cowherd, seen only in the framing sequences of the film.

That would be too simple, and the poetry of Mambéty's genius lies in his complex manipulation of sound and image, reality and the fantastic. A viewer might think that Mambéty's use of soundtrack derives directly from the practice of a European director like Godard, running against the image-track, dropping in subtle and beautiful moments, working parodically. As a child, Mambéty crept out of his home at night to listen to Westerns and Hindu films playing in the local open-air cinema – the Westerns were his favourite – but was unable to buy a ticket: 'Maybe this is why I attach a lot of importance to sound in my films, as I heard films for a number of years before I saw them' (Givanni 2011). Mambéty, a poet and sceptical filmmaker who once said that he had never made a film, took what he needed from European cinema courtesy of the Institute Française in Dakar, but his attitude to the work of the great directors as a model for African film was highly ambivalent. As a youth, like Mory and Anta, he had stowed away on a ship to Europe (but returned immediately), and he railed against Africans who 'are pining for Europe ['malades de l'Europe'], Africans who consider that Europe is the door to Africa and that one must have gone there in order to come back home and gain respect. In some sense it is about going to Europe for a training program in civilization' (Cottenet-Hage 2004: 118). Anta and Mory's illusory notion of Paris is undermined even by the haunting theme sung by the (black) chanteuse, Joséphine Baker, '*Paris, Paris, Paris, C'est sur la terre entière le paradis*', because the phrase recurs, on a very tightly edited loop, which parodies the sentiment even as it moves the listener. 'I do not choose the music, I choose the sound. All movement is accompanied by a sense .... sound is not something foreign to adorn the film. It is intrinsic to the film; it magnifies the action' (Ukadike 1999: 4).

From the moment that Mory and Anta ride out of Aunt Oumi's village entrance, they are a 'couple on the run', joining a long, dishonourable tradition in cinema: *They Live by Night* (1949), *Pierrot le Fou* (1965), *Bonnie and Clyde* (1967), *Easy Rider* (1969) and, released in the same year as *Touki-Bouki*, *Badlands* (1973). After a series of picaresque adventures, some of which are persuasively realistic, and others 'surreal' in the strict sense of the word, fantastic if not fantasist, Anta and Mory finally manage to book passage on a liner to France. The other travellers are mostly black Senegalese young men, also hoping to find their fortune, or at least a living, in France. There are also a small number of distinctly unappealing European travellers, white settlers returning to France. A sequence very reminiscent of Godard's anti-imperialist satire in *Pierrot le Fou* collages racist and neo-colonial opinion from these European passengers – 'African art is a joke made up by journalists in need of copy' – to which the film provides its own response.

Anta manages to board the vessel without difficulty, but as Mory approaches the gangplank we hear a Tannoy announcement, 'Mr Diop is requested to see the Captain at once'. Most commentary on the film argues that Mory chooses to abandon Anta at this point because he loses his nerve, but if 'Diop' is his false identity (Mambéty's own middle name, just as he gave his surname to a divisional commander of police in an earlier episode), then Mory realises that he is about to be arrested, and so has no choice but to run. The penultimate image of *Touki-Bouki* is of a small fishing boat slowly moving out of shot on the sunlit ocean, the craft that gave inspiration to Mory in the first place. As Mambéty put it, 'When a story ends – or "falls into the ocean", as we say – it creates dreams' (Ukadike 1999: 4).

Further reading

Madeleine Cottenet-Hage, 'Images of France in Francophone African Films (1978–1998)' in Françoise Pfaff (ed.), *Focus on African Films*, Bloomington, Indiana University Press, 2004, pp. 107–23.

Vlad Dima, 'Sound Moves: Displacement and Modernity in French and Senegalese Cinemas' (DPhil. dissertation, University of Minnesota, 2010). Available at http://conservancy.umn.edu/bitstream/94324/1/Dima_umn_0130E_11275.pdf (accessed 12 November 2012).

June Givanni, 'The Master, the Rebel, and the Artist: The Films of Ousmane Sembène, Djibril Diop Mambéty, and Mousa Sene Absa' (Museum of the Moving Image, 2011). Available at www.movingimage.us/films/2011/04/02/detail/the-master-the-rebel-and-the-artist-the-films-of-ousmane-sembne-djibril-diop-mambty-and-moussa-sene-absa/ (accessed 12 November 2012).

Jean Narboni and Tom Milne (eds) *Godard on Godard*, New York, Secker and Warburg, 1972.

'Laughter of a Celluloid Shaman', Staff Reporter, *Mail & Guardian*, 23 August 1996. Available at http://mg.co.za/article/1996-08-23-laughter-of-a-celluloid-shaman (accessed 12 November 2012).

Sada Niang, *Djibril Diop Mambéty: un cinéaste à contre-courant*, Paris, Editions L'Harmattan, 2002. (Quotation translated by Nigel Wheale.)

Bunmi John Oloruntoba, *Constructing a Postcolonial-surrealist Framework for West African Cinema: The Cinemas of Jean Rouch and Djibril Diop Mambéty*, Regent University, 2008.

Alessandra Speciale, 'Djibril, the Prince and Poet of African Cinema', *Écrans d'Afrique*, 24, 1998. Available at www.africultures.com/revue_africultures/articles/ecrans_afrique/24/24_6.pdf (accessed 12 November 2012).

N. Frank Ukadike, 'The Hyena's Last Laugh. An Interview with Djibril Diop Mambéty', *Transition 78*, 8:2, 1999, pp. 136–53. Available at www.worldcat.org/title/hyenas-last-laugh-a-conversation-with-djibril-diop-mambety/oclc/58439307 (accessed 12 November 2012).

Nigel Wheale

Trois couleurs/The Colors Trilogy (1993/4)

Trois couleurs: bleu (1993)

[Country: France, Switzerland, Poland. Production Company: MK2, CED Productions, France 3, CAB Productions, TOR production. Director: Krzysztof Kieślowski. Producer: Marin Karmitz.

Screenwriters: Krzysztof Kieślowski, Krzysztof Piesiewicz. Cinematographer: Sławomir Idziak. Editor: Jacques Witta. Music: Zbigniew Preisner. Cast: Juliette Binoche (Julie); Benoir Régent (Olivier); Florence Pernel (Sandrine); Charlotte Very (Lucille); Emanuelle Riva (mother); Julie Delpy (Dominique); Zbigniew Zamachowski (Karol Karol).]

Trois couleurs: blanc (1994)

[Country: France, Switzerland, Poland. Production Company: France 3 Cinema, MK2 Productions, CED Productions, France 3, CAB Productions, TOR Productions, Canal +. Director: Krzysztof Kieślowski. Producer: Marin Karmitz. Screenwriters: Krzysztof Kieślowski, Krzysztof Piesiewicz. Cinematographer: Edward Kłosiński. Editor: Urszula Lesiak. Music: Zbigniew Preisner. Cast: Zbigniew Zamachowski (Karol Karol), Julie Delpy (Dominique), Janusz Gajos (Mikołaj), Jerzy Stuhr (Jurek), Aleksander Bardini (lawyer), Jerzy Nowak (old farmer), Cezary Pazura (foreign exchange shop owner), Juliette Binoche (Julie).]

Trois couleurs: rouge (1994)

[Country: France, Switzerland, Poland. Production Company: France 3 Cinema, MK2 Productions, CED Productions, France 3, CAB Productions, TOR Productions, Canal + Productions, Télévision Suisse Romande. Director: Krzysztof Kieślowski. Producer: Marin Karmitz. Screenwriters: Krzysztof Kieślowski, Krzysztof Piesiewicz. Cinematographer: Piotr Sobociński. Editor: Jacques Witta. Music: Zbigniew Preisner. Cast: Irène Jacob (Valentine Dussaut), Jean-Louis Trintignant (judge Joseph Kern), Frédérique Feder (Karin), Jean-Pierre Lorit (Auguste Bruner), Samuel Lebihan (photographer), Juliette Binoche (Julie), Zbigniew Zamachowski (Karol Karol), Julie Delpy (Dominique), Benoir Régent (Olivier).]

Synopsis: *Blue:* A car accident causes the death of a well-known composer and his young daughter. Julie, the composer's wife and the girl's mother, survives the crash but withdraws into isolation and silence. She is slowly brought back to a social existence by small claims on her attention in her immediate proximity, and then by the revelation that a child will be born out of the dead husband's affair with another woman. She finally returns to composing music.

White: A humiliating divorce from a French hairdresser forces the emigrant Karol to sneak from Paris back home to Poland, impoverished and crushed. Having eventually hustled his way up the economic ladder, he stages his own death as a trap to lure his ex-wife to Poland, jail, and sweet revenge.

Red: Valentine, a student and occasional model, is distracted from her fretful daily life in Geneva by a chance encounter with a reclusive, charismatic, judge. Their acquaintance deepens in the course of a series of minor, seemingly unrelated events and conversations: Valentine's attempts to curb the old man's intrusive behaviour toward his morally suspect neighbours; her criss-crossing of paths with a law student and future judge in her neighbourhood; the young man's discovery of a girlfriend's deceit; Valentine's chagrin at her brother's descent into drug dependency; the old judge's confession of a traumatic end of a love affair in England. As Valentine travels to England to visit her distant boyfriend, her ferry capsizes but she is one of the few survivors; another one is the law student, coincidentally on the same ship.

The place of Krzysztof Kieślowski's trilogy in film history can be anchored by a two-part proposition: that, in the wake of the post-1989 folding of the Iron Curtain, this loosely connected series provides a unique and ingenious cinematic embodiment of the encounter of 'East' with 'West', and that it at the same time represents the culmination of a major auteur's oeuvre, the final work produced before his untimely death in 1996 – work that has prompted, and lives on, in a substantial body of critical and theoretical writing.

When in 1992 the fabled French producer Marin Karmitz announced the production of the three films that make up the *Trilogy*, he was delivering a trifecta of the best the contemporary 'European' cinema had to offer: 1) a powerful authorial name underwritten by nearly three decades of original, courageous and politically committed filmmaking; 2) the promise of a relevant and intellectually responsible set of stories addressing the convulsive political and social changes the continent was undergoing in the wake of the recent opening of the Iron Curtain, 3) made not only palatable but positively irresistible by a distinct visual style, refracted in all three films through a luminous (and French) female star whose inward-outward beauty could well compete with the brassier sex appeal of global Hollywood. These promises were delivered in quick succession between 1993 and 1994, making *The Colors Trilogy*, as it came to be known, mandatory viewing on the world film fest circuit as well as a serial winner of dozens of international and national awards. Then, in early 1996, its director Kieślowski died unexpectedly – from overwork, it was hinted: almost exactly like Weronika, the Polish heroine of one of his earlier films, his heart appeared to have burst in a transcendent sprint to heed a creative vision. The Trilogy thus became a kind of headstone, securing Kieślowski a place in the pantheon of Europe's benchmark authors, an equal now of an Antonioni, a Bergman, a Tarkovsky.[1]

While the trilogy came to be celebrated as Kieślowski's *summa*, it was at the time of its release also understood as a triumphant career upgrade. Starting in the late 1960s as a near-solo documentarian, Kieślowski developed during his feature-making years a unique collaborative style, becoming, together with Krzysztof Zanussi, the acting head of the fabled TOR production group, the studio that became synonymous with 'cinema of moral anxiety', Polish culture's ethical compass during the darkest years of post-Solidarity repression in the People's Republic.[2] With the totalitarian regime's dissolution in early 1989, that lifelong stance of social responsibility led Kieślowski to search for a new production model in a film industry that overnight lost both the protection of a state-buffered economy and the constraints of the State censor's heavy political hand. How, then, to reorganise a national film industry that would at once reconnect the Polish nation to its European roots, whatever they might be (for that was the political master narrative of the post-1989 'Wende', 'return', as the Berlin Wall was being dismantled, and the many fault-lines and scars of Europe's pre-1948 histories were being revisited)? How to do this even while updating it, instantly, for the global capitalist economy, criss-crossed now by the cables of new media and the noise of pervasive communication systems? This Gordian knot of intertwined temporalities, the national desire to get through the difficult present by coordinating its distant past with the urgently pressing future – that was the real challenge the *Trilogy* needed to resolve in the new production circumstances; indeed this temporal compression was, in the view of the English critic Emma Wilson, also one of the trilogy's major themes.[3]

This is not to say that Kieślowski's challenge was unique: more than in any of the East European countries, co-productions accounted for up to 50 per cent of all the films made in Poland in the immediate post-socialist period.[4] And France, long Poland's principal historical filiation in Europe, and long its staunchest ally against the pincers of two enemy neighbours, Germany and Russia, was also the main manager of the EurImages funds, parlaying its long history of co-productions into a role as the principal dispatcher agency for 'new Europe's' cinemas.[5] The tricolour motif was thus at once France's triumphant flag rising – some said – over the Polish red-and-white, and at the same time a claim-staking for the emergent cinema of the European Union. Beyond simply celebrating the abstract ideals of the Enlightenment – fraternity, equality, brotherhood – symbolised by the three colours (as the press releases relentlessly offered), the plot of each of the three films was centred on, and discreetly allegorised, the conditions of creative labour in Europe's new transnational economy.

The EU is thus the political entity whose triumph is being awkwardly feted (and whose flag is occasionally glimpsed) in the musical backstory of *Blue*, in the form of an anthem commissioned, at great expense, from Juliette's cheating composer husband before he meets his untimely end in the opening scene. Similarly, the plot of *White* could be paraphrased as a comic tale of a bumbling Polish leisure-industry employee trying to set up shop inside Fortress Europe, in Paris, on the strength of a modest previous success at an international festival in an East European backwater, and who then makes it his mission to raise enough domestic capital to frame, trap and neutralise the sexy French expert-competitor in his line of work (Julie Delpy) inside a bleak Polish public institution – aka jail – and who finally succeeds by making her smile for the camera at the prospect of a future collaboration. *Red* in turn can be said to allegorise its production circumstances by literally rescuing its greatest filmic asset, an exquisite and soulful model, from a mass grave and anonymous demise in the icy waters of shallow commerce (an empty bubble coming out of her mouth on a soft drink billboard her biggest accomplishment) inside a narrative driven – if only barely – by a quest for ethics, moral decency, and emotional authenticity.

A different reading of Kieślowski's strategies for balancing 'the Polish' inside 'the French' has been proposed by Emma Wilson, who parses the complex temporalities in Kieślowski's 'French films' along Deleuzian time-image lines, tracking the trilogy's reliance on and deployment of icons from the French New Wave (Emmanuelle Riva in *Blue*, Brigitte Bardot in *White*, and Jean-Louis Trintignant in *Red*) to claim that this strategy has much to teach us about 'how national cinemas are always open to infiltration and identificatory mechanisms where what is alien is absorbed, repeated and reproduced', concluding that Kieślowski may be 'mak[ing] films abroad, but stays resolutely at home'.[6]

Such critical (and later academic) appreciation on the part of 'Western' scholars wasn't necessarily shared by critics in Poland. Having supported Kieślowski during the lean decades of totalitarianism, and celebrated his subtle elaboration of the 'cinema of moral anxiety' in his features *Camera Buff*, *Blind Chance*, *No End*, and especially *Decalogue*, in the newly opened post-1989 atmosphere many saw the *Trilogy* as a sellout to the glossy values of the marketplace, and claimed it to be kitschy, maudlin, and bargain-basement metaphysical, not to mention sexist.[7]

In either case, however, the famously luxuriant look of *Trilogy* is the most marked difference against Kieślowski's earlier work, much of it documentary and austere, an uncompromising (in the sense of market-indifferent) investigation of the ethical consequences of a camera turning its prying gaze on a singular, unique, human being. If nothing else, this wholesale stylistic upgrade (already mobilised in *The Double Life of Véronique*) was one obvious way of securing the attention of a world cinema audience accustomed to sample its ethical quandaries in the framework of entertainment (commonly referred to by the oxymoron 'art film genre').[8] For all their shared audiovisual bravura, the three films were shot by three different cinematographers (Idziak, Sobociński, Kłosiński), each of whom had previously worked on a Kieślowski project in Poland. Interviews record not just the unusually active participation of the cameramen as well as other production team members in the filmmaking process, but also the efforts on Kieślowski's part to inflect the labour division customary in the heavily unionised French system in favour of a more collectivist mode of work. Such difference in modes of production signals that the emblematic concept of authorship, long an export hallmark of 'European cinema', might deserve a geopolitical revision informed by the sub-field of 'production studies' emerging in particular in the new 'post-East European' film historiography.[9]

Formally, all three films build their distinct mood and structure by a dramaturgical focus on a single and inward human being working her or his way through a trauma of some kind. This protagonist is a listener and observer more than she or he is a speaker or, so it appears, a doer. In *Blue*, Julie survives the loss of her family by practicing a kind of worldly ascesis, withdrawing into silence and looking to cut contact with as many living creatures as possible. In *White*, after suffering public humiliation on every imaginable front, the protagonist Karol appears to be recovering, enjoying a somewhat comical and unexpectedly stellar rise in Poland's sprouting capitalist economy, yet the real plot, his working-through of his initial Parisian dejection by capturing his former tormentor (and wife), is planned tacitly and off-screen, without anyone's knowledge, so that the final turn surprises the viewer as much as it does Karol's few friends. In *Red*, the single-protagonist scheme is somewhat modified. Here the viewer is not so much following one introvert character as s/he is led through a pattern of uncanny encounters and never-quite-explained parallels between a character-function and a double of sorts (the old and the young judge, Valentine and the old judge's lost lover, etc.). In these encounters time slows down and events lack closure, losing ground to contingency but retaining the uncanny power of possibility.

As is appropriate for modernist/time-image cinema, then, plotting is not where the viewer finds her satisfaction. Julie's final overcoming of her death-wish phase and tentative embrace of music and life with Oliver produces no change in the film's emotional tone; Karol's life after the triumphal revenge appears as pointless as it seemed when he was still hustling his way up; and though Valentine and Auguste are supposedly predetermined for a future happy life, as per the old judge's dream, that flaccid and possibly self-serving fantasy is all we have to go on as the film stills on the final shot. In this respect it is fair to say, with the Polish critics, that none of the three films – in fact, none of Kieślowski's 'Western' films – takes a real crack at a moral dilemma in a political sense. Instead, their narrative resolution is at most a hint at some alternative, virtual, reality, a dim glimpse of one or several other possible pathways in which the transpired events might be recombined. Assessing Kieślowski's legacy, a number of critics have traced the seed of the now so commonplace 'multivalent narratives' like Haneke's *Code: Unknown*, Iñárritu's *Babel* or the Wachowskis' *Cloud Atlas* to the open, hesitant, even haunted causalities structuring Kieślowski's films.[10]

Instead, the seductiveness of these late films derives from their unique array of optical and acoustic techniques of intimacy and inwardness. On a descriptive level, critics have highlighted their colour and light compositions as borrowed from painting and still photography, along with the highly elliptical editing and camera work that combines documentary and tightly controlled, 'predictive', movement so as to 'collaborate' with the viewer without dictating his or her reactions.[11] On a more theoretical level, the look of these films has been translated into a distinct ethics of seeing. Pointing to a recurrence of 'impossible' shots, in which a character sees herself seeing (with the help of an optical device such as a glass ball, a reflective surface, or even the iris itself), Slavoj Žižek has argued that in Kieślowski's editing philosophy such constructions, or 'interfaces', go beyond standard art cinema's familiar and comfortable bare-it-all self-reflexivity, and instead let the viewer indirectly glimpse a more radical recognition of alternative and mutually exclusive selves. In this sense, then, *The Color Trilogy* would represent one final missive of non-commercial cinema's 'non-pornographic' way of looking.[12]

Notes

1. Moreover, the trilogy format itself has been argued as the epitome of authorial power. See Claire Perkins and Constantine Verevis (eds), *Film Trilogies: New Critical Approaches*, New York: Palgrave, 2012.
2. In Danusia Stok (ed.), *Kieślowski on Kieślowski*, London, Faber & Faber, 1993, pp. 127–9, the director talks about his role as a cameraman-witness at the political trials against Solidarity activists, and his subsequent lifelong collaboration with their lawyer Krzysztof Piesowski – also a screenwriter on the *Trilogy*. On Zanussi and TOR, see Stok, p. 144.
3. Emma Wilson, *Memory and Survival: the French Films of Krzysztof Kieślowski*, Oxford, European Humanities Research Centre, 2000.
4. Marek Haltof, *The Cinema of Krzysztof Kieślowski: Variations on Destiny and Chance*, London, Wallflower, 2004, p. 110.
5. On France's politics in the global film market see for instance Martin O'Shaughnessy 'French Cinema: Counter-model, Cultural Exception, Resistances', in J. Kapur and K. B. Wagner (eds), *Neoliberalism and Global Cinema: Capital, Culture and Marxist Critiques*, New York, Routledge, 2011.
6. Wilson, p. 119.
7. Haltof, p. 125.
8. For the definitive discussion of the vicissitudes of this problematic see Thomas Elsaesser, *European Cinema Face to Face with Hollywood*, Amsterdam, University of Amsterdam Press, 2005.
9. For an introduction to 'Production Studies', see http://widescreenjournal.org/index.php/journal/issue/view/4.

10. Joseph Kickasola, 'Kieślowski Crosses the Atlantic', in Steven Woodward (ed.), *After Kieślowski: The Legacy of Krzysztof Kieślowski*, Detroit: Wayne State University Press, 2009, pp. 165–7.
11. See for instance Charles Eidsvik, 'Kieślowski's Visual Legacy', in Woodward (ed.).
12. Slavoj Žižek, *The Fright of Real Tears: Krzysztof Kieślowski Between Theory and Post-Theory*, London, BFI, 2001, pp. 75–7.

Nataša Ďurovičová

Tsotsi (2005)

[Country: South Africa, UK. Production Company: The UK Film and TV Production Company PLC, Industrial Development Corporation of South Africa, The National Film and Video Foundation of SA, Moviworld. Director: Gavin Hood. Producer: Peter Fudakowski. Screenwriter: Gavin Hood (based on the novel by Athol Fugard). Cinematographer: Lance Gewer. Music: Paul Hepker, Mark Kilian. Editor: Megan Gill. Cast: Presley Chweneyagae (Tsotsi), Terry Pheto (Miriam), Kenneth Nkosi (Aap), Mothusi Magano (Boston), Zenzo Ngqobe (Butcher), Zola (Fela), Rapulana Seiphemo (John Dube), Nambitha Mpumlwana (Pumla Dube), Ian Roberts (Captain Smit), Jerry Mofokeng (Morris).]

Synopsis: Tsotsi, a gang member living in a township, makes a living mugging and carjacking more affluent people. One day, while hijacking a car, he finds a baby on the back seat and takes him home. Identifying with the baby, he forces a young mother in the township to take care of him. Slowly remembering his own childhood, and his mother who had died from AIDS, he ends up returning the baby to his affluent parents.

A major success in both South Africa and around the world, winner of the 2005 Oscar for Best Foreign Language Film, *Tsotsi* took some risks: it featured no stars, but for the most part young unknown actors, was shot on location in Soweto, and its dialogue is mostly in *tsotistaal*, a hybrid of languages, such as Afrikaans, Sotho, Zwana and Zulu, spoken in the townships around Johannesburg. At the same time the film sparked much debate and controversy as far as its politics are concerned.

Tsotsi is based on the novel by the same name written by accomplished South African playwright Athol Fugard. Fugard had started the novel after the 1960 Sharpeville massacre, during which 69 people protesting pass laws restricting the movement of black South Africans were shot by apartheid police. Not published until 1980, four years after the Soweto uprising, during which police shot numerous students protesting the introduction of Afrikaans as the language of instruction, the novel is set in Sophiatown in the 1950s, shortly before this black cultural hub where non-whites could own property was razed to make room for the white suburb Triomf. The film updates the setting: Tsotsi's mother does not die because of apartheid, but of AIDS, and the baby is not 'historyless' (Rijsdijk and Haupt 2007: 38) but has affluent black South African parents, which introduces an entirely new storyline.

Critics have thus rightfully pointed out that in the film economic apartheid has replaced racial apartheid. The affluent black father is comfortable speaking up against the police and making a claim on the State. Within such economic apartheid, the film explores different kinds of violence, domestic, criminal and systemic (Dovey 2007: 155), but does not necessarily offer possible solutions to the violence. Within this context, the film's ending is important: Hood shot two versions, one in which Tsotsi escapes and another in which he gets shot by the police, but decided to use neither. Instead the film ends with a confrontation between the affluent black father and poor Tsotsi, leaving 'the final critique of Tsoti's violence to contemporary viewers' (Dovey 2007: 160). But a pirated version with the ending in which Tsotsi is shot by the police circulated widely in South Africa, allowing for a very different reading of the film.

It may therefore not be surprising that the film has divided critics: South African critics have generally been much harsher with the film, while foreign commentators tend to defend it. Disagreements concern the film's (un)willingness to critique the state as well as its representation of class, race and gender. Daniel Lehman, for instance, argues that the film critiques the economic and AIDS policies of then President Thabo Mbeki, who encouraged black economic empowerment for a select few but did little about widespread poverty, and who refused effective HIV treatment, which he saw as an 'assault on ... black male sexuality' (Mark Gevisser quoted in Lehman 2011a: 97). By contrast, South African critics argue that the film legitimises the State, by having fairly sympathetic white cops, by allowing the AIDS issue to be lost in the background of the plot, and above all by insisting on Tsotsi's positive, but entirely internal change that leaves all the responsibility up to the protagonist, apparently suggesting that individual initiative is enough and that economic, health and other state policies do not have to be changed (see Dovey 2007; Barnard 2008).

At the heart of these debates is the question of how important – or how unimportant – the film's relatively conventional, Hollywood-style narrative is. Gavin Hood himself has said that he filmed a classic story of redemption that he thinks has universal appeal (see Archibald and Hood 2006). His camera movements, he suggests, are minimal, driven by characters (Gunn 2009: 49). In classical Hollywood stories, (usually male, white) protagonists drive the plot. In *Tsotsi*, Tsotsi (a word meaning thug) starts out as a nameless, expressionless character tortured by flashbacks. In the course of the story, as he identifies with the baby (whom he gives his own name), he remembers more and more of his childhood. Emotionally driven flashbacks tell his traumatising story: after his father – who, misinformed about AIDS, would not let his son near his dying mother (though he probably infected her with the virus) – kicks and paralyzes his dog, David, as he was then called, runs away, becoming a homeless child and a nameless thug. While the film tells the story about how Tsotsi, through the baby and by remembering his traumatic past, finds respect and decency, critics have pointed out that such a transformation is both unlikely and problematic. In the film, Tsotis's maturation, or *Bildung*, happens all too easily. By contrast, Rita Barnard argues, the novel is a 'meditation on the socio-political preconditions for a coherent subjectivity and narration', a meditation, that is, on how the apartheid state makes telling one's story, and thus one's maturation and social mobility, difficult if not impossible (Barnard 2008: 549).

More specifically, *Tsotsi* is part of the gangster film genre. The word tsotsi, possibly derived from the English zoot suit, first emerged in 1930s Sophiatown, and represents an appropriation and transposition of the American gangster into a South African context. Not exactly unlike the American gangsters who often emerged in poor, ethnic environments, the tsotsi stands for mobility, violence, fashion – in short everything poor blacks were not allowed to be under the apartheid regime. As Rosalind Morris has it, the tsotsi 'invest[s] the township with commodity desire' (Morris 2010: 99). But while stylishness can sometimes be marshalled for radical politics, as it was for instance in the zoot suit riots of 1943, the connection between stylishness and critique is not always obvious. Barnard complains that 'gangsterism purely as style ... [is] not a real threat to the status quo' (Barnard 2008: 561). Such stylishness also approaches *Tsotsi* to film noir, a film movement often noted for its sense of style and fashion, and in this context one could easily look in more detail at the film's careful use of colours and lighting.

But fashion and stylishness are not everything. Dovey helpfully points out that from the 1950s onward, there were two different kinds of *tsotsis*, 'smartly dressed gangsters who tend to operate on big money from whites or Asians (represented in *Tsotsi* by Fela) … [and] marginalised boys who operate out of the desperation of poverty and who tend to serve the former kind of *tsotsi*' (Dovey 2007: 154–4). Tsotsi/David belongs more clearly to the latter kind, and in this context, it would be interesting to think of another of Hood's stylistic choices: his widescreen images place faces in landscapes, emphasising how much Tsotsi/David belongs to the township, as well as the gulf that separates the township from the modern city. Tsotsi/David remains embedded in the landscape, unable to escape the township (Dovey 2007: 154).

No discussion of *Tsotsi* would be complete without a discussion of its soundtrack. Many have noted the marked presence of kwaito music by South African artist Zola who also plays Fela in the film. Many of these tracks were pre-existing hits, and Zola's celebrity was used to market the film and its music (Rijsdijk and Haupt 2007: 33). Kwaito was first developed by gangsters in 1950s Sophiatown, and has been influenced by gangsta rap. Ian-Malcolm Rijsdijk and Adam Haupt have argued that the use of Zola's kwaito music 'constantly re-affirms a homogeneous black urban masculinity by not offering musical diversity' (Rijsdijk and Haupt 2007: 36). But kwaito is not the only music in the film, there are also 'choral arrangements, and … the combination of low bass notes, rattles and percussion that accompany scenes of action or tension in the film' (Rijsdijk and Haupt, 2007: 31). In the course of the film, we see a shift from the 'urban, fast-paced, heterosexist, aggressive and lyrically violent music of Zola to the soulful choral style of Mahlasela and Maphumulo' (Rijsdijs and Haupt 2007: 31). Tsotsi/David's emotional transformation gets associated with choral themes.

As becomes evident in this discussion of the film's music, questions of gender have lurked everywhere in the critical debate surrounding *Tsotsi*. Rijsdijk and Haupt conclude that the film runs the risk of 'essentialising conventional gender roles in which women are nurturers and men are violent plunderers' (Rijsdijk and Haupt 2007: 41). As noted earlier, the upper-middle-class couple is an addition in the film; in the novel, Tsotsi does not hijack a car but encounters a frightened, black woman in a grove and comes close to raping her. The topic of rape has disappeared from the film, although, Dovey reminds us, there was a 400 per cent increase in child rape in South Africa from 1988 to 2003, and that in 2003 children under 12 made up 40 per cent of South Africa's annual 1 million rape victims, in part because of the myth that raping a virgin would cure HIV/AIDS (Dovey 2007: 157). By contrast, Lehman focuses on the character of Miriam who takes on 'an increasingly proactive function', whose encounters with Tsotsi suggest that Hood does not avoid the topic of potential sexual violence (Lehman 2011b: 118). Along with the baby, she nudges Tsotsi toward a less aggressive masculinity, an alternative to the masculine violence also embodied by his father. Not coincidentally, when the film came out, real tsotis objected that Tsotis/David looked too soft and sloppy (Dovey 2007: 153).

Tsotsi can be located in the context of the post-apartheid flourishing of South African films, which often have high production values and run the risk of being 'Hollywoodised'. The NFVF (National Film and Video Foundation) specifically allocates funding to films that are adaptations of South African literature, which tends to privilege texts by white South Africans. Likewise, white directors have been more enamoured by the themes of reconciliation and redemptions than black or coloured directors. At the same time, *Tsotsi* also participates in a wave of internationally acclaimed films about gangsters and hoods, including the Brazilian film, *City of God* (2002) and the Anglo-Indian film, *Slumdog Millionaire* (2008). Like these other films, *Tsotsi* toys with the tradition of neo-realism, famous from films such as *Bicycle Thieves* (1948), which employed non-professional actors, yet, at the same time, the film's production values and narrative resemble Hollywood melodrama. These different legacies certainly help explain some of the contradictions of the film, which have generated so much debate.

Further reading

David Archibald and Gavin Hood, 'Violence and Redemption: An Interview with Gavin Hood', *Cineaste*, Vol. 31, No. 2, Spring 2006, pp. 44–47.

Rita Barnard, 'Tsotsis: On Law, the Outlaw, and the Postcolonial State', *Contemporary Literature,* Vol. 49, No. 4, Winter 2008, pp. 541–72.

Lindiwe Dovey, 'Redeeming Features: From "Tsotsi" (1980) to "Tsotsi" (2006)', in *Journal of African Cultural Studies,* Vol. 19, No. 2, December 2007, pp. 143–64.

Judith Gunn, *Studying Tsotsi,* Leighton Buzzard, Auteur, 2009.

Daniel W. Lehman, 'Tsotsi Transformed: Retooling Athol Fugard for the Thabo Mbeki Era', in *Research in African Literatures,* Vol. 42, No. 1, Spring 2011a, pp. 87–101.

Daniel W. Lehman, 'When We Remembered Zion: The Oscar, the Tsotsi, and the Contender', *English in Africa,* Vol. 38, No. 3, October 2011b, pp. 113–29.

Rosalind C. Morris, 'Style, *Tsotsi*-Style, and *Tsotistaal:* The Histories, Aesthetics and Politics of a South African Figure', *Social Text,* Vol. 28, No. 2, Summer 2010, pp. 85–112.

Ian-Malcolm Rijsdijk and Adam Haupt, 'Redemption to a kwaito beat: Gavin Hood's Tsotsi', in *Journal of the Musical Arts in Africa,* Vol. 4, No. 1, 2007, pp. 29–46.

Sabine Haenni

Ugetsu monogatari/Ugetsu (1953)

[Country: Japan. Production Company: Daiei's Kyoto Studio. Producer: Masaichi Nagata. Director: Kenji Mizoguchi. Screenwriters: Matsutaro Kawaguchi and Yoshikata Yoda (based on stories by Akinari Ueda). Sound: Iwao Otani. Cinematographer: Kazuo Miyagawa. Lighting: Kenichi Okamoto. Art Director: Kisaku Ito. Music: Fumio Hayasaka. Cast: Kinuyo Tanaka (Miyagi), Machiko Kyo (Wakasa), Mitsuko Mita (Ohama), Masayuki Mori (Genjuro), Sakae Ozawa (Tobei).]

Synopsis: In the sixteenth century, Japan is in a chaotic time of social upheaval and constant military conflict between warlords. Farmers Genjuro and Tobei realise that the pottery they make can sell well at the market in town. Seduced by prospects of wealth and social mobility, they embark on a dangerous trip through war zones, taking their family with them. While Tobei succeeds in becoming a samurai and then, by chance, a commanding officer, his wife Ohama is raped by soldiers and becomes a prostitute. They eventually reunite, reconcile, and go back to the village together. Genjuro is invited to Princess Wakasa's mansion and becomes her lover. After days of pleasure, he discovers that she is a ghost, escapes her spell, and returns home, where his wife Miyagi and their son welcome him. The next morning it turns out that Miyagi has been murdered by soldiers and yet come back as a ghost. Genjuro promises her spirit to lead a simple life in the village.

Kenji Mizoguchi took his first trip to Europe when he brought *Ugetsu* to the 1953 Venice International Film Festival. For the opening ceremony, he wore a *montsuki* (formal kimono with one's crest printed) made of white linen deliberately sans *haori* jacket. Mizoguchi and his company, including the leading lady Kinuyo Tanaka in an exquisite, contemporary arrangement of the sixteenth-century kimono, paraded a couple of blocks from the Excelsior Palace to the Cinema Palace. As they entered the Palace, applause and sighs of admiration arose. An accompanying film critic noted: 'That was an effective publicity'.[1] Mizoguchi's staging of a self-Orientalising spectacle of a kimono in Venice, in retrospect, epitomises how Mizoguchi's – and Japanese cinema's – relationship with the world was mediated through the idea of Japaneseness in the early post-Second World War period. At the same time, we must acknowledge that Mizoguchi's choice of white linen, rather than formal black, as well as Tanaka's revisionist kimono, added a twist to the straightforward presentation of ethnic authenticity, even though very few, if any, Western spectators in Venice could tell those fine differences. The film *Ugetsu*, like its director's image control, can be seen as a negotiation of Japanese culture in global modernity.

Ugetsu received thunderous applause at the screening and eventually a Silver Lion at the closing ceremony on the 4th of September. It solidified Mizoguchi's reputation within the international film circuit, following *The Life of Oharu* (1952), a Silver Lion winner of the previous year. It is well known that the younger Akira Kurosawa's unanticipated triumph with *Rashomon* (1950) in Venice in 1951 directly stimulated Mizoguchi to crave for international recognition.[2] Yet, in effect, another ghost story Mizoguchi had made in 1926, titled *The Passion of a Woman Teacher* (*Kyoren no onna shisho*), had been exported to France in 1929 and screened privately to an audience.[3] Even though recent research suggests that the film was never commercially distributed, and then presumably was shelved, lost and forgotten, it never left Mizoguchi's mind.[4] For his part, three Silver Lions (the third for *Sansho the Bailiff* in 1954) were tokens of a fair recognition that belatedly and finally arrived.

For our part, of interest is what may have caused the marked gap in the European reception of these two films, *The Passion of a Woman Teacher* and *Ugetsu*. I do not think it is a matter of some intrinsic artistic quality. Judging from the contemporary Japanese reviews, *The Passion of a Woman Teacher*, a dark, erotic tale of obsessive love and vengeance, was probably a brilliant film. Rather, a paradigm change in geopolitics of international film culture and industry that took place between 1929 and 1953 made 'world cinema' possible, and thus determined the respective fates of the two ghost stories.

Three interconnected factors were at play in this paradigm change. First, what Dudley Andrew, with much attention to Mizoguchi and Japanese cinema, aptly called 'federalism' emerged in Europe, taking shape most explicitly at international film festivals such as Cannes or post-war Venice. The 'federal model' of film culture, like the United Nations or UNESCO, was envisioned in the aftermath of the disastrous consequences of nationalism during the Second World War by local (i.e. European) alliances and communities of filmmakers, critics, and enthusiasts. 'Often explicitly commanding high moral ground, festivals claimed to be utopias where the appreciation of difference and similarity would contribute to tolerance, coexistence, and, of course, a richer cinema' (Andrew 2010: 71). Without the establishment of this phase, a film from a non-Western nation like *Ugetsu* would not have been recognised and evaluated in the name of film art.

Second, from the late 1940s throughout the 1950s, in the United States – the largest film market where 'films' had been synonymous with Hollywood products – art-house film circuits were established and played foreign films. As Douglas Gomery points out, several historical factors were at play behind this change. For instance, the GI bill produced an unparalleled number of educated audience members who developed familiarity with and interest in foreign culture through their service during the Second World War. Also, as the Paramount decision in 1948 weakened the major studios' control over movie theatres, independent theatre owners were pushed to look for a niche audience. And, of course, the contents mattered. In the post-war world, foreign films, starting with *Rome, Open City* (1946), took the lead in redefining film art (Gomery 1992: 180–93). Thus, producer and screenwriter Matsutaro Kawaguchi was approached by a young representative at Venice and sealed a contract for *Ugetsu*'s American distribution, even before the film officially received the prize.[5]

Third, the confluence of the European vision of federalism at international film festivals and the establishment of art-house film circuits in the US increased transatlantic traffic in film, generating a historically specific way of film-viewing called *cinephilia* and its accompanying mode of film criticism, the *politique des auteurs,* in the auditorium of the Cinémathèque française in Paris. Mizoguchi was assigned a position within the canon of world cinema wrought by auteurist critics, such as Alexandre Astruc, Jean-Luc Godard, Luc Moulet, Jacques Rivette, and Eric Rohmer (McDonald 1993: 123–4, 131–3; Rivette 1985: 264). They found Mizoguchi's cinema 'universal' not through its roots in the particular, i.e. Japanese culture, but through its mise en scène. In effect, Mizoguchi's films were indispensable in and constitutive of the formation of the universalist ground that has supported the *politique des auteurs*'s global operation across language and culture. Thus, the obscurity of *The Passion of a Woman Teacher* and the glory of *Ugetsu* were thoroughly historically determined.

It is well known that *Ugetsu* emerged, in the collaborative writing process by the screenwriters Yoshikata Yoda and Kawaguchi and Mizoguchi, as a patchwork of several originals, which were not necessarily 'Japanese': short stories from the Tokugawa-era author Akinari Ueda's collection *Ugetsu monogatari* (*Tales of Moonlight and Rain,* 1776), 'The House Amid the Thickets', 'The Lust of the White Serpent', and possibly 'The Chrysanthemum Vow', all of which were further based on Chinese ghost stories written in the Ming period, as well as Guy de Maupassant's short story 'The Legion of Honor' (1883) (McDonald 1993: 79–112). According to Yoda, the script underwent several rewrites. In the torturous process, a sarcastic allegory in which a man who called himself the 'spirit of money' parades with jingling noise of coins, and where Tobei and Ohama triumph in their respective worldly success as a warlord and a courtesan, was turned into the serious humanist drama we know today.[6] The Japanese film mogul Masaichi Nagata, having produced *Rashomon* (winner of the 1951 Venice Grand-Prix), clearly had his eye on another prize and on distribution contracts in Europe and North America in working on the *Ugetsu* project. Nagata believed that in order for a Japanese film to succeed on the international film market, it must have a 'universal' theme, a small number of protagonists, and a simple storyline.[7] It is very likely that *Ugetsu*'s script was made palatable to the international audience, as the Daiei president-producer imagined it.

Ugetsu's heterogeneous materials, however, worked productively for Mizoguchi in creating a new kind of visual narration inspired by a Japanese aesthetic tradition, the handscroll (*emakimono*). It seems obvious to compare Mizoguchi's film style to the handscroll; Noël Burch has drawn on this trope in order to highlight two distinctive devices in Mizoguchi's 1930s style: lateral traveling shots which pass and penetrate partitions, and higher-than-eye-level camera angles (Burch 1979: 228–9). Mizoguchi's own explanation, however, indicates a different set of devices. Kazuo Miyagawa, the cinematographer on *Ugetsu* and seven other Mizoguchi films, recalled the director's words: 'Miyagawa, I'd like to make a film like a handscroll (*emakimono*). My films from now on should be, above all, straight and irreversible like a handscroll, which you can look through successively, and don't have to return to the beginning again once you finish looking. You can smoothly follow the story of this handscroll in sequence until the end, and its pictures consist of climactic moments, some strong touches and other weaker ones'.[8] Judging from what he and Miyagawa did and considering the handscroll's narrative technique, Mizoguchi seems to have meant a particular kind of continuity and irreversibility that swiftly connects two or more different objects, locations, and temporalities.

Mizoguchi is known for the long take. The unblinking look at the murder of Miyagi testifies for such reputation, as Robin Wood brilliantly put it (McDonald 1993: 148–9). Most critics would agree, therefore, to place his style on the side of spatio-temporal continuity in opposition to montage in the taxonomy of film aesthetics. *Ugetsu*, however, in some of its best moments, connects and smoothly merges two or more heterogeneous or even incongruous parts with each other through montage, camera movements, or just change of lighting. The famous one shot where Genjuro reunites with Miyagi's ghost offers a good example: the circular movement of the camera and the changes of lighting and setting transform an abandoned house into a welcoming home, and thereby connect the realm of reality with that of fantasy and the supernatural in a seamless manner. And, at the end of this sequence, as Miyagi sits sewing by the sleeping Genjuro and their son, a few seconds in the fixed shot represents the passage of a few hours from night to morning by means of the magic of lighting and otherwordly music. *Ugetsu*'s generic, intermedial, and transnational connections with horror and fantasy provided Mizoguchi with an opportunity to bridge different realms: reality and fantasy, natural and supernatural, and this and other worlds.

Godard finely described another brilliant example of such bridging in *Ugetsu*:

> Genjuro is bathing with the fatal enchantress who has caught him in her net; the camera leaves the rock pool where they are disporting themselves, pans along the overflow which becomes a stream disappearing into the fields; at this point there is a swift dissolve to the furrows, other furrows seem to take their place, the camera continues tranquilly on its way, rises, and discovers a vast plain, then a garden in which we discover the two lovers again, a few months later, enjoying a picnic. Only masters of the cinema can make use of a dissolve to create a feeling which is here the very Proustian one of pleasure and regrets.
>
> (Godard 1972: 71)

Originally written in 1958 by the future master of montage of incongruous fragments through dissolves, this passage effectively highlights *Ugetsu*'s tour de force.

Mizoguchi was a modernist; he carefully picked stories and aesthetic idioms from a repository of Japanese and transnational traditions available to him, took them out of context, put them together through 'montage', and presented an innovative, eerie continuity as 'Japanese'. Even though he was painfully aware of the asymmetrical power relations of the 'world cinema' paradigm, he probably knew that nothing would start without becoming a player in it.

Notes

1. Chiyota Shimizu, 'Yoroppa eiga kiko: Venisu Eigasai ni shusseki shite', *Kinema junpo*, 15 September 1953, p. 28.
2. Yoda Yoshikata, *Mizoguchi Kenji no hito to geijutsu*, Tokyo, Tabata Shoten, 1970, p. 193.

3. Kuninosuke Matsuo, 'Nikkastsu eiga no Furansu yuki', *Kinema junpo* March 1st, 1929, 70, Matsuo, *Pari monogatari*, Tokyo: Shakai Hyoronsha, 2010, pp. 208–9. For *The Passion of a Woman Teacher*'s synopsis, its relationship to the original story, *Shinkei kasanegafuchi*, and contemporary reception, see Tsutomu Saso, *Mizoguchi Kenji zen sakuhin kaisetsu*, Vol. 4, Tokyo, Kindai Bungeisha, 2005, pp. 258–309. Hideo Nakata (*Ringu*, *Ring 2*) was highly conscious of this lineage in adapting the same original into his costume horror *Kaidan* (2007) at the height of his international fame.
4. Tamaki Tsuchida, 'Senzenki no Nihon eiga ni okeru "kokusaisei" no gainen: *Nippon* ni miru Kawakita Nagamasa no yume', *Cre Biz*, No. 7, 2012. Available at www.toho-univ.ac.jp/univ_info/_pdf/crebiz07_02.pdf (accessed 6 October 2013). Kenji Mizoguchi, 'Jisaku o kataru', Tsutomu Saso ed., *Mizoguchi Kenji chosakushu*, Tokyo, Omuro, 2013, p. 362.
5. Matsutaro Kawaguchi, 'Sekai isshu nikki', 4 September 1953, Nihon Kindai Bungakukan, Kawaguchi Matsutaro Collection.
6. I confirmed this account in Yoda's memoirs with the first draft of the script in the Kazuo Miyagawa collection. My deep gratitude goes to Jiro Miyagawa.
7. Masaichi Nagata, *Eigado masshigura*, Tokyo, Surugadai Shobo, 1953.
8. Kaneto Shindo, *Aru eiga kantoku no shôgai: Mizoguchi Kenji no kiroku*, 1st ed., Tokyo, Eijinsha, 1975, p. 313.

Further reading

Dudley Andrew, 'Time Zones and Jetlag: The Flows and Phases of World Cinema', in Nataša Durovicová and Kathleen Newman (eds), *World Cinemas, Transnational Perspectives*, New York, Routledge, 2010, pp. 59–89.

Noël Burch, *To the Distant Observer: Form and Meaning in the Japanese Cinema*, Berkeley, University of California Press, 1979.

Jean-Luc Godard, *Godard on Godard*, trans. and ed. Tom Milne, New York, Da Capo Press, 1972.

Douglas Gomery, *Shared Pleasures: A History of Movie Presentation in the United States*, Madison, University of Wisconsin Press, 1992.

Keiko I. McDonald (ed.), *Ugetsu: Kenji Mizoguchi, Director*, New Brunswick, NJ, Rutgers University Press, 1993.

Jacques Rivette, 'Mizoguchi Viewed from Here', trans. Liz Heron, in Jim Hillier (ed.), *Cahiers du cinema the 1950s: Neo-Realism, Hollywood, New Wave*, Cambridge, MA, Harvard University Press, 1985, p. 264.

Chika Kinoshita

Utomlennye solntsem/Burnt By The Sun (1994)

[Country: Russia, France. Production Company: Camera One, Canal+, and Studio TriTe. Director: Nikita Mikhalkov. Producers: Leonid Vereshchagin, Nikita Mikhalkov and Michel Seydoux. Screenwriters: Rustam Ebragimbekov and Nikita Mikhalkov. Cinematographer: Vilen Kaliuta. Music: Eduard Artemiev. Editor: Enzo Meniconi. Cast: Nikita Mikhalkov (Commander Sergei Kotov), Ingeborga Dapkunaite (Marusia), Nadezhda Mikhalkova (Nadia), Oleg Men'shikov (Dmitrii (Mitia)), Viacheslav Tikhonov (Vsevolod Konstantinovich), Vladimir Il'in (Kirik), Alla Kazanskaia (Lidia Stepanovna), Nina Arkhipova (Elena Mikhailovna), Avangard Leont'ev (the driver).]

Synopsis: The events in *Burnt by the Sun* take place on one summer day in 1936. This day becomes a turning point in the lives of two men, a revolutionary hero, Sergei Kotov and NKVD secret agent Dmitrii (Mitia). By the end of the day, Kotov is arrested and, as a result, loses his prestigious social position and perfect family; Dmitrii commits suicide. The events of the film elucidate the complexities of the early Soviet period and the onset of the Stalinist terror.

In the early 1990s, the Russian film industry underwent a rapid decline, resulting in the fall of film production from 300 films in 1990 to a mere 36 in 1996. This decrease in the number of annually produced films can be explained by a variety of reasons: the collapse of Soviet centralised distribution networks; a flood of low-priced foreign films into the Russian cinema market; the dilapidated condition and outdated equipment of Soviet-era cinema halls; widespread video piracy; and the economic crises that closed off government subsidies for the film industry.[1] Despite these unfavourable conditions, Nikita Mikhalkov's *Burnt by the Sun* became one of the first post-Soviet blockbusters.

Several factors led to the film's success. Mikhalkov was personally involved in the film's production and distribution.[2] Moreover, the film gained international recognition: it shared the Grand Jury Prize at the 1994 Cannes Film Festival (with Zhang Yimou's *To Live*), and in 1995 it attracted additional audiences as only the third Russian language film to win the Academy Award (Oscar) for Best Foreign Language Film. The film's international recognition, its elaborate Moscow premiere (it was the first film to be shown in the Kremlin in 20 years), and the celebrity of its director contributed to its blockbuster status.[3] Because of its critical acclaim, popular appeal and setting in Stalinist 1930s, the film contributed to contemporary post-Soviet debates on the nature of individual responsibility and the role of personality in history.[4]

The film's title draws on the name of the tango 'The Weary Sun' ('Utomlennoe solntse'), popular in the 1930s. The song is the film's central musical motif that is played on the gramophone and hummed by the characters. However, the film's title changes the grammatical correlation of the song to 'Utomlennye solntsem', in which 'the weary sun' turns into 'worn out by the sun' or even 'burnt by the sun' in the English translation. The title is connected to the film's dedication to all victims of the Revolution of 1917 – the film's postscript reads 'to those who were burnt by the sun of the Revolution'. As critics immediately noticed, this title is reminiscent of Hollywood's *Gone with the Wind* (in Russian *Unesennye vetrom*), which similarly uses the personal lives of its characters to illustrate dramatic events of American history.[5]

Personal responsibility or guilt under the pressure of history is one of the film's central themes. The words of the song 'Weary Sun' that serves as the film's musical motif, 'you and I are both guilty', refer to the feeling of mutual guilt in the death of love. The events in *Burnt by the Sun* take place on a Sunday in June 1936, at the beginning of Stalin's repressions. Secret service (NKVD) officer Mitia receives a phone call that informs him of a mission to arrest the Red Army Commander Sergei Kotov at his *dacha* (country cottage) near Moscow. Mitia arrives at the dacha, where Kotov spends the weekend with his family, his wife Marusia and their daughter Nadia. Mitia's arrival is disruptive not only because of his mission, but also because of his past relationship with Marusia's family. Mitia was the favourite pupil of Marusia's father, and Marusia's first love. The personal past of these two men are closely related. Kotov is not only married to a woman who Mitia loves, he has also enlisted Mitia in the NKVD and has sent him abroad as a double agent. Mitia believes that Kotov has done this intentionally, thereby removing a competitor for Marusia's affections. Thus, when Mitia brings arrested Kotov to Moscow, his actions can be interpreted as both an accomplishment of a secret mission and personal revenge.

In addition to their intertwined personal histories, both men share a connection to the NKVD and Stalin. Kotov knows Stalin's personal phone number by heart, and Stalin's portrait as well as family photos with Stalin decorate the walls of Kotov's dacha. While Kotov's connection to Stalin is personal, Mitia's association is primarily symbolic: Mitia appears at the beginning of the film following the portraits of Stalin, Lenin, Marx, and Engels. Arriving at Kotov's dacha, Mitia enters from under the portrait of Stalin carried by the group of pioneers. Mitia's apartment overlooking the Kremlin – the famous house on the Embankment of the party elite – similarly symbolises his privileged position within the Stalinist system.

The clash of these 'guilty' men occurs in the dacha that is contrasted to Moscow – the centre of the Stalinist state. The first scene at the dacha depicts Kotov's family in a Russian steam bath. This scene combines the family idyll with a traditional past, thus allowing for nostalgic contemplation of Russian traditions. Belonging to Mitia's lover and Kotov's wife, the dacha represents the Russian past and family life that the two men value, but eventually destroy through their connection to the system – their involvement with the secret police.

The theme of mutual guilt is interrelated with the themes of fate and the inevitability of Stalin's terror that is symbolised by the fireballs with their capacity for unpredictable destruction. The unexpectedly appearing fireballs are mentioned at the beginning of the film: While Mitia is trying to commit suicide through the game of Russian roulette, his former tutor, Philip, reads an article about fireballs that suddenly increase in number. Significantly, the article blames this phenomenon on sabotage, the work of anti-Soviet spies, thus showing that even natural phenomena could be incorporated in the logic of Stalin's terror. Similarly, the logic of terror destroys both Mitia and Commander Kotov, using their interconnected and complicated past to realise their destruction. The real fireballs then appear twice in the film: as Mitia retells Marusia and Nadia the story of his life in fairy-tale form, and, at the end of the film, as Mitia finally succeeds in his suicide. The emphasis on fate, symbolised by fireballs and Russian roulette, undermines the notions of mutual guilt and personal responsibility.

With its emphasis on mutual guilt, *Burnt by the Sun* initially proposes a tragic interpretation of the protagonists' personal history. However, it instead turns into an epic melodrama with a clear moral code.[6] In the final analysis, the film is quite direct in its evaluation of moral character: both men might be guilty, but one is clearly guiltier than the other. Kotov holds the moral high ground due to his love of the motherland and the Russian people. Recognised and loved by everyone, he even competes with the authority of Stalin in his popular appeal. Kotov is associated with the family and Russian tradition that Mitia comes to destroy.[7] In contrast to Kotov, Mitia represents the shiftless 'cosmopolitan intelligentsia', tainted by their prolonged contact with the West.[8] Their lack of conviction led to the destruction of the pre-revolutionary Russia that Mitia used to love, and Kotov directly accuses Mitia to be unable to defend his ideals. Having become a Soviet double agent, Mitia further undermines his ideals, and turns into a trickster figure. Lacking any solid identity, he plays an infinite number of roles.

Masculine conflicts and communities are central to *Burnt by the Sun*. This community is contrasted to the world of the family, women and children. Both Kotov's daughter, Nadia, and his wife, Marusia, are in need of protection. The two are often equated, since Marusia appears as childlike to both Mitia and Kotov. She is much younger than both men, and Mitia's fondest memories of Marusia are of her childhood years. The world of the family is characterised by innocence and simple pleasures, while the masculine world is contaminated by the system. At the same time, only the men have to make moral choices and are responsible for their fate, whereas the family becomes their passive victim. From the film's postscript we learn that as a wife of 'the enemy of the people', Marusia dies in the Gulag, and, as a result, Nadia loses both parents. Both real and symbolic father figures also play a prominent role in the film. Kotov is most sympathetic as Nadia's father. Stalin appears as a problematic father figure to both Mitia and Kotov, and he is also a surrogate father of the Soviet people – his portrait carried by the air balloon dominates the landscape at the end of the film.

The film has a circular structure, where the episodes in Mitia's apartment near the Kremlin frame the events in the rest of the film. The apartment stands in opposition to Kotov's dacha. While these spaces appear as clear contrasts in the film, they also represent the limitations of the film's social scope. Thus, the film focuses on the spaces connected to the past and present elites, while associating the larger Russian countryside with anonymity and chaos. The film's central conflict similarly brings together the representatives of Russian and Soviet elites.[9] In different ways, both Kotov and Mitia bridge the divide between pre-revolutionary and post-revolutionary elites,

Mitia is able to maintain a privileged life style because of his professional life – his service in the NKVD – and Kotov connects pre-revolutionary and Soviet privileged classes, since, through his marriage to Marusia, he enters her aristocratic and cultured family.

From the perspective of gender, class, and national identity, *Burnt by the Sun* is consistent with Mikhalkov's other films.[10] It does not deviate from Mikhalkov's ideology of 'enlightened conservatism', in that it combines nostalgia and nationalism in its presentation of the Soviet 1930s.[11]

Notes

1. See Birgit Beumers, 'Cinemarket, or the Russian Film Industry in "Mission Possible"', *Europe-Asia Studies*, Vol. 51, No. 5, 1999, pp. 871–96; Susan Larsen, 'In Search of an Audience: The New Russian Cinema in Reconciliation', in Adele Marie Barker (ed.), *Consuming Russia: Popular Culture, Sex and Society since Gorbachev*, Durham, NC, Duke University Press, 1999, pp. 192–200.
2. In *Nikita Mikhalkov: between nostalgia and nationalism*, Birgit Beumers points out that Mikhalkov personally managed the film's distribution with the help of TriTe (p. 113). On the film's distribution, also see Iuliia Khomiakova, '"Oskar", "Nika" i "Feliks" vstrechaiutsia na Malom Kozikhinskom' (interview with Leonid Vereshchagin), *Kino-glaz*, Vol. 3, 1995, p. 35.
3. On the film's premiere, see Tat'iana Cherednichenko, '"Utomlennye solntsem" v "Rossii"' *Iskusstvo kino*, Vol. 3, 1995, pp. 19–20.
4. On the discussions surrounding the film, see Stephen M. Norris, 'Utomlennye solntsem', in E. Vasil'eva and N. Braginskii, *Noev kovcheg Russkogo kino: ot 'Sten'ki Razina' do 'stiliag'*, Moscow, Globus Press, 2013, pp. 443–4.
5. For example, Andrei Plakhov describes *Burnt by the Sun* as 'our Gone with the Wind'. See 'Mikhalkov protiv Mikhalkova', *Seans*, Vol. 9, 1994, p. 21.
6. Susan Larsen interprets *Burnt by the Sun* as an epic melodrama, due to its insistence on 'moral clarity', seen in the 'polarization of ethical opposites', and its 'stylistic, emotional, and narrative "excess"'. See Susan Larson, 'National identity, cultural authority, and the post-Soviet blockbuster: Nikita Mikhalkov and Aleksei Balabanov', *Slavic Review* Vol. 62, No. 3, 2003, pp. 493–4.
7. Birgit Beumers argues that Mikhalkov does not blame Bolshevism for the destruction of the Russian past. As a result, he 'sways between neo-Leninist and Russophile tradition'. The commander of the Red Army, Kotov, perfectly embodies these contradictory ideals (2003: 104, 112).
8. Mikhalkov is often explicitly anti-Western in his films. This anti-Western position is especially evident in his later film, *The Barber of Siberia* (1998).
9. In *Imperial Trace: Recent Russian Cinema*, Nancy Condee argues that Mikhalkov's films create an illusion of 'elite cohesion', in which the pre-revolutionary country estate is indistinguishable from the Soviet dacha (p. 85).
10. For Condee, Mikhalkov's oeuvre is 'explicitly traditionalist in its political orientation, Orthodox in its belief system, and patriarchal in its sexual order' (*Imperial Trace*, p. 86).
11. See Beumers, *Nikita Mikhalkov: between nostalgia and nationalism*.

Further reading

Anna Lawton, *Imaging Russia 2000: Film and Facts*, Washington, DC, New Academia Publishing, 2004.

Birgit Beumers, *Burnt by the Sun, Kinofile 3*, London, I.B Tauris, 2000.

Birgit Beumers, *Nikita Mikhalkov: Between Nostalgia and Nationalism*, London, I.B. Tauris, 2003.

Birgit Beumers (ed.), *Russia on Reels: The Russian Idea in Post-Soviet Cinema*, London, New York, I. B. Tauris, 1999.

Nancy Condee, *Imperial Trace: Recent Russian Cinema*, Oxford, Oxford University Press, 2009.

Irina Anisimova

Uzak/Distant (2002)

[Country: Turkey. Production Company: NBC Ajans. Producer, Director, Cinematographer: Nuri Bilge Ceylan. Editors: Ayhan Ergürsel and Nuri Bilge Ceylan. Cast: Muzaffer Özdemir (Mahmut), Emin Toprak (Yusuf), Zuhal Gencer (Nasan).]

Synopsis: After his wife leaves him, a photographer has an existential crisis and tries to cope with his cousin's visit.

A cockerel crows and a Man From The Country traipses through a field covered in deep snow, a small silhouette making its slow, unsteady way across the white. Behind him the thin white tower of a minaret stands out against the greys and brown-greens of an Anatolian hillside dotted haphazardly with uninspiring downbeat houses, unfinished building-works and untended stone terraces, a bland landscape of rural conventionality from which this solitary black figure is seeking to put some distance. Dogs bark, sheep bleat and cars can be heard driving by, all unseen as the Man From The Country walks further away from the village until, for a few moments, beneath the lip of an embankment he too disappears, briefly, only to re-emerge first just as a bobbing head of curly black hair and then as a thick-set leather-jacketed 27-year-old climbing up the snowy verge. Breathing heavy from his exertions he stops in front of the static camera and takes one last look back at the same landscape that we ourselves have been contemplating this past minute-and-a-half and then, hitching his faux-American athletics bag over one shoulder he walks off-screen and out of the crisp chill of the tableaux. After a moment or two more at rest on this rural vista completely devoid now of human presence, the camera pans slowly left to reveal more of the ramshackle village nestling in the snowy foothills, finally coming to a stop framing a shot of a tarmac road that snakes its way back into the snow-covered distance, flanked on its left side by a leafless black tree reaching up to touch a pale and clear morning sky.

The Man From the Country is Mehmet Emin Toprak, a manual worker from a provincial ceramics factory who has once again been given leave by his bosses to help his cousin from Istanbul make another film. This the third time in four years that Toprak has taken a sabbatical from his job manufacturing tiles to join the man in the blue puffa jacket bent over the Aaton 35mm film camera by the side of another rural Turkish highway. Nuri Bilge Ceylan is photographer, screenwriter, director, cameraman, editor, producer and devotee of that poetic realist strand of Slavonic high culture epitomised by Chekhov, Dostoevsky and by Tarkovsky the Russian cine-literateur *par excellence* of impressionistic space and time. Toprak plays Yusef, The Man From The Country, recently laid-off from his factory job and heading for the big city to find work on a merchantship and to make his fortune on the high seas far away from this empty backwater. The provincial migrant plans to stay for a few days in Istanbul with his cousin, the metropolitan Mahmut, a commercial photographer of ceramic tiles who once harboured dreams 'of making movies like Tarkovsky' and whose bookcases are decorated with portraits of the bearded authors of *Ward No.6* and *Crime and Punishment*. Mahmut is played by Muzaffer Ozdemir, an architect not an actor and a friend of Ceylan's who, with his sullen, jaded demeanour and hangdog expression behind a permanent beard of stubble exudes ennui both here and in *Clouds of May* (1999), the preceding film in Ceylan's autobiographical trilogy.

Ceylan's first three features, in each of which Toprak enacts variations on the same restless country-boy archetype yenning for release from his small-town confines, form a loose triad of melancholy and starkly beautiful films meditating lyrically on the theme of nostalgia. The films detail rural life through a stylised and contemplative high art mode, an aesthetic embodiment of the cosmopolitan cineaste Ceylan's return to those intertwined provincial social realities and personal histories that, as a successful art cinema auteur, he has since left behind. Ceylan's cinema of nostalgia, both stylised and sad, subdued yet celebratory, abstract yet at times emotionally brutal, has something of Terence Davies' painful and poetic return to the working-class neighbourhoods of his Liverpool youth in *Distant Voices, Still Lives* (1988). For Davies and Ceylan nostalgia is not a longing for some lost, imagined past, whether in the sing-song communality of Northern pubs or the night picnics shared in Anatolian fields by three generations of a village family. It is instead, an etymologically faithful pain (*algia*) upon having to return home once again (*nostos = homecoming*), it is the experience of an exilic state at the very site one most expects, or rather is most *expected,* to experience a profound sense of affective belonging. *Uzak*, we could argue in line with Turkish film scholar Asumen Suner, is visually, as well as thematically, 'a film not so much about mobility and displacement, as the sense of getting stuck in an engulfing place where one is *supposed* to belong' (2006, emphasis added).

Eschewing flamboyant camera movements, *le travelling* of Theo Angelopoulos and the filigree cinematography of Davies' ornamentalism, Ceylan's gaze on the run-down mise en scène of provincial life is pared down, minimalist. The basic unit of his austere aesthetic is the achingly poetic long-take-in-stasis, the perfectly balanced static composition taken with his photographer's eye for leading lines and layers of pulled focus, an aesthetic of quotidian beauty that partakes in what Jonathon Romney calls the 'haunted ruralism of Tarkovsky's *Mirror*' (2004), while simultaneously attending to the melancholy lyricism to be found in the rusted detritus of urban living and post-industrial decay as pointed to in *Stalker*. For Yusef, Istanbul is The City, the national destination of choice of post-war migration from the countryside, a place that accepts all newcomers, regardless of their ugly sweaters, stinking shoes and naff leathers, but a place that very quickly becomes for The Man From The Country an extension of the cold and lonely snowfield he seeks to escape. Ceylan's opening shot is a portrait of isolation, a lone figure shod in inappropriate shoes leaving behind friends and family without fanfare or farewell, and when Toprak's Man From The Country re-enters the frame to flag down a passing car the screen cuts to black before we even see him negotiate the hitch in silence, leaving the audience to read the film's opening credits to the sound of car doors opening and closing and an engine revving up and pulling away but without a single word being exchanged. This image of a man completely isolated, unable either alone or in company to connect or communicate is one that Ceylan repeats throughout the film, both in Yusef's interactions in the snowy streets of Istanbul and mirrored in the icy misanthropy of his cousin Mahmut's world-weary cynicism.

'The winter wonderland of *Distant* could be a snowy park in Moscow,' writes Diane Sippl, 'if it weren't for the minarets of mosques in lieu of crosses on golden cupolas' (2005). Ploughing through the whiteout and chill winds of a snowbound Istanbul in a cramped jeep with his skeleton crew of family and friends in tow, Ceylan is able to imbue his Photographer of Ceramics and The Man From The Country with the tragi-comic emptiness of a Levantine Chekhov or the naive aimlessness of a Dostoevskian Idiot as they both seek out some impossible warmth in the solitary city. Just as this accident of freak weather conditions draws out the film's Russian antecedents, Ceylan's filmmaking announces both explicitly and more allusively its cinematic influences, as noted in the oft-made citing of the inspirational example of Tarkovsky. Both in name and through clips of his films watched within the diegesis, references to Tarkovsky abound, but there are more oblique intertextual allusions dotted within Ceylan's text to the work of the Russian filmmaker. The opening shot recalls the first view of the provincial doctor making his way slowly across a grassy field in *Mirror* and Yusef's hypnogogic vision of a light emanating from his bedroom radiator is a Tarkovskian manipulation of film speed to create a moment of temporal disquiet. Mahmut's dream of the falling lamp recalls the dreams of deluge and collapse and the falling apart of domestic space in *Mirror,* while the slow peregrinations of a ceramic egg rolling on the floor of Mahmut's studio has the unsettling beauty of Tarkovsky's famous shot of the fading imprint of an arm on a polished tabletop. Reading Diane Sippl's description of Yusef's first foray to find work on a ship, echoes of Tarkovsky's *Stalker* are clearly discernible:

> In the foreground a single freight hook, crusted with ice, swings like a pendulum as a man in the distance traverses an empty stretch of snow in astonishment. Half-sunk against the embankment on the Sea of Marmara, an enormous ocean vessel is

> tipped on its side like a beached whale ignored and abandoned. Hoping for work as a sailor, Yusuf walks by the ship, caked with snow and white as a phantom as it creaks and groans. A loud splash caps the spell, and Yusuf runs off, suddenly overwhelmed.
>
> (Sippl 2005)

The dockyard, like The Zone in *Stalker*, has become an uncanny site of huge almost extraterrestrial artifice abandoned to the vicissitudes of awesome nature, and even for Anthony Lane in *The New Yorker*, whose reading of the scene is that Yusef 'hardly notices' the overhauled ship, Lane too recognises its uncanny presence, 'like some relic of a forgotten civilization, or a frozen mammoth' (2004). The strangeness of this image, however, goes beyond its transformation in Ceylan's masterly tracking shot from beached shipwreck to unheimlich behemoth, his *bricoleur's* virtuosic appropriation of *found objects* on an epic scale. The strangeness of this image is its precise literalness, its actuality as an image of material catastrophe otherwise glossed over in the film. After all, the inciting incident of Ceylan's narrative is the closure of the factory where Yusef, his father and a thousand other men were formerly employed, a factory closure that has put an entire community out of work. The creaking hulk caked in ice is an index of Turkey's economic collapse, of the 2001 financial crisis that left the country in a state of social ruin teetering on the verge of total submersion. The ship stands in for the manipulation of the stock markets and banking sector, the rapacious privatisation of public services and the imposition of damaging welfare reforms by the International Monetary Fund. As Ceylan himself notes in conversation with Geoff Andrew when discussing the urban alienation that economic self-sufficiency engenders:

> You don't want anything from other people, and in return you don't give anything to people. It's as if you've earned the right not to help others, by having become economically strong enough not to need the help of others.
>
> (2004)

Despite its obvious artistic debts to a cosmopolitan intellectual culture, Ceylan's filmmaking praxis is testimony to a more communal, more parochial culture of shared doing. City friends and family from the country double up as cast and crew, the Art Director Ebru Yapici (who will go on to marry Ceylan) playing the neighbourhood girl or Feridun Koç in the dual roles of the diminutive caretaker of Mahmut's apartment building while also caretaking each day's shoot as the film's Line Producer. This artisanal mode of production is both a matter of economic and artistic necessity, of keeping down costs and maintaining control, as well as a lived corrective to the isolation of urban existence and the atomism of intellectual culture. Ceylan's austere approach is as much an aesthetics of austerity and a collective mode of co-operative interdependence that look back to rural ways of working, of barn-raising, of shared olive presses and communal harvests. It is an economy of reciprocal exchange, a mutuality of kindness rewarding kindness in which neither Mahmut nor Yusef are able to feel truly at home.

Further reading

Geoff Andrew, 'Beyond the Clouds: An Interview with Nuri Bilge Ceylan', 2004. Available at http://sensesofcinema.com/2004/feature-articles/nuri_bilge_ceylan/ (accessed 9 April 2013).

Anthony Lane, 'Men's Secrets' *The New Yorker Magazine*, 15 March 2004. Available at www.newyorker.com/archive/2004/03/15/040315crci_cinema (accessed 9 April 2013).

Jonathon Romney, 'A Silky Sadness', *Sight & Sound*, June 2004. Available at www.nbcfilm.com/uzak/press_sightsoundjonathan.php (accessed 9 April 2013).

Diane Sippl, 'Ceylan and Company: Autobiographical Trajectories of Cinema', *CineAction*, June 2005. Available at www.nbcfilm.com/uzak/press_cineaction.php (accessed 9 April 2013).

Asuman Suner, 'Outside in: "accented cinema" at large', *Inter-Asia Cultural Studies*, Volume 7, Number 3, 2006. Available at www.nbcfilm.com/uzak/press_screenasuman2.php (accessed 9 April 2013).

Asuman Suner, *New Turkish Cinema: Belonging, Identity and Memory*, London & New York: I.B. Tauris, 2010.

Nick Potamitis

Il vangelo secondo Matteo/The Gospel According to St. Matthew (1964)

[Country: Italy. Production Company: Arco Films and Lux Compagnie Cinematographique de France. Producer: Alfredo Bini. Director: Pier Paolo Pasolini. Screenwriter: Pier Paolo Pasolini. Cinematographer: Tonino Delli Colli. Music: Luis Bacalov. Editor: Nino Baragli. Production Design: Luigi Scaccianoce. Costume Designer: Danilo Donati. Cast: Enrique Irazoqui (Christ), Margherita Caruso (Young Mary), Susanna Pasolini (Old Mary), Marcello Morante (Joseph), Mario Socrate (John the Baptist), Otello Sestili (Judas Iscariot), Settimio Di Porto (Peter), Alfonso Gatto (Andrew), Luigi Barbini (James), Giacomo Morante (John).]

Synopsis: The film is based on the events related in Saint Matthew's Gospel. It begins with the angel Gabriel telling Joseph about the Immaculate Conception and goes on to recreate the Nativity, the flight into Egypt and the Slaughter of the Innocents before moving forward to Christ's baptism by John the Baptist, Christ's temptation in the wilderness, the gathering of the disciples, the Sermon on the Mount, John's execution by King Herod, Christ's miracles and entry into Jerusalem, Jesus in the temple, the anointing, the Last Supper, Christ's arrest, Crucifixion and finally the Resurrection.

One of the most important, controversial and divisive figures in post-war Italian culture, Pier Paolo Pasolini was a filmmaker, poet, painter, novelist, cultural theorist and political activist. An *agent provocateur* par excellence, Pasolini was a committed Communist who was at one point ejected from the party due to his homosexuality and who sided with the police during the events of 1968. He was an avowed atheist whose films *La ricotta* (1963) and *Teorema* (1968) were officially condemned by the Catholic Church and whose final work, *Salò* (1975), an adaptation of the Marquis de Sade's *The 120 Days of Sodom*, was banned in numerous countries for decades. However, *Il vangelo secondo Matteo*, his adaptation of Saint Matthew's Gospel was unironically dedicated to Pope John XXIII and won the OCIC (Catholic Organisation of Cinema and Audiovisual Culture) Award at the Venice film festival. Indeed, it is widely considered to be the greatest film about the life of Jesus ever made, and features on the Vatican's official list of important movies.

This is perhaps less of a contradiction than it as first seems, for although he was an atheist, Pasolini was a cultural Catholic whose vision of the world, by his own admission, was essentially religious. Furthermore, as Oswald Stack has argued, the two commanding ideologies which dominate Italian intellectual life are Catholicism and Marxism and this film attempts to bring these two seemingly opposing forces together (Stack 1969: 7). Inspired by Pope John XXIII's opening of the Second Vatican Council, and influenced by the Italian Marxist Antonio Gramsci to create national-popular myths that could lead people to political engagement and social reform, Pasolini made his Christ a 'total revolutionary' and the key note of his adaptation can be found in Matthew 10:34: 'I came not to send peace, but a sword'. For Pasolini, Jesus is a messenger who has come to spur on a 'world of poor people ready for revolution'. To this end, this cinematic incarnation of Christ continually addresses the audience. For example, during the reconstruction of the Sermon on the Mount the disciples are never seen and Christ is framed in close ups and medium shots throughout, looking directly into the camera at the viewer.

Despite having scouted locations in Palestine (a journey recorded in the 1963 short documentary, Sopralluoghi in Palestina), Pasolini finally elected to shoot the entire film in southern Italy. While this decision may partly have been made for budgetary reasons, the areas of Italy he chose where often poor and had changed little since the time of the Romans, which perhaps made them a closer approximation of ancient Israel than modern-day Palestine. However, Pasolini was not overly concerned with historical authenticity, and instead sought to tell the story of the Gospel through subtle analogies with recent history. Therefore, his images of Joseph and Mary fleeing to Egypt with the baby Jesus were inspired by photographs of Spanish Civil War refugees crossing the border into France on donkeys in 1939, while the uniforms of the Roman soldiers have echoes of those worn by the Italian police.

Pasolini also made it clear that his film is a version of Matthew's Gospel, not a film about the life of Christ (many such films, from *King of Kings* to *Jesus of Nazareth* to *The Passion of the Christ* combine material from all four Gospels in a way which Pasolini refused to do). His decision to focus his film solely on Matthew's Gospel was both aesthetic and political. The director found Mark's Gospel too 'crude', John's too 'mystical' and Luke's too 'sentimental and bourgeois'. Matthew, on the other hand, he found to be the most poetically written and the most radical. Convinced that he could not emulate the language of the original, Pasolini was careful only to have his characters speak words which came directly from the Gospel (with the exception of a few lines taken from the Book of Isaiah). However, his claim to have simply followed the story without omissions or additions is not strictly true. While adapting the text, he cut and rearranged the material to suit his ideological and aesthetic ends, and ultimately, only around two-thirds of the incidents described by Matthew end up in the finished film.

It would be wrong, however, to view the film as merely a visualisation of the one Gospel. Rather, Pasolini also wanted to 'tell the story of Christ plus two thousand years of Christian tradition, because it took two thousand years to mythologise that biography' (Stack 1969: 83). As the film is also about 2,000 years of storytelling about the life of Christ, Pasolini's mise en scène and soundtrack draws from an eclectic array of paintings, films and music.

One of the key sources of inspiration for *The Gospel According to St Matthew* was Roberto Rossellini's *Francis, God's Jester* (1950). This neo-realist depiction of the life of St. Francis, in which the Saint and his followers are played by genuine Franciscan monks, deliberately eschewed the spectacle, special effects and piety that characterised most previous biblical films. Like Rossellini, Pasolini shoots his film in a near documentary style, and avoids elaborate depictions of Christ's miracles. He also utilised non-actors in all roles. At first, in keeping with Pasolini's view of Christ as a revolutionary figure, he considered casting Yevgeny Yevtushenko, the Russian poet, or the American Beat writer, Jack Kerouac. In the end, however, he cast a Spanish student, Enrique Irazoqui, as his central character. Judas was played by a Roman lorry driver, while the part of the older Virgin Mary went to the director's own mother. This casting of unknowns similarly went against the Hollywood trend for using a roster of stars in biblical epics, such as the appearance of John Wayne as a Roman Centurion with only a single line of dialogue in George Stevens' *The Greatest Story Ever Told* (1965).

The British filmmaker, Derek Jarman, who was a great admirer of Pasolini, frequently compared his Italian forebear to Caravaggio, the great Italian painter who frequently paid prostitutes and petty criminals to pose for his religious canvases. Pasolini reversed the trend by making films about prostitutes and petty criminals and filming them in a reverential way, as he did in works such as *Accattone* (1961), in which he went as far as to liken his sub-proletarian protagonist to an angel by Gian Lorenzo Bernini. In addition, he underscores Accattone's mundane and unsavoury activities with a chorus from Bach's *St. Matthew Passion.* However, when filming his life of Christ, Pasolini concluded that this reverential style was simply a case of gilding the lily, and he rethought his shooting strategy. He began employing frequent zooms, handheld shots, and some techniques that went against conventional film grammar. He frequently contravenes the 180 degree rule and keeps 'mistakes' in the final cut, such as obvious focus pulls and pans that do not initially hit their mark. On the one hand, the inclusion of these elements adds to the film's documentary quality and makes the film seem as if it was comprised of found footage. At the same time, however, these techniques call attention to themselves and make the viewer constantly aware that they are watching a film. *The Gospel According to St Matthew* is therefore the most overtly realistic film about the life of Christ, but also the most modernist.

The use of music has attracted particular attention. Rather than commission a new score, Pasolini compiled an eclectic soundtrack. Perhaps least surprisingly, he made use of several excerpts from Bach's *Saint Matthew Passion*, as well as the composer's Mass in B Minor. In addition to Bach, he also uses snippets from Mozart's 'Dissonance' Quartet and *Masonic Funeral Music*, while the Slaughter of the Innocents plays out to part of Prokofiev's *Alexander Nevsky* cantata. More unusually, he repeatedly used the Gloria from the *Missa Luba*, a Congolese version of the Latin Mass (the Sanctus from the same piece features prominently in Lindsay Anderson's *If*...) and Blind Willie Johnson's haunting slide-guitar driven 'Dark Was the Night, Cold was the Ground' accompanies Christ's trial and the walk up to Calvary. However, the most surprising choice was Pasolini's use of a recording of the Blues singer, Odetta, performing 'Sometimes I Feel like a Motherless Child' during the Nativity. While some have found the inclusion of more contemporary music jarring and anachronistic, many more have found it highly effective and often very moving. Moreover, despite the seemingly different idioms, almost all the music in the film is of a sacred or religious nature, and the use of works from three different continents helps emphasise the universality of Christ's story.

In the 1940s Pasolini studied under the noted Italian art historian Roberto Longhi, and his interest in painting is apparent in all of his films; *The Gospel According to St. Matthew* is no exception. As with the music, Pasolini draws from a wide frame of reference which spans six centuries of representations of Christ. For example, the unusual woven hats worn by the Pharisees and Sadducees were in fact modelled on those in Piero della Francesca's *Exaltation of the Cross* (1466), while the first appearance of the pregnant virgin in the film recalls the same artist's *Madonna del Parto* (1460). Pasolini also seems to have cast his leading actor based on his physical resemblance to Christ as depicted by both El Greco (1541–1615) and the French painter Georges Rouault (1871–1958).

Ironically, many of the same Italian locations used in Pasolini's film where also used in Mel Gibson's *The Passion of the Christ*, a Catholic Jesus film that is radically different from Pasolini's in tone and ideology (Gibson has spoken out against the reforms of the Second Vatican Council which were such an inspiration to Pasolini). Rather, the true successor to *The Gospel According to St Matthew* is Denys Arcand's 1989 film *Jesus of Montreal*, which updates the story to contemporary Canada. Arcand's film is also the work of a non-believer with an essentially Christian worldview. It is also derived from a single Gospel (that of Saint Mark), and similarly presents viewers with an angry Christ-figure whose story is used to make political points about advertising, materialism and decadence in contemporary society.

Finally, although he was keen to stress that his film was the work of an atheist, Pasolini was also adamant that *The Gospel According to St Matthew* was not intended to deconsecrate the story of Christ. He noted that this was a fashion he hated. Rather Pasolini claimed to want to 're-consecrate things as much as possible ... to re-mythicize them'. It is perhaps Pasolini's ability to combine this sense of the sacred with a distinct lack of piety and a clear political purpose that makes *The Gospel According to St Matthew* the most important and lasting of all the Jesus films.

Further reading

Lloyd Baugh, *Imaging the Divine: Jesus and Christ Figures in Film*, Kansas City, Sheed and Ward, 1997.

Naomi Greene, *Pier Paolo Pasolini: Cinema as Heresy*, Princeton, Princeton University Press, 1992.

Sam Rohdie, *The Passion of Pier Paolo Pasolini*, London, BFI, 1996.

Oswald Stack, *Pasolini on Pasolini: Conversations with Oswald Stack*, London, Thames and Hudson, 1969.

Brian Hoyle

Varastettu kuolema/The Stolen Death (1938)

[Country: Finland. Production Company: Erik Blomberg. Director: Nyrki Tapiovaara. Producer: Erik Blomberg. Screenwriters: Eino Mäkinen, Erik Blomberg. Dialogue: Matti Kurjensaari. Cinematographers: Olavi Gunnari, Erik Blomberg. Music: George de Godzinsky. Editors: Erik Blomberg, Nyrki Tapiovaara. Cast: Tuulikki Paananen (Manja), Ilmari Mänty alias Ralph Enckell (Robert Hedman), Santeri Karilo (Jonni Claesson), Annie Mörk (Madam Johansson), Bertha Lindberg (Robert's Mother).]

Synopsis: In 1905, a young law student, Robert Hedman, belongs a group of Finnish activists striving for independence from the Russian Empire. He purchases weapons for the rebels from a shady businessman called Jonni. Jonni agrees to deliver a machine gun but also plans to blackmail the group. Jonni's girlfriend Manja and Robert fall in love with each other and Manja volunteers to help the activists to steal the weapon. When Jonni finds out about the theft, he reports the rebels to the Tsarist militia. Robert is imprisoned but escapes and is chased by the military. During the chase, Manja is wounded and dies in Robert's arms whereas he manages to sail out of the country.

When *The Stolen Death/ Varastettu kuolema* was released in September 1938, it was perceived as confusing. The film that had been widely advertised as an experiment within the action genre, an 'amazing example of innovative cinematic thinking' and a star vehicle promoting the beautiful Tuulikki Paananen – an actress with experience filming in Hollywood – was pronounced a disappointment. The reviews were unfavourable in several ways, and the box office a serious setback. Therefore, the film was moved from the first-run theatres in Helsinki to the smaller cinemas at the fringes of the capital after only a week. The marketing strategy was changed as well, addressing now to a more limited group of audiences interested in foreign and avant-garde films.

The Stolen Death was an independent production by a younger generation of intellectuals in Helsinki. The director Nyrki Tapiovaara – a dropout law student – was a member of a leftist-oriented group of writers and artists called *Kiila*.[1] His first feature-length film, *Juha* (1937), had been very successful, and he was offered to direct *The Stolen Death* by the photographer Erik Blomberg. Blomberg had written the script with another filmmaker, Eino Mäkinen, and planned to produce, shoot and edit the film as well. It seems he was quite eager to transfer the story into moving pictures but did not really trust his skills since, apart from a co-writer, he also engaged a dialogue writer and co-photographer. In fact, many other members of the cast and crew were recruited among friends of the producers.

The film is based on a novella from 1919, *Köttkvarn*, by a Swedish-speaking Finn, Runar Schldt.[2] The novella depicts a story from the Finnish Civil War waged in the winter of 1917–18 between the revolutionary 'Red' socialist workers sympathising with the Russian Bolsheviks, and the conservative, patriotic 'Whites' striving for Finnish independence. In the novella, the young White rebels, among them Robert Hedman, plan an attack on the Finnish Red Army that governed Helsinki at one point. Robert obtains weapons from a shady businessman Jonni Claesson, who promises to deliver a machine gun but plans, too, to blackmail the young men's rich parents: the Red Army would immediately execute Robert and his friends if they found out about the group. Jonni's accomplice Manja, who has fallen in love with Robert, helps the young man steal the machine gun. Jonni finds out about the scheme and reports Robert who is arrested and killed. The novella ends with Manja fainting of grief and exhaustion next to his dead body abandoned on the street.

Upon completion of the film, both producers and critics felt that not much was left of the original story except for the names of the characters. The changes made are a multifaceted example of how the political situation in a country may affect a film's content. The novella was published only two years after the Civil War, but after 20 years it was still considered much too delicate a topic for a film. Instead, the story was set in an earlier but equally precarious period in Finnish history, namely the Russo-Japanese war of 1905. In the late 30s it seemed politically 'safer' to depict the more clear-cut conflict between the Russian imperial oppressor and the Finnish patriots. Likewise, it seemed less provocative in regard to the leaders of the Bolshevik Soviet Union who were closely monitoring Finnish sentiments.[3]

Indeed, not just the context but the plot was altered. The novella is mainly constructed from the point of view of the woman, Manja. Its ominous atmosphere is a result of a net of arbitrary coincidences that seem to have a clandestine logic with fatal consequences for the characters. The film version foregrounds Robert and the political conflict reflected in his family relations, while Manja's situation, relations and motivations are pushed to the fringes of the story. Furthermore, in the film version Robert is imprisoned after a tip from Jonni to the Tsarist militia but he manages to escape, and the film includes a thrilling scene with Robert's Mother and a prison guard examining her bag. During the flight in the last scene of the film – another 'cinematic' supplement to the story – Manja gets lethally wounded and dies in Robert's arms.

On the whole, the film's storyline stresses and expands on the scenes typical for the action genre – such as chases, the transport of the stolen machine gun, and preparations for Robert's escape. However the editing and photographic work both differ from the shot/countershot mode of narrative technique typical for the period. This perhaps was an attempt to create the 'atmosphere' of the novella that many contemporary critics referred to, but it also pays a tribute to the Russian and European expressionist cinema in the 20s.

The criticism that followed the film premiere may be divided in rather clear-cut camps: the leftist and Swedish-speaking papers were favourable, while the right-wing and conservative papers criticised the film's lack of a proper ideological standpoint. They were quite merciless while accusing the producers of lack of patriotism, judgement and good taste: 'The lack of the Finnish spirit was obvious, as were the signs of love for the Fatherland and the claim for freedom felt by the Finnish people', writes alias –T. in an extreme right-wing paper.[4] However, almost every review, no matter how stern otherwise, considered the photographic work as genuinely excellent stating that the genre aspect of the film and the depiction of the city of Helsinki as a place of thrill and suspense were realised in a 'masterly manner'. The French influence in the visual style was spotted, and if such an influence was not perceived as 'unfinnish', the film's style was triumphantly declared 'as good as' in a French or, for that matter, British genre film.

An unusual aspect for the period is that in *The Stolen Death* the characters actually speak three different languages: Finnish, Swedish and Russian.[5] Language thus becomes a significant element: Jonni who betrays the cause of the Finnish, strikes us as quite promiscuous language-wise as he freely blends German and English expressions with his Finnish and Swedish. The major language in the film, also spoken between Robert and Manja, is Finnish. However, Robert speaks Swedish with his Mother and aunt. Robert's mother in her turn speaks all three languages, a feature indicative of the power position but also opportunism of the Finnish-born upper class. While the language issue was ignored by the Finns, Swedish-speaking journalists took offense: in their minds the hardcore conservatism and submissive politics represented by Robert's family did not give a truthful image of the general sentiments among the Swedish-speaking Finns.[6]

Nyrki Tapiovaara completed two more films and left one unfinished when he died during the last days of the Winter War, at the age of 29. His uncompleted *oeuvre*, his reputation as a war hero and the general appraisal of his work as ambitious and formally innovative contributed to the myth surrounding his person, well in line with the expanding post-Second World War view of the film director as an *auteur*.

As elsewhere in Europe recovering after the Second World War, film archives were established in Helsinki for the showing of art-house cinema. *The Stolen Death* was screened in a cinematheque in 1952. It was now hailed as a true masterpiece of Finnish film history. Voices were raised that it should be shown publicly again, and a new premiere was arranged in the spring of 1954. Before the release, Erik Blomberg – the producer, editor and photographer – re-edited the film that now became roughly ten minutes shorter. Blomberg himself said that he had cut the 'more blatant expressionist influences'.[7] The version of *The Stolen Death* that has been available for audiences since 1954 is the version re-edited by him.

When saying that he had cut the more blatant expressionist influences, Blomberg seems to have meant that he reduced the length of certain shots, mainly close-ups on faces expressing horror, surprise or excitement. A lengthy part in the beginning of the film was removed. It is a montage sequence on a newspaper mill accompanied by a suggestive music composed for the film by George de Godzinsky. The arrangement reminds us of the city symphonies of the 20s, but it also depicts a political situation, during which the Russian censorship authorities and the military closed down newspapers in Finland. Manually operated underground printing machines are being used, and the workers instruct the students to set up office in a scene that shows both intellectuals and workers working together against the Russian military. The dialogue begins at the moment when the activists decide to move from pamphlets to weapons.

Reviews of the 50s focused on the visual style and the contrasts of light and shadow; the critics suggested that Tapiovaara had chosen his camera angles 'with a shocking audacity'. These were choices that 'gave proof of his natural sense for cinema as an art form'.[8] This time the critics also reflected on the irony and sense of humour expressed in the film, whereas the pathos and solemnity of patriotic sentiments as well as the language issue were long gone. The reviews also paid attention to the early Russian and French influences in the film, especially those of René Clair. They referred to Tapiovaara's travels in Europe and his interest in modern literature. Tapiovaara's earlier film production was mentioned along with the heroic details surrounding his death. His unfinished film was called *Miehen Tie/One Man's Fate/The Man's Way* (1940), now seen as an omen of his fate in the service of the Fatherland. In 1954, Erik Blomberg had quite recently made an international success with his film *Valkoinen peura/White reindeer* (1953). He played a seminal role in the genesis of *The Stolen Death* – which nobody denied – and he got quite a lot of publicity in relation to the new premiere. But still, Nyrki Tapiovaara was hailed as the genius, the real artist and the instigator of the film. So mesmerising is the power of the myth.

The Stolen Death has since been screened at numerous film festivals, in cinematheques and of course on Finnish television. It has been valued as one of the county's few real art films and a valuable document for the youthful enthusiasm and spirit among the pre-war intellectuals in Finland. Every film chronicle or historical overview worth the name mentions *The Stolen Death* and its director. However, it seems another re-evaluation is on its way. Sentiments of disappointment and overtly critical reviews may be found among critics of the younger generations who also criticise the mythology and 'auteurism' surrounding Nyrki Tapiovaara.

Notes

1. English: a wedge.
2. English: 'meat grinder' – in the story a code name for a machine gun.
3. Kari Uusitalo, *Lavean tien sankarit, Suomalainen elokuva 1931–1939*, Helsinki, Otava, 1975, p. 121.
4. *Ajan Suunta*, 6 September 1938.
5. Swedish is a minority tongue in Finland that (wrongly) has been considered as the language of the upper classes. Russian was the official language of the military and civil servants during the Tsarist occupation.
6. *Åbo Underrättelser*, 7 September 1938.
7. Uusitalo, *Lavean tien sankarit*, p. 122.
8. *Nya Pressen*, 3 May 1954.

Tytti Soila

Varieté/Variety (1925)

[Country: Germany. Production Company: Universum-Film (UFA). Director: E. A. Dupont. Producer: Erich Pommer. Screenwriters: Leo Birinski, E. A. Dupont (based on Felix Holländer's novel *The Oath of Stephan Huller*). Cinematographer: Karl Freund, Carl Hoffmann. Music: Ernö Rapée. Cast: Emil Jannings (Boss Huller), Lya de Putti (Berta-Marie), Warwick Ward (Artinelli), Georg Baselt (variety agent), The Three Codonas (trapeze scenes).]

Synopsis: After many years in prison, with friends and family petitioning for his pardon, Prisoner 28 (Jannings) tells of his crime to a judge. In flashback, we learn that he is Boss Huller and that, years before, he had a carnival trapeze act along with his wife, Berta-Marie (de Putti). Invited to collaborate with Artinelli, a more famous trapeze artist, the Hullers move into the glamorous realms of spectacular variety entertainment. When Huller learns that Artinelli and Berta-Marie's friendship has turned into an affair, he contemplates murdering Artinelli by 'accidentally' dropping him in mid-performance. Instead, he confronts him and in the ensuing struggle, stabs him to death. Having heard Huller's story, the judge pronounces a pardon and releases him from prison.

On its release, E. A. Dupont's *Variety* was among the most talked about films in the world, both a box office and a critical success.[1] It was one of few interwar German films – *The Cabinet of Dr. Caligari* and *The Last Laugh* were others – to achieve substantial success in America, where it was the 1926 winner of the annual Film Critics poll. In the *New York Times*, it was hailed as no less than the greatest film ever made, 'the strongest and most inspiring drama that has ever been told by the evanescent shadows.'[2] Today, however, it is perhaps the least well known of well-known Weimar films; unlike *Metropolis* or *Pandora's Box*, its images have not been absorbed into the canon of cultural memory, either general or cinephile. Its place in film history has largely been reduced to one stunning visual effect: sequences shot from a camera on a moving circus trapeze, images which gave audiences the giddy sensation of swinging and soaring, and of falling and plunging to earth.

More than 80 years on, *Variety*'s visual impact remains startling, but the film is and was much more than a vehicle for photo-technical virtuosity. The film's look – encompassing its mobile camera, dynamic editing and a mise en scène teeming with the play of motion and light – forms an inseparable part of its closely observed psychological miniature, a triangle of desire and jealousy, masochism and murder. *Variety* borrows generic conventions from popular Weimar formats like the 'street film' and the 'chamber film'. In its general thematic preoccupations too, it is very much of its time, first, in its simultaneous fascination with and horror at urban modernity and its burgeoning mass cultural forms, second in its preoccupation with scenes of looking and technologies of vision, and third, in the ambiguity of its representation of gender and sexuality. Finally, *Variety* is medially self-reflexive, both a product and a representation of the booming popular entertainment industry, and a document of the complex intermedial relations between film and popular performance at the time.

Although film and – broadly speaking – theatre have often been depicted as rival media, in fact their relations were, and are, much more complex than simple opposition or competition. The exhibition of moving images on film, of course, began as a kind of variety act, just another fairground attraction. Significantly, although *Variety* does not directly allude to this, the first public film projections in Germany took place in the Wintergarten, here the location of the Three Artinellis' aerialist performances. While cinema in time moved out of this milieu, becoming an autonomous medium and industry, this expansion did not come directly at the expense of popular performance and variety theatre. As cinema developed into a central element in a culture of mass leisure and consumption, variety theatre experienced its own boom, with dozens of new locations opening in the early 1920s (Guerin 2005: 192–231).

This boom rested, to no small degree, on electricity. Electric technologies of illumination and amplification expanded the possibilities of popular entertainment, but they needed significant capital investment. A steeper hierarchy emerged, topped by a tier of wealthy venues and prestigious acts. *Variety* makes this stratification visible, both onstage and backstage. The Wintergarten spectacle – with its huge indoor arena, elaborate lighting, considerable publicity apparatus – contrasts with more rudimentary fairground entertainment. The hierarchy is also to be seen in the contrast between glamorous, upscale bohemia and the life of carnival's proletarian milieu; this sharpened distinction is also an important motivation for the characters, underlying Berta-Marie's ambition to ascend to higher showbiz echelons and Artinelli's initial repugnance at dealing with 'mere carnival performers'. And there is always further to go, higher to climb, another culture industry to conquer: Artinelli partly engineers his seduction of Berta-Marie with hints of offers from America.

E. A. Dupont, the film's director, knew these overlapping worlds of variety and film as well as anyone. Before moving into the film business around 1916, he was a newspaper reporter covering film *and* popular theatre, writing a column entitled 'Film and Variety'. Even after establishing himself as an important director and film writer, he kept ties to variety, even spending a year as a theatre manager in 1924.[3] After *Variety* made his name internationally – it was his calling card to a later career in Hollywood, England and France – he returned repeatedly to the world of popular performance in films like *Piccadilly* and *Moulin Rouge.* But it would be wrong to regard Dupont as an all-powerful, all-determining *auteur.* Other figures and larger forces were just as important in determining the film's form, meaning and impact. Above all, *Variety* bears the imprint of the man who hand-picked Dupont for the job: Erich Pommer, then head of production at the UFA studio, arguably the most important person in the German film business in the early 1920s.

Variety exemplified Pommer's belief that the German film industry could assert itself against Hollywood by producing films that combined artistic credibility with high production values, especially in their use of innovative technology and spectacular special effects.[4] Sometimes these 'quality films' borrowed from high art, as in Murnau's *Faust,* which added dazzling, expensive special effects to a version of Goethe's play; sometimes they were drawn from mass culture, as with *Variety*'s adaptation of a popular novel, Felix Hollaender's *The Oath of Stephan Huller.* Whatever the source material, Pommer's vision was of superior vernacular artworks, profitable enough to maintain German production against Hollywood competition, and even to make inroads in America itself.[5] The relative transatlantic success of Murnau's *Last Laugh* in 1924 seemed to confirm the model, and – looking to build on that success – *Variety* reprises two key elements of that film. The first was Jannings' unusual leading-man persona, which successfully combined a bulky, graceful physicality with sexualised abjection and the pathos of humiliation. The second, just as important, was the visceral thrill of Karl Freund's 'liberated camera' – *die entfesselte Kamera* – a shorthand name for techniques of mobility and portability that enabled startling visual sensations.[6]

In *Variety*, Freund and Dupont used camera mobilisation in more radical ways than in Murnau's film. As Thomas Brandlmeier points out, where camera movement in *The Last Laugh* functions largely along linear vertical and horizontal axes, *Variety*'s placement of the camera on suspended, swinging objects lent a qualitatively new fluidity to spatial representation (2008: 72). The *viewpoint* and *vanishing point* established in linear perspective are here dynamised, with vaulting, shifting horizons creating a giddy sense of groundlessness, foreshadowing the media theorist Paul Virilio's later formulation that 'cinema is not "I see", it is "I fly"'.[7]

But these moments of photoscopic hyperkinesis are actually used comparatively sparingly – they do not stand alone, but combine with other effects of motion to create the dynamic visual spectacle. Thus, in a number of set-piece scenes, the camera becomes only one moving object within a dizzying extravaganza of moving bodies and objects. In the opening carnival scene – a tutor-text for watching and understanding the film – the vaulting movement of the camera on a swingboat feeds into a still more extravagant play of movement, vibration and motility. This encompasses the Brownian motion of crowds, the turning of carousels, the shuttling of roller-coaster cars, the lights of distant trains cutting through the frame, even the resonant shudder of human muscles and performed facial twitches. We even see some of this photo-dynamism – reminiscent of contemporary formalist experiments by Walter Ruttmann or László Moholy-Nagy – through the close-up blur of a rotating fairground ride. Later, the film will reprise this veil of unfocussed movement in another famous shot, when the performers' party is seen through the blades of a rotating ceiling fan.

Crucially, this complex movement is not simply a visual thrill: it comes with an acute thematic, dramatic and psychological point. The thrills of the fairground and spectacular performance here are a concentrated node of a world in exciting, dangerous flux. Visual dynamism is used to characterise urban life as a place of upheaval and uncertainty, temptation and sensation, full of motion and excitement, but also overstimulation and excessive spectacle. Modernity exudes a nervousness and shallowness that threatens to destabilise moral certainties along with perceptual norms. The film underlines the link between variety's dynamism and larger phenomena of mobility by emphasising the Wintergarten's location in Berlin. We see theatrical performers arriving by train from all over Europe, walking en masse through the crowded streets to the nearby theatre. This passage through geographical space is in turn inseparable from the display of moving bodies on stage, celebrated in a hectic montage sequence of chorus lines, acrobats, spinning plates, slapstick artists, unicycling jugglers and more.

This dynamic environment is more than simply context for the film's action. It structurally pervades what is, on the face of it, a simple narrative constellation: a love triangle between two men and a woman, with a sequence of events leading from temptation to betrayal, concealment to discovery, from jealousy to murderous rage. The triangle is of a specific kind: the Oedipal triangle, a frequent Weimar story structure, understood in broad terms as sexual competition over a woman between an older and a younger man, often a father and son.[8] But *Variety* renders even this structure unstable and hard to read. The relation established between Berta-Marie, Boss and Artinelli forms a dangerously uncertain and ambiguous space, with gender, sexuality and age unmoored from simple definition. It is as if, at the level of the story too, all is in motion, the triangle's lines and points in dynamic relation.

The fluctuating relation of the three main characters has a proper name, appropriately paradoxical. Their act is 'The Three Artinellis', a formation that replaces the 'natural' fraternity of the 'Artinelli Brothers', put out of action when a second brother broke a leg. Artinelli is temporarily emasculated – forced to watch the performances of others from the audience – and in response constructs a quasi-family bearing his name, a grouping teeming with undefined, shifting and ultimately fatal desires. On the trapeze, the three are dressed in homogenous, androgynous white suits, marked with a black death's head, collectively performing for the audience's voyeuristic gaze, but internally pervaded with desire, riven with panic and death-fantasies. The group is described as the *kings of the air*, but from the outset, power is not shared equally, and neither the gender nor the relations of these three 'kings' are simple or clear.

Among the three, Berta-Marie is a noticeably underdeveloped character, perhaps pointing to her more abstract – and lesser – role as Dangerous Woman, primarily a trigger of desire's disturbance of fixed identities and relations. But additionally, as many viewers have noted, both Boss and Artinelli, in their different ways, are also partly feminised figures. In the fairground household, Boss performs the domestic role, cooking and cleaning, joining the women's queue to buy milk. In this context, Jannings's strength and physicality seems less traditionally masculine than proletarian-female. But his erotic relation to Berta-Marie is abject, almost infantile: in the scenes between the two, Jannings' facial performance emphasises his attitude of childish supplication. Artinelli, by contrast, is the suave upper-class heterosexual seducer, but at the same time his slight frame, fastidious manners and elegant dress position him as effeminate, particularly in comparison to Jannings' bulky presence. Ultimately the most intense side of the desiring-triangle is perhaps between Boss and Artinelli: it might be argued that Berta-Marie's key role is less as a subject or object of desire in her own right, but rather as a medium between the two men. At one point, Boss literally throws her into Artinelli's arms; in urging the two to attend the fireworks display together, Boss seems to conspire in his own cuckolding, drawing him ever closer to Artinelli. Their relation culminates in a murder scene that is also a bedroom scene: the struggle over the knife not hard to read as the final fatal consummation of repressed desire.

The film works hard to control the energies of visual dynamism, moral ambiguity and erotic transgression. Many commentators have noted a tension between the attractions of the film itself – the intensity of light and movement, the sheer visual spectacle – and the emphatic moralism of its frame story. By virtue of this outer story, the film situates the entire main narrative as deposition before a judge: the story is Boss's sign of repentance, and a plea for mercy. Having heard him out, the judge, a white-bearded man seated beneath a crucifix, declares him forgiven in the eyes of the law and of God. The final image of the film, the last frame of the frame story, is telling. We are shown another visual representation of motion, not the flux of urban modernity now, but a movement at once natural and highly controlled – trees blowing in the wind, framed within the outline of a prison gate.[9] Fluid energies are safely put back in their box, sensation subordinated to a rigid code of meaning, modernity's temptations contained within a moralistic frame.

Notes

1. The original, longer German version of the film contains significant differences to the American-released version currently available on DVD. In this original film, Boss is shown to leave his wife and family to form a professional and personal couple with Berta-Marie, whose role as exotic seductress is much more heavily underlined.
2. Morduant Hall, 'A German Masterpiece', *New York Times*, 28 June 1926.
3. In the nine years to 1925, Dupont scripted 32 films and directed 25, as well as, in 1919, writing an important early work on screenwriting, *Wie ein Film geschrieben wird und wie man ihn verwertet* (How to write and evaluate a film).
4. See Erich Pommer, 'Geschäftsfilm und künstlerischer Film' [1922], reprinted in Wolfgang Jacobsen, *Erich Pommer: ein Produzent macht Filmgeschichte*, Berlin, Argon, 1989, pp. 44–5.
5. The strategy left behind a considerable artistic legacy, but the investment required – above all the runaway costs of *Metropolis* – left UFA an easy takeover target for right-wing interests in the late 1920s. Hollywood happily bought up the talent. Within a few years, Dupont, Freund and the film's designers and architects would all be working there; even Pommer himself tried his hand across the Atlantic.
6. The film's visual innovations were a major selling point overseas. Dupont wrote about them in detail for the *New York Times*, explaining, for example, how the fall was simulated with a slow-cranked camera lowered on cables, with footage sped up in the final film. E.W. Dupont, 'Camera Work on Scenes in "Variety"', *New York Times*, 11 July 1926, p. X2.
7. Paul Virilio, *War and Cinema: The Logistics of Perception*, London: Verso, 2009 [1997], p. 15. Virilio describes the formulation as his 'paraphrase' of unspecified texts by the media artist Nam June Paik.
8. The structure recurs in different ways, for example, in Lang's *Metropolis*, Papst's *Pandora's Box*, Murnau's *Nosferatu*, among others. See Elsaesser 2000: 73–88.
9. This might even, given the Wintergarten's place as origin of the German moving image, be read as a containment of the 'cinema of attractions' within a 'cinema of narrative integration'.

Further reading

Thomas Brandlmeier, *Kameraautoren: Technik und Ästhetik*, Marburg, Schüren, 2008.

Jürgen Bretschneider, *Ewald André Dupont, Autor und Regisseur*, Munich, Edition Text + Kritik, 1992.

Thomas Elsaesser, *Weimar Cinema and after: Germany's Historical Imaginary*, London, Routledge, 2000.
Frances Guerin, *A Culture of Light: Cinema and Technology in 1920s Germany*, Minneapolis, MN, University of Minnesota Press, 2005.
Klaus Kreimeier, *The Ufa Story: a History of Germany's Greatest Film Company, 1918–1945*, New York, Hill & Wang, 1996.
Richard McCormick, 'The Carnival of Humiliation: Sex, Spectacle, and Self-Reflexivity in E. A. Dupont's *Variety* (1925)', in Randall Halle and Margaret McCarthy (eds), *Light Motives: German Popular Film in Perspective*, Detroit, MI, Wayne State University Press, 2003, pp. 41–60.
Paul Matthew St. Pierre, *E. A. Dupont and His Contribution to British Film*, Madison, NJ, Fairleigh Dickinson University Press, 2010.
Kristin Thompson, *Herr Lubitsch Goes to Hollywood: German and American Film after World War I*, Amsterdam, Amsterdam University Press, 2005.

Brían Hanrahan

Viagem ao princípio do mundo/ Voyage to the Beginning of the World (1997)

[Country: Portugal, France. Production Company: Madragoa Filmes and Gemini Filmes. Director: Manoel de Oliveira. Producer: Paulo Branco. Screenwriter: Manoel de Oliveira. Cinematographer: Renato Berta. Music: Emmanuel Nunes. Editor: Valérie Loiseleux. Cast: Marcello Mastroianni (Manoel), Leonor Silveira (Judite), Jean-Yves Gautier (Afonso), Diogo Dória (Duarte), Isabel de Castro (Maria Afonso), Cécile Sanz de Alba (Cristina), Isabel Ruth (Olga), José Pinto (José Afonso), Manoel de Oliveira (the chauffeur).]

Synopsis: *Viagem* is a road movie of sorts. Three actors and an aging director, on a day off from making an unnamed film, are being driven across Northern Portugal. Oliveira himself plays their chauffeur. The ostensible reason for their journey is for Afonso, a Frenchman of Portuguese descent, to visit his father's native village, Lugar do Teso, which Afonso knows only from stories, and meet his aunt, his only direct relative left in Portugal. Afonso's story, based on that of real-life actor Yves Afonso, only takes centre stage in the second half of the film. The first part is dominated by the experiences of the director Manoel. The group stops at a series of locations that evoke memories of Manoel's youth, listen to his reminiscences and debate questions of personal and national identity and history. The other two actors are Duarte, prompter of questions and source of information about Portugal and Judite, whose beauty, youth and wilfulness contrast with Manoel's frailty, age and wistful reflections.

No appreciation of Manoel de Oliveira's films, it seems, can avoid mentioning the director's longevity. Born in 1908, Oliveira made his first film in 1931 and, aged well over 100, is still active at the time of writing. Besides inspiring awe, Oliveira's age is also a reminder that the particular characteristics of his work – anti-realism, self-reflexivity, disinterest in the kinetic – stem from an experience of cinema almost coterminous with the medium itself. Nowhere is the director's elderliness more pertinent than in *Viagem ao princípio do mundo*, with its themes of aging, memory, origins and identity.

The role of Manoel turned out to be Mastroianni's last, a fact that both adds poignancy to his performance and reinforces the metafilmic dimensions of *Viagem*. Mastroianni, sporting

Oliveira's first name, his trademark floppy brimmed hat and appropriate biographemes, is presented as an alter ego of the director. The mise-en-scène reinforces this proxy status when, at one point, Oliveira appears in the background aligned with Mastroianni's character. The shadowy presence of the director in what Bénard da Costa calls Oliveira's 'most autobiographical film' (in Overhoff Ferreira, 2008: 40) invites us to consider the relation between *auteur* and creation, experience and memory, reality and diegesis. In a mind-spinning parallel, the reason the real-life Yves Afonso's visited Portugal was to play a chauffeur in the film *O Desejado* by Paulo Rocha.

First stop for the group is Caminha, a small town on the banks of the river Minho, which forms the northern border between Portugal and Spain. Manoel had once attended boarding school on the far bank. Of note here is that, at first, the party cannot see the school across the waters. It is too far away. Only when the chauffeur brings Manoel a pair of binoculars can he discern the building and begin the process of recollection. Film, and art in general, Oliveira seems to be suggesting, are powerful technologies for multiplying the force of memory. At the same time, in a doleful paradox that runs throughout the film, the reality which memory records (however subjectively) is as irrecoverable as youth is to the aged. This idea is later rendered visually when the group visit the Grande Hotel do Pezo, a deluxe hotel when Manoel was young but now little more than a derelict shell. While they visit its grounds, Manoel reaches up to pluck a flower growing from the overhanging branch of a tree but is unable to raise his arm high enough. If the Grande Hotel do Pezo scene asks us to consider the parallels between ruins, memories and the aging body, it is also where the theme of *saudade* is first broached openly, when Manoel quotes a verse by a little-known Brazilian poet. Said to be an untranslatable word for a universally felt concept, *saudade* evokes ideas of melancholy, longing and nostalgia. Whether this emotion is universal or not, it pervades *Viagem*.

The group's discussions at the boarding school and the Grande Hotel do Pezo raise issues surrounding the relationship of mnemonics to place and of identity to the body. It is common in Oliveira films for a character to conceive a sort of motto or axiom that is then repeated at key moments. In *Viagem*, this function is performed by Duarte's tongue-twisting comment that 'un temps sépare un autre temps qui avec le temps devient présent' (which is rendered prosaically in the subtitles as 'between eras there lies a time which becomes the present'). This question of the relationship between the past and the present is crucial to *Viagem*, as it is to most of Oliveira's later work.

Just as recurrent in his filmography is an interrogation of the link within cinema between word and image. The discussions woven around the various episodes of the first half of the film and the interaction between the characters that takes place in the interior of their vehicle are echoed and expanded by scenes that function as visual metaphors. The most recurrent is that of the road sliding away behind the car. Shot with a fixed camera, the movement takes place uniquely within the frame as so often in Oliveira's films. Seen from the rear-view perspective of the chauffeur, this image has many symbolic resonances: the march of time, the orientation of experience and the unspooling of film itself.

Words and image come together most powerfully in a scene where the party stops off to visit a statue Manoel remembers from his youth. It still stands, though its position has changed and it has been vandalised, a status that figures both the persistence and fragility of memory. As the group stares up at the statue, which represents a kneeling figure carrying a heavy beam of wood, a passing countrywoman tells them its history. The figure has a folk poem associated with it: 'Eu sou o Pedro Macau/E às costas tenho um pau/Aqui passa muito patego/Uns de focinho branco. outros de focinho negro/Mas ninguém me tira deste degredo' (My name is Pedro Macau/And I have a beam on my back/Many pass by here/Some white-nosed, some black/But none of them sets me free). Though Afonso is greatly moved by the figure – in exile high up on a wall, shouldering a burden no one can share – he is unable to understand the woman's explanation in Portuguese and has to rely upon his friends to translate. Judite later tries to teach him the poem in Portuguese but he is only able to repeat the translation in French. The local woman is bemused to discover the actor is 'um homem estangeiro' (a foreign man). Afonso's emotional fascination yet cultural distance introduces the themes of rurality and cosmopolitanism, ethnic identity and cultural misunderstanding that dominate the second half of the film.

After the scene at the derelict hotel, Afonso tells Manoel that, fascinating as his memories have been, they bear no relation to the story of his father, in another telling parallelism also called Manoel. The director belongs to a privileged bourgeoisie that formed only a tiny percentage of the population. Afonso's father, born in a remote village, experiencing the hardships of agricultural life before seeking a better existence abroad, is perhaps more representative of the countless Portuguese who have emigrated ever since the first caravels left Lisbon.

When the party arrives in Lugar do Teso, Afonso's aunt refuses to believe the stranger is her nephew as he 'não fala a nossa fala' (a rusticated form of 'he cannot speak our language'). The various members of the party intercede in Portuguese on Afonso's behalf, as does Maria's daughter-in-law, herself a Frenchwoman, but to no avail. The fact that Afonso is a famous actor in France makes no impression at all on the old lady. At no point do their worlds seem to touch. At length, Afonso rolls up his sleeve and asks his aunt to touch his arm, to feel their shared blood. On one level, this scene is a testament to the powerful effect of perceived ancestral ties. On the other, despite the emotional visits to the house where his father was born and the cemetery where his ancestors are buried, we can wonder whether Afonso has achieved his aim of better understanding the father who, we learn, died young. Before Afonso leaves, Maria asks him to bring his brother Yves (the other half of the real-life Yves Afonso?) to visit her before she dies. We are left in doubt as to whether this visit will ever occur.

It is important to bear in mind the ambiguity of the titular words 'princípio do mundo'. In Portuguese, 'princípio' means both 'beginning' and 'principle'. If Maria's life in Lugar do Teso represents an earlier, premodern world from which our modern day emerged, the fate of all the characters (Manoel so close to death, Afonso able to visit but not inhabit his origins, Maria perhaps the last generation of true peasants) display the 'principle' of a world conditioned by entropy.

Romney has called *Viagem* an 'unsentimental enquiry into an endangered national identity' (1998: 33). While the subordinate position of the Portuguese language and culture in the world system is often referenced – significantly almost all of the dialogue takes place in French – we might think instead that the fragile identity is in fact Afonso's, the second-generation immigrant caught between his life and his history, unable to speak Portuguese but gripped by *saudade*. Neither Duarte nor Judite evince any lack of cultural confidence. At several points in the film the spectre of the war in ex-Yugoslavia is evoked, establishing a resonance between the existential anxiety of the individual and the tragic political events preceding the film. Here *Viagem* hints at the dangers attendant when atavism displaces culture. Can the fiction of blood underwrite a stable identity? Or is its fragility what prompts tribalism's violence against the Other?

Viagem has divided critical opinion. Johnson holds that, though 'Manoel's journey to the beginning of the world is a journey towards death', Oliveira's film 'does not end on a sombre note. Rather it recognises death as the last act of life, which is characterised by multiple and constant transformations and modulations around a core whose roots are deeper than one might realise' (2007: 102). Wheeler Dixon, on the other hand, argues that 'Oliveira's initial vision of the world as a kind, forgiving entity is gradually transformed into a landscape of primitive violence, in which the dreams of youth are crushed by the burdens of history, poverty and hopelessness' (2005). One way of deciding how we read the film as a whole is to form a judgment of the short final scene. We find Afonso in his dressing room getting ready for the film he has come to Portugal to make. Dressed in costume traditional to his father's region, with a false moustache pasted to his lip, he is a simulacrum of Pedro Macau. As he strikes the statue's pose and intones its poem, the other members of the group burst out laughing at his seriousness. Afonso remarks that no one tells stories like that of Pedro Macau. He then looks into the mirror and says 'Toi non plus, Afonso. T'es pas tout à fait le meme' (You neither, Afonso. You're not quite the same). The story concludes with Afonso talking to the director. *Viagem* has come to an end; the film *outside* the film is yet to begin.

Further reading

Randal Johnson, *Manoel de Oliveira*, Urbana, University of Illinois Press, 2007.
Carolin Overhoff Ferreira, *On Manoel de Oliveira*, London, Wallflower, 2008.
Winston Wheeler Dixon, 'Voyage to the Beginning of the World', *Senses of Cinema*, issue 37, 20th October 2005. Available at: http://sensesofcinema.com/2005/cteq/voyage_beginning_world/ (accessed 2 July 2012).
Jonathan Romney, 'Eye Travel', *Sight and Sound*, July, 1998, 33–5.

Paul Melo e Castro

Videodrome (1983)

[Country: Canada. Production Company: Filmplan International. Director: David Cronenberg. Producer: Pierre David. Screenwriter: David Cronenberg. Cinematographer: Mark Irwin. Music: Howard Shore. Editor: Ronald Sanders. Cast: James Woods (Max Renn), Deborah Harry (Nicki Brand), Sonja Smits (Bianca O'Blivion), Peter Dvorsky (Harlan), Jack Creley (Brian O'Blivion).]

Synopsis: *Videodrome* tells the story of Max Renn (Woods), the sleazy programmer of a soft-core television channel who discovers a mysterious signal broadcasting a snuff TV show called 'Videodrome'. Increasingly obsessed with tracing the source of the rogue signal, Max crosses paths with media philosophy guru, Professor Brian O'Blivion (Creley) and his daughter Bianca (Smits). After a series of strange encounters and unsettling visions, he learns that 'Videodrome' is transmitted via a frequency that induces malignant tumours in the brain, which in turn cause vivid hallucinations that are indistinguishable from reality. The film's ambiguous ending imagines a violent and visceral takeover of technology by 'the New Flesh'. The question of what this 'New Flesh' might be is at the heart of the film's philosophical investigations into the influence and effects of media forms.

Although *Videodrome* was considered a critical and commercial failure upon its initial release in 1983, the film has since become a cult classic. There are many factors to consider when evaluating how *Videodrome* has achieved this status. From the perspective of debates in genre and auteur studies, it is often cited as the quintessential example of director David Cronenberg's distinctive philosophical approach to the body-horror genre. From a star studies approach, Deborah Harry's star turn as Max Renn's masochistic love interest, Nicki Brand, played a major role in consolidating the film's cult status. However, the film's sphere of influence extends far beyond considerations of stardom, authorship and genre. *Videodrome*'s prescient account of the role of media technologies in contemporary Western societies has influenced a number of other debates, including discussions about screen violence, censorship, and media effects and postmodernity. Finally, *Videodrome* raises important questions about gender and sexuality and, like Cronenberg's work more generally, has tended to divide critical opinion when it comes to its implications for feminism.

Perhaps more than any other contemporary filmmaker, Cronenberg's early work has come to embody the conventions of the body-horror genre, in which horror is derived from gory depictions of the human body's monstrous mutability. Cronenberg's early films, *Shivers* (1975), *Rabid* (1977), and *The Brood* (1979), use bodies in this way as the main motor for horror, as they become unwitting hosts to gruesome plagues, parasites, psychoses, and other aberrations. In keeping with these concerns, *Videodrome* focuses on the monstrous capacities of the human body, as Max Renn's physique begins to mutate in highly disturbing ways. In the film's most famous sequence, achieved in collaboration with renowned special effects artist Rick Baker, Max develops a lurid, vagina-like opening in his torso, to which he responds with equal parts disbelief, horror, and tentative fascination. With its emphasis on Max's grotesque bodily transformations, *Videodrome* can be seen as a natural extension of Cronenberg's early career in exploitation filmmaking.

However, *Videodrome* also anticipates the new, overtly philosophical turn that characterises Cronenberg's later work. More explicitly than his previous films, *Videodrome* is concerned with thinking through the terms of embodiment, and can be seen to offer a critique of Cartesian mind–body dualism, a philosophical tenet that holds that the mind is separate from the body.[1] *Videodrome* explicitly plays with and subverts this idea by presenting Max's body as possessing an agency of its own, as it begins to actively anticipate his needs. For instance, towards the end of the film, Max's hand morphs into a slimy and tentacled appendage fused with metal to form a pistol that allows him to defend himself against his foes. Later, the slit in his chest becomes another weapon of sorts, as it mutilates his opponent's hand. While, on one level, we are invited to write off these bodily mutations either as hallucinations or as an extension of a conspiracy subplot, Max's predicament gestures towards an understanding of human embodiment that is at the heart of Cronenberg's authorial vision. This vision is summed up in the film's evocation of 'the New Flesh'. While the question of what this 'New Flesh' might be remains ambiguous, it clearly involves an overturning of clear divisions and hierarchies between mind and body, human and technology, male and female, and a tentative embrace of the new image of humanity that such a levelling of binaries might presage. Cronenberg has commented that 'the most accessible version of the "New Flesh" in *Videodrome* would be that you can actually change what it means to be a human being in a physical way. We are physically different from our forefathers, partly because of what we take into our bodies, and partly because of things like glasses and surgery. But there is a further step that could happen, which would be that you could grow another arm, that you could actually physically change the way you look – mutate'.[2] *Videodrome*'s enigmatic ending, in which Max holds a gun to his head and utters, 'Long live the New Flesh', suggests that this 'further step' will involve a retreat from the physical world and a reincarnation as pure electronic presence in the video arena. But the film's abrupt ending and ambiguous tone make it difficult to know how we are meant to interpret this brave new world. Does the 'New Flesh' presage a bold evolutionary leap forward for mankind? Or is it a nihilistic ending, refusing any kind of transcendence? And what are we to make of this promise of a disembodied future, given the film's emphasis throughout on the visceral and the corporeal against the cerebral and the immaterial?[3]

Videodrome directs such questions toward a wide-ranging analysis of media technology and censorship in contemporary society. Through its basic plotline about the deadly effects of exposure to the Videodrome signal, the film stages a series of questions about the influence and effects of media, which have important corollaries within the context of the film's release. Fears about the effects of media content had been raging in several North American and European contexts, due to the expansion of new communications technologies in the 1970s and 1980s. Notable examples include the approval of pay cable television by the CRTC in Canada in 1982 and the widespread availability of domestic VCRs across America and Europe by the mid-1980s. In Britain, the film seemed oddly prophetic in the context of the 'video nasties' debates in 1985, which concerned the need to impose restrictions on graphic films that were readily available for home viewing on videocassette.[4] *Videodrome*'s central conceit, in which 'video itself becomes the monster', seemed to capitalise on this burgeoning cultural fear about the effects of these new technologies.[5] The film plays out these concerns in a typically hyperbolic fashion, as Max is drawn into a right-wing, moralistic conspiracy led by Spectacular Optical to rid North America of spectators of such morally corrupting images. Professor Brian O'Blivion and his daughter Bianca are representatives of a more progressive vision for the media, which includes a 'Cathode Ray Mission' that serves up TV to the disenfranchised and homeless as a means of patching them back into 'the world's mixing board'. As Professor O'Blivion tells Max at one point, 'the battle for the mind of North America will be fought in the video arena – the videodrome'. Brian O'Blivion serves as a thinly veiled alter-ego of Canadian media theorist Marshall McLuhan, whose expression 'the medium is the message' forms the basis of the film's critique of media censorship. In keeping with this dictum, it is significant that the malignant tumours that Max develops are induced through exposure to the signal itself, irrespective of what is actually depicted on the sadistic show. Far from suggesting the utility of social controls and moral limits, Cronenberg's dystopian vision suggests that it is the medium's relation to disciplinary structures, and its ability to be manipulated by those in power, which makes it dangerous.

Videodrome has likewise been taken up as a classic text within debates about postmodernism. The film makes explicit reference to postmodern theorists such as Jean Baudrillard, Guy Debord and Marshall McLuhan. These theories were relatively new at the time of the film's release, but had become highly fashionable by the late 1980s and early 1990s. This burgeoning interest in postmodernity helped to secure the film's reputation belatedly as a cult classic, as scholars began to turn their attention to the film's iterations of postmodern themes. Key from this perspective is the way that the film engages with concepts such as simulacrum and simulation, the increasing virtualisation and disappearance of the real through communications technologies, and the steady breakdown between objective reality and subjective perception. Max's exposure to the Videodrome signal leaves him unable to tell the difference between reality and his own hallucinations. The opening in his stomach leaves him vulnerable to external manipulation and overt control, as he in effect is 'transformed into a human video machine' and is programmed and reprogrammed to carry out the bidding of different factions.[6] As several commentators have pointed out, Max's situation closely resembles that of the postmodern schizophrenic, as theorised by Jean Baudrillard and Fredric Jameson.[7] The film also enacts this condition of schizophrenia for its spectators, since it emulates Max's point of view closely without any clear indication of where Max's visions depart from diegetic reality. Indeed, the film is postmodern precisely because it confuses our ability to tell the difference between such things in the first place.[8] If critics agree that *Videodrome* is a classic postmodern text, there have been frequent disagreements over what exactly the film suggests *about* postmodernity. Fredric Jameson argues that while *Videodrome* may diagnose a postmodern schizophrenic subject who is unable to master the complexity of his own situation, the film remains complicit with the mass cultural forms that it would attempt to critique.[9] Steven Shaviro argues that the film counters the notion that postmodernity involves a move towards disembodiment; rather, media technologies such as television and the VCR do not lead to the disappearance of the body, so much as they invest in the body in new and particularly intense ways.[10] Scott Bukatman's reading of the film, meanwhile, excavates the range of postmodern references in *Videodrome*, and underscores its essential complexity and ambiguity with respect to postmodernity.[11]

Finally, the film is also significant for its relation to debates about gender and sexuality. Cronenberg's work has been seen as problematic for feminism. He has been criticised for the way that his films often seem to equate femininity with monstrousness.[12] Some critics have argued that his films express misogynistic disgust toward feminine sexuality, and can be seen as a backlash against the liberalisation of sex more generally.[13] Along similar lines, Tania Modleski has argued that *Videodrome* presents media technology as horrible precisely 'because of the way it feminises its audience', noting that Max is in essence 'raped with a video cassette'.[14] Others, however, have argued that such images need to be carefully considered within the context of Cronenberg's interest in monstrousness and bodily transformation more generally. Steven Shaviro has argued that by emphasising the mutability of gender and of sexual desire, Cronenberg's films help us to see gender and sexuality as social constructs. While the vagina-like opening in Max's chest undoubtedly amounts to a feminisation, there is little to suggest that the sleazy, stereotypically masculine qualities that he embodies prior to this transformation are necessarily preferable. It can be argued that in staging gender constructions in a particularly literal way, *Videodrome* helps to demystify such discourses.

Notes

1. David M. Rosenthal, 'Dualism' in *Concise Routledge Encyclopedia of Philosophy* London, Routledge, 2000, p. 218.
2. David Cronenberg cited in Chris Rodley, *Cronenberg on Cronenberg*, London, Faber & Faber, 1992, p. 82.
3. See Steven Shaviro, 'Bodies of Fear: David Cronenberg' in *The Cinematic Body*, Minneapolis, University of Minnesota Press, 1993, pp. 138–41.
4. Rodley, p. 106.
5. Tania Modleski, 'The Terror of Pleasure: The Contemporary Horror Film and Postmodern Theory' in Ken Gelder (ed.) *The Horror Reader*, London, Routlege, 2000, p. 288.
6. Shaviro, p. 139.
7. See Modleski, Shaviro, and Scott Bukatman, 'Who Programs You? The Science Fiction of the Spectacle' in Annette Kuhn (ed.), *Alien Zone: Cultural Theory and Contemporary Science Fiction Cinema*, London, Verso, 1990, pp. 196–213.
8. Bukatman, p. 207.
9. Fredric Jameson, 'Totality as Conspiracy' in *The Geopolitical Aesthetic: Cinema and Space in the World System*, Bloomington, University of Indiana Press, 1992, pp. 9–86.
10. Shaviro, pp. 127–58.
11. Bukatman, pp. 196–213.
12. See Robin Wood, 'Cronenberg: A Dissenting View' in Piers Handling (ed.), *The Shape of Rage: The Films of David Cronenberg*, Toronto, Academy of Canadian Cinema, General Publishing Company, 1983, pp. 115–35, and Barbara Creed, *The Monstrous Feminine: Film, Feminism, Psychoanalysis*, London, Routledge, 1993, pp. 43–58.
13. See Wood, pp. 115–35.
14. Modleski, p. 292.

Further reading

Martin Barker and Julian Petley, (eds), *Ill Effects: The Media/Violence Debate*, London, Routledge, 1997.

Tina Kendall

Le violon rouge/The Red Violin (1998)

[Country: Canada, Italy and UK. Production Company: Rhombus Media, Mikado Film. Director: François Girard. Screenwriters: François Girard and Don McKellar. Producer: Niv Fichman. Cinematographer: Alain Dostie. Music: John Corigliano. Cast: Jean-Luc Bideau (Georges Poussin, Vienna), Carlo Cecchi (Nicolo Bussotti, Cremona), Sylvia Chang (Xiang Pei, Shanghai), Samuel L. Jackson (Charles Morritz, Montreal), Greta Scacchi (Victoria Byrd, Oxford).]

The Red Violin was written by François Girard and Don McKellar. Girard also directed this international co-production between Canada, the UK and Italy, which was released in theatres in 1998. The film won an Oscar for Best Original Musical Score, and the Canadian equivalent in the following Genie Awards: Best Picture, Best Director and Best Screenplay, amongst others. It also received numerous international awards and nominations like the Golden Globes (nominated for Best Foreign Language film), the Grammy Awards (nominated for Best Instrumental Composition) and the Tokyo International Film Festival (Best Artistic Contribution Award). This international recognition of *The Red Violin* reflects the global appeal of the film, which is the result of a co-produced feature with inherent qualities suitable for the international market. The story of *The Red Violin* spans centuries and many countries: thus, creating a narrative that interweaves several plot lines and addresses the universal theme of music appreciation. This is further emphasised by a composition by John Corigliano, which underscores the film and serves as a key framing device. The film was produced during the height of co-production activities between Canada and European partners. It is therefore representative of a new direction in Canadian cinema: namely, the focus on high-budget productions for international distribution in the global market.

Treaty co-productions provide the means for pooling resources in the form of finances, government subsidies, labour and talent. As a result, co-produced films tend to have higher budgets as is evidenced in the production of *The Red Violin*, which remains one of the most expensive Canadian films ever made. Co-productions became a focal point in the 1990s for Canadian film funding agencies in order to increase feature film production, international distribution, revenues and cultural capital. The signing of over 50 international co-production treaties between the Canadian government and countries around the world were meant to ensure that a global focus in cultural production would result in the proliferation of Canada's audiovisual industries. Indeed, Canadian co-productions increased dramatically during the 1990s and early 2000s until changing priorities of co-production partners in Europe toppled the Canadian agenda. From a political-economy perspective, *The Red Violin's* production context therefore exemplifies the increasing commercialisation of publicly funded media and the internationalisation of a country's cultural goods. Furthermore, the film's musical score reflects the expansion of media production ecologies into adjacent cultural industries. For *The Red Violin*, producers collaborated from the outset with the Sony Corporation to reap profits from ancillary revenue streams through the co-release of the soundtrack.

Co-productions tend to exhibit narrative structures that transcend time and space. In most instances this results from having to abide by official guidelines and treaty stipulations, which mandate that the involvement of talent and crew have to correspond in equal amounts to the financial participation of all co-producing parties. This also includes production, location shooting or post-production in the counties that partake in the co-production. The consequent mixing and matching has led to contrived narratives in films that garnered the label 'Euro-puddings'. A common aspect of many co-productions therefore tends to be a lacking sense of place and cultural identity. This 'uprootedness' in co-produced narratives resonates in theories of globalisation, which link the dis-embedding of social relations from local contexts to processes of time-space distanciation (Giddens 1990). Whereas in premodern eras space was linked to an individual's physical environment, today's societies are transformed by their restructuring across time and space. Equally important is Mosco's (2009) notion of spatialisation in global capitalism, which entails the process of overcoming the constraints of time and space in social life. This includes the global restructuring of media industries, integrated markets based on digital technologies, and the division of cultural labour, which reflect the transcendence of temporal and spatial relations in a global economy. Key examples of spatialisation also include co-productions, joint ventures, strategic alliances and emerging media ecologies, which integrate short-term or long-term project management across the cultural industries.

These dynamics are apparent in the production context of *The Red Violin*, as well as in its themes, narrative development and key framing devices. More specifically, *The Red Violin* has two main narratives: a tarot reading set in the past and a future auction in Montreal, which act as framing devices for four stories that unfold in a predominantly linear fashion in Italy, Austria, England and China between the seventeenth and twentieth centuries. Another key framing mechanism is Corigliano's musical score, which ties all narrative strands together through serving as a transitioning device as well as setting the overall tone for the film. As *The Red Violin* is a journey through several cultures, Girard and McKellar kept the dialogue in the native languages of the countries the stories are set in: therefore, shifting from Italian, German, English, Chinese to French. To address official co-production guidelines, Girard also used locations across Europe, China and Canada to shoot the film.

The film begins in Cremona, Italy, in 1681, where the violin-maker Nicolo Bussotti is building a new instrument in anticipation of the birth of his first child. His wife Anna consults a tarot reader to quell her anxiety about the future. But in spite of a promising future, and the prediction of a long life, she dies during childbirth. Nicolo bereft and filled with grief mixes Anna's blood into the varnish of the violin; thus, imbuing it with her soul. These events set the following plot lines in motion: the violin travels across Europe and finds a temporary home at a monastery near seventeenth-century Vienna, where it is played by the talented but frail orphan Kaspar Weiss. When Kaspar is faced with being separated from his beloved violin, he collapses during a rehearsal. After his death, the violin changes hands for many decades until it finds its way to Oxford, England. Here it becomes the focal point for a passionate but fated love affair between the musician Frederick Pope and a writer.

Each of the stories represents a different life cycle as played out by the characters, who are obsessed with the violin. Beginning in childhood, as embodied by Kaspar, the following events in Oxford mark the transition into young adulthood. The violin's arrival in China completes the cycle as, metaphorically, the stage of maturity, and political consciousness, is reached. In the hands of Xiang Pei, the violin becomes embroiled in upheavals of the cultural revolution and needs to be hidden in a secret place – the attic of the music teacher Chou Yan. The violin is discovered only three decades later, upon which it is sent to Montreal by a present-day Chinese government for appraisal and to be auctioned off. Throughout the film, scenes are intercut with flashbacks of the tarot reading, which predicts the violin's journey – and the affect of Anna's soul on the main characters – over the course of 300 years. The final tarot card, signifying rebirth, initiates the last story, set in a Montreal auction house. This story, which is foreshadowed throughout the film in the form of flash-forwards, concludes all narrative strands in the present. Representatives tied to previous plots, such as the monks from an Austrian monastery, an agent of the Pope foundation and Pei's son, are all present to bid on the violin. However, in a final twist the violin ends up in the hands of the appraiser Charles Morritz, who switches the real violin for a copy. He intends to give the violin to his musically gifted daughter; thus, potentially setting a new cycle in motion.

In spite of several plotlines, flashbacks and flash-forwards, the narrative of *The Red Violin* unfolds in a logical and easy-to-follow fashion. The narrative arc is maintained through the musical score as well as through the framing devices of the tarot reading and the Montreal auction. However, due to multiple storylines and changing locations the film's characters remain underdeveloped. And in spite of historical references, the stories appear to be uprooted rather than linked to cultural identities. This schematic referencing of time and place therefore transcends geographical boundaries and becomes reminiscent of what Appardurai (1990) has referred to in his globalisation theory as the existence of 'multiple worlds' which are comprised of historically situated 'imaginations of people' tied to economic, political and cultural spheres. Globalisation processes are thus marked by disjunctures, in which different configurations such as 'ethnoscapes' and the distribution of mobile individuals are no longer confined to actual geographies. In *The Red Violin* references to geographical destinations are therefore less relevant than the interconnection between cultures through their shared experience – in this case their encounter with the violin.

As a result, *The Red Violin's* narrative appears to unfold nowhere or anywhere, since a sense of place and cultural identity is never truly established. Moreover, as Longfellow (2001) points out, the obsession the film's characters express for the violin embodies a form of 'commodity fetishism' where the object is exalted to such an extent that it mediates and transforms all social relations. The final story about the Montreal auction, at which all descendants of former characters congregate, further emphasises the market as a binding and unifying force for the film's multiple storylines. As an international co-production *The Red Violin* therefore exemplifies the confluence of globalisation and increasing commercialisation of cultural goods, in its production context as well as in its diegetic and non-diegetic story worlds.

The Red Violin represents a key stage in the development of Canadian cinema, which became increasingly international during the 1990s. Through the development of co-production treaties with partners around the world, Canada's cultural agencies sought to generate revenues and increase the global profile of its cultural industries. However, this global focus came at the cost of the local arts and public media sectors, which, after a series of budgets cutbacks, were forced to adopt a more commercially driven agenda. In addition, co-production has proven to be an unreliable production technology for Canadian filmmakers, who had to face a challenging situation in the late 2000s when filmmakers in Europe shifted their attention towards pan-European collaborations and co-ventures with the USA, leading to a rapid decline of Canadian co-productions (Baltruschat 2010).

In the case of *The Red Violin*, co-production mandates became manifest in the film's production context as well as in its narrative development. Within the context of Canada's cultural globalisation in the 1990s, the film epitomises how co-production facilitates the integration of a country's film industry in the global market. It also reveals that a growing focus on international production and distribution channels often coincides with the commercialisation of publicly funded cultural goods.

Further reading

Arjun Appadurai, 'Disjuncture and Differences in the Global Cultural Economy', in Mike Featherstone (ed.), *Global Culture. Nationalism, Globalization and Modernity*, London, Sage, 1990, pp. 295–310.

Doris Baltruschat, 'International Film and TV Co-productions: A Canadian Case Study', in Simon Cottle (ed.), *Media Organization and Production*, London, Sage, 2003, pp. 181–207.

Doris Baltruschat, *Global Media Ecologies: Networked Production in Film and Television*, New York, London, Routledge, 2010.

Anthony Giddens, *The Consequences of Modernity*, Stanford, CA, Stanford University Press, 1990.

Brenda Longfellow, '*The Red Violin*, commodity fetishism and globalization', *Canadian Journal of Film Studies*, 10 (2), 2001, pp. 6–20.

Toby Miller, Nitin Govil, John McMurria and Richard Maxwell, *Global Hollywood*, London, BFI, 2001.

N. Morawetz, J. Hardy, C. Haslam and K. Randle, 'Finance, policy and industrial dynamics – The rise of co-productions in the film industry', *Industry and Innovation*, 14 (4), 2007, pp. 421–43.

Vincent Mosco, *The Political Economy of Communication: Rethinking and Renewal*, (2nd ed.), London, Sage, 2009.

Graham Murdock, 'Trading Places: The Cultural Economy of Co-production', in Sofia Blind and Gerd Hallenberger (eds), *European Co-productions in Television and Film*, Heidelberg, Germany, Universitätsverlag C, Winter, 1996, pp. 103–14.

Doris Baltruschat

Viridiana (1961)

[Country: Spain and Mexico. Production Company: Unión Industrial Cinematográfica (UNINCI), Gustavo Alatriste and Films 59. Director: Luis Buñuel. Producer: Gustavo Alatriste. Screenwriters: Luis Buñuel and Julio Alejandro. Cinematographer: Jose F. Aguayo. Music: Gustavo Pittaluga. Editor: Pedro del Rey. Cast: Silvia Pinal (Viridiana), Francisco Rabal (Jorge), Fernando Rey (Don Jaime), Margarita Lozano (Ramona), José Calvo (Beggar).]

Synopsis: *Viridiana* tells the story of a novice nun who, in the film's opening scenes, is asked by her Mother Superior to visit her widowed Uncle Jaime. She has not seen him for many years but he has asked to meet her before she takes her vows.

Spending the night at the farm where he lives with a handful of servants, she initially gives in to his request that she wears his late wife's wedding dress, but is horrified when she later discovers that he wants to marry her. He drugs her but cannot go through with his plan to rape her. In the morning he first claims that he has taken her virginity but then admits that this was a lie contrived to force her to stay with him. Faced with her departure and his own disgrace, Jaime hangs himself and Viridiana finds that she has inherited the property along with Jaime's illegitimate son, Jorge. In an act of Christian kindness Viridiana installs a group of vagrants and beggars in the farm's outbuildings but while she and Jorge are away they break into the main house and help themselves to wine and food. Returning, Jorge is attacked and Viridiana is nearly raped, but the arrival of the police brings the violence to an end. However, these combined events have brought about a profound change in Viridiana, who, at the film's close, seems to accept a ménage a trois with Jorge and one of the female servants, Ramona.

Luis Buñuel is cinema's great iconoclast. In a career stretching for nearly 50 years, and including over 30 films made in France, Spain and Mexico, he mounted a consistent assault on his two principle targets: the bourgeoisie and the Catholic Church. In works that are coolly satirical and sometimes cruelly lacerating, he exposed human weakness, not least in the area of sexual appetite. With his roots in the surrealist movement of the 1920s and 1930s, he never lost his eye for the arresting image or his awareness of the bizarre and the wayward. For many, *Viridiana* is the perfect distillation of his favourite themes and methods as an auteur. Winner of the Palme d'Or at the 1961 Cannes Film Festival, it was subsequently banned outright in his native Spain (only receiving its premiere there in 1977) and was condemned by the Vatican as blasphemous. Provocation was always at the heart of the director's vision.

To appreciate the intricacies of *Viridiana*, it's worth placing it first within the chronology of Buñuel's oeuvre. Buñuel was born in 1900 in Calanda, Spain to wealthy parents and was educated by the Jesuits. At 17 he went to live and study in the Residencia Estudiantes in Madrid where he remained for eight years enjoying its rich cross-fertilisation of ideas and creativity. He met Federico García Lorca and Salvador Dalí, who both had a profound influence on him. Moving to Paris he made his first film, the 17-minute *Un Chien Andalou* (1929) in partnership with Dalí. From its unforgettable opening image of a man (played by Buñuel himself) slashing a woman's eyeball, the film is one of cinema's purest essays in surrealism, dredging ideas from its creators' collective subconscious. Buñuel and Dali fell out during the making of *L'Age d'Or* (1930) but the film proved successful in offending the forces of reaction, resulting in attacks by right wing groups on the cinema where it was shown. In 1932 he made his first film in Spain with *Las Hurdes*, an experimental documentary exposing poverty and injustice in a remote rural area. The film suffered censorship by both the Republicans and later by Franco's regime.

Unusually for a major filmmaker, he spent 14 years without releasing a feature film. For a period in the early 1930s he worked developing Spanish film production under the Republicans but by the end of the decade, and with their defeat in the Civil War, he had gone into a reluctant exile in America. Unsurprisingly, considering his instinctive antipathy towards conformity, he never found a suitable place within Hollywood's studio system, working largely in the dubbing facilities at Warner Brothers. Eventually he decamped to Mexico where, between 1946 and 1965, he directed 19 films, re-establishing himself as a key creative figure in international cinema. Although some of his Mexican films were relatively conventional mainstream projects, he brought his characteristic irreverence to memorable work such as *Los Olvidados/The Young and the Damned* (1950) and the darkly satirical *El Ángel Exterminador/The Exterminating Angel* (1962).

In 1960 Buñuel was encouraged by the director Carlos Saura to return to Spain to make *Viridiana*. The Spanish film industry was under the tight regulation of the Franco regime but as a Mexican-Spanish co-production Buñuel was able to retain control of its content under the noses of the Fascists. They were, however, to take their revenge. Despite its initial success at Cannes, the authorities used the condemnation by the Vatican as their excuse to ban the film from cinemas at home and to disown the film's Spanish nationality; it was released internationally as a Mexican film. They also instigated a backlash against the more liberal elements within Spanish film production in the wake of the 'scandal' (Jordan and Allinson 2005: 20).

At the centre of the narrative of *Viridiana* is the theme of l'amour fou, much beloved of the surrealists of the 1930s. Providing an exact definition for the term remains difficult but its roots lie in Freud's notion of repressed desire. L'amour fou is the urge of the primitive within us which, due to societal pressures, finds distorted expression through fetishistic obsession. Uncle Jaime has never recovered from the shock of his wife's death in his arms on their wedding night. In secret he caresses her clothes and tries to put on her shoes. Viridiana's resemblance to her aunt causes Jaime to partially lose control of his inhibitions. He pressures her into wearing his wife's wedding dress. When she declines his proposal of marriage, he drugs her and carries her to his bed where he partially undresses her and kisses her breasts. Yet his conscience, or his sense of propriety, keeps pulling him back. Caught between desire and guilt he eventually takes his own life. But he is not the only one affected by l'amour fou. Ramona cannot resist Jorge, despite his obvious disregard for women. Sexual violence seems constantly just beneath the surface and erupts when two of the vagrants assault Viridiana. Even she is not exempt. Her religious observations are decidedly fetishistic too; she carries with her to her Uncle's house a wooden cross, nails and a hammer, and her own crown of thorns.

Religion is clearly a target in the film, but so are the middle classes who are invariably depicted as hypocritical and greedy. Viridiana is sent back to her Uncle's house because he has sent her dowry to the convent; in other words, he buys her back. Despite his acts of kindness, it is obvious that Jaime lives in great wealth whereas his servants are poor. Ramona is forced to become complicit in his plans to deflower Viridiana because she feels grateful that he has taken in both her and her daughter. The final orgy of destruction is brought about when the gang of beggars has access to the wealth of the big house, something that the feckless Jorge has inherited by birth. Hypocrisy is also a target in relation to the church, something we are reminded of during the beggar's feast when they play a gramophone record so that they can dance drunkenly only for the recording to be Handel's *Messiah*. The prevalence of double standards is symbolised by Jorge's discovery of a crucifix owned by his father, which also contains a retractable knife. Viridiana rescues the poor vagrants partly as an expression of her Christian ideals, but also because she feels a quite groundless guilt over her uncle's death; the Mother Superior points out her pride. We see further evidence when she feeds the beggars, as she appears as much pleased for her own sake as for theirs. When one of them is angered by her rules (the men and women sleep in separate dormitories, they must work, and bedtime is set at eight in the evening), he has to accept her commands or leave.

However, the attack on religion goes much further than this. Viridiana's acts of Christian charity are shown to be futile. The beggars take advantage of her, just as her uncle had tried to do, and end by stealing from the house, tying up Jorge and almost raping her. Her progression through the film is one of utter disillusionment, culminating in her discarding her crown of thorns, which Ramona's daughter then throws on the fire. By the end, she admits that she has changed. Our last sight of her is when she joins Jorge and Ramona in the kitchen in a game of cards and he tells her, 'All cats are grey at night'. Buñuel later revealed in his memoirs that the Spanish censor objected to the original ending which depicted Viridiana entering Jorge's bedroom with the door closing behind her (Buñuel 1985: 237). With appropriate irony, the revised ending, which satisfied the censors, is actually more suggestive in its possible sexual connotations. Despite the parody of Leonardo's Last Supper, the film seems less blasphemous than utterly nihilistic. The tone is not celebratory but deadpan and sardonic. The final recognition that Viridiana's ideals have come to nothing is not a cause for satisfaction but for desolate recognition of the inevitable. This theme is encapsulated in one short sequence when Jorge rescues a dog from a passing traveller who has the poor creature tied to the back of his wagon. Shocked by the neglect that has left the animal exhausted he buys it from its owner. However, as he happily sets off across the fields he doesn't notice a further wagon passing behind him with another dog tied to it. With complete disregard for his own actions, he later tells Viridiana that she will never end suffering and injustice by trying to save a few beggars. The bleak inference being that it's a waste of time to try to change the world for the better.

The power of Buñuel's vision is amplified by the restraint of his technique. There is little in the way of showy cinematic devices, with the exception of a rapid montage contrasting Viridiana leading her flock of vagrants in prayer with the mundane world of progress around them as Jorge's hired workers set about modernising the farm. As Gwynne Edwards observes, 'Buñuel exposes the inner life, the desires and unconscious urges of his characters', not through overtly Freudian imagery but by quietly observing their responses, such as Jaime surreptitiously looking at Viridiana's bare legs or Viridiana herself wanting to milk a cow but struggling to handle its udders (Edwards 1985: 164). Instead of obviously directing the viewer's gaze, Buñuel allows his camera to pan and track towards his point of attention, almost casually finding the revealing detail. He invariably keeps the camera back, never allowing us too close to his characters. We have little choice but to coolly observe their moral failure.

Further reading

Luis Buñuel, *My Last Breath*, London: Flamingo, 1985. Originally published as *Mon Dernier Soupir* (1982). English translation by Abigail Israel.

Gwynne Edwards, *The Discreet Art of Luis Buñuel: A Reading of his Films*, London: Marion Boyars, 1985.

Peter William Evans, *The Films of Luis Buñuel: Subjectivity and Desire*, Oxford: Clarendon Press, 1995.

Peter William Evans and Isabel Santaolalla (eds), *Luis Bunuel: New Readings*, London: BFI, 2003.

Graham Harper and Rob Stone (eds), *The Unsilvered Screen: Surrealism on Film*, London: Wallflower, 2007.

Barry Jordan and Mark Allinson, *Spanish Cinema: A Student's Guide*, London: Hodder and Arnold, 2005.

Robert Shail

Voskhozhdenie/The Ascent (1977)

[Country: USSR. Production Company: Mosfilm (Third Creative Unit). Director: Larisa Shepitko. Scriptwriters: Iurii Klepikov, Larisa Shepitko. Cinematographers: Vladimir Chukhnov, Pavel Lebeshev. Music: Alfred Shnitke. Cast: Vladimir Gostiukhin (Rybak), Boris Plotnikov (Sotnikov), Anatoloy Solonitsyn (Portnov).]

Synopsis: The film is set in Nazi-occupied Belarus and follows the story of two partisans (Soviet resistance fighters): Nikolai Rybak (Gostiukhin) and Boris Sotnikov (Plotnikov). A German counterinsurgency detachment surrounds the starving partisans and refugees in a frozen forest. The partisans' commander sends Rybak to get food for the insurgents from neighbouring farms. Sotnikov volunteers to help Rybak. While the latter is a career serviceman, the former is a school teacher who seems to be unfit for the challenges of the war. After the Germans wound Sotnikov, he and his partner find refuge first in the house of an elderly couple and later in the hut of a widow with three children. The Germans eventually capture Rybak and Sotnikov, sentencing not only them to death but also everyone who gave them refuge. The only way to save one's life is to agree to serve in a Nazi auxiliary police unit. Interrogated and tortured by the local collaborator Pavlo Portnov (Solonitsyn), Sotnikov perseveres through all the torments and dies like a hero. Rybak, on the other hand, breaks under torture and agrees to serve the Nazis. The film's narrative is a psychological suspense story examining the darker sides of the individual's psyche and the effect of social terror on an individual's integrity.

Having based her script on Vasil Bykov's short novel *Sotnikov* (1970), Shepitko altered the relative significance of characters in her adaptation in order to express more clearly her *auteurist* understanding of the moral choices that individuals faced during the Second World War. If in Bykov's book the contrast between Sotnikov and Rybak creates the major narrative tension, in Shepitko's film three characters play key roles in the plot. Sotnikov and Portnov struggle for the soul of Rybak. As a result, the story centres on Rybak rather than Sotnikov. In order to survive he makes a moral compromise that destroys him as an individual.

Shepitko juxtaposes Rybak's physical stamina to Sotnikov's physical weakness. His strength is of a different nature. When Portnov questions Sotnikov and Rybak, he decides to start with Sotnikov assuming that he will be able to break the physically exhausted man. But Portnov is mistaken. Sotnikov may be weak physically but he is strong spiritually. The interrogator hopes that a standard torture method used by Germans against captured partisans will make Sotnikov talk. With a branding iron shaped like a star he burns the communist 'red star' on Sotnikov's chest. The destruction of Sotnikov's flesh, however, only strengthens Sotnikov's spirit. To depict Sotnikov's transformation, Shepitko changes the mise en scène. At the beginning of the torture scene, Sotnikov and Portnov talk in a room with a window boarded by planks. After the torture, the planks disappear from the window. Sotnikov sees the light that not only makes things more visible in the room, but also clarifies what the two men stand for spiritually. This light fills Sotnikov's eyes (they literally become larger, like the eyes of the Saviour on the icon of 'Christ Made Without Hands') and gives him the power to pass the ultimate test of his values.

As it is clear from the film's title, Shepitko's picture pays homage to Christian iconography and the Gospel story. This layer of intertextual references comes to the filmmaker via Andrei Tarkovsky's films about the protagonist's spiritual journey amidst war and destruction in Russia. Critics noted that the mise en scène in Shepitko's film remind us of the mise en scène of *Ivan's Childhood* (1962) and *Andrei Rublev* (1966). The ascent of Sotnikov and other martyrs to the hill where they will be executed is modelled on the story of Christ going to his snowy, Russian-style Golgotha in *Andrei Rublev*. In the scenes of Sotnikov's Christ-like torture and execution, the filmmaker uses extreme close-ups of Sotnikov's face lit with a holy glow. Just in case the viewers missed the parallel between Sotnikov and the Saviour, a peasant woman appears on the side of the road, crosses herself, and bows to the martyr. After Sotnikov's hanging, another peasant woman calls Rybak 'Judas' for betraying his fellow soldier. The war story acquires the significance of a religious parable about the holy war between Good and Evil. Not surprisingly, Shepitko chose black and white film stock for her film. The moments of ultimate moral choices do not allow much space for compromises and shades of grey.

Like the major novels of Fedor Dostoevsky, Shepitko's film offers its viewers a quasi-religious narrative of fall and redemption. The filmmaker actually reaches out even beyond Russian literature, back to the kenotic ethics of the Russian orthodox tradition. The kenotic view of Christ's life celebrates the Saviour as a humble martyr dying for the sins of man. The first Russian saints, St Boris and St Gleb, were canonised for their humble acceptance of their martyrdom when they refused to take up arms against their power-thirsty brother, eventually stopping the bloodshed. Sotnikov accepts his martyrdom passively, like St Boris, and at the film's end, right before the execution, the viewers learn that Sotnikov's first name is Boris. If in Bykov's novel Sotnikov never reveals his real name, in the film Shepitko wants the viewers and especially Sotnikov's enemies to know the name of their martyr-opponent and to think about the power of Christian humility. Shepitko's Germans are obviously beyond any comprehension of whom they are fighting with, but Portnov catches Sotnikov's gaze before his death and realises that even Nazi atrocities cannot rival the power of kenotic humility.

With the help of Alfred Shnitke's music, the filmmaker also makes her story of Sotnikov's self-sacrifice audible to the viewers. The sound structure of Shepitko's film underscores perfectly Sotnikov's spiritual ascent. At the beginning of the film viewers hear only noises: the sound of the snowstorm and gunshots. Human voices appear much later. Only when Sotnikov and Rybak are captured and on their way to the place of their last trial, and we see the face of Sotnikov (the close-up like 'The Saviour Made without Hands'), does music emerge from behind the background noise. The music is diegetic, subjective, and only audible to Sotnikov who looks up at the sky/heaven and starts comprehending the meaning of this last stretch of his earthly existence. Eventually a clear and deeply sad main musical theme of Sotnikov's ascent muffles all other noises and meaningless rejoinders of the dialogue.

Made in the Soviet Union, Shepitko's film pays homage to Soviet ideology and iconography as well. Before his heroic death Sotnikov tells his tormentors that he was born in 1917, the year of the Bolshevik Revolution, and this matters for him a lot because he knows what he dies for. He looks at the crowd who gathered around the gallows, and the camera cuts to the face of a child wearing a 'Budyonnyi hat' with a faded communist star – a reference to the Red Cavalry leader and the ideals of the revolution.

The execution scene, witnessed by a child who learns a higher moral lesson at the moment of the martyr's demise, is reminiscent of the closing scene in Roberto Rossellini's *Rome, Open City* (1945). Like Don Pietro, Sotnikov is a spiritual teacher who passes the baton to the future generation. Children in Shepitko's film are not only watching us, they are the paragons of higher moral standards. They earned this position because they suffered a lot like their parents, but unlike the adults they are not implicated in the atrocities that many of the adults committed.

In her treatment of the communist and the Christian faiths Shepitko seems to follow the ideological model offered in Rossellini's *Rome, Open City* where communism and Christianity become allied ideologies in their struggle against fascism. Shepitko, however, has a different point of view on the communist faith. She has profound misgivings about the redemptive power of communism. The major carrier of communist ideology in the film is not Sotnikov but the Nazi interrogator Portnov. Before the war he was the head of the local community centre where he taught communist ideology to adults and Bolshevik propaganda songs to children. When Nazis moved in, he turned out to be the best enforcer of the new order. He kills his former adult students and rapes his former child student. Portnov explains his credo to Sotnikov: 'Terror will replace everything. You'll finally become true self, an ordinary human, full of shit. I know what a human is really like'. In Sheptiko's film, the ex-communist Portnov has more in common with the Nazis in his practice than with Sotnikov. The latter ends up on the gallows next to a deeply religious local peasant, who gave him shelter, and finds answers to his moral quest in the Gospel story.

Most likely because of Soviet censorship, Shepitko downplays the theme of Nazi genocide against Jews. In Bykov's novel, a Jewish girl, Basia, dies next to Sotnikov. Bykov makes a point to talk about Nazi extermination of Jews because the official Soviet histories of the Second World War omitted the Shoah. Without prior knowledge of the novel, Soviet viewers would have a hard time figuring out why Basia has been hiding from the Nazis and why the police make such a big deal about those locals who gave her shelter. She is neither a partisan, nor did she aid them. In the film, neither Germans, nor local collaborators allow themselves any anti-Semitic slurs against Basia in order not to invoke the Holocaust and disturb Soviet censors. The film, however, does not erase Basia from the narrative completely; rather, it blurs her identity with other Soviet martyrs.

The official heroic myth of the united Soviet nation defeating the Nazis in the Great Patriotic War did not allow any nationality or religious denomination the right to have its own individual story of martyrdom and struggle against the Nazis. For this reason the destruction of European Jews by the Nazis has been a taboo topic in Soviet cultural texts until the fall of the Soviet Union in 1991. The few moments in Soviet history when prominent artists mentioned the Holocaust in their works and challenged the official narrative of the Great Patriotic War, like the publication of Evgeny Evtushenko's poem 'Babyi Yar' in 1961, usually caused a major controversy and paranoid reaction on the part of Soviet cultural authorities. The official story of the great victory did not allow any splintering or competing narratives of martyrdom or victory. Shepitko's film follows this official Soviet line of the quiet denial of genocide against Jews and its representation as part of Nazi atrocities against all Soviet citizens.

Sheptiko, however, incorporates several conflicting narratives of the war in her film: the Soviet narrative of victory, the hagiographic story of martyrdom, and even hints at the forbidden story of the Holocaust. These narratives do not fit perfectly into the artistic structure of the film and make Shepitko's picture a site of ideological crisis. This crisis-driven structure of the film did not meet the demands of Soviet cultural authorities but created a complex artistic text that brought Shepitko domestic and international acclaim. The film won the Golden Bear at the Berlin International Film Festival in 1977.

While the quasi-hagiographic story of Christ-like teacher Sotnikov provides viewers with an example of martyrdom, few can live up to such moral heights; the story of Rybak, I would argue, provides the viewer with an experience one can identify with. Rybak is an average human being confronted with the test of his integrity that few can pass. Shepitko does not judge her character. However, she does not exonerate Rybak from the responsibility for his choices. And as it fits a modern narrative, the ordeal of the flawed individual, not the ascent of the martyr, becomes the major narrative interest for the viewer.

While the film is titled *The Ascent,* Shepitko does not close her picture with the scene of Sotnikov's superhuman feat. Instead she takes the viewer back to Rybak who tries and fails to commit suicide in an outhouse next to Nazi headquarters and is cursed to continue his physical existence with a memory of his betrayal. In a way, the film poses a question about everyone who survived the terrible war. What kind of choices did these people have to make in order to save their lives? Contemporary critics discussed the film a lot because it offered a fresh perspective on the war, different from standard Soviet celebrations of military hardware and the superiority of Soviet ideology. In the September 1977 issue of Russia's premier film journal *Art of Cinema,* Elena Stishova wrote the most insightful review of the film. She argued that the film condemns the war as a social situation that forces people to make impossible choices, such as the choice between life and conscience. Rybak is secondary to this bigger anti-war message of the film. Stishova does not judge Rybak and she thinks that Shepitko condemns only the war.

Shepitko's film left a lasting legacy in Russian cinema and culture. In the 1970s it triggered a discussion about *who* and *how* is allowed to commemorate the Great Patriotic War. Most importantly, the filmmaker depicted the community ruled by total terror and its corrosive impact on the individual. What Shepitko presented as a community created by the Nazi occupation, in retrospect, looks a lot like a community too familiar to Russians from their Stalinist past.

Further reading

Denise Youngblood, *Russian War Films. On the Cinema Front, 1914–2005,* Lawrence, Kansas University Press, 2005, pp. 180–4.

Alexander Prokhorov

W. R.: Misterije organizma/*WR: Mysteries of the Organism* (1971)

[Country: Yugoslavia, Germany. Production Company: Neoplanta Film, Novi Sad and Telepool, Munich. Director: Dušan Makavejev. Producer: Svetozar Udovički. Screenwriter: Dušan Makavejev. Cinematographers: Aleksandar Petrović and Pega Popović. Music arranged by: Bojana Marijan. Editor: Ivanka Vukasović. Cast: Milena Dravić (Milena), Jagoda Kaloper (Jagoda), Ivica Vidović (Vladimir Ilyich), Zoran Radmilović (Radmilović), Miodrag Andrić (Soldier Ljuba), Tuli Kupferberg, Jackie Curtis, Živka Matić, etc.]

Synopsis: The film is a collage of different materials, mainly documentary footage from the US, and fictional events taking place in Belgrade, Serbia. The 'American' section also contains various materials: interviews that attempt to shed light on the life and the theories on the relation between sex and politics espoused by psychoanalyst Wilhelm Reich, reflections by the transvestite Jackie Curtis, and various other pieces of footage. The 'Yugoslav' story depicts events surrounding a love affair between Milena, a Yugoslav communist activist and Soviet art ice skater Vladimir Ilyich, which ends with Milena's brutal death. Without attempting to coherently link these varied events, the movie strives to lead viewers towards abstract conclusions about hidden links between sex and politics.

Sex is fun, and sex is funny. This is certainly one of the basic premises of *WR: Mysteries of the Organism.*[1] Wilhelm Reich, German psychoanalyst, Freud's apprentice, who died in a US penitentiary in Louisburg, Pennsylvania, in 1957, would in all probability agree with the first part of this statement, although not with the second. This is the main difference between Makavejev and Reich. Much criticism of Makavejev's movie stems from this distinction, for many took the director's amusement and amazement with the topic of sex as his misinterpretation of Reich's work.[2] Reich took sex very seriously, and built his career trying to connect sexual energy with political and historical issues, which is what Makavejev attempted to do, tongue-in-cheek.

The film consists of two main intertwined parts. One is a documentary about Reich's work and testimony of the people who knew him, as well as about topics connected with sexuality in the United States, at the time the movie was made (1968–1971). The other is a feature made in Yugoslavia at the same time, which describes events surrounding the main character, Milena, her political activity, and her love affair with the People's Artist from the Soviet Union, ice skater Vladimir Ilyich. Interspersed is archival footage from various sources, documentary as well as fictional events, songs, poems, music. This structure has often led critics to describe this and other of Makavejev's films as works deploying the technique of collage.

Reich, convinced that personal freedom is a precondition for social revolution, worked in Germany during the 1930s where he initiated the movement *Sexpol* connected with the Communist party, with the aim of reaching young people. He was quite influential, but a few months before Hitler came to power, the conservatives in the Communist party, in line with Moscow, took a traditionalist line regarding sexuality, and Reich was expelled from the party as well as from the German psychoanalytic society. Reich persisted and claimed that the fight against fascism could not be led on a 'strictly rational level of political analysis', that it was futile.[3] He fled Germany when the Nazis came to power and settled in the United States, where he claimed to have discovered 'orgon energy', which connects matter, body, and mind. He developed 'orgon boxes' to collect this energy from the atmosphere, and sold them across the US. Officially, this is what brought him in conflict with the FDA (Food and Drug Administration), which ultimately ended with his imprisonment, and two years later, his death.

In his documentary footage, Makavejev approaches Reich very cautiously. Although excited by Reich's work, as an experienced documentary filmmaker (from 1958–1964 he made 13 documentaries), he circles around the centre of his investigation, shedding light from various directions. Makavejev is a passionate, but irreverent follower, which can be irritable. Nevertheless, he can hardly be called disrespectful or misleading. We never really know what he thinks of orgon boxes and the somewhat fanciful theories of Reich's. But his belief in the importance of Reich's effort in general cannot be doubted. Makavejev does not have ready answers, but assumes that the topic of sexuality is worthy of elaborate investigation, which this film represents. If it can be claimed that Makavejev's *Love Affair: The Case of the Missing Switchboard Operator* (1967) is 'one of the best movies Godard has ever made', as Lopate and Zavatsky say, *WR* is certainly one of the most intriguing film essays on politics, which is what Godard saw himself doing in his politically committed movies.[4] But Jean-Luc Godard, who is of crucial importance for Makavejev's work, rarely has patience to so carefully, consistently probe one topic as Makavejev does in *WR*. Rather than working from adopted premises, and then interpreting reality according to them, Makavejev investigates the basis of his research that is Reich's ideas themselves. It is hard to agree or not agree with him, when there is very little that we can take as definite conclusions in this film. However, Makavejev is more pronounced on certain matters than on others. For example, it is evident what he thinks of Stalinism. Footage from Chiaureli's features glorifying Stalin is readily juxtaposed with pictures of psychiatric patients being maltreated; one even repeatedly bangs his head against the doorframe. On another occasion, Stalin is compared with an erected plastic penis, which Nancy Godfrey makes from a live model, or 'Lily Marleen' is played against inserts from Chiaureli's *The Fall of Berlin*. The whole of *WR* is a montage of various pieces of footage that comes from seemingly very disparate sources. This allows for associations that quickly arise, and sometimes even faster disappear, which makes it difficult to pinpoint their connections and draw conclusions. However, on Stalin they are crystal clear.

In addition, the contemporary communist regime in the Soviet Union, through the character of Vladimir Ilyich, is represented in very unfavourable light. He is vein, arrogant, and intolerant. He preaches the doctrine of realist socialism, glorifies the Soviet Union not only in relation to the West, but also in the context of the system of socialist self-management, which existed at the time in Yugoslavia, and which his hosts in Belgrade represent. Here we come to see the global disposition established by Makavejev concerning the contemporary political and psychoanalytic stage. On one side are the West, Reich's disciples, New York, Jackie Curtis, Tuli Kupferberg, anti-communist hysteria, and the Vietnam War. On the other is Vladimir Ilyich, the Soviet Union, while in between lies Yugoslavia with the chaotic private and public lives of its heroes. China is only briefly, but significantly present. This description is, surprisingly, very close to how Tito and his entourage saw themselves and the world at the time the movie was made.[5] They criticised the West, of course, trying to keep the equidistance from the Soviet Union that had just invaded Czechoslovakia. The Soviet system of state control over the economy, art, and political life was seen as contrary to the liberating potentials, which socialism as a superior political system should bring to the people. On the other side, at least in theory, the system of socialist self-management, developed in Yugoslavia, should allow social life not subjected to the demands of the all mighty centralised state, as was the case in the Eastern bloc. This experiment, which often was not more than a litany of good wishes, did not survive, and it disappeared from the world stage at the same time as the Berlin wall fell and as communist regimes of Eastern Europe tumbled one after the other. We cannot say that Makavejev spoke for the system; in *WR* he readily mocked even the holy cows, Tito, the Communist party, and the JNA (Yugoslav People's Army), but with all its limits he saw it much more conducive to implementing Reich's ideas of a liberated society than the communism of Eastern Europe.[6]

It has been well noted that humour in *WR* possesses somewhat crude, vulgar, peasant features.[7] This we can connect to the uninhibited, 'uncivilised' character of Serbian peasantry, whose more than Rabelais-esque relationship to sexuality is visible in its long-suppressed verses of folk poetry.[8] This is most visible in the rapport between Jagoda and Ljuba, and in their dialogues, which are difficult to translate into English. Milena, by contrast, is a well-developed, exceptional character. She is an apprentice in a beauty parlour, and has finished a Party course, which made her aware of the pitiful state of the working class. Dressed in a short sleeping shirt and Ljuba's military jacket, army cap with the red star on her head, boots on her legs, she preaches to the dissatisfied, hostile crowd of workers and citizens in one of Belgrade's old-fashioned apartment buildings. She is ecstatic about the need for sexual liberation that will complement worker's self-management. But Milena herself falls in love with Vladimir Ilyich in a completely traditional way. She is impressed with his art, his looks, and his imperial demeanour. He does not respond, and she throws herself at him. He finally takes action, but he cannot stand making love, just like he cannot listen to music – it is too emotional for him. He decapitates her with his skating boot, and the film finishes with him stumbling along the banks of a river with his bloody hands outstretched, singing the song of Bulat Okudzhava. The words of this poem may be confusing, but it seems that they are a fitting end for what Makavejev wanted to say. In the end, human desires, wishes, hopes, aspirations are so complex, diverse, and often obscure, that all that helps is a prayer to God for some happiness and good luck in life.

As the film develops, the rhythm of cutting quickens, getting more complex. The choice of music plays a very important role. Makavejev (or his wife, who did it) is very inventive in this regard. His use of lively Balkan folk music well complements various scenes of *WR*. We move from one type of footage to another, while cuts are often motivated by a movement, or a sound, often shrieks. Various footage contributes to the rich field of associations. For example, what is the connection between Radmilović and Kupferberg, except for the crouched position of their bodies as they move? Or, what do the cries caused by electro-shock psychiatric treatment have in common with the cries produced at the mass therapeutic session of one of Reich's followers? These are not precisely formulated propositions, but allusions, inklings, the beginnings of thoughts the viewer is invited to further develop (or not). The medium of film with its rich arsenal offers here an idiosyncratic opportunity to do so. Also, this is what makes *WR* more than just an apt compendium of the problems and issues that the world faced during the 1960s.

Notes

1. WR here stands for Wilhelm Reich, but also for World Revolution.
2. The American theatre release version begins with the inserted designation: 'This film is, in part, a personal response to the life and teachings of Dr Wilhelm Reich (1897–1957)'. This was added to allay the fierce criticism of some of Reich's followers from New York who claimed that the movie severely distorted Reich's ideas.
3. See James Roy MacBean, 'Sex and Politics: Wilhelm Reich, World Revolution and Makavejev's WR', *Film Quarterly*, Vol. 25, No. 3, Spring 1972, p. 3.
4. This didn't stop the regime from practically, although not officially, banning the movie as soon as it was finished. It was shown in Yugoslavia for the first time in 1986.
5. Josip Broz Tito was a communist dictator of Yugoslavia from 1945–1980. He broke relations with Stalin in 1948 to set up a system of socialist self-management, and was one of the founders of the non-aligned movement of states, which tried to keep equidistance from the West and the East during the Cold War.
6. See Dušan Makavejev and Wilhelm Reich, *WR: Mysteries of the Organism: A Cinematic Testament to the Life and Teachings of Wilhelm Reich*, New York, Avon Books, 1972. The book contains Phillip Lopate and Bill Zavatsky, 'An Interview with Dušan Makavejev'.
7. See Lorraine Mortimer, *Terror and Joy: The Films of Dušan Makavejev*, Minneapolis, London, University of Minnesota Press, 2009.
8. Vuk Stefanović Karadžić, a Serbian language reformer from the nineteenth century collected these songs, but they were published in Serbia as late as 1979. English translation: Vuk Stefanović Karadžić, *Red Knight: Serbian Women's Songs*, edited and translated by Daniel Weissbort and Tomislav Longinović,

London, Menard Press / King's College London, 1992.

Further reading

Raymond Durgnat, *WR – Mysteries of the Organism*, London, British Film Institute, 1999.
Daniel J. Goulding, *Five Filmmakers: Tarkovsky, Forman, Polanski, Szabó, Makavejev*, Bloomington, Indiana University Press, 1994.
Kurt Jacobsen, 'Interview with Dušan Makavejev', *Left Curve*, Vol. 19, 1995.
David W. Paul (ed.), *Politics, Art and Commitment in the East European Cinema*, London, Macmillan, 1983.
Nevenka Stanković, 'The Cities of Play and Disclosure: WR: Mysteries of the Organism', *Third Text*, Vol. 19, No. 4, July 2005, pp. 385–98.

Saša Milić

West Side Story (1961)

[Country: USA. Production Company: The Mirisch Corporation/Beta Productions/Seven Arts Productions. Directors: Jerome Robbins/Robert Wise. Screenwriter: Ernest Lehman (based on the play by Arthur Laurents). Producer: Robert Wise. Music: Leonard Bernstein. Cinematographer: Daniel L. Fapp. Editor: Thomas Stanford. Choreographer: Jerome Robbins. Cast: Natalie Wood (Maria), Richard Beymer (Tony), George Chakiris (Bernardo), Rita Moreno (Anita), Russ Tamblin (Riff), Jose de Vega (Chino), Eliot Feld (Baby John), Susan Oakes (Anybodys), Gina Trikonis (Graziella), Carole D'Andrea (Velma), Ned Glass (Doc), Simon Oakland (Lieutenant Schrank), William Bramely (Officer Krupke).]

Synopsis: On New York's West Side, two gangs, the white Jets and the Puerto Rican Sharks, fight over turf. At a dance, the tensions are palpable, but Tony, a former Jet, and Maria, the little sister of Bernardo, the Sharks' leader, fall in love at first sight. While they meet secretly, the Jets and the Sharks agree on a rumble under the highway. Tony gets them to agree not to use weapons, but Maria asks him to prevent the rumble altogether. Things go bad, Bernardo kills Riff, the Jets' leader, and Tony kills Bernardo. Maria and Tony want to run a way, and Anita wants to help but stops doing so when she is humiliated and aggressed by the Jets. In the end, Maria is left to grieve over Tony's dead body.

Based on the successful Broadway musical first staged in 1957, a modern adaptation of Shakespeare's *Romeo and Juliet*, the musical expressed a number of ambivalences, about youth culture, social and urban change, high and low culture. Critics were divided about the film, some hailing it as a masterpiece lauding its choreography and pulsating rhythm, while others deplored the film's romanticisation of the heterosexual couple and of the street gangs as well as the tensions between stylisation and realism. In many ways, the stage musical and the film picked up on a subversive trend in the fifties, on an emerging youth culture, and, with its unhappy ending, anticipated the edgier films of the late 60s. At the same time, however, it remained committed to utopian (and romantic) thinking so typical of musicals.

West Side Story is an urban musical, a form that puts it in the context of films such as *42nd Street* (Lloyd Bacon, 1933), *On the Town* (Stanley Donen/Gene Kelly, 1949), *The Band Wagon* (Vincente Minnelli, 1953) and *Guys and Dolls* (Joseph L. Mankiewicz, 1955), and which may be distinguished from more rural, folkloristic musicals such as *Oklahoma!* (Fred Zinnemann, 1955) and *The Music Man* (Morton DaCosta, 1962). The urban context for *West Side Story*, however, was very specific, referencing post-war urban renewal. After the overture, the film opens with a sequence shot on location in Manhattan, and we see the gangs run through a number of non-continuous spaces, including a heap of construction rubble. The latter is an indication that the film commemorates what was about to be destroyed: the tenements in the San Juan Hill neighbourhood, which were about to be razed to make way for the construction of the Lincoln Center for the Performing Arts (among others home of the Metropolitan Opera). This replacement of working-class, ethnic neighbourhoods with a monument to high art – what was generally understood as slum clearance – was part of Robert Moses' plan for New York City. It was controversial not least because of the number of people it displaced. Another gesture towards a changing New York can be found in the rumble taking place under a highway overpass (represented by a set). Moses was also famous for razing blocks of apartments in order to make space for highways, in a misguided attempt to adapt New York City for the automobile. While the film is hardly a critique of Moses' policies, it nonetheless suggests that the restructuring of New York City created a number of deadly spaces.

Likewise, the film's take on New York City urban culture and its Puerto Rican inhabitants is ambivalent at best. The original idea for the musical had a different ethnic cast: located on New York City's East Side, the story was to be about Catholics and Jews feuding at Passover time. (A trace of Jewishness can be discerned in the Doc's Yiddish-inflected English, which casts the film's most reasonable character as a former immigrant.) During a stay in Hollywood, Leonard Bernstein and Arthur Laurents read about gang fights between Mexican immigrants and native-born Americans, and decided to relocate the story into New York City's Puerto Rican context (Garebian 1995: 30, 35). Immigration from Puerto Rico, which had been invaded by the United States during the Spanish–American War of 1898, whose inhabitants have US citizenship, but not the right to vote, surged in the 1950s. Since its release the film has often been criticised for its stereotypical depiction of Puerto Ricans, which was not helped by the fact that apart from Rita Moreno as Anita (who was made to assume an over-exaggerated accent), the cast was mostly non-Puerto Rican, a fact the producers were trying to make up for with hair dye and make-up. Puerto Ricans protested early on, though the objections to the original stage musical had to do less with the depiction of Puerto Rican juvenile delinquents (or of Puerto Ricans as delinquents) than with the characterisation of Puerto Rico in the song 'America' (Garebian 1995: 138). Part of the ambivalent response to the film may have to do with the film's own ambivalence. Casting a conflict between ethnic strife and romantic love, the film's choreography of urban space is simultaneously celebratory and martial, as becomes visible, for instance, in the opening encounter between the Jets and the Sharks.

West Side Story combined these urban and ethnic contexts with a theme that had proven profitable for Hollywood in the 1950s: youth culture, more specifically juvenile delinquency. The 1950s in general saw an increased targeting of younger movie audiences, in part because cinema was now locked into a competition with television, which turned out to be more family oriented. By contrast, cinema now sought out niche markets (such as teenagers in drive-ins). Movie stars tapping into a newly emerging youth culture, such as James Dean or Elvis Presley, proved incredibly popular. *Rebel without a Cause* (Nicholas Ray, 1955) had definitely established juvenile delinquency as a sellable product. To some extent, *West Side Story* can be understood as the transposition of this issue into a more working-class, ethnic context. Coming several years after *Rebel*, and after a wave of popularising the psychological theories of Sigmund Freud in Hollywood, *West Side Story* is very aware of the psychological contexts of juvenile delinquency. The most hilarious moment in this regard may be 'Officer Krupke', a musical number in which the Jets make fun of police officers, judges, psychotherapists and social workers. 'See them cops, they believe everything they read in the papers about us JDs. So that's what we give 'em, somethin' to believe in', Riff says. These self-consciously ironic moments provide a comic counterpart to the film's more romantic longings, and place the film in-between the melodramatic earnestness of films such as *Rebel without a Cause* and the more nihilistic scepticism of youth-culture films from the late 1960s, such as *Bonnie and Clyde* (Arthur Penn, 1967) and *Easy Rider* (Dennis Hopper, 1969).

West Side Story may thus be seen as a transitional film, originating in the 1950s and pointing toward a more youth-oriented film culture. This liminal status – and the ambivalences it entails – is crucially connected to its status as a musical. Rick Altman has argued that musicals are 'dual-focus' narratives, playing things against but also alongside each other. The most obvious version of such a dual focus may be the heterosexual couple – in *West Side Story* Tony and Maria – who get solos as well as duets. In a related issue, within musical criticism, the relationship between the musical numbers and the rest of the narrative has always been considered important. There are many different kinds of musicals – from the revue (which essentially strung together a series of musical numbers with little plot connecting them), to the backstage musical (where the stage setting justifies the inclusion of musical numbers), to the integrated musical (in which songs and dances advance plot and develop characters). Though not the first integrated musical, the original stage version of *West Side Story* was hailed as a landmark show, conceived around movement, with dances advancing plotlines even as the choreography allowed for interruptions, asymmetries and youthful freedom (Garebian 1995: 13).

West Side Story thus seemed to develop a musical form that was particularly good at staging and choreographing conflicts. One of these conflicts may well be the one between comedy and tragedy, irony and sincerity already mentioned in the discussion of the 'Officer Krupke' number. But other tensions abound, for instance between realism (the location shots) and fantasy (the fantastically coloured and stylised sets). Indeed, part of the film's conflict is brought out through subtle uses of colour, as the gangs are colour-coded, with the Jets wearing clothes ranging from yellow to brown while the Sharks' clothing ranges from purple to red. In this context, Maria's clothing is particularly interesting to watch, because she goes back and forth between the two groups. The film's gorgeous colours, however, also gesture toward another conflict. On the one hand, by the 1950s, the film industry was invested in colour movies and widescreen formats, so as to offer something more spectacular than the new televisual medium. On the other hand, the colour play during the overture also suggests another ambition. The film's solemn beginning reveals the high aspirations of film at the time – the attempt to become a highbrow art. The show's composer, Leonard Bernstein, son of Jewish immigrants, who had written a BA thesis titled 'The Absorption of Race Elements into American Music', was well known for his enthusiasm for American music, especially jazz, his eclecticism, and for mixing high and low, the classical and the vernacular (Garebian 1995: 24). The film's overture, though, clashes with its lowly subject as well as with the graffiti at the end of the film.

At the same time, however, the musical's impulse often is to try to transcend and resolve such conflicts. Richard Dyer has argued that musical entertainment has a profoundly utopian dimension. Musical numbers, through representational and non-representational signs (such as colour, movement, etc.), seek to overcome limitations, for instance replacing scarcity with abundance, exhaustion with energy, dreariness with intensity, fragmentation with community. In *West Side Story*, Tony's and Maria's romance – and duets – are part of the utopia – in 'Somewhere' Tony dreams of a 'place for us', 'peace and quiet and open air', and later he tells Doc about his fantasy of having 'lots of kids' with Maria in the country. But this place seems to play on the original meaning of utopia, a 'non-place'. This seems fairly conventional – conceiving of the nuclear family as utopian – and yet it is interesting that it does not exist in the film. One of the more intriguing minor characters is 'Anybodys', the girl who rejects conventional gender norms. She is thoroughly ridiculed, according to dominant sentiments of the time, but it is nonetheless worth asking to what extent the film registers, negotiates and responds to unstable or changing gender and sexual roles. ('My sister wears a mustache, my brother wears a dress', Riff sings in 'Officer Krupke'.) In addition to the question of gender utopia, the issue of national utopia may be most prevalent, staged as a disagreement between Puerto Rican men and women in 'America'. The song does not only comment on the comparative merits of the two 'islands' – Puerto Rico and Manhattan – but registers profound ambivalence about US consumerism – and capitalism more generally – because of how racism and unequal access are structured into the system. Because utopia always seems elsewhere in *West Side Story*, it becomes easier to read social issues against the grain – the film proposing the critique of gender or national norms as utopian. It is this ability to play both sides – to champion simultaneously critique and affirmation – that makes it one of the greatest American musicals.

Further reading

Richard Altman, *The American Film Musical*, Bloomington, Indiana University Press, 1987.

Hillary Ballon and Kenneth T. Jackson (eds), *Robert Moses and the Modern City: The Transformation of New York*, New York, Norton, 2007.

Thomas Patrick Doherty, *Teenagers and Teenpics: The Juvenilization of American Movies in the 1950s*, Philadelphia, Temple University Press, 2002.

Richard Dyer, 'Entertainment and Utopia', in Bill Nichols (ed.), *Movies and Methods*, Vol. II, Berkeley, University of California Press, 1985, pp. 220–32.

Keith Garebian, *The Making of* West Side Story, Toronto, ECW Press, 1995.

Sabine Haenni

Whale Rider (2002)

[Country: New Zealand, Germany. Production Company: South Pacific Pictures, ApolloMedia Distribution, Pandora Filmproduktion. Director and Screenwriter: Niki Caro. Cinematographer: Leon Narbey. Editor: David Coulson. Cast: Keisha Castle-Hughes (Paikea), Rawiri Paratene (Koro), Cliff Curtis (Porourangi), Grant Roa (Rawiri).]

Synopsis: The opening sequence presents a powerful juxtaposition between contemporary culture and Maori heritage, with a modern hospital birth-scene intercut with mysterious shots of a whale and a female narrator recounting the Maori tale of *Paikea*: a mythical descendant of the Ngati Konohi tribe who discovered Whangara on the back of a humpback whale after his canoe had capsized off the coast of Hawaiki – the ancient Maori homeland. By Maori tradition, the tribe's chief must be a direct descendant of the mythical Paikea, with first-born sons continuing this custom ever since. The film opens with Porourangi, eldest son of Koro, the current chief, anxiously supporting his wife who is in labour. She gives birth to a baby girl, but things soon take a turn for the worse as the narrator reveals, 'When I was born, my twin brother died and took our mother with him'. Unable to cope with the loss of his wife and son, Porourangi emigrates to Europe to pursue a career as an artist, turning his back on his Maori heritage and repurposing his traditional carving skills towards a more international and commercial market. To make matters worse, he names his daughter 'Paikea', which angers Koro who sees this as a mockery of Ngati Konohi customs and tradition. Koro had believed that Porourangi's first-born was destined to be 'the boy who would be chief', responsible for leading the community into a new age of prosperity, and he initially refuses to acknowledge his granddaughter.

The story then leaps forward 11 years, by which time Koro has developed a strong, (albeit slightly belligerent) affection for his granddaughter, who he only ever calls 'Pai', denying the true power and meaning of her full name. Despite his love for Pai, his passion to restore the tribe through a firstborn male leader is aggravated by her very presence. When Pai asks where her people come from, in what can be considered a key scene, Koro likens their ancestral line to the intertwining strands of a rope he is using to fix a boat motor. The rope proceeds to break when he tests it, which is further indication to Koro that the sacred line of the tribe is broken, that their ancestors have abandoned them in the face of modernity. However, Pai fixes the rope and the motor runs fine, much to Koro's frustration; frustrated that a young girl managed to repair something he couldn't, and for what it symbolises, that a female could become chief and restore the tribe. *Whale Rider*, then, challenges the lineage of male dominance, with Paikea's plight serving as 'symbolic indictment of the mores of patriarchy, and a call for greater inclusiveness' (Sison 2012: 129). Indeed, as Ryan Mottesheard (2003) argues, the film should be understood 'less as anthropological study of the Maori people, than a universal story of female empowerment', thus highlighting the film's global appeal.

Based on Witi Ihimaera's novel of the same name, Niki Caro's *Whale Rider* is a moving depiction of a young Maori girl battling to overturn the patriarchal traditions of her Ngati Konohi tribal community. Marginalised from contemporary New Zealand society, the Maori community is ostensibly struggling in rural poverty and obscurity; rusting car wrecks and abandoned machinery litter the otherwise idyllic Whangara coastline (the northeast region of New Zealand's North Island where the film was shot), emphasising the intrusion of Western/Pakeha culture and the effects of modernity. *Whale Rider*, then, brings into question the notion of postcolonial identity within New Zealand, with a renewal of tribal values being presented as the means by which the Maori people learn to adapt to the modern-day demands of urbanisation. Indeed, as Sison suggests, 'the cultural milieu of *Whale Rider* is characterised by the ongoing Maori quest for soul and identity in the postcolonial aftermath' (Sison 2012: 122), and it is these themes, as well as female empowerment, which underpin the narrative.

Koro's teachings of earlier cultural practices, ceremonies and mythologies help to shore up community identity in the present, with the effects of colonialism being implied as possible cause of the tribe's present day problems, such as youthful apathy, lack of direction and urban drift (Wilson 2011: 204). Similarly, Smith (2006: 110) suggests the imposition of Pakeha culture and 'opportunities of modernity' has created a 'lost generation' amongst the Maori people, with several characters portraying the effects of this modern allure. For example, Porourangi uses international travel to escape the pain of losing his loved ones, as well as the responsibility to produce a male son that Koro believes will lead his people 'out of the darkness'. Porourangi's unfinished *te waka* (ceremonial canoe) is left abandoned on the beach, acting as a 'constant reminder to Koro of his unfulfilled mission to anoint another male heir to tribal leadership' (Sison 2012: 122). Koro takes it upon himself to arrange another partner for his son, a teacher from Pai's school, who he believes will deliver Porourangi a male child. Koro is bitterly disappointed when Porourangi announces to his family that he already has a pregnant lover in Germany and will not be returning home with the child, putting an end to Koro's aspirations. Porourangi offers to take Paikea with him back to Europe, but as she looks out to sea she feels the pull of her ancestors and cannot abandon her heritage. Whereas the majority of her community appear disrespectful of Maori customs and traditions, Pai shows a deep affinity to 'the old ways' and demonstrates her passion publicly. Koro's youngest son Rawiri, meanwhile, has turned to drugs and alcohol as a form of escape, whilst the younger children of the tribe laugh and joke as Maori rituals are performed on the *marea*, more concerned with football and cigarettes. Even the elder women of the community are shown playing cards and smoking. For Bill Ashcroft *et al.* (1998: 139), this highlights a form of colonial *mimicry*, whereby the indigenous population adopts the coloniser's cultural habits. Furthermore, such a portrayal of a Maori tribe in their contemporary setting highlights post-colonial ambivalence in New Zealand, indicating that Maoris are not fully opposed to the *hybridisation* that has occurred during the colonial process. Koro's adoption of Western/Pakeha clothing and his noticeable reliance on modern technologies (i.e. the speedboat and tractor) connotes 'the complex mix of attraction and repulsion that characterises the relationship between the coloniser and colonised' (Ashcroft *et al.*, 1998: 12). This relationship is ambivalent since the colonised subject is never completely opposed to the coloniser.

In response to Porourangi's announcement and the realisation that he has failed to anoint a suitable heir to leadership, Koro gathers all firstborn males from the tribe to teach them ancient Ngati Konohi culture and traditions, with the intention that one of these boys will become the tribe's next chief. They initially find this strange in comparison to their modern lives but they gradually become more accustomed to Maori customs, especially the *taiahi* – a ritual fighting stick. When Paikea expresses her interest she is excluded by her grandfather, who is adamant that a woman should not be involved in learning about tribal leadership. This highlights the tensions between the traditional and the modern in Maori culture, with Koro's stringent following of the tribe's ancient traditions leading him to alienate his own kin, despite the fact that Pai shows more promise than any of the other boys. It is also implied that Koro had previously alienated Pai's uncle Rawiri, who, given the fact he was not Koro's firstborn son, was never considered a suitable leader for the tribe, leading him to lose touch with his Maori heritage. Paikea's grandmother, Nanny Flowers, reveals that Rawiri was once a champion *taiahi* fighter, and asks him to tutor Pai. Upon accepting Rawiri undergoes a transformation, immediately feeling 'at one' with his ancient tribal heritage:

> This artefact of tradition has an almost sacramental character and seems to immediately recall him to himself, to remind him of not only who he is but who is called to be. Rawiri takes up the challenge with fervour and not only trains Paikea to be the best in the tribe but also recovers his own sense of identity and self worth.
>
> (Smith 2006: 113).

Paikea trains in secret, eavesdropping on Koro's classes, determined to learn all she can of her ancestral customs. In one scene, Hami, the most promising student in Koro's school, challenges Pai to a *taiahi* duel, which Pai eventually wins. When Koro finds out he chastises Paikea, warning her that by tampering with sacred traditions she has shamed her community. Koro's frustration is plain to see as he proceeds to exclude both Hami and Pai from his final challenge to determine who will become the next chief. He takes the remaining boys out to sea in his speedboat and throws his whale-tooth necklace overboard stating that he needs someone to demonstrate the 'spirit' needed to recover the necklace (which symbolises the tribe's connection to their ancestors). Much to his dismay, none of the boys retrieve the pendant and Koro returns to shore, despondent. Unbeknown to Koro, Rawiri later takes Pai out in the boat, who not only finds the necklace, but also manages to catch a lobster as a present for her grandfather.

Pai sympathises with Koro and prays to her ancestors for help, with a voice-over revealing, 'They heard me', initiating the film's most iconic and emotional sequence. One night Paikea delivers a speech to the rest of the tribe that traces the history of her people and the significance of the Paikea legend, which she tearfully dedicates to her grandfather. Only Koro had failed to turn up; distant cries had drawn him to the beach where a pod of whales lay dying. For Koro, this symbolises the tribe's contemporary crisis of identity, a loss of spiritual connection to their ancestors. Eventually the rest of the tribe make their way to the shore, with the beached whales igniting in them a communal strength they believed was forgotten as they work tirelessly to lure the whales back towards the ocean. They attempt to move the largest bull whale using a tractor, but it is a problem that cannot be resolved by modern technology. Paikea, realising what she was destined to do, proceeds to ride the large whale, sparking it into life, followed by the rest of the pod. Fearing that his granddaughter has drowned Koro finally understands that it was Pai all along who was destined to be the tribe's new leader, finally accepting that he must adapt his cultural beliefs. Pai is found alive and the film closes with the whole tribe embracing their Maori culture, celebrating through traditional Maori rituals. What is more, Porourangi has returned with his German fiancé to finish his *waka* and celebrate with his people. As such, the film does not present a simple rejection of modernity, rather 'it is the recovery of tradition *in* modernity, and sometimes against identity, that makes possible the renewal of identity of Paikea's people' (Smith 2006: 116). Sison (2012: 134) proposes that this ending follows a particular theological trajectory, with Paikea's symbolic 'reincarnation' having a transformative impact on the community. Therefore, *Whale Rider* emphasises the benefits of bicultural cooperation, incorporating what Duncan Petrie

(2007: 172) describes as a 'utopian embrace of common humanity as an alternative strategy of dealing with the trauma of the past'.

Further reading

Bill Ashcroft, Gareth Griffiths and Helen Tiffin, *Key Concepts in Post-Colonial Studies*, London and New York, Routledge, 1998.

Ryan Mottesheard, 'Girl Power: New Zealand Writer/ Director Niki Caro Talks About "Whale Rider"', *IndieWire*, June 6, 2003. Available at www.indie-wire.com/article/girl_power_new_zealand_ wri-terdirector_niki_caro_talks_about_whale_ rider.

Duncan Petrie, 'New Zealand', in M. Hjort, D. Petrie (ed), *The Cinema of Small Nations*, Edinburgh: Edinburgh University Press, 2007.

Antonio Sison, *World Cinema, Theology, and the Human: Humanity in Deep Focus*, New York, Routledge, 2012.

James K A Smith, *Who's Afraid of Postmodernism?: Taking Derrida, Lyotard, and Foucault to Church*, MI, Baker Academic, 2006.

Janet Wilson, 'Re-representing Indigeneity: Approaches to History in recent New Zealand Australian Films', in Alistair Fox, Barry Keith Grant and Hilary Radner, (eds), *New Zealand Cinema: Interpreting the Past*, Bristol, Intellect, 2011, pp. 197–216.

Martyn Thayne

Whisky (2004)

[Country: Uruguay, Germany, Argentina, Spain. Production Company: Pandora Filmproduktion, Ctrl Z Films, Rizoma Films, Wanda Visión S.A. Directors: Juan Pablo Rebella and Pablo Stoll. Producer: Fernando Epstein. Screenwriters: Gonzalo Delgado, Juan Pablo Rebella and Pablo Stoll. Cinematographer: Bárbara Álvarez. Music: Pequeña Orquesta Reincidentes. Editor: Fernando Epstein. Cast: Andrés Pazos (Jacobo), Mirella Pascual (Marta), Jorge Bolani (Herman), Ana Katz (Newly married wife), Daniel Hendler (Newly married husband), Verónica Perrota (Factory worker 1), Mariana Velásquez (Factory worker 2), Dumas Lerena (Don Isaac), Damián Barrera (Andrés), Alfonso Tort (Juan Carlos), Francisca Barreira (Singer), Adrián Biniez (Dardo).]

Synopsis: Jacobo Köller is the owner of a small outdated factory in Uruguay's grey and quiet port of Montevideo. A year after his mother's death, his brother Herman visits from Brazil to attend the ceremony of the setting of the stone in the cemetery. Jacobo asks Marta, his loyal chief employee, to pretend they are a married couple while his brother is visiting. After the ceremony, Herman invites the couple to take a brief holiday in a seaside resort. Jacobo reluctantly agrees. Herman gives Jacobo money as compensation for his absence during their mother's illness and death. Jacobo gambles with it in the hotel casino with the intention to lose it, but he doubles the money. Herman flies back to Brazil and Jacobo and Marta separate once more. Jacobo gives Marta the money he won at the casino in exchange for her services. The next morning, Jacobo goes about his regular routine. He gets up, goes to the factory and opens it. This time, Marta is not there.

Every morning, Jacobo (Andrés Pazos), a monotone and austere Jewish man of maybe 70, meticulously repeats the same routine: he gets up, gets in an old automobile that takes a while to turn on, and rides through an almost deserted and still dark Montevideo to arrive at his modest sock factory where Marta (Mirella Pascual) awaits him, a timid middle-aged woman who is his loyal employee. After a frugal greeting, Jacobo brings up the workshop's metal shutter and turns on the machines. While Marta puts on her work apron and makes herself some tea, Jacobo tries fruitlessly to adjust the blinds in his office. Marta remains in the machine room all day, inspecting socks off the conveyer belt and managing two other employees. By day's end, she checks the bags of the other workers, marks their time sheets, and meets Jacobo outside as he closes the gates to the factory. In the first half of Whisky the actors barely speak. 'Excuse me' as she enters his office and a lugubrious 'See you tomorrow, God willing'. The two exchange the usual courtesies and depart only to return the next day to continue the monotony.

On several occasions the camera repeats the same sequence of images and sounds to account for Jacobo and Marta's routine. Fragments of the quotidian routine structured through repetition and the small rituals of a disaffected existence make up the story of *Whisky* (2004), the second film of Uruguayan filmmakers Pablo Stoll and Juan Pablo Rebella.[1] The conflict or, better yet, the latent tension which justifies the development of the story arises precisely from a situation which destabilises the routine that is presented in the introductory scenes. Jewish tradition dictates placing the headstone on a tomb one year after a person's death. On the first anniversary of the death of Jacobo's mother, Herman (Jorge Bolani), Jacobo's brother who lives in Brazil, decides to travel to Montevideo to attend the ceremony. In order to keep up appearances and almost without exchanging words, Jacobo asks Marta to pretend to be his wife during Herman's visit. Marta agrees and before Herman's arrival she manages a small transformation: she does her hair, she cleans Jacobo's apartment, she schedules a photo shoot in order to produce a portrait of the newlyweds, and she improvises an imagined honeymoon to Iguazú Falls.

Herman's visit is deliciously uncomfortable. There is a constant and silent confrontation between the two brothers. We learn that Jacobo had to handle the burden of his mother's illness and that Herman's sock factory in Sao Paulo is more modern and successful. The contrast between Marta's minimalist enthusiasm, Jacobo's emphatic apathy, and Herman's enterprising yet naïve character transform the visit into a low-intensity comedy. The trivialities that are commented on and the superficial and contained performances produce a dry and absurd humour.

However, the film is not only a model of narrative economy with regard to the execution of the characters. The modest *mise-en-scène* presents images where the objects and spaces exactly describe those who inhabit them. The moment in which Jacobo and Marta pose for their wedding picture condenses the *mise-en-scène* of the entire film. Jacobo's imperturbable head comes out of the frame, prompting the photographer to insist that he crouch down to Marta's height before asking them both to say 'whisky' (the Uruguayan version of the English 'cheese'). Nonetheless, the photographer is only able to incite the hint of a smile from the apathetic couple. On a purely cinematographic narrative level, Rebella and Stoll's entire film is a succession of equally static shots. The whole story is told through the singular point of view of one camera, always immobile, that steadfastly registers characters with dull interior lives in slightly absurd situations.[2]

The choice of tonality in the film reinforces this sort of atmosphere. Herman's visit happens during winter such that greys and browns abound in exterior shots. However, interior spaces and objects also have the same tonality. In a film where the characters hardly speak, the narration is articulated through objects. The oxygen tank and the wheelchair in Jacobo's apartment make his mother's absence fiercely present. The ugliness of the objects from the past not only inhabits Jacobo's apparently tedious and repetitive day-to-day life, but also responds to a social world that is stuck. Everything in the universe of *Whisky* revolves around the dilapidated or rundown. The machines in Jacobo's factory are old, the socks that come out of the conveyer belts have imperfections, the blinds in his office do not function properly, and his car does not start. In the bar that he visits daily, the fluorescent lights never really turn on and the businesses where he offers up his wares seem stuck in the past.

After the ceremony in the cemetery, Herman invites Marta and Jacobo to spend a few days in Piriápolis, a resort on the Uruguayan coast that the brothers frequented as kids with their parents. In the off-season, with a hotel casino that is practically vacant, the place of their childhood holidays also becomes a desolate world. However, while Jacobo remains cold and distant from the other characters, the melancholy atmosphere of Piriápolis becomes the backdrop for a minimal union between Marta and Herman, which is never fully realised. In the airport, when they say their goodbyes, Marta gives Herman a note to read on the plane, but we never see its content.

Given the modest gestures of the actors and the absurd humour of some situations, *Whisky*'s aesthetic brings to mind the films of Aki Kaurismaki, while the attention to mechanisms of repetition and the minimal *mise-en-scène* signal the influence of the cinematography of the Argentine director, Martín Rejtman. At the same time, the *mise-en-scène* of *Whisky* could be a response to the social and cultural context of Uruguay. The story of the film is not only the story of two brothers that make socks and a dull and loyal employee; *Whisky* is a portrait of Uruguay as a country that remained immobile in some part of history. If the contrast between the socks that Jacobo makes in his factory in Montevideo, brown and with rhombi, and the more modern socks that Herman makes in Brazil and exports to Chile suggests this backwardness, the scene in which Jacobo bets all the money his brother gives him to modernise his factory in the hope of losing it all speaks of stagnation as a certain option. According to Adrián Singer, the decadence of Jacobo's factory works as a metonymy of the decadence of Uruguayan society, where everything works with the minimum conditions and in the lowest possible intensity.[3]

In this 'comedy without joy', Jacobo maintains his bitter character, resistant to changing times, but Herman's warmer presence produces a certain sense of humour and fun in Marta. With the arrival of Jacobo's brother, Marta's personality begins to emerge: she dresses up, she wears make up, she shares Herman's strange ability to repeat any sentence with an inverse meaning, and she loves Leonardo Favio's music. While the story does not finalise Marta's romantic rebirth, it does gradually demonstrate both the profundity of her tranquil desperation and her unexpected capacity for change. After returning from the resort and once Herman has left, Marta bids Jacobo farewell with the same monotonous expression that she repeats throughout her routine life: 'Hasta mañana, si Dios quiere' ('Until tomorrow, God willing'). However, Jacobo arrives to his workshop the next day and finds himself alone.

Notes

1. *Whisky* won awards at various festivals, among others at those of Huelva, Havana, Lima, Tokyo, and Greece. It won a Goya in Spain and also the Prix du Regard Original at Cannes. Like *25 Watts* (2001), Stoll and Rebella's first film, *Whisky* had a good public reception and paved the way for *La perrera* (2005), *Acné* (2007) and *Gigante* (2008), first films by other directors that were also produced by Control Z Films, the production house for the Rebella-Stoll duo.
2. In an interview, the director, Juan Pablo Rebella, admitted that he found that visual concept for *Whisky* in the graphic novel 'Jimmy Corrigan, the Smartest Kid on Earth'. See: 'Whisky, de Juan Pablo Rebella y Pablo Stoll', Junio de 2004, 'Como Hacer Cine'. Available at www.comohacercine.com/articulo.php?id_art=706&id_cat = 3.
3. Uruguay is a very small country with just three million people situated between the two biggest countries in South America: Argentina and Brazil. In his reading of the film, Adrián Singer refers to what Héctor Achúgar defines as 'país petizo' (dwarf country), a concept that embodies a particular Uruguayan culture of impotence, as if the country sees itself as destined to be insignificant. This concept helps Singer to explain the resignation revealed in the film in the character of Jacobo but also in the use of the static camera emphasising the stagnation of Uruguay.

Further reading

Soledad Montañez and David Martin-Jones, 'Cinema in Progress: New Uruguayan Cinema', *Screen*, Vol. 50, No. 3, 2009, pp. 334–40.

Adrián Singer, 'Influence of the Italian Neorealism on Uruguayan Contemporary Cinema', *Iberoamerica Global*, Vol. 3, No. 1, March 2010, pp. 36–52.

Irene Depetris Chauvin

The Wild Bunch (1969)

[Country: USA. Production Company: Warner Bros-Seven Arts. Director: Sam Peckinpah. Producer: Phil Feldman. Cinematographer: Lucien Ballard. Editor: Lou Lombardo. Cast: William Holden (Pike Bishop), Robert Ryan (Deke Thornton), Ernest Borgnine (Dutch Engstrom), Edmond O'Brien (Freddie Sykes), Warren Oates (Lyle Gorch), Ben Johnson (Tector Gorch), Jamie Sánchez (Angel), Emilio Fernández (General Mapache), Bo Hopkins (Clarence 'Crazy' Lee), Alfonso Arau (Lieutenant Herrera), Sonia Amelio (Teresa).]

Synopsis: Set in 1913 during the Mexican Revolution, along the Mexican-Texan border, *The Wild Bunch* tells the story of an aging gang of outlaws led by Pike, and chased by bounty hunters led by a former gang member, Deke Thornton. They rob a bank, which turns out to be a set-up by the railroad company to capture the gang, and escape to a Mexican village, home of Angel, one of their gang members. The village was attacked by General Mapache, who also kidnapped Angel's girlfriend. After they get to Agua Verde, Angel sees his former girlfriend with the General and shoots her. Pike agrees to steal a US military shipment for Mapache in exchange for gold. Though the hold-up is successful, the train also carries the bounty hunters, who chase Pike and his group, only to be foiled again. When Mapache realises that Angel has stolen a crate of weapons, he captures and tortures Angel. In a bloody shootout between Mapache and Pike, almost everybody, including Pike, is killed. Thornton and the bounty hunters arrive, and Thornton rides off with one surviving gang member, the old Sykes, and a group of Mexican rebels.

From the very beginning *The Wild Bunch* produced strong and passionate reactions. During a preview in Kansas City in 1969, 60 per cent of the audience had negative reactions to it; one irate woman wrote her congressman who in turn wrote Jack Valenti, head of MPAA (The Motion Picture Association of America). Still, some 20 per cent of the audience rated the movie as excellent or outstanding. That the producers went ahead with the film had much to do with the crisis in which Hollywood found itself, and with the fact that the viewers who liked the film were predominantly in their late teens and early twenties. While it didn't gross as much as some other quintessential films of the late sixties – such as *Bonnie and Clyde* (Arthur Penn, 1967) and *Easy Rider* (Dennis Hopper, 1969) – like these latter films, *The Wild Bunch* simultaneously captured a historical moment and profoundly influenced future generations of filmmakers. Not just famous for its level of violence, *The Wild Bunch* revised the myth of the Western, reflected on the difficulty of (male) community and solidarity, reframed Mexican-American politics, and commented on the advance of modernisation and the effects of capitalism.

The violence for which *The Wild Bunch* – and Sam Peckinpah's films in general – has become famous cannot be quite understood outside the context of the late sixties. Major changes, transformations and upheavals occurred while the film was being shot on location in Mexico, from March to June 1968. The Production Code, which had regulated what could be shown on screen and what was deemed unacceptable, was revised in 1966 and in November 1968 replaced by the Code and Rating Administration (CARA), which installed the ratings system, giving *The Wild Bunch* an R-rating. That *The Wild Bunch* could get away with an R-rating – rather than an X-rating – was at least partially connected to the social and political violence occurring in American streets. While the film was being shot, Martin Luther King, Jr. and Bobby Kennedy were assassinated (in April and June 1968 respectively). Right before shooting for the film had started, in March 1968, American soldiers massacred over 300 unarmed Vietnamese, including women and children, at My Lai, a story that broke in November 1969, after the film had been released. As Vivian Sobchack has pointed out, the incredible violence that erupted on the screens in the late sixties reflected the general social climate, from urban riots, to the images of death and violence in Vietnam that appeared on the evening news, to anti-war protests. The emergence of 'ultraviolent' movies can thus be understood as a way of reflecting, negotiating and transforming the social violence of the late sixties.

While reviewers were divided about the effects of violence when *The Wild Bunch* first came out – middlebrow critics were appalled while intellectuals loved the film (Weddle, 1994: 366) – more recent critics have tended to agree with Peckinpah himself that the violence in the film conveys the sense of 'horror and agony' inherent in violence (Prince 1998: 33). Critics of the film usually presume its focus on frequently violent action: 'No one [in the film] thinks ... they all just act', Wheeler Winston Dixon writes.[1] Such a focus on violent action seems justified by the film's unprecedented numbers of cuts. Peckinpah was much influenced by the films of Akira Kurosawa. In a careful analysis of all of Peckinpah's films, Stephen Prince has isolated three types of montage that translate violence into a filmic language: slow-motion inserts, as in the opening massacre, that aestheticise violence but can also be understood as the human body's loss of control over its actions or as a way of slowing down – and paying tribute – to the last moments of somebody's life (Prince 1998: 63; Seydor 1997: 192); extended montages using crosscutting; and poetic or psychological montages that are connected to Peckinpah's use of flashbacks – such as when Deke is captured in the bordello – in *The Wild Bunch* (Prince 1998: 67–73). Part of the problem of translating violence into an aesthetic language has to do with how it turns violence into a commodity, making it available for (excited) consumption. But Peckinpah, Prince argues, tempers that possibility by complementing the aesthetics of violence, by also showing what emotional pain violence inflicts, and by producing moments of ironic and intellectual distance.

In this sense, violence in *The Wild Bunch* can be understood as joining the era's critique of US society, a critique that was often manifested in the cinema's attempt to revise – and thus critique – mythological histories, in this case the Western. Many classical Hollywood Westerns were set between 1865 and 1893 – between the end of the Civil War and the moment when Frederick Jackson Turner famously declared the frontier 'closed' – and featured conflicts between 'civilisation' and 'wilderness', in which a righteous cowboy often helped stabilise law and order – 'civilisation' – in an emerging Western settlement. While many so-called 'adult' Westerns of the 1950s often took a more sceptical view, *The Wild Bunch* pushed things to an altogether different level. Like other films from the period invested in revising notions of masculinity, *The Wild Bunch* dismantles the myth of the Western hero, as its characters are aging, frequently incompetent, and unethical (working for whomever pays best). At the same time, there are remnants of an ethical code – 'He gave his word' Pike says, and 'That ain't what counts! It's who you give it to', Dutch angrily responds – and the characters' flashbacks investigate their depth of character as well as their morality. Set in 1913, during the Mexican Revolution, the characters themselves are painfully aware of the passing of the 'old' – or mythological – West, something they often comment on and that is visually brought out most poignantly when the cowboys have their first encounter with an automobile.

The film's revision of the Western formula extends well beyond a critique of the genre and the mythological history attached to it – it can also be used to comment on larger political, social, and economic issues. For instance, we can understand it as a complex and ambivalent commentary on the American war in Vietnam – as a so-called 'Vietnam Western'. Thus, the savage robbery and killing of innocent civilians that opens the film can be understood as an 'essentially impotent outrage and despair' about the US involvement in Vietnam.[2] Such a reading becomes more complex when we consider how the film's final, extended massacre appears to reaffirm violent military intervention. An economic, rather than political avenue of interpretation is opened up by the importance of the railroad in the film. As a corporation hiring bounty hunters, the railroad represents 'a narrowing of possibilities', as experienced by Thornton, for instance, a sense of 'entrapment', 'arbitrary violence' and 'fateful inevitability'. 'The film's violence is capitalist violence', Michael Bliss has provocatively argued.[3]

If the film's commentary on difficult contemporary issues – such as Vietnam and capitalism – is complex and ambivalent, then its more apparent object of engagement – the US relationship with Mexico – seems even more vexed. Set during the Mexican Revolution, much of this history remains absent from the film, most notably revolutionary leader Pancho Villa and the United States government, which occludes not only the revolutionary struggle, but also the complex US involvement with a military dictatorship – the ways the US had helped General Huerta come into power in 1913, even if they later refused to recognise him as a legitimate leader. Instead of revealing the complexity of the political situation, the film sets up two key Mexican locations, the village where Angel, a Mexican member of the gang, comes from, and Agua Verde, a village under the command of Mapache, an ally of General Huerta who terrorises Angel's village. While Agua Verde is seen as brutal, Angel's village is understood as primitive, a lush place where toddlers play and youngsters dive into the water. Things get even more complicated after Mapache tortures and ultimately kills Angel, when the gang transfers its political loyalties from Huerta to the oppressed villagers, deciding to fight their former patron even if such a shift remains full of problems because motivations remain unclear and because it leaves most people dead.

The film has even more unsettling aspects. Critics have often noted how the film often seems to attack its viewers, leaving them no safe vantage point from where to observe the action, the characters and the setting, instead pulling them into different directions. One of the more unsettling techniques used in the film can be found in the moments of unrestrained laughter, for instance after the gang escapes across the border and rests in a small Mexican settlement, only to fight about shares and to discover they had been set up. Laughter here comes after a tense moment of confrontation – between the generations, between Americans and Mexicans – the danger that the group and camaraderie may 'fall apart'. The scene ends with a tenuous resolution to stick together – one of the main obsessions and difficulties in the film – and the laughter registers the discomfort attending such sticking together. In this context, the film's ending, after Sykes says, 'It ain't like it use to be, but it'll do', and romantic music is mixed with superimpositions of the dead laughing, may be one of the most difficult sequences to read.

While *The Wild Bunch* is important for both its aesthetic accomplishment – the ways in which it uses editing, slow motion, allegorical images, etc. – and for its social commentaries, its most complicated legacy might concern the history of screen violence. When the film was restored and re-released in 1994 it got an NC-17 rating (introduced in 1990) before the original R-rating was reinstated because no new footage had been added (Seydor 1997: 147–8). Upon the film's original release, Martin Scorsese was one of the film's avid viewers whose aesthetics of violence was much influenced by *The Wild Bunch*. Likewise, the film – as well as Peckinpah's other films – broke crucial ground for the representation and aestheticisation of violence for filmmakers such as Quentin Tarantino and Oliver Stone. Some critics worry that while Peckinpah's screen violence was a reaction to the social violence of the period – and was thus not only justified but had an ethical and moral component – today's screen violence seems decontextualised, disconnected from any urgent social, political and cultural issues, and thus potentially not only meaningless but hurtful. The current debates surrounding screen violence – which sometimes too easily assume that we know what effect screen violence has on spectators – certainly confirm the importance of the issue. While *The Wild Bunch* may offer no solution, it can nonetheless sustain a profound engagement and conversation about a crucial contemporary issue.

Notes

1. Wheeler Winston Dixon, 'Re-Visioning the Western: Code, Myth and Genre in Peckinpah's *The Wild Bunch*', in Prince 1999: 173.
2. Robert Torry, 'Therapeutic Narrative: *The Wild Bunch*, *Jaws*, and Vietnam', *The Velvet Light Trap*, Vol. 31, Spring 1993, p. 27.
3. Michael Bliss, '"Back Off to What?" Enclosure, Violence, and Capitalism in Sam Peckinpah's *The Wild Bunch*', in Prince 1999: 107–8, 124.

Further reading

Michael Bliss (ed.), *Doing it Right: The Best Criticism on Sam Peckinpah's* The Wild Bunch, Carbondale, Southern Illinois University Press, 1994.

Edward Buscombe, 'The Western', in Geoffrey Nowell-Smith (ed.), *The Oxford History of World Cinema*, Oxford, Oxford University Press, 1996, pp. 286–94.

Christine Gledhill, 'The Western', in Pam Cook and Mieke Bernink (eds), *The Cinema Book*, 2nd ed., London, BFI, 1999, pp. 147–56.

Stephen Prince, *Savage Cinema: Sam Peckinpah and the Rise of Ultraviolent Movies*, Austin, University of Texas Press, 1998.

Stephen Prince (ed.), *Sam Peckinpah's* The Wild Bunch, Cambridge, Cambridge University Press, 1999.

Paul Seydor, *Peckinpah: The Western Films, a Reconsideration*, foreword by David Weddle, Urbana, University of Illinois Press, 1997.

Vivian C. Sobchack, 'The Violent Dance: A Personal Memoir of Death in the Movies', in Stephen Prince (ed.), *Screening Violence*, New Brunswick, NJ, Rutgers University Press, 2000, pp. 110–24.

David Weddle, *'If They Move ... Kill 'Em!': The Life and Times of Sam Peckinpah*, New York, Grove Press, 1994.

Sabine Haenni

Wutai jiemei/Two Stage Sisters (1965)

[Country: China. Production Company: Shanghai Tianma Film Studio. Director: Xie Jin. Producer: Ding Li. Screenwriters: Lin Gu, Xu Jin and Xie Jin. Cinematographers: Zhou Damin and Chen Zhenxiang. Music: Huang Zhun. Editor: Zhang Liqun. Cast: Xie Fang (Chunhua), Cao Yindi (Yuehong), Feng Qi (Master Xing), Gao Aisheng (Jiang Bo), Shangguan Yunzhu (Shang Shuihua), Li Wei (Manager Tang), Deng Nan (Monk Ah-xin), Shen Hao (Auntie Shen), Dong Lin (Lord Ni).]

Synopsis: Against the backdrop of the evolution of Shanghai-based Yueju (aka Shaoxing opera), *Two Stage Sisters* unfolds around Chunhua, a child bride who runs away from her arranged marriage in 1935. Taking refuge with an itinerant Yueju company, Chunhua becomes an apprentice in that opera troupe and befriends the master's daughter, Yuehong. On stage Chunhua and Yuehong play duets together, while the troupe travels from village to village in the countryside. After the demise of the troupe master in 1940, however, Chunhua and Yuehong find themselves sold to an opera theatre in Shanghai, where all-female Yueju has recently attained an enormous popularity. Both Chunhua and Yuehong rise to stardom in the following years. However, Yuehong then falls for the manipulative stage manager, Tang, and gradually recedes from the performance scene. Chunhua, by contrast, is firmly dedicated to her career, and is gradually drawn to left-wing politics under the tutelage of female journalist Jiang Bo. Adding a political flavour to her performances, Chunhua irritates those in power, namely the KMT Nationalists at the time, whose failed attempt to blind and ruin Chunhua instead infuriates the public. To alleviate public anger, Tang forces Yuehong to bear the responsibility of the attack and give false testimony in court. Yet the public does not fall for the ruse, and the court falls into chaos. Then, there comes the Liberation. In deep remorse, Yuehong disappears into the countryside, but Chunhua manages to track her down, and the two stage sisters ultimately reconcile and reunite.

In English language scholarship director Xie Jin's films have been predominantly assessed through a melodramatic approach.[1] Nick Browne in particular challenges the applicability of Western 'family melodrama' in a Chinese context while proposing the idea of 'political melodrama' to better appreciate Xie's work after the Cultural Revolution (1966–76). Browne defines political melodrama as 'an expression of a mode of injustice ... in which gender as a mark of difference is a limited, mobile term activated by distinctive social powers and historical circumstances', while it addresses 'the relation of the individual to the social as a fully public matter' mediated by both 'the expectations of an ethical system' constituted by Confucianism and 'the demands of a political system' dominated by socialism.[2] While Browne's elucidation foregrounds the changed dynamic between the ethical system and the political system in the post-Cultural Revolution era, we can borrow the idea of 'political melodrama' to highlight the very marriage between a melodramatic format and a blatant political agenda, particularly the socialist revolutionary ideology hardly challenged in the People's Republic of China (PRC) until the late 1970s. As a form of melodrama, China's political melodrama, too, aroused emotions like sympathy and righteous indignation in the audience, providing the latter with 'both the depraved intrigues of villainy and the pathetic suffering of its innocent and helpless victims', to paraphrase Paul Pickowicz.[3] If, as Peter Brooks argues, '[m]elodramatic good and evil are highly personalized', then political melodrama shows its viewers 'the highly personalized human faces of virtue and evil', wherein the meaning of the self and the fate of the family are articulated *through* the public and the political.[4]

There is no doubt that in *Two Stage Sisters* the antagonistic forces are affiliated with those contradicting the political-economic interests of the Chinese Communist Party (CCP) and the 'people' it allegedly represents. Such antagonistic forces include the Japanese intruders (against the parameters of Chinese nationalism), the KMT Nationalists (adversary to the 'progressive' politics represented by the CCP), the rich and the landlords (opposed to the proletarian class), and the USA (evoked in the film as the 'big brother' behind the Nationalists and the ultimate representative of capitalism and Western imperialism). In a highly *personalised* manner, these oppositional forces are vividly embodied by such characters as Lord Ni, Manager Tang, and Auntie Shen.

Lord Ni, a gentry-landowner in the Zhejian countryside, appears early in the film. Watching Yuehong and Chunhua perform on a public stage, Ni lusts after the two sisters, and engages the troupe for an all-night small-scale performance in his residence. However, his demand that Yuehong stay over after the performance is declined, which in turn leads to the local police interrupting their public performance under the banner of 'maintaining social morality'. Though the police action aims at abducting Yuehong for Ni, it ends with arresting Chunhua for her effective intervention. Under the rhetoric of 'disobeying laws' and 'assaulting policemen', Chunhua is sentenced with a 'public exhibition' on a public square. Clearly, Ni represents someone who not only possesses land and wealth, but who is also salacious, immoral and affiliated with the local police, who, unfortunately, are equally venal and corrupt. These happenings manifest, in melodramatic terms, a high dramatisation of a series of events, the suffering of the innocent, and an intense moral and emotional appeal to the audience. Given the police abusing their power in public for evil, the suffering of an innocent individual, importantly, transcends the personal, and is translated into a public matter with a political overtone.

Aside from Lord Ni, the antagonistic forces are also personalised in two opportunistic characters: Manager Tang and Monk Ah-xin. Originally the manager of the opera troupe tutored by Yuehong's father, Ah-xin is responsible for hooking up the two sisters with Ni. Soon after Yuehong's father's death, Ah-xin makes a profit by selling the two sisters to Manager Tang, while he himself becomes one of Tang's henchmen. Whilst Ah-xin is an opportunist who gravitates toward whoever possesses wealth, Tang is an opportunist who, with wealth, gravitates toward whoever is in power: the Japanese and the Nationalists. In a sequence dated 1944, we find in Tang's office a doll in a kimono in a glass case. Though the Japanese (alongside the Americans) remain off-screen, this Japanese-styled ornament indicates Tang's rapport with the Japanese, and thus Tang's treacherous character. After the Sino-Japanese war, however, Tang's liaisons with the Japanese are replaced by those with the Nationalists, as epitomised by Commissioner Pan and a Nationalist agent who inspects the political activities in Shanghai. At one point, the Nationalist agent demands that Tang take action in thwarting Chunhua bringing to stage 'New Year's Sacrifice' – Lu Xun's acclaimed novella highly critical of society. Tang's action is deemed as returning a favour to the Nationalists, who supposedly have helped Tang cover up the scandal concerning his unpatriotic relations with the Japanese. It is evident that Tang is conceived as the character central to reactionary influences in this political melodrama.

Notably, among all the aforementioned male antagonists comes a female character – the wealthy, middle-aged Auntie Shen – who is also portrayed as negative and reactionary. The characterisation of Shen reveals some intriguing ramifications about gender. In the episode where Shen tries to dissuade Chunhua from performing 'New Year's Sacrifice', Shen's image as an amicable woman effectively facilitates her approaching Chunhua (while male characters Tang and Ah-xin, with their tough looks, stay behind). Shen's mediation between Tang and the actresses, with Shen's resort to the rhetoric of 'woman', eventually proves, from the film's dominant perspective, to be an intrigue that leads the sisters astray from the route of righteousness and, by extension, away from socialist revolution. As something that can be appropriated by the reactionaries to perpetuate their interests, gender in *Two Stage Sisters* is strategically conceived as a category secondary to class. The point of Auntie Shen in this political melodrama is therefore not so much about gender itself as about class and, specifically, class struggle under the guise of gender. Complicit with Tang in reactionary behaviour, Shen personalises foremost a force adverse to the class-based socialist revolution. It is under the influence of Tang and Shen that Yuehong, with her inclination to vanity and vulnerability to material temptation, eventually marries Tang and gives up her stage career. Though she still preserves some feelings for Chunhua, Yuehong becomes a member of the anti-revolutionary camp.

Contrary to Manager Tang, Auntie Shen and the antagonistic forces they represent, female journalist Jiang Bo personalises the positive and righteous influence around Chunhua. Under the guidance of Jiang Bo, Chunhua is introduced to movies and spoken dramas that represent a more 'progressive' political stance than that of traditional Yueju. In Jiang's company, Chunhua also visits the exhibition commemorating Lu Xun, which indicates a more direct impact of leftist politics on Chunhua, as evidenced by her subsequent adaptation of 'New Year's Sacrifice'. Chunhua's identification with the novella's protagonist, Xianglin's wife, resonates with the perceived tragic fate of women in feudal China. In a pivotal montage-sequence, through the technique of superimposition, the images of Chunhua's contemplative gaze, the woodcut of Xianglin's wife, Chunhua's humiliation in public, as well as Little Chunhua – a miserable child bride also named Chunhua – powerfully come together to solicit empathy from the spectators of this political melodrama.

While Chunhua has told Little Chunhua that she would never return to the village where she has been unjustly punished, towards the end of the film, Chunhua nevertheless revisits the very location of her persecution, which is made possible by the communist revolution. Chunhua's revisit indicates that the once wronged is now rectified with the repudiation of the *class* enemies as represented by Lord Ni. If, as noted, the interplay between Chunhua and Auntie Shen is implicated in the ideology that privileges class over gender in China's proletarian revolution, this finale seems to reiterate the same idea from another angle. That is, despite the fact that the proletarian revolution does not specifically focus on gender issues, women's emancipation would 'automatically' follow the victory of the political mobilisation against forms of class-based oppression. Symbolically, when revisiting the place of her past persecution, Chunhua is depicted on tour performing *The White-Haired Girl*, arguably the most famous revolutionary drama of the People's Republic. In terms of gender and the state politics, *The White-Haired Girl* – like *Two Stage Sisters* – also narrates the fate of a proletarian girl through the sociopolitical vicissitudes from the Republican era into the Liberation.

The tension between women's liberation and class-based state politics has nonetheless been pointed out by critics. For instance, Meng Yue, in her study of the adaptations of *White-Haired Girl*, identifies two axes along which the story has evolved. One is 'a gradual strengthening of [the protagonist's] political instincts', and the other 'a gradual erasure of [her] body and her sexual situation'. With the female protagonist's body and sexuality fading from the story, the term 'class', Meng notes, has gradually displaced 'the sexual code' in significance and becomes the constituent most essential to the story.[5] Symptomatic of this in *Two Stage Sisters* is Chunhua's plain dress when off-stage and lack of interest in men throughout the film, in contrast to her growing enthusiasm for revolutionary politics.[6] Writing on women's representation in mainland Chinese cinema, Dai Jinhua likewise suggests that the decline of a desiring male 'gaze' (characteristic of classical Hollywood cinema) in the revolutionary narratives does not translate into women's autonomy, for the gender binary between the characters is simply 'replaced by class antagonism and political difference'.[7] Of the same proletarian class, men and women *alike* are the children of the same 'spiritual father – the Communist Party, the socialist system, and the project of communism', but women are still subjugated to a kind of gaze that, though not strictly male, is nevertheless paternal and patriarchal.[8]

This being said, the images of 'new women' are significant to the classical revolutionary canon, according to Dai. They represent either those who are saved and 'turned over' (*fanshen*) by the CCP, or those who grow up into heroic woman warriors. In revolutionary narratives women are generally caught up in the political struggle between the glorious Communist Party and the abysmal Nationalist Party until the arrival of a male Communist who saves and mentors the suffering women. Although Jiang Bo manifests an altered gender dynamic in the apprenticeship structure, *Two Stage Sisters* pretty much fits in the larger scheme of Chinese revolutionary cinema, wherein the two kinds of 'new women' Dai observes are vividly embodied by Chunhua and Little Chunhua, respectively. With the practice of child marriage abolished and the yoke of her enslavement thereby shattered, Little Chunhua represents the women redeemed by the CCP. Although Chunhua and Yuehong are both caught up in the political struggle, and Yuehong temporarily chooses the dark side, Chunhua, under the impact of Jiang Bo and leftist politics, successfully transforms herself into a valiant heroine. With her resolute devotion to performing revolutionary dramas, Chunhua demonstrates a 'selfless' woman warrior in service of socialist nation-building, embodying the pedagogical function of the socialist political melodrama.

Notes

1. See, for instance, Ma Ning, 'Spatiality and Subjectivity in Xie Jin's Film Melodrama of the New Period', in Nick Browne, Paul G. Pickowicz, Vivian Sobchack, Esther Yau (eds), *New Chinese Cinemas: Forms, Identities, Politics*, New York, Cambridge University Press, 1994, pp. 15–39; Nick Browne, 'Society and Subjectivity: On the Political Economy of Chinese Melodrama', in Nick Browne *et al.*, *New Chinese Cinemas*, pp. 40–56; Paul G. Pickowicz, 'Melodramatic Representation and the "May Fourth" Tradition of Chinese Cinema', in Ellen Widmer and David Der-wei Wang (eds), *From May Fourth to June Fourth: Fiction and Film in Twentieth-Century China*, Cambridge, MA, Harvard University Press, 1993; Jerome Silbergeld, 'The Force of Labels: Melodrama in the Postmodern Era: *Hibiscus Town*', *China into Film: Frames of Reference in Contemporary Chinese Cinema*, London, Reaktion Books, 1999, pp. 188–233; Robert Chi, '*The Red Detachment of Women*: Resenting, Regendering, Remembering', in Chris Berry (ed.), *Chinese Films in Focus: 25 Takes*, New York, BFI Publishing, 2003, pp. 152–59.
2. Nick Browne, 'Society and Subjectivity', pp. 43, 46–7.
3. Pickowicz, 'Melodramatic Representation' p. 322.
4. Peter Brooks, *The Melodramatic Imagination: Balzac, Henry James, Melodrama, and the Mode of Excess*, New Haven, CT, Yale University Press, 1976, p. 16; Pickowicz, 'Melodramatic Representation', p. 322.
5. Meng Yue, 'Female Images and National Myth', in Tani E. Barlow (ed.), *Gender Politics on Modern China: Writing and Feminism*, Durham, NC, Duke University Press, 1993, p. 121.

6. Although Chunhua shows no interest in men, her persistent emotional attachment to Yuehong potentially bears a homoerotic overtone.
7. Dai Jinhua, 'Invisible Women: Contemporary Chinese Cinema and Women's Film', translated by Mayfair Yang, *Positions* Vol. 3, No. 1, Spring 1995, p. 262.
8. Ibid, pp. 262–3. In *Patriarchy and Socialist Revolution in China*, Judith Stacey sees the Confucian tradition and the socialist order as two patriarchal systems that function together in the PRC. While the former maintains the family as the basic socioeconomic unit of the society, the latter places the family under the leadership of the CCP. Judith Stacey, *Patriarchy and Socialist Revolution in China*, Berkeley, CA, University of California Press, 1983.

Further reading

Chris Berry, *Postsocialist Cinema in Post-Mao China: The Cultural Revolution after the Cultural Revolution*, New York, Routledge, 2004.

Paul Clark, *Chinese Cinema: Culture and Politics since 1949*, New York, Cambridge University Press, 1987.

Gina Marchetti. '*Two Stage Sisters*: The Blooming of a Revolutionary Aesthetic', in Sheldon Hsiao-peng Lu (ed.), *Transnational Chinese Cinemas: Identity, Nationhood, Gender*, Honolulu, University of Hawai'i Press, 1997, pp. 59–80.

Shanghai wenyi chubanshe (ed.), *Wutai jiemei: cong tigang dao yingpian* (Two Stage Sisters: *From Story to Film)*, Shanghai, Shanghai wenyi chubanshe, 1982.

Yingjin Zhang, *Chinese National Cinema*, New York, Routledge, 2004.

Shi-Yan Chao

Wuya yu maque/Crows and Sparrows (1949)

[Country: China. Production Company: Kun Lun. Director: Zheng Junli. Producers: Xia Yunhu, Ren Zongde. Screenwriters: Chen Baichen, Zheng Junli, Zhao Dan, Shen Fu, Xu Tao, Wang Lingu. Cinematographers: Miao Zhenhua, Hu Zhenhua. Music: Wang Yunjie. Sound: Li Liehong. Art Design: Ding Chen, Niu Baorong, Xu Xing. Editor: Wu Yanfang. Cast: Zhao Dan (Little Broadcaster/Mr Xiao), Wu Yin (Mrs Xiao), Sun Daolin (Mr Hua), Shangguan Yunzhu (Mrs Hua), Huang Zongying (Yu Xiaoying), Li Tianji (Mr Hou), Wei Heling (Mr Kong), Wang Pei (A-mei).]

Synopsis: The story takes place in Shanghai at the end of 1948. Hou, an official of the Republican government takes possession of Mr Kong's property, a residential house, driving the old man into a tiny corner room downstairs, while he and his concubine occupy the top level. Two other families, the Huas and the Xiaos, rent the other two rooms. However, the Republican army is soon defeated by the Communists, making Hou decide to sell this building and flee to Taiwan. He demands that all of the residents move out immediately. Unwilling to become homeless, Mr and Mrs Xiao propose to buy the house from Hou. They mortgage all their valuables with Hou to trade gold, but end up losing all the money. Meanwhile, Mr Hua is arrested for his unintended involvement in a strike. In order to rescue him, Mrs Hua asks Hou for help, yet is taken advantage by him. When the residents are finally outraged by Hou's exploitation and get ready for a confrontation, the Republican government collapses and Hou hurries to escape. Mr Kong gets his house back. On New Year's Eve, the three families gather happily, looking forward to the new world ahead of them.

Crows and Sparrows is a realistic film accented with satirical comic relief. It was made during the post-Second World War period when political power underwent intense redistribution worldwide and regional warfare continued to be waged from time to time. For Chinese nationals, the spring of 1949 saw the final battles between the republicans (KMT, aka, Kuomintang) and the communists (CCP, aka, Chinese Communist Party) over the future of the country. Such military competition inevitably affected the cultural arena. Life-on-a-thread dramas and dreadful guerrilla warfare were played out not only on battlefields but also on sound stages. The film project of *Crows and Sparrows* was initiated in Shanghai – the capital of cinema in China – among a group of filmmakers sympathising with the Communists. Both the film text and its production history witnessed and testified to the ongoing cultural war. The city was still under the control of the republican government; therefore, the filmmakers had to piece together fragments of resources and wrestle with the censors in order to push their shooting through. The film was finished and released in 1950, after socialist China declared its sovereignty. Having etched the time and its ethos onto celluloid, *Crows and Sparrows* became one of the classics of Chinese leftist cinema.

Once a popular film star in the 1930s, Zheng Junli turned to directing in the 1940s. In 1947, he was given the chance to be in charge of the shooting of *A Spring River Flows East* (another well-known Chinese leftist masterpiece) when the director Cai Chusheng was suffering from chronic illness.[1] *Crows and Sparrows* is the first film Zheng directed independently. The film adopts a classical allegorical device, using architectural space as the metaphor for class difference and class struggle. The story is staged in a tenement house (*shi ku men*, the typical residential architecture of urban Shanghai), where four families from different social strata reside. A crane shot early in the film reveals the 'vertical' relationship among the residents. Mr Hou (the 'crow' figure), a high-ranking official of the KMT and head of a company, sets up his concubine, Xiaoying, on the top floor of a tenement house, after robbing this property from its original owner, Mr Kong. The dispossessed Kong is driven to a cramped and messy room connected to the back door on the ground floor. A street vendor couple, Mr Xiao (also known as Little Broadcaster) and his wife, also lives on the same level with their three boys. Their warehouse-like room (converted from the living room) matches the family's low social status (it turns out later that the Xiao's family is also to be economically exploited by Mr Hou). In the small bedroom located in between the master's room and the ground floor (known as *ting zi jian*, a decent yet relatively cheap part of a tenement house) lives the Hua family. A middle school teacher, Mr Hua is representative of the kind of petty intellectuals who were awkwardly suspended in the mid-air either politically or economically – discontent with the status quo, yet too lofty to take sides or make an intervention. As the film unfolds, we see how economic power relationships can also translate into sexual exploitation. Mr Hou is always seeking opportunities to take advantage of Mrs Hua, which is foreshadowed (and made easy) by the spatial proximity between the two couples. Ownership of the house and its frequent inversion could be read as a metaphor of the corrupted and chaotic social order during the civil war.

The film adopts conventional dramaturgy to drive the plot. It opens with a crisis: the KMT has lost three key battles in a row; as the result, Mr Hou has to sell all his goods and properties (including the tenement house) before fleeing to Taiwan. He intends to drive out all the tenants on short notice. The unprepared tenants are thus turned into goal-oriented characters, each searching for his/her own solution before the deadline. What follows are naïve expectations, futile attempts, and frustrating incidents. The politics of the upstairs/downstairs become most obvious in a scene towards the end of the film, when accumulated contradictions between Hou and the renters finally explode. Three families gather at the bottom of the stairs, about to directly confront the greedy and abusive 'crow', who is standing on top and overlooking the 'little sparrows'. This visual metaphor charged with tension has clearly left its mark in Chinese film history.

Crows and Sparrows won its fame not only because it tells an allegorical drama that is timely and socially important, but also because its production history testifies to the clash among different cultural and ideological institutions.

As we know, Shanghai was a cosmopolitan centre for Chinese language film production and consumption since the early twentieth century.

However, during the Japanese occupation between the end of 1941 and 1945, once privately owned film studios were turned into imperialist propaganda machines. After the Second World War, many resources were given back, not to their original owners, but to the republican government. Most sound stages, filming equipment, and talents were managed and supervised by two state-run mega studios. Suffering from scarcity of capital and resources as well as an ever more stringent wartime censorship, a few private and leftist film companies still managed to survive on the margin. The Kun Lun Company, which produced *Crows and Sparrows*, was among them. Kun Lun was a post-Second World War company founded and funded by entrepreneurs Xia Yunhu and Ren Zongde. Due to the lack of film talent, the company hardly made any films until it merged with the left-leaning Lianhua Film Association, whose filmmakers and actors had direct connections with the underground CCP organisation. In other words, Kun Lun's films can be seen as *de facto* anti-KMT cultural statements. In order to make the film's screenplay pass the KMT censors, the crew prepared two different versions of the script; however, the satirical trope of the crow and several well-known leftist artists' involvement (especially the screenwriter Chen Baichen who was already named on the KMT's blacklist and had to hide himself) would not go unnoticed.[2] In early April, 1949, Kun Lun had to start shooting without a permit, while the producer, Meng Junmou, kept mediating between the company and the censor. Nevertheless, by the end of the month, the censor demanded termination of the film project and took away the finished footage for an investigation. The filmmakers shut down the studio in order to preserve the sound stage and settings, but, rather than giving up, they made use of this 'interval' to further revise the script. In order to cope with unexpected government inspections, the filmmakers adopted guerrilla tactics, for example pretending to play bridge and mahjong when actually having screenplay meetings, and hiding the script either in the ceiling above the sound stage, or in-between bags of straw (they used straw wall as a cheap soundproofing device). *Crows and Sparrows* (along with other unfinished Kun Lun films such as *The Winter of Three Hairs* (1949) and *Life of Wu Xun* (1950)) resumed production in September, 1949, after the CCP army took over Shanghai.

The kind of realistic concern and naturalism of *Crows and Sparrows* have been frequently invoked in film history books as comparable to that of Italian Neorealist works such as *Bicycle Thieves* (1948) and *Rome, Open City* (1945).[3] Similarities are very easy to find, for example in the systematic and attentive representation of working-class urbanites and the overwhelming wartime/post-war social reality; or in the acute perception of class domination and resistance. In terms of aesthetics, though, most of the shooting of *Crows and Sparrows* occurred in the studio rather than on location, even though its naturalist mise-en-scène (low-key lighting, casually picking out costumes from the crew members' own wardrobe and using everyday objects as props due to financial difficulty, encouraging improvisation and natural acting, etc.) delivers realistic texture and details of life.

However, in comparison to many Italian neorealist films which address the ambiguity of life with less dramatic narrative and more open endings, *Crows and Sparrows* appears to be a sonata dedicated more to victory than the poetry of everyday reality. According to Zhao Dan's memoir, the revision made to the script by September 1949 was enormous. The filmmakers 'passionately studied Mao's works, learning to analyze the characters using Marxist theory, therefore were able to give [the film] a more adequately proportioned dose of sympathy and critique'.[4] As a result, for most of the film, we see these imperfect yet quite 'real' tenants struggling with many problems in life (power abuse, ridiculous inflation, sexual harassment, and many more); yet, all these troubles are suddenly dissolved by the victory of the CCP over the KMT. In the happy ending of the film, the New Year celebration coincides with the 'rebirth' of the house (and the country, of course). A brief self-criticising speech is given by Mr Hua, further elevating the symbolism to the spiritual level. As a critic points out, this ending is bold and incongruous with the rest of the film, an idealist or romantic finale attached to the previous realistic and satirical treatment.[5] But ending with the victory of the CCP was common to many Chinese films finished after October 1949.

To a large extent, we could see it as a natural response of the leftist filmmakers to the triumph they had been expecting, rather than just a mannered ideological gesture.

Filmmakers enjoyed a certain level of artistic freedom at the time. Although they were influenced greatly by the communist ideology, they did not opt to simply use some so-called 'progressive figures' to illustrate political ideals. The ending aside, within an allegorical narrative framework, all the characters have interesting and quite subtle personalities, which gives the audience a feeling of flesh and blood. This may have something to do with the filmmakers' approaches in making the film. For example, the script was a collective endeavour of six contributors, including Chen Baichen, the director Zheng Junli, and the male lead Zhao Dan. It is said that they came up with the characters first, then added the filmmakers' own observations and experiences of the status quo to form the storyline (Zhao Dan had a lot of input of this kind). The satirical tone was fleshed out by Chen Baichen, who had been consistently representing 'the spiritual pursuit of freedom from repression and enslavement by human being' through 'laughter'.[6] Naturalism was also delivered through acting. *Crows and Sparrows* consciously challenged previous typecasting of its main actors and actresses, Zhao Dan, Huang Zongying, and Shangguan Yunzhu.[7] Before *Crows and Sparrows*, Zhao had been almost always playing positive (if not perfect) and well-groomed parts, but he was cast as the sloppy and talkative Little Broadcaster this time. He ended up playing this role through the internalisation of life experience in a Stanislavskian way (Little Broadcaster is modelled after Zhao's old neighbour). Some key performances in the film were the result of numerous rehearsals and reshootings (for instance, the scene in which Little Broadcaster fantasised about trading gold), even at a time of material scarcity. In Zhao's own words, his performance 'came from many feelings of life', through which 'the embodied life experiences infiltrated into the making of the film, as snow melts into earth', so that 'it was as if I had got real freedom; I and the character merged into one'.[8]

To sum up, the historical context of *Crows and Sparrows* makes its realism one of a kind. It is a complex style charged with contradiction. In 1957, the film won the first prize of 'best fiction made during 1949–1955', however, it was soon accused as an opportunist work by the 'Gang of Four', since the new doctrine of the Cultural Revolution did not allow ambiguous characters with imperfections, in other words 'real people', to be at the centre of cinematic representation. *Crows and Sparrows* was not re-evaluated and restored back to the classics of Chinese cinema until the 1980s.

Notes

1. Cai Chusheng was one of the best-known film pioneers of China. He entered the film business in the 1920s, working as Zheng Zhengqiu's assistant for a while. Cai joined the Lian Hua Film Co. in 1931. After several melodramatic and sentimental films, he made a 'left turn'. His works include *The Fisherman's Ballad* (1934), *New Woman* (1935) and *A Spring River Flows East* (1947).
2. Chen Baichen had been a member of 'the Left-Wing Dramatist's League' since 1930. While being an active revolutionist, he also worked in several progressive theatrical troupes and wrote a series of novels and screenplays.
3. See for example Jay Leyda, *Dianying: An Account of Films and the Film Audience in China*, Cambridge, MA, MIT Press, 1972, p. 177.
4. Dan Zhao, 'How did I play Little Broadcaster', *Searching for Artistic Gems in Hell and Heaven* [Diyu Tiantang suo Yizhu], Nanjing, Jiangsu Literature and Arts Press, 2011, pp. 118–19.
5. See Yongyuan Cui, *Crows and Sparrows: Up-down the Stairs* (documentary/in Chinese), 2006, in *Film Legends* (Dianying Chuanqi) series.
6. Baichen Chen, *I've Come along like This* (Wo Zheyang Zou Guolai), Nanjing, Jiangsu Fine Arts Press, 2008, p. 97.
7. Huang and Shangguan were popularly known by the audience as the lovely 'sweetheart' and 'evil mistress' respectively through their characters in previous films. To challenge typecasting, Huang played the concubine, Xiaoying, in *Crows and Sparrows*, while

Shangguan played the meek and harassed young mother, Mrs Hua.

8. Zhao, pp. 119–23.

Further reading

Paul Clark, 'Film and Chinese Society before 1949' and 'Yan'an and Shanghai', in *Chinese Cinema: Culture and Politics since 1949*, Cambridge, Cambridge University Press, 1987.

Jay Leyda, 'Between Victories: 1945–1949', in *Dianying: An Account of Films and the Film Audience in China*, Cambridge, MA, MIT Press, 1972.

Jihua Cheng, Shaobai, Li and Zuwen Xing, *Zhongguo Dianying Fazhanshi*, Vol. 2, Beijing, China Film Press, 1963.

Chaoguang Wang, 'Film Cersorship of the Kuomingtang Nationalist Government after the War of Resistance against Japan', *Journal of Nanjing University*, Vol. 38, No. 6, 2001, pp. 113–23.

Dan Gao

Xia nu/A Touch of Zen (1971)

[Country: Taiwan. Production Company: Union Film. Director and Screenwriter: King Hu (Hu Jinquan). Cinematographer: Hua Huiying. Director of martial arts: Han Yingjie. Cast: Shi Jun (Ku Shengzhai), Xu Feng (Yang Huizen), Roy Chiao (Abbot Hui Yuan), Han Yingjie (Hsu).]

Synopsis: An artist, Ku, lives with his mother near an abandoned fort, reputed to be haunted. One night, investigating strange noises, he meets the beautiful Yang who is living there, and finds himself caught up in her struggle to survive attacks by agents of an imperial noble who murdered her family.

The Chinese wuxia (martial chivalry) genre is familiar to Western audiences largely through Ang Lee's *Crouching Tiger/Hidden Dragon* (2000) with its characteristic code-bound warriors, their mastery with weapons and ability to scale walls or trees via great leaps. In Mainland China, the Communist Party banned the genre for romanticising feudalism and anti-authoritarianism, forcing it underground until the end of the last century. Meanwhile in nationalist Taiwan and colonialist Hong Kong, wuxia thrived where the subtext of the underdog's fight for traditional values against oppressive rule was unsubtle.[1] While wuxia's mythic history links a literary and cultural heritage across a politically scattered Chinese diaspora, director King Hu himself provides the film's transnational crux. A Beijing-born citizen whose career shifted from Hong Kong to Taiwan, Hu gained international recognition when *A Touch of Zen* became the first Chinese film to win a prize at the Cannes Film Festival in 1975.

However, just to consider *A Touch of Zen* as a genre film is limiting. Hu's direction, particularly of the dazzling combat sequences, is that of an innovative auteur at work. Moreover, the film's complex gender representation and deliberately elusive narrative structure underpin the intangible philosophy summed up by the English title.

The plot of this long film is complex and the following outline cursory: Gu Shengzhai, a painter and failed scholar is disturbed by events that at first seem ghostly. Gradually, it is revealed that his attractive new neighbour, Yang Huizen, is a powerful female warrior and fugitive from the corrupt eunuch ruling class. Gu is left holding the baby that results from his union with Yang as a series of battles ensues, climaxing with a showdown between Hsu, a powerful eunuch general, and Yang's mentor, the Buddhist monk Hui Yuan.

In an extended analysis of the film, Stephen Teo outlines the influence of Beijing opera on Hu's direction. This highly stylised synthesis of traditional dance, song and drama is utilised in conjunction with the possibilities offered by cinema and contrasts with the mimetic styles of Occidental screen performance. Teo suggests that, 'the idiosyncrasy of the synthesis may perhaps best be grasped as cinemaopera' (2009: 120). Throughout, stylised stance and movement indicate a non-realist, ritualised mode of performance that integrates the performers with their surroundings. See, for example, Yang's ceremonial seduction of Gu or the highly choreographed battle scenes where the frame is filled with carefully positioned tree branches or waving goldenrod that compliment the movement of his combatants. Chris Berry and Mary Farquhar suggest that the result is neither a Chinese appropriation of Western-style cinema nor a new medium for an old genre but a distinctively 'sinicised' style of cinema, 'at once culturally familiar, hybrid and locally distinct' (2006: 48).

Additionally, instead of wuxia's more familiar deployment of actors on wires, special effects or the typical long, sustained shots that demonstrate a martial artist's expertise, Hu's editing style stretches the possibilities of the medium, using a method that the formalist critic David Bordwell refers to as 'the glimpse'. Where other wuxia directors slow down action sequences in order to show off a star's proficiency, Hu edits in such a way that we witness only fleetingly key moments from the combat. This method has more in common with the montage style favoured by Sergei Eisenstein in the 1920s than Hu's contemporaries and prioritises dramatic impact over continuity. Bordwell notes: 'Hu's task was to dignify and beautify these feats without tipping them into implausibility and sheer fantasy. The solution was to stress certain qualities of these feats – their abruptness, their speed, their mystery. And he chose to do so by treating these feats as only partly visible' (2000: 118).

A striking example comes in the epic battle between Hsu and Hui Yuan. Hu structures a shot with the back of the monk's neck dominating the foreground. Hsu faces him, tiny within the frame. The characters pause and remain still before Hsu leaps to attack. Suddenly, a bravura jump cut shows Hsu large in the frame, nearly upon the monk, and also from this perspective, the spectator. Hui Yan knocks him back, a blow we don't actually see. Instead, the camera dwells for some time on Hsu reeling from the impact. As a perfect example of Bordwell's 'glimpse', we have been part of an anticipation-inducing build-up and given witness to the aftermath but the blow itself is only impressed upon us.

Just as with Eisenstein, this use of montage dispenses with logical continuity in favour of impact.[2] Consequently, a character may display preternatural prowess in combat by appearing to attack from more than one direction at once. Overall, Bordwell proposes that 'the opacities of setting, the play with the bounding frame, the overinformative long shots, the disorienting whip-pans, and the elliptical cutting create a teasing degree of indiscernibility' (2000: 134).

'Indiscernibility' also aptly characterises the film's philosophical intentions. Hu wanted to evoke the elusive nature of Zen enlightenment itself, rather than through a scripted element of the narrative and his method facilitates this. 'Zen could not be described, only felt and intuited. Any dialogue that attempted to explain Zen would be to rationalise it. Hu decided to go ahead and 'take a chance', as he put it, by expressing Zen visually' (Teo 2007: 133). Perhaps, to continue Bordwell's metaphor, we should consider this only 'partly visible' or 'glimpsed' also, mirroring how mere mortals might experience a moment of Zen insight. The English title accurately conveys the experience as 'a touch'.

Hence, the film's key recurring Zen motifs – the spider and dazzling sunlight – are integrated into image, gesture, symbolism, narrative and character throughout. The leisurely montage of spider webs that opens the film gradually leads us out of the woodland into civilisation; the rest of the film essentially takes us on the reverse journey. The spider image takes on multiple possible meanings (such as the female archetype) and is linked explicitly to Yang, from scenes of her weaving to her gravity-defying suspension between roof beams when she needs to hide. In combat, she darts quickly between trees, again evoking the spider. Elsewhere, the significance of the web suggests entrapment, such as the ambush that Gu sets for Yang's enemies or the later binding of Hsu with ropes, or even the inescapability of destiny.

Meanwhile, the blinding sun suggests enlightenment itself and is consistently associated with Hui Yuan, who frequently appears haloed with dappling beams. This dazzles his unenlightened enemies and points to the film's transcendental conclusion where he finally becomes one with the sun, indicating his achievement of nirvana. Gu and Yang's characters are similarly transitory. The film's Mandarin title *Xia Nü* translates as 'The Magnanimous Girl' and is based on a seventeenth-century story by Pu Songling that portrays a bisexual male character who becomes drawn from his male lover by the girl of the title. He gives up his life of sexual pleasure to take on the more complex demands of parenthood through heterosexual union. Although any open portrayal of homosexuality is absent, the film harks back to this source material as gender subversion and ambiguity abound and character sexuality is complex. The female knight is an archetype that appears elsewhere in Hu's wuxia films but Yang is at key moments particularly defeminised, whether constructing arrows with a makeshift foundry or dominating her relationship with Gu and abandoning their baby in order to pursue her own destiny.

In turn, Gu completes a journey from poor scholar and artist to military tactician to questing lover to single parent. He is, however, consistent in his difference to traditional masculine traits: he refuses to advance himself in society, shows intuition and never directly engages in combat. Notably, Yang begins her seduction of Gu by piquing his interest when she dresses as a young man, initiating his pursuit of her.

Transitory personality and the recurring motifs of spider and sun are brought together when Gu has his first moment of self-awareness after the battle at the 'haunted' fort. Through a series of gradually revealing tracking shots, we share Gu's revelation, shifting from delight at his cunning that has led to a victory in battle against the Eunuchs' soldiers to dawning realisation at the deadly consequences of slaughtered and dying men surrounding what had been his home. Spying the monk, he gazes at the sky. A point of view shot of the blazing sun reveals a web-like pattern that suggests both illumination and inevitable fate are revealed to our erstwhile hero.

The narrative structure equally peels back layers of perception. In the above sequence, we have glided from a ghost tale to an action/romance story to a deadly reality. Yang now mysteriously vanishes and Gu is revealed not as a victorious hero and lover, but a mass killer. The plot will advance as Gu searches for her, a journey that will result in further enlightenment and the adoption of yet another new persona: as an oddly feminised father in need of Yang's rescue.

While the nature of the two central figures is in flux, several others reveal hidden personae. Thus, character identity, including personality, sexuality and skills are transient throughout. It is thanks to the film's long running time that this seems to be progression, rather than inconsistency. The character resolutions Gu and Yang eventually make are connected by their child, yet, in narrative terms, they are wholly separate. Stephen Teo links the film's shifting narrative to the overall motif of Zen as an 'improvisation in the act of self-fashioning within the film text. The process involves ceaseless narrative invention because one is not forever fixd in a single, divinely sanctioned identity' (2009: 131).

The film's climax is also notable for its attempt to express the sensation of Zen, rather than offer a liminal explanation or logical narrative closure. Hui Yuan is tricked by Hsu's feigned repentance and is stabbed. Gu and Yang witness the monk bleeding gold, signifying his imminent enlightenment as Hsu endures psychedelic insanity, torment and death. The esoteric culmination that frames the holy monk Hui Yuan with a gigantic, blinding sun suggests that he has become the Buddha himself. Meanwhile, the main protagonists who have been practically absent bar brief reaction shots for the final half an hour, look on in amazement.

A Touch of Zen is a clear influence on more recent examples of transnational Chinese cinema, where talents have been drawn from the various regions to present a unified image to the world, including *Crouching Tiger/Hidden Dragon* and Zhang Yimou's *House of Flying Daggers* (2004). Both wuxia films recall the elusive female warrior and draw inspiration from Hu's bamboo forest sequence. However, *A Touch of Zen* is a wuxia film inasmuch as Stanley Kubrick's *2001: A Space Odyssey* (1968) or Andrei Tarkovsky's *Solaris* (1972) are science fiction. Recalling the plot for each is reductive. Each has a climax that is intuited, rather than explanatory. Each uses genre as a springboard for something more personal, challenging, elusive and extraordinary. At the heart of *A Touch of Zen* is a vivid transnationality that filters its cultural tradition through the sensibilities of its ambitious and singular director.

Notes

1. Until Zhang Yimou's post-unification *Hero* (2000) brought a seemingly pro-authoritarian bent to the genre.
2. A howling continuity error near the end of the film shows Yang's combat wound shift to various positions around her face.

Further reading

Chris Berry and Mary Farquhar, *China on Screen*, New York, Columbia University Press, 2006.

David Bordwell, 'Richness Through Imperfection: King Hu and the "Glimpse"' in Poshek Fu and David Desser (eds), *The Cinema of Hong Kong: History, Arts, Identity*, Cambridge, Cambridge University Press, 2000, pp. 113–36.

Stephen Teo, *King Hu's A Touch of Zen*, Hong Kong University Press, 2007.

Stephen Teo, *Chinese Martial Arts Cinema, The Wuxia Tradition*, Edinburgh, Edinburgh University Press, 2009.

Phil Lloyd

Y tu mamá también (2001)

[Country: Mexico. Production Company: Anhelo Producciones, Besame Mucho Pictures. Producer and Director: Alfonso Cuarón. Screenwriters: Alfonso Cuarón, Carlos Cuarón. Cinematographer: Emmanuel Lubezki. Editor: Alfonso Cuarón, Alex Rodríguez. Cast: Diego Luna (Tenoch Iturbide), Gael García Bernal (Julio Zapata), Maribel Verdú (Luisa Cortéz).]

Synopsis: The film's young male protagonists, Tenoch and Julio are just leaving high school and embarking on their adult life; they spend their time getting drunk, taking drugs, having sex and "whacking off". When they meet an attractive older woman, Luisa, at a family wedding they flirt with her and invite her to come on a trip to the beach with them. Luisa, in her late twenties, is married to Tenoch's cousin Juno and, although she doesn't take the invitation seriously at first, when she discovers that her husband has been unfaithful she takes the boys up on their offer. The trio travel through the Mexican countryside en route to the mythical Heaven's Mouth.

On the surface *Y tu mamá también* is a stylish road movie. Whilst the film borrows from the Hollywood genre, it does not employ a classical Hollywood style. *Y tu mamá también* has a distinctly documentary feel, employing long takes and fluid camera moves, which follow the action mostly in wide shots. The opening shot of the film, which shows Tenoch and his girlfriend Ana having sex before Ana heads off to Italy for the summer is more than two minutes long and in the bar scene towards the end of the film there is one take of over seven minutes. The use of this technique puts great pressure on the actors to deliver authentic performances. Luna (Tenoch) and Bernal (Julio) had worked together several times before and knew each other as children and so were very much at ease with one another from the outset, but they did not know Verdú (Luisa) who came over from Spain to shoot the film. To facilitate veracity in the performances, director Alfonso Cuarón shot the main action of the film in chronological order so that the development of relationships on screen was reflected in the developing relationships between the actors, who became more comfortable with one another as shooting progressed.[1]

Cuarón has asserted that context and character are equally important in the film.[2] Julio and Tenoch are self-absorbed and pay little attention to what is happening around them and so the social and cultural context of the story is brought to the audience through use of a wandering camera and voiceover. The context is a society in a state of flux. Mexico underwent rapid change in the late 1990s, largely instigated by the implementation of the North American Free Trade Agreement (NAFTA). In the wake of the agreement, new prosperity generated by increased trade with the US was concentrated in wealthy cities and Mexico experienced intense urbanisation, which placed pressure on rural communities and increased the inequities in society. In 2000 a new right wing government was elected ending the 71-year rule of the Institutional Revolutionary Party (PRI). This broader narrative is revealed when the camera moves away from the main action of the film and follows events, which are seemingly irrelevant to the main story. So at the family wedding the camera follows a tray of leftover food being carried to the car park where it is shared among the bodyguards and, on a rural road the camera leaves the car to dwell on a group of peasants being 'hassled' by the police. Using the camera in this way also reinforces the veracity of the action, giving the impression that the viewer is happening upon events rather than viewing scenes set up for the camera.

Diversions from the main story are often used to disclose inequalities in societal structure and the displacement of people in the face of economic progress. This occurs not just through the distracted camera but also in the use of voiceover. For example, in voiceover we are told that the lifestyle of the family who take Julio, Tenoch and Luisa on a boat tour around the bay of Heaven's Mouth will be lost due to the building of a tourist resort and in the city we are told that the cause of a traffic jam is an accident in which a migrant worker was killed whilst taking a short cut across a busy road because of a poorly positioned pedestrian bridge. The delivery of the voice-over is deadpan, without emotion, and it deals with very specific and detailed facts; we are told exact lengths of time, amounts of money and distances, so that it sounds like a news report. It also often cuts into the soundtrack silencing the diegetic sound. The effect of this is to distance the audience from the central narrative and to create a reflective space to consider the wider context of what we are seeing.

Mexico is presented as a class-riven society and class is an important factor in the relationship between Tenoch and Julio. Tenoch is from an upper-middle-class family and this is made clear through the camera's exploration of his palatial home and the lavish family wedding. On one occasion we see Tenoch's Nanny bringing him a sandwich from the kitchen. The journey to Tenoch is lengthy, she hands over the sandwich and he barely acknowledges her. She then answers the phone (that has been ringing for a while and is right next to Tenoch) and hands it to him. Tenoch is clearly comfortable being served by others. Julio, by contrast lives in a modest apartment in a built-up part of town. The camera takes us on a tour of the apartment and shows us the view from the window, while the voice-over tells us that Julio lives with his single mother. The friendship between Julio and Tenoch seems unfettered by this difference in status; however, when tensions develop between the boys the insults they throw at one another are bound up in class prejudice. One of the central themes of the film is the search for identity.[3] The boys are finding their identity as adults, Luisa is finding her identity as a free woman, and Mexico is finding its identity as a 'grown-up country'.

Throughout the film, Luisa's sadness is contrasted with the youthful exuberance of Julio and Tenoch. They are carefree and self-absorbed, interested only in having sex and getting high. In one scene this contrast takes place within a single frame: we see Luisa through the window in the telephone booth crying whilst on the phone to Juno, and next to the window in a mirror we see the reflection of Julio and Tenoch playing table football. Luisa develops throughout the film from a lonely wife whose husband is unfaithful, to a liberated and assertive woman. We learn near the beginning of the film that she has received the results of some medical tests but it is not fully revealed until the end that she has terminal cancer.[4] However, reminders of death follow her through the film as the trio pass by crosses and a funeral procession on the side of the road, and an old woman gives her a toy mouse that belonged to her dead granddaughter. Luisa's terminal illness is an additional motivation for taking the road trip that gives her journey greater import.

The boys are clearly attracted to Luisa from the start. She adopts a motherly tone with them but then seduces Tenoch when he comes to her room to borrow some shampoo. This sexual encounter, which is observed by Julio, is the start of tension between the two 'Charolastras',[5] and Julio then tells Tenoch that he has slept with his girlfriend. Luisa then sleeps with Julio seemingly in an attempt to even things up, but it just makes the situation worse and the relationship between the boys deteriorates until Luisa takes charge and sets out her own rules for the trip. The sex within the film is passionate but not romanticised. The boy's inept fumblings are comic and sweet, but ultimately unsatisfying for Luisa who reverts to mothering them in the aftermath.

In the climax of the road trip, Luisa seduces both boys placing them in a sexual encounter with one another. The sexual potential in their relationship is alluded to throughout the film, (we see them masturbating together at the swimming pool and chasing one another around the shower after Tenoch comments that Julio has 'one ugly dick'), but when sex becomes a reality the boys head back to the city and stop being friends. While Luisa is the catalyst for the break-up of their relationship, she is not the reason for it. The film presents this outcome as almost inevitable. The boys are from different strata of Mexican society and will follow different paths. When they bump into each other in the city and go for a coffee some time later, it is clear that they have now taken their predestined places in the adult world. Tenoch has given up dreams of writing and capitulated to his father's wishes to study economics and Julio is studying biology at college. The voice-over tells us they will never meet again and the final words in the film are Julio's, asking for the bill.

Although Cuarón asserts that the film does not make political points and is merely observing developments within Mexico, there is a clear indication that progress comes at a cost, which will be paid by the poor and powerless. The film can also be interpreted as an allegory of the role of Spain within Mexico. Luisa Cortéz is Spanish and the boys first encounter her at a family wedding held in a bullring emphasising the influence of Spanish culture within Mexico. She is clearly portrayed as an outsider; on several occasions she asks the boys to translate their slang phrases and has a tourist's interest in the culture of the people they encounter on their road trip. She is also named after the Spanish conqueror of Mexico[6] and is from the outset a 'contaminated' character;[7] she has a terminal cancer that remains hidden from the boys until her death is revealed after the trip. Her presence disrupts their friendship, she lures them into sexual transgression and order is only restored once she is gone. However, in this restored order, although sexual conformity returns, a new social conformity also emerges as Tenoch and Julio end their inter-class friendship and take their places in the adult world.

Notes

1. The film was shot chronologically except for the final scene in the café which was shot first. At this point in the film, the friendship between Julio and Tenoch is over.
2. See Alfonso Cuaron, 'Interview', *Y tu mamá también* (2001) DVD Extras.
3. Ibid.
4. The door of the consulting room is closed to the camera as the doctor gives her the news literally shutting out the audience.
5. Julio and Tenoch dub themselves 'Charolastra', which means astral cowboy. The small band of 'Charolastras' have a Manifesto which includes not sleeping with one another's girlfriends.
6. Names have significance within the film: Julio Zapata is named after a Mexican revolutionary and Tenoch is given an Aztec name by his politician father who was 'affected by a sudden nationalism' in the year he was born.
7. See E. Hind, 'Post NATFA Mexican Cinema 1998–2002', in *Studies in Latin American Popular Culture*, Vol. 23, University of Texas Press, 2004, pp. 95–111.

Further reading

Jeff Menne, 'A Mexican Nouvelle Vague: The Logic of New Waves under Globalization', *Cinema Journal* 47, No 1, Austin, University of Texas Press, 2007, pp. 70–92.

Laura Podalsky, 'The Young, the Damned and the Restless: Youth in Contemporary Mexican Cinema', *Framework* 49, No 1, Detroit, Wayne State University Press, 2008, pp. 144–60.

María Josefina Saldaña-Portillo, 'In the Shadow of NATFA: *Y tu mamá también* Revisits the National Allegory of Mexican Sovereignty', *American Quarterly* Vol. 57, Issue 3, 2005, pp. 751–78.

Paul Julian Smith, 'Heaven's Mouth', *Sight and Sound*, Vol. 12, Issue 4, 2002, pp. 16–19.

Janice Kearns

Yeelen (1987)

[Country: Mali, Burkina Faso, France, Germany. Production Company: Les Films Cissé, Atriascop, Les Films du Carrosse, CNC, WDR. Director, Producer and Screenwriter: Souleymane Cissé. Cinematographers: Jean-Noël Ferragut and Jean-Michel Humeau. Music: Salif Keita and Michael Portal. Editor: Dounamba Coulibaly. Cast: Issiaka Kane (Nianankoro Diarra), Niamanto Sanogo (Soma Diarra/Djigui Diarra), Balla Moussa Keita (Rouma Boll), Aoua Sangare (Attou), Soumba Traore (Mah).]

Synopsis: A young man, Nianankoro, embarks on a journey across ancient Mali to fulfil his destiny and challenge his tyrannical father Soma, a member of the Komo society which holds the secrets of a divine cosmic force. Nianankoro's power matures with the help of the Peul and Dogon peoples, and after acquiring the sacred Wing of Kore, he engages in an epic battle with his father for the fate of the entire country.

Yeelen stands as one of the most acclaimed African films of the twentieth century, largely due to its striking portrayal of the peoples and pre-colonial culture of Mali.[1] This status inevitably raises questions about how to judge the film in relation to the pervasive representation of Africa as 'a paradigm of difference', the ultimate 'Other' of Western modernity.[2] Does the film's vibrant portrayal of pre-colonial myth and culture make it an African film *par excellence*, or does the universal appeal of its political allegory and its sheer beauty allow it to transcend its 'African-ness'? Can the complexity of the film's politics and reception be understood outside of its distinction as *African* cinema?

One approach to answering these questions involves considering the nuances of the film's allegory in relation to viewers' access to the distinct cultural knowledge of the Bambara. The narrative is rather straightforward: a young man (Nianankoro Diarra) embarks on a journey to fulfil his destiny and challenge his tyrannical father Soma, a member of a society which holds the secrets of a magical cosmic power (*Komo*). However, the prologue explains that the Komo is not a fictional construct but an actual source of 'divine knowledge' in Malian cosmology, obliging spectators to regard the film through this lens.

Although set in an unspecified time period, it is widely believed that the film is based on the legend of Sundiata Keita, the thirteenth-century founder of the Malian empire who used magic to defeat an oppressive ruler. With this framing, we might interpret the film's political allegory as mere indictment of tyranny. Soma's despotic rule over the knowledge of the *Komo* is juxtaposed with the generous leadership of the Peul (Fulani) king, who spares Nianankoro's life; the Dogon priest, who shares the secrets of rain divination; and Soma's twin Djigui, whose desire to share the secrets of the Komo resulted in his exile and blindness.

The film is also regarded as an indictment of the violent authoritarian rule of President Moussa Traoré, still at the helm of the nation at the time of its release. *Yeelen* can be read as an appropriation of the history and myth of Mali as inspiration for post-colonial resistance. It can be grouped with other 'return to the source' African films of the 1980s that avoided censorship by advocating a return to indigenous, pre-colonial knowledge to solve contemporary problems.[3] Nianankoro's journey across the country symbolically unites the Bambara, Fulani and Dogon peoples and suggests that the indigenous knowledge of all segments of Malian society is needed to combat a common oppressor.

However, film scholar Suzanne MacRae has successfully argued that the more appropriate pre-colonial setting of the film is the late nineteenth century, on the cusp of the decline of the Diarra dynasty over the Segou kingdom and the colonisation of the country by the French (1995: 57). This reading is confirmed by the protagonist's surname, the explicit rebuke of the Diarras by the voice of the *Kore* in the apocalyptic standoff between father and son, and the implicit reference to colonisation in Djigui's prophecy.

Thus, while the Sundiata legend provides an important mythical context, *Yeelen* also resonates with the endless political upheaval that characterised the Segou kingdom. The film's title, translated as 'brightness' or 'the light', references this philosophy, presented through Bambara symbology in the opening moments: 'Heat (*Goniya*) makes fire (*Ta*) and the two worlds–earth and sky–exist through light (*Dye fia*)'. Blinding light plays an important role in the film, particularly in the climactic confrontation between Nianankoro and Soma. Cissé considers this endless cycle of the consolidation, destruction and recreation of knowledge by each generation *Yeelen*'s most 'universal aspect' (Diawara 1998: 15) While the film certainly indicts Soma for his refusal to share power, the sense of destiny guiding Nianankoro's actions suggests a more spiritual than political claim about the principle of infinite renewal.

The layered meanings of the film make it difficult to tie the film to a single mode of discourse. If understood as a political statement against tyrannical rule built upon the Sundiata myth, then

Yeelen can be considered a *Bildungsroman*, a rite-of-passage narrative about an ordinary man who matures as a wielder of magic, even though it lacks the psychological overtones we might expect from the genre. The spiritual interpretation suggests we read the film as an epic with archetypal characters.

It is the distinctive cultural knowledge of Mali that allows both readings to coexist, and our attempts to appropriate that knowledge, or our inability to do so, mirrors the struggle over access to the secrets of the Komo in the film. Our access to *Yeelen*'s depth of meaning is tied to our comprehension of its dense cultural source material. For example, MacRae's research suggests that the name Soma references a type of competitive sorcerer intent on vanquishing rivals, a fact with which Malian audiences might be familiar and which would support an understanding of the film as a retelling of a common myth or of the characters as familiar types (1995: 61).

On the one hand, *Yeelen* discloses the inner workings of a culture and universalises them. On the other, it presents a distinctive narrative whose deeper allegorical meanings may remain inaccessible to viewers outside of that culture, further exoticising African cultures. In this sense, *Yeelen* can be regarded as an anthropological film, immersing audiences in a world view that can only be fully comprehended through extensive study. The mere complexity of the rituals of sorcery, which include spitting, powerful wooden boards and amulets, various symbolic human and animal figures, and distinctive patterns of speech and mimicry, to name a few elements, invites audiences to linger over the foreignness and inherent beauty of Bambara culture. The film's deliberate pacing, achieved through long takes, minimal editing and shots that highlight mise en scène and natural elements over faces and character reactions, also accomplishes Cissé's goal to keep viewers 'busy looking, interpreting [and] discovering' the intricacies of Bambara culture (Diawara 1998: 15). Cissé can also be considered a cinematic griot, serving as a repository and source of transmission for oral knowledge.

The most explicit disclosure in the film, however, is lost on audiences unfamiliar with Malian popular culture, as issues of language and translation prevent them from perceiving the film's spiritual and affective dimensions. The characters of *Yeelen* speak in the Bambara and Fula languages, and audiences outside of these linguistic groups must mediate the film through woefully inadequate subtitles, particularly given the minimalist speech of many scenes. By presenting the intricacies of its ceremonies, Cissé not only introduced Malians to clandestine rites they had heard about but never seen, but he also 'decode[d] the secret ritual described by the song [Malians] usually hear on the radio'; these spectators are encouraged to 'look for the codic meaning of the song, which [contains] the secrets of the universe' (Diawara 1998: 15). For the unfamiliar spectator mediating the film through subtitles, the significance of this moment and this depth of meaning are lost.

Frank Ukadike's affirmation that Cissé succeeds in 'holding the middle ground between the Western ethnographic conception of the moving image, which seeks out the misery of the Third World, and the falsehood of repressing it on the grounds of cultural intrusion' begs the question: For whom is this true (Ukadike, 1994: 255)? Which audiences are able to fully access the knowledge that Cissé, like the Dogon priest, appears to freely share? How does the perception of Africa as other enter into this perception of the film? Is the film, ultimately, an allegory about the challenges of viewing African cinema?

Cissé acknowledges that one of his aims in making the film was to 'erase from people's mind the disdain they have for Black people and their culture', and we might argue that the film succeeds in opposing depictions of pre-colonial Africa as 'primitive' by humanising its characters and valorising their world view (Diawara 1998: 15). However, framing the film in this manner raises criticism of its appeal to authenticity that reaffirms binary oppositions between Africa and 'the West' or the primitive and the modern, while also obscuring its exposition of the underlying power structure and contemporary concerns in Malian society.

The politics of the film's aesthetic reception echoes these tensions. Although Cissé displays directorial skill that counters any notions of African cinema as aesthetically unsophisticated, we cannot assume that viewers do not see its stunning visuals as further exoticising African cultures. Long, artful shots of the natural elements and lengthy takes of purification rites are experienced as innovative, due to the content of the image as much as the cinematography.

Ultimately, the film reveals a thematic repetition of imagery that allows the visuals to operate symbolically. When Attou takes her turn bathing in the purifying springs of the Dogon territory, we may recall the visual effect of a prior scene of ritual purification, as Nianankoro's mother prays for her son's protection. The recognition of this pattern might lead viewers to ask critical questions about the idealistic framing of motherhood in these scenes, moving beyond, or least engaging in a less explicit way, the film's distinction as an example of African culture. We cannot assume, however, that this is naturally the case. As noted earlier, Cissé walks a fine line between cultural specificity and universal appeal that could be defined as the film's 'political unconscious'.[4]

Certainly, every film reflects a distinctive cultural orientation that many spectators fail to access, but the interpretive struggle between filmmaker and spectator of African cinema resonates at the level of allegory in films like *Yeelen*, whose subtle politics and experimental indigeneity cannot be grasped without also grappling with the politics of mainstream discourse about Africa. *Yeelen*'s greatest success may be that it challenges viewers to explore their own preconceptions of African cinema. In this sense, Cissé serves as an analogue to Nianankoro, attempting to expose stagnant and oppressive knowledge of Africa to the light in a fresh set of eyes.

Notes

1. *Yeelen* won the Jury Prize at the Cannes Film Festival in 1987, making Cissé the first African to place at the prestigious festival and giving the film an enduring international acclaim.
2. V.Y. Mudimbe, *The Idea of Africa*, Bloomington, Indiana University Press, 1994, p. xii.
3. Diawara 1998: 13. Cissé considers *Yeelen* his most political film, but admits political pressure forced him to tone down the criticism of the government in his films. For a further definition of the 'return to the source' genre, see Diawara 1992: 160–5.
4. The term, as used by Frederic Jameson, suggests that all texts have a political dimension that incorporates a philosophy of history beyond the literal political interpretation of their narratives.

Further reading

Manthia Diawara, *African Cinema: Politics and Culture*, Bloomington, Indiana University Press, 1992.

John Downing, 'Post-Tricolor African Cinema: Toward a Richer Vision', in Dina Sherzer (ed.), *Cinema, Colonialism, Postcolonialism: Perspectives from the French and Francophone Worlds*, Austin: University of Texas Press, 1996, pp. 188–228.

Manthia Diawara, 'Souleymane Cisse's Light on Africa', *Black Film Review*, Fall 1998.

Suzanne H. MacRae, '*Yeelen*: A Political Fable of the *Komo* Blacksmith Sorcerers', *Research in African Literatures*, Vol. 26, No. 3, Fall 1995, pp. 57–66.

N. Frank Ukadike, *Black African Cinema*, Berkeley and Los Angeles, University of California Press, 1994.

Jamicia Lackey

Yin shi nan nu/Eat Drink Man Woman (1994)

[Country: Taiwan. Production Company: Ang Lee Productions, Central Motion Picture Corporation and Good Machine. Director: Ang Lee. Producers: Kong Hsu and Li-Kong Su. Screenwriters: Ang Lee, James Schamus and Hui-Ling Wang. Cinematographer: Lin Jong. Music: Mader. Editor:

Time Squyres. Cast: Sihung Lung (Chu), Kuei-mei Yang (Jia-jen), Chien-lien Wu (Jia-chien), Yu-wen Wang (Jia-ning), Sylvia Chang (Jin-rong), Winston Chao (Li Kai), Lester Chit-Man Chan (Raymond), Chin-cheng Lu (Ming-dao Chou), Guo Lun (Chao-jung Chen), Ya-lei Juei (Mrs Liang), Jui Wang (Old Wen), Yu-chien Tang (Shan-Shan).][1]

Synopsis: Mr Chu (Lung) is a retired hotel chef in Taipei, Taiwan, who still shares the family home with his three adult daughters. Jia-jen (Yang), the oldest, is a Christian chemistry teacher who falls in love with the new school coach, Ming-dao Chou (Lu). The next daughter, Jia-chien (Wu), whose relationship with her father is the main focus of the film, is a successful executive at an expanding airline company who moves on from her modern, no-strings sex relationship with Raymond (Chan) when the suave Li Kai (Chao) arrives at her office. The youngest, 20-year-old Jia-ning (Wang), gets pregnant by her best friend's ex-boyfriend. Chu himself keeps secret his developing relationship with their neighbour Jin-rong (Chang) while preparing school-meals for her young daughter, Shan-Shan (Tang). Chu's oldest friend and colleague Old Wen (Wang) dies suddenly. Jia-jen and Jia-ning marry their lovers while Chu and Jia-chien, his favourite daughter, are finally able to express their strong emotional attachment as he leaves to live with Jin-rong. Throughout the film, food and its preparation both punctuates and enables the development of these relationships.

Eat Drink Man Woman is Ang Lee's third feature film and forms the final part of his 'Father Knows Best' trilogy, following *Pushing Hands / Tui shou* (1991) and *The Wedding Banquet/ Xi yan* (1993). All three films depict a clash between cultures: between youth and old age; between China and Taiwan; between tradition and progress; between East and West and investigate the freedoms and constraints inherent in family structures particularly those between fathers, daughters and sons. In each film the father is played by veteran martial arts actor Sihung Lung (here as Mr Chu, a retired master chef) and it is through his gentle and surprisingly progressive persona that contradictions and conflict are finally resolved. The trilogy also takes the repression of individual desire in the face of social pressure as one of its central themes and it is this overarching concern that informs all of Ang Lee's films to date.

The English title of *Eat Drink Man Woman* is a literal translation of the Chinese proverb 'yin shi nan nü' which suggests the interdependence of contrasting elements such as 'the difference between male and female' and that 'between eating and drinking' (Dilley 2007: 72). Dilley goes on to argue that in Lee's film this saying is ironised by Chu who uses the phrase to reflect on the complications inherent in even the simplest of relationships. The complex nature of human existence, the film suggests, cannot be summed up by the cliché of yin and yang.

Many of the shots in the film are framed as posed photographs with groups of characters closely clustered together in medium and close shots. While these shots emphasise the faces of the characters, the other dominant style of framing is of hands working with food. This second type of shot tends to avoid the face of the cook, not least because the actors are not the ones dextrously chopping, skinning, decanting or frying. The actual cooking was performed by three talented Taiwanese chefs. Regardless of the practicalities behind this aesthetic, the concentration on craft and ingredients lends these sequences a timeless property reflecting the ancestral nature of these actions. Many cooks have performed these same actions over many centuries – no modern electrical gadgets are used in any of the preparations – and we are made aware of continuity between the modern and the ancient. Lee however problematises this continuity by stressing the fragility of this tradition and the inevitability of change.

After the death of Old Wen, his hotel kitchen comrade, Chu explains that his own expertise in the traditional cooking of mainland China is no longer needed or even wanted as all has become an indistinguishable melange. The film is an elegy for a certain purity of culture but it is an elegy that is not necessarily nostalgic as Lee does not romanticise the iniquities and repression that is an essential part of those traditions. While food and its preparation could be seen in the film as a 'metaphor for love', Ma argues that it 'is poorly produced as the chef can no longer control the right amount of seasoning and is poorly received as the daughters contemplate a move away from the family prison' (Ma 1996: 195). The weekly feasts that Chu prepares for his daughters, what they call 'the Sunday torture ritual', are his attempts at shoring up the ruins of his own decline – his loss of smell and taste – and that of his family, and by extension of his culture and history, which is the history of China itself. As Dariotis puts it, the 'orgy of cooking belies the repression of appetites' (Dariotis and Fung 1997: 208). Food becomes not a celebration of life and community but a symbol of death and chaos.

At the centre of *Eat Drink Man Woman* is one of the tenets of Confucianism: filial piety, the duty of respect and care owed to one's parents (see Fairlamb 2007; Laine, 2005: 106). In a 2000 interview Ang Lee says, 'The essence of morality in the East is "filial piety": loyalty to your parents, to your family. It's where you come from. It's where your heritage comes from.' As in many of Lee's other films, the drama here is in the conflict between social duty and individual desire: 'Had [Jia-chien] left the family home rather than take care of her elderly father, she would have been acting in opposition to traditional expectations. Likewise, had she remained, she would have opposed the "modern" sensibilities of the "West", which place individual satisfaction over the welfare of the family,' (Dariotis and Fung 1997: 210). For Lee this contradiction leads inevitably to a state of 'total guilt' (quoted in Chan 2004: 8) and this phrase points to the importance of Freudian psychoanalysis in Lee's thought. While discussing *Crouching Tiger, Hidden Dragon* (2000), Lee says, 'But you have to use Freudian or Western techniques, to dissect what I think is hidden in a repressed society – the sexual tension, the prohibited feelings' (quoted in Chan 2004: 6). The conflict between Superego and Id, between obligation and desire, between 'the perennial cultural desire for individual freedom and rights versus a concern with social and communal responsibility' (Chan 2004: 7) is one that runs through all his films.

It is accent that marks this contradiction between new and old, East and West, since, according to Ma, Sihung Lung's 'near-perfect Beijing accent' aligns Chu clearly with the old order of China, but by 'contrast all the younger, white-collar Taiwanese immigrant-children speak Taiwanese Mandarin and English, symbolising their distance from the imagined Chinese core' (Ma 1996: 197). Chu is literally and figuratively out of time and stands as well for the impossible possibility of a non-communist China: what if Mao Zedong had not helped establish the People's Republic of China in 1949? It is perhaps no coincidence that the Grand Hotel in *Eat Drink Man Woman* is a pastiche of traditional Chinese architecture, constructed in 1952 on the site of a Shinto temple. The hotel, like Chu, is imposing and fiercely traditional, but in the film it floats alone in the darkness, adrift from history and taste.

The clash of cultures and histories in *Eat Drink Man Woman* is also evident in its own production history. Lee's first two feature films, *Pushing Hands* and *The Wedding Banquet*, were financed by the American independent company Good Machine and all three scripts were written or co-written by its head, the non-Chinese speaking James Schamus (see Pidduck 2006: 397). While the first two films are set in the United States, all three star Sihung Lung as the elderly Chinese traditionalist who reveals a surprisingly progressive attitude towards the end of each film: in *Pushing Hands* he accepts his Western daughter-in-law; in *The Wedding Banquet* he acknowledges his gay son; and in *Eat Drink Man Woman* he allows his daughter to cook for him. Chu leaves with his pregnant young wife for a modern apartment, while Jia-chien decides to stay in the family home. In the final scene, he arrives alone for a final meal cooked by his daughter, and at the very moment in which he accepts his daughter's cooking, he regains his sense of taste (this part of the script coming apparently from Schamus – a *bona ex machine* if there ever was one). As the daughter now feeds the father, so the traditional roles are both reversed and endorsed: the father cedes his power but the daughter accepts her father as her responsibility. The end of the film manages to simultaneously upset and reconfirm the established order.

There are two main ideological readings given of the film. The majority opinion seems to be that the film is finally conservative and a betrayal of Taiwanese values in favour of Western tastes and colonial-global politics with a rather noxious playing up to stereotypes of the exotic and inscrutable oriental. There is however a minority view, as expressed by Dariotis and Fung and by Laine among others, that the film challenges easy dichotomies between East and West, between the family and the individual and even between rights and duties. Perhaps we can see this latter reading more clearly when considering the changes made in *Tortilla Soup* (Maria Ripoll) the 2001 remake of *Eat Drink Man Woman* which relocates the action to the Mexican diaspora in Los Angeles. While *Tortilla Soup* is in many ways an uncanny replication of the original film, with scenes and dialogue reproduced almost word for word and shot for shot (with the Californian-Mexican cooking overseen by popular chefs Mary Sue Milliken and Susan Feniger), the ambiguous ending of *Eat Drink Man Woman* is replaced by a family celebration bringing together all generations in the Jia-chien equivalent daughter's successful new restaurant. It is clear that the remake aims to shut down the ambivalence of the original ending where father and daughter establish only a fraught temporary alliance. *Tortilla Soup*'s anxiety about this provisional solution indicates that *Eat Drink Man Woman* is perhaps more complex than its critics imagine.

Note

I have used the English tradition of placing the first names – usually hyphenated – first. When a character only has one name, this is generally the family name.

Further reading

Kenneth Chan, 'The Global Return of the Wu Xia Pian (Chinese Sword-Fighting Movie): Ang Lee's *Crouching Tiger, Hidden Dragon*', *Cinema Journal*, 43 (4), 2004, pp. 3–17.

Wei Ming Dariotis and Eileen Fung, 'Breaking the Soy Sauce Jar: Diaspora and Displacement in the Films of Ang Lee' in Sheldon Hsiao-peng Lu (ed.) *Transnational Chinese Cinemas: Identity, Nationhood, Gender*, Honolulu: University of Hawai'i Press, 1997, pp. 187–220.

Whitney Crothers Dilley, *The Cinema of Ang Lee: The Other Side of the Screen*, London and New York: Wallflower Press, 2007.

Horace L. Fairlamb, 'Romancing the Tao: How Ang Lee Globalized Ancient Chinese Wisdom', symploke, 15 (1), 2007, pp. 190–205.

Tarja Laine, 'Family Matters in *Eat Drink Man Woman*: Food Envy, Family Longing, or Intercultural Knowledge through the Senses' in Patricia Pisters and Wim Staat (eds) *Shooting the Family: Transnational Media and Intercultural Values*, Amsterdam: University of Amsterdam Press, 2005, pp. 103–15.

Sheng-mei Ma, 'Ang Lee's Domestic Tragicomedy: Immigrant Nostalgia, Exotic/Ethnic Tour, Global Market', *The Journal of Popular Culture* 30 (1), 1996, pp. 191–201.

Julianne Pidduck, 'The Transnational Cinema of Ang Lee', in Dimitris Eleftheriotis and Gary Needham (eds) *Asian Cinemas: A Reader and Guide*, Edinburgh: Edinburgh University Press, 2006, pp. 393–404.

Ming-Yeh T. Rawnsley, 'Cultural Representation of Taste in Ang Lee's *Eat, Drink, Man, Woman*' in Lawrence C. Rubin (ed.) *Food for Thought: Essays on Eating and Culture*, Jefferson, NC: McFarland, 2008, pp. 225–37.

Ti Wei, 'Generational/Cultural Contradiction and Global Incorporation: Ang Lee's *Eat Drink Man Woman*', in Chris Berry and Feii Lu (eds) *Island on the Edge: Taiwan New Cinema and After*, Hong Kong: Hong Kong University Press, 2005, pp. 101–12.

David Sorfa

Zangiku monogatari/The Story of the Last Chrysanthemum (1939)

[Country: Japan. Production Company: Shochiku's Shimogamo (Kyoto) Studio. Executive Producer: Shintaro Shirai. Director: Kenji Mizoguchi. Based on a short story by Shofu Matsumura. Adaptation: Matsutaro Kawaguchi. Screenwriter: Yoshikata Yoda. Cinematographer: Shigeto Miki. Art Director: Hiroshi Mizutani. Music: Shiro Fukai. Cast: Shotaro Hanayagi (Kikunosuke Onoe), Kakuko Mori (Otoku), Kokichi Takada (Fukusuke 'Fuku' Nakamura), Gonjuro Kawarazaki (Kikugoro V), Yoko Umemura (his wife Sato).]

Synopsis: In late nineteenth-century Tokyo, young kabuki actor Kikunosuke meets Otoku, his baby brother's wet nurse. Otoku candidly tells him how bad his acting is; her honesty impresses him, and love and trust develops between the two. Kikunosuke's adoptive father and mentor, the great Kikugoro V, however, does not approve of their relationship, let alone their marriage, and disowns him. Kikunosuke starts afresh in the Osaka kabuki world. One year later, Otoku joins him. Four years pass. Kikunosuke now plays in travelling troupes and, even if his acting itself has improved, the couple struggle to survive and often quarrel. She confides in Fuku, Kikunosuke's friend and fellow kabuki actor of privilege. Fuku and the impresario Morita promise Otoku to give Kikunosuke a chance in exchange for her leaving him. Kikunosuke makes a spectacular comeback performance and is received by his family in Tokyo, and Otoku disappears. Several months later, when Kikunosuke, together with his family, visits Osaka for a triumphant tour, he finally reunites with Otoku on her deathbed. While he parades in the procession boat and greets the public, she takes her last breath.

The Story of the Last Chrysanthemum is, as the synopsis shows, a quintessential backstage melodrama. And yet, it goes far beyond that in two respects. First, aesthetically, the film has been celebrated as one of the high points of Kenji Mizoguchi's career and one of the landmarks of Japanese cinema. It systematically draws on long takes and long shots, developing an elaborate mise en scène style within the spatiotemporal continuum. Formalist film scholars have argued that this style produces 'decentring' effects that challenge the classical Hollywood paradigm that is predominantly motivated by character psychology (Burch 1979: 230–6; Bordwell 1983; Kirihara 1992: 137–57). The director's recourse to a film style that could hinder the spectator's emotional involvement with the characters produced fascinating disjunctions with the story, which was remade twice in the post-Second World War period as straightforward melodrama (director Koji Shima, 1956; director Hideo Ooba, 1963).

Second, historically, *The Story of the Last Chrysanthemum* marked a turning point in Japanese film history. On the one hand, it showed off what the national cinema's first 'golden age' in the 1930s had achieved in its technical bravura, psychological complexity, and exquisite recreation of historical settings. At its closing moment, the 'cinema of flourishes' (Bordwell 1992: 328–46) celebrated its audacity and maturity through an adult melodrama set in the world of performing arts. On the other hand, the militarist government and its ideologues praised and promoted *The Story of the Last Chrysanthemum* as a model film that inaugurated a new era, selecting it for the first Minister of Education prize. Indeed, the Film Law (*Eigahô*) that legislated for the state's intervention in film culture and industry came into effect on 1 October 1939, just ten days before the film's release.

At various levels, *The Story of the Last Chrysanthemum* is split into polarities: the detached or even alienating style and the melodramatic mode, entertainment and propaganda, rebellion against and endorsement of the 'traditional' family system. These seemingly contradictory polarities are all connected to a historically specific configuration of high/low and art/entertainment in Japan in 1939. A close look at this configuration reveals why this film succeeded as a quality film with mass-appeal on all conceivable fronts – at the box office, in critical reception, and at the Ministry of Education.

Furthermore, the film's negotiations of high and low and different value systems resulted in its complex representation of family and gender issues. The film acknowledges and sympathetically portrays the hero Kikunosuke's revolt against kabuki's patrimony system and his desire for romantic love and independence, and yet, in the end, it seems, embraces his return to the family's tradition. Otoku, on the one hand, has been called a quintessentially self-sacrificing heroine of melodrama.[1] On the other hand, perceptive critics have noted her strength, rebellion, and far-sightedness (Ehrlich 1989: 156). She is the one who educates Kikunosuke and shapes his acting career; she is bold enough to reason with her master and mistress.

The Story of the Last Chrysanthemum was based on a true story about the household of Kikugoro V (1844–1903), one of the most celebrated actors of modern kabuki history. In fact, the real-life Kikunosuke Onoe (1868–1897) did not live long enough to become a true master after he made a comeback and parted with Otoku as depicted at the end of the film. Instead, the baby Ko in the film grew up to become Kikugoro VI (1884–1949) and was at the prime of his magnificent career when the film was made. Shofu Muramatsu's short story about the tragic romance of Kikunosuke and Otoku, *The Story of the Last Chrysanthemum* (*Zangiku monogatari*), was immediately adapted for *shinpa* production in 1937. *Shinpa* is a modern theatrical form, stylistically an amalgam of kabuki and Western bourgeois theatre. While most *shinpa* plays are domestic melodramas set in modern times (post-1868 Meiji Restoration) with more or less colloquial dialogue, they retain female impersonators and components of dance-based spectacles like kabuki. The *shinpa* version, featuring Shotaro Hanayagi and Yaeko Mizutani, the two top stars of the troupe, proved immensely popular.[2] Thus, from the start, the film version, produced at Shochiku, a company that virtually monopolised kabuki exhibition, was conceived as an intermedial project that embraced and capitalised on multiple references to theatrical traditions of Japanese modernity.

At the time of its release, the media celebrated that the film version made Hanayagi's first screen performance possible. Film industry and culture hoped that the *shinpa*-film collaboration like this would broaden Japanese films' audience, which had been predominantly young and working class, to include middle-class adults such as *shinpa* connoisseurs.[3] In the mid-1930s the Japanese government started its program of active involvement with and reform of the film industry, a program that eventually materialised as the 1939 Film Law. Japan had a long history of film censorship and regulation, and, since 1925, had established a centralised censorship system at the Home Ministry. Yet, as historian Atsuko Kato demonstrates, the mid-1930s program differed from earlier practice in two respects. First, the new national policy aimed at controlling, regulating, and developing the film industry as an industry, rather than censoring individual films. Second, it acknowledged cinema as a legitimate sphere of cultural production with potential use value for enlightenment and propaganda, rather than as mere entertainment. Japan started the invasion of China in 1931, and its growing international visibility and self-consciousness as an Asian empire motivated the state to intervene in the production of a national image for both domestic and international audiences.[4] To be sure, making the licensing of all the film personnel as well as pre-production censorship of all the scripts mandatory, the Film Law was an oppressive state apparatus, as many filmmakers and critics liked to point out in the post-war period; and yet, in 1939, the film industry embraced this 'first cultural legislation' as the state's gesture of recognition and legitimisation.

The Story of the Last Chrysanthemum, made at the time of the Film Law's promulgation, embodied its ideal of uplift and reform. Film critics agreed that its unconventionally long takes did not bother them, since they were combined with rich mise en scène and worked to show the actors beautifully, covering the flaws of their appearance (Hanayagi was 20 years older than the role, and Mori was considered plain). A writer, at the end of an essay praising the film's exquisite handling of a popular subject matter, an actor's life, commented on a scene at the movie theatre: two young army officers whispering, 'It's good, isn't it?', with tears in their eyes, when Otoku comes back to Kikunosuke to apologise after their fight in a rain-leaking rural theatre.[5] *The Story of the Last Chrysanthemum* was not received as an esoteric work, but highly praised as a popular film of quality.

The complex mise en scène and camera movement in the shot-sequence where Kikugoro disowns Kikunosuke has produced fine-grained analyses by formalist film scholars (Burch 1979: 233; Kirihara 1992: 146; Davis 1996: 118–20). This is arguably one of the best-discussed, albeit not best-known, sequences of any Japanese film. The sequence, in effect, showcases how Mizoguchi orchestrated actors' gestures and movements within multiple planes and separate spaces by specifically cinematic means of aperture shooting and the camera's mobility, precisely because it was a film about the world of kabuki enacted by *shinpa* and kabuki actors.

The sequence in question takes place in Kikugoro's mansion. Kikunosuke, having just returned from a clandestine meeting with Otoku, is summoned to the living room (*zashiki*) where Kikugoro awaits. His stepmother Sato and his birth brother and kabuki musician Enju are also present at this father-son meeting, acting as mediators. The six-minute long take can be divided into three phases. (1) Kikugoro examines Kikunosuke's true intention in the living room; (2) Enju and Sato attempt to persuade Kikunosuke to give up Otoku in an adjacent room; (3) Kikunosuke returns to the living room, confronts Kikugoro, and begs him to approve his relationship with Otoku. The sequence abruptly ends with Kikunosuke's exit, which takes place off-screen and is suggested by the rustling of clothing and the clatter of the door that follow a tense exchange between father and son, and finally by the opened door revealed by the panning camera.

In this sequence, Mizoguchi deliberately allocates the off-screen space to the patriarch Kikugoro. In (1), he initially remains offscreen, and even after the camera reveals his dominating presence, Enju often blocks our view of him; in most of (2), the camera captures Kikunosuke, Sato, and Enju retreating to the next room, supposedly in order to discuss the matter more frankly. Despite, or rather because of the invisibility, his offscreen presence, invoked by his short speeches delivered in a brisk Tokyo dialect, his knocking of his pipe against the ashtray, and, above all, the silence, is at the centre of the whole mise en scène in this long take. It manipulates the economy of sympathy between the characters, between the characters and the spectator. While the spectatorial sympathy stays with Kikunosuke throughout the shot, we feel Sato's fear of Kikugoro's reaction and worry about its consequences most acutely because the camera shows her anxious face and repeated glances at the offscreen space. Darrell Davis, having described this shot with great care, remarks: 'The displaced camerawork in this instance is … an interrogation of the nature of observation, sympathy, and judgment' (Davis 1996: 120). In other words, Mizoguchi's mise en scène and the camera enable the spectator to examine and feel conflicting values and sentiments, without total absorption into any one of them.

Whether *The Story of the Last Chrysanthemum* criticises or endorses conservative values of the 'traditional' family is an interesting question. Feminist sociologists and historians have shown that the household (*ie*) system itself was not an abiding tradition but a modern invention of the Meiji era. Furthermore, in this film, the fact that family in the kabuki world is a professional unit with a hierarchical structure of mentor/disciple, maintained through the frequent practice of adoption, as in the case of Kikunosuke, complicates the matter. Consequently, unlike the classical Hollywood musical in which the protagonist's pursuit of professional success and romantic love produces a dual-focus narrative that typically converges in the creation of a couple (Altman 1987: 16–58), in *geido-mono*, that is, melodrama set in the world of performing arts in the Meiji or Tokugawa period, romantic love sharply contradicts both his/her professional life and family. *The Story of the Last Chrysanthemum* and Mikio Naruse's *Tsuruhachi and Tsurujirô* (1938) were largely responsible for establishing *geido-mono* as popular entertainment at the time of mobilisation for total war, acknowledging and then channelling multiple contradictions between private and public, life and art, romantic love and family.

Stylistically, *The Story of the Last Chrysanthemum* claimed cinema's status as art against the backdrop of its strong intermedial connections to the world of theatre. The long take has often been labelled as 'theatrical' in contrast to montage. And yet, the techniques Mizoguchi effectively used in conjunction with it, such as aperture shooting, manipulation of offscreen space, and precision blocking, capitalise on cinema's specificity vis-à-vis theatre. For these techniques require the fixed point of view provided by the camera. This particular logic of medium specificity explains the reason that all the three kabuki scenes in *The Story of the Last Chrysanthemum* are heavily edited: they are performed not for the camera's eye but for the diegetic audience.

Notes

1. Mikiro Kato, 'Shisen no shuchu houka: *Gubijinsô* kara *Zangiku monogatari* e', in Inuhiko Yomota (ed.), *Eiga kantoku Mizoguchi Kenji*, Tokyo, Shinyosha, 1999, pp. 144–9.
2. *Engei gaho*, November 1937, pp. 38–45.
3. Tsuneo Hazumi, Ju'ichiro Tomoda, Seiji Mizumachi *et al.*, '*Zangkiku monogatari* gappyo', *Kinema junpo*, 11 October 1939, p. 23.
4. Atsuko Kato, *Sodoin taisei to eiga*, Tokyo, Shinyosha, 2003, pp. 28–30.
5. Haruo Sato, 'Kisewata: *Zangiku monogatari* o mite', *Nippon eiga*, December 1939, pp. 20–2.

Further reading

Rick Altman, *The American Film Musical*, Bloomington, Indiana University Press, 1987.
David Bordwell, 'Mizoguchi and the Evolution of Film Language', in Stephen Heath and Patricia Mellencamp (eds), *Cinema and Language*, Frederick, MD, University Publications of America, 1983, pp. 107–15.
David Bordwell, 'A Cinema of Flourishes: Japanese Decorative Classicism of the Prewar Era', in Arthur Nolletti, Jr., and David Desser (eds), *Reframing Japanese* Cinema, Bloomington, Indiana University Press, 1992, pp. 328–46.
Noël Burch, *To the Distant Observer: Form and Meaning in the Japanese Cinema*, Berkeley, University of California Press, 1979.
Darrell William Davis, *Picturing Japaneseness: Monumental Style, National Identity, Japanese Film*, New York: Columbia University Press, 1996.
Linda C. Ehrlich, 'The Artist's Desire: Eight Films of Mizoguchi Kenji', PhD diss., University of Hawai'i, 1989.
Donald Kirihara, *Patterns of Time: Mizoguchi and the 1930s*, Madison, WI, University of Wisconsin Press, 1992.

Chika Kinoshita

Zemlya/Earth (1930)

[Country: USSR. Production Company: WUFKU. Director, Screenwriter, Editor: Alexander Dovzhenko. Cinematographer: Danylo Demutsky. Cast: Stepan Shkurat (Opanas), Semyon Svashenko (Vasili).]

Synopsis: The film begins with the final moments of grandfather Semyon Opanas beneath a pear tree. Locals, including Arkhyp Bilokin, contemplate the process of collectivisation and declare their resistance to it, while elsewhere Semyon's grandson Vasyl and his friends meet to discuss collectivisation. That night a dark figure attacks and kills Vasyl. At the cemetery, Bilokin's son Khoma arrives to declare that he was the one who killed Vasyl, but the villagers pay him no attention. One declares that Vasyl's glory will fly around the world like a new communist airplane. The film ends with a downpour of rain over fruit and vegetables.

Earth shares several characteristics with many of the most influential Soviet films of its era. It follows the Communist Party line by depicting a proletarian collective as a united and heroic force against bourgeois self-interest, while its formalist experimentation with the effects of montage editing is the film's primary cinematic technique. On this level, Ukrainian director, Alexander Dovzhenko, stands shoulder to shoulder with contemporary filmmakers, such as Dziga Vertov and Sergei Eisenstein.

However, far from the urban centres of Russian industry that largely inspired his peers, *Earth* is marked by an overwhelmingly rural sensibility. While it bears a glancing resemblance to Eisenstein's The Old and the New (1929), the similarities are superficial. *Earth*'s aesthetic eludes simplistic readings, while its study of the sacrifices its proletarian characters have to make was, in a period of early Stalinism, politically ambiguous. A synopsis reveals a narrative at odds with the usually straightforward tales of Bolsheviks good/Tsarists bad that characterises the work of Dovzhenko's generation. Usually experimental in form but straightforward in theme, their style often disguises simplicity of narrative structure. They were, after all, propaganda films with an unwavering message of bolshevism at their heart. Dovzhenko's story is multifaceted and mysterious, circular in construction and in presentation of life and the land.

Following the death of a grandfather, who had dedicated his life to pulling oxen, a collective farming community takes delivery of a new tractor. Their landowning Kulak neighbours express dismay as this greatly increases the collective's capabilities. Vasili, the community spokesman, is mysteriously killed and his father demands a secular, communist burial. The film climaxes with interlocking sequences running in parallel: the funeral takes place while Vasili's Kulak murderer madly confesses his guilt, unnoticed by the crowd; Vasili's lover despairs alone; a priest curses the godless community; Vasili's mother gives birth.

Dovzhenko strongly diverges from the typically frenetic energy of his peers and *Earth* frequently dwells on moments of immobility. While individual shot duration isn't unusually long for the period, there is great emphasis on the lack of physical movement within many of the shots themselves. The critic Siegfried Kracauer (1960) refers to this as 'nascent motion', a contrast between movement and motionlessness, producing:

> a shock effect, as if all of a sudden we found ourselves within a vacuum. (But) even though the moving images on the screen come to a standstill, the thrust of their movement is too powerful to be discontinued simultaneously ... the suspended movement nevertheless perpetuates itself by changing from inner motion to outer motion.
>
> (in Braudy and Cohen 1999: 295)

Thus, a frequent deferral of what is fundamental to cinema – movement – becomes in Kracauer's view, a point of extreme tension, affecting the spectator in a manner that becomes at once both poignant and tense. It is as if the film is pausing for dramatic effect before continuing.

However, Kracauer calls these moments 'stills', a word that implies that the film stock itself is motionless, rather than the subject being presented. On the contrary, Dovzhenko's often fixed camera instead seems to scrutinise 'stillness' and in doing so observes the tiniest of motions: a blink or a breath from a human subject, a slight movement of leaves in the wind for the many shots of fruit. Thus, a series of dramatic moments result as the tension between rolling camera and motionless subject becomes heightened, as if engaged in a staring contest. Andy Warhol would take to this area of compositional conflict much later in his Screen Test films of the 1960s.

Earth opens with a sequence of images of wheat blowing in the breeze. Dovzhenko dwells on this for some time, asking us to contemplate the beauty of nature. It is this that dominates the characters we are about to meet and, as consistently throughout, we are presented with connections between the characters and the land.[1] Further descriptions of an abundant harvest abound before we arrive at the first of many shots of unmoving farmers. The group is waiting for the old man to die. Their motionlessness contrasts strongly with the vivid activity of the crops and completely reverses how life on screen is usually presented. Dovzhenko indicates the overall harvest through singling out fruit as examples of the whole. He then reverses this with the introduction of the human characters, framing each one singly at first, making us gradually piece together the crowd gathered around the dying man from individual shots, emphasising that it is a collection of individuals which forms a multitude.

Throughout, Dovzhenko explicitly connects the farmers to their environment: they are often framed low in the shot at the very bottom of the screen, standing tiny against a vast sky or in different ways allied with the nature that surrounds them. Children eat fruit, mirroring the old man's final act before dying, emphasising the cycle of life and death and harmonising the group with nature. In one shot, a young woman stands immobile as a giant sunflower by her head bows in the breeze. The gesture of respect to the dying man is unmistakable.

'Dovzhenko strongly engages the sense of touch in images that vividly render the fullness and self-sufficiency, the rounded steadfastness of solid forms,' states Gilberto Pérez in a 1998 lyrical analysis of *Earth* (1998: 172). It is usual to focus on a single thing to illustrate an example of a larger whole, particularly in Soviet cinema of the period where a face singled out in the crowd is an indication of coactivity as a whole. However, Pérez posits that Dovzhenko builds up the sense of a community and their collectivism (and by extension, their wider connection with the earth on which they depend) from the individual upwards. Whether it is a person, an apple or a sunflower, each thing has its own, vivid life and intensity as well as being part of a wider whole. In the sequence where the tractor arrives, the large crowd who eagerly await its arrival is again only gradually constructed from several separate, similarly framed shots of different people. A more typical filmmaker would use an establishing shot of the group as a whole, before picking out individuals.

Dovzhenko's unusual composition supports the unexpected turns of his narrative. In contrast to the usually limited depth of characterisation found in the work of his contemporaries, the sequence where Vasili holds his Bolshevik meeting in his home shows an interest in wry subtlety. The father's rejection of the son's communist idealism leads to a mutual turning of backs. Their conversation is then framed with the actors shot separately and facing away from the camera, linking the physical similarities between the pair. The scene leads neither to a hackneyed conversion of the father or a drawing of ideological battle lines, but to a still sulking father turning his face back to the spectator after the group leave, admitting a grudging respect in their absence. It is this feeling for a portrait of humanity that makes the father's later demand for his son's secular funeral rite more powerful.

After some comedy where the tractor runs dry, leading the men to urinate in the radiator to get it going again, we see a sequence that celebrates the process from harvest to baking. This is directly comparable to a sequence from one of Dziga Vertov's Kino-Eye newsreels and recalls that director's method of rhythmic montage that links mechanical action and labour. However, where Vertov transforms manual effort into something modernist and motorised, Dovzhenko makes the machinery seem fluid and human or earthy. The tempo evokes an organic (even erotic, according to Pérez) approach to the rhythms of work (1998: 178).

The film's most notably unusual sequence comes with the presentation of Vasili's murder, which follows a montage of shots of different loving couples, all standing in a near-identical, motionless embrace. Dovzhenko largely frames them as individuals, counter-intuitively suggesting separation, at least in thought, during this tender moment. A dark look seems to cross Vasili's face, unseen by his lover. Next, we see her, also framed separately, her eyes darting as if afraid of something unknown.

Subsequently, as Vasili walks home, he begins to dance, quickly becoming more ecstatic in his joyful expression. This is extraordinary: the character is alone, making this moment of rapturous physical display a striking contrast to the previous static images of him in the arms of his lover. The joy is expressed separate from the moment that prompted it.

What further makes this sequence bizarre is its outcome: Vasili collapses as if suddenly shot. Dovzhenko avoids the development of suspense in this sequence altogether. No cutaway reveals a weapon, nothing is given to suggest a cause for danger; Vasili simply drops dead. We are left to assume that it has been by a bullet, though the silence gives us no clue. This is startling, as if Stanley Donen ended the title song sequence from *Singin' in the Rain* (1952) by murdering Gene Kelly. Anticipating another famous screen shock, here Dovzhenko eliminates his lead character halfway through the story a full 30 years before *Psycho* (1960).

Having begun with the peaceful death of the old man, the film reaches its tragic pinnacle with the sudden death of a man in his prime. The event shocks both characters and spectator and leads Dovzhenko to further invoke the cycles of life and nature. Brushing past the hanging apples during the funeral procession, the branches seem to bow their condolence, linking back to the sunflowers from the opening sequence. As the father buries his son, the mother simultaneously goes into labour, producing new life. Again, there is no clear, socialist meaning to be received here, the juxtaposition of life and death is enough.

Pérez notes that the parallel climactic sequences depicting the guilty man, the grieving father, the anguished lover, the birthing mother and the furious priest do not physically communicate; it is a thematic interaction, drawing on the interconnectedness of all things (1998: 186). Parallels abound: frenzy, loss, anguish, agony and fury all merge in the painful ecstasies of overwhelming guilt, grief, torment, labour and devout wrath. Emotional extremes, unconnected by ideology, intertwine as individual, yet universal, unified.

Subsequent events were to quickly render *Earth* a period piece: the idealistic representations of collective farming and declarations that the class enemy is doomed are unintentionally chilling given Stalin's immanent liquidation of the landowning Kulak class. The Soviet authorities were also suspicious of the film's loyalties, which portray death and sadness, rather than simplistic martyrdom, as part of the process of revolution. Increasing state control of the film industry and the Soviet Premier's personal suspicion of formalist experimentation would enforce a new regime of Socialist Realism that was to dominate the arrival of sound cinema. Dovzhenko's own work would henceforth toe the Stalinist line.

The film's tension between stillness and movement is exploited fully in the film's final sequence. Here we see a long series of shots of rain falling on abundant fruit harvests. The nascent motion of nature, immobile yet moving, long decayed in time yet captured alive on celluloid in all its earthy fecundity was clearly in Dovzhenko's soul. With its celebration of renewal and the cyclical, the era of great experimentation that characterises the best of Soviet cinema of the 1920s comes to an end with the release of *Earth*.

Note

1. The wind in the wheat is acknowledged as having been an influence on Andrei Tarkovsky's similar shots in *Mirror* (1975).

Further reading

David Gillespie, *Early Soviet Cinema*, London, Wallflower, 2000.

Sigfried Kracauer, 'The Establishment of Physical Existence', in Leo Braudy & Marshall Cohen (eds), *Film Theory and Criticism*, New York & Oxford, Oxford University Press, 1999, pp. 41–59.

Jay Leyda, *Kino: A History of the Russian and Soviet Film*, Sydney, Allen & Unwin, 1960.

Gilberto Pérez, *The Material Ghost: Films and their Medium*, Baltimore, John Hopkins, 1998.

Phil Lloyd

Zerkalo/Mirror (1974)

[Country: USSR. Production Company: Mosfilm. Director: Andrei Tarkovsky. Screenwriters: Alexander Misharin, Andrei Tarkovsky. Cinematographer: Georgy Rerberg. Editor: Lyudmila Feiginova. Music: Eduard Artemiev. Cast: Cast: Margarita Terekhova (Natalya/Maroussia – the Mother); Ignat Daniltsev (Ignat/Alexei – 12 years old); Oleg Yankovsky (the Father); Anatoloy

Solonitsyn (Doctor); Larisa Tarkovskaya (Nadezha); Innokenty Smoktunovsky (adult Alexei – voice only); Arseny Tarkovsky (Narrator/Poet – voice only).

Synopsis: A jumbled series of dramatised scenes, dream sequences and newsreel excerpts reveal the memories and present-day experiences of unseen protagonist-narrator Alexei. The traumas of Alexei's rural childhood and experiences of war are mirrored in his urban adult life. His estranged relations with his ex-wife, Natalia, and son, Ignat, reflect the abandonment he suffered from his own father. A myriad of motifs echo across generations melding dream with reality and the personal with the political. Transcending autobiography, elements drawn from Tarkovsky's own experiences (and those of his mother and father, who both feature in the film) are implicated within the wider traumatic socio-historical experiences of Soviet Russia from 1930 to 1970.

> What is this film about? It is about a Man. No, not the particular man whose voice we hear. It's a film about you, your father, your grandfather, about someone who will live after you and who is still 'you'. There is no mathematical logic here, for it cannot explain what man is or what is the meaning of his life.[1]

Although Tarkovsky died after completing only seven feature films, his oeuvre is nevertheless both substantial and remarkably complete. Each of Tarkovsky's films warrants serious study and contemplation, both for their philosophical dimensions and for their formal accomplishments. A master of film form, Tarkovsky stands with a handful of others as an artistic genius of narrative cinema. More than striving for formal cinematic perfection in each individual film, Tarkovsky created (intuitively perhaps) an imaginative web of interlocking images, sounds, motifs and ideas that stretches across and unifies his oeuvre into a singular vision or pattern. The consistencies are indeed extraordinary. The outline left by Tarkovsky's work resembles something like a cycle; birth with *Ivan's Childhood* arching round to death with *The Sacrifice*.

In the middle of this creative cycle stands *Mirror*, Tarkovsky's most explicitly autobiographical film and also his most formally complex. *Mirror* is indicative of all of Tarkovsky's work for its sublime, even miraculous imagery, as equally real as it is surreal. But the film is also unique in the director's oeuvre for its radically disjointed structure. As Tarkovsky scholar Robert Bird notes, 'at first screening it can be very difficult to work out the connections between the sequences.'[2] *Mirror* bears no obvious logical narrative or temporal structure, features an unseen protagonist, uses actors to play multiple roles, alludes to a host of historical, artistic and religious references, utilises colour and black and white film in highly unreliable ways and incorporates documentary sequences, poetry and long dream sequences as well as dramatised scenes.

In spite of these difficulties there is in *Mirror* an emotional immediacy and power that other modernist art films of comparable formal ingenuity conspicuously lack. In an age of intellectualism, Tarkovsky valued emotion (often in a spiritual sense) as the source of creativity. In Tarkovsky's own words:

> The empirical process of intellectual cognition cannot explain how an artistic image comes into being – unique, indivisible, created and existing on some plane other than that of the intellect.
>
> (1986: 40)

Let this not be read as implying that Tarkovsky was intellectually ignorant or wilfully naive, but rather that he let his developed sense of intuition guide the course of his very complex and intellectually sophisticated work. One thinks of the guide in *Stalker* (Tarkovsky, 1979) leading the two intellectuals through the mysterious Zone.

In *Mirror* Tarkovsky took this intuitive approach to creativity to an almost paradoxically methodological extreme. Rather than first completing a scenario and shooting script for the film, Tarkovsky conscientiously allowed for *Mirror*'s content and form to develop through the creative process of its realisation. As early as 1967, in the first proposal for the film, Tarkovsky and his collaborator Alexander Misharin stated their case:

> [The film's] concept seems especially interesting to us also because for the first time, cinema … comes directly into contact with the process of creation. that is, when the

> entire creative process deepens the original concept, shapes it and gives it its final features only at the very end of the rough cut.[3]

In other words, neither Tarkovsky nor Misharin pre-formulated the eventual narrative *Mirror* was to become. The film's scenario was purposefully allowed to remain, in Tarkovsky's words, 'a fragile, living, ever-changing structure' (1986: 131). *Mirror* was to grow, like a tree, into the form appropriate to it.

Such an open creative process comes with its complexities however. Throughout the more than decade-long process of *Mirror*'s realisation this principle of continual organic development left virtually nothing in the film unaltered, rearranged or significantly re-envisioned. Key aspects of the film's scenario drafts were removed while substantial elements were introduced very late in the production process. (A long interview with Tarkovsky's mother was scrapped, while the role of Alexei's estranged wife Natalia was only introduced six months *after* shooting began.) The principal actors themselves knew very little of their parts. They were given their lines piecemeal, restricting their knowledge of the character to the here and now. Most significant were the major variations made in the editing suite to the overall structure of the film: the organisation of dramatic scenes, flashbacks, dreams and documentary sequences. Tarkovsky writes:

> There were some twenty or more variants. I don't mean changes in the order of certain shots, but major alterations in the actual structure, in the sequence of episodes. At moments it looked as if the film could not be edited ... it had no unity, no necessary inner connection, no logic. And then, one fine day. the material came to life. the film held together.[4]

So what is it that unifies this radically disjointed film? What makes it whole? The answer is far from self-evident, and yet key to comprehending *Mirror*. It certainly isn't a causally linked chain of events (as is the case in conventional narratives). It isn't really even the psychological centrality of the supposed narrator, Alexei, whose memories and dreams we seem to be witnessing. Other subjectivities, especially the Mother's and Father's, clearly take over the narration at different points in the film. (Tarkovsky was to reflect after completing the film that what had started as an autobiography became a story about his mother.)

In the search for the film's unifying principle, some commentaries have suggested *Mirror* obeys a kind of musical form. Natasha Synessios writes:

> More than anything it resembles a musical composition; it is polyphonic in its use of disparate parts, but the sense of wholeness and harmony it creates makes it akin to a symphony .... emphasis is placed not on the *logic*, but the *form*, of the flow of events.[5]

No one seriously claims to intellectually comprehend the formal unity of a piano prelude by Bach while experiencing the music. It is more accurate to say that we 'feel' the unity of these musical pieces through the listening experience. The principle is perhaps similar in *Mirror*, although in this case we are asked to watch and listen. Giving some scientific framework for these ideas the Soviet critic, Maya Turovskaya, suggests that Tarkovsky attempted to 'beam his message directly to the [brain's] right hemisphere, thereby evading control of the later established, now dominant, left hemisphere.'[6] 'The right brain,' to quote Colin Wilson, 'deals with intuitions, "with overall meanings", with patterns ... [while] the left brain deals with language, with logic.'[7] Such explanations would seem to imply that the intuitive method by which *Mirror* was made prevents it from being comprehended by the audience in any logical or cognitive manner. Indeed, if the filmmaker himself did not intellectually formulate a narrative while making the film, what narrative could there be for the audience to comprehend?

If, however, the film is to be approached intellectually, as a narrative or at least as a cinematic poem worthy of analysis, perhaps the best way to conceive of it is as a pattern of motific imagery. Like Tarkovsky's oeuvre as a whole *Mirror* is unified by a collection of motific images and sounds, ideas and themes. Although it is not within the scope of this essay to point these motifs out, close attention to the film will reveal an ocean of carefully placed repetitions, which endow the film with perceptible form. The task for the spectator here is not so much to *follow* the film as to chart its correlations, to map out its narrative and find a poetic image.

For Tarkovsky *Mirror*'s highly unconventional motific narrative unity represented the discovery of a specifically cinematic language. Interviewed a year before his death, he explained:

> A film consists of separate shots like a mosaic, of separate fragments of different colour and texture. And it may be that each fragment on its own is, it would seem, of no significance. But within that whole it becomes an absolutely necessary element, it exists only within that whole. That's why *Mirror* is in a sense the closest to my theoretical conception of cinema.[8]

It may seem wilfully paradoxical that Tarkovsky should describe an unformulated exercise in intuitive filmmaking in such theoretical terms. However, by allowing himself the freedom to develop *Mirror* without the strictures of narrative convention Tarkovsky was able to crystallise the filmic language of motific imagery that his earlier films aspire to and his later films refine. In this sense *Mirror* represents the high-water mark of Tarkovsky's filmmaking ambition. After *Mirror*, Tarkovsky would consciously return to the traditional laws of narrative by engaging with a scenario of the strictest spatial, temporal and causal limitations, which he would then transgress by means of cinematic language. That next film was *Stalker*, a definably narrative film that marks both a return to the ground covered in *Solaris* and a further movement out into uncharted territory.

Perhaps most importantly, *Mirror* is a film about each of us, for it is we who individually construct the film's story and endow it with meaning. We make it whole. We make the image. The fact that we are required to make such an effort to do this only intensifies the personal significance of the film's meaning. As a worker from a Leningrad factory put it in a letter to Tarkovsky: 'I can't even talk about [Mirror] because I am living it.'[9]

Notes

1. From an anonymous note published in the Institute of Physics and Academy of Sciences wall-newspaper. Quoted in Andrei Tarkovsky, *Sculpting in Time*, trans. Kitty Hunter-Blair, Austin, TX, University of Texas Press, 1986, p. 9.
2. Robert Bird, '*Mirror*' in Birgit Beumers, (ed.) *Directory of World Cinema*, Bristol and Chicago, IL, Intellect, 2011, p. 205.
3. Andrei Tarkovsky and Aleksandr Misharin, 'Proposal for the film "Confession"' in Andrei Tarkovsky, *Collected Screenplays*, p. 260.
4. Andrei Tarkovsky, *Sculpting in Time*, p. 116.
5. Natasha Synessios, *Mirror*, p. 4.
6. M. Turovskaya, *Tarkovsky: Cinema as Poetry*, London, Faber, 1989, p. 98.
7. C. Wilson, *Rudolf Steiner: The Man and his Vision*, London, Aeon, 2005, p. 73.
8. Andrei Tarkovsky, in Jerzy Illg and Leonard Neuger, 'Andrei Tarkowskim Rozmawiaja', *Res Publica*, 1987 (1), p. 137.
9. Quoted in Andrei Tarkovsky, *Sculpting in Time*, p. 10.

Further reading

Robert Bird, *Andrei Tarkovsky: Elements of Cinema*, London, Reaktion, 2008.

Thorsten Botz-Bornstein, *Film and Dreams: Tarkovsky, Bergman, Sokurov, Kubrick and Wong Kar-Wai*, New York, Lexington Books, 2008.

Nathan Dunne (ed.), *Tarkovsky*, London, Black Dog, 2008.

Geoff Dyer, *ZONA: A Book About a Film About a Journey to a Room*, London, Text Publishing, 2012.

John Gianvito (ed.), *Andrei Tarkovsky: Interviews*, Jackson, MS, University Press of Mississippi, 2006.

Peter Green, *Andrei Tarkovsky: The Winding Quest*, London, Macmillan, 1993.

Vida Johnson and Graham Petrie, *The Films of Andrei Tarkovsky*, Bloomington, IN, Indiana University Press, 1994.

Mark Le Fanu, *The Cinema of Andrey Tarkovsky*, London, BFI, 1987.

Herbert Marshall, 'Andrey Tarkovsky's *The Mirror*' *Sight and Sound*, Spring, 1976, pp. 92–5.

Natasha Synessios, *Mirror*, London, I. B. Taurus, 2001.

Andrei Tarkovsky, *Collected Screenplays*, trans. William Powell and Natasha Synessios, London, Faber, 1998.

Andrei Tarkovsky, *Time Within Time: The Diaries 1970–1986*, trans. Kitty Hunter-Blair, London, Faber, 1994.

Andrei Tarkovsky, *Sculpting in Time*, trans. Kitty Hunter-Blair, Austin, TX, University of Texas Press, 1986.

Maya Turovskaya, *Tarkovsky: Cinema as Poetry*, trans. Natasha Ward, London, Faber, 1989.

Peter Wuss, 'Dreamlike Images in Fellini's *8½* and Tarkovsky's *Mirror*: A Cognitive Approach', *The Journal of Moving Image Studies*, Vol. 2, No. 1, Fall, 2003.

Thomas Redwood

Index

Note: 'N' after a page number indicates a note.